CONTEMPORARY MORAL PROBLEMS

SIXTH EDITION

James E. White
St. Cloud State University

Wadsworth Publishing Company

An International Thomson Publishing Company

Belmont, CA • Albany, New York • Boston • Cincinnati • Detroit • Johannesburg • London • Madrid • Melbourne
Mexico City • New York • Pacific Grove, CA • Scottsdale, AZ • Singapore • Tokyo • Toronto

Philosophy Editor: Peter Adams
Assistant Editor: Kerri Abdinoor
Editorial Assistant: Mindy Newfarmer
Marketing Manager: Dave Garrison
Print Buyer: Stacey Weinberger
Permissions Editor: Susan Walters
Production: Matrix Productions
Copy Editor: Carole Crouse
Cover Design: Liz Harasymczuk

Cover Image: Robert Motherwell,
American, 1915–1991, *In Grey with
Parasol,* 1947, collage and oil on
board 120.7 × 90.2 cm, Art Gallery of
Ontario, Toronto, Gift from the
Women's Committee Fund, 1962.
Compositor: TBH Typecast, Inc.
Printer: R.R Donnelley

For permission to use material from this text, contact us:
web   *www.thomsonrights.com*
fax   1-800-730-2215
phone   1-800-730-2214

Printed in the United States of America
    3   4   5   6   7   8   9   10

Wadsworth Publishing Company
10 Davis Drive
Belmont, CA 94002

International Thomson Publishing Europe
Berkshire House
168-173 High Holborn
London, WC1V7AA, United Kingdom

Nelson ITP, Australia
102 Dodds Street
South Melbourne
Victoria 3205 Australia

Nelson Canada
1120 Birchmount Road
Scarborough, Ontario
Canada M1K 5G4

International Thomson Editores
Seneca, 53
Colonia Polanco
11560 México D.F. México

International Thomson Publishing Asia
60 Albert Street #15-01
Albert Complex
Singapore 189969

International Thomson Publishing Japan
Hirakawa-cho Kyowa Building, 3F
2-2-1 Hirakawa-cho, Chiyoda-ku
Tokyo 102, Japan

International Thomson Publishing Southern Africa
Building 18, Constantia Square
138 Sixteenth Road, P.O. Box 2459
Halfway House, 1685 South Africa

Library of Congress Cataloging-in-Publication Data

Contemporary moral problems / [edited by] James E. White. — 6th ed.
        p.   cm.
    Includes bibliographical references and index.
    ISBN 0-534-51724-2 (alk. paper)
    1. Ethical problems.   2. Applied ethics.   3. Civilization,
Modern—1950–   I. White, James E.
BJ1031.C6 1999
170—dc21   99-18200

Contents

Preface

The sixth edition has been extensively revised from the previous edition; it has thirty-eight new readings and five new or refocused topics. The choice of topics was determined by consulting students and reviewers. As a result, corporate responsibility, welfare, and war were dropped as topics, not because they are unimportant, but because they did not generate as much interest as sexuality, pornography, and hate speech. Abortion, euthanasia, capital punishment, and affirmative action continue to be topics of interest. Animals and the environment are treated in separate chapters. The chapter on ethical theories provides a basic theoretical background for the readings; many of them assume or apply a moral theory such as utilitarianism, Kant's theory, or a feminist theory.

The choice of particular readings for each topic was influenced by a variety of considerations. First, there was an attempt to find readings of high quality. All the readings have been previously published, and some are regarded as classics, such as Mary Anne Warren's "On the Moral and Legal Status of Abortion." Some of the readings were chosen for their historical importance—for example, the Supreme Court decisions on abortion and capital punishment. There was an attempt to balance the readings, to allow different and conflicting points of view to be expressed. Thus, in the chapter on abortion, we see a variety of viewpoints, from Noonan's strict pro-life position to Warren's radical pro-choice view. But the readings also were chosen to be read together; they respond to one another as in a conversation. This is seen in the abortion chapter, where the articles can be read as replying to one another. Finally, feminist articles or articles by women have been included in most chapters. For example, in the abortion chapter, there are two feminist articles, one defending the pro-life position and one attacking it.

Suitability for students was another important consideration. The book is intended to be an introductory-level textbook that can be read and understood by most college or junior college students. But finding the right level can be difficult, as most practicing teachers know. No doubt some will find the book too easy, and others will say it is too hard. For those who need it, several student aids have been provided:

1. *Chapter Introductions*. With the exception of the first chapter, on ethical theories, each chapter introduction is divided into three sections: factual background, the readings, and philosophical issues. The emphasis on factual background is new in this edition; an attempt has been made to provide accurate and up-to-date information on each topic. Next, there are brief summaries of the readings, and finally a discussion of the main philosophical issues.

2. *Reading Introductions.* An author biography and a brief summary of the author's main conclusions and arguments precede each reading.

3. *Study Questions.* Two types of study questions follow each reading. First are rather detailed and pedestrian review questions that test the student's grasp of the main points in the reading. These are intended for students wanting help in following the text. Second are more difficult discussion questions that probe deeper into the subject. These are aimed at the student who has understood the reading and is ready to discuss it.

4. *Problem Cases.* The problem cases at the end of each chapter require the student to apply the arguments and theories discussed in the chapter to hard cases, either actual or hypothetical. This case-study method, as it is called in law schools and business schools, can produce lively discussion and is a good way to get students to think about the issues. The problem cases also can be assigned as short paper topics or used for essay tests. More problem cases can be found at the book site in The Wadsworth Philosophy Shoppe website (http://philosophy.wadsworth.com).

5. *Suggested Readings.* At the end of each chapter is an extensive list of annotated suggestions for further reading. Sometimes websites are included, usually as sources of more factual information.

In revising the book for the sixth edition, I have benefited from the help and advice of many people. My colleague Jordan Curnutt made several useful suggestions. Janice Daurio helped me select a pro-life feminist article on abortion. Ronnie Hawkins advised me on abortion terminology as well as providing a provocative article on abortion. Peter Adams, the philosophy editor at Wadsworth, was a source of sound advice and encouragement. Jake Warde collected and summarized the reviews. Dave Garrison had useful insights on how to revise. Matrix Productions was invaluable in dealing with the permissions and production. Finally, I am grateful to the following reviewers for their thoughtful advice and criticisms: Kate Rogers (University of Delaware), Allen Hance (University of Illinois at Urbana-Champaign), Daniel M. Farrell (The Ohio State University), Ray Wright (University of Houston), Robert Hollinger (Iowa State University), Eleanor Katz (Orange Coast College, California), and Christine Cuomo (University of Cincinnati).

Chapter 1

Ethical Theories

Introduction

This chapter presents the basic moral theories that are the background for the subsequent readings in the book. For the sake of discussion, we can divide the theories into five types: theory of the right, theory of the good, virtue theory, rights theory, and feminist theory.

Theory of the Right

A theory of the right tries to tell us what is morally right and what is morally wrong. Such a theory is obviously relevant to moral problems in the book such as abortion, euthanasia, and the death penalty.

Theories of the right are usually subdivided into two different types: teleological and deontological theories. Teleological theories focus on consequences; they can be said to be forward-looking. Deontological theories do not do this but, rather, look backward at some nonconsequential feature, such as a motive or God's commands.

One standard teleological theory is ethical egoism, the view that everyone ought to act in his or her rational self-interest. This view is often defended by an appeal to psychological egoism, the thesis that, as a matter of fact, everyone does act in a self-interested way. But if this is so, then it is impossible for us to act unselfishly; all we can do is act selfishly. It seems to follow that ethical egoism is the only option available to us.

In the first reading, Rachels attacks both psychological and ethical egoism. He argues that psychological egoism is false and confused. It is false because people do act unselfishly, and in ways contrary to self-interest. It is confused because it fails to distinguish between selfishness and self-interest, it falsely assumes that every action is done either from self-interest or from other-regarding motives, and it ignores the fact that concern for one's own welfare is compatible with concern for the welfare of others.

As for ethical egoism, Rachels admits that it is not inconsistent and that it cannot be decisively refuted. But he thinks there are considerations that count against it. Most people do care about others; genuine egoists who really do not care about others are rare. And saying that an action will benefit others is giving a complete and sufficient reason for doing it. No further reason needs to be given.

Perhaps the most famous and widely discussed teleological theory is utilitarianism. The standard formulation of this theory is presented by John Stuart Mill in the fifth reading for the chapter. The most basic principle of utilitarianism is the Principle of Utility, which Mill states as follows: "Actions are right in proportion as they tend to promote happiness, wrong as they tend to produce the reverse of happiness." But what is happiness? Mill's answer is that happiness (or what is good) is pleasure and the absence of pain. Here Mill adopts a standard theory of the good, called hedonism, the view that the good is pleasure. We will examine this theory and alternatives to it in the next section.

In considering the happiness or unhappiness (or the good or evil) produced, utilitarianism counts everyone equally. But who counts? The answer of Mill and his followers is radical and important: We should consider everyone who is capable of suffering, including nonhuman animals. In Chapter 8 we see Singer and others arguing that it is wrong to discriminate against animals. This is in sharp contrast to the conventional view (defended by Noonan in Chapter 2) that only human beings count, or at least human beings count more than nonhumans.

Now let us turn to the other main kind of theory of the right, deontological theory. One popular view is the divine command theory, discussed by Arthur in the second reading for the chapter. This theory says that an act is right if it is commanded by God and wrong if God forbids it. No doubt this theory is accepted by millions of religious people, but only a few philosophers try to defend it. According to Arthur, it faces a host of difficulties. It assumes that there is a personal God who issues commands, and this is difficult to prove. Even assuming there is a personal God, there is the practical problem of discovering His or Her commands. Do we find them in the Old Testament, the New Testament, or the Koran? And how do we interpret these commands? For example, how do we follow Jesus' command to love your neighbor as yourself? Does this require us to actively help needy people, or is it good enough to leave them alone? Finally, Arthur brings up the famous question posed by Socrates in Plato's dialogue *Euthyphro:* Is something holy (or right) because God commands it, or does God command it because it is holy (or right)? As Arthur demonstrates in his discussion, this question raises some fundamental difficulties for the divine command theory.

In the third reading for the chapter, Nietzsche mounts a different sort of attack on the divine command theory, and indeed on any moral theory or religion making obedience a virtue. He calls any such theory or religion a "slave-morality" because it emphasizes slave virtues, such as obedience, humility, sympathy, and friendliness. Nietzsche thinks these virtues are contemptible; they are suitable only for weak and servile people. The noble person rejects them in favor of the "master-morality," a morality that focuses on superior virtues, such as power, strength, pride, vanity, and egoism.

Another standard deontological theory is cultural relativism. This is the view that moral rightness is relative to the beliefs of a culture. But different cultures have different moral beliefs; it seems to follow that what is right in one culture may not be right in another culture, and that we cannot legitimately criticize cultures that do not share our beliefs. In the fourth reading for the chapter, Mary Midgley presents a vivid example of this, the Japanese custom of trying out one's new samurai sword on a chance wayfarer. Although this seems to be obviously wrong from a Western moral perspective, can we justifiably criticize it? Midgley argues that we can and that cultural relativism, with its implication that we cannot criticize other cultures, is unacceptable. The problem with cultural relativism, says Midgley, is that it results in a moral isolationism that forbids moral reasoning. It is essentially a program of im-moralism that wants to put moralizing out of business.

Subjectivism is the view that moral beliefs are relative to a person's subjective feelings and beliefs. It says, in effect, that what is right or wrong is merely what I believe is right or wrong; or putting it another way, what is right is only what is right for me, and not for you. This view is vulnerable to the same objection that Midgley makes to cultural relativism. We can and do criticize the moral beliefs of other peo-ple. To rule this out is to forbid moral reasoning and its requirement of consistency.

The most influential deontological theory in the readings is Kant's theory. Kant believes that by pure reasoning we can discover one supreme moral principle that is binding on all rational beings. By "pure reasoning" he means reasoning that does not appeal to anything else, such as religious faith or popular opinion; it is like rea-soning in geometry and mathematics. The category of "rational beings" excludes animals in Kant's view (see his reading in Chapter 8); it includes not just human beings but also God and angels. The supreme moral principle uncovered by pure reasoning is called the categorical imperative because it commands absolutely, as dis-tinguished from hypothetical imperatives that command only if you have certain desires.

Kant formulates the categorical imperative in several different ways, but commen-tators usually focus on two distinct versions. The first one is that you should "act only on that maxim through which you can at the same time will that it should become a universal law." This principle gives you a way of deciding whether an act is wrong or not. You ask yourself what rule you would be following if you did some-thing; this rule is the "maxim" of your act. If you are not willing to have this rule become a universal law that everyone follows, then the act is wrong. To take one of Kant's examples, suppose you want to lie to someone. The rule you would be proposing (the "maxim" of your act) would be "It is not wrong to lie to someone." But you would not be willing to have everyone follow this rule, Kant claims, because it would be self-defeating. If everyone lied at will, then your lie would be pointless because nobody would believe you. According to Kant, these considera-tions prove that lying is always wrong. In Kant's terminology, it is a perfect duty that admits no exceptions.

Many philosophers have thought that this first formulation of the categorical imperative is problematic. One problem is that you can formulate the rule under which an act falls in different ways. Some of these rules could be made universal and others not. For example, instead of a general rule about lying, you could have a more specific rule about lying, such as "It is not wrong to lie to save someone's life." This seems to be a rule about lying that we would be willing to have as a uni-versal law.

Another objection attacks Kant's notion of perfect duty, the idea that there are duties that admit no exceptions. The objection is that there are always possible exceptions, exceptions that arise when there is a conflict between duties. Suppose, for example, that there is a conflict between the duty to not lie and the duty to not harm others. A terrorist asks you for a loaded gun to use in killing innocent hostages. You know where there is a gun handy, but should you tell the truth? It seems obvious enough that you should not tell the truth in this case because the duty to not harm others overrides the duty to not lie.

Kant formulated the categorical imperative in a second way, which commentators such as O'Neill (in the reading following Kant's reading) find more plausible. This second formulation, called the formula of the end in itself, recommends that you "act in such a way that you always treat humanity, whether in your own person or in the person of any other, never simply as a means, but always at the same time as an end." According to O'Neill, treating others as a mere means is to engage them in an activity to which they could not, in principle, consent, e.g. a deception. Treating people as ends in themselves requires that we treat them not only as mere means, but that we help them with their projects and activities. This gives us a duty to help or a duty of beneficence, but this duty is only imperfect. That is, it is a duty that cannot always be satisfied (as a perfect duty can) but requires us to exercise judgment and discretion.

Kant's theory has had an important impact on three of the moral problems covered in the book. First, Kant is a stern defender of capital punishment. In the reading in Chapter 4, Kant condemns the "serpent-windings of utilitarianism" and insists that the only appropriate punishment for murderers is death. They must be paid back for their crimes, and the consequences of the punishment are irrelevant. Kant is one of the main sources of the retributive theory of punishment, which holds that guilty people should be punished and that the punishment should fit the crime.

Second, according to Kant, we do not have any direct duties to animals. (See the reading in Chapter 8.) We have only indirect duties based on the effect the treatment of animals has on the treatment of humans. We should not be cruel to animals because this makes us likely to be cruel to humans. Animals are not subjects of direct moral concern because they are not rational beings. Kant's view, then, stands in sharp contrast to the utilitarians such as Mill and Singer, who believe that animals do have the status of moral subjects who deserve moral consideration.

Third, there is the abortion controversy. Kant does not discuss abortion. But it seems clear that fetuses are not rational beings, and thus an implication of Kant's view is that they have no more moral status than animals. This is the position that Warren takes in the reading in Chapter 2.

Theory of the Good

A theory of the good tries to tell us what is good and what is bad. Teleological theories seem to require some theory of the good in order to evaluate consequences. We noted above that Mill accepts hedonism, the theory that the good is pleasure. Hedonism is usually defended by making two important distinctions. First, there is a distinction between intrinsic and instrumental value. Something has intrinsic value if it is good or bad in itself apart from its use or consequences. By contrast, something has instrumental value if it is good or bad depending on how it is used. Hedonists allow that things such as knowledge and beauty can be instrumentally good but insist that only pleasure is intrinsically good. Similarly, things such as ignorance and ugliness can be instrumentally bad, but hedonists claim that only pain is intrinsically bad.

Critics of Mill and hedonism argue, however, that other things besides pleasure can be intrinsically good—for example, unexperienced beauty that is not instrumentally good because no one experiences it. And things besides pain can be intrinsically bad—for example, the injustice of punishing an innocent person. Indeed, the fact that utilitarianism does not seem to give a satisfactory account of retributive or distributive justice is seen as a serious defect. This has led modern philosophers to formulate theories of justice that are independent of utilitarianism—for example, Rawls's theory of justice in the readings for this chapter.

Another criticism of hedonism (which can be found in the reading by Aristotle) is that pleasure is an appropriate goal for animals but not for humans. According to Aristotle, the highest good for humans is found in contemplation because this involves the use of reason, and reasoning is what humans are naturally suited to do. The reply that Mill makes in the reading rests on the second distinction made by hedonists, a distinction between higher and lower pleasures. Roughly, higher pleasures involve the use of the intellect, whereas lower pleasures involve the senses. The higher pleasures are better than the lower pleasures, Mills argues, because the person who has experienced both will prefer the higher pleasures. Whether this is true or not is a matter of debate. In any event, Mill's view about the good life turns out to be not much different from Aristotle's view; on both views intellectual activities have a central role.

There are alternatives to hedonism. One is Kant's position that the only thing that is good without qualification is the good will, the desire to do one's duty for its own sake. Kant denied, by the way, that pleasure is always intrinsically good. He thought that the pleasure of a wicked person is not good; for example, in Kant's view the pleasure the sadist gets from torturing others is both instrumentally and intrinsically evil.

Another main source of alternatives to hedonism is religion. The monotheistic religions (Judaism, Christianity, and Islam) agree that the highest good involves God in some way. It might be obedience to God's will (emphasized in Islam), or love of God (recommended by Jesus), or a mystical union with God in this life, or a beatific vision of God in heaven. Aristotle says that the highest good for humans is found in the contemplation of God. Although we will not be concerned with religion as such, there is no doubt that religion has played an important role in ethics. Arthur discusses some of the connections between ethics and religion in the reading. We have already discussed the divine command theory, which is tacitly adopted in the monotheistic religions. (There are, of course, religions that do not worship God —for example, Buddhism, Taoism, and Confucianism.) Other religious doctrines come up in various contexts. In the readings on abortion, Noonan mentions ensoulment, the doctrine that the immortal soul enters the fetus (or technically, the zygote) at the moment of conception. Traditionally, philosophers have defended our lack of moral concern for animals by maintaining that animals do not have souls

(although it should be mentioned that in Hinduism and Jainism, animals are believed to have souls; indeed, some of them have the reincarnated souls of humans!)

Virtue Theory

Virtue theory is included in this chapter because it offers an important alternative to the theories that dwell on moral rightness and duty. We have already mentioned one such theory—namely, Nietzsche's distinction between the master- and slave-moralities with their corresponding virtues. The classical source of virtue theory, however, is Aristotle. Aristotle makes several important points about virtues. First, there is a distinction between intellectual and moral virtue. Intellectual virtue involves the use of what is best in humans—namely, reasoning—and the highest form of reasoning is self-sufficient, pure contemplation of God. Moral virtues involve a mean between the extremes of excess and deficiency. This is sometimes called the doctrine of the golden mean. To use one of Aristotle's examples, courage is a mean between the excess of foolhardiness and the deficiency of cowardliness. Second, Aristotle claims that some actions do not involve any means but are always wrong. This is an important point, for if there are such actions, then it seems to follow that some of the theories we have just discussed are problematic. Consider, for example, the action of torturing a small child to death. It seems obvious that this is wrong even if a person or a culture believes it is right, and even if God commands it, and even if it produces good consequences for others or the person doing the torturing. If so, then egoism, cultural relativism, the divine command theory, and utilitarianism all have a serious problem.

Rights Theory

Many of the readings in the book do not appeal to virtues or to duties, but to rights. We find references to the rights of fetuses, newborn infants, the terminally ill, animals, and even the environment. Most often mentioned are the rights to life and liberty. But what is the basis for moral rights? In his reading, Dworkin says that moral rights are based on the Kantian idea that humans who are members of the moral community should be treated with respect; Dworkin also appeals to the utilitarian idea of political equality.

The traditional basis for moral rights, however, is not utility or respect for persons, but rather the fact that they are given to us by God. Locke and Jefferson talk about God-given rights that are inalienable, that cannot be taken away by other people or the government. But most philosophers today do not want to appeal to God; they want a theory that appeals to nonbelievers too. The traditional secular view that is used to provide a foundation for rights is the social contract theory of Hobbes and Rousseau. According to this theory, it is in everyone's self-interest to live together in a society rather than alone in a state of nature. Life in a state of nature would be short, nasty, and brutish. But to live in a society, people must agree to follow certain rules (don't steal, don't murder, etc.), and these rules imply corresponding rights. Every citizen tacitly makes such an agreement (the social contract) to get the benefits of living in society. Without this social contract, society would be impossible.

Rawls's theory of justice is a type of social contract theory. We are asked to imagine what rules free, rational, and informed people would accept for a society. To make sure that the contractors are fair and unbiased, we are to imagine them operating under a "veil of ignorance" that hides from them personal facts such as their gender, race, and class. The rules such contractors would accept in the hypothetical original position, according to Rawls, are a principle giving people an equal right to liberty and a principle concerning social and economic inequalities.

But what rights do people have besides the right to liberty? In the reading, Dworkin says that United States citizens have certain fundamental rights that they hold against other people as well as the government. These are negative rights, or rights that imply that other people or the government should not interfere with them. These rights include the right to free speech, the right to a free press, and the right to bear arms. The basis for these rights is the Constitution of the United States; they are moral rights that have been turned into legal rights.

In the reading following Dworkin, Charlotte Bunch complains that this Western conception of rights as civil and political liberties is too narrow and impedes the advancement of women's rights. Bunch argues that the concept of rights needs to be expanded to include women's rights. These women's rights include socioeconomic rights to food, shelter, medical care, and employment where these are positive rights. That is, these rights or entitlements imply that the government has a duty to supply food, shelter, medical care, and employment. Bunch is also concerned about the right of women to not be abused, raped, enslaved, oppressed, or discriminated against.

Feminist Theory

In general, feminist theory is critical of the male theories discussed so far. They display a male bias that ignores the experience of women and contributes to the oppression of women in a male-dominated society. For example, Bunch says that the emphasis on the right to freedom we find in Rawls, Dworkin, Kant, and the other male philosophers is of little help to poor and oppressed women who lack basic necessities such as food, shelter, and medical care. Baier claims that the justice perspective of Kant, Rawls, and other male philosophers ignores the experience of women who care for children. The experience of these women involves emotions such as love, and not reasoning about abstract principles such as the categorical imperative. The parent-child relationship is between unequals, not the equal rational moral agents assumed by Kant, Rawls, and Dworkin. According to Baier, the best moral theory is not found in the justice perspective of the male philosophers but, rather, in a theory that includes the care perspective that is based on the experience of women.

Held agrees with Baier that male philosophers have ignored and discounted the emotions. Instead of seeing emotions as the enemy of reason, as Kant does, feminist philosophers think that morality requires the development of moral emotions such as love and sympathy. They are required for an understanding of moral relationships such as the parent-child relationship, and they are essential for the practice of morality.

Held goes on to attack two more biases of male philosophers. First, they assume a distinction between a public, male realm of war, politics, and business, and a private, female realm of domestic life, and then concentrate on the public realm. Feminists reject this artificial distinction and apply the care perspective of the so-called private realm to all areas of life. Second, the male philosophers assume that individuals are separate, isolated selves with conflicting interests. These conflicts have to be resolved by a social contract or some abstract moral rule such as the categorical imperative or the principle of utility. Feminist philosophers reject this view of the isolated self and replace it with a relational view of the self. That is, the self is constituted by its relationships with others, with parents, family, and friends, and ideally these relationships are trusting and cooperative and do not involve conflicting interests.

Egoism and Moral Scepticism

JAMES RACHELS

James Rachels is university professor of philosophy at the University of Alabama at Birmingham. He is the author of *The End of Life: Euthanasia and Morality* (1986), *Created from Animals: The Moral Implications of Darwinism* (1990), and *The Elements of Moral Philosophy* (1986; 2d ed., 1993).

Rachels examines psychological egoism and ethical egoism, two popular views used to attack conventional morality. Psychological egoism holds that all human actions are self-interested, whereas ethical egoism says that all actions ought to be self-interested. After discussing two arguments used to defend psychological egoism, Rachels concludes that it is both false and confused. But he is unable to refute ethical egoism. All that can be said is that genuine egoists are rare, and that it is a fundamental fact of human psychology that humans care about others and not just about themselves.

Source: James Rachels, "Egoism and Moral Skepticism,"
from *A New Introduction to Philosophy,* ed. Steven M. Cahn
(Harper & Row, 1971). Reprinted with permission.

1. OUR ORDINARY THINKING about morality is full of assumptions that we almost never question. We assume, for example, that we have an obligation to consider the welfare of other people when we decide what actions to perform or what rules to obey; we think that we must refrain from acting in ways harmful to others, and that we must respect their rights and interests as well as our own. We also assume that people are in fact capable of being motivated by such considerations, that is, that people are not wholly selfish and that they do sometimes act in the interests of others.

Both of these assumptions have come under attack by moral sceptics, as long ago as by Glaucon in Book II of Plato's *Republic*. Glaucon recalls the legend of Gyges, a shepherd who was said to have found a magic ring in a fissure opened by an earthquake. The ring would make its wearer invisible and thus would enable him to go anywhere and do anything undetected. Gyges used the power of the ring to gain entry to the Royal Palace where he seduced the Queen, murdered the King, and subsequently seized the throne. Now Glaucon asks us to determine that there are two such rings, one given to a man of virtue and one given to a rogue. The rogue, of course, will use his ring unscrupulously and do anything necessary to increase his own wealth and power. He will recognize no moral constraints on his conduct, and, since the cloak of invisibility will protect him from discovery, he can do anything he pleases without fear of reprisal. So, there will be no end to the mischief he will do. But how will the so-called virtuous man behave? Glaucon suggests that he will behave no better than the rogue: "No one, it is commonly believed, would have such iron strength of mind as to stand fast in doing right or keep his hands off other men's goods, when he could go to the market-place and fearlessly help himself to anything he wanted, enter houses and sleep with any woman he chose, set prisoners free and kill men at his pleasure, and in a word go about among men

with the powers of a god. He would behave no better than the other; both would take the same course."[1] Moreover, why shouldn't he? Once he is freed from the fear of reprisal, why shouldn't a man simply do what he pleases, or what he thinks is best for himself? What reason is there for him to continue being "moral" when it is clearly not to his own advantage to do so?

These sceptical views suggested by Glaucon have come to be known as *psychological egoism* and *ethical egoism* respectively. Psychological egoism is the view that all men are selfish in everything that they do, that is, that the only motive from which anyone ever acts is self-interest. On this view, even when men are acting in ways apparently calculated to benefit others, they are actually motivated by the belief that acting in this way is to their own advantage, and if they did not believe this, they would not be doing that action. Ethical egoism is, by contrast, a normative view about how men *ought* to act. It is the view that, regardless of how men do in fact behave, they have no obligation to do anything except what is in their own interests. According to the ethical egoist, a person is always justified in doing whatever is in his own interests, regardless of the effect on others.

Clearly, if either of these views is correct, then "the moral institution of life" (to use Butler's well-turned phrase) is very different than what we normally think. The majority of mankind is grossly deceived about what is, or ought to be, the case, where morals are concerned.

2. Psychological egoism seems to fly in the face of the facts. We are tempted to say: "Of course people act unselfishly all the time. For example, Smith gives up a trip to the country, which he would have enjoyed very much, in order to stay behind and help a friend with his studies, which is a miserable way to pass the time. This is a perfectly clear case of unselfish

1 *The Republic of Plato,* translated by F. M. Cornford (Oxford, 1941), p. 45.

behavior, and if the psychological egoist thinks that such cases do not occur, then he is just mistaken." Given such obvious instances of "unselfish behavior," what reply can the egoist make? There are two general arguments by which he might try to show that all actions, including those such as the one just outlined, are in fact motivated by self-interest. Let us examine these in turn:

A. The first argument goes as follows. If we describe one person's action as selfish, and another person's action as unselfish, we are overlooking the crucial fact that in both cases, assuming that the action is done voluntarily, *the agent is merely doing what he most wants to do.* If Smith stays behind to help his friend, that only shows that he wanted to help his friend more than he wanted to go to the country. And why should he be praised for his "unselfishness" when he is only doing what he most wants to do? So, since Smith is only doing what he wants to do, he cannot be said to be acting unselfishly.

This argument is so bad that it would not deserve to be taken seriously except for the fact that so many otherwise intelligent people have been taken in by it. First, the argument rests on the premise that people never voluntarily do anything except what they want to do. But this is patently false; there are at least two classes of actions that are exceptions to this generalization. One is the set of actions which we may not want to do, but which we do anyway as a means to an end which we want to achieve; for example, going to the dentist in order to stop a toothache, or going to work every day in order to be able to draw our pay at the end of the month. These cases may be regarded as consistent with the spirit of the egoist argument, however, since the ends mentioned are wanted by the agent. But the other set of actions are those which we do, not because we want to, nor even because there is an end which we want to achieve, but because we feel ourselves *under an obligation* to do them. For example, someone may do something because he has promised to

do it, and thus feels obligated, even though he does not want to do it. It is sometimes suggested that in such cases we do the action because, after all, we want to keep our promises; so, even here, we are doing what we want. However, this dodge will not work: if I have promised to do something, and if I do not want to do it, then it is simply false to say that I want to keep my promise. In such cases we feel a conflict precisely because we do *not* want to do what we feel obligated to do. It is reasonable to think that Smith's action falls roughly into this second category: he might stay behind, not because he wants to, but because he feels that his friend needs help.

But suppose we were to concede, for the sake of the argument, that all voluntary action is motivated by the agent's wants, or at least that Smith is so motivated. Even if this were granted, it would not follow that Smith is acting selfishly or from self-interest. For if Smith wants to do something that will help his friend, even when it means forgoing his own enjoyments, that is precisely what makes him *un-selfish.* What else could unselfishness be, if not wanting to help others? Another way to put the same point is to say that it is the *object* of a want that determines whether it is selfish or not. The mere fact that I am acting on *my* wants does not mean that I am acting selfishly; that depends on *what it is* that I want. If I want only my own good, and care nothing for others, then I am selfish; but if I also want other people to be well-off and happy, and if I act on *that* desire, then my action is not selfish. So much for this argument.

B. The second argument for psychological egoism is this. Since so-called unselfish actions always produce a sense of self-satisfaction in the agent,[2] and since this sense of satisfaction is a

---

2 Or, as it is sometimes said, "It gives him a clear conscience," or "He couldn't sleep at night if he had done otherwise," or "He would have been ashamed of himself for not doing it," and so on.

pleasant state of consciousness, it follows that the point of the action is really to achieve a pleasant state of consciousness, rather than to bring about any good for others. Therefore, the action is "unselfish" only at a superficial level of analysis. Smith will feel much better with himself for having stayed to help his friend—if he had gone to the country, be would have felt terrible about it—and that is the real point of the action. According to a well-known story, this argument was once expressed by Abraham Lincoln:

> Mr. Lincoln once remarked to a fellow-passenger on an old-time mud-coach that all men were prompted by selfishness in doing good. His fellow-passenger was antagonizing this position when they were passing over a corduroy bridge that spanned a slough. As they crossed this bridge they espied an old razor-backed sow on the bank making a terrible noise because her pigs had got into the slough and were in danger of drowning. As the old coach began to climb the hill, Mr. Lincoln called out, "Driver, can't you stop just a moment?" Then Mr. Lincoln jumped out, ran back, and lifted the little pigs out of the mud and water and placed them on the bank. When he returned, his companion remarked: "Now, Abe, where does selfishness come in on this little episode?" "Why, bless your soul, Ed, that was the very essence of selfishness. I should have had no peace of mind all day had I gone on and left that suffering old sow worrying over those pigs. I did it to get peace of mind, don't you see?"[3]

This argument suffers from defects similar to the previous one. Why should we think that merely because someone derives satisfaction from helping others this makes him selfish? Isn't the unselfish man precisely the one who *does* derive satisfaction from helping others, while the

3 Frank C. Sharp, *Ethics* (New York, 1928), pp. 74–75. Quoted from the Springfield (Ill.) *Monitor* in the *Outlook*, vol. 56, p. 1059.

selfish man does not? If Lincoln "got peace of mind" from rescuing the piglets, does this show him to be selfish, or, on the contrary, doesn't it show him to be compassionate and good-hearted? (If a man were truly selfish, why should it bother his conscience that *others* suffer—much less pigs?) Similarly, it is nothing more than shabby sophistry to say, because Smith takes satisfaction in helping his friend, that he is behaving selfishly. If we say this rapidly, while thinking about something else, perhaps it will sound all right; but if we speak slowly, and pay attention to what we are saying, it sounds plain silly.

Moreover, suppose we ask *why* Smith derives satisfaction from helping his friend. The answer will be, it is because Smith cares for him and wants him to succeed. If Smith did not have these concerns, then he would take no pleasure in assisting him; and these concerns, as we have already seen, are the marks of unselfishness, not selfishness. To put the point more generally: if we have a positive attitude toward the attainment of some goal, then we may derive satisfaction from attaining that goal. But the *object* of our attitude is *the attainment of that goal;* and we must want to attain the goal *before* we can find any satisfaction in it. We do not, in other words, desire some sort of "pleasurable consciousness" and then try to figure out how to achieve it; rather, we desire all sorts of different things—money, a new fishing-boat, to be a better chess-player, to get a promotion in our work, etc.—and because we desire these things, we derive satisfaction from attaining them. And so, if someone desires the welfare and happiness of another person, he will derive satisfaction from that; but this does not mean that this satisfaction is the object of his desire, or that he is in any way selfish on account of it.

It is a measure of the weakness of psychological egoism that these insupportable arguments are the ones most often advanced in its favor. Why, then, should anyone ever have thought it a true view? Perhaps because of a desire for theoretical simplicity: In thinking about human conduct, it would be nice if there were some simple formula that would unite the diverse phenomena of human behavior under a single explanatory principle, just as simple formulae in physics bring together a great many apparently different phenomena. And since it is obvious that self-regard is an overwhelmingly important factor in motivation, it is only natural to wonder whether all motivation might not be explained in these terms. But the answer is clearly No; while a great many human actions are motivated entirely or in part by self-interest, only by a deliberate distortion of the facts can we say that all conduct is so motivated. This will be clear, I think, if we correct three confusions which are commonplace. The exposure of these confusions will remove the last traces of plausibility from the psychological egoist thesis.

The first is the confusion of selfishness with self-interest. The two are clearly not the same. If I see a physician when I am feeling poorly, I am acting in my own interest but no one would think of calling me "selfish" on account of it. Similarly, brushing my teeth, working hard at my job, and obeying the law are all in my self-interest but none of these are examples of selfish conduct. This is because selfish behavior is behavior that ignores the interests of others, in circumstances in which their interests ought not to be ignored. This concept has a definite evaluative flavor; to call someone "selfish" is not just to describe his action but to condemn it. Thus, you would not call me selfish for eating a normal meal in normal circumstances (although it may surely be in my self-interest); but you would call me selfish for hoarding food while others about are starving.

The second confusion is the assumption that every action is done *either* from self-interest or from other-regarding motives. Thus, the egoist concludes that if there is no such thing as genuine altruism then all actions must be done from self-interest. But this is certainly a false dichotomy. The man who continues to smoke cigarettes, even after learning about the connection between smoking and cancer, is surely not acting from self-interest, not even by his own standards—self-interest would dictate that he quit smoking at once—and he is not acting altruistically either. He *is*, no doubt, smoking for the pleasure of it, but all that this shows is that undisciplined pleasure-seeking and acting from self-interest are very different. This is what led Butler to remark that "The thing to be lamented is, not that men have so great regard to their own good or interest in the present world, for they have not enough."[4]

The last two paragraphs show (*a*) that it is false that all actions are selfish, and (*b*) that it is false that all actions are done out of self-interest. And it should be noted that these two points can be made, and were, without any appeal to putative examples of altruism.

The third confusion is the common but false assumption that a concern for one's own welfare is incompatible with any genuine concern for the welfare of others. Thus, since it is obvious that everyone (or very nearly everyone) does desire his own well-being, it might be thought that no one can really be concerned with others. But again, this is false. There is no inconsistency in desiring that everyone, including oneself *and* others, be well-off and happy. To be sure, it may happen on occasion that our own interests conflict with the interests of others, and in these cases we will have to make hard choices. But even in these cases we might sometimes opt for the interests of others, especially when the others involved are our family or friends. But more importantly, not all cases are like this: sometimes we are able to promote the welfare of others

4 *The Works of Joseph Butler*, edited by W. E. Gladstone (Oxford, 1896), vol. II, p. 26. It should be noted that most of the points I am making against psychological egoism were first made by Butler. Butler made all the important points; all that is left for us is to remember them.

Dichotomy; division into two parts or kinds.

when our own interests are not involved at all. In these cases not even the strongest self-regard need prevent us from acting considerately toward others.

Once these confusions are cleared away, it seems to me obvious enough that there is no reason whatever to accept psychological egoism. On the contrary, if we simply observe people's behavior with an open mind, we may find that a great deal of it is motivated by self-regard, but by no means all of it; and that there is no reason to deny that "the moral institution of life" can include a place for the virtue of beneficence.[5]

3. The ethical egoist would say at this point, "Of course it is possible for people to act altruistically, and perhaps many people do act that way —but there is no reason why they *should* do so. A person is under no obligation to do anything except what is in his own interests."[6] This is really quite a radical doctrine. Suppose I have an urge to set fire to some public building (say, a department store) just for the fascination of watching the spectacular blaze: according to this view, the fact that several people might be burned to death provides no reason whatever why I should not do it. After all, this only concerns *their* welfare, not my own, and according to the ethical egoist the only person I need think of is myself.

Some might deny that ethical egoism has any such monstrous consequences. They would point out that it is really to my own advantage not to set the fire—for, if I do that I may be caught and put into prison (unlike Gyges, I have

no magic ring for protection). Moreover, even if I could avoid being caught it is still to my advantage to respect the rights and interests of others, for it is to my advantage to live in a society in which people's rights and interests are respected. Only in such a society can I live a happy and secure life; so, in acting kindly toward others, I would merely be doing my part to create and maintain the sort of society which it is to my advantage to have.[7] Therefore, it is said, the egoist would not be such a bad man; he would be as kindly and considerate as anyone else, because he would see that it is to his own advantage to be kindly and considerate.

This is a seductive line of thought, but it seems to me mistaken. Certainly it is to everyone's advantage (including the egoist's) to preserve a stable society where people's interests are generally protected. But there is no reason for the egoist to think that merely because *he* will not honor the rules of the social game, decent society will collapse. For the vast majority of people are not egoists, and there is no reason to think that they will be converted by his example—especially if he is discreet and does not unduly flaunt his style of life. What this line of reasoning shows is not that the egoist himself must act benevolently, but that he must encourage *others* to do so. He must take care to conceal from public view his own self-centered method of decision-making, and urge others to act on precepts very different from those on which he is willing to act.

The rational egoist, then, cannot advocate that egoism be universally adopted by everyone. For he wants a world in which his own interests are maximized; and if other people adopted the egoistic policy of pursuing their own interests to the exclusion of his interests, as he pursues his interests to the exclusion of theirs, then such a world would be impossible. So he himself will be an egoist, but he will want others to be altruists.

---

5 The capacity for altruistic behavior is not unique to human beings. Some interesting experiments with rhesus monkeys have shown that these animals will refrain from operating a device for securing food if this causes other animals to suffer pain. See Masserman, Wechkin, and Terris, "'Altruistic' Behavior in Rhesus Monkeys," *The American Journal of Psychiatry*, vol. 121 (1964), 584–585.

6 I take this to be the view of Ayn Rand, in so far as I understand her confusing doctrine.

7 Cf. Thomas Hobbes, *Leviathan* (London, 1651), chap. 17.

This brings us to what is perhaps the most popular "refutation" of ethical egoism current among philosophical writers—the argument that ethical egoism is at bottom inconsistent because it cannot be universalized.[8] The argument goes like this:

To say that any action or policy of action is *right* (or that it *ought* to be adopted) entails that it is right for *anyone* in the same sort of circumstances. I cannot, for example, say that it is right for me to lie to you, and yet object when you lie to me (provided, of course, that the circumstances are the same). I cannot hold that it is all right for me to drink your beer and then complain when you drink mine. This is just the requirement that we be consistent in our evaluations; it is a requirement of logic. Now it is said that ethical egoism cannot meet this requirement because, as we have already seen, the egoist would not want others to act in the same way that he acts. Moreover, suppose he *did* advocate the universal adoption of egoistic policies: he would be saying to Peter, "You ought to pursue your own interests even if it means destroying Paul"; and he would be saying to Paul, "You ought to pursue your own interests even if it means destroying Peter." The attitudes expressed in these two recommendations seem clearly inconsistent—he is urging the advancement of Peter's interest at one moment, and countenancing their defeat at the next. Therefore, the argument goes, there is no way to maintain the doctrine of ethical egoism as a consistent view about how we ought to act. We will fall into inconsistency whenever we try.

What are we to make of this argument? Are we to conclude that ethical egoism has been refuted? Such a conclusion, I think, would be unwarranted; for I think that we can show, contrary to this argument, how ethical egoism can

be maintained consistently. We need only to interpret the egoist's position in a sympathetic way: we should say that he has in mind a certain kind of world which he would prefer over all others; it would be a world in which his own interests were maximized, regardless of the effects on other people. The egoist's primary policy of action, then, would be to act in such a way as to bring about, as nearly as possible, this sort of world. Regardless of however morally reprehensible we might find it, there is nothing *inconsistent* in someone's adopting this as his ideal and acting in a way calculated to bring it about. And if someone did adopt this as his ideal, then he would not advocate universal egoism; as we have already seen, he would want other people to be altruists. So, if he advocates any principles of conduct for the general public, they will be altruistic principles. This would not be inconsistent; on the contrary, it would be perfectly consistent with his goal of creating a world in which his own interests are maximized. To be sure, he would have to be deceitful; in order to secure the good will of others, and a favorable hearing for his exhortations to altruism, he would have to pretend that he was himself prepared to accept altruistic principles. But again, that would be all right; from the egoist's point of view, this would merely be a matter of adopting the necessary means to the achievement of his goal—and while we might not approve of this, there is nothing inconsistent about it. Again, it might be said: "He advocates one thing, but does another. Surely *that's* inconsistent." But it is not; for what he advocates and what he does are both calculated as means to an end (the *same* end, we might note); and as such, he is doing what is rationally required in each case. Therefore, contrary to the previous argument, there is nothing inconsistent in the ethical egoist's view. He cannot be refuted by the claim that he contradicts himself.

Is there, then, no way to refute the ethical egoist? If by "refute" we mean show that he has made some *logical* error, the answer is that there

8 See, for example, Brian Medlin, "Ultimate Principles and Ethical Egoism," *Australasian Journal of Philosophy*, vol. 35 (1957), 111–118; and D. H. Monro, *Empiricism and Ethics* (Cambridge, 1967), chap. 16.

is not. However, there is something more that can be said. The egoist challenge to our ordinary moral convictions amounts to a demand for an explanation of why we should adopt certain policies of action, namely policies in which the good of others is given importance. We can give an answer to this demand, albeit an indirect one. The reason one ought not to do actions that would hurt other people is: other people would be hurt. The reason one ought to do actions that would benefit other people is: other people would be benefited. This may at first seem like a piece of philosophical sleight-of-hand, but it is not. The point is that the welfare of human beings is something that most of us value *for its own sake,* and not merely for the sake of something else. Therefore, when *further* reasons are demanded for valuing the welfare of human beings, we cannot point to anything further to satisfy this demand. It is not that we have no reason for pursuing these policies, but that our reason *is* that these policies are for the good of human beings.

So: if we are asked "Why shouldn't I set fire to this department store?" one answer would be "Because if you do, people may be burned to death." This is a complete, sufficient reason which does not require qualification or supplementation of any sort. If someone seriously wants to know why this action shouldn't be done, that's the reason. If we are pressed further and asked the sceptical question "But why shouldn't I do actions that will harm others?" we may not know what to say—but this is because the questioner has included in his question the very answer we would like to give: "Why shouldn't you do actions that will harm others? Because, doing those actions would harm others."

The egoist, no doubt, will not be happy with this. He will protest that *we* may accept this as a reason, but *he* does not. And here the argument stops: there are limits to what can be accomplished by argument, and if the egoist really doesn't care about other people—if he honestly doesn't care whether they are helped or hurt by his actions—then we have reached those limits. If we want to persuade him to act decently toward his fellow humans, we will have to make our appeal to such other attitudes as he does possess, by threats, bribes, or other cajolery. That is all that we can do.

Though some may find this situation distressing (we would like to be able to show that the egoist is just *wrong*), it holds no embarrassment for common morality. What we have come up against is simply a fundamental requirement of rational action, namely, that the existence of reasons for action always depends on the prior existence of certain attitudes in the agent. For example, the fact that a certain course of action would make the agent a lot of money is a reason for doing it only if the agent wants to make money; the fact that practicing at chess makes one a better player is a reason for practicing only if one wants to be a better player; and so on. Similarly, the fact that a certain action would help the agent is a reason for doing the action only if the agent cares about his own welfare, and the fact that an action would help others is a reason for doing it only if the agent cares about others. In this respect ethical egoism and what we might call ethical altruism are in exactly the same fix: both require that the agent *care* about himself, or about other people, before they can get started.

So a nonegoist will accept "It would harm another person" as a reason not to do an action simply because he cares about what happens to that other person. When the egoist says that he does *not* accept that as a reason, he is saying something quite extraordinary. He is saying that he has no affection for friends or family, that he never feels pity or compassion, that he is the sort of person who can look on scenes of human misery with complete indifference, so long as he is not the one suffering. Genuine egoists, people who really don't care at all about anyone other than themselves, are rare. It is important to keep this in mind when thinking about ethical egoism; it is easy to forget just how fundamental to human psychological makeup the feeling of sympathy is. Indeed, a man without any sympathy at all would scarcely be recognizable as a man; and that is what makes ethical egoism such a disturbing doctrine in the first place.

4. There are, of course, many different ways in which the sceptic might challenge the assumptions underlying our moral practice. In this essay I have discussed only two of them, the two put forward by Glaucon in the passage that I cited from Plato's *Republic*. It is important that the assumptions underlying our moral practice should not be confused with particular judgments made within that practice. To defend one is not to defend the other. We may assume—quite properly, if my analysis has been correct—that the virtue of beneficence does, and indeed should, occupy an important place in "the moral institution of life"; and yet we may make constant and miserable errors when it comes to judging when and in what ways this virtue is to be exercised. Even worse, we may often be able to make accurate moral judgments, and know what we ought to do, but not do it. For these ills, philosophy alone is not the cure.

Review Questions

1. Explain the legend of Gyges. What questions about morality are raised by the story?
2. Distinguish between psychological and ethical egoism.
3. Rachels discusses two arguments for psychological egoism. What are these arguments, and how does he reply to them?
4. What three commonplace confusions does Rachels detect in the thesis of psychological egoism?
5. State the argument for saying that ethical egoism is inconsistent. Why doesn't Rachels accept this argument?
6. According to Rachels, why shouldn't we hurt others, and why should we help others? How can the egoist reply?

Discussion Questions

1. Has Rachels answered the question raised by Glaucon, namely, "Why be moral?" If so, what exactly is his answer?
2. Are genuine egoists rare, as Rachels claims? Is it a fact that most people care about others, even people they don't know?
3. Suppose we define ethical altruism as the view that one should always act for the benefit of others and never in one's own self-interest. Is such a view immoral or not?

Religion, Morality, and Conscience

JOHN ARTHUR

What is morality? Does it need religion in some way? Or is it purely social? In this essay, John Arthur first discusses, and rejects, three ways morality has been thought to depend on religion: that without religious motivation people could not be expected to do the right thing; that religion is necessary to provide guidance to people in their search for the correct course of action; and that religion is essential for there even to be a right and wrong. Arthur then considers another conception of morality, suggested by John Dewey, which claims "morality is social." He concludes with some brief comments on the importance of these reflections for moral deliberation and for education. John Arthur is professor of philosophy and director of the Program in Philosophy, Politics, and Law at Binghamton University.

MY FIRST AND PRIME CONCERN in this paper is to explore the connections, if any, between morality and religion. I will argue that although there are a variety of ways the two can be connected, in fact religion is not necessary for morality. Despite the lack of any logical or other necessary connection, I will claim, there remain important respects in which the two are related. In the concluding section I will discuss the notion of moral conscience, and then look briefly at the various respects in which morality is "social" and the implications of that idea for moral education. First, however, I want to say something about the subjects: Just what are we referring to when we speak of morality and of religion?

1. MORALITY AND RELIGION

A useful way to approach the first question—the nature of morality—is to ask what it would mean for a society to exist without a social moral code. How would such people think and behave? What would that society look like? First, it seems clear that such people would never feel guilt or resentment. For example, the notions that I ought to remember my parents' anniversary, that he has a moral responsibility to help care for his children after the divorce, that she has a right to equal pay for equal work, and that discrimination on the basis of race is unfair would be absent in such a society. Notions of duty, rights, and obligations would not be present, except perhaps in the legal sense; concepts of justice and fairness would also be foreign to these people. In short, people would have no tendency to evaluate or criticize the behavior of others, nor to feel remorse about their own behavior. Children would not be taught to be ashamed when they steal or hurt others, nor would they be allowed to complain when others treat them badly. (People might, however, feel regret at a decision that didn't turn out as they had hoped; but that would only be because their expectations were frustrated, not because they feel guilty.)

Such a society lacks a moral code. What, then, of religion? Is it possible that a society

Source: John Arthur, "Religion, Morality, and Conscience," from *Morality and Moral Controversies* 4/e, ed. John Arthur (Prentice Hall, 1996), pp. 21–28. Reprinted with permission.

such as the one I have described would have religious beliefs? It seems clear that it is possible. Suppose every day these same people file into their place of worship to pay homage to God (they may believe in many gods or in one all-powerful creator of heaven and earth). Often they can be heard praying to God for help in dealing with their problems and thanking Him for their good fortune. Frequently they give sacrifices to God, sometimes in the form of money spent to build beautiful temples and churches, other times by performing actions they believe God would approve, such as helping those in need. These practices might also be institutionalized, in the sense that certain people are assigned important leadership roles. Specific texts might also be taken as authoritative, indicating the ways God has acted in history and His role in their lives or the lives of their ancestors.

To have a moral code, then, is to tend to evaluate (perhaps without even expressing it) the behavior of others and to feel guilt at certain actions when we perform them. Religion, on the other hand, involves beliefs in supernatural power(s) that created and perhaps also control nature, the tendency to worship and pray to those supernatural forces or beings, and the presence of organizational structures and authoritative texts. The practices of morality and religion are thus importantly different. One involves our attitudes toward various forms of behavior (lying and killing, for example), typically expressed using the notions of rules, rights, and obligations. The other, religion, typically involves prayer, worship, beliefs about the supernatural, institutional forms, and authoritative texts.

We come, then, to the central question: What is the connection, if any, between a society's moral code and its religious practices and beliefs? Many people have felt that morality is in some way dependent on religion or religious truths. But what sort of "dependence" might there be? In what follows, I distinguish various ways in which one might claim that religion is necessary for morality, arguing against those

who claim morality depends in some way on religion. I will also suggest, however, some other important ways in which the two are related, concluding with a brief discussion of conscience and moral education.

2. RELIGIOUS MOTIVATION AND GUIDANCE

One possible role which religion might play in morality relates to motives people have. Religion, it is often said, is necessary so that people will DO right. Typically, the argument begins with the important point that doing what is right often has costs: refusing to shoplift or cheat can mean people go without some good or fail a test; returning a billfold means they don't get the contents. Religion is therefore said to be necessary in that it provides motivation to do the right thing. God rewards those who follow His commands by providing for them a place in heaven or by ensuring that they prosper and are happy on earth. He also punishes those who violate the moral law. Others emphasize less self-interested ways in which religious motives may encourage people to act rightly. Since God is the creator of the universe and has ordained that His plan should be followed, they point out, it is important to live one's life in accord with this divinely ordained plan. Only by living a moral life, it is said, can people live in harmony with the larger, divinely created order.

The first claim, then, is that religion is necessary to provide moral motivation. The problem with that argument, however, is that religious motives are far from the only ones people have. For most of us, a decision to do the right thing (if that is our decision) is made for a variety of reasons: "What if I get caught? What if somebody sees me—what will he or she think? How will I feel afterwards? Will I regret it?" Or maybe the thought of cheating just doesn't arise. We were raised to be a decent person, and that's what we are—period. Behaving fairly and treating others well is more important than whatever we might gain from stealing or cheating, let alone seriously harming another person. So it seems clear that many motives for doing the right thing have nothing whatsoever to do with religion. Most of us, in fact, do worry about getting caught, being blamed, and being looked down on by others. We also may do what is right just because it's right, or because we don't want to hurt others or embarrass family and friends. To say that we need religion to act morally is mistaken; indeed, it seems to me that many of us, when it really gets down to it, don't give much of a thought to religion when making moral decisions. All those other reasons are the ones that we tend to consider, or else we just don't consider cheating and stealing at all. So far, then, there seems to be no reason to suppose that people can't be moral yet irreligious at the same time.

A second argument that is available for those who think religion is necessary to morality, however, focuses on moral guidance and knowledge rather than on people's motives. However much people may want to do the right thing, according to this view, we cannot ever know for certain what is right without the guidance of religious teaching. Human understanding is simply inadequate to this difficult and controversial task; morality involves immensely complex problems, and so we must consult religious revelation for help.

Again, however, this argument fails. First, consider how much we would need to know about religion and revelation in order for religion to provide moral guidance. Besides being aware that there is a God, we'd also have to think about which of the many religions is true. How can anybody be sure his or her religion is the right one? But even if we assume the Judeo-Christian God is the real one, we still need to find out just what it is He wants us to do, which means we must think about revelation.

Revelation comes in at least two forms, and not even all Christians agree on which is the best way to understand revelation. Some hold that revelation occurs when God tells us what he wants by providing us with His words: The Ten Commandments are an example. Many even believe, as evangelist Billy Graham once said, that the entire Bible was written by God using thirty-nine secretaries. Others, however, doubt that the "word of God" refers literally to the words God has spoken, but believe instead that the Bible is an historical document, written by human beings, of the events or occasions in which God revealed himself. It is an especially important document, of course, but nothing more than that. So on this second view, revelation is not understood as *statements* made by God but rather as His *acts,* such as leading His people from Egypt, testing Job, and sending His son as an example of the ideal life. The Bible is not itself revelation, it's the historical account of revelatory actions.

If we are to use revelation as a moral guide, then, we must first know what is to count as revelation—words given us by God, historical events, or both? But even supposing that we could somehow answer those questions, the problems of relying on revelation are still not over since we still must interpret that revelation. Some feel, for example, that the Bible justifies various forms of killing, including war and capital punishment, on the basis of such statements as "An eye for an eye." Others, emphasizing such sayings as "Judge not lest ye be judged" and "Thou shalt not kill," believe the Bible demands absolute pacifism. How are we to know which interpretation is correct? It is likely, of course, that the answer people give to such religious questions will be influenced in part at least by their own moral beliefs; if capital punishment is thought to be unjust, for example, then an interpreter will seek to read the Bible in a way that is consistent with that moral truth. That is not, however, a happy conclusion for those wishing to rest morality on revelation, for it means that their understanding of what God has revealed is itself dependent on their prior moral views. Rather than revelation serving as a guide for morality, morality is serving as a guide for how we interpret revelation.

So my general conclusion is that far from providing a short-cut to moral understanding, looking to revelation for guidance often creates more questions and problems. It seems wiser under the circumstances to address complex moral problems like abortion, capital punishment, and affirmative action directly, considering the pros and cons of each side, rather than to seek answers through the much more controversial and difficult route of revelation.

3. THE DIVINE COMMAND THEORY

It may seem, however, that we have still not really gotten to the heart of the matter. Even if religion is not necessary for moral motivation or guidance, it is often claimed, religion is necessary in another more fundamental sense. According to this view, religion is necessary for morality because without God there could BE no right or wrong. God, in other words, provides the foundation or bedrock on which morality is grounded. This idea was expressed by Bishop R. C. Mortimer:

> God made us and all the world. Because of that He has an absolute claim on our obedience...
> From [this] it follows that a thing is not right simply because we think it is. It is right because God commands it.[1]

What Bishop Mortimer has in mind can be seen by comparing moral rules with legal ones. Legal statutes, we know, are created by legislatures; if the state assembly of New York had not passed a law limiting the speed people can travel, then there would be no such legal obligation. Without the statutory enactments, such a law simply would not exist. Mortimer's view, the *divine command theory,* would mean that God has the same sort of relation to moral law as the legislature has to statutes it enacts: without God's commands there would be no moral rules, just as without a legislature there would be no statutes.

Defenders of the divine command theory often add to this a further claim, that only by assuming God sits at the foundation of morality can we explain the objective difference between right and wrong. This point was forcefully argued by F. C. Copleston in a 1948 British Broadcasting Corporation radio debate with Bertrand Russell.

Copleston: ... The validity of such an interpretation of man's conduct depends on the recognition of God's existence, obviously. ... Let's take a look at the Commandant of the [Nazi] concentration camp at Belsen. That appears to you as undesirable and evil and to me too. To Adolph Hitler we suppose it appeared as something good and desirable. I suppose you'd have to admit that for Hitler it was good and for you it is evil.

Russell: No, I shouldn't go so far as that. I mean, I think people can make mistakes in that as they can in other things. If you have jaundice you see things yellow that are not yellow. You're making a mistake.

Copleston: Yes, one can make mistakes, but can you make a mistake if it's simply a question of reference to a feeling or emotion? Surely Hitler would be the only possible judge of what appealed to his emotions.

Russell: ... You can say various things about that; among others, that if that sort of thing makes that sort of appeal to Hitler's emotions, then Hitler makes quite a different appeal to my emotions.

Copleston: Granted. But there's no objective criterion outside feeling then for condemning the conduct of the Commandant of Belsen, in your view. ... The human being's idea of the content of the moral law depends certainly to a large extent on education and environment, and a man has to use his reason in assessing the validity of the actual moral ideas of his social group. But the possibility of criticizing the accepted moral code presupposes that there is an objective standard, that there is an ideal moral order, which imposes itself. ... It implies the existence of a real foundation of God.[2]

---

1 R. C. Mortimer, *Christian Ethics* (London: Hutchinson's University Library, 1950), pp. 7–8.

2 This debate was broadcast on the Third Program of the British Broadcasting Corporation in 1948.

Against those who, like Bertrand Russell, seek to ground morality in feelings and attitudes, Copleston argues that there must be a more solid foundation if we are to be able to claim truly that the Nazis were evil. God, according to Copleston, is able to provide the objective basis for the distinction, which we all know to exist, between right and wrong. Without divine commands at the root of human obligations, we would have no real reason for condemning the behavior of anybody, even Nazis. Morality, Copleston thinks, would then be nothing more than an expression of personal feeling.

To begin assessing the divine command theory, let's first consider this last point. Is it really true that only the commands of God can provide an objective basis for moral judgments? Certainly many philosophers have felt that morality rests on its own perfectly sound footing, be it reason, human nature, or natural sentiments. It seems wrong to conclude, automatically, that morality cannot rest on anything but religion. And it is also possible that morality doesn't have any foundation or basis at all, so that its claims should be ignored in favor of whatever serves our own self-interest.

In addition to these problems with Copleston's argument, the divine command theory faces other problems as well. First, we would need to say much more about the relationship between morality and divine commands. Certainly the expressions "is commanded by God" and "is morally required" do not *mean* the same thing. People and even whole societies can use moral concepts without understanding them to make any reference to God. And while it is true that God (or any other moral being for that matter) would tend to want others to do the right thing, this hardly shows that being right and being commanded by God are the same thing. Parents want their children to do the right thing, too, but that doesn't mean parents, or anybody else, can make a thing right just by commanding it!

I think that, in fact, theists should reject the divine command theory. One reason is what it implies. Suppose we were to grant (just for the sake of argument) that the divine command theory is correct, so that actions are right just because they are commanded by God. The same, of course, can be said about those deeds that we believe are wrong. If God hadn't commanded us not to do them, they would not be wrong.

But now notice this consequence of the divine command theory. Since God is all-powerful, and since right is determined solely by His commands, is it not possible that He might change the rules and make what we now think of as wrong into right? It would seem that according to the divine command theory the answer is "yes": it is theoretically possible that tomorrow God would decree that virtues such as kindness and courage have become vices while actions that show cruelty and cowardice will henceforth be the right actions. (Recall the analogy with a legislature and the power it has to change law.) So now rather than it being right for people to help each other out and prevent innocent people from suffering unnecessarily, it would be right (God having changed His mind) to create as much pain among innocent children as we possibly can! To adopt the divine command theory therefore commits its advocate to the seemingly absurd position that even the greatest atrocities might be not only acceptable but morally required if God were to command them.

Plato made a similar point in the dialogue *Euthyphro*. Socrates is asking Euthyphro what it is that makes the virtue of holiness a virtue, just as we have been asking what makes kindness and courage virtues. Euthyphro has suggested that holiness is just whatever all the gods love.

Socrates: Well, then, Euthyphro, what do we say about holiness? Is it not loved by all the gods, according to your definition?
Euthyphro: Yes.

Socrates: Because it is holy, or for some other reason?

Euthyphro: No, because it is holy.

Socrates: Then it is loved by the gods because it is holy: it is not holy because it is loved by them?

Euthyphro: It seems so.

Socrates: . . . Then holiness is not what is pleasing to the gods, and what is pleasing to the gods is not holy as you say, Euthyphro. They are different things.

Euthyphro: And why, Socrates?

Socrates: Because we are agreed that the gods love holiness because it is holy: and that it is not holy because they love it.[3]

This raises an interesting question. Why, having claimed at first that virtues are merely what is loved (or commanded) by the gods, would Euthyphro contradict this and agree that the gods love holiness *because* it's holy, rather than the reverse? One likely possibility is that Euthyphro believes that whenever the gods love something, they do so with good reason, not without justification and arbitrarily. To deny this and say that it is merely the gods' love that makes holiness a virtue would mean that the gods have no basis for their attitudes, that they are arbitrary in what they love. Yet—and this is the crucial point—it's far from clear that a religious person would want to say that God is arbitrary in that way. If we say that it is simply God's loving something that makes it right, then what sense would it make to say God wants us to do right? All that could mean, it seems, is that God wants us to do what He wants us to do; He would have no reason for wanting it. Similarly, "God is good" would mean little more than "God does what He pleases." The divine command theory therefore leads us to the results that God is morally arbitrary, and that His wishing us to do good or even God's being just mean nothing more than that God does what He does and wants whatever He wants. Religious people who

reject that consequence would also, I am suggesting, have reason to reject the divine command theory itself, seeking a different understanding of morality.

This now raises another problem, however. If God approves kindness because it is a virtue and hates the Nazis because they were evil, then it seems that God discovers morality rather than inventing it. So haven't we then identified a limitation on God's power, since He now, being a good God, must love kindness and command us not to be cruel? Without the divine command theory, in other words, what is left of God's omnipotence?

But why, we may ask, is such a limitation on God unacceptable? It is not at all clear that God really can do anything at all. Can God, for example, destroy Himself? Or make a rock so heavy that He cannot lift it? Or create a universe which was never created by Him? Many have thought that God cannot do these things, but also that His inability to do them does not constitute a serious limitation on His power since these are things that cannot be done at all: to do them would violate the laws of logic. Christianity's most influential theologian, Thomas Aquinas, wrote in this regard that "whatever implies contradiction does not come within the scope of divine omnipotence, because it cannot have the aspect of possibility. Hence it is more appropriate to say that such things cannot be done than that God cannot do them."[4]

How, then, ought we to understand God's relationship to morality if we reject the divine command theory? Can religious people consistently maintain their faith in God the Creator and yet deny that what is right is right because He commands it? I think the answer to this is "yes." Making cruelty good is not like making a universe that wasn't made, of course. It's a moral limit on God rather than a logical one. But why suppose that God's limits are only logical?

---

3 Plato, *Euthyphro*, trans. H. N. Fowler (Cambridge, MA: Harvard University Press, 1947).

4 Thomas Aquinas, *Summa Theologica*, Part I, Q. 25, Art. 3.

One final point about this. Even if we agree that God loves justice or kindness because of their nature, not arbitrarily, there still remains a sense in which God could change morality even having rejected the divine command theory. That's because if we assume, plausibly, I think, that morality depends in part on how we reason, what we desire and need, and the circumstances in which we find ourselves, then morality will still be under God's control since God could have constructed us or our environment very differently. Suppose, for instance, that he created us so that we couldn't be hurt by others or didn't care about freedom. Or perhaps our natural environment were created differently, so that all we have to do is ask and anything we want is given to us. If God had created either nature or us that way, then it seems likely our morality might also be different in important ways from the one we now think correct. In that sense, then, morality depends on God whether or not one supports the divine command theory.

4. "MORALITY IS SOCIAL"

I have argued here that religion is not necessary in providing moral motivation or guidance, and that the religious person should not subscribe to the divine command theory's claim that God is necessary for there to be morality. In this last section, I want first to look briefly at how religion and morality sometimes *do* influence each other. Then I will consider briefly the important ways in which morality might correctly be thought to be "social."

Nothing I have said so far means that morality and religion are independent of each other. But in what ways are they related, assuming I am correct in claiming morality does not *depend* on religion? First, of course, we should note the historical influence religions have had on the development of morality as well as on politics and law. Many of the important leaders of the abolitionist and civil rights movements were religious

leaders, as are many current members of the pro-life movement. The relationship is not, however, one-sided: morality has also influenced religion, as the current debate within the Catholic [C]hurch over the role of women, abortion, and other social issues shows. In reality, then, it seems clear that the practices of morality and religion have historically each exerted an influence on the other.

But just as the two have shaped each other historically, so, too, do they interact at the personal level. I have already suggested how people's understanding of revelation, for instance, is often shaped by morality as they seek the best interpretations of revealed texts. Whether trying to understand a work of art, a legal statute, or a religious text, interpreters regularly seek to understand them in the best light—to make them as good as they can be, which requires that they bring moral judgment to the task of religious interpretation and understanding.

The relationship can go the other direction as well, however, as people's moral views are shaped by their religious training and their current religious beliefs. These relationships are often complex, hidden even from ourselves, but it does seem clear that our views on important moral issues, from sexual morality and war to welfare and capital punishment, are often influenced by our religious outlook. So not only are religious and moral practices and understandings historically linked, but for many religious people the relationship extends to the personal level—to their understanding of moral obligations as well as their sense of who they are and their vision of who they wish to be.

Morality, then, is influenced by religion (as is religion by morality), but morality's social character extends deeper even than that, I want to argue. First, of course, the existence of morality assumes that we possess a socially acquired language within which we think about our choices and which alternatives we ought to follow. Second, morality is social in that it governs relationships among people, defining our responsibilities to others and theirs to us. Morality provides the standards we rely on in gauging our interactions with family, lovers, friends, fellow citizens, and even strangers. Third, morality is social in the sense that we are, in fact, subject to criticism by others for our actions. We discuss with others what we should do, and often hear from them concerning whether our decisions were acceptable. Blame and praise are a central feature of morality.

While not disputing any of this, John Dewey has suggested another important sense in which morality is social. Consider the following comments about the origins of morality and conscience taken from an article he titled "Morality Is Social":

> In language and imagination we rehearse the responses of others just as we dramatically enact other consequences. We foreknow how others will act, and the foreknowledge is the beginning of judgment passed on action. We know *with* them; there is conscience. An assembly is formed within our breast which discusses and appraises proposed and performed acts. The community without becomes a forum and tribunal within, a judgment-seat of charges, assessments and exculpations. Our thoughts of our own actions are saturated with the ideas that others entertain about them. . . . Explicit recognition of this fact is a prerequisite of improvement in moral education. . . . Reflection is morally indispensable.[5]

So in addition to the three points I already mentioned, Dewey also wants to make another, and in some ways more important suggestion about morality's social character. This fourth idea depends on appreciating the fact that to think from the moral point of view, as opposed to the selfish one, for instance, demands that we reject our private, subjective perspective in favor of the perspective of others, envisioning how they might respond to various choices we might make. Far from being private and unrelated to others, moral conscience is in that sense "public." To consider a decision from the moral perspective requires envisioning what Dewey terms an "assembly of others" that is "formed within our breast." In that way, conscience cannot even be distinguished from the social: conscience invariably brings with it, or constitutes, the perspective of the other. "Is this right?" and "What would this look like were I to have to defend it to others?" are not separate questions.[6]

It is important not to confuse Dewey's point here, however. He is *not* saying that what is right is finally to be determined by the reactions of actually existing other people, or even by the reaction of society as a whole. To the contrary, what is right, and accords with the true dictates of conscience, might in fact not meet the approval of others. Conscience is "social" not in the sense that morality is determined by surveying what others in society think. Understood as the voice of an "assembly" of others within each of us, conscience cannot be reduced to the expected reaction of any existing individual or group. But what then does Dewey mean? The answer is that the assembly Dewey is describing is not an actual one but instead an hypothetical, "ideal" one; the actual "community without" is transformed into a "forum and tribunal within, a judgment seat of charges, assessments and exculpations." Only through the powers of imagination can we exercise our moral powers, envisioning with the powers of judgment what conscience requires.

Morality is therefore *inherently* social, in a variety of ways. It depends on socially learned language, is learned from interactions with others,

---

5 John Dewey, "Morality Is Social," in *The Moral Writings of John Dewey*, rev. ed., ed. James Gouinlock (Amherst, NY: Prometheus Books, 1994), pp. 182–4.

6 Obligations to animals raise an interesting problem for this conception of morality. Is it wrong to torture animals only because other *people* could be expected to disapprove? Or is it that the animal itself would disapprove? Or, perhaps, that duties to animals rest on sympathy and compassion while human moral relations are more like Dewey describes, resting on morality's inherently social nature and on the dictates of conscience viewed as an assembly of others?

and governs our interactions with others in society. But it also demands, as Dewey put it, that we know "with" others, envisioning for ourselves what their points of view would require along with our own. Conscience demands we occupy the positions of others.

Viewed in this light, God might play a role in moral reflection and conscience. That is because it is unlikely a religious person would wish to exclude God from the "forum and tribunal" that constitutes conscience. Rather, for the religious person conscience would almost certainly include the imagined reaction of God along with the reactions of others who might be affected by the action. So it seems that for a religious person morality and God's will cannot be separated, though the connection between them is not as envisioned by the divine command theory.

This leads to my final point, about moral education. If Dewey is correct, then it seems clear there is an important sense in which morality not only can be taught but must be. Besides early moral training, moral thinking depends on our ability to imagine others' reactions and to imaginatively put ourselves into their shoes. "What would somebody (including, perhaps, God) think if this got out?" expresses more than a concern with being embarrassed or punished; it is also the voice of conscience and indeed of morality itself. But that would mean, thinking of education, that listening to others, reading about what others think and do, and reflecting within ourselves about our actions and whether we could defend them to others are part of the practice of morality itself. Morality cannot exist without the broader, social perspective introduced by others, and this social nature ties it, in that way, with education and with public discussion, both actual and imagined. "Private" moral reflection taking place independently of the social world would be no moral reflection at all; and moral education is not only possible, but essential.

Review Questions

1. According to Arthur, how are morality and religion different?
2. Why isn't religion necessary for moral motivation?
3. Why isn't religion necessary as a source of moral knowledge?
4. What is the divine command theory? Why does Arthur reject this theory?
5. According to Arthur, how are morality and religion connected?
6. Dewey says that morality is social. What does this mean, according to Arthur?

Discussion Questions

1. Has Arthur refuted the divine command theory? If not, how can it be defended?
2. If morality is social, as Dewey says, then how can we have any obligations to nonhuman animals? (Arthur mentions this problem and some possible solutions to it in footnote 6.)
3. What does Dewey mean by moral education? Does a college ethics class count as moral education?

Master- and Slave-Morality

FRIEDRICH NIETZSCHE

Friedrich Nietzsche (1844–1900) was a German philosopher and poet who is often viewed as a source of modern Existentialism and Deconstructionism. Some of his most famous works are *The Birth of Tragedy* (1872), *The Gay Science* (1882), and *Thus Spake Zarathustra* (1891). Our reading is taken from *Beyond Good and Evil* (1886).

Nietzsche argues that a healthy society should allow superior individuals to exercise their "will to power," their drive toward domination and exploitation of the inferior. The superior person follows a "master-morality" that emphasizes power, strength, egoism, and freedom, as distinguished from a "slave-morality" that calls for weakness, submission, sympathy, and love.

257

EVERY ELEVATION of the type "man," has hitherto been the work of an aristocratic society—and so will it always be—a society believing in a long scale of gradations of rank and differences of worth among human beings, and requiring slavery in some form or other. Without the *pathos of distance,* such as grows out of the incarnated difference of classes, out of the constant outlooking and downlooking of the ruling caste on subordinates and instruments, and out of their equally constant practice of obeying and commanding, of keeping down and keeping at a distance—that other more mysterious pathos could never have arisen, the longing for an ever new widening of distance within the soul itself, the formation of ever higher, rarer, further, more extended, more comprehensive states, in short, just the elevation of the type "man," the continued "self-surmounting of man," to use a moral formula in a supermoral sense. To be sure, one must not resign oneself to any humanitarian illusions about the history of the origin of an aristocratic society (that is to say, of the preliminary condition for the elevation of the type "man"): the truth is hard. Let us acknowledge unprejudicedly how every higher civilisation hitherto has *originated!* Men with a still natural nature, barbarians in every terrible sense of the word, men of prey, still in possession of unbroken strength of will and desire for power, threw themselves upon weaker, more moral, more peaceful races (perhaps trading or cattle-rearing communities), or upon old mellow civilisations in which the final vital force was flickering out in brilliant fireworks of wit and depravity. At the commencement, the noble caste was always the barbarian caste: their superiority did not consist first of all in their physical, but in their psychical power—they were more *complete* men (which at every point also implies the same as "more complete beasts").

Source: Friedrich Nietzsche, *Beyond Good and Evil,* translated by Helen Zimmern, pp. 223–232 (Amherst, NY: Prometheus Books). Copyright 1989. Reprinted by permission of the publisher.

258

Corruption—as the indication that anarchy threatens to break out among the instincts, and that the foundation of the emotions, called "life," is convulsed—is something radically different according to the organisation in which it manifests itself. When, for instance, an aristocracy like that of France at the beginning of the Revolution, flung away its privileges with sublime disgust and sacrificed itself to an excess of its moral sentiments, it was corruption:—it was really only the closing act of the corruption which had existed for centuries, by virtue of which that aristocracy had abdicated step by step its lordly prerogatives and lowered itself to a *function* of royalty (in the end even to its decoration and parade-dress). The essential thing, however, in a good and healthy aristocracy is that it should *not* regard itself as a function either of the kingship or the commonwealth, but as the *significance* and highest justification thereof—that it should therefore accept with a good conscience the sacrifice of a legion of individuals, who, *for its sake,* must be suppressed and reduced to imperfect men, to slaves and instruments. Its fundamental belief must be precisely that society is *not* allowed to exist for its own sake, but only as a foundation and scaffolding, by means of which a select class of beings may be able to elevate themselves to their higher duties, and in general to a higher *existence:* like those sun-seeking climbing plants in Java—they are called *Sipo Matador,*—which encircle an oak so long and so often with their arms, until at last, high above it, but supported by it, they can unfold their tops in the open light, and exhibit their happiness.

259

To refrain mutually from injury, from violence, from exploitation, and put one's will on a par with that of others: this may result in a certain rough sense in good conduct among individuals when the necessary conditions are given (namely, the actual similarity of the individuals in amount of force and degree of worth, and their co-relation within one organisation). As soon, however, as one wished to take this principle more generally, and if possible even as *the fundamental principle of society,* it would immediately disclose what it really is—namely, a Will to the *denial* of life, a principle of dissolution and decay. Here one must think profoundly to the very basis and resist all sentimental weakness: life itself is *essentially* appropriation, injury, conquest of the strange and weak, suppression, severity, obtrusion of peculiar forms, incorporation, and at the least, putting it mildest, exploitation;—but why should one for ever use precisely these words on which for ages a disparaging purpose has been stamped? Even the organisation within which, as was previously supposed, the individuals treat each other as equal—it takes place in every healthy aristocracy—must itself, if it be a living and not a dying organisation, do all that towards other bodies, which the individuals within it refrain from doing to each other: it will have to be the incarnated Will to Power, it will endeavour to grow, to gain ground, attract to itself and acquire ascendency—not owing to any morality or immorality, but because it *lives,* and because life *is* precisely Will to Power. On no point, however, is the ordinary consciousness of Europeans more unwilling to be corrected than on this matter; people now rave everywhere, even under the guise of science, about coming conditions of society in which "the exploiting character" is to be absent:—that sounds to my ears as if they promised to invent a mode of life which should refrain from all organic functions. "Exploitation" does not belong to a depraved, or imperfect and primitive society: it belongs to the *nature* of the living being as a primary organic function; it is a consequence of the intrinsic Will to Power, which is precisely the Will to Life.—Granting that as a theory this is a novelty—as a reality it is the *fundamental fact* of all history: let us be so far honest towards ourselves!

260

In a tour through the many finer and coarser moralities which have hitherto prevailed or still prevail on the earth, I found certain traits recurring regularly together and connected with one another, until finally two primary types revealed themselves to me, and a radical distinction was brought to light. There is *master-morality* and *slave-morality;*—I would at once add, however, that in all higher and mixed civilisations, there are also attempts at the reconciliation of the two moralities; but one finds still oftener the confusion and mutual misunderstanding of them, indeed, sometimes their close juxtaposition—even in the same man, within one soul. The distinctions of moral values have either originated in a ruling caste, pleasantly conscious of being different from the ruled—or among the ruled class, the slaves and dependents of all sorts. In the first case, when it is the rulers who determine the conception "good," it is the exalted, proud disposition which is regarded as the distinguishing feature, and that which determines the order of rank. The noble type of man separates from himself the beings in whom the opposite of this exalted, proud disposition displays itself: he despises them. Let it at once be noted that in this first kind of morality the antithesis "good" and "bad" mean practically the same as "noble" and "despicable";—the antithesis "good" and "*evil*" is of a different origin. The cowardly, the timid, the insignificant, and those thinking merely of narrow utility are despised; moreover, also, the distrustful, with their constrained glances, the self-abasing, the dog-like kind of men who let themselves be abused, the mendicant flatterers, and above all the liars:—it is a fundamental belief of all aristocrats that the common people are untruthful. "We truthful ones"—the nobility in ancient Greece called themselves. It is obvious that everywhere the designations of moral value were at first applied to *men,* and were only derivatively and at a later period applied to *actions;* it is a gross mistake, therefore, when historians of

morals start with questions like, "Why have sympathetic actions been praised?" The noble type of man regards *himself* as a determiner of values; he does not require to be approved of; he passes the judgment: "What is injurious to me is injurious in itself"; he knows that it is he himself only who confers honour on things; he is a *creator of values.* He honours whatever he recognises in himself: such morality is self-glorification. In the foreground there is the feeling of plenitude, of power, which seeks to overflow, the happiness of high tension, the consciousness of a wealth which would fain give and bestow:—the noble man also helps the unfortunate, but not—or scarcely—out of pity, but rather from an impulse generated by the superabundance of power. The noble man honours in himself the powerful one, him also who has power over himself, who knows how to speak and how to keep silence, who takes pleasure in subjecting himself to severity and hardness, and has reverence for all that is severe and hard. "Wotan placed a hard heart in my breast," says an old Scandinavian Saga: it is thus rightly expressed from the soul of a proud Viking. Such a type of man is even proud of *not* being made for sympathy; the hero of the Saga therefore adds warningly: "He who has not a hard heart when young, will never have one." The noble and brave who think thus are the furthest removed from the morality which sees precisely in sympathy, or in acting for the good of others, or in *désintéressement,* the characteristic of the moral; faith in oneself, pride in oneself, a radical enmity and irony towards "selflessness," belong as definitely to noble morality, as do a careless scorn and precaution in presence of sympathy and the "warm heart."—It is the powerful who *know* how to honour, it is their art, their domain for invention. The profound reverence for age and for tradition —all law rests on this double reverence,—the belief and prejudice in favour of ancestors and unfavourable to newcomers, is typical in the morality of the powerful; and if, reversely, men of "modern ideas" believe almost instinctively in "progress" and the "future," and are more and more lacking in respect for old age, the ignoble origin of these "ideas" has complacently betrayed itself thereby. A morality of the ruling class, however, is more especially foreign and irritating to present-day taste in the sternness of its principle that one has duties only to one's equals; that one may act towards beings of a lower rank, towards all that is foreign, just as seems good to one, or "as the heart desires," and in any case "beyond good and evil": it is here that sympathy and similar sentiments can have a place. The ability and obligation to exercise prolonged gratitude and prolonged revenge—both only within the circle of equals,—artfulness in retaliation, *raffinement* of the idea in friendship, a certain necessity to have enemies (as outlets for the emotions of envy, quarrelsomeness, arrogance—in fact, in order to be a good *friend*): all these are typical characteristics of the noble morality, which, as has been pointed out, is not the morality of "modern ideas," and is therefore at present difficult to realise, and also to unearth and disclose.—It is otherwise with the second type of morality, *slave-morality*. Supposing that the abused, the oppressed, the suffering, the unemancipated, the weary, and those uncertain of themselves, should moralise, what will be the common element in their moral estimates? Probably a pessimistic suspicion with regard to the entire situation of man will find expression, perhaps a condemnation of man, together with his situation. The slave has an unfavourable eye for the virtues of the powerful; he has a scepticism and distrust, a *refinement* of distrust of everything "good" that is there honoured—he would fain persuade himself that the very happiness there is not genuine. On the other hand, *those* qualities which serve to alleviate the existence of sufferers are brought into prominence and flooded with light; it is here that sympathy, the kind, helping hand, the warm heart, patience, diligence, humility, and friendliness attain to honour; for here these are the most useful qualities, and almost the only means of supporting the burden of existence. Slave-morality is essentially the morality of utility. Here is the seat of the origin of the famous antithesis "good" and

"*evil*":—power and dangerousness are assumed to reside in the evil, a certain dreadfulness, subtlety, and strength, which do not admit of being despised. According to slave-morality, therefore, the "evil" man arouses fear; according to master-morality, it is precisely the "good" man who arouses fear and seeks to arouse it, while the bad man is regarded as the despicable being. The contrast attains its maximum when, in accordance with the logical consequences of slave-morality, a shade of depreciation—it may be slight and well-intentioned—at last attaches itself even to the "good" man of this morality; because, according to the servile mode of thought, the good man must in any case be the *safe* man: he is good-natured, easily deceived, perhaps a little stupid, *un bonhomme*. Everywhere that slave-morality gains the ascendancy, language shows a tendency to approximate the significations of the words "good" and "stupid."—A last fundamental difference: the desire for *freedom*, the instinct for happiness and the refinements of the feeling of liberty belong as necessarily to slave-morals and morality, as artifice and enthusiasm in reverence and devotion are the regular symptoms of an aristocratic mode of thinking and estimating. —Hence we can understand without further detail why love *as a passion*—it is our European speciality—must absolutely be of noble origin; as is well known, its invention is due to the Provençal poet-cavaliers, those brilliant ingenious men of the "*gai saber*," to whom Europe owes so much, and almost owes itself.

265

At the risk of displeasing innocent ears, I submit that egoism belongs to the essence of a noble soul, I mean the unalterable belief that to a being such as "we," other beings must naturally be in subjection, and have to sacrifice themselves. The noble soul accepts the fact of his egoism without question, and also without consciousness of harshness, constraint, or arbitrariness therein, but rather as something that may have its basis in the primary law of things:—if he sought a designation for it he would say: "It is justice itself." He acknowledges under certain circumstances, which made him hesitate at first, that there are other equally privileged ones; as soon as he has settled this question of rank, he moves among those equals and equally privileged ones with the same assurance, as regards modesty and delicate respect, which he enjoys in intercourse with himself—in accordance with an innate heavenly mechanism which all the stars understand. It is an *additional* instance of his egoism, this artfulness and self-limitation in intercourse with his equals—every star is a similar egoist; he honours *himself* in them, and in the rights which he concedes to them, he has no doubt that the exchange of honours and rights, as the *essence* of all intercourse, belongs also to the natural condition of things. The noble soul gives as he takes, prompted by the passionate and sensitive instinct of requital, which is at the root of his nature. The notion of "favour" has, *inter pares,* neither significance nor good repute; there may be a sublime way of letting gifts as it were light upon one from above, and of drinking them thirstily like dew-drops; but for those arts and displays the noble soul has no aptitude. His egoism hinders him here: in general, he looks "aloft" unwillingly—he looks either *forward,* horizontally and deliberately, or downwards—*he knows that he is on a height.*

Review Questions

1. How does Nietzsche characterize a good and healthy society?
2. What is Nietzsche's view of injury, violence, and exploitation?
3 Distinguish between master-morality and slave-morality.
4. Explain the Will to Power.

Discussion Questions

1. Some people view Nietzsche's writings as harmful and even dangerous. For example, some have charged Nietzsche with inspiring Nazism. Are these charges justified or not? Why or why not?
2. What does it mean to be "a creator of values"?

Trying Out One's New Sword

MARY MIDGLEY

Mary Midgley taught philosophy at the University of Newcastle-upon-Tyne in England for twenty years. She is now retired. She is the author of numerous books, including *Animals and Why They Matter* (1984), *Beast and Man: The Roots of Human Nature* (1995), *Can't We Make Moral Judgements?* (1993), and *Heart and Mind: The Varieties of Moral Experience* (1981), from which our reading is taken.

Source: Mary Midgley, "Trying Out One's New Sword" from *Heart and Mind* (St. Martin's Press, 1981), pp. 69–75. Reprinted with permission from St. Martin's Press, Inc.

Midgley attacks moral isolationism, the view of anthropologists and others that we cannot criticize cultures that we do not understand—for example, the Japanese culture that has the practice of trying out a new samurai sword on a chance wayfarer. She argues that moral isolationism is essentially a doctrine of immoralism because it forbids any moral reasoning. Furthermore, it falsely assumes that cultures are separate and unmixed, whereas, most cultures are in fact formed out of many influences.

ALL OF US ARE, more or less, in trouble today about trying to understand cultures strange to us. We hear constantly of alien customs. We see changes in our lifetime which would have astonished our parents. I want to discuss here one very short way of dealing with this difficulty, a drastic way which many people now theoretically favour. It consists in simply denying that we can ever understand any culture except our own well enough to make judgements about it. Those who recommend this hold that the world is sharply divided into separate societies, sealed units, each with its own system of thought. They feel that the respect and tolerance due from one system to another forbids us ever to take up a critical position to any other culture. Moral judgement, they suggest, is a kind of coinage valid only in its country of origin.

I shall call this position 'moral isolationism'. I shall suggest that it is certainly not forced upon us, and indeed that it makes no sense at all. People usually take it up because they think it is a respectful attitude to other cultures. In fact, however, it is not respectful. Nobody can respect what is entirely unintelligible to them. To respect someone, we have to know enough about him to make a *favourable* judgement, however general and tentative. And we do understand people in other cultures to this extent. Otherwise a great mass of our most valuable thinking would be paralysed.

To show this, I shall take a remote example, because we shall probably find it easier to think calmly about it than we should with a contemporary one, such as female circumcision in Africa or the Chinese Cultural Revolution. The

principles involved will still be the same. My example is this. There is, it seems, a verb in classical Japanese which means 'to try out one's new sword on a chance wayfarer'. (The word is *tsuji-giri*, literally 'crossroads-cut'.) A samurai sword had to be tried out because, if it was to work properly, it had to slice through someone at a single blow, from the shoulder to the opposite flank. Otherwise, the warrior bungled his stroke. This could injure his honour, offend his ancestors, and even let down his emperor. So tests were needed, and wayfarers had to be expended. Any wayfarer would do—provided, of course, that he was not another Samurai. Scientists will recognize a familiar problem about the rights of experimental subjects.

Now when we hear of a custom like this, we may well reflect that we simply do not understand it; and therefore are not qualified to criticize it at all, because we are not members of that culture. But we are not members of any other culture either, except our own. So we extend the principle to cover all extraneous cultures, and we seem therefore to be moral isolationists. But this is, as we shall see, an impossible position. Let us ask what it would involve.

We must ask first: Does the isolating barrier work both ways? Are people in other cultures equally unable to criticize *us*? This question struck me sharply when I read a remark in *The Guardian* by an anthropologist about a South American Indian who had been taken into a Brazilian town for an operation, which saved his life. When he came back to his village, he made several highly critical remarks about the white Brazilians' way of life. They may very well have been justified. But the interesting point was that the anthropologist called these remarks 'a damning indictment of Western civilization'. Now the Indian had been in that town about two weeks. Was he in a position to deliver a damning indictment? Would we ourselves be qualified to deliver such an indictment on the Samurai, provided we could spend two weeks in ancient Japan? What do we really think about this?

My own impression is that we believe that outsiders can, in principle, deliver perfectly good indictments—only, it usually takes more than two weeks to make them damning. Understanding has degrees. It is not a slapdash yes-or-no matter. Intelligent outsiders can progress in it, and in some ways will be at an advantage over the locals. But if this is so, it must clearly apply to ourselves as much as anybody else.

Our next question is this: Does the isolating barrier between cultures block praise as well as blame? If I want to say that the Samurai culture has many virtues, or to praise the South American Indians, am I prevented from doing *that* by my outside status? Now, we certainly do need to praise other societies in this way. But it is hardly possible that we could praise them effectively if we could not, in principle, criticize them. Our praise would be worthless if it rested on no definite grounds, if it did not flow from some understanding. Certainly we may need to praise things which we do not *fully* understand. We say 'there's something very good here, but I can't quite make out what it is yet'. This happens when we want to learn from strangers. And we can learn from strangers. But to do this we have to distinguish between those strangers who are worth learning from and those who are not. Can we then judge which is which?

This brings us to our third question: What is involved in judging? Now plainly there is no question here of sitting on a bench in a red robe and sentencing people. Judging simply means forming an opinion, and expressing it if it is called for. Is there anything wrong about this? Naturally, we ought to avoid forming—and ex-

pressing—*crude* opinions, like that of a simple-minded missionary, who might dismiss the whole Samurai culture as entirely bad, because non-Christian. But this is a different objection. The trouble with crude opinions is that they are crude, whoever forms them, not that they are formed by the wrong people. Anthropologists, after all, are outsiders quite as much as missionaries. Moral isolationism forbids us to form *any* opinions on these matters. Its ground for doing so is that we don't understand them. But there is much that we don't understand in our own culture too. This brings us to our last question: If we can't judge other cultures, can we really judge our own? Our efforts to do so will be much damaged if we are really deprived of our opinions about other societies, because these provide the range of comparison, the spectrum of alternatives against which we set what we want to understand. We would have to stop using the mirror which anthropology so helpfully holds up to us.

In short, moral isolationism would lay down a general ban on moral reasoning. Essentially, this is the programme of immoralism, and it carries a distressing logical difficulty. Immoralists like Nietzsche are actually just a rather specialized sect of moralists. They can no more afford to put moralizing out of business than smugglers can afford to abolish customs regulations. The power of moral judgement is, in fact, not a luxury, not a perverse indulgence of the self-righteous. It is a necessity. When we judge something to be bad or good, better or worse than something else, we are taking it as an example to aim at or avoid. Without opinions of this sort, we would have no framework of comparison for our own policy, no chance of profiting by other people's insights or mistakes. In this vacuum, we could form no judgements on our own actions.

Now it would be odd if Homo sapiens had really got himself into a position as bad as this—a position where his main evolutionary asset, his brain, was so little use to him. None of us is going to accept this sceptical diagnosis. We cannot do so, because our involvement in moral isolationism does not flow from apathy, but from a rather acute concern about human hypocrisy and other forms of wickedness. But we polarize that concern around a few selected moral truths. We are rightly angry with those who despise, oppress or steamroll other cultures. We think that doing these things is actually *wrong*. But this is itself a moral judgement. We could not condemn oppression and insolence if we thought that all our condemnations were just a trivial local quirk of our own culture. We could still less do it if we tried to stop judging altogether.

Real moral scepticism, in fact, could lead only to inaction, to our losing all interest in moral questions, most of all in those which concern other societies. When we discuss these things, it becomes instantly clear how far we are from doing this. Suppose, for instance, that I criticize the bisecting Samurai, that I say his behaviour is brutal. What will usually happen next is that someone will protest, will say that I have no right to make criticisms like that of another culture. But it is most unlikely that he will use this move to end the discussion of the subject. Instead, he will justify the Samurai. He will try to fill in the background, to make me understand the custom, by explaining the exalted ideals of discipline and devotion which produced it. He will probably talk of the lower value which the ancient Japanese placed on individual life generally. He may well suggest that this is a healthier attitude than our own obsession with security. He may add, too, that the wayfarers did not seriously mind being bisected, that in principle they accepted the whole arrangement.

Now an objector who talks like this is implying that it *is* possible to understand alien customs. That is just what he is trying to make me do. And he implies, too, that if I do succeed in understanding them, I shall do something better than giving up judging them. He expects me to change my present judgement to a truer one —namely, one that is favourable. And the standards I must use to do this cannot just be Samurai standards. They have to be ones current in my own culture. Ideals like discipline and devotion will not move anybody unless he himself accepts them. As it happens, neither discipline nor devotion is very popular in the West at present. Anyone who appeals to them may well have to do some more arguing to make *them* acceptable, before he can use them to explain the Samurai. But if he does succeed here, he will have persuaded us, not just that there was something to be said for them in ancient Japan, but that there would be here as well.

Isolating barriers simply cannot arise here. If we accept something as a serious moral truth about one culture, we can't refuse to apply it— in however different an outward form—to other cultures as well, wherever circumstance admit it. If we refuse to do this, we just are not taking the other culture seriously. This becomes clear if we look at the last argument used by my objector— that of justification by consent of the victim. It is suggested that sudden bisection is quite in order, *provided* that it takes place between consenting adults. I cannot now discuss how conclusive this justification is. What I am pointing out is simply that it can only work if we believe that *consent* can make such a transaction respectable—and this is a thoroughly modern and Western idea. It would probably never occur to a Samurai; if it did, it would surprise him very much. It is *our* standard. In applying it, too, we are likely to make another typically Western demand. We shall ask for good factual evidence that the wayfarers actually do have this rather surprising taste—that they are really willing to be bisected. In applying Western standards in this way, we are not being confused or irrelevant. We are asking the questions which arise *from where we stand,* questions which we can see the sense of. We do this because asking questions which you can't see the sense of is humbug. Certainly we can extend our questioning by imaginative effort. We can come to understand other societies better. By doing so, we may make their questions our own, or we may see that they are really forms of the questions which we are asking already. This is not impossible. It is just very hard work. The obstacles which often prevent it are simply those of ordinary ignorance, laziness and prejudice.

If there were really an isolating barrier, of course, our own culture could never have been formed. It is no sealed box, but a fertile jungle of different influences—Greek, Jewish, Roman, Norse, Celtic and so forth, into which further influences are still pouring—American, Indian, Japanese, Jamaican, you name it. The moral isolationist's picture of separate, unmixable cultures is quite unreal. People who talk about British history usually stress the value of this fertilizing mix, no doubt rightly. But this is not just an odd fact about Britain. Except for the very smallest and most remote, all cultures are formed out of many streams. All have the problem of digesting and assimilating things which, at the start, they do not understand. All have the choice of learning something from this challenge, or alternatively, of refusing to learn, and fighting it mindlessly instead.

This universal predicament has been obscured by the fact that anthropologists used to concentrate largely on very small and remote cultures, which did not seem to have this problem. These tiny societies, which had often forgotten their own history, made neat, self-contained subjects for study. No doubt it was valuable to emphasize their remoteness, their extreme strangeness, their independence of our cultural tradition. This emphasis was, I think, the root of moral isolationism. But, as the tribal studies themselves showed, even there the anthropologists were able to interpret what they saw and make judgements—often favourable—about the tribesmen. And the tribesmen, too, were quite equal to making judgements about the anthropologists—and about the tourists and Coca-Cola salesmen who followed them. Both sets of judgements, no doubt, were somewhat hasty, both have been refined in the light of further experience. A similar transaction between us and the Samurai might take even longer. But that is no reason at all for deeming it impossible. Morally as well as physically, there is only one world, and we all have to live in it.

Review Questions

1. What is "moral isolationism"?
2. Explain the Japanese custom of *tsujigiri*. What questions does Midgley ask about this custom?
3. What is wrong with moral isolationism, according to Midgley?
4. What does Midgley think is the basis for criticizing other cultures?

Discussion Questions

1. Midgley says that Nietzsche is an immoralist. Is that an accurate and fair assessment of Nietzsche? Why or why not?
2. Do you agree with Midgley's claim that the idea of separate and unmixed cultures is unreal? Explain your answer.

Utilitarianism

JOHN STUART MILL
Consequentialist.

John Stuart Mill (1806–1873) was one of the most important and influential British philosophers. His most important works in ethics are *On Liberty* (1859) and *Utilitarianism* (1861), from which the reading is taken.

Mill sets forth the basic principles of Utilitarianism, including the Principle of Utility (or the Greatest Happiness Principle) and the hedonistic principle that happiness is pleasure. He explains the theory by replying to various objections, and concludes with an attempt to prove the Principle of Utility.

THE CREED which accepts as the foundation of morals, Utility, or the Greatest Happiness Principle, holds that actions are right in proportion as they tend to promote happiness, wrong as they tend to produce the reverse of happiness. By happiness is intended pleasure, and the absence of pain; by unhappiness, pain, and the privation of pleasure. To give a clear view of the moral standard set up by the theory, much more requires to be said; in particular, what things it includes in the ideas of pain and pleasure; and to what extent this is left an open question. But these supplementary explanations do not affect the theory of life on which this theory of morality is grounded—namely, that pleasure, and freedom from pain, are the only things desirable as ends; and that all desirable things (which are as numerous in the utilitarian as in any other scheme) are desirable either for the pleasure inherent in themselves, or as means to the promotion of pleasure and the prevention of pain.

Now, such a theory of life excites in many minds, and among them in some of the most estimable in feeling and purpose, inveterate dislike. To suppose that life has (as they express it) no higher end than pleasure—no better and nobler object of desire and pursuit—they designate as utterly mean and groveling; as a doctrine worthy only of swine, to whom the followers of Epicurus were, at a very early period, contemptuously likened; and modern holders of the doctrine are occasionally made the subject of equally polite comparison by its German, French, and English assailants.

When thus attacked, the Epicureans have always answered, that it is not they, but their accusers, who represent human nature in a degrading light; since the accusation supposes human beings to be capable of no pleasures except those of which swine are capable. If this supposition were true, the charge could not be gainsaid, but would then be no longer an imputation; for if the sources of pleasure were precisely the same to human beings and to swine, the rule of life which is good enough for the one would be good enough for the other. The comparison of the Epicurean life to that of beasts is felt as degrading, precisely because a beast's pleasures do not satisfy a human being's conceptions of happiness. Human beings have faculties more

Source: John Stuart Mill, from *Utilitarianism* (1861), Chapters 12 and 17.

elevated than the animal appetites, and when once made conscious of them, do not regard anything as happiness which does not include their gratification. I do not, indeed, consider the Epicureans to have been by any means faultless in drawing out their scheme of consequences from the utilitarian principle. To do this in any sufficient manner, many Stoic, as well as Christian elements require to be included. But there is no known Epicurean theory of life which does not assign to the pleasures of the intellect, of the feelings and imagination, and of the moral sentiments, a much higher value as pleasures than to those of mere sensation. It must be admitted, however, that utilitarian writers in general have placed the superiority of mental over bodily pleasures chiefly in the greater permanency, safety, uncostliness, etc., of the former—that is, in their circumstantial advantages rather than in their intrinsic nature. And on all these points utilitarians have fully proved their case; but they might have taken the other and, as it may be called, higher ground, with entire consistency. It is quite compatible with the principle of utility to recognize the fact, that some *kinds* of pleasure are more desirable and more valuable than others. It would be absurd that while, in estimating all other things, quality is considered as well as quantity, the estimation of pleasures should be supposed to depend on quantity alone.

If I am asked, what I mean by difference of quality in pleasures, or what makes one pleasure more valuable than another, merely as a pleasure, except its being greater in amount, there is but one possible answer. Of two pleasures, if there be one to which all or almost all who have experience of both give a decided preference, irrespective of any feeling of moral obligation to prefer it, that is the more desirable pleasure. If one of the two is, by those who are competently acquainted with both, placed so far above the other that they prefer it, even though knowing it to be attended with a greater amount of discontent, and would not resign it for any quantity of the other pleasure which their nature is capable of, we are justified in ascribing to the preferred enjoyment a superiority in quality, so far outweighing quantity as to render it, in comparison, of small account.

Now it is an unquestionable fact that those who are equally acquainted with, and equally capable of appreciating and enjoying, both, do give a most marked preference to the manner of existence which employs their higher faculties. Few human creatures would consent to be changed into any of the lower animals, for a promise of the fullest allowance of a beast's pleasures; no intelligent human being would consent to be a fool, no instructed person would be an ignoramus, no person of feeling and conscience would be selfish and base, even though they should be persuaded that the fool, the dunce, or the rascal is better satisfied with his lot than they are with theirs. They would not resign what they possess more than he for the most complete satisfaction of all the desires which they have in common with him. If they ever fancy they would, it is only in cases of unhappiness so extreme, that to escape from it they would exchange their lot for almost any other, however undesirable in their own eyes. A being of higher faculties requires more to make him happy, is capable probably of more acute suffering, and certainly accessible to it at more points, than one of an inferior type; but in spite of these liabilities, he can never really wish to sink into what he feels to be a lower grade of existence. We may give what explanation we please of this unwillingness; we may attribute it to pride, a name which is given indiscriminately to some of the most and to some of the least estimable feelings of which mankind are capable; we may refer it to the love of liberty and personal independence, an appeal to which was with the Stoics one of the most effective means for the inculcation of it; to the love of power, or to the love of excitement, both of which do really enter into and contribute to it: but its most appropriate appellation is a sense of dignity, which all human beings possess in one form or other, and in some, though by no means in exact, proportion to their higher faculties, and which is so essential a part of the happiness of those in whom it is strong, that nothing which conflicts with it could be, otherwise than momentarily, an object of desire to them. Whoever supposes that this preference takes place at a sacrifice of happiness—that the superior being, in anything like equal circumstances, is not happier than the inferior—confounds the two very different ideas, of happiness, and content. It is indisputable that the being whose capacities of enjoyment are low, has the greatest chance of having them fully satisfied; and a highly endowed being will always feel that any happiness which he can look for, as the world is constituted, is imperfect. But he can learn to bear its imperfections, if they are at all bearable; and they will not make him envy the being who is indeed unconscious of the imperfections, but only because he feels not at all the good which those imperfections qualify. It is better to be a human being dissatisfied than a pig satisfied; better to be Socrates dissatisfied than a fool satisfied. And if the fool, or the pig, are of a different opinion, it is because they only know their own side of the question. The other party to the comparison knows both sides.

It may be objected, that many who are capable of the higher pleasures, occasionally, under the influence of temptation, postpone them to the lower. But this is quite compatible with a full appreciation of the intrinsic superiority of the higher. Men often, from infirmity of character, make their election for the nearer good, though they know it to be the less valuable; and this no less when the choice is between two bodily pleasures, than when it is between bodily and mental. They pursue sensual indulgence to the injury of health, though perfectly aware that health is the greater good. It may be further objected, that many who begin with youthful enthusiasm for everything noble, as they advance in years sink into indolence and selfishness. But I do not believe that those who undergo this very common change, voluntarily choose the lower description of pleasures in preference to the higher. I believe that before they devote themselves exclusively to the one, they have already become incapable of the other. Capacity for the nobler feelings is in most natures a very tender plant, easily killed, not only by hostile influences, but by mere want of sustenance; and in the majority of young persons it speedily dies away if the occupations to which their position in life has devoted them, and the society into which it has thrown them, are not favourable to keeping that higher capacity in exercise. Men lose their high aspirations as they lose their intellectual tastes, because they have not time or opportunity for indulging them; and they addict themselves to inferior pleasures, not because they deliberately prefer them, but because they are either the only ones to which they have access or the only ones which they are any longer capable of enjoying. It may be questioned whether any one who has remained equally susceptible to both classes of pleasures, ever knowingly and calmly preferred the lower; though many, in all ages, have broken down in an ineffectual attempt to combine both.

From this verdict of the only competent judges, I apprehend there can be no appeal. On a question which is the best worth having of two pleasures, or which of two modes of existence is the most grateful to the feelings, apart from its moral attributes and from its consequences, the judgment of those who are qualified by knowledge of both, or, if they differ, that of the majority among them, must be admitted as final. And there needs be the less hesitation to accept this judgment respecting the quality of pleasures, since there is no other tribunal to be referred to even on the question of quantity. What means are there of determining which is the acutest of two pains, or the intensest of two pleasurable sensations, except the general suffrage of those who are familiar with both? Neither pains nor pleasures are homogeneous, and pain is always heterogeneous with pleasure. What is there to decide whether a particular pleasure is worth purchasing at the cost of a particular pain, except the feelings and judgment of the experienced? When, therefore, those feelings and judgment declare the pleasures derived from the higher faculties to be preferable *in kind,* apart from the question of intensity, to those of which the animal nature, disjoined from the higher faculties, is susceptible, they are entitled on this subject to the same regard.

I have dwelt on this point, as being a necessary part of a perfectly just conception of Utility or Happiness, considered as the directive rule of human conduct. But it is by no means an indispensable condition to the acceptance of the utilitarian stand; for that standard is not the agent's own greatest happiness, but the greatest amount of happiness altogether; and if it may possibly be doubted whether a noble character is always the happier for its nobleness, there can be no doubt that it makes other people happier, and that the world in general is immensely a gainer by it. Utilitarianism, therefore, could only attain its end by the general cultivation of nobleness of character, even if each individual were only benefited by the nobleness of others, and his own, so far as happiness is concerned, were a sheer deduction from the benefit. But the bare enunciation of such an absurdity as this last, renders refutation superfluous.

According to the Greatest Happiness Principle, as above explained, the ultimate end, with reference to and for the sake of which all other things are desirable (whether we are considering our own good or that of other people), is an existence exempt as far as possible from pain, and as rich as possible in enjoyments, both in point of quantity and quality; the test of quality, and the rule for measuring it against quantity, being the preference felt by those who in their opportunities of experience, to which must be added their habits of self-consciousness and self-observation, are best furnished with the means

of comparison. This, being, according to the utilitarian opinion, the end of human action, is necessarily also the standard of morality; which may accordingly be defined, the rules and precepts for human conduct, by the observance of which an existence such as has been described might be, to the greatest extent possible, secured to all mankind; and not to them only, but, so far as the nature of things admits, to the whole sentient creation. . . .

I must again repeat what the assailants of utilitarianism seldom have the justice to acknowledge, that the happiness which forms the utilitarian standard of what is right in conduct, is not the agent's own happiness, but that of all concerned. As between his own happiness and that of others, utilitarianism requires him to be as strictly impartial as a disinterested and benevolent spectator. In the golden rule of Jesus of Nazareth, we read the complete spirit of the ethics of utility. To do as you would be done by, and to love your neighbor as yourself, constitute the ideal perfection of utilitarian morality. As the means of making the nearest approach to this ideal, utility would enjoin, first, that laws and social arrangements should place the happiness, or (as, speaking practically it may be called) the interest, of every individual, as nearly as possible in harmony with the interest of the whole; and secondly that education and opinion, which have so vast a power over human character, should so use that power as to establish in the mind of every individual an indissoluble association between his own happiness and the good of the whole; especially between his own happiness and the practice of such modes of conduct, negative and positive, as regard for the universal happiness prescribes; so that not only he may be unable to conceive the possibility of happiness to himself, consistently with conduct opposed to the general good, but also that a direct impulse to promote the general good may be in every individual one of the habitual motives of action, and the sentiments connected therewith may fill a large and prominent place in every human being's sentient existence. If the impugners of the utilitarian morality represented it to their own minds in this its true character, I know not what recommendation possessed by any other morality they could possibly affirm to be wanting to it; what more beautiful or more exalted developments of human nature any other ethical system can be supposed to foster, or what springs of action, not accessible to the utilitarian, such systems rely on for giving effect to their mandates. . . .

OF WHAT SORT OF PROOF THE PRINCIPLE OF UTILITY IS SUSCEPTIBLE

It has already been remarked, that questions of ultimate ends do not admit of proof, in the ordinary acceptation of the term. To be incapable of proof by reasoning is common to all first principles; to the first premises of our knowledge, as well as to those of our conduct. But the former, being matters of fact, may be the subject of a direct appeal to the faculties which judge of fact—namely, our senses, and our internal consciousness. Can an appeal be made to the same faculties on questions of practical ends? Or by what other faculty is cognizance taken of them?

Questions about ends, in other words, question what things are desirable. The utilitarian doctrine is, that happiness is desirable, and the only thing desirable, as an end; all other things being only desirable as means to that end. What ought to be required of this doctrine—what conditions is it requisite that the doctrine should fulfil—to make good its claim to be believed?

The only proof capable of being given that an object is visible, is that people actually see it. The only proof that a sound is audible, is that people hear it: and so of the other sources of our experience. In like manner, I apprehend, the sole evidence it is possible to produce that anything is desirable, is that people do actually desire it. If the end which the utilitarian doctrine proposes to itself were not, in theory and in practice, acknowledged to be an end, nothing could ever convince any person that it was so. No reason can be given why the general happiness is desirable, except that each person, so far as he believes it to be attainable, desires his own happiness. This, however, being a fact, we have not only all the proof which the cases admits of, but all which it is possible to require, that happiness is a good: that each person's happiness is a good to that person, and the general happiness, therefore, a good to the aggregate of all persons. Happiness has made out its title as one of the ends of conduct, and consequently one of the criteria of morality.

But it has not, by this alone, proved itself to be the sole criterion. To do that, it would seem, by the same rule, necessary to show, not only that people desire happiness, but that they never desire anything else. Now it is palpable that they do desire things which, in common language, are decidedly distinguished from happiness. They desire, for example, virtue, and the absence of vice, no less really than pleasure and the absence of pain. The desire of virtue is not as universal, but it is as authentic a fact, as the desire of happiness. And hence the opponents of the utilitarian standard deem that they have a right to infer that there are other ends of human action besides happiness, and that happiness is not the standard of approbation and disapprobation.

But does the utilitarian doctrine deny that people desire virtue, or maintain that virtue is not a thing to be desired? The very reverse. It maintains not only that virtue is to be desired, but that it is to be desired disinterestedly, for itself. Whatever may be the opinion of utilitarian moralists as to the original conditions by which virtue is made virtue; however they may believe (as they do) that actions and dispositions are only virtuous because they promote another end than virtue; yet this being granted, and it having been decided, form considerations of this description, what *is* virtuous, they not only place virtue at the very head of the things which are good as means to the ultimate end, but they also recognise as a psychological fact that possibility of its being, to the individual, a good in itself, without looking to any end beyond it; and hold, that the mind is not in a right state, not in a state conformable to Utility, not in the state most conducive to the general happiness, unless it does love virtue in this manner—as a thing desirable in itself, even although, in the individual instance, it should not produce those other desirable consequences which it tends to produce, and on account of which it is held to be virtue. This opinion is not, in the smallest degree, a departure from the Happiness principle. The ingredients of happiness are very various, and each of them is desirable in itself, and not merely when considered as swelling an aggregate. The principle of utility does not mean that any given pleasure, as music, for instance, or any given exemption from pain, as for example health, is to be looked upon as means to a collective something termed happiness, and to be desired on that account. They are desired and desirable in and for themselves; besides being means, they are a part of the end. Virtue, according to the utilitarian doctrine, is not naturally and originally part of the end, but it is capable of becoming so; and in those who love it disinterestedly it has become so, and is desired and cherished, not as a means to happiness, but as a part of their happiness.

To illustrate this farther, we may remember that virtue is not the only thing, originally a means, and which if it were not a means to anything else, would be and remain indifferent, but which by association with what it is a means to, comes to be desired for itself, and that too with the utmost intensity. What, for example, shall we say of the love of money? There is nothing originally more desirable about money than about any heap of glittering pebbles. Its worth is solely that of the things which it will buy; the desires for other things than itself, which it is a means of gratifying. Yet the love of money is not only one of the strongest moving forces of human life, but money is, in many cases, desired in and for itself; the desire to possess it is often stronger than the desire to use it, and goes on increasing when all the desires which point to ends beyond it, to be compassed by it, are falling off. It may, then, be said truly, that money is desired not for the sake of an end, but as part of the end. From being a means to happiness, it has come to be itself a principal ingredient of the individual's conception of happiness. The same may be said of the majority of the great objects of human life—power, for example, or fame; except that to each of these there is a certain amount of immediate pleasure annexed, which has at least the semblance of being naturally inherent in them; a thing which cannot be said of money. Still, however, the strongest natural attraction, both of power and of fame, is the immense aid they give to the attainment of our other wishes; and it is the strong association thus generated between them and all our objects of desire, which gives to the direct desire of them the intensity it often assumes, so as in some characters to surpass in strength all other desires. In these cases the means have become a part of the end, and a more important part of it than any of the things which they are means to. What was once desired as an instrument for the attainment of happiness, has come to be desired for its own sake. In being desired for its own sake it is, however, desired as *part* of happiness. The person is made, or thinks he would be made, happy by its mere possession; and is made unhappy by failure to obtain it. The desire of it is not a different thing from the desire of happiness, any more than the love of music, or the desire of health. They are included in happiness. They are some of the elements of which the desire of happiness is made up. Happiness is not an abstract idea, but a concrete whole; and these are some of its parts. And the utilitarian standard sanctions and approves their being so. Life would be a poor thing, very ill provided with sources of happiness, if there were not this provision of nature, by which things originally indifferent, but conducive to, or otherwise associated with, the satisfaction of our primitive desires, become in themselves sources of pleasure more valuable than the primitive pleasures, both in permanency, in the space of human existence that they are capable of covering, and even in intensity.

Virtue, according to the utilitarian conception, is a good of this description. There was no original desire of it, or motive to it, save its conduciveness to pleasure, and especially to protection from pain. But through the association thus formed, it may be felt a good in itself, and desired as such with as great intensity as any other good; and with this difference between it and the love of money, of power, or of fame, that all of these may, and often do, render the individual noxious to the other members of the society to which he belongs, whereas there is nothing which makes him so much a blessing to them as the cultivation of the disinterested love of virtue. And consequently, the utilitarian standard, while it tolerates and approves those other acquired desires, up to the point beyond which they would be more injurious to the general happiness than promotive of it, enjoins and requires the cultivation of the love of virtue up to the greatest strength possible, as being above all things important to the general happiness.

It results from the preceding considerations, that there is in reality nothing desired except happiness. Whatever is desired otherwise than as a means to some end beyond itself, and ultimately to happiness, is desired as itself a part of happiness, and is not desired for itself until it has become so. Those who desire virtue for its own sake, desire it either because the consciousness of it is a pleasure, or because the consciousness of being without it is a pain, or for both reasons united; as in truth the pleasure and pain seldom exist separately, but almost always together, the same person feeling pleasure in the degree of virtue attained, and pain in not having attained more. If one of these gave him no pleasure, and the other no pain, he would not love or desire virtue, or would desire it only for the other benefits which it might produce to himself or to persons whom he cared for. . . .

Review Questions

1. State and explain the Principle of Utility. Show how it could be used to justify actions that are conventionally viewed as wrong, such as lying and stealing.
2. How does Mill reply to the objection that Epicureanism is a doctrine worthy only of swine?
3. How does Mill distinguish between higher and lower pleasures?
4. According to Mill, whose happiness must be considered?
5. Carefully reconstruct Mill's proof of the Principle of Utility.

Discussion Questions

1. Is happiness nothing more than pleasure, and the absence of pain? What do you think?
2. Does Mill convince you that the so-called higher pleasures are better than the lower ones? What about the person of experience who prefers the lower pleasures over the higher ones?

3. Mill says, "In the golden rule of Jesus of Nazareth, we read the complete spirit of the ethics of utility." Is this true or not?
4. Many commentators have thought that Mill's proof of the Principle of Utility is defective. Do you agree? If so, then what mistake or mistakes does he make? Is there any way to reformulate the proof so that it is not defective?

The Categorical Imperative

IMMANUEL KANT

Immanuel Kant (1724–1804), a German, was one of the most important philosophers of all time. He made significant contributions to all areas of philosophy. He wrote many books; the most important ones are *Critique of Pure Reason, Prolegomena to All Future Metaphysics, Critique of Practical Reason, Critique of Judgment,* and *The Foundations of the Metaphysics of Morals,* from which the reading is taken.

Kant believes that our moral duty can be formulated in one supreme rule, the Categorical Imperative, from which all our duties can be derived. Although he says that there is just one rule, he gives different versions of it, and two of them seem to be distinct. He arrives at the supreme rule or rules by considering the nature of the good will and duty.

THE GOOD WILL

IT IS IMPOSSIBLE to conceive anything at all in the world, or even out of it, which can be taken as good without qualification, except a *good will.* Intelligence, wit, judgment, and any other *talents* of the mind we may care to name, or courage, resolution, and constancy of purpose, as qualities of *temperament,* are without doubt

Source: Immanuel Kant, "The Categorical Imperative" from *The Moral Law: Kant's Groundwork of the Metaphysic of Morals,* trans. H. J. Paton (New York: Barnes & Noble, Inc., 1948).

good and desirable in many respects; but they can also be extremely bad and hurtful when the will is not good which has to make use of these gifts of nature, and which for this reason has the term '*character*' applied to its peculiar quality. It is exactly the same with *gifts of fortune.* Power, wealth, honour, even health and that complete well-being and contentment with one's state which goes by the name of '*happiness,*' produce boldness, and as a consequence often over-boldness as well, unless a good will is present by which their influence on the mind—and so too the whole principle of action—may be corrected and adjusted to universal ends; not to mention that a rational and impartial spectator can never feel approval in contemplating the uninterrupted prosperity of a being graced by no touch of a pure and good will, and that consequently a good will seems to constitute the indispensable condition of our very worthiness to be happy.

Some qualities are even helpful to this good will itself and can make its task very much easier. They have none the less no inner unconditioned worth, but rather presuppose a good will which sets a limit to the esteem in which they are rightly held and does not permit us to regard them as absolutely good. Moderation in affections and passions, self-control, and sober reflexion are not only good in many respects: they may even seem to constitute part of the *inner worth of a person*. Yet they are far from being properly described as good without qualification (however unconditionally they have been commended by the ancients). For without the principles of a good will they may become exceedingly bad; and the very coolness of a scoundrel makes him, not merely more dangerous, but also immediately more abominable in our eyes than we should have taken him to be without it.

THE GOOD WILL
AND ITS RESULTS

A good will is not good because of what it effects or accomplishes—because of its fitness for attaining some proposed end: it is good through its willing alone—that is, good in itself. Considered in itself it is to be esteemed beyond comparison as far higher than anything it could ever bring about merely in order to favour some inclination or, if you like, the sum total of inclinations. Even if, by some special disfavour of destiny or by the niggardly endowment of stepmotherly nature, this will is entirely lacking in power to carry out its intentions; if by its utmost effort it still accomplishes nothing, and only good will is left (not, admittedly, as a mere wish,

but as the straining of every means so far as they are in our control); even then it would still shine like a jewel for its own sake as something which has its full value in itself. Its usefulness or fruitlessness can neither add to, nor subtract from, this value. Its usefulness would be merely, as it were, the setting which enables us to handle it better in our ordinary dealings or to attract the attention of those not yet sufficiently expert, but not to commend it to experts or to determine its value. . . .

THE GOOD WILL AND DUTY

We have now to elucidate the concept of a will estimable in itself and good apart from any further end. This concept, which is already present in a sound natural understanding and requires not so much to be taught as merely to be clarified, always holds the highest place in estimating the total worth of our actions and constitutes the condition of all the rest. We will therefore take up the concept of *duty*, which includes that of a good will, exposed, however, to certain subjective limitations and obstacles. These, so far from hiding a good will or disguising it, rather bring it out by contrast and make it shine forth more brightly.

THE MOTIVE OF DUTY

I will here pass over all actions already recognized as contrary to duty, however useful they may be with a view to this or that end; for about these the question does not even arise whether they could have been done *for the sake of duty* inasmuch as they are directly opposed to it. I will also set aside actions which in fact accord with duty, yet for which men have *no immediate inclination*, but perform them because impelled to do so by some other inclination. For there it is easy to decide whether the action which accords with duty has been done *from duty* or from some purpose of self-interest. This distinction is far more difficult to perceive when the action accords with duty and the subject has in addition an *immediate* inclination to the action. For example, it certainly accords with duty that a grocer should not overcharge his inexperienced customer; and where there is much competition a sensible shopkeeper refrains from so doing and keeps to a fixed and general price for everybody so that a child can buy from him just as well as anyone else. Thus people are served *honestly;* but this is not nearly enough to justify us in believing that the shopkeeper has acted in this way from duty or from principles of fair dealing; his interests required him to do so. We cannot assume him to have in addition an immediate inclination towards his customers, leading him, as it were out of love, to give no man preference over another in the matter of price. Thus the action was done neither from duty nor from immediate inclination, but solely from purposes of self-interest.

On the other hand, to preserve one's life is a duty, and besides this every one has also an immediate inclination to do so. But on account of this the often anxious precautions taken by the greater part of mankind for this purpose have no inner worth, and the maxim of their action is without moral content. They do protect their lives *in conformity with duty*, but not *from the motive of duty.* When on the contrary, disappointments and hopeless misery have quite taken away the taste for life; when a wretched man, strong in soul and more angered at his fate than faint-hearted or cast down, longs for death and still preserves his life without loving it—not from inclination or fear but from duty; then indeed his maxim has a moral content.

To help others where one can is a duty, and besides this there are many spirits of so sympathetic a temper that, without any further motive of vanity or self-interest, they find an inner pleasure in spreading happiness around them and

can take delight in the contentment of others as their own work. Yet I maintain that in such a case an action of this kind, however right and however amiable it may be, has still no genuinely moral worth. It stands on the same footing as other inclinations—for example, the inclination for honour, which if fortunate enough to hit on something beneficial and right and consequently honourable, deserves praise and encouragement, but not esteem; for its maxim lacks moral content, namely, the performance of such actions, not from inclination, but *from duty.* Suppose then that the mind of this friend of man were overclouded by sorrows of his own which extinguished all sympathy with the fate of others, but that he still had power to help those in distress, though no longer stirred by the need of others because sufficiently occupied with his own; and suppose that, when no longer moved by any inclination, he tears himself out of this deadly insensibility and does the action without any inclination for the sake of duty alone; then for the first time his action has its genuine moral worth. Still further: if nature had implanted little sympathy in this or that man's heart; if (being in other respects an honest fellow) he were cold in temperament and indifferent to the sufferings of others—perhaps because, being endowed with the special gift of patience and robust endurance in his own sufferings, he assumed the like in others or even demanded it; if such a man (who would in truth not be the worst product of nature) were not exactly fashioned by her to be a philanthropist, would he not still find in himself a source from which he might draw a worth far higher than any that a good-natured temperament can have? Assuredly he would. It is precisely in this that the worth of character begins to show—a moral worth and beyond all comparison the highest—namely, that he does good, not from inclination, but from duty. . . .

Thus the moral worth of an action does not depend on the result expected from it, and so too does not depend on any principle of action that needs to borrow its motive from this expected result. For all these results (agreeable states and even the promotion of happiness in others) could have been brought about by other causes as well, and consequently their production did not require the will of a rational being, in which, however, the highest and unconditioned good can alone be found. Therefore nothing but the *idea of the law* in itself, *which admittedly is present only in a rational being*—so far as it, and not an expected result, is the ground determining the will—can constitute that preeminent good which we call moral, a good which is already present in the person acting on this idea and has not to be awaited merely from the result.

THE CATEGORICAL IMPERATIVE

But what kind of law can this be the thought of which, even without regard to the results expected from it, has to determine the will if this is to be called good absolutely and without qualification? Since I have robbed the will of every inducement that might arise for it as a consequence of obeying any particular law, nothing is left but the conformity of actions to universal law as such, and this alone must serve the will as its principle. That is to say, I ought never to act except in such a way *that I can also will that my maxim should become a universal law*. Here bare conformity to universal law as such (without having as its base any law prescribing particular actions) is what serves the will as its principle, and must so serve it if duty is not to be everywhere an empty delusion and a chimerical concept. The ordinary reason of mankind also agrees with this completely in its practical judgements and always has the aforesaid principle before its eyes. . . .

When I conceive a *hypothetical imperative* in general, I do not know beforehand what it will contain—until its condition is given. But if I conceive a *categorical imperative*, I know at once what it contains. For since besides the law this imperative contains only the necessity that our maxim[1] should conform to this law, while the law, as we have seen, contains no condition to limit it, there remains nothing over to which the maxim has to conform except the universality of a law as such; and it is this conformity alone that the imperative properly asserts to be necessary.

There is therefore only a single categorical imperative and it is this: '*Act only on that maxim through which you can at the same time will that it should become a universal law*'.

Now if all imperatives of duty can be derived from this one imperative as their principle, then even although we leave it unsettled whether what we call duty may not be an empty concept, we shall still be able to show at least what we understand by it and what the concept means. . . .

ILLUSTRATIONS

We will now enumerate a few duties, following their customary division into duties towards self and duties towards others and into perfect and imperfect duties.[2]

1. A man feels sick of life as the result of a series of misfortunes that has mounted to the

---

1 A *maxim* is a subjective principle of action and must be distinguished from an *objective principle*—namely, a practical law. The former contains a practical rule determined by reason in accordance with the conditions of the subject (often his ignorance or again his inclinations): it is thus a principle on which the subject *acts*. A law, on the other hand, is an objective principle valid for every rational being; and it is a principle on which he *ought to act*—that is, an imperative.

2 It should be noted that I reserve my division of duties entirely for a future *Metaphysic of Morals* and that my present division is therefore put forward as arbitrary (merely for the purpose of arranging my examples). Further, I understand here by a perfect duty one which allows no exception in the interests of inclination, and so I recognize among *perfect duties*, not only outer ones, but also inner. This is contrary to the accepted usage of the schools, but I do not intend to justify it here, since for my purpose it is all one whether this point is conceded or not.

point of despair, but he is still so far in possession of his reason as to ask himself whether taking his own life may not be contrary to his duty to himself. He now applies the test 'Can the maxim of my action really become a universal law of nature?' His maxim is 'From self-love I make it my principle to shorten my life if its continuance threatens more evil than it promises pleasure'. The only further question to ask is whether this principle of self-love can become a universal law of nature. It is then seen at once that a system of nature by whose law the very same feeling whose function (*Bestimmung*) is to stimulate the furtherance of life should actually destroy life would contradict itself and consequently could not subsist as a system of nature. Hence this maxim cannot possibly hold as a universal law of nature and is therefore entirely opposed to the supreme principle of all duty.

2. Another finds himself driven to borrowing money because of need. He well knows that he will not be able to pay it back; but he sees too that he will get no loan unless he gives a firm promise to pay it back within a fixed time. He is inclined to make such a promise; but he has still enough conscience to ask 'Is it not unlawful and contrary to duty to get out of difficulties in this way?' Supposing, however, he did resolve to do so, the maxim of his action would run thus: 'Whenever I believe myself short of money, I will borrow money and promise to pay it back, though I know that this will never be done'. Now this principle of self-love or personal advantage is perhaps quite compatible with my own entire future welfare; only there remains the question 'Is it right?' I therefore transform the demand of self-love into a universal law and frame my question thus: 'How would things stand if my maxim became a universal law?' I then see straight away that this maxim can never rank as a universal law of nature and be self-consistent, but must necessarily contradict itself. For the universality of a law that every one believing himself to be in need can make any promise he pleases with the intention not to

keep it would make promising, and the very purpose of promising, itself impossible, since no one would believe he was being promised anything, but would laugh at utterances of this kind as empty shams.

3. A third finds in himself a talent whose cultivation would make him a useful man for all sorts of purposes. But he sees himself in comfortable circumstances, and he prefers to give himself up to pleasure rather than to bother about increasing and improving his fortunate natural aptitudes. Yet he asks himself further 'Does my maxim of neglecting my natural gifts, besides agreeing in itself with my tendency to indulgence, agree also with what is called duty?' He then sees that a system of nature could indeed always subsist under such a universal law, although (like the South Sea Islanders) every man should let his talents rust and should be bent on devoting his life solely to idleness, indulgence, procreation, and, in a word, to enjoyment. Only he cannot possibly *will* that this should become a universal law of nature or should be implanted in us as such a law by a natural instinct. For as a rational being he necessarily wills that all his powers should be developed, since they serve him, and are given him, for all sorts of possible ends.

4. Yet a *fourth* is himself flourishing, but he sees others who have to struggle with great hardships (and whom he could easily help); and he thinks 'What does it matter to me? Let every one be as happy as Heaven wills or as he can make himself; I won't deprive him of anything; I won't even envy him; only I have no wish to contribute anything to his well-being or to his support in distress!' Now admittedly if such an attitude were a universal law of nature, mankind could get on perfectly well—better no doubt than if everybody prates about sympathy and goodwill, and even takes pains, on occasion, to practise them, but on the other hand cheats where he can, traffics in human rights, or violates them in other ways. But although it is possible that a universal law of nature could subsist in harmony with this maxim, yet it is impossible

to *will* that such a principle should hold everywhere as a law of nature. For a will which decided in this way would be in conflict with itself, since many a situation might arise in which the man needed love and sympathy from others, and in which, by such a law of nature sprung from his own will, he would rob himself of all hope of the help he wants for himself. . . .

THE FORMULA
OF THE END IN ITSELF

The will is conceived as a power of determining oneself to action *in accordance with the idea of certain laws.* And such a power can be found only in rational beings. Now what serves the will as a subjective ground of its self-determination is an *end;* and this, if it is given by reason alone, must be equally valid for all rational beings. What, on the other hand, contains merely the ground of the possibility of an action whose effect is an end is called a *means.* . . .

Now I say that man, and in general every rational being, *exists* as an end in himself, *not merely as a means* for arbitrary use by this or that will: he must in all his actions, whether they are directed to himself or to other rational beings, always be viewed *at the same time as an end.* All the objects of inclination have only a conditioned value; for if there were not these inclinations and the needs grounded on them, their object would be valueless. Inclinations themselves, as sources of needs, are so far from having an absolute value to make them desirable for their own sake that it must rather be the universal wish of every rational being to be wholly free from them. Thus the value of all objects that can *be produced* by our action is always conditioned. Beings whose existence depends, not on our will, but on nature, have none the less, if they are non-rational beings, only a relative value as

means and are consequently called *things.* Rational beings, on the other hand, are called *persons* because their nature already marks them out as ends in themselves—that is, as something which ought not to be used merely as a means—and consequently imposes to that extent a limit on all arbitrary treatment of them (and is an object of reverence). Persons, therefore, are not merely subjective ends whose existence as an object of our actions has a value *for us:* they are *objective ends*—that is, things whose existence is in itself an end, and indeed an end such that in its place we can put no other end to which they should serve *simply* as means; for unless this is so, nothing at all of *absolute* value would be found anywhere. But if all value were conditioned—that is, contingent—then no supreme principle could be found for reason at all.

If then there is to be a supreme practical principle and—so far as the human will is concerned—a categorical imperative, it must be such that from the idea of something which is necessarily an end for every one because it is an *end in itself* it forms an *objective* principle of the will and consequently can serve as a practical law. The ground of this principle is: *Rational nature exists as an end in itself.* This is the way in which a man necessarily conceives his own existence: it is therefore so far a *subjective* principle of human actions. But it is also the way in which every other rational being conceives his existence on the same rational ground which is valid also for me; hence it is at the same time an *objective* principle, from which, as a supreme practical ground, it must be possible to derive all laws for the will. The practical imperative will therefore be as follows: *Act in such a way that you always treat humanity, whether in your own person or in the person of any other, never simply as a means, but always at the same time as an end.* . . .

Review Questions

1. Explain Kant's account of the good will.
2. Distinguish between hypothetical and categorical imperatives.

3. State the first formulation of the Categorical Imperative (using the notion of a universal law), and explain how Kant uses this rule to derive some specific duties toward self and others.
4. State the second version of the Categorical Imperative (using the language of means and end), and explain it.

Discussion Questions

1. Are the two versions of the Categorical Imperative just different expressions of one basic rule, or are they two different rules? Defend your view.
2. Kant claims that an action that is not done from the motive of duty has no moral worth. Do you agree or not? If not, give some counterexamples.
3. Some commentators think that the Categorical Imperative (particularly the first formulation) can be used to justify nonmoral or immoral actions. Is this a good criticism?

A Simplified Account of Kant's Ethics

ONORA O'NEILL

Onora O'Neill is Principal of Newnham College, Cambridge, England. She is the author of *Acting on Principle* (1975), *Faces of Hunger* (1986), and *Constructions of Reason: Exploration of Kant's Practical Philosophy* (1989).

O'Neill interprets and explains the formulation of the Categorical Imperative called the Formula of the End in Itself, and then compares the Kantian and utilitarian moral theories on the value of human life.

KANT'S MORAL THEORY has acquired the reputation of being forbiddingly difficult to understand and, once understood, excessively demanding in its requirements. I don't believe that this reputation has been wholly earned, and

I am going to try to undermine it. . . . I shall try to reduce some of the difficulties. . . . Finally, I shall compare Kantian and utilitarian approaches and assess their strengths and weaknesses.

The main method by which I propose to avoid some of the difficulties of Kant's moral theory is by explaining only one part of the theory. This does not seem to me to be an irresponsible approach in this case. One of the things that makes Kant's moral theory hard to understand is that he gives a number of different versions of the principle that he calls the Supreme Principle of Morality, and these different versions don't look at all like one another. They also don't look at all like the utilitarians' Greatest Happiness Principle. But the Kantian principle is supposed to play a similar role in arguments about what to do.

Kant calls his Supreme Principle the *Categorical Imperative;* its various versions also have sonorous names. One is called the *Formula of Universal Law;* another is the *Formula of the Kingdom of Ends.* The one on which I shall concentrate is known as the *Formula of the End in Itself.* To understand why Kant thinks that these picturesquely named principles are equivalent to one another takes quite a lot of close and detailed analysis of Kant's philosophy. I shall avoid this and concentrate on showing the implications of this version of the Categorical Imperative.

THE FORMULA
OF THE END IN ITSELF

Kant states the Formula of the End in Itself as follows:

> Act in such a way that you always treat humanity, whether in your own person or in the person of any other, never simply as a means but always at the same time as an end.[1]

To understand this we need to know what it is to treat a person as a means or as an end. According to Kant, each of our acts reflects one or more *maxims*. The maxim of the act is the principle on which one sees oneself as acting. A maxim expresses a person's policy, or if he or she has no settled policy, the principle underlying the particular intention or decision on which he or she acts. Thus, a person who decides "This year I'll give 10 percent of my income to famine relief" has as a maxim the principle of tithing his

1 [See the end of the reading from Kant—Ed.]

or her income for famine relief. In practice, the difference between intentions and maxims is of little importance, for given any intention, we can formulate the corresponding maxim by deleting references to particular times, places, and persons. In what follows I shall take the terms 'maxim' and 'intention' as equivalent.

Whenever we act intentionally, we have at least one maxim and can, if we reflect, state what it is. (There is of course room for self-deception here —"I'm only keeping the wolf from the door" we may claim as we wolf down enough to keep ourselves overweight, or, more to the point, enough to feed someone else who hasn't enough food.)

When we want to work out whether an act we propose to do is right or wrong, according to Kant, we should look at our maxims and not at how much misery or happiness the act is likely to produce, and whether it does better at increasing happiness than other available acts. We just have to check that the act we have in mind will not use anyone as a mere means, and, if possible, that it will treat other persons as ends in themselves.

USING PERSONS AS MERE MEANS

To use someone as a *mere means* is to involve them in a scheme of action *to which they could not in principle consent.* Kant does not say that there is anything wrong about using someone as a means. Evidently we have to do so in any cooperative scheme of action. If I cash a check I use the teller as a means, without whom I could not lay my hands on the cash; the teller in turn uses me as a means to earn his or her living. But in this case, each party consents to her or his part in the transaction. Kant would say that though they use one another as means, they do not use one another as *mere* means. Each person assumes that the other has maxims of his or her own and is not just a thing or a prop to be manipulated.

But there are other situations where one person uses another in a way to which the other could not in principle consent. For example, one person may make a promise to another with every intention of breaking it. If the promise is accepted, then the person to whom it was given must be ignorant of what the promisor's intention (maxim) really is. If one knew that the promisor did not intend to do what he or she was promising, one would, after all, not accept or rely on the promise. It would be as though there had been no promise made. Successful false promising depends on deceiving the person to whom the promise is made about what one's real maxim is. And since the person who is deceived doesn't know that real maxim, he or she can't in principle consent to his or her part in the proposed scheme of action. The person who is deceived is, as it were, a prop or a tool—a mere means—in the false promisor's scheme. A person who promises falsely treats the acceptor of the promise as a prop or a thing and not as a person. In Kant's view, it is this that makes false promising wrong.

One standard way of using others as mere means is by deceiving them. By getting someone involved in a business scheme or a criminal activity on false pretenses, or by giving a misleading account of what one is about, or by making a false promise or a fraudulent contract, one involves another in something to which he or she in principle cannot consent, since the scheme requires that he or she doesn't know what is going on. Another standard way of using others as mere means is by coercing them. If a rich or powerful person threatens a debtor with bankruptcy unless he or she joins in some scheme, then the creditor's intention is to coerce; and the debtor, if coerced, cannot consent to his or her part in the creditor's scheme. To make the example more specific: If a moneylender in an Indian village threatens not to renew a vital loan unless he is given the debtor's land, then he uses the debtor as a mere means. He coerces the debtor, who cannot truly consent to this "offer he can't refuse." (Of course the outward form of such transactions may look

like ordinary commercial dealings, but we know very well that some offers and demands couched in that form are coercive.)

In Kant's view, acts that are done on maxims that require deception or coercion of others, and so cannot have the consent of those others (for consent precludes both deception and coercion), are wrong. When we act on such maxims, we treat others as mere means, as things rather than as ends in themselves. If we act on such maxims, our acts are not only wrong but unjust: such acts wrong the particular others who are deceived or coerced.

TREATING PERSONS AS ENDS IN THEMSELVES

Duties of justice are, in Kant's view (as in many others'), the most important of our duties. When we fail in these duties, we have used some other or others as mere means. But there are also cases where, though we do not use others as mere means, still we fail to use them as ends in themselves in the fullest possible way. To treat someone as an end in him or herself requires in the first place that one not use him or her as mere means, that one respect each as a rational person with his or her own maxims. But beyond that, one may also seek to foster others' plans and maxims by sharing some of their ends. To act beneficently is to seek others' happiness, therefore to intend to achieve some of the things that those others aim at with their maxims. If I want to make others happy, I will adopt maxims that not merely do not manipulate them but that foster some of their plans and activities. Beneficent acts try to achieve what others want. However, we cannot seek everything that others want; their wants are too numerous and diverse, and, of course, sometimes incompatible. It follows that beneficence has to be selective.

There is then quite a sharp distinction between the requirements of justice and of beneficence in Kantian ethics. Justice requires that we act on *no* maxims that use others as mere means. Beneficence requires that we act on *some* maxims that foster others' ends, though it is a matter for judgment and discretion which of their ends we foster. Some maxims no doubt ought not to be fostered because it would be unjust to do so. Kantians are not committed to working interminably through a list of happiness-producing and misery-reducing acts; but there are some acts whose obligatoriness utilitarians may need to debate as they try to compare total outcomes of different choices, to which Kantians are stringently bound. Kantians will claim that they have done nothing wrong if none of their acts is unjust, and that their duty is complete if in addition their life plans have in the circumstances been reasonably beneficent.

In making sure that they meet all the demands of justice, Kantians do not try to compare all available acts and see which has the best effects. They consider only the proposals for action that occur to them and check that these proposals use no other as mere means. If they do not, the act is permissible; if omitting the act would use another as mere means, the act is obligatory. Kant's theory has less scope than utilitarianism. Kantians do not claim to discover whether acts whose maxims they don't know fully are just. They may be reluctant to judge others' acts or policies that cannot be regarded as the maxim of any person or institution. They cannot rank acts in order of merit. Yet, the theory offers more precision than utilitarianism when data are scarce. One can usually tell whether one's act would use others as mere means, even when its impact on human happiness is thoroughly obscure.

THE LIMITS OF KANTIAN ETHICS: INTENTIONS AND RESULTS

Kantian ethics differs from utilitarian ethics both in its scope and in the precision with which it guides action. Every action, whether of a person or of an agency, can be assessed by utilitarian methods, provided only that information is available about all the consequences of the act. The theory has unlimited scope, but owing to lack of data, often lacks precision. Kantian ethics has a more restricted scope. Since it assesses actions by looking at the maxims of agents, it can only assess intentional acts. This means that it is most at home in assessing individuals' acts; but it can be extended to assess acts of agencies that (like corporations and governments and student unions) have decision-making procedures. It can do nothing to assess patterns of action that reflect no intention or policy, hence it cannot assess the acts of groups lacking decision-making procedures, such as the student movement, the women's movement, or the consumer movement.

It may seem a great limitation of Kantian ethics that it concentrates on intentions to the neglect of results. It might seem that all conscientious Kantians have to do is to make sure that they never intend to use others as mere means, and that they sometimes intend to foster others' ends. And, as we all know, good intentions sometimes lead to bad results and correspondingly, bad intentions sometimes do no harm, or even produce good. If Hardin is right, the good intentions of those who feed the starving lead to dreadful results in the long run. If some traditional arguments in favor of capitalism are right, the greed and selfishness of the profit motive have produced unparalleled prosperity for many.

But such discrepancies between intentions and results are the exception and not the rule. For we cannot just *claim* that our intentions are good and do what we will. Our intentions reflect what we expect the immediate results of our action to be. Nobody credits the "intentions" of a couple who practice neither celibacy nor contraception but still insist "we never meant to have (more) children." Conception is likely (and known to be likely) in such cases. Where people's expressed intentions ignore the normal and predictable results of what they do, we infer that (if they are not amazingly ignorant) their words do not express their true intentions. The Formula of the End in Itself applies to the intentions on which one acts—not to some prettified version that one may avow. Provided this intention—the agent's real intention—uses no other as mere means, he or she does nothing unjust. If some of his or her intentions foster others' ends, then he or she is sometimes beneficent. It is therefore possible for people to test their proposals by Kantian arguments even when they lack the comprehensive causal knowledge that utilitarianism requires. Conscientious Kantians can work out whether they will be doing wrong by some act even though it blurs the implications of the theory. If we peer through the blur, we see that the utilitarian view is that lives may indeed be sacrificed for the sake of a greater good even when the persons are not willing. There is nothing wrong with using another as a mere means provided that the end for which the person is so used is a happier result than could have been achieved any other way, taking into account the misery the means have caused. In utilitarian thought persons are not ends in themselves. Their special moral status derives from their being means to the production of happiness. Human life has therefore a high though derivative value, and one life may be taken for the sake of greater happiness in other lives, or for ending of misery in that life. Nor is there any deep difference between ending a life for the sake of others' happiness by not helping (e.g., by triaging) and doing so by harming. Because the distinction between justice and beneficence is not sharply made within utilitarianism, it is not possible to say that triaging is a matter of not benefiting, while other interventions are a matter of injustice.

Utilitarian moral theory has then a rather paradoxical view of the value of human life. Living, conscious humans are (along with other sentient beings) necessary for the existence of everything utilitarians value. But it is not their being alive but the state of their consciousness that is of value. Hence, the best results may require certain lives to be lost—by whatever means—for the sake of the total happiness and absence of misery that can be produced.

KANT AND RESPECT FOR PERSONS

Kantians reach different conclusions about human life. Human life is valuable because humans (and conceivably other beings, e.g., angels or apes) are the bearers of rational life. Humans are able to choose and to plan. This capacity and its exercise are of such value that they ought not to be sacrificed for anything of lesser value. Therefore, no one rational or autonomous creature should be treated as mere means for the enjoyment or even the happiness of another. We may in Kant's view justifiably—even nobly—risk or sacrifice our lives for others. For in doing so we follow our own maxim and nobody uses us as mere means. But no others may use either our lives or our bodies for a scheme that they have either coerced or deceived us into joining. For in doing so they would fail to treat us as rational beings; they would use us as mere means and not as ends in ourselves.

It is conceivable that a society of Kantians, all of whom took pains to use no other as mere means, would end up with less happiness or with fewer persons alive than would some societies of complying utilitarians. For since the Kantians would be strictly bound only to justice, they might without wrongdoing be quite selective in their beneficence and fail to maximize either survival rates or happiness, or even to achieve as much of either as a strenuous group of utilitarians, who they know that their foresight is limited and that they may cause some harm or fail to cause some benefit. But they will not cause harms that they can foresee without this being reflected in their intentions.

UTILITARIANISM
AND RESPECT FOR LIFE

From the differing implications that Kantian and utilitarian moral theories have for our actions towards those who do or may suffer famine, we can discover two sharply contrasting views of the value of human life. Utilitarians value happiness and the absence or reduction of misery. As a utilitarian one ought (if conscientious) to devote one's life to achieving the best possible balance of happiness over misery. If one's life plan remains in doubt, this will be because the means to this end are often unclear. But whenever the causal tendency of acts is clear, utilitarians will be able to discern the acts they should successively do in order to improve the world's balance of happiness over unhappiness.

This task is not one for the faint-hearted. First, it is dauntingly long, indeed interminable. Second, it may at times require the sacrifice of happiness, and even of lives, for the sake of a greater happiness. Such sacrifice may be morally required not only when the person whose happiness or even whose life is at stake volunteers to make the sacrifice. It may be necessary to sacrifice some lives for the sake of others. As our control over the means of ending and preserving human life has increased, analogous dilemmas have arisen in many areas for utilitarians.

Should life be preserved at the cost of pain when modern medicine makes this possible? Should life be preserved without hope of consciousness? Should triage policies, because they may maximize the number of survivors, be used to determine who should be left to starve? Should population growth be fostered wherever it will increase the total of human happiness—or on some views so long as average happiness is not reduced? All these questions can be fitted into utilitarian frameworks and answered *if* we have the relevant information. And sometimes the answer will be that human happiness demands the sacrifice of lives, including the sacrifice of unwilling lives. Further, for most utilitarians, it makes no difference if the unwilling sacrifices involve acts of injustice to those whose lives are to be lost. It might, for example, prove necessary for maximal happiness that some persons have their allotted rations, or their hard-earned income, diverted for others' benefit. Or it might turn out that some generations must sacrifice comforts or liberties and even lives to rear "the fabric of felicity" for their successors. Utilitarians do not deny these possibilities, though the imprecision of our knowledge of consequences often somehow makes the right calculations. On the other hand, nobody will have been made an instrument of others' survival or happiness in the society of complying Kantians.

Review Questions

1. According to O'Neill, what is involved in using someone as a mere means? Give some examples. Why is this wrong?
2. On O'Neill's interpretation, how does one treat people as ends in themselves? Give examples.
3. Distinguish between the requirements of justice and beneficence.
4. According to O'Neill, how does Kantian ethics differ from utilitarian ethics?

Discussion Questions

1. Does Kantian ethics require us to help strangers or people in other countries? Why or why not?

2. As O'Neill explains it, Kant's view is that a life is valuable because it is rational. This seems to imply that the life of a fetus or a comatose person is not valuable because it is not rational—it involves no choosing or planning. Do you agree with this?

3. Which theory is more acceptable to you, utilitarianism or Kant's theory? Why?

Happiness and Virtue

ARISTOTLE

Aristotle (384–322 B.C.E.) made important contributions to all areas of philosophy, including the formulation of traditional logic. Along with his teacher Plato, he is regarded as one of the founders of western philosophy.

Aristotle argues that all human beings seek happiness, and that happiness is not pleasure, honor, or wealth, but an activity of the soul in accordance with virtue. Virtue is of two kinds: moral and intellectual. Moral virtue comes from training and habit, and generally is a state of character that is a mean between the vices of excess and deficiency. For example, Aristotle portrays the virtue of courage as a mean between the extremes of rashness (an excess) and cowardice (a deficiency). Intellectual virtue produces the most perfect happiness and is found in the activity of reason or contemplation.

OUR DISCUSSION WILL BE ADEQUATE if it has as much clearness as the subject-matter admits of, for precision is not to be sought for alike in all discussions, any more than in all the products of the crafts. Now fine and just actions, which political science investigates, admit of much variety and fluctuation of opinion, so that they may be thought to exist only by convention, and not by nature. And goods also give rise to a similar fluctuation because they bring harm to many people; for before now men have been undone by reason of their wealth, and others by reason of their courage. We must be content, then, in speaking of such subjects and with such premises to indicate the truth roughly and in outline, and in speaking about things which are only for the most part true and with premises of the same kind to reach conclusions that are no better. In the same spirit, therefore, should each type of statement be received; for it is the mark of an educated man to look for precision in each class of things just so far as the nature of the subject admits; it is evidently equally foolish

Source: Aristotle, *Happiness and Virtue*, Books I: 3–5, 7–9, 13; II: 1,6,7,9; and X: 7,8 from *Ethica Nicomachea*, trans. W. D. Ross in *The Oxford Translation of Aristotle*, vol. 9 (Oxford: Oxford University Press, 1925).

to accept probable reasoning from a mathematician and to demand from a rhetorician scientific proofs.

Now each man judges well the things he knows, and of these he is a good judge. And so the man who has been educated in a subject is a good judge of that subject, and the man who has received an all-round education is a good judge in general. Hence a young man is not a proper hearer of lectures on political science; for he is inexperienced in the actions that occur in life, but its discussions start from these and are about these; and, further, since he tends to follow his passions, his study will be vain and unprofitable, because the end aimed at is not knowledge but action. And it makes no difference whether he is young in years or youthful in character; the defect does not depend on time, but on his living, and pursuing each successive object, as passion directs. For to such persons, as to the incontinent, knowledge brings no profit; but to those who desire and act in accordance with a rational principle knowledge about such matters will be of great benefit.

These remarks about the student, the sort of treatment to be expected, and the purpose of the inquiry, may be taken as our preface.

Let us resume our inquiry and state, in view of the fact that all knowledge and every pursuit aims at some good, what it is that we say political science aims at and what is the highest of all goods achievable by action. Verbally there is very general agreement; for both the general run of men and people of superior refinement say that it is happiness, and identify living well and doing well with being happy; but with regard to what happiness is they differ, and the many do not give the same account as the wise. For the former think it is some plain and obvious thing, like pleasure, wealth, or honour; they differ, however, from one another—and often even the same man identifies it with different things, with health when he is ill, with wealth when he is poor; but, conscious of their ignorance, they admire those who proclaim some great ideal that is above their comprehension. Now some thought that apart from these many goods there is another which is self-subsistent and causes the goodness of all these as well. To examine all the opinions that have been held were perhaps somewhat fruitless; enough to examine those that are most prevalent or that seem to be arguable. . . .

Let us, however, resume our discussion from the point at which we digressed. To judge from the lives that men lead, most men, and men of the most vulgar type, seem (not without some ground) to identify the good, or happiness, with pleasure; which is the reason why they love the life of enjoyment. For there are, we may say, three prominent types of life—that just mentioned, the political, and thirdly the contemplative life. Now the mass of mankind are evidently quite slavish in their tastes, preferring a life suitable to beasts, but they get some ground for their view from the fact that many of those in high places share the tastes of Sardanapallus. A consideration of the prominent types of life shows that people of superior refinement and of active disposition identify happiness with honour; for this is, roughly speaking, the end of the political life. But it seems too superficial to be what we are looking for, since it is thought to depend on those who bestow honour rather than on him who receives it, but the good we divine to be something proper to a man and not easily taken from him. Further, men seem to pursue honour in order that they may be assured of their goodness; at least it is by men of practical wisdom that they seek to be honoured, and among those who know them, and on the ground of their virtue; clearly, then, according to them, at any rate, virtue is better. And perhaps one might even suppose this to be, rather than honour, the end of the political life. But even this appears somewhat incomplete; for possession of virtue seems actually compatible with being asleep, or with life-long inactivity, and, further, with the greatest sufferings and misfortunes; but a man who was living so no one would call happy, unless he were maintaining a thesis at all costs. But enough of this; for the subject has been sufficiently treated even in the current discussions. Third comes the contemplative life, which we shall consider later.

The life of money-making is one undertaken under compulsion, and wealth is evidently not the good we are seeking; for it is merely useful and for the sake of something else. And so one might rather take the aforenamed objects to be ends; for they are loved for themselves. But it is evident that not even these are ends; yet many arguments have been thrown away in support of them. . . .

Let us again return to the good we are seeking, and ask what it can be. It seems different in different actions and arts; it is different in medicine, in strategy, and in the other arts likewise. What then is the good of each? Surely that for whose sake everything else is done. In medicine this is health, in strategy victory, in architecture a house, in any other sphere something else, and in every action and pursuit the end; for it is for the sake of this that all men do whatever else they do. Therefore, if there is an end for all that we do, this will be the good achievable by action, and if there are more than one, these will be the goods achievable by action.

So the argument has by a different course reached the same point; but we must try to state this even more clearly. Since there are evidently more than one end, and we choose some of these (e.g. wealth, flutes, and in general instruments) for the sake of something else, clearly not all ends are final ends; but the chief good is evidently something final. Therefore, if there is only one final end, this will be what we are seeking, and if there are more than one, the most final of these will be what we are seeking. Now we call that which is in itself worthy of pursuit more final than that which is worthy of pursuit for the sake of something else, and that which is never desirable for the sake of something else more final than the things that are desirable both in themselves and for the sake of

that other thing, and therefore we call final without qualification that which is always desirable in itself and never for the sake of something else.

Now such a thing happiness, above all else, is held to be; for this we choose always for itself and never for the sake of something else, but honour, pleasure, reason, and every virtue we choose indeed for themselves (for if nothing resulted from them we should still choose each of them), but we choose them also for the sake of happiness, judging that by means of them we shall be happy. Happiness, on the other hand, no one chooses for the sake of these, nor, in general, for anything other than itself. . . .

Presumably, however, to say that happiness is the chief good seems a platitude, and a clearer account of what it is is still desired. This might perhaps be given, if we could first ascertain the function of man. For just as for a fluteplayer, a sculptor, or any artist, and, in general, for all things that have a function or activity, the good and the 'well' is thought to reside in the function, so would it seem to be for man, if he has a function. Have the carpenter, then, and the tanner certain functions or activities, and has man none? Is he born without a function? Or as eye, hand, foot, and in general each of the parts evidently has a function, may one lay it down that man similarly has a function apart from all these? What then can this be? Life seems to be common even to plants, but we are seeking what is peculiar to man. Let us exclude, therefore, the life of nutrition and growth. Next there would be a life of perception, but *it* also seems to be common even to the horse, the ox, and every animal. There remains, then, an active life of the element that has a rational principle; of this, one part has such a principle in the sense of being obedient to one, the other in the sense of possessing one and exercising thought. And, as 'life of the rational element' also has two meanings, we must state that life in the sense of activity is what we mean; for this seems to be the more proper sense of the term. Now if the function of man is an activity of soul which follows or implies a rational principle, and if we say 'a so-and-so' and 'a good so-and-so' have a function which is the same in kind, e. g. a lyre-player and a good lyre-player, and so without qualification in all cases, eminence in respect of goodness being added to the name of the function (for the function of a lyre-player is to play the lyre, and that of a good lyre-player is to do so well): if this is the case, [and we state the function of man to be a certain kind of life, and this to be an activity or actions of the soul implying a rational principle, and the function of a good man to be the good and noble performance of these, and if any action is well performed when it is performed in accordance with the appropriate excellence: if this is the case,] human good turns out to be activity of soul in accordance with virtue, and if there are more than one virtue, in accordance with the best and most complete.

But we must add 'in a complete life.' For one swallow does not make a summer, nor does one day; and so too one day, or a short time, does not make a man blessed and happy. . . .

We must consider it, however, in the light not only of our conclusion and our premisses, but also of what is commonly said about it; for with a true view all the data harmonize, but with a false one the facts soon clash. Now goods have been divided into three classes, and some are described as external, others as relating to soul or to body; we call those that relate to soul most properly and truly goods, and psychical actions and activities we class as relating to soul. Therefore our account must be sound, at least according to this view, which is an old one and agreed on by philosophers. It is correct also in that we identify the end with certain actions and activities; for thus it falls among goods of the soul and not among external goods. Another belief which harmonizes with our account is that the happy man lives well and does well; for we have practically defined happiness as a sort of good life and good action. The characteristics that are looked for in happiness seem also, all of them, to belong to what we have defined happiness as being. For some identify happiness with virtue, some with practical wisdom, others with a kind of philosophic wisdom, others with these, or one of these, accompanied by pleasure or not without pleasure; while others include also external prosperity. Now some of these views have been held by many men and men of old, others by a few eminent persons; and it is not probable that either of these should be entirely mistaken, but rather that they should be right in at least some one respect or even in most respects.

With those who identify happiness with virtue or some one virtue our account is in harmony; for to virtue belongs virtuous activity. But it makes, perhaps, no small difference whether we place the chief good in possession or in use, in state of mind or in activity. For the state of mind may exist without producing any good result, as in a man who is asleep or in some other way quite inactive, but the activity cannot; for one who has the activity will of necessity be acting, and acting well. And as in the Olympic Games it is not the most beautiful and the strongest that are crowned but those who compete (for it is some of these that are victorious), so those who act win, and rightly win, the noble and good things in life.

Their life is also in itself pleasant. For pleasure is a state of *soul*, and to each man that which he is said to be a lover of is pleasant; e. g. not only is a horse pleasant to the lover of horses, and a spectacle to the lover of sights, but also in the same way just acts are pleasant to the lover of justice and in general virtuous acts to the lover of virtue. Now for most men their pleasures are in conflict with one another because these are not by nature pleasant, but the lovers of what is noble find pleasant the things that are by nature pleasant; and virtuous actions are such, so that these are pleasant for such men as well as in their own nature. Their life, therefore, has no further need of pleasure as a sort of adventitious charm, but has its pleasure in itself. For, besides what we have said, the man who does not rejoice in noble actions is not even good; since no one would call a man just who did not enjoy acting justly, nor any man liberal who did not enjoy liberal actions; and similarly in all other cases. If this is so, virtuous actions must be in themselves pleasant. But they are also *good* and *noble,* and have each of these attributes in the highest degree, since the good man judges well about these attributes; his judgment is such as we have described. Happiness then is the best, noblest, and most pleasant thing in the world. . . .

Yet evidently, as we said, it needs the external goods as well; for it is impossible, or not easy, to do noble acts without the proper equipment. In many actions we use friends and riches and political power as instruments; and there are some things the lack of which takes the lustre from happiness, as good birth, goodly children, beauty; for the man who is very ugly in appearance or ill-born or solitary and childless is not very likely to be happy, and perhaps a man would be still less likely if he had thoroughly bad children or friends or had lost good children or friends by death. As we said, then, happiness seems to need this sort of prosperity in addition; for which reason some identify happiness with good fortune, though others identify it with virtue.

For this reason also the question is asked, whether happiness is to be acquired by learning or by habituation or some other sort of training, or comes in virtue of some divine providence or again by chance. Now if there is *any* gift of the gods to men, it is reasonable that happiness should be god-given, and most surely god-given of all human things inasmuch as it is the best. But this question would perhaps be more appropriate to another inquiry; happiness seems, however, even if it is not god-sent but comes as a result of virtue and some process of learning or training, to be among the most god-like things; for that which is the prize and end of virtue seems to be the best thing in the world, and something godlike and blessed.

It will also on this view be very generally shared; for all who are not maimed as regards their potentiality for virtue may win it by a certain kind of study and care. But if it is better to be happy thus than by chance, it is reasonable that the facts should be so, since everything that depends on the action of nature is by nature as good as it can be, and similarly everything that depends on art or any rational cause, and especially if it depends on the best of all causes. To entrust to chance what is greatest and most noble would be a very defective arrangement.

The answer to the question we are asking is plain also from the definition of happiness; for it has been said to be a virtuous activity of soul, of a certain kind. Of the remaining goods, some must necessarily pre-exist as conditions of happiness, and others are naturally co-operative and useful as instruments. And this will be found to agree with what we said at the outset; for we stated the end of political science to be the best end, and political science spends most of its pains on making the citizens to be of a certain character, viz. good and capable of noble acts.

It is natural, then, that we call neither ox nor horse nor any other of the animals happy; for none of them is capable of sharing in such activity. For this reason also a boy is not happy; for he is not yet capable of such acts, owing to his age; and boys who are called happy are being congratulated by reason of the hopes we have for them. For there is required, as we said, not only complete virtue but also a complete life, since many changes occur in life, and all manner of chances, and the most prosperous may fall into great misfortunes in old age, as is told of Priam in the Trojan Cycle; and one who has experienced such chances and has ended wretchedly no one calls happy. . . .

Since happiness is an activity of soul in accordance with perfect virtue, we must consider the nature of virtue; for perhaps we shall thus see better the nature of happiness. . . .

Virtue, then, being of two kinds, intellectual and moral, intellectual virtue in the main owes both its birth and its growth to teaching (for which reason it requires experience and time), while moral virtue comes about as a result of habit. . . . From this it is also plain that none of the moral virtues arises in us by nature; for nothing that exists by nature can form a habit contrary to its nature. For instance the stone which by nature moves downwards cannot be habituated to move upwards, not even if one tries to train it by throwing it up ten thousand times; nor can fire be habituated to move downwards, nor can anything else that by nature behaves in one way be trained to behave in another. Neither by nature, then, nor contrary to nature do the virtues arise in us; rather we are adapted by nature to receive them, and are made perfect by habit. . . .

We must, however, not only describe virtue as a state of character, but also say what sort of state it is. We may remark, then, that every virtue or excellence both brings into good condition the thing of which it is the excellence and makes the work of that thing be done well; e. g. the excellence of the eye makes both the eye and its work good; for it is by the excellence of the eye that we see well. Similarly the excellence of the horse makes a horse both good in itself and good at running and at carrying its rider and at awaiting the attack of the enemy. Therefore, if this is true in every case, the virtue of man also will be the state of character which makes a man good and which makes him do his own work well.

How this is to happen we have stated already, but it will be made plain also by the following consideration of the specific nature of virtue. In everything that is continuous and divisible it is possible to take more, less, or an equal amount, and that either in terms of the thing itself or relatively to us; and the equal is an intermediate between excess and defect. By the intermediate in the object I mean that which is equidistant from each of the extremes, which is one and the same for all men; by the intermediate relatively

to us that which is neither too much nor too little—and this is not one, nor the same for all. For instance, if ten is many and two is few, six is the intermediate, taken in terms of the object; for it exceeds and is exceeded by an equal amount; this is intermediate according to arithmetical proportion. But the intermediate relatively to us is not to be taken so; if ten pounds are too much for a particular person to eat and two too little, it does not follow that the trainer will order six pounds; for this also is perhaps too much for the person who is to take it, or too little—too little for Milo, too much for the beginner in athletic exercises. The same is true of running and wrestling. Thus a master of any art avoids excess and defect, but seeks the intermediate and chooses this—the intermediate not in the object but relatively to us.

If it is thus, then, that every art does its work well—by looking to the intermediate and judging its works by this standard (so that we often say of good works of art that it is not possible either to take away or to add anything, implying that excess and defect destroy the goodness of the works of art, while the mean preserves it; and good artists, as we say, look to this in their work), and if, further, virtue is more exact and better than any art, as nature also is, then virtue must have the quality of aiming at the intermediate. I mean moral virtue; for it is this that is concerned with passions and actions, and in these there is excess, defect, and the intermediate. For instance, both fear and confidence and appetite and anger and pity and in general pleasure and pain may be felt both too much and too little, and in both cases not well; but to feel them at the right times, with reference to the right objects, towards the right people, with the right motive, and in the right way, is what is both intermediate and best, and this is characteristic of virtue. Similarly with regard to actions also there is excess, defect, and the intermediate. Now virtue is concerned with passions and actions, in which excess is a form of failure, and so is defect, while the intermediate is praised and is a form of success; and being praised and being successful are both characteristics of virtue. Therefore virtue is a kind of mean, since, as we have seen, it aims at what is intermediate.

Again, it is possible to fail in many ways (for evil belongs to the class of the unlimited, as the Pythagoreans conjectured, and good to that of the limited), while to succeed is possible only in one way (for which reason also one is easy and the other difficult—to miss the mark easy, to hit it difficult); for these reasons also, then, excess and defect are characteristic of vice, and the mean of virtue;

> For men are good in but one way, but bad in many.

Virtue, then, is a state of character concerned with choice, lying in a mean, i. e. the mean relative to us, this being determined by a rational principle, and by that principle by which the man of practical wisdom would determine it. Now it is a mean between two vices, that which depends on excess and that which depends on defect; and again it is a mean because the vices respectively fall short of or exceed what is right in both passions and actions, while virtue both finds and chooses that which is intermediate. Hence in respect of its substance and the definition which states its essence virtue is a mean, with regard to what is best and right an extreme.

But not every action nor every passion admits of a mean; for some have names that already imply badness, e. g. spite, shamelessness, envy, and in the case of actions adultery, theft, murder; for all of these and suchlike things imply by their names that they are themselves bad, and not the excesses or deficiencies of them. It is not possible, then, ever to be right with regard to them; one must always be wrong. Nor does goodness or badness with regard to such things depend on committing adultery with the right woman, at the right time, and in the right way, but simply to do any of them is to go wrong. It

would be equally absurd, then, to expect that in unjust, cowardly, and voluptuous action there should be a mean, an excess, and a deficiency; for at that rate there would be a mean of excess and of deficiency, an excess of excess, and deficiency of deficiency. But as there is no excess and deficiency of temperance and courage because what is intermediate is in a sense an extreme, so too of the actions we have mentioned there is no mean nor any excess and deficiency, but however they are done they are wrong; for in general there is neither a mean of excess and deficiency, nor excess and deficiency of a mean.

We must, however, not only make this general statement, but also apply it to the individual facts. For among statements about conduct those which are general apply more widely, but those which are particular are more genuine, since conduct has to do with individual cases, and our statements must harmonize with the facts in these cases. We may take these cases from our table. With regard to feelings of fear and confidence courage is the mean; of the people who exceed, he who exceeds in fearlessness has no name (many of the states have no name), while the man who exceeds in confidence is rash, and he who exceeds in fear and falls short in confidence is a coward. With regard to pleasures and pains—not all of them, and not so much with regard to the pains—the mean is temperance, the excess self-indulgence. Persons deficient with regard to the pleasures are not often found; hence such persons also have received no name. But let us call them "insensible."

With regard to giving and taking of money the mean is liberality, the excess and the defect prodigality and meanness. In these actions people exceed and fall short in contrary ways; the prodigal exceeds in spending and falls short in taking, while the mean man exceeds in taking and falls short in spending. (At present we are giving a mere outline or summary, and are satisfied with this; later these states will be more exactly determined.) With regard to money there are also other dispositions—a mean, magnificence (for the magnificent man differs from the liberal man; the former deals with large sums, the latter with small ones), and excess, tastelessness, and vulgarity, and a deficiency, niggardliness; these differ from the states opposed to liberality. . . .

That moral virtue is a mean, then, and in what sense it is so, and that it is a mean between two vices, the one involving excess, the other deficiency, and that it is such because its character is to aim at what is intermediate in passions and in actions, has been sufficiently stated. Hence also it is no easy task to be good. For in everything it is no easy task to find the middle, e. g. to find the middle of a circle is not for every one but for him who knows; so, too, any one can get angry—that is easy—or give or spend money; but to do this to the right person, to the right extent, at the right time, with the right motive, and in the right way, *that* is not for every one, nor is it easy; wherefore goodness is both rare and laudable and noble. . . .

If happiness is activity in accordance with virtue, it is reasonable that it should be in accordance with the highest virtue; and this will be that of the best thing in us. Whether it be reason or something else that is this element which is thought to be our natural ruler and guide and to take thought of things noble and divine, whether it be itself also divine or only the most divine element in us, the activity of this in accordance with its proper virtue will be perfect happiness. That this activity is contemplative we have already said.

Now this would seem to be in agreement both with what we said before and with the truth. For, firstly, this activity is the best (since not only is reason the best thing in us, but the objects of reason are the best of knowable objects); and, secondly, it is the most continuous, since we can contemplate truth more continuously than we can do anything. And we think happiness has pleasure mingled with it, but the

activity of philosophic wisdom is admittedly the pleasantest of virtuous activities; at all events the pursuit of it is thought to offer pleasures marvellous for their purity and their enduringness, and it is to be expected that those who know will pass their time more pleasantly than those who inquire. And the self-sufficiency that is spoken of must belong most to the contemplative activity. For while a philosopher, as well as a just man or one possessing any other virtue, needs the necessaries of life, when they are sufficiently equipped with things of that sort the just man needs people towards whom and with whom he shall act justly, and the temperate man, the brave man, and each of the others is in the same case, but the philosopher, even when by himself, can contemplate truth, and the better the wiser he is; he can perhaps do so better if he has fellow-workers, but still he is the most self-sufficient. And this activity alone would seem to be loved for its own sake; for nothing arises from it apart from the contemplating, while from practical activities we gain more or less apart from the action. And happiness is thought to depend on leisure; for we are busy that we may have leisure, and make war that we may live in peace. Now the activity of the practical virtues is exhibited in political or military affairs, but the actions concerned with these seem to be unleisurely. Warlike actions are completely so (for no one chooses to be at war, or provokes war, for the sake of being at war; any one would seem absolutely murderous if he were to make enemies of his friends in order to bring about battle and slaughter); but the action of the statesman is also unleisurely, and—apart from the political action itself—aims at despotic power and honours, or at all events happiness, for him and his fellow citizens—a happiness different from political action, and evidently sought as being different. So if among virtuous actions political and military actions are distinguished by nobility and greatness, and these are unleisurely and aim at an end and are not desirable for their own sake, but the activity of reason, which is contemplative, seems both to be superior in serious worth and to aim at no end beyond itself, and to have its pleasure proper to itself (and this augments the activity), and the self-sufficiency, leisureliness, unweariedness (so far as this is possible for man), and all the other attributes ascribed to the supremely happy man are evidently those connected with this activity, it follows that this will be the complete happiness of man, if it be allowed a complete term of life (for none of the attributes of happiness is *in*complete).

But such a life would be too high for man; for it is not in so far as he is man that he will live so, but in so far as something divine is present in him; and by so much as this is superior to our composite nature is its activity superior to that which is the exercise of the other kind of virtue. If reason is divine, then in comparison with man, the life according to it is divine in comparison with human life. But we must not follow those who advise us, being men, to think of human things, and, being mortal, of mortal things, but must, so far as we can, make ourselves immortal, and strain every nerve to live in accordance with the best thing in us; for even if it be small in bulk, much more does it in power and worth surpass everything. This would seem, too, to be each man himself, since it is the authoritative and better part of him. It would be strange, then, if he were to choose not the life of his self but that of something else. And what we said before will apply now; that which is proper to each thing is by nature best and most pleasant for each thing; for man, therefore, the life according to reason is best and pleasantest, since reason more than anything else is man. This life therefore is also the happiest.

But in a secondary degree the life in accordance with the other kind of virtue is happy; for the activities in accordance with this befit our human estate. Just and brave acts, and other virtuous acts, we do in relation to each other, observing our respective duties with regard to contracts and services and all manner of actions and with regard to passions; and all of these seem to be typically human. Some of them seem even to arise from the body, and virtue of character to be in many ways bound up with the passions. Practical wisdom, too, is linked to virtue of character, and this to practical wisdom, since the principles of practical wisdom are in accordance with the moral virtues and rightness in morals is in accordance with practical wisdom. Being connected with the passions also, the moral virtues must belong to our composite nature; and the virtues of our composite nature are human; so, therefore, are the life and the happiness which correspond to these. The excellence of the reason is a thing apart; we must be content to say this much about it, for to describe it precisely is a task greater than our purpose requires. It would seem, however, also to need external equipment but little, or less than moral virtue does. Grant that both need the necessaries, and do so equally, even if the statesman's work is the more concerned with the body and things of that sort; for there will be little difference there; but in what they need for the exercise of their activities there will be much difference. The liberal man will need money for the doing of his liberal deeds, and the just man too will need it for the returning of services (for wishes are hard to discern, and even people who are not just pretend to wish to act justly); and the brave man will need power if he is to accomplish any of the acts that correspond to his virtue, and the temperate man will need opportunity; for how else is either he or any of the others to be recognized? It is debated, too, whether the will or the deed is more essential to virtue, which is assumed to involve both; it is surely clear that its perfection involves both; but for deeds many things are needed, and more, the greater and nobler the deeds are. But the man who is contemplating the truth needs no such thing, at least with a view to the exercise of his activity; indeed they are, one may say, even hindrances, at all events to his contemplation; but in so far as he is a man and lives with a number of people, he chooses to do virtuous acts; he will therefore need such aids to living a human life.

But that perfect happiness is a contemplative activity will appear from the following consideration as well. We assume the gods to be above all other beings blessed and happy; but what sort of actions must we assign to them? Acts of justice? Will not the gods seem absurd if they make contracts and return deposits, and so on? Acts of a brave man, then, confronting dangers and running risks because it is noble to do so? Or liberal acts? To whom will they give? It will be strange if they are really to have money or anything of the kind. And what would their temperate acts be? Is not such praise tasteless, since they have no bad appetites? If we were to run through them all, the circumstances of action would be found trivial and unworthy of gods. Still, every one supposes that they *live* and therefore that they are active; we cannot suppose them to sleep like Endymion. Now if you take away from a living being action, and still more production, what is left but contemplation? Therefore the activity of God, which surpasses all others in blessedness, must be contemplative; and of human activities, therefore, that which is most akin to this must be most of the nature of happiness.

This is indicated, too, by the fact that the other animals have no share in happiness, being completely deprived of such activity. For while the whole life of the gods is blessed, and that of men too in so far as some likeness of such activity belongs to them, none of the other animals is happy, since they in no way share in contemplation. Happiness extends, then, just so far as contemplation does, and those to whom contemplation more fully belongs are more truly happy, not as a mere concomitant but in virtue of the contemplation; for this is in itself precious. Happiness, therefore, must be some form of contemplation.

But, being a man, one will also need external prosperity; for our nature is not self-sufficient for the purpose of contemplation, but our body also must be healthy and must have food and other attention. Still, we must not think that the man who is to be happy will need many things or great things, merely because he cannot be supremely happy without external goods; for self-sufficiency and action do not involve excess, and we can do noble acts without ruling earth and sea; for even with moderate advantages one can act virtuously (this is manifest enough; for private persons are thought to do worthy acts no less than despots—indeed even more); and it is enough that we should have so much as that; for the life of the man who is active in accordance with virtue will be happy. . . .

Review Questions

1. What is happiness, according to Aristotle? How is it related to virtue? How is it related to pleasure?
2. How does Aristotle explain moral virtue? Give some examples.
3. Is it possible for everyone in our society to be happy, as Aristotle explains it? If not, who cannot be happy?

Discussion Questions

1. Aristotle characterizes a life of pleasure as suitable for beasts. But what, if anything, is wrong with a life of pleasure?
2. Aristotle claims that the philosopher will be happier than anyone else. Why is this? Do you agree or not?

Taking Rights Seriously

RONALD DWORKIN

Ronald Dworkin is university professor of jurisprudence, Oxford University, and professor of law, New York University. He is the author of *A Matter of Principle* (1985), *Law's Empire* (1986), *A Bill of Rights for Britain* (1990), and *Taking Rights Seriously* (1978), from which our reading is taken.

On Dworkin's view, if a people have a right to do something, then it is wrong to interfere with them. For example, if citizens have a right to free speech, then it is wrong for the government to interfere with the exercise of this right (unless this is necessary to protect other rights). This notion of rights, Dworkin believes, rests on the Kantian idea of treating people with dignity as members of the moral community, and also on the idea of political equality.

THE RIGHTS OF CITIZENS

THE LANGUAGE OF RIGHTS now dominates political debate in the United States. Does the Government respect the moral and political rights of its citizens? Or does the Government's foreign policy, or its race policy, fly in the face of these rights? Do the minorities whose rights have been violated have the right to violate the law in return? Or does the silent majority itself have rights, including the right that those who break the law be punished? It is not surprising that these questions are now prominent. The concept of rights, and particularly the concept of rights against the Government, has its most natural use when a political society is divided, and appeals to co-operation or a common goal are pointless.

The debate does not include the issue of whether citizens have *some* moral rights against their Government. It seems accepted on all sides

that they do. Conventional lawyers and politicians take it as a point of pride that our legal system recognizes, for example, individual rights of free speech, equality, and due process. They base their claim that our law deserves respect, at least in part, on that fact, for they would not claim that totalitarian systems deserve the same loyalty.

Some philosophers, of course, reject the idea that citizens have rights apart from what the law happens to give them. Bentham thought that the idea of moral rights was 'nonsense on stilts'. But that view has never been part of our orthodox political theory, and politicians of both parties appeal to the rights of the people to justify a great part of what they want to do. I shall not be concerned, in this essay, to defend the thesis that citizens have moral rights against their governments; I want instead to explore the implications of that thesis for those, including the present United States Government, who profess to accept it.

It is much in dispute, of course, what *particular* rights citizens have. Does the acknowledged right to free speech, for example, include the right to participate in nuisance demonstrations? In practice the Government will have the

Source: Reprinted by permission of the publisher from *Taking Rights Seriously* by Ronald Dworkin (Cambridge, Mass.: Harvard University Press), pp. 184–205. Copyright © 1977, 1978, 1985 by Ronald Dworkin.

last word on what an individual's rights are, because its police will do what its officials and courts say. But that does not mean that the Government's view is necessarily the correct view; anyone who thinks it does must believe that men and women have only such moral rights as Government chooses to grant, which means that they have no moral rights at all.

All this is sometimes obscured in the United States by the constitutional system. The American Constitution provides a set of individual *legal* rights in the First Amendment, and in the due process, equal protection, and similar clauses. Under present legal practice the Supreme Court has the power to declare an act of Congress or of a state legislature void if the Court finds that the act offends these provisions. This practice has led some commentators to suppose that individual moral rights are fully protected by this system, but that is hardly so, nor could it be so.

The Constitution fuses legal and moral issues, by making the validity of a law depend on the answer to complex moral problems, like the problem of whether a particular statute respects the inherent equality of all men. This fusion has important consequences for the debates about civil disobedience. . . . But it leaves open two prominent questions. It does not tell us whether the Constitution, even properly interpreted, recognizes all the moral rights that citizens have, and it does not tell us whether, as many suppose, citizens would have a duty to obey the law even if it did invade their moral rights. . . .

Even if the Constitution were perfect, of course, and the majority left it alone, it would not follow that the Supreme Court could guarantee the individual rights of citizens. A Supreme Court decision is still a legal decision, and it must take into account precedent and institutional considerations like relations between the Court and Congress, as well as morality. And no judicial decision is necessarily the right decision. Judges stand for different positions on controversial issues of law and morals and, as the

fights over Nixon's Supreme Court nominations showed, a President is entitled to appoint judges of his own persuasion, provided that they are honest and capable.

So, though the constitutional system adds something to the protection of moral rights against the Government, it falls far short of guaranteeing these rights, or even establishing what they are. . . .

RIGHTS AND THE RIGHT TO BREAK THE LAW

. . . In most cases when we say that someone has a 'right' to do something, we imply that it would be wrong to interfere with his doing it, or at least that some special grounds are needed for justifying any interference. I use this strong sense of right when I say that you have the right to spend your money gambling, if you wish, though you ought to spend it in a more worthwhile way. I mean that it would be wrong for anyone to interfere with you even though you propose to spend your money in a way that I think is wrong.

There is a clear difference between saying that someone has a right to do something in this sense and saying that it is the 'right' thing for him to do, or that he does no 'wrong' in doing it. Someone may have the right to do something that is the wrong thing for him to do, as might be the case with gambling. Conversely, something may be the right thing for him to do and yet he may have no right to do it, in the sense that it would not be wrong for someone to interfere with his trying. If our army captures an enemy soldier, we might say that the right thing for him to do is to try to escape, but it would not follow that it is wrong for us to try to stop him. . . .

These distinctions enable us to see an ambiguity in the orthodox question: Does a man ever have a right to break the law? Does that question mean to ask whether he ever has a right to break the law in the strong sense, so that the Government would do wrong to stop him, by arresting and prosecuting him? Or does it mean to ask whether he ever does the right thing to break the law, so that we should all respect him even though the Government should jail him? . . .

Conservatives and liberals do agree that sometimes a man does not do the wrong thing to break a law, when his conscience so requires. They disagree, when they do, over the different issue of what the State's response should be. Both parties do think that sometimes the State should prosecute. But this is not inconsistent with the proposition that the man prosecuted did the right thing in breaking the law. . . .

I said that in the United States citizens are supposed to have certain fundamental rights against their Government, certain moral rights made into legal rights by the Constitution. If this idea is significant, and worth bragging about, then these rights must be rights in the strong sense I just described. The claim that citizens have a right to free speech must imply that it would be wrong for the Government to stop them from speaking, even when the Government believes that what they will say will cause more harm than good. The claim cannot mean, on the prisoner-of-war analogy, only that citizens do no wrong in speaking their minds, though the Government reserves the right to prevent them from doing so.

This is a crucial point, and I want to labour it. Of course a responsible government must be ready to justify anything it does, particularly when it limits the liberty of its citizens. But normally it is a sufficient justification, even for an act that limits liberty, that the act is calculated to increase what the philosophers call general utility—that it is calculated to produce more over-all benefit than harm. So, though the New York City government needs a justification for forbidding motorists to drive up Lexington Avenue, it is sufficient justification if the proper officials believe, on sound evidence, that the gain to the many will outweigh the inconvenience to

the few. When individual citizens are said to have rights against the Government, however, like the right of free speech, that must mean that this sort of justification is not enough. Otherwise the claim would not argue that individuals have special protection against the law when their rights are in play, and that is just the point of the claim.

Not all legal rights, or even Constitutional rights, represent moral rights against the Government. I now have the legal right to drive either way on Fifty-seventh Street, but the Government would do no wrong to make that street one-way if it thought it in the general interest to do so. I have a Constitutional right to vote for a congressman every two years, but the national and state governments would do no wrong if, following the amendment procedure, they made a congressman's term four years instead of two, again on the basis of a judgment that this would be for the general good.

But those Constitutional rights that we call fundamental like the right of free speech, are supposed to represent rights against the Government in the strong sense; that is the point of the boast that our legal system respects the fundamental rights of the citizen. If citizens have a moral right of free speech, then governments would do wrong to repeal the First Amendment that guarantees it, even if they were persuaded that the majority would be better off if speech were curtailed.

I must not overstate the point. Someone who claims that citizens have a right against the Government need not go so far as to say that the State is *never* justified in overriding that right. He might say, for example, that although citizens have a right to free speech, the Government may override that right when necessary to protect the rights of others, or to prevent a catastrophe, or even to obtain a clear and major public benefit (though if he acknowledged this last as a possible justification he would be treating the right in question as not among the most important or fundamental). What he cannot do is to say that the Government is justified in over-riding a right on the minimal grounds that would be sufficient if no such right existed. He cannot say that the Government is entitled to act on no more than a judgment that its act is likely to produce, overall, a benefit to the community. That admission would make his claim of a right pointless, and would show him to be using some sense of 'right' other than the strong sense necessary to give his claim the political importance it is normally taken to have. . . .

I said that any society that claims to recognize rights at all must abandon the notion of a general duty to obey the law that holds in all cases. This is important, because it shows that there are no short cuts to meeting a citizen's claim to right. If a citizen argues that he has a moral right not to serve in the Army, or to protest in a way he finds effective, then an official who wants to answer him, and not simply bludgeon him into obedience, must respond to the particular point he makes, and cannot point to the draft law or a Supreme Court decision as having even special, let alone decisive, weight. Sometimes an official who considers the citizen's moral arguments in good faith will be persuaded that the citizen's claim is plausible, or even right. It does not follow, however, that he will always be persuaded or that he always should be.

I must emphasize that all these propositions concern the strong sense of right, and they therefore leave open important questions about the right thing to do. If a man believes he has the right to break the law, he must then ask whether he does the right thing to exercise that right. He must remember that reasonable men can differ about whether he has a right against the Government, and therefore the right to break the law, that he thinks he has; and therefore that reasonable men can oppose him in good faith. He must take into account the various consequences his acts will have, whether they involve violence, and such other considerations as the context makes relevant; he must not go beyond the rights he can in good faith claim, to acts that violate the rights of others. . . .

CONTROVERSIAL RIGHTS

The argument so far has been hypothetical: if a man has a particular moral right against the Government, that right survives contrary legislation or adjudication. But this does not tell us what rights he has, and it is notorious that reasonable men disagree about that. There is wide agreement on certain clearcut cases; almost everyone who believes in rights at all would admit, for example, that a man has a moral right to speak his mind in a non-provocative way on matters of political concern, and that this is an important right that the State must go to great pains to protect. But there is great controversy as to the limits of such paradigm rights; and the so-called 'anti-riot' law involved in the famous Chicago Seven trial of the last decade is a case in point.

The defendants were accused of conspiring to cross state lines with the intention of causing a riot. This charge is vague—perhaps unconstitutionally vague—but the law apparently defines as criminal emotional speeches which argue that violence is justified in order to secure political equality. Does the right of free speech protect this sort of speech? That, of course, is a legal issue, because it invokes the free-speech clause of the First Amendment of the Constitution. But it is also a moral issue, because, as I said, we must treat the First Amendment as an attempt to protect a moral right. It is part of the job of governing to 'define' moral rights through statutes and judicial decisions, that is, to declare officially the extent that moral rights will be taken to have in law. Congress faced this task in voting on the anti-riot bill, and the Supreme Court has faced it in countless cases. How should the different departments of government go about defining moral rights?

They should begin with a sense that whatever they decide might be wrong. History and their descendants may judge that they acted unjustly when they thought they were right. If they take their duty seriously, they must try to limit their mistakes, and they must therefore try to discover where the dangers of mistake lie.

They might choose one of two very different models for this purpose. The first model recommends striking a balance between the rights of the individual and the demands of society at large. If the Government *infringes* on a moral right (for example, by defining the right of free speech more narrowly than justice requires), then it has done the individual a wrong. On the other hand, if the Government *inflates* a right (by defining it more broadly than justice requires) then it cheats society of some general benefit, like safe streets, that there is no reason it should not have. So a mistake on one side is as serious as a mistake on the other. The course of government is to steer to the middle, to balance the general good and personal rights, giving to each its due. . . .

The first model, described in this way, has great plausibility, and most laymen and lawyers, I think, would respond to it warmly. The metaphor of balancing the public interest against personal claims is established in our political and judicial rhetoric, and this metaphor gives the model both familiarity and appeal. Nevertheless, the first model is a false one, certainly in the case of rights generally regarded as important, and the metaphor is the heart of its error.

The institution of rights against the Government is not a gift of God, or an ancient ritual, or a national sport. It is a complex and troublesome practice that makes the Government's job of securing the general benefit more difficult and more expensive, and it would be a frivolous and wrongful practice unless it served some point. Anyone who professes to take rights seriously, and who praises our Government for respecting them, must have some sense of what that point is. He must accept, at the minimum,

one or both of two important ideas. The first is the vague but powerful idea of human dignity. This idea, associated with Kant, but defended by philosophers of different schools, supposes that there are ways of treating a man that are inconsistent with recognizing him as a full member of the human community, and holds that such treatment is profoundly unjust.

The second is the more familiar idea of political equality. This supposes that the weaker members of a political community are entitled to the same concern and respect of their government as the more powerful members have secured for themselves, so that if some men have freedom of decision whatever the effect on the general good, then all men must have the same freedom. I do not want to defend or elaborate these ideas here, but only to insist that anyone who claims that citizens have rights must accept ideas very close to these.[1]

It makes sense to say that a man has a fundamental right against the Government, in the strong sense, like free speech, if that right is necessary to protect his dignity, or his standing as equally entitled to concern and respect, or some other personal value of like consequence. It does not make sense otherwise.

So if rights make sense at all, then the invasion of a relatively important right must be a very serious matter. It means treating a man as less than a man, or as less worthy of concern than other men. The institution of rights rests on the conviction that this is a grave injustice,

---

1 He need not consider these ideas to be axiomatic. He may, that is, have reasons for insisting that dignity or equality are important values, and these reasons may be utilitarian. He may believe, for example, that the general good will be advanced, *in the long run*, only if we treat indignity or inequality as very great injustices, and never allow our *opinions* about the general good to justify them. I do not know of any good arguments for or against this sort of 'institutional' utilitarianism, but it is consistent with my point, because it argues that we must treat violations of dignity and equality as special moral crimes, beyond the reach of ordinary utilitarian justification.

and that it is worth paying the incremental cost in social policy or efficiency that is necessary to prevent it. But then it must be wrong to say that inflating rights is as serious as invading them. If the Government errs on the side of the individual, then it simply pays a little more in social efficiency than it has to pay; it pays a little more, that is, of the same coin that it has already decided must be spent. But if it errs against the individual it inflicts an insult upon him that, on its own reckoning, it is worth a great deal of that coin to avoid. . . .

It cannot be an argument for curtailing a right, once granted, simply that society would pay a further price for extending it. There must be something special about that further cost, or there must be some other feature of the case, that makes it sensible to say that although great social cost is warranted to protect the original right, this particular cost is not necessary. Otherwise, the Government's failure to extend the right will show that its recognition of the right in the original case is a sham, a promise that it intends to keep only until that becomes inconvenient.

How can we show that a particular cost is not worth paying without taking back the initial recognition of a right? I can think of only three sorts of grounds that can consistently be used to limit the definition of a particular right. First, the Government might show that the values protected by the original right are not really at stake in the marginal case, or are at stake only in some attenuated form. Second, it might show that if the right is defined to include the marginal case, then some competing right, in the strong sense I described earlier, would be abridged. Third, it might show that if the right were so defined, then the cost to society would not be simply incremental, but would be of a degree far beyond the cost paid to grant the original right, a degree great enough to justify whatever assault on dignity or equality might be involved. . . .

But what of the individual rights of those who will be destroyed by a riot, of the passerby who will be killed by a sniper's bullet or the shopkeeper who will be ruined by looting? To put the issue in this way, as a question of competing rights, suggests a principle that would undercut the effect of uncertainty. Shall we say that some rights to protection are so important that the Government is justified in doing all it can to maintain them? Shall we therefore say that the Government may abridge the rights of others to act when their acts might simply increase the risk, by however slight or speculative a margin, that some person's right to life or property will be violated?

Some such principle is relied on by those who oppose the Supreme Court's recent liberal rulings on police procedure. These rulings increase the chance that a guilty man will go free, and therefore marginally increase the risk that any particular member of the community will be murdered, raped, or robbed. Some critics believe that the Court's decisions must therefore be wrong.

But no society that purports to recognize a variety of rights, on the ground that a man's dignity or equality may be invaded in a variety of ways, can accept such a principle. If forcing a man to testify against himself, or forbidding him to speak, does the damage that the rights against self-incrimination and the right of free speech assume, then it would be contemptuous for the State to tell a man that he must suffer this damage against the possibility that other men's risk of loss may be marginally reduced. If rights make sense, then the degrees of their importance cannot be so different that some count not at all when others are mentioned.

Of course the Government may discriminate and may stop a man from exercising his right to speak when there is a clear and substantial risk that his speech will do great damage to the person or property of others, and no other means of preventing this are at hand, as in the case of the man shouting 'Fire!' in a theater. But we must reject the suggested principle that the Government can simply ignore rights to speak when life and property are in question. So long as the impact of speech on these other rights remains speculative and marginal, it must look elsewhere for levers to pull.

WHY TAKE RIGHTS SERIOUSLY?

I said at the beginning of this essay that I wanted to show what a government must do that professes to recognize individual rights. It must dispense with the claim that citizens never have a right to break its law, and it must not define citizens' rights so that these are cut off for supposed reasons of the general good. Any Government's harsh treatment of civil disobedience, or campaign against vocal protest, may therefore be thought to count against its sincerity.

One might well ask, however, whether it is wise to take rights all that seriously after all. America's genius, at least in her own legend, lies in not taking any abstract doctrine to its logical extreme. It may be time to ignore abstractions, and concentrate instead on giving the majority of our citizens a new sense of their Government's concern for their welfare, and of their title to rule.

That, in any event, is what former Vice-President Agnew seemed to believe. In a policy statement on the issue of 'weirdos' and social misfits, he said that the liberals' concern for individual rights was a headwind blowing in the face of the ship of state. That is a poor metaphor, but the philosophical point it expresses is very well taken. He recognized, as many liberals do not, that the majority cannot travel as fast or as far as it would like if it recognizes the rights of individuals to do what, in the majority's terms, is the wrong thing to do.

Spiro Agnew supposed that rights are divisive, and that national unity and a new respect for law may be developed by taking them more skeptically. But he is wrong. America will continue to be divided by its social and foreign policy, and if the economy grows weaker again the divisions will become more bitter. If we want our laws and our legal institutions to provide the ground rules within which these issues will be contested then these ground rules must not be the conqueror's law that the dominant class imposes on the weaker, as Marx supposed the law of a capitalist society must be. The bulk of the law—that part which defines and implements social, economic, and foreign policy—cannot be neutral. It must state, in its greatest part, the majority's view of the common good. The institution of rights is therefore crucial, because it represents the majority's promise to the minorities that their dignity and equality will be respected. When the divisions among the groups are most violent, then this gesture, if law is to work, must be most sincere.

The institution requires an act of faith on the part of the minorities, because the scope of their rights will be controversial whenever they are important, and because the officers of the majority will act on their own notions of what these rights really are. Of course these officials will disagree with many of the claims that a minority makes. That makes it all the more important that they take their decisions gravely. They must show that they understand what rights are, and they must not cheat on the full implications of the doctrine. The Government will not reestablish respect for law without giving the law some claim to respect. It cannot do that if it neglects the one feature that distinguishes law from ordered brutality. If the Government does not take rights seriously, then it does not take law seriously either.

Review Questions

1. What does Dworkin mean by right in the strong sense? What rights in this sense are protected by the U.S. Constitution?

2. Distinguish between legal and moral rights. Give some examples of legal rights that are not moral rights, and moral rights that are not legal rights.
3. What are the two models of how a government might define the rights of its citizens? Which does Dworkin find more attractive?
4. According to Dworkin, what two important ideas are behind the institution of rights?

Discussion Questions

1. Does a person have a right to break the law? Why or why not?
2. Are rights in the strong sense compatible with Mill's Utilitarianism? (See the footnote about Institutional Utilitarianism.)
3. Do you think that Kant would accept rights in the strong sense or not?

Women's Rights as Human Rights: Toward a Re-Vision of Human Rights

CHARLOTTE BUNCH

Charlotte Bunch is the director of the Center for Global Issues and Women's Leadership at Rutgers University. She is the author of *Passionate Politics: Feminist Theory in Action* (1987).

   Bunch argues that the Western conception of human rights as involving civil and political liberties is too narrow; it leaves out women's rights. Women's rights include reproductive rights and socioeconomic rights—that is, the rights to food, shelter, medical care, and work. Violence against women and the oppression of women should be considered violations of women's rights. Bunch discusses four approaches to making women's rights into human rights: (1) the political and civil rights approach, (2) the socioeconomic approach, (3) the legal approach, and (4) the feminist transformation of human rights. She concludes that the four approaches are overlapping and that all four are necessary to achieve women's rights.

Source: Charlotte Bunch, "Women's Rights and Human Rights: Toward a Re-Vision of Human Rights," from *Human Rights Quarterly*, Vol. 12, No. 4 (November 1990), pp. 486–98. Copyright © 1990 The Johns Hopkins University Press.

SIGNIFICANT NUMBERS of the world's population are routinely subjected to torture, starvation, terrorism, humiliation, mutilation and even murder simply because they are female. Crimes such as these against any group other than women would be recognized as a civil and political emergency as well as a gross violation of the victims' humanity. Yet, despite a clear record of deaths and demonstrable abuse, women's rights are not commonly classified as human rights. This is problematic both theoretically and practically, because it has grave consequences for the way society views and treats the fundamental issues of women's lives. This paper questions why women's rights and human rights are viewed as distinct, looks at the policy implications of this schism, and discusses different approaches to changing it.

Women's human rights are violated in a variety of ways. Of course, women sometimes suffer abuses such as political repression that are similar to abuses suffered by men. In these situations, female victims are often invisible, because the dominant image of the political actor in our world is male. However, many violations of women's human rights are distinctly connected to being female—that is, women are discriminated against and abused on the basis of gender. Women also experience sexual abuse in situations where their other human rights are being violated, as political prisoners or members of persecuted ethnic groups, for example. In this paper I address those abuses in which gender is a primary or related factor because gender-related abuse has been most neglected and offers the greatest challenge to the field of human rights today.

The concept of human rights is one of the few moral visions ascribed to internationally. Although its scope is not universally agreed upon, it strikes deep chords of response among many. Promotion of human rights is a widely accepted goal and thus provides a useful framework for seeking redress of gender abuse. Further it is one of the few concepts that speaks to the need for transnational activism and concern about the lives of people globally. The Universal Declaration of Human Rights,[1] adopted in 1948, symbolizes this world vision and defines human rights broadly. While not much is said about women, Article 2 entitles all to "the rights and freedoms set forth in this Declaration, without distinction of any kind, such as race, colour, sex, language, religion, political or other opinion, national or social origin, property, birth or other status." Eleanor Roosevelt and the Latin American women who fought for the inclusion of sex in the Declaration and for its passage clearly intended that it would address the problem of women's subordination.[2]

Since 1948 the world community has continuously debated varying interpretations of human rights in response to global developments. Little of this discussion, however, has addressed questions of gender, and only recently have significant challenges been made to a vision of human rights which excludes much of women's experiences. The concept of human rights, like all vibrant visions, is not static or the property of any one group; rather, its meaning expands as people reconceive of their needs and hopes in relation to it. In this spirit, feminists redefine human rights abuses to include the degradation and violation of women. The specific experiences of women must be added to traditional approaches to human rights in order to make women more visible and to transform the concept and practice of human rights in our culture so that it takes better account of women's lives.

1 Universal Declaration of Human Rights, *adopted* 10 December 1948, G.A. Res. 217A(III), U.N. Doc. A/810 (1948).
2 Blanche Wiesen Cook, "Eleanor Roosevelt and Human Rights: The Battle for Peace and Planetary Decency," Edward P. Crapol, ed. *Women and American Foreign Policy: Lobbyists, Critics and Insiders* (New York: Greenwood Press, 1987), 98–118; Georgina Ashworth. "Of Violence and Violation: Women and Human Rights," *Change Thinkbook II* (London, 1986).

In the next part of this article, I will explore both the importance and the difficulty of connecting women's rights to human rights, and then I will outline four basic approaches that have been used in the effort to make this connection.

BEYOND RHETORIC: POLITICAL IMPLICATIONS

Few governments exhibit more than token commitment to women's equality as a basic human right in domestic or foreign policy. No government determines its policies toward other countries on the basis of their treatment of women, even when some aid and trade decisions are said to be based on a country's human rights record. Among nongovernmental organizations, women are rarely a priority, and Human Rights Day programs on 10 December seldom include discussion of issues like violence against women or reproductive rights. When it is suggested that governments and human rights organizations should respond to women's rights as concerns that deserve such attention, a number of excuses are offered for why this cannot be done. The responses tend to follow one or more of these lines: (1) sex discrimination is too trivial, or not as important, or will come after larger issues of survival that require more serious attention; (2) abuse of women, while regrettable, is a cultural, private, or individual issue and not a political matter requiring state action; (3) while appropriate for other action, women's rights are not human rights per se; or (4) when the abuse of women is recognized, it is considered inevitable or so pervasive that any consideration of it is futile or will overwhelm other human rights questions. It is important to challenge these responses.

The narrow definition of human rights, recognized by many in the West as solely a matter of state violation of civil and political liberties, impedes consideration of women's rights. In the United States the concept has been further limited by some who have used it as a weapon in the cold war almost exclusively to challenge human rights abuses perpetrated in communist countries. Even then, many abuses that affected women, such as forced pregnancy in Romania, were ignored.

Some important aspects of women's rights do fit into a civil liberties framework, but much of the abuse against women is part of a larger socioeconomic web that entraps women, making them vulnerable to abuses which cannot be delineated as exclusively political or solely caused by states. The inclusion of "second generation" or socioeconomic human rights to food, shelter, and work—which are clearly delineated as part of the Universal Declaration of Human Rights—is vital to addressing women's concerns fully. Further, the assumption that states are not responsible for most violations of women's rights ignores the fact that such abuses, although committed perhaps by private citizens, are often condoned or even sanctioned by states. I will return to the question of state responsibility after responding to other instances of resistance to women's rights as human rights.

The most insidious myth about women's rights is that they are trivial or secondary to the concerns of life and death. Nothing could be farther from the truth: sexism kills. There is increasing documentation of the many ways in which being female is life-threatening. The following are a few examples:

- Before birth: Amniocentesis is used for sex selection leading to the abortion of more female fetuses at rates as high as 99 percent in Bombay, India; in China and India, the two most populous nations, more males than females are born even though natural birth ratios would produce more females.[3]

- During childhood: The World Health Organization reports that in many coun-

3 Vibhuti Patel. *In Search of Our Bodies: A Feminist Look at Women, Health, and Reproduction in India* (Shakti, Bombay, 1987); Lori Heise, "International Dimensions of Violence Against Women," *Response*, vol. 12, no. 1 (1989): 3.

tries, girls are fed less, breast fed for shorter periods of time, taken to doctors less frequently, and die or are physically and mentally maimed by malnutrition at higher rates than boys.[4]

• In adulthood: The denial of women's rights to control their bodies in reproduction threatens women's lives, especially where this is combined with poverty and poor health services. In Latin America, complications from illegal abortions are the leading cause of death for women between the ages of fifteen and thirty-nine.[5]

Sex discrimination kills women daily. When combined with race, class, and other forms of oppression, it constitutes a deadly denial of women's right to life and liberty on a large scale throughout the world. The most pervasive violation of females is violence against women in all its manifestations, from wife battery, incest, and rape, to dowry deaths,[6] genital mutilation,[7] and female sexual slavery. These abuses occur in every country and are found in the home and in the workplace, on streets, on campuses, and in prisons and refugee camps. They cross class, race, age, and national lines; and at the same time, the forms this violence takes often reinforce other oppressions such as racism, "able-bodyism," and imperialism. Case in point: in order to feed their families, poor women in brothels around U.S. military bases in places like the Philippines bear the burden of sexual, racial, and national imperialism in repeated and often brutal violation of their bodies.

Even a short review of random statistics reveals that the extent of violence against women globally is staggering:

• In the United States, battery is the leading cause of injury to adult women, and a rape is committed every six minutes.[8]

• In Peru, 70 percent of all crimes reported to police involve women who are beaten by their partners; and in Lima (a city of seven million people), 168,970 rapes were reported in 1987 alone.[9]

• In India, eight out of ten wives are victims of violence, either domestic battery, dowry-related abuse, or among the least fortunate, murder.[10]

• In France, 95 percent of the victims of violence are women; 51 percent at the hands of a spouse or lover. Similar statistics from places as diverse as Bangladesh, Canada, Kenya, and Thailand demonstrate that more than 50 percent of female homicides were committed by family members.[11]

Where recorded, domestic battery figures range from 40 percent to 80 percent of women

---

4 Sundari Ravindran, *Health Implications of Sex Discrimination in Childhood* (Geneva: World Health Organization, 1986). These problems and proposed social programs to counter them in India are discussed in detail in "Gender Violence: Gender Discrimination Between Boy and Girl in Parental Family," paper published by CHETNA (Child Health Education Training and Nutrition Awareness), Ahmedabad, 1989.

5 Debbie Taylor, ed., *Women: A World Report, A New Internationalist Book* (Oxford: Oxford University Press, 1985), 10. See Joni Seager and Ann Olson, eds., *Women In The World: An International Atlas* (London: Pluto Press, 1986) for more statistics on the effects of sex discrimination.

6 Frequently a husband will disguise the death of a bride as suicide or an accident in order to collect the marriage settlement paid him by the bride's parents. Although dowry is now illegal in many countries, official records for 1987 showed 1,786 dowry deaths in India alone. See Heise, note 3, 5.

7 For an in-depth examination of the practice of female circumcision see Alison T. Slack, "Female Circumcision: A Critical Appraisal," *Human Rights Quarterly* 10 (1988): 439.

8 C. Everett Koop, M.D. "Violence Against Women: A Global Problem," presentation by the Surgeon General of the U.S., Public Health Service, Washington D.C., 1989.

9 Ana Maria Portugal, "Cronica de Una Violación Provocada?", *Fempress* especial 'Contraviolencia,' Santiago, 1988; Seager and Olson, note 5, 37.

10 Ashworth, note 2, 9.

11 "Violence Against Women in the Family" Centre for Social Development and Humanitarian Affairs, United Nations Office at Vienna, 1989.

beaten, usually repeatedly, indicating that the home is the most dangerous place for women and frequently the site of cruelty and torture. As the Carol Stuart murder in Boston demonstrated, sexist and racist attitudes in the United States often cover up the real threat to women; a woman is murdered in Massachusetts by a husband or lover every 22 days.[12]

Such numbers do not reflect the full extent of the problem of violence against women, much of which remains hidden. Yet rather than receiving recognition as a major world conflict, this violence is accepted as normal or even dismissed as an individual or cultural matter. Georgina Ashworth notes that:

> The greatest restriction of liberty, dignity and movement and at the same time, direct violation of the person is the threat and realization of violence. . . . However violence against the female sex, on a scale which far exceeds the list of Amnesty International victims, is tolerated publicly; indeed some acts of violation are not crimes in law, others are legitimized in custom or court opinion, and most are blamed on the victims themselves.[13]

Violence against women is a touchstone that illustrates the limited concept of human rights and highlights the political nature of the abuse of women. As Lori Heise states: "This is not random violence. . . . [T]he risk factor is being female."[14] Victims are chosen because of their gender. The message is domination: Stay in your place or be afraid. Contrary to the argument that such violence is only personal or cultural, it is profoundly political. It results from the structural relationships of power, domination, and privilege between men and women in society. Violence against women is central to maintain-

ing those political relations at home, at work, and in all public spheres.

Failure to see the oppression of women as political also results in the exclusion of sex discrimination and violence against women from the human rights agenda. Female subordination runs so deep that it is still viewed as inevitable or natural, rather than seen as a politically constructed reality maintained by patriarchal interests, ideology, and institutions. But I do not believe that male violation of women is inevitable or natural. Such a belief requires a narrow and pessimistic view of men. If violence and domination are understood as a politically constructed reality, it is possible to imagine deconstructing that system and building more just interactions between the sexes.

The physical territory of this political struggle over what constitutes women's human rights is women's bodies. The importance of control over women can be seen in the intensity of resistance to laws and social changes that put control of women's bodies in women's hands: reproductive rights, freedom of sexuality whether heterosexual or lesbian, laws that criminalize rape in marriage, etc. Denial of reproductive rights and homophobia are also political means of maintaining control over women and perpetuating sex roles and thus have human rights implications. The physical abuse of women is a reminder of this territorial domination and is sometimes accompanied by other forms of human rights abuse such as slavery (forced prostitution), sexual terrorism (rape), imprisonment (confinement to the home), and torture (systematic battery). Some cases are extreme, such as the women in Thailand who died in a brothel fire because they were chained to their beds. Most situations are more ordinary like denying women decent educations or jobs which leaves them prey to abusive marriages, exploitative work, and prostitution.

This raises once again the question of the state's responsibility for protecting women's human rights. Feminists have shown how the distinction between private and public abuse is a

---

12 Bella English, "Stereotypes Led Us Astray," *The Boston Globe,* 5 Jan. 1990, 17, col. 3. See also the statistics in *Women's International Network News,* 1989; United Nations Office, note 11 above; Ashworth, note 2; Heise, note 3; and *Fempress,* note 9.

13 Ashworth, note 2, 8.

14 Heise, note 3, 3.

dichotomy often used to justify female subordination in the home. Governments regulate many matters in the family and individual spheres. For example, human rights activists pressure states to prevent slavery or racial discrimination and segregation even when these are conducted by nongovernmental forces in private or proclaimed as cultural traditions as they have been in both the southern United States and in South Africa. The real questions are: (1) who decides what are legitimate human rights; and (2) when should the state become involved and for what purposes. Riane Eisler argues that:

> the issue is what types of private acts are protected by the right to privacy and/or the principle of family autonomy. Even more specifically, the issue is whether violations of human rights within the family such as genital mutilation, wife beating, and other forms of violence designed to maintain patriarchal control should be within the purview of human rights theory and action. . . . [T]he underlying problem for human rights theory, as for most other fields of theory, is that the yardstick that has been developed for defining and measuring human rights has been based on the male as the norm.[15]

The human rights community must move beyond its male defined norms in order to respond to the brutal and systematic violation of women globally. This does not mean that every human rights group must alter the focus of its work. However it does require examining patriarchal biases and acknowledging the rights of women as human rights. Governments must seek to end the politically and culturally constructed war on women rather than continue to perpetuate it. Every state has the responsibility to intervene in the abuse of women's rights within its borders and to end its collusion with the forces that perpetrate such violations in other countries.

15 Riane Eisler, "Human Rights: Toward an Integrated Theory for Action," *Human Rights Quarterly* 9 (1987):297. See also Alida Brill, *Nobody's Business: The Paradoxes of Privacy* (New York: Addison-Wesley, 1990).

TOWARD ACTION: PRACTICAL APPROACHES

The classification of human rights is more than just a semantics problem because it has practical policy consequences. Human rights are still considered to be more important than women's rights. The distinction perpetuates the idea that the rights of women are of a lesser order than the "rights of man," and, as Eisler describes it, "serves to justify practices that do not accord women full and equal status."[16] In the United Nations, the Human Rights Commission has more power to hear and investigate cases than the Commission on the Status of Women, more staff and budget, and better mechanisms for implementing its findings. Thus it makes a difference in what can be done if a case is deemed a violation of women's rights and not of human rights.[17]

The determination of refugee status illustrates how the definition of human rights affects people's lives. The Dutch Refugee Association, in its pioneering efforts to convince other nations to recognize sexual persecution and violence against women as justifications for granting refugee status, found that some European governments would take sexual persecution into account as an aspect of other forms of political repression, but none would make it the grounds for refugee status per se.[18] The implications of such a distinction are clear when examining a situation like that of the Bangladeshi women, who having been raped during the Pakistan–Bangladesh war, subsequently faced death at the hands of male relatives to preserve "family

16 Eisler, note 15, 291.
17 Sandra Coliver, "United Nations Machineries on Women's Rights: How Might They Better Help Women Whose Rights Are Being Violated?" in Ellen L. Lutz, Hurst Hannum, and Kathryn J. Burke, eds., *New Directions in Human Rights* (Philadelphia: Univ. of Penn. Press, 1989).
18 Marijke Meyer, "Oppression of Women and Refugee Status," unpublished report to NGO Forum, Nairobi, Kenya, 1985 and "Sexual Violence Against Women Refugees" Ministry of Social Affairs and Labour, The Netherlands, June 1984.

honor." Western powers professed outrage but did not offer asylum to these victims of human rights abuse.

I have observed four basic approaches to linking women's rights to human rights. These approaches are presented separately here in order to identify each more clearly. In practice, these approaches often overlap, and while each raises questions about the others, I see them as complementary. These approaches can be applied to many issues, but I will illustrate them primarily in terms of how they address violence against women in order to show the implications of their differences on a concrete issue.

1. Women's Rights as Political and Civil Rights

Taking women's specific needs into consideration as part of the already recognized "first generation" political and civil liberties is the first approach. This involves both raising the visibility of women who suffer general human rights violations as well as calling attention to particular abuses women encounter because they are female. Thus, issues of violence against women are raised when they connect to other forms of violation such as the sexual torture of women political prisoners in South America.[19] Groups like the Women's Task Force of Amnesty International have taken this approach in pushing for Amnesty to launch a campaign on behalf of women political prisoners which would address the sexual abuse and rape of women in custody, their lack of maternal care in detention, and the resulting human rights abuse of their children.

Documenting the problems of women refugees and developing responsive policies are other illustrations of this approach. Women and children make up more than 80 percent of those in refugee camps, yet few refugee policies are specifically shaped to meet the needs of these vulnerable populations who face considerable sexual abuse. For example, in one camp where men were allocated the community's rations, some gave food to women and their children in exchange for sex. Revealing this abuse led to new policies that allocated food directly to the women.[20]

The political and civil rights approach is a useful starting point for many human rights groups; by considering women's experiences, these groups can expand their efforts in areas where they are already working. This approach also raises contradictions that reveal the limits of a narrow civil liberties view. One contradiction is to define rape as a human rights abuse only when it occurs in state custody but not on the streets or in the home. Another is to say that a violation of the right to free speech occurs when someone is jailed for defending gay rights, but not when someone is jailed or even tortured and killed for homosexuality. Thus while this approach of adding women and stirring them into existing first generation human rights categories is useful, it is not enough by itself.

2. Women's Rights as Socioeconomic Rights

The second approach includes the particular plight of women with regard to "second generation" human rights such as the rights to food, shelter, health care, and employment. This is an approach favored by those who see the dominant Western human rights tradition and international law as too individualistic and identify women's oppression as primarily economic.

This tendency has its origins among socialists and labor activists who have long argued that political human rights are meaningless to many

19 Ximena Bunster describes this in Chile and Argentina in "The Torture of Women Political Prisoners: A Case Study in Female Sexual Slavery," in Kathleen Barry, Charlotte Bunch, and Shirley Castley, eds., *International Feminism: Networking Against Female Sexual Slavery* (New York: IWTC, 1984).

20 Report given by Margaret Groarke at Women's Panel, Amnesty International New York Regional Meeting, 24 Feb. 1990.

without economic rights as well. It focuses on the primacy of the need to end women's economic subordination as the key to other issues including women's vulnerability to violence. This particular focus has led to work on issues like women's right to organize as workers and opposition to violence in the workplace, especially in situations like the free trade zones which have targeted women as cheap, nonorganized labor. Another focus of this approach has been highlighting the feminization of poverty or what might better be called the increasing impoverishment of females. Poverty has not become strictly female, but females now comprise a higher percentage of the poor.

Looking at women's rights in the context of socioeconomic development is another example of this approach. Third world peoples have called for an understanding of socioeconomic development as a human rights issue. Within this demand, some have sought to integrate women's rights into development and have examined women's specific needs in relation to areas like land ownership or access to credit. Among those working on women in development, there is growing interest in violence against women as both a health and development issue. If violence is seen as having negative consequences for social productivity, it may get more attention. This type of narrow economic measure, however, should not determine whether such violence is seen as a human rights concern. Violence as a development issue is linked to the need to understand development not just as an economic issue but also as a question of empowerment and human growth.

One of the limitations of this second approach has been its tendency to reduce women's needs to the economic sphere which implies that women's rights will follow automatically with third world development, which may involve socialism. This has not proven to be the case. Many working from this approach are no longer trying to add women into either the Western capitalist or socialist development mod-

els, but rather seek a transformative development process that links women's political, economic, and cultural empowerment.

3. Women's Rights and the Law

The creation of new legal mechanisms to counter sex discrimination characterizes the third approach to women's rights as human rights. These efforts seek to make existing legal and political institutions work for women and to expand the state's responsibility for the violation of women's human rights. National and local laws which address sex discrimination and violence against women are examples of this approach. These measures allow women to fight for their rights within the legal system. The primary international illustration is the Convention on the Elimination of All Forms of Discrimination Against Women.[21]

The Convention has been described as "essentially an international bill of rights for women and a framework for women's participation in the development process . . . [which] spells out internationally accepted principles and standards for achieving equality between women and men."[22] Adopted by the UN General Assembly in 1979, the Convention has been ratified or acceded to by 104 countries as of January 1990. In theory these countries are obligated to pursue policies in accordance with it and to report on their compliance to the Committee on the Elimination of Discrimination Against Women (CEDAW).

While the Convention addresses many issues of sex discrimination, one of its shortcomings is failure to directly address the question of violence against women. CEDAW passed a resolution at its eighth session in Vienna in 1989 expressing concern that this issue be on its

21 Convention on the Elimination of All Forms of Discrimination Against Women, G.A. Res. 34/180, (1980).
22 International Women's Rights Action Watch. "The Convention on the Elimination of All Forms of Discrimination Against Women" (Minneapolis: Humphrey Institute of Public Affairs, 1988), 1.

agenda and instructing states to include in their periodic reports information about statistics, legislation, and support services in this area.[23] The Commonwealth Secretariat in its manual on the reporting process for the Convention also interprets the issue of violence against women as "clearly fundamental to the spirit of the Convention," especially in Article 5 which calls for the modification of social and cultural patterns, sex roles, and stereotyping that are based on the idea of the inferiority or the superiority of either sex.[24]

The Convention outlines a clear human rights agenda for women which, if accepted by governments, would mark an enormous step forward. It also carries the limitations of all such international documents in that there is little power to demand its implementation. Within the United Nations, it is not generally regarded as a convention with teeth, as illustrated by the difficulty that CEDAW has had in getting countries to report on compliance with its provisions. Further, it is still treated by governments and most nongovernmental organizations as a document dealing with women's (read "secondary") rights, not human rights. Nevertheless, it is a useful statement of principles endorsed by the United Nations around which women can organize to achieve legal and political change in their regions.

4. Feminist Transformation of Human Rights

Transforming the human rights concept from a feminist perspective, so that it will take greater account of women's lives, is the fourth approach. This approach relates women's rights and human rights, looking first at the viola-

tions of women's lives and then asking how the human rights concept can change to be more responsive to women. For example, the GABRIELA women's coalition in the Philippines simply stated that "Women's Rights are Human Rights" in launching a campaign last year. As Ninotchka Rosca explained, coalition members saw that "human rights are not reducible to a question of legal and due process. . . . In the case of women, human rights are affected by the entire society's traditional perception of what is proper or not proper for women"[25] Similarly, a panel at the 1990 International Women's Rights Action Watch conference asserted that "Violence Against Women is a Human Rights Issue." While work in the three previous approaches is often done from a feminist perspective, this last view is the most distinctly feminist with its woman-centered stance and its refusal to wait for permission from some authority to determine what is or is not a human rights issue.

This transformative approach can be taken toward any issue, but those working from this approach have tended to focus most on abuses that arise specifically out of gender, such as reproductive rights, female sexual slavery, violence against women, and "family crimes" like forced marriage, compulsory heterosexuality, and female mutilation. These are also the issues most often dismissed as not really human rights questions. This is therefore the most hotly contested area and requires that barriers be broken down between public and private, state and nongovernmental responsibilities.

Those working to transform the human rights vision from this perspective can draw on the work of others who have expanded the understanding of human rights previously. For example, two decades ago there was no concept of "disappearances" as a human rights abuse. However, the women of the Plaza de Mayo in

23 CEDAW Newsletter, 3rd Issue (13 Apr. 1989), 2 (summary of U.N. Report on the Eighth Session, U.N.Doc. A/44/38, 14 April 1989).
24 Commonwealth Secretariat, "The Convention on the Elimination of All Forms of Discrimination Against Women: The Reporting Process—A Manual for Commonwealth Jurisdictions," London, 1989.

25 Speech given by Ninotchka Rosca at Amnesty International New York Regional Conference, 24 Feb. 1990, 2.

Argentina did not wait for an official declaration but stood up to demand state accountability for these crimes. In so doing, they helped to create a context for expanding the concept of responsibility for deaths at the hands of paramilitary or right-wing death squads which, even if not carried out by the state, were allowed by it to happen. Another example is the developing concept that civil rights violations include "hate crimes," violence that is racially motivated or directed against homosexuals, Jews or other minority groups. Many accept that states have an obligation to work to prevent such rights abuses, and getting violence against women seen as a hate crime is being pursued by some.

The practical applications of transforming the human rights concept from feminist perspectives need to be explored further. The danger in pursuing only this approach is the tendency to become isolated from and competitive with other human rights groups because they have been so reluctant to address gender violence and discrimination. Yet most women experience abuse on the grounds of sex, race, class, nation, age, sexual preference, and politics as interrelated, and little benefit comes from separating them as competing claims. The human rights community need not abandon other issues but should incorporate gender perspectives into them and see how these expand the terms of their work. By recognizing issues like violence against women as human rights concerns, human rights scholars and activists do not have to take these up as their primary tasks. However, they do have to stop gatekeeping and guarding their prerogative to determine what is considered a "legitimate" human rights issue.

As mentioned before, these four approaches are overlapping and many strategies for change involve elements of more than one. All of these approaches contain aspects of what is necessary to achieve women's rights. At a time when dualist ways of thinking and views of competing economic systems are in question, the creative task is to look for ways to connect these approaches and to see how we can go beyond exclusive views of what people need in their lives. In the words of an early feminist group, we need bread and roses, too. Women want food and liberty and the possibility of living lives of dignity free from domination and violence. In this struggle, the recognition of women's rights as human rights can play an important role.

Review Questions

1. According to Bunch, why do governments and human rights organizations ignore women's rights?
2. What is the narrow Western conception of human rights that Bunch attacks?
3. Explain the political and civil rights approach to women's rights. Why is it inadequate?
4. What is the socioeconomic approach to women's rights? What are the limitations of this approach, in Bunch's view?
5. The legal approach is the third approach to making women's rights into human rights. What is it, and what are its shortcomings?
6. Explain the feminist transformation of women's rights. What issues does the approach address? What are the dangers of this approach?

Discussion Questions

1. Are there rights or entitlements to food, shelter, employment, and health care? If so, who should provide these goods? Are only women entitled to these goods? Should men get them too?

2. If there is a right to be free from violence and oppression, then why not say that both men and women have this right? And while we are at it, why not say that nonhuman animals have this right too?

A Theory of Justice

JOHN RAWLS

John Rawls is professor of philosophy at Harvard University. Our reading is taken from his well-known book *A Theory of Justice* (1971).

Rawls's theory states that there are two principles of justice: The first principle involves equal basic liberties, and the second principle concerns the arrangement of social and economic inequalities. According to Rawls's theory, these are the principles that free and rational persons would accept in a hypothetical original position where there is a veil of ignorance hiding from the contractors all the particular facts about themselves.

THE MAIN IDEA
OF THE THEORY OF JUSTICE

MY AIM IS TO PRESENT a conception of justice which generalizes and carries to a higher level of abstraction the familiar theory of the social contract as found, say, in Locke, Rousseau, and Kant.[1] In order to do this we are not to think of the original contract as one to enter a particular society or to set up a particular form of government. Rather, the guiding idea is that the principles of justice for the basic structure of society are the object of the original agreement. They are the principles that free and rational persons concerned to further their own interests would accept in an initial position of equality as defining the fundamental terms of their association. These principles are to regulate all further agreements; they specify the kinds of social cooperation that can be entered into and the forms of government that can be established. This way of regarding the principles of justice I shall call justice as fairness.

Source: Reprinted by permission of the publisher from *A Theory of Justice* by John Rawls (Cambridge, Mass.: Harvard University Press), pp. 11–16, 60–65. Copyright © 1971 by the President and Fellows of Harvard College. Footnotes renumbered.

1. As the text suggests, I shall regard Locke's *Second Treatise of Government,* Rousseau's *The Social Contract,* and Kant's ethical works beginning with *The Foundations of the Metaphysics of Morals* as definitive of the contract tradition. For all of its greatness, Hobbe's *Leviathan* raises special problems. A general historical survey is provided by J. W. Gough, *The Social Contract,* 2nd ed. (Oxford, The Clarendon Press, 1957), and Otto Gierke, *Natural Law and the* *Theory of Society,* trans. with an introduction by Ernest Barker (Cambridge, The University Press, 1934). A presentation of the contract view as primarily an ethical theory is to be found in G. R. Grice, *The Grounds of Moral Judgment* (Cambridge, The University Press, 1967). See also §19, note 30.)

Thus we are to imagine that those who engage in social cooperation choose together, in one joint act, the principles which are to assign basic rights and duties and to determine the division of social benefits. Men are to decide in advance how they are to regulate their claims against one another and what is to be the foundation charter of their society. Just as each person must decide by rational reflection what constitutes his good, that is, the system of ends which it is rational for him to pursue, so a group of persons must decide once and for all what is to count among them as just and unjust. The choice which rational men would make in this hypothetical situation of equal liberty, assuming for the present that this choice problem has a solution, determines the principles of justice.

In justice as fairness the original position of equality corresponds to the state of nature in the traditional theory of the social contract. This original position is not, of course, thought of as an actual historical state of affairs, much less as a primitive condition of culture. It is understood as a purely hypothetical situation characterized so as to lead to a certain conception of justice.[2] Among the essential features of this situation is that no one knows his place in society, his class position or social status, nor does any one know his fortune in the distribution of natural assets and abilities, his intelligence, strength, and the like. I shall even assume that the parties do not know their conceptions of the good or their special psychological propensities. The principles of justice are chosen behind a veil of ignorance. This ensures that no one is advantaged or disadvantaged in the choice of principles by the outcome of natural chance or the contingency of social circumstances. Since all are similarly situated and no one is able to design principles to favor his particular condition, the principles of justice are the result of a fair agreement or bargain. For given the circumstances of the original position, the symmetry of everyone's relations to each other, this initial situation is fair between individuals as moral persons, that is, as rational beings with their own ends and capable, I shall assume, of a sense of justice. The original position is, one might say, the appropriate initial status quo, and thus the fundamental agreements reached in it are fair. This explains the propriety of the name "justice as fairness": it conveys the idea that the principles of justice are agreed to in an initial situation that is fair. The name does not mean that the concepts of justice and fairness are the same, any more than the phrase "poetry as metaphor" means that the concepts of poetry and metaphor are the same.

Justice as fairness begins, as I have said, with one of the most general of all choices which persons might make together, namely, with the choice of the first principles of a conception of justice which is to regulate all subsequent criticism and reform of institutions. Then, having chosen a conception of justice, we can suppose that they are to choose a constitution and a legislature to enact laws, and so on, all in accordance with the principles of justice initially agreed upon. Our social situation is just if it is such that by this sequence of hypothetical agreements we would have contracted into the general system of rules which defines it. Moreover, assuming that the original position does determine a set of principles (that is, that a particular conception of justice would be chosen), it will then be true that whenever social institutions satisfy these principles those engaged in them can say to one another that they are cooperating on terms to which they would agree if

---

2 Kant is clear that the original agreement is hypothetical. See *The Metaphysics of Morals,* pt. I (*Rechtslehre*), especially §47, 52; and pt. II of the essay "Concerning the Common Saying: This May Be True in Theory but It Does Not Apply in Practice," in *Kant's Political Writings,* ed. Hans Reiss and trans. by H. B. Nisbet (Cambridge, The University Press, 1970), pp. 73–87. See Georges Vlachos, *La Pensée politique de Kant* (Paris, Presses Universitaires de France, 1962), pp. 326–335; and J. G. Murphy, *Kant: The Philosophy of Right* (London, Macmillan, 1970), pp. 109–112, 133–136, for a further discussion.

they were free and equal persons whose relations with respect to one another were fair. They could all view their arrangements as meeting the stipulations which they would acknowledge in an initial situation that embodies widely accepted and reasonable constraints on the choice of principles. The general recognition of this fact would provide the basis for a public acceptance of the corresponding principles of justice. No society can, of course, be a scheme of cooperation which men enter voluntarily in a literal sense; each person finds himself placed at birth in some particular position in some particular society, and the nature of this position materially affects his life prospects. Yet a society satisfying the principles of justice as fairness comes as close as a society can to being a voluntary scheme, for it meets the principles which free and equal persons would assent to under circumstances that are fair. In this sense its members are autonomous and the obligations they recognize self-imposed.

One feature of justice as fairness is to think of the parties in the initial situation as rational and mutually disinterested. This does not mean that the parties are egoists, that is, individuals with only certain kinds of interests, say in wealth, prestige, and domination. But they are conceived as not taking an interest in one another's interests. They are to presume that even their spiritual aims may be opposed, in the way that the aims of those of different religions may be opposed. Moreover, the concept of rationality must be interpreted as far as possible in the narrow sense, standard in economic theory, of taking the most effective means to given ends. I shall modify this concept to some extent . . . but one must try to avoid introducing into it any controversial ethical elements. The initial situation must be characterized by stipulations that are widely accepted.

In working out the conception of justice as fairness one main task clearly is to determine which principles of justice would be chosen in the original position. To do this we must describe this situation in some detail and formulate with care the problem of choice which it presents. . . . It may be observed, however, that once the principles of justice are thought of as arising from an original agreement in a situation of equality, it is an open question whether the principle of utility would be acknowledged. Offhand it hardly seems likely that persons who view themselves as equals, entitled to press their claims upon one another, would agree to a principle which may require lesser life prospects for some simply for the sake of a greater sum of advantages enjoyed by others. Since each desires to protect his interests, his capacity to advance his conception of the good, no one has a reason to acquiesce in an enduring loss for himself in order to bring about a greater net balance of satisfaction. In the absence of strong and lasting benevolent impulses, a rational man would not accept a basic structure merely because it maximized the algebraic sum of advantages irrespective of its permanent effects on his own basic rights and interests. Thus it seems that the principle of utility is incompatible with the conception of social cooperation among equals for mutual advantage. It appears to be inconsistent with the idea of reciprocity implicit in the notion of a well-ordered society. Or, at any rate, so I shall argue.

I shall maintain instead that the persons in the initial situation would choose two rather different principles: the first requires equality in the assignment of basic rights and duties, while the second holds that social and economic inequalities, for example inequalities of wealth and authority, are just only if they result in compensating benefits for everyone, and in particular for the least advantaged members of society. These principles rule out justifying institutions on the grounds that the hardships of some are offset by a greater good in the aggregate. It may be expedient but it is not just that some should have less in order that others may prosper. But there is no injustice in the greater benefits earned by a few provided that the situation of persons not so fortunate is thereby improved. The intuitive idea is that since everyone's well-being depends upon a scheme of cooperation without which no one could have a satisfactory life, the division of advantages should be such as to draw forth the willing cooperation of everyone taking part in it, including those less well situated. Yet this can be expected only if reasonable terms are proposed. The two principles mentioned seem to be a fair agreement on the basis of which those better endowed, or more fortunate in their social position, neither of which we can be said to deserve, could expect the willing cooperation of others when some workable scheme is a necessary condition of the welfare of all.[3] Once we decide to look for a conception of justice that nullifies the accidents of natural endowment and the contingencies of social circumstance as counters in quest for political and economic advantage, we are led to these principles. They express the result of leaving aside those aspects of the social world that seem arbitrary from a moral point of view.

The problem of the choice of principles, however, is extremely difficult. I do not expect the answer I shall suggest to be convincing to everyone. It is, therefore, worth noting from the outset that justice as fairness, like other contract views, consists of two parts: (1) an interpretation of the initial situation and of the problem of choice posed there, and (2) a set of principles which, it is argued, would be agreed to. One may accept the first part of the theory (or some variant thereof), but not the other, and conversely. The concept of the initial contractual situation may seem reasonable although the particular principles proposed are rejected. To be sure, I want to maintain that the most appropriate conception of this situation does lead

to principles of justice contrary to utilitarianism and perfectionism, and therefore that the contract doctrine provides an alternative to these views. . . .

A final remark. Justice as fairness is not a complete contract theory. For it is clear that the contract idea can be extended to the choice of more or less an entire ethical system, that is, to a system including principles for all the virtues and not only for justice. Now for the most part I shall consider only principles of justice and others closely related to them; I make no attempt to discuss the virtues in a systematic way. Obviously if justice as fairness succeeds reasonably well, a next step would be to study the more general view suggested by the name "rightness as fairness." But even this wider theory fails to embrace all moral relationships, since it would seem to include only our relations with other persons and to leave out of account how we are to conduct ourselves toward animals and the rest of nature. I do not contend that the contract notion offers a way to approach these questions which are certainly of the first importance; and I shall have to put them aside. We must recognize the limited scope of justice as fairness and of the general type of view that it exemplifies. How far its conclusions must be revised once these other matters are understood cannot be decided in advance. . . .

TWO PRINCIPLES OF JUSTICE

I shall now state in a provisional form the two principles of justice that I believe would be chosen in the original position. In this section I wish to make only the most general comments, and therefore the first formulation of these principles is tentative. As we go on I shall run through several formulations and approximate step by step the final statement to be given much later. I believe that doing this allows the exposition to proceed in a natural way.

The first statement of the two principles reads as follows.

3 For the formulation of this intuitive idea I am indebted to Allan Gibbard.

First: Each person is to have an equal right to the most extensive basic liberty compatible with a similar liberty for others.

Second: Social and economic inequalities are to be arranged so that they are both (a) reasonably expected to be to everyone's advantage, and (b) attached to positions and offices open to all. . . .

By way of general comment, these principles primarily apply, as I have said, to the basic structure of society. They are to govern the assignment of rights and duties and to regulate the distribution of social and economic advantages. As their formulation suggests, these principles presuppose that the social structure can be divided into two more or less distinct parts, the first principle applying to the one, the second to the other. They distinguish between those aspects of the social system that define and secure the equal liberties of citizenship and those that specify and establish social and economic inequalities. The basic liberties of citizens are, roughly speaking, political liberty (the right to vote and to be eligible for public office) together with freedom of speech and assembly; liberty of conscience and freedom of thought; freedom of the person along with the right to hold (personal) property; and freedom from arbitrary arrest and seizure as defined by the concept of the rule of law. These liberties are all required to be equal by the first principle, since citizens of a just society are to have the same basic rights.

The second principle applies, in the first approximation, to the distribution of income and wealth and to the design of organizations that make use of differences in authority and responsibility, or chains of command. While the distribution of wealth and income need not be equal, it must be to everyone's advantage, and at the same time, positions of authority and offices of command must be accessible to all. One applies the second principle by holding positions open, and then, subject to this constraint, arranges social and economic inequalities so that everyone benefits.

These principles are to be arranged in a serial order with the first principle prior to the second. This ordering means that a departure from the institutions of equal liberty required by the first principle cannot be justified by, or compensated for, by greater social and economic advantages. The distribution of wealth and income, and the hierarchies of authority, must be consistent with both the liberties of equal citizenship and equality of opportunity.

It is clear that these principles are rather specific in their content, and their acceptance rests on certain assumptions that I must eventually try to explain and justify. A theory of justice depends upon a theory of society in ways that will become evident as we proceed. For the present, it should be observed that the two principles (and this holds for all formulations) are a special case of a more general conception of justice that can be expressed as follows.

All social values—liberty and opportunity, income and wealth, and the bases of self-respect—are to be distributed equally unless an unequal distribution of any, or all, of these values is to everyone's advantage.

Injustice, then, is simply inequalities that are not to the benefit of all. Of course, this conception is extremely vague and requires interpretation.

As a first step, suppose that the basic structure of society distributes certain primary goods, that is, things that every rational man is presumed to want. These goods normally have a use whatever a person's rational plan of life. For simplicity, assume that the chief primary goods at the disposition of society are rights and liberties, powers and opportunities, income and wealth. . . . These are the social primary goods. Other primary goods such as health and vigor, intelligence and imagination, are natural goods; although their possession is influenced by the basic structure, they are not so directly under its control. Imagine, then, a hypothetical initial arrangement in which all the social primary goods are equally distributed: everyone has similar rights and duties, and income and wealth are evenly shared. This state of affairs provides a benchmark for judging improvements. If certain inequalities of wealth and organizational powers would make everyone better off than in this hypothetical starting situation, then they accord with the general conception.

Now it is possible, at least theoretically, that by giving up some of their fundamental liberties men are sufficiently compensated by the resulting social and economic gains. The general conception of justice imposes no restrictions on what sort of inequalities are permissible; it only requires that everyone's position be improved. We need not suppose anything so drastic as consenting to a condition of slavery. Imagine instead that men forego certain political rights when the economic returns are significant and their capacity to influence the course of policy by the exercise of these rights would be marginal in any case. It is this kind of exchange which the two principles as stated rule out; being arranged in serial order they do not permit exchanges between basic liberties and economic and social gains. The serial ordering of principles expresses an underlying preference among primary social goods. When this preference is rational so likewise is the choice of these principles in this order.

In developing justice as fairness I shall, for the most part, leave aside the general conception of justice and examine instead the special case of the two principles in serial order. The advantage of this procedure is that from the first the matter of priorities is recognized and an effort made to find principles to deal with it. One is led to attend throughout to the conditions under which the acknowledgment of the absolute weight of liberty with respect to social and economic advantages, as defined by the lexical order of the two principles, would be reasonable. Offhand, this ranking appears extreme and too special a case to be of much interest; but there is more justification for it than would appear at first sight. Or at any rate, so I shall main-

tain. . . . Furthermore, the distinction between fundamental rights and liberties and economic and social benefits marks a difference among primary social goods that one should try to exploit. It suggests an important division in the social system. Of course, the distinctions drawn and the ordering proposed are bound to be at best only approximations. There are surely circumstances in which they fail. But it is essential to depict clearly the main lines of a reasonable conception of justice; and under many conditions anyway, the two principles in serial order may serve well enough. When necessary we can fall back on the more general conception.

The fact that the two principles apply to institutions has certain consequences. Several points illustrate this. First of all, the rights and liberties referred to by these principles are those which are defined by the public rules of the basic structure. Whether men are free is determined by the rights and duties established by the major institutions of society. Liberty is a certain pattern of social forms. The first principle simply requires that certain sorts of rules, those defining basic liberties, apply to everyone equally and that they allow the most extensive liberty compatible with a like liberty for all. The only reason for circumscribing the rights defining liberty and making men's freedom less extensive than it might otherwise be is that these equal rights as institutionally defined would interfere with one another.

Another thing to bear in mind is that when principles mention persons, or require that everyone gain from an inequality, the reference is to representative persons holding the various social positions, or offices, or whatever, established by the basic structure. Thus in applying the second principle I assume that it is possible to assign an expectation of well-being to representative individuals holding these positions. This expectation indicates their life prospects as viewed from their social station. In general, the expectations of representative persons depend upon the distribution of rights and duties throughout the basic structure. When this changes, expectations change. I assume, then, that expectations are connected: by raising the prospects of the representative man in one position we presumably increase or decrease the prospects of representative men in other positions. Since it applies to institutional forms, the second principle (or rather the first part of it) refers to the expectations of representative individuals. As I shall discuss below, neither principle applies to distributions of particular goods to particular individuals who may be identified by their proper names. The situation where someone is considering how to allocate certain commodities to needy persons who are known to him is not within the scope of the principles. They are meant to regulate basic institutional arrangements. We must not assume that there is much similarity from the standpoint of justice between an administrative allotment of goods to specific persons and the appropriate design of society. Our common sense institutions for the former may be a poor guide to the latter.

Now the second principle insists that each person benefit from permissible inequalities in the basic structure. This means that it must be reasonable for each relevant representative man defined by this structure, when he views it as a going concern, to prefer his prospects with the inequality to his prospects without it. One is not allowed to justify differences in income or organizational powers on the ground that the disadvantages of those in one position are outweighed by the greater advantages of those in another. Much less can infringements of liberty be counterbalanced in this way. Applied to the basic structure, the principle of utility would have us maximize the sum of expectations of representative men (weighed by the number of persons they represent, on the classical view); and this would permit us to compensate for the losses of some by the gains of others. Instead, the two principles require that everyone benefit from economic and social inequalities. It is obvious, however, that there are indefinitely many ways in which all may be advantaged when the initial arrangement of equality is taken as a benchmark. How then are we to choose among these possibilities? The principles must be specified so that they yield a determinate conclusion. I now turn to this problem. . . .

Review Questions

1. Carefully explain Rawls's conception of the original position.
2. State and explain Rawls's first principle of justice.
3. State and explain the second principle. Which principle has priority such that it cannot be sacrificed?

Discussion Questions

1. On the first principle, each person has an equal right to the most extensive basic liberty as long as this does not interfere with a similar liberty for others. What does this allow people to do? Does it mean, for example, that people have a right to engage in homosexual activities as long as they don't interfere with others? Can people produce and view pornography if it does not restrict anyone's freedom? Are people allowed to take drugs in the privacy of their homes?
2. Is it possible for free and rational persons in the original position to agree upon different principles than those given by Rawls? For example, why wouldn't they agree to an equal distribution of wealth and income rather than an unequal distribution? That is, why wouldn't they adopt socialism rather than capitalism? Isn't socialism just as rational as capitalism?

The Need for More Than Justice

ANNETTE BAIER

Annette Baier teaches philosophy at the University of Pittsburgh. She is the author of many articles on feminist theory and other topics in ethics.

Following Carol Gilligan, Baier distinguishes between the justice perspective of philosophers such as Kant and Rawls, and the care perspective Gilligan found in her studies of the moral development of women. Baier argues that the justice perspective by itself is inadequate as a moral theory. It overlooks inequalities between people (as in parent-child relationships), it has an unrealistic view of freedom of choice, and it ignores the importance of moral emotions such as love. The best moral theory, she claims, is one that harmonizes justice and care.

IN RECENT DECADES in North American social and moral philosophy, alongside the development and discussion of widely influential theories of justice, taken as Rawls takes it as the "first virtue of social institutions,"[1] there has been a counter-movement gathering strength, one coming from some interesting sources. For some of the most outspoken of the diverse group who have in a variety of ways been challenging the assumed supremacy of justice among the moral and social virtues are members of those sections of society whom one might have expected to be especially aware of the supreme importance of justice, namely blacks and women. Those who have only recently won recognition of their equal rights, who have only recently seen the correction or partial correction of long-standing racist and sexist injustices to their race and sex, are among the philosophers now suggesting that justice is only one virtue among many, and one that may need the presence of the others in order to deliver its own undenied value. Among these philosophers of the philosophical counterculture, as it were—but an increasingly large counterculture—I include Alasdair MacIntyre,[2] Michael Stocker,[3] Lawrence Blum,[4] Michael Slote,[5] Laurence Thomas,[6] Claudia Card,[7] Alison Jaggar,[8] Susan

Source: Annette C. Baier, "The Need for More than Justice," from *Canadian Journal of Philosophy,* Supplementary Vol. 13, 1988, published by University of Calgary Press. Reprinted with permission.

1 John Rawls, *A Theory of Justice* (Harvard University Press).

2 Alasdair MacIntyre, *After Virtue* (Notre Dame: Notre Dame University Press).

3 Michael Stocker, "The Schizophrenia of Modern Ethical Theories," *Journal of Philosophy* 73, 14, 453–66, and "Agent and Other: Against Ethical Universalism," *Australasian Journal of Philosophy* 54, 206–20.

4 Lawrence Blum, *Friendship, Altruism and Morality* (London: Routledge & Kegan Paul 1980).

5 Michael Slote, *Goods and Virtues* (Oxford: Oxford University Press 1983).

6 Laurence Thomas, "Love and Morality" in *Epistemology and Sociobiology,* James Fetzer, ed. (1985) and "Justice, Happiness and Self Knowledge," *Canadian Journal of Philosophy* (March, 1986). Also "Beliefs and the Motivation to be Just," *American Philosophical Quarterly* 22 (4), 347–52.

7 Claudia Card, "Mercy," *Philosophical Review* 81, 1, and "Gender and Moral Luck," [in *Identity Characters, and Morality: Essays in Moral Psychology,* Owen Flanagan, ed. (Cambridge: MIT Press, 1990.)].

8 Alison Jaggar, *Feminist Politics and Human Nature* (London: Rowman and Allenheld 1983).

Wolf[9] and a whole group of men and women, myself included, who have been influenced by the writings of Harvard educational psychologist Carol Gilligan, whose book *In a Different Voice* (Harvard 1982; hereafter D.V.) caused a considerable stir both in the popular press and, more slowly, in the philosophic journals.[10]

Let me say quite clearly at this early point that there is little disagreement that justice is *a* social value of very great importance, and injustice an evil. Nor would those who have worked on theories of justice want to deny that other things matter besides justice. Rawls, for example, incorporates the value of freedom into his account of justice, so that denial of basic freedoms counts as injustice. Rawls also leaves room for a wider theory of the right, of which the theory of justice is just a part. Still, he does claim that justice is the "first" virtue of social institutions, and it is only that claim about priority that I think has been challenged. It is easy to exaggerate the differences of view that exist, and I want to avoid that. The differences are as much in emphasis as in substance, or we can say that they are differences in tone of voice. But these differences do tend to make a difference in approaches to a wide range of topics not just in moral theory but in areas like medical ethics, where the discussion used to be conducted in terms of patients' rights, of informed consent, and so on, but now tends to get conducted in an enlarged moral vocabulary, which draws on what Gilligan calls the ethics of *care* as well as that of *justice*.

For "care" is the new buzz-word. It is not, as Shakespeare's Portia demanded, mercy that is to season justice, but a less authoritarian humanitarian supplement, a felt concern for the good of others and for community with them. The "cold jealous virtue of justice" (Hume) is found to be too cold, and it is "warmer" more communitarian virtues and social ideals that are being called in to supplement it. One might say that liberty and equality are being found inadequate without fraternity, except that "fraternity" will be quite the wrong word, if as Gilligan initially suggested, it is *women* who perceive this value most easily. ("Sorority" will do no better, since it is too exclusive, and English has no gender-neuter word for the mutual concern of siblings.) She has since modified this claim, allowing that there are two perspectives on moral and social issues that we all tend to alternate between, and which are not always easy to combine, one of them what she called the justice perspective, the other the care perspective. It is increasingly obvious that there are many male philosophical spokespersons for the care perspective (Laurence Thomas, Lawrence Blum, Michael Stocker) so that it cannot be the prerogative of women. Nevertheless Gilligan still wants to claim that women are most unlikely to take *only* the justice perspective, as some men are claimed to, at least until some mid-life crisis jolts them into "bifocal" moral vision (see D.V., ch. 6).

Gilligan in her book did not offer any explanatory theory of why there should be any difference between female and male moral outlook, but she did tend to link the naturalness to women of the care perspective with their role as primary caretakers of young children, that is with their parental and specifically maternal role. . . . Later, both in "The Conquistador and the Dark Continent: Reflections on the Nature of Love" (*Daedalus* [Summer 1984]), and "The Origins of Morality in Early Childhood" (Chicago: University of Chicago Press, 1987), she develops this explanation. She postulates two evils that any infant may become aware of, the evil of detachment or isolation from others whose love one needs, and the evil of relative powerlessness and weakness. Two dimensions of moral development are thereby set—one aimed at achieving satisfying community with others,

9 Susan Wolf, "Moral Saints," *Journal of Philosophy* 79 (August, 1982), 419–39.

10 For a helpful survey article see Owen Flanagan and Kathryn Jackson, "Justice, Care and Gender: The Kohlberg-Gilligan Debate Revisited, *Ethics*.

the other aiming at autonomy or equality of power. The relative predominance of one over the other development will depend both upon the relative salience of the two evils in early childhood, and on early and later reinforcement or discouragement in attempts made to guard against these two evils. This provides the germs of a theory about *why,* given current customs of childrearing, it should be mainly women who are not content with only the moral outlook that she calls the justice perspective, necessary though that was and is seen by them to have been to their hard won liberation from sexist oppression. They, like the blacks, used the language of rights and justice to change their own social position, but nevertheless see limitations in that language, according to Gilligan's findings as a moral psychologist. She reports the "discontent with the individualist more or less Kantian moral framework that dominates Western moral theory and which influenced moral psychologists such as Lawrence Kohlberg,[11] to whose conception of moral maturity she seeks an alternative. Since the target of Gilligan's criticism is the dominant Kantian tradition, and since that has been the target also of moral philosophers as diverse in their own views as Bernard Williams,[12] Alasdair MacIntyre, Philippa Foot,[13] Susan Wolf, Claudia Card, her book is of interest as much for its attempt to articulate an alternative to the Kantian justice perspective as for its implicit raising of the question of male bias in Western moral theory, especially liberal democratic theory. For whether the supposed blind spots of that outlook are due to male bias, or to nonparental bias, or to early traumas of powerlessness or to early resignation to "detachment" from others, we need first to be persuaded that they *are* blind spots before we

11 Lawrence Kohlberg, *Essays in Moral Development,* vols. I & II (New York: Harper and Row 1981, 1984).
12 Bernard Williams, *Ethics and the Limits of Philosophy* (Cambridge: Cambridge University Press 1985).
13 Philippa Foot, *Virtues and Vices* (Berkeley: University of California Press 1978).

will have any interest in their cause and cure. Is justice blind to important social values, or at least only one-eyed? What is it that comes into view from the "care perspective" that is not seen from the "justice perspective"?

Gilligan's position here is most easily described by contrasting it with that of Kohlberg, against which she developed it. Kohlberg, influenced by Piaget and the Kantian philosophical tradition as developed by John Rawls, developed a theory about typical moral development which saw it to progress from a pre-conventional level, where what is seen to matter is pleasing or not offending parental authority-figures, through a conventional level in which the child tries to fit in with a group, such as a school community, and conform to its standards and rules, to a post-conventional critical level, in which such conventional rules are subjected to tests, and where those tests are of a Utilitarian, or, eventually, a Kantian sort—namely ones that require respect for each person's individual rational will, or autonomy, and conformity to any implicit social contract such wills are deemed to have made, or to any hypothetical ones they would make if thinking clearly. What was found when Kohlberg's questionnaires (mostly by verbal response to verbally sketched moral dilemmas) were applied to female as well as male subjects, Gilligan reports, is that the girls and women not only scored generally lower than the boys and men, but tended to *revert* to the lower stage of the conventional level even after briefly (usually in adolescence) attaining the post-conventional level. Piaget's finding that girls were deficient in "the legal sense" was confirmed.

These results led Gilligan to wonder if there might not be a quite different pattern of development to be discerned, at least in female subjects. She therefore conducted interviews designed to elicit not just how far advanced the subjects were towards an appreciation of the nature and importance of Kantian autonomy, but also to find out what the subjects themselves saw as progress or lack of it, what conceptions of moral maturity they came to possess by the time they were adults. She found that although the Kohlberg version of moral maturity as respect for fellow persons, and for their rights as equals (rights including that of free association), did seem shared by many young men, the women tended to speak in a different voice about morality itself and about moral maturity. To quote Gilligan, "Since the reality of interconnexion is experienced by women as given rather than freely contracted, they arrive at an understanding of life that reflects the limits of autonomy and control. As a result, women's development delineates the path not only to a less violent life but also to a maturity realized by interdependence and taking care" (D.V., 172). She writes that there is evidence that "women perceive and construe social reality differently from men, and that these differences center around experiences of attachment and separation . . . because women's sense of integrity appears to be intertwined with an ethics of care, so that to see themselves as women is to see themselves in a relationship of connexion, the major changes in women's lives would seem to involve changes in the understanding and activities of care" (D.V., 171). She contrasts this progressive understanding of care, from merely pleasing others to helping and nurturing, with the sort of progression that is involved in Kohlberg's stages, a progression in the understanding, not of mutual care, but of mutual *respect*, where this has its Kantian overtones of distance, even of some fear for the respected, and where personal autonomy and *in*dependence, rather than more satisfactory interdependence, are the paramount values.

This contrast, one cannot but feel, is one which Gilligan might have used the Marxist language of alienation to make. For the main complaint about the Kantian version of a society with its first virtue justice, construed as respect for equal rights to formal goods such as having contracts kept, due process, equal opportunity including opportunity to participate in political activities leading to policy and law-making, to basic liberties of speech, free association and assembly, religious worship, is that none of these goods do much to ensure that the people who have and mutually respect such rights will have any other relationships to one another than the minimal relationship needed to keep such a "civil society" going. They may well be lonely, driven to suicide, apathetic about their work and about participation in political processes, find their lives meaningless and have no wish to leave offspring to face the same meaningless existence. Their rights, and respect for rights, are quite compatible with very great misery, and misery whose causes are not just individual misfortunes and psychic sickness, but social and moral impoverishment. . . .

Let me try to summarize the main differences, as I see them, between on the one hand Gilligan's version of moral maturity and the sort of social structures that would encourage, express and protect it, and on the other the orthodoxy she sees herself to be challenging. I shall from now on be giving my own interpretation of the significance of her challenges, not merely reporting them.[14] The most obvious point is the challenge to the individualism of the Western tradition, to the fairly entrenched belief in the possibility and desirability of each person pursuing his own good in his own way, constrained only by a minimal formal common good, namely a working legal apparatus that enforces contracts and protects individuals from undue interference by others. Gilligan reminds us that noninterference can, especially for the relatively powerless, such as the very young, amount to neglect, and even between equals can be isolating and alienating. On her less individualist version of individuality, it becomes defined

14 I have previously written about the significance of her findings for moral philosophy in "What Do Women Want in a Moral Theory?" *Noûs* 19 (March 1985), "Trust and Antitrust," *Ethics* 96 (1986), and in "Hume the Women's Moral Theorist?" in *Women and Moral Theory*, Kittay and Meyers, ed., [Totowa, N.J.: Rowman & Littlefield, 1987].

by responses to dependency and to patterns of interconnexion, both chosen and unchosen. It is not something a person *has,* and which she then chooses relationships to suit, but something that develops out of a series of dependencies and interdependencies, and responses to them. This conception of individuality is not flatly at odds with, say, Rawls' Kantian one, but there is at least a difference of tone of voice between speaking as Rawls does of each of us having our own rational life plan, which a just society's moral traffic rules will allow us to follow, and which may or may not include close association with other persons, and speaking as Gilligan does of a satisfactory life as involving "progress of affiliative relationship" (D.V., 170) where "the concept of identity expands to include the experience of interconnexion" (D.V., 173). Rawls can allow that progress to Gilligan-style moral maturity may be *a* rational life plan, but not a moral constraint on every life-pattern. The trouble is that it will not do just to say "let this version of morality be an optional extra. Let us agree on the essential minimum, that is on justice and rights, and let whoever wants to go further and cultivate this more demanding ideal of responsibility and care." For, first, it cannot be satisfactorily cultivated without closer cooperation from others than respect for rights and justice will ensure, and, second, the encouragement of some to cultivate it while others do not could easily lead to exploitation of those who do. It obviously *has* suited some in most societies well enough that others take on the responsibilities of care (for the sick, the helpless, the young) leaving them free to pursue their own less altruistic goods. Volunteer forces of those who accept an ethic of care, operating within a society where the power is exercised and the institutions designed, redesigned, or maintained by those who accept a less communal ethic of minimally constrained self-advancement, will not be the solution. The liberal individualists may be able to "tolerate" the more communally minded, if they keep the lib-

erals' rules, but it is not so clear that the more communally minded can be content with just those rules, not be content to be tolerated and possibly exploited.

For the moral tradition which developed the concept of rights, autonomy and justice is the same tradition that provided "justifications" of the oppression of those whom the primary right-holders depended on to do the sort of work they themselves preferred not to do. The domestic work was left to women and slaves, and the liberal morality for right-holders was surreptitiously supplemented by a different set of demands made on domestic workers. As long as women could be got to assume responsibility for the care of home and children, and to train their children to continue the sexist system, the liberal morality could continue to be the official morality, by turning its eyes away from the contribution made by those it excluded. The long unnoticed moral proletariat were the domestic workers, mostly female. Rights have usually been for the privileged. Talking about laws, and the rights those laws recognize and protect, does not in itself ensure that the group of legislators and rights-holders will not be restricted to some elite. Bills of rights have usually been proclamations of the rights of some in-group, barons, landowners, males, whites, non-foreigners. The "justice perspective," and the legal sense that goes with it, are shadowed by their patriarchal past. What did Kant, the great prophet of autonomy, say in his moral theory about women? He said they were incapable of legislation, not fit to vote, that they needed the guidance of more "rational" males.[15] Autonomy was not for them, only for first class, really rational, persons. It is ironic that Gilligan's original findings in a way confirm Kant's views—it seems that autonomy really may not be for women. Many of them reject that ideal (D.V., 48), and have been found not as good at making rules as are men. But where Kant concludes

15 Immanuel Kant, *Metaphysics of Morals,* sec. 46.

—"so much the worse for women," we can conclude—"so much the worse for the male fixation on the special skill of drafting legislation, for the bureaucratic mentality of rule worship, and for the male exaggeration of the importance of independence over mutual interdependence."

It is however also true that the moral theories that made the concept of a person's rights central were not just the instruments for excluding some persons, but also the instruments used by those who demanded that more and more persons be included in the favored group. Abolitionists, reformers, women, used the language of rights to assert their claims to inclusion in the group of full members of a community. The tradition of liberal moral theory has in fact developed so as to include the women it had for so long excluded, to include the poor as well as rich, blacks and whites, and so on. Women like Mary Wollstonecraft used the male moral theories to good purpose. So we should not be wholly ungrateful for those male moral theories, for all their objectionable earlier content. They were undoubtedly patriarchal, but they also contained the seeds of the challenge, or antidote, to this patriarchal poison.

But when we transcend the values of the Kantians, we should not forget the facts of history—that those values were the values of the oppressors of women. The Christian church, whose version of the moral law Aquinas codified, in his very legalistic moral theory, still insists on the maleness of the God it worships, and jealously reserves for males all the most powerful positions in its hierarchy. Its patriarchical prejudice is open and avowed. In the secular moral theories of men, the sexist patriarchal prejudice is today often less open, not as blatant as it is in Aquinas, in the later natural law tradition, and in Kant . . . , but is often still there. No moral theorist today would say that women are unfit to vote, to make laws, or to rule a nation without powerful male advisors (as most queens had), but the old doctrines die hard. . . . Traces of the old patriarchal poison still remain in even

the best contemporary moral theorizing. Few may actually say that women's place is in the home, but there is much muttering, when unemployment figures rise, about how the relatively recent flood of women into the work force complicates the problem, as if it would be a good thing if women just went back home whenever unemployment rises, to leave the available jobs for the men. We still do not really have a wide acceptance of the equal right of women to employment outside the home. Nor do we have wide acceptance of the equal duty of men to perform those domestic tasks which in no way depend on special female anatomy, namely cooking, cleaning, and the care of weaned children. All sorts of stories (maybe true stories), about children's need for one "primary" parent, who must be the mother if the mother breast feeds the child, shore up the unequal division of domestic responsibility between mothers and fathers, wives and husbands. If we are really to transvalue the values of our patriarchal past, we need to rethink all of those assumptions, really test those psychological theories. And how will men ever develop an understanding of the "ethics of care" if they continue to be shielded or kept from that experience of caring for a dependent child, which complements the experience we all have had of being cared for as dependent children? These experiences form the natural background for the development of moral maturity as Gilligan's women saw it.

Exploitation aside, why would women, once liberated, not be content to have their version of morality merely tolerated? Why should they not see themselves as voluntarily, for their own reasons, taking on *more* than the liberal rules demand, while having no quarrel with the content of those rules themselves, nor with their remaining the only ones that are expected to be generally obeyed? To see why, we need to move on to three more differences between the Kantian liberals (usually contractarians) and their critics. These concern the relative weight put on relationships between equals, and the relative weight put on freedom of choice, and on the authority of intellect over emotions. It is a typical feature of the dominant moral theories and traditions . . . that relationships between equals or those who are deemed equal in some important sense, have been the relations that morality is concerned primarily to regulate. Relationships between those who are clearly unequal in power, such as parents and children, earlier and later generations in relation to one another, states and citizens, doctors and patients, the well and the ill, large states and small states, have had to be shunted to the bottom of the agenda, and then dealt with by some sort of "promotion" of the weaker so that an appearance of virtual equality is achieved. Citizens collectively become equal to states, children are treated as adults-to-be, the ill and dying are treated as continuers of their earlier more potent selves, so that their "rights" could be seen as the rights of equals. This pretense of an equality that is in fact absent may often lead to desirable protection of the weaker, or more dependent. But it somewhat masks the question of what our moral relationships are to those who are our superiors or our inferiors in power. A more realistic acceptance of the fact that we begin as helpless children, that at almost every point of our lives we deal with both the more and the less helpless, that equality of power and interdependency, between two persons or groups, is rare and hard to recognize when it does occur, might lead us to a more direct approach to questions concerning the design of institutions structuring these relationships between unequals (families, schools, hospitals, armies) and of the morality of our dealings with the more and the less powerful. . . .

The recognition of the importance for all parties of relations between those who are and cannot but be unequal, both of these relations in themselves and for their effect on personality formation and so on other relationships, goes along with a recognition of the plain fact that not all morally important relationships can or should be freely chosen. So far I have discussed three reasons women have not to be content to pursue their own values within the framework of the liberal morality. The first was its dubious record. The second was its inattention to relations of inequality or its pretence of equality. The third reason is its exaggeration of the scope of choice, or its inattention to unchosen relations. Showing up the partial myth of equality among actual members of a community, and of the undesirability of trying to pretend that we are treating all of them as equals, tends to go along with an exposure of the companion myth that moral obligations arise from freely *chosen* associations between such equals. Vulnerable future generations do not choose their dependence on earlier generations. The unequal infant does not choose its place in a family or nation, nor is it treated as free to do as it likes until some association is freely entered into. Nor do its parents always choose their parental role, or freely assume their parental responsibilities any more than we choose our power to affect the conditions in which later generations will live. Gilligan's attention to the version of morality and moral maturity found in women, many of whom had faced a choice of whether or not to have an abortion, and who had at some point become mothers, is attention to the perceived inadequacy of the language of rights to help in such choices or to guide them in their parental role. It would not be much of an exaggeration to call the Gilligan "different voice" the voice of the potential parents. The emphasis on care goes with a recognition of the often unchosen nature of the responsibilities of those who give care, both of children who care for their aged or infirm parents, and of parents who care for the children they in fact have. Contract soon ceases to seem the paradigm source of moral obligation once we attend to parental responsibility, and justice as a virtue of social institutions will come to seem at best only first equal with the virtue, whatever its name, that ensures that each

Paradigm; an example serving as a model; Pattern

new generation is made appropriately welcome and prepared for their adult lives.

. . . The fourth feature of the Gilligan challenge to liberal orthodoxy is a challenge to its typical *rationalism,* or intellectualism, to its assumption that we need not worry what passions persons have, as long as their rational wills can control them. This Kantian picture of a controlling reason dictating to possibly unruly passions also tends to seem less useful when we are led to consider what sort of person we need to fill the role of parent, or indeed want in any close relationship. It might be important for father figures to have rational control over their violent urges to beat to death the children whose screams enrage them, but more than control of such nasty passions seems needed in the mother or primary parent, or parent-substitute, by most psychological theories. They need to love their children, not just to control their irritation. So the emphasis in Kantian theories on rational control of emotions, rather than on cultivating desirable forms of emotion, is challenged by Gilligan, along with the challenge to the assumption of the centrality of autonomy, or rela-

tions between equals, and of freely chosen relations. . . .

It is clear, I think, that the best moral theory has to be a cooperative product of women and men, has to harmonize justice and care. The morality it theorizes about is after all for all persons, for men and for women, and will need their combined insights. As Gilligan said (D.V., 174), what we need now is a "marriage" of the old male and the newly articulated female insights. If she is right about the special moral aptitudes of women, it will most likely be the women who propose the marriage, since they are the ones with more natural empathy, with the better diplomatic skills, the ones more likely to shoulder responsibility and take moral initiative, and the ones who find it easiest to empathize and care about how the other party feels. Then, once there is this union of male and female moral wisdom, we maybe can teach each other the moral skills each gender currently lacks, so that the gender difference in moral outlook that Gilligan found will slowly become less marked.

Review Questions

1. Distinguish between the justice and care perspectives. According to Gilligan, how do these perspectives develop?
2. Explain Kohlberg's theory of moral development. What criticisms do Gilligan and Baier make of this theory?
3. Baier says there are three important differences between Kantian liberals and their critics. What are these differences?
4. Why does Baier attack the Kantian view that the reason should control unruly passions?

Discussion Questions

1. What does Baier mean when she speaks of the need "to transvalue the values of our patriarchal past"? Do new values replace the old ones? If so, then do we abandon the old values of justice, freedom, and rights?
2. What is wrong with the Kantian view that extends equal rights to all rational beings, including women and minorities? What would Baier say? What do you think?
3. Baier seems to reject the Kantian emphasis on freedom of choice. Granted, we do not choose our parents, but still don't we have freedom of choice about many things, and isn't this very important?

Feminist Transformations of Moral Theory

VIRGINIA HELD

Virginia Held is professor of philosophy at Hunter College and the Graduate School of the City University of New York. She is the author of *Rights and Goods: Justifying Social Action* (1989) and *Feminist Morality: Transforming Culture, Society, and Politics* (1993).

   Held examines three topics that have been transformed by feminist philosophers: the split between reason and emotion, the distinction between the public and the private realms, and the concept of the self. On each topic, feminists have rejected traditional male views and have formulated new theories based on the experience of women.

THE HISTORY OF PHILOSOPHY, including the history of ethics, has been constructed from male points of view, and has been built on assumptions and concepts that are by no means gender-neutral.[1] Feminists characteristically begin with different concerns and give different emphases to the issues we consider than do non-feminist approaches. And, as Lorraine Code expresses it, "starting points and focal points shape the impact of theoretical discussion."[2] Within philosophy, feminists often start with, and focus on, quite different issues than those found in standard philosophy and ethics, however "standard" is understood. Far from providing mere additional insights which can be incorporated into traditional theory, feminist explorations often require radical transformations of existing fields of inquiry and theory.[3] From a feminist point of view, moral theory along with almost all theory will have to be transformed to take adequate account of the experience of women.

   I shall in this paper begin with a brief examination of how various fundamental aspects of the history of ethics have not been gender-neutral. And I shall discuss three issues where feminist rethinking is transforming moral concepts and theories.

THE HISTORY OF ETHICS

Consider the ideals embodied in the phrase "the man of reason." As Genevieve Lloyd has told the story, what has been taken to characterize

This paper is based in part on my Truax Lectures on "The Prospect of Feminist Morality" at Hamilton College on November 2 and 9, 1989. Early versions were also presented at Colgate University; at Queens University in Kingston, Ontario; at the University of Kentucky; and at the New School for Social Research. I am grateful to all who made possible these occasions and commented on the paper at these times, and to Alison Jaggar, Laura Purdy, and Sara Ruddick for additional discussion. Source: Virginia Held, "Feminist Transformations of Moral Theory," from *Philosophy and Phenomenological Research*, Fall 1990 (supplement), pp. 321–344. Reprinted with permission.

1 See e.g. Cheshire Calhoun, "Justice, Care, Gender Bias," *The Journal of Philosophy* 85 (September, 1988): 451–63.
2 Lorraine Code, "Second Persons," in *Science, Morality and Feminist Theory*, ed. Marsha Hanen and Kai Nielsen (Calgary: University of Calgary Press, 1987), p. 360.

3 See e.g. *Revolutions in Knowledge: Feminism in the Social Sciences*, ed. Sue Rosenberg Zalk and Janice Gordon-Kelter (Boulder: Westview Press, forthcoming).

the man of reason may have changed from historical period to historical period, but in each, the character ideal of the man of reason has been constructed in conjunction with a rejection of whatever has been taken to be characteristic of the feminine. "Rationality," Lloyd writes, "has been conceived as transcendence of the 'feminine,' and the 'feminine' itself has been partly constituted by its occurrence within this structure."[4]

This has of course fundamentally affected the history of philosophy and of ethics. The split between reason and emotion is one of the most familiar of philosophical conceptions. And the advocacy of reason "controlling" unruly emotion, of rationality guiding responsible human action against the blindness of passion, has a long and highly influential history, almost as familiar to non-philosophers as to philosophers. We should certainly now be alert to the ways in which reason has been associated with male endeavor, emotion with female weakness, and the ways in which this is of course not an accidental association. As Lloyd writes, "From the beginnings of philosophical thought, femaleness was symbolically associated with what Reason supposedly left behind—the dark powers of the earth goddesses, immersion in unknown forces associated with mysterious female powers. The early Greeks saw women's capacity to conceive as connecting them with the fertility of Nature. As Plato later expressed the thought, women 'imitate the earth.'"[5]

Reason, in asserting its claims and winning its status in human history, was thought to have to conquer the female forces of Unreason. Reason and clarity of thought were early associated with maleness, and as Lloyd notes, "what had to be shed in developing culturally prized rationality was, from the start, symbolically associated with femaleness."[6] In later Greek philosophical thought, the form/matter distinction was articulated, and with a similar hierarchical and gendered association. Maleness was aligned with active, determinate, and defining form; femaleness with mere passive, indeterminate, and inferior matter. Plato, in the *Timaeus*, compared the defining aspect of form with the father, and indefinite matter with the mother; Aristotle also compared the form/matter distinction with the male/female distinction. To quote Lloyd again, "This comparison . . . meant that the very nature of knowledge was implicitly associated with the extrusion of what was symbolically associated with the feminine."[7]

The associations, between Reason, form, knowledge, and maleness, have persisted in various guises, and have permeated what has been thought to be moral knowledge as well as what has been thought to be scientific knowledge, and what has been thought to be the practice of morality. The associations between the philosophical concepts and gender cannot be merely dropped, and the concepts retained regardless of gender, because gender has been built into them in such a way that without it, they will have to be different concepts. As feminists repeatedly show, if the concept of "human" were built on what we think about "woman" rather than what we think about "man," it would be a very different concept. Ethics, thus, has not been a search for universal, or truly human guidance, but a gender-biased enterprise.

Other distinctions and associations have supplemented and reinforced the identification of reason with maleness, and of the irrational with the female; on this and other grounds "man"

---

4 Genevieve Lloyd, *The Man of Reason: 'Male' and 'Female' in Western Philosophy* (Minneapolis: University of Minnesota Press, 1984), p. 104.
5 Ibid., p. 2.

6 Ibid., p. 3.
7 Ibid., p. 4. For a feminist view of how reason and emotion in the search for knowledge might be reevaluated, see Alison M. Jaggar, "Love and Knowledge: Emotion in Feminist Epistemology," *Inquiry* 32 (June, 1989): 151–76.

has been associated with the human, "woman" with the natural. Prominent among distinctions reinforcing the latter view has been that between the public and the private, because of the way they have been interpreted. Again, these provide as familiar and entrenched a framework as do reason and emotion, and they have been as influential for non-philosophers as for philosophers. It has been supposed that in the public realm, man transcends his animal nature and creates human history. As citizen, he creates government and law; as warrior, he protects society by his willingness to risk death; and as artist or philosopher, he overcomes his human mortality. Here, in the public realm, morality should guide human decision. In the household, in contrast, it has been supposed that women merely "reproduce" life as natural, biological matter. Within the household, the "natural" needs of man for food and shelter are served, and new instances of the biological creature that man is are brought into being. But what is distinctively human, and what transcends any given level of development to create human progress, are thought to occur elsewhere.

This contrast was made highly explicit in Aristotle's conceptions of polis and household; it has continued to affect the basic assumptions of a remarkably broad swath of thought ever since. In ancient Athens, women were confined to the household; the public sphere was literally a male domain. In more recent history, though women have been permitted to venture into public space, the associations of the public, historically male sphere with the distinctively human, and of the household, historically a female sphere, with the merely natural and repetitious, have persisted. These associations have deeply affected moral theory, which has often supposed the transcendent, public domain to be relevant to the foundations of morality in ways that the natural behavior of women in the household could not be. To take some recent and representative examples, David Heyd, in his discussion

of supererogation, dismisses a mother's sacrifice for her child as an example of the supererogatory because it belongs, in his view, to "the sphere of natural relationships and instinctive feelings (which lie outside morality)."[8] J. O. Urmson had earlier taken a similar position. In his discussion of supererogation, Urmson said, "Let us be clear that we are not now considering cases of natural affection, such as the sacrifice made by a mother for her child; such cases may be said with some justice not to fall under the concept of morality. . . ."[9] And in a recent article called "Distrusting Economics," Alan Ryan argues persuasively about the questionableness of economics and other branches of the social sciences built on the assumption that human beings are rational, self-interested calculators; he discusses various examples of non self-interested behavior, such as of men in wartime, which show the assumption to be false, but nowhere in the article is there any mention of the activity of mothering, which would seem to be a fertile locus for doubts about the usual picture of rational man.[10] Although Ryan does not provide the kind of explicit reason offered by Heyd and Urmson for omitting the context of mothering from consideration as relevant to his discussion, it is difficult to understand the omission without a comparable assumption being implicit here, as it so often is elsewhere. Without feminist insistence on the relevance for morality of the experience in mothering, this context is

---

8 David Heyd, *Supererogation: Its Status in Ethical Theory* (New York: Cambridge University Press, 1982), p. 134.
9 J. O. Urmson, "Saints and Heroes," in *Essays in Moral Philosophy,* ed. A. I. Melden (Seattle: University of Washington Press, 1958), p. 202. I am indebted to Marcia Baron for pointing out this and the previous example in her "Kantian Ethics and Supererogation," *The Journal of Philosophy* 84 (May, 1987): 237–62.
10 Alan Ryan, "Distrusting Economics," *New York Review of Books* (May 18, 1989): 25–27. For a different treatment, see *Beyond Self-Interest,* ed. Jane Mansbridge (Chicago: University of Chicago Press, 1990).

largely ignored by moral theorists. And yet, from a gender-neutral point of view, how can this vast and fundamental domain of human experience possibly be imagined to lie "outside morality"?

The result of the public/private distinction, as usually formulated, has been to privilege the points of view of men in the public domains of state and law, and later in the marketplace, and to discount the experience of women. Mothering has been conceptualized as a primarily biological activity, even when performed by humans, and virtually no moral theory in the history of ethics has taken mothering, as experienced by women, seriously as a source of moral insight, until feminists in recent years have begun to.[11] Women have been seen as emotional rather than as rational beings, and thus as incapable of full moral personhood. Women's behavior has been interpreted as either "natural" and driven by instinct, and thus as irrelevant to morality and to the construction of moral principles, or it has been interpreted as, at best, in need of instruction and supervision by males better able to know what morality requires and better able to live up to its demands.

The Hobbesian conception of reason is very different from the Platonic or Aristotelian conceptions before it, and from the conceptions of Rousseau or Kant or Hegel later; all have in common that they ignore and disparage the experience and reality of women. Consider Hobbes's account of man in the state of nature contracting with other men to establish society. These men hypothetically come into existence fully formed and independent of one another, and decide on entering or staying outside of civil society. As Christine Di Stefano writes, "What we find in Hobbes's account of human nature and political order is a vital concern with the survival of a self conceived in masculine terms. . . . This masculine dimension of Hobbes's atomistic egoism is powerfully underscored in his state of nature, which is effectively built on the foundation of denied maternity."[12] In *The Citizen,* where Hobbes gave his first systematic exposition of the state of nature, he asks us to "consider men as if but even now sprung out of the earth, and suddenly, like mushrooms, come to full maturity, without all kinds of engagement with each other."[13] As Di Stefano says, it is a most incredible and problematic feature of Hobbes's state of nature that the men in it "are not born of, much less nurtured by, women, or anyone else."[14] To abstract from the complex web of human reality an abstract man for rational perusal, Hobbes has, Di Stefano continues, "expunged human reproduction and early nurturance, two of the most basic and typically female-identified features of distinctively human life, from his account of basic human nature. Such a strategy ensures that he can present a thoroughly atomistic subject. . . ."[15] From the point of view of women's experience, such a subject or self is unbelievable and misleading, even as a theoretical construct. The Leviathan, Di Stefano writes, "is effectively comprised of a body politic of orphans who have reared themselves, whose desires are situated within and reflect nothing but independently generated movement. . . . These essential elements are natural human beings conceived along masculine lines."[16]

Rousseau, and Kant, and Hegel, paid homage to the emotional power, the aesthetic sensi-

---

11 See especially *Mothering: Essays in Feminist Theory,* ed. Joyce Trebilcot (Totowa, New Jersey: Rowman and Allanheld, 1984); and Sara Ruddick, *Maternal Thinking: Toward a Politics of Peace* (Boston: Beacon Press, 1989).

12 Christine Di Stefano, "Masculinity as Ideology in Political Theory: Hobbesian Man Considered," *Women's Studies International Forum* (Special Issue: *Hypatia*), Vol. 6, No. 6 (1983): 633–44, p. 637.

13 Thomas Hobbes, *The Citizen: Philosophical Rudiments Concerning Government and Society,* ed. B. Gert (Garden City, New York: Doubleday, 1972 (1651)), p. 205.

14 Di Stefano, op. cit., p. 638.

15 Ibid.

16 Ibid., p. 639.

bility, and the familial concerns, respectively, of women. But since in their views morality must be based on rational principle, and women were incapable of full rationality, or a degree or kind of rationality comparable to that of men, women were deemed, in the view of these moralists, to be inherently wanting in morality. For Rousseau, women must be trained from childhood to submit to the will of men lest their sexual power lead both men and women to disaster. For Kant, women were thought incapable of achieving full moral personhood, and women lose all charm if they try to behave like men by engaging in rational pursuits. For Hegel, women's moral concern for their families could be admirable in its proper place, but is a threat to the more universal aims to which men, as members of the state, should aspire.[17]

These images, of the feminine as what must be overcome if knowledge and morality are to be achieved, of female experience as naturally irrelevant to morality, and of women as inherently deficient moral creatures, are built into the history of ethics. Feminists examine these images, and see that they are not the incidental or merely idiosyncratic suppositions of a few philosophers whose views on many topics depart far from the ordinary anyway. Such views are the nearly uniform reflection in philosophical and ethical theory of patriarchal attitudes pervasive throughout human history. Or they are exaggerations even of ordinary male experience, which exaggerations then reinforce rather than temper other patriarchal conceptions and institutions. They distort the actual experience and aspirations of many men as well as of women. Annette Baier recently speculated about why it is that moral philosophy has so seriously overlooked the trust between human beings that in her view is an utterly central aspect of moral life. She noted that "the great moral theorists in our tradition not only are all men, they are mostly men who had minimal adult dealings with (and so were then minimally influenced by) women."[18] They were for the most part "clerics, misogynists, and puritan bachelors," and thus it is not surprising that they focus their philosophical attention "so single-mindedly on cool, distanced relations between more or less free and equal adult strangers. . . ."[19]

As feminists, we deplore the patriarchal attitudes that so much of philosophy and moral theory reflect. But we recognize that the problem is more serious even than changing those attitudes. For moral theory as so far developed is incapable of correcting itself without an almost total transformation. It cannot simply absorb the gender that has been "left behind," even if both genders would want it to. To continue to build morality on rational principles opposed to the emotions and to include women among the rational will leave no one to reflect the promptings of the heart, which promptings can be moral rather than merely instinctive. To simply bring women into the public and male domain of the polis will leave no one to speak for the household. Its values have been hitherto unrecognized, but they are often moral values. Or to continue to seek contractual restraints on the pursuits of self-interest by atomistic individuals, and to have women join men in devotion to these pursuits, will leave no one involved in the nurturance of children and cultivation of social relations, which nurturance and cultivation can be of greatest moral import.

17 For examples of relevant passages, see *Philosophy of Woman: Classical to Current Concepts,* ed. Mary Mahowald (Indianapolis: Hackett, 1978); and *Visions of Women,* ed. Linda Bell (Clifton, New Jersey: Humana, 1985). For discussion, see Susan Moller Okin, *Women in Western Political Thought* (Princeton, New Jersey: Princeton University Press, 1979); and Lorenne Clark and Lynda Lange, eds., *The Sexism of Social and Political Theory* (Toronto: University of Toronto Press, 1979).

18 Annette Baier, "Trust and Anti-Trust," *Ethics* 96 (1986): 231–60, pp. 247–48.
19 Ibid.

There are very good reasons for women not to want simply to be accorded entry as equals into the enterprise of morality as so far developed. In a recent survey of types of feminist moral theory, Kathryn Morgan notes that "many women who engage in philosophical reflection are acutely aware of the masculine nature of the profession and tradition, and feel their own moral concerns as women silenced or trivialized in virtually all the official settings that define the practice."[20] Women should clearly not agree, as the price of admission to the masculine realm of traditional morality, to abandon our own moral concerns as women.

And so we are groping to shape new moral theory. Understandably, we do not yet have fully worked out feminist moral theories to offer. But we can suggest some directions our project of developing such theories is taking. As Kathryn Morgan points out, there is not likely to be a "star" feminist moral theorist on the order of a Rawls or Nozick: "There will be no individual singled out for two reasons. One reason is that vital moral and theoretical conversations are taking place on a large dialectical scale as the feminist community struggles to develop a feminist ethic. The second reason is that this community of feminist theoreticians is calling into question the very model of the individualized autonomous self presupposed by a star-centered male-dominated tradition. . . . We experience it as a common labour, a common task."[21]

The dialogues that are enabling feminist approaches to moral theory to develop are proceeding. As Alison Jaggar makes clear in her useful overview of them, there is no unitary view of ethics that can be identified as "feminist ethics." Feminist approaches to ethics share a commitment to "rethinking ethics with a view to correcting whatever forms of male bias it may contain."[22] While those who develop these approaches are "united by a shared project, they diverge widely in their views as to how this project is to be accomplished."[23]

Not all feminists, by any means, agree that there are distinctive feminist virtues or values. Some are especially skeptical of the attempt to give positive value to such traditional "feminine virtues" as a willingness to nurture, or an affinity with caring, or reluctance to seek independence. They see this approach as playing into the hands of those who would confine women to traditional roles.[24] Other feminists are skeptical of all claims about women as such, emphasizing that women are divided by class and race and sexual orientation in ways that make any conclusions drawn from "women's experience" dubious.[25]

Still, it is possible, I think, to discern various important focal points evident in current feminist attempts to transform ethics into a theoretical and practical activity that could be acceptable from a feminist point of view. In the glimpse I have presented of bias in the history of ethics, I focused on what, from a feminist point of view, are three of its most questionable aspects: (1) the split between reason and emotion and the devaluation of emotion; (2) the public/private distinction and the relegation of the private to

20 Kathryn Pauly Morgan, "Strangers in a Strange Land: Feminists Visit Relativists" in *Perspectives on Relativism,* ed. D. Odegaard and Carole Stewart (Toronto: Agathon Press, 1990).

21 Kathryn Morgan, "Women and Moral Madness," in *Science, Morality and Feminist Theory,* ed. Hanen and Nielsen, p. 223.

22 Alison M. Jaggar, "Feminist Ethics: Some Issues For The Nineties," *Journal of Social Philosophy* 20 (Spring/Fall 1989), p. 91.

23 Ibid.

24 One well-argued statement of this position is Barbara Houston, "Rescuing Womanly Virtues: Some Dangers of Moral Reclamation," in *Science, Morality and Feminist Theory,* ed. Hanen and Nielsen.

25 See e.g. Elizabeth V. Spelman, *Inessential Woman: Problems of Exclusion in Feminist Thought* (Boston: Beacon Press, 1988). See also Sarah Lucia Hoagland, *Lesbian Ethics: Toward New Value* (Palo Alto, California: Institute of Lesbian Studies, 1989); and Katie Geneva Cannon, *Black Womanist Ethics* (Atlanta, Georgia: Scholars Press, 1988).

the natural; and (3) the concept of the self as constructed from a male point of view. In the remainder of this article, I shall consider further how some feminists are exploring these topics. We are showing how their previous treatment has been distorted, and we are trying to reenvision the realities and recommendations with which these aspects of moral theorizing do and should try to deal.

I. Reason and Emotion

In the area of moral theory in the modern era, the priority accorded to reason has taken two major forms. (A) On the one hand has been the Kantian, or Kantian-inspired search for very general, abstract, deontological, universal moral principles by which rational beings should be guided. Kant's Categorical Imperative is a foremost example: it suggests that all moral problems can be handled by applying an impartial, pure, rational principle to particular cases. It requires that we try to see what the general features of the problem before us are, and that we apply an abstract principle, or rules derivable from it, to this problem. On this view, this procedure should be adequate for all moral decisions. We should thus be able to act as reason recommends, and resist yielding to emotional inclinations and desires in conflict with our rational wills.

(B) On the other hand, the priority accorded to reason in the modern era has taken a Utilitarian form. The Utilitarian approach, reflected in rational choice theory, recognizes that persons have desires and interests, and suggests rules of rational choice for maximizing the satisfaction of these. While some philosophers in this tradition espouse egoism, especially of an intelligent and long-term kind, many do not. They begin, however, with assumptions that what are morally relevant are gains and losses of utility to theoretically isolatable individuals, and that the outcome at which morality should aim is the maximization of the utility of individuals. Rational calculation about such an outcome will, in this view, provide moral recommendations to guide all our choices. As with the Kantian approach, the Utilitarian approach relies on abstract general principles or rules to be applied to particular cases. And it holds that although emotion is, in fact, the source of our desires for certain objectives, the task of morality should be to instruct us on how to pursue those objectives most rationally. Emotional attitudes toward moral issues themselves interfere with rationality and should be disregarded. Among the questions Utilitarians can ask can be questions about which emotions to cultivate, and which desires to try to change, but these questions are to be handled in the terms of rational calculation, not of what our feelings suggest.

Although the conceptions of what the judgments of morality should be based on, and of how reason should guide moral decision, are different in Kantian and in Utilitarian approaches, both share a reliance on a highly abstract, universal principle as the appropriate source of moral guidance, and both share the view that moral problems are to be solved by the application of such an abstract principle to particular cases. Both share an admiration for the rules of reason to be appealed to in moral contexts, and both denigrate emotional responses to moral issues.

Many feminist philosophers have questioned whether the reliance on abstract rules, rather than the adoption of more context-respectful approaches, can possibly be adequate for dealing with moral problems, especially as women experience them.[26] Though Kantians may hold that complex rules can be elaborated for specific contexts, there is nevertheless an assumption in this approach that the more abstract the reasoning applied to a moral problem, the more satisfactory. And Utilitarians suppose that one highly

26 For an approach to social and political as well as moral issues that attempts to be context-respectful, see Virginia Held, *Rights and Goods. Justifying Social Action* (Chicago: University of Chicago Press, 1989).

abstract principle, the Principle of Utility, can be applied to every moral problem no matter what the context.

A genuinely universal or gender-neutral moral theory would be one which would take account of the experience and concerns of women as fully as it would take account of the experience and concerns of men. When we focus on the experience of women, however, we seem to be able to see a set of moral concerns becoming salient that differs from those of traditional or standard moral theory. Women's experience of moral problems seems to lead us to be especially concerned with actual relationships between embodied persons, and with what these relationships seem to require. Women are often inclined to attend to rather than to dismiss the particularities of the context in which a moral problem arises. And we often pay attention to feelings of empathy and caring to suggest what we ought to do rather than relying as fully as possible on abstract rules of reason.

Margaret Walker, for instance, contrasts feminist moral "understanding" with traditional moral "knowledge." She sees the components of the former as involving "attention, contextual and narrative appreciation, and communication in the event of moral deliberation."[27] This alternative moral epistemology holds that "the adequacy of moral understanding decreases as its form approaches generality through abstraction."[28]

The work of psychologists such as Carol Gilligan and others has led to a clarification of what may be thought of as tendencies among women to approach moral issues differently. Rather than interpreting moral problems in terms of what could be handled by applying abstract rules of justice to particular cases, many of the women studied by Gilligan tended to be more concerned with preserving actual human relationships, and with expressing care for those for whom they felt responsible. Their moral reasoning was typically more embedded in a context of particular others than was the reasoning of a comparable group of men.[29] One should not equate tendencies women in fact display with feminist views, since the former may well be the result of the sexist, oppressive conditions in which women's lives have been lived. But many feminists see our own consciously considered experience as lending confirmation to the view that what has come to be called "an ethic of care" needs to be developed. Some think it should supersede "the ethic of justice" of traditional or standard moral theory. Others think it should be integrated with the ethic of justice and rules.

In any case, feminist philosophers are in the process of reevaluating the place of emotion in morality in at least two respects. First, many think morality requires the development of the moral emotions, in contrast to moral theories emphasizing the primacy of reason. As Annette Baier notes, the rationalism typical of traditional moral theory will be challenged when we pay attention to the role of parent. "It might be important," she writes, "for father figures to have rational control over their violent urges to beat to death the children whose screams enrage them, but more than control of such nasty passions seems needed in the mother or primary parent, or parent-substitute, by most psychological theories. They need to love their children, not just to control their irritation."[30] So the emphasis in many traditional theories on rational

27 Margaret Urban Walker, "Moral Understandings: Alternative 'Epistemology' for a Feminist Ethics," *Hypatia* 4 (Summer, 1989): 15–28, p. 19.
28 Ibid., p. 20. See also Iris Marion Young, "Impartiality and the Civic Public. Some Implications of Feminist Critiques of Moral and Political Theory," in Seyla Benhabib and Drucilla Cornell, *Feminism as Critique* (Minneapolis: University of Minnesota Press, 1987).

29 See especially Carol Gilligan, *In a Different Voice. Psychological Theory and Women's Development* (Cambridge, Massachusetts: Harvard University Press, 1988); and Eva Feder Kittay and Diana T. Meyers eds., *Women and Moral Theory* (Totowa, New Jersey: Rowman and Allanheld, 1987).
30 Annette Baier, "The Need for More Than Justice," in *Science, Morality and Feminist Theory,* ed. Hanen and Nielsen, p. 55.

control over the emotions, "rather than on cultivating desirable forms of emotion,"[31] is challenged by feminist approaches to ethics.

Secondly, emotion will be respected rather than dismissed by many feminist moral philosophers in the process of gaining moral understanding. The experience and practice out of which feminist moral theory can be expected to be developed will include embodied feeling as well as thought. In a recent overview of a vast amount of writing, Kathryn Morgan states that "feminist theorists begin ethical theorizing with embodied, gendered subjects who have particular histories, particular communities, particular allegiances, and particular visions of human flourishing. The starting point involves valorizing what has frequently been most mistrusted and despised in the western philosophical tradition. . . ."[32] Among the elements being reevaluated are feminine emotions. The "care" of the alternative feminist approach to morality appreciates rather than rejects emotion. The caring relationships important to feminist morality cannot be understood in terms of abstract rules or moral reasoning. And the "weighing" so often needed between the conflicting claims of some relationships and others cannot be settled by deduction or rational calculation. A feminist ethic will not just acknowledge emotion, as do Utilitarians, as giving us the objectives toward which moral rationality can direct us. It will embrace emotion as providing at least a partial basis for morality itself, and for moral understanding.

Annette Baier stresses the centrality of trust for an adequate morality.[33] Achieving and maintaining trusting, caring, relationships is quite different from acting in accord with rational principles, or satisfying the individual desires of either self or other. Caring, empathy, feeling with others, being sensitive to each other's feelings, all may be better guides to what morality requires in actual contexts than may abstract rules of reason, or rational calculation, or at least they may be necessary components of an adequate morality.

The fear that a feminist ethic will be a relativistic "situation ethic" is misplaced. Some feelings can be as widely shared as are rational beliefs, and feminists do not see their views as reducible to "just another attitude."[34] In her discussion of the differences between feminist medical ethics and nonfeminist medical ethics, Susan Sherwin gives an example of how feminists reject the mere case by case approach that has come to predominate in nonfeminist medical ethics. The latter also rejects the excessive reliance on abstract rules characteristic of standard ethics, and in this way resembles feminist ethics. But the very focus on cases in isolation from one another deprives this approach from attending to general features in the institutions and practices of medicine that, among other faults, systematically contribute to the oppression of women.[35] The difference of approach can be seen in the treatment of issues in the new reproductive technologies, where feminists consider how the new technologies may further decrease the control of women over reproduction. This difference might be thought to be one of substance rather than of method, bur Sherwin shows the implications for method also. With respect to reproductive technologies one can see especially clearly the deficiencies of the case by case approach: what needs to be considered is not only choice in the purely individualistic interpretation of the case by case approach, but control at a more general level and how it affects the structure of gender in society. Thus, a feminist perspective does not always counsel attention to specific case vs. appeal to general considerations, as some sort of methodological rule.

---

31 Ibid.
32 Kathryn Pauly Morgan, "Strangers in a Strange Land . . . ," p. 2.
33 Annette Baier, "Trust and Anti-Trust."

34 See especially Kathryn Pauly Morgan, "Strangers in a Strange Land. . . ."
35 Susan Sherwin, "Feminist and Medical Ethics: Two Different Approaches to Contextual Ethics," *Hypatia* 4 (Summer, 1989): 57–72.

Bur the general considerations are often not the purely abstract ones of traditional and standard moral theory, they are the general features and judgments to be made about cases in actual (which means, so far, patriarchal) societies. A feminist evaluation of a moral problem should never omit the political elements involved; and it is likely to recognize that political issues cannot be dealt with adequately in purely abstract terms any more than can moral issues.

The liberal tradition in social and moral philosophy argues that in pluralistic society and even more clearly in a pluralistic world, we cannot agree on our visions of the good life, on what is the best kind of life for humans, but we can hope to agree on the minimal conditions for justice, for coexistence within a framework allowing us to pursue our visions of the good life.[36] Many feminists contend that the commitment to justice needed for agreement *in actual conditions* on even minimal requirements of justice is as likely to demand relational feelings as a rational recognition of abstract principles. Human beings can and do care, and are capable of caring far more than at present, about the sufferings of children quite distant from them, about the prospects for future generations, and about the well-being of the globe. The liberal tradition's mutually disinterested rational individualists would seem unlikely to care enough to take the actions needed to achieve moral decency at a global level, or environmental sanity for decades hence, as they would seem unable to represent caring relationships within the family and among friends. As Annette Baier puts it, "A moral theory, it can plausibly be claimed, cannot regard concern for new and future persons as an optional charity left for those with a taste for it. If the morality the theory endorses is to sustain itself, it must provide for its own continuers, not just take out a loan on a carefully encouraged maternal instinct or on the enthusiasm of a self-

selected group of environmentalists, who make it their business or hobby to be concerned with what we are doing to mother earth."[37]

The possibilities as well as the problems (and we are well aware of some of them) in a feminist reenvisioning of emotion and reason need to be further developed, but we can already see that the views of nonfeminist moral theory are unsatisfactory.

II. *The Public and the Private*

The second questionable aspect of the history of ethics on which I focused was its conception of the distinction between the public and the private. As with the split between reason and emotion, feminists are showing how gender-bias has distorted previous conceptions of these spheres, and we are trying to offer more appropriate understandings of "private" morality and "public" life.

Part of what feminists have criticized has been the way the distinction has been accompanied by a supposition that what occurs in the household occurs as if on an island beyond politics, whereas the personal is highly affected by the political power beyond, from legislation about abortion to the greater earning power of men, to the interconnected division of labor by gender both within and beyond the household, to the lack of adequate social protection for women against domestic violence.[38] Of course we recognize that the family is not identical to the state, and we need concepts for thinking about the private or personal, and the public or political. Bur they will have to be very different from the traditional concepts.

37 Annette Baier, "The Need for More Than Justice," pp. 53–54.

38 See e.g. Linda Nicholson, *Gender and History. The Limits of Social Theory in the Age of the Family* (New York: Columbia University Press, 1986); and Jean Bethke Elshtain, *Public Man, Private Woman* (Princeton, New Jersey: Princeton University Press, 1981). See also Carole Pateman, *The Sexual Contract* (Stanford, California: Stanford University Press, 1988).

36 See especially the work of John Rawls and Ronald Dworkin; see also Charles Larmore, *Patterns of Moral Complexity* (Cambridge: Cambridge University Press, 1987).

Feminists have also criticized deeper assumptions about what is distinctively human and what is "natural" in the public and private aspects of human life, and what is meant by "natural" in connection with women.[39] Consider the associations that have traditionally been built up: the public realm is seen as the distinctively human realm in which man transcends his animal nature, while the private realm of the household is seen as the natural region in which women merely reproduce the species.[40] These associations are extraordinarily pervasive in standard concepts and theories, in art and thought and cultural ideals, and especially in politics.

Dominant patterns of thought have seen women as primarily mothers, and mothering as the performance of a primarily biological function. Then it has been supposed that while engaging in political life is a specifically human activity, women are engaged in an activity which is not specifically human. Women accordingly have been thought to be closer to nature than men,[41] to be enmeshed in a biological function involving processes more like those in which other animals are involved than like the rational discussion of the citizen in the polis, or the glorious battles of noble soldiers, or the trading and rational contracting of "economic man." The total or relative exclusion of women from the domain of public life has then been seen as either inevitable or appropriate.

The view that women are more determined by biology than are men is still extraordinarily prevalent. It is as questionable from a feminist perspective as many other traditional misinterpretations of women's experience. Human mothering is an extremely different activity from the mothering engaged in by other animals. The work and speech of men is recognized as very different from what might be thought of as the "work" and "speech" of other animals. Human mothering is fully as different from animal mothering. Of course all human beings are animal as well as human. But to whatever extent it is appropriate to recognize a difference between "man" and other animals, so would it be appropriate to recognize a comparable difference between "woman" and other animals, and between the activities—including mothering—engaged in by women and the behavior of other animals.

Human mothering shapes language and culture, it forms human social personhood, it develops morality. Animal behavior can be highly impressive and complex, but it does not have built into it any of the consciously chosen aims of morality. In creating human social persons, human mothering is different in kind from merely propagating a species. And human mothering can be fully as creative an activity as those activities traditionally thought of as distinctively human, because to create *new* persons, and new types of *persons,* can surely be as creative as to make new objects, products, or institutions. *Human* mothering is no more "natural" or "primarily biological" than is any other human activity.

Consider nursing an infant, often thought of as the epitome of a biological process with which mothering is associated and women are identified. There is no reason to think of human nursing as any more simply biological than there is to think of, say, a businessmen's lunch this way. Eating is a biological process, but what and how and with whom we eat are thoroughly cultural. Whether and how long and with whom a woman nurses an infant, are also human, cultural matters. If men transcend the natural by conquering new territory and trading with their

39 See e.g. Susan Moller Okin, *Women in Western Political Thought*. See also Alison M. Jaggar, *Feminist Politics and Human Nature* (Totowa, New Jersey: Rowman and Allanheld, 1983).

40 So entrenched is this way of thinking that it was even reflected in Simone de Beauvoir's path-breaking feminist text *The Second Sex,* published in 1949. Here, as elsewhere, feminists have had to transcend our own early searches for our own perspectives.

41 See e.g. Sherry B. Ortner, "Is Female to Male as Nature Is to Culture?" in *Woman, Culture, and Society,* ed. Michelle Z. Rosaldo and Louise Lamphere (Stanford: Stanford University Press, 1974).

neighbors and making deals over lunch to do so, women can transcend the natural by choosing not to nurse their children when they could, or choosing to nurse them when their culture tells them not to, or singing songs to their infants as they nurse, or nursing in restaurants to overcome the prejudices against doing so, or thinking human thoughts as they nurse, and so forth. Human culture surrounds and characterizes the activity of nursing as it does the activities of eating, or governing, or writing, or thinking.

We are continually being presented with images of the humanly new and creative as occurring in the public realm of the polis, or the realms of marketplace or of art and science outside the household. The very term 'reproduction' suggests mere repetition, the "natural" bringing into existence of repeated instances of the same human animal. But human reproduction is not repetition.[42] This is not to suggest that bringing up children in the interstices of patriarchal society, in society structured by institutions supporting male dominance, can achieve the potential of transformation latent in the activity of human mothering. But the activity of creating new social persons and new kinds of persons is potentially the most transformative human activity of all. And it suggests that morality should concern itself first of all with this activity, with what its norms and practices ought to be, and with how the institutions and arrangements throughout society and the world ought to be structured to facilitate the right kinds of development of the best kinds of new persons. The flourishing of children ought to be at the very center of moral and social and political and economic and legal thought, rather than, as at present, at the periphery, if attended to at all.

Revised conceptions of public and private have significant implications for our conceptions of human beings and relationships between them. Some feminists suggest that instead of seeing human relationships in terms of the impersonal ones of the "public" sphere, as standard political and moral theory has so often done, we might consider seeing human relationships in terms of those experienced in the sphere of the "private," or of what these relationships could be imagined to be like in post-patriarchal society.[43] The traditional approach is illustrated by those who generalize, to other regions of human life than the economic, assumptions about "economic man" in contractual relations with other men. It sees such impersonal, contractual relations as paradigmatic, even, on some views, for moral theory. Many feminists, in contrast, consider the realm of what has been misconstrued as the "private" as offering guidance to what human beings and their relationships should be like even in regions beyond those of family and friendship. Sara Ruddick looks at the implications of the practice of mothering for the conduct of peace politics.[44] Marilyn Friedman and Lorraine Code consider friendship, especially as women understand it, as a possible model for human relationships.[45] Others see society as non-contractual rather than as contractual.

Clearly, a reconceptualization is needed of the ways in which every human life is entwined with personal and with social components. Feminist theorists are contributing imaginative work to this project.

III. The Concept of Self

Let me turn now to the third aspect of the history of ethics which I discussed and which femi-

---

42 For further discussion and an examination of surrounding associations, see Virginia Held, "Birth and Death," in *Ethics* 99 (January 1989): 362–88.

43 See e.g. Virginia Held, "Non-contractual Society: A Feminist View," in *Science, Morality and Feminist Theory*, ed. Hanen and Nielson.

44 Sara Ruddick, *Maternal Thinking*.

45 See Marilyn Friedman, "Feminism and Modern Friendship: Dislocating the Community," *Ethics* 99 (January 1989): 275–90; and Lorraine Code, "Second Persons."

nists are re-envisioning: the concept of self. One of the most important emphases in a feminist approach to morality is the recognition that more attention must be paid to the domain between, on the one hand, the self as ego, as self-interested individual, and, on the other hand, the universal, everyone, others in general.[46] Traditionally, ethics has dealt with these poles of individual self and universal all. Usually, it has called for impartiality against the partiality of the egoistic self; sometimes it has defended egoism against claims for a universal perspective. But most standard moral theory has hardly noticed as morally significant the intermediate realm of family relations and relations of friendship, of group ties and neighborhood concerns, especially from the point of view of women. When it has noticed this intermediate realm it has often seen its attachments as threatening to the aspirations of the Man of Reason, or as subversive of "true" morality. In seeing the problems of ethics as problems of reconciling the interests of the self with what would be right or best for "everyone," standard ethics has neglected the moral aspects of the concern and sympathy which people actually feel for particular others, and what moral experience in this intermediate realm suggests for an adequate morality.

The region of "particular others" is a distinct domain, where what can be seen to be artificial and problematic are the very egoistic "self" and the universal "all others" of standard moral theory. In the domain of particular others, the self is already constituted to an important degree by relations with others, and these relations may be much more salient and significant than the interests of any individual self in isolation.[47] The "others" in the picture, however, are not the "all others," or "everyone," of traditional moral theory; they are not what a universal point of view or a view from nowhere could provide.[48] They are, characteristically, actual flesh and blood other human beings for whom we have actual feelings and with whom we have real ties.

From the point of view of much feminist theory, the individualistic assumptions of liberal theory and of most standard moral theory are suspect. Even if we would be freed from the debilitating aspects of dominating male power to "be ourselves" and to pursue our own interests, we would, as persons, still have ties to other persons, and we would at least in part be constituted by such ties. Such ties would be part of what we inherently are. We are, for instance, the daughter or son of given parents, or the mother or father of given children, and we carry with us at least some ties to the racial or ethnic or national group within which we developed into the persons we are.

If we look, for instance, at the realities of the relation between mothering person (who can be female or male) and child, we can see that what we value in the relation cannot be broken down into individual gains and losses for the individual members in the relation. Nor can it be understood in universalistic terms. Self-development apart from the relation may be much less important than the satisfactory development of the relation. What matters may often be the health and growth of and the development of the relation-and-its members in ways that cannot be understood in the individualistic terms of standard moral theories designed to maximize the satisfaction of self-interest. The universalistic terms of moral theories grounded in what would

---

46 See Virginia Held, "Feminism and Moral Theory," in *Women and Moral Theory,* ed. Kittay and Meyers.

47 See Seyla Benhabib, "The Generalized and the Concrete Other. The Kohlberg-Gilligan Controversy and Moral Theory," in *Women and Moral Theory,* ed. Kittay and Meyers. See also Caroline Whitbeck, "Feminist Ontology: A Different Reality," in *Beyond Domination,* ed. Carol Gould (Totowa, New Jersey: Rowman and Allanheld, 1983).

48 See Thomas Nagel, *The View from Nowhere* (New York: Oxford University Press, 1986). For a feminist critique, see Susan Bordo, "Feminism, Postmodernism, and Gender-Skepticism," in *Feminism/Postmodernism,* ed. Linda Nicholson (New York: Routledge, 1989).

be right for "all rational beings" or "everyone" cannot handle, either, what has moral value in the relation between mothering person and child.

Feminism is of course not the only locus of criticism of the individualistic and abstractly universalistic features of liberalism and of standard moral theory. Marxists and communitarians also see the self as constituted by its social relations. But in their usual form, Marxist and communitarian criticisms pay no more attention than liberalism and standard moral theory to the experience of women, to the context of mothering, or to friendship as women experience it.[49] Some recent nonfeminist criticisms, such as offered by Bernard Williams, of the impartiality required by standard moral theory, stress how a person's identity may be formed by personal projects in ways that do not satisfy universal norms, yet ought to be admired. Such views still interpret morality from the point of view of an individual and his project, not a social relationship such as that between mothering person and child. And recent nonfeminist criticisms in terms of traditional communities and their moral practices, as seen for instance in the work of Stuart Hampshire and Alasdair MacIntyre, often take traditional gender roles as given, or provide no basis for a radical critique of them.[50]

49 On Marxist theory, see e.g. *Women and Revolution,* ed. Lydia Sargent (Boston: South End Press, 1981); Alison Jaggar, *Feminist Politics and Human Nature;* and Ann Ferguson, *Blood at the Root. Motherhood, Sexuality and Male Dominance* (London: Pandora, 1989). On communitarian theory, see Marilyn Friedman, "Feminism and Modern Friendship. . . ." and also her paper "The Social Self and the Partiality Debates," presented at the Society for Women in Philosophy meeting in New Orleans, April 1990.

50 Bernard Williams, *Moral Luck* (Cambridge: Cambridge University Press, 1981); *Public and Private Morality,* ed. Stuart Hampshire (Cambridge: Cambridge University Press, 1978); Alasdair MacIntyre, *After Virtue. A Study in Moral Theory* (Notre Dame, Indiana: University of Notre Dame Press, 1981). For discussion see Susan Moller Okin, *Justice, Gender, and the Family* (New York: Basic Books, 1989).

There is no substitute, then, for feminist exploration of the area between ego and universal, as women experience this area, or for the development of a refocused concept of relational self that could be acceptable from a feminist point of view.

Relationships can be evaluated as trusting or mistrustful, mutually considerate or selfish, harmonious or stressful, and so forth. Where trust and consideration are appropriate, which is not always, we can find ways to foster them. But understanding and evaluating relationships, and encouraging them to be what they can be at their best, require us to look at relationships between actual persons, and to see what both standard moral theories and their nonfeminist critics often miss. To be adequate, moral theories must pay attention to the neglected realm of particular others in the actual relationships and actual contexts of women's experience. In doing so, problems of individual self-interest vs. universal rules may recede to a region more like background, out-of-focus insolubility or relative unimportance. The salient problems may then be seen to be how we ought best to guide or to maintain or to reshape the relationships, both close and more distant, that we have, or might have, with actual other human beings. Particular others can be actual children in need in distant continents, or the anticipated children of generations not yet even close to being born. But they are not "all rational beings" or "the greatest number," and the self that is in relationships with particular others and is composed to a significant degree by such relations is not a self whose ego must be pitted against abstract, universal claims. Developing the needed guidance for maintaining and reshaping relationships presents enormous problems, but a first step is to recognize how traditional and nonfeminist moral theory of both an individualistic and communitarian kind falls short in providing it.

The concept of the relational self which is evolving within feminist thought is leading to interesting inquiry in many fields. An example is the work being done at the Stone Center at Wellesley College.[51] Psychologists there have posited a self-in-relation theory and are conducting empirical inquiries to try to establish how the female self develops. They are working with a theory that a female relational self develops through a mutually empathetic mother-daughter bond.

The work has been influenced by Jean Baker Miller's re-evaluation of women's psychological qualities as strengths rather than weaknesses. In her book *Toward a New Psychology of Women,* published in 1976, Miller identified women's "great desire for affiliation" as one such strength.[52] Nancy Chodorow's *The Reproduction of Mothering,* published in 1978, has also had a significant influence on the work done at the Stone Center, as it has on much feminist inquiry.[53] Chodorow argued that a female affiliative self is reproduced by a structure of parenting in which mothers are the primary caretakers, and sons and daughters develop differently in relation to a parent of the same sex, or a parent of different sex, as primary caretaker. Daughters develop a sense of self by identifying themselves with the mother; they come to define themselves as connected to or in relation with others. Sons, in contrast, develop a sense of self by differentiating themselves from the mother; they come to define themselves as separate from or unconnected to others. An implication often drawn from Chodorow's work is that parenting should be shared equally by fathers and mothers so that children of either sex can develop with caretakers of both same and different sex.

In 1982, Carol Gilligan, building on both Miller and Chodorow, offered her view of the "different voice" with which girls and women express their understanding of moral problems.[54] Like Miller and Chodorow, Gilligan valued tendencies found especially in women to affiliate with others and to interpret their moral responsibilities in terms of their relationships with others. In all, the valuing of autonomy and individual independence over care and concern for relationships, was seen as an expression of male bias. The Stone Center has tried to elaborate and to study a feminist conception of the relational self. In a series of Working Papers, researchers and clinicians have explored the implications of this conception for various issues in women's psychology (e.g. power, anger, work inhibitions, violence, eating patterns) and for therapy.

The self as conceptualized in these studies is seen as having both a need for recognition and a need to understand the other, and these needs are seen as compatible. They are created in the context of mother-child interaction, and are satisfied in a mutually empathetic relationship. This does not require a loss of self, but a relationship of mutuality in which self and other both express intersubjectivity. Both give and take in a way that not only contributes to the satisfaction of their needs as individuals, but also affirms the "larger relational unit" they compose.[55] Maintaining this larger relational unit then becomes a goal, and maturity is seen not in terms of individual autonomy but in terms of competence in creating and sustaining relations of empathy and mutual intersubjectivity.

---

51 On the Stone Center concept of the self see especially Jean Baker Miller, "The Development of Women's Sense of Self," Wellesley, Massachusetts: Stone Center Working Paper No. 12; Janet Surrey, "The 'Self-in-Relation': A Theory of Women's Development" (Wellesley, Massachusetts: Stone Center Working Paper No. 13); and Judith Jordan, "The Meaning of Mutuality" (Wellesley, Massachusetts: Stone Center Working Paper No. 23). For a feminist but critical view of this work, see Marcia Westkott, "Female Relationality and the Idealized Self," *American Journal of Psychoanalysis* 49 (September, 1989): 239–50.

52 Jean Baker Miller, *Toward a New Psychology of Women* (Boston: Beacon Press, 1976).

53 Nancy Chodorow, *The Reproduction of Mothering: Psychoanalysis and the Sociology of Gender* (Berkeley: University of California Press, 1978).

54 Carol Gilligan, *In a Different Voice.*

55 J. V. Jordan, "'The Meaning of Mutuality," p. 2.

The Stone Center psychologists contend that the goal of mutuality is rarely achieved in adult male-female relationships because of the traditional gender system. The gender system leads men to seek autonomy and power over others, and to undervalue the caring and relational connectedness that is expected of women. Women rarely receive the nurturing and empathetic support they provide. Accordingly, these psychologists look to the interaction that occurs in mother-daughter relationships as the best source of insight into the promotion of the healthy, relational self. This research provides an example of exploration into a refocused, feminist conception of the self, and into empirical questions about its development and implications.

In a quite different field, that of legal theory, a refocused concept of self is leading to reexaminations of such concepts as property and autonomy and the role these have played in political theory and in constitutional law. For instance, the legal theorist Jennifer Nedelsky questions the imagery that is dominant in constitutional law and in our conceptions of property: the imagery of a bounded self, a self contained within boundaries and having rights to property within a wall allowing it to exclude others and to exclude government. The boundary metaphor, she argues, obscures and distorts our thinking about human relationships and what is valuable in them. "The boundedness of selves," Nedelsky writes, "may seem to be a self-evident truth, but I think it is a wrongheaded and destructive way of conceiving of the human creatures law and government are created for."[56] In the domain of the self's relation to the state, the central problem, she argues, is not "maintaining a sphere into which the state cannot penetrate, but fostering autonomy when people are already within the sphere of state control or responsibility."[57] What we can from a feminist perspective think

of as the male "separative self" seems on an endless quest for security behind such walls of protection as those of property. Property focuses the quest for security "in ways that are paradigmatic of the efforts of separative selves to protect themselves through boundaries. . . ."[58] But of course property is a social construction, not a thing; it requires the involvement of the state to define what it is and to defend it. What will provide what it seeks to offer will not be boundaries and exclusions, but constructive relationships.

In an article on autonomy, Nedelsky examines the deficiencies in the concept of self with which so much of our political and legal thinking about autonomy has been developed. She well recognizes that of course feminists are centrally concerned with freedom and autonomy, with enabling women to live our own lives. But we need a language with which to express these concerns which will also reflect "the equally important feminist precept that any good theorizing will start with people in their social contexts. And the notion of social context must take seriously its constitutive quality; social context cannot simply mean that individuals will, of course, encounter one another."[59] The problem, then, is how to combine the claim of the constitutiveness of social relations with the value of self-determination. Liberalism has been the source of our language of freedom and self-determination, but it lacks the ability to express comprehension of "the reality we know: the centrality of relationships in constituting the self."[60]

In developing a new conception of autonomy that avoids positing self-sufficient and thus highly artificial individuals, Nedelsky points out first that "the capacity to find one's own law can develop only in the context of relations with

56 Jennifer Nedelsky, "Law, Boundaries, and the Bounded Self," *Representations* 30 (Spring, 1990): 162–89, at 167.
57 Ibid., p. 169.

58 Ibid., p. 181.
59 Jennifer Nedelsky, "Reconceiving Autonomy: Sources, Thoughts and Possibilities," *Yale Journal of Law and Feminism* 1 (Spring, 1989): 7–36, p. 9. See also Diana T. Meyers, *Self, Society, and Personal Choice* (New York: Columbia University Press, 1989).
60 Ibid.

others (both intimate and more broadly social) that nurture this capacity, and second, that the 'content' of one's own law is comprehensible only with reference to shared social norms, values, and concepts."[61] She sees the traditional liberal view of the self as implying that the most perfectly autonomous man is the most perfectly isolated, and finds this pathological.

Instead of developing autonomy through images of walls around one's property, as does the Western liberal tradition and as does U.S. constitutional law, Nedelsky suggests that "the most promising model, symbol, or metaphor for autonomy is not property, but childrearing. There we have encapsulated the emergence of autonomy through relationship with others. . . . Interdependence [is] a constant component of autonomy."[62] And she goes on to examine how law and bureaucracies can foster autonomy within relationships between citizen and government. This does not entail extrapolating from intimate relations to largescale ones; rather, the insights gained from experience with the context of childrearing allow us to recognize the relational aspects of autonomy. In work such as Nedelsky's we can see how feminist reconceptualizations of the self can lead to the rethinking of fundamental concepts even in terrains such as law, thought by many to be quite distant from such disturbances.

To argue for a view of the self as relational does not mean that women need to remain enmeshed in the ties by which they are constituted.

In recent decades, especially, women have been breaking free of relationships with parents, with the communities in which they grew up, and with men, relationships in which they defined themselves through the traditional and often stifling expectations of others.[63] These quests for self have often involved wrenching instability and painful insecurity. But the quest has been for a new and more satisfactory relational self, not for the self-sufficient individual of liberal theory. Many might share the concerns expressed by Alison Jaggar that disconnecting ourselves from particular others, as ideals of individual autonomy seem to presuppose we should, might make us *in*capable of morality, rather than capable of it, if, as so many feminists think, "an ineliminable part of morality consists in responding emotionally to particular others."[64]

I have examined three topics on which feminist philosophers and feminists in other fields are thinking anew about where we should start and how we should focus our attention in ethics. Feminist reconceptualizations and recommendations concerning the relation between reason and emotion, the distinction between public and private, and the concept of the self, are providing insights deeply challenging to standard moral theory. The implications of this work are that we need an almost total reconstruction of social and political and economic and legal theory in all their traditional forms as well as a reconstruction of moral theory and practice at more comprehensive, or fundamental, levels.

---

61 Ibid., p. 11.
62 Ibid., p. 12. See also Mari J. Matsuda, "Liberal Jurisprudence and Abstracted Visions of Human Nature," *New Mexico Law Review* 16 (Fall, 1986): 613–30.

63 See e.g. *Women's Ways of Knowing. The Development of Self, Voice, and Mind,* by Mary Field Belenky, Blyth McVicker Clinchy, Nancy Rule Goldberger, and Jill Mattuck Tarule (New York: Basic Books, 1986).
64 Alison Jaggar, "Feminist Ethics: Some Issues for the Nineties," p. 11.

Review Questions

1. According to Held, how has male philosophy and ethics viewed reason and emotion? Give examples of male philosophers.
2. What is the traditional male distinction between public and private realms? Why doesn't Held accept this distinction?
3. How do feminist philosophers transform the male distinction between reason and emotion?

4. How do they view public and private realms?
5. Explain the feminist theory of the relational self, as distinguished from the egoist self and "all others" of standard moral theory.

Discussion Questions

1. Is it true, as Held claims, that human beings can and do care about distant children, future generations, and the well-being of the globe?
2. Try to imagine a feminist post-patriarchal society. What would it be like?
3. Does feminist moral theory allow for full freedom and autonomy? Why or why not?

Problem Cases

1. The Colt Sporter and Handguns

The Colt Sporter is one of the most popular semiautomatic assault rifles. A semi-automatic weapon fires one bullet with each pull of the trigger, as distinguished from a fully automatic weapon, which fires a stream of bullets with one trigger pull. Fully automatic weapons are banned by the federal government, but semiautomatic weapons are legal in most states. In 1993 a Connecticut law banned thirty kinds of semiautomatic guns, including the Colt Sporter. The Sporter is made by Colt's Manufacturing Company, based in Hartford, Connecticut. Even though it looks just like a Colt-made M16 (a standard military weapon), Colt officials say the Sporter is made for target practice and hunting. Furthermore, the Colt officials insist that people have a right to own and use rifles such as the Sporter. Critics claim that the Sporter can be converted into a fully automatic weapon and that it is used mostly in urban gang and drug shootings.

Do citizens have a right to own and use semiautomatic weapons? What about fully automatic weapons? What is your position?

Most gun owners have handguns, not semiautomatic or fully automatic weapons. It is estimated that there are 70 million handguns owned by private citizens in the United States. Those who support more gun control or even the elimination of all these guns point to statistics. Each year about 39,000 Americans are killed with guns: There are 19,000 suicides, 18,000 homicides, and some 2,000 people killed in gun accidents. In addition, there are about 40,000 injuries from accidents with guns each year, and probably millions of crimes committed using guns. By contrast, countries with strict handgun control have much lower rates of homicide. In 1990 there were 87 people killed by handguns in Japan, 13 in Sweden, 10 in Australia, and 22 in Great Britain.

Given these facts, why not have strict gun control in the United States? What would Mill say? How about Kant?

The opposition to gun control comes mainly from the National Rifle Association and its members. The NRA defends each person's right to own and use handguns in self-defense. The NRA claims that the homicide statistics are inflated and that the most important statistic is that there are 645,000 defensive uses of handguns each year. As for accidental deaths and injuries, the NRA solution is to teach principles of safe use of weapons.

Do you agree with the NRA position? Why or why not?

2. A New Drug

Suppose you are a poor and uneducated person from Chicago. Your only chance for success in life is through athletics, particularly distance running. You have trained hard, and you have placed high in 10-kilometer and marathon races, but you have never won a major race. You need to be just a little faster to win. In one month, there is the Chicago Marathon, with a cash prize of $50,000 for the winner. There is a good chance that the winner will also get a lucrative contract with a major shoe company, such as Nike. A friend who is an athletic trainer tells you she has obtained a limited supply of a new drug that dramatically improves endurance by preventing the buildup of lactic acid in the muscles. The drug is the result of genetic research on human growth hormones, and thus far it has been tested on animals with no bad side effects. It seems to be much safer and more effective than steroids or the human growth hormones used by some runners. Your friend offers you a month's supply of the drug. She assures you that it is not on the list of banned drugs and that it will not show up on drug tests, or at least the drug tests currently used. In return for giving you the drug, your friend wants $5,000, but only if you win the race and collect the $50,000 cash prize. If you do not win, you owe her nothing.

Should you take the drug or not? Why or why not?

3. Tobacco and Marijuana

In the United States it is legal for adults to smoke tobacco in cigars, cigarettes, and pipes. Even though the tobacco companies deny it, most doctors agree that smoking tobacco is unhealthy. Tobacco contains nicotine, a poisonous drug that is as addictive as cocaine and is associated with coronary heart disease and peripheral vascular disease. In addition, the tar in tobacco smoke damages the lung tissue and causes lung cancer. Despite these facts, smokers and the tobacco companies insist that people have a right to smoke.

Do people have a right to smoke? If so, do they have a right to smoke in public places?

Is it morally wrong to smoke? What would Mill say? How about Kant and Ross?

Is smoking a moral vice? Why or why not?

Should smoking be illegal for minors?

Even though it is legal for adults to smoke tobacco, it is illegal to smoke marijuana in the United States. When smoked, marijuana produces physical effects such as a dry mouth, mild reddening of the eyes, slight clumsiness, and increased appetite. The main psychological effects are feelings of well-being and calmness, and more vivid visual and auditory perceptions. In large doses it may cause panicky states or illusions. In rare cases, large doses may cause psychosis or loss of contact with reality. Prolonged use has been associated with apathy and loss of motivation. But all things considered, marijuana does not seem to be any more dangerous or unhealthy than tobacco, and is perhaps less so. If you agree that smoking should be legal for adults and that they have a right to smoke, then why not legalize marijuana for adults? On the other hand, if you think that marijuana should be illegal, then why shouldn't tobacco be illegal too?

Suggested Readings

1. Joseph Butler makes the classical attack on egoism in *Fifteen Sermons upon Human Nature* (London, 1729). Ayn Rand explains and defends egoism in *The Virtue of Selfishness* (Signet, 1964). Paul W. Taylor argues that ethical egoism contains an inconsistency in *Principles of Ethics: An Introduction* (Wadsworth, 1975).
2. *The Divine Command Theory of Ethics,* ed. Paul Helm (Oxford University Press, 1979), contains several articles on the divine command theory. Robert M. Adams defends the theory in "A Modified Divine Command Theory of Ethical Wrongness," in *The Virtue of Faith* (Oxford University Press, 1987). Philip L. Quinn gives a sophisticated defense and explanation of the theory using deontic logic in *Divine Commands and Moral Requirements* (Clarendon Press, 1978). Kai Nielson, *Ethics Without God* (Pemberton Books, 1973), argues that ethics can exist without belief in God.
3. To sample more of Nietzsche's writings, see *From Basic Writings of Nietzsche,* trans. and ed. Walter Kaufmann (The Modern Library, 1968). *On the Genealogy of Morals* contains Nietzsche's attack on Judeo-Christian morality, utilitarianism, and Kant's ethics of duty. In his critique, he uses "genealogy"—that is, the "unmasking" of beliefs by uncovering their seedy origin in psychological motivations. For commentary on Nietzsche, see *Reading Nietzsche,* ed. R. C. Solomon and K. M. Higgins (Oxford University Press, 1988).
4. *Ethical Relativism,* ed. John Ladd (Wadsworth, 1973), has readings on cultural relativism. James Rachels criticizes cultural relativism and subjectivism in *The Elements of Moral Philosophy* (Random House, 1993). William H. Shaw dismisses subjectivism as implausible and raises objections to cultural relativism in "Relativism and Objectivity in Ethics," in *Morality and Moral Controversies,* ed. John Arthur (Prentice Hall, 1981), pp. 31–50. J. L. Mackie presents a subjectivist theory in *Ethics* (Penguin, 1977). Gilbert Harman defends a version of relativism in *The Nature of Morality: An Introduction to Ethics* (Oxford University Press, 1977).
5. J. J. C. Smart defends utilitarianism and Bernard Williams attacks it in J. J. C. Smart and Bernard Williams, *Utilitarianism: For and Against* (Cambridge University Press, 1973). *Utilitarianism and Beyond,* ed. A. Sen and Bernard Williams (Cambridge University Press, 1973), is a collection of articles on utilitarianism. *Ethics,* ed. Peter Singer (Oxford University Press, 1994), has a selection of classical and modern readings on utilitarianism.
6. Kant's work on ethics is difficult. A good place to begin is his *Lectures on Ethics,* trans. Louis Infield (Harper, 1963). His ethical theory is developed in *Critique of Practical Reason,* trans. Lewis White Beck (Bobbs-Merrill, 1956); *The Metaphysical Elements of Justice,* trans. John Ladd (Bobbs-Merrill, 1965); and *The Metaphysical Principles of Virtue,* trans. James Ellington (Bobbs-Merrill, 1964). For commentaries on Kant's moral philosophy,

see H. J. Paton, *The Categorical Imperative* (Harper, 1967), and H. B. Acton, *Kant's Moral Philosophy* (Macmillan, 1970).

7. W. D. Ross explains Aristotle's ethics in his *Aristotle* (Meridan Books, 1959), Chapter 7. John M. Cooper defends Aristotelian ethics in *Reason and the Human Good in Aristotle* (Harvard University Press, 1975). For articles on virtue theory by classical and contemporary philosophers, see *Vice and Virtue in Everyday Life,* third edition, ed. Christina Sommers and Fred Sommers (Harcourt Brace Jovanovich, 1993). James Rachels raises objections to virtue theory in *The Elements of Moral Philosophy* (McGraw-Hill, 1993). Peter Geach discusses classical virtues such as courage in *The Virtues* (Cambridge University Press, 1977).

8. *Human Rights,* ed. Ellen Paul, Fred Mill, and Jeffrey Paul (Blackwell, 1948), is a collection of articles on rights. Another anthology on rights is *Theories of Rights,* ed. Jeremy Waldron (Oxford University Press, 1984). Joel Feinberg explains the nature and importance of rights in "The Nature and Value of Rights," *The Journal of Value Inquiry* 4 (1970), pp. 243–257. Judith Jarvis Thomson, *The Realm of Rights* (Harvard University Press, 1990), develops a systematic theory of the nature and foundation of rights. John Locke's classical theory of God-given natural rights is found in his *Two Treatises* (1690).

9. The clasical formulations of the social contract theory are Thomas Hobbes's *Leviathan* (1651), John Locke's *The Second Treatise of Government* (1690), and Jean-Jacques Rousseau's *The Social Contract* (1762).

10. Since it first appeared in 1971, Rawls's theory of justice has been widely discussed. One of the first books on the theory to appear was Brian Barry, *The Liberal Theory of Justice* (Oxford University Press, 1973). Another useful critical discussion is Robert Paul Wolff, *Understanding Rawls* (Princeton University Press, 1977). The journal *Ethics* devoted its entire July 1989 issue to a symposium on developments in the Rawlsian theory of justice.

11. Feminist theory has been much discussed in recent years. A big anthology that covers the application of feminist theory to current issues such as affirmative action, abortion, reproductive technology, meat-eating, militarism, and environmentalism is *Living with Contradictions,* ed. Allison M. Jaggar (Westview Press, Inc., 1994). Another recent collection of readings on feminist theory and its applications is *Woman and Values,* second edition, ed. Marilyn Pearsall (Wadsworth, 1993). For a comprehensive introduction to different feminist theories, see *Feminist Thought,* ed. Rosemarie Tong (Westview Press, 1989). Another comprehensive anthology is *Feminism and Philosophy,* ed. Nancy Tuana and Rosemarie Tong (Westview Press, 1995). This book covers liberal, Marxist, radical, psychoanalytic, socialist, ecological, phenomenological, and postmodern feminist perspectives.

Chapter 2

Abortion

Introduction

Factual Background

Abortion is usually defined as the intentional termination of pregnancy. Although the term "fetus" is often used to describe the prenatal organism from conception to birth, the prenatal organism is, strictly speaking, an embryo until the eighth week and a zygote when it is a fertilized egg. No doubt, in the future it will be possible to terminate pregnancy at any stage without causing the fetus to die; the fetus could be kept alive in an artificial womb. Then the decision to terminate pregnancy would be separate from the decision about the life of the fetus. But given the present state of medical technology, the decision to terminate pregnancy is also a decision to kill the fetus or let it die.

In 1994 an estimated 1.4 million abortions were performed in the United States, down from 1.5 million in 1992. From 1973 through 1994, more than 31 million legal abortions were obtained in the United States. It is estimated that 50 million abortions occur worldwide each year. (For sources of statistics on abortion, see the Suggested Readings at the end of the chapter.)

In the United States, about 55 percent of the women obtaining abortions each year are younger than age 25, and about 22 percent of them are teenagers. Two-thirds of all abortions are obtained by never-married women. Three-fourths of the women having abortions say that having a baby would interfere with work, school, or other responsibilities. About two-thirds say that they cannot afford a child. About 15,000 women have abortions each year because they became pregnant after rape or incest.

Before the Supreme Court decision in *Roe v. Wade* in 1973, the number of illegal abortions in the United States was 1.2 million a year. After the *Roe* decision made abortion legal, the number of abortions increased to 1.4 million a year in 1994. The latest figures, however, show that the number of abortions in the United States has decreased to the number before *Roe*. Worldwide, about 20 million illegal abortions are performed every year.

When performed by a qualified doctor, abortion is a reasonably safe procedure. Less than 1 percent of all abortion patients experience complications such as infection or hemorrhage requiring a blood transfusion. The risk of death from abortion increases with length of pregnancy, however, with 1 death for every 600,000 abortions at eight or fewer weeks to 1 death per 6,000 at twenty-one or more weeks. But the risk of death from childbirth is ten times as high as that associated with all abortions.

The law has treated abortion differently at different times. As Justice Blackmun notes in the first reading, English common law did not treat abortion before "quickening" as a criminal offense. "Quickening," or the first movement of the fetus, usually occurs between the sixteenth and the eighteenth weeks of pregnancy. This traditional view of abortion was widely accepted up to the mid–nineteenth century, but it was rejected in 1828, when Connecticut made abortion before quickening a crime.

Other states followed the example of Connecticut, and by the 1960s, most states had laws restricting abortion. All fifty states and the District of Columbia, however, allowed abortion to save the life of the mother, and Colorado and New Mexico permitted abortion to prevent serious harm to the mother.

These laws restricting abortion were overturned by the Supreme Court in the landmark decision of *Roe v. Wade* in 1973. Our first reading for the chapter is taken from this decision. In this case, the Court ruled that restrictive abortion laws, except in certain narrowly defined circumstances, are unconstitutional. This decision made abortion before viability legally available to women who could afford it and who could find a doctor willing to perform the procedure. It is not accurate to say, as critics do, that the Court legalized "abortion on demand." In fact, the Court has allowed a number of restrictions on the abortion right, as we shall see.

The decision has been very controversial, and it has been repeatedly challenged. Opponents of the decision have proposed to amend the Constitution with the Human Life Bill, which affirms that human life begins at conception and that every human life has intrinsic worth and equal value under the Constitution. As Blackmun notes in the reading, the Constitution says that the bearers of rights are "persons" and not "human lives."

A recent legal challenge to the decision was the case of *Webster v. Reproductive Health Services* (1989). In a 5-to-4 decision, the Court did not overturn *Roe* but allowed as constitutional certain restrictions placed on abortion by a Missouri law, namely, (1) banning the use of public funds for abortion and abortion counseling, (2) banning abortions in public hospitals and clinics, and (3) forbidding public employees to assist in the performance of an abortion.

The latest challenge to *Roe* was the case of *Planned Parenthood v. Casey* (1992). In a complicated and controversial decision that left people on both sides of the issue unsatisfied, the Court again reaffirmed the essential holding of *Roe* that a woman has a right to abortion. However, it permitted states to impose further restrictions on abortion, provided they do not impose an undue burden on the woman. The majority of the present Supreme Court has indicated that they do not intend to reconsider the basic abortion right, but given the ongoing controversy about abortion, it seems likely that it will be revisited by the Court in the future.

The Readings

With the exception of the reading from *Roe,* the readings are not concerned with the legal aspects of the abortion controversy, but instead concentrate on the moral problem of whether abortion is wrong or not. There are at least four views of the matter: (1) the pro-life view, (2) the pro-choice view, (3) "moderate" views, and (4) "feminist" views. Let us consider each in turn.

The pro-life view is that abortion is wrong, or almost always wrong, because it is the killing of an innocent person, or at least a potentially innocent person. It seems more accurate to call this the "anti-abortion" view rather than a "pro-life" view, since defenders of this view are rarely in favor of preserving all life, including the lives of murderers or those engaging in an unjust war or, for that matter, the lives of animals. (Ronnie Zoe Hawkins emphasizes this point.) Nevertheless, those who hold this view prefer the label "pro-life" rather than "anti-abortion"; so I will continue to refer to it as the "pro-life" view.

The representatives of the pro-life view in the readings are Noonan and Marquis. Although they are both opposed to abortion, they are willing to grant some exceptions. Noonan mentions the cases of ectopic pregnancy and cancer in the uterus. The most common form of ectopic pregnancy (where the fetus is not in the usual position) is tubal pregnancy; in this condition the zygote does not descend to the uterus but remains lodged in the fallopian tube. The mother will die if the abortion is not performed in this situation, and there is no hope for the survival of the zygote at the present stage of medical technology. Noonan grants that abortion is not wrong in this case, and so does Marquis, since he allows abortion to save the mother's life. In addition, Marquis is willing to permit abortions in cases of rape, when the fetus is anencephalic (partially or completely lacking a brain), and when the abortion is performed during the first fourteen days after conception. (Given the number of these exceptions, it is tempting to say that Marquis is really a "moderate" rather than strictly "pro-life," but since his emphasis is on the claim that abortion is seriously wrong, I will put him in the pro-life camp.)

The pro-choice view is that abortion is morally permissible whenever the mother chooses it. It would not be fair to call this the "pro-abortion" view, since those who hold it do not believe that every mother ought to get an abortion; they merely defend the option to have one. Perhaps it would be better to call it the "pro-abortion-choice" view, since defenders of this view certainly do not endorse any and all choices, including the choice to murder innocent adult humans. With these qualifications in mind, I will continue to refer to the view in question as "pro-choice."

Instead of viewing the fetus as a person with rights, or as a potential person, the pro-choice view defended by Mary Anne Warren in the readings adopts the Kantian view that only rational beings are persons with a moral status, and because fetuses are not rational, self-conscious beings, they have no moral status, or at least not the moral status of persons. She takes seriously the fact that in the later stages of development the fetus resembles a person, and she seems to accept this as a reason for not killing it. Thus she holds that an early abortion is preferable to a late one. But Warren's position is that in the early stages of development, when the fetus does not resemble a person, abortion should be permitted whenever the mother chooses it.

Those who defend the pro-choice view do not agree about infanticide. In a classic article (see the Suggested Readings), Michael Tooley argues that there is no moral difference between abortion and infanticide; both are morally acceptable on his view. Warren does not agree. She gives several reasons for making a moral distinction between abortion and infanticide. One important difference, she says, is that the fetus can pose a threat to the woman's life or health, whereas the newborn infant cannot pose such a threat, since the mother can put it up for adoption or place it in foster care.

Both Judith Jarvis Thomson and the Supreme Court decision in *Roe* represent what I am calling moderate views. Moderates agree in rejecting both the pro-life and the pro-choice views, but they disagree about when abortion should be morally permitted. Thomson appeals to the woman's rights. Even assuming that the fetus is a person with rights, the woman's rights (for example, her right to life, her right to self-defense, and her right to control her own body) are strong enough to override the right to life of the fetus, at least in some cases. But Thomson maintains that the fetus's right to life is not always overridden, or even usually overridden. In cases where an abortion is desired merely for the sake of convenience, and this is statistically the majority of the cases, the mother has a duty to have the child.

The majority decision in *Roe* takes a different approach, a dividing-line approach. That is, Blackmun tries to draw a line in the development of the fetus before which abortion is justified, and after which it is much harder to justify. The dividing line adopted by Blackmun in the *Roe* decision is viability. Viability occurs when the fetus is capable of surviving outside the womb. Just when this occurs is the subject of debate. Blackmun puts viability at the twenty-eighth week of pregnancy, but many doctors say it occurs at twenty-four weeks, or perhaps as early as twenty weeks. In any case, Blackmun holds that abortion is legal before viability but that after viability, the state may impose restrictions or even proscribe it except when it is necessary to save the life or the health of the mother.

Thomson rejects the dividing-line approach. One problem is that such an approach allows early abortions merely for the sake of convenience—say, to avoid postponing a trip to Europe (to use Thomson's example)—and Thomson holds that such an abortion would not be justified. Noonan also objects to lines drawn in the development of the fetus separating what is a person and what is a nonperson. These lines, he argues, are always arbitrary and inadequate. For example, viability is a shifting point. The development of artificial incubation will make the fetus viable at any time, even shortly after conception. Furthermore, the time at which the fetus is viable varies according to circumstances such as its weight, age, and race.

Opponents of dividing lines also use what are called slippery slope arguments; that is, they argue that a line cannot be securely drawn at any point in the development of the fetus because such a line inevitably slides down the slope of development to conception. They insist that the only place to draw the line is at conception. This argument is discussed by Thomson in the readings.

The views discussed so far do not exhaust the views on abortion. There remain the feminist views taken by Celia Wolf-Devine and Ronnie Zoe Hawkins. Both are feminists who seem to agree about the domination of women in our patriarchal society, and both appeal to ecofeminism to support their positions; yet, they come to completely different conclusions about abortion. Hawkins is pro-choice. She sees abortion as necessary to control population growth and to reduce poverty and environmental degradation. She thinks that a concern for all life, both human and nonhuman, supports the pro-choice view of abortion. In sharp contrast to Hawkins, Wolf-Devine is pro-life. She argues that the "feminine voice" in ethics, which includes ecofeminsim and the care ethic, strongly supports the view that abortion should be avoided.

Philosophical Issues

How can we resolve the moral issue about the wrongness of abortion? Most writers agree that settling this issue requires solving some very difficult problems in ethics. One is formulating an acceptable principle about the wrongness of killing. Such a principle is relevant not only in the abortion controversy but also in dealing with questions about euthanasia, capital punishment, war, and killing nonhuman animals. But it is hard to find a moral principle about killing that does not have scope problems—that is, that is not too broad or too narrow or subject to counterexamples. For example, the principle that it is wrong to take a human life is obviously too broad since it makes it wrong to kill a human cancer-cell culture (since it is both human and living). The alternative principle that it is wrong to kill a human being is too narrow; it doesn't seem to apply to the fetus in the early stages of development. The Kantian principle that it is wrong to kill persons or rational beings has similar problems; for example, it doesn't seem to apply to newborn infants or the retarded or the mentally ill.

In the reading, Don Marquis suggests that "killing someone is wrong, in general, when it deprives her of a future like ours." This principle forbids killing someone because it inflicts on the victim the loss of a future containing valuable experiences, activities, projects, and enjoyments. But this principle seems to have scope problems similar to those of the other principles about killing. It may be too broad because it seems to imply that killing nonhuman animals such as pigs is wrong, and this is very problematic in our meat-eating society. (See the discussion of animals rights in Chapter 8.) Marquis's principle may be too narrow, as well, for it seems to imply that active euthanasia of those facing unhappy or meaningless lives, such as the mentally ill or the severely retarded or the incurably diseased, is not wrong, and this is surely debatable.

Another focus of the debate about abortion has been the nature and status of the fetus. Is it a person or not, and how do we tell if a living being is a person or not? One common approach to these problems is to search for a criterion of personhood —that is, some one feature, such as human genetic coding or rationality, that is both a necessary and a sufficient condition for being a person. Utilitarians, for example, say that consciousness is the criterion for personhood or moral standing, whereas followers of Kant, such as Warren, hold that rationality is essential. (Warren adds six other features—sentience, emotionality, reason, the capacity to communicate, self-awareness, and moral agency—but these seem to be built into the concept of rationality.) Noonan thinks that human genetic coding is the criterion for personhood.

In the reading, Marquis argues that these criteria for personhood have scope problems, problems like the ones plaguing the principles about killing we just discussed. For example, the genetic criterion is too broad because it includes human cancer cells that are biologically human but not persons. Warren's criterion, on the other hand, is too narrow, since it excludes from the class of persons infants, the severely retarded, and some of the mentally ill.

In an important article listed in the Suggested Readings, Jane English makes a different objection to the search for a criterion of personhood. The search is doomed from the outset because the concept of "person" has fuzzy borders; that is, there are borderline cases in which we cannot say whether a living being is a person or not, and the fetus constitutes just such a case.

If we cannot conclusively determine the nature and moral status of the fetus, then how can we answer the moral question about abortion? The tactic of Thomson is to shift the focus of debate from the status of the fetus to the rights of the pregnant woman. She argues that even if the fetus is a person with a right to life, it still does not follow that abortions are never justified. The rights of the mother can outweigh those of the fetus. These rights include the mother's right to life, her right to self-defense, and the right to control her own body.

Thomson's method is open to criticism, however. She relies heavily on puzzling imaginary cases, such as the case of the famous violinist who is plugged into another person. She asks us what we would say or think in such cases; that is, she seems to appeal to our moral intuitions. But we cannot assume that everyone will have the same intuitions, particularly when we are dealing with a difficult subject like abortion. Those who are pro-life and those who are pro-choice will no doubt have different intuitions in these cases, and appealing to intuition will not produce agreement.

Feminist theory offers another approach to the abortion controversy, but it does not provide any clear answers. Even though feminists may agree about the oppression of women, and that male theories in ethics should be rejected, they do not seem to agree on any positive theory, and even when they do, they still disagree about how to apply it. Thus in our readings Celia Wolf-Devine and Ronnie Zoe Hawkins both accept ecofeminism and apply it to the abortion problem, and yet they end up with completely different views of abortion. Wolf-Devine and Ned Noddings (discussed by Wolf-Devine) both adopt the care ethic, but they disagree about how it applies to abortion. Noddings takes the position that the obligation to care for others in personal relationships does not extend to the fetus because it is not part of the "inner circle" formed by love and friendship, and the fetus does not count as a "proximate stranger." Wolf-Devine disagrees. She argues that this interpretation of the care ethic would allow us to kill not only fetuses but also persons in deep but reversible comas.

Excerpts from *Roe v. Wade* (1973)

THE SUPREME COURT

Harry B. Blackmun (1909–1999) was an associate justice of the United States Supreme Court. He was appointed to the Court in 1970 and retired in 1994.

Byron R. White was appointed to the Supreme Court in 1962 and retired in 1993.

In the case of *Roe v. Wade,* a pregnant single woman challenged a Texas abortion law making abortion (except to save the mother's life) a crime punishable by a prison sentence of two to five years. ("Jane Roe" was a pseudonym for Norma McCorvey, a woman who now says she is pro-life.) By a 7-to-2 vote, the Court ruled that the Texas law was unconstitutional.

The reading includes excerpts from the majority opinion, written by Justice Blackmun, and from the dissenting opinion, written by Justice White.

After an interesting survey of historical views of abortion, Justice Blackmun argues that the abortion decision is included in the right of personal privacy. But this right is not absolute; it must yield at some point to the state's legitimate interest in protecting potential life, and this interest becomes compelling at the point of viability.

In his dissenting opinion, Justice White claims that the Court has no constitutional basis for its decision and that it incorrectly values the convenience of the mother more than the existence and development of human life.

IT PERHAPS IS NOT GENERALLY APPRECIATED that the restrictive criminal abortion laws in effect in a majority of States today are of relatively recent vintage. Those laws, generally proscribing abortion or its attempt at any time during pregnancy except when necessary to preserve the pregnant woman's life, are not of ancient or even of common-law origin. Instead, they derive from statutory changes effected, for the most part, in the latter half of the 19th century.

ANCIENT ATTITUDES

These are not capable of precise determination. We are told that at the time of the Persian Empire, abortifacients were known and that criminal abortions were severely punished. We are also told, however, that abortion was practiced in Greek times as well as in the Roman Era, and that "it was resorted to without scruple." The Ephesian, Soranos, often described as the greatest of the ancient gynecologists, appears to have been generally opposed to Rome's prevailing free abortion practices. He found it necessary to think first of the life of the mother, and he resorted to abortion when, upon this standard, he felt the procedure advisable. Greek and Roman law afforded little protection to the unborn. If abortion was prosecuted in some places, it seems to have been based on a concept of a violation of the father's right to his offspring. Ancient religion did not bar abortion.

Source: The Supreme Court, *Roe v. Wade* (1973).

THE HIPPOCRATIC OATH

What then of the famous Oath that has stood so long as the ethical guide of the medical profession and that bears the name of the great Greek (460(?)–377(?) B.C.E.), who has been described as the Father of Medicine, the "wisest and the greatest practitioner of his art," and the "most important and most complete medical personality of antiquity," who dominated the medical schools of his time, and who typified the sum of the medical knowledge of the past? The Oath varies somewhat according to the particular translation, but in any translation the content is clear: "I will give no deadly medicine to anyone if asked, nor suggest any such counsel; and in like manner I will not give to a woman a pessary to produce abortion," or "I will neither give a deadly drug to anybody if asked for it, nor will I make a suggestion to this effect. Similarly, I will not give to a woman an abortive remedy."

Although the Oath is not mentioned in any of the principal briefs in this case or in *Doe v. Bolton, post,* p. 179, it represents the apex of the development of strict ethical concepts in medicine, and its influence endures to this day. Why did not the authority of Hippocrates dissuade abortion practice in his time and that of Rome? The late Dr. Edelstein provides us with a theory: The Oath was not uncontested even in Hippocrates' day; only the Pythagorean school of philosophers frowned upon the related act of suicide. Most Greek thinkers, on the other hand, commended abortion, at least prior to viability. See Plato, Republic, V, 461; Aristotle, Politics, VII, 1335b 25. For the Pythagoreans, however, it was a matter of dogma. For them the embryo was animate from the moment of conception, and abortion meant destruction of living being. The abortion clause of the Oath, therefore, "echoes Pythagorean doctrines," and "[i]n no other stratum of Greek opinion were such views held or proposed in the same spirit of uncompromising austerity."

Dr. Edelstein then concludes that the Oath originated in a group representing only a small segment of Greek opinion and that it certainly was not accepted by all ancient physicians. He points out that medical writings down to Galen (130–200 C.E.) "give evidence of the violation of almost every one of its injunctions." But with the end of antiquity a decided change took place. Resistance against suicide and against abortion became common. The Oath came to be popular. The emerging teachings of Christianity were in agreement with the Pythagorean ethic. The Oath "became the nucleus of all medical ethics" and "was applauded as the embodiment of truth." Thus, suggests Dr. Edelstein, it is "a Pythagorean manifesto and not the expression of an absolute standard of medical conduct."

This, it seems to us, is a satisfactory and acceptable explanation of the Hippocratic Oath's apparent rigidity. It enables us to understand, in historical context, a long-accepted and revered statement of medical ethics.

THE COMMON LAW

It is undisputed that at common law, abortion performed *before* "quickening"—the first recognizable movement of the fetus *in utero,* appearing usually from the 16th to the 18th week of pregnancy—was not an indictable offense. The absence of a common-law crime for pre-quickening abortion appears to have developed from a confluence of earlier philosophical, theological, and civil and canon law concepts of when life begins. These disciplines variously approached the question in terms of the point at which the embryo or fetus became "formed" or recognizably human, or in terms of when a "person" came into being, that is, infused with a "soul" or "animated." A loose consensus evolved in early English law that these events occurred at some point between conception and live birth. This was "mediate animation." Although Christian theology and the canon law came to fix the point of animation at 40 days for a male and 80 days for a female, a view that persisted until the 19th century, there was otherwise little agreement about the precise time of formation or animation. There was agreement, however, that prior to this point the fetus was to be regarded as part of the mother, and its destruction, therefore, was not homicide. Due to continued uncertainty about the precise time when animation occurred, or to the lack of any empirical basis for the 40–80-day view, and perhaps to Aquinas' definition of movement as one of the two first principles of life, Bracton focused upon quickening as the critical point. The significance of quickening was echoed by later common-law scholars and found its way into the received common law in this country.

Whether abortion of a *quick* fetus was a felony at common law, even a lesser crime, is still disputed. Bracton, writing early in the 13th century, thought it homicide. But the later and predominant view, following the great common-law scholars, has been that it was, at most, a lesser offense. In a frequently cited passage, Coke took the position that abortion of a woman "quick with childe" is "a great misprision, and no murder." Blackstone followed, saying that while abortion after quickening had once been considered manslaughter (though not murder), "modern law" took a less severe view. A recent review of the common-law precedents argues, however, that those precedents contradict Coke and that even post-quickening abortion was never established as a common-law crime. This is of some importance because while most American courts ruled, in holding or dictum, that abortion of an unquickened fetus was not criminal under their received common law, others followed Coke in stating that abortion of a quick fetus was a "misprision," a term they translated to mean "misdemeanor." That their reliance on Coke on this aspect of the law was uncritical and, apparently in all the reported cases, dictum (due probably to the paucity of common-law prosecutions for post-quickening abortion), makes it now appear doubtful that abortion was ever firmly established as a

common-law crime even with respect to the destruction of a quick fetus. . . .

THE AMERICAN LAW

In this country, the law in effect in all but a few States until mid-19th century was the pre-existing English common law. Connecticut, the first State to enact abortion legislation, adopted in 1821 that part of Lord Ellenborough's Act that related to a woman "quick with child." The death penalty was not imposed. Abortion before quickening was made a crime in that State only in 1860. In 1828, New York enacted legislation that, in two respects, was to serve as a model for early anti-abortion statutes. First, while barring destruction of an unquickened fetus as well as a quick fetus, it made the former only a misdemeanor, but the latter second-degree manslaughter. Second, it incorporated a concept of therapeutic abortion by providing that an abortion was excused if it "shall have been necessary to preserve the life of such mother, or shall have been advised by two physicians to be necessary for such purpose." By 1840, when Texas had received the common law, only eight American States had statutes dealing with abortion. It was not until after the War Between the States that legislation began generally to replace the common law. Most of these initial statutes dealt severely with abortion after quickening but were lenient with it before quickening. Most punished attempts equally with completed abortions. While many statutes included the exception for an abortion thought by one or more physicians to be necessary to save the mother's life, that provision soon disappeared and the typical law required that the procedure actually be necessary for that purpose.

Gradually, in the middle and late 19th century the quickening distinction disappeared from the statutory law of most States and the degree of the offense and the penalties were increased. By the end of the 1950s, a large majority of the jurisdictions banned abortion, however and whenever performed, unless done to save or preserve the life of the mother. The exceptions, Alabama and the District of Columbia, permitted abortion to preserve the mother's health. Three States permitted abortions that were not "unlawfully" performed or that were not "without lawful justification," leaving interpretation of those standards to the courts. In the past several years, however, a trend toward liberalization of abortion statutes has resulted in adoption, by about one-third of the States, of less stringent laws, most of them patterned after the ALI Model Penal Code, § 230.3.

It is thus apparent that common law, at the time of the adoption of our Constitution, and throughout the major portion of the 19th century, viewed abortion with less disfavor than most American statutes currently in effect. Phrasing it another way, a woman had a substantially broader right to terminate a pregnancy than she does in most states today. At least with respect to the early stage of pregnancy and very possibly without such a limitation, the opportunity to make this choice was present in this country well into the 19th century. Even later, the law continued for some time to treat less punitively an abortion procured in early pregnancy. . . .

Three reasons have been advanced to explain historically the enactment of criminal abortion laws in the 19th century and to justify their continued existence.

It has been argued occasionally that these laws were the product of a Victorian social concern to discourage illicit sexual conduct. Texas, however, does not advance this justification in the present case, and it appears that no court or commentator has taken the argument seriously. The appellants and *amici* contend, moreover, that this is not a proper state purpose at all and suggest that, if it were, the Texas statutes are overbroad in protecting it since the law fails to distinguish between married and unwed mothers.

A second reason is concerned with abortion as a medical procedure. When most criminal abortion laws were first enacted, the procedure was a hazardous one for the woman. This was particularly true prior to the development of antisepsis. Antiseptic techniques, of course were based on discoveries by Lister, Pasteur, and others first announced in 1867, but were not generally accepted and employed until about the turn of the century. Abortion mortality was high. Even after 1900, and perhaps until as late as the development of antibiotics in the 1940's, standard modern techniques such as dilation and curettage were not nearly so safe as they are today. Thus, it has been argued that a State's real concern in enacting a criminal abortion law was to protect the pregnant woman, that is, to restrain her from submitting to a procedure that placed her life in serious jeopardy.

Modern medical techniques have altered this situation. Appellants and various *amici* refer to medical data indicating that abortion in early pregnancy, that is, prior to the end of the first trimester, although not without its risk, is now relatively safe. Mortality rates for women undergoing early abortions, where the procedure is legal, appear to be as low as or lower than the rates for normal childbirth. Consequently, any interest of the State in protecting the women from an inherently hazardous procedure, except when it would be equally dangerous for her to forgo it, has largely disappeared. Of course, important state interests in the areas of health and medical standards do remain. The State has a legitimate interest in seeing to it that abortion, like any other medical procedure, is performed under circumstances that insure maximum safety for the patient. This interest obviously extends at least to the performing physician and his staff, to the facilities involved, to the availability of after-care, and to adequate provision for any complication or emergency that might arise. The prevalence of high mortality rates at illegal "abortion mills" strengthens, rather than weakens, the State's interest in regulating the conditions under which abortions are performed. Moreover, the risk to the woman increases as her pregnancy continues. Thus the

State retains a definite interest in protecting the woman's own health and safety when an abortion is proposed at a late stage of pregnancy.

The third reason is the State's interest—some phrase it in terms of duty—in protecting prenatal life. Some of the argument for this justification rests on the theory that a new human life is present from the moment of conception. The State's interest and general obligation to protect life then extends, it is argued, to prenatal life. Only when the life of the pregnant mother herself is at stake, balanced against the life she carries within her, should the interest of the embryo or fetus not prevail. Logically, of course, a legitimate state interest in this area need not stand or fall on acceptance of the belief that life begins at conception or at some other point prior to live birth. In assessing the State's interest, recognition may be given to the less rigid claim that as long as at least *potential* life is involved, the State may assert interests beyond the protection of the pregnant woman alone.

Parties challenging state abortion laws have sharply disputed in some courts the contention that a purpose of these laws, when enacted, was to protect prenatal life. Pointing to the absence of legislative history to support the contention, they claim that most state laws were designed solely to protect the woman. Because medical advances have lessened this concern, at least with respect to abortion in early pregnancy, they argue that with respect to such abortions the laws can no longer be justified by any state interest. There is some scholarly support for this view of original purpose. The few state courts called upon to interpret their laws in the late 19th and early 20th centuries did focus on the State's interest in protecting the woman's health rather than in preserving the embryo and fetus. Proponents of this view point out that in many States, including Texas, by statute or judicial interpretation, the pregnant woman herself could not be prosecuted for self-abortion or for cooperating in an abortion performed upon her by another. They claim that adoption of the "quickening" distinction through received common law and state statutes tacitly recognizes the greater health hazards inherent in late abortion and impliedly repudiates the theory that life begins at conception.

It is with these interests, and the weight to be attached to them, that this case is concerned.

The Constitution does not explicitly mention any right of privacy. In a line of decisions, however, going back perhaps as far as *Union Pacific R. Co. v. Botsford*, 141 U.S. 250, 251 (1891), the Court has recognized that a right of personal privacy, or a guarantee of certain areas or zones of privacy does exist under the Constitution. In carrying contexts, the Court or individual justices have, indeed, found at least the roots of that right in the First Amendment, in the Fourth and Fifth Amendments, in the penumbras of the Bill of Rights, in the Ninth Amendment, or in the concept of liberty guaranteed by the first section of the Fourteenth Amendment. These decisions make it clear that only personal rights that can be deemed "fundamental" or "implicit in the concept of ordered liberty," are included in this guarantee of personal privacy. They also make it clear that the right has some extension to activities relating to marriage, procreation, contraception, family relationships, and child rearing and education.

This right of privacy, whether it be founded in the Fourteenth Amendment's concept of personal liberty and restrictions upon state action, as we feel it is, or, as the District Court determined, in the Ninth Amendment's reservation of rights to the people, is broad enough to encompass a woman's decision whether or not to terminate her pregnancy. The detriment that the State would impose upon the pregnant woman by denying this choice altogether is apparent. Specific and direct harm medically diagnosable even in early pregnancy may be involved. Maternity, or additional offspring, may force upon the woman a distressful life and future. Psychological harm may be imminent. Mental and physical health may be taxed by child care. There is also the distress, for all concerned, associated with the unwanted child, and there is the problem of bringing a child into a family already unable, psychologically and otherwise, to care for it. In other cases, as in this one, the additional difficulties and continuing stigma of unwed motherhood may be involved. All these are factors the woman and her responsible physician necessarily will consider in consultation.

On the basis of elements such as these, appellant and some *amici* argue that the woman's right is absolute and that she is entitled to terminate her pregnancy at whatever time, in whatever way, and for whatever reason she alone chooses. With this we do not agree. Appellant's arguments that Texas either has no valid interest at all in regulating the abortion decision, or no interest strong enough to support any limitation upon the woman's sole determination, are unpersuasive. The Court's decisions recognizing a right of privacy also acknowledge that some state regulation in areas protected by that right is appropriate. As noted above, a State may properly assert important interests in safeguarding health, in maintaining medical standards, and in protecting potential life. At some point in pregnancy, these respective interests become sufficiently compelling to sustain regulation of the factors that govern the abortion decision. The privacy right involved, therefore, cannot be said to be absolute. In fact, it is not clear to us that the claim asserted by some *amici* that one has an unlimited right to do with one's body as one pleases bears a close relationship to the right of privacy previously articulated in the Court's decisions. The Court has refused to recognize an unlimited right of this kind in the past.

We, therefore, conclude that the right of personal privacy includes the abortion decision, but that this right is not unqualified and must be considered against important state interests in regulation.

We note that those federal and state courts that have recently considered abortion law challenges have reached the same conclusion. Although the results are divided, most of these courts have agreed that the right of privacy, however based, is broad enough to cover

the abortion decision, that the right, nonetheless, is not absolute and is subject to some limitations; and that at some point the state interests as to protection of health, medical standards, and prenatal life, become dominant. We agree with this approach.

Where certain "fundamental rights" are involved, the Court has held that regulation limiting these rights may be justified only by a "compelling state interest," and that legislative enactments must be narrowly drawn to express only the legitimate state interests at stake.

In the recent abortion cases, cited above, courts have recognized these principles. Those striking down state laws have generally scrutinized the State's interests in protecting health and potential life, and have concluded that neither interest justified broad limitations on the reasons for which a physician and his pregnant patient might decide that she should have an abortion in the early stages of pregnancy. Courts sustaining state laws have held that the State's determinations to protect health or prenatal life are dominant and constitutionally justifiable.

The District Court held that the appellee failed to meet his burden demonstrating that the Texas statute's infringement upon Roe's rights was necessary to support a compelling state interest, and that, although the appellee presented "several compelling justifications for state presence in the area of abortions," the statutes outstripped these justifications and swept "far beyond any areas of compelling state interest." Appellant and appellee both contest that holding. Appellant, as has been indicated, claims an absolute right that bars any state imposition of criminal penalties in the area. Appellee argues that the State's determination to recognize and protect prenatal life from and after conception constitutes a compelling state interest. As noted above, we do not agree fully with either formulation.

A. The appellee and certain *amici* argue that the fetus is a "person" within the language and meaning of the Fourteenth Amendment. In support of this, they outline at length and in detail the well-known facts of fetal development. If this suggestion of personhood is established, the appellant's case, of course, collapses, for the fetus' right to life would then be guaranteed specifically by the Amendment. The appellant conceded as much on reargument. On the other hand, the appellee conceded on reargument that no case could be cited that holds that a fetus is a person within the meaning of the Fourteenth Amendment.

The Constitution does not define "person" in so many words. Section 1 of the Fourteenth Amendment contains three references to "person." In nearly all these instances, the use of the word is such that it has application only postnatally. None indicates, with any assurance, that it has any possible pre-natal application.

All this, together with our observation, *supra,* that throughout the major portion of the 19th century prevailing legal abortion practices were far freer than they are today, persuades us that the word "person," as used in the Fourteenth Amendment, does not include the unborn. This is in accord with the results reached in those few cases where the issue has been squarely presented. Indeed, our decision in *United States v. Vuitch,* 402 U.S. 62 (1971), inferentially is to the same effect, for we there would not have indulged in statutory interpretation favorable to abortion in specified circumstances if the necessary consequence was the termination of life entitled to Fourteenth Amendment protection.

This conclusion, however, does not of itself fully answer the contentions raised by Texas, and we pass on to other considerations.

B. The pregnant woman cannot be isolated in her privacy. She carried an embryo and, later, a fetus, if one accepts the medical definitions of the developing young in the human uterus. See Dorland's Illustrated Medical Dictionary 478–479, 547 (24th ed. 1965). The situation therefore is inherently different from marital intimacy, or bedroom possession of obscene material, or marriage, or procreation, or education, with which *Eisenstadt* and *Griswold, Stanley, Loving, Skinner,* and *Pierce* and *Meyer* were respectively concerned. As we have intimated above, it is reasonable and appropriate for a State to decide that at some point in time another interest, that of health of the mother or that of potential human life, becomes significantly involved. The woman's privacy is no longer sole and any right of privacy she possesses must be measured accordingly.

Texas urges that, apart from the Fourteenth Amendment, life begins at conception and is present throughout pregnancy, and that, therefore, the State has a compelling interest in protecting that life from and after conception. We need not resolve the difficult question of when life begins. When those trained in the respective disciplines of medicine, philosophy, and theology are unable to arrive at any consensus, the judiciary, at this point in the development of man's knowledge, is not in a position to speculate as to the answer.

It should be sufficient to note briefly the wide divergence of thinking on this most sensitive and difficult question. There has always been strong support for the view that life does not begin until live birth. This was the belief of the Stoics. It appears to be the predominant, though not the unanimous, attitude of the Jewish faith. It may be taken to represent also the position of a large segment of the Protestant community, insofar as that can be ascertained; organized groups that have taken a formal position on the abortion issue have generally regarded abortion as a matter for the conscience of the individual and her family. As we have noted, the common law found greater significance in quickening. Physicians and their scientific colleagues have regarded that event with less interest and have tended to focus either upon conception, upon live birth, or upon the interim point at which the fetus becomes "viable," that is, potentially able to live outside the mother's womb, albeit with artificial aid. Viability is usually placed at about seven months (28 weeks) but may occur earlier, even at 24 weeks. The Aristotelian theory of "mediate animation," that held sway throughout the Middle Ages and the Renaissance in Europe, continued to be official Roman Catholic dogma until the 19th century, despite opposition to this "ensoulment" theory from those in the Church who would recognize the existence of life from the moment of conception. The latter is now, of course, the official belief of the Catholic Church. As one brief *amicus* discloses, this is a view strongly held by many non-Catholics as well, and by many physicians. Substantial problems for precise definition of this view are posed, however, by new embryological data that purport to indicate that conception is a "process" over time, rather than an event, and by new medical techniques such as menstrual extraction, the "morning-after" pill, implantation of embryos, artificial insemination, and even artificial wombs.

In areas other than criminal abortion, the law has been reluctant to endorse any theory that life, as we recognize it, begins before live birth or to accord legal rights to the unborn except in narrowly defined situations and except when the rights are contingent upon live birth. For example, the traditional rule of tort law denied recovery for prenatal injuries even though the child was born alive. That rule has been changed in almost every jurisdiction. In most States, recovery is said to be permitted only if the fetus was viable, or at least quick, when the injuries were sustained, though few courts have squarely so held. In a recent development, generally opposed by the commentators, some States permit the parents of a stillborn child to maintain an action for wrongful death because of prenatal injuries. Such an action, however, would appear to be one to vindicate the parents' interest and is thus consistent with the view that the fetus, at most, represents only the potentiality of life. Similarly, unborn children have been recognized as acquiring rights or interests by way of inheri-

tance or other devolution of property, and have been represented by guardians *ad litem*. Perfection of the interests involved, again, has generally been contingent upon live birth. In short, the unborn have never been recognized in the law as persons in the whole sense.

In view of all this, we do not agree that, by adopting one theory of life, Texas may override the rights of the pregnant woman that are at stake. We repeat, however, that the State does have an important and legitimate interest in preserving and protecting the health of the pregnant woman, whether she be a resident of the State or a nonresident who seeks medical consultation and treatment there, and that it has still *another* important and legitimate interest in protecting the potentiality of human life. These interests are separate and distinct. Each grows in substantiality as the woman approaches term and, at a point during pregnancy, each becomes "compelling."

With respect to the State's important and legitimate interest in the health of the mother, the "compelling" point, in the light of present medical knowledge, is at approximately the end of the first trimester. This is so because of the now-established medical fact, referred to above, that until the end of the first trimester mortality in abortion may be less than mortality in normal childbirth. It follows that, from and after this point, a State may regulate the abortion procedure to the extent that the regulation reasonably relates to the preservation and protection of maternal health. Examples of permissible state regulation in this area are requirements as to the qualifications of the person who is to perform the abortion; as to the licensure of that person; as to the facility in which the procedure is to be performed, that is, whether it must be a hospital or may be a clinic or some other place of less-than-hospital status; as to the licensing of the facility; and the like.

This means, on the other hand, that, for the period of pregnancy prior to this "compelling" point, the attending physician, in consultation with his patient, is free to determine, without regulation by the State, that, in his medical judgment, the patient's pregnancy should be terminated. If that decision is reached, the judgment may be effectuated by an abortion free of interference by the State.

With respect to the State's important and legitimate interest in potential life, the "compelling" point is at viability. This is so because the fetus then presumably has the capability of meaningful life outside the mother's womb. State regulation protective of fetal life after viability thus has both logical and biological justifications. If the State is interested in protecting fetal life after viability, it may go so far as to proscribe abortion during that period, except when it is necessary to preserve the life or health of the mother.

To summarize and to repeat:

1. A state criminal abortion statute of the current Texas type, that excepts from criminality only a *lifesaving* procedure on behalf of the mother, without regard to pregnancy stage and without recognition of the other interests involved, is violative of the Due Process Clause of the Fourteenth Amendment.

   (a) For the stage prior to approximately the end of the first trimester, the abortion decision and its effectuation must be left to the medical judgment of the pregnant woman's attending physician.

   (b) For the stage subsequent to approximately the end of the first trimester, the State, in promoting its interest in the health of the mother, may, if it chooses, regulate the abortion procedure in ways that are reasonably related to maternal health.

   (c) For the stage subsequent to viability, the State in promoting its interest in the potentiality of human life may, if it chooses, regulate, and even proscribe, abortion except where it is necessary, in appropriate medical judgment, for the preservation of the life or health of the mother.

2. The State may define the term "physician" as it has been employed in the preceding paragraphs of this Part XI of this opinion, to mean only a physician currently licensed by the State, and may proscribe any abortion by a person who is not a physician as so defined.

In *Doe v. Bolton, post*, p. 179, procedural requirements contained in one of the modern abortion statutes are considered. That opinion and this one, of course, are to be read together.

This holding, we feel, is consistent with the relative weights of the respective interests involved, with the lessons and examples of medical and legal history, with the lenity of the common law, and with the demands of the profound problems of the present day. The decision leaves the State free to place increasing restrictions on abortion as the period of pregnancy lengthens, so long as those restrictions are tailored to the recognized state interests. The decision vindicates the right of the physician to administer medical treatment according to his professional judgment up to the points where important state interests provide compelling justifications for intervention. Up to those points, the abortion decision in all its aspects is inherently, and primarily, a medical decision, and basic responsibility for it must rest with the physician. If an individual practitioner abuses the privilege of exercising proper medical judgment, the usual remedies, judicial and intraprofessional, are available.

MR. JUSTICE WHITE, DISSENTING

At the heart of the controversy in these cases are those recurring pregnancies that pose no danger whatsoever to the life or health of the mother but are nevertheless unwanted for any one or more of a variety of reasons—convenience, family planning, economics, dislike of children, the embarrassment of illegitimacy, etc. The common claim before us is that for any one of such reasons, or for no reason at all, and without asserting or claiming any threat to life or health, any woman is entitled to an abortion at her request if she is able to find a medical advisor willing to undertake the procedure.

The Court for the most part sustains this position: During the period prior to the time the fetus becomes viable, the Constitution of the United States values the convenience, whim or caprice of the putative mother more than the life or potential life of the fetus; the Constitution, therefore, guarantees the right to an abortion as against any state law or policy seeking to protect the fetus from an abortion not prompted by more compelling reasons of the mother.

With all due respect, I dissent. I find nothing in the language or history of the Constitution to support the Court's judgment. . . . As an exercise of raw judicial power, the Court perhaps has authority to do what it does today; but in my view its judgment is an improvident and extravagant exercise of the power of judicial review which the Constitution extends to this Court.

The Court apparently values the convenience of the pregnant mother more than the continued existence and development of the life or potential life which she carries. . . .

It is my view, therefore, that the Texas statute is not constitutionally infirm because it denies abortions to those who seek to serve only their convenience rather than to protect their life or health. . . .

Review Questions

1. Justice Blackmun discusses three reasons for the enactment of criminal abortion laws. Why doesn't he accept these reasons?
2. Where does the Constitution guarantee a right of privacy according to Justice Blackmun?
3. Is the fetus a person in the legal sense according to Justice Blackmun?
4. According to Justice Blackmun, when is the *compelling* point in the state's interest in the health of the mother?
5. When, according to Justice Blackmun, is the *compelling* point in the state's interest in potential life?
6. Explain Justice Blackmun's conclusions.
7. What are Justice White's objections?

Discussion Questions

1. What is the right to privacy? Try to define it.
2. What do you think is properly included in the right to privacy, and what is properly excluded?
3. Do you think that the fetus has any legal rights or any moral rights? Defend your view.
4. Justice White complains that Justice Blackmun's opinion allows a woman to get an abortion "without asserting or claiming any threat to life or health" provided she is able to find a doctor willing to undertake the procedure. Do you think that women should be allowed to get such abortions? Explain your answer. Do you believe that doctors have any obligation to perform such abortions? Why or why not?

An Almost Absolute Value in History

JOHN T. NOONAN, JR.

John T. Noonan, Jr., is professor of law at the University of California, Berkeley. His books include *Contraception: A History of Its Treatment by the Catholic Theologians and Canonists* (1965), (1970), and *Persons and Masks of the Law* (1976).

Noonan begins with the question, How do you determine the humanity of a being? The answer he defends is what he says is the view of traditional Christian theology, namely, that you are human if you are conceived by human parents. This view is compared with other alleged criteria of humanity, such as viability, experience, feelings of adults, sensations of adults, and social visibility. Each of these is rejected as inadequate and arbitrary. In his defense of the traditional view, Noonan does not appeal to the medieval theory of ensoulment, that is, the theory that the soul enters the body at conception. Instead, he rests his case on the fact that at conception the fetus (or strictly speaking, the zygote) receives the full genetic code of a human being. He assumes that anything with human genetic coding is a human being with rights equal to those of other humans. It follows that the fetus is a human being with rights from the moment of conception. Once this has been granted, we can see that abortion is morally wrong except in rare cases where it is necessary to save the mother's life.

THE MOST FUNDAMENTAL QUESTION involved in the long history of thought on abortion is: How do you determine the humanity of a being? To phrase the question that way is to put in comprehensive humanistic terms what the theologians either dealt with as an explicitly theological question under the heading of "ensoulment" or dealt with implicitly in their treatment of abortion. The Christian position as it originated did not depend on a narrow theological or philosophical concept. It had no relation to theories of infant baptism.[1] It appealed to no special theory of instantaneous ensoulment. It took the world's view on ensoulment as that view changed from Aristotle to Zacchia. There was, indeed, theological influence affecting the theory of ensoulment finally adopted, and, of course, ensoulment itself was a theological con-

Source: John T. Noonan, Jr., "An Almost Absolute Value in History," reprinted by permission of the publisher from *The Morality of Abortion* John T. Noonan, Jr., ed. (Cambridge, Mass.: Harvard University Press), pp. 51–59. Copyright © 1970 by the President and Fellows of Harvard College.

1 According to Glanville William (*The Sanctity of Human Life supra* n. 169, at 193), "The historical reason for the Catholic objection to abortion is the same as for the Christian Church's historical opposition to infanticide: the horror of bringing about the death of an unbaptized child." This statement is made without any citation of evidence. As had been seen, desire to administer baptism could, in the Middle Ages, even be urged as a reason for procuring an abortion. It is highly regrettable that the American Law Institute was apparently misled by Williams' account and repeated after him the same baseless statement. See American Law Institute, *Model Penal Code: Tentative Draft No. 9* (1959), p. 148, n. 12.

cept, so that the position was always explained in theological terms. But the theological notion of ensoulment could easily be translated into humanistic language by substituting "human" for "rational soul"; the problem of knowing when a man is a man is common to theology and humanism.

If one steps outside the specific categories used by the theologians, the answer they gave can be analyzed as a refusal to discriminate among human beings on the basis of their varying potentialities. Once conceived, the being was recognized as man because he had man's potential. The criterion for humanity, thus, was simple and all-embracing: if you are conceived by human parents, you are human.

The strength of this position may be tested by a review of some of the other distinctions offered in the contemporary controversy over legalizing abortion. Perhaps the most popular distinction is in terms of viability. Before an age of so many months, the fetus is not viable, that is, it cannot be removed from the mother's womb and live apart from her. To that extent, the life of the fetus is absolutely dependent on the life of the mother. This dependence is made the basis of denying recognition to its humanity.

There are difficulties with this distinction. One is that the perfection of artificial incubation may make the fetus viable at any time: it may be removed and artificially sustained. Experiments with animals already show that such a procedure is possible. This hypothetical extreme case relates to an actual difficulty: there is considerable elasticity to the idea of viability. Mere length of life is not an exact measure. The viability of the fetus depends on the extent of its anatomical and functional development. The weight and length of the fetus are better guides to the state of its development than age, but weight and length vary. Moreover, different racial groups have different ages at which their fetuses are viable. Some evidence, for example, suggests that Negro fetuses mature more quickly than white fetuses. If viability is the norm, the standard would vary with race and with many individual circumstances.

The most important objection to this approach is that dependence is not ended by viability. The fetus is still absolutely dependent on someone's care in order to continue existence; indeed a child of one or three or even five years of age is absolutely dependent on another's care for existence; uncared for, the older fetus or the younger child will die as surely as the early fetus detached from the mother. The unsubstantial lessening in dependence at viability does not seem to signify any special acquisition of humanity.

A second distinction has been attempted in terms of experience. A being who has had experience, has lived and suffered, who possesses memories, is more human than one who has not. Humanity depends on formation by experience. The fetus is thus "unformed" in the most basic human sense.

This distinction is not serviceable for the embryo which is already experiencing and reacting. The embryo is responsive to touch after eight weeks and at least at that point is experiencing. At an earlier stage the zygote is certainly alive and responding to its environment. The distinction may also be challenged by the rare case where aphasia has erased adult memory: has it erased humanity? More fundamentally, this distinction leaves even the older fetus or the younger child to be treated as an unformed inhuman thing. Finally, it is not clear why experience as such confers humanity. It could be argued that certain central experiences such as loving or learning are necessary to make a man human. But then human beings who have failed to love or to learn might be excluded from the class called man.

A third distinction is made by appeal to the sentiments of adults. If a fetus dies, the grief of the parents is not the grief they would have for a living child. The fetus is an unnamed "it" till birth, and is not perceived as personality until at least the fourth month of existence when movements in the womb manifest a vigorous presence demanding joyful recognition by the parents.

Yet feeling is notoriously an unsure guide to the humanity of others. Many groups of humans have had difficulty in feeling that persons of another tongue, color, religion, sex, are as human as they. Apart from reactions to alien groups, we mourn the loss of a ten-year-old boy more than the loss of his one-day-old brother or his 90-year-old grandfather. The difference felt and the grief expressed vary with the potentialities extinguished, or the experience wiped out; they do not seem to point to any substantial difference in the humanity of baby, boy, or grandfather.

Distinctions are also made in terms of sensation by the parents. The embryo is felt within the womb only after about the fourth month. The embryo is seen only at birth. What can be neither seen nor felt is different from what is tangible. If the fetus cannot be seen or touched at all, it cannot be perceived as man.

Yet experience shows that sight is even more untrustworthy than feeling in determining humanity. By sight, color became an appropriate index for saying who was a man, and the evil of racial discrimination was given foundation. Nor can touch provide the test; a being confined by sickness, "out of touch" with others, does not thereby seem to lose his humanity. To the extent that touch still has appeal as a criterion, it appears to be a survival of the old English idea of "quickening"—a possible mistranslation of the Latin *animatus* used in the canon law. To that extent touch as a criterion seems to be dependent on the Aristotelian notion of ensoulment, and to fall when this notion is discarded.

Finally, a distinction is sought in social visibility. The fetus is not socially perceived as human. It cannot communicate with others. Thus, both subjectively and objectively, it is not a member of society. As moral rules are rules for the behavior of members of society to each other, they cannot be made for behavior toward what is not yet a

member. Excluded from the society of men, the fetus is excluded from the humanity of men.[2]

By force of the argument from the consequences, this distinction is to be rejected. It is more subtle than that founded on an appeal to physical sensation, but it is equally dangerous in its implications. If humanity depends on social recognition, individuals or whole groups may be dehumanized by being denied any status in their society. Such a fate is fictionally portrayed in *1984* and has actually been the lot of many men in many societies. In the Roman empire, for example, condemnation to slavery meant the practical denial of most human rights; in the Chinese Communist world, landlords have been classified as enemies of the people and so treated as nonpersons by the state. Humanity does not depend on social recognition, though often the failure of society to recognize the prisoner, the alien, the heterodox as human has led to the destruction of human beings. Anyone conceived by a man and a woman is human. Recognition of this condition by society follows a real event in the objective order, however imperfect and halting the recognition. Any attempt to limit humanity to exclude some group runs the risk of furnishing authority and precedent for excluding other groups in the name of the consciousness or perception of the controlling group in the society.

A philosopher may reject the appeal to the humanity of the fetus because he views "humanity" as a secular view of the soul and because he doubts the existence of anything real and objective which can be identified as humanity. One answer to such a philosopher is to ask how he reasons about moral questions without supposing that there is a sense in which he and the oth-

---

2 . . . Thomas Aquinas gave an analogous reason against baptizing a fetus in the womb: "As long as it exists in the womb of the mother, it cannot be subject to the operation of the ministers of the Church as it is not known to men" (*In sententias Petri Lombardi* 4.6 1.1.2).

ers of whom he speaks are human. Whatever group is taken as the society which determines who may be killed is thereby taken as human. A second answer is to ask if he does not believe that there is a right and wrong way of deciding moral questions. If there is such a difference, experience may be appealed to: to decide who is human on the basis of the sentiment of a given society has led to consequences which rational men would characterize as monstrous.

The rejection of the attempted distinctions based on viability and visibility, experience and feeling, may be buttressed by the following considerations: Moral judgments often rest on distinctions, but if the distinctions are not to appear arbitrary *fiat,* they should relate to some real difference in probabilities. There is a kind of continuity in all life, but the earlier stages of the elements of human life possess tiny probabilities of development. Consider, for example, the spermatozoa in any normal ejaculate: there are about 200,000,000 in any single ejaculate, of which one has a chance of developing into a zygote. Consider the oocytes which may become ova: there are 100,000 to 1,000,000 oocytes in a female infant, of which a maximum of 390 are ovulated. But once spermatozoon and ovum meet and the conceptus is formed, such studies as have been made show that roughly in only 20 percent of the cases will spontaneous abortion occur. In other words, the chances are about 4 out of 5 that this new being will develop. At this stage in the life of the being there is a sharp shift in probabilities, an immense jump in potentialities. To make a distinction between the rights of spermatozoa and the rights of the fertilized ovum is to respond to an enormous shift in possibilities. For about twenty days after conception the egg may split to form twins or combine with another egg to form a chimera, but the probability of either event happening is very small.

It may be asked, What does a change in biological probabilities have to do with establishing humanity? The argument from probabilities is not aimed at establishing humanity but at establishing an objective discontinuity which may be taken into account in moral discourse. As life itself is a matter of probabilities, as most moral reasoning is an estimate of probabilities, so it seems in accord with the structure of reality and the nature of moral thought to found a moral judgment on the change in probabilities at conception. The appeal to probabilities is the most commonsensical of arguments; to a greater or smaller degree all of us base our actions on probabilities, and in morals, as in law, prudence and negligence are often measured by the account one has taken of the probabilities. If the chance is 200,000,000 to 1 that the movement in the bushes into which you shoot is a man's, I doubt if many persons would hold you careless in shooting; but if the chances are 4 out of 5 that the movement is a human being's, few would acquit you of blame. Would the argument be different if only one out of ten children conceived came to term? Of course this argument would be different. This argument is an appeal to probabilities that actually exist, not to any and all states of affairs which may be imagined.

The probabilities as they do exist do not show the humanity of the embryo in the sense of a demonstration in logic any more than the probabilities of the movement in the bush being a man demonstrate beyond all doubt that the being is a man. The appeal is a "buttressing" consideration, showing the plausibility of the standard adopted. The argument focuses on the decisional factor in any moral judgment and assumes that part of the business of a moralist is drawing lines. One evidence of the nonarbitrary character of the line drawn is the difference of probabilities on either side of it. If a spermatozoon is destroyed, one destroys a being which had a chance of far less than 1 in 200 million of developing into a reasoning being, possessed of the genetic code, a heart and other organs, and capable of pain. If a fetus is destroyed, one destroys a being already possessed of the genetic code, organs, and sensitivity to pain, and one which had an 80 percent chance of developing further into a baby outside the womb who, in time, would reason.

The positive argument for conception as the decisive moment of humanization is that at conception the new being receives the genetic code. It is this genetic information which determines his characteristics, which is the biological carrier of the possibility of human wisdom, which makes him a self-evolving being. A being with a human genetic code is man.

This review of current controversy over the humanity of the fetus emphasizes what a fundamental question the theologians resolved in asserting the inviolability of the fetus. To regard the fetus as possessed of equal rights with other humans was not, however, to decide every case where abortion might be employed. It did decide the case where the argument was that the fetus should be aborted for its own good. To say a being was human was to say it had a destiny to decide for itself which could not be taken from it by another man's decision. But human beings with equal rights often come in conflict with each other, and some decision must be made as to whose claims are to prevail. Cases of conflict involving the fetus are different only in two respects: the total inability of the fetus to speak for itself and the fact that the right of the fetus regularly at stake is the right to life itself.

The approach taken by the theologians to these conflicts was articulated in terms of "direct" and "indirect." Again, to look at what they were doing from outside their categories, they may be said to have been drawing lines or "balancing values." "Direct" and "indirect" are spatial metaphors; "line-drawing" is another. "To weigh" or "to balance" values is a metaphor of a more complicated mathematical sort hinting at the process which goes on in moral judgments. All the metaphors suggest that, in the moral judgments made, comparisons were necessary, that no value completely controlled. The principle of double effect was no doctrine

fallen from heaven, but a method of analysis appropriate where two relative values were being compared. In Catholic moral theology, as it developed, life even of the innocent was not taken as an absolute. Judgments on acts affecting life issued from a process of weighing. In the weighing, the fetus was always given a value greater than zero, always a value separate and independent from its parents. This valuation was crucial and fundamental in all Christian thought on the subject and marked it off from any approach which considered that only the parents' interests needed to be considered.

Even with the fetus weighed as human, one interest could be weighed as equal or superior: that of the mother in her own life. The casuists between 1450 and 1895 were willing to weigh this interest as superior. Since 1895, that interest was given decisive weight only in the two special cases of the cancerous uterus and the ectopic pregnancy. In both of these cases the fetus itself had little chance of survival even if the abortion were not performed. As the balance was once struck in favor of the mother whenever her life was endangered, it could be so struck again. The balance reached between 1895 and 1930 attempted prudentially and pastorally to forestall a multitude of exceptions for interests less than life.

The perception of the humanity of the fetus and the weighing of fetal rights against other human rights constituted the work of the moral analysts. But what spirit animated their abstract judgments? For the Christian community it was the injunction of Scripture to love your neighbor as yourself. The fetus as human was a neighbor; his life had parity with one's own. The commandment gave life to what otherwise would have been only rational calculation.

The commandment could be put in humanistic as well as theological terms: Do not injure your fellow man without reason. In these terms, once the humanity of the fetus is perceived, abortion is never right except in self-defense. When life must be taken to save life, reason alone cannot say that a mother must prefer a child's life to her own. With this exception, now of great rarity, abortion violates the rational humanist tenet of the equality of human lives.

For Christians the commandment to love had received a special imprint in that the exemplar proposed of love was the love of the Lord for his disciples. In the light given by this example, self-sacrifice carried to the point of death seemed in the extreme situations not without meaning. In the less extreme cases, preference for one's own interests to the life of another seemed to express cruelty or selfishness irreconcilable with the demands of love.

Review Questions

1. According to Noonan, what is the simple Christian criterion for humanity?
2. Noonan discusses five distinctions (starting with viability) used by defenders of abortion. Explain Noonan's critique of these distinctions.
3. State and explain Noonan's argument from probabilities.
4. What is Noonan's positive argument for saying that conception is "the decisive moment of humanization"?
5. In Noonan's view, why does the fetus have rights equal to those of other human beings?
6. According to Noonan, how do Christian theologians resolve conflicts of rights such as that between the mother's right to life and the fetus's right to life?
7. According to the traditional view defended by Noonan, in which cases does the fetus's right to life outweigh the mother's right to life?

Discussion Questions

1. Consider the following objection to Noonan's claim that "a being with a human genetic code is a man." A human cell also is a being with a human genetic code, but obviously it is not a man in the sense of being a human being; therefore, Noonan's claim is false. How could Noonan respond to this objection?
2. Is it possible for a nonhuman being—for example, an angel or an intelligent alien being—to have rights equal to those of human beings? Defend your answer.
3. Noonan admits that abortion can be justified by appealing to the right of self-defense. Does this right justify an abortion in a case of rape? Why or why not?

A Defense of Abortion

JUDITH JARVIS THOMSON

Judith Jarvis Thomson is professor of philosophy at Massachusetts Institute of Technology and author of *Rights, Restitution, and Risk* (1986), *Acts and Other Events* (1977), and *The Realm of Rights* (1990).

Thomson assumes, just for the sake of argument, that the fetus is a person from the moment of conception. It does not follow, she argues, that the fetus's right to life always outweighs the mother's rights. Using a series of imaginary examples (such as being plugged into a famous violinist), she tries to convice us that the mother's rights—for example, her right to control her own body—are strong enough to justify abortion in cases of rape, of threat to her life, or when she has taken reasonable precautions not to get pregnant. Abortion is not justified in all cases, however. The moral requirement to be a Minimally Decent Samaritan (as she puts it) makes abortion wrong if it is done just for the sake of convenience. To use her example, it would be wrong for a woman in her seventh month of pregnancy to get an abortion just to avoid the nuisance of postponing a trip abroad.

Source: Judith Jarvis Thomson, "A Defense of Abortion," from *Philosophy & Public Affairs,* Vol. 1, No. 1 (Fall 1971), pp. 47–66. Copyright © 1971 by Princeton University Press. Reprinted by permission of Princeton University Press.

MOST OPPOSITION TO abortion relies on the premise that the fetus is a human being, a person, from the moment of conception. The premise is argued for, but, as I think, not well. Take, for example, the most common argument. We are asked to notice that the development of a human being from conception through birth into childhood is continuous; then it is said that to draw a line, to choose a point in this development and say "before this point the thing is not a person, after this point it is a person" is to make an arbitrary choice, a choice for which in the nature of things no good reason can be given. It is concluded that the fetus is, or anyway that we had better say it is, a person from the moment of conception. But this conclusion does not follow. Similar things might be said about the development of an acorn into an oak tree, and it does not follow that acorns are oak trees, or that we had better say they are. Arguments of this form are sometimes called "slippery slope arguments"—the phrase is perhaps self-explanatory—and it is dismaying that opponents of abortion rely on them so heavily and uncritically.

I am inclined to agree, however, that the prospects for "drawing a line" in the development of the fetus look dim. I am inclined to think also that we shall probably have to agree that the fetus has already become a human person well before birth. Indeed, it comes as a surprise when one first learns how early in its life it begins to acquire human characteristics. By the tenth week, for example, it already has a face, arms and legs, fingers and toes; it has internal organs, and brain activity is detectable.[1] On the other hand, I think that the premise is false, that the fetus is not a person from the moment of conception. A newly fertilized ovum, a newly implanted clump of cells, is no more a person than an acorn is an oak tree. But I shall not discuss any of this. For it seems to me to be of great interest to ask what happens if, for the sake of argument, we allow the premise. How, precisely, are we supposed to get from there to the conclusion that abortion is morally impermissible? Opponents of abortion commonly spend most of their time establishing that the fetus is a person, and hardly any time explaining the step from there to the impermissibility of abortion. Perhaps they think the step too simple and obvious to require much comment. Or perhaps instead they are simply being economical in argument. Many of those who defend abortion rely on the premise that the fetus is not a person, but only a bit of tissue that will become a person at birth; and why pay out more arguments than you have to? Whatever the explanation, I suggest that the step they take is neither easy nor obvious, that it calls for closer examination than it is commonly given, and that when we do give it this closer examination we shall feel inclined to reject it.

I propose, then, that we grant that the fetus is a person from the moment of conception. How does the argument go from here? Something like this, I take it. Every person has a right to life. So the fetus has a right to life. No doubt the mother has a right to decide what shall happen in and to her body; everyone would grant that. But surely a person's right to life is

stronger and more stringent than the mother's right to decide what happens in and to her body, and so outweighs it. So the fetus may not be killed; an abortion may not be performed.

It sounds plausible. But now let me ask you to imagine this. You wake up in the morning and find yourself back to back in bed with an unconscious violinist. A famous unconscious violinist. He has been found to have a fatal kidney ailment, and the Society of Music Lovers has canvassed all the available medical records and found that you alone have the right blood type to help. They have therefore kidnapped you, and last night the violinist's circulatory system was plugged into yours, so that your kidneys can be used to extract poisons from his blood as well as your own. The director of the hospital now tells you, "Look, we're sorry the Society of Music Lovers did this to you—we would never have permitted it if we had known. But still, they did it, and the violinist now is plugged into you. To unplug you would be to kill him. But never mind, it's only for nine months. By then he will have recovered from his ailment, and can safely be unplugged from you." Is it morally incumbent on you to accede to this situation? No doubt it would be very nice of you if you did, a great kindness. But do you *have* to accede to it? What if it were not nine months, but nine years? Or longer still? What if the director of the hospital says, "Tough luck, I agree, but you've now got to stay in bed, with the violinist plugged into you, for the rest of your life. Because remember this. All persons have a right to life, and violinists are persons. Granted you have a right to decide what happens in and to your body, but a person's right to life outweighs your right to decide what happens in and to your body. So you cannot ever be unplugged from him." I imagine you would regard this as outrageous, which suggests that something really is wrong with that plausible-sounding argument I mentioned a moment ago.

In this case, of course, you were kidnapped; you didn't volunteer for the operation that

1 Daniel Callahan, *Abortion: Law, Choice and Morality* (New York, 1970), p. 373. This book gives a fascinating survey of the available information on abortion. The Jewish tradition is surveyed in David M. Feldman, *Birth Control in Jewish Law* (New York, 1968), Part 5, the Catholic tradition in John T. Noonan, Jr., "An Almost Absolute Value in History," in *The Morality of Abortion*, ed. John T. Noonan, Jr. (Cambridge, Mass., 1970).

plugged the violinist into your kidneys. Can those who oppose abortion on the ground I mentioned make an exception for a pregnancy due to rape? Certainly. They can say that persons have a right to life only if they didn't come into existence because of rape; or they can say that all persons have a right to life, but that some have less of a right to life than others, in particular, that those who came into existence because of rape have less. But these statements have a rather unpleasant sound. Surely the question of whether you have a right to life at all, or how much of it you have, shouldn't turn on the question of whether or not you are the product of a rape. And in fact the people who oppose abortion on the ground I mentioned do not make this distinction, and hence do not make an exception in case of rape.

Nor do they make an exception for a case in which the mother has to spend the nine months of her pregnancy in bed. They would agree that would be a great pity, and hard on the mother; but all the same, all persons have a right to life, the fetus is a person, and so on. I suspect, in fact, that they would not make an exception for a case in which, miraculously enough, the pregnancy went on for nine years, or even the rest of the mother's life.

Some won't even make an exception for a case in which continuation of the pregnancy is likely to shorten the mother's life; they regard abortion as impermissible even to save the mother's life. Such cases are nowadays very rare, and many opponents of abortion do not accept this extreme view. All the same, it is a good place to begin: a number of points of interest come out in respect to it.

1. Let us call the view that abortion is impermissible even to save the mother's life "the extreme view." I want to suggest first that it does not issue from the argument I mentioned earlier without the addition of some fairly powerful premises. Suppose a woman has become pregnant, and now learns that she has a cardiac condition such that she will die if she carries the baby to term. What may be done for her? The fetus, being a person, has a right to life, but as the mother is a person too, so has she a right to life. Presumably they have an equal right to life. How is it supposed to come out that an abortion may not be performed? If mother and child have an equal right to life, shouldn't we perhaps flip a coin? Or should we add to the mother's right to life her right to decide what happens in and to her body, which everybody seems to be ready to grant—the sum of her rights now outweighing the fetus' right to life?

The most familiar argument here is the following. We are told that performing the abortion would be directly killing[2] the child, whereas doing nothing would not be killing the mother, but only letting her die. Moreover, in killing the child, one would be killing an innocent person, for the child has committed no crime, and is not aiming at his mother's death. And then there are a variety of ways in which this might be continued. (1) But as directly killing an innocent person is always and absolutely impermissible, an abortion may not be performed. Or (2) as directly killing an innocent person is murder, and murder is always and absolutely impermissible, an abortion may not be performed.[3] Or (3) as one's duty to refrain from directly killing an innocent person is more stringent than one's duty to keep a person from dying, an abortion may not be performed. Or (4) if one's only options are directly

2 The term "direct" in the arguments I refer to is a technical one. Roughly, what is meant by "direct killing" is either killing as an end in itself, or killing as a means to some end, for example, the end of saving someone else's life. See note 5 for an example of its use.

3 Cf. *Encyclical Letter of Pope Pius XI on Christian Marriage*, St. Paul Editions (Boston, n.d.), p. 32: "however much we may pity the mother whose health and even life is gravely imperiled in the performance of the duty alloted to her by nature, nevertheless what could ever be a sufficient reason for excusing in any way the direct murder of the innocent? This is precisely what we are dealing with here." Noonan (*The Morality of Abortion*, p. 43) reads this as follows: "What cause can ever avail to excuse in any way the direct killing of the innocent? For it is a question of that."

killing an innocent person or letting a person die, one must prefer letting the person die, and thus an abortion may not be performed.[4]

Some people seem to have thought that these are not further premises which must be added if the conclusion is to be reached, but that they follow from the very fact that an innocent person has a right to life.[5] But this seems to me to be a mistake, and perhaps the simplest way to show this is to bring out that while we must certainly grant that innocent persons have a right to life, the theses in (1) through (4) are all false. Take (2), for example. If directly killing an innocent person is murder, and thus is impermissible, then the mother's directly killing the innocent person inside her is murder, and thus is impermissible. But it cannot seriously be thought to be murder if the mother performs an abortion on herself to save her life. It cannot seriously be said that she *must* refrain, that she *must* sit passively by and wait for her death. Let us look again at the case of you and the violinist. There you are, in bed with the violinist, and the director of the hospital says to you, "It's all most distressing, and I deeply sympathize, but you see this is putting an additional strain on your kidneys, and you'll be dead within the month. But you *have* to stay where you are all

the same. Because unplugging you would be directly killing an innocent violinist, and that's murder, and that's impermissible." If anything in the world is true, it is that you do not commit murder, you do not do what is impermissible, if you reach around to your back and unplug yourself from that violinist to save your life.

The main focus of attention in writings on abortion has been on what a third party may or may not do in answer to a request from a woman for an abortion. This is in a way understandable. Things being as they are, there isn't much a woman can safely do to abort herself. So the question asked is what a third party may do, and what the mother may do, if it is mentioned at all, is deduced, almost as an afterthought, from what it is concluded that third parties may do. But it seems to me that to treat the matter in this way is to refuse to grant to the mother that very status of person which is so firmly insisted on for the fetus. For we cannot simply read off what a person may do from what a third party may do. Suppose you find yourself trapped in a tiny house with a growing child. I mean a very tiny house, and a rapidly growing child— you are already up against the wall of the house and in a few minutes you'll be crushed to death. The child on the other hand won't be crushed to death; if nothing is done to stop him from growing he'll be hurt, but in the end he'll simply burst open the house and walk out a free man. Now I could well understand it if a bystander were to say, "There's nothing we can do for you. We cannot choose between your life and his, we cannot be the ones to decide who is to live, we cannot intervene." But it cannot be concluded that you too can do nothing, that you cannot attack it to save your life. However innocent the child may be, you do not have to wait passively while it crushes you to death. Perhaps a pregnant woman is vaguely felt to have the status of house, to which we don't allow the right of self-defense. But if the woman houses the child, it should be remembered that she is a person who houses it.

---

4 The thesis in (4) is in an interesting way weaker than those in (1), (2), and (3): they rule out abortion even in cases in which both mother *and* child will die if the abortion is not performed. By contrast, one who held the view expressed in (4) could consistently say that one needn't prefer letting two persons die to killing one.

5 Cf. The following passage from Pius XII, *Address to the Italian Catholic Society of Midwives:* "The baby in the maternal breast has the right to life immediately from God. Hence there is no man, no human authority, no science, no medical, eugenic, social, economic or moral 'indication' which can establish or grant a valid juridical ground for a direct deliberate disposition of an innocent human life, that is, a disposition which looks to its destruction either as an end or as a means to another end perhaps in itself not illicit. The baby, still not born, is a man in the same degree and for the same reason as the mother" (quoted in Noonan, *The Morality of Abortion,* p. 45).

I should perhaps stop to say explicitly that I am not claiming that people have a right to do anything whatever to save their lives. I think, rather, that there are drastic limits to the right of self-defense. If someone threatens you with death unless you torture someone else to death, I think you have not the right, even to save your life, to do so. But the case under consideration here is very different. In our case there are only two people involved, one whose life is threatened, and one who threatens it. Both are innocent: the one who is threatened is not threatened because of any fault, the one who threatens does not threaten because of any fault. For this reason we may feel that we bystanders cannot intervene. But the person threatened can.

In sum, a woman surely can defend her life against the threat to it posed by the unborn child, even if doing so involves its death. And this shows not merely that the theses in (1) through (4) are false; it shows also that the extreme view of abortion is false, and so we need not canvass any other possible ways of arriving at it from the argument I mentioned at the outset.

2. The extreme view could of course be weakened to say that while abortion is permissible to save the mother's life, it may not be performed by the third party, but only by the mother herself. But this cannot be right either. For what we have to keep in mind is that the mother and the unborn child are not like two tenants in a small house which has, by an unfortunate mistake, been rented to both: the mother *owns* the house. The fact that she does adds to the offensiveness of deducing that the mother can do nothing from the supposition that third parties can do nothing. But it does more than this: it casts a bright light on the supposition that third parties can do nothing. Certainly it lets us see that a third party who says "I cannot choose between you" is fooling himself if he thinks this is impartiality. If Jones has found and fastened on a certain coat, which he needs to keep him from freezing, but which Smith also needs to keep him from freezing, then it is not impartiality that says "I cannot choose between you" when Smith owns the coat. Women have said again and again "This body is *my* body!" and they have reason to feel angry, reason to feel that it has been like shouting into the wind. Smith, after all, is hardly likely to bless us if we say to him, "Of course it's your coat, anybody would grant that it is. But no one may choose between you and Jones who is to have it." . . .

3. Where the mother's life is not at stake, the argument I mentioned at the outset seems to have a much stronger pull. "Everyone has a right to life, so the unborn person has a right to life." And isn't the child's right to life weightier than anything other than the mother's own right to life, which she might put forward as ground for an abortion?

This argument treats the right to life as if it were unproblematic. It is not, and this seems to me to be precisely the source of the mistake.

For we should now, at long last, ask what it comes to, to have a right to life. In some views having a right to life includes having a right to be given at least the bare minimum one needs for continued life. But suppose that what in fact *is* the bare minimum a man needs for continued life is something he has no right at all to be given? If I am sick unto death, and the only thing that will save my life is the touch of Henry Fonda's cool hand on my fevered brow, then all the same, I have no right to be given the touch of Henry Fonda's cool hand on my fevered brow. It would be frightfully nice of him to fly in from the West Coast to provide it. It would be less nice, though no doubt well meant, if my friends flew out to the West Coast and carried Henry Fonda back with them. But I have no right at all against anybody that he should do this for me. Or again, to return to the story I told earlier, the fact that for continued life that violinist needs the continued use of your kidneys does not establish that he has a right to be given the continued use of your kidneys. He certainly has no right against you that *you* should give him continued use of your kidneys. For nobody has any right to use your kidneys unless you give him such a right; and nobody has the right against you that you shall give him this right—if you do allow him to go on using your kidneys, this is kindness on your part, and not something he can claim from you as his due. Nor has he any right against anybody else that *they* should give him continued use of your kidneys. Certainly he had no right against the Society of Music Lovers that they should plug him into you in the first place. And if you now start to unplug yourself, having learned that you will otherwise have to spend nine years in bed with him, there is nobody in the world who must try to prevent you, in order to see to it that he is given something he has a right to be given.

Some people are rather stricter about the right to life. In their view, it does not include the right to be given anything, but amounts to, and only to, the right not to be killed by anybody. But here a related difficulty arises. If everybody is to refrain from killing that violinist, then everybody must refrain from doing a great many different sorts of things. Everybody must refrain from slitting his throat, everybody must refrain from shooting him—and everybody must refrain from unplugging you from him. But does he have a right against everybody that they shall refrain from unplugging you from him? To refrain from doing this is to allow him to continue to use your kidneys. It could be argued that he has a right against us that *we* should allow him to continue to use your kidneys. That is, while he had no right against us that we should give him the use of your kidneys, it might be argued that he anyway has a right against us that we shall not now intervene and deprive him of the use of your kidneys. I shall come back to third-party interventions later. But certainly the violinist has no right against you that *you* shall allow him to continue to use

your kidneys. As I said, if you do allow him to use them, it is a kindness on your part, and not something you owe him.

The difficulty I point to here is not peculiar to the right to life. It reappears in connection with all the other natural rights; and it is something which an adequate account of rights must deal with. For present purposes it is enough just to draw attention to it. But I would stress that I am not arguing that people do not have a right to life—quite to the contrary, it seems to me that the primary control we must place on the acceptability of an account of rights is that it should turn out in that account to be a truth that all persons have a right to life. I am arguing only that having a right to life does not guarantee having either a right to be given the use of or a right to be allowed continued use of another person's body—even if one needs it for life itself. So the right to life will not serve the opponents of abortion in the very simple and clear way in which they seem to have thought it would.

4. There is another way to bring out the difficulty. In the most ordinary sort of case, to deprive someone of what he has a right to is to treat him unjustly. Suppose a boy and his small brother are jointly given a box of chocolates for Christmas. If the older boy takes the box and refuses to give his brother any of the chocolates, he is unjust to him, for the brother has been given a right to half of them. But suppose that, having learned that otherwise it means nine years in bed with that violinist, you unplug yourself from him. You surely are not being unjust to him, for you gave him no right to use your kidneys, and no one else can have given him any such right. But we have to notice that in unplugging yourself, you are killing him; and violinists, like everybody else, have a right to life, and thus in the view we were considering just now, the right not to be killed. So here you do what he supposedly has a right you shall not do, but you do not act unjustly to him in doing it.

The emendation which may be made at this point is this: the right to life consists not in the right not to be killed, but rather in the right not to be killed unjustly. This runs a risk of circularity, but never mind: it would enable us to square the fact that the violinist has a right to life with the fact that you do not act unjustly toward him in unplugging yourself, thereby killing him. For if you do not kill him unjustly, you do not violate his right to life, and so it is no wonder you do him no injustice.

But if this emendation is accepted, the gap in the argument against abortion stares us plainly in the face: it is by no means enough to show that the fetus is a person, and to remind us that all persons have a right to life—we need to be shown also that killing the fetus violates its right to life, i.e., that abortion is unjust killing. And is it?

I suppose we may take it as a datum that in a case of pregnancy due to rape the mother has not given the unborn person a right to the use of her body for food and shelter. Indeed, in what pregnancy could it be supposed that the mother has given the unborn person such a right? It is not as if there were unborn persons drifting about the world, to whom a woman who wants a child says "I invite you in."

But it might be argued that there are other ways one can have acquired a right to the use of another person's body than by having been invited to use it by that person. Suppose a woman voluntarily indulges in intercourse, knowing of the chance it will issue in pregnancy, and then she does become pregnant; is she not in part responsible for the presence, in fact the very existence, of the unborn person inside her? No doubt she did not invite it in. But doesn't her partial responsibility for its being there itself give it a right to the use of her body?[6] If so, then her aborting it would be more like the

boy's taking away the chocolates, and less like your unplugging yourself from the violinist—doing so would be depriving it of what it does have a right to, and thus would be doing it an injustice.

And then, too, it might be asked whether or not she can kill it even to save her own life: If she voluntarily called it into existence, how can she now kill it, even in self-defense?

The first thing to be said about this is that it is something new. Opponents of abortion have been so concerned to make out the independence of the fetus, in order to establish that it has a right to life, just as its mother does, that they have tended to overlook the possible support they might gain from making out that the fetus is *dependent* on the mother, in order to establish that she has a special kind of responsibility for it, a responsibility that gives it rights against her which are not possessed by any independent person—such as an ailing violinist who is a stranger to her.

On the other hand, this argument would give the unborn person a right to its mother's body only if her pregnancy resulted from a voluntary act, undertaken in full knowledge of the chance a pregnancy might result from it. It would leave out entirely the unborn person whose existence is due to rape. Pending the availability of some further argument, then, we would be left with the conclusion that unborn persons whose existence is due to rape have no right to the use of their mothers' bodies, and thus that aborting them is not depriving them of anything they have a right to and hence is not unjust killing.

And we should also notice that it is not at all plain that this argument really does go even as far as it purports to. For there are cases and cases, and the details make a difference. If the room is stuffy, and I therefore open a window to air it, and a burglar climbs in, it would be absurd to say, "Ah, now he can stay, she's given him a right to the use of her house—for she is partially responsible for his presence there, having voluntarily done what enabled him to get in, in full

6 The need for a discussion of this argument was brought home to me by members of the Society for Ethical and Legal Philosophy, to whom this paper was originally presented.

knowledge that there are such things as burglars, and that burglars burgle." It would be still more absurd to say this if I had had bars installed outside my windows, precisely to prevent burglars from getting in, and a burglar got in only because of a defect in the bars. It remains equally absurd if we imagine it is not a burglar who climbs in, but an innocent person who blunders or falls in. Again, suppose it were like this: people-seeds drift about in the air like pollen, and if you open your windows, one may drift in and take root in your carpets or upholstery. You don't want children, so you fix up your windows with fine mesh screens, the very best you can buy. As can happen, however, and on very, very rare occasions does happen, one of the screens is defective; and a seed drifts in and takes root. Does the person-plant who now develops have a right to the use of your house? Surely not—despite the fact that you voluntarily opened your windows, you knowingly kept carpets and upholstered furniture, and you knew that screens were sometimes defective. Someone may argue that you are responsible for its rooting, that it does have a right to your house, because after all you *could* have lived out your life with bare floors and furniture, or with sealed windows and doors. But this won't do—for by the same token anyone can avoid a pregnancy due to rape by having a hysterectomy, or anyway by never leaving home without a (reliable!) army.

It seems to me that the argument we are looking at can establish at most that there are *some* cases in which the unborn person has a right to the use of its mother's body, and therefore *some* cases in which abortion is unjust killing. There is room for much discussion and argument as to precisely which, if any. But I think we should sidestep this issue and leave it open, for at any rate the argument certainly does not establish that all abortion is unjust killing.

5. There is room for yet another argument here, however. We surely must all grant that there may be cases in which it would be morally indecent to detach a person from your body at the cost of his life. Suppose you learn that what the violinist needs is not nine years of your life, but only one hour: all you need do to save his life is to spend one hour in that bed with him. Suppose also that letting him use your kidneys for that one hour would not affect your health in the slightest. Admittedly you were kidnapped. Admittedly you did not give anyone permission to plug him into you. Nevertheless it seems to me plain you *ought* to allow him to use your kidneys for that hour—it would be indecent to refuse.

Again, suppose pregnancy lasted only an hour, and constituted no threat to life or health. And suppose that a woman becomes pregnant as a result of rape. Admittedly she did not voluntarily do anything to bring about the existence of a child. Admittedly she did nothing at all which would give the unborn person a right to the use of her body. All the same it might well be said, as in the newly emended violinist story, that she *ought* to allow it to remain for that hour—that it would be indecent in her to refuse.

Now some people are inclined to use the term "right" in such a way that it follows from the fact that you ought to allow a person to use your body for the hour he needs, that he has a right to use your body for the hour he needs, even though he has not been given that right by any person or act. They may say that it follows also that if you refuse, you act unjustly toward him. This use of the term is perhaps so common that it cannot be called wrong; nevertheless it seems to me to be an unfortunate loosening of what we would do better to keep a tight rein on. Suppose that box of chocolates I mentioned earlier had not been given to both boys jointly, but was given only to the older boy. There he sits, stolidly eating his way through the box, his small brother watching enviously. Here we are likely to say "You ought not to be so mean. You ought to give your brother some of those chocolates." My own view is that it just does not follow from the truth of this that the brother has any right to any of the chocolates. If the boy refuses to give his brother any, he is greedy, stingy, callous—but not unjust. I suppose that the people I have in mind will say it does follow that the brother has a right to some of the chocolates, and thus that the boy does act unjustly if he refuses to give his brother any. But the effect of saying this is to obscure what we should keep distinct, namely the difference between the boy's refusal in this case and the boy's refusal in the earlier case, in which the box was given to both boys jointly, and in which the small brother thus had what was from any point of view clear title to half.

A further objection to so using the term "right" that from the fact that A ought to do a thing for B, it follows that B has a right against A that A do it for him, is that it is going to make the question of whether or not a man has a right to a thing turn on how easy it is to provide him with it; and this seems not merely unfortunate, but morally unacceptable. Take the case of Henry Fonda again. I said earlier that I had no right to the touch of his cool hand on my fevered brow, even though I needed it to save my life. I said it would be frightfully nice of him to fly in from the West Coast to provide me with it, but that I had no right against him that he should do so. But suppose he isn't on the West Coast. Suppose he has only to walk across the room, place a hand briefly on my brow—and lo, my life is saved. Then surely he ought to do it, it would be indecent to refuse. Is it to be said "Ah, well, it follows that in this case she has a right to the touch of his hand on her brow, and so it would be an injustice in him to refuse"? So that I have a right to it when it is easy for him to provide it, though no right when it's hard? It's rather a shocking idea that anyone's rights should fade away and disappear as it gets harder and harder to accord them to him.

So my own view is that even though you ought to let the violinist use your kidneys for the one hour he needs, we should not conclude that he has a right to do so—we should say that

if you refuse, you are, like the boy who owns all the chocolates and will give none away, self-centered and callous, indecent in fact, but not unjust. And similarly, that even supposing a case in which a woman pregnant due to rape ought to allow the unborn person to use her body for the hour he needs, we should not conclude that he has a right to do so; we should conclude that she is self-centered, callous, indecent, but not unjust, if she refuses. The complaints are no less grave; they are just different. However, there is no need to insist on this point. If anyone does wish to deduce "he has a right" from "you ought," then all the same he must surely grant that there are cases in which it is not morally required of you that you allow that violinist to use your kidneys, and in which he does not have a right to use them, and in which you do not do him an injustice if you refuse. And so also for mother and unborn child. Except in such cases as the unborn person has a right to demand it— and we were leaving open the possibility that there may be such cases—nobody is morally *required* to make large sacrifices, of health, of all other interests and concerns, of all other duties and commitments, for nine years, or even for nine months, in order to keep another person alive. . . .

6. My argument will be found unsatisfactory on two counts by many of those who want to regard abortion as morally permissible. First, while I do argue that abortion is not impermissible, I do not argue that it is always permissible. There may well be cases in which carrying the child to term requires only Minimally Decent Samaritanism of the mother, and this is a standard we must not fall below. I am inclined to think it a merit of my account precisely that it does *not* give a general yes or a general no. It allows for and supports our sense that, for example, a sick and desperately frightened fourteen-year-old schoolgirl, pregnant due to rape, may *of course* choose abortion, and that any law which rules this out is an insane law. And it also allows for and supports our sense that in other

cases resort to abortion is even positively indecent. It would be indecent in the woman to request an abortion, and indecent in a doctor to perform it, if she is in her seventh month, and wants the abortion just to avoid the nuisance of postponing a trip abroad. The very fact that the arguments I have been drawing attention to treat all cases of abortion, or even all cases of abortion in which the mother's life is not at stake, as morally on a par ought to have made them suspect at the outset.

Secondly, while I am arguing for the permissibility of abortion in some cases, I am not arguing for the right to secure the death of the unborn child. It is easy to confuse these two things in that up to a certain point in the life of the fetus it is not able to survive outside the mother's body; hence removing it from her body guarantees its death. But they are importantly different. I have argued that you are not morally required to spend nine months in bed, sustaining the life of that violinist; but to say this is by no means to say that if, when you unplug yourself, there is a miracle and he survives, you

then have a right to turn round and slit his throat. You may detach yourself even if this costs him his life; you have no right to be guaranteed his death, by some other means, if unplugging yourself does not kill him. There are some people who will feel dissatisfied by this feature of my argument. A woman may be utterly devastated by the thought of a child, a bit of herself, put out for adoption and never seen or heard of again. She may therefore want not merely that the child be detached from her, but more, that it die. Some opponents of abortion are inclined to regard this as beneath contempt —thereby showing insensitivity to what is surely a powerful source of despair. All the same, I agree that the desire for the child's death is not one which anybody may gratify, should it turn out to be possible to detach the child alive.

At this place, however, it should be remembered that we have only been pretending throughout that the fetus is a human being from the moment of conception. A very early abortion is surely not the killing of a person, and so is not dealt with by anything I have said here.

Review Questions

1. What are "slippery slope arguments," and why does Thomson reject them?
2. Explain the example about the famous violinist.
3. What is the "extreme view," and what argument is used to defend it? How does Thomson attack this argument?
4. What is the point of the example about the tiny house and the growing child?
5. Why do women say, "This body is *my* body"? Do they say this?
6. Explain the example about "Henry Fonda's cool hand on my fevered brow."
7. What is the point of the example about people-seeds taking root in the carpet?
8. What are Thomson's conclusions? When is abortion justified and when is it not justified?

Discussion Questions

1. Is the case of the famous violinist really analogous to a case of pregnancy due to rape?
2. What are the limits to the right to self-defense? Do these limits apply to abortion in cases of rape?
3. What obligations do we have to people who have a right to life? Do we have an obligation, for example, to take care of them and feed them?
4. Does a woman who is accidentally pregnant have a right to get an abortion?

On the Moral and Legal Status of Abortion

MARY ANNE WARREN

Mary Anne Warren teaches philosophy at San Francisco State University. She is the author of *The Nature of Woman: An Encyclopedia and Guide to the Literature* (1980), *Gendercide: The Implications of Sex Selection* (1985), and numerous articles on topics in ethics.

In the first part of her article, Warren argues that Thomson's argument about the famous violinist proves that abortion is justified in cases of rape but fails to demonstrate that abortion is permissible when pregnancy is not due to rape and is not life-threatening. Warren thinks that more argument is needed to show the permissibility of abortion in those cases.

In the second part, Warren begins by distinguishing between two senses of the term "human being," a genetic sense and a moral sense. She criticizes Noonan for not providing an argument for saying that whatever is genetically human is also morally human. Then she suggests six criteria for personhood: sentience, emotionality, reason, the capacity to communicate, self-awareness, and moral agency. She claims that the fetus has none of these characteristics of a person in the early stages of development, and thus it is not a person with moral rights in those stages. The fact that a late-term fetus resembles a person is taken seriously by Warren, and she recommends that women wanting an abortion get one before the third trimester. But she is not impressed by an appeal to the fetus's potential for becoming a person because she thinks that the rights of an actual person—namely, the mother—will always outweigh the rights of a merely potential person when they conflict. Warren concludes with a reply to the objection that her view justifies infanticide. She argues that there are several reasons why infanticide is more difficult to justify than abortion.

FOR OUR PURPOSES, abortion may be defined as the act a woman performs in deliberately terminating her pregnancy before it comes to term, or in allowing another person to terminate it. Abortion usually entails the death of a fetus.[1] Nevertheless, I will argue that it is morally permissible, and should be neither legally prohibited nor made needlessly difficult to obtain, e.g., by obstructive legal regulations.[2]

Some philosophers have argued that the moral status of abortion cannot be resolved by

Source: Mary Anne Warren, "On the Moral and Legal Status of Abortion," from *Ethics in Practice,* ed. Hugh LaFollette, pp. 79–90. Copyright © 1997 Blackwell Publishers. Reprinted with permission.

1 Strictly speaking, a human conceptus does not become a fetus until the primary organ systems have formed, at about six to eight weeks gestational age. However, for simplicity I shall refer to the conceptus as a fetus at every stage of its prenatal development.

2 The views defended in this article are set forth in greater depth in my book *Moral Status,* which is forthcoming from Oxford University Press.

rational means.[3] If this is so then liberty should prevail; for it is not a proper function of the law to enforce prohibitions upon personal behavior that cannot clearly be shown to be morally objectionable, and seriously so. But the advocates of prohibition believe that their position is objectively correct, and not merely a result of religious beliefs or personal prejudices. They argue that the humanity of the fetus is a matter of scientific fact, and that abortion is therefore the moral equivalent of murder, and must be prohibited in all or most cases. (Some would make an exception when the woman's life is in danger, or when the pregnancy is due to rape or incest; others would prohibit abortion even in these cases.)

In response, advocates of a right to choose abortion point to the terrible consequences of prohibiting it, especially while contraception is still unreliable, and is financially beyond the reach of much of the world's population. Worldwide, hundreds of thousands of women die each year from illegal abortions, and many more suffer from complications that may leave them injured or infertile. Women who are poor, under-age, disabled, or otherwise vulnerable, suffer most from the absence of safe and legal abortion. Advocates of choice also argue that to deny a woman access to abortion is to deprive her of the right to control her own body—a right so fundamental that without it other rights are often all but meaningless.

These arguments do not convince abortion opponents. The tragic consequences of prohibition leave them unmoved, because they regard the deliberate killing of fetuses as even more tragic. Nor do appeals to the right to control one's own body impress them, since they deny that this right includes the right to destroy a fetus. We cannot hope to persuade those who

equate abortion with murder that they are mistaken, unless we can refute the standard antiabortion argument: that because fetuses are human beings, they have a right to life equal to that of any other human being. Unfortunately, confusion has prevailed with respect to the two important questions which that argument raises: (1) Is a human fetus really a human being at all stages of prenatal development? and (2) If so, what (if anything) follows about the moral and legal status of abortion?

John Noonan says that "the fundamental question in the long history of abortion is: How do you determine the humanity of a being?"[4] His antiabortion argument is essentially that of the Roman Catholic Church. In his words,

> . . . it is wrong to kill humans, however poor, weak, defenseless, and lacking in opportunity to develop their potential they may be. It is therefore morally wrong to kill Biafrans. Similarly, it is morally wrong to kill embryos.[5]

Noonan bases his claim that fetuses are human beings from the time of conception upon what he calls the theologians' criterion of humanity: that whoever is conceived of human beings is a human being. But although he argues at length for the appropriateness of this criterion of humanity, he does not question the assumption that if a fetus is a human being then abortion is almost always immoral.[6]

Judith Thomson has questioned this assumption. She argues that, even if we grant the antiabortionist the claim that a fetus is a human

3 For example, Roger Wertheimer argues, in "Understanding the Abortion Argument," *Philosophy and Public Affairs*, 1 (Fall, 1971), that the moral status of abortion is not a question of fact, but only of how one responds to the facts.

4 John Noonan, "Abortion and the Catholic Church: A Summary History," *Natural Law Forum*, 12 (1967), p. 125.

5 John Noonan, "Deciding Who Is Human," *Natural Law Forum*, 13 (1968), p. 134.

6 Noonan deviates from the current position of the Roman Catholic Church in that he thinks that abortion is morally permissible when it is the only way of saving the woman's life. See "An Almost Absolute Value in History," in *Contemporary Issues in Bioethics*, edited by Tom L. Beauchamp and LeRoy Walters (Belmont, California: Wadsworth, 1994), p. 283.

being with the same right to life as any other human being, we can still demonstrate that women are not morally obliged to complete every unwanted pregnancy.[7] Her argument is worth examining, because if it is sound it may enable us to establish the moral permissibility of abortion without having to decide just what makes an entity a human being, or what entitles it to full moral rights. This would represent a considerable gain in the power and simplicity of the pro-choice position.

Even if Thomson's argument does not hold up, her essential insight—that it requires *argument* to show that if fetuses are human beings then abortion is murder—is a valuable one. The assumption that she attacks is invidious, for it requires that in our deliberations about the ethics of abortion we must ignore almost entirely the needs of the pregnant woman and other persons for whom she is responsible. This will not do; determining what moral rights a fetus has is only one step in determining the moral status of abortion. The next step is finding a just solution to conflicts between whatever rights the fetus has, and the rights and responsibilities of the woman who is unwillingly pregnant.

My own inquiry will also have two stages. In Section I, I consider whether abortion can be shown to be morally permissible even on the assumption that a fetus is a human being with a strong right to life. I argue that this cannot be established, except in special cases. Consequently, we cannot avoid facing the question of whether or not a fetus has the same right to life as any human being.

In Section II, I propose an answer to this question, namely, that a fetus is not a member of the moral community—the set of beings with full and equal moral rights. The reason that a fetus is not a member of the moral community is that it is not yet a person, nor is it enough like

a person in the morally relevant respects to be regarded the equal of those human beings who are persons. I argue that it is personhood, and not genetic humanity, which is the fundamental basis for membership in the moral community. A fetus, especially in the early stages of its development, satisfies none of the criteria of personhood. Consequently, it makes no sense to grant it moral rights strong enough to override the woman's moral rights to liberty, bodily integrity, and sometimes life itself. Unlike an infant who has already been born, a fetus cannot be granted full and equal moral rights without severely threatening the rights and well-being of women. Nor, as we will see, is a fetus's *potential* personhood a threat to the moral permissibility of abortion, since merely potential persons do not have a moral right to become actual—or none that is strong enough to override the fundamental moral rights of actual persons.

I

Judith Thomson argues that, even if a fetus has a right to life, abortion is often morally permissible. Her argument is based upon an imaginative analogy. She asks you to picture yourself waking up one day, in bed with a famous violinist, who is a stranger to you. Imagine that you have been kidnapped, and your bloodstream connected to that of the violinist, who has an ailment that will kill him unless he is permitted to share your kidneys for nine months. No one else can save him, since you alone have the right type of blood. Consequently, the Society of Music Lovers has arranged for you to be kidnapped and hooked up. If you unhook yourself, he will die. But if you remain in bed with him, then after nine months he will be cured and able to survive without further assistance from you.

Now, Thomson asks, what are your obligations in this situation? To be consistent, the antiabortionist must say that you are obliged to stay in bed with the violinist: for violinists are human beings, and all human beings have a right to life.[8] But this is outrageous; thus, there must be something very wrong with the same argument when it is applied to abortion. It would be extremely generous of you to agree to stay in bed with the violinist; but it is absurd to suggest that your refusal to do so would be the moral equivalent of murder. The violinist's right to life does not oblige you to do whatever is required to keep him alive; still less does it justify anyone else in forcing you to do so. A law which required you to stay in bed with the violinist would be an unjust law, since unwilling persons ought not to be required to be Extremely Good Samaritans, i.e., to make enormous personal sacrifices for the sake of other individuals towards whom they have no special prior obligation.

Thomson concludes that we can grant the antiabortionist his claim that a fetus is a human being with a right to life, and still hold that a pregnant woman is morally entitled to refuse to be an Extremely Good Samaritan toward the fetus. For there is a great gap between the claim that a human being has a right to life, and the claim that other human beings are morally obligated to do whatever is necessary to keep him alive. One has no duty to keep another human being alive *at great personal cost,* unless one has somehow contracted a special obligation toward that individual; and a woman who is pregnant may have done nothing that morally obliges her to make the burdensome personal sacrifices necessary to preserve the life of the fetus.

This argument is plausible, and in the case of pregnancy due to rape it is probably conclusive. Difficulties arise, however, when we attempt to specify the larger range of cases in which abortion can be justified on the basis of this argument. Thomson considers it a virtue of her argument that it does not imply that abortion is *always* morally permissible. It would, she says, be indecent for a woman in her seventh month of pregnancy to have an abortion in order to embark on a trip to Europe. On the other hand, the violinist analogy shows that, "a sick and desperately frightened fourteen-year-old schoolgirl, pregnant due to rape, may *of course* choose abortion, and that any law which rules this out is an insane law."[9] So far, so good; but what are we to say about the woman who becomes pregnant not through rape but because she and her partner did not use available forms of contraception, or because their attempts at contraception failed? What about a woman who becomes pregnant intentionally, but then re-evaluates the wisdom of having a child? In such cases, the violinist analogy is considerably less useful to advocates of the right to choose abortion.

It is perhaps only when a woman's pregnancy is due to rape, or some other form of coercion, that the situation is sufficiently analogous to the violinist case for our moral intuitions to transfer convincingly from the one case to the other. One difference between a pregnancy caused by rape and most unwanted pregnancies is that only in the former case is it perfectly clear that the woman is in no way responsible for her predicament. In the other cases, she *might* have been able to avoid becoming pregnant, e.g., by taking birth control pills (more faithfully), or insisting upon the use of high-quality condoms, or even avoiding heterosexual intercourse altogether throughout her fertile years. In contrast, if you are suddenly kidnapped by strange music lovers and hooked up to a sick violinist, then you are in no way responsible for your situation, which you could not have foreseen or prevented. And responsibility does seem to matter here. If a person behaves in a way which she could have avoided, and which she knows might bring into existence a human being who will depend upon her for survival, then it is not entirely clear that if and when that happens she may rightly refuse to do what she must in order to keep that human being alive.

8 Ibid., p. 174.

9 Ibid., p. 187.

This argument shows that the violinist analogy provides a persuasive defense of a woman's right to choose abortion only in cases where she is in no way morally responsible for her own pregnancy. In all other cases, the assumption that a fetus has a strong right to life makes it necessary to look carefully at the particular circumstances in order to determine the extent of the woman's responsibility, and hence the extent of her obligation. This outcome is unsatisfactory to advocates of the right to choose abortion, because it suggests that the decision should not be left in the woman's own hands, but should be supervised by other persons, who will inquire into the most intimate aspects of her personal life in order to determine whether or not she is entitled to choose abortion.

A supporter of the violinist analogy might reply that it is absurd to suggest that forgetting her pill one day might be sufficient to morally oblige a woman to complete an unwanted pregnancy. And indeed it is absurd to suggest this. As we will see, a woman's moral right to choose abortion does not depend upon the extent to which she might be thought to be morally responsible for her own pregnancy. But once we allow the assumption that a fetus has a strong right to life, we cannot avoid taking this absurd suggestion seriously. On this assumption, it is a vexing question whether and when abortion is morally justifiable. The violinist analogy can at best show that aborting a pregnancy is a deeply tragic act, though one that is sometimes morally justified.

My conviction is that an abortion is not always this deeply tragic, because a fetus is not yet a person, and therefore does not yet have a strong moral right to life. Although the truth of this conviction may not be self-evident, it does, I believe, follow from some highly plausible claims about the appropriate grounds for ascribing moral rights. It is worth examining these grounds, since this has not been adequately done before.

II

The question we must answer in order to determine the moral status of abortion is: How are we to define the moral community, the set of beings with full and equal moral rights? What sort of entity has the inalienable moral rights to life, liberty, and the pursuit of happiness? Thomas Jefferson attributed these rights to all *men*, and he may have intended to attribute them *only* to men. Perhaps he ought to have attributed them to all human beings. If so, then we arrive, first, at Noonan's problem of defining what makes an entity a human being, and second, at the question which Noonan does not consider: What reason is there for identifying the moral community with the set of all human beings, in whatever way we have chosen to define that term?

On the Definition of "Human"

The term "human being" has two distinct, but not often distinguished, senses. This results in a slide of meaning, which serves to conceal the fallacy in the traditional argument that, since (1) it is wrong to kill innocent human beings, and (2) fetuses are innocent human beings, therefore (3) it is wrong to kill fetuses. For if "human being" is used in the same sense in both (1) and (2), then whichever of the two senses is meant, one of these premises is question-begging. And if it is used in different senses then the conclusion does not follow.

Thus, (1) is a generally accepted moral truth,[10] and one that does not beg the question about abortion, only if "human being" is used to mean something like "a full-fledged member of the moral community, who is also a member of the human species." I will call this the *moral*

10 The principle that it is always wrong to kill innocent human beings may be in need of other modifications, e.g., that it may be permissible to kill innocent human beings in order to save a larger number of equally innocent human beings; but we may ignore these complications here.

sense of "human being." It is not to be confused with what I will call the *genetic* sense, i.e., the sense in which any individual entity that belongs to the human species is a human being, regardless of whether or not it is rightly considered to be an equal member of the moral community. Premise (1) avoids begging the question only if the moral sense is intended; while premise (2) avoids it only if what is intended is the genetic sense.

Noonan argues for the classification of fetuses with human beings by pointing, first, to the presence of the human genome in the cell nuclei of the human conceptus from conception onwards; and secondly, to the potential capacity for rational thought.[11] But what he needs to show, in order to support his version of the traditional antiabortion argument, is that fetuses are human beings in the moral sense—the sense in which all human beings have full and equal moral rights. In the absence of any argument showing that whatever is genetically human is also morally human—and he gives none—nothing more than genetic humanity can be demonstrated by the presence of human chromosomes in the fetus's cell nuclei. And, as we will see, the strictly potential capacity for rational thought can at most show that the fetus may later *become* human in the moral sense.

Defining the Moral Community

Is genetic humanity sufficient for moral humanity? There are good reasons for not defining the moral community in this way. I would suggest that the moral community consists, in the first instance, of all *persons,* rather than all genetically human entities.[12] It is persons who invent moral

11 Noonan, "Deciding Who Is Human," p. 135.
12 From here on, I will use "human" to mean "genetically human," since the moral sense of the term seems closely connected to, and perhaps derived from, the assumption that genetic humanity is both necessary and sufficient for membership in the moral community.

rights, and who are (sometimes) capable of respecting them. It does not follow from this that only persons can have moral rights. However, persons are wise not to ascribe to entities that clearly are not persons moral rights that cannot in practice be respected without severely undercutting the fundamental moral rights of those who clearly are.

What characteristics entitle an entity to be considered a person? This is not the place to attempt a complete analysis of the concept of personhood; but we do not need such an analysis to explain why a fetus is not a person. All we need is an approximate list of the most basic criteria of personhood. In searching for these criteria, it is useful to look beyond the set of people with whom we are acquainted, all of whom are human. Imagine, then, a space traveler who lands on a new planet, and encounters organisms unlike any she has ever seen or heard of. If she wants to behave morally toward these organisms, she has somehow to determine whether they are people and thus have full moral rights, or whether they are things that she need not feel guilty about treating, for instance, as a source of food.

How should she go about making this determination? If she has some anthropological background, she might look for signs of religion, art, and the manufacturing of tools, weapons, or shelters, since these cultural traits have frequently been used to distinguish our human ancestors from prehuman beings, in what seems to be closer to the moral than the genetic sense of "human being." She would be right to take the presence of such traits as evidence that the extraterrestrials were persons. It would, however, be anthropocentric of her to take the absence of these traits as proof that they were not, since they could be people who have progressed beyond, or who have never needed, these particular cultural traits.

I suggest that among the characteristics which are central to the concept of personhood are the following:

1. *Sentience*—the capacity to have conscious experiences, usually including the capacity to experience pain and pleasure;

2. *Emotionality*—the capacity to feel happy, sad, angry, loving, etc.;

3. *Reason*—the capacity to solve new and relatively complex problems;

4. *The capacity to communicate,* by whatever means, messages of an indefinite variety of types; that is, not just with an indefinite number of possible contents, but on indefinitely many possible topics;

5. *Self-awareness*—having a concept of oneself, as an individual and/or as a member of a social group; and finally

6. *Moral agency*—the capacity to regulate one's own actions through moral principles or ideals.

It is difficult to produce precise definitions of these traits, let alone to specify universally valid behavioral indications that these traits are present. But let us assume that our explorer knows approximately what these six characteristics mean, and that she is able to observe whether or not the extraterrestrials possess these mental and behavioral capacities. How should she use her findings to decide whether or not they are persons?

An entity need not have *all* of these attributes to be a person. And perhaps none of them is absolutely necessary. For instance, the absence of emotion would not disqualify a being that was personlike in all other ways. Think, for instance, of two of the *Star Trek* characters, Mr Spock (who is half human and half alien), and Data (who is an android). Both are depicted as lacking the capacity to feel emotion; yet both are sentient, reasoning, communicative, self-aware moral agents, and unquestionably persons. Some people are unemotional; some cannot communicate well; some lack self-awareness; and some are not moral agents. It should not surprise us that many people do not

meet all of the criteria of personhood. Criteria for the applicability of complex concepts are often like this: none may be logically necessary, but the more criteria that are satisfied, the more confident we are that the concept is applicable. Conversely, the fewer criteria are satisfied, the less plausible it is to hold that the concept applies. And if none of the relevant criteria are met, then we may be confident that it does not.

Thus, to demonstrate that a fetus is not a person, all I need to claim is that an entity that has *none* of these six characteristics is not a person. Sentience is the most basic mental capacity, and the one that may have the best claim to being a necessary (though not sufficient) condition for personhood. Sentience can establish a claim to moral considerability, since sentient beings can be harmed in ways that matter to them; for instance, they can be caused to feel pain, or deprived of the continuation of a life that is pleasant to them. It is unlikely that an entirely insentient organism could develop the other mental and behavioral capacities that are characteristic of persons. Consequently, it is odd to claim that an entity that is not sentient, and that has never been sentient, is nevertheless a person. Persons who have permanently and irreparably lost all capacity for sentience, but who remain biologically alive, arguably still have strong moral rights by virtue of what they have been in the past. But small fetuses, which have not yet begun to have experiences, are not persons yet and do not have the rights that persons do.

The presumption that all persons have full and equal basic moral rights may be part of the very concept of a person. If this is so, then the concept of a person is in part a moral one; once we have admitted that X is a person, we have implicitly committed ourselves to recognizing X's right to be treated as a member of the moral community.[13] The claim that X is a *human being*

13 Alan Gewirth defends a similar claim, in *Reason and Morality* (University of Chicago Press, 1978).

may also be voiced as an appeal to treat X decently; but this is usually either because "human being" is used in the moral sense, or because of a confusion between genetic and moral humanity.

If 1–6 are the primary criteria of personhood, then genetic humanity is neither necessary nor sufficient for personhood. Some genetically human entities are not persons, and there may be persons who belong to other species. A man or woman whose consciousness his been permanently obliterated but who remains biologically alive is a human entity who may no longer be a person; and some unfortunate humans, who have never had any sensory or cognitive capacities at all, may not be people either. Similarly, an early fetus is a human entity which is not yet a person. It is not even minimally sentient, let alone capable of emotion, reason, sophisticated communication, self-awareness, or moral agency.[14] Thus, while it may be greatly valued as a future child, it does not yet have the claim to moral consideration that it may come to have later.

Moral agency matters to moral status, because it is moral agents who invent moral rights, and who can be obliged to respect them. Human beings have become moral agents from social necessity. Most social animals exist well enough, with no evident notion of a moral right. But human beings need moral rights, because we are not only highly social, but also sufficiently clever and self-interested to be capable of undermining our societies through violence and duplicity. For human persons, moral rights are essential for peaceful and mutually beneficial social life. So long as some moral agents are denied basic rights, peaceful existence is difficult, since moral agents justly resent being treated as something less. If animals of some terrestrial

species are found to be persons, or if alien persons come from other worlds, or if human beings someday invent machines whose mental and behavioral capacities make them persons, then we will be morally obliged to respect the moral rights of these nonhuman persons—at least to the extent that they are willing and able to respect ours in turn.

Although only those persons who are moral agents can participate directly in the shaping and enforcement of moral rights, they need not and usually do not ascribe moral rights only to themselves and other moral agents. Human beings are social creatures who naturally care for small children, and other members of the social community who are not currently capable of moral agency. Moreover, we are all vulnerable to the temporary or permanent loss of the mental capacities necessary for moral agency. Thus, we have self-interested as well as altruistic reasons for extending basic moral rights to infants and other sentient human beings who have already been born, but who currently lack some of these other mental capacities. These human beings, despite their current disabilities, are persons and members of the moral community.

But in extending moral rights to beings (human or otherwise) that have few or none of the morally significant characteristics of persons, we need to be careful not to burden human moral agents with obligations that they cannot possibly fulfill, except at unacceptably great cost to their own well-being and that of those they care about. Women often cannot complete unwanted pregnancies, except at intolerable mental, physical, and economic cost to themselves and their families. And heterosexual intercourse is too important a part of the social lives of most men and women to be reserved for times when pregnancy is an acceptable outcome. Furthermore, the world cannot afford the continued rapid population growth which is the inevitable consequence of prohibiting abortion, so long as contraception is neither very reliable nor available to everyone. If fetuses were persons, then

14 Fetal sentience is impossible prior to the development of neurological connections between the sense organs and the brain, and between the various parts of the brain involved in the processing of conscious experience. This stage of neurological development is currently thought to occur at some point in the late second or early third trimester.

they would have rights that must be respected, even at great social or personal cost. But given that early fetuses, at least, are unlike persons in the morally relevant respects, it is unreasonable to insist that they be accorded exactly the same moral and legal status.

Fetal Development and the Right to Life

Two questions arise regarding the application of these suggestions to the moral status of the fetus. First, if indeed fetuses are not yet persons, then might they nevertheless have strong moral rights based upon the degree to which they *resemble* persons? Secondly, to what extent, if any, does a fetus's potential to *become* a person imply that we ought to accord to it some of the same moral rights? Each of these questions requires comment.

It is reasonable to suggest that the more like a person something is—the more it appears to meet at least some of the criteria of personhood—the stronger is the case for according it a right to life, and perhaps the stronger its right to life is. That being the case, perhaps the fetus gradually gains a stronger right to life as it develops. We should take seriously the suggestion that, just as "the human individual develops biologically in a continuous fashion . . . the rights of a human person . . . develop in the same way."[15]

A seven-month fetus can apparently feel pain, and can respond to such stimuli as light and sound. Thus, it may have a rudimentary form of consciousness. Nevertheless, it is probably not as conscious, or as capable of emotion, as even a very young infant is; and it has as yet little or no capacity for reason, sophisticated intentional communication, or self-awareness. In these respects, even a late-term fetus is arguably less like a person than are many nonhuman animals.

Many animals (e.g., large-brained mammals such as elephants, cetaceans, or apes) are not only sentient, but clearly possessed of a degree of reason, and perhaps even of self-awareness. Thus, on the basis of its resemblance to a person, even a late-term fetus can have no more right to life than do these animals.

Animals may, indeed, plausibly be held to have some moral rights, and perhaps rather strong ones.[16] But it is impossible in practice to accord full and equal moral rights to all animals. When an animal poses a serious threat to the life or well-being of a person, we do not, as a rule, greatly blame the person for killing it; and there are good reasons for this species-based discrimination. Animals, however intelligent in their own domains, are generally not beings with whom we can reason; we cannot persuade mice not to invade our dwellings or consume our food. That is why their rights are necessarily weaker than those of a being who can understand and respect the rights of other beings.

But the probable sentience of late-term fetuses is not the only argument in favor of treating late abortion as a morally more serious matter than early abortion. Many—perhaps most—people are repulsed by the thought of needlessly aborting a late-term fetus. The late-term fetus has features which cause it to arouse in us almost the same powerful protective instinct as does a small infant.

This response needs to be taken seriously. If it were impossible to perform abortions early in pregnancy, then we might have to tolerate the mental and physical trauma that would be occasioned by the routine resort to late abortion. But where early abortion is safe, legal, and readily available to all women, it is not unreasonable to expect most women who wish to end a pregnancy to do so prior to the third trimester. Most women strongly prefer early to late abortion, because it is far less physically painful and emo-

---

15 Thomas L. Hayes, "A Biological View," *Commonweal*, 85 (March 17, 1967), pp. 677–8; cited by Daniel Callahan, in *Abortion: Law, Choice, and Morality* (London: Macmillan, 1970).

16 See, for instance, Tom Regan, *The Case for Animal Rights* (Berkeley: University of California Press, 1983).

tionally traumatic. Other things being equal, it is better for all concerned that pregnancies that are not to be completed should be ended as early as possible. Few women would consider ending a pregnancy in the seventh month in order to take a trip to Europe. If, however, a woman's own life or health is at stake, or if the fetus has been found to be so severely abnormal as to be unlikely to survive or to have a life worth living, then late abortion may be the morally best choice. For even a late-term fetus is not a person yet, and its rights must yield to those of the woman whenever it is impossible for both to be respected.

Potential Personhood and the Right to Life

We have seen that a presentient fetus does not yet resemble a person in ways which support the claim that it has strong moral rights. But what about its *potential*, the fact that if nurtured and allowed to develop it may eventually become a person? Doesn't that potential give it at least some right to life? The fact that something is a potential person may be a reason for not destroying it; but we need not conclude from this that potential people have a strong right to life. It may be that the feeling that it is better not to destroy a potential person is largely due to the fact that potential people are felt to be an invaluable resource, not to be lightly squandered. If every speck of dust were a potential person, we would be less apt to suppose that all potential persons have a right to become actual.

We do not need to insist that a potential person has no right to life whatever. There may be something immoral, and not just imprudent, about wantonly destroying potential people, when doing so isn't necessary. But even if a potential person does have some right to life, that right could not outweigh the right of a woman to obtain an abortion; for the basic moral rights of an actual person outweigh the rights of a merely potential person, whenever the two conflict. Since this may not be immediately obvious in the case of a human fetus, let us look at another case.

Suppose that our space explorer falls into the hands of an extraterrestrial civilization, whose scientists decide to create a few thousand new human beings by killing her and using some of her cells to create clones. We may imagine that each of these newly created women will have all of the original woman's abilities, skills, knowledge, and so on, and will also have an individual self-concept; in short, that each of them will be a bona fide (though not genetically unique) person. Imagine, further, that our explorer knows all of this, and knows that these people will be treated kindly and fairly. I maintain that in such a situation she would have the right to escape if she could, thus depriving all of these potential people of their potential lives. For her right to life outweighs all of theirs put together, even though they are all genetically human, and have a high probability of becoming people, if only she refrains from acting.

Indeed, I think that our space traveler would have a right to escape even if it were not her life which the aliens planned to take, but only a year of her freedom, or only a day. She would not be obliged to stay, even if she had been captured because of her own lack of caution—or even if she had done so deliberately, knowing the possible consequences. Regardless of why she was captured, she is not obliged to remain in captivity for *any* period of time in order to permit merely potential people to become actual people. By the same token, a woman's rights to liberty and the control of her own body outweigh whatever right to life a fetus may have merely by virtue of its potential personhood.

The Objection from Infanticide

One objection to my argument is that it appears to justify not only abortion, but also infanticide. A newborn infant is not much more personlike than a nine-month fetus, and thus it might appear that if late-term abortion is sometimes justified, then infanticide must also sometimes be justified. Yet most people believe that infanticide is a form of murder, and virtually never justified.

This objection is less telling than it may seem. There are many reasons why infanticide is more difficult to justify than abortion, even though neither fetuses nor newborn infants are clearly persons. In this period of history, the deliberate killing of newborns is virtually never justified. This is in part because newborns are so close to being persons that to kill them requires a very strong moral justification—as does the killing of dolphins, chimpanzees, and other highly personlike creatures. It is certainly wrong to kill such beings for the sake of convenience, or financial profit, or "sport." Only the most vital human needs, such as the need to defend one's own life and physical integrity, can provide a plausible justification for killing such beings.

In the case of an infant, there is no such vital need, since in the contemporary world there are usually other people who are eager to provide a good home for an infant whose own parents are unable or unwilling to care for it. Many people wait years for the opportunity to adopt a child, and some are unable to do so, even though there is every reason to believe that they would be good parents. The needless destruction of a viable infant not only deprives a sentient human being of life, but also deprives other persons of a source of great satisfaction, perhaps severely impoverishing *their* lives.

Even if an infant is unadoptable (e.g., because of some severe physical disability), it is still wrong to kill it. For most of us value the lives of infants, and would greatly prefer to pay taxes to support foster care and state institutions for disabled children, rather than to allow them to be killed or abandoned. So long as most people feel this way, and so long as it is possible to provide care for infants who are unwanted, or who have special needs that their parents cannot meet without assistance, it is wrong to let any infant die who has a chance of living a reasonably good life.

If these arguments show that infanticide is wrong, at least in today's world, then why don't they also show that late-term abortion is always wrong? After all, third-trimester fetuses are almost as personlike as infants, and many people value them and would prefer that they be preserved. As a potential source of pleasure to some family, a fetus is just as valuable as an infant. But there is an important difference between these two cases: once the infant is born, its continued life cannot pose any serious threat to the woman's life or health, since she is free to put it up for adoption or to place it in foster care. While she might, in rare cases, prefer that the child die rather than being raised by others, such a preference would not establish a right on her part.

In contrast, a pregnant woman's right to protect her own life and health outweighs other people's desire that the fetus be preserved—just as, when a person's life or health is threatened by an animal, and when the threat cannot be removed without killing the animal, that person's right to self-defense outweighs the desires of those who would prefer that the animal not be killed. Thus, while the moment of birth may mark no sharp discontinuity in the degree to which an infant resembles a person, it does mark the end of the mother's right to determine its fate. Indeed, if a late abortion can be safely performed without harming the fetus, she has in most cases no right to insist upon its death, for the same reason that she has no right to insist that a viable infant be killed or allowed to die.

It remains true that, on my view, neither abortion nor the killing of newborns is obviously a form of murder. Perhaps our legal system is correct in its classification of infanticide as murder, since no other legal category adequately expresses the force of our disapproval of this action. But some moral distinction remains, and it has important consequences. When a society cannot possibly care for all of the children who are born, without endangering the survival of adults and older children, allowing some infants to die may be the best of a bad set of options. Throughout history, most societies—from those that lived by gathering and hunting to the highly civilized Chinese, Japanese, Greeks, and Romans—have permitted infanticide under such unfortunate circumstances, regarding it as a necessary evil. It shows a lack of understanding to condemn these societies as morally benighted for this reason alone, since in the absence of safe and effective means of contraception and abortion, parents must sometimes have had no morally better options.

CONCLUSION

I have argued that fetuses are neither persons nor members of the moral community. Furthermore, neither a fetus's resemblance to a person, nor its potential for becoming a person, provides an adequate basis for the claim that it has a full and equal right to life. At the same time, there are medical as well as moral reasons for preferring early to late abortion when the pregnancy is unwanted.

Women, unlike fetuses, are undeniably persons and members of the human moral community. If unwanted or medically dangerous pregnancies never occurred, then it might be possible to respect women's basic moral rights, while at the same time extending the same basic rights to fetuses. But in the real world such pregnancies do occur—often despite the woman's best efforts to prevent them. Even if the perfect contraceptive were universally available, the continued occurrence of rape and incest would make access to abortion a vital human need. Because women are persons, and fetuses are not, women's rights to life, liberty, and physical integrity morally override whatever right to life it may be appropriate to ascribe to a fetus. Consequently, laws that deny women the right to obtain abortions, or that make safe early abortions difficult or impossible for some women to obtain, are an unjustified violation of basic moral and constitutional rights.

Review Questions

1. According to Warren, what is the standard anti-abortion argument, and what is the standard pro-choice response?
2. What objection does Warren make to Thomson's argument about the famous violinist?
3. Warren distinguishes between two senses of the term "human being." What are these two senses?
4. What are the characteristics of a person, according to Warren? Why isn't the fetus a person?
5. Besides saying that the fetus is not a person, what other reasons does Warren give for allowing abortions?
6. Warren grants that there are two problems with her account of the moral status of the fetus. What are these two problems, and how does she respond to them?

Discussion Questions

1. What is the moral status of a brain-dead human who is biologically alive but permanently unconscious? What is Warren's view? What do you think?
2. Explain Warren's position on the moral status of nonhuman animals. Do you agree with her? Why or why not?
3. Warren believes that there can be nonhuman persons—for example, alien beings, androids, and even robots—who think and act like humans. Are these beings persons with moral rights? Explain your position.
4. Do the rights of an actual person always outweigh the rights of a merely potential person? Can you think of any counterexamples?

An Argument That Abortion Is Wrong

DON MARQUIS

Don Marquis is professor of philosophy at the University of Kansas.

Marquis wants to show why abortion is seriously wrong, but he begins by granting a number of cases in which it is not wrong, including cases of rape, of abortion during the first fourteen days after conception, of threat to the woman's life, and an anencephalic fetus. After showing why the standard arguments fail to resolve the debate about abortion, he proceeds to his own argument: that abortion is wrong for the same reason that killing us is wrong; it is wrong because it deprives the fetus of a "future like ours," a future having valuable experiences, activities, projects, and enjoyments.

THE PURPOSE OF THIS ESSAY is to set out an argument for the claim that abortion, except perhaps in rare instances, is seriously wrong.[1] One reason for these exceptions is to eliminate from consideration cases whose ethical analysis should be controversial and detailed for clear-headed opponents of abortion. Such cases include abortion after rape and abortion during the first fourteen days after conception when there is an argument that the fetus is not definitely an individual. Another reason for making these exceptions is to allow for those cases in which the permissibility of abortion is compatible with the argument of this essay. Such cases include abortion when continuation of a pregnancy endangers a woman's life and abortion when the fetus is anencephalic. When I speak of the wrongness of abortion in this essay, a reader should presume the above qualifications. I mean by an abortion an action intended to bring about the death of a fetus for the sake of the woman who carries it. (Thus, as is standard on the literature on this subject, I eliminate spontaneous abortions from consideration.) I mean by a fetus a developing human being from the time of conception to the time of birth. (Thus, as is standard, I call embryos and zygotes, fetuses.)

The argument of this essay will establish that abortion is wrong for the same reason as killing a reader of this essay is wrong. I shall just assume, rather than establish, that killing you is seriously wrong. I shall make no attempt to offer a complete ethics of killing. Finally, I shall make no attempt to resolve some very fundamental and difficult general philosophical issues into which this analysis of the ethics of abortion might lead.

WHY THE DEBATE OVER ABORTION SEEMS INTRACTABLE

Symmetries that emerge from the analysis of the major arguments on either side of the abortion debate may explain why the abortion debate seems intractable. Consider the following standard anti-abortion argument: Fetuses are both

Source: Don Marquis, "An Argument that Abortion Is Wrong," from *Ethics in Practice,* ed. Hugh LaFollette, pp. 91–102. Copyright © 1997 Blackwell Publishers. Reprinted with permission.

1 This essay is an updated version of a view that first appeared in the *Journal of Philosophy* (1989). This essay incorporates attempts to deal with the objections of McInerney (1990), Norcross (1990), Shirley (1995), Steinbock (1992), and Paske (1994) to the original version of the view.

human and alive. Humans have the right to life. Therefore, fetuses have the right to life. Of course, women have the right to control their own bodies, but the right to life overrides the right of a woman to control her own body. Therefore, abortion is wrong.

Thomson's View

Judith Thomson (1971) has argued that even if one grants (for the sake of argument only) that fetuses have the right to life, this argument fails. Thomson invites you to imagine that you have been connected while sleeping, bloodstream to bloodstream, to a famous violinist. The violinist, who suffers from a rare blood disease, will die if disconnected. Thomson argues that you surely have the right to disconnect yourself. She appeals to our intuition that having to be in bed with a violinist for an indefinite period is too much for morality to demand. She supports this claim by noting that the body being used is *your* body, not the violinist's body. She distinguishes the right to life, which the violinist clearly has, from the right to use someone else's body when necessary to preserve one's life, which it is not at all obvious the violinist has. Because the case of pregnancy is like the case of the violinist, one is no more morally obligated to remain attached to a fetus than to remain attached to the violinist.

It is widely conceded that one can generate from Thomson's vivid case the conclusion that abortion is morally permissible when a pregnancy is due to rape (Warren, 1973, p. 49; and Steinbock, 1992, p. 79). But this is hardly a general right to abortion. Do Thomson's more general theses generate a more general right to an abortion? Thomson draws our attention to the fact that in a pregnancy, although a fetus uses a woman's body as a life-support system, a pregnant woman does not use a fetus's body as a life-support system. However, an opponent of abortion might draw our attention to the fact that in an abortion the life that is lost is the fetus's, not the woman's. This symmetry seems to leave us with a stand-off.

Thomson points out that a fetus's right to life does not entail its right to use someone else's body to preserve its life. However, an opponent of abortion might point out that a woman's right to use her own body does not entail her right to end someone else's life in order to do what she wants with her body. In reply, one might argue that a pregnant woman's right to control her own body doesn't come to much if it is wrong for her to take any action that ends the life of the fetus within her. However, an opponent of abortion can argue that the fetus's right to life doesn't come to much if a pregnant woman can end it when she chooses. The consequence of all of these symmetries seems to be a stand-off. But if we have the stand-off, then one might argue that we are left with a conflict of rights: a fetal right to life versus the right of a woman to control her own body. One might then argue that the right to life seems to be a stronger right than the right to control one's own body in the case of abortion because the loss of one's life is a greater loss than the loss of the right to control one's own body in one respect for nine months. Therefore, the right to life overrides the right to control one's own body and abortion is wrong. Considerations like these have suggested to both opponents of abortion and supporters of choice that a Thomsonian strategy for defending a general right to abortion will not succeed (Tooley, 1972; Warren, 1973; and Steinbock, 1992). In fairness, one must note that Thomson did not intend her strategy to generate a general moral permissibility of abortion.

Do Fetuses Have the Right to Life?

The above considerations suggest that whether abortion is morally permissible boils down to the question of whether fetuses have the right to life. An argument that fetuses either have or lack the right to life must be based upon some general criterion for having or lacking the right to life. Opponents of abortion, on the one hand, look around for the broadest possible plausible criterion, so that fetuses will fall under it. This explains why classic arguments against abortion appeal to the criterion of being human (Noonan, 1970; Beckwith, 1993). This criterion appears plausible: The claim that all humans, whatever their race, gender, religion or *age,* have the right to life seems evident enough. In addition, because the fetuses we are concerned with do not, after all, belong to another species, they are clearly human. Thus, the syllogism that generates the conclusion that fetuses have the right to life is apparently sound.

On the other hand, those who believe abortion is morally permissible wish to find a narrow, but plausible, criterion for possession of the right to life so that fetuses will fall outside of it. This explains, in part, why the standard pro-choice arguments in the philosophical literature appeal to the criterion of being a person (Feinberg, 1986; Tooley, 1972; Warren, 1973; Benn, 1973; Engelhardt, 1986). This criterion appears plausible: The claim that only persons have the right to life seems evident enough. Furthermore, because fetuses neither are rational nor possess the capacity to communicate in complex ways nor possess a concept of self that continues through time, no fetus is a person. Thus, the syllogism needed to generate the conclusion that no fetus possesses the right to life is apparently sound. Given that no fetus possesses the right to life, a woman's right to control her own body easily generates the general right to abortion. The existence of two apparently defensible syllogisms which support contrary conclusions helps to explain why partisans on both sides of the abortion dispute often regard their opponents as either morally depraved or mentally deficient.

Which syllogism should we reject? The anti-abortion syllogism is usually attacked by attacking its major premise: the claim that whatever is biologically human has the right to life. This premise is subject to scope problems because the class of the biologically human includes too much: human cancer-cell cultures are biologically human, but they do not have the right to life. Moreover, this premise also is subject to moral-relevance problems: the connection between the biological and the moral is merely assumed. It is hard to think of a good *argument* for such a connection. If one wishes to consider the category of "human" a moral category, as some people find it plausible to do in other contexts, then one is left with no way of showing that the fetus is fully human without begging the question. Thus, the classic anti-abortion argument appears subject to fatal difficulties.

These difficulties with the classic anti-abortion argument are well known and thought by many to be conclusive. The symmetrical difficulties with the classic pro-choice syllogism are not as well recognized. The pro-choice syllogism can be attacked by attacking its major premise: Only persons have the right to life. This premise is subject to scope problems because the class of persons includes too little: infants, the severely retarded, and some of the mentally ill seem to fall outside the class of persons as the supporter of choice understands the concept. The premise is also subject to moral-relevance problems: Being a person is understood by the pro-choicer as having certain psychological attributes. If the pro-choicer questions the connection between the biological and the moral, the opponent of abortion can question the connection between the psychological and the moral. If one wishes to consider "person" a moral category, as is often done, then one is left with no way of showing that the fetus is not a person without begging the question.

Pro-choicers appear to have resources for dealing with their difficulties that opponents of abortion lack. Consider their moral-relevance problem. A pro-choicer might argue that morality rests on contractual foundations and that only those who have the psychological attributes of persons are capable of entering into the moral contract and, as a consequence, being a member of the moral community. [This is essentially Engelhardt's (1986) view.] The great advantage of this contractarian approach to morality is that it seems far more plausible than any approach the anti-abortionist can provide. The great disadvantage of this contractarian approach to morality is that it adds to our earlier scope problems by leaving it unclear how we can have the duty not to inflict pain and suffering on animals.

Contractarians have tried to deal with their scope problems by arguing that duties to some individuals who are not persons can be justified even though those individuals are not contracting members of the moral community. For example, Kant argued that, although we do not have direct duties to animals, we "must practice kindness towards animals, for he who is cruel to animals becomes hard also in his dealings with men" (Kant, 1963, p. 240). Feinberg argues that infanticide is wrong, not because infants have the right to life, but because our society's protection of infants has social utility. If we do not treat infants with tenderness and consideration, then when they are persons they will be worse off and we will be worse off also (Feinberg, 1986, p. 271).

These moves only stave off the difficulties with the pro-choice view; they do not resolve them. Consider Kant's account of our obligations to animals. Kantians certainly know the difference between persons and animals. Therefore, no true Kantian would treat persons as she would treat animals. Thus, Kant's defense of our duties to animals fails to show that Kantians have a duty not to be cruel to animals. Consider Feinberg's attempt to show that infanticide is wrong even though no infant is a person. All Feinberg really shows is that it is a good idea to treat with care and consideration the infants we intend to keep. That is quite compatible with killing the infants we intend to discard. This point can be supported by an analogy with which any pro-choicer will agree. There are plainly good reasons to treat with care and consideration the fetuses we intend to keep. This is quite compatible with aborting those fetuses we intend to discard. Thus, Feinberg's account of the wrongness of infanticide is inadequate.

Accordingly, we can see that a contractarian defense of the pro-choice personhood syllogism fails. The problem arises because the contractarian cannot account for our duties to individuals who are not persons, whether these individuals are animals or infants. Because the pro-choicer wishes to adopt a narrow criterion for the right to life so that fetuses will not be included, the scope of her major premise is too narrow. Her problem is the opposite of the problem the classic opponent of abortion faces.

The argument of this section has attempted to establish, albeit briefly, that the classic anti-abortion argument and the pro-choice argument favored by most philosophers both face problems that are mirror images of one another. A stand-off results. The abortion debate requires a different strategy.

THE "FUTURE LIKE OURS" ACCOUNT OF THE WRONGNESS OF KILLING

Why do the standard arguments in the abortion debate fail to resolve the issue? The general principles to which partisans in the debate appeal are either truisms most persons would affirm in the absence of much reflection, or very general moral theories. All are subject to major problems. A different approach is needed.

Opponents of abortion claim that abortion is wrong because abortion involves killing someone like us, a human being who just happens to be very young. Supporters of choice claim that ending the life of a fetus is not in the same moral category as ending the life of an adult human being. Surely this controversy cannot be resolved in the absence of an account of what it is about killing us that makes killing us wrong. On the one hand, if we know what property we possess that makes killing us wrong, then we can ask whether fetuses have the same property. On the other hand, suppose that we do not know what it is about us that makes killing us wrong.

If this is so, we do not understand even easy cases in which killing is wrong. Surely, we will not understand the ethics of killing fetuses, for if we do not understand easy cases, then we will not understand hard cases. Both pro-choicer and anti-abortionist agree that it is obvious that it is wrong to kill us. Thus, a discussion of what it is about us that makes killing us not only wrong, but seriously wrong, seems to be the right place to begin a discussion of the abortion issue.

Who is primarily wronged by a killing? The wrong of killing is not primarily explained in terms of the loss to the family and friends of the victim. Perhaps the victim is a hermit. Perhaps one's friends find it easy to make new friends. The wrong of killing is not primarily explained in terms of the brutalization of the killer. The great wrong to the victim explains the brutalization, not the other way around. The wrongness of killing us is understood in terms of what killing does to us. Killing us imposes on us the misfortune of premature death. That misfortune underlies the wrongness.

Premature death is a misfortune because when one is dead, one has been deprived of life. This misfortune can be more precisely specified. Premature death cannot deprive me of my past life. That part of my life is already gone. If I die tomorrow or if I live thirty more years my past life will be no different. It has occurred on either alternative. Rather than my past, my death deprives me of my future, of the life that I would have lived if I had lived out my natural life span.

The loss of a future biological life does not explain the misfortune of death. Compare two scenarios: In the former I now fall into a coma from which I do not recover until my death in thirty years. In the latter I die now. The latter scenario does not seem to describe a greater misfortune than the former.

The loss of our future conscious life is what underlies the misfortune of premature death.

Not any future conscious life qualifies, however. Suppose that I am terminally ill with cancer. Suppose also that pain and suffering would dominate my future conscious life. If so, then death would not be a misfortune for me.

Thus, the misfortune of premature death consists of the loss to us of the future goods of consciousness. What are these goods? Much can be said about this issue, but a simple answer will do for the purposes of this essay. The goods of life are whatever we get out of life. The goods of life are those items toward which we take a "pro" attitude. They are completed projects of which we are proud, the pursuit of our goals, aesthetic enjoyments, friendships, intellectual pursuits, and physical pleasures of various sorts. The goods of life are what makes life worth living. In general, what makes life worth living for one person will not be the same as what makes life worth living for another. Nevertheless, the list of goods in each of our lives will overlap. The lists are usually different in different stages of our lives.

What makes the goods of my future good for me? One possible, but wrong, answer is my desire for those goods now. This answer does not account for those aspects of my future life that I now believe I will later value, but about which I am wrong. Neither does it account for those aspects of my future that I will come to value, but which I don't value now. What is valuable to the young may not be valuable to the middle-aged. What is valuable to the middle-aged may not be valuable to the old. Some of life's values for the elderly are best appreciated by the elderly. Thus it is wrong to say that the value of my future to me is just what I value now. What makes my future valuable to me are those aspects of my future that I will (or would) value when I will (or would) experience them, whether I value them now or not.

It follows that a person can believe that she will have a valuable future and be wrong. Furthermore, a person can believe that he will not have a valuable future and also be wrong. This is confirmed by our attitude toward many of the suicidal. We attempt to save the lives of the suicidal and to convince them that they have made an error in judgment. This does not mean that the future of an individual obtains value from the value that others confer on it. It means that, in some cases, others can make a clearer judgment of the value of a person's future *to that person* than the person herself. This often happens when one's judgment concerning the value of one's own future is clouded by personal tragedy. (Compare the views of McInerney, 1990, and Shirley, 1995.)

Thus, what is sufficient to make killing us wrong, in general, is that it causes premature death. Premature death is a misfortune. Premature death is a misfortune, in general, because it deprives an individual of a future of value. An individual's future will be valuable to that individual if that individual will come, or would come, to value it. We know that killing us is wrong. What makes killing us wrong, in general, is that it deprives us of a future of value. Thus, killing someone is wrong, in general, when it deprives her of a future like ours. I shall call this "an FLO."

ARGUMENTS IN FAVOR OF THE FLO THEORY

At least four arguments support this FLO account of the wrongness of killing.

The Considered Judgment Argument

The FLO account of the wrongness of killing is correct because it fits with our considered judgment concerning the nature of the misfortune of death. The analysis of the previous section is an exposition of the nature of this considered judgment. This judgment can be confirmed. If one were to ask individuals with AIDS or with incurable cancer about the nature of their misfortune, I believe that they would say or imply

that their impending loss of an FLO makes their premature death a misfortune. If they would not, then the FLO account would plainly be wrong.

The Worst of Crimes Argument

The FLO account of the wrongness of killing is correct because it explains why we believe that killing is one of the worst of crimes. My being killed deprives me of more than does my being robbed or beaten or harmed in some other way because my being killed deprives me of all of the value of my future, not merely part of it. This explains why we make the penalty for murder greater than the penalty for other crimes.

As a corollary the FLO account of the wrongness of killing also explains why killing an adult human being is justified only in the most extreme circumstances, only in circumstances in which the loss of life to an individual is outweighed by a worse outcome if that life is not taken. Thus, we are willing to justify killing in self-defense, killing in order to save one's own life, because one's loss if one does not kill in that situation is so very great. We justify killing in a just war for similar reasons. We believe that capital punishment would be justified if, by having such an institution, fewer premature deaths would occur. The FLO account of the wrongness of killing does not entail that killing is always wrong. Nevertheless, the FLO account explains both why killing is one of the worst of crimes and, as a corollary, why the exceptions to the wrongness of killing are so very rare. A correct theory of the wrongness of killing should have these features.

The Appeal to Cases Argument

The FLO account of the wrongness of killing is correct because it yields the correct answers in many life-and-death cases that arise in medicine and have interested philosophers.

Consider medicine first. Most people believe that it is not wrong deliberately to end the life of a person who is permanently unconscious.

Thus we believe that it is not wrong to remove a feeding tube or a ventilator from a permanently comatose patient, knowing that such a removal will cause death. The FLO account of the wrongness of killing explains why this is so. A patient who is permanently unconscious cannot have a future that she would come to value, whatever her values. Therefore, according to the FLO theory of the wrongness of killing, death could not, *ceteris paribus*, be a misfortune to her. Therefore, removing the feeding tube or ventilator does not wrong her.

By contrast, almost all people believe that it is wrong, *ceteris paribus*, to withdraw medical treatment from patients who are temporarily unconscious. The FLO account of the wrongness of killing also explains why this is so. Furthermore, these two unconsciousness cases explain why the FLO account of the wrongness of killing does not include present consciousness as a necessary condition for the wrongness of killing.

Consider now the issue of the morality of legalizing active euthanasia. Proponents of active euthanasia argue that if a patient faces a future of intractable pain and wants to die, then, *ceteris paribus*, it would not be wrong for a physician to give him medicine that she knows would result in his death. This view is so universally accepted that even the strongest *opponents* of active euthanasia hold it. The official Vatican view (Sacred Congregation, 1980) is that it is permissible for a physician to administer to a patient morphine sufficient (although no more than sufficient) to control his pain even if she foresees that the morphine will result in his death. Notice how nicely the FLO account of the wrongness of killing explains this unanimity of opinion. A patient known to be in severe intractable pain is presumed to have a future without positive value. Accordingly, death would not be a misfortune for him and an action that would (foreseeably) end his life would not be wrong.

Contrast this with the standard emergency medical treatment of the suicidal. Even though the suicidal have indicated that they want to die, medical personnel will act to save their lives. This supports the view that it is not the mere *desire* to enjoy an FLO which is crucial to our understanding of the wrongness of killing. *Having* an FLO is what is crucial to the account, although one would, of course, want to make an exception in the case of fully autonomous people who refuse life-saving medical treatment. Opponents of abortion can, of course, be willing to make an exception for fully autonomous fetuses who refuse life support.

The FLO theory of the wrongness of killing also deals correctly with issues that have concerned philosophers. It implies that it would be wrong to kill (peaceful) persons from outer space who come to visit our planet even though they are biologically utterly unlike us. Presumably, if they are persons, then they will have futures that are sufficiently like ours so that it would be wrong to kill them. The FLO account of the wrongness of killing shares this feature with the personhood views of the supporters of choice. Classical opponents of abortion who locate the wrongness of abortion somehow in the biological humanity of a fetus cannot explain this.

The FLO account does not entail that there is another species of animals whose members ought not to be killed. Neither does it entail that it is permissible to kill any non-human animal. On the one hand, a supporter of animals' rights might argue that since some non-human animals have a future of value, it is wrong to kill them also, or at least it is wrong to kill them without a far better reason than we usually have for killing non-human animals. On the other hand, one might argue that the futures of non-human animals are not sufficiently like ours for the FLO account to entail that it is wrong to kill them. Since the FLO account does not specify which properties a future of another individual must possess so that killing that individual is wrong, the FLO account is indeterminate with respect to this issue. The fact that the FLO account of the wrongness of killing does not give a determinate answer to this question is not a flaw in the theory. A sound ethical account should yield the right answers in the obvious cases; it should not be required to resolve every disputed question.

A major respect in which the FLO account is superior to accounts that appeal to the concept of person is the explanation the FLO account provides of the wrongness of killing infants. There was a class of infants who had futures that included a class of events that were identical to the futures of the readers of this essay. Thus, reader, the FLO account explains why it was as wrong to kill you when you were an infant as it is to kill you now. This account can be generalized to almost all infants. Notice that the wrongness of killing infants can be explained in the absence of an account of what makes the future of an individual sufficiently valuable so that it is wrong to kill that individual. The absence of such an account explains why the FLO account is indeterminate with respect to the wrongness of killing non-human animals.

If the FLO account is the correct theory of the wrongness of killing, then because abortion involves killing fetuses and fetuses have FLOs for exactly the same reasons that infants have FLOs, abortion is presumptively seriously immoral. This inference lays the necessary groundwork for a fourth argument in favor of the FLO account that shows that abortion is wrong.

The Analogy with Animals Argument

Why do we believe it is wrong to cause animals suffering? We believe that, in our own case and in the case of other adults and children, suffering is a misfortune. It would be as morally arbitrary to refuse to acknowledge that animal suffering is wrong as it would be to refuse to acknowledge that the suffering of persons of another race is wrong. It is, on reflection, suffering

that is a misfortune, not the suffering of white males or the suffering of humans. Therefore, infliction of suffering is presumptively wrong no matter on whom it is inflicted and whether it is inflicted on persons or nonpersons. Arbitrary restrictions on the wrongness of suffering count as racism or speciesism. Not only is this argument convincing on its own, but it is the only way of justifying the wrongness of animal cruelty. Cruelty toward animals is clearly wrong. (This famous argument is due to Singer, 1979.)

The FLO account of the wrongness of abortion is analogous. We believe that, in our own case and the cases of other adults and children, the loss of a future of value is a misfortune. It would be as morally arbitrary to refuse to acknowledge that the loss of a future of value to a fetus is wrong as to refuse to acknowledge that the loss of a future of value to Jews (to take a relevant twentieth-century example) is wrong. It is, on reflection, the loss of a future of value that is a misfortune; not the loss of a future of value to adults or loss of a future of value to non-Jews. To deprive someone of a future of value is wrong no matter on whom the deprivation is inflicted and no matter whether the deprivation is inflicted on persons or nonpersons. Arbitrary restrictions on the wrongness of this deprivation count as racism, genocide or ageism. Therefore, abortion is wrong. This argument that abortion is wrong should be convincing because it has the same form as the argument for the claim that causing pain and suffering to non-human animals is wrong. Since the latter argument is convincing, the former argument should be also. Thus, an analogy with animals supports the thesis that abortion is wrong.

REPLIES TO OBJECTIONS

The four arguments in the previous section establish that abortion is, except in rare cases, seriously immoral. Not surprisingly, there are objections to this view. There are replies to the four most important objections to the FLO argument for the immorality of abortion.

THE POTENTIALITY OBJECTION

The FLO account of the wrongness of abortion is a potentiality argument. To claim that a fetus *has* an FLO is to claim that a fetus now has the potential to be in a state of a certain kind in the future. It is not to claim that all ordinary fetuses *will* have FLOs. Fetuses who are aborted, of course, will not. To say that a standard fetus has an FLO is to say that a standard fetus either will have or would have a life it will or would value. To say that a standard fetus would have a life it would value is to say that it will have a life it will value if it does not die prematurely. The truth of this conditional is based upon the nature of fetuses (including the fact that they naturally age) and this nature concerns their potential.

Some appeals to potentiality in the abortion debate rest on unsound inferences. For example, one may try to generate an argument against abortion by arguing that because persons have the right to life, potential persons also have the right to life. Such an argument is plainly invalid as it stands. The premise one needs to add to make it valid would have to be something like: "If Xs have the right to Y, then potential Xs have the right to Y." This premise is plainly false. Potential presidents don't have the rights of the presidency; potential voters don't have the right to vote.

In the FLO argument potentiality is not used in order to bridge the gap between adults and fetuses as is done in the argument in the above paragraph. The FLO theory of the wrongness of killing adults is based upon the adult's potentiality to have a future of value. Potentiality is in the argument from the very beginning. Thus, the plainly false premise is not required. Accordingly, the use of potentiality in

the FLO theory is not a sign of an illegitimate inference.

The Argument from Interests

A second objection to the FLO account of the immorality of abortion involves arguing that even though fetuses have FLOs, nonsentient fetuses do not meet the minimum conditions for having any moral standing at all because they lack interests. Steinbock (1992, p. 5) has presented this argument clearly:

> Beings that have moral status must be capable of caring about what is done to them. They must be capable of being made, if only in a rudimentary sense, happy or miserable, comfortable or distressed. Whatever reasons we may have for preserving or protecting nonsentient beings, these reasons do not refer to their own interests. For without conscious awareness, beings cannot have interests. Without interests, they cannot have a welfare of their own. Without a welfare of their own, nothing can be done for their sake. Hence, they lack moral standing or status.

Medical researchers have argued that fetuses do not become sentient until after 22 weeks of gestation (Steinbock, 1992, p. 50). If they are correct, and if Steinbock's argument is sound, then we have both an objection to the FLO account of the wrongness of abortion and a basis for a view on abortion minimally acceptable to most supporters of choice.

Steinbock's conclusion conflicts with our settled moral beliefs. Temporarily unconscious human beings are nonsentient, yet no one believes that they lack either interests or moral standing. Accordingly, neither conscious awareness nor the capacity for conscious awareness is a necessary condition for having interests.

The counter-example of the temporarily unconscious human being shows that there is something internally wrong with Steinbock's argument. The difficulty stems from an ambiguity. One cannot *take* an interest in something without being capable of caring about what is done to it. However, something can be *in* someone's interest without that individual being capable of caring about it, or about anything. Thus, life support can be *in* the interests of a temporarily unconscious patient even though the temporarily unconscious patient is incapable of *taking* an interest in that life support. If this can be so for the temporarily unconscious patient, then it is hard to see why it cannot be so for the temporarily unconscious (that is, nonsentient) fetus who requires placental life support. Thus the objection based on interests fails.

The Problem of Equality

The FLO account of the wrongness of killing seems to imply that the degree of wrongness associated with each killing varies inversely with the victim's age. Thus, the FLO account of the wrongness of killing seems to suggest that it is far worse to kill a five-year-old than an 89-year-old because the former is deprived of far more than the latter. However, we believe that all persons have an equal right to life. Thus, it appears that the FLO account of the wrongness of killing entails an obviously false view (Paske, 1994).

However, the FLO account of the wrongness of killing does not, strictly speaking, imply that it is worse to kill younger people than older people. The FLO account provides an explanation of the wrongness of killing that is sufficient to account for the serious presumptive wrongness of killing. It does not follow that killings cannot be wrong in other ways. For example, one might hold, as does Feldman (1992, p. 184), that in addition to the wrongness of killing that has its basis in the future life of which the victim is deprived, killing an individual is also made wrong by the admirability of an individual's past behavior. Now the amount of admirability will presumably vary directly with age, whereas the amount of deprivation will vary inversely with age. This tends to equalize the wrongness of murder.

However, even if, *ceteris paribus,* it is worse to kill younger persons than older persons, there are good reasons for adopting a doctrine of the

legal equality of murder. Suppose that we tried to estimate the seriousness of a crime of murder by appraising the value of the FLO of which the victim had been deprived. How would one go about doing this? In the first place, one would be confronted by the old problem of interpersonal comparisons of utility. In the second place, estimation of the value of a future would involve putting oneself, not into the shoes of the victim at the time she was killed, but rather into the shoes the victim would have worn had the victim survived, and then estimating from that perspective the worth of that person's future. This task seems difficult, if not impossible. Accordingly, there are reasons to adopt a convention that murders are equally wrong.

Furthermore, the FLO theory, in a way, explains why we do adopt the doctrine of the legal equality of murder. The FLO theory explains why we regard murder as one of the worst of crimes, since depriving someone of a future like ours deprives her of more than depriving her of anything else. This gives us a reason for making the punishment for murder very harsh, as harsh as is compatible with civilized society. One should not make the punishment for younger victims harsher than that. Thus, the doctrine of the equal legal right to life does not seem to be incompatible with the FLO theory.

The Contraception Objection

The strongest objection to the FLO argument for the immorality of abortion is based on the claim that, because contraception results in one less FLO, the FLO argument entails that contraception, indeed, abstention from sex when conception is possible, is immoral. Because neither contraception nor abstention from sex when conception is possible is immoral, the FLO account is flawed.

There is a cogent reply to this objection. If the argument of the early part of this essay is correct, then the central issue concerning the morality of abortion is the problem of whether fetuses are individuals who are members of the class of individuals whom it is seriously presumptively wrong to kill. The properties of being human and alive, of being a person, and of having an FLO are criteria that participants in the abortion debate have offered to mark off the relevant class of individuals. The central claim of this essay is that having an FLO marks off the relevant class of individuals. A defender of the FLO view could, therefore, reply that since, at the time of contraception, there is no individual to have an FLO, the FLO account does not entail that contraception is wrong. The wrong of killing is primarily a wrong to the individual who is killed; at the time of contraception there is no individual to be wronged.

However, someone who presses the contraception objection might have an answer to this reply. She might say that the sperm and egg are the individuals deprived of an FLO at the time of contraception. Thus, there are individuals whom contraception deprives of an FLO and if depriving an individual of an FLO is what makes killing wrong, then the FLO theory entails that contraception is wrong.

There is also a reply to this move. In the case of abortion, an objectively determinate individual is the subject of harm caused by the loss of an FLO. This individual is a fetus. In the case of contraception, there are far more candidates (see Norcross, 1990). Let us consider some possible candidates in order of the increasing number of individuals harmed: (1) The single harmed individual might be the combination of the particular sperm and the particular egg that would have united to form a zygote if contraception had not been used. (2) The two harmed individuals might be the particular sperm itself, and, in addition, the ovum itself that would have physically combined to form the zygote. (This is modeled on the double homicide of two persons who would otherwise in a short time fuse. (1) is modeled on harm to a single entity some of whose parts are not physically contiguous, such as a university.) (3) The many harmed individuals might be the millions of *combina-*

tions of sperm and the released ovum whose (small) chances of having an FLO were reduced by the successful contraception. (4) The even larger class of harmed individuals (larger by one) might be the class consisting of all of the individual sperm in an ejaculate and, in addition, the individual ovum released at the time of the successful contraception. (1) through (4) are all candidates for being the subject(s) of harm in the case of successful contraception or abstinence from sex. Which should be chosen? Should we hold a lottery? There seems to be no non-arbitrarily determinate subject of harm in the case of successful contraception. But if there is no such subject of harm, then no determinate thing was harmed. If no determinate thing was harmed, then (in the case of contraception) no wrong has been done. Thus, the FLO account of the wrongness of abortion does not entail that contraception is wrong.

CONCLUSION

This essay contains an argument for the view that, except in unusual circumstances, abortion is seriously wrong. Deprivation of an FLO explains why killing adults and children is wrong. Abortion deprives fetuses of FLOs. Therefore, abortion is wrong. This argument is based on an account of the wrongness of killing that is a result of our considered judgment of the nature of the misfortune of premature death. It accounts for why we regard killing as one of the worst of crimes. It is superior to alternative accounts of the wrongness of killing that are intended to provide insight into the ethics of abortion. This account of the wrongness of killing is supported by the way it handles cases in which our moral judgments are settled. This account has an analogue in the most plausible account of the wrongness of causing animals to suffer. This account makes no appeal to religion. Therefore, the FLO account shows that abortion, except in rare instances, is seriously wrong.

References

Beckwith, F. J., *Politically Correct Death: Answering Arguments for Abortion Rights* (Grand Rapids, Michigan: Baker Books, 1993).

Benn, S. I., "Abortion, infanticide, and respect for persons," *The Problem of Abortion,* ed. J. Feinberg (Belmont, California: Wadsworth, 1973), pp. 92–104.

Engelhardt, Jr, H. T., *The Foundations of Bioethics* (New York: Oxford University Press, 1986).

Feinberg, J., "Abortion," *Matters of Life and Death: New Introductory Essays in Moral Philosophy,* ed. T. Regan (New York: Random House, 1986).

Feldman, F., *Confrontations with the Reaper: A Philosophical Study of the Nature and Value of Death* (New York: Oxford University Press, 1992).

Kant, I., *Lectures on Ethics,* tr. L. Infeld (New York: Harper, 1963).

Marquis, D. B., "A future like ours and the concept of person: a reply to McInerney and Paske," *The Abortion Controversy: A Reader,* ed. L. P. Pojman and F. J. Beckwith (Boston: Jones and Bartlett, 1994), pp. 354–68.

———, "Fetuses, futures and values: a reply to Shirley," *Southwest Philosophy Review,* 11 (1995): 263–5.

———, "Why abortion is immoral," *Journal of Philosophy,* 86 (1989): 183–202.

McInerney, P., "Does a fetus already have a future like ours?," *Journal of Philosophy,* 87 (1990): 264–8.

Noonan, J., "An almost absolute value in history," in *The Morality of Abortion,* ed. J. Noonan (Cambridge, Massachusetts: Harvard University Press).

Norcross, A., "Killing, abortion, and contraception: a reply to Marquis," *Journal of Philosophy,* 87 (1990): 268–77.

Paske, G., "Abortion and the neo-natal right to life: a critique of Marquis's futurist argument," *The Abortion Controversy: A Reader,* ed. L. P. Pojman and F. J. Beckwith (Boston: Jones and Bartlett, 1994), pp. 343–53.

Sacred Congregation for the Propagation of the Faith, *Declaration on Euthanasia* (Vatican City, 1980).

Shirley, E. S., "Marquis' argument against abortion: a critique," *Southwest Philosophy Review,* 11 (1995): 79–89.

Singer, P., "Not for humans only: the place of nonhumans in environmental issues," *Ethics and Problems of the 21st Century,* ed. K. E. Goodpaster and K. M. Sayre (South Bend: Notre Dame University Press, 1979).

Steinbock, B., *Life Before Birth: The Moral and Legal Status of Embryos and Fetuses* (New York: Oxford University Press, 1992).

Thomson, J. J., "A defense of abortion," *Philosophy and Public Affairs,* 1 (1971): 47–66.

Tooley, M., "Abortion and infanticide," *Philosophy and Public Affairs,* 2 (1972): 37–65.

Warren, M. A., "On the moral and legal status of abortion," *Monist,* 57 (1973): 43–61.

Review Questions

1. What exceptions does Marquis allow to his claim that abortion is seriously wrong? Why does he make these exceptions?
2. What "symmetries" does Marquis find in the abortion debate? Why do these make the debate seem intractable?
3. Why is killing a person wrong according to Marquis?
4. State and explain the four arguments Marquis uses to support his account of the wrongness of killing.
5. What is the potentiality objection, and how does Marquis respond to it?
6. State and explain Steinbock's argument from interests. How does Marquis reply?

7. What is the problem of equality? How does Marquis deal with it?
8. Explain the contraception objection and Marquis's reply.

Discussion Questions

1. There seem to be a number of cases in which the fetus does not have a "future like ours" besides the case of the anencephalic fetus that Marquis mentions. For example, the fetus can be deformed in other ways or have a genetic disease. Or perhaps the child will have abusive parents and a life full of suffering. Does Marquis have to grant that abortion is not wrong in all these cases where the fetus does not have a "future like ours"? Explain your answer.

2. Is the wrongness of killing a matter of degree, such that killing a person at the end of her life is not as wrong as killing a young person? Or is killing the old and the young equally wrong? What is Marquis's position on this? What do you think?

3. Is it wrong to kill nonhuman animals? Why doesn't Marquis take a position on this? What is your view?

4. In his reply to the contraception objection, Marquis assumes that the fetus is one individual. But when the zygote divides into twins there are two individuals, not one. Does twinning pose a problem for Marquis or not? Why or why not?

Abortion and the "Feminine Voice"

CELIA WOLF-DEVINE

Celia Wolf-Devine is professor of philosophy at Stonehill College in Massachusetts.

Wolf-Devine argues that the "feminine voice" in morality that rejects the male emphasis on individuality, autonomy, justice, and rights, and instead is concerned with an ethics of care for particular others, says that abortion is clearly to be avoided. In defending this position, Wolf-Devine attacks Thomson, Warren, Nel Noddings, and other women who support the right of women to have abortions.

A GROWING NUMBER of feminists now seek to articulate the "feminine voice," to draw attention to women's special strengths, and to correct the systematic devaluation of these by our

Source: Celia Wolf-Devine, "Abortion and the 'Feminine Voice'," from *Public Affairs Quarterly*, Vol. 3, No. 3 (July 1989). Reprinted with permission.

male-dominated society. Carol Gilligan's book, *In a Different Voice,* was especially important to the emergence of this strain of feminist thought. It was her intention to help women identify more positively with their own distinctive style of reasoning about ethics, instead of feeling that there is something wrong with them because they do not think like men (as Kohlberg's and

Freud's theories would imply). Inspired by her work, feminists . . . have tried to articulate further the feminine voice in moral reasoning. . . . When properly transformed by a feminist consciousness, women's different characteristics can, they suggest, be productive of new social visions.

Similar work is also being done by feminists who try to correct for masculine bias in other areas such as our conception of human nature, the way we view the relationship between people and nature, and the kinds of paradigms we employ in thinking about society.

Some of those engaged in this enterprise hold that women *by nature* possess certain valuable traits that men do not, but more frequently, they espouse the weaker position that, on the whole, the traits they label "feminine" are more common among women (for reasons which are at least partly cultural), but that they also can be found in men, and that they should be encouraged as good traits for a human being to have, regardless of sex.

Virtually all of those feminists who are trying to reassert the value of the feminine voice, also express the sort of unqualified support for free access to abortion which has come to be regarded as a central tenet of feminist "orthodoxy." What I wish to argue in this paper is that: (1) abortion is, by their own accounts, clearly a masculine response to the problems posed by an unwanted pregnancy, and is thus highly problematic for those who seek to articulate and defend the "feminine voice" as the proper mode of moral response, and that (2) on the contrary the "feminine voice" as it has been articulated generates a strong presumption against abortion as a way of responding to an unwanted pregnancy.[1]

---

1 A strong presumption against abortion is not, of course, the same thing as an absolute ban on all abortions. I do not attempt here to resolve the really hard cases; it is not clear that the feminine voice (at least as it has been articulated so far) is sufficiently fine-grained to tell us exactly where to draw the line in such cases.

These conclusions, I believe, can be argued without relying on a precise determination of the moral status of the fetus. A case at least can be made that the fetus is a person since it is biologically a member of the human species and will, in time, develop normal human abilities. Whether the burden of proof rests on those who defend the personhood of the fetus, or on those who deny it, is a matter of moral methodology, and for that reason will depend in part on whether one adopts a masculine or feminine approach to moral issues.

I. MASCULINE VOICE/ FEMININE VOICE

A. Moral Reasoning

According to Gilligan, girls, being brought up by mothers, identify with them, while males must define themselves through separation from their mothers. As a result, girls have "a basis for empathy built into their primary definition of self in a way that boys do not."[2] Thus while masculinity is defined by separation and threatened by intimacy, femininity is defined through attachment and threatened by separation; girls come to understand themselves as imbedded within a network of personal relationships.

A second difference concerns attitudes toward general rules and principles. Boys tend to play in larger groups than girls, and become "increasingly fascinated with the legal elaboration of rules, and the development of fair procedures for adjudicating conflicts."[3] We thus find men conceiving of morality largely in terms of adjudicating fairly between the conflicting rights of self-assertive individuals.

Girls play in smaller groups, and accord a greater importance to relationships than to following rules. They are especially sensitive to the

---

2 See Carol Gilligan, *In a Different Voice* (Cambridge, MA: Harvard University Press, 1982), p. 8.
3 Ibid., p. 10.

needs of the particular other, instead of emphasizing impartiality, which is more characteristic of the masculine perspective. They think of morality more in terms of having responsibilities for taking care of others, and place a high priority upon preserving the network of relationships which makes this possible. While the masculine justice perspective requires detachment, the feminine care perspective sees detachment and separation as themselves the moral problem. . . .

The feminine voice in ethics attends to the particular other, thinks in terms of responsibilities to care for others, is sensitive to our interconnectedness, and strives to preserve relationships. It contrasts with the masculine voice, which speaks in terms of justice and rights, stresses consistency and principles, and emphasizes the autonomy of the individual and impartiality in one's dealings with others.

B. Mind, Body, and Nature

Feminist writers have also discovered a masculine bias in the way we think of mind and body and the relationship between them. A large number of feminists, for example, regard radical mind-body dualism as a masculine way of understanding human nature. Alison Jaggar, for example, criticizes what she calls "normative dualism" for being "male biased,"[4] and defines "normative dualism" as "the belief that what is especially valuable about human beings is a particular 'mental' capacity, the capacity for rationality."[5] . . .

Many feminists hold that mind-body dualism which sees mind as transcendent to and superior to the body, leads to the devaluation of both women and nature. For the transcendent mind is conceived as masculine, and women, the body and nature assigned an inferior and subservient status. As Rosemary Radford Reuther puts it:

The woman, the body and the world are the lower half of a dualism that must be declared posterior to, created by, subject to, and ultimately alien to the nature of (male) consciousness in whose image man made his God.[6]

Women are to be subject to men, and nature may be used by man in any way he chooses. Thus the male ideology of transcendent dualism sanctions unlimited technological manipulation of nature; nature is an alien object to be conquered. . . .

Feminists who stress the deep affinities between feminism and the ecology movement are often called "ecofeminists." Stephanie Leland, radical feminist and co-editor of a recent collection of ecofeminist writings, has explained that:

Ecology is universally defined as the study of the balance and interrelationship of all life on earth. The motivating force behind feminism is the expression of the feminine principle. As the essential impulse of the feminine principle is the striving towards balance and interrelationship, it follows that feminism and ecology are inextricably connected.[7]

The masculine urge is, she says, to "separate, discriminate and control," while the feminine impulse is "towards belonging, relationship and letting be."[8] The urge to discriminate leads, she thinks, to the need to dominate "in order to feel secure in the choice of a particular set of differences."[9] The feminine attitude springs from a more holistic view of the human person and sees us as imbedded in nature rather than standing over and above it. It entails a more egalitarian attitude, regarding the needs of other creatures as important and deserving of consideration. It seeks to "let be" rather than to control, and

4 AIison Jaggar, *Feminist Politics and Human Nature* (Totowa, N.J.: Rowman & Alanheld, 1983), p. 46.
5 Ibid., p. 28.

6 Rosemary Radford Reuther, *New Woman, New Earth* (New York: The Seabury Press, 1975), p. 195.
7 Stephanie Leland and Leonie Caldecott (eds.), *Reclaim the Earth: Women Speak out for Life on Earth* (London: The Women's Press, 1983), p. 72. . . .
8 Ibid., p. 71.
9 Ibid., p. 69.

maintains a pervasive awareness of the interconnectedness of all things and the need to preserve this if all are to flourish.

Interconnectedness, which we found to be an important theme in feminist ethics, thus reappears in the writings of the ecofeminists as one of the central aspects of the feminine attitude toward nature.

C. Paradigms of Social Life

Feminists' descriptions of characteristically masculine and feminine paradigms of social life center around two different focuses. Those influenced by Gilligan tend to stress the contrast between individualism (which they take to be characteristic of the masculine "justice tradition") and the view of society as "a web of relationships sustained by a process of communication" (which they take to characterize the feminine "care perspective"). According to them, the masculine paradigm sees society as a collection of self-assertive individuals seeking rules which will allow them to pursue their own goals without interfering with each other. The whole contractarian tradition from Locke and Hobbes through Rawls is thus seen as a masculine paradigm of social life; we are only connected to others and responsible to them through our own choice to relinquish part of our autonomy in favor of the state. The feminine care perspective guides us to think about societal problems in a different way. We are already imbedded in a network of relationships, and must never exploit or hurt the other. We must strive to preserve those relationships as much as possible without sacrificing the integrity of the self.

The ecofeminists, pacifist feminists, and those whose starting point is a rejection of dualism, tend to focus more on the contrast between viewing social relationships in terms of hierarchy, power, and domination (the masculine paradigm) and viewing them in a more egalitarian and nonviolent manner (the feminine one).

Feminists taking this position range from the moderate ones who believe that masculine social thought tends to be more hierarchical than feminine thought, to the extreme radicals who believe males are irredeemably aggressive and dominating, and prone to violence in order to preserve their domination.

The more moderate characterization of masculine social thought would claim that men tend to prefer a clear structure of authority; they want to know who is in control and have a clear set of procedures or rules for resolving difficult cases. The more extreme view, common among ecofeminists and a large number of radical feminists, is that males seek to establish and maintain patriarchy (systematic domination by males) and use violence to maintain their control. These feminists thus see an affinity between feminism (which combats male violence against women) and the pacifist movement (which does so on a more global scale). . . . .

II. ABORTION

A person who had characteristically masculine traits, attitudes and values as defined above would very naturally choose abortion, and justify it ethically in the same way in which most feminists do. Conversely, a person manifesting feminine traits, attitudes and values would not make such a choice, or justify it in that way.

According to the ecofeminists, the masculine principle is insensitive to the interconnectedness of all life; it strives to discriminate, separate and control. It does not respect the natural cycles of nature, but objectifies it, and imposes its will upon it through unrestrained technological manipulation. Such a way of thinking would naturally lead to abortion. If the woman does not *want* to be pregnant, she has recourse to an operation involving highly sophisticated technology in order to defend her control of her body. This fits the characterization of the masculine principle perfectly.

Abortion is a separation—a severing of a life-preserving connection between the woman and the fetus. It thus fails to respect the interconnectedness of all life. Nor does it respect the natural cycles of nature. The mother and the developing child together form a delicately balanced ecosystem with the woman's entire hormonal system geared towards sustaining the pregnancy. The abortionist forces the cervical muscles (which have become thick and hard in order to hold in the developing fetus) open and disrupts her hormonal system by removing it.

Abortion has something further in common with the behavior ecofeminists and pacifist feminists take to be characteristically masculine; it shows a willingness to use violence in order to maintain control. The fetus is destroyed by being pulled apart by suction, cut in pieces, or poisoned. It is not merely killed inadvertently as fish might be by toxic wastes, but it is deliberately targeted for destruction. . . . This point was recently brought home to me by a Quaker woman who had reached the conclusion that the abortion she had had was contrary to her pacifist principles. She said, "we must seek peaceableness both within and without."

In terms of social thought, again, it is the masculine models which are most frequently employed in thinking about abortion. If masculine thought is naturally hierarchical and oriented towards power and control, then the interests of the fetus (who has no power) would naturally be suppressed in favor of the interests of the mother. But to the extent that feminist social thought is egalitarian, the question must be raised of why the mother's interests should prevail over the child's.

Feminist thought about abortion has, in addition, been deeply pervaded by the individualism which they so ardently criticize. The woman is supposed to have the sole authority to decide the outcome of the pregnancy. But what of her interconnectedness with the child and with others? Both she and the unborn child already exist within a network of relationships ranging from the closest ones—the father, grandparents, siblings, uncles and aunts, and so on—to ones with the broader society—including the mother's friends, employer, employees, potential adoptive parents, taxpayers who may be asked to fund the abortion or subsidize the child, and all the numerous other people affected by her choice. To dismiss this already existing network of relationships as irrelevant to the mother's decision is to manifest the sort of social atomism which feminist thinkers condemn as characteristically masculine.

Those feminists who are seeking to articulate the feminine voice in ethics also face a *prima facie* inconsistency between an ethics of care and abortion. Quite simply, abortion is a failure to care for one living being who exists in a particularly intimate relationship to oneself. If empathy, nurturance, and taking responsibility for caring for others are characteristic of the feminine voice, then abortion does not appear to be a feminine response to an unwanted pregnancy. If, as Gilligan says, "an ethic of care rests on the premise of non-violence—that no one should be hurt,"[10] then surely the feminine response to an unwanted pregnancy would be to try to find a solution which does not involve injury to anyone, including the unborn.

"Rights" have been invoked in the abortion controversy in a bewildering variety of ways, ranging from the "right to life" to the "right to control one's body." But clearly those who defend unrestricted access to abortion in terms of such things as the woman's right to privacy or her right to control her body are speaking the language of an ethics of justice rather than an ethics of care. For example, Judith Jarvis Thomson's widely read article "A Defense of Abortion"[11] treats the moral issue involved in abortion as a conflict between the rights of the fetus and the mother's rights over her own

10 Gilligan, op. cit., p. 174.
11 Judith Jarvis Thomson, "A Defense of Abortion," *Philosophy and Public Affairs,* vol. 1 (1971), pp. 47–66.

body. Mary Anne Warren also sees the issue in terms of a conflict of rights, but since the fetus does not meet her criteria for being a person, she weighs the woman's rights to "freedom, happiness and self-determination" against the rights of other people in the society who would like to see the fetus preserved for whatever reason.[12] And, insofar as she appeals to consciousness, reasoning, self-motivated activity, the capacity to communicate, and the presence of self-concepts and self-awareness as criteria of personhood, she relies on the kind of opposition between mind and nature criticized by many feminists as masculine. In particular, she is committed to what Jaggar calls "normative dualism"—the view that what is especially valuable about humans is their mental capacity for rational thought.

It is rather striking that feminists defending abortion lapse so quickly into speaking in the masculine voice. Is it because they feel they must do so in order to be heard in our male dominated society, or is it because no persuasive defense of abortion can be constructed from within the ethics of care tradition? We now consider several possible "feminine voice" defenses of abortion.

III. POSSIBLE RESPONSES AND REPLIES

Among the feminists seeking to articulate and defend the value of the feminine voice, very few have made any serious attempt to grapple with abortion. The writings of the ecofeminists and the pacifist feminists abound with impassioned defenses of such values as non-violence, a democratic attitude towards the needs of all living things, letting others be and nurturing them, and so on, existing side by side with impassioned defenses of "reproductive rights." They

see denying women access to abortion as just another aspect of male domination and violence against women.

This will not do for several reasons. First, it is not true that males are the chief opponents of abortion. Many women are strongly opposed to it. The pro-life movement at every level is largely composed of women. For example, as of May 1988, 38 of the state delegates to the National Right to Life Board of Directors were women, and only 13 were men. Indeed . . . the pro-life movement has mobilized into political action an enormous number of women who were never politically active before. And a Gallup poll in 1981 found that 51% of women surveyed believed a person is present at conception, compared with only 33% of the men. The pro-life movement, thus, cannot be dismissed as representing male concerns and desires only. Granted, a pro-choice feminist could argue that women involved in the pro-life movement suffer from "colonized minds," but this sort of argument clearly can be made to cut both directions. After all, many of the strongest supporters of "reproductive rights" have been men—ranging from the Supreme Court in *Roe v. Wade* to the Playboy Philosopher.

Secondly, terms like violence and domination are used far too loosely by those who condemn anti-abortion laws. If there are laws against wife abuse, does this mean that abusive husbands are being subjected to domination and violence? One does not exercise violence against someone merely by crossing his or her will, or even by crossing his or her will and backing this up by threats of legal retribution.

Finally, those who see violence and domination in laws against abortion, but not in abortion itself, generally fail to look at the nature of the act itself, and thus fail to judge that act in light of their professed values and principles. This is not surprising; abortion is a bloody and distressing thing to contemplate. But one cannot talk about it intelligently without being willing to look concretely at the act itself.

12 Mary Anne Warren, "On the Moral and Legal Status of Abortion," *The Monist*, vol. 57 (January, 1973), reprinted in Wasserstrom, *Today's Moral Problems* (New York: Macmillan, 1985), p. 448.

One line of thought is suggested by Gilligan, who holds that at the highest level of moral development, we must balance our responsibility to care for others against our need to care for ourselves. Perhaps we could, then, see the woman who has an abortion as still being caring and nurturing in that she is acting out of a legitimate care for herself. This is an implausible view of the actual feelings of women who undergo abortions. They may believe they are "doing something for themselves" in the sense of doing what they must do to safeguard their legitimate interests. But the operation is more naturally regarded as a violation of oneself than as a nurturing of oneself. This has been noted, even by feminists who support permissive abortion laws. For example, Carolyn Whitbeck speaks of "the unappealing prospect of having someone scraping away at one's core," and Adrienne Rich says that "Abortion is violence: a deep, desperate violence inflicted by a woman upon, first of all, herself."

We here come up against the problem that a directive to care, to nurture, to take responsibility for others, and so on, provides a moral orientation, but leaves unanswered many important questions and hence provides little guidance in problem situations. What do we do when caring for one person involves being uncaring toward another? How widely must we extend our circle of care? Are some kinds of not caring worse than others? Is it caring to give someone what they want even though it may be bad for them?

Thinking in terms of preserving relationships suggests another possible "feminine" defense of abortion—namely that the woman is striving to preserve her interconnectedness with her family, husband, or boyfriend. Or perhaps she is concerned to strengthen her relationship with her other children by having enough time and resources to devote to their care. To simply tell a woman to preserve *all* her existing relationships is not the answer. Besides the fact that it may not be possible (women *do* sometimes have to sever relationships), it is not clear that it would be desirable even if it were possible. Attempting

to preserve our existing relationships has conservative tendencies in several unfortunate ways. It fails to invite us to reflect critically on whether those relationships are good, healthy or worthy of preservation. It also puts the unborn at a particular disadvantage, since the mother's relationship with him or her is just beginning, while her relationships with others have had time to develop. And not only the unborn, but any needy stranger who shows up at our door can be excluded on the grounds that caring for them would disrupt our existing pattern of relationships. Thus the care perspective could degenerate into a rationalization for a purely tribal morality; I take care of myself and my friends.

But how are decisions about severing relationships to be made? One possibility is suggested by Gilligan in a recent article. She looks at the network of connections within which the woman who is considering abortion finds herself entangled, and says "to ask what actions constitute care or are more caring directs attention to the parameters of connection and the *costs of detachment* . . . (emphasis added)."[13] Thus, the woman considering abortion should reflect upon the comparative costs of severing various relationships. This method of decision, however, makes her vulnerable to emotional and psychological pressure from others, by encouraging her to sever whichever connection is easiest to break (the squeaky wheel principle).[14]

But perhaps we can lay out some guidelines (or, at least, rules of thumb) for making these difficult decisions. One way we might reason, from the point of view of the feminine voice, is that since preserving interconnectedness is good, we should prefer a short term estrangement to an irremediable severing of relation-

13 Carol Gilligan, "Moral Orientation and Moral Development" in Kittay and Meyers, (eds.) *Women and Moral Theory* (Minneapolis: University of Minnesota, 1987), p. 24.
14 This was evident in the reasoning of the women in Gilligan's case studies, many of whom had abortions in order to please or placate other significant persons in their lives. ED.

ship. And we should choose an action which *may* cause an irremediable break in relationship over one which is certain to cause such a break. By either of these criteria, abortion is clearly to be avoided.[15]

Another consideration suggested by Gilligan's work is that since avoiding hurt to others (or non-violence) is integral to an ethics of care, severing a relationship where the other person will be only slightly hurt would be preferable to severing one where deep or lasting injury will be inflicted by our action. But on this criterion, again, it would seem she should avoid abortion, since loss of life is clearly a graver harm than emotional distress.

Two other possible criteria which would also tell against abortion are: (1) that it is permissible to cut ties with someone who behaves unjustly and oppressively toward one, but not with someone who is innocent of any wrong against one, or (2) we have special obligations to our own offspring, and thus should not sever relationship with them. . . .

It seems that the only way open to the person who seeks to defend abortion from the point of view of the feminine voice is to deny that a relationship (or at least any morally significant relationship) exists between the embryo/fetus and the mother. The question of how to tell when a relationship (or a morally significant relationship) exists is a deep and important one, which has, as yet, received insufficient attention from those who are trying to articulate the feminine voice in moral reasoning. The whole ecofeminist position relies on the assumption that our relationship with nature and with other species is a real and morally significant one. They, thus, have no basis at all for excluding the unborn from moral consideration.

There are those, however, who wish to define morally significant relationships more narrowly —thus effectively limiting our obligation to extend care. While many philosophers within the "justice tradition" (for example, Kant) have seen moral significance only where there is some impact upon rational beings, Nel Noddings, coming from the "care perspective," tries to limit our obligation to extend care in terms of the possibility of "completion" or "reciprocity" in a caring relationship. Since she takes the mother-child relationship to be paradigmatic of caring, it comes as something of a surprise that she regards abortion as a permissible response to an unwanted pregnancy.[16]

There are, on Noddings' view, two different ways in which we may be bound, as caring persons, to extend our care to one for whom we do not already have the sort of feelings of love and affection which would lead us to do the caring action naturally. One is by virtue of being connected with our "inner circle" of caring (which is formed by natural relations of love and friendship) through "chains" of "personal or formal relations."[17] As an example of a person appropriately linked to the inner circle, she cites her daughter's fiancé. It would certainly *seem* that the embryo in one's womb would belong to one's "inner circle" (via natural caring), or at least be connected to it by a "formal relation" (that is, that of parenthood). But Noddings does not concede this. Who is part of my inner circle, and who is connected to it in such a way that I am obligated to extend care to him or her seems to be, for Noddings, largely a matter of my feelings toward the person and/or my choice to include him or her. Thus the mother *may* "confer sacredness" upon the "information speck" in her womb, but need not if, for example, her relationship with the father is not a stable and loving one.

---

15 Some post-abortion counselors find the sense of irremediable break in relationship to be one of the most painful aspects of the post-abortion experience, and try to urge the woman to imaginatively re-create a relationship with the baby in order to be better able to complete the necessary grieving process. . . . ED.

16 Noddings' discussion of abortion occurs on pp. 87–90 of *Caring: A Feminine Approach to Ethics* (Berkeley: University of California Press, 1984), and all quotes are from these pages unless otherwise noted.

17 Ibid., p. 47.

During pregnancy "many women recognize the relation as established when the fetus begins to move about. It is not a question of when life begins, but of when relation begins."

But making the existence of a relation between the unborn and the mother a matter of her choice or feelings, seems to run contrary to one of the most central insights of the feminine perspective in moral reasoning—namely that we already *are* interconnected with others, and thus have responsibilities to them. The view that we are connected with others only when we choose to be or when we *feel* we are, presupposes the kind of individualism and social atomism which Noddings and other feminists criticize as masculine.

Noddings also claims that we sometimes are obligated to care for "the proximate stranger." She says:

> We cannot refuse obligation in human affairs by merely refusing to enter relation; we are, by virtue of our mutual humanity, already and perpetually in potential relation.

Why, then, are we not obligated to extend care to the unborn? She gives two criteria for when we have an obligation to extend care: there must be "the existence of or potential for present relation" and the "dynamic potential for growth in relation, including the potential for increased reciprocity. . . ." Animals are, she believes, excluded by this second criterion since their response is nearly static (unlike a human infant).

She regards the embryo/fetus as not having the potential for present relationships of caring and reciprocity, and thus as having no claim upon our care. As the fetus matures, he or she develops increasing potential for caring relationships, and thus our obligation increases also. There are problems with her position, however.

First of all, the only relationships which can be relevant to *my* obligation to extend care, for Noddings, must be relationships with *me*. Whatever the criteria for having a relationship are, it must be that at a given time, an entity either has a relationship with me or it does not. If it does not, it may either have no potential for a morally

significant relationship with me (for example, my word processor), or it may have such potential in several ways: (1) The relationship may become actual at the will of one or both parties (for example, the stranger sitting next to me on the bus). (2) The relationship may become actual only after a change in relative spatial locations which will take time, and thus can occur only in the future (for example, walking several blocks to meet a new neighbor, or traveling to Tibet to meet a specific Tibetan). Or (3) The relationship may become actual only after some internal change occurs within the other (for example by waiting for a sleeping drug to wear off, for a deep but reversible coma to pass, or for the embryo to mature more fully) and thus can also happen only in the future.

In all three of these cases there is present now in the other the potential for relations of a caring and reciprocal sort. In cases (1) and (2) this is uncontroversial, but (3) requires some defense in the case of the unborn. The human embryo differs now from a rabbit embryo in that it possesses potential for these kinds of relationships although neither of them is presently able to enter into relationships of any sort. That potential becomes actualized only over time, but it can become actualized only because it is there to be actualized (as it is not in the rabbit embryo). Noddings fails to give any reason why the necessity for some internal change to occur in the other before relation can become actual has such moral importance that we are entitled to kill the other in case (3), but not in the others, especially since my refraining from killing it is a sufficient condition for the actualization of the embryo's potential for caring relationships. Her criterion as it stands would also seem to imply that we may kill persons in deep but predictably reversible comas.

Whichever strand of Noddings' thought we choose, then, it is hard to see how the unborn can be excluded from being ones for whom we ought to care. If we focus on the narrow, tribal morality of "inner circles" and "chains," then an objective connection exists tying the unborn to the mother and other relatives. If we are to be open to the needy stranger because of the real potential for relationship and reciprocity, then we should be open to the unborn because he or she also has the real and present potential for a relationship of reciprocity and mutuality which comes with species membership.

Many feminists will object to my argument so far on the grounds that they do not, after all, consider abortion to be a *good* thing. They aren't pro-abortion in the sense that they encourage women to have abortions. They merely regard it as something which must be available as a kind of "grim option"—something a woman would choose only when the other alternatives are all immeasurably worse. . . .

Feminists standardly hold that absolutely no restrictions may be placed on a woman's right to choose abortion. This position cannot be supported by the grim options argument. One who believes something is a grim option will be inclined to try to avoid or prevent it, and thus be willing, at least in principle, to place some restrictions on what counts as a grim option. Granted, practical problems exist about how such decisions are to be made and by whom. But someone who refuses in principle to allow any restrictions on women's right to abort, cannot in good faith claim that they regard abortion only as a grim option.

Some feminists will say: yes, feminine virtues are a good thing for any person to have, and yes, abortion is a characteristically masculine way of dealing with an unwanted pregnancy, but in the current state of things we live in a male dominated society, and we must be willing to use now weapons which, ideally, in a good, matriarchal society, we would not use. But there are no indications that an ideal utopian society is just around the corner; thus we are condemned to a constant violation of our own deepest commitments. If the traits, values and attitudes characteristic of the "feminine voice" are asserted to be good ones, we ought to act according to them. And such values and attitudes simply do not lend support to either the choice of abortion as a way of dealing with an unwanted pregnancy in individual cases, or to the political demand for unrestricted[18] access to abortion which has become so entrenched in the feminist movement. Quite the contrary.

18 Restrictions can take many forms, including laws against abortion, mandatory counseling which includes information about the facts of fetal development and encourages the woman to choose other options, obligatory waiting periods, legal requirements to notify (and/or obtain the consent of) the father, or in the case of a minor the girl's parents, etc. To defend the appropriateness of any particular sort of restrictions goes beyond the scope of this paper.

Review Questions

1. Carol Gilligan claims that the "feminine voice" in ethics is different from the "masculine voice." What are the differences?
2. How do feminists view social relations?
3. According to Wolf-Devine, why do masculine traits, attitudes, and values naturally favor abortion?
4. What general criticisms does Wolf-Devine make of feminist thought about abortion? In particular, how does she criticize Judith Jarvis Thomson and Mary Anne Warren?
5. What is Gilligan's approach to abortion? How does this support the view that abortion should be avoided, on Wolf-Devine's view?
6. Explain Nel Noddings' view of abortion. Why doesn't Wolf-Devine agree?

Discussion Questions

1. Does the care ethic require women to have children and care for them? Does it require women to play the role of wife and mother that so many feminists find oppressive?

2. How do you think Thomson, Warren, and Noddings would reply to Wolf-Devine? Do they have good replies or not?
3. Does the "masculine voice" in ethics naturally support the pro-choice view, as Wolf-Devine says? If so, why are so many men opposed to abortion?
4. Ecofeminists complain that male thinking in ethics is dualistic. Is Wolf-Devine guilty of dualistic thinking or not? Explain your answer.

Reproductive Choices: The Ecological Dimension

RONNIE ZOE HAWKINS

Ronnie Zoe Hawkins teaches philosophy at the University of Central Florida in Orlando, Florida.

After presenting empirical evidence about the causal relations between population growth, poverty, and environmental degradation, and the importance of abortion in population control, Hawkins uses ecofeminism to attack the standard pro-life position and to defend a pro-choice view that is concerned with both human and non-human welfare.

WHILE MUCH HAS BEEN SAID about the morality of choosing to abort a human fetus, too little attention has been given to the moral implications, from an ecological perspective, of deciding whether or not to add a new human life to the planet. In this essay I will argue that environmental considerations are relevant to the abortion debate and, conversely, that the abortion dispute ought to enter into a discussion of feminism and the environment. Speaking from a perspective of concern for *life* in a broadly inclusive sense, referring to the diversity of all life-forms on the planet, I will conclude that, when the ecological dimension is added to discussions of reproductive choice, the term "pro-life" might most properly undergo a dramatic change in usage.

ENVIRONMENTAL CONSIDERATIONS IN THE ABORTION DEBATE: POPULATION, POVERTY, AND ENVIRONMENTAL DEGRADATION

From a size of less than one billion throughout all our previous history, over the last two centuries the human population has swelled to a present total of 6 billion people worldwide and

Source: Ronnie Zoe Hawkins, "Reproductive Choices: The Ecological Dimension" from *APA Newsletters*, Vol. 19, No. 1 (Spring 1992), pp. 66–73. Additional comments and revisions by the author, copyright 1994 and 1999.

is continuing to expand logarithmically. The latest United Nations projections for future growth include a "medium" scenario, in which women give birth to an average of 2 children worldwide and the population grows to 9.4 billion by 2050 and then stabilizes at 11 billion in the following century, and a "high" scenario, wherein women average 2.5 children and the population rises to 11.2 billion by 2050 with no signs of leveling off, exceeding 27 billion by 2150.[1] Estimates of the maximum number of people the planet's resources will support with intensive management vary widely, as do assessments of the quality of life the majority of people will experience.[2] The links between population growth, poverty, and environmental degradation are becoming increasingly well documented, however, the combination frequently producing what is termed a "downward spiral" —a growing number of poor people are forced to make a living on increasingly marginal land, resulting in deforestation, overgrazing, soil erosion, or an assortment of other environmental problems further exacerbating their poverty and often leading them to move on and repeat the process elsewhere.[3] At least 1.2 billion people around the world are presently estimated to be living in absolute poverty, of which about half are thought to be trapped in such a self-reinforcing process of increasing environmental degradation.[4] Unequal access to land and resources, ill-conceived development schemes, local and national politics, and the international economic power structure may all contribute prominently to the maintenance of their poverty, but continued population growth heightens the desperateness of the situation.

While the poor may seek to have large families as a way of coping with their immediate economic conditions, to provide more hands to work and to offer an increased chance that parents will be cared for in their old age, the long-term trade-off parallels that of employing ecologically damaging farming practices because of today's need to eat: tomorrow, the overall needs will be greater, while the resources for

1 See *1998 World Population Data Sheet,* book edition (Washington, DC: Population Reference Bureau, 1998), p. 9. Paul Demeny, in "The World Demographic Situation," *World Population and U.S. Policy: The Choices Ahead,* ed. J. Menken (New York: W. W. Norton, 1986), pp. 29–39, presents an examination of population growth curves projected earlier for growth beyond 1985. For three projections making the simple assumption of a fixed growth rate, the "low" rate of 0.5% per year (the average rate of growth in the nineteenth century), yields 8.6 billion people by the end of the twenty-first century, the "medium" rate of 1% per year (the average rate between 1920 and 1950) yields 15.3 billion by that time, and the "high" rate of 1.65% (the rate estimated for 1985) leads to "a world population of over 32 billion people, an outcome implausible on its face" (p. 34); Demeny notes that the assumptions needed to generate the lower figures imply "a discontinuous break from the pre-1985 growth path." "More realistic" extrapolations mesh with earlier growth rates but trace an S-curve showing a progressive leveling off of growth rates over time, though an inflection point in the late 1960s—apparently our only evidence for such an overall leveling off thus far—is "not obvious at a casual glance." Demeny cautions that "the range of alternative long-term demographic futures is wide, and implications of possible policy choices that may influence the path actually followed are far-reaching" (p. 36).

2 Expectations range from the dire predictions of famine and social collapse early in the twenty-first century made in *The Limits to Growth,* by Donella Meadows et al. (New York: Universe Books, 1972), to the wild optimism proclaiming great improvement in life and environmental quality of *The Resourceful Earth,* by Julian Simon and Herman Kahn (Oxford: Basil Blackwell, 1984). A report by the U.S. National Academy of Sciences in 1969 arrived at a figure of 10 billion as "the upper limit of what an intensively managed world might support with some degree of comfort and choice"; see David Western, "Population, Resources, and Environment in the Twenty-first Century," in *Conservation for the Twenty-first Century,* ed. D. Western and M. C. Pearl (New York: Oxford University Press, 1989), pp. 13–14, for a discussion of the various scenarios within a context of the outlook for wildlife in the coming century, which is generally conceded to be "more uniformly dismal" by all predictors.

3 Alan B. Durning, *Poverty and the Environment: Reversing the Downward Spiral,* Worldwatch Paper 92 (Washington, DC: Worldwatch Institute, 1989).

4 Ibid., p. 45.

meeting them will be proportionally less. Women, bearing a large and growing share of the burden of poverty, are increasingly seeking to limit their family sizes, but all too often, for institutional or social reasons, they are denied access to the means for doing so.[5]

POPULATION, CONSUMPTION, AND THE TOLL ON NONHUMAN LIFE

Human beings are far from the only victims of the interaction between population growth and environmental degradation, however, and poor people are not the only actors in the ecological tragedy. As more and more land is radically altered to meet growing human needs and its biotic components are converted into resources for human use, nonhuman organisms also are experiencing limitations on their growth, movements, and interactions, deprivation of access to the necessities of life, and frequently loss of life itself. With destruction of habitats and fragmentation of populations, entire species are dwindling and disappearing as a result of human activities. In contrast to natural extinctions, which are relatively rare occurrences that are mitigated by the emergence of new species, anthropogenic or human-caused species extinctions are occurring at several hundred times the natural, background rate and, since they are the result of abrupt and often total destruction of

habitats, are not offset by new speciation.[6] The changes are so enormous that scientists working within a "crisis discipline" attempting to stem the massive loss of species from the planet have even begun discussing a possible *end to evolution;* conservation biologist Michael Soulé assesses the situation as follows:

> At best, the planet's macrobiota is entering a kind of pause, an evolutionary lacuna, caused by the human usurpation of the land surface. For the survivors, the pause will last until the human population declines to a biologically tolerable level—a level at which land appropriated by humans is returned to nature, and extinction rates return to the (paleontological) background level.[7]

When we come to grips with the massive scale on which conditions for human and nonhuman life alike are increasingly deteriorating we must acknowledge that planetary life itself, construed in the larger sense as encompassing all the diverse extant as well as potential future forms arising through the evolutionary process, is faced with a crisis of unprecedented proportions. This crisis is in large part an undeniable if unintended result of the disproportionate expansion in human numbers occurring over very recent time.

---

5 Surveys show that 50–60% of couples in Latin America, 60–80% in nonaffluent Asian countries (excluding China), 75% in North Africa and the Middle East, and 90% in sub-Saharan Africa presently use no form of modern birth control. The same research, however, shows that a majority in Latin America and Asia desire to limit their family size, and a growing number do so in the Middle East and Africa, though "the desire to maintain male dominance" on the part of the husband remains a major factor in keeping birth rates in Africa high. See Jodi L. Jacobson, *The Global Politics of Abortion,* Worldwatch Paper 97 (Washington, DC: Worldwatch Institute, 1990), pp. 22–37.

6 Anthropogenic, or human-caused, extinction must be clearly differentiated from natural extinction, which is "part of the process of replacing less well-adapted gene pools with better adapted ones"; natural extinctions are "rare events on a human time scale," with "few, if any," of the hundreds of vertebrate extinctions incurred over the last several centuries being the result of factors other than human activities, according to Michael Soulé, "What Is Conservation Biology?" *Bioscience* 35 (1985): 730. The rate of species loss in the present anthropogenic extinction event is "about 400 times that recorded through recent geological time and is accelerating rapidly"; the event is "the most extreme for 65 million years," since the end of the dinosaur era, and it is far more severe with respect to the loss of plant diversity. See Edward O. Wilson, "The Biological Diversity Crisis," *Bioscience* 35 (1985): 703.

7 Michael Soulé, "Conservation Biology in the Twenty-first Century: Summary and Outlook," in Western and Pearl, p. 303.

Perhaps the suddenness of its onset accounts for the relative philosophical neglect it has received heretofore, but continued inattention is no longer acceptable in the face of difficulties that grow more severe with each passing day.

While not overlooking the multiple contributory factors leading to our present predicament, we must clearly define its inescapable biological dimension: the global "balance" of lifeforms has been changed dramatically, and individual and societal decisions that further increase the human preponderance relative to other forms of life, in augmenting the imbalance, serve to aggravate its untoward consequences. And while technological advances may appear to maintain the quality of human life at a much higher carrying capacity than prevailed throughout millennia—at least for certain groups of humans over a finite period of time[8]—the existence and continued evolution of other forms of life, and

hence the well-being of life in the larger sense, require a reversal of the present trend and an eventual reduction in the size of the human population.[9]

THE IMPORTANCE OF ABORTION IN POPULATION LIMITATION

If only for anthropocentric and sometimes even nationalistic or ethnocentric reasons, many people will agree that some form of human population limitation is needed. Often, however, in the industrialized nations the population problem is construed as something "out there," a pressing issue for the poorer nations of the tropics perhaps but of little concern within a wealthy country. Just as frequently, abortion is seen as isolable from the larger picture of population limitation, something quite different from the "acceptable" methods of family planning. But those familiar with the empirical evidence present a somewhat different picture of these issues.

According to the 1998 World Population Data Sheet,[10] the rate of natural increase for the world as a whole is currently 1.4% per year, a growth rate that, if sustained, would result in a doubling of the size of the human population every 49 years.[11] It is true that the "more developed" regions of the world, comprising North

---

8 The carrying capacity is a measure of the number of human beings (or individuals of other species) an environment can sustain over a period of time, usually taken to be the indefinite future—i.e., without causing harm to the environment. It should be noted that "overpopulation" is being defined in recent works not in terms of population density but in terms of the *long-term carrying capacity* of the region. In *The Population Explosion* (New York: Simon & Schuster, 1990), Paul and Anne Ehrlich maintain that an area is overpopulated "when its population can't be maintained without rapidly depleting nonrenewable resources . . . and without degrading the capacity of the environment to support the population," or "in short, if the long-term carrying capacity is clearly being degraded by its current inhabitants," pp. 38–39. By this definition, virtually all rich and poor nations alike are overpopulated, since virtually all are depleting their resources faster than they can be renewed—the process may be just a little less obvious in the case of the rich nations because they are drawing upon resources that lie largely outside their own boundaries. The Netherlands, for example, often presented as an example of a country with both a high population density and a high standard of living, maintains its 1,031 people per square mile by importing raw materials from around the world, far exceeding the carrying capacity of its own land base (Ehrlich and Ehrlich, 1990). For an extended examination of the planet's carrying capacity for human beings, see Joel E. Cohen, *How Many People Can the Earth Support?* (New York: W. W. Norton, 1995).

9 The "deep ecology platform" proposed by philosopher Arne Naess recognizes that, for the "continuing evolution" of, for instance, "mammals defending vast territory," not just a stabilization of the human population but an eventual reduction will be needed; he criticizes traditional discussions that refer only to "'carrying capacity' for humans," not "carrying capacity for humans and non-humans.'" See Naess, "Sustainable Development and Deep Ecology," in *Ethics of Environment and Development,* ed. J. R. Engel and J. G. Engel (Tucson: University of Arizona Press, 1990), pp. 88–91.

10 Compiled annually by the Population Reference Bureau, Inc, 1875 Connecticut Avenue NW, Suite 520, Washington, DC 20009; http://www.prb.org.

11 The present expansion of the human population is an example of *exponential* growth, the kind of growth that is said

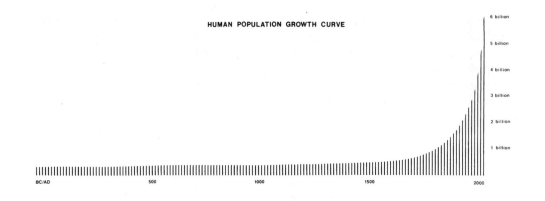

HUMAN POPULATION GROWTH CURVE

America, Europe, Australia, Japan, New Zealand and the former USSR, have a considerably lower annual rate of increase and a longer doubling time overall, 0.1% and 548 years, respectively, as opposed to a growth rate of 2.0% and a doubling time of 35 years for the "lesser developed" regions (excluding China); it must be noted, however, that the United States has one of the highest rates of natural increase of all the industrialized nations, 0.6%, and is currently growing so as to double in size every 116 years —in striking contrast to the common misconception that "zero population growth" has already been achieved in this country.

Even where populations are increasing at a relatively small rate, however, such countries should by no means be considered innocent of the toll being taken on the planet's living systems. Estimates of the consumption of world resources and generation of stress to the global environment have ranged from twelve to several hundred times as great per capita for citizens of the industrialized nations relative to those of the

poorer regions of the world.[12] One group of authors construes population and consumption as intertwined in a *multiplicative* relationship, the total adverse effect of an increase in human numbers in certain regions of the globe thus being greatly amplified, as follows (where $\times$ indicates the multiplication sign):

> environmental impact = population $\times$ consumption of goods per person $\times$ environmental impact per quantity of goods consumed[13]

According to this formula, the environmental toll taken by each new human born within the

---

to occur when a quantity is increasing by a fixed percentage of its size per interval of time. A simple mathematical relationship holds between the percent growth per unit time and the time it takes for that quantity to double in size: the *doubling time* is equal to 70 divided by the percent growth, or $T_2 = 70/P$. Hence, if the world population is growing by 1.7% per year (as it was in 1972), its doubling time is 70/1.7 or a little over 41 years. See Albert A. Bartlett, "Forgotten Fundamentals of the Energy Crisis," *Focus* 1 (Winter 1992), 26–40, for a discussion of exponential growth in relation to both population size and resource depletion.

12 According to the "ecological footprint analysis" of Mathis Wackernagel and William Rees in *Our Ecological Footprint: Reducing Human Impact on the Earth,* Philadelphia: New Society Publishers, 1996), a citizen of the United States consumes more than 12 times the resources of a citizen of India, p. 85. F. E. Trainer, in *Abandon Affluence* (London: Zed Books, 1985), estimates the average per capita resource consumption of persons living in the rich nations of the world to be about 15 times that of those living in the poor nations, p. 3; Paul and Anne Ehrlich (*National Geographic* 174 [1988], 914–17) estimate that the birth of a baby within the United States will "impose more than a hundred times the stress on the world's resources and environment than a baby born in a developing nation"; and the "Demographic Facts of Life in the U.S.A." fact sheet prepared by Zero Population Growth (Washington, DC, August 1991) maintains that "the average American's energy use is equivalent to the consumption of 3 Japanese, 6 Mexicans, 13 Chinese, 35 Indians, 153 Bangladeshis, or 499 Ethiopians."

13 For a discussion see Paul R. Ehrlich, Anne H. Ehrlich and John P. Holdren, *Ecoscience: Population, Resources, Environment* (San Francisco: W. H. Freeman and Company,

"developed" world will be very much greater than that of one born elsewhere. By the same token, those of us living in the industrialized nations can lower our overall destructive effect on the natural environment both by reducing the amount and nature of our consumption and by reducing the number of us that consume the planet's precious resources.

Projections that foresee the world population leveling off at a total far less than what can be calculated by simply taking today's number through several doubling times (which, at our current rate of growth, yields over forty billion people just past the end of the next century)[14] are dependent in part upon the assumption that the rate of population increase will fall substantially in the less industrialized countries as they undergo the "demo-graphic transition"[15] from a state of high fertility and high mortality to a state where both fertility and mortality rates are low. In the process of making that transition, however, a large gap often develops between the fall in death rate and the decline in birth rate, generating a great increase in absolute numbers before stabilization can be attained. It is at this critical period of time, when smaller family sizes are becoming desirable but contraceptive use is unfamiliar or unavailable, that abortion plays a

prominent and necessary role in fertility reduction, with abortion rates later declining as contraceptive use increases.[16] The abortion rates in Japan and in South Korea, for example, countries which underwent rapid transitions to a low birth rate during this century, rose when fertility was declining most sharply, then fell dramatically as the rate of contraceptive use increased; without abortion, it is estimated that South Korea's birth rate during the transition would have been 22% higher.[17] And since even small changes in the birth rate during this period will result in substantial differences in the size of the reproducing population base and therefore in ultimate population size, abortion has an important role to play in the long-term welfare of many developing nations.

In the industrialized world, too, where each additional "place at life's table" results in consumption of a significantly greater slice of the resource pie, abortion continues to contribute substantially to reducing environmental destruction; termination of almost a million and a half undesired pregnancies every year in the United States, for instance, has served to lessen significantly the toll on the global ecosystem, however small a part such concerns may play in an individual woman's decision to choose abortion. Figures for the 1990s show that, worldwide, while the total population increased by more than 80 million, an estimated 36–53 million abortions were performed; in 1995, while the population of the United States grew by almost 2.5 million, 1.2 million abortions were performed.[18] Abortion, therefore, far from

---

1977), p. 720. Also see Ehrlich and Ehrlich, *The Population Explosion,* pp. 58–59, where the equation is summarized as Impact = Population × Affluence × Technology, or $I = PAT$.

14 If the total world population is 6 billion in 2000 and is growing at a rate of 1.4% per year, as per the current World Population Data Sheet, its doubling time is slightly over 49 years, and maintaining this rate of growth through 3 doubling times would yield 12 billion in 2048, 24 billion in 2098, and 48 billion by 2147. See note 1 for an indication of the assumptions made in order to reach projections for leveling off that fall far short of these figures.

15 It should be noted that the theory holding that a "demographic transition" to lower birth rates follows automatically upon economic "development" of a region is controversial in the field of population studies. See, for example, Garrett Hardin, "Mythic Aspects of the Demographic Transition," *Population and Environment* 12 (1990): 41–42.

16 Jacobson, *The Global Politics of Abortion,* p. 23.

17 Ibid.

18 See Wendy R. Ewart and Beverly Winikoff, "Toward Safe and Effective Medical Abortion," *Science* 281 (1998): 520–21, and Lisa M. Koonin, Jack C. Smith, Merrell Ramick, and Lilo T. Strauss, "Abortion Surveillance—United States, 1995," in *Morbidity and Mortality Weekly Report* 47 (1998): 31–68. Also see Population Crisis Committee, *Access to Birth Control: A World Assessment,* Population Briefing Paper No. 19 (October 1987), as reported in brief for Population–Environment Balance, et al., as *Amici Curiae* supporting appellees in *Webster v. Reproductive Health*

being a minor contributor where population limitation is concerned, is currently serving to reduce the yearly population increase, both in this country and overall, by between 30 and 40%. As a backup to contraception, abortion plays a major role in limiting the ecologically damaging effects of continued human population growth in all parts of the globe.

RELEVANCE OF THE ABORTION ISSUE TO FEMINIST CONCERNS ABOUT THE ENVIRONMENT

The above, drawing heavily on empirical material, is intended to illustrate the practical importance of ecological considerations to the abortion debate. Expanding the focus of discussion to include the ecological dimension also serves, as will be shown, to illuminate certain issues of theoretical importance. A certain construal of the emerging position known as *ecofeminism* will be shown to provide additional grounding for a woman's right to choose abortion, while clarifying such an approach to the abortion issue may lead to greater consistency in feminist thinking about the environment.

WOMEN, NATURE, DUALISM AND DOMINATION

While there have been various formulations of ecofeminism, perhaps the dominant theme of ecofeminism as a philosophical position is the

recognition of connections existing between the domination of women, the domination of certain groups of human beings by other groups, and the domination of nonhuman animals or of "nature" in general. The common root of such domination is often traced to what has been identified as patriarchal thinking, a type of thinking that has been characterized by various authors as predominantly dualistic, hierarchical, atomistic, abstract, and rationalistic.[19] According to ecofeminist philosopher Karen Warren, underlying all forms of domination is an "oppressive conceptual framework" that sanctions differential power relationships according to a "logic of domination" having its basis in dualism: a dichotomous split is postulated to exist between polar opposites determined by possession or lack of a particular characteristic; one side of the dichotomy is assumed to be morally superior to the other; and this assumption in turn is taken to justify the domination of the side considered inferior by that considered superior.[20] Examples bearing out this analysis abound: mind/body, man/woman, white/black, "developed" society/"undeveloped" society, culture/nature, and human being/non-

---

Services, Supreme Court of the United States, October Term, 1988. The interest of the *Amici Curiae* preparing the brief, which included the Sierra Club, the Worldwatch Institute and Zero Population Growth among others, was stated to be "the potential detrimental impact on family planning programs both here and abroad of the provision of the Missouri statute at issue that prohibits 'encouraging or counseling a woman to have an abortion not necessary to save her life,'" in light of the fact that "if abortion were not an option, the strains on the environment would be even greater" than they are at present.

19 For characterizations of patriarchal thinking as seen from an ecofeminist perspective, see Karen J. Warren, "Feminism and Ecology: Making Connections," *Environmental Ethics* 9 (1987): 3–20; Jim Cheney, "Eco-feminism and Deep Ecology," *Environmental Ethics* 9 (1987):115–45; and Michael E. Zimmerman, "Feminism, Deep Ecology, and Environmental Ethics," *Environmental Ethics* 9 (1987): 21–44.

20 See Karen J. Warren, "The Power and the Promise of Ecological Feminism," *Environmental Ethics* 12 (1990): 125–46, and also Warren, "Feminism and Ecology," [note 19]. A conceptual framework is a socially constructed set of assumptions about the nature of the world and ourselves that tends to structure the way we form our beliefs and judgments; its nature is likely to be in large part a result of the characteristics of those involved in its construction, including their gender and other socially relevant variables, but this nature becomes "invisible" to those seeing all things through its coloring lenses. See also Elizabeth Dodson Gray, *Green Paradise Lost* (Wellesley, MA: Roundtable Press, 1981) and *Patriarchy as a Conceptual Trap* (Wellesley, MA: Roundtable Press, 1982). ·

human organism are examples of socially constructed dualisms that, through operation of a logic of domination that assigns unequal value to the two components of each pair and sanctions subjugation of one to the other, can be understood to undergird not only patriarchy but Western (or Northern) imperialism and much ecological destruction as well.

It is claimed by some ecofeminists that women have historically been identified with the physical side of the mind/body dualism and with nature as opposed to culture, and that, through linkage with the "inferior" poles of such traditionally accepted dichotomies, their subordination to men has been reinforced.[21] Many contemporary feminists have rejected these identifications, some recasting liberation in terms of women taking their place alongside men in a separate, nature-transcending realm of the mental or spiritual. In a critical review of the ecofeminist literature, however, Val Plumwood criticizes such a rejection as an incomplete solution to the problem of domination and stresses the need to challenge the dualistic framework itself.[22] She maintains that, since we have heretofore been employing a "basically masculine" model of what it means to be human, a rethinking of the man/woman split must be linked with a reexamination of the mind/body and human/nonhuman dichotomies also, as well as of "the notion of humanity itself."[23]

DUALISM AND
THE ABORTION DEBATE

Our conception of what it means to be human is something that lies deep at the heart of the abortion debate, and inspection of some of the underlying assumptions involved provides fur-

ther support for an ecofeminist critique targeting dualism. Constructed almost entirely within the framework of patriarchal thought, the present "pro-life" stance is riddled with dualisms. At the social level, for instance, many antiabortion activists reportedly profess a belief in "intrinsic differences" existing between the nature of men and that of women, a belief not shared by their pro-choice counterparts.[24] On a more metaphysical plane, the current majority position of Catholic theologians upholds a belief in "ensoulment" occurring at the moment of conception of a human being, a "theory of immediate animation" that is rooted in the Cartesian dichotomy between the mind or soul and the body and that makes the origin of a new human life an abrupt crossing of an absolute threshold.[25] And, clearly, even abortion opponents who would withhold explicit endorsement of the Cartesian view or of strictly separate male and female spheres appear to embrace without reservation the existence of an unbridgeable gap between human life and other forms of life. Without such an assumption, condemnation of the taking of an "innocent life" in "pro-life" arguments would have to address issues of meat-eating, animal experimentation, and the destruction of wildlife as well as the aborting of a human fetus.[26]

21 See, for instance, Warren, "The Power and the Promise of Ecological Feminism," 129–31.
22 Val Plumwood, "Ecofeminism: An Overview and Discussion of Positions and Arguments," *Australasian Journal of Philosophy,* Supplement to Vol. 64 (June 1986): 120–37.
23 Ibid., 134.

24 For a thoughtful examination of the contrasting attitudes of "pro-life" and "pro-choice" women, as expressed in their own words, see Kristin Luker, "Abortion and the Meaning of Life," in *Abortion: Understanding Differences,* ed. S. Callahan and D. Callahan (New York and London: Plenum Press, 1984), pp. 31–45.
25 For a critical discussion of this point, see Joseph F. Donceel, "A Liberal Catholic's View," in *Abortion and Catholicism,* ed. P. B. Jung and T. A. Shannon (New York: Crossroad Publishing Company, 1988), pp. 48–53.
26 The status of nonhuman life has indeed been recognized as problematic for certain approaches to interpretation of the proscription "thou shalt not kill" and for the phrase "the sanctity of life"; see Carol A. Tauer, "Probabilism and the Moral Status of the Early Embryo," in Jung and Shannon, pp. 78–79, and Marjorie Reiley Maguire, "Personhood, Covenant, and Abortion" in the same volume, p. 104.

DOES NATURE ABHOR A DUALISM?

Rising to the challenge of Plumwood and others, ecological and other feminists may choose to reject all the dualisms lying at the core of the "pro-life" position, working instead to develop a nondualistic understanding of humanness and, indeed, of *life* in the broader sense. The traditional view postulating radical differences between men and women has been under siege for some time, of course, and perhaps increasing self-determination of gender roles by individuals will be most effective in loosening the grip of this particular conceptual split on our collective consciousness. The other two sharp divisions mentioned above are, however, also increasingly open to challenge, spurred on in part by developments in the empirical and technological sciences demonstrating that graded differences, not abrupt discontinuities, seem to be the rule rather than the exception in nature.

The controversy surrounding the "abortion pill" mifepristone (RU 486),[27] can, for instance, be interpreted as in part a fight over the need to keep our dichotomies sharp in the face of yet another threat to our time-honored distinctions. An obvious worry to abortion foes is that a medical as well as surgical option will make abortion seem "easier," less traumatic, and perhaps more a matter of "menstrual regulation" than a termination of pregnancy; as a method that can take place in a greater variety of settings and that is less delimited in time than uterine aspiration or curettage, abortion by administration of mifepristone may be somewhat less likely to be perceived as an act that definitively crosses over a line.[28]

In addition, the growing availability of medical abortion as well as the other new reproductive technologies serves to underscore the gradualness of development from the fertilized egg or zygote to the newborn infant—medically recognized as "a continuous process of becoming."[29] Approximately six days are required for the zygote, fertilized in the fallopian tube, to

---

27 Mifepristone, developed by Roussel-Uclaf under the designation RU 486 and now produced by Exelgyn and Danco, is a steroid that blocks the action of progesterone, the hormone essential for the establishment and maintenance of pregnancy. Clinical studies in both industrialized and "developing" countries have shown mifepristone, in combination with a prostaglandin such as misoprostol, to be safe, effective, and acceptable to most women seeking abortion. Expulsion of uterine contents usually occurs within hours after the administration of the prostaglandin, which is given around 2 days after the mifepristone, and bleeding usually lasts for a little over a week. Possible adverse effects, including excessive bleeding, cramping, abdominal pain and incomplete abortion, indicate a need for medical supervision during the course of treatment but generally have been mild or confined to a small percentage of cases. Mifepristone may also be of benefit for postcoital contraception, induction of labor, and treatment of endometriosis, breast cancer, and premenstrual syndromes, among other conditions. See Etienne-Emile Baulieu, "Contragestion and Other Clinical Applications of RU 486, An Antiprogesterone at the Receptor," *Science* 245 (1989): 1351–56; Louise Silvestre et al., "Voluntary Interruption of Pregnancy with Mifepristone (RU 486) and a Prostaglandin Analogue: A Large-Scale French Experience," *New England Journal of Medicine* 322 (1990): 645–48; "Mifepristone (RU 486)" in *The Medical Letter on Drugs and Therapeutics* 32 (1990): 112–13; Etienne-Emile Baulieu, "Editorial: RU486 and the Early Nineties," *Endocrinology* 127 (1990): 2043–46; Beverly Winikoff, Irving Sivin, Kurus J. Coyaji, Evelio Cabezas, Xiao Bilian, Gu Sujuan, Du Ming-kun, Usha R. Krishna, Andrea Eschen, and Charlotte Ellertson, "Safety, Efficacy, and Acceptability of Medical Abortion in China, Cuba, and India: A Comparative Trial of Mifepristone-Misoprostol versus Surgical Abortion," *American Journal of Obstetrics and Gynecology* 176 (1997): 431–37.

28 See G. W. K. Tang, "A Pilot Study of Acceptability of RU 486 and ONO 802 in a Chinese Population," *Contraception* 44 (1991): 523–32, for an examination of contrasting attitudes toward medical and surgical abortion. Reasons for favoring medical over surgical abortion included its lesser association with injury or trauma to the body, its being "a more natural means to interrupt a pregnancy," and its being akin to "a menstrual regulation," while some negative perceptions were related to the longer time interval required for the medical procedure and a sense of guilt arising from "actively taking part" in the abortion by the act of swallowing the tablets, as opposed to playing a "passive" role in undergoing the surgical procedure.

29 Committee on Ethics of the American Fertility Society, "Ethical Considerations of New Reproductive Technolo-

reach a position where it can implant in the lining of the uterus, and another 6 to 8 days are needed for implantation to be completed, with pregnancy, on its medical definition, said to have begun only at this time.[30] While the zygote is recognized as unquestionably "both alive and human" and possessing the potential to develop into an adult human being, this potential is noted to be only "theoretic and statistical," since only about one in three actually succeeds in fulfilling it, a high percentage of conceptions ending in spontaneous abortions that frequently pass unnoticed.[31] Furthermore, since, before implantation, the developing entity has the potential to become either less (through fusion) or more (twinning) than a complete individual, and since its first cellular differentiation involves establishment of what become the placental tissues, it is termed a "preembryo" through the first 14 days after fertilization; the term "embryo" is applied from implantation through the end of the eighth week, during which time the major organ systems are being formed, and the term "fetus" from the second month onward, with the potential being recognized for differentiation in the "status" of the developing entity at various different times along this continuum.[32]

It may be, then, that questions as to whether or not a woman is pregnant or has undergone abortion have answers that are gray rather than black or white. Mifepristone, for instance, has been shown in some experimental studies to be effective in preventing implantation as well as inducing abortion after implantation has taken place, and, thus, can be construed as potentially a contraceptive as well as an abortifacient;[33] making this distinction depends, however, on accepting some such differentiation between the embryo and the preembryo, since the zygote has been formed by the time of action of the agent—as it has by the time of action of other accepted methods of "contraception," including the IUD, progestin implants, and other postcoital methods. In view of the spectrum of time periods during which actions to prevent pregnancy may be undertaken, one of the scientists involved in the development of mifepristone, Etienne-Emile Baulieu, has coined the word "contragestion" (a shortening of "contra-gestation") to emphasize the continuity of the processes at work and of the possibilities for choosing to interrupt them, "stressing the quite natural aspects of fertility and the control thereof."[34]

An understanding of embryological development leads one to an appreciation of another kind of continuity as well, one that speaks against the third type of dualism mentioned earlier, the assumed gap between the human and the nonhuman. The earliest phases of development are very similar for all vertebrate embryos. By the fifth week after fertilization, for example —three weeks after a missed period, around the time many women will be discovering their pregnancies and deciding whether or not to continue them—the embryo, about a quarter of an inch in size, shows rather undifferentiated paddle-shaped limb buds, an extremely rudimentary facial structure, and the same kind of skin all vertebrates initially share; it has the type of kidney that is functional in fishes and amphibians and a set of pharyngeal pouches resembling the early stages of the gills formed in these creatures; and, while indeed possessed of a brain

gies," *Fertility and Sterility* 46 Supplement 1 (1986), 26S; a detailed discussion of the early phases of development is presented in chapter 11, "The Biologic Characteristics of the Preembryo," 26S–28S.

30 See Rebecca J. Cook, "Antiprogestin Drugs: Medical and Legal Issues," *Family Planning Perspectives* 21 (1989): 267.

31 Committee on Ethics of the American Fertility Society, *Fertility and Sterility* 46 Supplement 1 (1986), 26S.

32 Ibid.; see also *Fertility and Sterility* 46 Supplement 1 (1986): vii for definition of the preembryo.

33 See E. E. Baulieu and A. Ulmann, "Antiprogesterone Activity of RU 486 and Its Contragestive and Other Applications," *Human Reproduction* 1 (1986):107–10, and Baulieu, "Contragestion and Other Clinical Applications" [note 27].

34 Baulieu, "Contragestion and Other Clinical Applications," *Science* 245 (1989): 1356.

and a beating heart, its early heart is two-chambered, like that of a fish, and its brain at this stage little more than a simple tubular structure that is much the same in developing amphibians, reptiles, birds and mammals.[35] The close resemblance of the developmental sequence among the different vertebrate classes is taken as an indication of a common evolutionary origin, and, indeed, Darwin is said to have considered embryology to provide some of the strongest evidence for his theory of natural selection.[36] (See Figures 2 and 3.)

Furthermore, while the human fetus may be genetically identifiable as human from the time of conception, all life on Earth is remarkably the same in its nucleic-acid basis. Humans and chimpanzees, in particular, are strikingly close in their genetic makeup, with DNA sequences differing by only a little over 1%—so close, in fact, that some taxonomists are proposing that humans and the two chimpanzee species should all share the same genus, *Homo*.[37] And, of perhaps even greater import to philosophers, those who study animal behavior are finding considerable empirical support for attributing mental states such as beliefs and desires to a variety of nonhuman animals, and even the question as to whether chimpanzees and other apes may have their own "theory of mind," the ability to attribute mental states to others, is currently under scrutiny.[38]

Biology thus presents little evidence for a sharp discontinuity between human and nonhuman, offering, instead, virtually overwhelming support for placing human life on a continuum with all other life. It would seem, then, that the burden of proof must fall on those arguing for a sharp division within this spectrum. And if empirical evidence alone falls short of entailing a need for similarity in our moral valuation of other forms of life, it can at the very least be taken as undermining the dualistic assumptions that undergird our currently accepted value hierarchy.[39]

HEALING THE SPLITS IS IN THE INTEREST OF ALL LIFE

In rejecting the dualistic thinking rife within our contemporary society, and in particular rejecting a stark division between human and nonhuman

35 See T. W. Sadler, *Langman's Medical Embryology*, 5th ed. (Baltimore: Williams & Wilkins, 1985), and Scott F. Gilbert, *Developmental Biology*, 2d ed. (Sunderland, MA: Sinauer Associates, Inc., 1988).

36 Gilbert, *Developmental Biology*, p. 154.

37 For a discussion of this point see Jared Diamond, *The Third Chimpanzee* (New York: HarperCollins, 1992), pp. 19–25.

38 Several recent, detailed explorations of this issue include Richard W. Byrne and Andrew Whiten, eds., *Machiavellian Intelligence: Social Expertise and the Evolution of Intellect in Monkeys, Apes, and Humans* (Oxford: Clarendon Press, 1988); Dorothy L. Cheney and Robert M. Seyfarth, *How Monkeys See the World* (Chicago and London: University of Chicago Press, 1990); Donald R. Griffin, *Animal Minds* (Chicago and London: University of Chicago Press, 1992);

Carolyn A. Ristau, ed., *Cognitive Ethology: The Minds of Other Animals* (Hillsdale, NJ: Lawrence Erlbaum Associates, 1991); and Andrew Whiten, ed., *Natural Theories of Mind: Evolution, Development, and Simulation of Everyday Mindreading* (Cambridge, MA: Basil Blackwell, 1991).

39 See James Rachels, *Created from Animals* (Oxford: Oxford University Press, 1990), for an extended discussion of the undermining effect of evolutionary theory on moral claims that assume a value discontinuity between humans and nonhuman animals. Rachels takes aim at the traditional Western concept of "human dignity," which he construes as involving "a sharp contrast between human and non-human life" (p. 86) and maintains that, whereas Darwinism does not entail "that the doctrine of human dignity is false," it "provides reason for doubting the truth of the considerations that support the doctrine," e.g., "that humans are morally special *because* they are made in the image of God, or because they are uniquely rational beings" (p. 97). Using somewhat similar terminology (though not an evolutionary argument), Peter Singer has criticized "the doctrine of the sanctity of human life," which he takes to mean, similarly, "the idea that there is a radical difference between the value of a human life and the value of the life of some other animal —a difference not merely in degree, but of quality or kind"; see Singer, "Unsanctifying Human Life," in *Philosophy and the Human Condition*, ed. T. L. Beauchamp, W. T. Blackstone, and J. Feinberg (Englewood Cliffs, NJ: Prentice-Hall, 1980), pp. 264–65. The aim of both arguments appears to be one not of lowering the value we place on human life but rather of elevating that which we accord nonhuman life, to "bring our attitudes to human and nonhuman animals closer together" (Singer, p. 273).

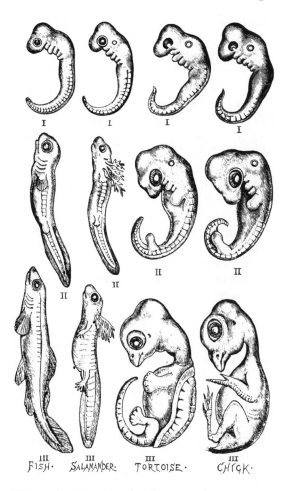

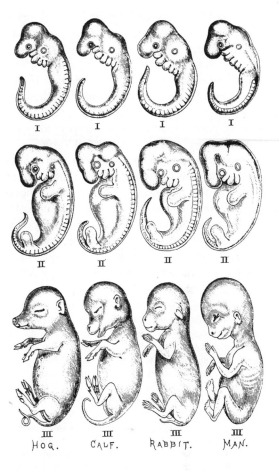

Figure 2 A series of embryos at three comparable and progressive stages of development (marked I, II, III), representing each of the classes of vertebrated animals below the Mammalia. (After Häckel.)

Figure 3 Another series of embryos, also at three comparable and progressive stages of development (marked I, II, III), representing four different divisions of the class Mammalia. (After Häckel.)

life, ecofeminists may draw upon the massive destruction of nonhuman organisms as well as mounting human misery for ample evidence of the need for a reversal of the current population trends among the planet's different species. Such a move shifts the context of the debate away from a pitting of the needs of a certain subset of human beings against those of another

(potential) subset and into a domain in which we must at least ask how the consequences of our reproductive choices will affect the needs of all planetary lifeforms.

An antiabortion stance stands as at best narrowly anthropocentric in this regard, at worst falling far short even of anthropocentrism when the long-range interests of humanity are considered.[40] At a more theoretical level, however, without the sharp human/nonhuman dichotomy, the "pro-life" position itself collapses, since the assumption of human separateness and superiority makes up its very foundation. If that great moral chasm cannot be defended, then the refusal to weigh human fetal life against other pressing considerations becomes open to question, especially in light of our society's great willingness to take nonhuman life for far more trivial reasons than are likely to underlie the choice of abortion. With a growing body of feminist moral theory developed around frameworks emphasizing continuity, difference without value disparity, relationship, contextual concreteness, and emotional responses such as loving and caring,[41] nondualistic criteria for deciding how, in particular situations, to favor one form of life over another —as all our reproductive choices ultimately do, in consequence of our living on a finite planet—can and must be found.

Abortion has recently received attention as a problematic issue for ecofeminists: it has been viewed as a "masculine" response to unwanted pregnancy that "fails to respect the interconnectedness of all life,"[42] and as a choice that is difficult to reconcile with "an abstract pro-nature stance"[43] that would allow "natural" events such as pregnancy to run their course (a stance which in itself would be highly problematic for most ecofeminists to embrace). As Plumwood maintains, there is a need to reconceptualize both the concept of the human and the concept of nature,[44] and part of meeting this challenge may lie in reconceiving ourselves as beings who are part of the natural world and simultaneously beings whose nature is to be active choosers of our own actions, responsible for the effect of those actions on each other and on other lifeforms, including the effects of our own reproductive activities. At the present time in history, recognition of our connectedness with all other life on the planet reinforces the need for the abortion option. When the interests of life in this larger sense are taken into consideration, the pro-choice position is actually the one most deserving of the adjective "pro-life."

40 Since abortion cannot be separated from its often important role in family planning, discussion of the global problems humanity is facing should also help turn attention to the underlying pronatalist orientation of many "pro-life" advocates. Outspoken antiabortionists such as Father Paul Marx, president of Human Life International, a U.S.-based organization acting to further restrict abortion rights in the less industrialized countries, and Judie Brown, president of the American Life Lobby, have gone on record in opposition to contraceptive use as well as abortion; see Jacobson, *The Global Politics of Abortion*, p. 54. Pronatalism is a position that requires a defense on its own merit, distinct from any connection it might exploit to the presumed rights of an unborn fetus. Appeal to "natural law" as a justification for unlimited human procreation in the face of our dramatic departure from the original "balance of nature" would seem a difficult task.

41 See Carol Gilligan's pioneering work in this area, *In a Different Voice. Psychological Theory and Women's Development* (Cambridge, MA: Harvard University Press, 1982), and, for instance, E. F. Kittay and D. T. Meyers, eds., *Women and Moral Theory* (Savage, MD: Rowman & Littlefield, 1987).

42 Celia Wolf-Devine, "Abortion and the 'Feminine Voice,'" *Public Affairs Quarterly* 3 (1989): 81–97.
43 Patricia Jagentowicz Mills, "Feminism and Ecology: On the Domination of Nature," *Hypatia* 6 (1991): 162– 78.
44 See Val Plumwood, "Nature, Self, and Gender: Feminism, Environmental Philosophy, and the Critique of Rationalism," *Hypatia* 6 (1991): 3–27.

Review Questions

1. How does Hawkins view "concern for life" and the term "pro-life"?
2. What are the links between population growth, poverty, and environmental degradation?
3. How is nonhuman life affected?
4. What role does abortion play in population control?
5. Explain ecofeminism. How does Hawkins apply ecofeminism to the pro-life position?

Discussion Questions

1. Is the zygote a potential person? What does Hawkins say? What do you think?
2. Hawkins suggests that before implantation (about fourteen days after conception), it is problematic whether or not the woman is pregnant or can undergo an abortion. Do you agree? Why or why not?
3. Hawkins challenges the claim that there is a sharp distinction between human and nonhuman vertebrate life. Can such a distinction be made? How?
4. Why does Hawkins think that the pro-choice position is the one most deserving of the label "pro-life"? Do you agree? Why or why not?

Problem Cases

1. Partial-Birth Abortions

(Reported by Deborah Sontag in *The New York Times*, March 21, 1997.) On March 21, 1997, the U.S. House of Representatives voted to ban "partial-birth abortions." This procedure is technically called "intact dilation and evacuation" and is done after twenty weeks of pregnancy. A doctor who has performed 200 such abortions describes it as follows: Twenty-four hours before the abortion, the woman's cervix is dilated through the use of laminaria, which are sterilized sticks of seaweed. The next day, the patient is given a local anesthetic and a sedative. Both the mother and the fetus are asleep during the procedure. The fetus is partly pulled out in a breach position, that is, with the feet first and the head remaining in the womb (thus the phrase "partial birth"). Then the skull of the fetus has to be crushed or perforated with forceps to get it out.

Doctors who perform the intact-dilation-and-evacuation procedure claim that it is safer for the woman than a classic D & C, where the fetus is scraped out with a serrated forceps, dismembering and killing it in the process. The woman's uterus can be perforated by the forceps or by fragments of bone as the fetus disintegrates. It is much safer to manually pull out the fetus intact, the doctors say.

No reliable statistics exist on the use of the intact dilation and extraction procedure. Groups opposing the ban originally claimed there were between 450 and 500 a year, but the Catholic bishops estimate that there are between 800 and 2,000 a year.

Ron Fitzsimmons, a representative of abortion providers, said he lied in February 1997, in a comment to *Nightline* that was never broadcast, by underestimating the number of these abortions performed a year. There are really several thousand, he said. But his critics said he was speaking without statistical evidence.

According to federal statistics, most late abortions are performed between twenty and twenty-four weeks, and about 86 percent are done by some kind of dilation-and-evacuation procedure. About 15,000 late abortions are performed a year, or about 1 percent of the 1.4 million abortions that occur in the United States each year.

Doctors who perform late abortions say that they are most often used on poor, young women choosing to end an unwanted pregnancy. But in some cases, they are done for medical reasons—for example, because the fetus is severely abnormal or the woman faces grave health risks. When President Clinton vetoed the ban in 1996, he surrounded himself with five women who had obtained partial-birth abortions for medical reasons.

Do you agree with President Clinton that partial-birth abortions should not be banned? Or do you agree with the House of Representatives that the procedure should be banned? Explain your position.

2. The Morning-After Pill

(Discussed in "The Morning-After Pill," by Jan Hoffman, in *The New York Times Magazine,* January 10, 1993.) Depending on when a woman takes it, the morning-after pill prevents either fertilization (occurring up to eighteen hours after intercourse) or implantation of the fertilized egg in the lining of the uterus (occurring about a week or two after conception). Because pregnancy tests do not register positive until a day or two after implantation, a woman who takes the pill after intercourse will not know if she has prevented conception or implantation.

The drug most often used as a morning-after pill is Ovral. It is also used as a birth-control pill, and it was approved as such by the FDA (the Federal Food and Drug Administration) in 1968. Other lower-dose pills that can be used as morning-after pills are Lo/Ovral, Nordette, Levlen, Triphasil, and Tri Levlen. All these pills combine estrogen and progestin. They affect a woman's hormones in such a way that the egg cannot be fertilized; or if it is, it cannot become implanted in the lining of the uterus. Instead the egg is sloughed off during menstruation.

The morning-after pill can be effectively taken up to seventy-two hours after intercourse, and it reduces the likelihood of pregnancy to below 8 percent. (On her most fertile day, a woman's chance of becoming pregnant is at most about 25 percent.) Although it certainly reduces the chances of becoming pregnant, it is not completely effective because it does not prevent tubal pregnancies. The side effects of the morning-after pill include temporary nausea and breast tenderness, and it is not recommended for women who should not take oral contraceptives.

According to the *Times* article, the morning-after pill is widely prescribed on college campuses, and it has been part of standard care for rape victims for more than a decade. Planned Parenthood affiliates have been offering it for about three years. Use of birth-control pills as morning-after pills has not received the approval of the FDA, largely because no drug company has sought approval, and without FDA approval they cannot be dispensed in federally supported Title X clinics that serve poor women.

Doctors estimate that by making the morning-after pill widely available, the number of unwanted pregnancies could be reduced by 1.7 million annually and the number of abortions could be reduced by 800,000 annually. Currently, there are about 3.5 million unwanted pregnancies per year in the United States and about 1.4 million abortions.

The morning-after pill raises several interesting questions:

Is preventing implantation an abortion, contraception, interception, or what?

Is the zygote or fertilized egg a person with rights before it becomes implanted?

The IUD (interuterine device) also prevents fertilization or implantation. Does using it amount to getting an abortion?

In the one or two weeks before implantation, many fertilized eggs are naturally sloughed off, and women don't usually think of this as miscarriage. So why should a woman think of preventing implantation as an abortion?

3. Mrs. Sherri Finkbine and Thalidomide

In 1962, Mrs. Sherri Finkbine, the mother of four normal children, became pregnant. During the pregnancy, Mrs. Finkbine had trouble sleeping, so without consulting her physician, she took some tranquilizers containing the drug thalidomide that her husband had brought back from a trip to Europe. In Europe, the sedative was widely used.

Later Mrs. Finkbine read that a number of severely deformed children had been born in Europe. These children's limbs failed to develop or developed in malformed ways; some were born blind and deaf or had seriously defective internal organs. The birth defects were traced to the use in pregnancy of a widely used tranquilizer whose active ingredient was thalidomide, the very tranquilizer that she had taken.

Mrs. Finkbine went to her physician, and he confirmed her fears. The tranquilizer did contain thalidomide, and she had a very good chance of delivering a seriously deformed baby. The physician recommended an abortion. Mrs. Finkbine then presented her case to the three-member medical board of Phoenix, and they granted approval for the abortion.

In her concern for other women who might have taken thalidomide, Mrs. Finkbine told her story to a local newspaper. The story made the front page, and it wasn't long before reporters had discovered and published Mrs. Finkbine's identity. She became the object of an intense anti-abortion campaign, and she was condemned as a murderer by the Vatican newspaper.

As a result of the controversy, the medical board decided that their approval for an abortion would not survive a court test because the Arizona statute at that time allowed abortion only to save the mother's life. So the board withdrew their approval.

Eventually Mrs. Finkbine found it necessary to get an abortion in Sweden. After the abortion, Mrs. Finkbine asked if the fetus was a boy or a girl. The doctor could not say because the fetus was too badly deformed.

Do you think that Mrs. Finkbine acted wrongly in having an abortion? Explain your answer.

Do you think that the government has a right to prohibit abortions in such cases? Why or why not?

Suggested Readings

1. The best source of statistics on all aspects of abortion and pregnancy is The Alan Guttmacher Institute (http://www.agi-usa.org). The federal Centers for Disease Control and Prevention also provides nationally valid data, but consistent with its function, it focuses on the safety of the procedure.

2. Michael Tooley, "Abortion and Infanticide," *Philosophy and Public Affairs* 2 (Fall 1972), pp. 47–66, presents a classic defense of the pro-choice view that neither a fetus nor a newborn infant has a serious right to continued existence and that both abortion and infanticide are morally acceptable. Tooley also has a book titled *Abortion and Infanticide* (Oxford University Press, 1974), in which he develops his position.

3. Gary M. Atkinson, "The Morality of Abortion," *International Philosophy Quarterly* 14 (Spring 1974), pp. 347–62, argues, like Tooley, that abortion and infanticide are morally equivalent, but he takes the argument a step further by claiming that each is equivalent to involuntary euthanasia. But since involuntary euthanasia is wrong, on Atkinson's view, it follows that abortion and infanticide are wrong too.

4. Jane English, "Abortion and the Concept of a Person," *Canadian Journal of Philosophy* 5, no. 2 (October 1975), pp. 233–43, argues that the question about whether the fetus is a person or not cannot be conclusively settled because the concept of "person" cannot be defined in terms of necessary and sufficient conditions. English goes on to argue that even if the fetus is a person, the mother's right to self-defense is strong enough to justify abortions to avoid death or serious harm.

5. L. W. Sumner, "Abortion," in *Health Care Ethics,* ed. Donald VanDeVeer and Tom Regan (Temple University Press, 1987), pp. 162–81, proposes a moderate view about the moral standing of the fetus: It acquires moral standing when it becomes sentient—that is, capable of feeling pleasure and pain. Before this dividing line in the development of the fetus (which occurs sometime in the second trimester), abortion is the moral equivalent of contraception, and after this line abortion is the moral equivalent of infanticide.

6. Susan Sherwin, "Abortion Through a Feminist Ethics Lens," *Dialogue* 30 (1991), pp. 327–42, presents a standard feminist view that freedom to choose abortion is essential for sexual and reproductive freedom, and without it, women will continue to be oppressed by men.

7. *Feminist Philosophies,* ed. Janet A. Kourany, James P. Sterba, and Rosemarie Tong (Prentice Hall, 1992), has four feminist articles on abortion and reproduction, including "Abortion: Is a Woman a Person?" by Ellen Willis. Willis claims that pro-lifers view the woman as a mere womb and not as a person with rights.

8. Angela Davis, *Women, Race, and Class* (Random House, 1981), Chapter 12, discusses the abortion-rights movement in the context of race, class, and the women's liberation movement.

9. Sally Markowitz, "Feminism and Abortion," *Social Theory and Practice* 16 (Spring 1990), pp. 1–17, maintains that women with unwanted pregnancies should be allowed to have abortions in a society where they suffer oppression and discrimination.

10. Ronald Dworkin, "A Critical Review of Feminist Analyses of Abortion," *The New York Review of Books* (June 10, 1993), attacks Catharine MacKinnon, Robin West, Carol Gilligan, and other feminists who emphasize the unique relationship between the pregnant woman and the fetus.

11. Jim Stone, "Why Potentiality Matters," *Canadian Journal of Philosophy* 17 (December 1987), pp. 815–30, argues that the fetus has a right to life because it is potentially an adult human being.

12. Louis P. Pojman and Francis J. Beckwith, eds., *The Abortion Controversy* (Wadsworth, 1988), is a comprehensive anthology that includes articles on the *Roe* decision, Thomson's appeal to the woman's right to her body, numerous articles about the personhood of the fetus, and feminist articles.

13. Alan Zaitchik, "Viability and the Morality of Abortion," *Philosophy and Public Affairs* 10, no. 1 (1981), pp. 18–24, defends the view that viability is a morally significant dividing line.

14. Tristram H. Engelhardt, Jr., "The Ontology of Abortion," *Ethics* 84 (April 1974), pp. 217–34, maintains that the fetus is not a person until the later stages of pregnancy, but after viability it can be treated as if it were a person.

15. Peter Singer, *Practical Ethics*, 2d ed. (Cambridge University Press, 1993), Chapter 6, presents a utilitarian view of abortion. The version of utilitarianism that Singer accepts is called preference utilitarianism.

16. Sissela Bok, "Ethical Problems of Abortion," *Hastings Center Studies* 2 (January 1974), pp. 33–52, rejects attempts to define humanity and suggests that various reasons for not getting an abortion become stronger as the fetus develops.

17. Daniel Callahan, *Abortion, Law, Choice and Morality* (Macmillan, 1970), defends the moderate view that the fetus has what he calls a partial moral status.

18. Joel Feinberg and Barbara Baum Levenbook, "Abortion," in *Matters of Life and Death*, third edition, ed. Tom Regan (Random House, 1993), provide a sophisticated discussion of various issues connected to abortion, and end up with a moderate position. But in a postscript they decide that a legal ban on abortion may be justified even if abortion is not generally morally wrong.

19. R. M. Hare, "Abortion and the Golden Rule," *Philosophy and Public Affairs* 4 (Spring 1975), pp. 201–22, attacks those, such as Judith Jarvis Thomson, who appeal to moral intuition, and uses the Golden Rule as a basic ethical principle to defend a moderate view of abortion.

20. Susan Nicholson, *Abortion and the Roman Catholic Church* (Religious Ethics, 1974), explains the position of the Catholic Church on abortion.

Chapter 3

Euthanasia and Sustaining Life

Introduction

Factual Background

Euthanasia is killing someone for the sake of mercy to relieve great suffering. But when a doctor helps an injured or ill person commit suicide, as Dr. Jack Kevorkian has done in 120 cases, it seems that there is little difference between doctor-assisted suicide and euthanasia. This point is made by Singer in the readings.

Statistics on euthanasia and physician-assisted suicide are difficult to obtain in the United States. Other than Dr. Kevorkian, few doctors come forward to talk about something that is illegal in every state except Oregon. It one study, 36 percent of the doctors said they would write lethal prescriptions if it were legal, and 24 percent said they would administer lethal injections. Another study, reported in the *Journal of the American Medical Association* (August 12, 1998), found in telephone interviews of 355 oncologists that almost 16 percent had participated in euthanasia or physician-assisted suicide. A national survey found that nearly one in five doctors who care for very ill and dying people said that they had been asked for help in dying, either by delivering a lethal injection or by writing a prescription for lethal drugs, but only 5 percent admitted to administering a lethal injection, and only 3 percent said they had ever written the prescription.

Since 1984 euthanasia in the Netherlands has been technically illegal but not prosecuted if certain conditions are satisfied. The request to die must be free and well considered, there must be unacceptable suffering, and the physician must consult with another doctor. If these conditions are met, then an infringement of the law that forbids euthanasia and assisted suicide can be justified. In 1994 a new law required physicians to accurately report death in cases of euthanasia and assisted suicide. As a result of this law, we have data on euthanasia practice in the Netherlands. In 1995 there were 3,200 cases of euthanasia and 400 cases of assisted suicide. In 15 cases the lives of newborns were terminated. There were over 14,000 cases where treatment was withdrawn or withheld with the intention to shorten life.

Oregon is the only state in the United States where doctor-assisted suicide for the terminally ill is legal. The state law, known officially as the Death with Dignity Act, took effect in November 1997. The law applies only to adults of sound mind who have, in the opinion of at least two doctors, less than six months to live. Doctors may prescribe but not administer the lethal dose. Those requesting death must fill out and sign a single-page form titled "Request for medication to end my life in a humane and dignified manner." According to *The New York Times* (August 19, 1998), eight people have died after taking lethal drugs according to the provisions of the law. All eight were suffering from cancer, all received a medical evaluation by at least two doctors confirming their terminal condition, all were judged to be of sound mind by the doctors, and all complied with the fifteen-day waiting period between the first and second requests for the lethal drugs.

In 1998 Michigan voters overwhelming rejected Proposal B, a ballot initiative that would have permitted doctors to administer lethal doses of medication to terminally ill patients. Previously, the state had outlawed assisted suicide for fifteen months in response to the practices of Dr. Kevorkian, but then it failed to convict him, even though he continued to violate the law. (See the first Problem Case.)

In June 1997 the Supreme Court ruled that laws in New York and Washington making doctor-assisted suicide a crime were not unconstitutional. But the 9-to-0 decision was tentative, and some of the justices seemed to grant that some terminally ill people in intractable pain might be able to claim a constitutional right to a doctor's assistance in hastening their deaths. Justice Sandra Day O'Connor, for example, said that it was still an open question whether "a mentally competent person who is experiencing great suffering" that cannot otherwise be controlled has a constitutionally based "interest in controlling the circumstances of his or her imminent death." (See the story by Linda Greenhouse in *The New York Times*, June 27, 1997.)

The Readings

Discussions of euthanasia often distinguish between different types of euthanasia. Voluntary euthanasia is mercy killing with the consent of the terminally ill or suffering person. Many writers include physician-assisted suicide as a type of voluntary euthanasia; for example, Singer seems to do this in the reading. Nonvoluntary euthanasia, by contrast, is mercy killing without the consent of the person killed, although the consent of others, such as parents or relatives, can be obtained. Writers who discuss nonvoluntary euthanasia usually have in mind the killing of those who are unable to give consent—for example, a comatose person such as Karen Quinlan or a defective infant. Obviously, such a person cannot commit suicide. There is another possibility, however, and that is the mercy killing of a person who is able to give consent but is not asked. If the person killed does not wish to die, it might be more accurate to call this involuntary euthanasia. This is not discussed in the readings, but it may be safely assumed that all the authors in this book would consider it wrong.

A further distinction is often made between active and passive euthanasia, or between killing and letting a patient die for the sake of mercy. Just how this distinction should be drawn and whether the distinction should be made at all is a focus of debate in the readings. As Rachels explains it in the reading, active euthanasia is taking a direct action designed to kill the patient, such as giving the patient a lethal injection of morphine. Passive euthanasia, by contrast, is allowing the patient to die by withholding treatment—not performing lifesaving surgery on a defective infant, for example.

Rachels believes that this distinction has no moral significance and that using it leads to pointless suffering and confused moral thinking. Callahan does not agree. From a moral perspective, he says, there is an important difference between killing a person directly with a fatal injection, where an action causes death, and letting a person die from disease, where it is the disease, not an action, that causes death. In the case of killing a person directly, the killer is morally culpable; but if the person dies from disease, then it seems that no one is morally culpable.

But there are still problems. Callahan admits that in cases where the doctor turns off a respirator or removes an artificial feeding tube, the distinction is problematic. Are these cases of killing a person directly with an act (the act of turning off the respirator or removing the feeding tube), or are they cases of letting the person die (from not breathing or lack of food)?

John Harris raises more problems for the distinction between killing and letting die in his discussion of the survival lottery. Suppose we can save two dying patients, Y and Z, by killing an innocent person, A. We take A's heart and give it to Y, who needs a new heart to survive, and we take A's lungs and give them to Z, who needs new lungs. No doubt we are guilty of killing an innocent person, but if we let Y and Z die by failing to perform the transplants, then aren't we still guilty, guilty of killing two innocent persons instead of one? After all, even Callahan seems to grant that if we allow someone to die when we could keep them alive, then we are guilty of killing them, just as guilty as if we had killed them directly.

It might be objected that Harris is not talking about real life; his survival lottery is pure fiction. But Susan Sherwin gives us some disturbing facts about the real world, where thousands of women and members of minorities die every year from lack of medical care. She says, for example, that black American women are four times more likely to die in childbirth and three times more likely to have their newborns die than are white women. Black women in the United States are twice as likely to die of heart disease as are white women; they are more likely than white women to die from breast cancer, despite having lower rates of incidence; and they are four times more likely than white women to die of homicide.

Why do we allow black women to die at much higher rates than white women? Why do we let minorities, women, and the poor die while we keep white men alive at great cost? According to Sherwin the answer is clear: The health care system is racist and sexist and classist; it discriminates against minorities, women, and the poor. To remedy the unfairness of the current delivery of health care, Sherwin thinks we should adopt an alternative feminist model that is more egalitarian, allows equal access to health care, and promotes health rather than merely treating injury and illness.

Philosophical Issues

One basic issue is whether voluntary euthanasia and physician-assisted suicide are wrong or not. The standard view, represented by the AMA statement and Callahan, is that both are wrong. The AMA statement quoted by Rachels says clearly that "the intentional termination of the life of one human being by another—mercy killing—is contrary to that for which the medical profession stands." Callahan agrees that doctors should not kill patients. He insists that the role of the physician is to cure and comfort, never to kill.

Rachels and Singer take a different view. Rachels argues that in some cases active euthanasia is preferable to passive euthanasia because it reduces suffering. If there is a choice between a quick and painless death and prolonged suffering, and no other alternative, then Rachels would prefer a quick and painless death. Singer appeals to the principle of respect for autonomy. This principle tells us to allow rational agents to live their lives according to their decisions, and if they choose to die, they should be allowed to do so and even should be assisted in carrying out their decision.

Another important issue, as we have seen, is whether or not there is a morally significant difference between killing and letting a patient die, or between active and passive euthanasia, or between intentionally causing death and merely permitting death. Rachels attacks such distinctions, and Callahan defends them. It seems obvious that most doctors make such distinctions; the statistics show that withholding or withdrawing lifesaving treatment is much more common than active euthanasia or physician-assisted suicide.

Another matter of controversy is the distinction between ordinary and extraordinary means of prolonging life. This distinction is found in the AMA statement that allows the cessation of the employment of extraordinary means to prolong the life of the body. Rachels thinks that the cessation of extraordinary means of treatment amounts to passive euthanasia because it is the intentional termination of life. But Callahan suggests a response to this. He points out that painful and excessive treatment (that is, extraordinary means of treatment) can be as detrimental to the welfare of the patient as inadequate treatment. But since the doctor's obligation is to promote the welfare of the patient, the cessation of this extraordinary treatment should be allowed, where the reason for doing this is not to cause death but to avoid the painful and excessive treatment.

Although he does not explicitly discuss it, Callahan seems to accept a traditional view about intentions called the Doctrine of Double Effect. (See the article by Philippa Foot cited in the Suggested Readings.) According to this doctrine, as long as the intended consequence of an act is good, a bad foreseen consequence (such as death) can be morally allowed, provided it is not intended and prevents a greater evil (such as great suffering). A common medical practice can be used to illustrate this. Suppose that a doctor gives a terminal cancer patient an overdose of morphine, that is, an amount sufficient to kill the patient. If the doctor intends only to reduce or eliminate the patient's pain, and not to kill the patient, and if the death of the patient is not as bad as the patient's suffering, then according to the Doctrine of Double Effect, the doctor's action is not wrong, even though the doctor foresees that the patient will die from the overdose.

This kind of reasoning seems fairly common among doctors. It seems to be suggested, for example, when the AMA statement says that it is *intentional* termination of life that is forbidden. Doesn't this allow for unintentional but foreseen death? In his successful legal defenses, Dr. Kevorkian has repeatedly said that his only intention is to reduce or eliminate great suffering, and not to cause death.

Critics of the Doctrine of Double Effect complain that no clear distinction can be made between the two effects, the intended one and the unintended but foreseen one. If Dr. Kevorkian intends to reduce the patient's suffering but also knows that the patient is getting a lethal dose of drugs when she turns the switch on the suicide machine, does it make sense to say that Dr. Kevorkian doesn't also intend to kill the patient with his machine?

Finally, there is the basic issue of how to make life-or-death decisions. One standard answer, given by Rachels, is to appeal to the quality of a person's life. If a person will have a bad life, then she should be allowed to end it; but if she will have a good life, then it is wrong to end it. But how do we distinguish between good and bad lives? That is a classical problem that resists easy solution. Hedonists would say that a life full of pleasure is good, and a life filled with suffering is bad. But Kant and many others would reject this view. It is not represented in the readings, but it is worth mentioning that the Christian view is that all life is sacred, all life is valuable, no matter how much suffering it contains.

Active and Passive Euthanasia

JAMES RACHELS

James Rachels is professor of philosophy at the University of Alabama at Birmingham. He is the author of *The Elements of Moral Philosophy,* (second edition 1993), *The End of Life: Euthanasia and Morality* (1986), and *Created from Animals: The Moral Implications of Darwinism* (1990).

Here Rachels attacks the distinction between active and passive euthanasia, and the doctrine apparently accepted by the American Medical Association that taking direct action to kill a patient (active euthanasia) is wrong, but withholding treatment and allowing a patient to die (passive euthanasia) is allowable. Rachels makes three criticisms of this doctrine. First, it results in unnecessary suffering for patients who die slowly and painfully rather than quickly and painlessly. Second, the doctrine leads to moral decisions based on irrelevant considerations. Third, the distinction between killing and letting die assumed by the doctrine is of no moral significance.

Source:James Rachels, "Active and Passive Euthanasia," from *The Elements of Moral Philosophy* (1986), pp. 90–103. Reprinted with the permission of The McGraw-Hill Companies.

THE DISTINCTION between active and passive euthanasia is thought to be crucial for medical ethics. The idea is that it is permissible, at least in some cases, to withhold treatment and allow a patient to die, but it is never permissible to take any direct action designed to kill the patient. This doctrine seems to be accepted by most doctors, and it is endorsed in a statement adopted by the House of Delegates of the American Medical Association on December 4, 1973:

> The intentional termination of the life of one human being by another—mercy killing—is contrary to that for which the medical profession stands and is contrary to the policy of the American Medical Association. The cessation of the employment of extraordinary means to prolong the life of the body when there is irrefutable evidence that biological death is imminent is the decision of the patient and/or his immediate family. The advice and judgment of the physician should be freely available to the patient and/or his immediate family.

However, a strong case can be made against this doctrine. In what follows I will set out some of the relevant arguments, and urge doctors to reconsider their views on this matter.

To begin with a familiar type of situation, a patient who is dying of incurable cancer of the throat is in terrible pain, which can no longer be satisfactorily alleviated. He is certain to die within a few days, even if present treatment is continued, but he does not want to go on living for those days since the pain is unbearable. So he asks the doctor for an end to it, and his family joins in the request.

Suppose the doctor agrees to withhold treatment, as the conventional doctrine says he may. The justification for his doing so is that the patient is in terrible agony, and since he is going to die anyway, it would be wrong to prolong his suffering needlessly. But now notice this. If one simply withholds treatment, it may take the patient longer to die, and so he may suffer more than he would if more direct action were taken and a lethal injection given. This fact provides strong reason for thinking that, once the initial decision not to prolong his agony has been made, active euthanasia is actually preferable to passive euthanasia, rather than the reverse. To say

otherwise is to endorse the option that leads to more suffering rather than less, and is contrary to the humanitarian impulse that prompts the decision not to prolong his life in the first place.

Part of my point is that the process of being "allowed to die" can be relatively slow and painful, whereas being given a lethal injection is relatively quick and painless. Let me give a different sort of example. In the United States about one in 600 babies is born with Down's syndrome. Most of these babies are otherwise healthy—that is, with only the usual pediatric care, they will proceed to an otherwise normal infancy. Some, however, are born with congenital defects such as intestinal obstructions that require operations if they are to live. Sometimes, the parents and the doctor will decide not to operate, and let the infant die. Anthony Shaw describes what happens then:

> . . . When surgery is denied [the doctor] must try to keep the infant from suffering while natural forces sap the baby's life away. As a surgeon whose natural inclination is to use the scalpel to fight off death, standing by and watching a salvageable baby die is the most emotionally exhausting experience I know. It is easy at a conference, in a theoretical discussion, to decide that such infants should be allowed to die. It is altogether different to stand by in the nursery and watch as dehydration and infection wither a tiny being over hours and days. This is a terrible ordeal for me and the hospital staff—much more so than for the parents who never set foot in the nursery.[1]

I can understand why some people are opposed to all euthanasia, and insist that such infants must be allowed to live. I think I can also understand why other people favor destroying these babies quickly and painlessly. But why should anyone favor letting "dehydration and infection wither a tiny being over hours and days"? The doctrine that says that a baby may be allowed to

1 A. Shaw: "Doctor, Do We Have a Choice?" *The New York Times Magazine,* January 30, 1972, p. 54.

dehydrate and wither, but may not be given an injection that would end its life without suffering, seems so patently cruel as to require no further refutation. The strong language is not intended to offend, but only to put the point in the clearest possible way.

My second argument is that the conventional doctrine leads to decisions concerning life and death made on irrelevant grounds.

Consider again the case of the infants with Down's syndrome who need operations for congenital defects unrelated to the syndrome to live. Sometimes, there is no operation, and the baby dies, but when there is no such defect, the baby lives on. Now, an operation such as that to remove an intestinal obstruction is not prohibitively difficult. The reason why such operations are not performed in these cases is, clearly, that the child has Down's syndrome and the parents and doctor judge that because of that fact it is better for the child to die.

But notice that this situation is absurd, no matter what view one takes of the lives and potentials of such babies. If the life of such an infant is worth preserving, what does it matter if it needs a simple operation? Or, if one thinks it better that such a baby should not live on, what difference does it make that it happens to have an unobstructed intestinal tract? In either case, the matter of life and death is being decided on irrelevant grounds. It is the Down's syndrome, and not the intestines, that is the issue. The matter should be decided, if at all, on that basis, and not be allowed to depend on the essentially irrelevant question of whether the intestinal tract is blocked.

What makes this situation possible, of course, is the idea that when there is an intestinal blockage, one can "let the baby die," but when there is no such defect there is nothing that can be done, for one must not "kill" it. The fact that this idea leads to such results as deciding life or death on irrelevant grounds is another good reason why the doctrine should be rejected.

One reason why so many people think that there is an important moral difference between active and passive euthanasia is that they think killing someone is morally worse than letting someone die. But is it? Is killing, in itself, worse than letting die? To investigate this issue, two cases may be considered that are exactly alike except that one involves killing whereas the other involves letting someone die. Then, it can be asked whether this difference makes any difference to the moral assessments. It is important that the cases be exactly alike, except for this one difference, since otherwise one cannot be confident that it is this difference and not some other that accounts for any variation in the assessments of the two cases. So, let us consider this pair of cases:

In the first, Smith stands to gain a large inheritance if anything should happen to his six-year-old cousin. One evening while the child is taking his bath, Smith sneaks into the bathroom and drowns the child, and then arranges things so that it will look like an accident.

In the second, Jones also stands to gain if anything should happen to his six-year-old cousin. Like Smith, Jones sneaks in planning to drown the child in his bath. However, just as he enters the bathroom Jones sees the child slip and hit his head and fall face down in the water. Jones is delighted; he stands by, ready to push the child's head back under if it is necessary, but it is not necessary. With only a little thrashing about the child drowns all by himself, "accidentally," as Jones watches and does nothing.

Now Smith killed the child, whereas Jones "merely" let the child die. That is the only difference between them. Did either man behave better, from a moral point of view? If the difference between killing and letting die were in itself a morally important matter, one should say that Jones's behavior was less reprehensible than Smith's. But does one really want to say that? I think not. In the first place, both men acted from the same motive, personal gain, and both had exactly the same end in view when they acted. It may be inferred from Smith's conduct that he is a bad man, although that judgment may be withdrawn or modified if certain further facts are learned about him—for example, that he is mentally deranged. But would not the very same thing be inferred about Jones from his conduct? And would not the same further considerations also be relevant to any modification of this judgment? Moreover, suppose Jones pleaded, in his own defense, "After all, I didn't do anything except just stand there and watch the child drown. I didn't kill him; I only let him die." Again, if letting die were in itself less bad than killing, this defense should have at least some weight. But it does not. Such a "defense" can only be regarded as a grotesque perversion of moral reasoning. Morally speaking, it is no defense at all.

Now, it may be pointed out, quite properly, that the cases of euthanasia with which doctors are concerned are not like this at all. They do not involve personal gain or the destruction of normally healthy children. Doctors are concerned only with cases in which the patient's life is of no further use to him, or in which the patient's life has become or will soon become a terrible burden. However, the point is the same in these cases: the bare difference between killing and letting die does not, in itself, make a moral difference. If a doctor lets a patient die, for humane reasons, he is in the same moral position as if he had given the patient a lethal injection for humane reasons. If his decision was wrong—if, for example, the patient's illness was in fact curable—the decision would be equally regrettable no matter which method was used to carry it out. And if the doctor's decision was the right one, the method used is not in itself important.

The AMA policy statement isolates the crucial issue very well; the crucial issue is "the intentional termination of the life of one human being by another." But after identifying this issue, and forbidding "mercy killing," the statement goes on to deny that the cessation of treatment is the intentional termination of a life. This is where the mistake comes in, for what is the cessation of treatment, in these circumstances, if it is not "the intentional termination of the life of one human being by another"? Of

course it is exactly that, and if it were not, there would be no point to it.

Many people will find this judgment hard to accept. One reason, I think, is that it is very easy to conflate the question of whether killing is, in itself, worse than letting die, with the very different question of whether most actual cases of killing are more reprehensible than most actual cases of letting die. Most actual cases of killing are clearly terrible (think, for example, of all the murders reported in the newspapers), and one hears of such cases every day. On the other hand, one hardly ever hears of a case of letting die, except for the actions of doctors who are motivated by humanitarian reasons. So one learns to think of killing in a much worse light than of letting die. But this does not mean that there is something about killing that makes it in itself worse than letting die, for it is not the bare difference between killing and letting die that makes the difference in these cases. Rather, the other factors—the murderer's motive of personal gain, for example, contrasted with the doctor's humanitarian motivation—account for different reactions to the different cases.

I have argued that killing is not in itself any worse than letting die; if my contention is right, it follows that active euthanasia is not any worse than passive euthanasia. What arguments can be given on the other side? The most common, I believe, is the following:

> The important difference between active and passive euthanasia is that, in passive euthanasia, the doctor does not do anything to bring about the patient's death. The doctor does nothing, and the patient dies of whatever ills already afflict him. In active euthanasia, however, the doctor does something to bring about the patient's death: he kills him. The doctor who gives the patient with cancer a lethal injection has himself caused his patient's death; whereas if he merely ceases treatment, the cancer is the cause of the death.

A number of points need to be made here. The first is that it is not exactly correct to say that in passive euthanasia the doctor does nothing, for he does do one thing that is very important: he lets the patient die. "Letting someone die" is certainly different, in some respects, from other types of action—mainly in that it is a kind of action that one may perform by way of not performing certain other actions. For example, one may let a patient die by way of not giving medication, just as one may insult someone by way of not shaking his hand. But for any purpose of moral assessment, it is a type of action nonetheless. The decision to let a patient die is subject to moral appraisal in the same way that a decision to kill him would be subject to moral appraisal: it may be assessed as wise or unwise, compassionate or sadistic, right or wrong. If a doctor deliberately let a patient die who was suffering from a routinely curable illness, the doctor would certainly be to blame for what he had done, just as he would be to blame if he had needlessly killed the patient. Charges against him would then be appropriate. If so, it would be no defense at all for him to insist that he didn't "do anything." He would have done something very serious indeed, for he let his patient die.

Fixing the cause of death may be very important from a legal point of view, for it may determine whether criminal charges are brought against the doctor. But I do not think that this notion can be used to show a moral difference between active and passive euthanasia. The reason why it is considered bad to be the cause of someone's death is that death is regarded as a great evil—and so it is. However, if it has been decided that euthanasia—even passive euthanasia—is desirable in a given case, it has also been decided that in this instance death is no greater an evil than the patient's continued existence.

And if this is true, the usual reason for not wanting to be the cause of someone's death simply does not apply.

Finally, doctors may think that all of this is only of academic interest—the sort of thing that philosophers may worry about but that has no practical bearing on their own work. After all, doctors must be concerned about the legal consequences of what they do, and active euthanasia is clearly forbidden by the law. But even so, doctors should also be concerned with the fact that the law is forcing upon them a moral doctrine that may well be indefensible, and has a considerable effect on their practices. Of course, most doctors are not now in the position of being coerced in this matter, for they do not regard themselves as merely going along with what the law requires. Rather in statements such as the AMA policy statement that I have quoted, they are endorsing this doctrine as a central point of medical ethics. In that statement, active euthanasia is condemned not merely as illegal but as "contrary to that for which the medical profession stands," whereas passive euthanasia is approved. However, the preceding considerations suggest that there is really no moral difference between the two, considered in themselves (there may be important moral differences in some cases in their *consequences*, but, as I pointed out, these differences may make active euthanasia, and not passive euthanasia, the morally preferable option). So, whereas doctors may have to discriminate between active and passive euthanasia to satisfy the law, they should not do any more than that. In particular, they should not give the distinction any added authority and weight by writing it into official statements of medical ethics.

Review Questions

1. According to Rachels, what is the distinction between active and passive euthanasia?
2. Why does Rachels think that being allowed to die is worse in some cases than a lethal injection?
3. What is Rachels's second argument against the conventional doctrine?
4. According to Rachels, why isn't killing worse than letting die?

Discussion Questions

1. The AMA statement quoted by Rachels does not use the terminology of active and passive euthanasia. Furthermore, so-called passive euthanasia could be the intentional termination of life rejected by the AMA. Does the AMA really accept this distinction? Why or why not?
2. Is the distinction between killing and letting die morally relevant? What do you think?
3. Should the law be changed to allow active euthanasia or not? Defend your view.

Killing and Allowing to Die

DANIEL CALLAHAN

Daniel Callahan serves on the staff of The Hastings Center after retiring as its president in 1996. He is the author of *Setting Limits: Medical Goals in an Aging Society* (1987), *What Kind of Life: The Limits of Medical Progress* (1990), and *The Troubled Dream of Life: Living with Mortality* (1993).

Callahan defends the distinction between killing and allowing to die attacked by Rachels in the previous reading. He argues that the distinction can be understood as expressing three overlapping perspectives on nature and human action: (1) a metaphysical perspective that distinguishes between the self and the external world, (2) a moral perspective that sees a difference between physical causality and moral culpability, and (3) a medical perspective that sees the physician as curing and comforting patients rather than killing them.

. . . NO VALID DISTINCTION, many now argue, can be made between killing and allowing to die, or between an act of commission and one of omission. The standard distinction being challenged rests on the commonplace observation that lives can come to an end as the result of: (a) the direct action of another who becomes the cause of death (as in shooting a person), and (b) the result of impersonal forces where no human agent has acted (death by lightning, or by dis-

Source: Daniel Callahan, "Killing and Allowing to Die," from the *Hastings Center Report*, Vol. 19 (January/February 1989), pp. 5–6. Copyright © The Hastings Center. Reprinted by permission.

ease). The purpose of the distinction has been to separate those deaths caused by human action, and those caused by nonhuman events. It is, as a distinction, meant to say something about human beings and their relationship to the world. It is a way of articulating the difference between those actions for which human beings can be held rightly responsible, or blamed, and those of which they are innocent. At issue is the difference between physical causality, the realm of impersonal events, and moral culpability, the realm of human responsibility.

The challenges encompass two points. The first is that people can become equally dead by our omissions as well as our commissions. We can refrain from saving them when it is possible to do so, and they will be just as dead as if we shot them. It is our decision itself that is the reason for their death, not necessarily how we effectuate that decision. That fact establishes the basis of the second point: if we *intend* their death, it can be brought about as well by omitted acts as by those we commit. The crucial moral point is not how they die, but our intention about their death. We can, then, be responsible for the death of another by intending that they die and accomplish that end by standing aside and allowing them to die.

Despite these criticisms—resting upon ambiguities that can readily be acknowledged—the distinction between killing and allowing to die remains, I contend, perfectly valid. It not only has a logical validity but, no less importantly, a social validity whose place must be central in moral judgments. As a way of putting the distinction into perspective, I want to suggest that it is best understood as expressing three different, though overlapping, perspectives on nature and human action. I will call them the metaphysical, the moral, and the medical perspectives.

METAPHYSICAL

The first and most fundamental premise of the distinction between killing and allowing to die is that there is a sharp difference between the self and the external world. Unlike the childish fantasy that the world is nothing more than a projection of the self, or the neurotic person's fear that he or she is responsible for everything that goes wrong, the distinction is meant to uphold a simple notion: there is a world external to the self that has its own, and independent, causal dynamism. The mistake behind a conflation of killing and allowing to die is to assume that the self has become master of everything within and outside of the self. It is as if the conceit that modern man might ultimately control nature has been internalized: that, if the self might be

able to influence nature by its actions, then the self and nature must be one.

Of course that is a fantasy. The fact that we can intervene in nature, and cure or control many diseases, does not erase the difference between the self and the external world. It is as "out there" as ever, even if more under our sway. That sway, however great, is always limited. We can cure disease, but not always the chronic illness that comes with the cure. We can forestall death with modern medicine, but death always wins in the long run because of the innate limitations of the body, inherently and stubbornly beyond final human control. And we can distinguish between a diseased body and an aging body, but in the end if we wait long enough they always become one and the same body. To attempt to deny the distinction between killing and allowing to die is, then, mistakenly to impute more power to human action than it actually has and to accept the conceit that nature has now fallen wholly within the realm of human control. Not so.

MORAL

At the center of the distinction between killing and allowing to die is the difference between physical causality and moral culpability. To bring the life of another to an end by an injection kills the other directly; our action is the physical cause of the death. To allow someone to die from a disease we cannot cure (and that we did not cause) is to permit the disease to act as the cause of death. The notion of physical causality in both cases rests on the difference between human agency and the action of external nature. The ambiguity arises precisely because we can be morally culpable for killing someone (if we have no moral right to do so, as we would in self-defense) and no less culpable for allowing someone to die (if we have both the possibility and the obligation of keeping that person alive). Thus there are cases where, morally speaking, it makes no difference whether we killed or allowed to die;

we are equally responsible. In those instances, the lines of physical causality and moral culpability happen to cross. Yet the fact that they can cross in some cases in no way shows that they are always, or even usually, one and the same. We can normally find the difference in all but the most obscure cases. We should not, then, use the ambiguity of such cases to do away altogether with the distinction between killing and allowing to die. The ambiguity may obscure, but does not erase, the line between the two.

There is one group of ambiguous cases that is especially troublesome. Even if we grant the ordinary validity between killing and allowing to die, what about those cases that combine (a) an illness that renders a patient unable to carry out an ordinary biological function (to breathe or eat on his own, for example), and (b) our turning off a respirator or removing an artificial feeding tube? On the level of physical causality, have we killed the patient or allowed him to die? In one sense, it is our action that shortens his life, and yet in another sense his underlying disease brings his life to an end. I believe it reasonable to say that, since his life was being sustained by artificial means (respirator or feeding tube) made necessary because of the fact that he had an incapacitating disease, his disease is the ultimate reality behind his death. But for its reality, there would be no need for artificial sustenance in the first place and no moral issue at all. To lose sight of the paramount reality of the disease is to lose sight of the difference between our selves and the outer world.

I quickly add, and underscore, a moral point: the person who, without good moral reason, turns off a respirator or pulls a feeding tube, can be morally culpable; that the patient has been allowed to die of his underlying condition does not morally excuse him. The moral question is whether we are obliged to continue treating a life that is being artificially sustained. To cease treatment may or may not be morally acceptable; but it should be understood, in either case, that the physical cause of death was the underlying disease.

MEDICAL

An important social purpose of the distinction between killing and allowing to die has been that of protecting the historical role of the physician as one who tries to cure or comfort patients rather than to kill patients. Physicians have been given special knowledge about the body, knowledge that can be used to kill or to cure. They are also given great privileges in making use of that knowledge. It is thus all the more important that physicians' social role and power be, and be seen to be, a limited power. It may be used only to cure or comfort, never to kill. They have not been given, nor should they be given, the power to use their knowledge and skills to bring life to an end. It would open the way for powerful misuse and, no less importantly, represent an intrinsic violation of what it has meant to be a physician.

Yet if it is possible for physicians to misuse their knowledge and power to kill people directly, are they thereby required to use that same knowledge always to keep people alive, always to resist a disease that can itself kill the patient? The traditional answer has been: not necessarily. For the physician's ultimate obligation is to the welfare of the patient, and excessive treatment can be as detrimental to that welfare as inadequate treatment. Put another way, the obligation to resist the lethal power of disease is limited—it ceases when the patient is unwilling to have it resisted, or where the resistance no longer serves the patient's welfare. Behind this moral premise is the recognition that disease (of some kind) ultimately triumphs and that death is both inevitable sooner or later and not, in any case, always the greatest human evil. To demand of the physician that he always struggle against disease, as if it was in his power always to conquer it, would be to fall into the same metaphysical trap mentioned above: that of assuming that no distinction can be drawn between natural and human agency.

A final word. I suggested [in an earlier discussion] that the most potent motive for active euthanasia and assisted suicide stems from a dread of the power of medicine. That power then seems to take on a drive of its own regardless of the welfare or wishes of patients. No one can easily say no—not physicians, not patients, not families. My guess is that happens because too many have already come to believe that it is their choice, and their choice alone, which brings about death; and they do not want to exercise that kind of authority. The solution is not to erase the distinction between killing and allowing to die, but to underscore its validity and importance. We can bring disease as a cause of death back into the care of the dying.

Review Questions

1. How does Callahan explain the distinction between killing and allowing to die?
2. What is the metaphysical perspective on the distinction, according to Callahan?
3. How is the distinction viewed from the moral perspective?
4. What is the medical perspective on the distinction?

Discussion Questions

1. When a doctor turns off a respirator or removes an artificial feeding tube, has the doctor killed the patient or merely allowed the patient to die? What is Callahan's answer? Do you agree? Why or why not?
2. What does Callahan mean when he talks about a "dread of the power of medicine"? Why can't the power of medicine be used to help the patient?

Justifying Voluntary Euthanasia

PETER SINGER

Peter Singer is professor of philosophy, codirector of the Institute of Ethics and Public Affairs, and deputy director of the Center for Human Bioethics at Monash University, Melbourne. He is the author and editor of many books. His best-known book is *Animal Liberation* (1975), which started the Animal Liberation movement. Our reading is taken from his *Practical Ethics,* second edition (1993).

   Singer argues that voluntary euthanasia and assisted suicide are morally justified in cases where a patient is suffering from an incurable and painful or very distressing condition. In such cases, utilitarianism, the theory of rights, and respect for autonomy all provide reasons for allowing voluntary euthanasia or assisted suicide.

Source: Peter Singer, "Justifying Voluntary Euthanasia," from *Practical Ethics* 2/e (Cambridge University Press, 1993), pp. 176–178, 193–200. Copyright © Cambridge University Press 1993. Reprinted with the permission of Cambridge University Press.

VOLUNTARY EUTHANASIA

MOST OF THE GROUPS currently campaigning for changes in the law to allow euthanasia are campaigning for voluntary euthanasia—that is, euthanasia carried out at the request of the person killed.

Sometimes voluntary euthanasia is scarcely distinguishable from assisted suicide. In *Jean's Way*, Derek Humphry has told how his wife Jean, when dying of cancer, asked him to provide her with the means to end her life swiftly and without pain. They had seen the situation coming and discussed it beforehand. Derek obtained some tablets and gave them to Jean, who took them and died soon afterwards.

Dr. Jack Kevorkian, a Michigan pathologist, went one step further when he built a 'suicide machine' to help terminally ill people commit suicide. His machine consisted of a metal pole with three different bottles attached to a tube of the kind used to provide an intravenous drip. The doctor inserts the tube in the patient's vein, but at this stage only a harmless saline solution can pass through it. The patient may then flip a switch, which will allow a coma-inducing drug to come through the tube; this is automatically followed by a lethal drug contained in the third bottle. Dr. Kevorkian announced that he was prepared to make the machine available to any terminally ill patient who wished to use it. (Assisting suicide is not against the law in Michigan.) In June 1990, Janet Adkins, who was suffering from Alzheimer's disease, but still competent to make the decision to end her life, contacted Dr. Kevorkian and told him of her wish to die, rather than go through the slow and progressive deterioration that the disease involves. Dr. Kevorkian was in attendance while she made use of his machine, and then reported Janet Adkin's death to the police. He was subsequently charged with murder, but the judge refused to allow the charge to proceed to trial, on the grounds that Janet Adkins had caused her own death. The following year Dr. Kevorkian

made his device available to two other people, who used it in order to end their lives.[1]

In other cases, people wanting to die may be unable to kill themselves. In 1973 George Zygmaniak was injured in a motorcycle accident near his home in New Jersey. He was taken to hospital, where he was found to be totally paralysed from the neck down. He was also in considerable pain. He told his doctor and his brother, Lester, that he did not want to live in this condition. He begged them both to kill him. Lester questioned the doctor and the hospital staff about George's prospects of recovery: he was told that they were nil. He then smuggled a gun into the hospital, and said to his brother: "I am here to end your pain, George. Is it all right with you?" George, who was not able to speak because of an operation to assist his breathing, nodded affirmatively. Lester shot him through the temple.

The Zygmaniak case appears to be a clear instance of voluntary euthanasia, although without some of the procedural safeguards that advocates of the legalisation of voluntary euthanasia propose. For instance, medical opinions about the patient's prospects of recovery were obtained only in an informal manner. Nor was there a careful attempt to establish, before independent witnesses, that George's desire for death was of a fixed and rational kind, based on the best available information about his situation. The killing was not carried out by a doctor. An injection would have been less distressing to others than shooting. But these choices were not open to Lester Zygmaniak, for the law in New Jersey, as in most other places, regards mercy killing as murder, and if he had made his plans known, he would not have been able to carry them out.

Euthanasia can be voluntary even if a person is not able, as Jean Humphry, Janet Adkins, and

---

1 Dr. Kevorkian was again charged with murder, and with providing a prohibited substance, in connection with the latter two cases, but was once more discharged.

George Zygmaniak were able, to indicate the wish to die right up to the moment the tablets are swallowed, the switch thrown, or the trigger pulled. A person may, while in good health, make a written request for euthanasia if, through accident or illness, she should come to be incapable of making or expressing a decision to die, in pain, or without the use of her mental faculties, and there is no reasonable hope of recovery. In killing a person who has made such a request, who has re-affirmed it from time to time, and who is now in one of the states described, one could truly claim to be acting with her consent.

There is now one country in which doctors can openly help their patients to die in a peaceful and dignified way. In the Netherlands, a series of court cases during the 1980s upheld a doctor's right to assist a patient to die, even if that assistance amounted to giving the patient a lethal injection. Doctors in the Netherlands who comply with certain guidelines (which will be described later in this chapter) can now quite openly carry out euthanasia and can report this on the death certificate without fear of prosecution. It has been estimated that about 2,300 deaths each year result from euthanasia carried out in this way. . . .

JUSTIFYING VOLUNTARY EUTHANASIA

Under existing laws in most countries, people suffering unrelievable pain or distress from an incurable illness who beg their doctors to end their lives are asking their doctors to risk a murder charge. Although juries are extremely reluctant to convict in cases of this kind the law is clear that neither the request, nor the degree of suffering, nor the incurable condition of the person killed, is a defence to a charge of murder. Advocates of voluntary euthanasia propose that this law be changed so that a doctor could legally act on a patient's desire to die without

further suffering. Doctors have been able to do this quite openly in the Netherlands, as a result of a series of court decisions during the 1980s, as long as they comply with certain conditions. In Germany, doctors may provide a patient with the means to end her life, but they may not administer the substance to her.

The case for voluntary euthanasia has some common ground with the case for non-voluntary euthanasia, in that death is a benefit for the one killed. The two kinds of euthanasia differ, however, in that voluntary euthanasia involves the killing of a person, a rational and self-conscious being and not a merely conscious being. (To be strictly accurate it must be said that this is not always so, because although only rational and self-conscious beings can consent to their own deaths, they may not be rational and self-conscious at the time euthanasia is contemplated—the doctor may, for instance, be acting on a prior written request for euthanasia if, through accident or illness, one's rational faculties should be irretrievably lost. For simplicity we shall, henceforth, disregard this complication.)

We have seen that it is possible to justify ending the life of a human being who lacks the capacity to consent. We must now ask in what way the ethical issues are different when the being is capable of consenting, and does in fact consent.

Let us return to the general principles about killing. . . . I [have] argued . . . that killing a self-conscious being is a more serious matter than killing a merely conscious being. I gave four distinct grounds on which this could be argued:

1. The classical utilitarian claim that since self-conscious beings are capable of fearing their own death, killing them has worse effects on others.

2. The preference utilitarian calculation that counts the thwarting of the victim's desire to go on living as an important reason against killing.

3. A theory of rights according to which to have a right one must have the ability to

desire that to which one has a right, so that to have a right to life one must be able to desire one's own continued existence.

4. Respect for the autonomous decisions of rational agents.

Now suppose we have a situation in which a person suffering from a painful and incurable disease wishes to die. If the individual were not a person—not rational or self-conscious—euthanasia would, as I have said, be justifiable. Do any of the four grounds for holding that it is normally worse to kill a person provide reasons against killing when the individual is a person who wants to die?

The classical utilitarian objection does not apply to killing that takes place only with the genuine consent of the person killed. That people are killed under these conditions would have no tendency to spread fear or insecurity, since we have no cause to be fearful of being killed with our own genuine consent. If we do not wish to be killed, we simply do not consent. In fact, the argument from fear points in favour of voluntary euthanasia, for if voluntary euthanasia is not permitted we may, with good cause, be fearful that our deaths will be unnecessarily drawn out and distressing. In the Netherlands, a nationwide study commissioned by the government found that 'Many patients want an assurance that their doctor will assist them to die should suffering become unbearable.' Often, having received this assurance, no persistent request for euthanasia eventuated. The availability of euthanasia brought comfort without euthanasia having to be provided.

Preference utilitarianism also points in favour of, not against, voluntary euthanasia. Just as preference utilitarianism must count a desire to go on living as a reason against killing, so it must count a desire to die as a reason for killing.

Next, according to the theory of rights we have considered, it is an essential feature of a right that one can waive one's rights if one so chooses. I may have a right to privacy; but I can,

if I wish, film every detail of my daily life and invite the neighbours to my home movies. Neighbours sufficiently intrigued to accept my invitation could do so without violating my right to privacy, since the right has on this occasion been waived. Similarly, to say that I have a right to life is not to say that it would be wrong for my doctor to end my life, if she does so at my request. In making this request I waive my right to life.

Lastly, the principle of respect for autonomy tells us to allow rational agents to live their own lives according to their own autonomous decisions, free from coercion or interference; but if rational agents should autonomously choose to die, then respect for autonomy will lead us to assist them to do as they choose.

So, although there are reasons for thinking that killing a self-conscious being is normally worse than killing any other kind of being, in the special case of voluntary euthanasia most of these reasons count for euthanasia rather than against. Surprising as this result might at first seem, it really does no more than reflect the fact that what is special about self-conscious beings is that they can know that they exist over time and will, unless they die, continue to exist. Normally this continued existence is fervently desired; when the foreseeable continued existence is dreaded rather than desired however, the desire to die may take the place of the normal desire to live, reversing the reasons against killing based on the desire to live. Thus the case for voluntary euthanasia is arguably much stronger than the case for non-voluntary euthanasia.

Some opponents of the legalisation of voluntary euthanasia might concede that all this follows, if we have a genuinely free and rational decision to die: but, they add, we can never be sure that a request to be killed is the result of a free and rational decision. Will not the sick and elderly be pressured by their relatives to end their lives quickly? Will it not be possible to commit outright murder by pretending that a person has requested euthanasia? And even if there is no pressure of falsification, can anyone who is ill, suffering pain, and very probably in a drugged and confused state of mind, make a rational decision about whether to live or die?

These questions raise technical difficulties for the legalisation of voluntary euthanasia, rather than objections to the underlying ethical principles; but they are serious difficulties nonetheless. The guidelines developed by the courts in the Netherlands have sought to meet them by proposing that euthanasia is acceptable only if

- It is carried out by a physician.
- The patient has explicitly requested euthanasia in a manner that leaves no doubt of the patient's desire to die.
- The patient's decision is well-informed, free, and durable.
- The patient has an irreversible condition causing protracted physical or mental suffering that the patient finds unbearable.
- There is no reasonable alternative (reasonable from the patient's point of view) to alleviate the patient's suffering.
- The doctor has consulted another independent professional who agrees with his or her judgment.

Euthanasia in these circumstances is strongly supported by the Royal Dutch Medical Association, and by the general public in the Netherlands. The guidelines make murder in the guise of euthanasia rather far-fetched, and there is no evidence of an increase in the murder rate in the Netherlands.

It is often said, in debates about euthanasia, that doctors can be mistaken. In rare instances patients diagnosed by two competent doctors as suffering from an incurable condition have survived and enjoyed years of good health. Possibly the legalisation of voluntary euthanasia would, over the years, mean the deaths of a few people who would otherwise have recovered from their immediate illness and lived for some extra years.

This is not, however, the knockdown argument against euthanasia that some imagine it to be. Against a very small number of unnecessary deaths that might occur if euthanasia is legalised we must place the very large amount of pain and distress that will be suffered if euthanasia is not legalised, by patients who really are terminally ill. Longer life is not such a supreme good that it outweighs all other considerations. (If it were, there would be many more effective ways of saving life—such as a ban on smoking, or a reduction of speed limits to 40 kilometres per hour—than prohibiting voluntary euthanasia.) The possibility that two doctors may make a mistake means that the person who opts for euthanasia is deciding on the balance of probabilities and giving up a very slight chance of survival in order to avoid suffering that will almost certainly end in death. This may be a perfectly rational choice. Probability is the guide of life, and of death, too. Against this, some will reply that improved care for the terminally ill has eliminated pain and made voluntary euthanasia unnecessary. Elisabeth Kübler-Ross, whose *On Death and Dying* is perhaps the best-known book on care for the dying, has claimed that none of her patients request euthanasia. Given personal attention and the right medication, she says, people come to accept their deaths and die peacefully without pain.

Kübler-Ross may be right. It may be possible, now, to eliminate pain. In almost all cases, it may even be possible to do it in a way that leaves patients in possession of their rational faculties and free from vomiting, nausea, or other distressing side-effects. Unfortunately only a minority of dying patients now receive this kind of care. Nor is physical pain the only problem. There can also be other distressing conditions, like bones so fragile they fracture at sudden movements, uncontrollable nausea and vomiting, slow starvation due to a cancerous growth, inability to control one's bowels or bladder, difficulty in breathing, and so on.

Dr. Timothy Quill, a doctor from Rochester, New York, has described how he prescribed barbiturate sleeping pills for "Diane," a patient with a severe form of leukaemia, knowing that she wanted the tablets in order to be able to end her life. Dr. Quill had known Diane for many years, and admired her courage in dealing with previous serious illnesses. In an article in the *New England Journal of Medicine,* Dr. Quill wrote:

> It was extraordinarily important to Diane to maintain control of herself and her own dignity during the time remaining to her. When this was no longer possible, she clearly wanted to die. As a former director of a hospice program, I know how to use pain medicines to keep patients comfortable and lessen suffering. I explained the philosophy of comfort care, which I strongly believe in. Although Diane understood and appreciated this, she had known of people lingering in what was called relative comfort, and she wanted no part of it. When the time came, she wanted to take her life in the least painful way possible. Knowing of her desire for independence and her decision to stay in control, I thought this request made perfect sense. . . . In our discussion it became clear that preoccupation with her fear of a lingering death would interfere with Diane's getting the most out of the time she had left until she found a safe way to ensure her death.

Not all dying patients who wish to die are fortunate enough to have a doctor like Timothy Quill. Betty Rollin has described, in her moving book *Last Wish,* how her mother developed ovarian cancer that spread to other parts of her body. One morning her mother said to her:

> I've had a wonderful life, but now it's over, or it should be. I'm not afraid to die, but I am afraid of this illness, what it's doing to me. . . . There's never any relief from it now. Nothing but nausea and this pain. . . . There won't be any more chemotherapy. There's no treatment anymore. So what happens to me now? I know what happens. I'll die slowly. . . . I don't want that. . . . Who does it benefit if I die slowly? If it

benefits my children I'd be willing. But it's not going to do you any good. . . . There's no point in a slow death, none. I've never liked doing things with no point. I've got to end this.

Betty Rollin found it very difficult to help her mother to carry out her desire: "Physician after physician turned down our pleas for help (How many pills? What kind?)." After her book about her mother's death was published, she received hundreds of letters, many from people, or close relatives of people, who had tried to die, failed, and suffered even more. Many of these people were denied help from doctors, because although suicide is legal in most jurisdictions, assisted suicide is not.

Perhaps one day it will be possible to treat all terminally ill and incurable patients in such a way that no one requests euthanasia and the subject becomes a non-issue; but this is now just a utopian ideal, and no reason at all to deny euthanasia to those who must live and die in far less comfortable conditions. It is, in any case, highly paternalistic to tell dying patients that they are now so well looked after that they need not be offered the option of euthanasia. It would be more in keeping with respect for individual freedom and autonomy to legalise euthanasia and let patients decide whether their situation is bearable.

Do these arguments for voluntary euthanasia perhaps give too much weight to individual freedom and autonomy? After all, we do not allow people free choices on matters like, for instance, the taking of heroin. This is a restriction of freedom but, in the view of many, one that can be justified on paternalistic grounds. If preventing people from becoming heroin addicts is justifiable paternalism, why isn't preventing people from having themselves killed?

The question is a reasonable one, because respect for individual freedom can be carried too far. John Stuart Mill thought that the state should never interfere with the individual except to prevent harm to others. The individual's own good, Mill thought, is not a proper reason for state intervention. But Mill may have had too high an opinion of the rationality of a human being. It may occasionally be right to prevent people from making choices that are obviously not rationally based and that we can be sure they will later regret. The prohibition of voluntary euthanasia cannot be justified on paternalistic grounds, however, for voluntary euthanasia is an act for which good reasons exist. Voluntary euthanasia occurs only when, to the best of medical knowledge, a person is suffering from an incurable and painful or extremely distressing condition. In these circumstances one cannot say that to choose to die quickly is obviously irrational. The strength of the case for voluntary euthanasia lies in this combination of respect for the preferences, or autonomy, of those who decide for euthanasia; and the clear rational basis of the decision itself. . . .

Review Questions

1. Distinguish between the cases of Janet Adkins and George Zygmaniak.
2. What are the four grounds for holding that killing a person is wrong? According to Singer, how do these grounds support voluntary euthanasia and assisted suicide?
3. What difficulties does Singer discuss? How does he reply?

Discussion Questions

1. Singer accepts the guidelines for voluntary euthanasia developed by the courts in the Netherlands. Are these acceptable? Why or why not?
2. Did Janet Adkins do anything wrong? How about Lester Zygmaniak?
3. Should the law be changed to allow voluntary euthanasia or assisted suicide for terminally ill patients?

The Survival Lottery

JOHN HARRIS

John Harris is a reader in philosophy at the University of Manchester, England. He is the author of *Violence and Responsibility* (1980), *The Value of Life: An Introduction to Medical Ethics* (1985), and *Wonderwoman and Superman: The Ethics of Human Biotechnology* (1992).

Harris proposes a lottery to decide who lives and who dies. Whenever there are two or more patients who can be saved by organ transplants, a lottery drawing randomly picks out a person to be sacrificed; this person is required to donate organs so

Source: John Harris, "The Survival Lottery," from *Philosophy, The Journal of the Royal Institute of Philosophy*, Vol. 50 (1975), pp. 87–95. Copyright © The Royal Institute of Philosophy 1975. Reprinted with permission of Cambridge University Press.

that others can live. Such a scheme seems to conflict with our moral intuition that it is wrong to kill an innocent person, even to save the lives of others. But Harris argues that such a lottery scheme can be defended against objections such as the claim that it is playing God, that killing is wrong but letting die is not wrong, that it violates the right of self-defense, and that it has bad side effects.

LET US SUPPOSE that organ transplant procedures have been perfected; in such circumstances if two dying patients could be saved by organ transplants then, if surgeons have the requisite organs in stock and no other needy patients, but nevertheless allow their patients to die, we would be inclined to say, and be justified in saying, that the patients died because the doctors refused to save them. But if there are no spare organs in stock and none otherwise available, the doctors have no choice, they cannot save their patients and so must let them die. In this case we would he disinclined to say that the doctors are in any sense the cause of their patients' deaths. But let us further suppose that the two dying patients, Y and Z, are not happy about being left to die. They might argue that it is not strictly true that there are no organs which could be used to save them. Y needs a new heart and Z new lungs. They point out that if just one healthy person were to be killed his organs could be removed and both of them be saved. We and the doctors would probably be alike in thinking that such a step, while technically possible, would be out of the question. We would not say that the doctors were killing their patients if they refused to prey upon the healthy to save the sick. And because this sort of surgical Robin Hoodery is out of the question we can tell Y and Z that they cannot be saved, and that when they die they will have died of natural causes and not of the neglect of their doctors. Y and Z do not agree, however, they insist that if the doctors fail to kill a healthy man and use his organs to save them, then the doctors will be responsible for their deaths.

Many philosophers have for various reasons believed that we must not kill even if by doing so we could save life. They believe that there is a moral difference between killing and letting die. On this view, to kill A so that Y and Z might live is ruled is out because we have a strict obligation not to kill but a duty of some lesser kind to save life. A. H. Clough's dictum "Thou shalt not kill but need'st not strive officiously to keep alive" expresses bluntly this point of view. The dying Y and Z may be excused for not being much impressed by Clough's dictum. They agree that it is wrong to kill the innocent and are prepared to agree to an absolute prohibition against so doing. They do not agree, however, that A is more innocent than they are. Y and Z might go on to point out that the currently acknowledged right of the innocent not to be killed, even where their deaths might give life to others, is just a decision to prefer the lives of the fortunate to those of the unfortunate. A is innocent in the sense that he has done nothing to deserve death, but Y and Z are also innocent in this sense. Why should they be the ones to die simply because they are so unlucky as to have diseased organs? Why, they might argue, should their living or dying be left to chance when in so many other areas of human life we believe that we have an obligation to ensure the survival of the maximum number of lives possible?

Y and Z argue that if a doctor refuses to treat a patient, with the result that the patient dies, he has killed that patient as sure as shooting, and that, in exactly the same way, if the doctors refuse Y and Z the transplants that they need, then their refusal will kill Y and Z, again as sure as shooting. The doctors, and indeed the society which supports their inaction, cannot defend themselves by arguing that they are neither expected, nor required by law or convention, to kill so that lives may be saved (indeed, quite the reverse) since this is just an appeal to custom or authority. A man who does his own moral thinking must decide whether, in these circumstances, he ought to save two lives at the cost of one, or one life at the cost of two. The fact that so-called "third parties" have never before been brought into such calculations, have never before been thought of as being involved, is not an argument against their now becoming so. There are, of course, good arguments against allowing doctors simply to haul passers-by off the streets whenever they have a couple of patients in need of new organs. And the harmful side-effects of such a practice in terms of terror and distress to the victims, the witnesses and society generally, would give us further reasons for dismissing the idea. Y and Z realize this and have a proposal, which they will shortly produce, which would largely meet objections to placing such power in the hands of doctors and eliminate at least some of the harmful side-effects.

In the unlikely event of their feeling obliged to reply to the reproaches of Y and Z, the doctors might offer the following argument: they might maintain that a man is only responsible for the death of someone whose life he might have saved, if, in all the circumstances of the case, he ought to have saved the man by the means available. This is why a doctor might be a murderer if he simply refused or neglected to treat a patient who would die without treatment, but not if he could only save the patient by doing something he ought in no circumstances to do—kill the innocent. Y and Z readily agree that a man ought not to do what he ought not to do, but they point out that if the doctors, and for that matter society at large, ought on balance to kill one man if two can thereby be saved, then failure to do so will involve responsibility for the consequent deaths. The fact that Y's and Z's proposal involves killing the innocent cannot be a reason for refusing to consider their proposal, for this would just be a refusal to face the question at issue and so avoid having to make a decision as to what ought to be done in circumstances like these. It is Y's and Z's claim that failure to adopt their plan will also involve killing the innocent, rather more of the innocent than the proposed alternative.

To back up this last point, to remove the arbitrariness of permitting doctors to select their donors from among the chance passers-by outside hospitals, and the tremendous power this would place in doctors' hands, to mitigate worries about side-effects and lastly to appease those who wonder why poor old A should be singled out for sacrifice, Y and Z put forward the following scheme: they propose that everyone be given a sort of lottery number. Whenever doctors have two or more dying patients who could be saved by transplants, and no suitable organs have come to hand through "natural" deaths, they can ask a central computer to supply a suitable donor. The computer will then pick the number of a suitable donor at random and he will be killed so that the lives of two or more others may be saved. No doubt if the scheme were ever to be implemented a suitable euphemism for "killed" would be employed. Perhaps we would begin to talk about citizens being called upon to "give life" to others. With the refinement of transplant procedures such a scheme could offer the chance of saving large numbers of lives that are now lost. Indeed, even taking into account the loss of the lives of donors, the numbers of untimely deaths each year might be dramatically reduced, so much so that everyone's chance of living to a ripe old age might be increased. If this were to be the consequence of the adoption of such a scheme, and it might well be, it could not be dismissed lightly. It might of course be objected that it is likely that more old people will need transplants to prolong their lives than will the young, and so the scheme would inevitably lead to a society dominated by the old. But if such a society is thought objectionable, there is no reason to suppose that a program could not be designed for the computer that would ensure the maintenance of whatever is considered to be an optimum age distribution throughout the population.

Suppose that inter-planetary travel revealed a world of people like ourselves, but who organized their society according to this scheme. No one was considered to have an absolute right to life or freedom from interference, but everything was always done to ensure that as many people as possible would enjoy long and happy lives. In such a world a man who attempted to escape when his number was up or who resisted on the grounds that no one had a right to take his life, might well be regarded as a murderer. We might or might not prefer to live in such a world, but the morality of its inhabitants would surely be one that we could respect. It would not be obviously more barbaric or cruel or immoral than our own.

Y and Z are willing to concede one exception to the universal application of their scheme. They realize that it would be unfair to allow people who have brought their misfortune on themselves to benefit from the lottery. There would clearly be something unjust about killing the abstemious B so that W (whose heavy smoking has given him lung cancer) and X (whose drinking has destroyed his liver) should be preserved to over-indulge again.

What objections could be made to the lottery scheme? A first straw to clutch at would be the desire for security. Under such a scheme we would never know when we would hear *them* knocking at the door. Every post might bring a sentence of death, every sound in the night might be the sound of boots on the stairs. But, as we have seen, the chances of actually being called upon to make the ultimate sacrifice might be slimmer than is the present risk of being killed on the roads, and most of us do not lie trembling abed, appalled at the prospect of being dispatched on the morrow. The truth is that lives might well be more secure under such a scheme.

If we respect individuality and see every human being as unique in his own way, we might want to reject a society in which it appeared that individuals were seen merely as interchangeable units in a structure, the value of which lies in its having as many healthy units as possible. But of course Y and Z would want to know why A's individuality was more worthy of respect than theirs.

Another plausible objection is the natural reluctance to play God with men's lives, the feeling that it is wrong to make any attempt to re-allot the life opportunities that fate has determined, that the deaths of Y and Z would be "natural," whereas the death of anyone killed to save them would have been perpetrated by men. But if we are able to change things, then to elect not to do so is also to determine what will happen in the world.

Neither does the alleged moral difference between killing and letting die afford a respectable way of rejecting the claims of Y and Z. For if we really want to counter proponents of the lottery, if we really want to answer Y and Z and not just put them off, we cannot do so by saying that the lottery involves killing and object to it for that reason, because to do so would, as we have seen, just beg the question as to whether the failure to save as many people as possible might not also amount to killing.

To opt for the society which Y and Z propose would be then to adopt a society in which saintliness would be mandatory. Each of us would have to recognize a binding obligation to give up his own life for others when called upon to do so. In such a society anyone who reneged upon this duty would be a murderer. The most promising objection to such a society, and indeed to any principle which required us to kill A in order to save Y and Z, is, I suspect, that we are committed to the right of self-defense. If I can kill A to save Y and Z then he can kill me to save P and Q, and it is only if I am prepared to agree to this that I will opt for the lottery or be prepared to agree to a man's being killed if doing so would save the lives of more than one other man. Of course, there is something paradoxical about basing objections to the lottery scheme on the right of self-defense since, *ex hypothesi*, each person would have a better chance of living to a ripe old age if the lottery scheme were to be implemented. None the less, the feeling that no man should be required to lay down his life for others makes many people shy away from such a scheme, even though it might be rational to accept it on prudential grounds, and perhaps even mandatory on utilitarian grounds. Again, Y and Z would reply that the right of self-defense must extend to them as much as to anyone else, and while it is true that they can only live if another man is killed, they would claim that it is also true that if they are left to die, then someone who lives on does so over their dead bodies.

It might be argued that the institution of the survival lottery has not gone far to mitigate the harmful side-effects in terms of terror and distress to victims, witnesses, and society generally, that would be occasioned by doctors simply snatching passers-by off the streets and disorganizing them for the benefit of the unfortunate. Donors would after all still have to be procured, and this process, however it was carried out, would still be likely to prove distressing to all concerned. The lottery scheme would eliminate the arbitrariness of leaving the life and death decisions to the doctors, and remove the possibility of such terrible power falling into the hands of any individuals, but the terror and distress would remain. The effect of having to apprehend presumably unwilling victims would give us pause. Perhaps only a long period of education or propaganda could remove our abhorrence. What this abhorrence reveals about the rights and wrongs of the situation is, however, more difficult to assess. We might be inclined to say that only monsters could ignore the promptings of conscience so far as to operate the lottery scheme. But the promptings of conscience are not necessarily the most reliable guide. In the present case Y and Z would argue that such promptings are mere squeamishness, an overnice self-indulgence that costs lives. Death, Y and Z would remind us, is a distressing experience whenever and to whomever it occurs, so the less it occurs the better. Fewer victims and witnesses will be distressed as part of the side-

effects of the lottery scheme than would suffer as part of the side-effects of not instituting it.

Lastly, a more limited objection might be made, not to the idea of killing to save lives, but to the involvement of "third parties." Why, so the objection goes, should we not give X's heart to Y or Y's lungs to X, the same number of lives being thereby preserved and no one else's life set at risk? Y's and Z's reply to this objection differs from their previous line of argument. To amend their plan so that the involvement of so called "third parties" is ruled out would, Y and Z claim, violate their right to equal concern and respect with the rest of society. They argue that such a proposal would amount to treating the unfortunate who need new organs as a class within society whose lives are considered to be of less value than those of its more fortunate members. What possible justification could there be for singling out one group of people whom we would be justified in using as donors but not another? The idea in the mind of those who would propose such a step must be something like the following: since Y and Z cannot survive, since they are going to die in any event, there is no harm in putting their names into the lottery, for the chances of their dying cannot thereby be increased and will in fact almost certainly be reduced. But this is just to ignore everything that Y and Z have been saying. For if their lottery scheme is adopted they are not going to die anyway—their chances of dying are no greater and no less than those of any other participant in the lottery whose number may come up. This ground for confining selection of donors to the unfortunate therefore disappears. Any other ground must discriminate against Y and Z as members of a class whose lives are less worthy of respect than those of the rest of society.

It might more plausibly be argued that the dying who cannot themselves be saved by transplants, or by any other means at all, should be the priority selection group for the computer program. But how far off must death be for a man to be classified as "dying"? Those so classified might argue that their last few days or weeks of life are as valuable to them (if not more valuable) than the possibly longer span remaining to others. The problem of narrowing down the class of possible donors without discriminating unfairly against some sub-class of society is, I suspect, insoluble.

Such is the case for the survival lottery. Utilitarians ought to be in favor of it, and absolutists cannot object to it on the ground that it involves killing the innocent, for it is Y's and Z's case that any alternative must also involve killing the innocent. If the absolutist wishes to maintain his objection he must point to some morally relevant difference between positive and negative killing. This challenge opens the door to a large topic with a whole library of literature, but Y and Z are dying and do not have time to explore it exhaustively. In their own case the most likely candidate for some feature which might make this moral difference is the malevolent intent of Y and Z themselves. An absolutist might well argue that while no one intends the deaths of Y and Z, no one necessarily wishes them dead, or aims at their demise for any reason, they do mean to kill A (or have him killed). But Y and Z can reply that the death of A is no part of their plan, they merely wish to use a couple of his organs, and if he cannot live without them . . . *tant pis!* None would be more delighted than Y and Z if artificial organs would do as well, and so render the lottery scheme otiose.

One form of absolutist argument perhaps remains. This involves taking an Orwellian stand on some principle of common decency. The argument would then be that even to enter into the sort of "macabre" calculations that Y and Z propose displays a blunted sensibility, a corrupted and vitiated mind. Forms of this argument have recently been advanced by Noam Chomsky (*American Power and the New Mandarins*) and Stuart Hampshire (*Morality and Pessimism*). The indefatigable Y and Z would of course deny that their calculations are in any sense "macabre," and would present them as the most humane course available in the circumstances. Moreover they would claim that the

Orwellian stand on decency is the product of a closed mind, and not susceptible to rational argument. Any reasoned defense of such a principle must appeal to notions like respect for human life, as Hampshire's argument in fact does, and these Y and Z could make conformable to their own position.

Can Y and Z be answered? Perhaps only by relying on moral intuition, on the insistence that we do feel there is something wrong with the survival lottery and our confidence that this feeling is prompted by some morally relevant difference between our bringing about the death of A and our bringing about the deaths of Y and Z. Whether we could retain this confidence in our intuitions if we were to be confronted by a society in which the survival lottery operated, was accepted by all, and was seen to save many lives that would otherwise have been lost, it would be interesting to know.

There would of course be great practical difficulties in the way of implementing the lottery. In so many cases it would be agonizingly difficult to decide whether or not a person had brought his misfortune on himself. There are numerous ways in which a person may contribute to his predicament, and the task of deciding how far, or how decisively, a person is himself responsible for his fate would be formidable. And in those cases where we can be confident that a person is innocent of responsibility for his predicament, can we acquire this confidence in time to save him? The lottery scheme would be a powerful weapon in the hands of someone willing and able to misuse it. Could we ever feel certain that the lottery was safe from unscrupulous computer programmers? Perhaps we should be thankful that such practical difficulties make the lottery an unlikely consequence of the perfection of transplants. Or perhaps we should be appalled.

It may be that we would want to tell Y and Z that the difficulties and dangers of their scheme would be too great a price to pay for its benefits. It is as well to be clear, however, that there is also a high, perhaps an even higher, price to be paid for the rejection of the scheme. That price is the lives of Y and Z and many like them, and we delude ourselves if we suppose that the reason why we reject their plan is that we accept the sixth commandment.

ACKNOWLEDGMENT

Thanks are due to Ronald Dworkin, Jonathan Glover, M. J. Inwood, and Anne Seller for helpful comments.

Review Questions

1. Explain the lottery scheme proposed by Harris. What are its advantages supposed to be?
2. How does Harris reply to the objection that the lottery is "playing God"?
3. What is his answer to those who appeal to the distinction between killing and letting die?
4. What about the right of self-defense? Why doesn't it provide a good objection to the lottery, according to Harris?
5. How does Harris deal with the objection that the lottery would have harmful side effects?

Discussion Questions

1. Harris excludes heavy smokers and drinkers from the lottery scheme. Do you agree that they do not deserve to be saved? Why or why not?
2. Harris challenges us to point out some morally relevant difference between positive and negative killing (as he calls it). Is there such a difference? What is it?
3. Is the lottery scheme immoral or not? Explain your answer.

Gender, Race, and Class in the Delivery of Health Care

SUSAN SHERWIN

Susan Sherwin is professor of philosophy and women's studies at Dalhousie University in Canada. She is the author of *No Longer Patient: Feminist Ethics and Health Care* (1992) and the coeditor of *Moral Problems in Medicine,* second edition (1983).

Sherwin discusses inequalities in the current system of health care in the United States, Canada, and the Developing (Third) World. She argues that it oppresses women, minorities, and poor people. Their health care needs are not being met. Also, the current structures of the health care system discriminate against women and minorities and the poor. Sherwin concludes with feminist proposals for correcting these problems.

Source: Susan Sherwin, "Gender, Race, and Class in the Delivery of Health Care" from *No Longer Patient: Feminist Ethics & Health Care* by Susan Sherwin. Reprinted by permission of Temple University Press. Copyright © 1992 by Temple University. All rights reserved.

OPPRESSION AND ILLNESS

IT IS WIDELY RECOGNIZED throughout the field of biomedical ethics that people's health care needs usually vary inversely with their power and privilege within society. Most bioethical discussions explain these differences solely in economic terms, observing that health and access to health resources are largely dependent on income levels. Poverty is an important determining factor in a person's prospects for health: being poor often means living without access to adequate nutrition, housing, heat, clean water, clothing, and sanitation, and each of these factors may have a negative impact on health (Lewis 1990). Further, the poor are more likely than others to work in industries that pose serious health risks (Stellman 1988) and to do without adequate health insurance (Tallon and Block 1988). And the poor suffer higher rates of mental illness and addiction (Paltiel 1988) than do other segments of the population. Financial barriers also often force the poor to let diseases reach an advanced state before they seek professional help; by the time these individuals do receive care, recovery may be compromised.

It is not sufficient, however, just to notice the effects of poverty on health; it is also necessary to consider who is at risk of becoming the victim of poverty. In a hierarchical society such as the one we live in, members of groups that are oppressed on the basis of gender, race, sexuality, and so forth are the people who are most likely to be poor. Moreover, not only does being oppressed lead to poverty and poverty to poor health but being oppressed is itself also a significant determining factor in the areas of health and health care. Those who are most oppressed in society at large are likely to experience the most severe and frequent health problems and have the least. adequate medical treatment.[1]

1 Writers who are concerned about oppression are likely to make the connection prominent; for example, Beverly Smith states: "The reason that Black women don't have good health in this country is because we are so oppressed. It's just that simple" (quoted in Lewis 1990, 174).

One reason for this vulnerability is that oppressed individuals are usually exposed to high levels of stress by virtue of their oppressed status, and excessive stress is responsible for many serious illnesses and is a complicating factor in most diseases. Another important factor to consider, as we shall see, is that the same prejudices that undermine the status of the oppressed members of society may affect the treatment they receive at the hands of health care workers.

North American society is characteristically sexist, racist, classist, homophobic, and frightened of physical or mental imperfections; we can anticipate, then, that those who are oppressed by virtue of their gender, race, class, sexual orientation, or disabilities—and especially, those who are oppressed in a number of different ways—will experience a disproportional share of illness and will often suffer reduced access to resources. Moreover, the connection between illness and oppression can run in both directions; because serious or chronic illness is often met with fear and hostility, it may also precipitate an individual's or family's slide into poverty and can therefore lead to oppression based on class.

The damaging connections between oppression and illness are profoundly unfair. Because this situation is ethically objectionable, bioethicists have a responsibility to consider ways in which existing medical institutions can be modified to challenge and undermine these connections, rather than contribute to them. Ethical analyses of the distribution of health and health care must take into consideration the role that oppression plays in a person's prospects for health and well-being.

PATIENTS AS MEMBERS OF OPPRESSED GROUPS

Throughout . . . I have argued that women constitute an oppressed group, which is at a clear disadvantage in the health care system. Women are the primary consumers of health care, but the care they receive does not always serve their overall health interests. In a report presented to the American Medical Association, Richard Mc-Murray (1990) reviewed recent studies on gender disparities in clinical decision-making; he found that although women are likely to undergo more medical procedures than do men when they present the same symptoms and condition, they have significantly less access than men do to some of the major diagnostic and therapeutic interventions that are considered medically appropriate for their conditions. In some cases the discrepancies were quite remarkable: for example, despite comparable physical needs, women were 30 percent less likely than men to receive kidney transplants, 50 percent as likely to be referred for diagnostic testing for lung cancer, and only 10 percent as likely to be referred for cardiac catheterization. The studies were unable to identify any biological difference that would justify these discrepancies. In addition, even though biological differences are sometimes significant in the course of various diseases and therapies, McMurray found that medical researchers have largely ignored the study of diseases and medications in women; for instance, cardiovascular disease is the leading cause of death in women in the United States, but research in this area has been almost exclusively conducted on men.

Therefore, as a group, it appears that women are particularly vulnerable to poor health care. Although they receive a great deal of medical treatment, the relevant research data are frequently missing, and specific treatment decisions seem to be biased against them. When women are medically treated, they are often overtreated, that is, subjected to excessive testing, surgery, and prescription drugs (Weaver and Garrett 1983). Sometimes they are simply not offered the treatment that physicians have judged to be preferable; for example, most professionals who work in the area of fertility control encourage women seeking birth control to go on the pill, despite its known risks. Interest-ingly, the majority of practitioners choose barrier methods for themselves and their spouses (Todd 1989); they do not seem to trust ordinary women to be conscientious in the use of the safer, less medically intrusive methods.

Physicians are trained in the stereotypical views of women as people who are excessively anxious, devious, and unintelligent; they are taught not to take all women's complaints seriously (Ehrenreich and English 1979; Corea 1985; Todd 1989). Researchers have found that physicians are often condescending toward their women patients, and many deliberately withhold medical information from them out of concern for their inability to interpret it correctly (Corea 1985; Todd 1989). Having medicalized the very condition of being female, many doctors have seized opportunities to intervene and modify those bodies in ways they are unwilling to apply to men—for example, psychosurgery, an exceedingly controversial therapy, is performed twice as often on women as on men, and ultrasound was widely practiced on women before being introduced as a therapy for men (Corea, 1985a).

Nevertheless, not all women experience the health care system in the same ways. There are many important differences among women that result in different sorts of experiences within the health care system; in particular, differences that are associated with race, economic class, and ethnicity compound the difficulties most women experience in their various encounters with health care workers. Alexandra Todd observed that "the darker a woman's skin and/or the lower her place on the economic scale, the poorer the care and efforts at explanation she received" (Todd 1989, 77). Other factors that contribute to the sort of health care a woman is likely to receive include age, sexuality, body size, intelligence, disabilities, and a history of mental illness. It is a matter of serious moral concern that social factors play a significant role in determining the quality of health care a woman receives.

If we expand our scope to that of a global perspective, then it is obvious that women in other parts of the world face distinct health problems, such as those created by malnutrition, often to the point of starvation, and by the absence of a safe source of drinking water; many women must cope with the ravages of war or the hazards of living under brutally repressive political regimes. Third World women must frequently rely on unsafe drugs, which have failed to meet minimum safety standards and therefore are dumped in developing countries by manufacturers determined to make a profit from them (McDonnell 1986). Some prominent concerns of bioethicists, such as the need to obtain informed consent for treatment and research, are deemed to be the products of Western ideals and are likely to go unrecognized in nations where all personal liberties are severely curtailed; elsewhere, the ethical "niceties" are often ignored in the face of the pressing demands posed by crippling poverty and illiteracy.

The injustice represented by the differing health options and standards of care based on different levels of power and privilege is not restricted to the Third World. Inadequate prenatal care and birth services are common to poor women everywhere, and the lack of safe, effective birth control and abortion services is more a matter of politics than of economics. In North America women of color are at a higher risk than white women for many life-threatening conditions; for example, black American women are four times more likely to die in childbirth and three times more likely to have their newborns die than are white women (Gordon-Bradshaw 1988, 256). Black women in the United States are twice as likely to die of hypertensive cardiovascular disease as are white women; they have three times the rate of high blood pressure and of lupus as do white women; they are more likely than white women to die from breast cancer (despite having lower rates of incidence); they are twelve times more likely than white women to contract the AIDS virus;

and they are four times more likely than white women to die of homicide (Davis 1990).

In the United States the poor usually have (at best) access only to inadequate health services. Many people who find themselves employed full time but receiving annual incomes well below established poverty lines fail to qualify for Medicaid support (Tallon and Block 1988). Those who do receive subsidized health care must confront the fact that many physicians and hospitals refuse to accept Medicaid patients. In 1985, for example, four out of ten physicians who provided obstetrical service refused to take Medicaid patients (McBarnette 1988).

Canadians have so far avoided the two-tiered system of private and public health care. In Canada poor women are not turned away from hospitals or doctors' offices,[2] but they may not be able to afford travel to these facilities. Rural women are often restricted from access to needed health care by lack of transportation. Many Canadian communities lack suitably qualified health care specialists, and some provinces simply refuse to provide needed services, especially abortion, thus making it unavailable to women who cannot travel to a private clinic in another jurisdiction. Despite its guaranteed payment for health care, then, the Canadian health care system still reflects the existence of differential patterns of health and illness, associated with both race and income level (York 1987; Paltiel 1988).

In both countries the services available to women through the health care system are predominantly those that meet the needs of the most privileged and articulate women, namely, those who are white, middle-class, educated, and urban. The health needs of other women are likely to be invisible or to slip through the cracks of the structures and funding of the

---

2 Nevertheless many provinces would like to reinstitute a "small" user fee. Quebec has recently announced plans to proceed with a five-dollar charge for each visit to a hospital emergency room.

system. In most cities, for example, prenatal programs, exercise counseling, mammography facilities, and hormone replacement therapy for menopausal women are available, but other urgent services, such as programs for alcohol or drug dependent women, are less easily found. Although some private programs exist for affluent women with substance-abuse problems, poor women have virtually no place to which they can turn. Further, if they should manage to find a program that is not too alienating to their experience to be of value, then they may face the problem of finding child care for the duration of the program, and if they are poor, then they are liable to lose custody of children to the state when they admit to having a problem with addiction.

Although most urban centers offer nutritional guidance to affluent women trying to lose weight (even if their main goal is to fit the cultural ideals and medically mandated norms of slimness), few programs help women on welfare learn how to stretch their inadequate welfare checks to provide nutritious meals or to locate the resources for a healthy diet. Battered women who arrive at emergency rooms are patched up by the specialists on duty and perhaps referred to local, short-term shelters—if space can be found.[3] Preventive health care, which would help the abuser find nonviolent ways of behaving, is usually not available. As a result, many women get trapped in the cycle of returning home to their violent partner, returning to hospital with increasingly severe injuries (where they encounter frustrated staff members, who frequently blame them for repeat episodes), and recuperating in a temporary shelter. In the meantime, their children become intimately acquainted with violence as a means of addressing

personal tensions and become primed to continue the pattern in the next generation.

In bioethics literature the issue of justice is often raised, but most discussions focus on whether or not everyone has a right to health care and, if so, what services this right might entail. Accessibility is viewed as the principal moral concern, but even where there is universal health insurance (for example, in Canada), the system is not designed to respond to the particular health needs of many groups of women. Being subject to violence, at risk of developing addictions to alcohol or other mood-altering drugs, and lacking adequate resources to obtain a nutritious food supply are all factors that affect peoples' prospects for health and their ability to promote their own well-being. Such threats to health are a result of the social system, which promotes oppression of some groups by others. Health care alone will not correct all these social effects, but as long as the damage of oppression continues, it is necessary to help its victims recover from some of the harms to their health that occur as a result of their oppressed status.

Bioethicists share with health care professionals and the rest of the community an ethical responsibility to determine how the health needs generated by oppressive structures can best be met. Medical care per se will not always be the most effective means of restoring or preserving the health of oppressed persons. Investigation of how best to respond to these socially generated needs is a topic that must be added to the traditional agenda of health care ethics.

THE ORGANIZATION OF HEALTH CARE

Much of the explanation for the different ways in which health care providers respond to the needs of different social groups can be found in the very structures of the health care delivery system. The dominance structures that are pervasive throughout society are reproduced in the medical context; both within and without the

3 Women who gain entry to shelters learn that there are limits to the amount of time any woman can stay; most also find that low-cost housing is not available for them to move into once their prescribed time is exhausted, especially if they have children in tow and welfare is their only means of support.

health care delivery system, sex, race, economic class, and able-bodied status are important predictors in determining someone's place in the hierarchy. The organization of the health care system does not, however, merely mirror the power and privilege structures of the larger society; it also perpetuates them.

Within existing health care structures, women do most of the work associated with health care, but they are, for the most part, excluded from making the policy decisions that shape the system. They are the principal providers of home health care, tending the ill members of their own families, but because this work is unpaid, it is unrecorded labor, not even appearing in statistical studies of health care delivery systems; it carries no social authority, and the knowledge women acquire in caring for the ill is often dismissed by those who have power in the system. Furthermore, support is not made available to provide some relief to women carrying out this vital but demanding work.

In the formal institutions of health care delivery, women constitute over 80 percent of paid health care workers, but men hold almost all the positions of authority.[4] Health policy is set by physicians, directors, and legislators, and these positions are filled overwhelmingly by men. Despite recent dramatic increases in female enrollment in medical schools, most physicians are men (78.8 percent in Canada and 84.8 percent in the United States as of 1986);[5] further, female physicians tend to cluster in less influential specialties, such as family practice and pediatrics, and they are seldom in positions of authority within their fields. Most medical textbooks are written by men, most clinical instructors are men, and most hospital

directors are men.[6] The professional fields that women do largely occupy in the health care system are ones associated with traditionally female skills, such as nursing, nutrition, occupational and physical therapy, and public health. Women who work in health administration tend to be situated in middle-management positions, where their mediating skills may be desirable but their influence on policy is limited.

Research, too, is largely concentrated in male hands. Few women have their own labs or the budgets to pursue projects of their own choosing. The standards by which research is evaluated are those that have been developed by privileged men to meet their needs. They do not incorporate considerations that some female scientists and most feminist philosophers of science find important, such as including space in the design of a project for a measure of participant control, reducing the separation between subject and object, and resisting restrictive, medicalized analysis.

When we focus directly on issues of race and economic class, the isolation of health care provider from consumer becomes even more pronounced. Although many members of minority races and plenty of poor people are involved in the delivery of health care, very few hold positions of authority. Working-class and minority employees are concentrated in the nonprofessional ranks of cleaners, nurses' aides, orderlies, kitchen staff, and so forth. Women from these groups generally have the lowest income and status in the whole health care system. They have no opportunity to shape health care policy or voice their concerns about their own health needs or those of persons for whom they are responsible. One result of this unbalanced representation is that there has been virtually no research into the distinct needs of minority

4 Canada census data statistics for 1986 list 104,315 men and 418,855 women employed in the areas of medicine and health. Brown (1983) reports that over 85 percent of all health-service and hospital workers in the United States are women.

5 The Canadian figure is from Statistics Canada census figures; the American figure is taken from Todd (1989).

6 To correct the apparently systematic gender bias in the provision of health care McMurray (1990) recommends that efforts be made to increase "the number of female physicians in leadership roles and other positions of authority in teaching, research and the practice of medicine" (10).

women (White 1990). Both those empowered to do medical research and those expected to respond to identified health needs come almost entirely from the socially defined groups and classes most removed from the experiences of women of color and poor and disabled women.

The gender and racial imbalances in the health care system are not accidental; they are a result of specific barriers designed to restrict access to women and minorities to the ranks of physicians. Regina Morantz-Sanchez (1985) documents how the medical profession organized itself over the last century to exclude and harass women who sought to become doctors, and Margaret Campbell (1973) shows that many of these mechanisms are still with us. Blacks, too, have been subject to systematic barriers, which keep them out of the ranks of physicians. For example, it is necessary to serve as an intern to become licensed to practice medicine, but until the 1960s, few American hospitals would grant internship positions to black physicians; those blacks who did manage to become qualified to practice medicine often encountered hospitals that refused to grant them the opportunity to admit patients (Blount 1990). Because black women must overcome both gender and race barriers, they face nearly insurmountable obstacles to pursuing careers as physicians (Weaver and Garrett 1983; Gamble 1990). Therefore, although blacks make up 12 percent of the population of the United States, they account for only 3 percent of the population of practicing doctors, and black women constitute only 1 percent of the nation's physicians; further, blacks represent only 2 percent of the faculty at medical schools (Gamble 1990).

Racism and sexism in health care have been exacerbated by the fact that different oppressed groups have long been encouraged to perceive their interests as in conflict, so that race often divides women who might otherwise be expected to unite. Darlene Clark Hine (1989) has shown that racial struggles have plagued the nursing profession since 1890. For much of that period, white nurses acted on their own racist views and fought to exclude black women from their ranks. Although their racism is not excusable, it is perhaps understandable: Hine explains that white nurses felt compelled to fight for professional status and autonomy. Acting within a predominantly racist culture, they feared that their claims for recognition would be undermined if they were to welcome black nurses into the profession on an equal footing. In other words, because the combined forces of racism and sexism made it especially difficult for black nurses to obtain respect as professionals, white nurses chose to accept the implicit judgments behind such attitudes and to distance themselves from their black colleagues, rather than joining them in the struggle to counter racial prejudice.

Moreover, the racial struggles of nurses are just one symptom of a larger problem. The hierarchical structures that operate throughout the health care system motivate each social group to pursue the pragmatic strategy of establishing its relative superiority over yet more disadvantaged groups, rather than working collectively to challenge the structures themselves. Although white nurses did seek to dissociate themselves from black nurses and claimed greater commonality with the higher-ranked (white) male physicians, black nurses were themselves driven to seek distance from other black women who were employed in the system as domestic staff or nurses' aides, by claiming an unreciprocated identity with white nurses. Within hierarchical structures, all participants have reason to foster connections with those ranked higher and to seek distance from those ranked lower. This motive breeds an attitude that encourages submission to those above and hostility and a sense of superiority toward those below; in this way, all but the most oppressed groups become complicit in maintaining the hierarchical structure of the health care system. Thus the organization of the health care system itself helps reinforce the oppressive structures and attitudes of society at large. . . .

The power and authority that society has entrusted to doctors give them the opportunity to destroy many of the patriarchal assumptions about women collectively and the racist, classist, homophobic, and other beliefs about various groups of women that are key to their oppression. Few physicians, however, have chosen to exercise their social power in this way. Many doctors have accepted uncritically the biases of an oppressive society, and some have offered evidence in confirmation of such values. As a group, physicians have held onto their own power and privilege by defending the primacy of the authoritarian medical model as a necessary feature of health care. Most have failed to listen honestly to the alternative perspectives of oppressed people who are very differently situated in society.

The medical model organizes our current attempts at defining and responding to health needs. It has been conceived as a structure that requires a hierarchically organized health care system, in which medical expertise is privileged over other sorts of knowledge. It grants license to an elite class of experts to formulate all matters of health and to determine the means of responding to them. As we have seen, however, there are several serious moral problems with this model. First, it responds differently to the health needs of different groups, offering less and lower-quality care to members of oppressed groups. Second, its structures and presuppositions support the patterns of oppression that shape our society. Finally, it rationalizes the principle of hierarchy in human interactions, rather than one of equality, by insisting that its authoritarian structures are essential to the accomplishment of its specific ends, and it tolerates an uneven distribution of positions within its hierarchy.

We need, then, different models to guide our thinking about ways to organize the delivery of health care. In addition to the many limits to the medical model that have been named in the bioethics literature, the traditional model reflects and perpetuates oppression in society. I conclude by summarizing some feminist suggestions that I believe should be incorporated into alternative models, if they are to be ethically acceptable.

A model that reflects the insights of feminist ethics would expand its conceptions of health and health expertise. It would recognize social as well as physiological dimensions of health. In particular, it would reflect an understanding of both the moral and the health costs of oppression. Thus it would make clear that those who are committed to improving the health status of all members of the population should assume responsibility for avoiding and dismantling the dominance structures that contribute to oppression.

Such a model would require a change in traditional understandings of who has the relevant knowledge to make decisions about health and health policy. Once we recognize the need to include oppression as a factor in health, we can no longer maintain the authoritarian medical model, in which physicians are the experts on all matters of health and are authorized to respond to all such threats. We need also to recognize that experiential knowledge is essential to understanding how oppression affects health and how the damage of oppression can be reduced. Both political and moral understandings may be necessary to address these dimensions of health and health care. Physiological knowledge is still important, but it is not always decisive.

Therefore, a feminist model would resist hierarchical structures and proclaim a commitment to egalitarian alternatives. Not only would these alternatives be more democratic in themselves and hence more morally legitimate, they would also help to produce greater social equality by empowering those who have been traditionally disempowered. They would limit the scope for domination that is available to those now accustomed to power and control.

More egalitarian structures would foster better health care and higher standards of health for those who are now oppressed in society; such structures would recognize voices that are now largely unheard and would be in a position to respond to the needs they express.

The current health care system is organized around the central ideal of pursuing a "cure" in the face of illness, wherein "cure" is interpreted with most of the requisite agency belonging to the health care providers. A feminist alternative would recommend that the health care system be principally concerned with empowering consumers in their own health by providing them with the relevant information and the means necessary to bring about the changes that would contribute to their health. The existing health care system, modeled as it is on the dominance structures of an oppressive society, is closed to many innovative health strategies that would increase the power of patients; a feminist model would be user-controlled and responsive to patient concerns.

Such a change in health care organization would require us to direct our attention to providing the necessities of healthy living, rather than trying only to correct the serious consequences that occur when the opportunities for personal care have been denied. Moreover, as an added benefit, a shift to a more democratized notion of health needs may help to evolve a less expensive, more effective health care delivery system; most patients seem to be less committed than are their professional health care providers to a costly high-tech, crisis-intervention focus in health care (York 1987).

A health care system that reflects feminist ideals would avoid or at least lessen the contribution that the system of health care makes in the maintenance of oppression. It would be significantly more egalitarian in both organization and effect than anything that we are now accustomed to. This system not only would be fairer in its provision of health services but would also help to undermine the ideological assumptions on which many of our oppressive practices rest. Such an alternative is required as a matter of both ethics and health.

To spell out that model in greater detail and with an appropriate understanding, it is necessary to democratize the discipline of bioethics itself—hence, bioethics, as an area of intellectual pursuit, must also recognize the value of incorporating diverse voices in its discussions and analyses. Like medicine or any other discipline, bioethics is largely defined by the perspective of its participants. If we hope to ensure a morally adequate analysis of the ethics of health care, then we should ensure the participation of many different voices in defining the central questions and exploring the promising paths to answers in the field.

References

Blount, Melissa. 1990. "Surpassing Obstacles: Pioneering Black Women Physicians." In *Black Women's Health Book*. See White.

Campbell, Margaret. 1973. *Why Would a Woman Go Into Medicine? Medical Education in the United States: A Guide for Women*. Old Westbury, NY: Feminist Press.

Corea, Gena. 1985. *The Hidden Malpractice: How American Medicine Mistreats Women*. rev. ed. New York: Harper Colophon Books.

Davis, Angela Y. 1990. "Sick and Tired of Being Sick and Tired: The Politics of Black Women's Health." In *Black Women's Health Book*. See White.

Ehrenreich, Barbara, and Deidre English. 1979. *For Her Own Good: 150 Years of the Experts' Advice to Women*. Garden City, NY: Anchor Books.

Gamble, Vanessa Northington. 1990. "On Becoming a Physician: A Dream Not Deferred." In *Black Women's Health Book*. See White.

Gordon-Bradshaw, Ruth H. 1988. "A Social Essay on Special Issues Facing Poor Women of Color." In *Too Little, Too Late*. See Stellman.

Hine, Darlene Clark. 1989. *Black Women in White: Racial Conflict and Cooperation in the Nursing Profession, 1890–1950*. Bloomington: Indiana University Press.

Lewis, Andrea. 1990. "Looking at the Total Picture: A Conversation with Health Activist Beverly Smith." In *Black Women's Health Book*. See White.

McBarnette, Lorna. 1988. "Women and Poverty: The Effects on Reproductive Status." In *Too Little, Too Late*. See Stellman.

McDonnell, Kathleen. 1984. *Not an Easy Choice: A Feminist Re-examines Abortion*, Toronto: Women's Press.

McMurray, Richard J. 1990. "Gender Disparities in Clinical Decision-Making." Report to the American Medical Association Council on Ethical and Judicial Affairs.

Morantz-Sanchez, Regina Markell. 1985. *Sympathy and Science: Women Physicians in American Medicine*. New York: Oxford University Press.

Paltiel, Freda L. 1988. "Is Being Poor a Mental Health Hazard?" In *Too Little, Too Late*. See Stellman, 1988.

Stellman, Jean Mager. 1988. "The Working Environment of the Working Poor: An Analysis based on Worker's Compensation Claims, Census Data and Known Risk Factors." In *Too Little, Too Late: Dealing with the Health Needs of Women in Poverty*, ed. Cesar Perales and Lauren Young. New York: Harrington Park Press.

Tallon, James R. Jr., and Rachel Block. 1988. "Changing Patterns of Health Insurance Coverage: Special Concerns for Women." In *Too Little, Too Late*. See Stellman, 1988.

Todd, Alexandra Dundas. 1989. *Intimate Adversaries: Cultural Conflict Between Doctors and Women Patients*. Philadelphia: University of Pennsylvania Press.

Weaver, Jerry L., and Sharon D. Garrett. 1983. "Sexism and Racism in the American Health Care Industry: A Comparative Analysis." In *Women and Health: The Politics of Sex in Medicine*, ed. Elizabeth Fee. Farmingdale, NY: Baywood.

White, Evelyn C., ed. 1990. *Black Women's Health Book: Speaking for Ourselves*. Seattle: Seal Press.

York, Geoffrey. 1987. *The High Price of Health: A Patient's Guide to the Hazards of Medical Politics*. Toronto: James Lorimer and Company.

Review Questions

1. Who is oppressed in North America and the Developing World, according to Sherwin?
2. How are women treated by the health care system in the United States and Canada? How are they treated in the Developing World?
3. Describe the sexism, racism, and classism in the structures of the existing health care system.
4. Explain the feminist model for improving health care proposed by Sherwin.

Discussion Questions

1. Sherwin claims that a more egalitarian, democratized system of health care would be less expensive and more efficient than the current high-tech and high-cost system. Do you agree? Explain your answer.
2. Sherwin rejects the "authoritarian model," wherein doctors are viewed as experts on all matters of health care. But what is the alternative? If doctors are not considered experts anymore, then whom do we consult about health care?

Problem Cases

1. Dr. Kevorkian

(Reported by Jack Lessenberry in *The New York Times,* May 15, 1996.) On May 14, 1996, Dr. Jack Kevorkian was found not guilty of violating a Michigan common law making assisted suicide a crime. That was the fifth time he had been acquitted at three different trials.

The latest acquittal was in a case involving the deaths of Majorie Wantz, 58, and Sherry Miller, 43. They died side by side on October 23, 1991, in a cabin in the Bald Mountain State Recreation Area in Michigan. Mrs. Miller died by breathing carbon monoxide through a mask. She had multiple sclerosis, which prosecutors said was not a terminal illness. Mrs. Wantz died by using a lethal injection from a machine invented by Dr. Kevorkian called the Mercitron. She had been in constant pain after a series of ineffective surgeries to remove her vulva, but her condition was not terminal, a fact conceded by Dr. Kevorkian.

Dr. Kevorkian's main defense was that "his only intent had been to relieve their pain and suffering," and that "their death was just an unfortunate but necessary consequence of the only way that could be done." He also argued that it was improper to try him for breaking a common law made up after the event by the courts, and not a law passed by the legislature.

These arguments persuaded the jury to acquit Dr. Kevorkian. Do you agree with their verdict? Should Dr. Kevorkian be allowed to assist people to commit suicide, even in a case where they are not suffering from a terminal illness? Is this wrong? Should there be a law against this? Explain your answers.

2. Cruzan v. Director, Missouri Department of Health (United States Supreme Court. 110 S. Ct. 2841 [1990])

In this case, the U.S. Supreme Court ruled on a petition to terminate the artificial nutrition and hydration of Nancy Cruzan, a 25-year-old woman existing in a persistent vegetative state following an automobile accident.

On the night of January 11, 1983, Cruzan rolled her car over while driving down Elm Road in Jasper County, Missouri. She was found lying in a ditch. She was not breathing, and her heart was not beating. Paramedics were able to restore her breathing and heartbeat, but she remained unconscious. She remained in a coma for about three weeks. To keep her alive, surgeons implanted a gastrostomy feeding and hydration tube; she remained in a persistent vegetative state—a condition in which a person exhibits motor reflexes but no sign of consciousness or cognitive function.

After it became clear that Cruzan had practically no chance of recovery, her parents asked the doctors to terminate the artificial feeding and hydration. The doctors and the parents agreed that this would cause Cruzan's death. The doctors refused to do this without a court order. The parents petitioned a court and received authorization to terminate treatment. But the Supreme Court of Missouri reversed the decision of the trial court and ruled that treatment could not be terminated without "clear and convincing evidence" that termination is what Cruzan would have wanted.

The case went to the U.S. Supreme Court, and it upheld the judgment of the Missouri Supreme Court that termination of treatment was unconstitutional in this case. The decision was 5 to 4, and the majority opinion was written by Justice William H. Rehnquist. In his opinion, Rehnquist granted that a competent person has a right to refuse lifesaving nutrition and hydration. But he ruled that in the case of an incompetent person such as Nancy Cruzan, it is constitutional for Missouri to require that feeding and hydration be terminated only if there is clear and convincing evidence that this is what Cruzan would have wanted. Because such evidence was not provided, the decision to deny the request for termination was upheld.

In later developments, the parents presented new evidence to show that Cruzan would have chosen termination of treatment, and the feeding and hydration were stopped. Nancy Cruzan finally died in December of 1990, seven years after the accident.

This case raises several troubling questions:

1. What would be the AMA position in this case? Are artificial feeding and hydration ordinary or extraordinary means of prolonging life? If they are ordinary means, then is cessation of treatment not allowed? If they are extraordinary means, then is cessation of treatment allowed? Is the AMA position defensible in this case?

2. Is termination of treatment in this case active or passive euthanasia? Is it an act that causes Cruzan's death, or does it just allow her to die from natural causes? Does it cause death or permit death?

3. Suppose that there were no "clear and convincing evidence" that termination of treatment is what Cruzan would have wanted. Does this mean that termination is wrong in this case? On the other hand, suppose that there were such evidence. Does this mean that termination is not wrong?

3. The Case of Baby Jane Doe

In October 1983, Baby Jane Doe (as the infant was called by the court to protect her anonymity) was born with spina bifida and a host of other congenital defects. According to the doctors consulted by the parents, the child would be severely mentally retarded, be bedridden, and suffer considerable pain. After consultations with doctors and religious counselors, Mr. and Mrs. A (as the parents were called in the court documents) decided not to consent to lifesaving surgery.

At this point, a right-to-life activist lawyer tried to legally force lifesaving surgery in the Baby Doe case, but two New York appeals courts and a state children's agency decided not to override the parents' right to make a decision in the case. Then the U.S. Justice Department intervened in the case. It sued to obtain records from the University Hospital in Stony Brook, New York, to determine if the hospital had violated a federal law that forbids discrimination against the handicapped. Dr.

C. Everett Koop, the U.S. surgeon general, appeared on television to express the view that the government has the moral obligation to intercede on behalf of such infants in order to protect their right to life.

Two weeks later, Federal District Judge Leonard Wexler threw out the Justice Department's unusual suit. Wexler found no discrimination. The hospital had been willing to do the surgery but had failed to do so because the parents refused to consent to the surgery. Wexler found the parents' decision to be a reasonable one in view of the circumstances.

The day after the ruling, the Justice Department appealed. On January 9, 1984, federal regulations were issued preventing federally funded hospitals from withholding treatment in such cases.

Do parents have a right to make life-or-death decisions for their defective children? Why or why not?

Do you agree with Dr. Koop that the government has a moral obligation to save the lives of such infants, even when their parents do not wish it? Explain your position.

If the government forces us to save the lives of defective infants like Baby Doe, then should it assume the responsibility for the cost of surgery, intensive care, and so on? If so, then how much money should be spent on this program? If not, then who is going to pay the bills?

Suggested Readings

1. Derek Humphry's *Final Exit* (The Hemlock Society, 1991) is a controversial book that tells you how to commit suicide or get assistance from a doctor. Critics of the book charge that there has been a 31 percent increase in plastic-bag suicides, the method recommended in the book.
2. St. Thomas Aquinas, *Summa Theologica* 2 (Benziger Brothers, 1925), part 2, question 64, argues that suicide is unnatural and immoral.
3. Richard B. Brandt, "On the Morality and Rationality of Suicide," in *A Handbook for the Study of Suicide,* ed. Seymour Perlin (Oxford University Press, 1975), maintains that it is not wrong, blameworthy, or irrational for a person suffering from a painful terminal illness to commit suicide. Brandt argues that it is morally right to actively terminate defective newborns in "Defective Newborns and the Morality of Termination," in *Infanticide and the Value of Life,* ed. Marvin Kohl (Prometheus Books, 1978).
4. Arthur J. Dyck, "An Alternative to the Ethic of Euthanasia," in *To Live and to Let Die,* ed. R. H. Williams (Springer-Verlag, 1973), attacks the ethic of euthanasia and defends an ethic of benemortasia that forbids suicide but allows a person to refuse medical interventions that prolong dying.
5. J. Gay-Williams, "The Wrongfulness of Euthanasia," in *Intervention and Reflection: Basic Issues in Medical Ethics,* fifth edition, ed. Ronald Munson (Wadsworth, 1996), argues that euthanasia is inherently wrong because it is unnatural, is contrary to self-interest, and has bad effects.
6. Bonnie Steinbock, "The Intentional Termination of Life," in *Ethics in Science and Medicine* 6, no. 1 (Pergamon Press, Ltd., 1979), defends the AMA policy statements from Rachels's

attack. She says that the statement rejects both active and passive euthanasia, since both are intentional killing, but it permits the cessation of the employment of extraordinary means of prolonging life, which is not the same as passive euthanasia.

7. Tristram H. Englehardt, Jr., "Ethical Issues in Aiding the Death of Young Children," in *Beneficient Euthanasia,* ed. Marvin Kohl (Prometheus Books, 1975), claims that adult euthanasia can be justified by the appeal to freedom but that children do not have the right to choose to die because they are not persons in the strict sense.

8. Philippa Foot, "The Problem of Abortion and the Doctrine of Double Effect," *Oxford Review,* no. 5 (1973), presents a classic discussion of the Doctrine of Double Effect. She discusses euthanasia in "Euthanasia," *Philosophy and Public Affairs* 6 (Winter 1977).

9. Jonathan Glover, *Causing Death and Saving Lives* (Penguin, 1977), applies utilitarianism to the problem of euthanasia and to other problems of killing, such as abortion and capital punishment.

10. *Infanticide and the Value of Life,* ed. Marvin Kohl (Prometheus Books, 1978), is an anthology that concentrates on the morality of euthanasia for severely defective newborns.

11. *Killing and Letting Die,* ed. Bonnie Steinbock (Prentice Hall, 1980), is a collection of readings that focus on the controversial distinction between killing and letting die.

12. Tom L. Beauchamp, "A Reply to Rachels on Active and Passive Euthanasia," in *Ethical Issues in Death and Dying,* ed. Tom L. Beauchamp and Seymour Perlin (Prentice Hall, 1978), defends the moral significance of the distinction between active and passive euthanasia.

13. Thomas D. Sullivan, "Active and Passive Euthanasia: An Impertinent Distinction?" *Human Life Review* 3 (Summer 1977), argues that Rachels's distinction between active and passive euthanasia is impertinent and irrelevant. Rachels's reply to Sullivan is titled "More Impertinent Distinctions," in *Biomedical Ethics,* ed. T. A. Mappes and J. S. Zembaty (McGraw-Hill, 1981).

14. John Ladd, "Positive and Negative Euthanasia," in *Ethical Issues Relating to Life and Death,* ed. John Ladd (Oxford University Press, 1979), argues that no clear distinction can be made between killing and letting die but that they are not morally equivalent, either. His own position is that the distinction always depends on the context.

15. James Rachels, "Euthanasia," in *Matters of Life and Death,* third edition, ed. Tom Regan (Random House, 1993), relates the history of euthanasia, discusses the arguments for and against active euthanasia, and concludes with a proposal of how to legalize active euthanasia.

16. James Rachels, *The End of Life: Euthanasia and Morality* (Oxford University Press, 1986), develops his view of euthanasia and defends it from criticism.

17. Robert Young, "Voluntary and Nonvoluntary Euthanasia," *The Monist* 59 (April 1976), reviews a number of arguments used to show that voluntary active euthanasia is not justified and concludes that none of them is successful.

18. John A. Robertson, "Involuntary Euthanasia of Defective Newborns," *Stanford Law Review* 27 (January 1975), argues that the utilitarian defense of euthanasia for defective newborns does not succeed in showing that it is justified.

19. Robert F. Weir, *Selective Nontreatment of Handicapped Newborns: Moral Dilemmas in Neonatal Medicine* (Oxford University Press, 1984), discusses moral issues relating to the care and treatment of defective or handicapped newborns.

20. "Cruzan: Clear and Convincing?" *Hastings Center Report* 20 (September/October 1990), has six articles discussing the Cruzan case.

Chapter 4

Capital Punishment

Introduction

Factual Background

There were 486 executions in the United States from 1976 to 1998. The number is increasing rapidly; there were 74 executions in 1997, compared with 45 in 1996, and 31 in 1994. There were only 11 executions in the years 1976 to 1983. Only three women have been executed; the case of one of them, a 38-year-old born-again Christian named Karla Faye Tucker, received worldwide attention. (See the first Problem Case.) As for minorities, a statistic cited by Amsterdam in the reading is that an almost equal number of whites and blacks have been executed since 1930, even though blacks constituted only about a tenth of the U.S. population during this period.

There are now 3,517 prisoners on death row awaiting capital punishment in the thirty-eight states having this punishment. Of these, 35 percent are black, 7 percent are Hispanic, and 57 percent are white. There are 43 women, including one who used to be a man. In the past twenty-five years, 74 men have been exonerated and freed from death row, and a number of men now on death row claim they are innocent. Since 1900, at least 23 innocent men have been executed.

As Amsterdam notes in the reading, the death penalty is expensive. California spends $90 million a year on capital punishment. In Florida the average total cost per executed prisoner is $3.2 million. In Texas the cost per case is $2.3 million, but this is still three times the cost of keeping a criminal in maximum security for forty years.

Currently, the most common method of execution is lethal injection; 330 people in thirty-four states have been executed using this method. Electrocution is used in ten states, and the gas chamber in six states. Hanging is used in two states, and the firing squad is used in two states.

The Eighth Amendment to the Constitution of the United States prohibits cruel and unusual punishment. For example, the medieval punishment of cutting off the hands of thieves seems to be cruel and unusual punishment. Is the death penalty another example of cruel and unusual punishment, and thus unconstitutional? The Supreme Court has given contradictory answers, saying it is unconstitutional in the cases of *Furman* (1972) and *Woodson* (1976), and then reversing itself and affirming that it is constitutional in *Gregg* (1976).

To be more specific, in the case of *Furman v. Georgia* (1972), the Supreme Court ruled (by a mere 5-to-4 majority) that the death penalty was unconstitutional because it was being administered in an arbitrary and capricious manner. Juries were allowed to impose the death sentence without any explicit guidelines or standards, and the result was that blacks were much more likely to receive the death penalty than whites.

After the *Furman* decision, states wishing to retain the death penalty reacted in two ways. One was to correct the arbitrary discretion of juries by making the death penalty mandatory for certain crimes. But in *Woodson v. North Carolina* (1976), the Court ruled (again by a 5-to-4 majority) that mandatory death sentences were unconstitutional.

The second attempt to counter the objection raised in *Furman* was to provide standards for juries. Georgia specified in its law ten statutory aggravating circumstances, one of which the jury had to find beyond reasonable doubt in order to render a death sentence. This second approach proved to be successful, for in *Gregg v. Georgia* (1976) the majority ruled, with Justices Marshall and Brennan dissenting, that the death penalty is not unconstitutional for the crime of murder, provided there are safeguards against any arbitrary or capricious imposition by juries.

The Readings

The first reading for the chapter is taken from *Gregg*, the landmark decision legalizing the death penalty. In their majority opinion, Justices Steward, Powell, and Stevens try to explain why the death penalty is not cruel and unusual, and thus not in violation of the Eighth Amendment. They begin with an explanation of the concept of cruel and unusual. In their view, a punishment is cruel and unusual if it either fails to accord with evolving standards of decency or fails to accord with the dignity of humans that is the basic concept underlying the Eighth Amendment. This second stipulation rules out excessive punishment that involves unnecessary pain or is disproportionate to the crime. They argue that the death penalty does not satisfy either of these stipulations. It is acceptable to the majority of people, since in 1976 there were thirty-five states with the death penalty (and now there are thirty-eight capital-punishment states). Furthermore, it is not excessive because it achieves two important social purposes, retribution and deterrence.

To fully understand the appeal to retribution, it is necessary to examine the theory on which it is based, namely, retributivism. The classical formulation of this theory is given by Immanuel Kant in the second reading. According to Kant, the only justification for punishing a person is guilt. If a person is guilty of a crime, then justice requires that he or she be punished; if a person is not guilty, then no punishment is justified. In other words, guilt is both a necessary and a sufficient condition for justified punishment. Furthermore, Kant's view is that the punishment must fit the crime (or be proportionate to the crime) according to the biblical principle of retaliation *(lex talionis)* that says "eye for eye, tooth for tooth, life for life." Now, what punishment fits the crime of murder using this principle? Kant insists that death, and only death, is the proper punishment for murder; no other punishment will satisfy the requirements of legal justice.

The other purpose of punishment that the justices appeal to in the majority opinion in *Gregg* is deterrence. Although the justices admit that the statistical evidence for deterrence seems inconclusive, they still believe that the death penalty is a deterrent for carefully contemplated murders, such as murder for hire, and for murder by a person already in prison.

In the third reading, van den Haag gives a different account of deterrence. The effectiveness of a punishment as a deterrent does not depend on or require calculations on the part of those deterred; rather, they need only be responsive to danger posed by the punishment. But the fact that the death penalty is irrevocable makes it more terrifying than revocable punishments such as life imprisonment, and since a terrifying punishment is more likely to deter than a less terrifying one, van den Haag concludes that we may expect the death penalty to deter more than alternative revocable punishments. Or at least the burden of proof lies on those who claim that execution does not deter.

Furthermore, the fact that we are uncertain about the deterrent effect of the death penalty is not a good reason for abandoning it, because we are also uncertain about the effect of *not* using the death penalty. Given these two uncertainties, van den Haag thinks it is better to execute murderers even if we are uncertain about the deterrent effect of doing this, for this involves risking the lives of the guilty murderers rather than the lives of innocent victims, lives that might be lost if we don't execute.

Jeffrey H. Reiman raises difficulties for both Kant and van den Haag. Even if we accept Kant's retributivist law of *lex talionis,* it does not follow that we ought to do to criminals exactly what they did to their victims. Such an exact application of *lex talionis* would require us to rape rapists and torture torturers, and such punishments are rejected by Reiman as horrible and uncivilized. As for van den Haag's appeal to deterrence, Reiman denies that we have any good reasons for thinking that execution deters more than life imprisonment. For one thing, Reiman claims that criminals committing crimes already face a substantial risk of death, and that doesn't deter them. In reply to van den Haag's argument that given the uncertainties about deterrence we should choose the death penalty, Reiman points out that there might be a deterrent effect produced by *not* executing that matches the deterrent effect of executing, and thus either way we risk innocent lives.

Anthony G. Amsterdam has more objections to capital punishment. It is intentionally killing a person, and as such it is wrong unless proven otherwise. Thus the burden of proof is on those who want to defend it. It results in innocent people being executed, and this injustice cannot be corrected. It is unfairly applied to minorities and the poor. Contrary to what van den Haag and the Supreme Court justices say, Amsterdam claims there is substantial evidence that it is not a better deterrent than life imprisonment, and in fact evidence that it acts as a counterdeterrent—that is, that it motivates suicidal people to commit murder.

Philosophical Issues

How do we justify punishment? This is the basic issue at the heart of the debate about capital punishment. There seem to be two main theories about this, utilitarianism and retributivism.

Utilitarians justify punishment by appealing to good consequences, such as rehabilitation, protection of society, and deterrence of crime. As van den Haag notes in the reading, however, capital punishment does not rehabilitate the person killed, and imprisonment would do the job of protecting society from criminals. Capital punishment is not necessary for protection of society. It seems, then, that deterrence of crime is the only possible justification of the death penalty for utilitarians, and indeed there has been much debate about the deterrence value of the death penalty.

Three main arguments have been used to demonstrate that execution deters criminals. First, there is the appeal to statistics. Even though the Supreme Court justices in the *Gregg* decision and van den Haag both think that the statistics are inconclusive, Amsterdam does not agree. He claims that there is "very, very substantial" evidence that refutes the claim that capital punishment is a better deterrent than life imprisonment.

Second, there are intuitive or commonsense arguments used by both the Supreme Court justices and van den Haag. The justices think that those who calculate their crimes will be deterred, and van den Haag believes that those who fear death as irrevocable punishment will be motivated to avoid it. Against this, Amsterdam claims that instead of being deterred, suicidal people will be motivated to commit capital crimes. Reiman also makes the point that criminals already face a substantial threat of death from police and citizens with guns, and this apparently does not deter them from crime.

Third, there is van den Haag's "best bet argument" (as I shall call it). Essentially, this is the argument that given uncertainties about whether execution deters, the best bet is to execute, for this involves gambling with guilty lives rather than innocent ones. The bet, of course, is that the executions will deter and thus save innocent lives. But there seem to be problems with the argument. Reiman thinks that not executing might also deter and thus save guilty lives; so perhaps not executing is the best bet. Amsterdam denies the uncertainty; we have substantial evidence that execution does not deter better than life imprisonment.

The other theory that is the focus of debate is retributivism. As Reiman says in the reading, there are two different retributive principles, *lex talionis* and the principle of proportionality. The principle of proportionality says that the punishment should fit the crime or be proportional to the crime, so that a serious crime should receive a harsh punishment. No doubt, murder is a serious crime, but is death the only punishment that fits this crime, as Kant says? Why isn't life imprisonment without a parole a punishment that fits this crime too? The trouble with the principle of proportionality is that it doesn't tell us which punishments fit which crimes. Not only is this a problem for the crime of murder, it is also a problem for crimes such as rape and torture and treason. Perhaps these crimes should be punished by execution too. Or maybe death is not harsh enough; perhaps those crimes should be punished by solitary confinement or castration or even torture.

The biblical principle of *lex talionis* requires us to do to the criminal what he or she has done, "an eye for an eye." This principle is attacked by both Amsterdam and Reiman. Amsterdam claims that this principle does not justify capital punishment because of the simple fact that most murderers are sent to prison, not executed. Clearly, we think that many crimes of murder do not deserve the death penalty; for example, we do not have the death sentence for homicides that are unpremeditated or accidental. Another objection is that we do have the death sentence for nonhomicidal crimes such as treason. This shows that the death sentence can be justified for crimes other than murder. As we have seen, Reiman has another objection to *lex talionis:* It would require us to torture torturers, and such punishment is horrible and unacceptable for civilized persons.

Gregg v. Georgia (1976)

THE SUPREME COURT

Potter Stewart (1915–1985) and Lewis F. Powell, Jr. (1908–1998), served as associate justices of the U.S. Supreme Court. John Paul Stevens continues to serve as an associate justice. Thurgood Marshall (1908–1993) retired from the Court in 1991; he was the first African American ever to be appointed.

The main issue before the Court in the case of *Gregg v. Georgia* (1976) was whether or not the death penalty violates the Eighth Amendment prohibition of cruel and unusual punishment. The majority of the Court, with Justice Marshall and Justice Brennan dissenting, held that the death penalty does not violate the Eighth Amendment because it is in accord with contemporary standards of decency. It serves both a deterrent and a retributive purpose, and in the case of the Georgia law being reviewed, it is no longer arbitrarily applied.

In his dissenting opinion, Justice Marshall objects that the death sentence is excessive because a less severe penalty—life imprisonment—would accomplish the legitimate purposes of punishment. In reply to the claim that the death sentence is necessary for deterrence, Marshall asserts that the available evidence shows that this is not the case. As for the appeal to retribution, Marshall argues that the justification for the death penalty is not consistent with human dignity.

THE ISSUE IN THIS CASE is whether the imposition of the sentence of death for the crime of murder under the law of Georgia violates the Eighth and Fourteenth Amendments.

Source: The Supreme Court, *Gregg v. Georgia* (1976).

I

The petitioner, Troy Gregg, was charged with committing armed robbery and murder. In accordance with Georgia procedure in capital cases, the trial was in two stages, a guilt stage and a sentencing stage. . . .

. . . The jury found the petitioner guilty of two counts of murder.

At the penalty stage, which took place before the same jury, . . . the trial judge instructed the jury that it could recommend either a death sentence or a life prison sentence on each count. . . . The jury returned verdicts of death on each count.

The Supreme Court of Georgia affirmed the convictions and the imposition of the death sentences for murder. . . . The death sentences imposed for armed robbery, however, were vacated on the grounds that the death penalty had rarely been imposed in Georgia for that offense. . . .

II

. . . The Georgia statute, as amended after our decision in *Furman v. Georgia* (1972), retains the death penalty for six categories of crime: murder, kidnapping for ransom or where the victim is harmed, armed robbery, rape, treason, and aircraft hijacking. . . .

III

We address initially the basic contention that the punishment of death for the crime of murder is, under all circumstances, "cruel and unusual" in violation of the Eighth and Fourteenth Amendments of the Constitution. In Part IV of this opinion, we will consider the sentence of death imposed under the Georgia statutes at issue in this case.

The Court on a number of occasions has both assumed and asserted the constitutionality of capital punishment. In several cases that assumption provided a necessary foundation for the decision, as the Court was asked to decide whether a particular method of carrying out a capital sentence would be allowed to stand under the Eighth Amendment. But until *Furman v. Georgia* (1972), the Court never confronted squarely the fundamental claim that the punishment of death always, regardless of the enormity of the offense or the procedure followed in imposing the sentence, is cruel and unusual punishment in violation of the Constitution. Although this issue was presented and addressed in *Furman,* it was not resolved by the Court. Four justices would have held that capital punishment is not unconstitutional *per se;* two justices would have reached the opposite conclusion; and three justices, while agreeing that the statutes then before the Court were invalid as applied, left open the question whether such punishment may ever be imposed. We now hold that the punishment of death does not invariably violate the Constitution.

A

The history of the prohibition of "cruel and unusual" punishment already has been reviewed at length. The phrase first appeared in the English Bill of Rights of 1689, which was drafted by Parliament at the accession of William and Mary. The English version appears to have been directed against punishments unauthorized by statute and beyond the jurisdiction of the sentencing court, as well as those disproportionate to the offense involved. The American draftsmen, who adopted the English phrasing in drafting the Eighth Amendment, were primarily concerned, however, with proscribing "tortures" and other "barbarous" methods of punishment.

In the earliest cases raising Eighth Amendment claims, the Court focused on particular methods of execution to determine whether they were too cruel to pass constitutional muster. The constitutionality of the sentence of death itself was not at issue, and the criterion used to evaluate the mode of execution was its similarity to "torture" and other "barbarous" methods. . . .

But the Court has not confined the prohibition embodied in the Eighth Amendment to "barbarous" methods that were generally outlawed in the 18th century. Instead, the Amendment has been interpreted in a flexible and dynamic manner. The Court early recognized that "a principle to be vital must be capable of wider application than the mischief which gave it birth." Thus the clause forbidding "cruel and unusual" punishments "is not fastened to the obsolete but may acquire meaning as public opinion becomes enlightened by a humane justice." . . .

It is clear from the foregoing precedents that the Eighth Amendment has not been regarded as a static concept. As Mr. Chief Justice Warren said, in an oftquoted phrase, "[t]he Amendment must draw its meaning from the evolving standards of decency that mark the progress of a maturing society." Thus, an assessment of contemporary values concerning the infliction of a challenged sanction is relevant to the application of the Eighth Amendment. As we develop below more fully, this assessment does not call for a subjective judgment. It requires, rather, that we look to objective indicia that reflect the public attitude toward a given sanction.

But our cases also make clear that public perceptions of standards of decency with respect to criminal sanctions are not conclusive. A penalty also must accord with "the dignity of man," which is the "basic concept underlying the Eighth Amendment." This means, at least, that the punishment not be "excessive." When a form of punishment in the abstract (in this case, whether capital punishment may ever be imposed as a sanction for murder) rather than in the particular (the propriety of death as a penalty to be applied to a specific defendant for a specific crime) is under consideration, the inquiry into "excessiveness" has two aspects. First, the punishment must not involve the unnecessary and wanton infliction of pain. Second, the punishment must not be grossly out of proportion to the severity of the crime.

B

Of course, the requirements of the Eighth Amendment must be applied with an awareness of the limited role to be played by the courts. This does not mean that judges have no role to play, for the Eighth Amendment is a restraint upon the exercise of legislative power. . . .

But, while we have an obligation to ensure that constitutional bounds are not over-reached, we may not act as judges as we might as legislators. . . .

Therefore, in assessing a punishment selected by a democratically elected legislature against the constitutional measure, we presume its validity. We may not require the legislature to select the least severe penalty possible so long as the penalty selected is not cruelly inhumane or disproportionate to the crime involved. And a heavy burden rests on those who would attack the judgment of the representatives of the people.

This is true in part because the constitutional test is intertwined with an assessment of contemporary standards and the legislative judgment weighs heavily in ascertaining such standards. [I]n a democratic society legislatures, not courts, are constituted to respond to the will and consequently the moral values of the people."

The deference we owe to the decisions of the state legislatures under our federal system is enhanced where the specification of punishments is concerned, for "these are peculiarly questions of legislative policy." Caution is necessary lest this Court become, "under the aegis of the Cruel and Unusual Punishment Clause, the ultimate arbiter of the standards of criminal responsibility . . . throughout the country." A decision that a given punishment is impermissible under the Eighth Amendment cannot be reversed short of a constitutional amendment. The ability of the people to express their preference through the normal democratic processes, as well as through ballot referenda, is shut off. Revisions cannot be made in the light of further experience.

C

In the discussion to this point we have sought to identify the principles and considerations that guide a court in addressing an Eighth Amendment claim. We now consider specifically whether the sentence of death for the crime of murder is a *per se* violation of the Eighth and Fourteenth Amendments to the Constitution. We note first that history and precedent strongly support a negative answer to this question.

The imposition of the death penalty for the crime of murder has a long history of acceptance both in the United States and in England. . . .

It is apparent from the text of the Constitution itself that the existence of capital punishment was accepted by the Framers. At the time the Eighth Amendment was ratified, capital punishment was a common sanction in every State. Indeed, the First Congress of the United States enacted legislation providing death as the penalty for specified crimes. . . .

For nearly two centuries, this Court, repeatedly and often expressly, has recognized that capital punishment is not invalid *per se*. . . .

Four years ago, the petitioners in *Furman* and its companion cases predicated their argument primarily upon the asserted proposition that standards of decency had evolved to the point where capital punishment no longer could be tolerated. The petitioners in those cases said, in effect, that the evolutionary process had come to an end, and that standards of decency required that the Eighth Amendment be construed finally as prohibiting capital punishment for any crime regardless of its depravity and impact on society. This view was accepted by two Justices. Three other Justices were unwilling to go so far; focusing on the procedures by which convicted defendants were selected for the death penalty rather than on the actual punishment inflicted, they joined in the conclusion that the statutes before the Court were constitutionally invalid.

The petitioners in the capital cases before the Court today renew the "standards of decency" argument, but developments during the four years since *Furman* have undercut substantially the assumptions upon which their argument rested. Despite the continuing debate, dating back to the nineteenth century, over the morality and utility of capital punishment, it is now evident that a large proportion of American society continues to regard it as an appropriate and necessary criminal sanction.

The most marked indication of society's endorsement of the death penalty for murder is the legislative response to *Furman*. The legislatures of at least thirty-five States have enacted new statutes that provide for the death penalty for at least some crimes that result in the death of another person. And the Congress of the United States, in 1974, enacted a statute providing the death penalty for aircraft piracy that results in death. These recently adopted statutes have attempted to address the concerns expressed by the Court in *Furman* primarily (i) by specifying the factors to be weighed and the procedures to be followed in deciding when to impose a capital sentence, or (ii) by making the death penalty mandatory for specified crimes. But all of the post-*Furman* statutes make clear that capital punishment itself has not been rejected by the elected representatives of the people. . . .

The jury also is a significant and reliable objective index of contemporary values because it is so directly involved. The Court has said that "one of the most important functions any jury can perform in making . . . a selection [between life imprisonment and death for a defendant convicted in a capital case] is to maintain a link between contemporary community values and the penal system." It may be true that evolving standards have influenced juries in recent decades to be more discriminating in imposing the sentence of death. But the relative infrequency of jury verdicts imposing death sentence does not indicate rejection of capital punishment *per se*. Rather, the reluctance of juries in many cases to impose the sentence may well reflect the humane feeling that this most irrevocable of sanctions should be reserved for a small number of extreme cases. Indeed, the actions of juries in many states since *Furman* are fully compatible with the legislative judgments, reflected in the new statutes, as to the continued utility and necessity of capital punishment in appropriate cases. At the close of 1974 at least 254 persons had been sentenced to death since *Furman,* and by the end of March 1976, more than 460 persons were subject to death sentences.

As we have seen, however, the Eighth Amendment demands more than that a challenged punishment be acceptable to contemporary society. The Court also must ask whether it comports with the basic concept of human dignity at the core of the amendment. Although we cannot "invalidate a category of penalties because we deem less severe penalties adequate to serve the ends of penology," the sanction imposed cannot be so totally without penological justification that it results in the gratuitous infliction of suffering.

The death penalty is said to serve two principal social purposes: retribution and deterrence of capital crimes by prospective offenders.[1]

In part, capital punishment is an expression of society's moral outrage at particularly offensive conduct. This function may be unappealing to many, but it is essential in an ordered society that asks its citizens to rely on legal processes rather than self-help to vindicate their wrongs.

> The instinct for retribution is part of the nature of man, and channeling that instinct in the administration of criminal justice serves an important purpose in promoting the stability of a society governed by law. When people begin to believe that organized society is unwilling or unable to impose upon criminal offenders the punishment they "deserve," then there are sown the seeds of anarchy—of self-help, vigilante justice, and lynch law. *Furman v. Georgia* (Stewart, J., concurring).

Retribution is no longer the dominant objective of the criminal law, but neither is it a forbidden

objective nor one inconsistent with our respect for the dignity of men. Indeed, the decision that capital punishment may be the appropriate sanction in extreme cases is an expression of the community's belief that certain crimes are themselves so grievous an affront to humanity that the only adequate response may be the penalty of death.

Statistical attempts to evaluate the worth of the death penalty as a deterrent to crimes of potential offenders have occasioned a great deal of debate. The results simply have been inconclusive. . . .

Although some of the studies suggest that the death penalty may not function as a significantly greater deterrent than lesser penalties, there is no convincing empirical evidence either supporting or refuting this view. We may nevertheless assume safely that there are murderers, such as those who act in passion, for whom the threat of death has little or no deterrent effect. But for many others, the death penalty undoubtedly is a significant deterrent. There are carefully contemplated murders, such as murder for hire, where the possible penalty of death may well enter into the cold calculus that precedes the decision to act. And there are some categories of murder, such as murder by a life prisoner, where other sanctions may not be adequate.

The value of capital punishment as a deterrent of crime is a complex factual issue the resolution of which properly rests with the legislatures, which can evaluate the results of statistical studies in terms of their own local conditions and with a flexibility of approach that is not available to the courts. Indeed, many of the post-*Furman* statutes reflect just such a responsible effort to define those crimes and those criminals for which capital punishment is most probably an effective deterrent.

In sum, we cannot say that the judgment of the Georgia Legislature that capital punishment may be necessary in some cases is clearly wrong. Considerations of federalism, as well as respect for the ability of a legislature to evaluate, in terms of its particular State, the moral consensus

---

1 Another purpose that has been discussed is the incapacitation of dangerous criminals and the consequent prevention of crimes that they may otherwise commit in the future.

concerning the death penalty and its social utility as a sanction, require us to conclude, in the absence of more convincing evidence, that the infliction of death as a punishment for murder is not without justification and thus is not constitutionally severe.

Finally, we must consider whether the punishment of death is disproportionate in relation to the crime for which it is imposed. There is no question that death as a punishment is unique in its severity and irrevocability. When a defendant's life is at stake, the Court has been particularly sensitive to insure that every safeguard is observed. But we are concerned here only with the imposition of capital punishment for the crime of murder, and when a life has been taken deliberately by the offender,[2] we cannot say that the punishment is invariably disproportionate to the crime. It is an extreme sanction, suitable to the most extreme of crimes.

We hold that the death penalty is not a form of punishment that may never be imposed, regardless of the circumstances of the offense, regardless of the character of the offender, and regardless of the procedure followed in reaching the decision to impose it.

IV

We now consider whether Georgia may impose the death penalty on the petitioner in this case.

A

While *Furman* did not hold that the infliction of the death penalty *per se* violates the Constitution's ban on cruel and unusual punishments, it did recognize that the penalty of death is different in kind from any other punishment imposed under our system of criminal justice. Because of the uniqueness of the death penalty, *Furman* held that it could not be imposed under sen-

tencing procedures that created a substantial risk that it would be inflicted in an arbitrary and capricious manner. . . .

Furman mandates that where discretion is afforded a sentencing body on a matter so grave as the determination of whether a human life should be taken or spared, that discretion must be suitably directed and limited so as to minimize the risk of wholly arbitrary and capricious action.

It is certainly not a novel proposition that discretion in the area of sentencing be exercised in an informed manner. We have long recognized that "[f]or the determination of sentences, justice generally requires . . . that there be taken into account the circumstances of the offense together with the character and propensities of the offender." . . .

Jury sentencing has been considered desirable in capital cases in order "to maintain a link between contemporary community values and the penal system—a link without which the determination of punishment could hardly reflect 'the evolving standards of decency that mark the progress of a maturing society.'" But it creates special problems. Much of the information that is relevant to the sentencing decision may have no relevance to the question of guilt, or may even be extremely prejudicial to a fair determination of that question. This problem, however, is scarcely insurmountable. Those who have studied the question suggest that a bifurcated procedure—one in which the question of sentence is not considered until the determination of guilt has been made—is the best answer. . . . When a human life is at stake and when the jury must have information prejudicial to the question of guilt but relevant to the question of penalty in order to impose a rational sentence, a bifurcated system is more likely to ensure elimination of the constitutional deficiencies identified in *Furman*.

But the provision of relevant information under fair procedural rules is not alone sufficient to guarantee that the information will be properly used in the imposition of punishment, especially if sentencing is performed by a jury. Since

---

2 We do not address here the question whether the taking of the criminal's life is a proportionate sanction where no victim has been deprived of life—for example, when capital punishment is imposed for rape, kidnapping, or armed robbery that does not result in the death of any human being.

the members of a jury will have had little, if any, previous experience in sentencing, they are unlikely to be skilled in dealing with the information they are given. To the extent that this problem is inherent in jury sentencing, it may not be totally correctable. It seems clear, however, that the problem will be alleviated if the jury is given guidance regarding the factors about the crime and the defendant that the State, representing organized society, deems particularly relevant to the sentencing decision. . . .

While some have suggested that standards to guide a capital jury's sentencing deliberations are impossible to formulate, the fact is that such standards have been developed. When the drafters of the Model Penal Code faced this problem, they concluded "that it is within the realm of possibility to point to the main circumstances of aggravation and of mitigation that should be weighed *and weighed against each other* when they are presented in a concrete case."[3] While such standards are by necessity somewhat general, they do provide guidance to the sentencing authority and thereby reduce the likelihood that it will impose a sentence that fairly can be called capricious or arbitrary. Where the sentencing authority is required to specify the factors it relied upon in reaching its decision, the further safeguard of meaningful appellate review is available to ensure that death sentences are not imposed capriciously or in a freakish manner.

In summary, the concerns expressed in *Furman* that the penalty of death not be imposed in an arbitrary or capricious manner can be met by a carefully drafted statute that ensures that the sentencing authority is given adequate information and guidance. As a general proposition these concerns are best met by a system that provides for a bifurcated proceeding at which the sentencing authority is apprised of the information relevant to the imposition of sentence and provided with standards to guide its use of the information.

We do not intend to suggest that only the above-described procedures would be permissible under *Furman* or that any sentencing system constructed along these general lines would inevitably satisfy the concerns of *Furman,* for each distinct system must be examined on an individual basis. Rather, we have embarked upon

3 The Model Penal Code proposes the following standards:

(3) Aggravating Circumstances.

(a) The murder was committed by a convict under sentence of imprisonment.

(b) The defendant was previously convicted of another murder or of a felony involving the use or threat of violence to the person.

(c) At the time the murder was committed the defendant also committed another murder.

(d) The defendant knowingly created a great risk of death to many persons.

(e) The murder was committed while the defendant was engaged or was an accomplice in the commission of, or an attempt to commit, or flight after committing or attempting to commit robbery, rape or deviate sexual intercourse by force or threat of force, arson, burglary or kidnapping.

(f) The murder was committed for the purpose of avoiding or preventing a lawful arrest or effecting an escape from lawful custody.

(g) The murder was committed for pecuniary gain.

(h) The murder was especially heinous, atrocious or cruel, manifesting exceptional depravity.

(4) Mitigating Circumstances.

(a) The defendant has no significant history of prior criminal activity.

(b) The murder was committed while the defendant was under the influence of extreme mental or emotional disturbance.

(c) The victim was a participant in the defendant's homicide conduct or consented to the homicidal act.

(d) The murder was committed under circumstances which the defendant believed to provide a moral justification or extenuation for his conduct.

(e) The defendant was an accomplice in a murder committed by another person and his participation in the homicide act was relatively minor.

(f) The defendant acted under duress or under the domination of another person.

(g) At the time of the murder, the capacity of the defendant to appreciate the criminality (wrongfulness) of his conduct or to conform his conduct to the requirements of law was impaired as a result of mental disease or defect or intoxication.

(h) The youth of the defendant at the time of the crime. (ALI Model Penal Code §210.6, Proposed Official Draft 1962).

this general exposition to make clear that it is possible to construct capital-sentencing systems capable of meeting *Furman's* constitutional concerns.

B

We now turn to consideration of the constitutionality of Georgia's capital-sentencing procedures. In the wake of *Furman,* Georgia amended its capital punishment statute, but chose not to narrow the scope of its murder provisions. Thus, now as before *Furman,* in Georgia "[a] person commits murder when he unlawfully and with malice aforethought, either express or implied, causes the death of another human being." All persons convicted of murder "shall be punished by death or by imprisonment for life."

Georgia did act, however, to narrow the class of murderers subject to capital punishment by specifying ten statutory aggravating circumstances, one of which must be found by the jury to exist beyond a reasonable doubt before a death sentence can ever be imposed. In addition, the jury is authorized to consider any other appropriate aggravating or mitigating circumstances. The jury is not required to find any mitigating circumstance in order to make a recommendation of mercy that is binding on the trial court, but it must find a *statutory* aggravating circumstance before recommending a sentence of death.

These procedures require the jury to consider the circumstances of the crime and the criminal before it recommends sentence. No longer can a Georgia jury do as Furman's jury did: reach a finding of the defendant's guilt and then, without guidance or direction, decide whether he should live or die. Instead, the jury's attention is directed to the specific circumstances of the crime: Was it committed in the course of another capital felony? Was it committed for money? Was it committed on a peace officer or judicial officer? Was it committed in a particularly heinous way or in a manner that endangered the lives of many persons? In addition,

the jury's attention is focused on the characteristics of the person who committed the crime: Does he have a record of prior convictions for capital offenses? Are there any special facts about this defendant that mitigate against imposing capital punishment (e.g., his youth, the extent of his cooperation with the police, his emotional state at the time of the crime)? As a result, while some jury discretion still exists, "the discretion to be exercised is controlled by clear and objective standards so as to produce nondiscriminatory application."

As an important additional safeguard against arbitrariness and caprice, the Georgia statutory scheme provides for automatic appeal of all death sentences to the State's Supreme Court. That court is required by statute to review each sentence of death and determine whether it was imposed under the influence of passion or prejudice, whether the evidence supports the jury's finding of statutory aggravating circumstance, and whether the sentence is disproportionate compared to those sentences imposed in similar cases.

In short, Georgia's new sentencing procedures require as a prerequisite to the imposition of the death penalty, specific jury findings as to the circumstances of the crime or the character of the defendant. Moreover, to guard further against a situation comparable to that presented in *Furman,* the Supreme Court of Georgia compares each death sentence with the sentences imposed on similarly situated defendants to ensure that the sentence of death in a particular case is not disproportionate. On their face these procedures seem to satisfy the concerns of *Furman.* No longer should there be "no meaningful basis for distinguishing the few cases in which [the death penalty] is imposed from the many cases in which it is not.". . .

V

The basic concern of *Furman* centered on those defendants who were being condemned to death capriciously and arbitrarily. Under the procedures before the Court in that case, sentencing authorities were not directed to give attention to the nature or circumstances of the crime committed or to the character or record of the defendant. Left unguided, juries imposed the death sentence in a way that could only be called freakish. The new Georgia sentencing procedures, by contrast, focus the jury's attention on the particularized nature of the crime and the particularized characteristics of the individual defendant. While the jury is permitted to consider any aggravating or mitigating circumstances, it must find and identify at least one statutory aggravating factor before it may impose a penalty of death. In this way the jury's discretion is channeled. No longer can a jury wantonly and freakishly impose the death sentence; it is always circumscribed by the legislative guidelines. In addition, the review function of the Supreme Court of Georgia affords additional assurance that the concerns that prompted our decision in *Furman* are not present to any significant degree in the Georgia procedure applied here.

For the reasons expressed in this opinion, we hold that the statutory system under which Gregg was sentenced to death does not violate the Constitution. Accordingly, the judgment of the Georgia Supreme Court is affirmed.

DISSENTING OPINION

In *Furman v. Georgia* (1972) (concurring opinion), I set forth at some length my views on the basic issue presented to the Court in [this case]. The death penalty, I concluded, is a cruel and unusual punishment prohibited by the Eighth and Fourteenth Amendments. That continues to be my view.

I have no intention of retracing the "long and tedious journey" that led to my conclusion in *Furman*. My sole purposes here are to consider the suggestion that my conclusion in *Furman* has been undercut by developments since

then, and briefly to evaluate the basis for my Brethren's holding that the extinction of life is a permissible form of punishment under the Cruel and Unusual Punishments Clause.

In *Furman*, I concluded that the death penalty is constitutionally invalid for two reasons. First, the death penalty is excessive. And second, the American people, fully informed as to the purposes of the death penalty and its liabilities, would in my view reject it as morally unacceptable.

Since the decision in *Furman*, the legislatures of thirty-five States have enacted new statutes authorizing the imposition of the death sentence for certain crimes, and Congress has enacted a law providing the death penalty for air piracy resulting in death. I would be less than candid if I did not acknowledge that these developments have a significant bearing on a realistic assessment of the moral acceptability of the death penalty to the American people. But if the constitutionality of the death penalty turns, as I have urged, on the opinion of an *informed* citizenry, then even the enactment of new death statutes cannot be viewed as conclusive. In *Furman*, I observed that the American people are largely unaware of the information critical to a judgment on the morality of the death penalty, and concluded that if they were better informed they would consider it shocking, unjust, and unacceptable. A recent study, conducted after the enactment of the post-*Furman* statutes, has confirmed that the American people know little about the death penalty, and that the opinions of an informed public would differ significantly from those of a public unaware of the consequences and effects of the death penalty.

Even assuming, however, that the post-*Furman* enactment of statutes authorizing the death penalty renders the prediction of the views of an informed citizenry an uncertain basis for a constitutional decision, the enactment of those statutes has no bearing whatsoever on the conclusion that the death penalty is unconstitutional because it is excessive. An excessive penalty is invalid under the Cruel and Unusual Punishments Clause "even though popular sentiment may favor" it. The inquiry here, then, is simply whether the death penalty is necessary to accomplish the legitimate legislative purposes in punishment, or whether a less severe penalty—life imprisonment—would do as well.

The two purposes that sustain the death penalty as nonexcessive in the Court's view are general deterrence and retribution. In *Furman,* I canvassed the relevant data on the deterrent effect of capital punishment. The state of knowledge at that point, after literally centuries of debate, was summarized as follows by a United Nations Committee:

> It is generally agreed between the retentionists and abolitionists, whatever their opinions about the validity of comparative studies of deterrence, that the data which now exist show no correlation between the existence of capital punishment and lower rates of capital crime.

The available evidence, I concluded in *Furman,* was convincing that "capital punishment is not necessary as a deterrent to crime in our society.". . .

The evidence I reviewed in *Furman* remains convincing, in my view, that "capital punishment is not necessary as a deterrent to crime in our society." The justification for the death penalty must be found elsewhere.

The other principal purpose said to be served by the death penalty is retribution. The notion that retribution can serve as a moral justification for the sanction of death finds credence in the opinion of my Brothers Stewart, Powell, and Stevens. . . . It is this notion that I find to be the most disturbing aspect of today's unfortunate [decision].

The concept of retribution is a multifaceted one, and any discussion of its role in the criminal law must be undertaken with caution. On one level, it can be said that the notion of retribution or reprobation is the basis of our insistence that only those who have broken the law be punished, and in this sense the notion is quite obviously central to a just system of criminal sanctions. But our recognition that retribution plays a crucial role in determining who may be punished by no means requires approval of retribution as a general justification for punishment. It is the question whether retribution can provide a moral justification for punishment—in particular, capital punishment—that we must consider.

My Brothers Stewart, Powell, and Stevens offer the following explanation of the retributive justification for capital punishments:

> The instinct for retribution is part of the nature of man, and channeling that instinct in the administration of criminal justice serves an important purpose in promoting the stability of a society governed by law. When people begin to believe that organized society is unwilling or unable to impose upon criminal offenders the punishment they "deserve," then there are sown the seeds of anarchy—of self-help, vigilante justice, and lynch law.

This statement is wholly inadequate to justify the death penalty. As my Brother Brennan stated in *Furman,* "[t]here is no evidence whatever that utilization of imprisonment rather than death encourages private blood feuds and other disorders." It simply defies belief to suggest that the death penalty is necessary to prevent the American people from taking the law into their own hands.

In a related vein, it may be suggested that the expression of moral outrage through the imposition of the death penalty serves to reinforce basic moral values—that it marks some crimes as particularly offensive and therefore to be avoided. The argument is akin to a deterrence argument, but differs in that it contemplates the individual's shrinking from antisocial conduct, not because he fears punishment, but because he has been told in the strongest possible way that the conduct is wrong. This contention, like the previous one, provides no support for the death penalty. It is inconceivable that any individual concerned about conforming his conduct to what society says is "right" would fail to realize that murder is "wrong" if the penalty were simply life imprisonment.

The foregoing contentions—that society's expression of moral outrage through the imposition of the death penalty preempts the citizenry from taking the law into its own hands and reinforces moral values—are not retributive in the purest sense. They are essentially utilitarian in that they portray the death penalty as valuable because of its beneficial results. These justifications for the death penalty are inadequate because the penalty is, quite clearly I think, not necessary to the accomplishment of those results.

There remains for consideration, however, what might be termed the purely retributive justification for the death penalty—that the death penalty is appropriate, not because of its beneficial effect on society, but because the taking of the murderer's life is itself morally good. Some of the language of the opinion of my Brothers Stewart, Powell, and Stevens . . . appears positively to embrace this notion of retribution for its own sake as a justification for capital punishment. They state:

> [T]he decision that capital punishment may be the appropriate sanction in extreme cases is an expression of the community's belief that certain crimes are themselves so grievous an affront to humanity that the only adequate response may be the penalty of death.

They then quote with approval from Lord Justice Denning's remarks before the British Commission on Capital Punishment:

> The truth is that some crimes are so outrageous that society insists on adequate punishment, because the wrong-doer deserves it, irrespective of whether it is a deterrent or not.

Of course, it may be that these statements are intended as no more than observations as to the popular demands that it is thought must be responded to in order to prevent anarchy. But the implication of the statements appears to me to be quite different—namely, that society's judgment that the murderer "deserves" death must be respected not simply because the preservation of order requires it, but because it is appropriate that society make the judgment and carry it out. It is the latter notion, in particular, that I consider to be fundamentally at odds with the Eighth Amendment. The mere fact that the community demands the murderer's life in return for the evil he has done cannot sustain the death penalty, for as justices Stewart, Powell, and Stevens remind us, "the Eighth Amendment demands more than that a challenged punishment be acceptable to contemporary society." To be sustained under the Eighth Amendment, the death penalty must "compor[t] with the basic concept of human dignity at the core of the Amendment"; the objective in imposing it must be "[consistent] with our respect for the dignity of [other] men." Under these standards, the taking of life "because the wrongdoer deserves it" surely must fail, for such a punishment has as its very basis the total denial of the wrongdoer's dignity and worth.

The death penalty, unnecessary to promote the goal of deterrence or to further any legitimate notion of retribution, is an excessive penalty forbidden by the Eighth and Fourteenth Amendments. I respectfully dissent from the Court's judgment upholding the [sentence] of death imposed upon the [petitioner in this case].

Review Questions

1. How did the justices rule in *Furman v. Georgia* (1972), and by contrast, how do they rule in this case?
2. According to the justices, what is the basic concept underlying the Eighth Amendment?

3. According to the justices, in what two ways may a punishment be excessive?
4. According to the justices, why doesn't the death penalty violate contemporary standards of decency?
5. The justices say that the death penalty serves two principal social purposes. What are they, and how are they supposed to work?
6. What safeguards against the arbitrary and capricious application of the death sentence are suggested by the justices?
7. Explain Justice Marshall's objections and his criticisms of the majority opinion.

Discussion Questions

1. The Georgia statute retains the death penalty for six crimes, including rape, armed robbery, and treason. Do you agree that persons guilty of these crimes should receive the death sentence? Explain your view.
2. Try to give a precise definition of the phrase "cruel and unusual." Can you do it?
3. How could it be conclusively proven that the death penalty deters potential criminals better than life imprisonment?
4. Should the instinct for retribution be satisfied? Defend your answer.

The Retributive Theory of Punishment

IMMANUEL KANT

For biographical information on Kant, see his reading in Chapter 1.

In Kant's retributive theory of punishment, punishment is justified not by any good results but simply by the criminal's guilt. Criminals must pay for their crimes; otherwise an injustice has occurred. Furthermore, the punishment must fit the crime. Kant asserts that the only punishment that is appropriate for the crime of murder is the death of the murderer. As he puts it, "Whoever has committed a murder must *die*."

JUDICIAL OR JURIDICAL punishment *(poena forensis)* is to be distinguished from natural punishment *(poena naturalis),* in which crime as vice punishes itself, and does not as such come within the cognizance of the legislator. Juridical punishment can never be administered merely as a means for promoting another good, either with regard to the criminal himself or to civil society, but must in all cases be imposed only because the individual on whom it is inflicted *has committed a crime.* For one man ought never to be dealt with merely as a means subservient to

Source: Immanuel Kant, "The Retributive Theory of Punishment" from *The Philosophy of Law,* Part II, trans. W. Hastie (1887).

the purpose of another, nor be mixed up with the subjects of real right. Against such treatment his inborn personality has a right to protect him, even although he may be condemned to lose his civil personality. He must first be found guilty and *punishable*, before there can be any thought of drawing from his punishment any benefit for himself or his fellow-citizens. The penal law is a categorical imperative; and woe to him who creeps through the serpent-windings of utilitarianism to discover some advantage that may discharge him from the justice of punishment, or even from the due measure of it, according to the pharisaic maxim: 'It is better that *one* man should die than that the whole people should perish.' For if justice and righteousness perish, human life would no longer have any value in the world. What, then, is to be said of such a proposal as to keep a criminal alive who has been condemned to death, on his being given to understand that if he agreed to certain dangerous experiments being performed upon him, he would be allowed to survive if he came happily through them? It is argued that physicians might thus obtain new information that would be of value to the commonweal. But a court of justice would repudiate with scorn any proposal of this kind if made to it by the medical faculty; for justice would cease to be justice, if it were bartered away for any consideration whatever.

But what is the mode and measure of punishment which public justice takes as its principle and standard? It is just the principle of equality, by which the pointer of the scale of justice is made to incline no more to the one side than the other. It may be rendered by saying that the undeserved evil which any one commits on another, is to be regarded as perpetrated on himself. Hence it may be said: 'If you slander another, you slander yourself; if you steal from another, you steal from yourself; if you strike another, you strike yourself; if you kill another, you kill yourself.' This is the right of retaliation (*jus talionis*); and properly understood, it is the only principle which in regulating a public court, as distinguished from mere private judgment, can definitely assign both the quality and the quantity of a just penalty. All other standards are wavering and uncertain; and on account of other considerations involved in them, they contain no principle comformable to the sentence of pure and strict justice. It may appear, however, that difference of social status would not admit the application of the principle of retaliation, which is that of 'like with like.' But although the application may not in all cases be possible according to the letter, yet as regards the effect it may always be attained in practice, by due regard being given to the disposition and sentiment of the parties in the higher social sphere. Thus a pecuniary penalty on account of a verbal injury, may have no direct proportion to the injustice of slander; for one who is wealthy may be able to indulge himself in this offense for his own gratification. Yet the attack committed on the honor of the party aggrieved may have its equivalent in the pain inflicted upon the pride of the aggressor, especially if he is condemned by the judgment of the court, not only to retract and apologize, but to submit to some meaner ordeal, as kissing the hand of the injured person. In like manner, if a man of the highest rank has violently assaulted an innocent citizen of the lower orders, he may be condemned not only to apologize but to undergo a solitary and painful imprisonment, whereby, in addition to the discomfort endured, the vanity of the offender would be painfully affected, and the very shame of his position would constitute an adequate retaliation after the principle of like with like. But how then would we render the statement: 'If you *steal* from another, you steal from yourself'? In this way, that whoever steals anything makes the property of all insecure; he therefore robs himself of all security in property, according to the right of retaliation. Such a one has nothing, and can acquire nothing, but he has the will to live; and this is only possible by others supporting him. But as the state should not do this gratuitously, he must for this purpose yield his powers to the state to be used in penal labour; and thus he falls for a time, or it may be for life, into a condition of slavery. But whoever has committed murder, must *die.* There is, in this case, no juridical substitute or surrogate, that can be given or taken for the satisfaction of justice. There is no *likeness* or proportion between life, however painful, and death; and therefore there is no equality between the crime of murder and the retaliation of it but what is judicially accomplished by the execution of the criminal. His death, however, must be kept free from all maltreatment that would make the humanity suffering in his person loathsome or abominable. Even if a civil society resolved to dissolve itself with the consent of all its members—as might be supposed in the case of a people inhabiting an island resolving to separate and scatter themselves throughout the whole world—the last murderer lying in the prison ought to be executed before the resolution was carried out. This ought to be done in order that everyone may realize the desert of his deeds, and that bloodguiltiness may not remain upon the people; for otherwise they might all be regarded as participators in the murder as a public violation of justice.

The equalization of punishment with crime, is therefore only possible by the cognition of the judge extending even to the penalty of death, according to the right of retaliation.

Review Questions

1. According to Kant, who deserves judicial punishment?
2. Why does Kant reject the maxim "It is better that *one* man should die than that the whole people should perish"?
3. How does Kant explain the principle of retaliation?

Discussion Questions

1. Does Kant have any good reason to reject the "serpent-windings of utilitarianism"?
2. Is death always a just punishment for murder? Can you think of any exceptions?

On Deterrence and the Death Penalty

ERNEST VAN DEN HAAG

Ernest van den Haag (now retired) was professor of jurisprudence and public policy at Fordham University. He is the author of *The Fabric of Society* (1957), *Political Violence and Civil Disobedience* (1973), and *Punishing Criminals: Concerning a Very Old and Painful Question* (1975).

Source: Ernest van den Haag, "On Deterrence and the Death Penalty," from *Journal of Criminal Law, Criminology, and Political Science,* Vol. 60, No. 2 (Northwestern University School of Law, 1969). Reprinted with permission.

After admitting that the death penalty cannot be justified by appealing to rehabilitation or protection of society, van den Haag turns to deterrence. He explains the deterrence effect of punishment in terms of a response to danger rather than any calculation on the part of the person being deterred. Legal threats deter actions that threaten society by being internalized; we develop a conscience that threatens us if we do wrong. But this conscience needs to be reinforced by external authority that punishes illegal behavior. The causes of criminal behavior on van den Haag's view are not slums, ghettos, or personality disorders, but rather simply desires that are stronger than the fear of punishment. Although we cannot conclusively prove that the death penalty deters crime, we cannot prove that it doesn't do this, either. Given these two uncertainties, van den Haag thinks it is preferable to use the death penalty. We should do this because it is better to risk the lives of the guilty than to risk the lives of the innocent victims who might be killed if we do not use the death penalty.

I

IF REHABILITATION and the protection of society from unrehabilitated offenders were the only purposes of legal punishment, the death penalty could be abolished: It cannot attain the first end, and is not needed for the second. No case for the death penalty can be made unless "doing justice" or "deterring others" is among our penal aims.[1] Each of these purposes can justify capital punishment by itself; opponents, therefore, must show that neither actually does, while proponents can rest their case on either.

Although the argument from justice is intellectually more interesting, and, in my view, decisive enough, utilitarian arguments have more appeal: The claim that capital punishment is useless because it does not deter others is most persuasive. I shall, therefore, focus on this claim. Lest the argument be thought to be unduly narrow, I shall show, nonetheless, that some claims of injustice rest on premises which the claimants reject when arguments for capital punishment are derived therefrom; while other claims of injustice have no independent standing: Their weight depends on the weight given to deterrence.

II

Capital punishment is regarded as unjust because it may lead to the execution of innocents, or because the guilty poor (or disadvantaged) are more likely to be executed than the guilty rich.

Regardless of merit, these claims are relevant only if "doing justice" is one purpose of punishment. Unless one regards it as good, or, at least, better, that the guilty be punished rather than the innocent, and that the equally guilty be punished equally,[2] unless, that is, one wants penalties to be just, one cannot object to them because they are not. However, if one does include justice among the purposes of punishment, it becomes possible to justify any one punishment—even death—on grounds of justice. Yet, those who object to the death penalty because of its alleged injustice usually deny not only the merits, or the sufficiency, of specific arguments based on justice, but the propriety of

1 Social solidarity of "community feeling" (here to be ignored) might be dealt with as a form of deterrence.

2 Certainly a major meaning of *suum cuique tribue*.

justice as an argument: They exclude "doing justice" as a purpose of legal punishment. If justice is not a purpose of penalties, injustice cannot be an objection to the death penalty, or to any other; if it is, justice cannot be ruled out as an argument for any penalty.

Consider the claim of injustice on its merits now. A convicted man may be found to have been innocent; if he was executed, the penalty cannot be reversed. Except for fines, penalties never can be reversed. Time spent in prison cannot be returned. However, a prison sentence may be remitted once the prisoner serving it is found innocent; and he can be compensated for the time served (although compensation ordinarily cannot repair the harm). Thus, though (nearly) all penalties are irreversible, the death penalty, unlike others, is irrevocable as well.

Despite all precautions, errors will occur in judicial proceedings: The innocent may be found guilty,[3] or the guilty rich may more easily escape conviction, or receive lesser penalties than the guilty poor. However, these injustices do not reside in the penalties inflicted but in their maldistribution. It is not the penalty—whether death or prison—which is unjust when inflicted on the innocent, but its imposition on the innocent. Inequity between poor and rich also involves distribution, not the penalty distributed.[4] Thus injustice is not an objection to the death penalty but to the distributive process—the trial. Trials are more likely to be fair when life is at stake—the death penalty is probably less often unjustly inflicted than others. It requires special consideration not because it is more, or more often, unjust than other penalties, but because it is always irrevocable.

Can any amount of deterrence justify the possibility of irrevocable injustice? Surely injustice is unjustifiable in each actual individual case; it must be objected to whenever it occurs. But we are concerned here with the process that may produce injustice, and with the penalty that would make it irrevocable—not with the actual individual cases produced, but with the general rules which may produce them. To consider objections to a general rule (the provision of any penalties by law) we must compare the likely net result of alternative rules and select the rule (or penalty) likely to produce the least injustice. For however one defines justice, to support it cannot mean less than to favor the least injustice. If the death of innocents because of judicial error is unjust, so is the death of innocents by murder. If some murders could be avoided by a penalty conceivably more deterrent than others—such as the death penalty—then the question becomes: Which penalty will minimize the number of innocents killed (by crime and by punishment)? It follows that the irrevocable injustice sometimes inflicted by the death penalty would not significantly militate against it, if capital punishment deters enough murders to reduce the total number of innocents killed so that fewer are lost than would be lost without it.

In general, the possibility of injustice argues against penalization of any kind only if the expected usefulness of penalization is less important than the probable harm (particularly to innocents) and the probable inequities. The possibility of injustice argues against the death penalty only inasmuch as the added usefulness (deterrence) expected from irrevocability is thought less important than the added harm. (Were my argument specifically concerned with justice, I could compare the injustice inflicted by the courts with the injustice—outside the courts—avoided by the judicial process. *I.e.*, "important" here may be used to include everything to which importance is attached.)

We must briefly examine now the general use and effectiveness of deterrence to decide

---

3 I am not concerned here with the converse injustice, *which I regard as no less grave.*

4 Such inequity, though likely, has not been demonstrated. Note that, since there are more poor than rich, there are likely to be more guilty poor; and, if poverty contributes to crime, the proportion of the poor who are criminals also should be higher than of the rich.

whether the death penalty could add enough deterrence to be warranted.

III

Does any punishment "deter others" at all? Doubts have been thrown on this effect because it is thought to depend on the incorrect rationalistic psychology of some of its 18th- and 19th-century proponents. Actually deterrence does not depend on rational calculation, on rationality or even on capacity for it; nor do arguments for it depend on rationalistic psychology. Deterrence depends on the likelihood and on the regularity—not on the rationality—of human responses to danger; and further on the possibility of reinforcing internal controls by vicarious external experiences.

Responsiveness to danger is generally found in human behavior; the danger can, but need not, come from the law or from society; nor need it be explicitly verbalized. Unless intent on suicide, people do not jump from high mountain cliffs, however tempted to fly through the air; and they take precautions against falling. The mere risk of injury often restrains us from doing what is otherwise attractive; we refrain even when we have no direct experience, and usually without explicit computation of probabilities, let alone conscious weighing of expected pleasure against possible pain. One abstains from dangerous acts because of vague, inchoate, habitual and, above all, preconscious fears. Risks and rewards are more often felt than calculated; one abstains without accounting to oneself, because "it isn't done," or because one literally does not conceive of the action one refrains from. Animals as well refrain from painful or injurious experiences presumably without calculation; and the threat of punishment can be used to regulate their conduct.

Unlike natural dangers, legal threats are constructed deliberately by legislators to restrain actions which may impair the social order. Thus legislation transforms social into individual dangers. Most people further transform external into internal danger: They acquire a sense of moral obligation, a conscience, which threatens them, should they do what is wrong. Arising originally from the external authority of rulers and rules, conscience is internalized and becomes independent of external forces. However, conscience is constantly reinforced in those whom it controls by the coercive imposition of external authority on recalcitrants and on those who have not acquired it. Most people refrain from offenses because they feel an obligation to behave lawfully. But this obligation would scarcely be felt if those who do not feel or follow it were not to suffer punishment.

Although the legislators may calculate their threats and the responses to be produced, the effectiveness of the threats neither requires nor depends on calculations by those responding. The predictor (or producer) of effects must calculate; those whose responses are predicted (or produced) need not. Hence, although legislation (and legislators) should be rational, subjects, to be deterred as intended, need not be: They need only be responsive.

Punishments deter those who have not violated the law for the same reasons—and in the same degrees (apart from internalization: moral obligation) as do natural dangers. Often natural dangers—all dangers not deliberately created by legislation (e.g., injury of the criminal inflicted by the crime victim) are insufficient. Thus, the fear of injury (natural danger) does not suffice to control city traffic; it must be reinforced by the legal punishment meted out to those who violate the rules. These punishments keep most people observing the regulations. However, where (in the absence of natural danger) the threatened punishment is so light that the advantage of violating rules tends to exceed the disadvantage of being punished (divided by the risk), the rule is violated (i.e., parking fines are too light). In this case the feeling of obligation tends to vanish as well. Elsewhere punishment deters.

To be sure, not everybody responds to threatened punishment. Non-responsive persons may be (a) self-destructive or (b) incapable of responding to threats, or even of grasping them. Increases in the size, or certainty, of penalties would not affect these two groups. A third group (c) might respond to more certain or more severe penalties.[5] If the punishment threatened for burglary, robbery, or rape were a $5 fine in North Carolina, and 5 years in prison in South Carolina, I have no doubt that the North Carolina treasury would become quite opulent until vigilante justice would provide the deterrence not provided by law. Whether to increase penalties (or improve enforcement) depends on the importance of the rule to society, the size and likely reaction of the group that did not respond before, and the acceptance of the added punishment and enforcement required to deter it. Observation would have to locate the points—likely to differ in different times and places—at which diminishing, zero, and negative returns set in. There is no reason to believe that all present and future offenders belong to the *a priori* non-responsive groups, or that all penalties have reached the point of diminishing, let alone zero returns.

IV

Even though its effectiveness seems obvious, punishment as a deterrent has fallen into disrepute. Some ideas which help explain this progressive heedlessness were uttered by Lester Pearson, then Prime Minister of Canada, when, in opposing the death penalty, he proposed that instead "the state seek to eradicate the causes of crime—slums, ghettos and personality disorders."[6]

"Slums, ghettos, and personality disorders" have not been shown, singly or collectively, to be "the causes" of crime.

(1) The crime rate in the slums is indeed higher than elsewhere; but so is the death rate in hospitals. Slums are no more "causes" of crime than hospitals are of death; they are locations of crime, as hospitals are of death. Slums and hospitals attract people selectively; neither is the "cause" of the condition (disease in hospitals, poverty in slums) that leads to the selective attraction.

As for poverty which draws people into slums, and, sometimes, into crime, any relative disadvantage may lead to ambition, frustration, resentment and, if insufficiently restrained, to crime. Not all relative disadvantages can be eliminated; indeed very few can be, and their elimination increases the resentment generated by the remaining ones; not even relative poverty can be removed altogether. (Absolute poverty—whatever that may be—hardly affects crime.) However, though contributory, relative disadvantages are not a necessary or sufficient cause of crime: Most poor people do not commit crimes, and some rich people do. Hence "eradication of poverty" would, at most, remove one (doubtful) cause of crime.

In the United States, the decline of poverty has not been associated with a reduction of crime. Poverty measured in dollars of constant purchasing power, according to present government standards and statistics, was the condition

---

5 I neglect those motivated by civil disobedience or, generally, moral or political passion. Deterring them depends less on penalties than on the moral support they receive, though penalties play a role. I also neglect those who may belong to all three groups listed, some successively, some even simultaneously, such as drug addicts. Finally, I must altogether omit the far-from-negligible role that problems of apprehension and conviction play in deterrence—beyond saying that, by reducing the government's ability to apprehend and convict, courts are able to reduce the risks of offenders.

6 I quote from *The New York Times* (November 24, 1967, p. 22). The actual psychological and other factors which bear on the disrepute—as distinguished from the rationalizations—cannot be examined here.

of ½ of all our families in 1920; of ⅕ in 1962; and of less than ⅙ in 1966. In 1967, 5.3 million families out of 49.8 million were poor—⅑ of all families in the United States. If crime has been reduced in a similar manner, it is a well-kept secret.

Those who regard poverty as a cause of crime often draw a wrong inference from a true proposition: The rich will not commit certain crimes—Rockefeller never riots; nor does he steal. (He mugs, but only on T.V.) Yet while wealth may be the cause of not committing (certain) crimes, it does not follow that poverty (absence of wealth) is the cause of committing them. Water extinguishes or prevents fire; but its absence is not the cause of fire. Thus, if poverty could be abolished, if everybody had all "necessities" (I don't pretend to know what this would mean), crime would remain, for, in the words of Aristotle, "the greatest crimes are committed not for the sake of basic necessities but for the sake of superfluities." Superfluities cannot be provided by the government; they would be what the government does not provide.

(2) Negro ghettos have a high, Chinese ghettos have a low crime rate. Ethnic separation, voluntary or forced, obviously has little to do with crime; I can think of no reason why it should.[7]

(3) 1 cannot see how the state could "eradicate" personality disorders even if all causes and cures were known and available. (They are not.) Further, the known incidence of personality disorders within the prison population does not exceed the known incidence outside—though our knowledge of both is tenuous. Nor are personality disorders necessary or sufficient causes for criminal offenses, unless these be identified by means of (moral, not clinical) definition with personality disorders. In this case, Mr. Pearson would have proposed to "eradicate" crime by eradicating crime—certainly a sound, but not a helpful idea.

Mr. Pearson's views are part as well of the mental furniture of the former U.S. Attorney General Ramsey Clark, who told a congressional committee that ". . . only the elimination of the causes of crime can make a significant and lasting difference in the incidence of crime." Uncharitably interpreted, Mr. Clark revealed that only the elimination of causes eliminates effects —a sleazy cliché and wrong to boot. Given the benefit of the doubt, Mr. Clark probably meant that the causes of crime are social; and that therefore crime can be reduced "only" by nonpenal (social) measures.

This view suggests a fireman who declines fire-fighting apparatus by pointing out that "in the long run only the elimination of the causes" of fire "can make a significant and lasting difference in the incidence" of fire, and that fire-fighting equipment does not eliminate "the causes" —except that such a fireman would probably not rise to fire chief. Actually, whether fires are checked depends on equipment and on the efforts of the firemen using it no less than on the presence of "the causes": inflammable materials. So with crimes. Laws, courts and police actions are no less important in restraining them than "the causes" are in impelling them. If firemen (or attorneys general) pass the buck and refuse to use the means available, we may all be burned while waiting for "the long run" and "the elimination of the causes."

Whether any activity—be it lawful or unlawful—takes place depends on whether the desire for it, or for whatever is to be secured by it, is stronger than the desire to avoid the costs involved. Accordingly people work, attend college, commit crimes, go to the movies—or refrain from any of these activities. Attendance at a theatre may be high because the show is entertaining and because the price of admission is low. Obviously the attendance depends on both

---

7 Mixed areas, incidentally, have higher crime rates than segregated ones. See, e.g., R. Ross and E. van den Haag, *The Fabric of Society* (New York: Harcourt, Brace & Co., 1957), pp. 102–4. Because slums are bad (morally) and crime is, many people seem to reason that "slums spawn crime"— which confuses some sort of moral with a causal relation.

—on the combination of expected gratification and cost. The wish, motive or impulse for doing anything—the experienced, or expected, gratification—is the cause of doing it; the wish to avoid the cost is the cause of not doing it. One is no more and no less "cause" than the other. (Common speech supports this use of "cause" no less than logic: "Why did you go to Jamaica?" "*Because* it is such a beautiful place." "Why didn't you go to Jamaica?" "*Because* it is too expensive." "Why do you buy this?"—"*Because* it is so cheap." "Why don't you buy that?" "*Because* it is too expensive.") Penalties (costs) are causes of lawfulness, or (if too low or uncertain) of unlawfulness, of crime. People do commit crimes because, given their conditions, the desire for the satisfaction sought prevails. They refrain if the desire to avoid the cost prevails. Given the desire, low cost (penalty) causes the action, and high cost restraint. Given the cost, desire becomes the causal variable. Neither is intrinsically more causal than the other. The crime rate increases if the cost is reduced or the desire raised. It can be decreased by raising the cost or by reducing the desire.

The cost of crime is more easily and swiftly changed than the conditions producing the inclination to it. Further, the costs are very largely within the power of the government to change, whereas the conditions producing propensity to crime are often only indirectly affected by government action, and some are altogether beyond the control of the government. Our unilateral emphasis on these conditions and our undue neglect of costs may contribute to an unnecessarily high crime rate.

V

The foregoing suggests the question posed by the death penalty: Is the deterrence added (return) sufficiently above zero to warrant irrevocability (or other, less clear, disadvantages)? The question is not only whether the penalty deters, but whether it deters more than alternatives and whether the difference exceeds the cost of irrevocability. (I shall assume that the alternative is actual life imprisonment so as to exclude the complication produced by the release of the unrehabilitated.)

In some fairly infrequent but important circumstances the death penalty is the only possible deterrent. Thus, in case of acute *coups d'état*, or of acute substantial attempts to overthrow the government, prospective rebels would altogether discount the threat of any prison sentence. They would not be deterred because they believe the swift victory of the revolution will invalidate a prison sentence and turn it into an advantage. Execution would be the only deterrent because, unlike prison sentences, it cannot be revoked by victorious rebels. The same reasoning applies to deterring spies or traitors in wartime. Finally, men who, by virtue of past acts, are already serving, or are threatened, by a life sentence could be deterred from further offenses only by the threat of the death penalty.[8]

What about criminals who do not fall into any of these (often ignored) classes? Prof. Thorsten Sellin has made a careful study of the available statistics: He concluded that they do not yield evidence for the deterring effect of the death penalty.[9] Somewhat surprisingly, Prof. Sellin seems to think that this lack of evidence for deterrence is evidence for the lack of deterrence. It is not. It means that deterrence has not been demonstrated statistically—not that nondeterrence has been.

8 Cautious revolutionaries, uncertain of final victory, might be impressed by prison sentences—but not in the acute stage, when faith in victory is high. And one can increase even the severity of a life sentence in prison. Finally, harsh punishment of rebels can intensify rebellious impulses. These points, though they qualify it, hardly impair the force of the argument.

9 Sellin considered mainly homicide statistics. His work may be found in his *Capital Punishment* (New York: Harper & Row, 1967); or, most conveniently, in H. A. Bedau, *The Death Penalty in America* (Garden City, N.Y.: Doubleday & Co., 1964), which offers other material, mainly against the death penalty.

It is entirely possible, indeed likely (as Prof. Sellin appears willing to concede), that the statistics used, though the best available, are nonetheless too slender a reed to rest conclusions on. They indicate that the homicide rate does not vary greatly between similar areas with or without the death penalty, and in the same area before and after abolition. However, the similar areas are not similar enough; the periods are not long enough; many social differences and changes, other than the abolition of the death penalty, may account for the variation (or lack of it) in homicide rates with and without, before and after abolition; some of these social differences and changes are likely to have affected homicide rates. I am unaware of any statistical analysis which adjusts for such changes and differences. And logically, it is quite consistent with the postulated deterrent effect of capital punishment that there be less homicide after abolition: With retention there might have been still less.

Homicide rates do not depend exclusively on penalties any more than do other crime rates. A number of conditions which influence the propensity to crime, demographic, economic or generally social changes or differences—even such matters as changes of the divorce laws or of the cotton price—may influence the homicide rate. Therefore variation or constancy cannot be attributed to variations or constancy of the penalties, unless we know that no other factor influencing the homicide rate has changed. Usually we don't. To believe the death penalty deterrent does not require one to believe that the death penalty, or any other, is the only or the decisive causal variable; this would be as absurd as the converse mistake that "social causes" are the only or always the decisive factor. To favor capital punishment, the efficacy of neither variable need be denied. It is enough to affirm that the severity of the penalty may influence some potential criminals, and that the added severity of the death penalty adds to deterrence, or may do so. It is quite possible that such a deterrent effect may be offset (or intensified) by non-penal factors which affect propensity; its presence or absence therefore may be hard, and perhaps impossible to demonstrate.

Contrary to what Prof. Sellin et al. seem to presume, I doubt that offenders are aware of the absence or presence of the death penalty state by state or period by period. Such unawareness argues against the assumption of a calculating murderer. However, unawareness does not argue against the death penalty if by deterrence we mean a preconscious, general response to a severe, but not necessarily specifically and explicitly apprehended, or calculated threat. A constant homicide rate, despite abolition, may occur because of unawareness and not because of lack of deterrence: People remain deterred for a lengthy interval by the severity of the penalty in the past, or by the severity of penalties used in similar circumstances nearby.

I do not argue for a version of deterrence which would require me to believe that an individual shuns murder while in North Dakota, because of the death penalty, and merrily goes to it in South Dakota since it has been abolished there; or that he will start the murderous career from which he had hitherto refrained, after abolition. I hold that the generalized threat of the death penalty may be a deterrent, and the more so, the more generally applied. Deterrence will not cease in the particular areas of abolition or at the particular times of abolition. Rather, general deterrence will be somewhat weakened, through local (partial) abolition. Even such weakening will be hard to detect owing to changes in many offsetting, or reinforcing, factors.

For all of these reasons, I doubt that the presence or absence of a deterrent effect of the death penalty is likely to be demonstrable by statistical means. The statistics presented by Prof. Sellin et al. show only that there is no statistical proof for the deterrent effect of the death penalty. But they do not show that there is no deterrent effect. Not to demonstrate presence of the effect is not the same as to demonstrate its absence; certainly not when there are plausible explanations for the nondemonstrability of the effect.

It is on our uncertainty that the case for deterrence must rest.[10]

VI

If we do not know whether the death penalty will deter others, we are confronted with two uncertainties. If we impose the death penalty, and achieve no deterrent effect thereby, the life of a convicted murderer has been expended in vain (from a deterrent viewpoint). There is a net loss. If we impose the death sentence and thereby deter some future murderers, we spared the lives of some future victims (the prospective murderers gain too; they are spared punishment because they were deterred). In this case, the death penalty has led to a net gain, unless the life of a convicted murderer is valued more highly than that of the unknown victim, or victims (and the non-imprisonment of the deterred non-murderer).

The calculation can be turned around, of course. The absence of the death penalty may harm no one and therefore produce a gain—the life of the convicted murderer. Or it may kill future victims of murderers who could have been deterred, and thus produce a loss—their life.

To be sure, we must risk something certain—the death (or life) of the convicted man, for something uncertain—the death (or life) of the victims of murderers who may be deterred. This is in the nature of uncertainty—when we invest, or gamble, we risk the money we have for an uncertain gain. Many human actions, most commitments—including marriage and crime—share this characteristic with the deterrent purpose of any penalization, and with its rehabilitative purpose (and even with the protective).

More proof is demanded for the deterrent effect of the death penalty than is demanded for the deterrent effect of other penalties. This is not justified by the absence of other utilitarian purposes such as protection and rehabilitation; they involve no less uncertainty than deterrence.[11]

Irrevocability may support a demand for some reason to expect more deterrence than revocable penalties might produce, but not a demand for more proof of deterrence, as has been pointed out above. The reason for expecting more deterrence lies in the greater severity, the terrifying effect inherent in finality. Since it seems more important to spare victims than to spare murderers, the burden of proving that the greater severity inherent in irrevocability adds nothing to deterrence lies on those who oppose capital punishment. Proponents of the death penalty need show only that there is no more uncertainty about it than about greater severity in general.

The demand that the death penalty be proved more deterrent than alternatives can not be satisfied any more than the demand that six years in prison be proved to be more deterrent than three. But the uncertainty which confronts us favors the death penalty as long as by imposing it we might save future victims of murder. This effect is as plausible as the general idea that penalties have deterrent effects which increase with their severity. Though we have no proof of the

---

10 In view of the strong emotions aroused (itself an indication of effectiveness to me: Might not murderers be as upset over the death penalty as those who wish to spare them?) and because I believe penalties must reflect community feeling to be effective, I oppose mandatory death sentences and favor optional, and perhaps binding, recommendations by juries after their finding of guilt. The opposite course risks the non-conviction of guilty defendants by juries who do not want to see them executed.

11 Rehabilitation or protection are of minor importance in our actual penal system (though not in our theory). We confine many people who do not need rehabilitation and against whom we do not need protection (e.g., the exasperated husband who killed his wife); we release many unrehabilitated offenders against whom protection is needed. Certainly rehabilitation and protection are not, and deterrence is, the main actual function of legal punishment if we disregard non-utilitarian ones.

positive deterrence of the penalty, we also have no proof of zero or negative effectiveness. I believe we have no right to risk additional future victims of murder for the sake of sparing convicted murderers; on the contrary, our moral obligation is to risk the possible ineffectiveness of executions. However rationalized, the opposite view appears to be motivated by the simple fact that executions are more subjected to social control than murder. However, this applies to all penalties and does not argue for the abolition of any.

Review Questions

1. Why doesn't rehabilitation or protection of society justify the death penalty?
2. How does van den Haag reply to the charges that capital punishment leads to the execution of innocents and falls unfairly on the poor rather than the rich?
3. According to van den Haag, how does deterrence work psychologically?
4. What is the difference between a natural danger and a legal threat, in van den Haag's view?
5. Why aren't slums, ghettos, and personality disorders the causes of crime, according to van den Haag?
6. What causes a person to commit a crime, in van den Haag's view?
7. Explain van den Haag's argument about the two uncertainties of the death penalty.

Discussion Questions

1. Is it true that slums and ghettos are no more causes of crime than hospitals are causes of death? Explain your view.
2. Van den Haag claims that rebels, spies, and traitors can be deterred only by the death penalty; there is no alternative punishment. Is this true? Can you think of any other punishments that might do the job? What are they?
3. The Supreme Court justices think cold calculation is involved in deterrence, whereas van den Haag denies this. Who is right and why?
4. Suppose that for each person we execute we save one innocent person who would otherwise be killed. Are the executions justified or not? Why or why not?

Justice, Civilization, and the Death Penalty

JEFFREY H. REIMAN

Jeffrey H. Reiman is William Fraser McDowell Professor of Philosophy at The American University in Washington, D.C. He is the author of *In Defense of Political Philosophy* (1972) and *The Rich Get Richer and the Poor Get Prison,* third edition, (1990).

Reiman begins with a careful discussion of retributivism. He distinguishes between two versions of the doctrine, *lex talionis* and proportional retributivism, and between two different retributive approaches to punishment, a Hegelian and a Kantian approach. Then he argues that it does not follow from the retributivist principle that we ought to impose the death penalty; like torture, it is too horrible to be used by civilized people. He concludes with a reply to van den Haag. He rejects van den Haag's commonsense argument that execution deters more than life imprisonment does, and he attacks van den Haag's argument for preferring the death penalty in the face of uncertainties about its deterrence value.

ON THE ISSUE OF CAPITAL PUNISHMENT, there is as clear a clash of moral intuitions as we are likely to see. Some (now a majority of Americans) feel deeply that justice requires payment in kind and thus that murderers should die; and others (once, but no longer, nearly a majority of Americans) feel deeply that the state ought not be in the business of putting people to death.[1] Arguments for either side that do not

Source: Jeffrey H. Reiman, "Justice, Civilization, and the Death Penalty: Answering van den Haag," from *Philosophy & Public Affairs,* Vol. 14 (Spring 1985), pp. 141–147.

1 Asked in a 1981 Gallup Poll, "Are you in favor of the death penalty for persons convicted of murder?" 66.25% were in favor, 25% were opposed, and 8.75% had no opinion. Asked the same question in 1966, 47.5% were opposed, 41.25% were in favor, and 11.25% had no opinion (Timothy J. Flanagan, David J. van Alstyne, and Michael R. Gottfredson, eds., *Sourcebook of Criminal Justice Statistics—1981,* U.S. Department of Justice, Bureau of Justice Statistics [Washington, D.C.: U.S. Government Printing Office, 1982], p. 209).

do justice to the intuitions of the other are unlikely to persuade anyone not already convinced. And, since, as I shall suggest, there is truth on both sides, arguments are easily refutable, leaving us with nothing but conflicting intuitions and no guidance from reason in distinguishing the better from the worse. In this context, I shall try to make an argument for the abolition of the death penalty that does justice to the intuitions on both sides. I shall sketch out a conception of retributive justice that accounts for the justice of executing murderers, and then I shall argue that *though the death penalty is a just punishment for murder,* abolition of the death penalty is a part of the civilizing mission of modern states. . . .

I. JUST DESERTS AND JUST PUNISHMENTS

In my view, the death penalty is a just punishment for murder because the *lex talionis,* an eye for an eye, and so on, is just, although, as I shall suggest at the end of this section, it can only be rightly applied when its implied preconditions are satisfied. The *lex talionis* is a version of retributivism. Retributivism—as the word itself suggests—is the doctrine that the offender should be *paid back* with suffering he deserves because of the evil he has done, and the *lex talionis* asserts that injury equivalent to that he imposed is what the offender deserves. But the *lex talionis* is not the only version of retributivism. Another, which I shall call "proportional retributivism," holds that what retribution requires is not equality of injury between crimes and punishments, but "fit" or proportionality, such that the worst crime is punished with the society's worst penalty, and so on, though the society's worst punishment need not duplicate the injury of the worst crime.[2] Later, I shall try to show how a form of proportional retributivism is compatible with acknowledging the justice of the *lex talionis*. Indeed, since I shall defend the justice of the *lex talionis,* I take such compatibility as a necessary condition of the validity of any form of retributivism.

There is nothing self-evident about the justice of the *lex talionis* nor, for that matter, of retributivism.[3] The standard problem confronting those who would justify retributivism is that of

overcoming the suspicion that it does no more than sanctify the victim's desire to hurt the offender back. Since serving that desire amounts to hurting the offender simply for the satisfaction that the victim derives from seeing the offender suffer, and since deriving satisfaction from the suffering of others seems primitive, the policy of imposing suffering on the offender for no other purpose than giving satisfaction to his victim seems primitive as well. Consequently, defending retributivism requires showing that the suffering imposed on the wrongdoer has some worthy point beyond the satisfaction of victims. In what follows, I shall try to identify a proposition—which I call the *retributivist principle*—that I take to be the nerve of retributivism. I think this principle accounts for the justice of the *lex talionis* and indicates the point of the suffering demanded by retributivism. Not to do too much of the work of the death penalty advocate, I shall make no extended argument for this principle beyond suggesting the considerations that make it plausible. I shall identify these considerations by drawing, with considerable license, on Hegel and Kant.

I think that we can see the justice of the *lex talionis* by focusing on the striking affinity between it and the *golden rule*. The *golden rule* mandates "Do unto others as you would have others do unto you," while the *lex talionis* counsels "Do unto others as they have done unto you." It would not be too far-fetched to say that the *lex talionis* is the law enforcement arm of the golden rule, at least in the sense that if people were actually treated as they treated others, then everyone would necessarily follow the golden rule because then people could only willingly act toward others as they were willing to have others act toward them. This is not to suggest that the *lex talionis* follows from the golden rule, but rather that the two share a common moral inspiration: the equality of per-

2 "The most extreme form of retributivism is the law of retaliation: 'an eye for an eye'" (Stanley I. Benn, "Punishment," *The Encyclopedia of Philosophy* 7. ed. Paul Edwards [New York: Macmillan. 19671, p. 32]. Hugo Bedau writes: "retributive justice need not be thought to consist of *lex talionis*. One may reject that principle as too crude and still embrace the retributive principle that the severity of punishments should be graded according to the gravity of the offense" (Hugo Bedau, "Capital Punishment," in *Matters of Life and Death,* ed. Tom Regan [New York: Random House, 1980], p. 177). See also, Andrew von Hirsch, "Doing Justice: The Principle of Commensurate Deserts," and Hyman Gross, "Proportional Punishment and Justifiable Sentences," in *Sentencing,* eds. H. Gross and A. von Hirsch (New York: Oxford University Press, 1981), pp. 243–56 and 272–83, respectively.

3 Stanley Benn writes: "to say 'it is fitting' or 'justice demands' that the guilty should suffer is only to affirm that

punishment is right, not to give grounds for thinking so" (Benn, "Punishment," p. 30).

sons. Treating others as you *would* have them treat you means treating others as equal to you, because adopting the golden rule as one's guiding principle implies that one counts the suffering of others to be as great a calamity as one's own suffering, that one counts one's right to impose suffering on others as no greater than their right to impose suffering on one, and so on. This leads to the *lex talionis* by two approaches that start from different points and converge.

I call the first approach "Hegelian" because Hegel held (roughly) that crime upsets the quality between persons and retributive punishment restores that equality by "annulling" the crime. As we have seen, acting according to the golden rule implies treating others as your equals. Conversely, violating the golden rule implies the reverse: Doing to another what you would *not* have that person do to you violates the equality of persons by asserting a right toward the other that the other does not possess toward you. Doing back to you what you did "annuls" your violation by reasserting that the other has the same right toward you that you assert toward him. Punishment according to the *lex talionis* cannot heal the injury that the other has suffered at your hands, rather it rectifies the indignity he has suffered, by restoring him to equality with you.

"Equality of persons" here does not mean equality of concern for their happiness, as it might for a utilitarian. On such a (roughly) utilitarian understanding of equality, imposing suffering on the wrongdoer equivalent to the suffering he has imposed would have little point. Rather, equality of concern for people's happiness would lead us to impose as little suffering on the wrongdoer as was compatible with maintaining the happiness of others. This is enough to show that retributivism (at least in this "Hegelian" form) reflects a conception of morality quite different from that envisioned by utilitarianism. Instead of seeing morality as administering doses of happiness to individual re-

cipients, the retributivist envisions morality as maintaining the relations appropriate to equally sovereign individuals. A crime, rather than representing a unit of suffering added to the already considerable suffering in the world, is an assault on the sovereignty of an individual that temporarily places one person (the criminal) in a position of illegitimate sovereignty over another (the victim). The victim (or his representative, the state) then has the right to rectify this loss of standing relative to the criminal by meting out a punishment that reduces the criminal's sovereignty in the degree to which he vaunted it above his victim's. It might be thought that this is a duty, not just a right, but that is surely too much. The victim has the right to forgive the violator without punishment, which suggests that it is by virtue of having the right to punish the violator (rather than the duty) that the victim's quality with the violator is restored.

I call the second approach "Kantian" since Kant held (roughly) that, since reason (like justice) is no respecter of the sheer difference between individuals, when a rational being decides to act in a certain way toward his fellows, he implicitly authorizes similar action by his fellows toward him. A version of the golden rule, then, is a requirement of reason: Acting rationally, one always acts as he would have others act toward him. Consequently, to act toward a person as he has acted toward others is to treat him as a rational being, that is, as if his act were the product of a rational decision. From this, it may be concluded that we have a duty to do to offenders what they have done, since this amounts to according them the respect due rational beings. Here too, however, the assertion of a duty to punish seems excessive, since, if this duty arises because doing to people what they have done to others is necessary to accord them the respect due rational beings, then we would have a duty to do to all rational persons *everything*—good, bad, or indifferent—that they do to others. The point rather is that, by his acts, a rational being *authorizes* others to do the same to him, he doesn't *compel* them to. Here too, then, the argument leads to a right, rather than a duty, to exact the *lex talionis.* And this is supported by the fact that we can conclude from Kant's argument that a rational being cannot validly complain of being treated in the way he has treated others, and where there is no valid complaint, there is no injustice, and where there is no injustice, others have acted within their rights. It should be clear that the Kantian argument also rests on the equality of persons, because a rational agent only implicitly authorizes having done to him action similar to what he has done to another, if he and the other are similar in the relevant ways.

The "Hegelian" and "Kantian" approaches arrive at the same destination from opposite sides. The "Hegelian" approach starts from the victim's equality with the criminal, and infers from it the victim's right to do to the criminal what the criminal has done to the victim. The "Kantian" approach starts from the criminal's rationality, and infers from it the criminal's authorization of the victim's right to do to the criminal what the criminal has done to the victim. Taken together, these approaches support the following proposition: The equality and rationality of persons implies that an offender deserves and his victim has the right to impose suffering on the offender equal to that which he imposed on the victim. This is the proposition I call the *retributivist principle,* and I shall assume henceforth that it is true. This principle provides that the *lex talionis* is the criminal's just desert and the victim's (or as his representative, the state's) right. Moreover, the principle also indicates the point of retributive punishment, namely, it affirms the equality and rationality of persons, victims and offenders alike.[4] And the point of this affirmation is, like any moral affirmation, to make a statement, to the criminal, to impress upon him his equality with his victim (which earns him a like fate) and his rationality (by which his actions are held to authorize his fate), and to the society, so that recognition of the equality and rationality of persons becomes a visible part of our shared moral environment that none can ignore in justifying their actions to one another. . . .

The truth of the retributivist principle establishes the justice of the *lex talionis,* but, since it establishes this as a right of the victim rather than a duty, it does not settle the question of whether or to what extent the victim or the state should exercise this right and exact the *lex talionis.* This is a separate moral question because strict adherence to the *lex talionis* amounts to allowing criminals, even the most barbaric of them, to dictate our punishing behavior. It seems certain that there are at least some crimes, such as rape or torture, that we ought not try to match. And this is not merely a matter of imposing an alternative punishment that produces an equivalent amount of suffering, as, say, some number of years in prison that might "add up" to the harm caused by a rapist or a torturer. Even if no amount of time in prison would add up to the harm caused by a torturer, it still seems that we ought not torture him even if this were the only way of making him suffer as much as he has made his victim suffer. Or, consider someone who has committed several murders in cold blood. On the *lex talionis,* it would seem that such a criminal might justly be brought to within an inch of death and then revived (or to within a moment of execution and then reprieved) as many times as he has killed (minus one), and then finally executed. But surely this is a degree of cruelty that would be monstrous.[5] . . .

---

4 Herbert Morris defends retributivism on parallel grounds. See his "Persons and Punishment," *The Monist* 52, no. 4 (October 1968): 475–501. Isn't what Morris calls "the right to be treated as a person" essentially the right of a rational being to be treated only as he has authorized, implicitly or explicitly, by his own free choices?

5 Bedau writes: "Where criminals set the limits of just methods of punishment, as they will do if we attempt to give

I suspect that it will be widely agreed that the state ought not administer punishments of the sort described above even if required by the letter of the *lex talionis,* and thus, even granting the justice of *lex talionis,* there are occasions on which it is morally appropriate to diverge from its requirements. . . .

This way of understanding just punishment enables us to formulate proportional retributivism so that it is compatible with acknowledging the justice of the *lex talionis:* If we take the *lex talionis* as spelling out the offender's just deserts, and if other moral considerations require us to refrain from matching the injury caused by the offender while still allowing us to punish justly, then surely we impose just punishment if we impose the closest morally acceptable approximation to the *lex talionis.* Proportional retributivism, then, in requiring that the worst crime be punished by the society's worst punishment and so on, could be understood as translating the offender's just desert into its nearest equivalent in the society's table of morally acceptable punishments. Then the two versions of retributivism (*lex talionis* and proportional) are related in that the first states what just punishment would be if nothing but the offender's just desert mattered, and the second locates just punishment at the meeting point of the offender's just deserts and the society's moral scruples. And since this second version only modifies the requirements of the *lex talionis* in light of other moral considerations, it is compatible with believing that the *lex talionis* spells out the offender's just deserts, much in the way that modifying the obligations of promisers in light

of other moral considerations is compatible with believing in the binding nature of promises. . . .

II. CIVILIZATION, PAIN, AND JUSTICE

As I have already suggested, from the fact that something is justly deserved, it does not automatically follow that it should be done, since there may be other moral reasons for not doing it such that, all told, the weight of moral reasons swings the balance against proceeding. The same argument that I have given for the justice of the death penalty for murderers proves the justice of beating assaulters, raping rapists, and torturing torturers. Nonetheless, I believe, and suspect that most would agree, that it would not be right for us to beat assaulters, rape rapists, or torture torturers, *even though it were their just deserts*—and even if this were the only way to make them suffer as much as they had made their victims suffer. Calling for the abolition of the death penalty, though it be just, then, amounts to urging that as a society we place execution in the same category of sanction as beating, raping, and torturing, and treat it as something it would not be right for us to do to offenders, *even if it were their just deserts.* . . .

Progress in civilization is characterized by a lower tolerance for one's own pain and that suffered by others. And this is appropriate, since, via growth in knowledge, civilization brings increased power to prevent or reduce pain and, via growth in the ability to communicate and interact with more and more people, civilization extends the circle of people with whom we empathize.[6] If civilization is characterized by lower

---

exact and literal implementation to *lex talionis,* society will find itself descending to the cruelties and savagery that criminals employ. But society would be deliberately authorizing such acts, in the cool light of reason, and not (as is often true of vicious criminals) impulsively or in hatred and anger or with an insane or unbalanced mind. Moral restraints, in short, prohibit us from trying to make executions perfectly retributive" (Bedau, "Capital Punishment," p. 176).

6 Van den Haag writes that our ancestors "were not as repulsed by physical pain as we are. The change has to do not with our greater smartness or moral superiority but with a new outlook pioneered by the French and American revolutions [namely, that assertion of human equality and with it 'universal identification'], and by such mundane things as the invention of anesthetics, which make pain much less of

tolerance for our own pain and that of others, then publicly refusing to do horrible things to our fellows both signals the level of our civilization *and, by our example, continues the work of civilizing*. And this gesture is all the more powerful if we refuse to do horrible things to those who deserve them. I contend then that the more things we are able to include in this category, the more civilized we are and the more civilizing. Thus we gain from including torture in this category, and if execution is especially horrible, we gain still more by including it. . . .

What can be said of reducing the horrible things that we do to our fellows even when deserved? First of all, given our vulnerability to pain, it seems clearly a gain. Is it however an unmitigated gain? That is, would such a reduction ever amount to a loss? It seems to me that there are two conditions under which it would be a loss, namely, if the reduction made our lives more dangerous, or if not doing what is justly deserved were a loss in itself. Let us leave aside the former, since, as I have already suggested and as I will soon indicate in greater detail, I accept that if some horrible punishment is necessary to deter equally or more horrible acts, then we may have to impose the punishment. Thus my claim is that reduction in the horrible things we do to our fellows is an advance in civilization *as long as our lives are not thereby made more dangerous,* and that it is only then that we are called upon to extend that reduction as part of the work of civilization. Assuming then, for the moment, that we suffer no increased danger by refraining from doing horrible things to our fellows when they justly deserve them, does such refraining to do what is justly deserved amount to a loss?

It seems to me that the answer to this must be that refraining to do what is justly deserved is only a loss where it amounts to doing an injustice. But such refraining to do what is just is not doing what is unjust, unless what we do instead falls below the bottom end of the range of just punishments. Otherwise, it would be unjust to refrain from torturing torturers, raping rapists, or beating assaulters. In short, I take it that if there is no injustice in refraining from torturing torturers, then there is no injustice in refraining to do horrible things to our fellows generally, when they deserve them, as long as what we do instead is compatible with believing that they do deserve them. And thus that if such refraining does not make our lives more dangerous, then it is no loss, and given our vulnerability to pain, it is a gain. Consequently, reduction in the horrible things we do to our fellows, when not necessary to our protection, is an advance in civilization that we are called upon to continue once we consciously take upon ourselves the work of civilization.

To complete the argument, however, I must show that execution is horrible enough to warrant its inclusion alongside torture. Against this it will be said that execution is not especially horrible since it only hastens a fate that is inevitable for us.[7] I think that this view overlooks

---

an everyday experience" ([Ernest van den Haag and John P. Conrad, *The Death Penalty: A Debate* (New York: Plenum Press, 1983)]. p. 215: cf. van den Haag's *Punishing Criminals* [New York: Basic Books, 1975], pp. 196–206).

7 Van den Haag seems to waffle on the question of the unique awfulness of execution. For instance. he takes it not to be revolting in the way that earcropping is, because "We all must die. But we must not have our ears cropped" (p. 190), and here he cites John Stuart Mill's parliamentary defense of the death penalty in which Mill maintains that execution only *hastens* death. Mill's point was to defend the claim that "There is not . . . any human infliction which makes an impression on the imagination so entirely out of proportion to its real severity as the punishment of death" (Mill, "Parliamentary Debate," p. 273). And van den Haag seems to agree since he maintains that, since "we cannot imagine our own nonexistence . . . , [t]he fear of the death penalty is in part the fear of the unknown. It . . . rests on a confusion" (pp. 258–59). On the other hand, he writes that "Execution sharpens our separation anxiety because death becomes clearly foreseen. . . . Further, and perhaps most important, when one is executed he does not just die, he is put to death, forcibly expelled from life. He is told that he is too depraved, unworthy of living with other humans" (p. 258).

important differences in the manner in which people reach their inevitable ends. I contend that execution is especially horrible, and it is so in a way similar to (though not identical with) the way in which torture is especially horrible. I believe we view torture as especially awful because of two of its features, which also characterize execution: intense pain and the spectacle of one human being completely subject to the power of another. This latter is separate from the issue of pain since it is something that offends us about unpainful things, such as slavery (even voluntarily entered) and prostitution (even voluntarily chosen as an occupation).[8] Execution shares this separate feature, since killing a bound and defenseless human being enacts the total subjugation of that person to his fellows. I think, incidentally, that this accounts for the general uneasiness with which execution by lethal injection has been greeted. Rather than humanizing the event, it seems only to have purchased a possible reduction in physical pain at the price of increasing the spectacle of subjugation—with no net gain in the attractiveness of the death penalty. Indeed, its net effect may have been the reverse.

In addition to the spectacle of subjugation, execution, even by physically painless means, is

also characterized by a special and intense psychological pain that distinguishes it from the loss of life that awaits us all. Interesting in this regard is the fact that although we are not terribly squeamish about the loss of life itself, allowing it in war, self-defense, as a necessary cost of progress, and so on, we are, as the extraordinary hesitance of our courts testifies, quite reluctant to execute. I think this is because execution involves the most psychologically painful features of deaths. We normally regard death from human causes as worse than death from natural causes, since a humanly caused shortening of life lacks the consolation of unavoidability. And we normally regard death whose coming is foreseen by its victim as worse than sudden death, because a foreseen death adds to the loss of life the terrible consciousness of that impending loss.[9] As a humanly caused death whose advent is foreseen by its victim, an execution combines the worst of both.

Thus far, by analogy with torture, I have argued that execution should be avoided because of how horrible it is to the one executed. But there are reasons of another sort that follow from the analogy with torture. Torture is to be avoided not only because of what it says about *what* we are willing to do to our fellows, but also because of what it says about *us* who are willing to do it. To torture someone is an awful spectacle not only because of the intensity of pain imposed, but because of what is required to be able to impose such pain on one's fellows. The tortured body cringes, using its full exertion to escape the pain imposed upon it—it literally begs for relief with its muscles as it does

I think, incidentally, that it is an overstatement to say that we cannot imagine our own nonexistence. If we can imagine any counterfactual experience, for example, how we might feel if we didn't know something that we do in fact know, then it doesn't seem impossible to imagine what it would "feel like" not to live. I think I can arrive at a pretty good approximation of this by trying to imagine how things "felt" to me in the eighteenth century. And, in fact, the sense of the awful difference between being alive and not that enters my experience when I do this makes the fear of death—not as a state, but as the absence of life—seem hardly to rest on a confusion.

8 I am not here endorsing this view of voluntarily entered slavery or prostitution. I mean only to suggest that it is *the belief* that these relations involve the extreme subjugation of one person to the power of another that is at the basis of their offensiveness. What I am saying is quite compatible with finding that this belief is false with respect to voluntarily entered slavery or prostitution.

9 This is no doubt partly due to modern skepticism about an afterlife. Earlier peoples regarded a foreseen death as a blessing allowing time to make one's peace with God. Writing of an early Middle Ages, Phillippe Aries says, "In this world that was so familiar with death, sudden death was a vile and ugly death; it was frightening; it seemed a strange and monstrous thing nobody dared talk about" (Phillippe Aries, *The Hour of Our Death* [New York: Vintage, 1982], p. 11).

with its cries. To torture someone is to demonstrate a capacity to resist this begging, and that in turn demonstrates a kind of hardheartedness that a society ought not parade.

And this is true not only of torture, but of all severe corporal punishment. Indeed, I think this constitutes part of the answer to the puzzling question of why we refrain from punishments like whipping, even when the alternative (some months in jail versus some lashes) seems more costly to the offender. Imprisonment is painful to be sure, but it is a reflective pain, one that comes with comparing what is to what might have been, and that can be temporarily ignored by thinking about other things. But physical pain has an urgency that holds body and mind in a fierce grip. Of physical pain, as Orwell's Winston Smith recognized, "you could only wish one thing: that it should stop."[10] Refraining from torture in particular and corporal punishment in general, we both refuse to put a fellow human being in this grip *and* refuse to show our ability to resist this wish. The death penalty is the last corporal punishment used officially in the modern world. And it is corporal not only because administered via the body, but because the pain of foreseen, humanly administered death strikes us with the urgency that characterizes intense physical pain, causing grown men to cry, faint, and lose control of their bodily functions. There is something to be gained by refusing to endorse the hardness of heart necessary to impose such a fate.

By placing execution alongside torture in the category of things we will not do to our fellow human beings even when they deserve them, we broadcast the message that totally subjugating a person to the power of others *and* confronting him with the advent of his own humanly administered demise is too horrible to

be done by civilized human beings to their fellows even when they have earned it: too horrible to do, and too horrible to be capable of doing. And I contend that broadcasting this message loud and clear would in the long run contribute to the general detestation of murder and be, to the extent to which it worked itself into the hearts and minds of the populace, a deterrent. In short, refusing to execute murderers though they deserve it both reflects and continues the taming of the human species that we call civilization. Thus, I take it that the abolition of the death penalty, though it is just punishment for murder, is part of the civilizing mission of modern states.

III. CIVILIZATION, SAFETY, AND DETERRENCE

Earlier I said that judging a practice too horrible to do even to those who deserve it does not exclude the possibility that it could be justified if necessary to avoid even worse consequences. Thus, were the death penalty clearly proven a better deterrent to the murder of innocent people than life in prison, we might have to admit that we had not yet reached a level of civilization at which we could protect ourselves without imposing this horrible fate on murderers, and thus we might have to grant the necessity of instituting the death penalty.[11] But this is far from proven. The available research by no means clearly indicates that the death penalty reduces the incidence of homicide more than life

---

10 George Orwell, *1984* (New York: New American Library, 1983; originally published in 1949), p. 197.

11 I say "might" here to avoid the sticky question of just how effective a deterrent the death penalty would have to be to justify overcoming our scruples about executing. It is here that the other considerations often urged against capital punishment—discrimination, irrevocability, the possibility of mistake, and so on—would play a role. Omitting such qualifications, however, my position might crudely be stated as follows: *Just desert limits what a civilized society may do to deter crime, and deterrence limits what a civilized society may do to give criminals their just deserts.*

imprisonment does. Even the econometric studies of Isaac Ehrlich, which purport to show that each execution saves seven or eight potential murder victims, have not changed this fact, as is testified to by the controversy and objections from equally respected statisticians that Ehrlich's work has provoked.[12]

Conceding that it has not been proven that the death penalty deters more murders than life imprisonment, van den Haag has argued that neither has it been proven that the death penalty does not deter more murders,[13] and thus we must follow common sense which teaches that

the higher the cost of something, the fewer people will choose it, and therefore at least some potential murderers who would not be deterred by life imprisonment will be deterred by the death penalty. Van den Haag writes:

> . . . our experience shows that the greater the penalty, the more it deters.
>   . . . Life in prison is still life, however unpleasant. In contrast, the death penalty does not just threaten to make life unpleasant—it threatens to take life altogether. This difference is perceived by those affected. We find that when they have the choice between life in prison and execution, 99% of all prisoners under sentence of death prefer life in prison. . . .

From this unquestioned fact a reasonable conclusion can be drawn in favor of the superior deterrent effect of the death penalty. Those who have the choice in practice . . . fear death more than they fear life in prison. . . . If they do, it follows that the threat of the death penalty, all other things equal, is likely to deter more than the threat of life in prison. One is most deterred by what one fears most. From which it follows that whatever statistics fail, or do not fail, to show, the death penalty is likely to be more deterrent than any other. [pp. 68–69]

Those of us who recognize how commonsensical it was, and still is, to believe that the sun moves around the earth, will be less willing than Professor van den Haag to follow common sense here, especially when it comes to doing something awful to our fellows. Moreover, there are good reasons for doubting common sense on this matter. Here are four:

1. From the fact that one penalty is more feared than another, it does not follow that the more feared penalty will deter more than the less feared, unless we know that the less feared

---

12 Isaac Ehrlich. "The Deterrent Effect of Capital Punishment: A Question of Life or Death," *American Economic Review* 65 (June 1975): 397–417. For reactions to Ehrlich's work, see Alfred Blumstein, Jacqueline Cohen, and Daniel Nagin, eds., *Deterrence and Incapacitation: Estimating the Effects of Criminal Sanctions on Crime Rates* (Washington, D.C.: National Academy of Sciences, 1978), esp. pp. 59–63 and 336–60; Brian E. Forst, "The Deterrent Effect on Capital Punishment: A Cross-State Analysis," *Minnesota Law Review* 61 (May 1977): 743–67, Deryck Beyleveld, "Ehrlich's Analysis of Deterrence," *British Journal of Criminology* 22 (April 1982): 101–23, and Isaac Ehrlich, "On Positive Methodology, Ethics and Polemics in Deterrence Research," *British Journal of Criminology* 22 (April 1982): 124–39. Much of the criticism of Ehrlich's work focuses on the fact that he found a deterrence impact of executions in the period from 1993–1969, which includes the period 1963–1969, a time when hardly any executions were carried out and crime rates rose for reasons that are arguably independent of the existence or nonexistence of capital punishment. When the 1963–1969 period is excluded, no significant deterrent effect shows. Prior to Ehrlich's work, research on the comparative deterrent impact of the death penalty versus life imprisonment indicated no increase in the incidence of homicide in states that abolished the death penalty and no greater incidence of homicide compared to similar states with the death penalty. See Thorsten Sellin, *The Death Penalty* (Philadelphia: American Law Institute, 1959).

13 Van den Haag writes: "Other studies published since Ehrlich's contend that his results are due to the techniques and periods he selected, and that different techniques and periods yield different results. Despite a great deal of research on all sides, one cannot say that the statistical evidence is conclusive. Nobody has claimed to have *disproved* that the death penalty may deter more than life imprison-

ment. But one cannot claim, either, that it has been proved statistically in a conclusive manner that the death penalty does deter more than alternative penalties. This lack of proof does not amount to disproof" (p. 65).

penalty is not fearful enough to deter everyone who can be deterred—and this is just what we don't know with regard to the death penalty Though I fear the death penalty more than life in prison, I can't think of any act that the death penalty would deter me from that an equal likelihood of spending my life in prison wouldn't deter me from as well. Since it seems to me that whoever would be deterred by a given likelihood of death would be deterred by an *equal* likelihood of life behind bars, I suspect that the common-sense argument only seems plausible because we evaluate it unconsciously assuming that potential criminals will face larger likelihoods of death sentences than of life sentences. if the likelihoods were equal, it seems to me that where life imprisonment was improbable enough to make it too distant a possibility to worry much about, a similar low probability of death would have the same effect. After all, we are undeterred by small likelihoods of death every time we walk the streets. And if life imprisonment were sufficiently probable to pose a real deterrent threat, it would pose as much of a deterrent threat as death. And this is just what most of the research we have on the comparative deterrent impact of execution versus life imprisonment suggests.

2. In light of the fact that roughly 500 to 700 suspected felons are killed by the police in the line of duty every year, and the fact that the number of privately owned guns in America is substantially larger than the number of households in America, it must be granted that anyone contemplating committing a crime *already* faces a substantial risk of ending up dead as a result.[14] It's hard to see why anyone *who is not already deterred by this* would be deterred by the addition of the more distant risk of death after apprehension, conviction, and appeal. Indeed, this suggests that people consider risks in a much crueler way than van den Haag's appeal to common sense suggests—which should be evident to anyone who contemplates how few people use seatbelts (14% of drivers, on some estimates), when it is widely known that wearing them can spell the difference between life (outside prison) and death.[15]

3. Van den Haag has maintained that deterrence doesn't work only by means of cost-benefit calculations made by potential criminals. It works also by the lesson about the wrongfulness of murder that is slowly learned in a society that subjects murderers to the ultimate punishment (p. 63). But if I am correct in claiming that the refusal to execute even those who deserve it has a civilizing effect, then the refusal to execute also teaches a lesson about the wrongfulness of murder. My claim here is admittedly speculative, but no more so than van den Haag's to the contrary. And my view has the added virtue of accounting for the failure of research to show an increased deterrent effect from executions *without having to deny the plausibility of van den Haag's common-sense argument that at least some additional potential murderers will be deterred by the prospect of the death penalty*. If there is a deterrent effect from *not executing,* then it is understandable that while executions will deter some murderers, this effect will be balanced out by the weakening of the deterrent effect of not executing, such that no net reduction in murders will result.[16] And this, by the way, also disposes of van den Haag's

14 On the number of people killed by the police, see Lawrence W. Sherman and Robert H. Langworthy, "Measuring Homicide by Police Officers," *Journal of Criminal Law and Criminology* 70, no. 4 (Winter 1979): 546–60; on the number of privately owned guns, see Franklin Zimring, *Firearms and Violence in American Life* (Washington, D.C.: U.S. Government Printing Office, 1968), pp. 6–7.

15 *AAA World* (Potomac ed.) 4, no. 3 (May–June 1984). pp. 18c and 18i.
16 A related claim has been made by those who defend the so-called brutalization hypothesis by presenting evidence to show that murders *increase* following an execution. See, for example, William J. Bowers and Glenn L. Pierce, "Deterrence or Brutalization: What Is the Effect of Executions?" *Crime & Delinquency* 26, no. 4 (October 1980): 453–84.

argument that, in the absence of knowledge one way or the other on the deterrent effect of executions, we should execute murderers rather than risk the lives of innocent people whose murders might have been deterred if we had. If there is a deterrent effect of not executing, it follows that we risk innocent lives either way. And if this is so, it seems that the only reasonable course of action is to refrain from imposing what we know is a horrible fate.[17]

4. Those who still think that van den Haag's common-sense argument for executing murderers is valid will find that the argument proves more than they bargained for. Van den Haag maintains that, in the absence of conclusive evidence on the relative deterrent impact of the death penalty versus life imprisonment, we must follow common sense and assume that if one punishment is more fearful than another, it will deter some potential criminals not deterred by the less fearful punishment. Since people sentenced to death will almost universally try to get their sentences changed to life in prison, it follows that death is more fearful than life imprisonment, and thus that it will deter some additional murderers. Consequently, we should institute the death penalty to save the lives

these additional murderers would have taken. But, since people sentenced to be tortured to death would surely try to get their sentences changed to simple execution, the same argument proves that death-by-torture will deter still more potential murderers. Consequently, we should institute death-by-torture to save the lives these additional murderers would have taken. Anyone who accepts van den Haag's argument is then confronted with a dilemma: Until we have conclusive evidence that capital punishment is a greater deterrent to murder than life imprisonment, we must grant *either* that we should not follow common sense and not impose the death penalty; *or* we should follow common sense and torture murderers to death. In short, either we must abolish the electric chair or reinstitute the rack. Surely, this is the *reductio ad absurdum* of van den Haag's common-sense argument.

CONCLUSION

I believe that, taken together, these arguments prove that we should abolish the death penalty though it is a just punishment for murder.

They conclude that each execution gives rise to two additional homicides in the month following and that these are real additions, not just a change in timing of the homicides (ibid. p. 481). My claim, it should be noted, is not identical to this, since, as I indicate in the text, what I call "the deterrence effect of not executing" is not something whose impact is to be seen immediately following executions but over the long haul, and, further, my claim is compatible with finding no net increase in murders due to executions. Nonetheless, should the brutalization hypothesis be borne out by further studies, it would certainly lend support to the notion that there is a deterrent effect of not executing.

17 Van den Haag writes: "If we were quite ignorant about the marginal deterrent effects of execution, we would have to choose—like it or not—between the certainty of the convicted murderer's death by execution and the likelihood of the survival of future victims of other murderers on the one hand, and on the other his certain survival and the likelihood of the death of new victims. I'd rather execute a man

convicted of having murdered others than put the lives of innocents at risk. I find it hard to understand the opposite choice" (p. 69). Conway was able to counter this argument earlier by pointing out that the research on the marginal deterrent effects of execution was not *inconclusive* in the sense of *tending to point both ways*, but rather in the sense of *giving us no reason to believe that capital punishment saves more lives than life imprisonment*. He could then answer van den Haag by saying that the choice is not between risking the lives of murderers and risking the lives of innocents, but between killing a murderer with no reason to believe lives will be saved and sparing a murderer with no reason to believe lives will be lost (Conway, "Capital Punishment and Deterrence." [*Philosophy & Public Affairs* 3, no. 4], pp. 442–43). This, of course, makes the choice to spare the murderer more understandable than van den Haag allows. Events, however, have overtaken Conway's argument. The advent of Ehrlich's research, contested though it may be, leaves us in fact with research that tends to point both ways.

Review Questions

1. What is Reiman's distinction between *lex talionis* and "proportional retributivism"?
2. Explain the affinity that Reiman sees between *lex talionis* and the golden rule.
3. What is the Hegelian approach to crime and punishment, as distinguished from the utilitarian view?
4. What is the Kantian view as Reiman explains it?
5. What is the retributivist principle? Why doesn't it settle the question about the application of *lex talionis* according to Reiman?
6. Why does Reiman reject the claim that we should rape rapists or torture torturers?
7. On Reiman's view, why is execution similar to torture?
8. How does Reiman reply to van den Haag?

Discussion Questions

1. What is the appropriate punishment for the crimes of rape and torture?
2. Is execution really similar to torture, as Reiman says? Why or why not?
3. How could van den Haag reply to Reiman's arguments?

Capital Punishment

ANTHONY G. AMSTERDAM

Anthony G. Amsterdam is a lawyer who has represented many clients who have received the death sentence.

Amsterdam begins by asserting that capital punishment is a great evil simply because it is intentionally killing a person. Furthermore, it is wrong because it results in killing people in error, and these errors cannot be corrected. Moreover, it is unfairly applied. The death sentence is disproportionately imposed on the poor and blacks.

Armstrong concludes with a discussion of retribution and deterrence. He argues that neither the appeal to retribution nor the appeal to deterrence justifies capital punishment.

[Source: Anthony G. Amsterdam, "Capital Punishment" from *Stanford Magazine* (Fall/Winter 1977). Copyright © Stanford Alumni Association.]

MY DISCUSSION OF CAPITAL PUNISHMENT will proceed in three stages.

First, I would like to set forth certain basic factual realities about capital punishment, like the fact that capital punishment is a fancy phrase for legally killing people. Please forgive me for beginning with such obvious and ugly facts. Much of our political and philosophical debate about the death penalty is carried on in language calculated to conceal these realities and their implications. The implications, I will suggest, are that capital punishment is a great evil—surely the greatest evil except for war that our society can intentionally choose to commit.

This does not mean that we should do away with capital punishment. Some evils, like war, are occasionally necessary, and perhaps capital punishment is one of them. But the fact that it is a great evil means that we should not choose to do it without some very good and solid reason of which we are satisfactorily convinced upon sufficient evidence. The conclusion of my first point simply is that the burden of proof upon the question of capital punishment rightly rests on those who are asking us to use our laws to kill people with, and that this is a very heavy burden.

Second, I want to review the justifications that have been advanced to support capital punishment. I want to explore with you concepts such as retribution and deterrence, and some of the assumptions and evidence about them. The conclusion of my second point will be that none of these reasons which we like to give ourselves for executing criminals can begin to sustain the burden of proof that rightfully rests upon them.

Third, I would like to say a word about history—about the slow but absolutely certain progress of maturing civilization that will bring an inevitable end to punishment by death. That history does not give us the choice between perpetrating and abolishing capital punishment, because we could not perpetuate it if we wanted to. A generation or two within a single nation can retard but not reverse a long-term, world-wide evolution of this magnitude. Our choice

is narrower although it is not unimportant: whether we shall be numbered among the last generations to put legal killing aside. I will end by asking you to cast your choice for life instead of death. But, first, let me begin with some basic facts about the death penalty.

I

The most basic fact, of course, is that capital punishment means taking living, breathing men and women, stuffing them into a chair, strapping them down, pulling a lever, and exterminating them. We have almost forgotten this fact because there have been no executions in this country for more than ten years, except for Gary Gilmore whose combined suicide and circus were so wildly extravagant as to seem unreal. For many people, capital punishment has become a sanitized and symbolic issue: Do you or do you not support your local police? Do you or do you not care enough about crime to get tough with criminals? These abstractions were never what capital punishment was about, although it was possible to think so during the ten-year moratorium on executions caused by constitutional challenges to the death penalty in the courts. That is no longer possible. The courts have now said that we can start up executions again, if we want to. Today, a vote for capital punishment is a vote to kill real, live people.

What this means is, first, that we bring men or women into court and put them through a trial for their lives. They are expected to sit back quietly and observe decent courtroom decorum throughout a proceeding whose purpose is systematically and deliberately to decide whether they should be killed. The jury hears evidence and votes; and you can always tell when a jury has voted for death because they come back into court and they will not look the defendant or defense counsel in the eyes. The judge pronounces sentence and the defendant is taken away to be held in a cell for two to six years, hoping that his appeals will succeed, not really knowing what they are all about, but knowing that if they fail, he will be taken out and cinched down and put to death. Most of the people in prison are reasonably nice to him, and even a little apologetic; but he realizes every day for that 700 or 2,100 days that they are holding him there helpless for the approaching slaughter; and that, once the final order is given, they will truss him up and kill him, and that nobody in that vast surrounding machinery of public officials and servants of the law will raise a finger to save him. This is why Camus once wrote that an execution

> . . . is not simply death. It is just as different . . . from the privation of life as a concentration camp is from prison. . . . It adds to death a rule, a public premeditation known to the future victim, an organization . . . which is itself a source of moral sufferings more terrible than death . . . *[Capital punishment] is . . . the most premeditated of murders, to which no criminal's deed, however calculated . . . can be compared. . . . For there to be an equivalency, the death penalty would have to punish a criminal who had warned his victim of the date at which he would inflict a horrible death on him and who, from that moment onward, had confined him at his mercy for months. Such a monster is not encountered in private life.*

I will spare you descriptions of the execution itself. Apologists for capital punishment commonly excite their readers with descriptions of extremely gruesome, gory murders. All murders are horrible things, and executions are usually a lot cleaner physically—although, like Camus, I have never heard of a murderer who held his victim captive for two or more years waiting as the minutes and hours ticked away toward his preannounced death. The clinical details of an execution are as unimaginable to me as they are to most of you. We have not permitted public executions in this country for over 40 years. The law in every state forbids more than a few people to watch the deed done behind prison walls. In January of 1977, a federal judge in Texas ruled that executions could be photographed for television, but the attorneys general of 25 states asked the federal Court of Appeals to set aside that ruling, and it did. I can only leave to your imagination what they are trying so very hard to hide from us. Oh, of course, executions are too hideous to put on television; we all know that. But let us not forget that it is the same hideous thing, done in secret, which we are discussing under abstract labels like "capital punishment" that permit us to talk about the subject in after-dinner conversation instead of spitting up.

In any event, the advocates of capital punishment can and do accentuate their arguments with descriptions of the awful physical details of such hideous murders as that of poor Sharon Tate. All of us naturally and rightly respond to these atrocities with shock and horror. You can read descriptions of executions that would also horrify you (for example, in Byron Eshelman's 1962 book, *Death Row Chaplain*, particularly pages 160–61), but I prefer not to insult your intelligence by playing "can you top this" with issues of life and death. I ask you only to remember two things, if and when you are exposed to descriptions of terrifying murders.

First, the murders being described are not murders that are being done by us, or in our name, or with our approval; and our power to stop them is exceedingly limited even under the most exaggerated suppositions of deterrence, which I shall shortly return to question. Every execution, on the other hand, is done by our paid servants, in our collective name, and we can stop them all. Please do not be bamboozled into thinking that people who are against executions are in favor of murders. If we had the individual or the collective power to stop murders, we would stop them all—and for the same basic reason that we want to stop executions. Murders and executions are both ugly, vicious things, because they destroy the same sacred and mysterious gift of life which we do not understand and can never restore.

Second, please remember therefore that descriptions of murders are relevant to the subject of capital punishment only on the theory that two wrongs make a right, or that killing murderers can assuage their victims' sufferings or bring them back to life, or that capital punishment is the best deterrent to murder. The first two propositions are absurd, and the third is debatable—although as I shall later show, the evidence is overwhelmingly against it. My present point is only that deterrence is debatable, whereas we *know* that persons whom we execute are dead beyond recall, no matter how the debate about deterrence comes out. That is a sufficient reason, I believe, why the burden of proof on the issue of deterrence should be placed squarely upon the executioners.

There are other reasons too. Let me try to state them briefly.

Capital punishment not merely kills people, it also kills some of them in error, and these are errors which we can never correct. When I speak about legal error, I do not mean only the question whether "they got the right man" or killed somebody who "didn't do it." Errors of that sort do occur: Timothy Evans, for example, an innocent man whose execution was among the reasons for the abolition of the death penalty in Great Britain. If you read Anthony Scaduto's recent book, *Scapegoat,* you will come away with unanswerable doubts whether Bruno Richard Hauptmann was really guilty of the kidnapping of the Lindbergh infant for which he was executed, or whether we killed Hauptmann, too, for a crime he did not commit.

In 1975, the Florida Cabinet pardoned two black men, Freddie Lee Pitts and Wilbert Lee, who were twice tried and sentenced to death and spent 12 years apiece on death row for a murder committed by somebody else. This one, I am usually glibly told, "does not count," because Pitts and Lee were never actually put to death. Take comfort if you will but I cannot, for I know that only the general constitutional attack which we were then mounting upon the death penalty in Florida kept Pitts and Lee alive long enough to permit discovery of the evidence of their innocence. Our constitutional attack is now dead, and so would Pitts and Lee be if they were tried tomorrow. Sure, we catch some errors. But we often catch them by extremely lucky breaks that could as easily not have happened. I represented a young man in North Carolina who came within a hair's breadth of being the Gary Gilmore of his day. Like Gilmore, he became so depressed under a death sentence that he tried to dismiss his appeal. He was barely talked out of it, his conviction was reversed, and on retrial a jury acquitted him in 11 minutes.

We do not know how many "wrong men" have been executed. We think and pray that they are rare—although we can't be sure because, after a man is dead, people seldom continue to investigate the possibility that he was innocent. But that is not the biggest source of error anyway.

What about *legal* error? In 1968, the Supreme Court of the United States held that it was unconstitutional to exclude citizens from capital trial juries simply because they had general conscientious or religious objections to the death penalty. That decision was held retroactive; and I represented 60 or 70 men whose death sentences were subsequently set aside for constitutional errors in jury selection. While researching their cases, I found the cases of at least as many more men who had already been executed on the basis of trials infected with identical errors. On June 29, 1977, we finally won a decision from the Supreme Court of the United States that the death penalty is excessively harsh and therefore unconstitutional for the crime of rape. Fine, but it comes too late for the 455 men executed for rape in this country since 1930—405 of them black.

In 1975, the Supreme Court held that the constitutional presumption of innocence forbids a trial judge to tell the jury that the burden of proof is on a homicide defendant to show provocation which reduces murder to manslaughter.

On June 17, 1977, the Court held that this decision was also retroactive. Jury charges of precisely that kind were standard forms for more than a century in many American states that punished murder with death. Can we even begin to guess how many people were unconstitutionally executed under this so-called retroactive decision?

Now what about errors of fact that go to the degree of culpability of a crime? In almost every state, the difference between first and second degree murder—or between capital and non-capital murder—depends on whether the defendant acted with something called "premeditation" as distinguished from intent to kill. Premeditation means intent formed beforehand, but no particular amount of time is required. Courts tell juries that premeditation "may be as instantaneous as successive thoughts in the mind." Mr. Justice Cardozo wrote that *he* did not understand the concept of premeditation after several decades of studying and trying to apply it as a judge. Yet this is the kind of question to which a jury's answer spells out life or death in a capital trial—this, and the questions of whether the defendant had "malice aforethought," or "provocation and passion," or "insanity," or the "reasonableness" necessary for killing in self-defense.

I think of another black client, Johnny Coleman, whose conviction and death sentence for killing a white truck driver named "Screwdriver" Johnson we twice got reversed by the Supreme Court of the United States. On retrial a jury acquitted him on the grounds of self-defense upon exactly the same evidence that an earlier jury had had when it sentenced him to die. When ungraspable legal standards are thus applied to intangible mental states, there is not merely the possibility but the actuarial certainty that juries deciding substantial volumes of cases are going to be wrong in an absolutely large number of them. If you accept capital punishment, you must accept the reality—not the risk, but the reality—that we shall kill people whom the law says that it is not proper to kill. No other outcome is possible when we presume to administer an infallible punishment through a fallible system.

You will notice that I have taken examples of black defendants as some of my cases of legal error. There is every reason to believe that discrimination on grounds of race and poverty fatally infect the administration of capital justice in this country. Since 1930, an almost equal number of white and black defendants has been executed for the crime of murder, although blacks constituted only about a tenth of the nation's population during this period. No sufficiently careful studies have been done of these cases, controlling variables other than race, so as to determine exactly what part race played in the outcome. But when that kind of systemic study *was* done in rape cases, it showed beyond the statistical possibility of a doubt that black men who raped white women were disproportionately sentenced to die on the basis of race alone. Are you prepared to believe that juries which succumbed to conscious or unconscious racial prejudices in rape cases were or are able to put those prejudices wholly aside where the crime charged is murder? Is it not much more plausible to believe that even the most conscientious juror—or judge, or prosecuting attorney—will be slower to want to inflict the death penalty on a defendant with whom he can identify as a human being; and that the process of identification in our society is going to be very seriously affected by racial identity?

I should mention that there have been a couple of studies—one by the *Stanford Law Review* and the other by the Texas Judicial Council—which found no racial discrimination in capital sentencing in certain murder cases. But both of these studies had methodological problems and limitations; and both of them also found death-sentencing discrimination against the economically poor, who come disproportionately from racial minorities. The sum of the evidence still stands where the National Crime Commission found it ten years ago, when it described the following discriminatory patterns. "The death sentence," said the Commission, "is disproportionately imposed and carried out on the poor, the Negro, and members of unpopular groups."

Apart from discrimination, there is a haphazard, crazy-quilt character about the administration of capital punishment that every knowledgeable lawyer or observer can describe but none can rationally explain. Some juries are hanging juries, some counties are hanging counties, some years are hanging years; and men live or die depending on these flukes.

However atrocious the crime may have been for which a particular defendant is sentenced to die, "[e]xperienced wardens know many prisoners serving life or less whose crimes were equally, or more atrocious." This is a quotation, by the way, from former Attorney General Ramsey Clark's statement to a congressional subcommittee; and wardens Lewis Lawes, Clinton Duffy, and others have said the same thing.

With it I come to the end of my first point. I submit that the deliberate judicial extinction of human life is intrinsically so final and so terrible an act as to cast the burden of proof for its justification upon those who want us to do it. But certainly when the act is executed through a fallible system which assures that we kill some people wrongly, others because they are black or poor or personally unattractive or socially unacceptable, and all of them quite freakishly in the sense that whether a man lives or dies for any particular crime is a matter of luck and happenstance, *then,* at the least, the burden of justifying capital punishment lies fully and heavily on its proponents.

II

Let us consider those justifications. The first and the oldest is the concept of *retribution:* an eye for an eye, a life for a life. You may or may not believe in this kind of retribution, but I will not waste your time debating it because it cannot

honestly be used to justify the only form of capital punishment that this country has accepted for the past half-century. Even before the judicial moratorium, executions in the United States had dwindled to an average of about 30 a year. Only a rare, sparse handful of convicted murderers are being sentenced to die or executed for the selfsame crimes for which many, many times as many murderers were sent away to prison. Obviously, as Professor Herbert Wechsler said a generation ago, the issue of capital punishment is no longer "whether it is fair or just that one who takes another person's life should lose his own. . . . [W]e do not and cannot act upon . . . [that proposition] generally in the administration of the penal law. The problem rather is whether a small and highly random sample of people who commit murder . . . ought to be despatched, while most of those convicted of . . . [identical] crimes are dealt with by imprisonment."

Sometimes the concept of retribution is modernized a little with a notion called *moral reinforcement*—the ideal that we should punish very serious crimes very severely in order to demonstrate how much we abhor them. The trouble with *this* justification for capital punishment, of course, is that it completely begs the question, which is *how severely* we ought to punish any particular crime to show appropriate abhorrence for it. The answer can hardly be found in a literal application of the eye-for-an-eye formula. We do not burn down arsonists' houses or cheat back at bunco artists. But if we ought not punish all crimes exactly according to their kind, then what is the fit moral reinforcement for murder? You might as well say burning at the stake or boiling in oil is as simple as gassing or electrocution.

Or is it not more plausible—if what we really want to say is that the killing of a human being is wrong and ought to be condemned as clearly as we can—that we should choose the punishment of prison as the fitting means to make this point? So far as moral reinforcement goes, the difference between life imprisonment and capital punishment is precisely that imprisonment continues to respect the value of human life. The plain message of capital punishment, on the other hand, is that life ceases to be sacred whenever someone with the power to take it away decides that there is a sufficiently compelling pragmatic reason to do so.

But there is still another theory of a retributive sort which is often advanced to support the death penalty, particularly in recent years. This is the argument that *we*—that is, the person making the argument—no longer believe in the outworn concept of retribution, but the *public*—they believe in retribution, and so we must let them have their prey or they will lose respect for law. Watch for this argument because it is the surest sign of demogragic depravity. It is disgusting in its patronizing attribution to "the public" of a primitive, uneducable bloodthirstiness which the speaker is unprepared to defend but is prepared to exploit as a means of sidestepping the rational and moral limitations of a *just* theory of retribution. It out-judases Judas in its abnegation of governmental responsibility to respond to popular misinformation with enlightenment, instead of seizing on it as a pretext for atrocity. This argument asserts that the proper way to deal with a lynch mob is to string its victim up before the mob does.

I don't think "the public" is a lynch mob or should be treated as one. People today are troubled and frightened by crime, and legitimately so. Much of the apparent increase of violent crime in our times is the product of intensified statistics keeping, massive and instantaneous and graphic news reporting, and manipulation of figures by law enforcement agencies which must compete with other sectors of the public economy for budget allocations. But part of the increase is also real, and very disturbing. Murders ought to disturb us all, whether or not they are increasing. Each and every murder is a terrible human tragedy. Nevertheless, it is irresponsible for public officials—particularly law enforcement officials whom the public views as experts—first to exacerbate and channel legitimate public concern about crime into public support for capital punishment by advertising unsupportable claims that capital punishment is an answer to the crime problem, and then to turn around and cite public support for capital punishment as justification when all other justifications are shown to be unsupportable. Politicians do this all the time, for excellent political reasons. It is much easier to advocate simplistic and illusory solutions to the crime problem than to find real and effective solutions. Most politicians are understandably afraid to admit that our society knows frighteningly little about the causes or cure of crime, and will have to spend large amounts of taxpayers' money even to begin to find out. The facile politics of crime do much to explain our national acceptance of capital punishment, but nothing to justify it.

Another supposed justification for capital punishment that deserves equally brief treatment is the notion of *isolation or specific deterrence*—the idea that we must kill a murderer to prevent him from murdering ever again. The usual forms that this argument takes are that a life sentence does not mean a life sentence—it means parole after 7, or 12, or 25 years; and that, within prisons themselves, guards and other prisoners are in constant jeopardy of death at the hands of convicted but unexecuted murderers.

It amazes me that these arguments can be made or taken seriously. Are we really going to kill a human being because we do not trust other people—the people whom we have chosen to serve on our own parole boards—to make a proper judgment in his case at some future time? We trust this same parole board to make far more numerous, difficult, and dangerous decisions: hardly a week passes when they do not consider the cases of armed robbers, for example, although armed robbers are much, much more likely statistically to commit future murders than any murderer is to repeat his crime. But if we really do distrust the public agencies of law—if we fear that they may make mistakes—then surely that is a powerful argument *against* capital punishment. Courts which hand out death sentences because they predict that a man will still be criminally dangerous 7 or 25 years in the future cannot conceivably make fewer mistakes than parole boards who release a prisoner after 7 or 25 years of close observation in prison have convinced them that he is reformed and no longer dangerous.

But pass this point. If we refuse to trust the parole system, then let us provide by law that the murderers whose release we fear shall be given sentences of life imprisonment without parole which *do* mean life imprisonment without parole. I myself would be against that, but it is far more humane than capital punishment, and equally safe.

As for killings inside prisons, if you examine them you will find that they are very rarely done by convicted murderers, but are almost always done by people imprisoned for crimes that no one would think of making punishable by death. Warden Lawes of Sing Sing and Governor Wallace of Alabama, among others, regularly employed murder convicts as house servants because they were among the very safest prisoners. There are exceptions, of course; but these can be handled by adequate prison security. You cannot tell me or believe that a society which is capable of putting a man on the moon is incapable of putting a man in prison, keeping him there, and keeping him from killing while he is there. And if anyone says that this is costly, and that we should kill people in order to reduce government expenditures, I can only reply that the cost of housing a man for life in prison is considerably less than the cost of putting the same man through all of the extraordinary legal proceedings necessary to kill him.

That brings me to the last supposed justification for the death penalty: *deterrence.* This is the subject that you most frequently hear debated, and many people who talk about capital punishment talk about nothing else. I have done otherwise here, partly for completeness, partly because it is vital to approach the subject of deterrence knowing precisely what question you want to ask and have answered. I have suggested that the proper question is *whether there is sufficiently convincing evidence that the death penalty deters murder better than does life imprisonment so that you are willing to accept responsibility for doing the known evil act of killing human beings—with all of the attending ugliness that I have described—on the faith of your conviction in the superior deterrent efficacy of capital punishment.*

If this is the question, then I submit that there is only one fair and reasonable answer. When the Supreme Court of the United States reviewed the evidence in 1976, it described that evidence as "inconclusive." Do not let anybody tell you—as death-penalty advocates are fond of doing—that the Supreme Court held the death penalty justifiable as a deterrent. What the Court's plurality opinion said, exactly, was that "there is no convincing evidence *either supporting or refuting* . . . [the] view" that "the death penalty may not function as a significantly greater deterrent than lesser penalties." *Because* the evidence was inconclusive, the Court held that the Constitution did not forbid judgment either way. But if the evidence is inconclusive, is it your judgment that we should conclusively kill people on a factual theory that the evidence does not conclusively sustain?

I hope not. But let us examine the evidence more carefully because—even though it is not conclusive—it is very, very substantial; and the overwhelming weight of it refutes the claims of those who say that capital punishment is a better deterrent than life imprisonment for murder.

For more than 40 years, criminologists have studied this question by a variety of means. They have compared homicide rates in countries and states that did and did not have capital punishment, or that actually executed people more and less frequently. Some of these studies compared large aggregates of abolitionist and retentionist states; others compared geographically adjacent pairs or triads of states, or states that were chosen because they were comparable in other socio-economic factors that might affect homicide. Other studies compared homicide rates in the same country or state before and after the abolition or reinstatement of capital punishment, or they compared homicide rates for the same geographic area during periods preceding and following well publicized executions. Special comparative studies were done relating to police killings and prison killings. All in all, there were dozens of studies. Without a single exception, *none* of them found that the death penalty had any statistically significant effect upon the rate of homicide or murder. Often I have heard advocates of capital punishment explain away its failures by likening it to a great lighthouse: "We count the ships that crash," they say, "but we never know how many saw the light and were saved." What these studies show, however, is that coastlines of the same shape and depth and tidal structure, with and without lighthouses, invariably have the same number of shipwrecks per year. On that evidence, would you invest your money in a lighthouse, or would you buy a sonar if you really wanted to save lives?

In 1975, the first purportedly scientific study ever to find that capital punishment *did* deter homicides was published. This was done by Issac Ehrlich of Chicago, who is not a criminologist but an economist. Using regression analysis involving an elaborate mathematical model, Ehrlich reported that every execution deterred something like eight murders. Naturally supporters of capital punishment hurriedly clambered on the Ehrlich bandwagon.

Unhappily, for them, the wagon was a factory reject. Several distinguished econometricians— including a team headed by Lawrence Klein,

president of the American Economy Association —reviewed Ehrlich's work and found it fatally flawed with numerous methodological errors. Some of these were technical: it appeared, for example, that Ehrlich had produced his results by the unjustified and unexplained use of a logarithmic form of regression equation instead of the more conventional linear form—which made his findings of deterrence vanish. Equally important, it was shown that Ehrlich's findings depended entirely on data from the post-1962 period, when executions declined and the homicide rate rose *as a part of a general rise, in the overall crime rate that Ehrlich incredibly failed to consider.*

Incidentally, the nonscientific proponents of capital punishment are also fond of suggesting that the rise in homicide rates in the 1960s and the 1970s, when executions were halted, proves that executions used to deter homicides. This is ridiculous when you consider that crime as a whole has increased during this period; that homicide rates have increased about *half* as much as the rates for all other FBI Index crimes; and that whatever factors are affecting the rise of most noncapital crimes (which *cannot* include cessation of executions) almost certainly affect the homicide-rate rise also.

In the event, Ehrlich's study was discredited and a second, methodologically inferior study by a fellow named Yunker is not even worth criticizing here. These are the only two scientific studies in 40 years, I repeat, which have ever purported to find deterrence. On the other hand, several recent studies have been completed by researchers who adopted Ehrlich's basic regression-analysis approach but corrected its defects. Peter Passell did such a study finding no deterrence. Kenneth Avio did such a study finding no deterrence. If you want to review all of these studies yourselves, you may find them discussed and cited in an excellent article in the 1976 *Supreme Court Review* by Hans Zeisel, on page 317. The conclusion you will have to draw is that—during 40 years and today—the scientific community has looked and looked and looked for any reliable evidence that capital punishment deters homicide better than does life imprisonment, and it has found no such evidence at all.

Proponents of capital punishment frequently cite a different kind of study, one that was done by the Los Angeles Police Department. Police officers asked arrested robbers who did not carry guns, or did not use them, *why* they did not; and the answers, supposedly, were frequently that the robber "did not want to get the death penalty." It is noteworthy that the Los Angeles Police Department has consistently refused to furnish copies of this study and its underlying data to professional scholars, apparently for fear of criticism. I finally obtained a copy of the study from a legislative source, and I can tell you that it shows two things. First, an arrested person will tell a police officer anything that he thinks the police officer wants to hear. Second, police officers, like all other human beings, hear what they want to hear. When a robber tries to say that he did not carry or use a gun because he did not wish to risk the penalties for homicide, he will describe those penalties in terms of whatever the law happens to be at the time and place. In Minnesota, which has no death penalty, he will say, "I didn't want to get life imprisonment." In Los Angeles, he will say, "I didn't want to get the death penalty." Both responses mean the same thing; neither tells you that death is a superior deterrent to life imprisonment.

The real mainstay of deterrence thesis, however, is not evidence but intuition. You and I ask ourselves: Are we not afraid to die? Of course! Would the threat of death, then, not intimidate us to forbear from a criminal act? Certainly! *Therefore,* capital punishment must be a deterrent. The trouble with this intuition is that the people who are doing the reasoning and the people who are doing the murdering are not the same people. You and I do not commit murder for a lot of reasons other than the death

penalty. The death penalty might perhaps also deter us from murdering—but altogether needlessly, since we would not murder with it or without it. Those who are sufficiently dissocialized to murder are not responding to the world in the same way that we are, and we simply cannot "intuit" their thinking processes from ours.

Consider, for example, the well-documented cases of persons who kill *because* there is a death penalty. One of these was Pamela Watkins, a babysitter in San Jose who had made several unsuccessful suicide attempts and was frightened to try again. She finally strangled two children so that the state of California would execute her. In various bizarre forms, this "suicide-murder" syndrome is reported by psychiatrists again and again. (Parenthetically, Gary Gilmore was probably such a case.) If you intuit that somewhere, sometime, the death penalty *does* deter some potential murders, are you also prepared to intuit that their numbers mathematically exceed the numbers of these wretched people who are actually induced to murder by the existence of capital punishment?

Here, I suggest, our intuition does—or should—fail, just as the evidence certainly does fail, to establish a deterrent justification for the death penalty. There is simply no credible evidence, and there is no rational way of reasoning about the real facts once you know them, which can sustain this or any other justification with the degree of confidence that should be demanded before a civilized society deliberately extinguishes human life.

III

I have only a little space for my final point, but it is sufficient because the point is perfectly plain. Capital punishment is a dying institution in this last quarter of the twentieth century. It has already been abandoned in law or in fact throughout most of the civilized world. England, Canada, the Scandinavian countries, virtually all of Western Europe except for France and Spain have abolished the death penalty. The vast majority of countries in the Western Hemisphere have abolished it. Its last strongholds in the world—apart from the United States—are in Asia and Africa, particularly South Africa. Even the countries which maintain capital punishment on the books have almost totally ceased to use it in fact. In the United States, considering only the last half century, executions have plummeted from 199 in 1935 to approximately 29 a year during the decade before 1967, when the ten-year judicial moratorium began.

Do you doubt that this development will continue? Do you doubt that it will continue because it is the path of civilization—the path up out of fear and terror and the barbarism that terror breeds, into self-confidence and decency in the administration of justice? The road, like any other built by men, has its detours, but over many generations it has run true, and will run true. And there will therefore come a time—perhaps in 20 years, perhaps in 50 or 100, but very surely and very shortly as the lifetime of nations is measured—when our children will look back at us in horror and unbelief because of what we did in their names

and for their supposed safety, just as we look back in horror and unbelief at the thousands of crucifixions and beheadings and live disembowelments that our ancestors practiced for the supposed purpose of making our world safe from murderers and robbers, thieves, shoplifters, and pickpockets.

All of these kinds of criminals are still with us, and will be with our children—although we can certainly decrease their numbers and their damage, and protect ourselves from them a lot better, if we insist that our politicians stop pounding on the whipping boy of capital punishment and start coming up with some real solutions to the real problems of crime. Our children will cease to execute murderers for the same reason that we have ceased to string up pickpockets and shoplifters at the public crossroads, although there are still plenty of them around. Our children will cease to execute murderers because executions are a self-deluding, self-defeating, self-degrading, futile, and entirely stupid means of dealing with the crime of murder, and because our children will prefer to be something better than murderers themselves. Should we not—can we not—make the same choice now?

Review Questions

1. Why does Amsterdam think that capital punishment is a great evil?
2. What additional reasons does Amsterdam give for saying that capital punishment is wrong?
3. Why does Amsterdam reject the oldest concept of retribution, an eye for an eye, a life for a life?
4. What is the notion of moral reinforcement, and why doesn't Amsterdam accept it?
5. How does Amsterdam reply to the argument that the public's desire for retribution must be satisfied?
6. What is wrong with the notion of specific deterrence, according to Amsterdam?
7. How does Amsterdam deal with the appeal to deterrence?

Discussion Questions

1. Do you agree with Amsterdam that capital punishment is a great evil? Why or why not?
2. Has Amsterdam successfully defeated the appeal to retribution?
3. Are you convinced that capital punishment is not a better deterrent than life imprisonment? Explain your answer.

Problem Cases

1. *Karla Fay Tucker*

(Reported by Daniel Pedersen in *Newsweek,* February 2, 1998.) On June 13, 1983, a few hours before dawn, Tucker used a pickax to kill two people who had annoyed her. The male victim, Jerry Lynn Dean, had once dripped motor oil on her living-room carpet and had cut up some photographs of Tucker's mother. The female victim, Deborah Thorton, just happened to be asleep beside Dean in his Houston apartment; Tucker didn't even know her. Tucker and her boyfriend hacked away at both victims until they were dead, and then left a two-foot blade imbedded seven inches into Thorton's chest. On a tape played at her trial, Tucker boasted that she had felt a surge of sexual pleasure with every swing of the pickax.

Tucker was found guilty and was sentenced to death by lethal injection. But fourteen years later, shortly before she was to be executed, Tucker launched an impressive last-minute campaign to have her sentence commuted to life imprisonment. Her appeal attracted worldwide media attention. One reason for all the publicity was Tucker's gender. Texas has had more executions than any other state, and the death penalty is popular in Texas, but a woman had not been executed there since the middle of the Civil War.

Tucker's appeal was not based on her gender, however. She claimed that when she committed the crime, she was a drug-addicted prostitute, but now she was a born-again Christian who was sincerely repentant and reformed. She was married to a prison minister. She was an active evangelist, writing essays and making antidrug videotapes. She appeared on Pat Robertson's Christian cable TV show, *The 700 Club.* She managed to muster the support of a wide variety of character witnesses and sympathizers, including Pope John Paul II, Bianca Jagger, the European Parliament, prison guards, former prosecutors, the detective who arrested her, one of the jurors in her case, and even the brother of the woman she murdered.

Tucker's appeal was unsuccessful. The Texas parole board voted 16 to 0 against commuting her sentence. Governor George Bush, Jr., the son of the former U.S. president, refused to grant a thirty-day reprieve, and the Supreme Court rejected Tucker's final appeal less than an hour before she was put to death.

At 6:45 P.M. on February 3, 1998, Tucker was pronounced dead, eight minutes after the injection of lethal drugs. In Europe, opinion writers called it a "barbaric act." In the United States, some feminists voiced approval that women had achieved equal rights in capital litigation; not like Russia, where the death penalty is used for men but not women.

Was the execution of Tucker justified or not? Why or why not?

If there is a death penalty, should it be applied equally to men and women? What is your view?

2. *Rickey Ray Rector*

(Reported by Marshall Frady, "Death in Arkansas," *The New Yorker,* February 22, 1993.) Rickey Ray Rector was a 40-year-old black man who was executed in

Arkansas in 1992. In 1981, after killing two men (one a policeman), he put a pistol to his temple and shot himself through the forehead. The shot did not kill him, but it blasted away some three inches from the front of his brain. The effect was similar to that of a frontal lobotomy, and it left him with the mental capacity of a young child. One psychologist testified that he had an I.Q. of 63 and no memory of his crime. Rector spent ten years on death row, during which time he showed little or no understanding of why he was there. He was executed after pardon appeals to Bill Clinton, then the governor of Arkansas, failed.

Did Rector deserve to die? What was the point of the death sentence in this case? Should suicidal criminals who request the death penalty be killed? Why or why not?

3. The Sacco-Vanzetti Case

On April 15, 1920, a paymaster for a shoe company in South Braintree, Massachusetts, and his guard were shot and killed by two men who escaped with more than $15,000. Witnesses thought the two men were Italians, and Nicola Sacco and Bartolomeo Vanzetti were arrested. Both men were anarchists, and had evaded the army draft. Upon their arrest, they made false statements. Both carried firearms; but neither had a criminal record, nor was there any evidence that they had the money. In July 1921 they were found guilty and sentenced to death. The conduct of the trial by Judge Webster Thayer was criticized, and indeed much of the evidence against them was later discredited. The court denied their appeal for a new trial, and Governor Alvan T. Fuller, after postponing the execution, allowed them to be executed on August 22, 1927. Many regarded them as innocent, prompting worldwide sympathy demonstrations. The case has been the subject of many books, most of which agree that Vanzetti was innocent but that Sacco may have been guilty. The gun found on Sacco was tested with modern ballistics equipment in 1961, and these tests seem to show that the gun had been used to kill the guard.

Was it morally right to execute these two men? Why or why not?

Suggested Readings

1. For extensive data on the death penalty, see the Death Penalty Information Center (http://www.essential.org/dpic/).
2. Ernest van den Haag, "The Ultimate Punishment: A Defense," *Harvard Law Review* 99 (1986), replies to various objections to capital punishment and defends it using a version of his "best bet argument."
3. Ernest van den Haag, "End the Death Penalty; Use Life Without Parole," *USA Today,* April 8, 1994, changes his mind and says that the evidence for abolition of capital punishment is "beyond dispute." He says, "The death penalty is a failure as a tool of law, justice or public safety."
4. Jonathan Glover, *Causing Death and Saving Lives* (Pelican Books, 1977), pp. 228–45, attacks Kant's retributive theory and argues for the abolition of the death penalty from a utilitarian point of view.

5. Hugo Adam Bedau, "How to Argue About the Death Penalty," *Israel Law Review* 25, nos. 2–4 (Summer/Autumn 1991), pp. 466–80, argues that a preponderance of reasons favors the abolition of the death penalty.

6. Hugo Adam Bedau, "Capital Punishment," in *Matters of Life and Death,* third edition, ed. Tom Regan (Random House, 1993), argues that neither the appeal to retribution nor the appeal to deterrence justifies the death penalty as opposed to the alternative punishment of life imprisonment.

7. Hugo Adam Bedau, ed., *The Death Penalty in America,* third edition (Oxford University Press, 1982), provides a number of useful articles on factual data relevant to the death penalty, and articles both for and against it.

8. Robert M. Baird and Stuart E. Rosenbaum, eds., *Punishment and the Death Penalty: The Current Debate* (Prometheus Books, 1995), is an anthology with readings on the justification of punishment and the death penalty.

9. Tom Sorell, *Moral Theory and Capital Punishment* (Blackwell, 1988), defends the death penalty.

10. Charles L. Black, Jr., *Capital Punishment: The Inevitability of Caprice and Mistake* (Norton, 1981), maintains that mistakes cannot be eliminated from the imposition of the death penalty, and for that reason it ought to be abolished.

11. Walter Berns, *For Capital Punishment* (Basic Books, 1979), defends a retributivist justification of capital punishment.

12. Robert S. Gerstein, "Capital Punishment—'Cruel and Unusual?' A Retributivist Response," *Ethics* 85 (January 1975), pp. 75–79, defends retributivism against the complaint that it is mere vengeance.

13. Steven Goldberg, "On Capital Punishment," *Ethics* 85 (October 1974), pp. 67–74, examines the factual issue of whether or not the death penalty is a uniquely effective deterrent. A revised version titled "Does Capital Punishment Deter?" appears in *Today's Moral Problems,* second edition, ed. Richard A. Wasserstrom (Macmillan, 1979).

14. Sidney Hook, "The Death Sentence," in *The Death Penalty in America,* ed. Hugo Adam Bedau (Doubleday, 1967), supports the retention of the death penalty in two cases: (1) defendants convicted of murder who choose death rather than life imprisonment, and (2) those who have been sentenced to prison for murder and then murder again while in prison.

15. Bruce N. Waller, "From Hemlock to Lethal Injection: The Case for Self-Execution," *International Journal of Applied Philosophy* 4 (Fall 1989), pp. 53–58, argues that prisoners condemned to death should be offered the chance to kill themselves.

16. Robert Johnson, "This Man Has Expired. Witness to an Execution," *Commonweal* (January 13, 1989), pp. 9–13, gives a detailed and graphic description of an electric-chair execution.

17. Stephen Nathanson, *An Eye for an Eye? The Morality of Punishing Death* (Roman & Littlefield, 1987), discusses issues surrounding the death penalty and develops a case for abolishing it.

18. Welsh S. White, *The Death Penalty in the Nineties* (University of Michigan Press, 1991), examines the way the death penalty has been administered in the nineties.

Chapter 5

Sexuality

Introduction

Factual Background

There are numerous studies of human sexuality containing a wealth of information. I will confine myself to a few basic facts. People are not either homosexual or heterosexual; another sexual orientation is bisexuality—that is, being sexually attracted to people of both sexes. Although Kinsey has been criticized, many authorities believe that the Kinsey studies in 1948 and 1953 still give us the most reliable figures on homosexuality. Kinsey reported that about 10 percent of white American males were exclusively homosexual for at least three years of their lives and 4 percent were exclusively homosexual throughout their lives. Only 2 to 3 percent of women reported being exclusively lesbian. The percentages of both sexes who are bisexual are believed to be about the same as those who are homosexual.

It is generally agreed that masturbation is common. One study found that 92 percent of males and 73 percent of females had masturbated by age 20. Oral sex is also common. According to the American Psychological Association, approximately 90 percent of all heterosexual married couples have engaged in oral sex. It is interesting to note that oral sex is currently illegal in eighteen states. These states have laws forbidding "sodomy," or "crimes against nature," usually defined as anal or oral sex. In five states the sodomy laws are aimed specifically at homosexuals, but in thirteen states they do not distinguish between heterosexual and homosexual couples.

In the *Bowers* case (see the Problem Cases), the Supreme Court ruled that Georgia's antisodomy law did not violate the U.S. Constitution. But in late November 1998, the Georgia Supreme Court struck down the state's ban on sodomy, ruling that the law violated privacy. In their 6-to-1 ruling, the Georgia court said, "We cannot think of any other activity that reasonable persons would rank as more private and more deserving of protection from government interference." Courts in Kentucky, Montana, and Tennessee previously had reached the same conclusion in striking down their antisodomy laws.

The Readings

The Judeo-Christian tradition holds that the main purpose of sex is the procreation of children within the context of marriage. Nonmarital sex—adultery, premarital sex, fornication, prostitution, masturbation, and homosexuality—is morally wrong. In the first reading, the Vatican Declaration on Sexual Ethics presents an influential statement of this traditional Christian view of sex.

To understand this traditional view of sex, it is necessary to know something about the natural law theory used to support it. Natural law is a set of prescriptive rules of conduct binding on all human beings because of their human nature. In natural law theory, human action is naturally directed toward certain goals and purposes, such as life and procreation. These natural goals and purposes are good, and to interfere with them is morally wrong. Accordingly, if the natural goal or purpose of sexual activity is reproduction within the context of marriage, then interfering with this natural goal is morally wrong.

The Vatican Declaration espouses this natural law theory. According to the Declaration, homosexuality is seriously disordered because it contradicts its finality; that is, it opposes the natural end of sex, which is procreation. Masturbation is also a serious disorder for the same reason. Premarital sexual relations are condemned because they often exclude the prospect of children, and even if children are produced, they will be deprived of a proper and stable environment.

In the second reading, Alan Goldman presents a different view of sex. To begin with, he rejects the "means-end analysis" of sex that sees sex as merely a means to some end such as reproduction. Instead, Goldman proposes the idea of "plain sex" —that is, sex that is not a means to some further end such as reproduction, communication, or the expression of love, but is simply the satisfaction of sexual desire. As Goldman defines it, sexual desire is simply the desire for contact with another person's body and for the pleasure such contact produces, and not the desire to reproduce, to communicate, or to express love. Given this account of sex, masturbation is not really sex at all; rather it is just an imaginary substitute for sex. But nongenital activities such as kissing, embracing, or massaging can be sexual on Goldman's view if they satisfy sexual desire as he defines it. As for homosexuality, Goldman would agree that it is a sexual perversion, but for him this just means that it is statistically abnormal, and not that it is morally wrong. In general, Goldman thinks that sexuality has no intrinsic morality; sexual behavior, like any other behavior, has to be morally evaluated in terms of moral principles, such as Kant's principle of reciprocity.

In sharp contrast to Goldman, John Finnis argues that homosexuality and masturbation are intrinsically immoral because they involve treating one's body as an instrument. This disintegrates oneself by treating the body as a mere instrument of the self and by making the choosing self a quasi slave of the experiencing self. Furthermore, this behavior is worthless because it does not actualize a real common good, namely, marriage, with its double blessing of procreation and friendship. In addition, it is deeply hostile to the self-understanding of members of the community who are committed to real marriage, with its shared responsibilities. For these reasons, Finnis thinks that the political community should do whatever it can to discourage such conduct.

In her reply to Finnis, Martha Nussbaum objects to his characterization of homosexual acts as only selfish or manipulative. After describing the celebration of male-male love in the dialogues of Plato and the writings of Aristotle, she asserts that male-male sexual relationships can produce love and friendship, undeniably important human goods. She complains that Finnis assumes without any argument or evidence that homosexual acts aim only at casual bodily pleasure rather than love or friendship, that procreative relationships cannot be selfish or manipulative, and that the only sort of community a sexual relationship can produce is a procreative one.

Goldman says that rape is always immoral because it violates the general moral prohibition against using other persons against their wills. It seems to follow that consensual sex is not wrong; at least it does not violate this moral prohibition. Finnis believes that consensual heterosexual sex in the context of marriage is good, since it can result in the goods of children and friendship. The Vatican Declaration also approves of heterosexual consensual sex between married people. In the last reading for the chapter, Robin West challenges this standard view of heterosexual consensual sex. She argues that such sex is frequently harmful to women. She thinks it injures a woman's self-assertiveness, her sense of self-possession, her autonomy, and her integrity. These harms are often unnoticed or not taken seriously for two reasons. First, they tend to have an effect on women such that they do not experience the harms as harmful or painful. Second, the feminist campaigns against rape seem to imply that if a woman is not raped, if she consents to sex, then she is not harmed.

Philosophical Issues

What counts as sex? This is a basic issue raised by the readings. The Vatican Declaration seems to assume that only genital sex counts; it speaks about "genital acts" and ignores nongenital acts, such as kissing or embracing. Goldman thinks that nongenital acts can satisfy a sexual desire as he defines it; indeed, he believes that the baby's desire to be cuddled is a sexual desire. But oddly enough, it seems that reproductive sex that is done solely because of the desire to procreate, and not because of any desire for contact with another person's body or any desire for the pleasure produced, would *not* be sexual, on Goldman's view.

What counts as sexual perversion? This is a related issue that comes up in the readings. The view of the Vatican Declaration seems to be that nonreproductive sex, such as masturbation and homosexual acts, is a perversion, and the fact that masturbation is statistically normal is irrelevant. Does this mean that kissing is a perversion because it is nonreproductive? What about sex between married couples who are infertile? On Goldman's view, what is sexually perverse is what is statistically abnormal. It seems to follow that masturbation is not perverse; it is normal. But reproductive sex in an unusual position would be perverse because it is statistically abnormal.

Are sexual perversions morally wrong? Goldman does not think so, since in his view the concept of sexual perversion is merely statistical, not evaluative. What is sexually perverse is what is statistically abnormal, but this does not mean that it is immoral. The Vatican Declaration has a different view; perversion involves unnaturalness, and what is unnatural is wrong. Homosexuality and masturbation are unnatural in that they contradict the finality or natural purpose of sex, which is reproduction, and for that reason they are not just wrong but also serious disorders.

But is reproduction the natural purpose of sex? Goldman agrees that this may be "nature's purpose," but he denies that it is always or usually our purpose. He mentions the analogy with eating. The natural purpose of eating may be nourishment, but that is not always our purpose in eating; we eat for enjoyment too. Similarly, the natural purpose of sex may be reproduction, but that is not always our goal; we usually have sex for enjoyment. Indeed, on Goldman's analysis sexual desire is the desire for contact with another person's body and for the pleasure produced; it is different from the desire for reproduction. Sexual activity satisfies sexual desire, a desire that is different from the desire to reproduce.

Declaration on Sexual Ethics

THE VATICAN

The Declaration on Sexual Ethics was issued in Rome by the Sacred Congregation for the Doctrine of the Faith on December 29, 1975.

The authors defend the Christian doctrine that "every genital act must be within the framework of marriage." Premarital sex, masturbation, and homosexuality are specifically condemned, and chastity is recommended as a virtue.

1. According to contemporary scientific research, the human person is so profoundly affected by sexuality that it must be considered as one of the factors which give to each individual's life the principal traits that distinguish it. In fact it is from sex that the human person receives the characteristics which, on the biological, psychological and spiritual levels, make that person a man or a woman, and thereby largely condition his or her progress towards maturity and insertion into society. Hence sexual matters, as is obvious to everyone, today constitute a theme frequently and openly dealt with in books, reviews, magazines, and other means of social communication.

In the present period, the corruption of morals has increased, and one of the most serious indications of this corruption is the unbridled exaltation of sex. Moreover, through the means of social communication and through public entertainment this corruption has reached the point of invading the field of education and of infecting the general mentality.

In this context certain educators, teachers, and moralists have been able to contribute to a better understanding and integration into life of the values proper to each of the sexes; on the other hand there are those who have put forward concepts and modes of behavior which are contrary to the true moral exigencies of the human person. Some members of the latter group have even gone so far as to favor a licentious hedonism.

As a result, in the course of a few years, teachings, moral criteria, and modes of living hitherto faithfully preserved have been very much unsettled, even among Christians. There are many people today who, being confronted

Source: The Vatican, "Declaration on Sexual Ethics."

with so many widespread opinions opposed to the teachings which they received from the Church, have come to wonder what they must still hold as true.

2. The Church cannot remain indifferent to this confusion of minds and relaxation of morals. It is a question, in fact, of a matter which is of the utmost importance both for the personal lives of Christians and for the social life of our time.[1]

The Bishops are daily led to note the growing difficulties experienced by the faithful in obtaining knowledge of wholesome moral teaching, especially in sexual matters, and of the growing difficulties experienced by pastors in expounding this teaching effectively. The Bishops know that by their pastoral charge they are called upon to meet the needs of their faithful in this very serious matter, and important documents dealing with it have already been published by some of them or by Episcopal Conferences. Nevertheless, since the erroneous opinions and resulting deviations are continuing to spread everywhere, the Sacred Congregation for the Doctrine of the Faith, by virtue of its function in the universal Church[2] and by a mandate of the Supreme Pontiff, has judged it necessary to publish the present Declaration.

3. The people of our time are more and more convinced that the human person's dignity and vocation demand that they should discover, by the light of their own intelligence, the values innate in their nature, that they should ceaselessly develop these values and realize them in their lives, in order to achieve an ever greater development.

In moral matters man cannot make value judgments according to his personal whim: "In the depths of his conscience, man detects a law which he does not impose on himself, but which holds him to obedience. . . . For man has in his heart a law written by God. To obey it is the very dignity of man; according to it he will be judged."[3]

Moreover, through his revelation God has made known to us Christians his plan of salvation, and he has held up to us Christ, the Saviour and Sanctifier, in his teaching and example, as the supreme and immutable law of life: "I am the light of the world; anyone who follows me will not be walking in the dark, he will have the light of life."[4]

Therefore there can be no true promotion of man's dignity unless the essential order of his nature is respected. Of course, in the history of civilization many of the concrete conditions and needs of human life have changed and will continue to change. But all evolution of morals and every type of life must be kept within the limits imposed by the immutable principles based upon every human person's constitutive elements and essential relations—elements and relations which transcend historical contingency.

These fundamental principles, which can be grasped by reason, are contained in "the divine law—eternal, objective, and universal—whereby God orders, directs, and governs the entire universe and all the ways of the human community, by a plan conceived in wisdom and love. Man has been made by God to participate in this law, with the result that, under the gentle disposition of divine Providence, he can come to perceive ever increasingly the unchanging truth."[5] This divine law is accessible to our minds.

4. Hence, those many people are in error who today assert that one can find neither in human nature nor in the revealed law any ab-

---

1 See Vatican II, *Pastoral Constitution on the Church in the World of Today*, no. 47: *Acta Apostolicae Sedis* 58 (1966) 1067 [*The Pope Speaks* XI, 289—290].

2 See the Apostolic Constitution *Regimini Ecclesiae Universae* (August 15, 1967), no. 29: *AAS* 59 (1967) 897 [*TPS* XII, 401–402].

3 *Pastoral Constitution on the Church in the World of Today*, no. 16: *AAS* 58 (1966) 1037 [*TPS* XI, 268].

4 *Jn* 8, 12.

5 *Declaration on Religious Freedom*, no. 3: *AAS* 58 (1966) 931 [*TPS* XI, 86].

solute and immutable norm to serve for particular actions other than the one which expresses itself in the general law of charity and respect for human dignity. As a proof of their assertion they put forward the view that so-called norms of the natural law or precepts of Sacred Scripture are to be regarded only as given expressions of a form of particular culture at a certain moment of history.

But in fact, divine Revelation and, in its own proper order, philosophical wisdom, emphasize the authentic exigencies of human nature. They thereby necessarily manifest the existence of immutable laws inscribed in the constitutive elements of human nature and which are revealed to be identical in all beings endowed with reason.

Furthermore, Christ instituted his Church as "the pillar and bulwark of truth."[6] With the Holy Spirit's assistance, she ceaselessly preserves and transmits without error the truths of the moral order, and she authentically interprets not only the revealed positive law but "also . . . those principles of the moral order which have their origin in human nature itself"[7] and which concern man's full development and sanctification. Now in fact the Church throughout her history has always considered a certain number of precepts of the natural law as having an absolute and immutable value, and in their transgression she has seen a contradiction of the teaching and spirit of the Gospel.

5. Since sexual ethics concern certain fundamental values of human and Christian life, this general teaching equally applies to sexual ethics.

In this domain there exist principles and norms which the Church has always unhesitatingly transmitted as part of her teaching, however much the opinions and morals of the world may have been opposed to them. These principles and norms in no way owe their origin to a certain type of culture, but rather to knowledge of the divine law and of human nature. They therefore cannot be considered as having become out of date or doubtful under the pretext that a new cultural situation has arisen.

It is these principles which inspired the exhortations and directives given by the Second Vatican Council for an education and an organization of social life taking account of the equal dignity of man and woman while respecting their difference.[8]

Speaking of "the sexual nature of man and the human faculty of procreation," the Council noted that they "wonderfully exceed the dispositions of lower forms of life."[9] It then took particular care to expound the principles and criteria which concern human sexuality in marriage, and which are based upon the finality of the specific function of sexuality.

In this regard the Council declares that the moral goodness of the acts proper to conjugal life, acts which are ordered according to true human dignity, "does not depend solely on sincere intentions or on an evaluation of motives. It must be determined by objective standards. These, based on the nature of the human person and his acts, preserve the full sense of mutual self-giving and human procreation in the context of true love."[10]

6 1 *Tm* 3, 15.
7 *Declaration on Religious Freedom,* no. 14: *AAS* 58 (1966) 940 [*TPS* XI, 93]. See also Pius XI, Encyclical *Casti Connubii* (December 31, 1930): *AAS* 22 (1930) 579–580; Pius XII, Address of November 2, 1954 *AAS* 46 (1954) 671–672 [*TPS* I 380–381]; John XXIII, Encyclical *Mater et Magistra* (May 25, 1961), no. 239: *AAS* 53 (1961) 457 [*TPS* VII, 388]; Paul VI, Encyclical *Humanae Vitae* (July 25, 1968), no. 4: *AAS* 60 (1968) 483 [*TPS* XIII, 331–332].

8 See Vatican II, *Declaration on Christian Education,* nos. 1 and 8: *AAS* 58 (1966) 729–730, 734–736 [*TPS* XI, 201–202, 206–207]; *Pastoral Constitution on the Church in the World of Today,* nos. 29, 60, 67: *AAS* 58 (1966) 1048–1049, 1080–181, 1088–1089 [*TPS* XI, 276–277, 299–300, 304–305].
9 *Pastoral Constitution on the Church in the World of Today,* no. 51: *AAS* 58 (1966) 1072 [*TPS* XI, 293].
10 *Loc. cit.;* see also no. 49: *AAS* 58 (1966) 1069–1070 [*TPS* XI, 291–292].

These final words briefly sum up the Council's teaching—more fully expounded in an earlier part of the same Constitution[11]—on the finality of the sexual act and on the principal criterion of its morality: it is respect for its finality that ensures the moral goodness of this act.

This same principle, which the Church holds from divine Revelation and from her authentic interpretation of the natural law, is also the basis of her traditional doctrine, which states that the use of the sexual function has its true meaning and moral rectitude only in true marriage."[12]

6. It is not the purpose of the present declaration to deal with all the abuses of the sexual faculty, nor with all the elements involved in the practice of chastity. Its object is rather to repeat the Church's doctrine on certain particular points, in view of the urgent need to oppose serious errors and widespread aberrant modes of behavior.

7. Today there are many who vindicate the right to sexual union before marriage, at least in those cases where a firm intention to marry and an affection which is already in some way conjugal in the psychology of the subjects require this completion, which they judge to be connatural. This is especially the case when the celebration of the marriage is impeded by circumstances or when this intimate relationship seems necessary in order for love to be preserved.

This opinion is contrary to Christian doctrine, which states that every genital act must be within the framework of marriage. However firm the intention of those who practice such premature sexual relations may be, the fact remains that these relations cannot ensure, in sincerity and fidelity, the interpersonal relationship between a man and a woman, nor especially can they protect this relationship from whims and caprices. Now it is a stable union that Jesus

willed, and he restored its original requirement, beginning with the sexual difference. "Have you not read that the creator from the beginning made them male and female and that he said: This is why a man must leave father and mother, and cling to his wife, and the two become one body? They are no longer two, therefore, but one body. So then, what God has united, man must not divide."[13] Saint Paul will be even more explicit when he shows that if unmarried people or widows cannot live chastely they have no other alternative than the stable union of marriage: ". . . it is better to marry than to be aflame with passion."[14] Through marriage, in fact, the love of married people is taken up into that love which Christ irrevocably has for the Church,[15] while dissolute sexual union[16] defiles the temple of the Holy Spirit which the Christian has become. Sexual union therefore is only legitimate if a definitive community of life has been established between the man and the woman.

This is what the Church has always understood and taught,[17] and she finds a profound agreement with her doctrine in men's reflection and in the lessons of history.

Experience teaches us that love must find its safeguard in the stability of marriage, if sexual intercourse is truly to respond to the requirements of its own finality and to those of human dignity. These requirements call for a conjugal contract sanctioned and guaranteed by society —a contract which establishes a state of life of capital importance both for the exclusive union of the man and the woman and for the good of their family and of the human community. Most

---

11 See *Pastoral Constitution on the Church in the World of Today*, nos. 49–50: *AAS* 58 (1966) 1069–1072 [*TPS* XI, 291–293].

12 The present Declaration does not review all the moral norms for the use of sex, since they have already been set forth in the encyclicals *Casti Connubii* and *Humanae Vitae*.

13 *Mt 19*, 4–6.

14 1 *Cor 7*, 9.

15 See *Eph 5*, 25–32.

16 Extramarital intercourse is expressly condemned in 1 *Cor* 5, 1; 6, 9; 7, 2; 10, 8; *Eph* 5, 5–7; 1 *Tm* 1, 10; *Heb* 13, 4; there are explicit arguments given in 1 *Cor* 6, 12–20.

17 See Innocent IV, Letter *Sub Catholicae professione* (March 6, 1254) (*DS* 835); Pius II, Letter *Cum sicut accepimus* (November 14, 1459) (*DS* 1367); Decrees of the Holy Office on September 24, 1665 (*DS* 2045) and March 2, 1679 (*DS* 2148); Pius XI, Encyclical *Casti Conubii* (December 31, 1930): *AAS* 22 (1930) 538–539.

often, in fact, premarital relations exclude the possibility of children. What is represented to be conjugal love is not able, as it absolutely should be, to develop into paternal and maternal love. Or, if it does happen to do so, this will be to the detriment of the children, who will be deprived of the stable environment in which they ought to develop in order to find in it the way and the means of their insertion into society as a whole.

The consent given by people who wish to be united in marriage must therefore be manifested externally and in a manner which makes it valid in the eyes of society. As far as the faithful are concerned, their consent to the setting up of a community of conjugal life must be expressed according to the laws of the Church. It is a consent which makes their marriage a Sacrament of Christ.

8. At the present time there are those who, basing themselves on observations in the psychological order, have begun to judge indulgently, and even to excuse completely, homosexual relations between certain people. This they do in opposition to the constant teaching of the Magisterium and to the moral sense of the Christian people.

A distinction is drawn, and it seems with some reason, between homosexuals whose tendency comes from a false education, from a lack of normal sexual development, from habit, from bad example, or from other similar causes, and is transitory or at least not incurable; and homosexuals who are definitively such because of some kind of innate instinct or a pathological constitution judged to be incurable.

In regard to this second category of subjects, some people conclude that their tendency is so natural that it justifies in their case homosexual relations within a sincere communion of life and love analogous to marriage insofar as such homosexuals feel incapable of enduring a solitary life.

In the pastoral field, these homosexuals must certainly be treated with understanding and sustained in the hope of overcoming their personal difficulties and their inability to fit into society.

Their culpability will be judged with prudence. But no pastoral method can be employed which would give moral justification to these acts on the grounds that they would be consonant with the condition of such people. For according to the objective moral order, homosexual relations are acts which lack an essential and indispensable finality. In Sacred Scripture they are condemned as a serious depravity and even presented as the sad consequence of rejecting God.[18] This judgment of Scripture does not of course permit us to conclude that all those who suffer from this anomaly are personally responsible for it, but it does attest to the fact that homosexual acts are intrinsically disordered and can in no case be approved.

9. The traditional Catholic doctrine that masturbation constitutes a grave moral disorder is often called into doubt or expressly denied today. It is said that psychology and sociology show that it is a normal phenomenon of sexual development, especially among the young. It is stated that there is real and serious fault only in the measure that the subject deliberately indulges in solitary pleasure closed in on self ("ipsation"), because in this case the act would indeed be radically opposed to the loving communion between persons of different sex which some hold is what is principally sought in the use of the sexual faculty.

This opinion is contradictory to the teaching and pastoral practice of the Catholic Church. Whatever the force of certain arguments of a biological and philosophical nature, which have sometimes been used by theologians, in fact

18 *Rom* 1:24–27: "in consequence, God delivered them up in their lusts to unclean practices; they engaged in the mutual degradation of their bodies, these men who exchanged the truth of God for a lie and worshipped and served the creature rather than the Creator—blessed be he forever, amen! God therefore delivered them to disgraceful passions. Their women exchanged natural intercourse for unnatural, and the men gave up natural intercourse with women and burned with lust for one another. Men did shameful things with men, and thus received in their own persons the penalty for their perversity." See also what St. Paul says of sodomy in 1 *Cor* 6, 9; 1 *Tm* 1, 10.

both the Magisterium of the Church—in the course of a constant tradition—and the moral sense of the faithful have declared without hesitation that masturbation is an intrinsically and seriously disordered act."[19] The main reason is that, whatever the motive for acting in this way, the deliberate use of the sexual faculty outside normal conjugal relations essentially contradicts the finality of the faculty. For it lacks the sexual relationship called for by the moral order, namely the relationship which realizes "the full sense of mutual self-giving and human procreation in the context of true love." [20] All deliberate exercise of sexuality must be reserved to this regular relationship. Even if it cannot be proved that Scripture condemns this sin by name, the tradition of the Church has rightly understood it to be condemned in the New Testament when the latter speaks of "impurity," "unchasteness," and other vices contrary to chastity and continence.

Sociological surveys are able to show the frequency of this disorder according to the places, populations, or circumstances studied. In this way facts are discovered, but facts do not constitute a criterion for judging the moral value of human acts.[21] The frequency of the phenomenon in question is certainly to be linked with man's innate weakness following original sin; but it is also to be linked with the loss of a sense of God, with the corruption of morals engendered by the commercialization of vice, with the unrestrained licentiousness of so many public entertainments and publications, as well as with the neglect of modesty, which is the guardian of chastity.

On the subject of masturbation modern psychology provides much valid and useful information for formulating a more equitable judgment on moral responsibility and for orienting pastoral action. Psychology helps one to see how the immaturity of adolescence (which can sometimes persist after that age), psychological imbalance, or habit can influence behavior, diminishing the deliberate character of the act and bringing about a situation whereby subjectively there may not always be serious fault. But in general, the absence of serious responsibility must not be presumed; this would be to misunderstand people's moral capacity.

In the pastoral ministry, in order to form an adequate judgment in concrete cases, the habitual behavior of people will be considered in its totality, not only with regard to the individual's practice of charity and of justice but also with regard to the individual's care in observing the particular precepts of chastity. In particular, one will have to examine whether the individual is using the necessary means, both natural and supernatural, which Christian asceticism from its long experience recommends for overcoming passions and progressing in virtue. . . .

19 See Leo IX, Letter *Ad splendidum nitentes* (1054) (*DS* 687–688); Decree of the Holy Office on March 2, 1679 (*DS* 2149); Pius XII, Addresses of October 8, 1953: *AAS* 45 (1953) 677–678, and May 19, 1956: *AAS* 48 (1956) 472–473.

20 *Pastoral Constitution on the Church in the World of Today*, no. 51: *AAS* 58 (1966) 1072 [*TPS* XI, 2931.]

21 See Paul VI, Apostolic Exhortation *Quinque iam anni* (December 8, 1970): *AAS* 63 (1971) 102 [*TPS* XV, 329]: "If sociological surveys are useful for better discovering the thought patterns of the people of a particular place, the anxieties and needs of those to whom we proclaim the word of God, and also the oppositions made to it by modern reasoning through the widespread notion that outside science there exists no legitimate form of knowledge, still the conclusions drawn from such surveys could not of themselves constitute a determining criterion of truth."

Review Questions

1. What is the traditional Christian doctrine about sex, according to the declaration?
2. Why does the declaration find premarital sexual relations to be immoral?
3. What is the declaration's objection to homosexuality?
4. What is wrong with masturbation, according to the declaration?

Discussion Questions

1. Is celibacy a violation of natural law? Explain your view.
2. Is contraception wrong too? Defend your answer.
3. Is procreation the only natural purpose of sex? Defend your position.

Plain Sex

ALAN H. GOLDMAN

Alan H. Goldman is professor of philosophy at the University of Miami, Coral Gables, Florida. Goldman defines sexual desire as the desire for contact with another person's body and for the pleasure such contact produces. Plain Sex fulfills sexual desire without being used to satisfy some other goal, such as reproduction. He attacks what he calls the "means-end" analysis of sex that requires sex to be a means to some further end, such as reproduction, expression of love, or communication. Furthermore, he claims that there is nothing intrinsically moral or immoral about sex; it should be evaluated like any other behavior—for example, by a Kantian principle of reciprocity. There is a distinction between normal and perverted sex, but this distinction is just a matter of statistics and has no moral significance.

I

SEVERAL RECENT ARTICLES on sex herald its acceptance as a legitimate topic for analytic philosophers (although it has been a topic in

Source: Alan Goldman, "Plain Sex," from *Philosophy & Public Affairs,* Vol. 6, No. 3 (Spring 1977). Copyright © 1977 by Princeton University Press. Reprinted by permission of Princeton University Press.

philosophy since Plato). One might have thought conceptual analysis unnecessary in this area; despite the notorious struggles of judges and legislators to define pornography suitably, we all might be expected to know what sex is and to be able to identify at least paradigm sexual desires and activities without much difficulty. Philosophy is nevertheless of relevance here if for no other reason than that the concept of sex remains at the center of moral and social consciousness in our, and perhaps any, society. Before we can get a sensible view of the relation of sex to morality, perversion, social regulation, and marriage, we require a sensible analysis of the concept itself; one which neither understates its animal pleasure nor overstates its importance within a theory or system of value. I say "before," but the order is not quite so clear, for questions in this area, as elsewhere in moral philosophy, are both conceptual and normative at the same time. Our concept of sex will partially determine our moral view of it, but as philosophers we should formulate a concept that will accord with its proper moral status. What we require here, as elsewhere, is "reflective equilibrium," a goal not achieved by traditional and recent analyses together with their moral implications. Because sexual activity, like other natural functions such as eating or exercising, has become imbedded in layers of cultural, moral, and superstitious superstructure, it is hard to conceive it in its simplest terms. But partially for this reason, it is only by thinking about plain sex that we can begin to achieve this conceptual equilibrium.

I shall suggest here that sex continues to be misrepresented in recent writings, at least in philosophical writings, and I shall criticize the predominant form of analysis which I term "means-end analysis." Such conceptions attribute a necessary external goal or purpose to sexual activity, whether it be reproduction, the expression of love, simple communication, or interpersonal awareness. They analyze sexual activity as a means to one of these ends, implying that sexual desire is a desire to reproduce, to love or be loved, or to communicate with others. All definitions of this type suggest false views of the relation of sex to perversion and morality by implying that sex which does not fit one of these models or fulfill one of these functions is in some way deviant or incomplete.

The alternative, simpler analysis with which I will begin is that sexual desire is desire for contact with another person's body and for the pleasure which such contact produces; sexual activity is activity which tends to fulfill such desire of the agent. Whereas Aristotle and Butler were correct in holding that pleasure is normally a byproduct rather than a goal of purposeful action, in the case of sex this is not so clear. The desire for another's body is, principally among other things, the desire for the pleasure that physical contact brings. On the other hand, it is not a desire for a particular sensation detachable from its causal context, a sensation which can be derived in other ways. This definition in terms of the general goal of sexual desire appears preferable to an attempt to more explicitly list or define specific sexual activities, for many activities such as kissing, embracing, massaging, or holding hands may or may not be sexual, depending upon the context and more specifically upon the purposes, needs, or desires into which such activities fit. The generality of the definition also represents a refusal (common in recent psychological texts) to overemphasize orgasm as the goal of sexual desire or genital sex as the only norm of sexual activity (this will be hedged slightly in the discussion of perversion below).

Central to the definition is the fact that the goal of sexual desire and activity is the physical contact itself, rather than something else which this contact might express. By contrast, what I term "means-end analyses" posit ends which I take to be extraneous to plain sex, and they view sex as a means to these ends. Their fault lies not in defining sex in terms of its general goal, but in seeing plain sex as merely a means to other separable ends. I term these "means-end analyses" for convenience, although "means-separable-end analyses," while too cumbersome, might be more fully explanatory. The desire for physical contact with another person is a minimal criterion for (normal) sexual desire, but is both necessary and sufficient to qualify normal desire as sexual. Of course, we may want to express other feelings through sexual acts in various contexts; but without the desire for the physical contact in and for itself, or when it is sought for other reasons, activities in which contact is involved are not predominantly sexual. Furthermore, the desire for physical contact in itself, without the wish to express affection or other feelings through it, is sufficient to render sexual the activity of the agent which fulfills it. Various activities with this goal alone, such as kissing and caressing in certain contexts, qualify as sexual even without the presence of genital symptoms of sexual excitement. The latter are not therefore necessary criteria for sexual activity.

This initial analysis may seem to some either over- or underinclusive. It might seem too broad in leading us to interpret physical contact as sexual desire in activities such as football and other contact sports. In these cases, however, the desire is not for contact with another body per se, it is not directed toward a particular person for that purpose, and it is not the goal of the activity—the goal is winning or exercising or knocking someone down or displaying one's prowess. If the desire is purely for contact with another specific person's body, then to interpret it as sexual does not seem an exaggeration. A slightly more difficult case is that of a baby's desire to be cuddled and our natural response in wanting to cuddle it. In the case of the baby, the desire may be simply for the physical contact, for the pleasure of the caresses. If so, we may characterize this desire, especially in keeping with Freudian theory, as sexual or protosexual. It will differ nevertheless from full-fledged sexual desire in being more amorphous, not directed outward toward another specific person's body. It may also be that what the infant unconsciously desires is not physical contact per se but signs of affection, tenderness, or security, in which case we have further reason for hesitating to characterize its wants as clearly sexual. The intent of our response to the baby is often the showing of affection, not the pure physical contact, so that our definition in terms of action which fulfills sexual desire *on the part of the agent* does not capture such actions, whatever we say of the baby. (If it is intuitive to characterize our response as sexual as well, there is clearly no problem here for my analysis.) The same can be said of signs of affection (or in some cultures polite greeting) among men or women: these certainly need not be homosexual when the intent is only to show friendship, something extrinsic to plain sex although valuable when added to it.

Our definition of sex in terms of the desire for physical contact may appear too narrow in that a person's personality, not merely her or his body, may be sexually attractive to another, and in that looking or conversing in a certain way can be sexual in a given context without bodily contact. Nevertheless, it is not the contents of one's thoughts per se that are sexually appealing, but one's personality as embodied in certain manners of behavior. Furthermore, if a person is sexually attracted by another's personality, he or she will desire not just further conversation, but actual sexual contact. While looking at or conversing with someone can be interpreted as sexual in given contexts it is so when intended as preliminary to, and hence parasitic upon, elemental sexual interest. Voyeurism or viewing a pornographic movie qualifies as a sexual activity, but only as an imaginative substitute for the real thing (otherwise a deviation from the norm as expressed in our definition). The same is true of masturbation as a sexual activity without a partner.

That the initial definition indicates at least an ingredient of sexual desire and activity is too obvious to argue. We all know what sex is, at least in obvious cases, and do not need philosophers to tell us. My preliminary analysis is meant to serve as a contrast to what sex is not, at least, not necessarily. I concentrate upon the physically manifested desire for another's body, and I take as central the immersion in the physical aspect of one's own existence and attention to the physical embodiment of the other. One may derive pleasure in a sex act from expressing certain feelings to one's partner or from awareness of the attitude of one's partner, but sexual desire is essentially desire for physical contact itself: it is a bodily desire for the body of another that dominates our mental life for more or less brief periods. Traditional writings were correct to emphasize the purely physical or animal aspect of sex; they were wrong only in condemning it. This characterization of sex as an intensely pleasurable physical activity and acute physical desire may seem to some to capture only its barest level. But it is worth distinguishing and focusing upon this least common denominator in order to avoid the false views of sexual morality and perversion which emerge from thinking that sex is essentially something else.

II

We may turn then to what sex is not, to the arguments regarding supposed conceptual connections between sex and other activities which it is necessary to conceptually distinguish. The most comprehensible attempt to build an extraneous purpose into the sex act identifies that purpose as reproduction, its primary biological function. While this may be "nature's" purpose, it certainly need not be ours (the analogy with eating, while sometimes overworked, is pertinent here). While this identification may once have had a rational basis which also grounded the identification of the value and morality of sex with that applicable to reproduction and childrearing, the development of contraception rendered the connection weak. Methods of contraception are by now so familiar and so widely used that it is not necessary to dwell upon the changes wrought by these developments in the concept of sex itself and in a rational sexual ethic dependent upon that concept. In the past, the ever present possibility of children rendered the concepts of sex and sexual morality different from those required at present. There may be good reasons, if the presence and care of both mother and father are beneficial to children, for restricting reproduction to marriage. Insofar as society has a legitimate role in protecting children's interests, it may be justified in giving marriage a legal status, although this question is complicated by the fact (among others) that children born to single mothers deserve no

penalties. In any case, the point here is simply that these questions are irrelevant at the present time to those regarding the morality of sex and its potential social regulation. (Further connections with marriage will be discussed below.)

It is obvious that the desire for sex is not necessarily a desire to reproduce, that the psychological manifestation has become, if it were not always, distinct from its biological roots. There are many parallels, as previously mentioned, with other natural functions. The pleasures of eating and exercising are to a large extent independent of their roles in nourishment or health (as the junk-food industry discovered with a vengeance). Despite the obvious parallel with sex, there is still a tendency for many to think that sex acts which can be reproductive are, if not more moral or less immoral, at least more natural. These categories of morality and "naturalness," or normality, are not to be identified with each other, as will be argued below, and neither is applicable to sex by virtue of its connection to reproduction. The tendency to identify reproduction as the conceptually connected end of sex is most prevalent now in the pronouncements of the Catholic church. There the assumed analysis is clearly tied to a restrictive sexual morality according to which acts become immoral and unnatural when they are not oriented towards reproduction, a morality which has independent roots in the Christian sexual ethic as it derives from Paul. However, the means-end analysis fails to generate a consistent sexual ethic: homosexual and oral-genital sex is condemned while kissing or caressing, acts equally unlikely to lead in themselves to fertilization, even when properly characterized as sexual according to our definition, are not.

III

Before discussing further relations of means-end analyses to false or inconsistent sexual ethics and concepts of perversion, I turn to other examples of these analyses. One common position views sex as essentially an expression of love or affection between the partners. It is generally recognized that there are other types of love besides sexual, but sex itself is taken as an expression of one type, sometimes termed "romantic" love.[1] Various factors again ought to weaken this identification. First, there are other types of love besides that which it is appropriate to express sexually, and "romantic" love itself can be expressed in many other ways. I am not denying that sex can take on heightened value and meaning when it becomes a vehicle for the expression of feelings of love or tenderness, but so can many other usually mundane activities such as getting up early to make breakfast on Sunday, cleaning the house, and so on. Second, sex itself can be used to communicate many other emotions besides love, and, as I will argue below, can communicate nothing in particular and still be good sex.

On a deeper level, an internal tension is bound to result from an identification of sex, which I have described as a physical-psychological desire, with love as a long-term, deep emotional relationship between two individuals. As this type of relationship, love is permanent, at least in intent, and more or less exclusive. A normal person cannot deeply love more than a few individuals even in a lifetime. We may be suspicious that those who attempt or claim to love many love them weakly if at all. Yet, fleeting sexual desire can arise in relation to a variety of other individuals one finds sexually attractive. It may even be, as some have claimed, that sexual desire in humans naturally seeks variety, while this is obviously false of love. For this reason, monogamous sex, even if justified, almost always represents a sacrifice or the exercise of self-control on the part of the spouses, while monogamous love generally does not. There is no such thing as casual love in the

sense in which I intend the term "love." It may occasionally happen that a spouse falls deeply in love with someone else (especially when sex is conceived in terms of love), but this is relatively rare in comparison to passing sexual desires for others; and while the former often indicates a weakness or fault in the marriage relation, the latter does not.

If love is indeed more exclusive in its objects than is sexual desire, this explains why those who view sex as essentially an expression of love would again tend to hold a repressive or restrictive sexual ethic. As in the case of reproduction, there may be good reasons for reserving the total commitment of deep love to the context of marriage and family—the normal personality may not withstand additional divisions of ultimate commitment and allegiance. There is no question that marriage itself is best sustained by a deep relation of love and affection; and even if love is not naturally monogamous, the benefits of family units to children provide additional reason to avoid serious commitments elsewhere which weaken family ties. It can be argued similarly that monogamous sex strengthens families by restricting and at the same time guaranteeing an outlet for sexual desire in marriage. But there is more force to the argument that recognition of a clear distinction between sex and love in society would help avoid disastrous marriages which result from adolescent confusion of the two when sexual desire is mistaken for permanent love, and would weaken damaging jealousies which arise in marriages in relation to passing sexual desires. The love and affection of a sound marriage certainly differs from the adolescent romantic variety, which is often a mere substitute for sex in the context of a repressive sexual ethic.

In fact, the restrictive sexual ethic tied to the means-end analysis in terms of love again has failed to be consistent. At least, it has not been applied consistently, but forms part of the double standard which has curtailed the freedom of women. It is predictable in light of this history that some women would now advocate using

---

1 Even Bertrand Russell, whose writing in this area was a model of rationality, at least for its period, tends to make this identification and to condemn plain sex in the absence of love: "sex intercourse apart from love has little value, and is to be regarded primarily as experimentation with a view to love." *Marriage and Morals* (New York: Bantam, 1959), p. 87.

sex as another kind of means, as a political weapon or as a way to increase unjustly denied power and freedom. The inconsistency in the sexual ethic typically attached to the sex-love analysis, according to which it has generally been taken with a grain of salt when applied to men, is simply another example of the impossibility of tailoring a plausible moral theory in this area to a conception of sex which builds in conceptually extraneous factors.

I am not suggesting here that sex ought never to be connected with love or that it is not a more significant and valuable activity when it is. Nor am I denying that individuals need love as much as sex and perhaps emotionally need at least one complete relationship which encompasses both. Just as sex can express love and take on heightened significance when it does, so love is often naturally accompanied by an intermittent desire for sex. But again love is accompanied appropriately by desires for other shared activities as well. What makes the desire for sex seem more intimately connected with love is the intimacy which is seen to be a natural feature of mutual sex acts. Like love, sex is held to lay one bare psychologically as well as physically. Sex is unquestionably intimate, but beyond that the psychological toll often attached may be a function of the restrictive sexual ethic itself, rather than a legitimate apology for it. The intimacy involved in love is psychologically consuming in a generally healthy way, while the psychological tolls of sexual relations, often including embarrassment as a correlate of intimacy, are too often the result of artificial sexual ethics and taboos. The intimacy involved in both love and sex is insufficient in any case in light of previous points to render a means-end analysis in these terms appropriate.

IV

In recent articles, Thomas Nagel and Robert Solomon, who recognize that sex is not merely a means to communicate love, nevertheless re-

tain the form of this analysis while broadening it. For Solomon, sex remains a means of communicating (he explicitly uses the metaphor of body language), although the feelings that can be communicated now include, in addition to love and tenderness, domination, dependence, anger, trust, and so on.[2] Nagel does not refer explicitly to communication, but his analysis is similar in that he views sex as a complex form of interpersonal awareness in which desire itself is consciously communicated on several different levels. In sex, according to his analysis, two people are aroused by each other, aware of the other's arousal, and further aroused by this awareness.[3] Such multileveled conscious awareness of one's own and the other's desire is taken as the norm of a sexual relation, and this model is therefore close to that which views sex as a means of interpersonal communication.

Solomon's analysis is beset by the same difficulties as those pointed out in relation to the narrower sex-love concept. Just as love can be communicated by many activities other than sex, which do not therefore become properly analyzed as essentially vehicles of communication (making breakfast, cleaning the house, and so on), the same is true of the other feelings mentioned by Solomon. Domination can be communicated through economic manipulation, trust by a joint savings account. Driving a car can be simultaneously expressing anger, pride, joy, and so on. We may, in fact, communicate or express feelings in anything we do, but this does not make everything we do into language. Driving a car is not to be defined as an automotive means of communication, although with a little ingenuity we might work out an automotive vocabulary (tailgating as an expression of aggression or impatience; beating another car away from a stoplight as expressing domination)

2 Robert Solomon, "Sex and Perversion" *Philosophy and Sex,* ed. R. Baker and F. Elliston (Buffalo: Prometheus, 1975).

3 Thomas Nagel, "Sexual Perversion," *The Journal of Philosophy* 66, no. 1 (16 January 1969).

to match the vocabulary of "body language." That one can communicate various feelings during sex acts does not make these acts merely or primarily a means of communicating.

More importantly, to analyze sex as a means of communication is to overlook the intrinsic nature and value of the act itself. Sex is not a gesture or series of gestures, in fact not necessarily a means to any other end, but a physical activity intensely pleasurable in itself. When a language is used, the symbols normally have no importance in themselves; they function merely as vehicles for what can be communicated by them. Furthermore skill in the use of language is a technical achievement that must be carefully learned; if better sex is more successful communication by means of a more skillful use of body language, then we had all better be well schooled in the vocabulary and grammar. Solomon's analysis, which uses the language metaphor, suggests the appropriateness of a sex-manual approach, the substitution of a bit of technological prowess for the natural pleasure of the unforced surrender to feeling and desire.

It may be that Solomon's position could be improved by using the analogy of music rather than that of language, as an aesthetic form of communication. Music might be thought of as a form of aesthetic communicating, in which the experience of the "phonemes" themselves is generally pleasing. And listening to music is perhaps more of a sexual experience than having someone talk to you. Yet, it seems to me that insofar as music is aesthetic and pleasing in itself, it is not best conceived as primarily a means for communicating specific feelings. Such an analysis does injustice to aesthetic experience in much the same way as the sex-communication analysis debases sexual experience itself.[4]

For Solomon, sex that is not a totally self-conscious communicative art tends toward vulgarity,[5] whereas I would have thought it the other way around. This is another illustration of the tendency of means-end analyses to condemn what appears perfectly natural or normal sex on my account. Both Solomon and Nagel use their definitions, however, not primarily to stipulate moral norms for sex, as we saw in earlier analyses, but to define norms against which to measure perversion. Once again, neither is capable of generating consistency or reflective equilibrium with our firm intuitions as to what counts as subnormal sex, the problem being that both build factors into their norms which are extraneous to an unromanticized view of normal sexual desire and activity. If perversion represents a breakdown in communication, as Solomon maintains, then any unsuccessful or misunderstood advance should count as perverted. Furthermore, sex between husband and wife married for several years, or between any partners already familiar with each other, would be, if not perverted, nevertheless subnormal or trite and dull, in that the communicative content would be minimal in lacking all novelty. In fact the pleasures of sex need not wear off with familiarity, as they would if dependent upon the communicative content of the feelings. Finally, rather than a release or relief from physical desire through a substitute imaginative outlet, masturbation would become a way of practicing or rehearsing one's technique or vocabulary on oneself, or simply a way of talking to oneself, as Solomon himself says.[6]

Nagel fares no better in the implications of his overintellectualized norm. Spontaneous and heated sex between two familiar partners may

---

4 Sex might be considered (at least partially) as communication in a very broad sense in the same way as performing ensemble music, in the sense that there is in both ideally a communion or perfectly shared experience with another. This is, however, one possible ideal view whose central feature is not necessary to sexual acts or desire per se. And in emphasizing the communication of specific feelings by means of body language, the analysis under consideration narrows the end to one clearly extrinsic to plain and even good sex.

5 Solomon, pp. 284–285.

6 Ibid., p. 283. One is reminded of Woody Allen's rejoinder to praise of his technique: "I practice a lot when I'm alone."

well lack the complex conscious multileveled interpersonal awareness of which he speaks without being in the least perverted. The egotistical desire that one's partner be aroused by one's own desire does not seem a primary element of the sexual urge, and during sex acts one may like one's partner to be sometimes active and aroused, sometimes more passive. Just as sex can be more significant when love is communicated, so it can sometimes be heightened by an awareness of the other's desire. But at other times this awareness of an avid desire of one's partner can be merely distracting. The conscious awareness to which Nagel refers may actually impede the immersion in the physical of which I spoke above, just as may concentration upon one's "vocabulary" or technique. Sex is a way of relating to another, but primarily a physical rather than intellectual way. For Nagel, the ultimate in degeneration or perversion would have to be what he calls "mutual epidermal stimulation"[7] without mutual awareness of each other's state of mind. But this sounds like normal, if not ideal, sex to me (perhaps only a minimal description of it). His model certainly seems more appropriate to a sophisticated seduction scene than to the sex act itself,[8] which according to the model would often have to count as a subnormal anticlimax to the intellectual foreplay. While Nagel's account resembles Solomon's means-end analysis of sex, here the sex act itself does not even qualify as a preferred or central means to the end of interpersonal communication.

V

I have now criticized various types of analysis sharing or suggesting a common means-end form. I have suggested that analyses of this form relate to attempts to limit moral or natural sex to that which fulfills some purpose or function extraneous to basic sexual desire. The attempts to brand forms of sex outside the idealized models as immoral or perverted fail to achieve consistency with intuitions that they themselves do not directly question. The reproductive model brands oral-genital sex a deviation, but cannot account for kissing or holding hands; the communication account holds voyeurism to be perverted but cannot accommodate sex acts without much conscious thought or seductive nonphysical foreplay; the sex-love model makes most sexual desire seem degrading or base. The first and last condemn extramarital sex on the sound but irrelevant grounds that reproduction and deep commitment are best confined to family contexts. The romanticization of sex and the confusion of sexual desire with love operate in both directions: sex outside the context of romantic love is repressed; once it is repressed, partners become more difficult to find and sex becomes romanticized further, out of proportion to its real value for the individual.

What all these analyses share in addition to a common form is accordance with and perhaps derivation from the Platonic-Christian moral tradition, according to which the animal or purely physical element of humans is the source of immorality, and plain sex in the sense I defined it is an expression of this element, hence in itself to be condemned. All the analyses examined seem to seek a distance from sexual desire itself in attempting to extend it conceptually beyond the physical. The love and communication analyses seek refinement or intellectualization of the desire; plain physical sex becomes vulgar, and too straightforward sexual encounters without an aura of respectable cerebral communicative content are to be avoided. Solomon explicitly argues that sex cannot be a "mere" appetite, his argument being that if it were, subway exhibitionism and other vulgar forms would be pleasing.[9] This fails to recognize that sexual desire can be focused or selective at the same time as being physical. Lower animals are not attracted by every other member of their species,

7 Nagel, p. 15.
8 Janice Moulton made the same point in a paper at the Pacific APA meeting, March 1976.

9 Solomon, p. 285.

either. Rancid food forced down one's throat is not pleasing, but that certainly fails to show that hunger is not a physical appetite. Sexual desire lets us know that we are physical beings and, indeed, animals; this is why traditional Platonic morality is so thorough in its condemnation. Means-end analyses continue to reflect this tradition, sometimes unwittingly. They show that in conceptualizing sex it is still difficult, despite years of so-called revolution in this area, to free ourselves from the lingering suspicion that plain sex as physical desire is an expression of our "lower selves," that yielding to our animal natures is subhuman or vulgar.

VI

Having criticized these analyses for the sexual ethics and concepts of perversion they imply, it remains to contrast my account along these lines. To the question of what morality might be implied by my analysis, the answer is that there are no moral implications whatever. Any analysis of sex which imputes a moral character to sex acts in themselves is wrong for that reason. There is no morality intrinsic to sex, although general moral rules apply to the treatment of others in sex acts as they apply to all human relations. We can speak of a sexual ethic as we can speak of a business ethic, without implying that business in itself is either moral or immoral or that special rules are required to judge business practices which are not derived from rules that apply elsewhere as well. Sex is not in itself a moral category, although like business it invariably places us into relations with others in which moral rules apply. It gives us opportunity to do what is otherwise recognized as wrong, to harm others, deceive them or manipulate them against their wills. Just as the fact that an act is sexual in itself never renders it wrong or adds to its wrongness if it is wrong on other grounds (sexual acts towards minors are wrong on other grounds, as will be argued below), so no wrong act is to be excused because done from a sexual motive. If a "crime of passion" is to be excused,

it would have to be on grounds of temporary insanity rather than sexual context (whether insanity does constitute a legitimate excuse for certain actions is too big a topic to argue here). Sexual motives are among others which may become deranged, and the fact that they are sexual has no bearing in itself on the moral character, whether negative or exculpatory, of the actions deriving from them. Whatever might be true of war, it is certainly not the case that all's fair in love or sex.

Our first conclusion regarding morality and sex is therefore that no conduct otherwise immoral should be excused because it is sexual conduct, and nothing in sex is immoral unless condemned by rules which apply elsewhere as well. The last clause requires further clarification. Sexual conduct can be governed by particular rules relating only to sex itself. But these precepts must be implied by general moral rules when these are applied to specific sexual relations or types of conduct. The same is true of rules of fair business, ethical medicine, or courtesy in driving a car. In the latter case, particular acts on the road may be reprehensible, such as tailgating or passing on the right, which seem to bear no resemblance as actions to any outside the context of highway safety. Nevertheless their immorality derives from the fact that they place others in danger, a circumstance which, when avoidable, is to be condemned in any context. This structure of general and specifically applicable rules describes a reasonable sexual ethic as well. To take an extreme case, rape is always a sexual act and it is always immoral. A rule against rape can therefore be considered an obvious part of sexual morality which has no bearing on nonsexual conduct. But the immorality of rape derives from its being an extreme violation of a person's body, of the right not to be humiliated, and of the general moral prohibition against using other persons against their wills, not from the fact that it is a sexual act.

The application elsewhere of general moral rules to sexual conduct is further complicated by the fact that it will be relative to the particular desires and preferences of one's partner (these may be influenced by and hence in some sense include misguided beliefs about sexual morality itself). This means that there will be fewer specific rules in the area of sexual ethics than in other areas of conduct, such as driving cars, where the relativity of preference is irrelevant to the prohibition of objectively dangerous conduct. More reliance will have to be placed upon the general moral rule, which in this area holds simply that the preferences, desires, and interests of one's partner or potential partner ought to be taken into account. This rule is certainly not specifically formulated to govern sexual relations; it is a form of the central principle of morality itself. But when applied to sex, it prohibits certain actions, such as molestation of children, which cannot be categorized as violations of the rule without at the same time being classified as sexual. I believe this last case is the closest we can come to an action which is wrong *because* it is sexual, but even here its wrongness is better characterized as deriving from the detrimental effects such behavior can have on the future emotional and sexual life of the naive victims, and from the fact that such behavior therefore involves manipulation of innocent persons without regard for their interests. Hence, this case also involves violation of a general moral rule which applies elsewhere as well.

Aside from faulty conceptual analyses of sex and the influence of the Platonic moral tradition, there are two more plausible reasons for thinking that there are moral dimensions intrinsic to sex acts per se. The first is that such acts are normally intensely pleasurable. According to a hedonistic, utilitarian moral theory they therefore should be at least prima facie morally right, rather than morally neutral in themselves. To me this seems incorrect and reflects unfavorably on the ethical theory in question. The pleasure intrinsic to sex acts is a good, but not, it seems to me, a good with much positive moral significance. Certainly I can have no duty to pursue such pleasure myself, and while it may be nice to

give pleasure of any form to others, there is no ethical requirement to do so, given my right over my own body. The exception relates to the context of sex acts themselves, when one partner derives pleasure from the other and ought to return the favor. This duty to reciprocate takes us out of the domain of hedonistic utilitarianism, however, and into a Kantian moral framework, the central principles of which call for just such reciprocity in human relations. Since independent moral judgments regarding sexual activities constitute one area in which ethical theories are to be tested, these observations indicate here, as I believe others indicate elsewhere, the fertility of the Kantian, as opposed to the utilitarian, principle in reconstructing reasoned moral consciousness.

It may appear from this alternative Kantian viewpoint that sexual acts must be at least prima facie wrong in themselves. This is because they invariably involve at different stages the manipulation of one's partner for one's own pleasure, which might appear to be prohibited on the formulation of Kant's principle which holds that one ought not to treat another as a means to such private ends. A more realistic rendering of this formulation, however, one which recognizes its intended equivalence to the first universalizability principle, admits no such absolute prohibition. Many human relations, most economic transactions for example, involve using other individuals for personal benefit. These relations are immoral only when they are one-sided, when the benefits are not mutual, or when the transactions are not freely and rationally endorsed by all parties. The same holds true of sexual acts. The central principle governing them is the Kantian demand for reciprocity in sexual relations. In order to comply with the principle, one must recognize the subjectivity of one's partner (not merely by being aroused by her or his desire, as Nagel describes). Even in an act which by its nature "objectifies" the other, one recognizes a partner as a subject with demands and desires by yielding to those desires, by allowing oneself to be a sexual object as well, by giving pleasure or ensuring that the pleasures of the acts are mutual. It is this kind of reciprocity which forms the basis for morality in sex, which distinguishes right acts from wrong in this area as in others. (Of course, prior to sex acts one must gauge their effects upon potential partners and take these longer range interests into account.)

VII

I suggested earlier that in addition to generating confusion regarding the rightness or wrongness of sex acts, false conceptual analyses of the means-end form cause confusion about the value of sex to the individual. My account recognizes the satisfaction of desire and the pleasure this brings as the central psychological function of the sex act for the individual. Sex affords us a paradigm of pleasure, but not a cornerstone of value. For most of us it is not only a needed outlet for desire but also the most enjoyable form of recreation we know. Its value is nevertheless easily mistaken by being confused with that of love, when it is taken as essentially an expression of that emotion. Although intense, the pleasures of sex are brief and repetitive rather than cumulative. They give value to the specific acts which generate them, but not the lasting kind of value which enhances one's whole life. The briefness of these pleasures contributes to their intensity (or perhaps their intensity makes them necessarily brief), but it also relegates them to the periphery of most rational plans for the good life.

By contrast, love typically develops over a long term relation; while its pleasures may be less intense and physical, they are of more cumulative value. The importance of love to the individual may well be central in a rational system of value. And it has perhaps an even deeper moral significance relating to the identification with the interests of another person, which broadens one's possible relationships with oth-

ers as well. Marriage is again important in preserving this relation between adults and children, which seems as important to the adults as it is to the children in broadening concerns which have a tendency to become selfish. Sexual desire, by contrast, is desire for another which is nevertheless essentially self-regarding. Sexual pleasure is certainly a good for the individual, and for many it may be necessary in order for them to function in a reasonably cheerful way. But it bears little relation to those other values just discussed, to which some analyses falsely suggest a conceptual connection.

VIII

While my initial analysis lacks moral implications in itself, as it should, it does suggest by contrast a concept of sexual perversion. Since the concept of perversion is itself a sexual concept, it will always be defined relative to some definition of normal sex; and any conception of the norm will imply a contrary notion of perverse forms. The concept suggested by my account again differs sharply from those implied by the means-end analyses examined above. Perversion does not represent a deviation from the reproductive function (or kissing would be perverted), from a loving relationship (or most sexual desire and many heterosexual acts would be perverted), or from efficiency in communicating (or unsuccessful seduction attempts would be perverted). It is a deviation from a norm, but the norm in question is merely statistical. Of course, not all sexual acts that are statistically unusual are perverted—a three-hour continuous sexual act would be unusual but not necessarily abnormal in the requisite sense. The abnormality in question must relate to the *form of the desire* itself in order to constitute sexual perversion; for example, desire, not for contact with another, but for merely looking, for harming or being harmed, for contact with items of clothing. This concept of sexual abnormality is that suggested by my definition of normal sex in terms of its typical desire. However not all unusual desires qualify either, only those with the typical physical sexual effects upon the individual who satisfies them. These effects, such as erection in males, were not built into the original definition of sex in terms of sexual desire, for they do not always occur in activities that are properly characterized as sexual, say, kissing for the pleasure of it. But they do seem to bear a closer relation to the definition of activities as perverted. (For those who consider only genital sex sexual, we could build such symptoms into a narrower definition, then speaking of sex in a broad sense as well as "proper" sex.)

Solomon and Nagel disagree with this statistical notion of perversion. For them the concept is evaluative rather than statistical. I do not deny that the term "perverted" is often used evaluatively (and purely emotively for that matter), or that it has a negative connotation for the average speaker. I do deny that we can find a norm, other than that of statistically usual desire, against which all and only activities that properly count as sexual perversions can be contrasted. Perverted sex is simply abnormal sex, and if the norm is not to be an idealized or romanticized extraneous end or purpose, it must express the way human sexual desires usually manifest themselves. Of course not all norms in other areas of discourse need be statistical in this way. Physical health is an example of a relatively clear norm which does not seem to depend upon the numbers of healthy people. But the concept in this case achieves its clarity through the connection of physical health with other clearly desirable physical functions and characteristics, for example, living longer. In the case of sex, that which is statistically abnormal is not necessarily incapacitating in other ways, and yet these abnormal desires with sexual effects upon their subject do count as perverted to the degree to which their objects deviate from usual ones. The connotations of the concept of perversion beyond those connected with abnormality or statistical deviation derive more from the attitudes of those likely to call certain acts perverted than from specifiable features of the acts themselves. These connotations add to the concept of abnormality that of *sub*normality, but there is no norm against which the latter can be measured intelligibly in accord with all and only acts intuitively called perverted.

The only proper evaluative norms relating to sex involve degrees of pleasure in the acts and moral norms, but neither of these scales coincides with statistical degrees of abnormality, according to which perversion is to be measured. The three parameters operate independently (this was implied for the first two when it was held above that the pleasure of sex is a good, but not necessarily a moral good). Perverted sex may be more or less enjoyable to particular individuals than normal sex, and more or less moral, depending upon the particular relations involved. Raping a sheep may be more perverted than raping a woman, but certainly not more condemnable morally.[10] It is nevertheless true that the evaluative connotations attaching to the term "perverted" derive partly from the fact that most people consider perverted sex highly immoral. Many such acts are forbidden by long standing taboos, and it is sometimes difficult to distinguish what is forbidden from what is immoral. Others, such as sadistic acts, are genuinely immoral, but again not at all because of their connection with sex or abnormality. The principles which condemn these acts would condemn them equally if they were common and nonsexual. It is not true that we properly could continue to consider acts perverted which were found to be very common practice across societies. Such acts, if harmful, might continue to be condemned properly as immoral, but it was just shown that the immorality of an act does not vary with its degree of perversion. If not harmful, common acts previously considered abnormal might continue to be called perverted for a

10 The example is like one from Sara Ruddick, "Better Sex," *Philosophy and Sex,* p. 96.

time by the moralistic minority; but the term when applied to such cases would retain only its emotive negative connotation without consistent logical criteria for application. It would represent merely prejudiced moral judgments.

To adequately explain why there is a tendency to so deeply condemn perverted acts would require a treatise in psychology beyond the scope of this paper. Part of the reason undoubtedly relates to the tradition of repressive sexual ethics and false conceptions of sex; another part to the fact that all abnormality seems to disturb and fascinate us at the same time. The former explains why sexual perversion is more abhorrent to many than other forms of abnormality; the latter indicates why we tend to have an emotive and evaluative reaction to perversion in the first place. It may be, as has been suggested according to a Freudian line,[11] that our uneasiness derives from latent desires we are loathe to admit, but this thesis takes us into psychological issues I am not competent to judge.

11 See Michael Slote, "Inapplicable Concepts and Sexual Perversion," *Philosophy and Sex*.

Whatever the psychological explanation, it suffices to point out here that the conceptual connection between perversion and genuine or consistent moral evaluation is spurious and again suggested by misleading means-end idealizations of the concept of sex.

The position I have taken in this paper against those concepts is not totally new. Something similar to it is found in Freud's view of sex, which of course was genuinely revolutionary, and in the body of writings deriving from Freud to the present time. But in his revolt against romanticized and repressive conceptions, Freud went too far—from a refusal to view sex as merely a means to a view of it as the end of all human behavior, although sometimes an elaborately disguised end. This pansexualism led to the thesis (among others) that repression was indeed an inevitable and necessary part of social regulation of any form, a strange consequence of a position that began by opposing the repressive aspects of the means-end view. Perhaps the time finally has arrived when we can achieve a reasonable middle ground in this area, at least in philosophy if not in society.

Review Questions

1. What is the "means-end analysis" of sex, and why does Goldman reject it?
2. Explain Goldman's alternative analysis of sex.
3. How does Goldman reply to the objection that his analysis is either too broad or too narrow?
4. What criticisms does Goldman make of the view that the purpose of sex is reproduction?
5. According to Goldman, why isn't sex the expression of romantic love?
6. How do Solomon and Nagel analyze sex? What are Goldman's objections to these analyses?
7. Why does Goldman think there is no morality intrinsic to sex?
8. What is Goldman's view of sexual perversion?

Discussion Questions

1. Is sex analogous to eating? Why or why not?
2. What is plain sex? Is there anything morally wrong with it? Explain.
3. On Goldman's view, the baby's desire to be cuddled is sexual. Do you agree that babies have sexual desires? Defend your answer.

4. Goldman says that masturbation is not real sexual activity, but only an "imaginary substitute." Is this right or not?
5. Goldman claims that rape is always a sexual act, but some people claim it is an act of violence, not sex. Who is right?

Homosexual Conduct Is Wrong

JOHN FINNIS

John Finnis is Fellow in Jurisprudence, University College, Oxford University, and Reader in Commonwealth and American Law, Oxford University. He is the author of *Natural Law and Natural Rights* (1994).

Finnis gives several reasons for condemning and discouraging masturbation and sodomy: They involve treating one's body as a mere instrument; they make the choosing self the quasi slave of the experiencing self; they are worthless and disintegrating because they fail to actualize the real common good of marriage, with its two goods of children and friendship; and they are deeply hostile to members of the community who are committed to real marriage and its responsibilities.

THE UNDERLYING THOUGHT is on the following lines. In masturbating, as in being masturbated or sodomized, one's body is treated as instrumental for the securing of the experiential satisfaction of the conscious self. Thus one disintegrates oneself in two ways, (1) by treating one's body as a mere instrument of the consciously operating self, and (2) by making one's choosing self the quasi-slave of the experiencing self which is demanding gratification. The worthlessness of the gratification, and the disintegration of oneself, are both the result of the fact that, in these sorts of behavior, one's conduct is not the actualizing and experiencing of a

real common good. Marriage, with its double blessing—procreation and friendship—is a real common good. Moreover, it is a common good that can be both actualized and experienced in the orgasmic union of the reproductive organs of a man and a woman united in commitment to that good. Conjugal sexual activity, and—as Plato and Aristotle and Plutarch and Kant all argue—*only* conjugal activity is free from the shamefulness of instrumentalization that is found in masturbating and in being masturbated or sodomized.

At the very heart of the reflections of Plato, Xenophon, Aristotle, Musonius Rufus, and Plutarch on the homoerotic culture around them is the very deliberate and careful judgment that homosexual *conduct* (and indeed all extramarital sexual gratification) is radically incapable

Source: John Finnis, "Why Homosexuality Is Wrong." Reprinted from the legal depositions from the trial in Colorado on the constitutionality of Amendment 2.

of participating in, or actualizing, the common good of friendship. Friends who engage in such conduct are following a natural impulse and doubtless often wish their genital conduct to be an intimate expression of their mutual affection. But they are deceiving themselves. The attempt to express affection by orgasmic nonmarital sex is the pursuit of an illusion. The orgasmic union of the reproductive organs of husband and wife really unites them biologically (and their biological reality is part of, not merely an instrument of, their *personal* reality); that orgasmic union therefore can actualize and allow them to experience their real common good—their marriage with the two goods, children and friendship, which are the parts of its wholeness as an intelligible common good. But the common good of friends who are not and cannot be married (man and man, man and boy, woman and woman) has nothing to do with their having children by each other, and their reproductive organs cannot make them a biological (and therefore a personal) unit. So their genital acts together cannot do what they may hope and imagine.

In giving their considered judgment that homosexual conduct cannot actualize the good of friendship, Plato and the many philosophers who followed him intimate an answer to the questions why it should be considered shameful to use, or allow another to use, one's body to give pleasure, and why this use of one's body differs from one's bodily participation in countless other activities (e.g., games) in which one takes and/or gets pleasure. Their response is that pleasure is indeed a good, when it is the experienced aspect of one's participation in some intelligible good, such as a task going well, or a game or a dance or a meal or a reunion. Of course, the activation of sexual organs with a view to the pleasures of orgasm is sometimes spoken of as if it were a game. But it differs from real games in that its point is not the exercise of skill; rather, this activation of reproductive organs is focused upon the body precisely as a source of pleasure for one's consciousness. So this is a "use of the body" in a strongly different sense of "use." The body now is functioning not in the way one, as a bodily person, acts to instantiate some other intelligible good, but precisely as providing a service to one's consciousness, to satisfy one's desire for satisfaction.

This disintegrity is much more obvious when masturbation is solitary. Friends are tempted to think that pleasuring each other by some forms of mutual masturbation could be an instantiation or actualization or promotion of their friendship. But that line of thought overlooks the fact that if their friendship is not marital . . . activation of their reproductive organs cannot be, in reality, an instantiation or actualization of their friendship's common good. In reality, whatever the generous hopes and dreams with which the loving partners surround their use of their genitals, *that use* cannot express more than is expressed if two strangers engage in genital activity to give each other orgasm, or a prostitute pleasures a client, or a man pleasures himself. Hence, Plato's judgment, at the decisive moment of the *Gorgias,* that there is no important distinction in essential moral worthlessness between solitary masturbation, being sodomized as a prostitute and being sodomized for the pleasure of it. . . .

Societies such as classical Athens and contemporary England (and virtually every other) draw a distinction between behavior found merely (perhaps extremely) offensive (such as eating excrement) and behavior to be repudiated as destructive of human character and relationships. Copulation of humans with animals is repudiated because it treats human sexual activity and satisfaction as something appropriately sought in a manner that, like the coupling of animals, is divorced from the expressing of an intelligible common good—and so treats human bodily life, in one of its most intense activities, as merely animal. The deliberate genital coupling of persons of the same sex is repudiated for a very similar reason. It is not simply that it is sterile and disposes the participants to an abdication of responsibility for the future of humankind. Nor is it simply that it cannot *really* actualize the mutual devotion that some homosexual persons hope to manifest and experience by it; nor merely that it harms the personalities of its participants by its disintegrative manipulation of different parts of their one personal reality. It is also that it treats human sexual capacities in a way that is deeply hostile to the self-understanding of those members of the community who are willing to commit themselves to real marriage [even one that happens to be sterile) in the understanding that its sexual joys are not mere instruments or accompaniments to, or mere compensation for, the accomplishments of marriage's responsibilities, but rather are the *actualizing and experiencing* of the intelligent commitment to share in those responsibilities. . . .

This pattern of judgment, both widespread and sound, concludes as follows. Homosexual orientation—the deliberate willingness to promote and engage in homosexual acts—is a standing denial of the intrinsic aptness of sexual intercourse to actualize and give expression to the exclusiveness and open-ended commitment

of marriage as something good in itself. All who accept that homosexual acts can be a humanly appropriate use of sexual capacities must, if consistent, regard sexual capacities, organs, and acts as instruments to be put to whatever suits the purposes of the individual "self" who has them. Such an acceptance is commonly (and in my opinion rightly) judged to be an active threat to the stability of existing and future marriages; it makes nonsense, for example, of the view that adultery is per se (and not merely because it may involve deception), and in an important way, inconsistent with conjugal love. A political community that judges that the stability and educative generosity of family life is of fundamental importance to the community's present and future can rightly judge that it has a compelling interest in denying that homosexual conduct is a valid, humanly acceptable choice and form of life, and in doing whatever it properly can, as a community with uniquely wide but still subsidiary functions, to discourage such conduct.

Review Questions

1. Try to state and explain Finnis's argument or arguments that masturbation and sodomy are wrong.
2. According to Finnis, what was the considered judgment of Plato and many philosophers on homosexuality?
3. Finnis claims that homosexuality is a threat to the stability of existing and future marriages. Why is this?

Discussion Questions

1. What exactly is the disintegration that Finnis talks about? Why is it bad or wrong?
2. Is it wrong for married heterosexual couples to engage in masturbation and sodomy? Why or why not?

Homosexual Conduct Is Not Wrong

MARTHA NUSSBAUM

Martha Nussbaum teaches philosophy at Brown University. She is the author of *Sex and Social Justice* (1998).

After a review of the celebrations of male-male love in the writings of Plato and Aristotle, Nussbaum charges Finnis with making false assumptions about the purpose of homosexual acts, about procreative acts, and about the sort of community sexual relations can produce.

FINNIS'S ARGUMENTS against homosexuality set themselves in a tradition of "natural law" argumentation that derives from ancient Greek traditions. The term "law of nature" was first used by Plato in his *Gorgias*. The approach is further developed by Aristotle, and, above all, by the Greek and Roman Stoics, who are usually considered to be the founders of natural law argumentation in the modern legal tradition, through their influence on Roman law. This being so, it is worth looking to see whether those traditions did in fact use "natural law" arguments to rule homosexual conduct morally or legally substandard.

Plato's dialogues contain several extremely moving celebrations of male-male love, and judge this form of love to be, on the whole, superior to male-female love because of its potential for spirituality and friendship. The *Symposium* contains a series of speeches, each expressing conventional views about this subject that Plato depicts in an appealing light. The speech by Phaedrus points to the military advantages derived by including homosexual couples in a fighting force: Because of their intense love, each will fight better, wishing to show himself in

the best light before his lover. The speech of Pausanias criticizes males who seek physical pleasure alone in their homosexual relationships, and praises those who seek in sex deeper spiritual communication. Pausanias mentions that tyrants will sometimes promulgate the view that same-sex relations are shameful in order to discourage the kind of community of dedication to political liberty that such relations foster. The speech of Aristophanes holds that all human beings are divided halves of formerly whole beings, and that sexual desire is the pursuit of one's lost other half; he points out that the superior people in any society are those whose lost "other half" is of the same sex—especially the male-male pairs —since these are likely to be the strongest and most warlike and civically minded people. Finally, Socrates's speech recounts a process of religious-mystical education in which male-male love plays a central guiding role and is a primary source of insight and inspiration into the nature of the good and beautiful.

Plato's *Phaedrus* contains a closely related praise of the intellectual, political, and spiritual benefits of a life centered around male-male love. Plato says that the highest form of human life is one in which a male pursues "the love of a young man along with philosophy," and is transported by passionate desire. He describes the experience of falling in love with another

Source: Martha Nussbaum, "Reply to Finnis." Reprinted from the legal depositions from the trial in Colorado on the constitutionality of Amendment 2.

male in moving terms, and defends relationships that are mutual and reciprocal over relationships that are one-sided. He depicts his pairs of lovers as spending their life together in the pursuit of intellectual and spiritual activities, combined with political participation. (Although no marriages for these lovers are mentioned, it was the view of the time that this form of life does not prevent its participants from having a wife at home, whom they saw only rarely and for procreative purposes.)

Aristotle speaks far less about sexual love than does Plato, but it is evident that he too finds in male-male relationships the potential for the highest form of friendship, a friendship based on mutual well-wishing and mutual awareness of good character and good aims. He does not find this potential in male-female relationships, since he holds that females are incapable of good character. Like Pausanias in Plato's *Symposium,* Aristotle is critical of relationships that are superficial and concerned only with bodily pleasure; but he finds in male-male relationships— including many that begin in this way—the potential for much richer developments.

The ideal city of the Greek Stoics was built around the idea of pairs of male lovers whose bonds gave the city rich sources of motivation for virtue. Although the Stoics wished their "wise man" to eliminate most passions from his life, they encouraged him to foster a type of erotic love that they defined as "the attempt to form a friendship inspired by the perceived beauty of young men in their prime." They held that this love, unlike other passions, was supportive of virtue and philosophical activity.

Furthermore, Finnis's argument . . . against homosexuality is a bad moral argument by any standard, secular or theological. First of all, it assumes that the purpose of a homosexual act is always or usually casual bodily pleasure and the instrumental use of another person for one's own gratification. But this is a false premise, easily disproved by the long historical tradition I have described and by the contemporary lives of real men and women. Finnis offers no evidence for this premise, or for the equally false idea that procreative relations cannot be selfish and manipulative. Second, having argued that a relationship is better if it seeks not casual pleasure but the creation of a community, he then assumes without argument that the only sort of community a sexual relationship can create is a "procreative community." This if, of course, plainly false. A sexual relationship may create, quite apart from the possibility of procreation, a community of love and friendship, which no religious tradition would deny to be important human goods. Indeed, in many moral traditions, including those of Plato and Aristotle, the procreative community is ranked beneath other communities created by sex, since it is thought that the procreative community will probably not be based on the best sort of friendship and the deepest spiritual concerns. That may not be true in a culture that values women more highly than ancient Greek culture did; but the possibility of love and friendship between individuals of the same sex has not been removed by these historical changes.

Review Questions

1. How do Plato's dialogues treat male-male love, according to Nussbaum? What is Aristotle's view of male-male relationships?
2. Why does Nussbaum think that Finnis's argument against homosexuality is a bad moral argument by any standard?

Discussion Questions

1. How might Finnis reply to Nussbaum?
2. Is there any evidence that homosexual relationships are always or usually founded on casual bodily pleasure while procreative relationships are not? What is this evidence?

The Harms of Consensual Sex

ROBIN WEST

Robin West is professor of law at Georgetown University Law Center. She is the author of *Narrative, Authority, and Law* (1993) and *Progressive Constitutionalism: Reconstructing the Fourteenth Amendment* (1994).

West argues that consensual sex frequently harms women; it produces injury to self-assertiveness, self-possession, autonomy, and integrity. These harms are such that they make it difficult for the women harmed to experience the harm. As a result, these harms go unnoticed or are not taken seriously. The liberal and radical feminist rape-reform campaigns have inadvertently contributed to the problem. By insisting that nonconsensual sex is bad, they mistakenly imply that consensual sex is not bad or not harmful.

ARE CONSENSUAL, non-coercive, non-criminal, and even non-tortious, heterosexual transactions ever harmful to women? I want to argue briefly that many (not all) consensual sexual transactions are, and that accordingly we should open a dialogue about what those harms might be. Then I want to suggest some reasons those harms may be difficult to discern, even by the women sustaining them, and lastly two ways in which the logic of feminist legal theory and practice itself might undermine their recognition.

Let me assume what many women who are or have been heterosexually active surely know

Source: Robin West, "The Harms of Consensual Sex" from *APA Newsletters*, Vol. 94 (Spring 1995), pp. 52–55.

to be true from their own experience, and that is that some women occasionally, and many women quite frequently, consent to sex even when they do not desire the sex itself, and accordingly have a good deal of sex that, although consensual, is in no way pleasurable. Why might a woman consent to sex she does not desire? There are, of course, many reasons. A woman might consent to sex she does not want because she or her children are dependent upon her male partner for economic sustenance, and she must accordingly remain in his good graces. A woman might consent to sex she does not want because she rightly fears that if she does not her partner will be put into a foul humor, and she simply decides that tolerating the undesired sex is less burdensome than tolerating the foul humor. A woman might consent to sex she does not want because she has been taught and has come to believe that it is her lot in life to do so, and that she has no reasonable expectation of attaining her own pleasure through sex. A woman might consent to sex she does not want because she rightly fears that her refusal to do so will lead to an outburst of violent behavior some time following—only if the violence or overt threat of violence is *very* close to the sexual act will this arguably constitute a rape. A woman may consent to sex she does not desire because she *does* desire a friendly man's protection against the very real threat of non-consensual violent rape by other more dangerous men, and she correctly perceives, or intuits, that to gain the friendly man's protection, she needs to give him in exchange for that protection, the means to his own sexual pleasure. A woman, particularly a young woman or teenager, may consent to sex she does not want because of peer expectations that she be sexually active, or because she cannot bring herself to hurt her partner's pride, or because she is uncomfortable with the prospect of the argument that might ensue, should she refuse.

These transactions may well be rational—indeed in some sense they all are. The women involved all trade sex for something they value more than they value what they have given up. But that doesn't mean that they are not harmed. Women who engage in unpleasurable, undesired, but consensual sex may sustain real injuries to their sense of selfhood, in at least four distinct ways. First, they may sustain injuries to their capacities for self-assertion: the "psychic connection," so to speak, between pleasure, desire, motivation, and action is weakened or severed. *Acting* on the basis of our own felt pleasures and pains is an important component of forging our own way in the world—of "asserting" our "selves." Consenting to *un*pleasurable sex—acting in spite of displeasure—threatens that means of self-assertion. Second,

women who consent to undesired sex may injure their sense of self-*possession*. When we consent to undesired penetration of our physical bodies we have in a quite literal way constituted ourselves as what I have elsewhere called "giving selves"—selves who cannot be violated, because they have been defined as (and define themselves as) being "for others." Our bodies to that extent no longer belong to ourselves. Third, when women consent to undesired and unpleasurable sex because of their felt or actual dependency upon a partner's affection or economic status, they injure their sense of autonomy: they have thereby neglected to take whatever steps would be requisite to achieving the self-sustenance necessary to their independence. And fourth, to the extent that these unpleasurable and undesired sexual acts are followed by contrary to fact claims that they enjoyed the whole thing—what might be called "hedonic lies"—women who engage in them do considerable damage to their sense of integrity.

These harms—particularly if multiplied over years or indeed over an entire adulthood—may be quite profound, and they certainly may be serious enough to outweigh the momentary or day-to-day benefits garnered by each individual transaction. Most debilitating, though, is their circular, self-reinforcing character: the more thorough the harm—the deeper the injury to self-assertiveness, self-possession, autonomy and integrity—the greater the likelihood that the woman involved will indeed *not* experience these harms as harmful, or as painful. A woman utterly lacking in self-assertiveness, self-possession, a sense of autonomy, or integrity will not experience the activities in which she engages that reinforce or constitute those qualities *as harmful,* because she, to that degree, lacks a self-asserting, self-possessed self who *could* experience those activities as a threat to her selfhood. But the fact that she does not experience these activities as harms certainly does not mean that they are not harmful. Indeed, that they are not felt as harmful is a consequence of the harm they have already caused. This phenomenon, of course, renders the "rationality" of these transactions tremendously and even tragically misleading. Although these women may be making rational calculations in the context of the particular decision facing them, they are by making those calculations, sustaining deeper and to some degree unfelt harms that undermine the very qualities that constitute the capacity for rationality being exercised.

Let me quickly suggest some reasons that these harms go so frequently unnoticed—or are simply not taken seriously—and then suggest in slightly more detail some ways that feminist legal theory and practice may have undermined their recognition. The first reason is cultural. There is a deep-seated U.S. cultural tendency to equate the legal with the good, or harmless: we are, for better or worse, an anti-moralistic, anti-authoritarian, and anti-communitarian people. When combined with the sexual revolution of the 1960s, this provides a powerful cultural explanation for our tendency to shy away from a sustained critique of the harms of consensual sex. Any suggestion that legal transactions to which individuals freely consent may be harmful, and hence *bad*, will invariably be met with skepticism —*particularly* where those transactions are sexual in nature. This tendency is even further underscored by more contemporary postmodern skeptical responses to claims asserting the pernicious consequences of false consciousness.

Second, at least our legal-academic discourses, and no doubt academic political discourses as well, have been deeply transformed by the "exchange theory of value," according to which, if I exchange A for B voluntarily, then I simply must be better off after the exchange than before, having, after all, agreed to it. If these exchanges *are* the source of value, then it is of course impossible to ground a *value* judgment that some voluntary exchanges are harmful. Although stated baldly this theory of value surely has more critics than believers, it nevertheless in some way perfectly captures the modern zeitgeist. It is certainly, for example, the starting and ending point of normative analysis for many, and perhaps most, law students. Obviously, given an exchange theory of value, the harms caused by consensual sexual transactions simply fade away into definitional oblivion.

Third, the exchange theory of value is underscored, rather than significantly challenged, by the continuing significance of liberal theory and ideology in academic life. To the degree that liberalism still rules the day, we continue to valorize individual choice against virtually anything with which it might seem to be in conflict, from communitarian dialogue to political critique, and continue to perceive these challenges to individual primacy as somehow on a par with threats posed by totalitarian statist regimes.

Fourth, and perhaps most obvious, the considerable harms women sustain from consensual but undesired sex must be downplayed if the considerable pleasure men reap from heterosexual transactions is morally justified—*whatever* the relevant moral theory. Men do have a psycho-sexual stake in insisting that voluntariness alone ought to be sufficient to ward off serious moral or political inquiry into the value of consensual sexual transactions.

Let me comment in a bit more detail on a further reason why these harms seem to be underacknowledged, and that has to do with the logic of feminist legal theory, and the efforts of feminist practitioners, in the area of rape law reform. My claim is that the theoretical conceptualizations of sex, rape, force, and violence that underscore both liberal and radical legal feminism undermine the effort to articulate the harms that might be caused by consensual sexuality. I will begin with liberal feminism and then turn to radical feminism.

First, and entirely to their credit, liberal feminist rape law reformers have been on the forefront of efforts to stiffen enforcement of the existing criminal sanction against rape, and to extend that sanction to include non-consensual sex which presently is not cognizable legally as rape but surely should be. This effort is to be applauded, but it has the *almost* inevitable consequence of valorizing, celebrating, or, to use the critical term, "legitimating" consensual sexual transactions. If rape is bad *because* it is non-consensual—which is increasingly the dominant liberal-feminist position on the badness of rape —then it seems to follow that *consensual* sex must be good because it is consensual. But appearances can be misleading, and this one certainly is. That non-consensual transactions—rape, theft, slavery—are bad because non-consensual, does *not* imply the value, worth or goodness of their consensual counterparts—sex, property, or work. It only follows that consensual sex, property, or work are not bad in the ways that non-consensual transactions are bad; they surely may be bad for some other reason. We need to explore, in the case of sex (as well as property and work) what those other reasons might be. Non-consensuality does not exhaust the types of harm we inflict on each other in social interactions, nor does consensuality exhaust the list of benefits.

That the liberal-feminist argument for extending the criminal sanction against rape to include non-consensual sex *seems* to imply the positive value of consensual sex is no doubt in part simply a reflection of the powers of the forces enumerated above—the cultural, economic, and liberal valorization of individualism against communal and authoritarian controls. Liberal feminists can obviously not be faulted for that phenomenon. What I want to caution against, is simply the ever present temptation to *trade* on those cultural and academic forces in putting forward arguments for reform of rape law. We need not trumpet the glories of consensual sex *in order to* make out a case for strengthening the criminal sanction against coercive sex. Coercion, violence, and the fear under which women live because of the threat of rape are sufficient evils to sustain the case for strengthening and extending the criminal law against those

harms. We need not and should not supplement the argument with the unnecessary and unwarranted celebration of consensual sex—which whatever the harms caused by coercion, does indeed carry its own harms.

Ironically, radical feminist rhetoric—which *is* aimed at highlighting the damage and harm done to women by ordinary, "normal" heterosexual transactions—*also* indirectly burdens the attempt to articulate the harms done to women by consensual heterosexual transactions, although it does so in a very different way. Consider the claim, implicit in a good deal of radical feminist writing, explicit in some, that "all sex is rape," and compare it for a moment with the rhetorical Marxist claim that "all property is theft." Both claims are intended to push the reader or listener to a reexamination of the ordinary, and both do so by blurring the distinction between consent and coercion. Both seem to share the underlying premise that which is coerced—and perhaps *only* that which is coerced —is bad, or as a strategic matter, is going to be perceived as bad. Both want us to reexamine the value of that which we normally think of as good or at least unproblematic because of its apparent consensuality—heterosexual transactions in the first case, property transactions in the second—and both do so by putting into doubt the reality of that apparent consensuality.

But there is a very real difference in the historical context and hence the practical consequences of these two rhetorical claims. More specifically, there are two pernicious, or at least counter-productive consequences of the feminist claim which are not shared, at least to the same degree, by the marxist. First, and as any number of liberal feminists have noted, the radical feminist equation of sex and rape runs the risk of undermining parallel feminist efforts in a way not shared by the marxist equation of property and theft. Marxists are for the most part not engaged in the project of attempting to extend the existing laws against *theft* so as to embrace non-consensual market transactions that are currently not covered by the laws against larceny and embezzlement. Feminists, however, *are* engaged in a parallel effort to extend the existing laws against rape to include all non-consensual sex, and as a result, the radical feminist equation of rape and sex is indeed undermining. The claim that all sex is in effect non-consensual runs the real risk of "trivializing," or at least confusing, the feminist effort at rape reform so as to include all truly non-consensual sexual transactions.

There is, though, a second cost to the radical feminist rhetorical claim, which I hope these comments have by now made clear. The radical feminist equation of rape and sex, no less than the liberal rape reform movement, gets its rhetorical force by trading on the liberal, normative-economic, and cultural assumptions that whatever is coercive is bad, and whatever is non-coercive is morally non-problematic. It has the effect, then, of further burdening the articulation of harms caused by consensual sex by forcing the characterization of those harms into a sort of "descriptive funnel" of non-consensuality. It requires us to say, in other words, that consensual sex is harmful, if it is, only because or to the extent that it shares in the attributes of non-consensual sex. But this might not be true—the harms caused by consensual sex might be just as important, just as serious, but nevertheless *different* from the harms caused by non-consensual sex. If so, then women are disserved, rather than served, by the equation of rape and sex, even were that equation to have the rhetorical effect its espousers clearly desire.

Liberal feminist rape reform efforts and radical feminist theory both, then, in different ways, undermine the effort to articulate the distinctive harms of consensual sex; the first by indirectly celebrating the value of consensual sex, and the latter by at least rhetorically denying the existence of the category. Both, then, in different ways, underscore the legitimation of consensual sex effectuated by non-feminist cultural and academic forces. My conclusion is simply that feminists could counter these trends in part by focusing attention on the harms caused women by consensual sexuality. . . .

Review Questions

1. According to West, why do women consent to sex they do not desire?
2. In what ways are women harmed by consensual sex, in West's view?
3. Why don't women who have been harmed by consensual sex experience the harms as harmful or painful?
4. Why does West think that the harms are frequently unnoticed or not taken seriously?
5. What are the liberal and radical feminist views of rape? Why does West find them misleading or pernicious?

Discussion Questions

1. How can women avoid the harms of consensual sex, and how can they become aware of them?
2. Are men also harmed by consensual sex? If so, how? If not, why not?
3. If a person who has supposedly been harmed does not even notice the harm, or does not experience it as harmful or painful, then is it a serious harm? Explain your answer.

Problem Cases

1. Same-Sex Marriage

In 1993, the state supreme court of Hawaii ruled that the state was violating its constitution in denying marriage licenses to gay men and lesbians. This ruling attracted media attention because it seemed to open the door to same-sex marriages. No such marriages have occurred in Hawaii yet because the court's ruling hedged and called for more debate on the matter. On November 3, 1998, voters in Hawaii approved a constitutional amendment (by a 69- to 20-percent margin) that would empower the state legislature to ban same-sex marriages.

The issue is not confined to Hawaii. Twenty-nine states have passed laws restricting marriage to opposite-sex couples. In addition, the Defense of Marriage Act, a federal law, was passed by both the House and the Senate by overwhelming majorities and was signed into law by President Clinton in 1996. This federal law defines marriage as "only a legal union between one man and one woman as husband and wife." It also allows states to refuse to recognize a marriage made in another state if the spouses are of the same sex.

Many legal experts believe that these restrictive marriage laws are clearly unconstitutional. Similar laws prohibiting interracial marriage (which existed as late as 1967) have been stricken down as unconstitutional. If gays and lesbians had been allowed to marry in Hawaii, they would have legal standing as married couples to challenge these laws.

Should same-sex marriages be illegal? Why or why not?

Are they immoral? Explain your answer.

Suppose a same-sex couple wants to adopt a child. Should they be allowed to do so?

2. Timothy R. McVeigh

Senior Chief Petty Officer McVeigh is a sailor stationed in Honolulu. (He is no relation to the convicted Oklahoma City bomber.) The Navy tried to discharge him, saying that he had violated the "don't ask, don't tell" policy on homosexuals by posting a profile page on America Online listing his first name, his residence in Honolulu, his birth date, and his marital status as "gay."

In January 1998 (see the story in *The New York Times,* May 9, 1998), U.S. District Judge Stanley Sporkin ruled that the Navy went too far in investigating McVeigh. The judge said that the Navy violated the 1986 Electronic Communications Privacy Act by obtaining confidential information about McVeigh from AOL without a warrant or a court order. In March, Sporkin told the Navy to comply with his order reinstating McVeigh and giving him the right to continue managing nuclear attack submarines. McVeigh had been assigned to clerical work instead of his management work.

The "don't ask, don't tell" policy was put in place after President Clinton ordered the Pentagon to review its long-time policy of banning homosexuals. But the official policy of the Pentagon still is to prohibit homosexuals and lesbians from serving in the military. The Pentagon stated its rationale for banning gays in the military in a policy statement issued in 1982. The statement claims that men or women who engage in homosexual conduct undermine "discipline, good order, and morale." The military has maintained this policy despite evidence that a large number of gays and lesbians now serve in the military.

Is the "don't ask, don't tell" policy a good one? Why or why not?

Is it true that gays or lesbians undermine "discipline, good order, and morale"? Explain your answer.

3. *Bowers v. Hardwick (1986)*

In August 1982, Michael Hardwick was drinking beer in a bar when police, in an attempt to harass gays, arrested him for displaying an open beer bottle. Hardwick paid the fine. But apparently the police did not know this, or ignored it, and a police officer went to Hardwick's house, supposedly to collect the fine. One of Hardwick's friends let the officer in, and the officer observed Hardwick in the bedroom engaged in sex with another man. The officer arrested Hardwick (but not the other male) and charged him with violating the sodomy law.

In 1986 the Georgia law stated that "a person commits the offense of sodomy when he performs or submits to any sexual act involving the sex organ of one person and the mouth or anus of another." The punishment for this crime was "imprisonment for not less than one nor more than 20 years."

Hardwick brought suit in federal district court challenging the constitutionality of the Georgia statute. He argued that the sodomy law was unconstitutional because it violated the Fourteenth Amendment. A federal appeals court agreed that the Fourteenth Amendment protected privacy, including sexual behavior. The court did not require that the Georgia statute be overturned, however; it just required Georgia to demonstrate that the law served a compelling state interest. It was the decision that Georgia be required to defend the sodomy law that was reviewed by the Supreme Court.

In a 5-to-4 decision, the Supreme Court ruled for Georgia, represented by Attorney General Michael Bowers. The majority opinion was written by associate justice Byron R. White. White argued that the constitution does not confer a fundamental right to engage in sodomy. White noted that prior cases, such as *Roe,* had recognized a right of privacy in cases of abortion, contraception, procreation, and marriage, but he denied that this right of privacy extended to consensual acts of sodomy, even if such acts occur in the privacy of the home. Furthermore, White maintained that the majority sentiments about the immorality of sodomy are an adequate basis for the law.

In his opinion White speaks only of homosexual sodomy, but the Georgia law made no distinction between homosexual and heterosexual sodomy; it applied to heterosexual sodomy as well. Should heterosexual sodomy be illegal? Is it immoral? If not, then why not say the same about homosexual sodomy?

Is it a good idea to have restrictive laws regulating the private sexual behavior of consenting adults? If so, how should they be enforced?

Is majority opinion an adequate basis for laws? What would be the consequences if our laws were based entirely on public sentiments?

Suggested Readings

1. Alfred C. Kinsey et. al., *Sexual Behavior in the Human Male* (W. B. Saunders, 1948). This is the classic study that remains authoritative despite attacks on Kinsey's own sexual behavior and his methods.
2. Alfred C. Kinsey et. al, *Sexual Behavior in the Human Female* (W. B. Saunders, 1953).
3. June M. Reinisch, *The Kinsey Institute New Report on Sex* (St. Martin's Press, 1991), claims to give accurate answers to the questions people ask most about sex, based on a new national survey.
4. James Howard Jones and Alfred C. Kinsey, *A Public/Private Life* (Norton, 1997), tells all about Kinsey, including his masochism, voyeurism, bisexuality, and active sex life. Jones argues that Kinsey's findings were not as objective as claimed but were biased in various ways.
5. Bruce M. King, *Human Sexuality Today,* second edition (Prentice Hall, 1996), is an up-to-date textbook that covers all aspects of human sexuality from anatomy to paraphilias.
6. Robert T. Michael et al., *Sex in America: A Definitive Survey* (Little, Brown, 1994), is a detailed report of a national survey of adult sexual behavior. An expanded version for professionals is *The Social Organization of Sexuality* (University of Chicago Press, 1994).
7. Paul Cameron, "A Case Against Homosexuality," *Human Life Review* 4 (Summer 1978), pp. 17–49, contends that homosexuality should be discriminated against as an undesirable lifestyle because it produces undesirable personality traits—a self-centered orientation, irresponsibility, and a tendency toward suicide and homicide.
8. Richard D. Mohr, *The Little Book of Gay Rights* (Beacon Press, 1994), attacks those, including Christians, who want to discriminate against homosexuals, and defends gay rights.
9. Robert Baird and Katherine Baird, eds., *Homosexuality: Debating the Issues* (Prometheus Books, 1995), is an anthology dealing with the morality of homosexuality.
10. William Dudley, ed., *Homosexuality—Opposing Viewpoints* (Greenhaven Press, 1993), is an anthology presenting arguments for and against allowing homosexuality.
11. Peter A. Bertocci, *Sex, Love, and the Person* (Sheed & Ward, 1967), defends conventional morality.
12. Vincent C. Punzo, *Reflective Naturalism* (Macmillan, 1969), argues against premarital sex. In his view, marriage is constituted by mutual and total commitment, and absent commitment, sexual unions are morally deficient.
13. Andrea Dworkin, *Intercourse* (The Free Press, 1987), presents the radical feminist view that heterosexual intercourse is a patriarchal institution that degrades and enslaves women.
14. Burton Leiser, *Liberty, Justice and Morals,* second edition (Macmillan, 1979). In Chapter 2, Leiser attacks arguments that homosexuality is immoral.
15. Michael Ruse, *Homosexuality: A Philosophical Inquiry* (Basil Blackwell, 1990), gives a careful and detailed discussion of various issues related to homosexuality. He argues that it is not unnatural, not immoral, and not a sexual perversion.
16. Michael Levin, "Why Homosexuality Is Abnormal," *The Monist* 67, no. 2 (1984), pp. 260–76, argues that homosexuality is inherently abnormal and immoral because it is a misuse of body parts.

17. Richard Taylor, *Having Love Affairs* (Prometheus Books, 1982), claims that people have a right to love affairs even if they are married. He also thinks there is nothing wrong with people living together without being legally married.

18. Jeffner Allen, ed., *Lesbian Philosophies* (State University of New York Press, 1990). This is a collection of articles on lesbianism by lesbians. It includes a candid account of lesbian sex by Marilyn Frye; one of the important features is the lack of phallocentricity (to use her term).

19. John Arthur, *The Unfinished Constitution* (Wadsworth, 1989), reviews and attacks the Supreme Court decision in *Bowers v. Hardwick* (1986).

20. Onora O'Neill, "Between Consenting Adults," *Philosophy and Public Affairs* 14, no. 3 (Summer 1985), examines sexual relations from a Kantian perspective that focuses on respect for persons.

21. Morris B. Kaplan, "Intimacy and Equality: The Question of Lesbian and Gay Marriage," *The Philosophical Forum* 25 (Summer 1994), pp. 333–60, argues that gays and lesbians should be granted the same rights as heterosexuals to marry or to form domestic partnerships.

Chapter 6

Pornography and Hate Speech

Introduction

Factual Background

There have been two extensive government reports on pornography, one in 1970 and another in 1986. The 1970 report was presented by the Commission on Obscenity and Pornography, an advisory commission appointed by President Johnson in 1968. It found that there is no evidence to support the claim that exposure to sexually explicit materials causes either social harm, such as crimes, or individual harms, such as emotional upset. It recommended that all legislation prohibiting the sale, exhibition, or distribution of sexually explicit materials to consenting adults be repealed. But the 1970 commission recommended continuing legislation to protect nonconsenting adults from being solicited through public displays or mailings. It also recommended prohibiting the distribution of sexually explicit materials to juveniles.

President Richard Nixon declared that the report was completely unsatisfactory, and many members of Congress agreed. It received little or no public support or approval, and as a result there was no movement to repeal or discontinue legislation restricting pornography.

The 1986 report was given by the Attorney General's Commission on Pornography, an eleven-member commission appointed by Attorney General Edwin Meese III to reexamine pornography. Unlike the 1970 report, the 1986 report found that some types of pornography do have a causal relationship to personal and social harms. Specifically, the 1986 report found that violent pornography and degrading pornography did produce undesirable changes in attitude and acts of sexual violence, and that nonviolent and nondegrading pornography did not do this. Also, the 1986 report condemned child pornography as a form of sexual exploitation and abuse of children.

There is debate about the harms caused by pornography. Although it seems clear that children and women are harmed in the making of violent and sadistic pornography, there is debate about whether or not the men viewing this material are caused to commit acts of sexual violence. For example, in his reading, Barry Lynn notes that two commissioners repudiated the 1986 report; they said their data did not demonstrate any causal connection between pornography and sexual assault. But when it comes to hate speech, the harmful effects seem obvious. In his reading, Charles R. Lawrence III gives numerous examples of racist speech and several examples of how it harms people. Perhaps a historical example will illustrate the harms of hate speech. In 1543 Martin Luther published an influential document called "On the Jews and Their Lies." Among other things, he said that the Jews are "wicked, venomous, and devilish," and recommended that Jewish synagogues and homes be destroyed and that the Jews be driven out like mad dogs. Christians have persecuted Jews for centuries, and it seems obvious that Luther's document contributed to the

338

persecution. Hitler greatly admired Luther and did as Luther recommended, and much more. Given the Holocaust and the history of persecution, it is no wonder that Jews react strongly to hate speech directed at them.

Today a great deal of hate speech targets gays. This produces psychological harm, violence against gays, and hate crimes. In the reading, Lawrence gives a vivid description of the effect being called a "faggot" had on a gay man, and Jonathan Rauch gives a similar account of his own experience. As a result of the Hate Crime Statistics Act, we have reliable statistics on hate crimes. The FBI estimates that anti-gay violence constitutes 11.6 percent of all hate crimes. In 1998, antigay assaults were up 81 percent in New York City, and they more than doubled in Chicago. Many people claim that the death of Matthew Shepard was the direct result of the widespread rhetoric of gay bashing. (For the details, see the Problem Cases.)

In response to the perceived harm of hate speech, some colleges instituted speech codes. Some were fairly narrow in scope. For example, the code at Stanford University (stated and discussed by Lawrence) prohibited speech that was intended to insult or stigmatize, that was addressed directly to the victims, and that employed terms conveying "visceral hate or contempt." Other speech codes were broad in scope. The University of Connecticut code prohibited, among other things, inconsiderate jokes, stereotyping people's skills, or imitating the speech and mannerisms of a targeted individual or group.

The First Amendment to the U.S. Constitution, however, provides that the government shall make no law abridging the freedom of speech, and the U.S. courts have made few exceptions. These exceptions include "fighting words," libelous speech, and lewd and obscene speech. In general, the U.S. courts have viewed speech codes with suspicion and have found most of them to be unconstitutional. The speech codes at the University of Michigan, the University of Wisconsin, and Stanford University were all found to be unconstitutional (in 1989, 1991, and 1995, respectively).

The Readings

In the first reading, John Stuart Mill presents what is often called the harm principle. This is the principle that the only justification for interfering with liberty is harm to others. Self-harm does not justify limiting liberty. As Mill explains it, this principle applies to adults, not children, and it includes liberty of thought and feeling, "absolute freedom of opinion and sentiment on all subjects," liberty of tastes and pursuits, and the freedom to unite with others for any purpose. Mill gives a utilitarian defense of this principle. A society in which these liberties are respected is better than one in which they are restricted. As he puts it, "Mankind are greater gainers by suffering each other to live as seems good to themselves, than by compelling each to live as seems good to the rest."

The application of the harm principle to pornography seems obvious. If it harms others, then it should be restricted. This is basically the position MacKinnon advocates in the second reading. She argues that pornography, defined as "the graphic sexually explicit subordination of women through pictures or words," harms women by promoting the domination and submission of women. It promotes sexual assault against women by first sexually using them to make materials presenting them as enjoying pain or humiliation or rape, being tied up, cut up, mutilated, bruised, and physically hurt in a context that makes these acts sexual, and then distributing these materials to consumers who are conditioned to a sexuality of <u>objectification</u> and abuse, and desensitized to violence against women, thus causing them to sexually assault women. It also is a form of sex discrimination because women are selected for victimization on the basis of their gender.

Barry Lynn disagrees about the harms of pornography. He claims that there is no scientific evidence to support the claim that pornography causes men to commit sexual assault. He admits, however, that there are "copycat" actions wherein people imitate in real life things they see on television or in films. To use one of his examples, Japanese teenagers commit suicide after they learn on the news that a pop music idol has committed suicide. But this is hardly a good reason for censorship. If it were, we would have to censor all violence in the media. Lynn also mentions the data showing that pornography produces short-term attitude changes, making some viewers see women in a more negative light. But he claims that attitude changes do not necessarily produce changes in behavior, and anyway, we should punish harmful behavior, not harmful thoughts. Furthermore, there is data from other countries (Japan, West Germany, and Denmark) to show that wide availability of pornography is correlated with low rates of rape and sexual assault. As for the subordination of women, the status of women in places such as Saudi Arabia, where there is virtually no pornography at all, is much lower than in countries such as the United States, where there is an 8-billion-dollar industry in pornography.

Charles R. Lawrence compares hate speech to pornography. Both are ubiquitous and both occur in a context of sexism and racism that makes the harms more difficult to see. But to recognize the harm of hate speech, we need only listen to the accounts of those who have been harmed, including Lawrence's own autobiographical accounts. To remedy the problem, Lawrence recommends limitations on hate speech, such as the Stanford speech code. He rejects the civil libertarians who appeal to an absolute First Amendment standard. The trouble with this, he claims, is that the prevalent racism in our society rules out a free and open exchange of ideas.

Jonathan Rauch disagrees with Lawrence on a number of points. He does not think that we are all racists or that racist speech constructs social reality. He attacks what he calls "the new purism" that attempts to eliminate all forms of prejudice from our society. The trouble with this is that it targets not just racism, sexism, and homophobia but also religious beliefs and unpopular beliefs. It confuses words with violence, whereas it is better to keep this distinction clear. Purism has bad consequences in the workplace and in universities, and ends up attacking the very minorities it is supposed to protect. Instead of purism, Rauch advocates an intellectual pluralism that allows the free expression of speech and tolerates expressions of hatred and bigotry. *what is this going to solve?*

Philosophical Issues

How should we define pornography? This is a basic issue addressed in the readings. According to the court in the *American Booksellers* decision, the word "pornography" is usually associated, and sometimes synonymous, with the word "obscenity."

The word "obscenity" has a special meaning in the law, laid down by Justice William Brennan in a 1973 decision, *Miller v. California*. The *Miller* definition sets three tests for legal obscenity: (1) whether "the average person, applying contemporary community standards" would find that the work, taken as a whole, appeals to prurient interest. . . . , (2) whether the work depicts or describes, in a patently offensive way, sexual conduct. . . . , and (3) whether the work, taken as a whole, lacks serious literary, artistic, political, or scientific value.

Critics of the *Miller* test complain that it provides no national standard of obscenity. Community standards vary from place to place, and so what is obscene will vary; what is obscene in Topeka will not be obscene in San Francisco. This means that a person's First Amendment rights may be restricted in one jurisdiction but not in another. Furthermore, the test is subjective, since what offends or appeals to the prurient interest of one person may not do so in a different person. Finally, in the case of *Ferber,* the Supreme Court notes that the *Miller* standard for legal obscenity does not satisfy the concerns posed by child pornography.

MacKinnon proposes a different definition of pornography—namely, "the graphic sexually explicit subordination of women, whether in pictures or in words." Both Barry Lynn and the court in *American Booksellers* find MacKinnon's definition unsatisfactory. Lynn thinks it includes "vast amounts of popular culture, from the writings of Erica Jong and Ernest Hemingway to feminist health-care and sex-education materials." Another problem is child pornography; that it shows only boys, and not girls, does not seem to be a good reason for saying it is not pornographic. The court in the *American Booksellers* case raises a further problem. The definition seems to open the door to censorship of any material that may exploit or discriminate, and this would include racist material, material with ethnic or religious slurs, material uncomplimentary to the handicapped, and so on, resulting in an unacceptable encroachment on First Amendment freedoms.

A similar definition problem arises with hate speech. What do we count as hate speech? Lawrence is concerned mainly with racist and homophobic language, but Rauch thinks that anti-Christian or antifamily remarks might be included too. In fact, there is no clear line dividing hate speech from criticism. Ultimately, what is hate speech is in the mind of the hearer. To paraphrase Rauch, the statement "God hates homosexuals" is merely a statement of biblical fact for Christians, but it is hate speech for most gays. — *no were in the Bible does "God" say he hates gays!*

What are the harms of pornography and hate speech? This is another issue debated in the readings. MacKinnon holds that pornography harms all women by maintaining and continuing the oppression and subordination of women, whereas Lynn raises doubts about the amount of harm pornography causes. Lawrence and Rauch agree that hate speech causes psychological harms; they both have stories to demonstrate this. But Lawrence wants to go on to say that hate speech amounts to acts of physical violence; Rauch denies this.

A related issue is whether pornography and hate speech may actually provide benefits. When Lynn cites facts to support the claim that women are better off in countries such as Denmark, that have pornography, than in countries such as Saudi Arabia, that do not, he seems to imply that accessibility to pornography may be beneficial to some degree. Rauch makes a similar point about hate speech with his

What bull shit!

example about the claim that the Holocaust never happened. The denier's claims that the Auschwitz gas chambers could not have worked led to closer study showing how they actually did work. Prejudice and stupidity led to more knowledge.

Finally, there is an issue about balancing the harms caused by pornography or hate speech with the benefits of allowing free speech. MacKinnon and Lawrence seem to agree that, all things considered, the harms of pornography or hate speech outweigh the good of free speech, that free speech must be restricted to remedy these harms. Lynn, Rauch, and the court in *American Booksellers* adopt the opposite position, that the goods produced by free speech outweigh the harms of pornography or hate speech, that these harms should be tolerated rather than interfere with free speech.

On Liberty

JOHN STUART MILL

For biographical information on Mill, see his reading in Chapter 1.

Mill begins with his principle of liberty, that the only justification for interfering with liberty is to prevent harm to others. Harming yourself never justifies restricting your liberty. Mill distinguishes between liberty of consciousness, liberty of tastes and pursuits, and liberty in meeting others. He argues on utilitarian grounds that freedom of expression on any opinion should be allowed.

THE OBJECT OF THIS ESSAY is to assert one very simple principle, as entitled to govern absolutely the dealings of society with the individual in the way of compulsion and control, whether the means used be physical force in the form of legal penalties, or the moral coercion of public opinion. That principle is, that the sole end for which mankind are warranted, individually or collectively, in interfering with the liberty of action of any of their number, is self-protection. That the only purpose for which power can be rightfully exercised over any member of a civilized community, against his will, is to prevent harm to others. His own good, either physical or moral, is not a sufficient warrant. He cannot rightfully be compelled to do or forbear because it will be better for him to do so, because it will make him happier, because, in the opinions of others, to do so would be wise, or even right. These are good reasons for remonstrating with him, or reasoning with him, or persuading him, or entreating him, but not for compelling him, or visiting him with any evil in case he do otherwise. To justify that, the conduct from which it is desired to deter him, must be calculated to

Source: John Stuart Mill, "On Liberty" from *Utilitarianism* (London, 1859).

produce evil to some one else. The only part of the conduct of any one, for which he is amenable to society, is that which concerns others. In the part which merely concerns himself, his independence is, of right, absolute. Over himself, over his own body and mind, the individual is sovereign.

It is, perhaps, hardly necessary to say that this doctrine is meant to apply only to human beings in the maturity of their faculties. We are not speaking of children, or of young persons below the age which the law may fix as that of manhood or womanhood. Those who are still in a state to require being taken care of by others, must be protected against their own actions as well as against external injury. . . .

But there is a sphere of action in which society, as distinguished from the individual, has, if any, only an indirect interest; comprehending all that portion of a person's life and conduct which affects only himself, or if it also affects others, only with their free, voluntary, and undeceived consent and participation. When I say only himself, I mean directly, and in the first instance: for whatever affects himself, may affect others through himself; and the objection which may be grounded on this contingency will receive consideration in the sequel. This, then, is the appropriate region of human liberty. It comprises, first, the inward domain of consciousness; demanding liberty of conscience, in the most comprehensive sense; liberty of thought and feeling; absolute freedom of opinion and sentiment on all subjects, practical or speculative, scientific, moral or theological. The liberty of expressing and publishing opinions may seem to fall under a different principle, since it belongs to that part of the conduct of an individual which concerns other people; but, being almost of as much importance as the liberty of thought itself, and resting in great part on the same reasons, is practically inseparable from it. Secondly, the principle requires liberty of tastes and pursuits; of framing the plan of our life to suit our own character; of doing as we like, subject to

such consequences as may follow: without impediment from our fellow creatures, so long as what we do does not harm them, even though they should think our conduct foolish, perverse, or wrong. Thirdly, from this liberty of each individual, follows the liberty, within the same limits, of combination among individuals; freedom to unite, for any purpose not involving harm to others: the persons combining being supposed to be of full age, and not forced or deceived.

No society in which these liberties are not, on the whole, respected, is free, whatever may be its form of government; and none is completely free in which they do not exist absolute and unqualified. The only freedom which deserves the name, is that of pursuing our own good in our own way, so long as we do not attempt to deprive others of theirs, or impede their efforts to obtain it. Each is the proper guardian of his own health, whether bodily, or mental and spiritual. Mankind are greater gainers by suffering each other to live as seems good to themselves, than by compelling each to live as seems good to the rest. . . .

ON THE LIBERTY OF THOUGHT AND DISCUSSION

. . . If all mankind minus one, were of one opinion, and only one person were of the contrary opinion, mankind would be no more justified in silencing that one person, than he, if he had the power, would be justified in silencing mankind. Were an opinion a personal possession of no value except to the owner; if to be obstructed in the enjoyment of it were simply a private injury, it would make some difference whether the injury was inflicted only on a few persons or on many. But the peculiar evil of silencing the expression of an opinion is, that it is robbing the human race; posterity as well as the existing generation; those who dissent from the opinion, still more than those who hold it. If the opinion is right, they are deprived of the opportunity of exchanging error for truth: if wrong, they lose, what is almost as great a benefit, the clearer perception and livelier impression of truth, produced by its collision with error.

It is necessary to consider separately these two hypotheses, each of which has a distinct branch of the argument corresponding to it. We can never be sure that the opinion we are endeavouring to stifle is a false opinion; and if we were sure, stifling it would be an evil still.

First: the opinion which it is attempted to suppress by authority may possibly be true. Those who desire to suppress it, of course deny its truth; but they are not infallible. They have no authority to decide the question for all mankind, and exclude every other person from the means of judging. To refuse a hearing to an opinion, because they are sure that it is false, is to assume that *their* certainty is the same thing as *absolute* certainty. All silencing of discussion is an assumption of infallibility. Its condemnation may be allowed to rest on this common argument, not the worse for being common.

Unfortunately for the good sense of mankind, the fact of their fallibility is far from carrying the weight in their practical judgement, which is always allowed to it in theory; for while every one well knows himself to be fallible, few think it necessary to take any precautions against their own fallibility, or admit the supposition that any opinion, of which they feel very certain, may be one of the examples of the error to which they acknowledge themselves to be liable. . . .

Let us now pass to the second division of the argument, and dismissing the supposition that any of the received opinions may be false, let us assume them to be true, and examine into the worth of the manner in which they are likely to be held, when their truth is not freely and openly canvassed. However unwillingly a person who has a strong opinion may admit the possibility that his opinion may be false, he ought to be moved by the consideration that however

true it may be, if it is not fully, frequently, and fearlessly discussed, it will be held as a dead dogma, not a living truth.

There is a class of persons (happily not quite so numerous as formerly) who think it enough if a person assents undoubtingly to what they think true, though he has no knowledge whatever of the grounds of the opinion, and could not make a tenable defence of it against the most superficial objections. Such persons, if they can once get their creed taught from authority, naturally think that no good, and some harm, comes of it being allowed to be questioned. Where their influence prevails, they make it nearly impossible for the received opinion to be rejected wisely and considerately, though it may still be rejected rashly and ignorantly; for to shut out discussion entirely is seldom possible, and when it once gets in, beliefs not grounded on conviction are apt to give way before the slightest semblance of an argument. Waiving, however, this possibility—assuming that the true opinion abides in the mind, but abides as a prejudice, a belief independent of, and proof against, argument—this is not the way in which truth ought to be held by a rational being. This is not knowing the truth. Truth, thus held, is but one superstition the more, accidentally clinging to the words which enunciate a truth.

If the intellect and judgement of mankind ought to be cultivated, a thing which Protestants at least do not deny, on what can these faculties be more appropriately exercised by any one, than on the things which concern him so much that it is considered necessary for him to hold opinions on them? If the cultivation of the understanding consists in one thing more than in another, it is surely in learning the grounds of one's own opinions. Whatever people believe, on subjects on which it is of the first importance to believe rightly, they ought to be able to defend against at least the common objections. But, some one may say, 'Let them be *taught* the grounds of their opinions. It does not follow that opinions must be merely parroted because they are never heard controverted. Persons who learn geometry do not simply commit the theorems to memory, but understand and learn likewise the demonstrations; and it would be absurd to say that they remain ignorant of the grounds of geometrical truths, because they never hear any one deny, and attempt to disprove them.' Undoubtedly: and such teaching suffices on a subject like mathematics, where there is nothing at all to be said on the wrong side of the question. The peculiarity of the evidence of mathematical truths is, that all the argument is on one side. There are no objections, and no answers to objections. But on every subject on which difference of opinion is possible, the truth depends on a balance to be struck between two sets of conflicting reasons. . . . He who knows only his own side of the case, knows little of that. His reasons may be good, and no one may have been able to refute them. But if he is equally unable to refute the reasons on the opposite side; if he does not so much as know what they are, he has no ground for preferring either opinion. The rational position for him would be suspension of judgement, and unless he contents himself with that, he is either led by authority, or adopts, like the generality of the world, the side to which he feels most inclination. Nor is it enough that he should hear the arguments of adversaries from his own teachers, presented as they state them, and accompanied by what they offer as refutations. That is not the way to do justice to the arguments, or bring them into real contact with his own mind. He must be able to hear them from persons who actually believe them; who defend them in earnest, and do their very utmost for them. He must know them in their most plausible and persuasive form; he must feel the whole force of the difficulty which the true view of the subject has to encounter and dispose of; else he will never really possess himself of the portion of truth which meets and removes that difficulty. . . .

. . .The fact, however, is, that not only the grounds of the opinion are forgotten in the absence of discussion, but too often the meaning of the opinion itself. The words which convey it, cease to suggest ideas, or suggest only a small portion of those they were originally employed to communicate. Instead of a vivid conception and a living belief, there remain only a few phrases retained by rote; or, if any part, the shell and husk only of the meaning is retained, the finer essence being lost. The great chapter in human history which this fact occupies and fills, cannot be too earnestly studied and meditated on.

It is illustrated in the experience of almost all ethical doctrines and religious creeds. They are all full of meaning and vitality to those who originate them, and to the direct disciples of the originators. Their meaning continues to be felt in undiminished strength, and is perhaps brought out into even fuller consciousness, so long as the struggle lasts to give the doctrine or creed an ascendancy over other creeds. At last it either prevails, and becomes the general opinion, or its progress stops; it keeps possession of the ground it has gained, but ceases to spread further. When either of these results has become apparent, controversy on the subject flags, and gradually dies away. . . .

It still remains to speak of one of the principal causes which make diversity of opinion advantageous, and will continue to do so until mankind shall have entered a stage of intellectual advancement which at present seems at an incalculable distance. We have hitherto considered only two possibilities: that the received opinion may be false, and some other opinion, consequently, true; or that, the received opinion being true, a conflict with the opposite error is essential to a clear apprehension and deep feeling of its truth. But there is a commoner case than either of these; when the conflicting doctrines, instead of being one true and the other false, share the truth between them; and the nonconforming opinion is needed to supply the remainder of the truth, of which the received doctrine embodies only a part. Popular opinions, on subjects not palpable to sense, are often true, but seldom or never the whole truth. They are a part of the truth; sometimes a greater, sometimes a smaller part, but exaggerated, distorted, and disjoined from the truths by which they ought to be accompanied and limited. Heretical opinions, on the other hand, are generally some of these suppressed and neglected truths, bursting the bonds which kept them down, and either seeking reconciliation with the truth contained in the common opinion, or fronting it as enemies, and setting themselves up, with similar exclusiveness, as the whole truth. The latter case is hitherto the most frequent, as, in the human mind, one-sidedness has always been the rule, and many-sidedness the exception. Hence, even in revolutions of opinion, one part of the truth usually sets while another rises. Even progress, which ought to superadd, for the most part only substitutes, one partial and incomplete truth for another; improvement consisting chiefly in this, that the new fragment of truth is more wanted, more adapted to the needs of the time, than that which it displaces. Such being the partial character of prevailing opinions, even when resting on a true foundation, every opinion which embodies somewhat of the portion of truth which the common opinion omits, ought to be considered precious, with whatever amount of error and confusion that truth may be blended. No sober judge of human affairs will feel bound to be indignant because those who force on our notice truths which we should otherwise have overlooked, overlook some of those which we see. Rather, he will think that so long as popular truth is one-sided, it is more desirable than otherwise that unpopular truth should have one-sided asserters too; such being usually the most energetic, and the most likely to compel reluctant attention to the fragment of wisdom which they proclaim as if it were the whole. . . .

We have now recognized the necessity to the mental well-being of mankind (on which all their other well-being depends) of freedom of opinion, and freedom of the expression of opinion, on four distinct grounds; which we will now briefly recapitulate.

First, if any opinion is compelled to silence, that opinion may, for aught we can certainly know, be true. To deny this is to assume our own infallibility.

Secondly, though the silenced opinion be an error, it may, and very commonly does, contain a portion of truth; and since the general or prevailing opinion on any subject is rarely or never the whole truth, it is only by the collision of adverse opinions that the remainder of the truth has any chance of being supplied.

Thirdly, even if the received opinion be not only true, but the whole truth; unless it is suffered to be, and actually is, vigorously and earnestly contested, it will, by most of those who receive it, be held in the manner of a prejudice, with little comprehension or feeling of its rational grounds. And not only this, but, fourthly, the meaning of the doctrine itself will be in danger of being lost, or enfeebled, and deprived of its vital effect on the character and conduct: the dogma becoming a mere formal profession, inefficacious for good, but cumbering the ground, and preventing the growth of any real and heartfelt conviction, from reason or personal experience. . . .

Review Questions

1. State and explain Mill's principle of liberty.
2. What are the three domains of liberty, according to Mill?
3. Why does Mill think that silencing the expression of opinion is evil?

Discussion Questions

1. Are there any opinions that should be censored? What are they?
2. Is Mill's principle of liberty compatible with his utilitarianism? Why or why not?

Pornography, Civil Rights, and Speech

CATHARINE MACKINNON

Catharine MacKinnon is professor of law at the University of Michigan. She is the author of *Toward a Feminist Theory of the State* (1989), *Only Words* (1993), and *Feminism Unmodified: Discourse on Life and Law* (1987), from which our reading is taken. MacKinnon defines pornography as "the graphic sexually explicit subordination of women." It harms women by violating them in its making and by mass-producing that violation through its use. It also harms women by promoting and maintaining the inferior status of women, and it violates their civil rights because it is sex discrimination; it targets women on the basis of their gender. The harm and the discrimination are hard to see, MacKinnon argues, because of the persuasiveness and potency of pornography. To the extent that pornography constructs social reality, it becomes invisible as harm.

THE CONTENT OF PORNOGRAPHY is one thing. There, women substantively desire dispossession and cruelty. We desperately want to be bound, battered, tortured, humiliated, and killed. Or, to be fair to the soft core, merely taken and used. This is erotic to the male point of view. Subjection itself, with self-determination ecstatically relinquished, is the content of women's sexual desire and desirability. Women are there to be violated and possessed, men to violate and possess us, either on screen or by camera or pen on behalf of the con-

Source: Catharine MacKinnon, "Pornography, Civil Rights, and Speech" from *Feminism Unmodified* (Harvard University Press, 1987), pp. 168–191.

sumer. On a simple descriptive level, the inequality of hierarchy, of which gender is the primary one, seems necessary for sexual arousal to work. Other added inequalities identify various pornographic genres or subthemes, although they are always added through gender: age, disability, homosexuality, animals, objects, race (including anti-Semitism), and so on. Gender is never irrelevant.

What pornography *does* goes beyond its content: it eroticizes hierarchy, it sexualizes inequality. It makes dominance and submission into sex. Inequality is its central dynamic; the illusion of freedom coming together with the reality of force is central to its working. Perhaps because this is a bourgeois culture, the victim must look free, appear to be freely acting. Choice is how she got there. Wining is what she is when she is being equal. It seems equally important that then and there she actually be forced and that forcing be communicated on some level, even if only through still photos of her in postures of receptivity and access, available for penetration. Pornography in this view is a form of forced sex, a practice of sexual politics, an institution of gender inequality.

From this perspective, pornography is neither harmless fantasy nor a corrupt and confused misrepresentation of an otherwise natural and healthy sexual situation. It institutionalizes the sexuality of male supremacy, fusing the erotization of dominance and submission with the social construction of male and female. To the extent that gender is sexual, pornography is part of constituting the meaning of that sexuality. Men treat women as who they see women as being. Pornography constructs who that is. Men's power over women means that the way men see women defines who women can be. Pornography is that way. Pornography is not imagery in some relation to a reality elsewhere constructed. It is not a distortion, reflection, projection, expression, fantasy, representation, or symbol either. It is a sexual reality.

In Andrea Dworkin's definitive work, *Pornography: Men Possessing Women*,[1] sexuality itself is a social construct gendered to the ground. Male dominance here is not an artificial overlay upon an underlying inalterable substratum of uncorrupted essential sexual being. Dworkin presents a sexual theory of gender inequality of which pornography is a constitutive practice. The way pornography produces its meaning constructs and defines men and women as such. Gender has no basis in anything other than the social reality its hegemony constructs. Gender is what gender means. The process that gives sexuality its male supremacist

1 Andrea Dworkin, *Pornography: Men Possessing Women* (1981).

meaning is the same process through which gender inequality becomes socially real.

In this approach, the experience of the (overwhelmingly) male audiences who consume pornography is therefore not fantasy or simulation or catharsis but sexual reality, the level of reality on which sex itself largely operates. Understanding this dimension of the problem does not require noticing that pornography models are real women to whom, in most cases, something real is being done; nor does it even require inquiring into the systematic infliction of pornography and its sexuality upon women, although it helps. What matters is the way in which the pornography itself provides what those who consume it want. Pornography *participates* in its audience's eroticism through creating an accessible sexual object, the possession and consumption of which *is* male sexuality, as socially constructed; to be consumed and possessed as which, *is* female sexuality, as socially constructed; pornography is a process that constructs it that way.

The object world is constructed according to how it looks with respect to its possible uses. Pornography defines women by how we look according to how we can be sexually used. Pornography codes how to look at women, so you know what you can do with one when you see one. Gender is an assignment made visually, both originally and in everyday life. A sex object is defined on the basis of its looks, in terms of its usability for sexual pleasure, such that both the looking—the quality of the gaze, including its point of view—and the definition according to use become eroticized as part of the sex itself. This is what the feminist concept "sex object" means. In this sense, sex in life is no less mediated than it is in art. Men have sex with their image of a woman. It is not that life and art imitate each other; in this sexuality, they *are* each other.

To give a set of rough epistemological translations, to defend pornography as consistent with the equality of the sexes is to defend the subordination of women to men as sexual equality. What in the pornographic view is love

Hegemony; predominant influence or domination

and romance looks a great deal like hatred and torture to the feminist. Pleasure and eroticism become violation. Desire appears as lust for dominance and submission. The vulnerability of women's projected sexual availability, that acting we are allowed (that is, asking to be acted upon), is victimization. Play conforms to scripted roles. Fantasy expresses ideology, is not exempt from it. Admiration of natural physical beauty becomes objectification. Harmlessness becomes harm. Pornography is a harm of male supremacy made difficult to see because of its pervasiveness, potency, and, principally, because of its success in making the world a pornographic place. Specifically, its harm cannot be discerned, and will not be addressed, if viewed and approached neutrally, because it *is* so much of "what is." In other words, to the extent pornography succeeds in constructing social reality, it becomes invisible as harm. If we live in a world that pornography creates through the power of men in a male-dominated situation, the issue is not what the harm of pornography is, but how that harm is to become visible.

Obscenity law provides a very different analysis and conception of the problem of pornography.[2] In 1973 the legal definition of obscenity became that which the average person, applying contemporary community standards, would find that, taken as a whole, appeals to the prurient interest; that which depicts or describes in a patently offensive way—you feel like you're a cop reading someone's *Miranda* rights—sexual conduct specifically defined by the applicable state law; and that which, taken as a whole, lacks serious literary, artistic, political or scientific value.[3] Feminism doubts whether the average person gender-neutral exists; has more questions about the content and process of defining

what community standards are than it does about deviations from them; wonders why prurience counts but powerlessness does not and why sensibilities are better protected from offense than women are from exploitation; defines sexuality, and thus its violation and expropriation, more broadly than does state law; and questions why a body of law that has not in practice been able to tell rape from intercourse should, without further guidance, be entrusted with telling pornography from anything less. Taking the work "as a whole" ignores that which the victims of pornography have long known: legitimate settings diminish the perception of injury done to those whose trivialization and objectification they contextualize. Besides, and this is a heavy one, if a woman is subjected, why should it matter that the work has other value? Maybe what redeems the work's value is what enhances its injury to women, not to mention that existing standards of literature, art, science, and politics, examined in a feminist light, are remarkably consonant with pornography's mode, meaning, and message. And finally—first and foremost, actually—although the subject of these materials is overwhelmingly women, their contents almost entirely made up of women's bodies, our invisibility has been such, our equation as a sex *with* sex has been such, that the law of obscenity has never even considered pornography a women's issue.

Obscenity, in this light, is a moral idea, an idea about judgments of good and bad. Pornography, by contrast, is a political practice, a practice of power and powerlessness. Obscenity is ideational and abstract; pornography is concrete and substantive. The two concepts represent two entirely different things. Nudity, excess of candor, arousal or excitement, prurient appeal, illegality of the acts depicted, and unnaturalness or perversion are all qualities that bother obscenity law when sex is depicted or portrayed. Sex forced on real women so that it can be sold at a profit and forced on other real women; women's bodies trussed and maimed and raped

2 For a fuller development of this critique, see "Not a Moral Issue" (Chapter 13 in original source).
3 *Miller v. California*, 413 U.S. 15, 24 (1973).

and made into things to be hurt and obtained and accessed, and this presented as the nature of women in a way that is acted on and acted out, over and over; the coercion that is visible and the coercion that has become invisible—this and more bothers feminists about pornography. Obscenity as such probably does little harm.[4] Pornography is integral to attitudes and behaviors of violence and discrimination that define the treatment and status of half the population.

At the request of the city of Minneapolis, Andrea Dworkin and I conceived and designed a local human rights ordinance in accordance with our approach to the pornography issue. We define pornography as a practice of sex discrimination, a violation of women's civil rights, the opposite of sexual equality. Its point is to hold those who profit from and benefit from that injury accountable to those who are injured. It means that women's injury—our damage, our pain, our enforced inferiority—should outweigh their pleasure and their profits, or sex equality is meaningless.

We define pornography as the graphic sexually explicit subordination of women through pictures or words that also includes women dehumanized as sexual objects, things, or commodities; enjoying pain or humiliation or rape; being tied up, cut up, mutilated, bruised, or physically hurt; in postures of sexual submission or servility or display; reduced to body parts, penetrated by objects or animals, or presented in scenarios of degradation, injury, torture; shown as filthy or inferior; bleeding, bruised, or hurt in a context that makes these conditions sexual.[5] Erotica, defined by distinction as not this, might be sexually explicit materials

premised on equality.[6] We also provide that the use of men, children, or transsexuals in the place of women is pornography.[7] The definition is substantive in that it is sex-specific, but it covers everyone in a sex-specific way, so is gender neutral in overall design.

There is a buried issue within sex discrimination law about what sex, meaning gender, is. If sex is a *difference*, social or biological, one looks to see if a challenged practice occurs along the same lines; if it does, or if it is done to both sexes, the practice is not discrimination, not inequality. If, by contrast, sex has been a matter of *dominance*, the issue is not the gender difference but the difference gender makes. In this more substantive, less abstract approach, the concern with inequality is whether a practice *subordinates* on the basis of sex. The first approach implies that marginal correction is needed; the second requires social change. Equality, in the first view, centers on abstract symmetry between equivalent categories; the asymmetry that occurs when categories are not equivalent is not inequality, it is treating unlikes differently. In the second approach, inequality centers on the substantive, cumulative disadvantagement of social hierarchy. Equality for the first is nondifferentiation; for the second, nonsubordination.[8] Although it is consonant with both approaches, our antipornography statute emerges largely from an analysis of the problem under the second approach.

To define pornography as a practice of sex discrimination combines a mode of portrayal that has a legal history—the sexually explicit—with an active term that is central to the inequality of the sexes—subordination. Among other things, subordination means to be in a position

---

4 See *The Report of the Presidential Commission on Obscenity and Pornography* (1970).
5 For the specific statutory language, see "Not a Moral Issue."

6 See, e.g., Gloria Steinem, "Erotica v. Pornography," in *Outrageous Acts and Everyday Rebellions* 219 (1983).
7 See Indianapolis Ordinance, "Not a Moral Issue."
8 See Catharine A. MacKinnon, *Sexual Harassment of Working Women* 101–41 (1979).

of inferiority or loss of power, or to be demeaned or denigrated.[9] To be someone's subordinate is the opposite of being their equal. The definition does not include all sexually explicit depictions *of* the subordination of women. That is not what it says. It says, this which *does* that: the sexually explicit that subordinates women. To these active terms to capture what the pornography *does,* the definition adds a list of what it must also contain. This list, from our analysis, is an exhaustive description of what must be in the pornography for it to do what it does behaviorally. Each item in the definition is supported by experimental, testimonial, social, and clinical evidence. We made a legislative choice to be exhaustive and specific and concrete rather than conceptual and general, to minimize problems of chilling effect, making it hard to guess wrong, thus making self-censorship less likely, but encouraging (to use a phrase from discrimination law) voluntary compliance, knowing that if something turns up that is not on the list, the law will not be expansively interpreted.

The list in the definition, by itself, would be a content regulation.[10] But together with the first part, the definition is not simply a content regulation. It is a medium-message combination that resembles many other such exceptions to First Amendment guarantees.[11]

9 For a lucid discussion of subordination, see Andrea Dworkin, "Against the Male Flood: Censorship, Pornography, and Equality," 8 *Harvard Women's Law Journal* 1 (1985).
10 If this part stood alone, it would, along with its support, among other things, have to be equally imposed—an interesting requirement for an equality law, but arguably met by this one. See *Carey v. Brown,* 447 U.S. 455 (1980); *Police Department of Chicago v. Mosley,* 408 U.S. 92 (1972); Kenneth Karst, "Equality as a Central Principle in the First Amendment," 43 *University of Chicago Law Review* 20 (1975).
11 See *KPNX Broadcasting Co. v. Arizona Superior Court,* 459 U.S. 1302 (1982) (Rehnquist as Circuit Justice denied application to stay Arizona judge's order that those involved with heavily covered criminal trial avoid direct contact with

To focus what our law is, I will say what it is not. It is not a prior restraint. It does not go to possession. It does not turn on offensiveness. It is not a ban, unless relief for a proven injury is a

press; mere potential confusion from unrestrained contact with press is held to justify order); *New York v. Ferber,* 458 U.S. 747 (1982) (child pornography, defined as promoting sexual performance by a child, can be criminally banned as a form of child abuse); *F.C.C. v. Pacifica Found.,* 438 U.S. 726 (1978) ("indecent" but not obscene radio broadcasts may be regulated by F.C.C. through licensing); *Young v. American Mini Theatres, Inc.,* 427 U.S. 50 (1976) (exhibition of sexually explicit "adult movies" may be restricted through zoning ordinances); *Gertz v. Robert Welch, Inc.,* 418 U.S. 323, 347 (1974) (state statute may allow private persons to recover for libel without proving actual malice so long as liability is not found without fault); *Pittsburgh Press Co. v. Human Relations Comm'n,* 413 U.S. 376 (1973) (sex-designated help-wanted columns conceived as commercial speech may be prohibited under local sex discrimination ordinance); *Miller v. California,* 413 U.S. 15, 18 (1973) (obscenity unprotected by First Amendment in case in which it was "thrust by aggressive sales action upon unwilling [viewers]. . . ."); *Red Lion Broadcasting Co. v. F.C.C.,* 395 U.S. 367, 387 (1969) (F.C.C. may require broadcasters to allow reply time to vindicate speech interests of the public: "The right of free speech of a broadcaster, the user of a sound truck, or any other individual does not embrace a right to snuff out the free speech of others."); *Ginzburg v. United States,* 383 U.S. 463, 470 (1966) (upholding conviction for mailing obscene material on "pandering" theory: "[T]he purveyor's sole emphasis [is] on the sexually provocative aspects of his publications."); *Roth v. United States,* 354 U.S. 476, 487 (1957) (federal obscenity statute is found valid; obscene defined as "material which deals with sex in a manner appealing to prurient interest"); *Beauharnais v. Illinois,* 343 U.S. 250 (1952) (upholding group libel statute); *Chaplinsky v. New Hampshire,* 315 U.S. 568 (1942) (a state statute outlawing "fighting words" likely to cause a breach of peace is not unconstitutional under the First Amendment); *Near v. Minnesota,* 283 U.S. 697 (1931) (Minnesota statute permitting prior restraint of publishers who regularly engage in publication of defamatory material is held unconstitutional; press freedom outweighs prior restraints in all but exceptional cases, such as national security or obscenity); for one such exceptional case, see *United States v. Progressive, Inc.,* 486 F. Supp. 5 (W. D. Wis. 1979) (prior restraint is allowed against publication of information on how to make a hydrogen bomb, partially under "troop movements" exception); *Schenck v. United States,* 249 U.S.

"ban" on doing that injury again. Its principal enforcement mechanism is the civil rights commission, although it contains an option for direct access to court as well as de novo judicial review of administrative determinations, to ensure that no case will escape full judicial scrutiny and full due process. I will also not discuss various threshold issues, such as the sources of municipal authority, preemption, or abstention, or even issues of overbreadth or vagueness, nor will I defend the ordinance from views that never have been law, such as First Amendment absolutism. I will discuss the merits: how pornography by this definition is a harm, specifically how it is a harm of gender inequality, and how that harm outweighs any social interest in its protection by recognized First Amendment standards.[12]

This law aspires to guarantee women's rights consistent with the First Amendment by making visible a conflict of rights between the equality guaranteed to all women and what, in some legal sense, is now the freedom of the pornographers to make and sell, and their consumers to have access to, the materials this ordinance defines. Judicial resolution of this conflict, if the judges do for women what they have done for others, is likely to entail a balancing of the rights of women arguing that our lives and opportunities, including our freedom of speech and action, are constrained by—and in many cases flatly precluded by, in, and through—pornography, against those who argue that the pornography is harmless, or harmful only in part but not in the whole of the definition; or that it is more important to preserve the pornography than it is to prevent or remedy whatever harm it does.

In predicting how a court would balance these interests, it is important to understand that this ordinance cannot now be said to be either conclusively legal or illegal under existing law or precedent,[13] although I think the weight of authority is on our side. This ordinance enunciates a new form of the previously recognized governmental interest in sex equality. Many laws make sex equality a governmental interest.[14]

---

13 After the delivery of the Biddle Lecture, an Indiana federal court declared the ordinance unconstitutional in a facial challenge brought by the "Media Coalition," an association of publishers and distributors. The ordinance is repeatedly misquoted, and the misquotations are underscored to illustrate its legal errors. Arguments not made in support of the law are invented and attributed to the city and found legally inadequate. Evidence of harm before the legislature is given no weight at all, while purportedly being undisturbed, as an absolutist approach is implicitly adopted, unlike any existing Supreme Court precedent. To the extent that existing law, such as obscenity law, overlaps with the ordinance, even it would be invalidated under this ruling. And clear law on sex equality is flatly misstated. The opinion permits a ludicrous suit by mostly legitimate trade publishers, parties whose interests are at most tenuously and remotely implicated under the ordinance, to test a law that directly and importantly would affect others, such as pornographers and their victims. The decision also seems far more permissive toward racism than would be allowed in a concrete case even under existing law, and displays blame-the-victim misogyny: "Adult women generally have the capacity to protect themselves from participating in and being personally victimized by pornography . . ." *American Booksellers v. Hudnutt*, 598 F. Supp. 1316, 1334 (S.D. Ind. 1984). For subsequent developments, see "The Sexual Politics of the First Amendment."

14 See, e.g., Title IX of the Educ. Amends. of 1972, 20 U.S.C. §§ 1681–1686 (1972); Equal Pay Act, 29 U.S.C. § 206(d) (1963); Title VII of the Civil Rights Act of 1964, 42 U.S.C. §§ 2000e to 2000e–17 (1976). Many states have equal rights amendments to their constitutions, see Barbara Brown and Ann Freedman, "Equal Rights Amendment: Growing Impact on the States," 1 *Women's Rights Law Reporter* 1.63, 1.63–1.64 (1974); many states and cities, including Minneapolis and Indianapolis, prohibit discrimination on the basis of sex. See also *Roberts v. United States Jaycees,* 468 U.S. 609 (1984) (recently recognizing that sex equality is a compelling state interest); *Frontiero v. Richardson,* 411 U.S. 677 (1973); *Reed v. Reed,* 404 U.S. 71 (1971); U.S. Const. amend. XIV.

47, 52 (1919) ("clear and present dangers" excepted from the First Amendment: "The most stringent protection of free speech would not protect a man in falsely shouting fire in a theatre and causing a panic").

12 See *Young v. American Mini Theatres, Inc.,* 427 U.S. 50 (1976); *Pittsburgh Press Co. v. Human Relations Comm'n,* 413 U.S. 376 (1973); *Konigsberg v. State Bar of California,* 366 U.S. 36, 49–51 (1961).

Our law is designed to further the equality of the sexes, to help make sex equality real. Pornography is a practice of discrimination on the basis of sex, on one level because of its role in creating and maintaining sex as a basis for discrimination. It harms many women one at a time and helps keep all women in an inferior status by defining our subordination as our sexuality and equating that with our gender. It is also sex discrimination because its victims, including men, are selected for victimization on the basis of their gender. But for their sex, they would not be so treated.[15]

15 See *City of Los Angeles v. Manhart*, 435 U.S. 702, 711 (1978) (City water department's pension plan was found discriminatory in its "treatment of a person in a manner which but for that person's sex would be different"). See also *Orr v. Orr*, 440 U.S. 268 (1979); *Barnes v. Costle*, 561 F.2d 983 (D.C. Cir. 1977).

Review Questions

1. How does MacKinnon describe the content of pornography? What does pornography do beyond this content? What parts of her ordinance are directed toward content, and what parts to what pornography does beyond content?
2. Explain Dworkin's theory of sexuality.
3. How does MacKinnon define "sex object" through the way she uses the term?
4. Why is the harm of pornography difficult to see, according to MacKinnon?
5. What objections does MacKinnon make to the 1973 legal definition of obscenity?
6. How does MacKinnon distinguish between obscenity and pornography?
7. How do MacKinnon and Dworkin define pornography? By contrast, what is erotica?
8. In MacKinnon's view, why is pornography a harm, and why is it a violation of civil rights?

Discussion Questions

1. Given MacKinnon's definition, how pervasive is pornography in our society, in newspapers, magazines, movies, novels, and so on? What should be done about this?
2. Are men victims of pornography too? Explain.
3. What is gender, as distinguished from biological sex?
4. Does the First Amendment protect pornography? Why or why not?

Pornography and Free Speech: The Civil Rights Approach

BARRY LYNN

Barry Lynn was a counsel to the American Civil Liberties Union in Washington, D.C., when he wrote this article.

Lynn attacks the civil rights approach to pornography advocated by MacKinnon in the previous reading. To begin with, he thinks that the definition proposed by MacKinnon is too broad, including vast amounts of popular culture that would be subject to censorship; and if adopted, it would produce a chilling effect on speech. As for the claim that pornography is harmful, Lynn claims that there is no general scientific evidence that pornography causes men to commit sexual assaults and that there is evidence to the contrary—namely, the fact that countries such as Denmark have low rates of rape and sexual assault despite the wide availability of pornography. Lynn also rejects as "dangerous fallacies" the other arguments used by feminists to justify the censorship of pornography—for example, that there is no "corrective" to pornography and that it is sex discrimination. He concludes that pornography should be protected by the First Amendment like any other speech.

MANY PRACTITIONERS OF "WICCA," a pre-Christian nature religion, have engaged in a lengthy public relations campaign against the filming of John Updike's *The Witches of Eastwick* because of the film's allegedly negative stereotyping of "witches" as Devil-worshipping fanatics. Some Arab-Americans and Asian-Americans have orchestrated well-publicized protests against *The Delta Force* and *Year of the Dragon*, respectively, because of those films' depictions of ethnic groups in an allegedly derogatory fashion. Black Americans in some communities continue to object to the use of Mark Twain's *The Adventures of Huckleberry Finn* in public school classrooms because, notwithstanding its au-

thor's apparent sympathy with abolitionism, the work contains characters using racial epithets considered demeaning and objectionable. Even Christian fundamentalists have launched objections against television networks in the United States for their supposed systematically unfavorable portrayal of members of the clergy.

In each of these cases, the often rightly indignant group has essentially argued that the imagery in the objectionable books or films would be interpreted by readers or viewers to reflect the general, or perhaps even total, experience of the class: that all "witches" are evil or all Arab nationals are terrorists. In essence, the protesters argue that the depictions "lie" by suggesting universality for the worst attributes of a few members of the group or, even worse, misrepresent the group by fabricating erroneous attributes. All this is of concern because of the belief that speech, written or visual, has the power to

Source: Barry Lynn, "Pornography and Free Speech: The Civil Rights Approach," from *Civil Liberties in Conflict*, ed. Larry Gostin (Routledge, 1988), pp. 170–184. Reprinted with permission.

alter (or at least reinforce) perceptions and thus to shape attitudes and, in the long run, actions.

Supporters of a free speech principle, guaranteed in the United States Constitution in the First Amendment which warrants that "Congress shall make no law . . . abridging the freedom of speech, or of the press," would resist any effort by any of these groups to use the coercive power of government to prohibit or "correct" the imagery and ideas contained in the offending productions. Nevertheless, few would argue that the chain of reasoning employed was wholly irrelevant, since free speech advocates recognize that one major significance of the principle is that speech may indeed persuade persons to view some issue differently, and perhaps to act in accordance with that worldview. If speech had no impact, there would be little but academic interest in protecting it. The communicative possibility of words and pictures is precisely why they must be so vigorously protected.

In a fashion akin to that of the ethnic and religious groups cited above, some feminist groups have picketed screenings of explicit "pornographic" films which "displayed" women, as well as helped shutter more "mainstream" horror films which depicted grotesque brutality against women.

Some feminists have taken their effort one step further, however. Although claiming to eschew "censorship," they have been promoting so-called "civil rights" laws which could make publishers, film-makers, distributors, and even retail merchants extremely cautious about creating or disseminating certain sexually oriented images and ideas. These laws are to replace existing regulation of sexual material under "obscenity" laws. . . .

In essence, this approach would permit civil lawsuits against those who create (and in most cases those who distribute) "pornographic" material in which women are coerced to appear, where the material is used to harass women in the workplace, or which is implicated in some act of sexual assault. Most also create liability for "trafficking" in certain forbidden material. The definition of "pornography" in recent county ordinances in Indianapolis, Indiana, and elsewhere, drafted by law professor Catharine MacKinnon and author Andrea Dworkin, was the "graphic sexually-explicit subordination of women, whether in pictures or words" which also include scenarios ranging from those in which women are "presented as sexual objects who enjoy pain or humiliation" to those which depict women in "postures or positions of servility or submission or display."[1]

Whether the rubric for analysis is "obscenity" law or newer "anti-pornography" approaches, the universe of material to be controlled is largely co-extensive. The definition of "pornography" is no more "objective" than that in "obscenity" law, and is therefore no less susceptible to abuse. In fact, the new definition is as subjective and fluid as that created by the *Miller* test, taking within its ambit vast amounts of popular culture, from the writings of Erica Jong and Ernest Hemingway to feminist health-care and sex-education materials. It poses the problems related to any vague statute, including inducing citizens to "steer far wider of the unlawful zone" than if the boundaries of the forbidden areas were clearly marked.[2] This is the so-called "chilling effect" which occurs where the fear of future sanction has the practical effect of influencing whether a product is created or distributed. Moreover, these new statutes generally reflect the mistaken view that the product called pornography is itself what "harms," when in fact it is the action of some who produce or consume it which is what should be regulated.

There is actually nothing which ought to distinguish pornography itself from other constitutionally protected speech. Although *Das Kapital*

---

1 Indianapolis, Ind., City-County General Ordinance 35 Sec. 16–3 (q) (6) (11 June 1984).
2 *Grayned v. City of Rockford*, 408 US 104, 108–9, quoting *Baggett v. Bullitt*, 377 US 360, 372 (1964), quoting *Speiser v. Randall* 357 US 513, 526 (1958).

is indeed different in form from a centerfold in *Hustler* magazine, rational discourse should not be treated as a matter of law as superior to even the rawest of emotional appeals. Producers of communicative material should have the opportunity to speak through whatever medium they choose. If someone wishes to argue the merits of oral sex, he or she should not be accorded lesser constitutional protection if the "argument" is made in a XXX-rated video than in the prose of an academic psychology journal.

It is important to re-emphasize that pornography is indeed "communicative." Religious opponents of the material quite correctly note that it often represents a dazzling assault on the concepts of traditional morality, urging a "pornotopic" vision filled with lack of commitment, abandon, non-procreational goals, and a search for pleasure for its own sake. Feminist opponents also recognize much of it as a powerful advocate for the view that women affirmatively desire domination in sexual relationships. If it were not successful in transmitting these views, no one would bother to find ways to suppress it. . . .

That pornography achieves its communication through primarily non-cognitive means should not distinguish it constitutionally, either. Even the Supreme Court, in a famous case in which it upheld the right of a war protestor to wear a jacket emblazoned with the words "Fuck the Draft," noted that

> We cannot sanction the view that the Constitution, while solicitous of the cognitive content of individual speech, has little or no regard for that emotive function which, practically speaking, may often be the more important element of the overall message sought to be communicated.[3]

The court also has upheld the claim that live nude dancing was "speech,"[4] and lower courts

have accorded First Amendment protection to the "emotive" (and sometimes even "wordless") communication of rock and roll, jazz, bagpiping, and even mime.[5] . . .

Of course, communication does not have value only if it has some role in a political debate. Pornography also has what may be characterized as a "self-actualization" function. Its "message" can be significant to the self-identity of some viewers, particularly to those in sexual minorities. Indeed, now that pornography has transcended its earlier nearly exclusive interest in the breasts of young women, there is a message that 50-year-old grandmothers, pregnant women, and other-abled persons may also be viewed as sexual beings. Perhaps the real tragedy is that it is only in sexually explicit materials that this message is likely to be found. Certainly, the acknowledgement of the sexual diversity of our society can be an important step in the direction of a healthier understanding of overall human sexuality.

Moreover, the material can simply legitimatize the exploration of fantasy, without any impact on conduct. The Feminist Anti-Censorship Taskforce has noted:

> Depictions of ways of living and acting that are radically different from our own can enlarge the range of human possibilities open to us and help us grasp the potentialities of human behavior, both good and bad. Rich fantasy imagery allows us to experience in imagination ways of being that we may not wish to experience in real life. Such an enlarged vision of possible realities enhances our human potential, and is highly relevant to our decision-making as citizens on a wide range of social and ethical issues.[6]

3 *Cohen v. California,* 403 US 15, 26 (1970).
4 *Schad v. Borough of Mount Ephraim,* 452 US 61, 65 (1981).

5 See *Cinevision Corp. v. City of Burbank,* 745 F. 2d 560, 569 (9th Cir. 1984) (music); *Fact Concerts, Inc. v. City of Newport,* 626 F. 2d 1060 (1st Cir. 1980) (jazz); *Davenport v. City of Alexandria,* 710 F. 2d 148 (4th Cir. 1983) (bagpiping); *Birkenshaw v. Haley,* 409 F. Supp. 13 (E. D. Mich. 1974) (mime).
6 *Amicus* brief of the Feminist Anti-Censorship Taskforce at

This "positive" value to sexually explicit material is yet another basis for rejecting the characterization as "low-value" speech.

Clearly, there is no serious basis for treating sexual speech differently than other speech. Moreover, the specific elements of these "civil rights" ordinances illustrate the dangerous fallacies generally utilized to justify the suppression of sexually oriented material.

The first component of such measures is a cause of action for assault "caused" by pornography. There is no question that there are "copycat" actions where people replicate in real life the things they see in a variety of pornographic and non-pornographic material. Children see stunts on television and attempt them with tragic results; Japanese teenagers commit suicide after they learn on the national news of the suicide of a pop music idol; a man who views the television movie *The Burning Bed* burns his sleeping wife to death that night, mirroring the action of the abused wife against her abusive husband in the film; and a boy dies of strangulation with a men's magazine containing an article (albeit critical) about autoerotic asphyxiation found open near his corpse. . . .

The argument of causation, of course, usually goes beyond the neat parallelism of anecdotal evidence. However, there is no general scientific evidence to support the view that pornography "causes" men to commit sexual assault. Even researchers whose work was cited in the recent Attorney General's Commission on Pornography *Final Report,* to buttress its conclusion that pornography was harmful, have now publicly repudiated any claim that their data demonstrate such causation.[7] Two commissioners, one a well-known sex offender therapist, writing in partial dissent, noted that "efforts to tease the current data into proof of a causal link between these acts simply cannot be accepted."[8] The most that scientific data can show is some short-term attitude change in some experimental subjects after significant exposure to certain kinds of pornography. That is, some viewers temporarily see women in a more "negative" light, or have a more "positive" attitude toward non-marital sexual activity, and indicate such opinions on attitudinal surveys.[9] This is hardly a surprising finding, since laboratory studies show short-term attitudinal alteration after exposing subjects to almost any "message," from those in anti-smoking films to those in movies portraying other-abled persons in a favorable light.[10] The longevity of these altered impressions is likely to be short, and even laboratory data on the effects of violent "anti-women" films demonstrate only brief alterations in opinions of subjects.[11]

The US Pornography Commission and other pornography critics allege that attitude changes obviously affect behavior. Although it is logically true that attitude change always precedes behavioral change, not every attitude shift results in behavior modification. There are literally thousands of passing thoughts which would get the average person in trouble, if not in jail, every

29, *American Booksellers Assn v. Hudnutt,* 771 F. 2d 323 (7th Cir. 1985).

7 *New York Times,* 17 May 1986, at A-1, col. 1.

8 *Attorney General's Commission on Pornography, US Department of Justice, Final Report* (1986) (statement of Ellen Levine and Judith Becker).

9 See e.g. N. Malamuth and J. V. P. Check, "The effects of mass media exposure on acceptance of violence against women: a field experiment," *Journal of Research in Personality* 15 (1981): 436 (acceptance of violence); *Transcript of Proceedings, US Dept of Justice, The Attorney General's Commission on Pornography,* public hearing, Houston, Texas (11 September 1985): 112 (statement of Dr. Dolf Zillman, summarizing his research in acceptance of non-marital sexual activity).

10 See e.g. Timothy R. Elliott and E. Keith Byrd, "Attitude change toward disability through television portrayal," *Journal of Applied Rehabilitation Counseling* 14 (1983):35; "Smoker's luck: can a shocking programme change attitudes to smoking?" *Addictive Behavior* 8 (1983):43.

11 J. Ceniti and N. Malamuth, "Effects of repeated exposure to sexually violent or sexually non-violent stimuli on sexual arousal to rape and non-rape depictions," *Research and Therapy* (1985).

ents were allowed to punish "bad ckily, however, this nation regu-houghts. In fact, were a demon-itude change itself sufficient to permit the regulation of speech, the First Amendment would lose all significance. Certainly the amendment at least means that persons shall have an unencumbered opportunity to alter the attitudes of others by presenting them with powerful ideas and images.

Measures of association between pornography circulation and rape incidents are also not viable as a justification for regulating this material. One widely publicized study, by Baron and Straus, has been interpreted as a demonstration that sexual assault rates correlate with circulation rates of adult magazines.[12] This study, however, has now been characterized by one of its authors as not indicating that pornography causes rape. Moreover, he has indicated that introducing new factors into the equation statistically invalidates the relationship between circulation and assault rates.[13] In other countries, there remain data supporting correlations between wide availability of "hardcore" material and low rape rates (Japan),[14] as well as decreased or stable rates of sexual assault and other "sex" crimes as material is decriminalized (West Germany and Denmark, respectively).[15]

In other words, there is nothing to demonstrate any measurable increase in the aggregate level of sexual violence in the nation due to the presence of pornography. One commentator argues that "it is highly plausible to believe that the general climate reinforced by pornography contributes to an increased level of sexual violence against women." Such a standard of "plausibility" is not only insufficient to regulate speech; such speculative conclusions would properly preclude even regulation of commodities like food products and medicine. If there was a clear connection between pornography and sexual violence it would be apparent, not "plausible." . . .

The civil rights approach also usually contains a remedy for the "forcing" of pornography on unwilling persons. Public display of this material is hardly a major problem for most Americans. Surveys show that a remarkably high percentage of persons have never seen it at all, as it remains invisible to most non-consumers.[16] Many who are bothered by the material actually see nothing more explicit than the covers of the monthly *Cosmopolitan* or the swimsuit issue of *Sports Illustrated* when they look at the cover of the pornographic item. They are really concerned about the internal contents, which they would view only were they to open the periodical or insert the video cassette into a player.

Unwanted presentation is not a trivial matter, but no tolerant society can impose legal sanctions on the basis of chance encounters with offensive images. The Supreme Court, in a decision regarding nudity occasionally spotted by drivers passing an outdoor movie theater, noted that, absent a showing that substantial privacy interests were being invaded in an "essentially intolerable manner, the burden normally falls upon the viewer to avoid further bombardment of [his] sensibilities by averting [his] eyes."[17] It is in fact possible to walk through the vast majority of streets in America without observing,

12 L. Baron and M. Straus, "Sexual stratification, pornography, and rape in the United States" in N. Malamuth and E. Donnerstein (eds.) *Pornography and Sexual Aggression* (London, 1984): 185.

13 *Final Report* (note 8): 950.

14 P. Abramson and H. Hayashi, "Pornography in Japan: cross-cultural and theoretical considerations in pornography and sexual aggression," in Malamuth and Donnerstein (note 12): 173.

15 B. Kutchinsky, "Pornography and its effects in Denmark and the United States: a rejoinder and beyond," in R. F. Tomasson (ed.) *Comparative Social Research* (1985): 8.

16 See Pornography Commission, *Transcript,* Houston hearing (note 9): 310-E (author's calculations from testimony of Diana Russell indicate that 58 percent of women had never seen pornography, and 56 percent of those who did were not "upset" by it).

17 *Erznoznik v. City of Jacksonville,* 422 US 205, 210 (1985), citing *Cohen v. California,* 403 US 15, 21 (1971).

even by happenstance, a single explicit sexual image.

Where there are truly occurrences of malicious harassment by forced exposure to pornography, tort laws in most states already provide an avenue for redress.[18] In addition, courts are increasingly allowing suits under Title VII of the 1964 Civil Rights Law where employers, for example, display graphic material in the workplace so that a specific woman worker is presented with an essentially intolerable work environment.[19] These legal remedies are often justified, but the mere presence of offensive material inside magazines or the black plastic cases of video cassettes must remain an uncompensated offense, a *damnum absque injuria,* that the law cannot be reasonably expected to redress. . . .

A final cause of action is the most amorphous of all, creating a remedy against those who "traffic" in pornography. This is an apparent effort to permit any woman who believes that pornography has led to discrimination against her to sue the publisher, distributor, or retailer. This is possibly the baldest effort in such laws simply to frighten people out of the business of sexually explicit material from fear of lawsuits, even by those who have never been coerced into performing, forced to observe it, or assaulted by a viewer. It is predicated, however, on the assumption that pornography plays some major role in sex discrimination, but this, like previous arguments, is untenable. The status of women in places like Saudi Arabia, where there is virtually no pornography, cannot be considered superior to the position of women in the United States, where there is possibly an $8 billion industry in the material. Likewise, measures of the economic status of women in various states correlate positively with the circulation rates of major pornographic magazines. The fact that there is statistical correlation between higher women's status and a large number of sexual magazines is certainly not the result of any causative relationship, but it also tends to disprove the significance of the material in causing social disparity between the sexes.[20]

One other facile argument which has been advanced to justify new restriction is that the First Amendment rights of anti-pornography activists (and, by extension, the women they purport to "represent" in their efforts) have somehow been abridged by the pornographers, and that the government therefore owed some affirmative duty to try to equalize the power of those competing voices.[21] In fact, a vast amount of public attention has been given to the feminist antipornography effort in every conceivable popular medium. The underlying critique of the "pornotopic" vision is also present in a large array of scholarly and mass-market books which are readily available. Feminism as a vital social critique can hardly be said to have generated equality, but it has certainly changed both the consciousness and culture of American society. It has always done so by a critique of existing patriarchal doctrine, and not by an effort to silence the patriarchs. There is no constitutional basis for demanding that government scrutinize speech about any subject in order to determine the relative volume expressing particular viewpoints, much less than to effect a balance by curtailing some expressions of the "majoritarian" speakers.

Another variation which infuses the "new" debate over pornography is that there is no "corrective" to the way in which women's sexuality is depicted in the material. However, responsible researchers like Edward Donnerstein have been careful to "debrief" their experimental subjects, who have been "taught" rape myths

18 See e.g. *Shaffer v. National Can Corp.,* 565 E Supp. 909 (E. D. Pa. 1983) ("pornographic entertainment" offered to female employee by supervisor can be element of claim for intentional infliction of emotional distress).

19 See e.g. *Kyriazi v. Western Electric Co.,* 461 Supp. 894 (D. NJ 1978).

20 Baron and Straus (note 12).

21 See e.g. A. Dworkin, "Against the male flood: censorship, pornography and equality," *Harvard Women's Law Journal* 8 (1985): 1, 13.

with certain visual material, by providing them with factual information about the nature of sexual assault. They consistently find significant improvement in the understanding of rape following the debriefings, a demonstration that erroneous viewpoints about sexuality can indeed be successfully combated through the presentation of alternative ideas.[22] "More speech" supplants even "pornographic" speech. There is no magical or mystical ability of this material to alter behavior, notwithstanding its general ability to cause erections. It is no better a conditioner than any other form of expression, and when its viewpoint is offensive it may be effectively rebutted in the same way one can challenge the views of witches, Arabs, Asians, blacks, or Christians with which this chapter began.

Regardless of the name given to the efforts to regulate pornographic images, it is hard to construe them as anything but efforts at governmental censorship. All require enlisting the state, directly or indirectly, in removing certain sexual views from the culture. It is the political or moral ideas expressed therein which are offensive, and therefore deemed dangerous. Although Catharine MacKinnon, the author of the Indianapolis ordinance, repeatedly claim that hers is not a "moral" crusade,[23] she is in fact enlisting the government's courts to support her view of correct sexuality. By frightening "incorrect" expressions from the scene for fear of civil sanction, she is attempting to hurt financially those who promote such attitudes. Ultimately, there is little difference between the goal of her ordinances and the goal of traditional obscenity law.

The treatment by the US Supreme Court of sexual materials as a unique content-circum-

scribed class clearly has a ripple effect of ominous proportions. The very existence of "obscenity" laws, predicated on the constitutional difference between explicit speech about sex and other speech, has helped legitimatize the premise of these new ordinances that some sexual material is entitled to no First Amendment protection. "Sexual speech" fuels local efforts of others to ban Judy Blume novels from the high-school shelves or to eliminate the feminist works on women's health care from the local library, because these materials too are "about" sex. Whether any individual effort succeeds or fails, censorship is no phantom danger. The goal of regulating or suppressing certain sexual viewpoints is, nearly, in turn, indistinguishable in purpose from that noted by justice William Brennan in his dissent in *Paris Adult Theatres v. Slaton:*

> If a state may, in an effort to maintain or create a moral tone, prescribe what its citizens cannot read or cannot see, then it would seem to follow that in pursuit of that same objective a state could decree that its citizens must read certain books or must view certain films.[24]

If the courts may tell us what is wrong or incorrect, why not tell us precisely what is right and correct as well?

The ferocity of the debate among feminists is strong evidence of the complexity and danger of the effort to constrain a correct female sexuality. The Feminist Anti-Censorship Taskforce, in its *amicus* brief challenging the Indianapolis ordinance, notes with irony that the ordinance

> delegitimates and makes socially invisible women who find sexually explicit images of women "in positions of display" or "penetrated by objects" to be erotic, liberating, or educational. These women are told that their perceptions are a product of "false consciousness" and

22 See e.g. E. Donnerstein and L. Berkowitz, "Victim reactions in aggressive erotic films as a factor in violence against women," *Journal of Personality and Social Psychology* 41 (1981): 710.

23 See e.g. C. MacKinnon, "Not a moral issue," *Yale Law and Policy Review* 2 (1984): 321.

24 413 US 110.

that such images are so inherently degrading that they may be suppressed by the state.[25]

The whole discussion of pornography and the law was substantially polluted in 1986 by the release of the *Final Report* of the Attorney General's Commission on Pornography, a curious mix of moralizing and pseudo-feminist musings which urged a nationwide crackdown on sexually oriented material. Since the commission's method of data-gathering was so intellectually irresponsible, it is regrettable that its data and conclusions have received any acceptance by responsible persons. Indeed, the conclusions of the commission were essentially embodied in the documents which created the body, most notably the serious problem posed by the material and the need for further regulation. When combined with a membership which had, for the most part, staked out an "anti-pornogra-

25 *Amicus* (note 6): 42.

phy" position before their appointment, the likelihood of serious inquiry was jeopardized.

Although the Pornography Commission's emphasis on enforcing existing (or slightly "improved") obscenity laws was rejected by feminist anti-pornography advocates, those groups generally endorsed the conclusions of the commission about the "harmfulness" of the material for women, including its implication in acts of sexual violence. Moreover, the commission's recurring conclusion that regulating much of this material had no serious free speech implications was also seen by some feminists as a boon to their analysis, particularly since the commission endorsed legislative examination of the new "civil rights" laws. . . .

The new approaches rest on unacceptable analytical principles and a legal philosophy that is antithetical to the civil liberties guarantee of free expression. It would hold speech about sexuality hostage to even the most unique and unintended response of the most susceptible viewer or reader.

Review Questions

1. How does Lynn interpret the First Amendment?
2. What are Lynn's objections to the MacKinnon-Dworkin definition of pornography?
3. Explain Lynn's view of pornography.
4. Why should pornography be given First Amendment protection, according to Lynn?
5. In Lynn's view, what does the evidence show about pornography and sexual assault?
6. What is Lynn's position on unsolicited pornography?
7. What are the feminist arguments, and why does Lynn reject them?
8. According to Lynn, what are the effects of ordinances banning pornography?
9. What is Lynn's view of the 1986 report on pornography?

Discussion Questions

1. Lynn admits that exposure to pornography causes short-term attitude changes. Why isn't this a reason for banning pornography? What does Lynn say? What do you think?
2. Does pornography play a role in sex discrimination or not? Why or why not?
3. Lynn complains that MacKinnon is trying to force her view of "correct sexuality" on us by means of the courts. Do you agree? Explain your answer.
4. If certain films should be banned, should other films be required viewing?

American Booksellers v. Hudnutt

UNITED STATES DISTRICT COURT AND COURT OF APPEALS

In this case, the court ruled that an Indianapolis ordinance prohibiting pornography was unconstitutional. Instead of being directed at discriminatory behavior, the ordinance was restricting speech protected by the First Amendment to the U.S. Constitution. Although the court recognized that there are compelling state interests for restricting speech in some cases—e.g. "fighting words," libel, and obscenity—no compelling state interest for restricting speech was found in this case. Furthermore, the court argued that broad limitations on speech such as the one contemplated by the ordinance produce a slippery slope of bad consequences, leading eventually to tyranny and injustice.

INDIANAPOLIS ENACTED AN ORDINANCE defining "pornography" as a practice that discriminates against women. "Pornography" is to be redressed through the administrative and judicial methods used for other discrimination. . . .

"Pornography" under the ordinance is "the graphic sexually explicit subordination of women, whether in pictures or in words, that also includes one or more of the following:

1. Women are presented as sexual objects who enjoy pain or humiliation; or
2. Women are presented as sexual objects who experience sexual pleasure in being raped; or
3. Women are presented as sexual objects tied up or cut up or mutilated or bruised or physically hurt, or as dismembered or truncated or fragmented or severed into body parts; or
4. Women are presented as being penetrated by objects or animals; or
5. Women are presented in scenarios of degradation, injury, abasement, torture, shown

as filthy or inferior, bleeding, bruised, or hurt in a context that makes these conditions sexual; or
6. Women are presented as sexual objects for domination, conquest, violation, exploitation, possession, or use, or through postures or positions of servility or submission or display." . . .

FIRST AMENDMENT REQUIREMENTS

This Ordinance cannot be analyzed adequately without first recognizing this: The drafters of the Ordinance have used what appears to be a legal term of art, "pornography," but have in fact given the term a specialized meaning which differs from the meanings ordinarily assigned to that word in both legal and common parlance. In Section 16-3(v) (page 6), the Ordinance states:

Pornography shall mean the sexually explicit subordination of women, graphically depicted, whether in pictures or in words, that includes one or more of the following: . . .

Source: United States District Court and Court of Appeals, *American Booksellers v. Hudnutt*.

There follows . . . a listing of five specific presentations of women in various settings which serve as examples of "pornography" and as such further define and describe that term under the Ordinance.

As is generally recognized, the word "pornography" is usually associated, and sometimes synonymous, with the word, "obscenity." "Obscenity" not only has its own separate and specialized meaning in the law, but in laymen's use also, and it is a much broader meaning than the definition given the word "pornography" in the Ordinance which is at issue in this action. There is thus a considerable risk of confusion in analyzing this Ordinance unless care and precision are used in that process.

The Constitutional analysis of this Ordinance requires a determination of several underlying issues: First, the Court must determine whether the Ordinance imposes restraints on speech or behavior (content versus conduct); if the Ordinance is found to regulate speech, the Court must next determine whether the subject speech is protected or not protected under the First Amendment; if the speech . . . regulated by this Ordinance is protected speech under the Constitution, the Court must then decide whether the regulation is constitutionally permissible . . . based on a compelling state interest justifying the removal of such speech from First Amendment protections.

Do the Ordinances Regulate Speech or Behavior (Content or Conduct)?

It appears to be central to the defense of the Ordinance by defendants that the Court accept their premise that the City-County Council has not attempted to regulate speech, let alone protected speech. Defendants repeat throughout their briefs the incantation that their Ordinance regulates conduct, not speech. They contend (one senses with a certain sleight of hand) that the production, dissemination, and use of sexually explicit words and pictures is the actual subordination of women and not an expression of ideas deserving of First Amendment protection. . . .

Defendants claim support for their theory by analogy, arguing that it is an accepted and established legal distinction that has allowed other courts to find that advocacy of a racially "separate but equal" doctrine in a civil rights context is protected speech under the First Amendment though "segregation" is not constitutionally protected behavior. Accordingly, defendants characterize their Ordinance here as a civil rights measure, through which they seek to prevent the distribution, sale, and exhibition of "pornography," as defined in the Ordinance, in order to regulate and control the underlying unacceptable conduct. The content-versus-conduct approach espoused by defendants is not persuasive, however, and is contrary to accepted First Amendment principles. Accepting as true the City-County Council's finding that pornography conditions society to subordinate women, the means by which the Ordinance attempts to combat this sex discrimination is nonetheless through the regulation of speech.

For instance, the definition of pornography, the control of which is the whole thrust . . . , states that it is "the sexually explicit subordination of women, graphically *depicted,* whether in *pictures* or in *words,* that includes one or more of the following:" (emphasis supplied) and the following five descriptive subparagraphs begin with . . . , "Women are *presented.* . . ."

The unlawful acts and discriminatory practices under the Ordinance are set out in Section 16-3(g):

> (4) Trafficking in pornography: the production, sale, exhibition, or distribution of pornography. . . .
> (5) Coercion into pornographic performance: coercing, intimidation or fraudulently inducing any person . . . into performing for pornography. . . .
> (6) Forcing pornography on a person: . . .
> (7) Assault or physical attack due to pornography: the assault, physical attack, or

injury of any woman, man, child or transsexual in a way that is directly caused by specific pornography. . . .

Section (7), *supra,* goes on to provide a cause of action in damages against the perpetrators, makers, distributors, sellers, and exhibitors of pornography and injunctive relief against the further exhibition, distribution or sale of pornography.

In summary, therefore, the Ordinance establishes through the legislative findings that pornography causes a tendency to commit these various harmful acts, and outlaws the pornography (that is, the "depictions"), the activities involved in the production of pornography, and the behavior caused by or resulting from pornography.

Thus, though the purpose of the Ordinance is cast in civil rights terminology—"to prevent and prohibit all discriminatory practices of sexual subordination or inequality through pornography" . . .—it is clearly aimed at controlling the content of the speech and ideas that the City-County Council has found harmful and offensive. Those words and pictures which depict women in sexually subordinate roles are banned by the Ordinance. Despite defendants' attempt to redefine offensive speech as harmful action, the clear wording of the Ordinance discloses that they seek to control speech, and those restrictions must be analyzed in light of applicable constitutional requirements and standards.

Is the Speech Regulated by the Ordinance Protected or Unprotected Speech Under the First Amendment?

The First Amendment provides that government shall make no law abridging the freedom of speech. However, "the First and Fourteenth Amendments have never been thought to give absolute protection to every individual to speak whenever or wherever he pleases or to

use any form of address in any circumstances that he chooses." *Cohen v. California* (1971). Courts have recognized only a "relatively few categories of instances," . . . where the government may regulate certain forms of individual expression. The traditional categories of speech subject to permissible government regulation include "the lewd and obscene, the profane, the libelous, and the insulting or 'fighting' words—those which by their very utterance inflict injury or tend to incite an immediate breach of the peace." *Chaplinsky v. State of New Hampshire* (1942). In addition, the Supreme Court has recently upheld legislation prohibiting the dissemination of material depicting children engaged in sexual conduct. *New York v. Ferber* (1982).

Having found that the Ordinance at issue here seeks to regulate speech (and not conduct), the next question before the Court is whether the Ordinance, which seeks to restrict the distribution, sale, and exhibition of "pornography" as a form of sex discrimination against women, falls within one of the established categories of speech subject to permissible government regulation, that is, speech deemed to be unprotected by the First Amendment.

It is clear that this case does not present issues relating to profanity, libel, or "fighting words." In searching for an analytical "peg," the plaintiffs argue that the Ordinance most closely resembles obscenity, and is, therefore, subject to the requirements set forth in *Miller v. California* (1973). . . . But the defendants admit that the scope of the Ordinance is not limited to the regulation of legally obscene material as defined in *Miller.* . . . In fact, defendants concede that the "pornography" they seek to control goes beyond obscenity, as defined by the Supreme Court and excepted from First Amendment protections. Accordingly, the parties agree that the materials . . . in the restrictions set out in the Ordinance include to some extent what have traditionally been protected materials.

The test under *Miller* for determining whether material is legal obscenity is:

(a) whether "the average person, applying contemporary community standards" would find that the work, taken as a whole, appeals to the prurient interest, . . . ; (b) whether the work depicts or describes, in a patently offensive way, sexual conduct specifically defined by the applicable state law; and (c) whether the work, taken as a whole, lacks serious literary, artistic, political, or scientific value. . . .

It is obvious that this three-step test is not directly applicable to the present case, because, as has been noted, the Ordinance goes beyond legally obscene material in imposing its controls. The restrictions in the Indianapolis ordinance reach what has otherwise traditionally been regarded as protected speech under the *Miller* test. Beyond that, the Ordinance does not speak in terms of a "community standard" or attempt to restrict the dissemination of material that appeals to the "prurient interest." Nor has the Ordinance been drafted in a way to limit only distributions of "patently offensive" materials. Neither does it provide for the dissemination of works which, though "pornographic," may have "serious literary, artistic, political or scientific value." Finally, the Ordinance does not limit its reach to "hard-core sexual conduct," though conceivably "hard-core" materials may be included in its proscriptions.

Because the Ordinance spans so much more . . . in its regulatory scope than merely "hard-core" obscenity by limiting the distribution of "pornography," the proscriptions in the Ordinance intrude with defendants' explicit approval into areas of otherwise protected speech. Under ordinary constitutional analysis, that would be sufficient grounds to overturn the Ordinance, but defendants argue that this case is not governed by any direct precedent, that it raises a new issue for the Court and even though the Ordinance regulates protected speech, it does so in a constitutionally permissible fashion.

Does Established First Amendment Law Permit the Regulation Provided for in the Ordinance of Otherwise Protected Speech?

In conceding that the scope of this Ordinance extends beyond constitutional limits, it becomes clear that what defendants actually seek by enacting this legislation is a newly defined class of constitutionally unprotected speech, labeled "pornography" and characterized as sexually discriminatory.

Defendants vigorously argue that *Miller* is not the "'constitutional divide' separating protected from unprotected expression in this area." . . . Defendants point to three cases which allegedly support their proposition that *Miller* is not the exclusive guideline for disposing of pornography/obscenity cases, and that the traditional obscenity test should not be applied in the present case. . . .

Defendants first argue that the Court must use the same reasoning applied by the Supreme Court in *New York v. Ferber,* . . . which upheld a New York statute prohibiting persons from promoting child pornography by distributing material which depicted such activity, and carve out another similar exception to protected speech under the First Amendment.

Defendants can properly claim some support for their position in *Ferber.* There the Supreme Court allowed the states "greater leeway" in their regulation of pornographic depictions of children in light of the State's compelling interest in protecting children who, without such protections, are extraordinarily vulnerable to exploitation and harm. The court stated in upholding the New York statute:

The prevention of sexual exploitation and abuse of children constitutes a government objective of surpassing importance. The legislative findings accompanying passage of the New York laws reflect this concern: . . .

The Supreme Court continued in *Ferber* by noting that the *Miller* standard for legal obscenity does not satisfy the unique concerns and issues posed by child pornography where children are involved; it is irrelevant, for instance, that the materials sought to be regulated contain serious literary, artistic, political, or scientific value. In finding that some speech, such as that represented in depictions of child pornography, is outside First Amendment protections, the *Ferber* court stated:

> When a definable class of material . . . bears so heavily and pervasively on the welfare of children engaged in its production, we think the balance of competing interests is clearly struck and that it is permissible to consider these materials as without the protection of the First Amendment.

Defendants, in the case at bar, argue that the interests of protecting women from sex-based discrimination are analogous to and every bit as compelling and fundamental as those which the Supreme Court upheld in *Ferber* for the benefit of children. But *Ferber* appears clearly distinguishable from the instant case on both the facts and law.

As has already been shown, the rationale applied by the Supreme Court in *Ferber* appears intended to apply solely to child pornography cases. In *Ferber*, the court recognized "that a state's interest in 'safeguarding the physical and psychological well-being of a minor' is 'compelling.'" . . . Also, the obscenity standard in *Miller* is appropriately abandoned in child pornography cases because it "[does] not reflect the State's particular and more compelling interest in prosecuting those who promote the sexual exploitations of children." . . . . Since a state's compelling interest in preventing child pornography outweighs an individual's First Amendment rights, the Supreme Court held that "the states are entitled to greater leeway in the regulation of pornographic depictions of children." . . .

In contrast, the case at bar presents issues more far reaching than those in *Ferber*. Here, the City-County Council found that the distri-

bution, sale, and exhibition of words and pictures depicting the subordination of women is a form of sex discrimination and as such is appropriate for governmental regulation. The state has a well-recognized interest in preventing sex discrimination, and, defendants argue, it can regulate speech to accomplish that end.

But the First Amendment gives primacy to free speech and any other state interest (such as the interest of sex-based equality under law) must be so compelling as to be fundamental; only then can it be deemed to outweigh the interest of free speech. This Court finds no legal authority or public policy argument which justifies so broad an incursion into First Amendment freedoms as to allow that which defendants attempt to advance here. *Ferber* does not open the door to allow the regulation contained in the Ordinance for the reason that adult women as a group do not, as a matter of public policy or applicable law, stand in need of the same type of protection which has long been afforded children. This is true even of women who are subject to the sort of inhuman treatment defendants have described and documented to the Court in support of this Ordinance. The Supreme Court's finding in *Ferber* of the uncontroverted state interest in "safeguarding the physical and psychological well-being of a minor" and its resultant characterization of that interest as "compelling," . . . is an interest that inheres to children and is not an interest which is readily transferrable to adult women as a class. Adult women generally have the capacity to protect themselves from participating in and being personally victimized by pornography, which make the State's interest in safeguarding the physical and psychological well-being of women by prohibiting "the sexually explicit subordination of women, graphically depicted, whether in pictures or in words" not so compelling as to sacrifice the guarantees of the First Amendment. In any case, whether a state interest is so compelling as to be a fundamental interest sufficient to warrant an exception from constitutional protections, therefore, surely must turn on something other than mere legislative dictate, which issue is discussed more fully further on in this Opinion. . . .

The second case relied upon by defendants to support their contention that Miller is not controlling in the present case is *FCC v. Pacifica Foundation* . . . (1978). According to defendants, *Pacifica* exemplifies the Supreme Court's refusal to make obscenity the sole legal basis for regulating sexually explicit conduct.

In *Pacifica,* the Supreme Court was faced with the question of whether a broadcast of patently offensive words dealing with sex and excretion may be regulated on the basis of their content. . . . The Court held that this type of speech was not entitled to absolute constitutional protection in every context. . . . Since the context of the speech in *Pacifica* was broadcasting, it was determined only to be due "the most limited First Amendment protection." . . . The reason for such treatment was two-fold:

> First, the broadcast media have established a uniquely pervasive presence in all the lives of all Americans. Patently offensive, indecent material presented over the airwaves confronts the citizen, not only in public, but also in the privacy of the home, where the individual's right to be left alone plainly outweighs the First Amendment rights of an intruder.
>
> Second, broadcasting is uniquely accessible to children, even those too young to read. . . .

Although the defendants correctly point out that the Supreme Court did not use the traditional obscenity test in *Pacifica,* this Court is not persuaded that the rule enunciated there is applicable to the facts of the present case. The Ordinance does not attempt to regulate the airwaves; in terms of its restrictions, it is not even remotely concerned with the broadcast media. The reasons for the rule in *Pacifica,* that speech in certain contexts should be afforded minimal First Amendment protection, are not present here, since we are not dealing with a medium that "invades" the privacy of the home. In con-

trast, if an individual is offended by "pornography," as defined in the Ordinance, the logical thing to do is avoid it, an option frequently not available to the public with material disseminated through broadcasting.

In addition, the Ordinance is not written to protect children from the distribution of pornography, in contrast to the challenged FCC regulation in *Pacifica.* Therefore, the peculiar state interest in protecting the "well-being of its youth," . . . does not underlie this Ordinance and cannot be called upon to justify a decision by this Court to uphold the Ordinance.

The third case cited by defendants in support of their proposition that the traditional obscenity standard in *Miller* should not be used to overrule the Ordinance is *Young v. American Mini Theatres, Inc.* . . . (1976). In *Young* the Supreme Court upheld a city ordinance that restricted the location of movie theatres featuring erotic films. The Court, in a plurality opinion, stated that "[e]ven though the First Amendment protects communication in this area from total suppression, we hold that the State may legitimately use the content of these materials as the basis for placing them in a different classification from other motion pictures." . . . The Court concluded that the city's interest in preserving the character of its neighborhoods justified the ordinance which required that adult theatres be separated, rather than concentrated, in the same areas as it is permissible for other theaters to do without limitation. . . .

Young is distinguishable from the present case because we are not here dealing with an attempt by the City-County Council to restrict the time, place, and manner in which "pornography" may be distributed. Instead, the Ordinance prohibits completely the sale, distribution, or exhibition of material depicting women in a sexually subordinate role, at all times, in all places and in every manner.

The Ordinance's attempt to regulate speech beyond one of the well-defined exceptions to protected speech under the First Amendment is not supported by other Supreme Court precedents. The Court must, therefore, examine the underlying premise of the Ordinance: That the State has so compelling an interest in regulating the sort of sex discrimination imposed and perpetuated through "pornography" that it warrants an exception to free speech.

Is Sex Discrimination a Compelling State Interest Justifying an Exception to First Amendment Protections?

It is significant to note that the premise of the Ordinance is the sociological harm, i.e., the discrimination, which results from "pornography" to degrade women as a class. The Ordinance does not presume or require specifically defined, identifiable victims for most of its proscriptions. The Ordinance seeks to protect adult women, as a group, from the diminution of their legal and sociological status as women, that is, from the discriminatory stigma which befalls women *as women* as a result of "pornography." On page one of the introduction to defendants' *Amicus Brief,* counsel explicitly argues that the harm which underlies this legislation is the "harm to the treatment and *status* of women . . . on the basis of sex." . . .

This is a novel theory advanced by the defendants, an issue of first impression in the courts. If this Court were to accept defendants' argument—that the State's interest in protecting women from the humiliation and degradation which comes from being depicted in a sexually subordinate context is so compelling as to warrant the regulation of otherwise free speech to accomplish that end—one wonders what would prevent the City-County Council (or any other legislative body) from enacting protections for other equally compelling claims against exploitation and discrimination as are presented here. Legislative bodies, finding support here, could also enact legislation prohibiting other unfair expression—the publication and distribution of racist material, for instance,

on the grounds that it causes racial discrimination,[1] or legislation prohibiting ethnic or religious slurs on the grounds that they cause discrimination against particular ethnic or religious groups, or legislation barring literary depictions which are uncomplimentary or oppressive to handicapped persons on the grounds that they cause discrimination against that group of people, and so on. If this Court were to extend to this case the rationale in *Ferber* to uphold the Amendment, it would signal so great a potential encroachment upon First Amendment freedoms that the precious liberties reposed within those guarantees would not survive. The compelling state interest, which defendants claim gives constitutional life to their Ordinance, though important and valid as that interest may be in other contexts, is not so fundamental an interest as to warrant a broad intrusion into otherwise free expression.

Defendants contend that pornography is not deserving of constitutional protection because its harms victimize all women. It is argued that "pornography" not only negatively affects women who risk and suffer the direct abuse of its production, but also, those on whom violent pornography is forced through such acts as compelled performances of "dangerous acts such as being hoisted upside down by ropes, bound by ropes and chains, hung from trees and

---

1 In *Beauharnais v. Illinois* . . . (1952), the Supreme Court upheld an Illinois libel statute prohibiting the dissemination of materials promoting racial or religious hatred and which tended to produce a breach of the peace and riots. It has been recognized that "the rationale of that decision turns quite plainly on the strong tendency of the prohibited utterances to cause violence and disorder." *Collin v. Smith* (7th Cir. 1978). The Supreme Court has recognized breach of the peace as the traditional justification for upholding a criminal libel statute. *Beauharnais* . . . Therefore, a law preventing the distribution of material that causes racial discrimination, an attitude, would be upheld under this analysis. Further, the underlying reasoning of the *Beauharnais* opinion, that the punishment of libel raises no constitutional problems, has been questioned in many recent cases. . . .

scaffolds or having sex with animals. . . ." It is also alleged that exposure to pornography produces a negative impact on its viewers, causing in them an increased willingness to aggress toward women, *ibid*. . . . , and experience self-generated rape fantasies, increases in sexual arousal and a rise in the self-reported possibility of raping. . . . In addition, it causes discriminatory attitudes and behavior toward all women. . . . The City-County Council, after considering testimony and social research studies, enacted the Ordinance in order to "combat" pornography's "concrete and tangible harms to women." . . .

Defendants rely on *Paris Adult Theatre I v. Slaton* . . . (1973) to justify their regulation of "pornography." In that case the Supreme Court held "there are legitimate state interests at stake in stemming the tide of commercialized obscenity . . . [that] include the interest of the public in the quality of life and the total community environment, the tone of commerce in the great city centers, and, possibly, . . . public safety itself." . . .

The Georgia Legislature had determined that in that case exposure to obscene material adversely affected men and women, that is to say, society as a whole. Although the petitioners argued in that case that there was no scientific data to conclusively prove that proposition, the Court said, "[i]t is not for us to resolve empirical uncertainties underlying state legislation, save in the exceptional case where that legislation plainly impinges upon rights protected by the constitution itself." . . .

Based on this reasoning, defendants argue that there is more than enough "empirical" evidence in the case at bar to support the City-County Council's conclusion that "pornography" harms women in the same way obscenity harms people, and, therefore, this Court should not question the legislative finding. As has already been acknowledged, it is not the Court's function to question the City-County Council's legislative finding. The Court's solitary duty is to ensure that the Ordinance accomplishes its purpose without violating constitutional standards or impinging upon constitutionally protected rights. In applying those tests, the Court finds that the Ordinance cannot withstand constitutional scrutiny.

It has already been noted that the Ordinance does not purport to regulate legal obscenity, as defined in *Miller*. Thus, although the City-County Council determined that "pornography" harms women, this Court must and does declare the Ordinance invalid without being bound by the legislative findings because "pornography," as defined and regulated in the Ordinance, is constitutionally protected speech under the First Amendment and such an exception to [its] protections is constitutionally unwarranted. This Court cannot legitimately embark on judicial policy making, carving out a new exception to the First Amendment simply to uphold the Ordinance, even when there may be many good reasons to support legislative action. To permit every interest group, especially those who claim to be victimized by unfair expression, their own legislative exceptions to the First Amendment so long as they succeed in obtaining a majority of legislative votes in their favor demonstrates the potentially predatory nature of what defendants seek through this Ordinance and defend in this lawsuit.

It ought to be remembered by defendants and all others who would support such a legislative initiative that, in terms of altering sociological patterns, much as alteration may be necessary and desirable, free speech, rather than being the enemy, is a long-tested and worthy ally. To deny free speech in order to engineer social change in the name of accomplishing a greater good for one sector of our society erodes the freedoms of all and, as such, threatens tyranny and injustice for those subjected to the rule of such laws. The First Amendment protections presuppose the evil of such tyranny and prevent a finding by this Court upholding the Ordinance. . . .

Review Questions

1. What is the usual meaning of the word "pornography," according to the court?
2. Does the Indianapolis ordinance regulate speech or conduct? What is the court's answer?
3. What does the First Amendment say? When does it protect speech, according to the court?
4. What is the three-step test for legal obscenity under *Miller*? Why does this test apply to the Indianapolis ordinance?
5. Why does the court reject the argument that protecting women is analogous to protecting children?
6. What was the *Pacifica* case about, and why wasn't it relevant, according to the court?
7. Describe the *Young* case. How was it different from the present case?
8. Why does the court reject the argument that sex discrimination justifies an exception to First Amendment protection of free speech?

Discussion Questions

1. Does pornography harm all women? Does it harm some women? Why don't people agree about the answers? How should we go about answering these questions?
2. Do you agree with the court's claim that restricting free speech produces tyranny and injustice? Explain your answer.

If He Hollers Let Him Go: Regulating Racist Speech on Campus

CHARLES R. LAWRENCE III

Charles R. Lawrence III is professor of law at Georgetown University. He is a co-author of *The Bakke Case: The Politics of Inequality* (1979).

Lawrence defends narrow speech codes such as the one at Stanford University. To show that they are constitutional, he appeals to the case of *Brown* and the Civil Rights Act of 1964. To demonstrate that hate speech produces real harms, he cites examples of hate speech and explains in detail why this speech harms people. He also explains why there is a tendency in our racist society to overlook or minimize these harms. He repudiates the arguments of civil libertarians who defend an absolute First Amendment standard that allows racist hate speech. These arguments all fail because they presuppose an ideal nonracist society with equality of opportunity. If we listen to the hate speech and its victims, we can see that our society is deeply infected with racism and that equality is an illusion.

Racist incidents occur at the University of Michigan, University of Massachusetts-Amherst, University of Wisconsin, University of New Mexico, Columbia University, Wellesley College, Duke University, and University of California-Los Angeles. (*Ms.* magazine, October, 1987)

The campus ought to be the last place to legislate tampering with the edges of first amendment protections.

University of Michigan: "Greek Rites of Exclusion": Racist leaflets distributed in dorms; white students paint themselves black and place rings in their noses at "jungle parties." (*The Nation,* July 1987)

Silencing a few creeps is no victory if the price is an abrogation of free speech. Remember censorship is an ugly word too.

Northwest Missouri State University: White Supremacists distribute flyers stating: "The Knights of the Ku Klux Klan are Watching You." (Klanwatch Intelligence Report No. 42, February 1988 [*Klanwatch*])

Kansas University: KKK members speak. (*Klanwatch*)

Temple University: White Student Union formed. (*Klanwatch*)

Stanford University: Aryan Resistance literature distributed. (*Klanwatch*)

Stockton State College (New Jersey): Invisible Empire literature distributed. (*Klanwatch*)

Memphis State University: Bomb threats at Jewish Student Union. (*Klanwatch*)

Arizona State University: Shot fired at Hillel Foundation building. (Klanwatch*)*

The harm that censors allege will result unless speech is forbidden rarely occurs.

Dartmouth College: Black professor called "a cross between a welfare queen and a bathroom attendant" and the *Dartmouth Review* purported to quote a Black student, "Dese boys be sayin' that we be comin' here to Dartmut an' not takin' the classics." (*The Nation,* February 27, 1989)

Source: Charles R. Lawrence III, "Regulating Racist Speech on Campus," from the *Duke University Law Review* (1990). Reprinted with permission.

Yes, speech is sometimes painful. Sometimes it is abusive. That is one of the prices of a free society.

Purdue University: Counselor finds "Death Nigger" scratched on her door. (*The Nation,* February 27, 1989)

More speech, not less, is the proper cure for offensive speech.

Smith College: African student finds message slipped under her door that reads, "African Nigger do you want some bananas? Go back to the Jungle." (*New York Times,* October 19, 1988).

Speech cannot be banned simply because it is offensive.

University of Michigan: Campus radio station broadcasts a call from a student who "joked": "Who are the most famous black women in history? Aunt Jemima and Mother Fucker." (*The Nation,* February 27, 1989)

Those who don't like what they are hearing or seeing should try to change the atmosphere through education. That is what they will have to do in the real world after they graduate.

University of Michigan: A student walks into class and sees this written on the blackboard: "A mind is a terrible thing to waste—especially on a nigger." (*Chicago Tribune,* April 23, 1989)

People of color, women, and gays and lesbians owe their vibrant political movements in large measure to their freedom to communicate. If speech can be banned because it offends someone, how long will it be before the messages of these groups are themselves found offensive?

Stanford University: "President Donald Kennedy refused yesterday to consider amnesty for students who took over his office last week. . . . Kennedy insisted that the probe of violations of the Stanford behavior code go forward. The students [who were demanding more minority faculty and ethnic studies reforms] consider the prospect of disciplinary action unfair in view of Stanford's decision earlier this year not to punish two white students who defaced a poster of 19th century composer Ludwig van Beethoven to portray a stereotypical black face, then tacked it up in a predominantly black dormitory. The two incidents differ sharply, Kennedy said. The poster was admittedly racially offensive. But its defacement probably was protected by constitutional freedoms. However, the office takeover was clearly a violation of Stanford's policy against campus disruption." (*San Francisco Chronicle,* May 25, 1989)

Now it's the left that is trying to restrict free speech. Though the political labels have shifted, the rationale is the same: Our adversaries are dangerous and therefore should not be allowed to speak.

IN RECENT YEARS, university campuses have seen a resurgence of racial violence and a corresponding rise in the incidence of verbal and symbolic assault and harassment to which blacks and other traditionally subjugated groups are subjected. The events listed above were gathered from newspapers and magazine reports of racist incidents on campuses. The accompanying italicized statements criticizing proposals to regulate racism on campus were garnered from conversations, debates, and panel discussions at which I was present. Some were recorded verbatim and are exact quotes; others paraphrase the sentiment expressed. I have heard some version of each of these arguments many times over. These incidents are but a small sampling of the hate speech to which minorities are subjected on a daily basis on our nation's college campuses. There is a heated debate in the civil liberties community concerning the proper response to incidents of racist speech on campus. Strong disagreements have arisen between those individuals who believe that racist speech such as that described above should be regulated by the university or some public body and those individuals who believe that racist expression should be protected from all public regulation. At the center of the controversy is a tension between the constitutional values of free speech and equality. Like the debate over affirmative action in university admissions, this issue has divided old allies and revealed unrecognized or unac-

knowledged differences in the experience, perceptions, and values of members of longstanding alliances. It also has caused considerable soul searching by individuals with longtime commitments to both the cause of political expression and the cause of racial equality.

I write this chapter from within the cauldron of this controversy. I make no pretense of dispassion or objectivity, but I do claim a deep commitment to the values that motivate both sides of the debate. I have spent the better part of my life as a dissenter. As a high school student I was threatened with suspension for my refusal to participate in a civil defense drill, and I have been a conspicuous consumer of my first amendment liberties ever since. I also have experienced the injury of the historical, ubiquitous, and continuous defamation of American racism. I grew up with Little Black Sambo and Amos and Andy, and I continue to receive racist tracts in the mail and shoved under my door. As I struggle with the tension between these constitutional values, I particularly appreciate the experience of both belonging and not belonging that gives to African Americans and other outsider groups a sense of duality. W. E. B. DuBois—scholar and founder of the National Association for the Advancement of Colored People (NAACP)—called the gift and burden inherent in the dual, conflicting heritage of all African Americans their "second-sight."[1]

The double consciousness of groups outside the ethnic mainstream is particularly apparent in the context of this controversy. Blacks know and value the protection the first amendment affords those of us who must rely upon our voices to petition both government and our neighbors for redress of grievances. Our political tradition has looked to "the word,"[2] to the moral power of ideas, to change the system when neither the power of the vote nor that of the gun were avail-

1 W. E. B. DuBois, *The Souls of Black Folk* 16–17 (1953).
2 V. Harding, *There Is a River* 82 (1981).

able. This part of us has known the experience of belonging and recognizes our common and inseparable interest in preserving the right of free speech for all. But we also know the experience of the outsider. The framers excluded us from the protection of the first amendment. The same Constitution that established rights for others endorsed a story that proclaimed our inferiority. It is a story that remains deeply ingrained in the American psyche. We see a different world than that seen by Americans who do not share this historical experience. We often hear racist speech when our white neighbors are not aware of its presence.

It is not my purpose to belittle or trivialize the importance of defending unpopular speech against the tyranny of the majority. There are very strong reasons for protecting even racist speech. Perhaps the most important reasons are that it reinforces our society's commitment to the value of tolerance, and that by shielding racist speech from government regulation, we are forced to combat it as a community These reasons for protecting racist speech should not be set aside hastily, and I will not argue that we should be less vigilant in protecting the speech and associational rights of speakers with whom most of us would disagree.

But I am deeply concerned about the role that many civil libertarians have played, or the roles we have failed to play, in the continuing, real-life struggle through which we define the community in which we live. I fear that by framing the debate as we have—as one in which the liberty of free speech is in conflict with the elimination of racism—we have advanced the cause of racial oppression and placed the bigot on the moral high ground, fanning the rising flames of racism. Above all, I am troubled that we have not listened to the real victims, that we have shown so little empathy or understanding for their injury, and that we have abandoned those individuals whose race, gender, or sexual orientation provokes others to regard them as

second-class citizens. These individuals' civil liberties are most directly at stake in the debate. In this chapter I focus on racism. Although I will not address violent pornography and homophobic hate speech directly, I will draw on the experience of women and gays as victims of hate speech where they operate as instructive analogues.

I have set two goals in constructing this chapter. The first goal is limited and perhaps overly modest, but it is nonetheless extremely important: I will demonstrate that much of the argument for protecting racist speech is based on the distinction that many civil libertarians draw between direct, face-to-face racial insults, which they think deserve first amendment protection, and all other fighting words, which they find unprotected by the first amendment. I argue that the distinction is false, that it advances none of the purposes of the first amendment, and that the time has come to put an end to the ringing rhetoric that condemns all efforts to regulate racist speech, even narrowly drafted provisions aimed at racist speech that results in direct, immediate, and substantial injury.

I also urge the regulation of racial epithets and vilification that do not involve face-to-face encounters—situations in which the victim is part of a captive audience and the injury is experienced by all members of a racial group who are forced to hear or see these words. In such cases, the insulting words are aimed at an entire group with the effect of causing significant harm to individual group members.

My second goal is more ambitious and more indeterminate. I propose several ways in which the traditional civil liberties position on free speech does not take into account important values expressed elsewhere in the Constitution. Further, I argue that even those values the first amendment itself is intended to promote are frustrated by an interpretation that is acontextual and idealized, by presupposing a world characterized by equal opportunity and the absence of societally created and culturally in-grained racism.

This chapter is divided into four parts: The first part explores whether our Constitution already commits us to some regulation of racist speech. I argue that it does; that this is the meaning of *Brown v. Board of Education*.[3] For the time being, I would ask only that the reader be open to considering this interpretation of *Brown*. This interpretation is useful even for those who believe the censorship of any expression cannot ultimately be condoned: *Brown* can help us better understand the injury of racist speech, an understanding that is vital to our discussion.

I also consider the implications of the state action doctrine in understanding *Brown* and argue that the public/private ideology promoted by that doctrine plays a critical role in advancing racism and clouding our vision of the appropriate role for the community in disestablishing systematic, societal group defamation.

The second part considers the debate over regulation of racial harassment on campus. I argue that carefully drafted regulations can and should be sustained without significant departures from existing first amendment doctrine. The regulation of racist fighting words should not be treated differently from the regulation of garden-variety fighting words, and captive audiences deserve no less protection when they are held captive by racist speakers. I also suggest that rules requiring civility and respect in academic discourse encourage rather than discourage the fullest exchange of ideas. Regulations that require minimal civility of discourse in certain designated forums are not incursions on intellectual and political debate.

The third part explores the nature of the injury inflicted by racist hate speech and examines the unstated assumptions that lie at the core of first amendment theory. In this part, I urge reconsideration of the history of racism in the United States; the ubiquity and continued vital-ity of culturally engendered conscious and unconscious beliefs about the inferiority of non-whites, and the effect of inequities of power on the marketplace of ideas.

In the last part, I argue that civil libertarians must examine not just the substance of our position on racist speech but also the ways in which we enter the debate. The way the debate has been framed makes heroes out of bigots and fans the flames of racial violence. I also consider the reasons for some civil libertarians' resistance to even minimal and narrowly drafted regulations of racist harassment.

BROWN V. BOARD OF EDUCATION: A CASE ABOUT REGULATING RACIST SPEECH

The landmark case of *Brown v. Board of Education* is not one we normally think of as concerning speech. As read most narrowly, the case is about the rights of Black children to equal educational opportunity. But *Brown* can also be read more broadly to articulate a principle central to any substantive understanding of the equal protection clause, the foundation on which all antidiscrimination law rests. This is the principle of equal citizenship. Under that principle, "Every individual is presumptively entitled to be treated by the organized society as a respected, responsible, and participating member."[4] The principle further requires the affirmative disestablishment of society practices that treat people as members of an inferior or dependent caste, as unworthy to participate in the larger community. The holding in *Brown*—that racially segregated schools violate the equal protection clause—reflects the fact that segregation amounts to a demeaning, caste-creating practice. The prevention of stigma was at the core of the Supreme Court's unanimous decision in *Brown* that segregated public

---

3 347 U.S. 483 (1954).

4 Karst, *Citizenship, Race and Marginality*, 30 Wm. & Mary L. Rev. 1, 1 (1988).

schools are inherently unequal. Observing that the segregation of Black pupils "generates a feeling of inferiority as to their status in the community,"[5] Chief Justice Earl Warren recognized what a majority of the Court had ignored almost sixty years earlier in *Plessy v. Ferguson*.[6] The social meaning of racial segregation in the United States is the designation of a superior and an inferior caste, and segregation proceeds "on the ground that colored citizens are . . . inferior and degraded."[7]

The key to this understanding of *Brown* is that the practice of segregation, the practice the Court held inherently unconstitutional, was *speech*. *Brown* held that segregation is unconstitutional not simply because the physical separation of Black and white children is bad or because resources were distributed unequally among Black and white schools. *Brown* held that segregated schools were unconstitutional primarily because of the *message* segregation conveys—the message that Black children are an untouchable caste, unfit to be educated with white children. Segregation serves its purpose by conveying an idea. It stamps a badge of inferiority upon Blacks, and this badge communicates a message to others in the community, as well as to Blacks wearing the badge, that is injurious to Blacks. Therefore, *Brown* may be read as regulating the content of racist speech. As a regulation of racist speech, the decision is an exception to the usual rule that regulation of speech content is presumed unconstitutional.

THE CONDUCT/ SPEECH DISTINCTION

Some civil libertarians argue that my analysis of *Brown* conflates speech and conduct. They maintain that the segregation outlawed in *Brown* was discriminatory conduct, not speech,

and the defamatory message conveyed by segregation simply was an incidental by-product of that conduct. This position is often stated as follows: "Of course segregation conveys a message, but this could be said of almost all conduct. To take an extreme example, a murderer conveys a message of hatred for his victim. But we would not argue that we cannot punish the murder—the primary conduct—merely because of this message, which is its secondary by-product."[8] The Court has been reluctant to concede that the first amendment has any relevance whatsoever in examples like this one, because the law would not be directed at anything resembling speech or at the views expressed. In such a case the regulation of speech is truly incidental to the regulation of the conduct.

These same civil libertarians assert that I suggest that all conduct with an expressive component should be treated alike—namely, as unprotected speech. This reading of my position clearly misperceives the central point of my argument. I do not contend that *all* conduct with an expressive component should be treated as unprotected speech. To the contrary, my suggestion that *racist* conduct amounts to speech is premised upon a unique characteristic of racism—namely its reliance upon the defamatory message of white supremacy to achieve its injurious purpose. I have not ignored the distinction between the speech and conduct elements of segregation, although, as the constitutional scholar Lawrence Tribe explained, "Any particular course of conduct may be hung almost randomly on the 'speech' peg or the 'conduct' peg as one sees fit."[9] Rather, my analysis turns on that distinction; I ask the question of whether there is a purpose to outlawing segregation that is unrelated to its message and conclude that the answer is no.

---

5 347 U.S. at 494.
6 163 U.S. 537 (1896).
7 Id. at 560 (J. Harlan, dissenting).

8 *See,* e.g., Strossen, *Regulating Racist Speech on Campus: A Modest Proposal?* Duke L. J. 484 at 541–43 (1990).
9 L. Tribe, *American Constitutional Law* §12–7 at 827 (2d ed. 1988).

If, for example, John W. Davis, counsel for the Board of Education of Topeka, Kansas, had been asked during oral argument in *Brown* to state the board's purpose in educating Black and white children in separate schools, he would have been hard pressed to answer in a way unrelated to the purpose of designating Black children as inferior. If segregation's primary goal is to convey the message of white supremacy, then *Brown's* declaration that segregation is unconstitutional amounts to a regulation of the message of white supremacy. Properly understood, *Brown* and its progeny require that the systematic group defamation of segregation be disestablished. Although the exclusion of Black children from white schools and the denial of educational resources and association that accompany exclusion can be characterized as conduct, these particular instances of conduct are concerned primarily with communicating the idea of white supremacy. The nonspeech elements are by-products of the main message rather than the message being simply a by-product of unlawful conduct.

The public accommodations provisions of the Civil Rights Act of 1964[10] illuminate why laws against discrimination also regulate racist speech. The legislative history and the Supreme Court's opinions upholding the act establish that Congress was concerned that Blacks have access to public accommodations to eliminate impediments to the free flow of interstate commerce, but this purpose could have been achieved through a regime of separate but equal accommodations. Title II of the Civil Rights Act goes farther; it incorporates the principle of the inherent inequality of segregation and prohibits restaurant owners from providing separate places at the lunch counter for "whites" and "coloreds." Even if the same food and the same service are provided, separate but equal facilities are unlawful. If the signs indicating separate facilities remain in place, then the statute is violated despite proof that restaurant patrons are free to disregard the signs. Outlawing these signs graphically illustrates my point that antidiscrimination laws are primarily regulations of the content of racist speech.

In the summer of 1966, Robert Cover and I were working as summer interns with C. B. King in Albany, Georgia. One day we stopped for lunch at a take-out chicken joint. The establishment was housed in a long diner-like structure with an awning extending from each of two doors in the side of the building. A sign was painted at the end of each awning. One said White, the other Colored. Bob and I entered the "white" side together, knowing we were not welcome to do so. When the proprietor took my order, I asked if he knew that the signs on his awnings were illegal under Title II of the Civil Rights Act of 1964. He responded, "People can come in this place through any door they want to." What this story makes apparent is that the signs themselves violate the antidiscrimination principle even when the conduct of denial of access is not present.

Another way to understand the inseparability of racist speech and discriminatory conduct is to view individual racist acts as part of a totality. When viewed in this manner, white supremacists' conduct or speech is forbidden by the equal protection clause. The goal of white supremacy is not achieved by individual acts or even by the cumulative acts of a group, but rather it is achieved by the institutionalization of the ideas of white supremacy. The institutionalization of white supremacy within our culture has created conduct on the society level that is greater than the sum of individual racist acts. The racist acts of millions of individuals are mutually reinforcing and cumulative because the status quo of institutionalized white supremacy remains long after deliberate racist actions subside.

Professor Kendall Thomas describes the way in which racism is simultaneously speech (a socially constructed meaning or idea) and conduct

10 42 U.S.C. §2000a (1982).

by asking us to consider the concept of "race" not as a noun but as a verb. He notes that race is a social construction. The meaning of "Black" or "white" is derived through a history of acted-upon ideology. Moreover, the cultural meaning of race is promulgated through millions of ongoing contemporaneous speech/acts. Thus, he says, "We are raced." The social construction of race is an ongoing process.[11]

It is difficult to recognize the institutional significance of white supremacy or how it *acts* to harm, partially because of its ubiquity. We simply do not see most racist conduct because we experience a world in which whites are supreme as simply "the world." Much racist conduct is considered unrelated to race or regarded as neutral because racist conduct maintains the status quo, the status quo of the world as we have known it. Catharine MacKinnon has observed that "To the extent that pornography succeeds in constructing social reality, it becomes invisible as harm." Thus, pornography "is more act-like than thought-like."[12] This truth about gender discrimination is equally true of racism.

Just because one can express the idea or message embodied by a practice such as white supremacy does not necessarily equate that practice with the idea. Slavery was an idea as well as a practice, but the Supreme Court recognized the inseparability of idea and practice in the institution of slavery when it held the enabling clause of the thirteenth amendment clothed Congress with the power to pass "all laws necessary and proper for abolishing all badges and incidents of slavery in the United States."[13] This understanding also informs the regulation of speech/conduct in the public accommodations

provisions of the Civil Rights Act of 1964 discussed above. When the racist restaurant or hotel owner puts a Whites Only sign in his window, his sign is more than speech. Putting up the sign is more than an act excluding Black patrons who see the sign. The sign is part of the larger practice of segregation and white supremacy that constructs and maintains a culture in which nonwhites are excluded from full citizenship. The inseparability of the idea and practice of racism is central to *Brown's* holding that segregation is inherently unconstitutional.

Racism is both 100 percent speech and 100 percent conduct. Discriminatory conduct is not racist unless it also conveys the message of white supremacy—unless it is interpreted within the culture to advance the structure and ideology of white supremacy. Likewise, all racist speech constructs the social reality that constrains the liberty of nonwhites because of their race. By limiting the life opportunities of others, this act of constructing meaning also makes racist speech conduct.

The Public/Private Distinction

There are critics who would contend that *Brown* is inapposite because the equal protection clause only restricts government behavior, whereas the first amendment protects the speech of private persons. They say, "Of course we want to prevent the state from defaming Blacks, but we must continue to be vigilant about protecting speech rights, even of racist individuals, from the government. In both cases our concern must be protecting the individual from the unjust power of the state."

At first blush, this position seems persuasive, but its persuasiveness relies upon the mystifying properties of constitutional ideology. In particular, I refer to the state action doctrine. Roughly stated,

> The [state action] doctrine holds that although someone may have suffered harmful treatment of a kind that one might ordinarily describe as a

---

11 K. Thomas, Comments at Frontiers of Legal Thought Conference, Duke Law School (Jan. 26, 1990).

12 C. MacKinnon, *Toward a Feminist Theory of the State*, 204 (1989).

13 *Jones v. Alfred H. Mayer Co.*, 392 U.S. 409, 439 (1968) (upholding Congress's use of the "badge of servitude" idea to justify federal legislation prohibiting racially discriminatory practices by private persons).

deprivation of liberty or a denial of equal protection of the laws, that occurrence excites no constitutional concern unless the proximate active perpetrators of the harm include persons exercising the special authority or power of the government of a state.[14]

By restricting the application of the fourteenth amendment to discrimination implicating the government, the state action rule immunizes private discriminators from constitutional scrutiny. In so doing, it leaves untouched the largest part of the vast system of segregation in the United States. The *Civil Rights Cases*[15] in which this doctrine was firmly established stands as a monument preserving American racial discrimination. Although the origin of state action is textual, countervailing values of privacy, freedom of association, and free speech all have been used to justify the rule's exculpation of private racism.

For example, it is argued that a white family's decision to send its children to private school or to move to a racially exclusive suburb should be accorded respect in spite of the fourteenth amendment's requirement of nondiscrimination because these decisions are part of the right to individual familial autonomy In this way, the state action rule's rather arbitrary limit on the scope of the antidiscrimination principle is transformed into a right of privacy—which is presented as the constitutional embodiment of an affirmative, neutral, and universally shared value. A new and positive image emerges—an image that has been abstracted from its original context.

In the abstract, the right to make decisions about how we will educate our children or with whom we will associate is an important value in American society But when we decontextualize

by viewing this privacy value in the abstract, we ignore the way it operates in the real world. We do not ask ourselves, for example, whether it is a value to which all people have equal access. And we do not inquire about who has the resources to send their children to private school or move to an exclusive suburb. The privacy value, when presented as an ideal, seems an appropriate limitation on racial justice because we naively believe that everyone has an equal stake in this value.

I do not mean to suggest that privacy or autonomy has no normative value; there is some point at which the balance ought to be struck in its favor *after full consideration of the inequities that might accompany that choice*. What is objectionable about the privacy language that I am discussing here is that it ignores inequities and assumes we all share equally in the value being promoted.

The Supreme Court's treatment of the abortion controversy provides the most striking example of the fact that the right of autonomous choice is not shared by rich and poor alike. In *Roe v. Wade*, the Court declared in no uncertain terms that the right of privacy "is broad enough to encompass a woman's decision whether or not to terminate her pregnancy."[16] Yet, in *Harris v. McRae*, the Court with equal certainty asserted, "It simply does not follow that a woman's freedom of choice carries with it a constitutional entitlement to the financial resources to avail herself of the full range of protected choices."[17]

The argument that distinguishes private racist speech from the government speech outlawed by *Brown* suffers from the same decontextualizing ideology. If the government is involved in a joint venture with private contractors to engage in the business of defaming Blacks, should it be able to escape the constitutional mandate that

---

14 Michelman, *Conceptions of Democracy in American Constitutional Argument: The Case of Pornography Regulation*, 56 Tenn. L. Rev. 291, 306 (1989).
15 109 U.S. 3 (1883).

16 410 U.S. 113 (1973).
17 448 U.S. 297, 316 (1980).

makes that business illegal simply by handing over the copyright and the printing presses to its partners in crime? I think not. And yet this is the essence of the position that espouses first amendment protection for those partners.

In an insightful article considering the constitutional implications of government regulation of pornography, the legal scholar Frank Michelman observed that the idea of state action plays a crucial, if unspoken, role for judges and civil libertarians who favor an absolute rule against government regulation of private pornographic publications (or racist speech), even when that expression causes "effects fairly describable . . . as deprivations of liberty and denials of equal protection of the laws."[18] He noted that judges and civil libertarians would not balance the evils of private subversions of liberty and equal protection against the evils of government censorship because "the Constitution, through the state action doctrine, in effects tells them not to." Michelman suggests that the state action doctrine, by directing us to the text of the fourteenth amendment, diverts our attention from the underlying issue—whether we should balance the evils of private deprivations of liberty against the government deprivations of liberty that may arise out of state regulations designed to avert those private deprivations.

A person who responds to the argument that *Brown* mandates the abolition of racist speech by reciting the state action doctrine fails to consider that the alternative to regulating racist speech is infringement of the claims of Blacks to liberty and equal protection. The best way to constitutionally protect these competing interests is to balance them directly. To invoke the state action doctrine is to circumvent our value judgment as to how these competing interests should be balanced.

The deference usually given to the first amendment values in this balance is justified using the argument that racist speech is unpopular speech, that like the speech of civil rights activists, pacifists, and religious and political dissenters, it is in need of special protection from majoritarian censorship. But for over three hundred years, racist speech has been the liturgy of the leading established religion of the United States, the religion of racism. Racist speech remains a vital and regrettably popular characteristic of the U.S. vernacular. It must be noted that there has not yet been satisfactory retraction of the government-sponsored defamation in the slavery clauses,[19] the *Dred Scott* decision,[20] the Black codes, the segregation statutes, and countless other group libels. The injury to Blacks is hardly redressed by deciding the government must no longer injure our reputation if one then invokes the first amendment to ensure that racist speech continues to thrive in an unregulated private market.

Consider, for example, the case of *McLaurin v. Oklahoma State Regents*,[21] in which the University of Oklahoma graduate school, under order by a federal court to admit McLaurin, a Black student, designated a special seat, roped off from other seats, in each classroom, the library, and the cafeteria. The Supreme Court held that this arrangement was unconstitutional because McLaurin could not have had an equal opportunity to learn and participate if he was humiliated and symbolically stigmatized as an untouchable. Would it be any less injurious if all McLaurin's classmates had shown up at class wearing blackface? Should this symbolic speech be protected by the Constitution? Yet, according to a *Time* magazine report, in the fall of 1988 at the University of Wisconsin, "Members of the Zeta Beta Tau fraternity staged a mock slave auction, complete with some pledges in

18 *See* Michelman, note 14, at 306–07.

19 U.S. Const. art. I, §2, cl. 3 and §9, cl. 1; art. IV, §2, cl. 3.
20 *Dred Scott v. Sanford*, 60 U.S. (19 How.) 393 (1857).
21 339 U.S. 637 (1950).

blackface."[22] More recently, at the same university, white male students trailed Black female students shouting, "I've never tried a nigger before."[23] These young women were no less severely injured than was McLaurin simply because the university did not directly sponsor their assault. If the university fails to protect them in their right to pursue their education free from this kind of degradation and humiliation, then surely there are constitutional values at stake.

It is a very sad irony that the first instinct of many civil libertarians is to express concern for possible infringement of the assailants' liberties while barely noticing the constitutional rights of the assailed. Shortly after *Brown,* many Southern communities tried to escape the mandate of desegregation by closing public schools and opening private (white) academies. These attempts to avoid the fourteenth amendment through the privatization of discrimination consistently were invalidated by the courts. In essence, the Supreme Court held that the defamatory message of segregation would not be insulated from constitutional proscription simply because the speaker was a nongovernment entity.

The Supreme Court also has indicated that Congress may enact legislation regulating private racist speech. In upholding the public accommodations provisions of Title II of the Civil Rights Act of 1964 in *Heart of Atlanta Motel v. United States,*[24] the Court implicitly rejected the argument that the absence of state action meant that private discriminators were protected by first amendment free speech and associational rights. Likewise in *Bob Jones University v. United States,*[25] the Court sustained the Internal Revenue Service decision to discontinue tax-exempt status for a college with a policy against interracial dating and marriage. The college framed its objection in terms of the free exercise of religion, arguing its policy was religiously motivated, but the Court found that the government had "a fundamental, overriding interest in eradicating racial discrimination in education" that "substantially outweighs whatever burden denial of tax benefits" placed on the college's exercise of its religious beliefs.[26] It is difficult to believe that the university would have fared any better under free speech analysis or if the policy had been merely a statement of principle rather than an enforceable disciplinary regulation. Regulation of private racist speech also has been held constitutional in the context of prohibition of race-designated advertisements for employees, home sales, and rentals.

Thus *Brown* and the antidiscrimination law it spawned provide precedent for my position that the content regulation of racist speech is not only permissible but may be required by the Constitution in certain circumstances. This precedent may not mean that we should advocate the government regulation of all racist speech, but it should give us pause in assuming absolutist positions about regulations aimed at the message or idea such speech conveys. If we understand *Brown*—the cornerstone of the civil rights movement and equal protection doctrine —correctly, and if we understand the necessity of disestablishing the system of signs and symbols that signal Blacks' inferiority, then we should not proclaim that all racist speech that stops short of physical violence must be defended.

RACIST SPEECH AS THE FUNCTIONAL EQUIVALENT OF FIGHTING WORDS

Much recent debate over the efficacy of regulating racist speech has focused on the efforts by

22 "A Step Toward Civility," *Time,* May 1, 1989, at 43.
23 Id.
24 *Heart of Atlanta Motel, Inc. v. United States,* 379 U.S. 241, 258 (1964); *see also Roberts v. United States Jaycees,* 468 U.S. 609, 624 (1984)(Court upheld the public accommodations provision of the Minnesota Human Rights Act).
25 461 U.S. 574, 595 (1983).

26 461 U.S. at 604.

colleges and universities to respond to the burgeoning incidents of racial harassment on their campuses. At Stanford, where I teach, there has been considerable controversy over whether racist and other discriminatory verbal harassment should be regulated and what form any regulation should take. Proponents of regulation have been sensitive to the danger of inhibiting expression, and the current regulation (which was drafted by my colleague Tom Grey) manifests that sensitivity. It is drafted somewhat more narrowly than I would have preferred, leaving unregulated hate speech that occurs in settings where there is a captive audience, but I largely agree with this regulation's substance and approach. I include it here as one example of a regulation of racist speech that I would argue violates neither first amendment precedent nor principle. The regulation reads as follows:

Fundamental Standard Interpretation: Free Expression and Discriminatory Harassment

1. Stanford is committed to the principles of free inquiry and free expression. Students have the right to hold and vigorously defend and promote their opinions, thus entering them into the life of the University, there to flourish or wither according to their merits. Respect for this right requires that students tolerate even expression of opinions which they find abhorrent. Intimidation of students by other students in their exercise of this right, by violence or threat of violence, is therefore considered to be a violation of the Fundamental Standard.

2. Stanford is also committed to principles of equal opportunity and nondiscrimination. Each student has the right to equal access to a Stanford education, without discrimination on the basis of sex, race, color, handicap, religion, sexual orientation, or national and ethnic origin.

Harassment of students on the basis of any of these characteristics tends to create a hostile environment that makes access to education for those subjected to it less than equal. Such discriminatory harassment is therefore considered to be a violation of the Fundamental Standard.

3. This interpretation of the Fundamental Standard is intended to clarify the point at which protected free expression ends and prohibited discriminatory harassment begins. Prohibited harassment includes discriminatory intimidation by threats of violence, and also includes personal vilification of students on the basis of their sex, race, color, handicap, religion, sexual orientation, or national and ethnic origin.

4. Speech or other expression constitutes harassment by vilification if it:
   a) is intended to insult or stigmatize an individual or a small number of individuals on the basis of their sex, race, color, handicap, religion, sexual orientation, or national and ethnic origin; and
   b) is addressed directly to the individual or individuals whom it insults or stigmatizes; and
   c) makes use of "fighting" words or nonverbal symbols.
   In the context of discriminatory harassment, "fighting" words or nonverbal symbols are words, pictures or symbols that, by virtue of their form, are commonly understood to convey direct and visceral hatred or contempt for human beings on the basis of their sex, race, color, handicap, religion, sexual orientation, and national and ethnic origin.[27]

---

[27] Interpretation of the Fundamental Standard defining when verbal or nonverbal abuse violates the student conduct code adopted by the Stanford University Student Conduct Legislative Council, March 14, 1990. *SCLC Offers Revised Reading of Standard,* Stanford Daily, Apr. 4, 1990, §1, col. 4.
   It is important to recognize that this regulation is not

This regulation and others like it have been characterized in the press as the work of "thought police," but the rule does nothing more than prohibit intentional face-to-face insults, a form of speech that is unprotected by the first amendment. When racist speech takes the form of face-to-face insults, catcalls, or other assaultive speech aimed at an individual or a small group of persons, then it falls within the "fighting words" exception to first amendment protection. The Supreme Court has held that words that "by their very utterance inflict injury or tend to incite an immediate breach of the peace"[28] are not constitutionally protected.

Face-to-face racial insults, like fighting words, are undeserving of first amendment protection for two reasons. The first reason is the immediacy of the injurious impact of racial insults. The experience of being called "nigger," "spic," "Jap," or "kike" is like receiving a slap in the face. The injury is instantaneous. There is neither an opportunity for intermediary reflection on the idea conveyed nor an opportunity for responsive speech. The harm to be avoided is both clear and present. The second reason that racial insults should not fall under protected speech relates to the purpose underlying the first amendment. The purpose of the first amendment is to foster the greatest amount of speech. Racial insults disserve that purpose. Assaultive racist speech functions as a preemptive strike. The racial invective is experienced as a

blow, not a proffered idea, and once the blow is struck, it is unlikely that dialogue will follow. Racial insults are undeserving of first amendment protection because the perpetrator's intention is not to discover truth or initiate dialogue, but to injure the victim.

The fighting words doctrine anticipates that the verbal slap in the face of insulting words will provoke a violent response, resulting in a breach of the peace. When racial insults are hurled at minorities, the response may be silence or flight rather than a fight, but the preemptive effect on further speech is the same. Women and minorities often report that they find themselves speechless in the face of discriminatory verbal attacks. This inability to respond is not the result of oversensitivity among these groups, as some individuals who oppose protective regulation have argued. Rather it is the product of several factors, all of which evidence the nonspeech character of the initial preemptive verbal assault. The first factor is that the visceral emotional response to personal attack precludes speech. Attack produces an instinctive, defensive psychological reaction. Fear, rage, shock, and flight all interfere with any reasoned response. Words like "nigger," "kike," and "faggot" produce physical symptoms that temporarily disable the victim, and the perpetrators often use these words with the intention of producing this effect. Many victims do not find words of response until well after the assault, when the cowardly assaulter has departed.

A second factor that distinguishes racial insults from protected speech is the preemptive nature of such insults—words of response to such verbal attacks may never be forthcoming because speech is usually an inadequate response. When one is personally attacked with words that denote one's subhuman status and untouchability, there is little, if anything, that can be said to redress either the emotional or reputational injury. This is particularly true when the message and meaning of the epithet resonates with beliefs widely held in society.

---

content neutral. It prohibits "discriminatory harassment" rather than just plain harassment, and it regulates only discriminatory harassment based on "sex, race, color, handicap, religion, sexual orientation, and national and ethnic origin." It is arguably viewpoint neutral with respect to these categories, although its reference to "words . . . that, by virtue of their form, are commonly understood to convey direct and visceral hatred or contempt" probably means that there will be many more epithets that refer to subordinated groups than words that refer to superordinate groups covered by the regulation.

28 *Chaplinsky v. New Hampshire*, 315 U.S. 568, 572 (1942).

This preservation of widespread beliefs is what makes the face-to-face racial attack more likely to preempt speech than other fighting words do. The racist name caller is accompanied by a cultural chorus of equally demeaning speech and symbols. Segregation and other forms of racist speech injure victims because of their dehumanizing and excluding message. Each individual message gains its power because of the cumulative and reinforcing effect of countless similar messages that are conveyed in a society where racism is ubiquitous.

The subordinated victims of fighting words also are silenced by their relatively powerless position in society. Because of the significance of power and position, the categorization of racial epithets as fighting words provides an inadequate paradigm; instead one must speak of their functional equivalent. The fighting words doctrine presupposes an encounter between two persons of relatively equal power who have been acculturated to respond to face-to-face insults with violence: The fighting words doctrine is a paradigm based on a white male point of view. It captures the "macho" quality of male discourse. It is accepted, justifiable, and even praiseworthy when "real men" respond to personal insult with violence. (Presidential candidate George Bush effectively emulated the most macho—and not coincidentally most violent—of movie stars, Clint Eastwood, when he repeatedly used the phrase, "Read my lips!" Any teenage boy will tell you the subtext of this message: "I've got nothing else to say about this and if you don't like what I'm saying we can step outside.") The fighting words doctrine's responsiveness to this male stance in the world and its blindness to the cultural experience of women is another example of how neutral principles of law reflect the values of those who are dominant.

Black men also are well aware of the double standard that our culture applies in responding to insult. Part of the culture of racial domination through violence—a culture of dominance manifested historically in thousands of lynchings in the South and more recently in the racial violence at Howard Beach and Bensonhurst—is the paradoxical expectation on the part of whites that Black males will accept insult from whites without protest, yet will become violent without provocation. These expectations combine two assumptions: First, that Blacks as a group—and especially Black men—are more violent; and second, that as inferior persons, Blacks have no right to feel insulted. One can imagine the response of universities if Black men started to respond to racist fighting words by beating up white students.

In most situations, minorities correctly perceive that a violent response to fighting words will result in a risk to their own life and limb. This risk forces targets to remain silent and submissive. This response is most obvious when women submit to sexually assaultive speech or when the racist name caller is in a more powerful position—the boss on the job or a member of a violent racist group. Certainly, we do not expect the Black woman crossing the Wisconsin campus to turn on her tormentors and pummel them. Less obvious, but just as significant, is the effect of pervasive racial and sexual violence and coercion on individual members of subordinated groups, who must learn the survival techniques of suppressing and disguising rage and anger at an early age.

One of my students, a white, gay male, related an experience that is quite instructive in understanding the fighting words doctrine. In response to my request that students describe how they experienced the injury of racist speech, Michael told a story of being called "faggot" by a man on a subway. His description included all of the speech-inhibiting elements I have noted previously. He found himself in a state of semishock, nauseous, dizzy, unable to muster the witty, sarcastic, articulate rejoinder he was accustomed to making. He was instantly aware of the recent spate of gay bashing in San Francisco and that many of these incidents had escalated from verbal encounters. Even hours later when the shock subsided and his facility with words returned, he realized that any response was inadequate to counter the hundreds of years of societal defamation that one word—"faggot"—carried with it. Like the word "nigger" and unlike the word "liar," it is not sufficient to deny the truth of the word's application, to say, "I am not a faggot." One must deny the truth of the word's meaning, a meaning shouted from the rooftops by the rest of the world a million times a day. The complex response "Yes, I am a member of the group you despise and the degraded meaning of the word you use is one that I reject" is not effective in a subway encounter. Although there are many of us who constantly and in myriad ways seek to counter the lie spoken in the meaning of hateful words like "nigger" and "faggot," it is a nearly impossible burden to bear when one is ambushed by a sudden, face-to-face hate speech assault.

But there is another part of my discussion with Michael that is equally instructive. I asked if he could remember a situation when he had been verbally attacked with reference to his being a white male. Had he ever been called a "honkey," a "chauvinist pig," or "mick"? (Michael is from a working-class Irish family in Boston.) He said that he had been called some version of all three and that although he found the last one more offensive than the first two, he had not experienced—even in that subordinated role—the same disorienting powerlessness he had experienced when attacked for his membership in the gay community. The question of power, of the context of the power relationships within which speech takes place, and the connection to violence must be considered as we decide how best to foster the freest and fullest dialogue within our communities. Regulation of face-to-face verbal assault in the manner contemplated by the proposed Stanford provision will make room for more speech than it chills. The provision is clearly within the spirit, if not the letter, of existing first amendment doctrine.

The proposed Stanford regulation, and indeed regulations with considerably broader reach, can be justified as necessary to protect a captive audience from offensive or injurious speech. Courts have held that offensive speech may not be regulated in public forums such as streets and parks where listeners may avoid the speech by moving on or averting their eyes,[29] but the regulation of otherwise protected speech has been permitted when the speech invades the privacy of unwilling listeners' homes or when unwilling listeners cannot avoid the speech.[30] Racist posters, flyers, and graffiti in dorms, classrooms, bathrooms, and other common living spaces would fall within the reasoning of these cases. Minority students should not be required to remain in their rooms to avoid racial assault. Minimally, they should find a safe haven in their dorms and other common rooms that are a part of their daily routine. I would argue that the university's responsibility for ensuring these students receive an equal educational opportunity provides a compelling justification for regulations that ensure them safe passage in all common areas. Black, Latino, Asian, or Native American students should not have to risk being the target of racially assaulting speech every time they choose to walk across campus. The regulation of vilifying speech that cannot be anticipated or avoided would not pre-

29 *See Cohen v. California,* 403 U.S. 15, 21 (1971) (holding that the state could not excise, as offensive conduct, particular epithets from public discourse); *Erznoznik v. City of Jacksonville,* 43 U.S. 205, 209 (1975) (overturning a city ordinance that deterred drive-in theaters from showing movies containing nudity).
30 *See Kovacks v. Cooper,* 336 U.S. 77, 86 (1949) (right to free speech not abridged by city ordinance outlawing use of sound trucks on city streets); *Federal Communication Comm'n v. Pacifica Found.,* 438 U.S. 726, 748 (1978) (limited first amendment protection of broadcasting that extends into privacy of home); *Rowan v. United States Post Office Dep't,* 397 U.S. 728, 736 (1970) (unwilling recipient of sexually arousing material had right to instruct Postmaster General to cease mailings to protect recipient from unwanted communication of "ideas").

clude announced speeches and rallies where minorities and their allies would have an opportunity to organize counterdemonstrations or avoid the speech altogether.

KNOWING THE INJURY AND STRIKING THE BALANCE: UNDERSTANDING WHAT IS AT STAKE IN RACIST SPEECH CASES

I argued in the last section that narrowly drafted regulations of racist speech that prohibit face-to-face vilification and protect captive audiences from verbal and written harassment can be defended within the confines of existing first amendment doctrine. Here I argue that many civil libertarians who urge that the first amendment prohibits any regulation of racist speech have given inadequate attention to the testimony of individuals who have experienced injury from such speech. These civil libertarians fail to comprehend both the nature and extent of the injury inflicted by racist speech. I further urge that understanding the injury requires reconsideration of the balance that must be struck between our concerns for racial equality and freedom of expression.

The arguments most commonly advanced against the regulation of racist speech go something like this: We recognize that minority groups suffer pain and injury as the result of racist speech, but we must allow this hate mongering for the benefit of society as a whole. Freedom of speech is the lifeblood of our democratic system. It is a freedom that enables us to persuade others to our point of view. Free speech is especially important for minorities because often it is their only vehicle for rallying support for redress of their grievances. Even though we do not wish anyone to be persuaded that racist lies are true, we cannot allow the public regulation of racist invective and vilification because any prohibition broad enough to prevent racist speech would catch in the same net forms of speech that are central to a democratic society.

Whenever we argue that racist epithets and vilification must be allowed, not because we would condone them ourselves but because of the potential danger the precedent of regulation would pose for the speech of all dissenters, we are balancing our concern for the free flow of ideas and the democratic process with our desire for equality. This kind of categorical balance is struck whenever we frame any rule—even an absolute rule. It is important to be conscious of the nature and extent of injury to both concerns when we engage in this kind of balancing. In this case, we must place on one side of the balance the nature and extent of the injury caused by racism. We must also consider whether the racist speech we propose to regulate is advancing or retarding the values of the first amendment.

Understanding the Injury Inflicted by Racist Speech

There can be no meaningful discussion about how to reconcile our commitment to equality and our commitment to free speech until we acknowledge that racist speech inflicts real harm and that this harm is far from trivial. I should state that more strongly: To engage in a debate about the first amendment and racist speech without a full understanding of the nature and extent of the harm of racist speech risks making the first amendment an instrument of domination rather than a vehicle of liberation. Not everyone has known the experience of being victimized by racist, misogynist, or homophobic speech, and we do not share equally the burden of the societal harm it inflicts. Often we are too quick to say we have heard the victims' cries when we have not; we are too eager to assure ourselves we have experienced the same injury and therefore can make the constitutional balance without danger of mismeasurement. For many of us who have fought for the rights of oppressed minorities, it is difficult to accept that by underestimating the injury from racist speech we too might be implicated in the vicious words we would never utter. Until we have eradicated racism and sexism and no longer share in the fruits of those forms of domination, we cannot legitimately strike the balance without hearing the protest of those who are dominated. My plea is simply that we listen to the victims.

Members of my own family were involved in a recent incident at a private school in Wilmington, Delaware, that taught me much about both the nature of the injury racist speech inflicts and the lack of understanding many whites have of that injury.

A good Quaker school dedicated to a deep commitment to and loving concern for all the members of its community, Wilmington Friends School also became a haven for white families fleeing the court-ordered desegregation of the Wilmington public schools. In recent years, the school strove to meet its commitment to human equality by enrolling a small (but significant) group of minority students and hiring an even smaller number of Black faculty and staff. My sister Paula, a gifted, passionate, and dedicated teacher, was the principal of the lower school. Her sons attended the high school. My brother-in-law, John, teaches geology at the University of Delaware. He is a strong, quiet, loving man, and he is white. My sister's family had moved to Wilmington, shouldering the extra burdens and anxieties borne by an interracial family moving to a town where, not long ago, the defamatory message of segregation graced the doors of bathrooms and restaurants. Within a year they had made a place as well-loved and respected members of the community, particularly the school community, where Paula was viewed as a godsend and my nephews made many good friends.

In May of their second year in Wilmington, an incident occurred that shook the entire school community, but was particularly painful to my sister's family and others who found themselves the objects of hateful speech. In a letter to the school community explaining a decision to expel four students, the school headmistress described the incident as follows:

> On Sunday evening, May 1, four students in the senior class met by prearrangement to paint the soccer kickboard, a flat rectangular structure, approximately 8 ft. by 25 ft., standing in the midst of the Wilmington Friends School playing fields. They worked for approximately one hour under bright moonlight and then went home.
>
> What confronted students and staff the following morning, depicted on the kickboard, were racist and anti-Semitic slogans and, most disturbing of all, threats of violent assault against one clearly identified member of the senior class. The slogans written on the kickboard included: "Save the land, join the Klan," and "Down with Jews"; among the drawings were at least twelve hooded Ku Klux Klansmen, Nazi swastikas, and a burning cross. The most frightening and disturbing depictions, however, were those that threatened violence against one of our senior Black students. He was drawn, in a cartoon figure, identified by his name, and his initials, and by the name of his mother. Directly to the right of his head was a bullet, and farther to the right was a gun with its barrel directed toward the head. Under the drawing of the student, three Ku Klux Klansmen were depicted, one of whom was saying that the student "dies." Next to the gun was a drawing of a burning cross under which was written "Kill the Tarbaby."[31]

When I visited my sister's family a few days after this incident, the injury they had suffered was evident. The wounds were fresh. My sister, a care giver by nature and vocation, was clearly in need of care. My nephews were quiet. Their faces betrayed the aftershock of a recently inflicted blow and a newly discovered vulnerability. I knew the pain and scars were no less enduring because the injury had not been phys-

---

31 Letter from Dulany O. Bennett to parents, alumni, and friends of the Wilmington Friends School (May 17, 1988).

ical. And when I talked to my sister, I realized the greatest part of her pain came not from the incident itself, but rather from the reaction of white parents who had come to the school in unprecedented numbers to protest the offending students' expulsion. "It was only a prank." "No one was physically attacked." "How can you punish these kids for mere words, mere drawings." Paula's pain was compounded by the failure of these people with whom she lived and worked to recognize that she had been hurt, to understand in even the most limited way the reality of her pain and that of her family.

Many people called the incident "isolated." But Black folks know that no racial incident is "isolated" in the United States. That is what makes the incidents so horrible, so scary. It is the knowledge that they are *not* the isolated unpopular speech of a dissident few that makes them so frightening. These incidents are manifestations of an ubiquitous and deeply ingrained cultural belief system, an American way of life. Too often in recent months, as I have debated this issue with friends and colleagues, I have heard people speak of the need to protect "offensive" speech. The word offensive is used as if we were speaking of a difference in taste, as if I should learn to be less sensitive to words that "offend" me. I cannot help but believe that those people who speak of offense—those who argue that this speech must go unchecked—do not understand the great difference between offense and injury. They have not known the injury my sister experienced, have not known the fear, vulnerability, and shame experienced by the Wisconsin students described at the beginning of this chapter. There is a great difference between the offensiveness of words that you would rather not hear because they are labeled dirty, impolite, or personally demeaning and the *injury* inflicted by words that remind the world that you are fair game for physical attack, that evoke in you all of the millions of cultural lessons regarding your inferiority that you have so painstakingly repressed, and that imprint

upon you a badge of servitude and subservience for all the world to see. It is instructive that the chief proponents of restricting people who inflict these injuries are women and people of color, and there are few among these groups who take the absolutist position that any regulation of this speech is too much.

Again, *Brown v. Board of Education* is a useful case for our analysis. *Brown* is helpful because it articulates the nature of the injury inflicted by the racist message of segregation. When one considers the injuries identified in the *Brown* decision, it is clear that racist speech causes tangible injury, and it is the kind of injury for which the law commonly provides, and even requires, redress.

Psychic injury is no less an injury than being struck in the face, and it often is far more severe. *Brown* speaks directly to the psychic injury inflicted by racist speech in noting that the symbolic message of segregation affected "the hearts and minds" of Negro children "in a way unlikely ever to be undone."[32] Racial epithets and harassment often cause deep emotional scarring and feelings of anxiety and fear that pervade every aspect of a victim's life. Many victims of hate propaganda have experienced physiological and emotional symptoms, such as rapid pulse rate and difficulty in breathing.

A second injury identified in *Brown,* and present in my example, is reputational injury. As Professor Tribe has noted, "Libelous speech was long regarded as a form of personal assault . . . that government could vindicate . . . without running afoul of the constitution."[33] Although *New York Times v. Sullivan* and its progeny have subjected much defamatory speech to constitutional scrutiny—on the reasoning that "debate on public issues should be uninhibited, robust, and wide-open"[34] and should not be "chilled" by the possibility of libel suits—these cases also demonstrate a concern for balancing the

32 347 U.S. at 494.
33 L. Tribe, note 9, at 861.
34 376 U.S. 254, 270.

public's interest in being fully informed with the competing interest of defamed persons in vindicating their reputation.

The interest of defamed persons is even stronger in racial defamation cases than in the *Sullivan* line of cases. The *Sullivan* rule protects statements of fact that are later proven erroneous. But persons who defame a racial group with racial epithets and stereotyped caricatures are not concerned that they may have "guessed wrong" in attempting to ascertain the truth. The racial epithet is the expression of a widely held belief. It is invoked as an assault, not as a statement of fact that may be proven true or false. Moreover, if the *Sullivan* rule protects erroneous speech because of an ultimate concern for the discovery of truth, then the rule's application to racial epithets must be based on an acceptance of the possible "truth" of racism, a position that, happily, most first amendment absolutists are reluctant to embrace. Furthermore, the rationale of *Sullivan* and its progeny is that public issues should be vigorously debated and that, as the Supreme Court held in *Gertz v. Robert Welch, Inc.*, there is "no such thing as a false idea."[35] But are racial insults ideas? Do they encourage wide-open debate?

Brown is a case about group defamation. The message of segregation was stigmatizing to Black children. To be labeled unfit to attend school with white children injured the reputation of Black children, thereby foreclosing employment opportunities and the right to be regarded as respected members of the body politic. An extensive discussion on the constitutionality or efficacy of group libel laws is beyond the scope of this chapter, and it must suffice for me to note that although *Beauharnais v. Illinois*,[36] which upheld an Illinois group libel statute, has fallen into disfavor with some commentators, *Brown* remains an instructive case. By identifying the inseparability of discrimina-

tory speech and action in the case of segregation, where the injury is inflicted by the meaning of the segregation, *Brown* limits the scope of *Sullivan. Brown* reflects the understanding that racism is a form of subordination that achieves its purposes through group defamation.

The third injury identified in *Brown* is the denial of equal educational opportunity. *Brown* recognized that even where segregated facilities are materially equal, Black children did not have an equal opportunity to learn and participate in the school community if they bore the additional burden of being subjected to the humiliation and psychic assault that accompanies the message of segregation. University students bear an analogous burden when they are forced to live and work in an environment where at any moment they may be subjected to denigrating verbal harassment and assault. The testimony of nonwhite students about the detrimental effect of racial harassment on their academic performance and social integration in the college community is overwhelming. A similar injury is recognized and addressed in the requirement of Title VII of the Civil Rights Act that employers maintain a nondiscriminatory, nonhostile work environment and in federal and state regulations prohibiting sexual harassment on campuses as well as in the workplace.

All three of these very tangible, continuing, and often irreparable forms of injury—psychic, reputational, and the denial of equal educational opportunity—must be recognized, accounted for, and balanced against the claim that a regulation aimed at the prevention of these injuries may lead to restrictions on important first amendment liberties.

The Other Side of the Balance: Does the Suppression of Racial Epithets Weigh for or Against Speech

In striking a balance, we also must think about what we are weighing on the side of speech. Most Blacks—unlike many white civil libertari-

35 418 U.S. 323, 339 (1974).
36 343 U.S. 250 (1952).

ans—do not have faith in free speech as the most important vehicle for liberation. The first amendment coexisted with slavery, and we still are not sure it will protect us to the same extent that it protects whites. It often is argued that minorities have benefited greatly from first amendment protection and therefore should guard it jealously We are aware that the struggle for racial equality has relied heavily on the persuasion of peaceful protest protected by the first amendment, but experience also teaches us that our petitions often go unanswered until protests disrupt business as usual and require the self-interested attention of those persons in power.

Paradoxically, the disruption that renders protest speech effective usually causes it to be considered undeserving of first amendment protection. Note the cruel irony in the news story cited at the beginning of this chapter that describes the Stanford president's justification for prosecuting students engaged in a peaceful sit-in for violation of the university's Fundamental Standard: The protesting students were punished, but the racist behavior the students were protesting went unpunished. This lack of symmetry was justified on the grounds that punishment might violate the bigots' first amendment rights—a particularly ironic result given Professor Derrick Bell's observation that it was Black students' civil rights protests that underlay the precedents upon which white students relied to establish their first amendment rights in school and university settings. As in so many other areas, a policy that Blacks paid the price for is used against them and on behalf of whites. Once one begins to doubt the existence of a symmetry between official reactions to racism and official reactions to protests against racism, the absolutist position loses credence: It becomes difficult for us to believe that fighting to protect speech rights for racists will ensure our own speech rights. Our experience is that the American system of justice has never been symmetrical where race is concerned. No wonder

we see equality as a precondition of free speech and place more weight on that side of the balance aimed at the removal of the badges and incidents of slavery that continue to flourish in our culture.

Blacks and other people of color are equally skeptical about the absolutist argument that even the most injurious speech must remain unregulated because in an unregulated marketplace of ideas the best ideas will rise to the top and gain acceptance. Our experience tells us the opposite. We have seen too many demagogues elected by appealing to U.S. racism. We have seen too many good, liberal politicians shy away from the issues that might brand them as too closely allied with us. The American marketplace of ideas was founded with the idea of the racial inferiority of nonwhites as one of its chief commodities, and ever since the market opened, racism has remained its most active item in trade.

But it is not just the prevalence and strength of the idea of racism that make the unregulated marketplace of ideas an untenable paradigm for those individuals who seek full and equal personhood for all. The real problem is that the idea of the racial inferiority of nonwhites infects, skews, and disables the operation of a market (like a computer virus, sick cattle, or diseased wheat). It trumps good ideas that contend with it in the market. It is an epidemic that distorts the marketplace of ideas and renders it dysfunctional.

Racism is irrational. Individuals do not embrace or reject racist beliefs as the result of reasoned deliberation. For the most part, we do not even recognize the myriad ways in which the racism that pervades our history and culture influences our beliefs. But racism is ubiquitous. We are all racists. Often we fail to see it because racism is so woven into our culture that it seems normal. In other words, most of our racism is unconscious. So it must have been with the middle-aged, white, male lawyer who thought he was complimenting a Mexican-American law student of mine who had applied for a job with his firm. "You speak very good English," he said. But she was a fourth-generation Californian, not the stereotypical poor immigrant he unconsciously imagined she must be.

The disruptive and disabling effect on the market of an idea that is ubiquitous and irrational, but seldom seen or acknowledged, should be apparent. If the community is considering competing ideas about providing food for children, shelter for the homeless, or abortions for pregnant women, and the choices made among the proposed solutions are influenced by the idea that some children, families, or women are less deserving of our sympathy because they are racially inferior, then the market is not functioning as either John Stuart Mill or Oliver Wendell Holmes envisioned it. In the term used by constitutional theorist John Ely, there is a "process defect."[37]

Professor Ely coined the term *process defect* in the context of developing a theory to identify instances in which legislative action should be subjected to heightened judicial scrutiny under the equal protection clause. Ely argued that the courts should interfere with the normal majoritarian political process when the defect of prejudice bars groups subject to widespread vilification from participation in the political process and causes governmental decisionmakers to misapprehend the costs and benefits of their actions. This same process defect that excludes vilified groups and misdirects the government operates in the marketplace of ideas. Mill's vision of truth emerging through competition in the marketplace of ideas relies on the ability of members of the body politic to recognize "truth" as serving their interest and to act on that recognition.[38] As such, this vision depends upon the same process that James Madison referred to when he described his vision of a democracy in which the numerous minorities within our society would form coalitions to create majorities with overlapping interests through pluralist wheeling and deal-

ing.[39] Just as the defect of prejudice blinds white voters to interests that overlap with those of vilified minorities, it also blinds them to the "truth" of an idea or the efficacy of solutions associated with that vilified group. And just as prejudice causes the governmental decisionmakers to misapprehend the costs and benefits of their actions, it also causes all of us to misapprehend the value of ideas in the market.

Prejudice that is unconscious or unacknowledged causes the most significant distortions in the market. When racism operates at a conscious level, opposing ideas may prevail in open competition for the rational or moral sensibilities of the market participant. But when individuals are unaware of their prejudice, neither reason nor moral persuasion will likely succeed.

Racist speech also distorts the marketplace of ideas by muting or devaluing the speech of Blacks and other despised minorities. Regardless of intrinsic value, their words and ideas become less salable in the marketplace of ideas. An idea that would be embraced by large numbers of individuals if it were offered by a white individual will be rejected or given less credence if its author belongs to a group demeaned and stigmatized by racist beliefs.

An obvious example of this type of devaluation is the Black political candidate whose ideas go unheard or are rejected by white voters, although voters would embrace the same ideas if they were championed by a white candidate. Once again, the experience of one of my gay students provides a paradigmatic example of how ideas are less acceptable when their authors are members of a group that has been victimized by hatred and vilification. Bob had not "come out" when he first came to law school. During his first year, when issues relating to heterosexism came up in class or in discussions with other students, he spoke to these issues as a sympathetic "straight" white male student. His arguments were listened to and taken seriously. In his second

---

37 J. Ely, Democracy and Distrust, 103–04,135–79 (1980).

38 J. S. Mill, On Liberty, ch. 2 (1859).

39 J. Madison. The Federalist No. 51, at 323–24 (C. Rossiter ed. 1961).

year, when he had come out and his classmates knew that he was gay, he found that he was not nearly as persuasive an advocate for his position as when he was identified as straight. He was the same person saying the same things, but his identity gave him less authority. Similarly, Catharine MacKinnon argues that pornography causes women to be taken less seriously as they enter the public arena.[40] Racial minorities have the same experiences on a daily basis as they endure the microaggression of having their words doubted, or misinterpreted, or assumed to be without evidentiary support, or when their insights are ignored and then appropriated by whites who are assumed to have been the original authority.

Finally, racist speech decreases the total amount of speech that reaches the market by coercively silencing members of those groups who are its targets. I noted earlier in this chapter the ways in which racist speech is inextricably linked with racist conduct. The primary purpose and effect of the speech/conduct that constitutes white supremacy is the exclusion of nonwhites from full participation in the body politic. Sometimes the speech/conduct of racism is direct and obvious. When the Klan burns a cross on the lawn of a Black person who joined the NAACP or exercised the right to move to a formerly all-white neighborhood, the effect of this speech does not result from the persuasive power of an idea operating freely in the market. It is a threat; a threat made in the context of a history of lynchings, beatings, and economic reprisals that made good on earlier threats; a threat that silences a potential speaker. Such a threat may be difficult to recognize because the tie between the speech and the threatened act is unstated. The tie does not need to he explicit because the promised violence is systemic. The threat is effective because racially motivated violence is a well-known historical and contemporary reality. The threat may be even more effective than a phone call that takes responsibil-

ity for a terrorist bomb attack and promises another, a situation in which we easily recognize the inextricable link between the speech and the threatened act. The Black student who is subjected to racial epithets, like the Black person on whose lawn the Klan has burned a cross, is threatened and silenced by a credible connection between racist hate speech and racist violence. Certainly the recipients of hate speech may be uncommonly brave or foolhardy and ignore the system of violence in which this abusive speech is only a bit player. But it is more likely that we, as a community, will be denied the benefit of many of their thoughts and ideas.

Again MacKinnon's analysis of how first amendment law misconstrues pornography is instructive. She notes that in concerning themselves only with government censorship, first amendment absolutists fail to recognize that whole segments of the population are systematically silenced by powerful private actors. "As a result, [they] cannot grasp that the speech of some silences the speech of others in a way that is not simply a matter of competition for airtime."[41]

Asking Victim Groups to Pay the Price

Whenever we decide that racist hate speech must be tolerated because of the importance of tolerating unpopular speech, we ask Blacks and other subordinated groups to bear a burden for the good of society—to pay the price for the societal benefit of creating more room for speech. And we assign this burden to them without seeking their advice or consent. This amounts to white domination, pure and simple. It is taxation without representation. We must be careful that the ease with which we strike the balance against the regulation of racist speech is in no way influenced by the fact the cost will be borne by others. We must be certain that the individuals who pay the price are fairly represented in our deliberation and that they are heard.

Even as our discussions concerning the efficacy of regulating racist speech on campuses

40 MacKinnon, *Not a Moral Issue,* 2 Yale L & Pol'y Rev. 321, 325–26, 335 (1984).

41 C. MacKinnon, note 12, at 206.

continue, they evidence our lack of attention to the costs of constitutional injury borne by the victims. I have had scores of conversations about this topic over the past several months with students, colleagues, university administrators, ACLU board members, reporters, friends, relatives, and strangers. By now there is an experience of déjà vu each time I am asked to explain how a good civil libertarian like myself—a veteran of 1960s sit-ins and demonstrations, a progressive constitutional law professor, and a person who has made antiestablishment speech his vocation—could advocate censorship. I try to be patient, articulate, and good natured as I set forth the concerns and the arguments explored in this chapter. I try to listen carefully, to remain open to others' experiences and to my own strong instincts against governmental incursion on individual liberty.

Often when I am at my best, even the most steadfast defenders of the first amendment faith will concede that these are persuasive arguments. They say they agree with much of what I have said, they recognize I am proposing narrowly framed restrictions on only the most abusive, least substantive forms of racist speech, and they understand the importance of hearing the victims' stories. Then they say, "But I'm afraid I still come out differently from you in the end. I still don't see how we can allow even this limited regulation of racist speech without running some risk of endangering our first amendment liberties."

One of these encounters occurred at a recent dinner with colleagues in New York. My good friend and former colleague John Powell—John is national legal director of the ACLU and he is Black—was in attendance. He told the following story:

> My family was having Thanksgiving dinner at the home of friends. We are vegetarians and my two kids were trying to figure out which of the two dressings on the table was the vegetarian dressing and which was the meat dressing. One of our hosts pointed to one of the dressings and said, "This is the regular dressing and the other is the vegetarian dressing." I corrected him saying, "There is no such thing as 'regular' dressing. There is meat dressing and there is vegetarian dressing, but neither one of them is regular dressing."

This incident reminded Powell of the discussions he has had with his colleagues on the subject of regulating racist speech. "Somehow," he said,

> I always come away from these discussions feeling that my white colleagues think about the first amendment the way my friend thought about "regular" [meat] dressing, as an amendment for regular people or all people, and that they think of the equal protection clause of the fourteenth amendment the way my friend thought about vegetarian dressing, as a special amendment for a minority of different people.

Inevitably, in these conversations, those of us who are nonwhite bear the burden of justification, of justifying our concern for protection under our "special" amendment. It is not enough that we have demonstrated tangible and continuing injury committed against the victims of racist speech. There can be no public remedy for our special fourteenth amendment injury until we have satisfied our interlocutors that there is no possible risk of encroachment on their first amendment—the "regular" amendment.

If one asks why we always begin by asking whether we can afford to fight racism rather than asking whether we can afford not to, or if one asks why my colleagues who oppose all regulation of racist speech do not feel that the burden is theirs to justify a reading of the first amendment that requires sacrificing rights guaranteed under the equal protection clause, then one sees an example of how unconscious racism operates in the marketplace of ideas.

Well-meaning individuals who are committed to equality without regard to race and who have demonstrated that commitment in many arenas do not recognize where the burden of persuasion has been placed in this discussion. When they do, they do not understand why. Even as I experienced the frustration of always bearing the burden of persuasion, I did not see the source of my frustration or understand its significance until Powell told his story about the Thanksgiving dressing. Unfortunately, our unconscious racism causes even those of us who are the direct victims of racism to view the first amendment as the "regular" amendment—an amendment that works for all people—and the equal protection clause and racial equality as a special-interest amendment important to groups that are less valued.

Derrick Bell has noted that often in our constitutional history the rights of Blacks have been sacrificed because sacrifice was believed necessary to preserve the greater interests of the whole.[42] It is not just the actual sacrifice that is racist but also the way the "whole with the greater interests" gets defined. Today in a world committed to the idea of equality, we rarely notice the sacrifice or how we have avoided noticing the sacrifice by defining the interests of whites as the whole, "the regular." When we think this way, when we see the potential danger of incursions on the first amendment but do not see existing incursions on the fourteenth amendment, our perceptions have been influenced by an entire belief system that makes us less sensitive to the injury experienced by nonwhites. Unaware, we have adopted a worldview that takes for granted Black sacrifice.

Richard Delgado has suggested there is another way in which those of us who abhor racist speech but insist that it cannot be regulated may be, perhaps unwittingly, benefiting from the presence of "a certain amount of low-grade racism" in the environment:

> I believe that racist speech benefits powerful white-dominated institutions. The highly educated, refined persons who operate the University of Wisconsin, other universities, major corporations, would never, ever themselves

42 D. Bell, Racism and American Law, 30 (2nd ed. 1980).

utter a racial slur. That is the last thing they would do.

> Yet, they benefit, and on a subconscious level they know they benefit, from a certain amount of low-grade racism in the environment. If an occasional bigot or redneck calls one of us a nigger or spick one night late as we're on our way home from the library, that is all to the good. Please understand that I am not talking about the very heavy stuff—violence, beatings, bones in the nose. That brings out the TV cameras and the press and gives the university a black eye. I mean the daily, low-grade largely invisible stuff, the hassling, cruel remarks, and other things that would be covered by rules. This kind of behavior keeps nonwhite people on edge, a little off balance. We get these occasional reminders that we are different, and not really wanted. It prevents us from digging in too strongly, starting to think we could really belong here. It makes us a little introspective, a little unsure of ourselves; at the right low-grade level it prevents us from organizing on behalf of more important things. It assures that those of us of real spirit, real pride, just plain leave—all of which is quite a substantial benefit for the institution.[43]

"WHICH SIDE ARE (WE) ON?"

However one comes out on the question of whether racist hate speech should be artificially distinguished from other fighting words and given first amendment protection, it is important to examine and take responsibility for the effects of how one participates in the debate. It is important to consider how our voice is heard. We must ask ourselves whether in our well-placed passion for preserving our first amendment freedoms we have been forceful enough in our personal condemnation of ideas we abhor,

43 R. Delgado, Address to State Historical Society, Madison, Wis. (Apr. 24, 1989). Delgado drew an analogy to Susan Brownmiller's observation that rape is the crime of all men against all women. Men who would never commit rape and who abhor it nonetheless benefit from the climate of terror that the experience of rape helps create.

whether we have neglected our alliances with victims of the oppressive manifestations of the continuing dominance of these racist ideas within our communities and within ourselves.

At the core of the argument that we should resist all government regulation of speech is the ideal that the best cure for bad speech is good speech and that ideas that affirm equality and the worth of all individuals ultimately will prevail over racism, sexism, homophobia, and anti-Semitism because they are better ideas. Despite an optimism regarding the human capacity for good that can only be explained by faith, I am skeptical of ideals that provide the vehicle for oppressive ideology. I do not believe that truth will prevail in a rigged game or in a contest where the referees are on the payroll of the proponents of falsity. The argument that good speech ultimately drives out bad speech rests on a false premise unless those of us who fight racism are vigilant and unequivocal in that fight.

There is much about the way many civil libertarians have participated in the debate over the regulation of racist speech that causes the victims of that speech to wonder which side the civil libertarians are on. Those who raise their voices in protest against public sanctions against racist speech have not organized private protests against the voices of racism. It has been people of color, women, and gays who have held vigils at offending fraternity houses, staged candlelight marches and counterdemonstrations, and distributed flyers calling upon their classmates and colleagues to express their outrage at pervasive racism, sexism, and homophobia in their midst and to show their solidarity with its victims.

Traditional civil libertarians have been conspicuous largely in their absence from these group expressions of condemnation. Their failure to participate in this marketplace response to speech with more speech is often justified, paradoxically, as concern for the principle of free speech. When racial minorities or other victims of hate speech hold counterdemonstrations or engage in picketing, leafleting, heckling, or booing of racist speakers, civil libertarians often accuse them of private censorship, of seeking to silence opposing points of view. When both public and private responses to racist speech are rejected as contrary to the principle of free speech, it is no wonder that the victims of racism do not consider first amendment absolutists allies.

Blacks and other racial minorities also are made skeptical by the resistance encountered when we approach traditional civil liberties groups like the ACLU with suggestions that they at least reconsider the ways in which they engage in this complex debate concerning speech and equality. Traditional civil liberties lawyers typically have elected to stand by as universities respond to the outbreak of hate speech by adopting regulations that often are drafted with considerable attention to appeasing various, widely diverging political constituencies with only passing concern for either free speech or equality. Not surprisingly, these regulations are vague and overbroad. I believe that there is an element of unconscious collusion in the failure of universities, some with top-notch legal staffs and fine law schools, to draft narrow, carefully crafted regulations. For example, it is difficult to believe that anyone at the University of Michigan Law School was consulted in drafting the regulation that was struck down at that university.[44] It is almost as if the university administrators purposefully wrote an unconstitutional regulation so that they could say to the Black students, "We tried to help you, but the courts just won't let us do it." Such sloppy regulations provide easy prey for the white-hatted defenders of the first amendment faith who dutifully march into court to have them declared unconstitutional. Nor do some civil liberties lawyers stop there. They go on to point to the regulations' inadequacies as evidence that any regulation against racist speech may chill expression that should be protected.

44 721 F. Supp. 852 (1989).

Minority delegates to the 1989 ACLU biennial convention proposed a different approach. Their approach was to have the ACLU offer its expertise to schools and universities at the beginning of the legislative process instead of waiting until the end to attack a predictably unacceptable regulation. In the view of minority delegates, hearings should be held on university campuses where the incidence and nature of the injury of racist speech could be carefully documented and responses that were least restrictive of protected speech could be recommended. Such an approach would serve two important purposes. It would give civil libertarians an opportunity to influence the process from the outset, ensuring that the regulation reflected their constitutional concerns. It also would signal to racial minorities and other hate speech victims that the civil liberties community is aware of and concerned about issues of equality as well as free speech. But this approach to racist speech incidents was rejected at the national convention and has faced strong opposition when proposed to regional ACLU boards.

There is also a propensity among some civil libertarians to minimize the injury to the victims of racist speech and distance themselves from it by characterizing individual acts of racial harassment as aberrations, as isolated incidents in a community that is otherwise free of racism. When those persons who argue against the regulation of racist speech speak of "silencing a few creeps" or argue that "the harm that censors allege will result unless speech is forbidden rarely occurs," they demonstrate an unwillingness even to acknowledge the injury. Moreover, they disclaim any responsibility for its occurrence. A recent conversation with a colleague about an incident at Stanford exemplifies this phenomenon. Two white freshmen had defaced a poster bearing the likeness of Beethoven. They had colored the drawing of Beethoven brown, given it wild curly hair, big lips, and red eyes and posted it on the door of a black student dorm room in Ujamaa, the Black theme house. An in-

vestigation of the incident revealed that the two white students involved had been in an argument with the same Black student the night before. The white students contested the Black student's assertion that Beethoven was of African descent. It appeared that the Sambo-like defacement of the portrait was the white students' final rebuttal to the Black student's claim of familial relationship with the great composer —that this caricature was meant to ridicule the idea that such a genius could be Black—could be "Sambo."

My colleague shared my outrage at these students' behavior but went on to say that he thought I had misinterpreted the import of the incident in viewing it as a manifestation of more widespread racism at Stanford. He was inclined to explain the students' behavior as that of two rather isolated, ignorant, misguided youths acting out against the dominant liberal culture. This hardly seemed an accurate description to me. The message conveyed by the defaced poster replicated, in a crude form, an argument that was being made by much of the Stanford faculty in the then-current debate over Stanford's course requirement in Western Civilization. The thrust of much of the argument for maintaining a Eurocentric curriculum that included no contributions of people of color was that there were no significant non-European contributions to be included. The students' defacement had added a graphic footnote to that argument. It seemed to me—contrary to my colleague's explanation of the students' behavior —that they were imitating their role models in the professorate, not rebelling against them.

In its most obvious manifestations, the recent outbreak of racism on our campuses provides an opportunity to examine the presence of less overt forms of racism within our educational institutions. But the debate that has followed these incidents has focused on the first amendment freedoms of the perpetrators rather than the university community's responsibility for creating an environment where such acts occur.

The resurgence of flagrant racist acts has not occurred in a vacuum. It is evidence of more widespread resistance to change by those holding positions of dominance and privilege in institutions, which until recently were exclusively white. An atmosphere that engenders virulent racist speech is inseparable from practices that exclude minorities from university professorships and attitudes that devalue their contributions to the culture. Those who are marginalized in these institutions—by their token inclusion on faculties and administrations, by the exclusion of their cultures from core curricula, and by an ideology of diversity and multiculturalism that seems to require assimilation more than real change in the university—see their colleagues' attention to free speech as an avoidance of these larger issues of equality.

I believe that the speech/acts that "race" us must all be fought simultaneously, for they are mutually dependent parts of a whole. At Stanford I have responded to some of my colleagues who have urged that we turn our attention from the relatively trivial concern of racist speech to more important concerns like affirmative action by suggesting that we tie the two efforts together. Why not hold the university responsible for individual violations of a regulation against racial harassment, much as the employer is held responsible under Title VII of the Civil Rights Act for the harassing acts of its employees? Each time a violation of the regulation against racist speech occurs there would be a public intervention in the form of a hearing and a public announcement of the judicial body's findings of fact. Instead of the university punishing the individuals involved, an affirmative remedy or reparation would be made by the university to the injured class. The university might set aside a slot for a minority professor or fund an additional full scholarship for a minority student, or cancel classes for a day and hold a university-wide teach-in on racism. Such a proposal would directly address the institution's responsibility for maintaining a discrimination-free environment; it would have the symbolic value provided by a clear university position against certain forms of racist speech, and it would avoid first amendment problems by placing public sanctions on the institution rather than the individual speaker. If minority students knew that concrete institutional resources were being spent to change the atmosphere of racism on campus, they would be less concerned that individual racist speakers were escaping punishment. As things are, minority students hear the call for focus on racist attitudes and practices rather than on racist speech as "just a lot of cheap talk."

When the ACLU enters the debate by challenging the University of Michigan's efforts to provide a safe harbor for its Black, Latino, and Asian students (in a climate that a colleague of mine compared unfavorably with Mississippi in the 1960s), we should not be surprised that nonwhite students feel abandoned. When we respond to Stanford students' pleas for protection by accusing them of seeking to silence all who disagree with them, we paint the harassing bigot as a martyred defender of democracy. When we valorize bigotry, we must assume some responsibility for the assaultive acts of those emboldened by their newfound status as defenders of the faith. We must find ways to engage actively in speech and action that resists and counters the racist ideas the first amendment protects. If we fail in this duty, the victims of hate speech rightly assume we are aligned with their oppressors.

We must also begin to think creatively as lawyers. We must embark upon the development of a first amendment jurisprudence that is grounded in the reality of our history and contemporary experience, particularly the experiences of the victims of oppression. We must eschew abstractions of first amendment theory that proceed without attention to the dysfunction in the marketplace of ideas created by racism and unequal access to that market. We must think hard about how best to launch legal attacks against the most assaultive and indefensible forms of hate speech. Good lawyers can create exceptions and narrow interpretations limiting the harm of hate speech without opening the floodgates of censorship. We must weigh carefully and critically the competing constitutional values expressed in the first and fourteenth amendments.

A concrete step in this direction is the abandonment of overstated rhetorical and legal attacks on individuals who conscientiously seek to frame a public response to racism that preserves our first amendment liberties. I have ventured a second step in this chapter by suggesting that the regulation of certain face-to-face racial vilification on university campuses may be justified under current first amendment doctrine as an analogy to the protection of certain classes of captive audiences. Most important, we must continue this discussion. It must be a discussion in which the victims of racist speech are heard. We must be attentive to the achievement of the constitutional ideal of equality as we are to the ideal of untrammeled expression. There can be no true free speech where there are still masters and slaves.

EPILOGUE

"Eeny, meeny, miney, mo."

It is recess time at the South Main Street School. It is 1952, and I am nine. Eddie Becker, Muck Makowski, John Thomas, Terry Flynn, Howie Martin, and I are standing in a circle, each with our right foot thrust forward. The toes of our black, high-top Keds sneakers touch, forming a tight hub of white rubber at the center, our skinny, blue-jeaned legs extending like spokes from the hub. Heads bowed, we are intently watching Muck, who is hunkered down on one knee so that he can touch our toes as he calls out the rhyme. We are enthralled and entranced by the drama of this boyhood ritual, this customary pregame incantation. It is no less important than the game itself.

But my mind is not on the ritual. I have lost track of the count that will determine whose foot must be removed from the hub, who will no longer have a chance to be a captain in this game. I hardly feel Muck's index finger as it presses through the rubber to my toes. My mind is on the rhyme. I am the only Black boy in this circle of towheaded prepubescent males. Time stands still for me. My palms are sweaty and I feel a prickly heat at the back of my neck. I know that Muck will not say the word.

"Catch a tiger by the toe."

The heads stay down. No one looks at me. But I know that none of them is picturing the capture of a large striped animal. They are thinking of me, imagining my toe beneath the white rubber of my Keds sneaker—my toe attached to a large, dark, thick-lipped, burr-headed American fantasy/nightmare.

"If he hollers let him go."

Tigers don't holler. I wish I could right now.

My parents have told me to ignore this word that is ringing unuttered in my ears. "You must not allow those who speak it to make you feel small or ugly" they say. They are proud, Mississippi-bred Black professionals and longtime political activists. Oft-wounded veterans of the war against the racist speech/conduct of Jim Crow and his many relations, they have, on countless occasions, answered the bad speech/conduct of racism with the good speech/conduct of their lives—representing the race; being smarter, cleaner, and more morally upright than white folk to prove that Black folk are equal, are fully human—refuting the lies of the cultural myth that is American racism. "You must know that it is their smallness, their ugliness of which this word speaks," they say.

I am struggling to heed their words, to follow their example, but I feel powerless before this word and its minions. In a moment's time it has made me an other. In an instant it has rebuilt the wall between my friends' humanity and my own, the wall that I have so painstakingly disassembled.

I was good at games, not just a good athlete, but a strategist, a leader. I knew how to make my teammates feel good about themselves so that they played better. It just came naturally to me. I could choose up a team and make the members feel like family. When other folks felt good, I felt good too. Being good at games was the main tool I used to knock down the wall I'd found when I came to this white school in this white town. I looked forward to recess because that was when I could do the most damage to the wall. But now this rhyme, this word, had undone all my labors.

"Eeny meeny, miney, mo."

I have no memory of who got to be captain that day or what game we played. I just wished Muck had used "One potato, two potato . . ." We always used that at home.

Review Questions

1. What does Lawrence mean by "the double consciousness" of groups outside the ethnic mainstream?
2. What reasons are given for protecting racist speech? Why doesn't Lawrence accept them?
3. How does Lawrence interpret the *Brown* case?
4. Why does the Civil Rights Act of 1964 regulate racist speech, on Lawrence's analysis?
5. According to Lawrence, why is it difficult to recognize white supremacy and how it acts to harm?
6. What is the state action doctrine, and how does Lawrence object to it?
7. Explain the Stanford speech code. Why is it constitutional, according to Lawrence?
8. Explain the double standard about responding to an insult that Lawrence finds in our society.
9. Lawrence identifies three injuries caused by racist speech. What are they?
10. Why doesn't Lawrence have much faith in free speech as a vehicle for liberation?
11. What is a "process defect"? How does it work in our society, according to Lawrence?
12. Why does the decision to tolerate racist hate speech amount to white domination, in Lawrence's view?
13. What is "low-grade racism," and how does it work, according to Richard Delgado?
14. Why does Lawrence reject the argument that good speech will drive out bad speech?
15. What positive suggestions does Lawrence make for combating hate speech and acts?

Discussion Questions

1. Does racist conduct amount to racist speech, as Lawrence contends? If so, how do we distinguish between conduct and speech?
2. Lawrence seems to hold that private choices—for example the choice to send a child to a private school—should be limited if they involve inequalities. Do you agree? Why or why not?
3. Does free speech actually encourage racism, sexism, and homophobia? Why or why not?
4. Lawrence compares racist hate speech to pornography. Are they similar or not?

In Defense of Prejudice:
Why Incendiary Speech Must Be Protected

JONATHAN RAUCH

Jonathan Rauch is a writer for *The Economist* and the author of *Kindly Inquisitors: The New Attacks on Free Thought* (1993).

   Rauch defends intellectual pluralism that tolerates expressions of bigotry, and attacks purism, the anti-pluralism campaign to eradicate expressions of prejudice in our society. He identifies at least three problems with purism. One, the concept of prejudice is vague and seems to include religious and controversial beliefs. Two, it has bad consequences in the law, in the workplace, and in the university. In the name of protecting minorities such as Rauch (who identifies himself as a gay Jew), it threatens to silence them too. Three, it confuses words with violence, and this is a mistake.

THE WAR ON PREJUDICE is now, in all likelihood, the most uncontroversial social movement in America. Opposition to "hate speech," formerly identified with the liberal left, has become a bipartisan piety. In the past year, groups and factions that agree on nothing else have agreed that the public expression of any and all prejudices must be forbidden. On the left, protesters and editorialists have insisted that Francis L. Lawrence resign as president of Rutgers University for describing blacks as "a disadvantaged population that doesn't have the genetic, hereditary background to have a higher average." On the other side of the ideological divide, Ralph Reed, the executive director of the Christian Coalition, responded to criticism of the religious right by calling a press conference to denounce a supposed outbreak of "namecalling, scapegoating, and religious bigotry." Craig Rogers, an evangelical Christian student at California State University, recently filed a $2.5 million sexual-harassment suit against a lesbian professor of psychology, claiming that antimale bias in one of her lectures violated campus rules and left him feeling "raped and trapped."

   In universities and on Capitol Hill, in workplaces and newsrooms, authorities are declaring that there is no place for racism, sexism, homophobia, Christian-bashing, and other forms of prejudice in public debate or even in private thought. "Only when racism and other forms of prejudice are expunged," say the crusaders for sweetness and light, "can minorities be safe and society be fair." So sweet, this dream of a world without prejudice. But the very last thing society should do is seek to utterly eradicate racism and other forms of prejudice.

   I suppose I should say, in the customary I-hope-I-don't-sound-too-defensive tone, that I am not a racist and that this is not an article favoring racism or any other particular prejudice.

It is an article favoring intellectual pluralism, which permits the expression of various forms of bigotry and always will. Although we like to hope that a time will come when no one will believe that people come in types and that each type belongs with its own kind, I doubt such a day will ever arrive. By all indications, *Homo sapiens* is a tribal species for whom "us versus them" comes naturally and must be continually pushed back. Where there is genuine freedom of expression, there will be racist expression. There will also be people who believe that homosexuals are sick or threaten children or—especially among teenagers—are rightful targets of manly savagery. Homosexuality will always be incomprehensible to most people, and what is incomprehensible is feared. As for anti-Semitism, it appears to be a hardier virus than influenza. If you want pluralism, then you get racism and sexism and homophobia, and communism and fascism and xenophobia and tribalism, and that is just for a start. If you want to believe in intellectual freedom and the progress of knowledge and the advancement of science and all those other good things, then you must swallow hard and accept this: for as thickheaded and wayward an animal as us, the realistic question is how to make the best of prejudice, not how to eradicate it.

Indeed, "eradicating prejudice" is so vague a proposition as to be meaningless. Distinguishing prejudice reliably and nonpolitically from non-prejudice, or even defining it crisply, is quite hopeless. We all feel we know prejudice when we see it. But do we? At the University of Michigan, a student said in a classroom discussion that he considered homosexuality a disease treatable with therapy. He was summoned to a formal disciplinary hearing, for violating the school's policy against speech that "victimizes" people based on "sexual orientation." Now, the evidence is abundant that this particular hypothesis is wrong, and any American homosexual can attest to the harm that the student's hypothesis has inflicted on many real people. But was it a statement of prejudice or of misguided belief? Hate speech or hypothesis? Many Americans who do not regard themselves as bigots or haters believe that homosexuality is a treatable disease. They may be wrong, but are they all bigots? I am unwilling to say so, and if you are willing, beware. The line between a prejudiced belief and a merely controversial one is elusive, and the harder you look the more elusive it becomes. "God hates homosexuals" is a statement of fact, not of bias, to those who believe it; "American criminals are disproportionately black" is a statement of bias, not of fact, to those who disbelieve it.

Who is right? You may decide, and so may others, and there is no need to agree. That is the great innovation of intellectual pluralism (which is to say, of post-Enlightenment science, broadly defined). We cannot know in advance or for sure which belief is prejudice and which is truth, but to advance knowledge we don't need to know. The genius of intellectual pluralism lies not in doing away with prejudices and dogmas but in channeling them—making them socially productive by pitting prejudice against prejudice and dogma against dogma, exposing all to withering public criticism. What survives at the end of the day is our base of knowledge.

What they told us in high school about this process is very largely a lie. The Enlightenment tradition taught us that science is orderly, antiseptic, rational, the province of detached experimenters and high-minded logicians. In the popular view, science stands for reason against prejudice, open-mindedness against dogma, calm consideration against passionate attachment—all personified by pop-science icons like the magisterially deductive Sherlock Holmes, the coolly analytic Mr. Spock, the genially authoritative Mr. Science (from our junior-high science films). Yet one of science's dirty secrets is that although science as a whole is as unbiased as anything human can be, scientists are just as biased as anyone else, sometimes more so. "One of the strengths of science," writes the philosopher of science David L. Hull, "is that it does not require that scientists be unbiased, only that different scientists have different biases." Another dirty secret is that, no less than the rest of us, scientists can be dogmatic and pigheaded. "Although this pigheadedness often damages the careers of individual scientists," says Hull, "it is beneficial for the manifest goal of science," which relies on people to invest years in their ideas and defend them passionately. And the dirtiest secret of all, if you believe in the antiseptic popular view of science, is that this most ostensibly rational of enterprises depends on the most irrational of motives—ambition, narcissism, animus, even revenge. "Scientists acknowledge that among their motivations are natural curiosity, the love of trust, and the desire to help humanity, but other inducements exist as well, and one of them is to 'get that son of a bitch,'" says Hull. "Time and again, scientists whom I interviewed described the powerful spur that 'showing that son of a bitch' supplied to their own research."

Many people, I think, are bewildered by this unvarnished and all too human view of science. They believe that for a system to be unprejudiced, the people in it must also be unprejudiced. In fact, the opposite is true. Far from eradicating ugly or stupid ideas and coarse or unpleasant motives, intellectual pluralism relies upon them to excite intellectual passion and redouble scientific effort. I know of no modern idea more ugly and stupid than that the Holocaust never happened, nor any idea more viciously motivated. Yet the deniers' claims that the Auschwitz gas chambers could not have worked led to closer study and in 1993, research showing, at last, how they actually did work. Thanks to prejudice and stupidity, another opening for doubt has been shut.

An enlightened and efficient intellectual regime lets a million prejudices bloom, including many that you or I may regard as hateful or grotesque. It avoids any attempt to stamp out prejudice, because stamping out prejudice really means forcing everyone to share the same prejudice, namely that of whatever is in authority. The great American philosopher Charles Sanders Peirce wrote in 1877: "When complete agreement could not otherwise be reached, a general massacre of all who have not thought in a certain way has proved a very effective means of settling opinion in a country." In speaking of "settling opinion," Peirce was writing about one of the two or three most fundamental problems that any human society must confront and solve. For most societies down through the centuries, this problem was dealt with in the manner he described: errors were identified by the authorities—priests, politburos, dictators—or by mass opinion, and then the error-makers were eliminated along with their putative mistakes. "Let all men who reject the established belief be terrified into silence," wrote Peirce, describing this system. "This method has, from the earliest times, been one of the chief means of upholding correct theological and political doctrines."

Intellectual pluralism substitutes a radically different doctrine: we kill our mistakes rather than each other. Here I draw on another great philosopher, the late Karl Popper, who pointed out that the critical method of science "consists in letting our hypotheses die in our stead." Those who are in error are not (or are not supposed to be) banished or excommunicated or forced to sign a renunciation or required to submit to "rehabilitation" or sent for psychological counseling. It is the error we punish, not the errant. By letting people make errors—even mischievous, spiteful errors (as, for instance, Galileo's insistence on Copernicanism was taken to be in 1633)—pluralism creates room to challenge orthodoxy, think imaginatively, experiment boldly. Brilliance and bigotry are empowered in the same stroke.

Pluralism is the principle that protects and makes a place in human company for that loneliest and most vulnerable of all minorities, the minority who is hounded and despised among blacks and whites, gays and straights, who is suspect or criminal among every tribe in every nation of the world, and yet on whom progress depends: the dissident. I am not saying that dissent is always or even usually enlightened. Most of the time it is foolish and self-serving. No dissident has the right to be taken seriously, and the fact that Aryan Nation racists or Nation of Islam anti-Semites are unorthodox does not entitle them to respect. But what goes around comes around. As a supporter of gay marriage, for example, I reject the majority's view of family, and as a Jew I reject its view of God. I try to be civil but the fact is that most Americans regard my views on marriage as a reckless assault on the most fundamental of all institutions, and many people are more than a little discomfited by the statement "Jesus Christ was no more divine than anybody else" (which is why so few people ever say it). Trap the racists and anti-Semites, and you lay a trap for me too. Hunt for them with eradication in your mind, and you have brought dissent itself within your sights.

The new crusade against prejudice waves aside such warnings. Like earlier crusades against antisocial ideas, the mission is fueled by good (if cocksure) intentions and a genuine sense of urgency. Some kinds of error are held to be intolerable, like pollutants that even in small traces poison the water for a whole town. Some errors are so pernicious as to damage real people's lives, so wrongheaded that no person of right mind or goodwill could support them. Like their forebears of other stripe—the Church in its campaigns against heretics, the Mc-Carthyites in their campaigns against Communists—the modern anti-racist and anti-sexist and anti-homophobic campaigners are totalists, demanding not that misguided ideas and ugly expressions be corrected or criticized but that they be eradicated. They make war not on errors but on error, and like other totalists they act in the name of public safety—the safety, especially, of minorities.

The sweeping implications of this challenge to pluralism are not, I think, well enough understood by the public at large. Indeed, the new brand of totalism has yet even to be properly named. "Multiculturalism," for instance, is much too broad. "Political correctness" comes closer but is too trendy and snide. For lack of anything else, I will call the new anti-pluralism "purism," since its major tenet is that society cannot be just until the last traces of invidious prejudice have been scrubbed away. Whatever you call it, the purists' way of seeing things has spread through American intellectual life with remarkable speed, so much so that many people will blink at you uncomprehendingly or even call you a racist (or sexist or homophobe, etc.) if you suggest that expressions of racism should be tolerated or that prejudice has its part to play.

The new purism sets out, to begin with, on a campaign against words, for words are the currency of prejudice, and if prejudice is hurtful then so must be prejudiced words. "We are not safe when these violent words are among us," wrote Mari Matsuda, then a UCLA law professor. Here one imagines gangs of racist words swinging chains and smashing heads in back alleys. To suppress bigoted language seems, at first blush, reasonable, but it quickly leads to a curious result. A peculiar kind of verbal shamanism takes root, as though certain expressions, like curses or magical incantations, carry in themselves the power to hurt or heal—as though words were bigoted rather than people. "Context is everything," people have always said. The use of the word "nigger" in *Huckleberry Finn* does not make the book an "act" of hate speech—or does it? In the new view, this is no longer so clear. The very utterance of the word "nigger" (at least by a non-black) is a racist act. When a *Sacramento Bee* cartoonist put the word "nigger" mockingly in the mouth of a white supremacist, there were howls of protest and 1,400 canceled subscriptions and an editorial apology, even though the word was plainly being invoked against racists, not against blacks.

Faced with escalating demands of verbal absolutism, newspapers issue lists of forbidden words. The expression "gyp" (derived from "Gypsy") and "Dutch treat" were among the dozens of terms stricken as "offensive" in a much-ridiculed (and later withdrawn) *Los Angeles Times* speech code. The University of Missouri journalism school issued a *Dictionary of Cautionary Words and Phrases* which included "*Buxom:* Offensive reference to a woman's chest. Do not use. See 'Woman.' *Codger:* Offensive reference to a senior citizen."

As was bound to happen, purists soon discovered that chasing around after words like "gyp" or "buxom" hardly goes to the roots of the problem. As long as they remain bigoted, bigots will simply find other words. If they can't call you a kike then they will say Jewboy, Judas, or Hebe, and when all those are banned they will press words like "oven" and "lampshade" into their service. The vocabulary of hate is potentially as rich as your dictionary, and all you do by banning language used by cretins is to let them decide what the rest of us may say. The problem, some purists have concluded, must therefore go much deeper than laws: it must go to the deeper level of ideas. Racism, sexism, homophobia, and the rest must be built into the very structure of American society and American patterns of thought, so pervasive yet so insidious that, like water to a fish, they are both omnipresent and unseen. The mere existence of prejudice constructs a society whose very nature is prejudiced.

This line of thinking was pioneered by feminists, who argued that pornography, more than just being expressive, is an act by which men construct an oppressive society. Racial activists quickly picked up the argument. Racist expressions are themselves acts of oppression, they said. "All racist speech constructs the social reality that constrains the liberty of nonwhites because of their race," wrote Charles R. Lawrence III, then a law professor at Stanford. From the purist point of view, a society with even one racist is a racist society, because the idea itself threatens and demeans its targets. They cannot feel wholly safe or wholly welcome as long as racism is present. Pluralism says: There will always be some racists. Marginalize them, ignore them, exploit them, ridicule them, take pains to make their policies illegal, but otherwise leave them alone. Purists say: That's not enough. Society cannot be just until these pervasive and oppressive ideas are searched out and eradicated.

And so what is now under way is a growing drive to eliminate prejudice from every corner of society. I doubt that many people have noticed how far-reaching this anti-pluralist movement is becoming.

In universities: Dozens of universities have adopted codes proscribing speech and other expression that (this is from Stanford's policy, which is more or less representative) "is intended to insult or stigmatize an individual or a small number of individuals on the basis of their sex, race, color, handicap, religion, sexual orientation or national and ethnic origin." Some codes punish only persistent harassment of a targeted individual, but many, following the purist doctrine that even one racist is too many, go much further. At Penn, an administrator declared: "We at the University of Pennsylvania have guaranteed students and the community that they can live in a community free of sexism, racism, and homophobia." Here is the purism that gives "political correctness" its distinctive combination of puffy high-mindedness and authoritarian zeal.

In school curricula: "More fundamental than eliminating racial segregation has to be the removal of racist thinking, assumptions, symbols, and materials in the curriculum," writes theorist Molefi Kete Asante. In practice, the effort to "remove racist thinking" goes well beyond striking egregious references from textbooks. In many cases it becomes a kind of mental engineering in which students are encouraged to see prejudice everywhere; it includes teaching identity politics as an antidote to internalized racism; it rejects mainstream science as "white male" thinking; and it tampers with history, installing such dubious notions as that the ancient Greeks stole their culture from Africa or that an ancient carving of a bird is an example of "African experimental aeronautics."

In criminal law: Consider two crimes. In each, I am beaten brutally; in each, my jaw is smashed and my skull is split in just the same way. However, in the first crime my assailant calls me an "asshole"; in the second he calls me a "queer." In most states, in many localities, and, as of September 1994, in federal cases, these two crimes are treated differently: the crime motivated by bias—or deemed to be so motivated by prosecutors and juries—gets a stiffer punishment. "Longer prison terms for bigots," shrilled Brooklyn Democratic Congressman Charles Schumer, who introduced the federal hate-crimes legislation, and those are what the law now provides. Evidence that the assailant holds prejudiced beliefs, even if he doesn't actually express them while committing an offense, can serve to elevate the crime. Defendants in hate-crimes cases may be grilled on how many black friends they have and whether they have told racist jokes. To increase a prison sentence only because of the defendant's "prejudice" (as gauged by prosecutor and jury) is, of course, to try minds and punish beliefs. Purists say, Well, they are dangerous minds and poisonous beliefs.

In the workplace: Though government cannot constitutionally suppress bigotry directly, it is now busy doing so indirectly by requiring employers to eliminate prejudice. Since the early 1980s, courts and the Equal Employment Opportunity Commission have moved to bar workplace speech deemed to create a hostile or abusive working environment for minorities. The law, held a federal court in 1988, "does require that an employer take prompt action to prevent . . . bigots from expressing their opinions in a way that abuses or offends their co-workers," so as to achieve "the goal of eliminating prejudices and biases from our society." So it was, as UCLA law professor Eugene Volokh notes, that the EEOC charged that a manufacturer's ads using admittedly accurate depictions of samurai, kabuki, and sumo were "racist" and "offensive to people of Japanese origin"; that a Pennsylvania court found that an employer's printing Bible verses on paychecks was religious harassment of Jewish employees; that an employer had to desist using gender-based job titles like "foreman" and "draftsman" after a female employee sued.

On and on the campaign goes, darting from one outbreak of prejudice to another like a cat chasing flies. In the American Bar Association, activists demand that lawyers who express "bias or prejudice" be penalized. In the Education Department, the civil-rights office presses for a ban on computer bulletin board comments that show hostility toward a person or group based on sex, race or color, including slurs, negative stereotypes, jokes or pranks." In its security checks for government jobs, the FBI takes to asking whether applicants are "free of biases against any class of citizens," whether, for instance, they have told racist jokes or indicated other "prejudices." Joke police! George Orwell, grasping the close relationship of jokes to dissent, said that every joke is a tiny revolution. The purists will have no such rebellions.

The purist campaign reaches, in the end, into the mind itself. In a lecture at the University of New Hampshire, a professor compared writing to sex ("You and the subject become one"); he was suspended and required to apologize, but what was most insidious was the order to undergo university-approved counseling to have his mind straightened out. At the University of Pennsylvania, a law lecturer said, "We have ex-slaves here who should know about the Thirteenth Amendment"; he was banished from campus for a year and required to make a public apology, and he, too, was compelled to attend a "sensitivity and racial awareness" session. Mandatory reeducation of alleged bigots is the natural consequence of intellectual purism. Prejudice must be eliminated.

Ah, but the task of scouring minds clean is Augean. "Nobody escapes," said a Rutgers University report on campus prejudice. Bias and prejudice, it found, cross every conceivable line, from sex to race to politics: "No matter who you are, no matter what the color of your skin, no matter what your gender or sexual orientation, no matter what you believe, no matter how you behave, there is somebody out there who doesn't like people of your kind." Charles Lawrence writes: "Racism is ubiquitous. We are all racists." If he means that most of us think racist thoughts of some sort at one time or another, he is right. If we are going to "eliminate prejudices and biases from our society" then the work of the prejudice police is unending. They are doomed to hunt and hunt and hunt, scour and scour and scour.

What is especially dismaying is that the purists pursue prejudice in the name of protecting minorities. In order to protect people like me (homosexual), they must pursue people like me (dissident). In order to bolster minority self-esteem, they suppress minority opinion. There are, of course, all kinds of practical and legal problems with the purists' campaign: the incursions against the first Amendment; the inevitable abuses by prosecutors and activists who define as "hateful" or "violent" whatever speech they dislike or can score points off of; the lack of any evidence that repressing prejudice eliminates rather than inflames it. But minorities, of all people, ought to remember that by definition we cannot prevail by numbers, and we generally cannot prevail by force. Against the power of ignorant mass opinion and group prejudice and superstition, we have only our voices. If you doubt that minorities' voices are powerful weapons, think of the lengths to which Southern officials went to silence the Reverend Martin Luther King Jr. (recall that the city commissioner of Montgomery, Alabama, won a $500,000 libel suit, later overturned in *New York Times v Sullivan* [1964], regarding an advertisement in the *Times* placed by civil-rights leaders who denounced the Montgomery

police). Think of how much gay people have improved their lot over twenty-five years simply by refusing to remain silent. Recall the Michigan student who was prosecuted for saying that homosexuality is a treatable disease, and notice that he was black. Under that Michigan speech code, more than twenty blacks were charged with racist speech, while no instance of racist speech by whites was punished. In Florida, the hate-speech law was invoked against a black man who called a policeman a "white cracker"; not so surprisingly, in the first hate-crimes case to reach the Supreme Court, the victim was white and the defendant black.

In the escalating war against "prejudice," the right is already learning to play by the rules that were pioneered by the purists activists of the left. [In 1994] leading Democrats, including the President, criticized the Republican Party for being increasingly in the thrall of the Christian right. Some of the rhetoric was harsh ("fire-breathing Christian radical right"), but it wasn't vicious or even clearly wrong. Never mind: when Democratic Representative Vic Fazio said Republicans were "being forced to the fringes by the aggressive political tactics of the religious right," the chairman of the Republican National Committee, Haley Barbour, said, "Christian-bashing" was "the left's preferred form of religious bigotry." Bigotry! Prejudice! "Christians active in politics are now on the receiving end of an extraordinary campaign of bias and prejudice," said the conservative leader William J. Bennett. One discerns, here, where the new purism leads. Eventually, any criticism of any group will be "prejudice."

Here is the ultimate irony of the new purism: words, which pluralists hope can be substituted for violence, are redefined by purists *as* violence.

"The experience of being called 'nigger,' 'spic,' 'Jap,' 'kike' is like receiving a slap in the face," Charles Lawrence wrote in 1990. "Psychic injury is no less an injury than being struck in the face, and it often is far more severe." This kind of talk is commonplace today. Epithets, insults, often even polite expressions of what's taken to be prejudice are called by purists "assaultive speech," "words that wound," "verbal violence." "To me, racial epithets are not speech," one University of Michigan law professor said. "They are bullets." In her speech accepting the 1993 Nobel Prize for Literature in Stockholm, Sweden, the author Toni Morrison said this: "Oppressive language does more than represent violence; it is violence."

It is not violence. I am thinking back to a moment on the subway in Washington, a little thing. I was riding home late one night and a squad of noisy kids, maybe seventeen or eighteen years old, noisily piled into the car. They yelled across the car and a girl said, "Where do we get off?"

A boy said, "Farragut North."

The girl: "*Faggot* North!"

The boy: "Yeah! Faggot North!"

General hilarity

First, before the intellect resumes control, there is a moment of fear, an animal moment. Who are they? How many of them? How dangerous? Where is the way out? All of these things are noted preverbally and assessed by the gut. Then the brain begins an assessment: they are sober, this is probably too public a place for them to do it, there are more girls than boys, they were just talking, it is probably nothing.

They didn't notice me and there was no incident. The teenage babble flowed on, leaving me to think. I became interested in my own reaction: the jump of fear out of nowhere like an alert animal, the sense for a brief time that one is naked and alone and should hide or run away. For a time, one ceases to be a human being and becomes instead a faggot.

The fear engendered by these words is real. The remedy is as clear and as imperfect as ever: protect citizens against violence. This, I grant, is something that American society has never done

very well and now does quite poorly. It is no solution to define words as violence or prejudice as oppression, and then by cracking down on words or thoughts pretend that we are doing something about violence and oppression. No doubt it is easier to pass a speech code or hate-crimes law and proclaim the streets safer than actually to make the streets safer, but the one must never be confused with the other. Every cop or prosecutor chasing words is one fewer chasing criminals. In the world rife with real violence and oppression, full of Rwandas and Bosnias and eleven-year-olds spraying bullets at children in Chicago and in turn being executed by gang lords, it is odious of Toni Morrison to say that words are violence.

Indeed, equating "verbal violence" with physical violence is a treacherous, mischievous business. Not long ago a writer was charged with viciously and gratuitously wounding the feelings and dignity of millions of people. He was charged, in effect, with exhibiting flagrant prejudice against Muslims and outrageously slandering their beliefs. "What is freedom of expression?" mused Salman Rushdie a year after the ayatollahs sentenced him to death and put a price on his head. "Without the freedom to offend, it ceases to exist." I can think of nothing sadder than that minority activists, in their haste to make the world better, should be the ones to forget the lesson of Rushdie's plight: for minorities, pluralism, not purism, is the answer. The campaigns to eradicate prejudice—all of them, the speech codes and workplace restrictions and mandatory therapy for accused bigots and all the rest—should stop, now. The whole objective of eradicating prejudice, as opposed to correcting and criticizing it, should be repudiated as a fool's errand. Salman Rushdie is right, Toni Morrison wrong, and minorities belong at his side, not hers.

Review Questions

1. Rauch says he is in favor of intellectual pluralism. What is it, and how does it deal with expressions of racism, sexism, and homophobia?

2. How does Rauch view science?
3. What are Rauch's objections to purism, the program of eradicating prejudice?
4. How does purism, or anti-pluralism, manifest itself in universities, school curricula, criminal law, and the workplace? What problems are created?
5. What is the ultimate irony of the new purism, according to Rauch?

Discussion Questions

1. How would Lawrence respond to Rauch's claim that what survives public criticism is "our base of knowledge"?
2. Does the attack on racists and homophobes also attack people such as Rauch? Why or why not?
3. Does racist speech "construct social reality," as Lawrence says? How does Rauch respond? Who is right and why?
4. Should hate crimes be treated differently from plain crimes? What does the law say? What is Rauch's view? What do you think?

Problem Cases

1. Cyberporn

The Communications Decency Act (CDA) was a last-minute Senate amendment to another bill, the Telecommunications Act of 1996. It was signed into law by President Clinton on February 8, 1996. Two provisions of the law made it a crime to put on the Internet material deemed "indecent" or "patently offensive" for minors.

The law was immediately challenged by a coalition of Internet users, computer-industry groups, and civil liberties organizations, and in June 1997, the Supreme Court in a unanimous decision held that the law was unconstitutional. The majority opinion in the case *(Reno v. American Civil Liberties Union)* was written by Justice John Paul Stevens. He argued that speech on the Internet, the global network that allows about 60 million people to communicate online, is entitled to the highest level of First Amendment protection, similar to the protection given to books and newspapers. (By contrast, the Court has allowed a wide array of governmental regulations of speech on broadcast and cable television.) Justice Stevens argued that although the goal of protecting children from indecent material is legitimate and important, the CDA goes too far in suppressing speech. He noted that it could include, among other things, discussions of birth control, homosexuality, or prison rape.

The latest law restricting online pornography, or cyberporn as it is called, is the Child Online Protection Act, passed by Congress as a small part of the huge budget bill and signed into law by President Clinton in October 1998. The act makes it a crime for operators of commercial websites to make graphic sexual material available to those under age 17.

Like the CDA, this latest statute was immediately challenged. Hours after President Clinton signed the bill, a coalition of seventeen organizations filed suit in the federal district court in Philadelphia. They argue that the act violates the free speech provisions of the First Amendment because it limits the free speech of adults.

Defenders of the law hope that it will be found to be constitutional. Instead of the vague term "indecent," the new act has the term "harmful to minors." This phrase is defined as material that is prurient for minors, depicts or describes sexual contact in a manner patently offensive for minors, and lacks serious artistic, political, literary, or scientific value for minors.

These attempts to censor cyberporn raise some interesting questions. What do terms such as "prurient," "patently offensive," "sexual contact," and "serious value" mean? Try to define them, or, failing that, try to give examples of what is and is not covered. For example, is information about condoms "harmful to minors"?

Isn't it ironic that the U.S. Congress put the report of independent counsel Kenneth W. Starr on the Internet even though it included graphic sexual references to oral sex? Was this material appropriate for minors?

Should the federal government try to censor the Internet at all? If so, what material should be censored, and how should this be done?

2. Corry v. Stanford University

In this case, the Superior Court of California ruled that the Stanford speech code was unconstitutional. (The speech code is quoted in the reading by Lawrence.) The court argued that the speech code, as drawn, was overbroad, that it went beyond fighting words (which are not protected by the First Amendment) and proscribed the expression of particular ideas on race, gender, handicap, religion, sexual orientation, and ethnic origin. The court rejected the view that such speech is conduct—namely, discriminatory harassment—as claimed by the defenders of the code. Rather, the court argued that Stanford's speech code targeted the content of certain speech, not fighting words or behavior, and as such it violated the First Amendment protection of free speech.

Does the Stanford speech code prohibit the expression of unpopular ideas, or does it merely target fighting words? Give examples of speech that would be prohibited by the code.

Consider what it says in Leviticus 20:13: "If a man lies with a man as one lies with a woman, both of them have done what is detestable. They must be put to death." Is this quotation from the Bible prohibited by the Stanford speech code? Why or why not?

3. National Endowment for the Arts v. Finley (1998)

In this case, the Supreme Court ruled that a Congressional decency test for grants awarded by the National Endowment for the Arts (NEA) did not violate the First Amendment and thus was constitutional.

The controversy about federal arts grants began in 1989 when the NEA awarded two grants, one to Robert Mapplethorpe for $30,000 and another one to Andres Serrano for $15,000. The works of both artists produced controversy. Mapplethorpe's photographs of homosexual and sadomasochistic acts, and of children with exposed genitals, offended some viewers. But they were exhibited in several art museums, and art experts defended them as the work of a serious and brilliant artist. Serrano photographed a crucifix immersed in his own urine and called the work "Piss Christ." Some Christians were deeply offended, but Serrano claimed that he was displaying the humanity of Jesus.

As a result of the controversy, Congress slashed the NEA's budget, and in 1990 a bill was passed placing a restriction on NEA grants, saying that the NEA had to take into consideration "general standards of decency and respect for the diverse beliefs and values of the American public." This restriction was the target of a lawsuit brought against the NEA by Karen Finley and three other performance artists whose request for grants had been denied. They argued that the decency proviso violated the First Amendment.

In 1996 a federal appeals court ruled that the decency proviso did violate the First Amendment. But this decision was appealed by the Clinton administration, and the case went to the Supreme Court. In an 8-to-1 decision, the Court ruled that the decency proviso did not violate the First Amendment after all. The majority opinion was written by Justice Sandra Day O'Connor. She argued that if the law imposed "a penalty on disfavored viewpoints," then it would violate the First Amendment. But if it was only "advisory language," then it was not unconstitutional because it would not actually prohibit federal grants for indecent art.

In the sole dissenting opinion, Justice David H. Souter argued that the decency proviso did violate the First Amendment. As he interpreted it, the decency proviso amounted to "viewpoint discrimination" and as such it was unconstitutional. As he put it, "Viewpoint discrimination in the exercise of public authority over expressive activity is unconstitutional."

This case raises some fundamental issues. What is decency? Can this vague word be clearly defined? Assuming it can, should indecent works of art be supported by federal grants? Should such works be banned? If so, why doesn't this amount to "viewpoint discrimination," as Justice Souter claims?

Suggested Readings

1. Studies of the effects of pornography (http://users.bigpond.com//ttguy/refs2.htm). This website is a good place to start if you want to examine the latest research on the effects of pornography. There are links to abstracts of numerous papers. Some of the papers seem to belabor the obvious—e.g. that watching pornography makes you think about sex. Some support the 1986 Final Report and others attack it, but none seems conclusive.
2. U.S. Department of Justice, Attorney General's Commission on Pornography. Final Report, July 1986. The commission surveyed and classified types of pornography. It found

a causal relationship between violent pornography and sexual aggression, but there was disagreement about the harmfulness of nonviolent pornography.

3. Brenda Cassman et al., *Bad Attitude/s on Trial: Pornography, Feminism, and the Bulter Decision* (University of Toronto Press, 1997). This book examines the effects of the *Bulter* decision in Canada. In the case of *Bulter* (1992), the Supreme Court of Canada ruled that obscenity (including material depicting women "as sexual playthings") could be criminalized.

4. Nadine Strossen, *Defending Pornography: Free Speech, Sex, and the Fight for Women's Rights* (Anchor, 1996), argues that state repression of obscenity subverts women's rights. For example, she points out that the recent Canadian ban on pornography has been used to ban gay, lesbian, and feminist literature, including the novels of Andrea Dworkin!

5. Catharine A. MacKinnon, *Only Words* (Harvard University Press, 1993), argues that pornography, sexual harassment, and hate speech are not "only words" but also acts of subordination and discrimination, and should be legally treated as such.

6. Catherine A. MacKinnon and Andrea Dworkin, eds., *In Harm's Way: The Pornography Civil Rights Hearings* (Harvard University Press, 1998), contains the verbal testimony of victims of pornography and introductions by MacKinnon and Dworkin.

7. Joel Feinberg, *Offense to Others* (Oxford University Press, 1985), discusses pornography in Chapters 10–12.

8. Mark R. Wicclair, "Feminism, Pornography, and Censorship," in Thomas A. Mappes and Jane S. Zembaty, eds., *Social Ethics,* fourth edition (McGraw-Hill, 1992), pp. 282–88, maintains that the causal connection between pornography and harm to women has not been established and that pornography may actually reduce harm to women.

9. Alan Soble, *Pornography* (Yale University Press, 1986), argues that pornography is not objectionable in a society that does not exploit women, but it is wrong in a society that does do this.

10. Andrea Dworkin, *Pornography: Men Possessing Women* (Perigee Press, 1981), holds that in a patriarchal society pornography depicting women necessarily degrades and subordinates them.

11. John Arthur, *The Unfinished Constitution* (Wadsworth, 1989), discusses the constitutional issues raised by pornography, including the proposed feminist ordinances in Minneapolis and Indianapolis that attempted to outlaw pornography.

12. Laura Lederer, ed., *Take Back the Night: Women on Pornography* (Morrow, 1980). This anthology presents the feminist view of pornography as degrading and harmful to women.

13. Robert M. Baird and Stuart E. Rosenbaum, eds., *Pornography: Private Right or Public Menace?* (Prometheus Books, 1991). This anthology includes discussions of the two commission reports on pornography and different views on pornography.

14. Judith W. DeCew, "Violent Pornography: Censorship, Morality, and Social Alternatives," *Journal of Applied Philosophy* 1 (1984), pp. 79–94, argues that violent pornography is immoral but should not be censored.

15. Richard L. Abel, *Speaking Respect, Respecting Speech* (University of Chicago Press, 1998), identifies problems with legislating speech and proposes intercommunity apology as a way of showing respect for cultural identities.

16. Milton Heumann and Thomas W. Church, eds., *Hate Speech on Campus: Cases, Case Studies, and Commentary* (Northeastern University Press, 1997), presents a number of cases involving hate speech and speech codes, together with commentaries by John Stuart Mill, Herbert Marcuse, Nadine Strosser, and others.

17. Owen M. Fiss, *The Irony of Free Speech* (Harvard University Press, 1996), argues that restrictions on hate speech and pornography can be defended in terms of the First Amendment.

18. Samuel E. Walker, *Hate Speech: The History of an American Controversy* (University of Nebraska Press, 1994), gives a history of the United States policy on hate speech. Most countries prohibit hate speech, but in the United States it has been allowed because of the importance of free speech.

19. Jonathan Rauch, *Kindly Inquisitors: The New Attacks on Free Thought* (University of Chicago Press, 1993), attacks those who try to limit thought by restricting free speech.

20. Rita Kirk Whillock and David Slayden, eds., *Hate Speech* (Sage Publications, 1995). This collection of nine essays explores hate speech in the media, popular culture, politics, and private realms.

21. Stanley Fish, *There's No Such Thing As Free Speech: And It's a Good Thing Too* (Oxford University Press, 1994). The basic argument given by Fish is that liberals trying to regulate speech create the very thing that they set out to avoid—namely, tyranny, discrimination, and censorship. He concludes that free speech can't and shouldn't be legislated.

22. Nicholas Wolfson, *Hate Speech, Sex Speech, Free Speech* (Praeger, 1997), argues that it is impossible to separate bad speech from good speech without compromising free speech. He thinks that even the most hateful of speech should be protected by the First Amendment.

23. Laura Lederer and Richard Delgado, eds., *The Price We Pay: The Case Against Racist Speech, Hate Propaganda, and Pornography* (Hill and Wang, 1995). This is a collection of forty essays dealing with connections between pornography and sexual harassment, and between hate speech and racism.

24. Timothy C. Shiell, *Campus Hate Speech on Trial* (University Press of Kansas, 1998), reviews campus speech codes and the resulting litigation. He argues that speech codes have tended to be overbroad, arbitrarily enforced, and used to protect only certain groups.

25. Lynn S. Chancer, *Reconcilable Differences: Confronting Beauty, Pornography, and the Future of Feminism* (University of California Press, 1998), examines pornography, beauty, prostitution, "victim feminism," and "third-wave feminism."

Chapter 7

Affirmative Action

Introduction

Factual Background

Affirmative action is an effort to remedy the injustice of racial and sexual discrimination, particularly in employment and admission to schools. Historically, women and minorities were mostly excluded from schools and professional employment as doctors or lawyers, but beginning in the 1950s, laws were passed to remedy some of the more obvious forms of discrimination. Perhaps the most important of these was the Civil Rights Act of 1964 (quoted by Pojman in the reading). Title VII of this law prohibited discrimination in employment on the basis of race, color, religion, sex, or national origin by private employers, employment agencies, and unions with fifteen or more employees. It also prohibited the sex segregation of jobs, and it required that there be a Bona Fide Occupational Qualification to allow preference for a specific group for certain jobs, such as wet nurse or male clothing model.

Despite antidiscrimination laws, sexual and racial discrimination have continued, although perhaps not quite as blatantly as before the laws were enacted. The evidence is enormous and difficult to summarize, but consider these statistics: (1) At all occupational levels, women make less money than men, even for the same work, despite the Equal Pay Act of 1963, which says that men and women have to be given equal pay for substantially equal work. According to the Economic Policy Institute in Washington, D.C., in the first half of 1993 women's wages reached 78 percent of men's, a "historic high" but hardly proving that there is no longer a problem of unequal pay for women. (2) The latest census statistics available indicate that the most desirable occupations (management and administration, professions, and technical jobs) are dominated by whites, whereas the less desirable jobs (service and farm work) are dominated by African Americans, Hispanics, and other ethnic minorities. Women predominate in the lowest-paying jobs: librarians, nurses, elementary-school teachers, sales clerks, secretaries, bank tellers, and waitresses. At the same time, men predominate in the highest-paying jobs: lawyers, doctors, U.S. senators, and so on. (3) In the well-known AT&T case, that enormous company signed a settlement giving tens of millions of dollars to women and minority workers, thus admitting to vast discrimination against women and minorities. (4) Female college teachers with identical credentials in publications and experience are promoted at almost exactly one-half the rate of their male counterparts. More evidence could be cited, but it seems clear enough that there is racial and sexual discrimination in employment and pay.

By giving preferences to minorities and women in employment and college admissions, affirmative action programs are designed to remedy the effects of discrimination. But do they work? A recent study reported in *The New York Times,*

October 8, 1997, provides interesting evidence about the effects of affirmative action. The study looked at doctors trained at the University of California at Davis over a twenty-year period. It compared those who were admitted with special consideration, such as race or ethnic origin, with those who had not received any special consideration in admission. It found that the two groups had remarkably similar postgraduate records and careers. They graduated at the same high rate, completed residency training at the same rate, received similar evaluations, selected their specialties in the same percentages, and established practices with almost the same racial mixes. (For comprehensive statistics on the effects of affirmative action on more than 60,000 white and African American students, see the first book in the Suggested Readings, titled *The Shape of the River: Long-Term Consequences of Considering Race in College and University Admissions.*)

What about the effects of ending affirmative action programs? In 1996 voters in California passed Proposition 209, an initiative banning the use of race and sex in college admissions, contracting, and public employment. We now have evidence about the effects of Proposition 209. According to a report in *The New York Times* (April 5, 1998), the number of minorities admitted to college has declined dramatically. The University of California at Berkeley reported a 40 percent decline in the number of Hispanic high school seniors admitted and a 57 percent drop in the number of blacks. The University of California at Los Angeles reported a decline of 43 percent for African American students and 33 percent for Hispanic Americans. Of course, admission to these elite schools is very competitive. The figures showed that Berkeley turned away 800 black applicants who had 4.0 grade point averages and had scored at least 1200 on the Scholastic Aptitude Test.

The U.C., Berkeley law school has also had a dramatic drop in the number of black students. Before Proposition 209 was passed, the school had 20 black students in a class of 270, but in 1997 the school reported that only 1 new black student planned to attend and that there would be no new black students in 1998. As the result of a Texas ban on affirmative action, the law school at the University of Texas reported that in 1997 they would have only 3 black students in a class of 500.

Opponents of affirmative action in school admissions claim that it is unfair to whites. The most famous example of this was Allan Bakke, a white male, who was denied admission to the Medical School at the University of California at Davis, a school that had a racial quota. Bakke's application was rejected even though minority applicants who were admitted had lower grade point averages and lower Medical College Admissions Test scores. Bakke sued and in a landmark case (see the second Problem Case), the Supreme Court ruled that his rights had been violated under Title VII of the Civil Rights Act of 1964 and the Equal Protection Clause of the Fourteenth Amendment.

In another famous case, *DeFunis v. Odegaard* (1973), Marco DeFunis, a nonminority applicant, was denied admission to the University of Washington Law School's class of 1971. He filed a suit claiming that he had been denied admission on the basis of race. Preferential treatment that year was accorded to African Americans, Native Americans, Chicanos, and Filipinos. Thirty-seven of these minority applicants were accepted, and eighteen actually enrolled. The Law School Admission

Test scores and projected grade point averages of almost all these minority students were lower than those of some of the rejected nonminority students. The Supreme Court of the state of Washington ruled against DeFunis. The court argued that racial classifications are not unconstitutional, that their use is acceptable if there is a compelling state interest, and that the shortage of minority attorneys constituted a compelling state interest. The case was appealed to the U.S. Supreme Court, but it did not hand down a ruling.

The Readings

What is affirmative action? In the first reading, Louis P. Pojman defines it as the effort to rectify the injustice of the past by special policies and goes on to distinguish between weak and strong forms. The weak form of affirmative action involves such measures as the elimination of segregation, advertisements to minorities, and special scholarships for the disadvantaged. The strong form involves such actions as hiring on the basis of race or gender to reach proportionate representation.

Pojman is opposed to both forms of affirmative action. He argues that both forms discriminate against innocent young white males, encourage mediocrity and incompetence, ignore merit, cannot be limited, and simply don't work to solve social problems. As for the arguments supporting affirmative action, Pojman argues that the seven arguments he considers are all defective. He denies that we need role models of the same race or gender, that we need affirmative action to eliminate false stereotypes of women and blacks, that inequality of results is evidence of inequality of opportunity, that blacks should be compensated for past injury, and that the value of diversity overrides considerations of merit and efficiency. He is particularly scathing in his attack on diversity. He says, "Diversity for diversity's sake is moral promiscuity, since it obfuscates rational distinctions."

In the next reading, however, Laurence Thomas defends an argument for diversity in faculty members. He does not defend the view that ethnic or gender composition of faculty members should be proportional to their numbers in society. And he agrees with Pojman that unqualified women and minorities should not be hired, although he points out that deciding who is best qualified is often a judgment call. But he insists that only diversity of faculty gives a woman or minority student the hope that trust, intellectual affirmation, and gratitude are possible for all people and not just for white males. It is not enough to merely talk about justice for all; the university must actually do something to demonstrate it.

Thomas defends affirmative action appointments of women and minorities at colleges and universities, but he does not address the broader issue of overcoming racism and sexism throughout our society. This problem is discussed by T. Alexander Aleinikoff. He argues that it is impossible and undesirable to try to achieve a color-blind society that does not recognize race, and pretending to do so just reinforces racial oppression and white domination. We must face the fact the we live in a world of racial inequality where blacks are worse off than whites in employment, income, life expectancy, infant mortality, crime victimization, and single-parent households. The solution is not color-blindness, but rather a race-consciousness that seeks racial justice; this requires race discrimination laws, including affirmative action.

Pojman is mainly concerned with affirmative action for blacks. He believes that much of what he says can be applied to women, but this is problematic. Mary Anne Warren argues that women are subject to a special kind of discrimination in employment that does not apply to men. This secondary sexism, as she calls it, comes about from the use of sex-correlated criteria that apply only to women. For example, the criterion of having an uninterrupted work record obviously puts women who interrupt their careers to have and raise children at a disadvantage. What about marital status? It is not unknown for faculty members to vote to hire or promote a man rather than a woman because he has a wife and children to support, whereas she has a husband to support her. To correct the injustice of both primary and secondary sexism, Warren recommends mandatory hiring quotas for women. These are of a minimum sort that are based on the proportion of women among qualified candidates; she agrees with Pojman that unqualified people should not be hired. Finally, in reply to the objection that men will be treated unfairly, she says that the men whose careers are set back will be the very ones who have benefited in the past and will benefit in the future from sexist discrimination against women.

Thomas E. Hill makes a useful distinction between two basic types of arguments used to defend affirmative action: forward-looking arguments, which look to future benefits, and backward-looking arguments, which are based on the principle of reparation for past injuries. Both Thomas and Aleinikoff have forward-looking arguments, whereas Mary Anne Warren has basically a backward-looking argument that seeks to compensate women for sexist hiring practices in the past. Hill argues that both types of argument give the wrong message. The forward-looking argument ignores merit and reparation, and the backward-looking argument ignores the fact that racism and sexism are insults, not injuries, and cannot be adequately measured and repaid with equivalents. As an alternative to these arguments, Hill suggests that the value of affirmative action is best seen as being "cross-time"—that is, as involving the past, the present, and the future—and that the appropriate message should be one of mutual trust and respect.

Philosophical Issues

The most basic issue in the readings is whether affirmative action is justified. As we have seen, Pojman gives several arguments for saying it is not justified, and attacks the arguments used to justify it. One of those arguments, the argument from diversity, is attacked by Pojman but defended by Thomas. Both Thomas and Warren give narrow defenses of affirmative action in the hiring of faculty members, whereas Aleinikoff and Hill give broader defenses that seem to apply to the whole society.

Do backward-looking arguments justify affirmative action? Pojman does not think so. He makes several objections to the argument that we should compensate blacks for the injury caused them in the past: Those compensated are not the ones who were harmed in the past; it is not clear that all blacks were harmed in the same way or even harmed as much as poor whites; and giving a high-level job to an unqualified person is not appropriate compensation. But Warren's argument seems to escape most of Pojman's objections, if not all of them. The women compensated may be the very ones who have been discriminated against in the past, and Warren is talking only about qualified women.

Do forward-looking arguments justify affirmative action? Although he does not attack them specifically, many of Pojman's objections seem to apply to forward-looking arguments. His basic objection is that affirmative action programs produce bad results —namely, mediocrity, incompetence, and deep resentment in white men who are victims of reverse discrimination. But what about the good results? Thomas thinks that women and minorities will develop trust, intellectual affirmation, and gratitude. Aleinikoff talks about racial justice. Hill speaks of trust and respect for all persons.

Do the benefits produced by affirmative action outweigh bad results? That is an important and divisive issue that is not easily resolved. To resolve it, we need factual data about the actual effects of affirmative action. But even if there is agreement about the facts, there still may be disagreement about values. For example, is merit more important than equality? Are trust and respect more valuable than mere competence?

The Moral Status of Affirmative Action

LOUIS P. POJMAN

Louis P. Pojman is currently teaching philosophy at Brigham Young University in Provo, Utah. He is the editor of numerous anthologies in philosophy.

Pojman begins by defining his terms. He distinguishes between weak and strong forms of affirmative action. The weak form involves measures such as the elimination of segregation, advertisements to underrepresented groups, and special scholarships for the disadvantaged. The strong form involves more positive steps, such as hiring on the basis of race or gender to reach proportionate representation. After presenting a brief history of affirmative action, Pojman examines the arguments for and against it. He attacks the arguments for affirmative action and defends the arguments against it. He concludes that affirmative action (both weak and strong) is unjustified.

"A ruler who appoints any man to an office, when there is in his dominion another man better quali- *fied for it, sins against God and against the State."* *(The Koran)*

"[Affirmative action] is the meagerest recompense for centuries of unrelieved oppression." (Quoted by Shelby Steele as the justification for affirmative action.)

Source: Louis P. Pojman, "The Moral Status of Affirmative Action," from *Public Affairs Quarterly,* Vol. 6 (1977), pp. 181–206. Reprinted with permission.

HARDLY A WEEK GOES BY but that the subject of affirmative action does not come up. Whether in the guise of reverse discrimination, preferential hiring, nontraditional casting, quotas, goals and timetables, minority scholarships, or race norming, the issue confronts us as a terribly perplexing problem. Last summer's Actor's Equity debacle over the casting of the British actor, Jonathan Pryce, as a Eurasian in Miss Saigon; Assistant Secretary of Education Michael Williams' judgment that Minority Scholarships are unconstitutional; the "Civil Rights Bill of 1991," reversing recent decisions of the Supreme Court which constrain preferential hiring practices; the demand that Harvard Law School hire a black female professor; grade stipends for black students at Pennsylvania State University and other schools; the revelations of race norming in state employment agencies; as well as debates over quotas, underutilization guidelines, and diversity in employment; all testify to the importance of this subject for contemporary society.

There is something salutary as well as terribly tragic inherent in this problem. The salutary aspect is the fact that our society has shown itself committed to eliminating unjust discrimination. Even in the heart of Dixie there is a recognition of the injustice of racial discrimination. Both sides of the affirmative action debate have good will and appeal to moral principles. Both sides are attempting to bring about a better society, one that is color blind, but they differ profoundly on the morally proper means to accomplish that goal.

And this is just the tragedy of the situation: Good people on both sides of the issue are ready to tear each other to pieces over a problem that has no easy or obvious solution. And so the voices become shrill and the rhetoric hyperbolic. The same spirit which divides the pro-choice movement from the right-to-life movement on abortion divides liberal pro-affirmative action advocates from liberal anti-affirmative action advocates. This problem, more than any other, threatens to destroy the traditional liberal consensus in our society. I have seen family members and close friends who until recently fought on the same side of the barricades against racial injustice divide in enmity over this issue. The anti-affirmative liberals ("liberals who've been mugged") have tended towards a form of neo-conservatism, and the pro-affirmative liberals have tended to side with the radical left to form the "politically correct ideology" movement.

In this paper I will confine myself primarily to affirmative action policies with regard to race, but much of what I say can be applied to the areas of gender and ethnic minorities.

I. DEFINITIONS

First let me define my terms:

Discrimination is simply judging one thing to differ from another on the basis of some criterion. "Discrimination" is essentially a good quality, having reference to our ability to make distinctions. As rational and moral agents we need to make proper distinctions. To be rational is to discriminate between good and bad arguments, and to think morally is to discriminate between reasons based on valid principles and those based on invalid ones. What needs to be distinguished is the difference between rational and moral discrimination on the one hand, and irrational and immoral discrimination on the other hand.

Prejudice is a discrimination based on irrelevant grounds. It may simply be an attitude which never surfaces in action, or it may cause prejudicial actions. A prejudicial discrimination in action is immoral if it denies someone a fair deal. So discrimination on the basis of race or sex where these are not relevant for job performance is unfair. Likewise, one may act prejudicially in applying a relevant criterion on insufficient grounds, as in the case where I apply the criterion of being a hard worker but then assume, on insufficient evidence, that the black man who applies for the job is not a hard worker.

There is a difference between *prejudice* and *bias*. Bias signifies a tendency towards one thing rather than another where the evidence is incomplete or is based on non-moral factors. For example, you may have a bias towards blondes and I towards redheads. But prejudice is an attitude (or action) where unfairness is present— where one *should* know or do better, as in the case where I give people jobs simply because they are redheads. Bias implies ignorance or incomplete knowledge, whereas prejudice is deeper, involving a moral failure—usually a failure to pay attention to the evidence. But note that calling people racist or sexist without good evidence is also an act of prejudice. I call this form of prejudice "defamism," for it unfairly defames the victim. It is a contemporary version of McCarthyism.

Equal opportunity is offering everyone a fair chance at the best positions that society has at its disposal. Only native aptitude and effort should be decisive in the outcome, not factors of race, sex, or special favors.

Affirmative action is the effort to rectify the injustice of the past by special policies. Put this way, it is Janus-faced or ambiguous, having both a backward-looking and a forward-looking feature. The backward-looking feature is its attempt to correct and compensate for past injustice. This aspect of affirmative action is strictly deontological. The forward-looking feature is its implicit ideal of a society free from prejudice; this is both deontological and utilitarian.

When we look at a social problem from a backward-looking perspective we need to determine who has committed or benefited from a wrongful or prejudicial act and to determine who deserves compensation for that act.

When we look at a social problem from a forward-looking perspective we need to determine what a just society (one free from prejudice) would look like and how to obtain that kind of society. The forward-looking aspect of affirmative action is paradoxically race-conscious, since it uses race to bring about a society which is not race-conscious, which is color-blind (in the morally relevant sense of this term).

It is also useful to distinguish two versions of affirmative action. *Weak affirmative action* involves such measures as the elimination of segregation (namely the idea of "separate but equal"), widespread advertisement to groups not previously represented in certain privileged positions, special scholarships for the disadvantaged classes (e.g., all the poor), using underrepresentation or a history of past discrimination as a tie breaker when candidates are relatively equal, and the like.

Strong affirmative action involves more positive steps to eliminate past injustice, such as reverse discrimination, hiring candidates on the basis of race and gender in order to reach equal or nearly equal results, and proportionate representation in each area of society.

II. A BRIEF HISTORY OF AFFIRMATIVE ACTION

1. After a long legacy of egregious racial discrimination the forces of civil justice came to a head during the decade of 1954–1964. In the 1954 U.S. Supreme Court decision, *Brown v. Board of Education,* racial segregation was declared inherently and unjustly discriminatory, a violation of the constitutional right to equal protection, and in 1964 Congress passed the Civil Rights Act which banned all forms of racial discrimination.

During this time the goal of the Civil Rights Movement was equal opportunity. The thinking was that if only we could remove the hindrances to progress, invidious segregation, discriminatory laws, and irrational prejudice against blacks, we could free our country from the evils of past injustice and usher in a just society in which the grandchildren of the slave could play together and compete with the grandchildren of the slave owner. We were after a color-blind society in which every child had an equal chance to attain the highest positions based not on his skin color but on the quality of his credentials. In the early 60s when the idea of reverse discrimination was mentioned in civil rights groups, it was usually rejected as a new racism. The Executive Director of the NAACP, Roy Wilkins, stated this position unequivocally during congressional consideration of the 1964 civil rights law. "Our association has never been in favor of a quota system. We believe the quota system is unfair whether it is used for [blacks] or against [blacks]. . . . [We] feel people ought to be hired because of their ability, irrespective of their color. . . . We want equality, equality of opportunity and employment on the basis of ability."[1]

So the Civil Rights Act of 1964 was passed outlawing discrimination on the basis of race or sex.

> Title VII, Section 703(a) Civil Rights Act of 1964: It shall be an unlawful practice for an employer (1) to fail or refuse to hire or to discharge any individual or otherwise to discriminate against any individual with respect to his compensation, terms, conditions, or privileges of employment, because of such individual's race, color, sex, or national origin; or
>
> (2) to limit, segregate, or classify his employees or applicants for employment in any way which would deprive or tend to deprive any individual of employment opportunities or otherwise adversely affect his status as an employee because of such individual's race, color, religion, sex, or national origin. [42 U.S.C. 2000e-2(a).]
>
> . . . Nothing contained in this title shall be interpreted to require any employer to grant preferential treatment to any individual or to any group on account of an imbalance which may exist with respect to the total numbers or percentage of persons of any race . . . employed by any employer . . . in comparison with the total or percentage of persons of such race . . . in any community, State, section, or other areas, or in the available work force in any community, State, section, or other area. [42 U.S.C.2000e-2(j)]

The Civil Rights Act of 1964 espouses a meritocratic philosophy, calling for equal opportunity and prohibiting reverse discrimination as just another form of prejudice. The Voting Rights Act (1965) was passed and Jim Crow laws throughout the South were overturned. Schools were integrated and public accommodations opened to all. Branch Rickey's promotion of Jackie Robinson from the minor leagues in 1947 to play for the Brooklyn Dodgers was seen as the paradigm case of this kind of equal opportunity—the successful recruiting of a deserving person.

2. But it was soon noticed that the elimination of discriminatory laws was not producing the fully integrated society that leaders of the civil rights movement had envisioned. Eager to improve the situation, in 1965 President Johnson went beyond equal opportunity to affirmative action. He issued the famous Executive Order 11246 in which the Department of Labor was enjoined to issue government contracts with construction companies on the basis of race. That is, it would engage in reverse discrimination in order to make up for the evils of the past. He explained the act in terms of the shackled runner analogy.

> Imagine a hundred yard dash in which one of the two runners has his legs shackled together. He has progressed ten yards, while the unshackled runner has gone fifty yards. How do they rectify the situation? Do they merely remove the shackles and allow the race to proceed? Then they could say that "equal opportunity" now prevailed. But one of the runners would still be forty yards ahead of the other. Would it not be the better part of justice to allow the previously shackled runner to make up the forty-yard gap; or to start the race

---

1 Quoted in William Bradford Reynolds, "Affirmative Action is Unjust" in D. Bender and B. Leone (eds.), *Social Justice* (St. Paul, MN, 1984), p. 23.

all over again? That would be affirmative action towards equality. (President Lyndon Johnson, 1965, inaugurating the affirmative action policy of Executive Order 11246).

In 1967 President Johnson issued Executive Order 11375 extending affirmative action (henceforth "AA") to women. Note here that AA originates in the executive branch of government. Until the Kennedy-Hawkins Civil Rights Act of 1990, AA policy was never put to a vote or passed by Congress. Gradually, the benefits of AA were extended to Hispanics, native Americans, Asians, and handicapped people.[2]

The phrase "An Equal Opportunity/Affirmative Action Employer" ("AA/EO") began to appear as official public policy. But few noticed an ambiguity in the notion of "AA" which could lead to a contradiction in juxtaposing it with "EO," for there are two types of AA. At first AA was interpreted as what I have called "weak affirmative action," in line with equal opportunity, signifying wider advertisement of positions, announcements that applications from blacks would be welcomed, active recruitment and hiring blacks (and women) over *equally* qualified men. While few liberals objected to these measures, some expressed fears of an impending slippery slope towards reverse discrimination.

However, except in professional sports—including those sponsored by universities—weak affirmative action was not working, so in the late 60s and early 70s a stronger version of affir-

mative action was embarked upon—one aimed at equal results, quotas (or "goals"—a euphemism for "quotas"). In *Swann v. Charlotte-Mecklenburg* (1971), regarding the busing of children out of their neighborhood . . . to promote integration, the Court, led by Justice Brennan, held that affirmative action was implied in *Brown* and was consistent with the Civil Rights Act of 1964. The NAACP now began to support reverse discrimination.

Thus began the search for minimally qualified blacks in college recruitment, hiring, and the like. Competence and excellence began to recede into second place as the quest for racial, ethnic, and gender diversity became the dominant goals. The slogan "We have to become race conscious in order to eliminate race consciousness" became the paradoxical justification for reverse discrimination.

3. In 1968 the Department of Labor ordered employers to engage in utilization studies as part of its policy of eliminating discrimination in the workplace. The office of Federal Contract Compliance of the U.S. Department of Labor (Executive Order 11246) stated that employers with a history of *underutilization* of minorities and women were required to institute programs that went beyond passive nondiscrimination through deliberate efforts to identify people of "affected classes" for the purpose of advancing their employment. Many employers found it wise to adopt policies of preferential hiring in order to preempt expensive government suits.

Employers were to engage in "utilization analysis" of their present work force in order to develop "specific and result-oriented procedures" to which the employer commits "*every good-faith effort*" in order to provide "relief for members of an '*affected class*,' who by virtue of *past discrimination* continue to suffer the present effects of that discrimination." This self-analysis is supposed to discover areas in which such affected classes are underused, considering their availability and skills. "*Goals and timetables*

---

2 Some of the material in this section is based on Nicholas Capaldi's *Out of Order: Affirmative Action and the Crisis of Doctrinaire Liberalism* (Buffalo, NY, 1985), chapters 1 and 2. Capaldi, using the shackled runner analogy, divides the history into three stages: a *platitude stage* "in which it is reaffirmed that the race is to be fair, and a fair race is one in which no one has either special disadvantages or special advantages (equal opportunity)"; a *remedial stage* in which victims of past discrimination are to be given special help overcoming their disadvantages; and a *realignment stage* "in which all runners will be reassigned to those positions on the course that they would have had if the race had been fair from the beginning" (p. 18f).

are to be developed to guide efforts to correct deficiencies in the employment of affected classes of people in each level and segment of the work force." Affirmative action also calls for "rigorous examination" of standards and criteria for job performance, not so as to "dilute necessary standards" but in order to ensure that "arbitrary and discriminatory employment practices are eliminated" and to eliminate unnecessary criteria which "have had the effect of eliminating women and minorities" either from selection or promotion.[3]

4. In 1969 two important events occurred. (a) The Philadelphia Plan—The Department of Labor called for "goals and timetables" for recruiting minority workers. In Philadelphia area construction industries, where these companies were all-white, family-run businesses, the contractor's union took the case to court on the grounds that Title VII of the Civil Rights Act prohibits quotas. The Third Circuit Court of Appeals upheld the Labor Department, and the Supreme Court refused to hear it. This case became the basis of the EEOC's aggressive pursuit of "goals and timetables" in other business situations.

(b) In the Spring of 1969 James Forman disrupted the service of Riverside Church in New York City and issued the Black Manifesto to the American Churches, demanding that they pay blacks $500,000,000 in reparations. The argument of the Black Manifesto was that for three and a half centuries blacks in America have been "exploited and degraded, brutalized, killed and persecuted" by whites; that this was part of the persistent institutional patterns of first, legal slavery and then, legal discrimination and forced segregation; and that through slavery and discrimination whites had procured enormous wealth from black labor with little return to blacks. These facts were said to constitute

grounds for reparations on a massive scale. The American churches were but the first institutions to be asked for reparations.[4]

5. The Department of Labor issued guidelines in 1970 calling for hiring representatives of *underutilized* groups. "*Nondiscrimination* requires the elimination of all existing discriminatory conditions, whether purposeful or inadvertent. . . . Affirmative action requires . . . the employer to make additional efforts to recruit, employ and promote qualified members of groups formerly excluded" (HEW Executive Order 22346, 1972). In December of 1971 Guidelines were issued to eliminate underutilization of minorities, aiming at realignment of job force at every level of society.

6. In *Griggs v. Duke Power Company* (1971) the Supreme Court interpreted Title VII of the Civil Rights Act as forbidding use of aptitude tests and high school diplomas in hiring personnel. These tests were deemed presumptively discriminatory, employers having the burden of proving such tests relevant to performance. The notion of *sufficiency* replaced that of excellence or best qualified, as it was realized (though not explicitly stated) that the social goal of racial diversity required compromising the standards of competence.

7. In 1977, the EEOC called for and *expected* proportional representation of minorities in every area of work (including universities).

8. In 1978 the Supreme Court addressed the Bakke case. Alan Bakke had been denied admission to the University of California at Davis Medical School even though his test scores were higher than the sixteen blacks who were admitted under the affirmative action quota program. He sued the University of California and the U.S. Supreme Court ruled (*University of California v. Bakke*, July 28, 1978) in a 5 to 4 vote that reverse discrimination and quotas are illegal

---

3 Wanda Warren Berry, "Affirmative Action Is Just" in D. Bender, op. cit., p. 18.

4 Robert Fullinwider, *The Reverse Discrimination Controversy* (Totowa, NJ, 1970), p. 25.

except (as Justice Powell put it) when engaged in for purposes of promoting diversity (interpreted as a means to extend free speech under the First Amendment) and restoring a situation where an institution has had a history of prejudicial discrimination. The decision was greeted with applause from anti-AA quarters and dismay from pro-AA quarters. Ken Tollett lamented, "The affirmance of Bakke would mean the reversal of affirmative action; it would be an officially sanctioned signal to turn against blacks in this country. . . . Opposition to special minority admissions programs and affirmative action is anti-black."[5]

But Tollett was wrong. The Bakke case only shifted the rhetoric from "quota" language to "goals and timetables" and "diversity" language. In the 80s affirmative action was alive and well, with preferential hiring, minority scholarships, and race norming prevailing in all walks of life. No other white who has been excluded from admission to college because of his race has even won his case. In fact only a year later, Justice Brennan was to write in *U.S. Steel v. Weber* that prohibition of racial discrimination against "any individual" in Title VII of the Civil Rights Act did not apply to discrimination against whites.[6]

9. Perhaps the last step in the drive towards equal results took place in the institutionalization of grading applicants by group-related standards, race norming. Race norming is widely practiced but most of the public is unaware of it, so let me explain it.

Imagine that four men come into a state employment office in order to apply for a job. One is black, one Hispanic, one Asian, and one white. They take the standard test (a version of the General Aptitude Test Battery or VG-GATB). All get a composite score of 300. None of them will ever see that score. Instead the numbers will be fed into a computer and the applicants' percentile ranking emerges. The scores are group-weighted. Blacks are measured against blacks, whites against whites, Hispanics against Hispanics. Since blacks characteristically do less well than other groups, the effect is to favor blacks. For example, a score of 300 as an accountant will give the black a percentile score of 87, a Hispanic a percentile score of 74 and a white or oriental a score of 47. The black will get the job as the accountant. (See the box on the facing page.)

This is known as race norming. Until an anonymous governmental employee recently blew the whistle, this practice was kept a secret in several state employment services. Prof. Linda Gottfredson of the University of Delaware, one of the social scientists to expose this practice, has since had her funding cut off. In a recent letter published to the *New York Times* she writes:

> One of America's best-kept open secrets is that the Employment Service of the Department of Labor has unabashedly promulgated quotas. In 1981 the service recommended that state employment agencies adopt a race-conscious battery to avoid adverse impact when referring job applicants to employers. . . . The score adjustments are not trivial. An unadjusted score that places a job applicant at the 15th percentile among whites would, after race-norming, typically place a black near the white 50th percentile. Likewise, unadjusted scores at the white 50th percentile would, after race-norming, typically place a black near the 85th percentile for white job applicants. . . . [I]ts use by 40 states in the last decade belies the claim that *Griggs* did not lead to quotas.[7]

---

5 Quoted in Fullinwider, op. cit., p. 4f.

6 See Lino A. Graglia, "'Affirmative Action,' the Constitution, and the 1964 Civil Rights Act," *Measure,* no. 92 (1991).

7 Linda Gottfredson, "Letters to the Editor," *New York Times,* Aug. 1, 1990 issue. Gender-norming is also a feature of the proponents of affirmative action. Michael Levin begins his book *Feminism and Freedom* (New Brunswick, 1987) with federal court case *Beckman v. NYFD* in which 88 women who failed the New York City Fire Department's entrance exam in 1977 filed a class-action sex discrimination

---

Percentile Conversion Tables

Jobs are grouped into five broad families: Family I includes, for example, machinists, cabinet makers, and tool makers; Family II includes helpers in many types of agriculture, manufacturing, and so on; Family III includes professional jobs such as accountant, chemical engineer, nurse, editor; Family IV includes bus drivers, bookkeepers, carpet layers; Family V includes exterminators, butchers, file clerks. A raw score of 300 would convert to the following percentile rankings:

	I	II	III	IV	V
Black	79	59	87	83	73
Hispanic	62	41	74	67	55
Other	39	42	47	45	42

Sources: Virginia Employment Commission: U.S. Department of Labor. Employment and Training Administration, Validity Generalization Manual (Section A: Job Family Scoring).

---

10. In the *Ward Cove, Richmond,* and *Martin* decisions of the mid-80s the Supreme Court limited preferential hiring practices, placing a greater burden of proof on the plaintiff, now required to prove that employers have discriminated. The Kennedy-Hawkins Civil Rights Act of 1990, which was passed by Congress last year, sought to reverse these decisions by requiring employers to justify statistical imbalances not only in the employment of racial minorities but also that of ethnic and religious minorities. Wherever underrepresentation of an "identified" group exists, the employer bears the burden of proving he is innocent of prejudicial behavior. In other words, the bill would make it easier for minorities to sue employers. President Bush vetoed the bill, deeming it a subterfuge for quotas. A revised bill is now in Congressional committee.

---

suit. The court found that the physical strength component of the test was not job-related, and thus a violation of Title VII of the Civil Rights Act, and ordered the city to hire forty-nine of the women. It further ordered the fire department to devise a special, less-demanding physical strength exam for women. Following EEOC guidelines, if the passing rate for women is less than 80 percent that of the passing rate of men, the test is presumed invalid.

Affirmative action in the guise of underutilized or "affected groups" now extends to American Indians and Hispanics (including Spanish nobles) but not Portuguese, Asians, the handicapped, and in some places Irish and Italians. Estimates are that 75 percent of Americans may obtain AA status as minorities: everyone except the white nonhandicapped male. It is a strange policy that affords special treatment to the children of Spanish nobles and illegal immigrants but not the children of the survivors of Russian pogroms or Nazi concentration camps.

Of course, there is nothing new about the notions of racial discrimination and preferential treatment. The first case of racial discrimination is the fall of man, as standardly interpreted, in which the whole race is held accountable and guilty of Adam's sin. The notion of collective responsibility also goes way back in our history. The first case of preferential treatment is God's choosing Abel's sacrifice of meat and rejecting Cain's vegetarian sacrifice—which should give all Jewish-Christian vegetarians something to think about! The first case of preferential treatment in Greek mythology is that of the Achaian horse race narrated in the 23rd book of the

Iliad. Achilles had two prizes to give out. First prize went to the actual winner. Antilochus, son of Nestor, came in second, but Achilles decided to give second prize to Eumelius because he was of a nobler rank, even though he had come in last. Antilochus complained, saying in effect, "If it is preordained that some other criterion than merit is to count for the award, why should we have a race at all?" Achilles was moved by this logic and gave the prize to Antilochus, offering Eumelius a treasure of his own.

Neither is affirmative action primarily an American problem. Thomas Sowell has recently written a book on the international uses of preferential treatment, *Preferential Policies: An International Perspective,* in which he analyzes government-mandated preferential policies in India, Nigeria, Malaysia, Sri Lanka, and the United States.[8] We will consider Sowell's study towards the end of this paper.

III. ARGUMENTS FOR AFFIRMATIVE ACTION

Let us now survey the main arguments typically cited in the debate over affirmative action. I will briefly discuss seven arguments on each side of the issue.

1. Need for Role Models

This argument is straightforward. We all have need of role models, and it helps to know that others like us can be successful. We learn and are encouraged to strive for excellence by emulating our heroes and role models.

However, it is doubtful whether role models of one's own racial or sexual type are necessary for success. One of my heroes was Gandhi, an Indian Hindu, another was my grade school science teacher, one Miss DeVoe, and another was Martin Luther King. More important than having role models of one's own type is having gen-

uinely good people, of whatever race or gender, to emulate. Furthermore, even if it is of some help to people with low self-esteem to gain encouragement from seeing others of their particular kind in leadership roles, it is doubtful whether this need is a sufficient condition to justify preferential hiring or reverse discrimination. What good is a role model who is inferior to other professors or business personnel? Excellence will rise to the top in a system of fair opportunity. Natural development of role models will come more slowly and more surely. Proponents of preferential policies simply lack the patience to let history take its own course.

2. The Need of Breaking the Stereotypes

Society may simply need to know that there are talented blacks and women, so that it does not automatically assign them lesser respect or status. We need to have unjustified stereotype beliefs replaced with more accurate ones about the talents of blacks and women. So we need to engage in preferential hiring of qualified minorities even when they are not the most qualified.

Again, the response is that hiring the less qualified is neither fair to those better qualified who are passed over nor an effective way of removing inaccurate stereotypes. If competence is accepted as the criterion for hiring, then it is unjust to override it for purposes of social engineering. Furthermore, if blacks or women are known to hold high positions simply because of reverse discrimination, then they will still lack the respect due to those of their rank. In New York City there is a saying among doctors, "Never go to a black physician under 40," referring to the fact that AA has affected the medical system during the past fifteen years. The police use "Quota Cops" and "Welfare Sergeants" to refer to those hired without passing the standardized tests. (In 1985 180 black and Hispanic policemen, who had failed a promotion test, were promoted anyway to the rank of sergeant.) The destruction of false stereotypes will come naturally as qualified blacks rise naturally in fair

8 Thomas Sowell, *Preferential Policies: An International Perspective* (New York, 1990).

competition (or if it does not—then the stereotypes may be justified). Reverse discrimination sends the message home that the stereotypes are deserved—otherwise, why do these minorities need so much extra help?

3. Equal Results Argument

Some philosophers and social scientists hold that human nature is roughly identical, so that on a fair playing field the same proportion from every race and gender and ethnic group would attain to the highest positions in every area of endeavor. It would follow that any inequality of results itself is evidence for inequality of opportunity. John Arthur, in discussing an intelligence test, Test 21, puts the case this way.

> History is important when considering governmental rules like Test 21 because low scores by blacks can be traced in large measure to the legacy of slavery and racism: Segregation, poor schooling, exclusion from trade unions, malnutrition, and poverty have all played their roles. Unless one assumes that blacks are naturally less able to pass the test, the conclusion must be that the results are themselves socially and legally constructed, not a mere given for which law and society can claim no responsibility.
>
> The conclusion seems to be that genuine equality eventually requires equal results. Obviously blacks have been treated unequally throughout U.S. history, and just as obviously the economic and psychological effects of that inequality linger to this day, showing up in lower income and poorer performance in school and on tests than whites achieve. Since we have no reason to believe that difference in performance can be explained by factors other than history, equal results are a good benchmark by which to measure progress made toward genuine equality.[9]

The result of a just society should be equal numbers in proportion to each group in the work force.

However, Arthur fails even to consider studies that suggest that there are innate differences between races, sexes, and groups. If there are genetic differences in intelligence and temperament within families, why should we not expect such differences between racial groups and the two genders? Why should the evidence for this be completely discounted?

Perhaps some race or one gender is more intelligent in one way than another. At present we have only limited knowledge about genetic differences, but what we do have suggests some difference besides the obvious physiological traits.[10] The proper use of this evidence is not to promote discriminatory policies but to be *open* to the possibility that innate differences may have led to an overrepresentation of certain groups in certain areas of endeavor. It seems that on average blacks have genetic endowments favoring them in the development of skills necessary for excellence in basketball.

Furthermore, on Arthur's logic, we should take aggressive AA against Asians and Jews since they are overrepresented in science, technology, and medicine. So that each group receives its fair share, we should ensure that 12 percent of U.S. philosophers are black, reduce the percentage of Jews from an estimated 15 percent to 2 percent—firing about 1,300 Jewish philosophers. The fact that Asians are producing 50 percent of Ph.D's in science and math and blacks less than 1 percent clearly shows, on this reasoning, that we are providing special secret advantages to Asians.

But why does society have to enter into this results game in the first place? Why do we have to decide whether all difference is environmental or genetic? Perhaps we should simply admit

---

9 John Arthur, *The Unfinished Constitution* (Belmont, CA, 1990), p. 238.

10 See Phillip E. Vernon's excellent summary of the literature in *Intelligence: Heredity and Environment* (New York, 1979) and Yves Christen "Sex Differences in the Human Brain" in Nicholas Davidson (ed.) *Gender Sanity* (Lanham, 1989) and T. Bouchard, et al., "Sources of Human Psychological Differences: The Minnesota Studies of Twins Reared Apart," *Science,* vol. 250 (1990).

that we lack sufficient evidence to pronounce on these issues with any certainty—but if so, should we not be more modest in insisting on equal results? Here is a thought experiment. Take two families of different racial groups, Green and Blue. The Greens decide to have only two children, to spend all their resources on them, to give them the best education. The two Green kids respond well and end up with achievement test scores in the 99th percentile. The Blues fail to practice family planning. They have fifteen children. They can only afford two children, but lack of ability or whatever prevents them from keeping their family down. Now they need help for their large family. Why does society have to step in and help them? Society did not force them to have fifteen children. Suppose that the achievement test scores of the fifteen children fall below the 25th percentile. They cannot compete with the Greens. But now enters AA. It says that it is society's fault that the Blue children are not as able as the Greens and that the Greens must pay extra taxes to enable the Blues to compete. No restraints are put on the Blues regarding family size. This seems unfair to the Greens. Should the Green children be made to bear responsibility for the consequences of the Blues' voluntary behavior?

My point is simply that Arthur needs to cast his net wider and recognize that demographics and child-bearing and -rearing practices are crucial factors in achievement. People have to take some responsibility for their actions. The equal results argument (or axiom) misses a greater part of the picture.

4. The Compensation Argument

The argument goes like this: Blacks have been wronged and severely harmed by whites. Therefore white society should compensate blacks for the injury caused them. Reverse discrimination in terms of preferential hiring, contracts, and scholarships is a fitting way to compensate for the past wrongs.

This argument actually involves a distorted notion of compensation. Normally, we think of compensation as owed by a specific person A to another person B whom A has wronged in a specific way C. For example, if I have stolen your car and used it for a period of time to make business profits that would have gone to you, it is not enough that I return your car. I must pay you an amount reflecting your loss and my ability to pay. If I have only made $5,000 and only have $10,000 in assets, it would not be possible for you to collect $20,000 in damages—even though that is the amount of loss you have incurred.

Sometimes compensation is extended to groups of people who have been unjustly harmed by the greater society. For example, the U.S. government has compensated the Japanese-Americans who were interred during the Second World War, and the West German government has paid reparations to the survivors of Nazi concentration camps. But here a specific people have been identified who were wronged in an identifiable way by the government of the nation in question.

On the face of it the demand by blacks for compensation does not fit the usual pattern. Perhaps Southern states with Jim Crow laws could be accused of unjustly harming blacks, but it is hard to see that the U.S. government was involved in doing so. Furthermore, it is not clear that all blacks were harmed in the same way or whether some were *unjustly* harmed or harmed more than poor whites and others (e.g. short people). Finally, even if identifiable blacks were harmed by identifiable social practices, it is not clear that most forms of affirmative action are appropriate to restore the situation. The usual practice of a financial payment seems more appropriate than giving a high-level job to someone unqualified or only minimally qualified, who, speculatively, might have been better qualified had he not been subject to racial discrimination. If John is the star tailback of our college team with a promising professional future, and I accidentally (but culpably) drive my pick-up truck over his legs, and so cripple him, John may be due compensation, but he is not due the tailback spot on the football team.

Still, there may be something intuitively compelling about compensating members of an oppressed group who are minimally qualified. Suppose that the Hatfields and the McCoys are enemy clans and some youths from the Hatfields go over and steal diamonds and gold from the McCoys, distributing it within the Hatfield economy. Even though we do not know which Hatfield youths did the stealing, we would want to restore the wealth, as far as possible, to the McCoys. One way might be to tax the Hatfields, but another might be to give preferential treatment in terms of scholarships and training programs and hiring to the McCoys.[11]

This is perhaps the strongest argument for affirmative action, and it may well justify some weak versions of AA, but it is doubtful whether it is sufficient to justify strong versions with quotas and goals and timetables in skilled positions. There are at least two reasons for this. First, we have no way of knowing how many people of group G would have been at competence level L had the world been different. Secondly, the normal criterion of competence is a strong prima facie consideration when the most important positions are at stake. There are two reasons for this: (1) Society has given people expectations that if they attain certain levels of excellence they will be awarded appropriately and (2) filling the most important positions with the best qualified is the best way to insure efficiency in job-related areas and in society in general. These reasons are not absolutes. They can be overridden. But there is a strong presumption in their favor so that a burden of proof rests with those who would override them.

At this point we get into the problem of whether innocent non-blacks should have to pay a penalty in terms of preferential hiring of blacks. We turn to that argument.

5. Compensation from Those Who Innocently Benefited from Past Injustice

White males as innocent beneficiaries of unjust discrimination of blacks and women have no grounds for complaint when society seeks to rectify the tilted field. White males may be innocent of oppressing blacks and minorities (and women), but they have unjustly benefited from that oppression or discrimination. So it is perfectly proper that less qualified women and blacks be hired before them.

The operative principle is: He who knowingly and willingly benefits from a wrong must help pay for the wrong. Judith Jarvis Thomson puts it this way. "Many [white males] have been direct beneficiaries of policies which have downgraded blacks and women . . . and even those who did not directly benefit . . . had, at any rate, the advantage in the competition which comes of the confidence in one's full membership [in the community], and of one's right being recognized as a matter of course."[12] That is, white males obtain advantages in self-respect and self-confidence deriving from a racist system that denies these to blacks and women.

Objection. As I noted in the previous section, compensation is normally individual and specific. If A harms B regarding x, B has a right to compensation from A in regards to x. If A steals B's car and wrecks it, A has an obligation to compensate B for the stolen car, but A's son has no obligation to compensate B. Furthermore, if A dies or disappears, B has no moral right to claim that society compensate him for the stolen car—though if he has insurance, he can make such a claim to the insurance company. Sometimes a wrong cannot be compensated, and we

---

11 See Michael Levin, "Is Racial Discrimination Special?" *Policy Review,* Fall issue (1982).

12 Judith Jarvis Thomson, "Preferential Hiring" in Marshall Cohen, Thomas Nagel and Thomas Scanlon (eds.), *Equality and Preferential Treatment* (Princeton, 1977).

just have to make the best of an imperfect world.

Suppose my parents, divining that I would grow up to have an unsurpassable desire to be a basketball player, bought an expensive growth hormone for me. Unfortunately, a neighbor stole it and gave it to little Lew Alcindor, who gained the extra 18 inches—my 18 inches—and shot up to an enviable 7 feet 2 inches. Alias Kareem Abdul Jabbar, he excelled in basketball, as I would have done had I had my proper dose.

Do I have a right to the millions of dollars that Jabbar made as a professional basketball player—the unjustly innocent beneficiary of my growth hormone? I have a right to something from the neighbor who stole the hormone, and it might be kind of Jabbar to give me free tickets to the Laker basketball games, and perhaps I should be remembered in his will. As far as I can see, however, he does not *owe* me anything, either legally or morally.

Suppose further that Lew Alcindor and I are in high school together and we are both qualified to play basketball, only he is far better than I. Do I deserve to start in his position because I would have been as good as he is had someone not cheated me as a child? Again, I think not. But if being the lucky beneficiary of wrongdoing does not entail that Alcindor (or the coach) owes me anything in regards to basketball, why should it be a reason to engage in preferential hiring in academic positions or highly coveted jobs? If minimal qualifications are not adequate to override excellence in basketball, even when the minimality is a consequence of wrongdoing, why should they be adequate in other areas?

6. The Diversity Argument

It is important that we learn to live in a pluralistic world, learning to get along with other races and cultures, so we should have fully integrated schools and employment situations. Diversity is an important symbol and educative device. Thus preferential treatment is warranted to perform this role in society.

But, again, while we can admit the value of diversity, it hardly seems adequate to override considerations of merit and efficiency. Diversity for diversity's sake is moral promiscuity, since it obfuscates rational distinctions, and unless those hired are highly qualified the diversity factor threatens to become a fetish. At least at the higher levels of business and the professions, competence far outweighs considerations of diversity. I do not care whether the group of surgeons operating on me reflect racial or gender balance, but I do care that they are highly qualified. And likewise with airplane pilots, military leaders, business executives, and, may I say it, teachers and professors. Moreover, there are other ways of learning about other cultures besides engaging in reverse discrimination.

7. Anti-Meritocratic (Desert) Argument to Justify Reverse Discrimination: "No One Deserves His Talents"

According to this argument, the competent do not deserve their intelligence, their superior character, their industriousness, or their discipline; thus they have no right to the best positions in society; therefore society is not unjust in giving these positions to less (but still minimally) qualified blacks and women. In one form this argument holds that since no one deserves anything, society may use any criteria it pleases to distribute goods. The criterion most often designated is social utility. Versions of this argument are found in the writings of John Arthur, John Rawls, Bernard Boxill, Michael Kinsley, Ronald Dworkin, and Richard Wasserstrom. Rawls writes, "No one deserves his place in the distribution of native endowments, any more than one deserves one's initial starting place in society. The assertion that a man deserves the superior character that enables him to make the effort to cultivate his abilities is equally problematic; for his character depends in large part upon fortunate family and social circumstances for which he can claim no credit. The notion of desert seems not to apply to these cases."[13] Michael Kinsley is even more adamant:

> Opponents of affirmative action are hung up on a distinction that seems more profoundly irrelevant: treating individuals versus treating groups. What is the moral difference between dispensing favors to people on their "merits" as individuals and passing out society's benefits on the basis of group identification?
>
> Group identifications like race and sex are, of course, immutable. They have nothing to do with a person's moral worth. But the same is true of most of what comes under the label "merit." The tools you need for getting ahead in a meritocratic society—not all of them but most: talent, education, instilled cultural values such as ambition—are distributed just as arbitrarily as skin color. They are fate. The notion that people somehow "deserve" the advantages of those characteristics in a way they don't "deserve" the advantage of their race is powerful, but illogical.[14]

It will help to put the argument in outline form.

1. Society may award jobs and positions as it sees fit as long as individuals have no claim to these positions.

2. To have a claim to something means that one has earned it or deserves it.

13 John Rawls, *A Theory of Justice* (Cambridge, 1971), p. 104; See Richard Wasserstrom "A Defense of Programs of Preferential Treatment," *National Forum* (Phi Kappa Phi Journal), vol. 58 (1978). See also Bernard Boxill, "The Morality of Preferential Hiring," *Philosophy and Public Affairs,* vol. 7 (1978).
14 Michael Kinsley, "Equal Lack of Opportunity," *Harper's,* June issue (1983).

3. But no one has earned or deserves his intelligence, talent, education or cultural values which produce superior qualifications.

4. If a person does not deserve what produces something, he does not deserve its products.

5. Therefore better qualified people do not deserve their qualifications.

6. Therefore, society may override their qualifications in awarding jobs and positions as it sees fit (for social utility or to compensate for previous wrongs).

So it is permissible if a minimally qualified black or woman is admitted to law or medical school ahead of a white male with excellent credentials or if a less qualified person from an "underutilized" group gets a professorship ahead of a far better qualified white male. Sufficiency and underutilization together outweigh excellence.

Objection. Premise 4 is false. To see this, reflect that just because I do not deserve the money that I have been given as a gift (for instance) does not mean that I am not entitled to what I get with that money. If you and I both get a gift of $100 and I bury mine in the sand for five years while you invest yours wisely and double its value at the end of five years, I cannot complain that you should split the increase 50/50 since neither of us deserved the original gift. If we accept the notion of responsibility at all, we must hold that persons deserve the fruits of their labor and conscious choices. Of course, we might want to distinguish moral from legal desert and argue that, morally speaking, effort is more important than outcome, whereas, legally speaking, outcome may be more important. Nevertheless, there are good reasons in terms of efficiency, motivation, and rough justice for holding a strong prima facie principle of giving scarce high positions to those most competent.

The attack on moral desert is perhaps the most radical move that egalitarians like Rawls and company have made against meritocracy, but the ramifications of their attack are far-reaching. The following are some of its implications. Since I do not deserve my two good eyes or two good kidneys, the social engineers may take one of each from me to give to those needing an eye or a kidney—even if they have damaged their organs by their own voluntary actions. Since no one deserves anything, we do not deserve pay for our labors or praise for a job well done or first prize in the race we win. The notion of moral responsibility vanishes in a system of levelling.

But there is no good reason to accept the argument against desert. We do act freely and, as such, we are responsible for our actions. We deserve the fruits of our labor, reward for our noble feats and punishment for our misbehavior.

We have considered seven arguments for affirmative action and have found no compelling case for Strong AA and only one plausible argument (a version of the compensation argument) for weak AA. We must now turn to the arguments against affirmative action to see whether they fare any better.[15]

---

15 There is one other argument which I have omitted. It is one from precedence and has been stated by Judith Jarvis Thomson in the article cited earlier:

"Suppose two candidates for a civil service job have equally good test scores, but only one job is available. We could decide between them by coin-tossing. But in fact we do allow for declaring for A straightaway, where A is a veteran, and B is not. It may be that B is a non-veteran through no fault of his own. . . . Yet the fact is that B is not a veteran and A is. On the assumption that the veteran has served his country, the country owes him something. And it is plain that giving him preference is not an unjust way in which part of that debt of gratitude can be paid" (p. 379f).

The two forms of preferential hiring are analogous. Veteran's preference is justified as a way of paying a debt of gratitude; preferential hiring is a way of paying a debt of compensation. In both cases innocent parties bear the burden of the community's debt, but it is justified.

My response to this argument is that veterans should not be hired in place of better qualified candidates, but that benefits like the GI scholarships are part of the contract with

IV. ARGUMENTS AGAINST AFFIRMATIVE ACTION

1. Affirmative Action Requires Discrimination Against a Different Group

Weak affirmative action weakly discriminates against new minorities, mostly innocent young white males, and strong affirmative action strongly discriminates against these new minorities. As I argued in III.5, this discrimination is unwarranted, since, even if some compensation to blacks were indicated, it would be unfair to make innocent white males bear the whole brunt of the payments. In fact, it is poor white youth who become the new pariahs on the job market. The children of the wealthy have no trouble getting into the best private grammar schools and, on the basis of superior early education, into the best universities, graduate schools, managerial and professional positions. Affirmative action simply shifts injustice, setting blacks and women against young white males, especially ethnic and poor white males. It does little to rectify the goal of providing equal opportunity to all. If the goal is a society where everyone has a fair chance, then it would be better to concentrate on support for families and early education and decide the matter of university admissions and job hiring on the basis of traditional standards of competence.

2. Affirmative Action Perpetuates the Victimization Syndrome

Shelby Steele admits that affirmative action may seem "the meagerest recompense for centuries of unrelieved oppression" and that it helps promote diversity. At the same time, though, notes Steele, affirmative action reinforces the spirit of victimization by telling blacks that they can gain more by emphasizing their suffering, degrada-

---

veterans who serve their country in the armed services. The notion of compensation only applies to individuals who have been injured by identifiable entities. So the analogy between veterans and minority groups seems weak.

tion and helplessness than by discipline and work. This message holds the danger of blacks becoming permanently handicapped by a need for special treatment. It also sends to society at large the message that blacks cannot make it on their own.

Leon Wieseltier sums up the problem this way.

> The memory of oppression is a pillar and a strut of the identity of every people oppressed. It is no ordinary marker of difference. It is unusually stiffening. It instructs the individual and the group about what to expect of the world, imparts an isolating sense of aptness. . . . Don't be fooled, it teaches, there is only repetition. For that reason, the collective memory of an oppressed people is not only a treasure but a trap.
>
> In the memory of oppression, oppression outlives itself. The scar does the work of the wound. That is the real tragedy: that injustice obtains the power to distort long after it has ceased to be real. It is a posthumous victory for the oppressors, when pain becomes a tradition. And yet the atrocities of the past must never be forgotten. This is the unfairly difficult dilemma of the newly emancipated and the newly enfranchised: An honorable life is not possible if they remember too little and a normal life is not possible if they remember too much.[16]

With the eye of recollection, which does not "remember too much," Steele recommends a policy that offers "educational and economic development of disadvantaged people regardless of race and the eradication from our society— through close monitoring and severe sanctions —of racial and gender discrimination."[17]

3. Affirmative Action Encourages Mediocrity and Incompetence

Last spring Jesse Jackson joined protesters at Harvard Law School in demanding that the Law School faculty hire black women. Jackson dismissed Dean of the Law School Robert C. Clark's standard of choosing the best qualified person for the job as "cultural anemia." "We cannot just define who is qualified in the most narrow vertical, academic terms," he said. "Most people in the world are yellow, brown, black, poor, non-Christian and don't speak English, and they can't wait for some white males with archaic rules to appraise them."[18] It might be noted that if Jackson is correct about the depth of cultural decadence at Harvard, blacks might be well advised to form and support their own more vital law schools and leave places like Harvard to their archaism.

At several universities, the administration has forced departments to hire members of minorities even when far superior candidates were available. Shortly after obtaining my Ph.D. in the late 70s I was mistakenly identified as a black philosopher (I had a civil rights record and was once a black studies major) and was flown to a major university, only to be rejected for a more qualified candidate when it [was] discovered that I was white.

Stories of the bad effects of affirmative action abound. The philosopher Sidney Hook writes that "At one Ivy League university, representatives of the Regional HEW demanded an explanation of why there were no women or minority students in the Graduate Department of Religious Studies. They were told that a reading knowledge of Hebrew and Greek was presupposed. Whereupon the representatives of HEW advised orally: 'Then end those old-fashioned programs that require irrelevant languages. And start up programs on relevant things which minority group students can study without learning languages.'"[19]

Nicholas Capaldi notes that the staff of HEW itself was one-half women, three-fifths members

---

16 Quoted in Jim Sleeper, *The Closest of Strangers* (New York, 1990), p. 209.
17 Shelby Steele, "A Negative Vote on Affirmative Action." *New York Times,* May 13, 1990 issue.

18 *New York Times,* May 10, 1990 issue.
19 Nicholas Capaldi, op. cit., p. 85.

of minorities, and one-half black—a clear case of racial over-representation.

In 1972 officials at Stanford University discovered a proposal for the government to monitor curriculum in higher education: the "Summary Statement . . . Sex Discrimination Proposed HEW Regulation to Effectuate Title IX of the Education Amendment of 1972" to "establish and use internal procedure for reviewing curricula, designed both to ensure that they do not reflect discrimination on the basis of sex and to resolve complaints concerning allegations of such discrimination, pursuant to procedural standards to be prescribed by the Director of the office of Civil Rights." Fortunately, Secretary of HEW Caspar Weinberger, when alerted to the intrusion, assured Stanford University that he would never approve of it.[20]

Government programs of enforced preferential treatment tend to appeal to the lowest possible common denominator. Witness the 1974 HEW Revised Order No. 14 on Affirmative Action expectations for preferential hiring: "Neither minorities nor female employees should be required to possess higher qualifications than those of the lowest qualified incumbents."

Furthermore, no tests may be given to candidates unless it is *proved* to be relevant to the job.

> No standard or criteria which have, by intent or effect, worked to exclude women or minorities as a class can be utilized, unless the institution can demonstrate the necessity of such standard to the performance of the job in question.
>
> Whenever a validity study is called for . . . the user should include . . . an investigation of suitable alternative selection procedures and suitable alternative methods of using the selection procedure which have as little adverse impact as possible. . . . Whenever the user is shown an alternative selection procedure with evidence of less adverse impact and substantial evidence of validity for the same job in similar circumstances, the user should investigate it to

determine the appropriateness of using or validating it in accord with these guidelines.[21]

At the same time Americans are wondering why standards in our country are falling and the Japanese are getting ahead. Affirmative action with its twin idols, Sufficiency and Diversity, is the enemy of excellence. I will develop this thought below (IV.6).

4. Affirmative Action Policies Unjustly Shift the Burden of Proof

Affirmative action legislation tends to place the burden of proof on the employer who does not have an "adequate" representation of "underutilized" groups in his work force. He is guilty until proven innocent. I have already recounted how in the mid-80s the Supreme Court shifted the burden of proof back onto the plaintiff, while Congress is now attempting to shift the burden back to the employer. Those in favor of deeming disproportional representation "guilty until proven innocent" argue that it is easy for employers to discriminate against minorities by various subterfuges, and I agree that steps should be taken to monitor against prejudicial treatment. But being prejudiced against employers is not the way to attain a just solution to discrimination. The principle: Innocent until proven guilty applies to employers as well as criminals. Indeed, it is clearly special pleading to reject this basic principle of Anglo-American law in this case of discrimination while adhering to it everywhere else.

5. An Argument from Merit

Traditionally, we have believed that the highest positions in society should be awarded to those who are best qualified—as the Koran states in the quotation at the beginning of this paper. Rewarding excellence both seems just to the individuals in the competition and makes for efficiency. Note that one of the most successful acts of integration, the recruitment of Jackie Robinson in the

---

20 Cited in Capaldi, op. cit., p. 95.

21 Ibid.

late 40s, was done in just this way, according to merit. If Robinson had been brought into the major league as a mediocre player or had batted .200 he would have been scorned and sent back to the minors where he belonged.

Merit is not an absolute value. There are times when it may be overridden for social goals, but there is a strong prima facie reason for awarding positions on its basis, and it should enjoy a weighty presumption in our social practices.

In a celebrated article Ronald Dworkin says that "Bakke had no case" because society did not owe Bakke anything. That may be, but then why does it owe anyone anything? Dworkin puts the matter in Utility terms, but if that is the case, society may owe Bakke a place at the University of California at Davis, for it seems a reasonable rule-utilitarian principle that achievement should be rewarded in society. We generally want the best to have the best positions, the best qualified candidate to win the political office, the most brilliant and competent scientist to be chosen for the most challenging research project, the best qualified pilots to become commercial pilots, only the best soldiers to become generals. Only when little is at stake do we weaken the standards and content ourselves with sufficiency (rather than excellence)—there are plenty of jobs where "sufficiency" rather than excellence is required. Perhaps we now feel that medicine or law or university professorships are so routine that they can be performed by minimally qualified people—in which case AA has a place.

But note, no one is calling for quotas or proportional representation of *underutilized* groups in the National Basketball Association where blacks make up 80 percent of the players. But if merit and merit alone reigns in sports, should it not be valued at least as much in education and industry?

6. The Slippery Slope

Even if strong AA or reverse discrimination could meet the other objections, it would face a tough question: Once you embark on this project, how do you limit it? Who should be excluded from reverse discrimination? Asians and Jews are over-represented, so if we give blacks positive quotas, should we place negative quotas on these other groups? Since white males, "WMs," are a minority which is suffering from reverse discrimination, will we need a new affirmative action policy in the twenty-first century to compensate for the discrimination against WMs in the late twentieth century?

Furthermore, affirmative action has stigmatized the *young* white male. Assuming that we accept reverse discrimination, the fair way to make sacrifices would be to retire *older* white males who are more likely to have benefited from a favored status. Probably the least guilty of any harm to minority groups is the young white male—usually a liberal who has been required to bear the brunt of ages of past injustice. Justice Brennan's announcement that the Civil Rights Act did not apply to discrimination against whites shows how the clearest language can be bent to serve the ideology of the moment.[22]

7. The Mounting Evidence Against the Success of Affirmative Action

Thomas Sowell of the Hoover Institute has shown in his book *Preferential Policies: An International Perspective* that preferential hiring almost never solves social problems. It generally builds in mediocrity or incompetence and causes deep resentment. It is a short-term solution which lacks serious grounding in social realities.

---

22 The extreme form of this New Speak is incarnate in the Politically Correct Movement ("PC" ideology) where a new orthodoxy has emerged, condemning white, European culture and seeing African culture as the new savior of us all. Perhaps the clearest example of this is Paula Rothenberg's book *Racism and Sexism* (New York, 1987) which asserts that there is no such thing as black racism; only whites are capable of racism (p. 6). Ms. Rothenberg's book has been scheduled as required reading for all freshmen at the University of Texas. See Joseph Salemi, "Lone Star Academic Politics," no. 87 (1990).

For instance, Sowell cites some disturbing statistics on education. Although twice as many blacks as Asian students took the nationwide Scholastic Aptitude Test in 1983, approximately fifteen times as many Asian students scored above 700 (out of a possible 800) on the mathematics half of the SAT. The percentage of Asians who scored above 700 in math was also more than six times higher than the percentage of American Indians and more than ten times higher than that of Mexican Americans—as well as more than double the percentage of whites. As Sowell points out, in all countries studied, "intergroup performance disparities are huge" (108).

> There are dozens of American colleges and universities where the median combined verbal SAT score and mathematics SAT score total 1200 or above. As of 1983 there were less than 600 black students in the entire US with combined SAT scores of 1200. This meant that, despite widespread attempts to get a black student "representation" comparable to the black percentage of the population (about 11 percent), there were not enough black students in the entire country for the Ivy League alone to have such a "representation" without going beyond this pool—even if the entire pool went to the eight Ivy League colleges.[23]

Often it is claimed that a cultural bias is the cause of the poor performance of blacks on SATs (or IQ tests), but Sowell shows that these test scores are actually a better predictor of college performance for blacks than for Asians and whites. He also shows the harmfulness of the effect on blacks of preferential acceptance. At the University of California, Berkeley, where the freshman class closely reflects the actual ethnic distribution of California high school students, more than 70 percent of blacks fail to graduate. All 312 black students entering Berkeley in 1987 were admitted under "affirmative action"

criteria rather than by meeting standard academic criteria. So were 480 out of 507 Hispanic students. In 1986 the median SAT score for blacks at Berkeley was 952, for Mexican Americans 1014, for American Indians 1082 and for Asian Americans 1254. (The average SAT for all students was 1181.)

The result of this mismatching is that blacks who might do well if they went to a second-tier or third-tier school where their test scores would indicate they belong, actually are harmed by preferential treatment. They cannot compete in the institutions where high abilities are necessary.

Sowell also points out that affirmative action policies have mainly assisted the middle-class blacks, those who have suffered least from discrimination. "Black couples in which both husband and wife are college-educated overtook white couples of the same description back in the early 1970s and continued to at least hold their own in the 1980s" (115).

Sowell's conclusion is that similar patterns of results obtained from India to the United States wherever preferential policies exist. "In education, preferential admissions policies have led to high attrition rates and substandard performances for those preferred students . . . who survived to graduate." In all countries the preferred tended to concentrate in less difficult subjects which lead to less remunerative careers. "In the employment market, both blacks and untouchables at the higher levels have advanced substantially while those at the lower levels show no such advancement and even some signs of retrogression. These patterns are also broadly consistent with patterns found in countries in which majorities have created preferences for themselves . . ." (116).

The tendency has been to focus at the high-level end of education and employment rather than on the lower level of family structure and early education. But if we really want to help the worst off improve, we need to concentrate on the family and early education. It is foolish to expect equal results when we begin with

23 Thomas Sowell, op. cit., p. 108.

grossly unequal starting points—and discriminating against young white males is no more just than discriminating against women, blacks or anyone else.

CONCLUSION

Let me sum up. The goal of the Civil Rights movement and of moral people everywhere has been equal opportunity. The question is: How best to get there? Civil Rights legislation removed the legal barriers to equal opportunity, but did not tackle the deeper causes that produced differential results. Weak affirmative action aims at encouraging minorities in striving for the highest positions without unduly jeopardizing the rights of majorities, but the problem of weak affirmative action is that it easily slides into strong affirmative action where quotas, "goals," and equal results are forced into groups, thus promoting mediocrity, inefficiency, and resentment. Furthermore, affirmative action aims at the higher levels of society—universities and skilled jobs—yet if we want to improve our society, the best way to do it is to concentrate on families, children, early education, and the like. Affirmative action is, on the one hand, too much, too soon and on the other hand, too little, too late.

Martin Luther said that humanity is like a man mounting a horse who always tends to fall off on the other side of the horse. This seems to be the case with affirmative action. Attempting to redress the discriminatory iniquities of our history, our well-intentioned social engineers engage in new forms of discriminatory iniquity and thereby think that they have successfully mounted the horse of racial harmony. They have only fallen off on the other side of the issue.[24]

---

24 I am indebted to Jim Landesman, Michael Levin, and Abigail Rosenthal for comments on a previous draft of this paper. I am also indebted to Nicholas Capaldi's *Out of Order* for first making me aware of the extent of the problem of affirmative action.

Review Questions

1. How does Pojman define discrimination, prejudice, and bias?
2. How does he explain equal opportunity and affirmative action? What are the two forms of affirmative action?
3. As Pojman describes it, what were the main events in the history of affirmative action?
4. What are the arguments for affirmative action, according to Pojman? How does he attack them?
5. What are Pojman's arguments against affirmative action?

Discussion Questions

1. Pojman's arguments focus on affirmative action policies with regard to race. Do they also apply to such policies that target gender, as he claims? Why or why not?
2. Even if Pojman's arguments show that the strong form of affirmative action is unjustified, do they also prove that the weak form is unjustified? What do you think?
3. How would the defender of affirmative action reply to Pojman's arguments against it? Is there a good reply?
4. Pojman makes some controversial factual claims—for example, that stereotypes of blacks may be justified, that one race or gender may be more intelligent than another, that affirmative action harms blacks rather than helping them, and that it encourages incompetence. Are these claims true? How do we find out?

What Good Am I?

LAURENCE THOMAS

Laurence Thomas is professor of philosophy at Syracuse University. He is the author of *Living Morally: A Psychology of Moral Character* (1989).

Thomas presents an argument for diversity in university faculty. He argues that having women and minorities as faculty produces an environment in which trust, intellectual affirmation, and accompanying gratitude are possible for all people, and not just white males. Furthermore, this diversity is needed to show that the commitment to gender and racial equality goes beyond mere verbal behavior; it includes nonverbal behavior as well.

WHAT GOOD AM I as a black professor? The raging debate over affirmative action surely invites me to ask this searching question of myself, just as it must invite those belonging to other so-called suspect categories to ask it of themselves. If knowledge is color blind, why should it matter whether the face in front of the classroom is a European white, a Hispanic, an Asian, and so on? Why should it matter whether the person is female or male?

One of the most well-known arguments for affirmative action is the role-model argument. It is also the argument that I think is the least satisfactory—not because women and minorities do not need role models—everyone does—but because as the argument is often presented, it comes dangerously close to implying that about the only thing a black, for instance, can teach a white is how not to be a racist. Well, I think better of myself than that. And I hope that all women and minorities feel the same about themselves. . . .

But even if the role-model argument were acceptable in some version or the other, affirmative action would still seem unsavory, as the implicit assumption about those hired as affirmative action appointments is that they are less qualified than those who are not. For, so the argument goes, the practice would be unnecessary if, in the first place, affirmative action appointees were the most qualified for the position, since they would be hired by virtue of their merits. I call this the counterfactual argument from qualifications.

Now, while I do not want to say much about it, this argument has always struck me as extremely odd. In a morally perfect world, it is no doubt true that if women and minorities were the most qualified they would be hired by virtue of their merits. But this truth tells me nothing about how things are in this world. It does not show that biases built up over decades and centuries do not operate in the favor of, say, white males over nonwhite males. It is as if one argued against feeding the starving simply on the grounds that in a morally perfect world starvation would not exist. Perhaps it would not. But this is no argument against feeding the starving now.

It would be one thing if those who advance the counterfactual argument from qualifications addressed the issue of built-up biases that operate against women and minorities. Then I could perhaps suppose that they are arguing in good faith. But for them to ignore these built-up biases in the name of an ideal world is sheer hypocrisy. It is to confuse what the ideal should be with the steps that should be taken to get there. Sometimes the steps are very simple or, in any case, purely procedural: instead of *A*, do *B;* or perform a series of well-defined steps that guarantee the outcome. Not so with nonbiased hiring, however, since what is involved is a change in attitude and feelings—not even merely a change in belief. After all, it is possible to believe something quite sincerely and yet not have the emotional wherewithal to act in accordance with that belief. It is this reality regarding sexism and racism that I believe is not fully appreciated in this volume.

The philosophical debate over affirmative action has stalled, as Lawrence C. Becker observes, because so many who oppose it, and some who do not, are unwilling to acknowledge the fact that sincere belief in equality does not entail a corresponding change in attitude and feelings in day-to-day interactions with women and minorities. Specifically, sincere belief does not eradicate residual and, thus, unintentional sexist and racist attitudes.[1] So, joviality among minorities may be taken by whites as the absence of intellectual depth or sincerity on the part of those minorities, since such behavior is presumed to be uncommon among high-minded intellectual whites. Similarly, it is a liability for academic women to be too fashionable in their attire, since fashionably attired women are often taken by men as aiming to be seductive.

[1] For a most illuminating discussion along this line, see Adrian M. S. Piper's very important essay, "Higher-Order Discrimination," in Owen Flanagan and Amelie Oksenberg Rorty, eds., *Identity, Character, and Morality: Essays in Moral Psychology* (Cambridge: MIT Press, 1990).

Lest there be any misunderstanding, nothing I have said entails that unqualified women and minorities should be hired. I take it to be obvious, though, that whether someone is the best qualified is often a judgment call. On the other hand, what I have as much as said is that there are built-up biases in the hiring process that disfavor women and minorities and need to be corrected. I think of it as rather on the order of correcting for unfavorable moral head winds. It is possible to be committed to gender and racial equality and yet live a life in which residual, and thus unintentional, sexism and racism operate to varying degrees of explicitness.

I want to return now to the question with which I began this essay: What good am I as a black professor? I want to answer this question because, insofar as our aim is a just society, I think it is extremely important to see the way in which it does matter that the person in front of the class is not always a white male, notwithstanding the truth that knowledge, itself, is color blind.

Teaching is not just about transmitting knowledge. If it were, then students could simply read books and professors could simply pass out tapes or lecture notes. Like it or not, teachers are the object of intense emotions and feelings on the part of students solicitous of faculty approval and affirmation. Thus, teaching is very much about intellectual affirmation; and there can be no such affirmation of the student by the mentor in the absence of deep trust between them, be the setting elementary or graduate school. Without this trust, a mentor's praise will ring empty; constructive criticism will seem mean-spirited; and advice will be poorly received, if sought after at all. A student needs to be confident that he can make a mistake before the professor without being regarded as stupid in the professor's eyes and that the professor is interested in seeing beyond his weaknesses to his strengths. Otherwise, the student's interactions with the professor will be plagued by uncertainty; and that uncertainty will fuel the self-doubts of the student.

Now, the position that I should like to defend, however, is not that only women can trust women, only minorities can trust minorities, and only whites can trust whites. That surely is not what we want. Still, it must be acknowledged, first of all, that racism and sexism have very often been a bar to such trust between mentor and student, when the professor has been a white male and the student has been either a woman or a member of a minority group. Of course, trust between mentor and student is not easy to come by in any case. This, though, is compatible with women and minorities having even greater problems if the professor is a white male.

Sometimes a woman professor will be necessary if a woman student is to feel the trust of a mentor that makes intellectual affirmation possible; sometimes a minority professor will be necessary for a minority student; indeed, sometimes a white professor will be necessary for a white student. (Suppose the white student is from a very sexist and racist part of the United States, and it takes a white professor to undo the student's biases.)

Significantly, though, in an academy where there is gender and racial diversity among the faculty, that diversity alone gives a woman or minority student the hope that intellectual affirmation is possible. This is so even if the student's mentor should turn out to be a white male. For part of what secures our conviction that we are living in a just society is not merely that we experience justice, but that we see justice around us. A diverse faculty serves precisely this end in terms of women and minority students believing that it is possible for them to have an intellectually affirming mentor relationship with a faculty member regardless of the faculty's gender or race.

Naturally, there are some women and minority students who will achieve no matter what the environment. Harriet Jacobs and Frederick Douglass were slaves who went on to accomplish more than many of us will who have never seen the chains of slavery. Neither, though, would have thought their success a reason to leave slavery intact. Likewise, the fact that there are some women and minorities who will prevail in spite of the obstacles is no reason to leave the status quo in place.

There is another part of the argument. Where there is intellectual affirmation, there is also gratitude. When a student finds that affirmation in a faculty member, a bond is formed, anchored in the student's gratitude, that can weather almost anything. Without such ties there could be no "ole boy" network—a factor that is not about racism, but a kind of social interaction running its emotional course. When women and minority faculty play an intellectually affirming role in the lives of white male students, such faculty undermine a nonracist and nonsexist pattern of emotional feelings that has unwittingly served the sexist and racist end of passing the intellectual mantle from white male to white male. For what we want, surely, is not just blacks passing the mantle to blacks, women to women, and white males to white males, but a world in which it is possible for all to see one another as proper recipients of the intellectual mantle. Nothing serves this end better than the gratitude between mentor and student that often enough ranges over differences between gender and race or both.

Ideally, my discussion of trust, intellectual affirmation, and gratitude should have been supplemented with a discussion of nonverbal behavior. For it seems to me that what has been ignored by all of the authors is the way in which judgments are communicated not simply by what is said but by a vast array of nonverbal behavior. Again, a verbal and sincere commitment to equality, without the relevant change in emotions and feelings, will invariably leave nonverbal behavior intact. Mere voice intonation and flow of speech can be a dead giveaway that the listener does not expect much of substance to come from the speaker. Anyone who doubts this should just remind her- or himself that it is a commonplace to remark to someone over the phone that he sounds tired or "down" or distracted, where the basis for this judgment, obviously, can only be how the individual sounds. One can get the clear sense that one called at the wrong time just by the way in which the other person responds or gets involved in the conversation. So, ironically, there is a sense in which it can be easier to convince ourselves that we are committed to gender and racial equality than it is to convince a woman or a minority person; for the latter see and experience our nonverbal behavior in a way that we ourselves do not. Specifically, it so often happens that a woman or minority can see that a person's nonverbal behavior belies their verbal support of gender and racial equality in faculty hiring—an interruption here, or an all too quick dismissal of a remark there. And this is to say nothing of the ways in which the oppressor often seems to know better than the victim how the victim is affected by the oppression that permeates her or his life, an arrogance that is communicated in a myriad of ways. This is not the place, though, to address the topic of social justice and nonverbal behavior.[2]

Before moving on let me consider an objection to my view. No doubt some will balk at the very idea of women and minority faculty intellectually affirming white male students. But this is just so much nonsense on the part of those balking. For I have drawn attention to a most powerful force in the lives of all individuals, namely trust and gratitude; and I have indicated that just as these feelings have unwittingly served racist and sexist ends, they can serve ends that are morally laudable. Furthermore, I have rejected the idea, often implicit in the role-model argument, that women and minority faculty are only good for their own kind. What is more, the position I have advocated is not one of subservience in the least, as I have spoken of an affirming role that underwrites an often unshakable debt of gratitude.

2 For an attempt, see my "Moral Deference," *Philosophical Forum* (forthcoming).

So, to return to the question with which I began this essay: I matter as a black professor and so do women and minority faculty generally, because collectively, if not in each individual case, we represent the hope, sometimes in a very personal way, that the university is an environment where the trust that gives rise to intellectual affirmation and the accompanying gratitude is possible for all, and between all peoples. Nothing short of the reality of diversity can permanently anchor this hope for ourselves and posterity.

This argument for diversity is quite different from those considered by Robert L. Simon. I do not advocate the representation of given viewpoints or the position that the ethnic and gender composition of faculty members should be proportional to their numbers in society. The former is absurd because it is a mistake to insist that points of view are either gender- or color-coded. The latter is absurd because it would actually entail getting rid of some faculty, since the percentage of Jews in the academy far exceeds their percentage in the population. If one day this should come to be true of blacks or Hispanics, they in turn would be fair game.

Francis rightly observes, though, that the continued absence of any diversity whatsoever draws attention to itself. My earlier remarks about nonverbal behavior taken in conjunction with my observations about trust, affirmation, and gratitude are especially apropos here. The complete absence of diversity tells departments more about themselves than no doubt they are prepared to acknowledge.

I would like to conclude with a concrete illustration of the way in which trust and gratitude can make a difference in the academy. As everyone knows, being cited affirmatively is an important indication of professional success. Now, who gets cited is not just a matter of what is true and good. On the contrary, students generally cite the works of their mentors and the work of others introduced to them by their mentors; and, on the other hand, mentors generally cite the work of those students of theirs for whom they have provided considerable intellectual affirmation. Sexism and racism have often been obstacles to faculty believing that women and minorities can be proper objects of full intellectual affirmation. It has also contributed to the absence of women and minority faculty which, in turn, has made it well-nigh impossible for white male students to feel an intellectual debt of gratitude to women and minority faculty. Their presence in the academy cannot help but bring about a change with regard to so simple a matter as patterns of citation, the professional ripple effect of which will be significant beyond many of our wildest dreams.

If social justice were just a matter of saying or writing the correct words, then equality would have long ago been a *fait accompli* in the academy. For I barely know anyone who is a faculty member who has not bemoaned the absence of minorities and women in the academy, albeit to varying degrees. So, I conclude with a very direct question: Is it really possible that so many faculty could be so concerned that women and minorities should flourish in the academy, and yet so few do? You will have to forgive me for not believing that it is. For as any good Kantian knows, one cannot consistently will an end without also willing the means to that end. Onora O'Neill writes: "Willing, after all, is not just a matter of wishing that something were the case, but involves committing oneself to doing something to bring that situation about when opportunity is there and recognized. Kant expressed this point by insisting that rationality requires that whoever wills some end wills the necessary means insofar as these are available."[3] If Kant is right, then much hand-wringing talk about social equality for women and minorities can only be judged insincere.

3 Onora O'Neill, *Constructions of Reason: Explorations of Kant's Practical Philosophy* (Cambridge University Press, 1989), p. 90.

Review Questions

1. What is the counterfactual argument from qualifications, as Thomas calls it? Why does he find it to be extremely odd?
2. According to Thomas, why has the debate about affirmative action stalled?
3. What is Thomas's answer to the question "What good am I as a black professor?"
4. How does Thomas reply to the objection that women and minority faculty cannot intellectually affirm white male students?
5. Explain Thomas's argument from diversity. How does it differ from the one given by Robert L. Simon?

Discussion Questions

1. Thomas speaks of "built-up biases in the hiring process that disfavor women and minorities." Explain these biases. Can you give examples? Is it possible for a white male to not have these biases? Why or why not?
2. Does hiring women and minorities result in less-qualified people, as Pojman claims in the previous reading? What is Thomas's reply?
3. Who counts as a minority? Thomas speaks only of blacks, but there are other minorities, such as Hispanics, Native Americans, Asians, and Muslims. Do they also have to be hired in order to satisfy the need for diversity?

A Case for Race-Consciousness

T. ALEXANDER ALEINIKOFF

T. Alexander Aleinikoff is a professor at the University of Michigan School of Law.

Aleinikoff attacks colorblindness as a social ideal and defends its opposite, race-consciousness. He distinguishes between a strong and a weak version of colorblindness. The strong version makes race just as irrelevant as eye color. Aleinikoff claims that this is impossible and undesirable. The weak version allows some recognition of race, but not when it comes to the distribution of resources or opportunities. This is not acceptable either, Aleinikoff argues, because it does not overcome white domination and thus it does not provide for racial justice. Racial justice requires race-conscious laws and programs like affirmative action.

I WANT, IN THIS ARTICLE, to consider and critique "colorblindness." . . .

Specifically, I will argue that we are not currently a colorblind society, and that race has a deep social significance that continues to disadvantage blacks and other Americans of color. While the legal strategy of colorblindness achieved great victories in the past, it has now become an impediment in the struggle to end racial inequality. At the base of racial injustice is a set of assumptions—a way of understanding the world—that so characterizes blacks as to make persistent inequality seem largely untroubling. A remedial regime predicated on colorblindness will have little influence at this deep level of social and legal consciousness because it cannot adequately challenge white attitudes or recognize a role for black self-definition. In the pages ahead I will explain and justify this somewhat paradoxical claim that a norm of colorblindness supports racial domination. I will conclude that in order to make progress in ending racial oppression and racism, our political and moral discourse must move from colorblindness to color-consciousness, from antidiscrimination to racial justice.

I. COLORBLINDNESS AND RACE-CONSCIOUSNESS: CLARIFYING THE CATEGORIES

. . . In the colorblind world, race is an arbitrary factor—one upon which it is doubly unfair to allocate benefits and impose burdens: one's race is neither voluntarily assumed nor capable of change. For nearly all purposes, it is maintained, the race of a person tells us nothing about an individual's capabilities and certainly nothing about her moral worth. Race-consciousness, from this perspective, is disfavored because it assigns a value to what should be a meaningless variable. To categorize on the basis of race is to miss the individual.

Adhering to a strategy of colorblindness does not make race a prohibited classification. Violations of the colorblind principle cannot be recognized and remedied without "noticing" the

Source: T. Alexander Aleinikoff, "A Case for Race-Consciousness." This article originally appeared at 91 *Columbia Law Review* 1060 (1991). Reprinted by permission.

race of the harmed individual or racial group. But, to be true to the model, race-conscious measures must be limited to identified instances of past discrimination.

The debate over colorblindness and race-consciousness has usually appeared in the cases and literature discussing programs that give preferences in employment or other opportunities to nonwhites. In now familiar terms, advocates of colorblindness characterize affirmative action programs as unjustifiably altering meritocratic standards and requiring a distribution of social goods that reflect the proportionate representation of minority groups in the population as a whole.

The presuppositions of supports of affirmative action may be closer to those of their opponents than is usually recognized. Many advocate "goals" of rough proportional representation upon the claim that since race is, or ought to be, an irrelevant factor in the distribution of the good in question, deviation from proportionate shares is the result either of present discrimination or the continuing effects of past discrimination. That is, the justification for affirmative action programs is usually stated in terms of remedying past and present violations of the colorblind principle. What separates most of the participants in the debate is not so much the goal of colorblindness, but rather differing views about the cause of current inequality and of the efficacy of race-blind or race-conscious remedies in reaching a colorblind future.[1]

In this article, I will use the term "race-consciousness" to apply to more than just "affirmative action" programs intended to help bring about a colorblind world or remedy past discrimination. There are many other situations in which race *qua* race might be seen as relevant to the pursuit of a legitimate and important gov-

ernmental goal. These include: ensuring the presence of persons of color on juries; taking race into account in allocating radio and television licenses; seeking nonwhites to fill positions in social service agencies that deal largely with minority populations; requiring voting rules and districts that improve the chances of electing minority representatives; fostering integration by adopting race-based school assignment plans and housing programs; taking measures to integrate police forces; adding the works of minority authors to the "literary canon" taught to college students; and giving weight to the race of applicants for teaching positions in higher education. In each of these situations, the race-consciousness of the program may be justified in other than remedial (and colorblind) terms.

II. THE DIFFERENCE THAT RACE MAKES

We live in a world of racial inequality. In almost every important category, blacks as a group are worse off than whites. Compared to whites, blacks have higher rates of unemployment, lower family incomes, lower life expectancy, higher rates of infant mortality, higher rates of crime victimization, and higher rates of teenage pregnancies and single-parent households. Blacks are less likely to go to college, and those who matriculate are less likely to graduate. Blacks are underrepresented in the professions, in the academy, and in the national government.[2]

Of course there has been progress. Comparing the situation of blacks half a century ago to their situation today shows a difference that is startling, and even encouraging, although the last decade evidences a slowing progress and some backsliding. But when the comparison is made between whites and blacks today, it is im-

---

1 See *Regents of the Univ. of Cal. v. Bakke,* 438 U.S. 265, 407 (1978) (Blackmun, J., dissenting). ("In order to get beyond racism, we must first take account of race. There is no other way.")

2 See *A Common Destiny: Blacks & American Society* 3–32 (G. Jaynes & R. Williams, Jr. eds. 1989). . . .

possible to ignore the deep and widening difference that race makes.[3]

To say that race makes a difference means more than simply identifying material disadvantages facing people of color in contemporary America. It also recognizes that race may have an influence on how members of society understand their worlds and each other, and how such understandings may serve to perpetuate racial inequalities in our society. The next two sections pursue these psychological and cultural claims.

A. Race and Cognition

Race matters. Race is among the first things that one notices about another individual. To be born black is to know an unchangeable fact about oneself that matters every day. [I]n my life," wrote W. E. B. Du Bois in his autobiography *Dusk of Dawn,* "the chief fact has been race —not so much scientific race, as that deep conviction of myriads of men that congenital differences among the main masses of human beings absolutely condition the individual destiny of every member of a group."[4] To be born white is to be free from confronting one's race on a daily, personal, interaction-by-interaction basis. Being white, it has been said, means not having to think about it. Understandably, white people have a hard time recognizing this difference.[5] Most blacks have to overcome, when meeting whites, a set of assumptions older than this nation about one's abilities, one's marriageability, one's sexual desires, and one's morality. Most whites, when they are being honest with themselves, know that these racial understandings are part of their consciousness.

Race matters with respect to the people we choose to spend time with or marry, the neighborhoods in which we choose to live, the houses of worship we join, our choice of schools for our children, the people for whom we vote, and the people we allow the state to execute. We make guesses about the race of telephone callers we do not know and about persons accused of crimes. While not every decision we make necessarily has a racial component, when race is present it almost invariably influences our judgments. We are intensely—even if subconsciously—race-conscious.

It is common to speak of racial attitudes as being based on "stereotypes"—an incorrect or unthinking generalization applied indiscriminately to individuals simply on the basis of group membership. From this perspective, stereotypes can be overcome by supplying more information about an individual or the group to which that individual belongs.

But this explanation fails to recognize race-consciousness as an entrenched structure of thought that affects how we organize and process information. Social science research suggests that stereotypes serve as powerful heuristics, supplying explanations for events even when evidence supporting nonstereotypical explanations exists, and leading us to interpret situations and actions differently when the race of the actors varies. It is often more likely that our mental schema will influence how we understand new information than it is that the new information will alter our mental schema.

A troubling example can be found in *Larry P. by Lucile P. v. Riles,*[6] a case challenging the use of IQ tests that disproportionately assigned black children to special classes for the "educable mentally retarded." In discussing the expert testimony presented on the adequacy of the tests, the court of appeals observed:

> Since the 1920's it has been generally known that black persons perform less well than white

3 For data to support the assertions in the preceding two paragraphs, see id. at 122–23, 278, 280–81, 293, 295, 302–03, 399, 416–17, 465, 524, 530.
4 W. E. B. Du Bois, *Dusk of Dawn* 139 (1940).
5 Much as men have a difficult time understanding the routine and ever-present fears that women have for their physical safety.

6 793 F. 2d 969 (9th Cir. 1984).

persons on the standardized intelligence tests. IQ tests had been standardized so that they yielded no bias because of sex. For example, when sample tests yielded different scores for boys and girls, the testing experts assumed such differences were unacceptable and modified the tests so that the curve in the standardization sample for boys and girls was identical. No such modification on racial grounds has ever been tried by the testing companies.[7]

The testing companies received two sets of data and chose to act on just one. Their assumptions made one set of data "surprising" and the other "expected" or "natural."

Because cognitive racial categories predispose us to select information that conforms to existing categories and to process information in such a way that it will fit into those categories, they are self-justifying and self-reinforcing. And because we adopt racial categories more through a process of cultural absorption than rational construction, we are likely to be unaware of the role that the categories play in the way we perceive the world. . . .

This deeply imbedded race-consciousness has a distressing effect on discourse between the races. In many ways, whites and blacks talk past each other. The stories that African-Americans tell about America—stories of racism and exclusion, brutality and mendacity—simply do not ring true to the white mind. Whites have not been trained to hear it, and to credit such accounts would be to ask whites to give up too much of what they "know" about the world. It would also argue in favor of social programs and an alteration in power relations that would fundamentally change the status quo. White versions of substantial progress on racial attitudes are also likely to ring hollow for many blacks. One might see an equality of missed communication here. But there is actually a great inequal-

ity because it is the white version that becomes the "official story" in the dominant culture.

B. The Power of Definition

In our society, race has not been a benign mode of classification. The designation of one's race has had a double function, both defining social categories and assigning characteristics to members of those categories. The predominant power of social and cultural definition has, from the start, been exercised by and for whites.

The theme of invisibility that permeates black literature portrays white erasure of black attempts at self-definition. Listen to Audre Lorde:

> . . . I can recall without counting
> eyes
> cancelling me out
> like an unpleasant appointment
> postage due
> stamped in yellow red purple
> any color
> except Black[8]

Blacks are "invisible" not in the sense that whites do not see them; they are "invisible" in the sense that whites see primarily what a white dominant culture has trained them to see. In a curious yet powerful way, whites create and reflect a cultural understanding of blackness that requires little contribution from blacks. The dominant and dominating story excludes or ignores black representations of blackness not out of vindictiveness or animus but because the black stories simply do not register. Robert Berkhofer's description of the process by which whites understand American Indians applies here: "preconception became conception and conception became fact."[9] . . .

7 Id. at 975–76; see generally S. Gould, *The Mismeasure of Man* (1981).

8 A. Lorde, "To the Poet Who Happens to Be Black and the Black Poet Who Happens to Be a Woman," in *Our Dead Behind Us* 6–7 (1986).

9 R. Berkhofer, *The White Man's Indian* 71 (1978).

Continued white ignorance of blacks and lack of contact in daily life makes white understandings of race difficult to alter.[10] Whites are only dimly aware of how blacks live or what it means to be black in America. Despite attempts to bring African-American history into the classroom, most whites do not understand the role of black slavery in the economic development of the United States, nor are they familiar with major trends in black political and social thought, or even the contributions of Frederick Douglass, W. E. B. Du Bois, and Malcolm X. Absence of knowledge is compounded by physical and social segregation. Blacks and whites rarely get to know each other in neighborhoods, schools, or churches; and interracial friendships remain surprisingly rare. As a result, most of what a white person in American knows about blacks is likely to have been learned from white family, friends, or the white-dominated media.

That the white-created image of African-Americans should remain largely unchallenged by black conceptions is troubling not only because the white version reflects stereotypes, myths, and half-truths, but also because of the role the white definition plays in explaining the historical treatment and current condition of blacks. Given strong incentives to absolve whites and blame blacks for existing social and economic inequalities, the white story about blacks has never been flattering. As Kimberle Crenshaw has powerfully argued, when the white image of blacks is combined with other American stories—such as equality of opportunity—it becomes "difficult for whites to see the Black situation as illegitimate or unnecessary." It works this way:

> Believing both that Blacks are inferior and that the economy impartially rewards the superior over the inferior, whites see that most Blacks are indeed worse off than whites are, which reinforces their sense that the market is operating "fairly and impartially"; those who should logically be on the bottom are on the bottom. This strengthening of whites' belief in the system in turn reinforces their beliefs that Blacks are *indeed* inferior. After all, equal opportunity is the rule, and the market is an impartial judge; if Blacks are on the bottom, it must reflect their relative inferiority.[11]

In sum, racial inequality has many faces. Social and economic statistics paint a clear and distressing picture of the differences among racial groups. Yet other inequalities are less obvious, based on nearly inaccessible and usually unchallenged assumptions that hide power and explain away domination. The next section examines alternative legal responses to this complex web of inequalities based on race. . . .

III. FROM COLORBLINDNESS TO RACE-CONSCIOUSNESS

Colorblindness may seem to be a sensible strategy in a world in which race has unjustly mattered for so long. Yet the claim that colorblindness today is the most efficacious route to colorblindness tomorrow has always been controversial. Justice Blackmun's paradoxical aphorism in *Bakke* reflects the usual counterclaim: "In order to get beyond racism, we must first take account of race. There is no other way. And

---

10 This is not to say that simply putting white and black folks together will end discrimination. As social science studies have suggested, such contacts may actually increase prejudice unless the contact occurs under particular conditions —such as when there are superordinate goals or institutional support in the form of superordinate norms and sanctions. For a review of the "contact" literature, see Amir, "The Role of Intergroup Contact in Change of Prejudice and Ethnic Relations," in *Towards the Elimination of Racism* 245, 245–308 (P. A. Katz ed. 1976).

11 Crenshaw, ["Race, Reform, and Retrenchment," 101 *Harv. L. Rev.* 1331], at 1380 (footnote omitted).

in order to treat some persons equally, we must treat them differently."[12] . . .

The claim I wish to press here is different from Blackmun's familiar stance in the affirmative action debate. I will argue in this section that a legal norm of colorblindness will not end race-consciousness; rather, it will simply make the unfortunate aspects and consequences of race-consciousness less accessible and thus less alterable. Furthermore, colorblind strategies are likely to deny or fail to appreciate the contribution that race-consciousness can make in creating new cultural narratives that would support serious efforts aimed at achieving racial justice.

Before these claims can be made, however, two varieties of colorblindness should be distinguished. The first, which I will call "strong colorblindness," argues that race should truly be an irrelevant, virtually unnoticed, human characteristic. Richard Wasserstrom has described this "assimilationist ideal";

> [A] nonracist society would be one in which the race of an individual would be the functional equivalent of the eye color of individuals in our society today. In our society no basic political rights and obligations are determined on the basis of eye color. No important institutional benefits and burdens are connected with eye color. Indeed, except for the mildest sort of aesthetic preferences, a person would be thought odd who even made private, social decisions by taking eye color into account.[13]

The second type, "weak colorblindness," would not outlaw all recognition of race, but would condemn the use of race as a basis for the distribution of scarce resources or opportunities and the imposition of burdens. Under "weak colorblindness," race might function like ethnicity: an attribute that could have significance for group members, and one that society as a whole

could recognize, but not one upon which legal distinctions could be based. Furthermore, individuals would be able to choose how important a role race would play in their associations and identifications, but their race would not be used by others to limit their opportunities or define their identities. Thus, college courses on "African-American literature" might well be permissible under a weak colorblindness regime, but such a regime would not tolerate allocating places in the class based on race or allowing race to be used as a factor in the choice of an instructor. In the sections that follow, I will argue that strong colorblindness is impossible and undesirable, and that weak colorblindness—although perhaps able to be implemented as a legal strategy—is an inadequate response to current manifestations of racial inequality.

A. Masking Race-Consciousness

It is apparently important, as a matter of widespread cultural practice, for whites to assert that they are strongly colorblind, in the sense that they do not notice or act on the basis of race. One can see this at work in such statements as: "I judge each person as an individual." Of course, it cannot be that whites do not notice the race of others. Perhaps what is being said is that the speaker does not begin her evaluation with any preconceived notions. But this too is difficult to believe, given the deep and implicit ways in which our minds are color-coded. To be truly colorblind in this way, as David Strauss has shown, requires color-consciousness: one must notice race in order to tell oneself not to trigger the usual mental processes that take race into account.

The denial of race-consciousness occasioned by the desire to be strongly colorblind is described in a recent study of a desegregated junior high school by psychologist Janet Schofield. She reports that teachers, apparently concerned that acknowledging racial awareness would be viewed as a sign of prejudice, claimed not to notice the race of their students. In pur-

12 *Regents of Univ. of Cal. v. Bakke,* 438 U.S. 265, 407 (1978) (Blackmun, J., dissenting).
13 R. Wasserstrom, *Philosophy and Social Issues* 24 (1980). . . .

suit of colorblindness, teachers rarely used the words "white" or "black," and avoided racial topics and identifications in class.[14]

This act of denial is troubling not only because it distorts reality, but also because it will make less accessible the ways in which color-consciousness influences our understanding of the world and of others. Strong colorblindness will perpetuate the white image of blacks by rendering irrelevant the kind of race-based discussion and data necessary for a serious critique of white definitions. Schofield's study documents how teachers' desires to act in a colorblind fashion harmed the educational experience by ignoring or denying race when it would have been appropriate to notice it:

> [One] teacher included George Washington Carver on a list of great Americans from which students could pick individuals to learn about but specifically decided not to mention he was black for fear of raising racial issues. In the best of all worlds, there would be no need to make such mention, because children would have no preconceptions that famous people are generally white. However, in a school where one white child was surprised to learn from a member of our research team that Martin Luther King was black, not white[!], it would seem reasonable to argue that highlighting the accomplishments of black Americans and making sure that students do not assume famous figures are white is a reasonable practice.[15]

Certainly such conduct creates possibilities for serious miscommunication. There is significant evidence of cultural differences between whites and blacks . . . When white teachers, unaware of such differences, ask questions in a way that conforms to white middle-class practice, they unwittingly disadvantage black school children.

But the problem runs deeper than the level of miscommunication. Whites believe that they can act in a colorblind fashion merely by acting as they always have. Colorblindness puts the burden on blacks to change; to receive "equal" treatment, they must be seen by whites as "white."[16] Hence, the "compliment" that some whites pay to blacks: "I don't think of you as black." Colorblindness is, in essence, not the absence of color, but rather monochromatism: whites can be colorblind when there is only one race—when blacks become white.

B. Local Knowledge: Race-Consciousness as Cultural Critique

Strong colorblindness, I have argued, is unlikely to produce the result it promises—a world in which race does not matter. In this section, I want to make the case for race-consciousness more direct by focusing on the benefits of race-consciousness in undermining and shifting deep cultural assumptions and ultimately, perhaps, making progress in overcoming racism. In presenting these claims, I hope also to undermine the case for weak colorblindness. To be effective, strategies for attacking racism may well demand affirmative race-conscious governmental policies. Clifford Geertz, in a collection of his essays entitled *Local Knowledge*, has stated that:

> To see ourselves as others see us can be eye-opening. To see others as sharing a nature with ourselves is the merest decency. But it is from the far more difficult achievement of seeing ourselves amongst others, as a local example of the forms human life has locally taken, a case among cases, a world among worlds, that the largeness of mind, without which objectivity is

14 Schofield, "Causes and Consequences of the Colorblind Perspective," in *Prejudice, Discrimination, and Racism* (J. Dovidio & S. Gaertner eds., 1986) at 231.
15 Id. at 249.

16 James Baldwin commented on the "tone of warm congratulation with which so many [white] liberals address their Negro equals. It is the Negro, of course, who is presumed to have become equal—an achievement that not only proves the comforting fact that perseverance has no color but also overwhelmingly corroborates the white man's sense of his own value." J. Baldwin. *The Fire Next Time* 127 (1962).

self-congratulation and tolerance a sham, comes.[17]

Colorblindness operates at Geertz's level of "merest decency." It begins and ends with the observation that there is something, under the skin, common to all human beings. . . . But Geertz clearly seeks more than this; he would reorient the usual hierarchical relationship between dominant and subordinate cultures by rotating the axis through its center point, making the vertical horizontal. This shift requires two related transformations: the first is to appreciate the contingency, the nonuniversalism of one's own culture—to view it as an example of "local knowledge"; the second is to recognize and credit the "local knowledges" of other groups. Of course, these two efforts are related. By valorizing the dominated, one is likely to cast doubts on the dominant group's characterizations or definition of the dominated group, which, in turn, tells us something new about the dominant group as well.

My claim outlined in the pages that follow is that race-consciousness can aid in these cultural transformations. . . .

Rotating the axis helps us to be open to other accounts and perspectives, and in doing so it reminds us of the fictional or constructed nature of "local knowledges"—including our own. Once white Americans shed the false assumption that "they know all they need to know" about African-Americans, they will begin to learn as much about themselves as about others.

1. Understanding Domination

The American Negro has the great advantage of having never believed that collection of myths to which white Americans cling. . . .[18]

James Baldwin

"[T]he quickest way to bring the reason of the world face to face [with white racism]," Du Bois

wrote, "is to listen to the complaint of those human beings today who are suffering most from white attitudes, from white habits, from the conscious and unconscious wrongs which white folk are today inflicting on their victims."[19] . . .

The claim here is limited, but important. One need not believe that subordinated groups hold world views thoroughly differentiated from the dominant culture in order to give credit to the claim that the views of subordinated groups on the extent and nature of subordination are likely to differ from those of majority groups. This is so for a number of reasons.

Dominant groups may have neither the inclination nor the ability to be fully aware of their domination. Dominant groups generally do not consider themselves to be oppressive, particularly in a society in which tolerance for diversity is valued, and they can provide descriptions of themselves and the disadvantaged that explain inequality as either justified or natural. To the extent that these descriptions effectively absolve dominant groups of responsibility for inequality, and therefore from bearing any of the costs of ameliorating inequality, there is little motivation for the dominant culture to question them.

Furthermore, the dominant culture's conceptions of the dominated are often not explicit. They are likely to be rooted, as Du Bois notes, in "long followed habits, customs, and folkways; [in] subconscious trains of reasoning and unconscious nervous reflexes."[20] These assumptions and mental structures, as noted above, may well have a significant influence on conduct and attitudes, yet they are rarely subjected to careful scrutiny because they seem so natural, so much a part of us.

Finally, since dominant groups are not the direct victims of their acts toward dominated groups, they may underestimate the burdens suffered by the dominated groups. This prob-

---

17 C. Geertz, *Local Knowledge: Further Essays in Interpretive Anthropology* 16 (1983).
18 J. Baldwin, [note 16], at 136.

19 W. E. B. Du Bois, [note 4], at 172.
20 W. E. B. Du Bois, [note 4], at 172. . . .

lem is compounded if dominant and dominated groups inhabit separate geographical and social spaces, so that the extent and harms of domination remain largely hidden from the dominant groups. . . .

2. Recognizing the Dominated Finally, recognizing race validates the lives and experiences of those who have been burdened because of their race. White racism has made "blackness" a relevant category in our society. Yet colorblindness seeks to deny the continued social significance of the category, to tell blacks that they are no different from whites, even though blacks as blacks are persistently made to feel that difference. Color-consciousness allows for recognition of the distinct and difficult difference that race has made; it facilitates white awareness of the efforts of African-Americans to describe and examine that difference. This is not simply the telling of a story of oppression. Color-consciousness makes blacks subjects and not objects, undermining the durability of white definitions of "blackness." It permits recognition of the strength and adaptive power of a black community able to survive slavery and oppression; and it acknowledges the contributions of black culture—not simply as windows on "the race question" but as distinct (if varied) voices and traditions, worthy of study in their own right. . . .

C. Weak Colorblindness and Its Costs

It is common for advocates of affirmative action to point out that a legal strategy dedicated to "equality of opportunity" is likely to replicate deeply imbedded inequalities. The familiar metaphor is of a race between two runners, one of whom starts many yards back from the starting line, or is encumbered by ankle weights. Color-conscious policies are said to remove the advantage that has for several centuries been granted to whites. The simplicity of this argument should not disguise its soundness or moral power. Unfortunately, however, affirmative ac-

tion programs based on the objective of overcoming past societal discrimination are deemed to run afoul of the Court's model of weak colorblindness.[21] To the extent race-conscious policies help ameliorate material disadvantage due to societal discrimination, the negative injunction of weak colorblindness imposes heavy costs.

Beyond this familiar terrain in the affirmative action debate, there are other advantages to race-conscious programs that also call into question the adequacy of weak colorblindness. As Justice Stevens has noted, there are a number of situations in which it seems eminently reasonable for government decision makers to take race into account.[22] For example:

> in a city with a recent history of racial unrest, the superintendent of policy might reasonably conclude that an integrated police force could develop a better relationship with the community and thereby do a more effective job of maintaining law and order than a force composed only of white officers.[23]

Similar claims could be made about integrated civil service and school administrations. That situations exist that could benefit from race-conscious policies should hardly be surprising, given the prominent role that race has played in allocating benefits and burdens throughout American history. Indeed, Justice Powell's famous "diversity" argument in *Bakke*[24] implicitly acknowledges the reasonableness of some manner of color-conscious decision making in a world in which race has mattered and continues to matter. To the extent that weak colorblindness makes these forms of race-consciousness

21 See, e.g., *City of Richmond v. J. A. Croson Co.,* 109 S. Ct. 706, 720–23 (1989); *Wygant v. Jackson Bd. of Educ.,* 476 U.S. 267, 277–78, 293–94 (1986). . . .
22 See *Wygant,* 476 U.S. at 314–15 (Stevens, J., dissenting). . . . (analysis of *Wygant* reveals that a forward-looking justification for affirmative action would be more effective than treating it as a remedy for past wrongs).
23 *Wygant,* 476 U.S. at 314 (Stevens, J., dissenting).
24 *Regents of Univ. of Cal. v. Bakke,* 438 U.S. 265, 315–19 (1978).

problematic, it is simply nearsighted social policy. . . .

Universities need more than African-American literature classes; they need a diversity of students in all literature classes, and not simply to show white students that students of color can perform as well as white students, but also to help all students become more self-conscious of the underlying assumptions with which they approach the world. To be sure, there are risks. Given the power of imbedded ways of thinking, new information may simply be "processed" in accordance with pre-existing views; or, white students may make the error of assuming that comments by black students express "the" black perspective. But to students and faculty open to a Geertzian moment, the intellectual rewards are enormous.

D. An Objection to Race-Consciousness

. . . [An] objection . . . that figures prominently in the attack on affirmative action is that race-consciousness is self-defeating to the extent that it reinforces rather than undermines racism. Affirmative action, it is argued, may have this effect because it inevitably creates the impression of a lowering of standards in order to benefit minorities. Furthermore, as Shelby Steele argues, the "implication of inferiority in racial preferences" has a demoralizing effect on blacks, contributing to "an enlargement of self doubt."[25]

One response is that we ought to run this claim by those who have been the victims of racism. Despite assertions by whites that race-conscious programs "stigmatize" beneficiaries, blacks remain overwhelmingly in favor of affirmative action.[26] Would we not expect blacks to

be the first to recognize such harms and therefore to oppose affirmative action if it produced serious stigmatic injury? It might be argued, however, that individual blacks are willing to participate in affirmative action programs because of the direct benefits they receive, yet those blacks who are not beneficiaries suffer the stigmatic harm without the compensating gains. But, again, one would expect that if this were the case, then blacks as a class would oppose affirmative action since the vast majority of blacks are not beneficiaries of affirmative action. Furthermore, Randall Kennedy provides a convincing argument that affirmative action, on balance, is more likely to reduce stigma than to impose it:

> It is unrealistic to think . . . that affirmative action causes most white disparagement of the abilities of blacks. Such disparagement, buttressed for decades by the rigid exclusion of blacks from educational and employment opportunities, is precisely what engendered the explosive crisis to which affirmative action is a response. . . . In the end, the uncertain extent to which affirmative action diminishes the accomplishments of blacks must be balanced against the stigmatization that occurs when blacks are virtually absent from important institutions in the society.[27]

Confident measures of the costs and benefits of affirmative action do not exist. Given the material gains afforded minorities by race-conscious programs and the fact that these gains are likely, as Kennedy notes, to counteract "conventional stereotypes about the place of the Negro,"[28] I would put the burden of proof on those who claim that affirmative action contributes more to racism than it diminishes racism. Significantly, the case for race-conscious-

---

25 S. Steele, *The Content of Our Character* 116–17 (1990).
26 D. Kinder & L. Sanders, "Pluralistic Foundations of American Opinion on Race," 9 & n. 6 (August 1987) (unpublished paper) (on file with *Columbia Law Review*).

27 Kennedy, "Persuasion and Distrust: A Comment on the Affirmative Action Debate," 99 *Harv. L. Rev.* 1327, 1331 (1986) (footnotes omitted)
28 Id.

ness suggested here would affect the evaluation of the costs and benefits because it would count as one of the benefits—as colorblindness cannot —the gains to white society of increased association with minorities and greater awareness of nondominant cultures. . . .

IV. FROM ANTIDISCRIMINATION TO RACIAL JUSTICE

Discussion about the appropriateness of race-conscious measures is but the doctrinal manifestation of a broader debate regarding the animating principle of race discrimination law. The strategy of colorblindness follows from an understanding of discrimination law that views the use of racial classifications as morally and politically objectionable. In contrast, support for broad race-conscious policies is usually imbedded in a description of race discrimination law as aimed at ending the second-class citizenship of African-Americans and other subordinated minorities. . . .

Starting fresh, it appears obvious that an antidiscrimination model that sees the use of racial classifications as the central problem to be addressed ill fits this society's current racial situation. There is no symmetry in either the use of racial classifications or the experiences of different racial groups. To see the problem of race discrimination as the problem of using racial criteria is to wrench legal theory out of social reality.[29] . . .

The choice among race discrimination law principles is, in the deepest sense, moral and political. Arrayed on the side of the antidiscrimination-as-colorblindness model is the knowledge of the terrible wrongs that color-consciousness

has wrought in our history, the ending of legal segregation effectuated by colorblindness, an ideology of individualists that stresses evaluation and rewards based on individual effort and personal characteristics over which a person has control, and the antagonisms that race-based preferences may breed. These, of course, are not trivial arguments, which suggests why colorblindness has had such significant appeal.

But the claim that race should be ignored would be far more persuasive if the difference that race had made in the past had been overcome. What cannot be denied—even if it is often ignored—is that blacks, as a class, have never attained economic or social equality with whites. Reconstruction ended long before it achieved its (some would say limited) set of goals. The "Second Reconstruction" of the 1960s wiped away some of the additional legal insults added by the race hysteria of the late nineteenth century, but it did little to fundamentally alter the material well-being of blacks. The narrowing of the economic gap between blacks and whites that occurred in the 1950s and 1960s—due primarily to the overall growth in the economy—stalled by the middle of the 1970s and did not improve during the Reagan years. A prodigious study sponsored by the National Academy of Sciences has recently concluded that the United States faces "an unfinished agenda: many black Americans remain separated from the mainstream of national life under conditions of great inequality." . . .

There are strong reasons for continuing the struggle to fulfill the initial goals of race discrimination law. Whether phrased as "anti-caste," "anti-group disadvantage," or "anti-subjugation," the task remains where it began: the ending of second class status of an historically oppressed group and the achieving of racial justice.

There are two interrelated aspects to this agenda for race discrimination law. The first supports programs that would produce material

---

29 To its advocates, colorblindness remains an instrumental strategy for achieving racial justice. I do not mean to imply that supporters of colorblindness have no regard for the real-world consequences of their theoretical positions.

improvements in the lives of black people: programs promoting jobs, medical care, and decent housing. Such programs, it should be noted, need not be race-based. A "racial justice" perspective need not entail explicitly race-conscious policies. It seems clear, however, that a racial justice perspective is friendly to race-conscious policies directed at overcoming the effects of past and present societal discrimination. . . . Set-aside programs . . . are modest examples of the kind of state intervention that is needed.

The second aspect of a racial justice perspective is an attack on the set of beliefs that makes existing inequalities untroubling. What must be addressed is not just old-fashioned racism, but also the deeply ingrained mental structures that categorize and define race to the disadvantage of blacks and other nonwhite groups. As suggested above, altering the image of blacks in the white mind requires paying attention to, and crediting, black voices, and to refashioning institutions in ways that will allow those voices to be heard. Here race-conscious programs may be crucial. . . .

V. CONCLUSION: TOWARD AN INCLUSIVE AMERICAN STORY

In the current political and social climate, a call for color-consciousness poses real risks. For several centuries of American history, noticing race provided the basis for a caste system that institutionalized second-class status for people of color. It was precisely this oppressive use of race that colorblindness sought to overcome. Furthermore, central to white opposition to affirmative action is the belief that blacks have attained equality of opportunity, and therefore any assistance directed to minorities qua minorities affords them an undeserved benefit and an unfair advantage. . . .[30]

30 See J. Kluegel & E. Smith, "Whites' Beliefs About Black Opportunity," 47 *Am. Soc. Rev.* 518, 523 (1982).

[But] race-neutral strategies simply postpone our society's inevitable rendezvous with its history of racism. Constant liminal and subliminal messages of the difference that race makes take their toll—no matter what justificatory rhetoric enshrouds official governmental action—and will ultimately breed a powerful claim of enough-is-enough. Such a call can take the form of a national commitment to end racial injustice, or it can take the form of "by any means necessary" in the minds and hands of the victims of discrimination who know that colorblindness is a descriptive lie and a normative mistake.

Race-conscious programs alone will not end racism. At best, they represent a small step toward changing social relations and structures of thought and perception. What is needed is direct, self-conscious scrutiny of the way we think and of the assumptions about race that each of us holds and upon which we act. Attention to black constructions of reality can provide a counterbalance to the white construction of blacks in the white mind. . . .

Racial equality will not be attainable until American myths include blacks as full members and equal partners in society. A new set of stories is needed to provide the impetus for self and social reexamination, and to provide the foundation upon which support for race-conscious measures can be based. For example, we might develop an historical narrative not about those who *chose* America, but rather about those who *built* America. This account would be about slaves and free blacks in the South in the nineteenth century and blacks in the twentieth century who migrated to work in Northern factories; about women who worked in the factories and (unnoticed and uncompensated) in the home and about Chinese laborers who built the railroads, Mexican workers who harvested the crops, and European immigrants who built the great cities of the East. Such a narrative would acknowledge the deep and lasting contributions of African-Americans and other groups usually marginalized in the traditional account and would focus attention on the injustice of continued inequalities founded on racial oppression.

Blacks as blacks have had a unique history in this country. It is a history that whites and blacks confront every day and will continue to confront into the indefinite future. In pretending to ignore race, this society denies itself the self-knowledge that is demanded for eradicating racism and achieving racial justice.

Review Questions

1. What does Aleinikoff mean by race-consciousness? Why does he think that race and race-consciousness are important in our society?
2. What is the strategy of color-blindness? Distinguish between the strong and the weak versions of color-blindness.
3. What are Aleinikoff's objections to strong color-blindness?
4. What is wrong with weak color-blindness?
5. How does Aleinikoff reply to Steele?
6. What is required for racial equality, according to Aleinikoff?

Discussion Questions

1. Does race-consciousness help eliminate racism or does it sustain it?
2. Is color-blindness really impossible to achieve and undesirable? Aren't there any situations where color-blindness might be more appropriate than race-consciousness? For example, shouldn't grading in school be color-blind?
3. Has Aleinikoff given an adequate response to Steele?
4. Which produces the best consequences for society, color-blindness or race-consciousness?

Secondary Sexism and Quota Hiring

MARY ANNE WARREN

For biographical information on Mary Anne Warren, see her reading in Chapter 2.

Warren begins by distinguishing between primary and secondary sexism. Primary sexism is simply unfair discrimination on the basis of sex. Secondary sexism involves the use of sex-correlated criteria that are not valid measures of merit. One such criterion is:

Source: Mary Anne Warren, "Secondary Sexism and Quota Hiring," from *Philosophy & Public Affairs*, Vol. 6, No. 3 (Spring 1977), pp. 240–261. Copyright © 1977 by Princeton University Press. Reprinted by permission of Princeton University Press.

Does the candidate have an uninterrupted work record? This criterion discriminates against women who have interrupted their careers to have and raise children. To counteract primary and secondary sexist hiring practices that have put women at a disadvantage, Warren favors mandatory hiring quotas of a minimum sort based on the proportion of women among qualified and available candidates. Even though employers may have to use weak discrimination in favor of women to meet these quotas, Warren does not think that this is especially unfair to men. She feels that men have benefited in the past and will benefit in the future from sexist discrimination against women.

I WANT TO CALL attention to a pervasive form of discrimination against women, one which helps to explain the continuing male monopoly of desirable jobs in the universities, as elsewhere. Discrimination of this sort is difficult to eliminate or even, in some cases, to recognize, because (1) it is not explicitly based on sex, and (2) it typically *appears* to be justified on the basis of plausible moral or practical considerations. The recognition of this form of discrimination gives rise to a new argument for the use of numerical goals or quotas in the hiring of women for college and university teaching and administrative positions.

I shall argue that because of these de facto discriminatory hiring practices, minimum numerical quotas for the hiring and promotion of women are necessary, not (just) to compensate women for past discrimination or its results, or to provide women with role models, but to counteract this *ongoing* discrimination and thus make the competition for such jobs more nearly fair. Indeed, given the problems inherent in the compensatory justice and role-model arguments for reverse discrimination, this may well be the soundest argument for the use of such quotas.

I. PRIMARY AND SECONDARY SEXISM

Most of us try not to be sexists; that is, we try not to discriminate unfairly in our actions or attitudes toward either women or men. But it is not a simple matter to determine just which actions or attitudes discriminate unfairly, and a sincere effort to avoid unfair discrimination is often not enough. This is true of both of the forms of sexism that I wish to distinguish.

In its primary sense, "sexism" means *unfair discrimination on the basis of sex*. The unfairness may be unintentional; but the cause or reason for the discrimination must be the sex of the victim, not merely some factor such as size or strength that happens to be correlated with sex. Primary sexism may be due to dislike, distrust, or contempt for women, or, in less typical cases, for men or hermaphrodites. Or it may be due to sincerely held but objectively unjustified beliefs about women's properties or capacities. It may also be due to beliefs about the properties women *tend* to have, which are objectively justified but inappropriately applied to a particular case, in which the woman discriminated against does not have those properties.

For instance, if members of a philosophy department vote against hiring or promoting a woman logician because they dislike women (logicians), or because they think that women cannot excel in logic, or because they know that most women do not so excel and wrongly conclude that this one does not, then they are guilty of primary sexism. This much, I think, is noncontroversial.

But what should we say if they vote to hire or promote a man rather than a woman because he has a wife and children to support, while she has a husband who is (capable of) supporting her? Or because they believe that the woman has childcare responsibilities which will limit the time she can spend on the job? What if they hire a woman at a lower rank and salary than is standard for a man with comparable qualifications, for one of the above reasons? These actions are not sexist in the primary sense because there is no discrimination on the basis of sex itself. The criteria used *can* at least be applied in a sex-neutral manner. For instance, it might be asserted that if the woman candidate had had a spouse and children who depended upon her for support, this would have counted in her favor just as much as it would in the case of a man.

Of course, appeals to such intrinsically sex-neutral criteria may, in some cases, be mere rationalizations of what is actually done from primary sexist motives. In reality, the criteria cited may not be applied in a sex-neutral manner. But let us assume for the sake of argument that the application of these criteria *is* sex-neutral, not merely a smoke screen for primary sexism. On this assumption, the use of such criteria discriminates against women only because of certain contingent features of this society, such as the persistence of the traditional division of labor in marriage and childrearing.[1]

Many people see nothing morally objectionable in the use of such intrinsically sex-neutral yet de facto discriminatory criteria. For not only may employers who use such criteria be free of primary sexism, but their actions may appear to be justified on both moral and pragmatic grounds. It might, for instance, be quite clear that a department will really do more to alleviate economic hardship by hiring or promoting a man with dependents rather than a woman with none, or that a particular woman's domestic responsibilities will indeed limit the time she can spend on the job. And it might seem perfectly appropriate for employers to take account of such factors. Nevertheless, I shall argue that the use of such considerations is unfair. It is an example of secondary sexism, which I define as comprising

all those actions, attitudes and policies which, while not using sex itself as a reason for discrimination, do involve sex-correlated factors or criteria and do result in an unfair impact upon (certain) women. In the case of university hiring policies, secondary sexism consists in the use of sex-correlated selection criteria which are not valid measures of academic merit, with the result that women tend to be passed over in favor of men who are not, in fact, better qualified. I call sexism of this sort *secondary*, not because it is any less widespread or harmful than primary sexism, but because (1) it is, in this way, indirect or covert, and (2) it is typically parasitic upon primary sexism, in that the injustices it perpetuates—for example, those apparent from the male monopoly of desirable jobs in the universities—are usually due in the first instance to primary sexism.

Two points need to be made with respect to this definition. First, it is worth noting that, although in the cases we will be considering the correlations between sex and the apparently independent but de facto discriminatory criteria are largely due to past and present injustices against women, this need not always be the case. The discriminatory impact of excluding pregnancy-related disabilities from coverage by employee health insurance policies, for example, probably makes this an instance of secondary sexism. Yet it is certainly not (human) injustice which is responsible for the fact that it is only women who become pregnant. The fact that the correlation is due to biology rather than prior injustice does not show that the exclusion is not sexist. Neither does the fact that pregnancy is often undertaken voluntarily. If such insurance programs fail to serve the needs of women employees as well as they serve those of men, then they can escape the charge of sexism only if—as seems unlikely—it can be shown that they cannot possibly be altered to include disabilities related to pregnancy without ceasing to serve their mutually agreed upon purposes, and/or producing an even greater injustice.

---

1 I mean, of course, the tradition that the proper husband earns (most of) the family's income, while the proper wife does (most of) the housekeeping and childrearing.

This brings us to the second point. It must be stressed that on the above definition the use of valid criteria of merit in hiring to university positions is not an instance of secondary sexism. Some might argue that merit criteria discriminate unfairly against women, because it is harder for women to earn the advanced degrees, to write the publications, and to obtain the professional experience that are the major traditional measures of academic merit. But it would be a mistake to suppose that merit criteria as such are therefore sexist. They are sexist only to the extent that they understate women's actual capacity to perform well in university positions; and to that extent, they are invalid as criteria of merit. To the extent that they are valid, that is, the most reliable available measurements of capacities which are indeed crucial for the performance of the job, they are not unjust, even though they may result in more men than women being hired.

If this seems less than obvious, the following analogy may help. It is surely not unjust to award first prize in a discus throwing contest to the contestant who actually makes the best throw (provided, of course, that none of the contestants have been unfairly prevented from performing up to their capacity on this particular occasion), even if some of the contestants have in the past been wrongly prevented from developing their skill to the fullest, say by sexist discrimination in school athletic programs. Such contestants may be entitled to other relevant forms of compensation, for example, special free training programs to help them make up for lost time, but they are not entitled to win this particular contest. For the very *raison d'être* of an athletic contest dictates that prizes go to the best performers, not those who perhaps *could* have been the best, had past conditions been ideally fair.

So too, a university's central reasons for being dictate that positions within it be filled by candidates who are as well qualified as can be found. Choosing less qualified candidates deprives students of the best available instruction, colleagues of a more intellectually productive environment, and—in the case of state-funded universities—the public of the most efficient use of its resources.[2] To appoint inferior candidates defeats the primary purposes of the university, and is therefore wrong-headed, however laudable its motivations. It is also, as we shall see, a weapon of social change which is apt to backfire against those in whose interest it is advocated.

II. SECONDARY SEXISM IN UNIVERSITY HIRING

Consider the following policies, which not infrequently influence hiring, retention, and promotion decisions in American colleges and universities:

1. Antinepotism rules, proscribing the employment of spouses of current employees.
2. Giving preference to candidates who (are thought to) have the greater financial need, where the latter is estimated by whether someone has, on the one hand, financial dependents, or, on the other hand, a spouse capable of providing financial support.

---

2 It might be argued that the hiring process ought not to be based on merit alone, because there are cases in which being a woman, or being black, might itself be a crucial job qualification. As Michael Martin points out, this might well be the case in hiring for, say, a job teaching history in a previously all white-male department which badly needs to provide its students with a more balanced perspective. See "Pedagogical Arguments for Preferential Hiring and Tenuring of Women Teachers in the University," *The Philosophical Forum* 5, no. 2: 325–333. I think it is preferable, however, to describe such cases, not as instances requiring a departure from the merit principle, but as instances in which sex or race itself, or rather certain interests and abilities that are correlated with sex or race, constitutes a legitimate qualification for a certain job, and hence a measure of merit, vis-à-vis that job.

3. The "last hired-first fired" principle, used in determining who shall be fired or not rehired as a result of staffing cutbacks.

4. Refusing promotions, tenure, retention seniority, or pro-rata pay to persons employed less than full time, where some are so employed on a relatively long-term basis and where there is no evidence that such persons are (all) less well qualified than full time employees.

5. Hiring at a rank and salary determined primarily by previous rank and salary rather than by more direct evidence of a candidate's competence, for example, degrees, publications, and student and peer evaluations.

6. Counting as a negative factor the fact that a candidate has or is thought to have, or to be more likely to have, childcare or other domestic responsibilities which may limit the time s/he can spend on the job.

7. Giving preference to candidates with more or less uninterrupted work records over those whose working careers have been interrupted (for example, by raising children) in the absence of more direct evidence of a present difference in competence.

8. Not hiring, especially to administrative or supervisory positions, persons thought apt to encounter disrespect or lack of cooperation from peers or subordinates, without regard for whether this presumed lack of respect may be itself unjustified, for example, as the result of primary sexism.

9. Discriminating against candidates on the grounds of probable mobility due to the mobility of a spouse, present or possible.

Each of these practices is an example of secondary sexism, in that while the criterion applied does not mention sex, its use nevertheless tends to result in the hiring and promotion of men in preference to women who are not otherwise demonstrably less well qualified. I suggest that in seeking to explain the continuing underrepresentation of women in desirable jobs in the universities, we need to look not only toward primary sexist attitudes within those institutions, and certainly not toward any intrinsic lack of merit on the part of women candidates,[3] but toward covertly, and often unintentionally, discriminatory practices such as these.

Of course, none of these practices operates to the detriment of women in every case; but each operates against women much more often than against men, and the cumulative effect is enormous. No doubt some of them are more widespread than others and some (for example, the use of antinepotism rules) are already declining in response to pressures to remove barriers to the employment of women. Others, such as policies 3 and 4, are still fairly standard and have barely begun to be seriously challenged in most places. Some are publicly acknowledged and may have been written into law or administrative policy, for example, policies 1, 3, 4, and 5. Others are more apt to be private policies on the part of individual employers, to which they may not readily admit or of which they may not even be fully aware, for example, policies 2, 6, 7, and 8. It is obviously much more difficult to demonstrate the prevalence of practices of the latter sort. Nevertheless, I am certain that all of these practices occur, and I strongly suspect that none is uncommon, even now.

This list almost certainly does not include all of the secondary sexist practices which influence university hiring. But these examples are typical, and an examination of certain of their features

---

3 With respect to one such measure, books and articles published, married women Ph.D.'s published as much or slightly more than men, and unmarried women only slightly less. See "The Woman Ph.D.: A Recent Profile," by R. J. Simon, S. M. Clark, and K. Galway, in *Social Problems* 15, no. 2 (Fall 1967): 231.

will shed light on the way in which secondary sexism operates in the academic world and on the reasons why it is morally objectionable.

In each of these examples, a principle is used in choosing between candidates that in practice acts to discriminate against women who may even be better qualified intrinsically than their successful rivals, on any reliable and acceptable measure of merit.[4] Nevertheless, the practice may *seem* to be justified. Nepotism rules, for instance, act to exclude women far more often than men, since women are more apt to seek employment in academic and/or geographical areas in which their husbands are already employed than vice versa. Yet nepotism rules may appear to be necessary to ensure fairness to those candidates and appointees, both male and female, who are *not* spouses of current employees and who, it could be argued, would otherwise be unfairly disadvantaged. Similarly, giving jobs or promotions to those judged to have the greatest financial need may seem to be simple humanitarianism, and the seniority system may seem to be the only practical way of providing job security to *any* portion of the faculty. For

policies 5 through 9, it could be argued that, although the criteria used are not entirely reliable, they may still have *some* use in predicting job performance.

Thus each practice, though discriminatory in its results, may be defended by reference to principles which are not intrinsically sex-biased. In the context of an otherwise sexually egalitarian society, these practices would probably not result in de facto discrimination against either sex. In such a society, for instance, men would not hold a huge majority of desirable jobs, and women would be under no more social or financial pressure than men to live where their spouses work rather than where they themselves work; thus they would not be hurt by nepotism rules any more often, on the average, than men.[5] The average earning power of men and women would be roughly equal, and no one could assume that women, any more than men, ought to be supported by their spouses, if possible. Thus the fact that a woman has an employed spouse would not be thought to reduce her need for a job any more—or less—than in the case of a man. We could proceed down the list; in a genuinely nonsexist society, few or none of the conditions would exist which cause these practices to have a discriminatory impact upon women. *Except we don't live in a nonsexist society!*

Of course, there may be other reasons for rejecting these practices, besides their discriminatory impact upon women. Nepotism rules might be unfair to married persons of both sexes, even in a context in which they were not *especially* unfair to women. My point is simply that these practices would not be instances of sexism in a society which was otherwise free of sexism and its results. Hence, those who believe that the test of the justice of a practice is whether or not it would unfairly disadvantage any group or individual *in the context of an otherwise just society* will see no sexual injustice whatever in these practices.

4 I am assuming that whether a candidate is married to a current employee, or has dependents, or a spouse capable of supporting her, whether she is employed on a part-time or a full-time basis, her previous rank and salary, the continuity of her work record, and so on, are not in themselves reliable and acceptable measures of merit. As noted in example 5, more direct and pertinent measures of merit can be obtained. Such measures as degrees, publications, and peer and student evaluations have the moral as well as pragmatic advantage of being based on the candidate's actual past performance, rather than on unreliable and often biased conjectures of various sorts. Furthermore, even if there is or were *some* correlation (it would surely not be a *reliable* one) between certain secondary sexist criteria and job performance, it could still be argued that employers are not morally entitled to use such criteria, because of the unfair consequences of doing so. As Mary Vetterling has observed, there might well be some correlation between having "a healthy and active sex life" and "the patience and good humor required of a good teacher"; yet employers are surely not entitled to take into account the quality of a person's sex life in making hiring and promotion decisions. "Some Common Sense Notes on Preferential Hiring," *The Philosophical Forum* 5, no. 2: 321.

5 Unless, perhaps, a significant average age difference between wives and husbands continued to exist.

But surely the moral status of a practice, as it operates in a certain context, must be determined at least in part by its actual consequences, in that context. The fact is that each of these practices acts to help preserve the male monopoly of desirable jobs, in spite of the availability of women who are just as well qualified on any defensible measure of merit. This may or may not suffice to show that these practices are morally objectionable. It certainly shows that they are inconsistent with the "straight merit" principle, that is, that jobs should go to those best qualified for them on the more reliable measures of merit. Hence, it is ironic that attempts to counteract such de facto discriminatory practices are often interpreted as attacks on the "straight merit" principle.

III. WHY SECONDARY SEXISM IS UNFAIR

Two additional points need to be stressed in order to show just why these practices are unfair. In the first place, the contingent social circumstances which explain the discriminatory impact of these practices are themselves morally objectionable, and/or due to morally objectionable practices. It is largely because men *are* more able to make good salaries, and because married women are still expected to remain financially dependent upon their husbands, if possible, that the fact that a woman has an employed husband can be seen as evidence that she doesn't "need" a job. It is because a disproportionate number of women must, because of family obligations and the geographical limitations these impose, accept part-time employment even when they would prefer full time, that the denial of tenure, promotion and pro-rata pay to part-time faculty has a discriminatory impact upon women. That women accept such obligations and limitations may seem to be their own free choice; but, of course, that choice is heavily conditioned by financial pressures—for example, the fact that the husband can usually make more money—and by sexually stereotyped social expectations.

Thus, the effect of these policies is to compound and magnify prior social injustices against women. When a woman is passed over on such grounds, it is rather as if an athlete who had without her knowledge been administered a drug to hamper her performance were to be disqualified from the competition for failing the blood-sample test. In such circumstances, the very least that justice demands is that the unfairly imposed handicap not be used as a rationale for the imposition of further handicaps. If the unfair handicaps that society imposes upon women cause them to be passed over by employers because of a lack of straight merit, that is one thing, and it is unfortunate, but it is not obvious that it involves unfairness on the part of the employers. But if those handicaps are used as an excuse for excluding them from the competition regardless of their merit, as all too often happens, this is quite another thing, and it is patently unfair.

In the second place, practices such as these often tend to perpetuate the very (unjust) circumstances which underlie their discriminatory impact, thus creating a vicious circle. Consider the case of a woman who is passed over for a job or promotion because of her childcare responsibilities. Given a (better) job, she might be able to afford day care, or to hire someone to help her at home, or even to persuade her husband to assume more of the responsibilities. Denying her a job because of her domestic responsibilities may make it almost impossible for her to do anything to lessen those responsibilities. Similarly, denying her a job because she has a husband who supports her may force him to continue supporting her and her to continue to accept that support.

Both of these points may be illustrated by turning to a somewhat different sort of example. J. R. Lucas has argued that there are cases in which women may justifiably be discriminated against on grounds irrelevant to their merit. He claims, for example, that it is "not so evidently wrong to frustrate Miss Amazon's hopes of a military career in the Grenadier Guards on the grounds not that she would make a bad soldier, but that she would be a disturbing influence in the mess room."[6]

But this is a paradigm case of secondary, and perhaps also primary, sexism; it is also quite analogous to practice 8. To exclude women from certain jobs or certain branches of the military on the grounds that certain third parties are not apt to accept them, when that nonacceptance is itself unreasonable and perhaps based on sexual bigotry, is to compound the injustice of that bigotry. If it is inappropriate for soldiers to be disturbed or to make a disturbance because there are women in the mess room, then it is wrong to appeal to those soldiers' attitudes as grounds for denying women the opportunities available to comparably qualified men. It is also to help ensure the perpetuation of those attitudes, by preventing male soldiers from having an opportunity to make the sorts of observations which might lead to their eventually accepting women as comrades.

Thus, these practices are morally objectionable because they compound and perpetuate prior injustices against women, penalizing them for socially imposed disadvantages which cannot be reliably shown to detract from their actual present capacities. We may conclude that the hiring process will never be fair to women, nor will it be based on merit alone, so long as such practices persist on a wide scale. But it remains to be seen whether numerical hiring quotas for women are a morally acceptable means of counteracting the effects of sexist hiring practices.

IV. WEAK QUOTAS

I shall discuss the case for mandatory hiring quotas of a certain very minimal sort: those based on the proportion of women, not in the population as a whole, but among qualified and available candidates in each academic field. Such a "weak" quota system would require that in each institution, and ideally within each department and each faculty and administrative rank and salary, women be hired and promoted at least in accordance with this proportion. If, for instance, a tenured or tenure-track position became available in a given department on an average of every other year, and if women were twenty percent of the qualified and available candidates in the field, then such a quota system would require that the department hire a woman to such a position at least once in ten years.[7]

Needless to say, this is not a formula for rapid change in the sexual composition of the universities. Suppose that the above department has twenty members, all male and all or almost all tenured, that it does not grow, and that it perhaps shrinks somewhat. Under these not atypical circumstances, it could easily take over forty years for the number of women in the department to become proportional to the number of qualified women available, even if the quota is strictly adhered to, and the proportion of qualified women does not increase in the meantime. Consequently, some would agree that such a quota system would be inadequate.[8]

Furthermore, it *could* be argued that if the job competition were actually based on merit, women would be hired and promoted at a *higher* rate than such a weak quota system would require, since the greater obstacles still

---

6 J. R. Lucas, "Because You Are a Woman," *Moral Problems,* ed. James Rachels (New York: Harper & Row, 1975), p. 139.

7 In practice problems of statistical significance will probably require that quotas be enforced on an institution-wide basis rather than an inflexible department-by-department basis. Individual departments, especially if they are small and if the proportion of qualified women in the field is low, may fail to meet hiring quotas, not because of primary or secondary sexism, but because the best qualified candidates happen in fact to be men. But if no real discrimination against women is occurring, then such statistical deviations should be canceled out on the institutional level, by deviations in the opposite direction.

8 See Virginia Held, "Reasonable Progress and Self-Respect," *The Monist* 57, no. 1: 19.

encountered by women on the way to obtaining qualifications ensure that only very able women make it.[9] Or, it might be argued that women should be hired and promoted in more than such proportional numbers, in order to compensate for past discrimination or to provide other women with role models. Indeed, some existing affirmative action plans, so I am told, already require that women be hired in more than proportional numbers. Nevertheless, I will not defend quotas higher than these minimal ones. For, as will be argued in Section VIII, higher quotas at least give the appearance of being unfair to male candidates, and it is not clear that either the compensatory justice or the role-model argument is sufficient to dispel that appearance.

V. QUOTAS OR GOALS?

Before turning to the case of such minimal hiring quotas, we need to comment on the "quotas vs. goals" controversy. Those who oppose the use of numerical guidelines in the hiring of women or racial minorities usually refer to such guidelines as *quotas,* while their defenders usually insist that they are not quotas but *goals.* What is at issue here? Those who use the term "quotas" pejoratively tend to assume that the numerical standards will be set so high or enforced so rigidly that strong reverse discrimination—that is, the deliberate hiring of demonstrably less well qualified candidates—will be necessary to implement them.[10] The term "goal," on the other hand, suggests that this will not be the case, and that good faith efforts to comply with the standards by means short of strong reverse discrimination will be acceptable.[11]

But whatever one calls such minimum numerical standards, and whether or not one suspects that strong reverse discrimination has in fact occurred in the name of affirmative action, it should be clear that it is not *necessary* for the implementation of a quota system such as I have described. Neither, for that matter, is weak reverse discrimination—that is, the deliberate hiring of women in preference to equally but not better qualified men.[12] For if hiring decisions are solely based on reliable measures of merit and wholly uncorrupted by primary or secondary sexist policies, then qualified women would *automatically* be hired and promoted at least in proportion to their numbers, except, of course, in statistically abnormal cases.[13] Consequently, reverse discrimination will *appear* to be necessary to meet proportional quotas only where the hiring process continues to be influenced by sexist practices—primary or secondary, public or private.

---

9 Gertrude Ezorsky cites in support of this point a study by L. R. Harmon for over 20,000 Ph.D.'s which showed that "Women . . . Ph.D.'s are superior to their male counterparts on all measures derived from high school records, in all . . . specializations." *High School Ability Patterns: A Backward Look from the Doctorate,* Scientific Manpower [*sic*] Report No. 6, 1965, pp. 27–28; cited by Ezorsky in "The Fight Over University Women," *The New York Review of Books* 21, no. 8 (16 May 1974): 32.

10 See, for instance, Paul Seaburg, "HEW and the Universities," *Commentary* 53, no. 2 (February 1972): 38–44.

11 In practice, strong reverse discrimination is specifically prohibited by HEW affirmative action guidelines, and good faith efforts to implement affirmative action programs without resorting to strong reverse discrimination have been accepted as adequate. Nevertheless, though I would not wish to see *these* features of affirmative action policies changed, I prefer the term "quota" for what I am proposing, because this term suggests a standard which will be enforced, in one way or another, while the term "goal" suggests—and affirmative action is in great danger of becoming—a mere expression of good intentions, compliance with which is virtually unenforceable.

12 The distinction between strong and weak reverse discrimination is explored by Michael Bayles in "Compensatory Reverse Discrimination in Hiring," *Social Theory and Practice* 2, no. 3: 303–304, and by Vetterling, "Common Sense Notes," pp. 320–323.

13 This conclusion can be avoided only by assuming either that qualified women would not want better jobs if these were available, or that they are somehow less meritorious than comparably qualified men. The first assumption is absurd, since women who do not want desirable jobs are not apt to take the trouble to become qualified for them; and the second assumption is amply refuted by empirical data. See, for instance, the studies cited in fn. 9.

In effect, the implementation of a minimum quota system would place a price upon the continued use of sexist practices. Employers would be forced to choose between eliminating sexist practices, thus making it possible for quotas to be met without discriminating for or against anyone on the basis of sex, and practicing reverse discrimination on an ad hoc basis in order to meet quotas without eliminating sexist practices. Ideally, perhaps, they would all choose the first course, in which case the quota system would serve only to promote an ongoing check upon, and demonstration of, the nonsexist nature of the hiring process.

In reality, however, not all secondary sexist practices can be immediately eliminated. Some forms of secondary sexism have probably not yet been recognized, and given the nature of the interests involved it is likely that new forms will tend to spring up to replace those which have been discredited. More seriously, perhaps, some secondary sexist policies, such as the seniority system, cannot be eliminated without an apparent breach of contract (or of faith) with present employees. Others—for example, hiring on the basis of need—may survive because they are judged, rightly or wrongly, to be on the whole the lesser evil. A quota system, however, would require that the impact of such secondary sexist practices be counterbalanced by preferential treatment of women in other instances. Furthermore, it would hasten the elimination of all sexist policies by making it in the interest of all employees, men as well as women, that this be done, since until it is done both will run the risk of suffering from (sexist or reverse) discrimination. Certainly their elimination would be more probable than it is at present, when it is primarily women who have a reason based on self-interest for opposing them, yet primarily men who hold the power to eliminate or preserve them.

The most crucial point, however, is that under such a quota system, even if (some) employers do use weak discrimination in favor of women to meet their quota, this will not render the job competition especially unfair to men. For, as I will argue, unfairness would result only if the average male candidate's chances of success were reduced to below what they would be in an ongoing, just society, one in which men and women had complete equality of opportunity and the competition was based on merit alone; and I will argue that the use of weak reverse discrimination to meet proportional hiring quotas will not have this effect.

VI. QUOTAS AND FAIRNESS

Now one way to support this claim would be to argue that in an ongoing, just society women would constitute a far higher proportion of the qualified candidates in most academic fields and that therefore the average male candidate's chances would, other things being equal, automatically be reduced considerably from what they are now. Unfortunately, however, the premise of this argument is overly speculative. It is possible that in a fully egalitarian society women would still tend to avoid certain academic fields and to prefer others, much as they do now, or even that they would fail to (attempt to) enter the academic profession as a whole in much greater numbers than at present.

But whatever the proportion of male and female candidates may be, it must at least be the case that in a just society the chances of success enjoyed by male candidates must be no greater, on the average, and no less than those enjoyed by comparably qualified women. Individual differences in achievement, due to luck or to differences in ability, are probably inevitable; but overall differences in the opportunities accorded to comparably qualified men and women, due to discrimination, would not be tolerated.

The question, then is: Would the use of weak discrimination in favor of women, to a degree just sufficient to offset continuing sexist discrimination against women and thus to meet minimum quotas, result in lowering the average chances of male candidates to below those of comparably qualified women? The answer, surely, is that it would not, since by hypothesis men would be passed over, in order to fill a quota, in favor of women no better qualified only as often as women continue to be passed over, because of primary or secondary sexism, in favor of men no better qualified.

In this situation, individual departures from the "straight merit" principle might be no less frequent than at present; indeed, their frequency might even be doubled. But since it would no longer be predominantly women who were repeatedly disadvantaged by those departures, the overall fairness of the competition would be improved. The average long-term chances of success of *both* men and women candidates would more closely approximate those they would enjoy in an ongoing just society. If individual men's careers are temporarily set back because of weak reverse discrimination, the odds are good that these same men will have benefited in the past and/or will benefit in the future —not necessarily in the job competition, but in *some* ways—from sexist discrimination against women. Conversely, if individual women receive apparently unearned bonuses, it is highly likely that these same women will have suffered in the past and/or will suffer in the future from primary or secondary sexist attitudes. Yet, the primary purpose of a minimum quota system would not be to compensate the victims of discrimination or to penalize its beneficiaries, but rather to increase the overall fairness of the situation—to make it possible for the first time for women to enjoy the same opportunity to obtain desirable jobs in the universities as enjoyed by men with comparable qualifications.

It is obvious that a quota system implemented by weak reverse discrimination is not the ideal long-term solution to the problem of sexist discrimination in academic hiring. But it would be a great improvement over the present situation, in which the rate of unemployment among women Ph.D.'s who are actively seeking employment is still far higher than among men with Ph.D.'s, and in which women's starting salaries and chances of promotion are still considerably lower than those of men.[14] Strong reverse discrimination is clearly the least desirable method of implementing quotas. Not only is it unfair to the men who are passed over, and to their potential students and colleagues, to hire demonstrably less well qualified women, but it is very apt to reinforce primary sexist attitudes on the part of all concerned, since it appears to presuppose that women cannot measure up on their merits. But to presume that proportional hiring quotas could not be met without strong reverse discrimination is also to make that discredited assumption. If, as all available evidence indicates, women in the academic world are on the average just as hard-working, productive, and meritorious as their male colleagues, then there can be no objection to hiring and promoting them at least in accordance with their numbers, and doing so will increase rather than decrease the extent to which success is based upon merit.

VII. ARE QUOTAS NECESSARY?

I have argued that minimum proportional quotas such as I have described would not make the job competition (especially) unfair to men. But it might still be doubted that quotas are necessary to make the competition fair to women. Why not simply attack sexist practices wherever they exist and then let the chips fall as they may? Alan Goldman argues that quotas are not necessary, since, he says, other measures—for example, "active recruitment of minority candidates,

14 Elizabeth Scott tells me that her survey of 1974–1976 figures reveals that, in spite of affirmative action policies, unemployment among women Ph.D.'s who are actively seeking work is about twice as high as among men Ph.D.'s and that the starting salaries of women Ph.D.'s average $1,200 to $1,500 lower than those of men.

the advertisement and application of nondiscriminatory hiring criteria . . . and the enforcement of these provisions by a neutral government agency"[15] would suffice to guarantee equal treatment for women. Goldman claims that if women candidates are as well qualified as men then, given these other measures, they will automatically be hired at least in proportion to their numbers. Indeed, he suggests that the only basis for doubting this claim is "an invidious suspicion of the real inferiority of women . . . even those with Ph.D.'s"[16] That discrimination against women might continue to occur in spite of such affirmative measures short of quotas, he regards as "an untested empirical hypothesis without much *prima facie* plausibility."[17]

In a similar vein, George Sher has argued that blacks, but not women, are entitled to reverse discrimination in hiring, since the former but not the latter have suffered from a poverty syndrome which has denied them the opportunity to obtain the qualifications necessary to compete on an equal basis with white men.[18] He views reverse discrimination—and presumably hiring quotas—as primarily a way of compensating those who suffer from present competitive disadvantages due to past discrimination, and claims that since women are not disadvantaged with respect to (the opportunity to obtain) qualifications, they are not entitled to reverse discrimination.

What both Goldman and Sher overlook, of course, is that women suffer from competitive disadvantages quite apart from any lack of qualifications. Even if primary sexism were to vanish utterly from the minds of all employers, secondary sexist practices such as those we have considered would in all likelihood suffice to per-

petuate the male monopoly of desirable jobs well beyond our lifetimes. Such practices cannot be expected to vanish quickly or spontaneously; to insist that affirmative action measures stop short of the use of quotas is to invite their continuation and proliferation.

VIII. THE COMPENSATORY JUSTICE AND ROLE-MODEL ARGUMENTS

Most of the philosophers who have recently defended the use of goals or quotas in the hiring of women and/or minority group members have assumed that this will necessarily involve at least weak and perhaps strong reverse discrimination, but have argued that it is nevertheless justified as a way of compensating individuals or groups for past injustices or for present disadvantages stemming from past injustices.[19] Others have argued that reverse discrimination is justified not (just) as a form of compensatory justice, but as a means of bringing about certain future goods—for example, raising the status of downtrodden groups,[20] or providing young women and blacks with role models and thus breaking the grip of self-fulfilling expectations which cause them to fail.[21]

If one is intent upon arguing for a policy which would give blacks or women "advantages in employment . . . greater than these same blacks or women would receive in an ongoing just society,"[22] then perhaps it is necessary to appeal to compensatory justice or to the role model or to other utilitarian arguments to justify the *prima facie* unfairness to white males which such a policy involves. But there is no

15 Alan H. Goldman, "Affirmative Action," *Philosophy & Public Affairs* 5, no. 2 (Winter 1976): 185.

16 Goldman, p. 186.

17 Goldman, p. 185.

18 George Sher, "Justifying Reverse Discrimination in Employment," *Philosophy & Public Affairs* 4, no. 2 (Winter 1975): 168.

19 See Bayles and Sher, respectively.

20 Irving Thalberg, "Reverse Discrimination and the Future," *The Philosophical Forum* 5, no. 2: 307.

21 See Marlene Gerber Fried, "In Defense of Preferential Hiring," *The Philosophical Forum* 5, no 2: 316.

22 Charles King, "A Problem Concerning Discrimination," *Reason Papers* no. 2 (Fall 1975), p. 92.

need to use these arguments in justifying a weak quota system such as the one described here, and indeed, it is somewhat misleading to do so. For, as we have seen, such a system would not lower the average male candidate's overall chances of success to below what they would be if the selection were based on merit alone. It would simply raise women's chances, and lower men's, to a closer approximation of what they would be in an ongoing just society, in which the "straight merit" principle prevailed. This being the case, the fact that quotas may serve to compensate some women for past or present wrongs, or to provide others with role models, must be seen as a fortuitous side effect of their use and not their primary reasons for being. The primary reason for weak quotas is simply to increase the present fairness of the competition.

Furthermore, there are problems with the compensatory justice and role-model arguments which make their use hazardous. It is not clear that either suffices to justify any use of reverse discrimination beyond what may in practice (appear to) be necessary to implement weak quotas. For, granted that society as a whole has some obligation to provide compensation to the victims of past discrimination, and assuming that at least some women candidates for university positions are suitable beneficiaries of such compensation, it is by no means clear that male candidates should be forced to bear most of the burden for providing that compensation. It would be plausible to argue on the basis of compensatory justice for, say, tax-supported *extra* positions for women, since then the burden would be distributed relatively equitably. But compensatory justice provides no case for placing an extra, and seemingly punitive, burden on male candidates, who are no more responsible for past and present discrimination against women that the rest of us.

Similarly, however badly women may need role models, it is not clear that male candidates should be disproportionately penalized in order to provide them. It can be argued on the basis of simple fairness that male candidates' chances should not be allowed to remain *above* what they would be in a just society; but to justify reducing them to *below* that point requires a stronger argument than simply appealing to compensatory justice or the need for role models.

Nor does it help to argue that the real source of the injustice to male candidates, if and when preferential hiring of women results in lowering the former's chances to below what they would be in a just society, is not the preferential hiring policy itself, but something else. Thomas Nagel, for instance, argues that reverse discrimination is not seriously unjust, even if it means that it is harder for white men to get certain sorts of jobs than it is for women and blacks who are no better qualified, since, he suggests, the real source of the injustice is the entire system of providing differential rewards on the basis of differential abilities.[23] And Marlene Fried argues that the root of the injustice is not preferential hiring, but the failure of those with the power to do so to expand job opportunities so that blacks and women could be hired in increasing numbers without hiring fewer men.[24]

Unfortunately, we cannot, on the one hand, reject secondary sexist practices because of their contingent and perhaps unintended discriminatory effects, and, on the other hand, accept extenuations such as these for a policy which would, in practice, discriminate unfairly against (white) men. These other sources of injustice are real enough: but this does not alter the fact that if reverse discrimination were practiced to the extent that certain men's chances of success were reduced to below those enjoyed, on the average, by comparably qualified women, then it would at least give every appearance of being unfair to those men. After all, the primary insight necessary for recognizing the injustice of

23 Thomas Nagel, "Equal Treatment and Compensatory Justice," *Philosophy & Public Affairs* 2, no. 4 (Summer 1973): 348–363, especially p. 353.
24 Fried, p. 318.

468   CHAPTER SEVEN: AFFIRMATIVE ACTION

secondary sexist polices is that a policy must be judged, at least in part, by its consequences in practice, regardless of whether or not these consequences are a stated or intended part of the policy. If a given policy results in serious and extensive injustice, then it is no excuse that this injustice has its roots in deeper social injustices which are not themselves easily amenable to change, at least not if there is any feasible way of altering the policy so as to lessen the resulting injustice.

I think we may conclude that while proportional quotas for the hiring of women are justified both on the basis of the merit principle and as a way of improving the overall fairness of the competition, it is considerably more difficult to justify the use of higher quotas. The distinction between such weak quotas and higher quotas is crucial, since although higher quotas have in practice rarely been implemented, the apparent injustice implied by what are typically *assumed* to be higher quotas has generated a backlash which threatens to undermine affirmative action entirely. If quotas are abandoned, or if they are nominally adopted but never enforced, then employers will be free to continue using secondary and even primary sexist hiring criteria, and it is probable that none of us will see the day when women enjoy job opportunities commensurate with their abilities and qualifications.

Review Questions

1. According to Warren, what is primary sexism?
2. What is secondary sexism, as it is explained by Warren?
3. Why does Warren think that secondary sexism is unfair?
4. What is the weak quota system recommended by Warren?
5. How does Warren characterize the quota vs. goals controversy?
6. According to Warren, why is the use of weak reverse discrimination to meet proportional hiring quotas not unfair?
7. Why does Warren think that quotas are necessary to make competition for jobs fair for women?
8. What are the compensatory justice and role-model arguments?
9. Why doesn't Warren accept these arguments?

Discussion Questions

1. Is the sort of weak reverse discrimination advocated by Warren unfair to men? Explain your position.
2. Is the use of hiring quotas really necessary, as Warren says? What do you think?

The Message of Affirmative Action

THOMAS E. HILL, JR.

Thomas E. Hill, Jr., is professor of philosophy at the University of North Carolina. He is the author of *Autonomy and Self-Respect* (1991).

Hill distinguishes between forward- and backward-looking arguments for affirmative action. He finds problems in both. Among other things, they convey the wrong messages to blacks and women who benefit from affirmative action, and to white males who are disadvantaged by the programs. As an alternative approach, Hill proposes that we see values as "cross-time wholes," with the past, present, and future connected in a narrative whole. Using this approach, he suggests that the appropriate message of affirmative action should emphasize the ideal of mutual respect and trust among human beings in a community over time.

AFFIRMATIVE ACTION PROGRAMS remain controversial, I suspect, partly because the familiar arguments for and against them start from significantly different moral perspectives. Thus I want to step back for a while from the details of debate about particular programs and give attention to the moral viewpoints presupposed in different *types* of argument. My aim, more specifically, is to compare the "messages" expressed when affirmative action is defended from different moral perspectives. Exclusively forward-looking (for example, utilitarian) arguments, I suggest, tend to express the wrong message, but this is also true of exclusively backward-looking (for example, reparation-based) arguments. However, a moral outlook that focuses on cross-temporal narrative values (such as mutually respectful social relations) suggests a more appropriate account of what affirmative action should try to express. Assessment of the message, admittedly, is only one aspect of a complex issue, but it is a relatively neglected one. My discussion takes for granted some common-sense ideas about the communicative function of action, and so I begin with these.

Actions, as the saving goes, often *speak* louder than words. There are times, too, when only actions can effectively communicate the message we want to convey and times when giving a message is a central part of the purpose of action. What our actions say to others depends largely, though not entirely, upon our avowed reasons for acting; and this is a matter for reflective decision, not something we discover later by looking back at what we did and its effects. The decision is important because "the same act" can have very different consequences, depending upon how we choose to justify it. In a sense, acts done for different reasons are not "the same act" even if they are otherwise similar, and so not merely the consequences but also the moral nature of our acts depends in part on our decisions about the reasons for doing them.

Source: Thomas E. Hill, Jr., "The Message of Affirmative Action," from *Social Philosophy & Policy*, Vol. 8, No. 2 (1991), pp. 108–129. Copyright © 1991 Social Philosophy and Policy Foundation. Reprinted with the permission of Cambridge University Press.

Unfortunately, the message actually conveyed by our actions does not depend only on our intentions and reasons, for our acts may have a meaning for others quite at odds with what we hoped to express. Others may misunderstand our intentions, doubt our sincerity, or discern a subtext that undermines the primary message. Even if sincere, well-intended, and successfully conveyed, the message of an act or policy does not by itself justify the means by which it is conveyed; it is almost always a relevant factor, however, in the moral assessment of an act or policy. . . .

I shall focus attention for a while upon this relatively neglected issue of the message of affirmative action. In particular, I want to consider what messages we *should try* to give with affirmative action programs and what messages we should try to avoid. What is the best way to convey the intended message, and indeed whether it is likely to be heard, are empirical questions that I cannot settle; but the question I propose to consider is nonetheless important, and it is a *prior* question. What do we want to say with our affirmative action programs, and why? Since the message that is received and its consequences are likely to depend to some extent on what we decide, in all sincerity, to be the rationale for such programs, it would be premature and foolish to try to infer or predict these outcomes without adequate reflection on what the message and rationale should be. Also, for those who accept the historical/narrative perspective described in [this essay], there is additional reason to focus first on the desired message; for that perspective treats the message of affirmative action not merely as a minor side effect to be weighed in, for or against, but rather as an important part of the legitimate purpose of affirmative action.

Much useful discussion has been devoted to the constitutionality of affirmative action programs, to the relative moral rights involved, and to the advantages and disadvantages of specific types of programs.[1] By deemphasizing these matters here, I do not mean to suggest that they are unimportant. Even more, my remarks are not meant to convey the message, "It doesn't matter what we do or achieve, all that matters is what we *say*." To the contrary, I believe that mere gestures are insufficient and that universities cannot even communicate what they should by affirmative action policies unless these are sincerely designed to result in increased opportunities for those disadvantaged and insulted by racism and sexism. . . .

STRATEGIES OF JUSTIFICATION: CONSEQUENCES AND REPARATIONS

Some arguments for affirmative action look exclusively to its future benefits. The idea is that what has happened in the past is not in itself relevant to what we should do; at most, it provides clues as to what acts and policies are likely to bring about the best future. The philosophical tradition associated with this approach is utilitarianism, which declares that the morally right act is whatever produces the best consequences.

1 See, for example, the following: John Arthur, ed., *Morality and Moral Controversies,* 2nd ed. (Englewood Cliffs: Prentice-Hall, Inc., 1986), ch. 11, pp. 305–47; William T. Blackstone and Robert D. Heslep. eds., *Social Justice and Preferential Treatment* (Athens: The University of Georgia Press, 1977); Bernard Boxill, *Blacks and Social Justice* (Totowa: Rowman and Allanheld, 1984); Marshall Cohen, Thomas Nagel, and Thomas Scanlon, eds., *Equality and Preferential Treatment* (Princeton: Princeton University Press, 1977); Robert K. Fullinwider, *The Reverse Discrimination Controversy* (Totowa: Rowman and Littlefield, 1980); Alan H. Goldman, *Justice and Reverse Discrimination* (Princeton: Princeton University Press, 1979); Kent Greenawalt, *Discrimination and Reverse Discrimination* (New York: Alfred A. Knopf, 1983), Barry R. Gross, ed., *Reverse Discrimination* (Buffalo: Prometheus Press, 1977); Thomas A. Mappes and Jane S. Zembaty, eds., *Social Ethics* (2nd ed.; New York: McGraw-Hill Book Company, 1982), ch. 5, pp. 159–98.

Traditionally, utilitarianism evaluated consequences in terms of happiness and unhappiness, but the anticipated consequences of affirmative action are often described more specifically. For example, some argue that affirmative action will ease racial tensions, prevent riots, improve services in minority neighborhoods, reduce unemployment, remove inequities in income distribution, eliminate racial and sexual prejudice, and enhance the self-esteem of blacks and women. Some have called attention to the fact that women and minorities provide alternative perspectives on history, literature, philosophy, and politics, and that this has beneficial effects for both education and research.

These are important considerations, not irrelevant to the larger responsibilities of universities. For several reasons, however, I think it is a mistake for advocates of affirmative action to rest their case exclusively on such forward-looking arguments. First, critics raise reasonable doubts about whether affirmative action is necessary to achieve these admirable results. The economist Thomas Sowell argues that a free-market economy can achieve the same results more efficiently; his view is therefore that even if affirmative action has beneficial results (which he denies), it is not necessary for the purpose.[2] Though Sowell's position can be contested, the controversy itself tends to weaken confidence in the entirely forward-looking defense of affirmative action.

An even more obvious reason why affirmative action advocates should explore other avenues for its defense is that the exclusively forward-looking approach must give equal consideration to possible negative consequences of affirmative action. It may be, for example, that affirmative action will temporarily increase racial tensions, especially if its message is misunderstood. Even

legitimate use of race and sex categories may encourage others to abuse the categories for unjust purposes. If applied without sensitive regard to the educational and research purposes of the university, affirmative action might severely undermine its efforts to fulfill these primary responsibilities. If affirmative action programs were to lower academic standards for blacks and women, they would run the risk of damaging the respect that highly qualified blacks and women have earned by leading others to suspect that these highly qualified people lack the merits of white males in the same positions. This could also be damaging to the self-respect of those who accept affirmative action positions. Even programs that disavow "lower standards" unfortunately arouse the suspicion that they don't really do so, and this by itself can cause problems. Although I believe that well-designed affirmative action programs can minimize these negative effects, the fact that they are a risk is a reason for not resting the case for affirmative action on a delicate balance of costs and benefits.

Reflection on the *message* of affirmative action also leads me to move beyond entirely forward-looking arguments. For if the sole purpose is to bring about a brighter future, then we give the wrong message to both the white males who are rejected and to the women and blacks who are benefited. To the latter what we say, in effect, is this: "Never mind how you have been treated. Forget about the fact that your race or sex has in the past been actively excluded and discouraged, and that you yourself may have had handicaps due to prejudice. Our sole concern is to bring about certain good results in the future, and giving you a break happens to be a useful means for doing this. Don't think this is a recognition of your rights as in individual or your disadvantages as a member of a group. Nor does it mean that we have confidence in your abilities. We would do the same for those who are privileged and academically inferior if it would have the same socially beneficial results."

2 Thomas Sowell, *Race and Economics* (New York: David McKay Co., 1975), ch. 6; *Markets and Minorities* (New York: Basic Books, Inc., 1981), pp. 114–15.

To the white male who would have had a university position but for affirmative action, the exclusively forward-looking approach says: "We deny you the place you otherwise would have had simply as a means to produce certain socially desirable outcomes. We have not judged that others are more deserving, or have a right, to the place we are giving them instead of you. Past racism and sexism are irrelevant. The point is just that the sacrifice of your concerns is a useful means to the larger end of the future welfare of others."

This, I think, is the wrong message to give. It is also unnecessary. The proper alternative, however, is not to ignore the possible future benefits of affirmative action but rather to take them into account as a part of a larger picture.

A radically different strategy for justifying affirmative action is to rely on backward-looking arguments. Such arguments call our attention to certain events in the past and assert that *because* these past events occurred, we have certain duties now. The modern philosopher who most influentially endorsed such arguments was W. D. Ross.[3] He argued that there are duties of fidelity, justice, gratitude, and reparation that have a moral force independent of any tendency these may have to promote good consequences. The fact that you have made a promise, for example, gives you a strong moral reason to do what you promised, whether or not doing so will on balance have more beneficial consequences. The Rossian principle that is often invoked in affirmative action debates is a principle of reparation. This says that those who wrongfully injure others have a (*prima facie*) duty to apologize and make restitution. Those who have wronged others owe reparation.

James Forman dramatically expressed this idea in New York in 1969 when he presented "The Black Manifesto," which demanded five hundred million dollars in reparation to American blacks from white churches and synagogues.[4] Such organizations, the Manifesto contends, contributed to our history of slavery and racial injustice; as a result, they incurred a debt to the black community that still suffers from its effects. Objections were immediately raised: for example, both slaves and slave-owners are no longer alive; not every American white is guilty of racial oppression; and not every black in America was a victim of slavery and its aftermath.

Bernard Boxill, author of *Blacks and Social Justice,* developed a more sophisticated version of the backward-looking argument with a view to meeting these objections.[5] Let us admit, he says, that both the perpetrators and the primary victims of slavery are gone, and let us not insist that contemporary whites are guilty of perpetrating further injustices. Some do, and some do not, and public administrators cannot be expected to sort out the guilty from the nonguilty. However, reparation, or at least some "compensation,"[6] is still owed, because contemporary whites have reaped the profits of past in-

---

3 W D. Ross, *The Right and the Good* (Oxford: Clarendon Press, 1930).

4 James Forman was at the time director of international affairs for SNCC (Student Nonviolent Coordinating Committee). The "Black Manifesto" stems from an economic development conference sponsored by the Interreligious Foundation for Community Organizations, April 26, 1969, and presented by Forman at the New York Interdenominational Riverside Church on May 4, 1969. Later the demand was raised to three billion dollars. See Robert S. Lecky and H. Elliot Wright, *Black Manifesto* (New York: Sheed and Ward Publishers, 1969), pp. vii, 114–26.

5 Bernard Boxill, "The Morality of Reparation," *Social Theory and Practice,* vol. 2, no. 1 (1972), pp. 113–22. and *Blacks and Social Justice,* ch. 7

6 In the article cited above, Boxill calls what is owed "reparation," but in the book (above) he calls it "compensation." The latter term, preferred by many, is used more broadly to cover not only restitution for wrongdoing but also "making up" for deficiencies and losses that are not anyone's fault (for example, naturally caused physical handicaps, or damages unavoidably resulting from legitimate and necessary activities). We could describe the backward-looking arguments

justice to blacks. He asks us to consider the analogy with a stolen bicycle. Suppose my parent stole your parent's bicycle some time ago, both have since died, and I "inherited" the bike from my parent, the thief. Though I may be innocent of any wrongdoing (so far), I am in possession of stolen goods rightfully belonging to you, the person who would have inherited the bike if it had not been stolen. For me to keep the bike and declare that I owe you nothing would be wrong, even if I was not the cause of your being deprived. By analogy, present-day whites owe reparations to contemporary blacks, not because they are themselves guilty of causing the disadvantages of blacks, but because they are in possession of advantages that fell to them as a result of the gross injustices of their ancestors. Special advantages continue to fall even to innocent whites because of the ongoing prejudice of their white neighbors.

Although it raises many questions, this line of argument acknowledges some important points missing in most exclusively forward-looking arguments: for example, it stresses the (intrinsic) relevance of past injustice and it calls attention to the rights and current disadvantages of blacks (in contrast with future benefits for others). When developed as an argument for affirmative action, it does not accuse all white males of prejudice and wrongdoing; at the same time, however, it sees the fundamental value as justice. As a result, it avoids giving the message to either rejected white males or reluctant affirmative action applicants that they are "mere means" to a social goal that is largely independent of their rights and interests as individuals.

There are, however, serious problems in trying to justify affirmative action by this backward-looking argument, especially if it is treated

presented here as demands for "compensation" rather than "reparation," so long as we keep in mind that the compensation is supposed to be due as the morally appropriate response to past wrongdoing.

as the exclusive or central argument. Degrees of being advantaged and disadvantaged are notoriously hard to measure. New immigrants have not shared our history of past injustices, and so the argument may not apply to them in any straightforward way. The argument appeals to controversial ideas about property rights, inheritance, and group responsibilities. Some argue that affirmative action tends to benefit the least disadvantaged blacks and women; though this does not mean that they are owed nothing, their claims would seem to have lower priority than the needs of the most disadvantaged. Some highly qualified blacks and women object that affirmative action is damaging to their reputations and self-esteem, whereas the reparation argument seems to assume that it is a welcome benefit to all blacks and women.

If we focus on the message that the backward-looking argument sends, there are also some potential problems. Though rightly acknowledging past injustice, the argument (by itself) seems to convey the message that racial and sexual oppression consisted primarily in the loss of tangible goods, or the deprivation of specific rights and opportunities, that can be "paid back" in kind. The background idea, which goes back at least to Aristotle, is that persons wrongfully deprived of their "due" can justly demand an "equivalent" to what they have lost.[7] But, while specific deprivations were an important part of our racist and sexist past, they are far from the whole story. Among the worst wrongs then, as now, were humiliations and contemptuous treatment of a type that cannot, strictly, be "paid back." The problem was, and is, not just that specific rights and advantages were denied, but that prejudicial attitudes damaged self-esteem, undermined motivations, limited realistic options, and made even "officially open" opportunities

7 Aristotle, *Nicomachean Ethics,* tr. A. K. Thomson (Baltimore: Penguin Books, Inc., 1955), bk. V, esp. pp. 143–55.

seem undesirable. Racism and sexism were (and are) *insults,* not merely tangible *injuries.*[8] These are not the sort of thing that can be adequately measured and repaid with equivalents. The trouble with treating insulting racist and sexist practices on a pure reparation model is not merely the practical difficulty of identifying the offenders, determining the degree of guilt, assessing the amount of payment due, etc. It is also that penalty payments and compensation for lost benefits are not the only, or primary, moral responses that are called for. When affirmative action is defended exclusively by analogy with reparation, it tends to express the misleading message that the evils of racism and sexism are all tangible losses that can be "paid off"; by being silent on the insulting nature of racism and sexism, it tends to add insult to insult.

The message suggested by the reparation argument, by itself, also seems objectionable because it conveys the idea that higher education, teaching, and doing research are mainly benefits awarded in response to self-centered demands. The underlying picture too easily suggested is that applicants are a group of self-interested, bickering people, each grasping for limited "goodies" and insisting on a right to them. When a university grants an opportunity through affirmative action, its message would seem to be this. "We concede that you have a valid claim to this benefit and we yield to your demand, though this is not to suggest that we have confidence in your abilities or any desire to have you here." This invitation seems too concessive, the atmosphere too adversarial, and the emphasis too much on the benefits rather than the responsibilities of being a part of the university.

PHILOSOPHICAL INTERLUDE: AN ALTERNATIVE PERSPECTIVE

Here I want to digress from the explicit consideration of affirmative action in order to consider more abstract philosophical questions about the ways we evaluate acts and policies. At the risk of oversimplifying, I want to contrast some assumptions that have, until recently, been dominant in ethical theory with alternatives suggested by contemporary philosophers who emphasize historical context, narrative unity, and community values.[9] Although these alternatives, in my opinion, have not yet been adequately developed, there seem to be at least four distinguishable themes worth considering.

First, when we reflect on what we deeply value, we find that we care not merely about the present moment and each future moment in isolation but also about how our past, present, and future cohere or fit together into a life and a piece of history. Some of our values, we might say, are cross-time wholes, with past, present, and future parts united in certain ways. Thus, for example, the commitments I have made, the projects I have begun, what I have shared with those I love, the injuries I have caused, and the hopes I have encouraged importantly affect both whether I am satisfied with my present and how I want the future to go.

Second, in reflecting on stretches of our lives and histories, we frequently use evaluative concepts drawn more from narrative literature than from accounting. Thus, for example, we think of our lives as having significant beginnings, crises, turning points, dramatic tension, character development, climaxes, resolutions, comic interludes, tragic disruptions, and eventually fitting

---

8 See Boxill, *Blacks and Social Justice,* pp. 132ff., and Ronald Dworkin, "Reverse Discrimination," in *Taking Rights Seriously* (Cambridge: Harvard University Press, 1978), pp. 231ff.

9 See, for example, Alasdair MacIntyre, *After Virtue* (Notre Dame: Notre Dame University Press, 1981). Similar themes are found in Carol Gilligan's *In A Different Voice* (Cambridge: Harvard University Press, 1982) and in Lawrence Blum, *Friendship, Altruism, and Morality* (Boston: Routledge and Kegan Paul, 1980).

(or unfitting) endings. The value of any moment often depends on what came before and what we anticipate to follow. And since our lives are intertwined with others in a common history, we also care about how our moments cohere with others' life stories. The past is seen as more than a time of accumulated debts and assets, and the future is valued as more than an opportunity for reinvesting and cashing in assets.

Third, evaluation must take into account one's particular historical context, including one's cultural, national, and ethnic traditions, and the actual individuals in one's life. Sometimes this point is exaggerated, I think, to suggest a dubious cultural relativism or "particularism" in ethics: for example, the thesis that what is valuable for a person is defined by the person's culture or that evaluations imply no general reasons beyond particular judgments, such as "That's *our* way" and "John is *my* son."[10] But, construed modestly as a practical or epistemological point, it seems obvious enough, on reflection, that we should take into account the historical context of our acts and that we are often in a better position to judge what is appropriate in particular cases than we are to articulate universally valid premises supporting the judgment. . . .

Fourth, when we evaluate particular acts and policies as parts of lives and histories, what is often most important is the value of the whole, which cannot always be determined by "summing up" the values of the parts. Lives, histo-

ries, and interpersonal relations over time are what G. E. Moore called "organic unities"— that is, wholes the value of which is not necessarily the sum of the values of the parts.[11] The point here is not merely the obvious practical limitation that we cannot measure and quantify values in this area. More fundamentally, the idea is that it would be a mistake even to try to evaluate certain unities by assessing different parts in isolation from one another, then adding up all their values. Suppose, for example, a woman with terminal cancer considered two quite different ways of spending her last days. One way, perhaps taking a world cruise, might seem best when evaluated in terms of the quality of each future moment, in isolation from her past and her present ties; but another way, perhaps seeking closure in projects and with estranged family members, might seem more valuable when seen as a part of her whole life.

Taken together, these ideas cast doubt on both the exclusively forward-looking method of assessment and the standard backward-looking alternative. Consequentialism, or the exclusively forward-looking method, attempts to determine what ought to be done at present by fixing attention entirely on future results. To be sure, any sensible consequentialist will consult the past for lessons and clues helpful in predicting future outcomes: for example, recalling that you offended someone yesterday may enable you to predict that the person will be cool to you tomorrow unless you apologize. But beyond this, consequentialists have no concern with the past, for their "bottom line" is always "what happens from now on," evaluated independently of the earlier chapters of our lives and histories. For the consequentialist, assessing a life or history from a narrative perspective becomes impossible or at least bizarre, as what must be evaluated at each shifting moment is "the story from now

---

10 Regarding cultural and moral relativism see, for example, David B. Wong, *Moral Relativity* (Berkeley and Los Angeles: University of California Press, 1984), with an excellent bibliography, and Richard B. Brandt, *Ethical Theory*, (Englewood Cliffs: Prentice-Hall Inc., 1959), ch. 11, pp. 271–94. Versions of particularism are presented in Andrew Oldenquist, " Loyalties," *The Journal of Philosophy*, vol. 79 (1982), pp. 173–93; Lawrence Blum, *Friendship, Altruism, and Morality;* and Bernard Williams, "Persons, Character and Morality" in *Moral Luck* (New York: Cambridge University Press, 1981), pp. 1–19.

11 G. E. Moore, *Principia Ethica* (Cambridge University Press, 1912), pp. 27ff.

on" independently of what has already been written.[12]

The standard Rossian alternative to this exclusively forward-looking perspective is to introduce certain (*prima facie*) *duties* to respond to certain past events in specified ways—for example, pay debts, keep promises, pay reparation for injuries. These duties are supposed to be self-evident and universal (though they are *prima facie*), and they do not hold because they tend to promote anything good or valuable. Apart from aspects of the acts mentioned in the principles (for example, fulfilling a promise, returning favors, not injuring, etc.), details of historical and personal context are considered irrelevant.

By contrast, the narrative perspective sketched above considers the past as an integral part of the valued unities that we aim to bring about, not merely as a source of duties. If one has negligently wronged another, Ross regards this past event as generating a duty to pay reparations even if doing so will result in nothing good. But from the narrative perspective, the past becomes relevant in a further way. One may say, for example, that the *whole* consisting of your life and your relationship with that person from the time of the injury into the future will be a better thing if you acknowledge the wrong and make efforts to restore what you have damaged. For Ross, the duty is generated by the past and unrelated to bringing about anything good; from the narrative perspective, however, the requirement is just what is required to bring about a valuable connected whole with past, present, and future parts—the best way to complete a chapter, so to speak, in two intersecting lifestories.

So far, neither the Rossian nor the narrative account has told us much about the ultimate reasons for their evaluations, but they reveal ways to consider the matter. The Rossian asks us to judge particular cases in the light of "self-evident" general principles asserting that certain past events tend to generate present (or future) duties. The alternative perspective calls for examining lives and relationships, over time, in context, as organic unities evaluated (partly) in narrative terms.

To illustrate, consider two persons, John and Mary. John values having Mary's trust and respect, and conversely, Mary values having John's; moreover, John values the fact that Mary values being trusted and respected by him, and conversely Mary values the same about John.[13]

Now suppose that other people have been abusive and insulting to Mary, and that John is worried that Mary may take things he had said and done as similarly insulting, even though he does not think that he consciously meant them this way. Though he is worried, Mary does not seem to suspect him; he fears that he may only make matters worse if he raises the issue, creating suspicions she did not have or focusing on doubts that he cannot allay. Perhaps, he thinks, their future relationship would be better served if he just remained silent, hoping that the trouble, if any, will fade in time. If so, consequentialist thinking would recommend silence. Acknowledging this, he might nonetheless feel that duties of friendship and fidelity demand that he raise the issue, regardless of whether or not the result will be worse. Then he would be thinking as a Rossian.

But, instead, he might look at the problem from an alternative perspective, asking himself what response best affirms and contributes to

---

12 That is, the evaluation is independent of the past in the sense that the past makes no intrinsic difference to the final judgment and the future is not evaluated as a part of a temporal whole including the past. As noted, however, consequentialists will still look to the past for lessons and clues about how to bring about the best future.

13 For an interesting illustration of reciprocal desires (e.g., A wanting B, B wanting A, A wanting B to want A, B wanting A to want B, A wanting B to want A to want B, etc.), see Thomas Nagel, "Sexual Perversion," *The Journal of Philosophy,* vol. 66 (1969).

the sort of ongoing relationship he has and wants to continue with Mary. Given their history together, it is important to him to do his part towards restoring the relationship if it indeed has been marred by perceived insults or suspicions. To be sure, he wants *future* relations of mutual trust and respect, but not at any price and not by just any means. Their history together is not irrelevant, for what he values is not merely a future of a certain kind, but that their relationship over time be of the sort he values. He values an ongoing history of mutual trust and respect that *calls for* an explicit response in this current situation, not merely as a means to a brighter future but as a present affirmation of what they value together. Even if unsure which course will be best for the future, he may be reasonably confident that the act that best expresses his respect and trust (and his valuing hers, etc.) is to confront the problem, express his regrets, reaffirm his respect, ask for her trust, be patient with her doubts, and welcome an open dialogue. If the insults were deep and it is not entirely clear whether or not he really associated himself with them, then mere words may not be enough to convey the message or even to assure himself of his own sincerity. Positive efforts, even at considerable cost, may be needed to express appropriately and convincingly what needs to be said. How the next chapter unfolds is not entirely up to him, and he would not be respectful if he presumed otherwise by trying to manipulate the best future unilaterally.

The example concerns only two persons and their personal values, but it illustrates a perspective that one can also take regarding moral problems involving many persons.

MUTUAL RESPECT, FAIR OPPORTUNITY, AND AFFIRMATIVE ACTION

Turning back to our main subject, I suggest that some of the values that give affirmative action its

point are best seen as cross-time values that fall outside the exclusively forward-looking and backward-looking perspectives. They include having a history of racial and gender relations governed, so far as possible, by the ideals of mutual respect, trust, and fair opportunity for all.

Our national history provides a context of increasing recognition and broader interpretation of the democratic ideal of the equal dignity of all human beings—an ideal that has been flagrantly abused from the outset, partially affirmed in the bloody Civil War, and increasingly extended in the civil rights movement, but is still far from being fully respected. More specifically, blacks and women were systematically treated in an unfair and demeaning way by public institutions, including universities, until quite recently, and few could confidently claim to have rooted out racism and sexism even now.[14] The historical context is not what grounds or legitimates democratic values, but it is the background of the current problem, the sometimes admirable and often ugly way the chapters up until now have been written.

Consider the social ideal of mutual respect and trust among citizens. The problem of implementing this in the current context is different from the problem in the two-person example discussed above, for the history of our racial and gender relations is obviously not an idyllic story of mutual respect and trust momentarily, interrupted by a crisis. Even so, the question to ask is not merely, "What will promote respectful and trusting racial and gender relations in future generations?", but rather, "Given our checkered past, how can we appropriately express the social value of mutual respect and trust that we want, so far as possible, to characterize our history?" We cannot change our racist and sexist past, but

---

14 Racism and sexism present significantly different problems, but I shall not try to analyze the differences here. For the most part my primary focus is on racism, but the relevance of the general type of moral thinking considered here to the problems of sexism should nonetheless be evident.

we also cannot express full respect for those present individuals who live in its aftermath if we ignore it. What is called for is not merely repayment of tangible debts incurred by past injuries, but also a message to counter the deep insult inherent in racism and sexism. . . .

CONCLUSION

The message is called for not just as a means to future good relations or a dutiful payment of a debt incurred by our past. It is called for by the ideal of being related to other human beings over time, so that our histories and biographies reflect the responses of those who deeply care about fair opportunity, mutual trust, and respect for all.

If so, what should public universities try to say to those offered opportunities through affirmative action? Perhaps something like this: "Whether we individually are among the guilty or not, we acknowledge that you have been wronged—if not by specific injuries which could be named and repaid, at least by the humiliating and debilitating attitudes prevalent in our country and our institutions. We deplore and denounce these attitudes and the wrongs that spring from them. We acknowledge that, so far, most of you have had your opportunities in life diminished by the effects of these attitudes, and we want no one's prospects to be diminished by injustice. We recognize your understandable grounds for suspicion and mistrust when we express these high-minded sentiments, and we want not only to ask respectfully for your trust but also to give concrete evidence of our sincerity. We welcome you respectfully into the university community and ask you to take a full share of the responsibilities as well as the benefits. By creating special opportunities, we recognize the disadvantages you have probably suffered; we show our respect for your talents and our commitment to the ideals of the university however, by not faking grades and honors for you. Given current

attitudes about affirmative action, accepting this position will probably have drawbacks as well as advantages.[15] It is an opportunity and a responsibility offered neither as charity nor as entitlement, but rather as part of a special effort to welcome and encourage minorities and women to participate more fully in the university at all levels. We believe that this program affirms some of the best ideals implicit in our history without violating the rights of any applicants. We hope that you will choose to accept the position in this spirit as well as for your own benefit."

The appropriate message is no doubt harder to communicate to those who stand to lose some traditional advantages under a legitimate affirmative action program. But if we set aside

---

15 How severe these drawbacks are will, of course, depend upon the particular means of affirmative action that are selected and how appropriate these are for the situation. For example, if, to meet mandated quotas, highly-ranked colleges and universities offer special admission to students not expected to succeed, then they may well be misleading those students into a wasteful and humiliating experience when those students could have thrived at lower-ranked educational institutions. This practice was explicitly rejected in the policies at Pomona College and at U.C.L.A.. but William Allen suggested to me in discussion that, in his opinion, the practice is quite common. The practice, I think, is unconscionable, and my argument in no way supports it.

Geoffrey Miller described in discussion another possible affirmative action program that would be quite inappropriate to the circumstances but is again not supported by the line of argument I have suggested. He asks us to imagine a "permanent underclass" of immigrants who are "genetically or culturally deficient" and as a result fail to succeed. Since we do not share a common social and cultural history of injustice resulting in their condition, the historical dimension of my case for affirmative action is missing. And since they are a "permanent" underclass, and thus the "genetic or cultural deficiencies" that result in their failure cannot be altered, one cannot argue that universities can help them or even can sincerely give them an encouraging "message" through affirmative action. This does not mean, however, that there are not other reasons for society to extend appropriate help. Also, any suggestion that certain urban populations that are now *called* a "permanent underclass" are accurately and fairly described by the "fictional" example is politically charged and needs careful examination.

practical difficulties and suppose that the proper message could be sincerely given and accepted as such, what would it say? Ideally, it would convey an understanding of the moral reasoning for the program; perhaps, in conclusion, it would say something like the following.

"These are the concerns that we felt made necessary the policy under which the university is temporarily giving special attention to women and minorities. We respect your rights to formal justice and to a policy guided by the university's education and research mission as well as its social responsibilities. Our policy in no way implies the view that your opportunities are less important than others', but we estimate (roughly, as we must) that as a white male you have probably had advantages and encouragement that for a long time have been systematically, unfairly, insultingly unavailable to most women and minorities. We deplore invidious race and gender distinctions; we hope that no misunderstanding of our program will prolong them. Unfortunately, nearly all blacks and women have been disadvantaged to some degree by bias against their groups, and it is impractical for universities to undertake the detailed investigations that would be needed to assess how much particular individuals have suffered or gained from racism and sexism. We appeal to you to share the historical values of fair opportunity and mutual respect that underlie this policy; we hope that, even though its effects may be personally disappoint-ing, you can see the policy as an appropriate response to the current situation."

Unfortunately, as interests conflict and tempers rise, it is difficult to convey this idea without giving an unintended message as well. White males unhappy about the immediate effects of affirmative action may read the policy as saying that "justice" is the official word for giving preferential treatment to whatever group one happens to favor. Some may see a subtext insinuating that blacks and women are naturally inferior and "cannot make it on their own." Such cynical readings reveal either misunderstanding or the willful refusal to take the moral reasoning underlying affirmative action seriously. They pose serious obstacles to the success of affirmative action—practical problems that may be more intractable than respectful moral disagreement and counter-argument. But some types of affirmative action invite misunderstanding and suspicion more than others. For this reason, anyone who accepts the general case for affirmative action suggested here would do well to reexamine in detail the means by which they hope to communicate its message.[16]

16 Although my aim in this paper has been to survey general types of arguments for thinking that some sort of affirmative action is needed, rather than to argue for any particular program, one cannot reasonably implement the general idea without considering many contextual factors that I have set aside here. Thus, the need for more detailed discussion is obvious.

Review Questions

1. What does Hill mean by the "message" of affirmative action programs? How do we determine what it is?
2. What are the forward-looking arguments for affirmative action, according to Hill? What problems does Hill detect in these arguments?
3. What is the basic principle in the backward-looking arguments for affirmative action, according to Hill? Hill sees serious problems in these arguments. What are they?
4. What does Hill mean by saying that some of our values are "cross-time wholes"? How is this related to narrative perspective and historical context?
5. What does Hill recommend as the appropriate message of affirmative action?

Discussion Questions

1. Is Hill's message to the white male who is denied admission to school acceptable? Why or why not?
2. What is Hill's message to the woman or the African American who does not want to benefit from affirmative action, who wants to be judged on merit alone? Is this an appropriate message? Explain your answer.
3. Hill talks only about blacks and women, but of course there are other disadvantaged minorities, such as Hispanics and Native Americans. Isn't it an insult to leave them out of consideration? If not, then what is Hill's message to them?

Problem Cases

1. Supreme Court Law Clerks

The law clerks hired by the Supreme Court justices play a very important behind-the-scenes role in screening cases and drafting court opinions; yet, very few of them are minorities. According to *USA Today* (December 11, 1998), 428 law clerks have been hired by the current Court; of these only 7 (or 1.6%) have been African American, and only 5 (or 1.2%) have been Hispanic. One quarter have been women.

Chief Justice William Rehnquist has never hired a black law clerk, and he has been targeted for criticism by black civil rights and labor activists. In October 1998, nearly one thousand protesters converged on the Court to voice their objections to the hiring practices of the Court, and particularly those of Justice Rehnquist. Roger Wilkins, a civil rights scholar, said, "If the chief justice can't find a single black law clerk in more than a quarter of a century, that speaks volumes about his soul."

Chief Justice Rehnquist refused to meet with the protesters, but about a month later, in December 1998, he issued a letter blaming the lack of minority law clerks on the scarcity of minorities among his preferred group, namely, Ivy League graduates who have already clerked for a federal judge.

Critics reply that Chief Justice Rehnquist needs to conduct a broader search. He could follow the example set by Justice Sandra Day O'Connor, who has hired six minorities and thirty-two women as law clerks.

Should Chief Justice Rehnquist hire a black law clerk? Why or why not?

Do you think the Supreme Court should practice affirmative action? Explain your answer.

2. The University of California v. Bakke (1978)

In the years 1973 and 1974, Allan Bakke, a white male, applied for admission to the Medical School of the University of California at Davis. In both years, his application was rejected even though other applicants who had lower grade point averages and lower Medical College Admissions Test scores were admitted under a special program. After the second rejection, in 1974, Bakke filed a lawsuit in the Superior Court of California. He alleged that the special program that admitted less-qualified minority students operated to exclude him from the school on the basis of race, in violation of his rights under Title VII of the Civil Rights Act of 1964 and the Equal Protection Clause of the Fourteenth Amendment. The trial court found that the special program operated as an unconstitutional racial quota because minority applicants were rated only against one another and sixteen places in the class of one hundred were reserved for them. But the court refused to order Bakke's admission. Bakke appealed, and the case went to the Supreme Court of the United States. The justices of the Supreme Court were divided 4 to 4 on the issues in the case with Justice Powell providing the decisive vote. Justice Powell sided with Chief Justice Warren Burger and three other justices in holding that the admissions program was unconstitutional and that Bakke must be admitted to the school. But Justice Powell also sided with the other four justices in holding that colleges and universities can consider race as a factor in the admissions process.

Are quotas based on race or ethnic status unjust? What is your view?

Is it acceptable to consider race or sex as a factor in admissions? Why or why not?

3. A Case of Academic Hiring

Suppose that the philosophy department of a state university has a tenure-track opening. The position is advertised and there are numerous applications, including one from a woman. It is not possible to determine the race of the applicants from the documents provided, and the department does not have the resources to interview the candidates. One of the male applicants has really outstanding credentials—a Ph.D. degree from Harvard with a dissertation on justice written under the direction of John Rawls (the dissertation is being published as a book by Harvard University Press), several articles published in leading journals, evidence of being an excellent teacher, and very flattering letters of recommendation. By comparison, the woman's credentials are good but not really outstanding. She does not yet have a Ph.D. degree, although she says that her dissertation on feminism is almost done, and she has not published any articles. However, she does possess evidence of being a good teacher, and she has positive letters of recommendation.

Should the department hire the apparently less-qualified woman or not? Why or why not?

Suppose that it is discovered that one of the candidates is a black man; this fact is mentioned in one of the letters of recommendation. This man's credentials seem to be roughly equal to those of the woman. Should he be hired rather than the woman? What choice should be made in this case?

Suppose that the woman's credentials seem roughly equal to that of the leading man; that is, she has a Ph.D. degree from a good school, has publications and good letters of recommendation, and so on. Should the department hire her rather than the man? What do you think?

Suggested Readings

1. William G. Bowen, Derek C. Bok, et al., *The Shape of the River: Long-Term Consequences of Considering Race in College and University Admissions* (Princeton University Press, 1998). This important book presents comprehensive statistics and analysis of the academic, employment, and personal histories of more than 60,000 white and African American students who attended elite universities between the 1970s and the 1990s. The findings give factual support for affirmative action policies and flatly refute some claims of the opponents of affirmative action—for example, that it produces mediocrity and incompetence.

2. Ellis Case, *Color-Blind: Seeing Beyond Race in a Race-Obsessed World* (HarperCollins, 1998), argues that racism will persist in the United States unless Americans actively work to eliminate it. Case concludes with a twelve-step program for producing a race-neutral nation.

3. George E. Curry, *The Affirmative Action Debate* (Addison Wesley Longman, 1996). This anthology covers various aspects of the debate about affirmative action, including its history, how programs work, recent Supreme Court rulings, and legislative initiatives. It includes the voices of Latinos and Asian Americans, who are often affected but usually ignored in the debate.

4. Barry R. Gross, "Is Turn About Fair Play?" *Journal of Critical Analysis* 5, no. 4 (January/February 1975), makes several objections to affirmative action, or reverse discrimination as he prefers to call it. The victims of past discrimination are not easily identified, reverse discrimination produces bad effects such as making people feel inferior, and it is unfair to white males.

5. Bernard R. Boxill, *Blacks and Social Justice,* revised edition (Roman and Littlefield, 1992), gives and defends both forward- and backward-looking arguments for preferential treatment of minorities in hiring and admission.

6. Shelby Steele, *The Content of Our Character* (St. Martin's Press, 1990), maintains that affirmative action is the product of white guilt and black power that is supposed to compensate blacks for past injustices, but does not do so. It has bad effects on blacks, including producing self-doubt, continuing the myth of black inferiority, causing more subtle discrimination against blacks, and resulting in a glass ceiling when considerations of competence come into play.

7. Thomas Sowell, *Civil Rights: Rhetoric or Reality* (Morrow, 1984), argues that we should strive for equal opportunity without regard to race or sex. Sowell rejects affirmative action because it helps those who need it least.

8. William Julius Wilson, *The Truly Disadvantaged: The Inner City, the Underclass, and Public Policy* (University of Chicago Press, 1987), claims that affirmative action ignores the real victims of discrimination, the truly disadvantaged, and instead benefits well-educated middle-class blacks who have no need for it.

9. Edward Tivan, *The Moral Imagination* (Simon & Schuster, 1995), Chapter 5, discusses the history of affirmative action and gives an emotional defense of it, arguing that whites must help blacks to avoid a race war.

10. Gertrude Ezorsky, *Racism and Justice: The Case for Affirmative Action* (Cornell University Press, 1991), maintains that preferential treatment of blacks (including those in the middle or upper class) is just compensation for past discrimination and enslavement.

11. Robert Nozick, *Anarchy, State, and Utopia* (Basic Books, 1974), defends the libertarian view that employers have the right to hire people who will do the best job without government interference.

12. Charles Murray, "Affirmative Racism," *New Republic* (December 31, 1984), argues that preferential treatment for blacks amounts to a new kind of racism that assumes that blacks are less competent than whites and thus continues the racism it is supposed to eliminate.

13. Charles Murray, *The Bell Curve* (Simon & Schuster, 1994), presents controversial evidence that blacks are inferior in intelligence to whites, and then considers the implications this has for social policy and programs.

14. Richard Wasserstrom, "Racism and Sexism," in *Today's Moral Problems,* third edition, ed. R. A. Wasserstrom (Macmillan, 1985), pp. 1–29, proposes a forward-looking solution to racism and sexism, namely an assimilationist ideal wherein race and sex are no more important than eye color.

15. Bernard R. Boxill, "Sexual Blindness and Sexual Equality," *Social Theory and Practice* 6, no. 3 (Fall 1980), pp. 281–98, attacks Wasserstrom's assimilationist ideal that a good and just society would be sex- and color-blind; his main objection is that this ideal has unacceptable costs.

16. Marshall Cohen, Thomas Nagel, and Thomas Scanlon, eds., *Equality and Preferential Treatment* (Princeton University Press, 1971). This collection of articles includes Nagel's well-known defense of preferential treatment titled "Equal Treatment and Compensatory Discrimination." Also included is Ronald Dworkin's article on two important legal decisions, one dealing with a 1945 policy that denied an African American man admission to law school, and the other dealing with a 1971 policy that denied a white male (DeFunis) admission to law school.

17. Ronald Dworkin, "Why Bakke Has No Case," *The New York Review of Books* (November 19, 1977), argues that Bakke's rights were not violated by the University of California at Davis policy of having a quota of sixteen places out of a class of one hundred reserved for minority students. Soon after this article was published, the Supreme Court ruled 5 to 4 that the quota system at Davis was unconstitutional. (See the second Problem Case.)

18. Cornel West, "Beyond Affirmative Action: Equality and Identity," in *Race Matters* (Beacon Press, 1993), argues that without affirmative action, discrimination would return with a vengeance.

19. Stephen Carter, *Reflections of an Affirmative Action Baby* (Basic Books, 1991), maintains that preferential treatment has become an embarrassment and an insult to competent blacks; they would rather be hired on their merits and not because of their skin color.

20. Tom Beauchamp, "The Justification of Reverse Discrimination," in *Social Justice and Preferential Treatment,* ed. William T. Blackstone and Robert Heslep (University of Georgia Press, 1976), argues that reverse discrimination in hiring is justified in order to eliminate present discriminatory practices.

21. Bernard R. Boxill, "The Morality of Preferential Hiring," *Philosophy and Public Affairs,* 7, no. 3 (Spring 1978), pp. 246–68, replies to two objections to preferential hiring: that it benefits those who do not deserve compensation and that it is unfair to young white men.

22. Lisa Newton, "Reverse Discrimination as Unjustified," *Ethics* 83 (1973), pp. 308–12, contends that reverse discrimination is as unjust as ordinary discrimination and as such it undermines the moral ideal of equality.

23. Barry Gross, ed., *Reverse Discrimination* (Prometheus Books, 1977), is an anthology that includes articles by Sidney Hook, Lisa Newton, Bernard Boxill, and Alan Goldman.

Chapter 8

Animals

Introduction

Factual Background

Humans cause a great deal of animal suffering. According to Peter Singer, the use and abuse of animals raised for food far exceeds, in numbers, any other kind of mistreatment. In his book *Animal Liberation,* he says that hundreds of millions of cattle, pigs, and sheep are raised and killed in the United States each year. The number of chickens killed is over 3 billion; in other words, about 5,000 chickens have been slaughtered in the time it takes to read this page.

But do these animals really suffer? Consider the treatment of veal calves, for example. To make their flesh pale and tender, these calves are given special treatment. They are put in narrow stalls and tethered with a chain so that they cannot turn around, lie down comfortably, or groom themselves. They are fed a totally liquid diet to promote rapid weight gain. This diet is deficient in iron, and, as a result, the calves lick the sides of the stall, which are impregnated with urine containing iron. They are given no water because thirsty animals eat more than ones that drink water.

Another cause of animal suffering is experimentation. Singer gives a graphic example of this. At the Lovelace Foundation in New Mexico, experimenters forced sixty-four beagles to inhale radioactive strontium 90. Twenty-five of the dogs died; initially, most of them were feverish and anemic, suffering from hemorrhages and bloody diarrhea. One of the deaths occurred during an epileptic seizure, and another resulted from a brain hemorrhage. In a similar experiment, beagles were injected with enough strontium 90 to produce early death in 50 percent of the group.

These dogs were the subject of what is called the LD50 Test. According to PETA Factsheet #6 (see the People for the Ethical Treatment of Animals website, http://www.peta-online.org/), this is a test that measures the amount of a toxic substance that will kill, in a single dose, 50 percent of the animals in a test group. It is a common test, used each year on about 5 million dogs, rabbits, rats, monkeys, and other animals in the United States. It is used to test cosmetics and household products such as weed killers, oven cleaners, insecticides, and food additives to satisfy the FDA (Food and Drug Administration) requirement that a product be "adequately substantiated for safety." But it is not actually required by the FDA. In the administration of the test, no painkillers are used. The experimental substance is forced into the animals' throats or is pumped into their stomachs by a tube, sometimes causing death by stomach rupture or from the sheer bulk of the chemical dose. Substances also are injected under the skin, into a vein, or into the lining of the stomach. They are also often applied to the eyes, rectum, and vagina, or forcibly inhaled through a gas mask.

The Readings

We begin with a classic statement of the view that animals should be treated differently from humans. Kant assumes that humans are self-conscious and rational, whereas animals are not. In Kant's view, this difference implies that we have no direct duties to animals; we have direct duties only to humans who are self-conscious and rational. Our duties to animals are indirect duties to humans. In other words, the moral treatment of animals is only a means of cultivating moral treatment of humans. We should not mistreat animals because this produces mistreatment of humans.

Kant's view is a clear example of what Singer calls "speciesism." As Singer defines it, speciesism is "a prejudice or attitude of bias toward the interests of members of one's own species and against those of members of other species." Singer goes on to argue that speciesism is analogous to racism and sexism. It is unjust to discriminate against blacks because of their skin color or against women because of their gender. Their interests—for example, their interest in voting—have to be considered equally with those of whites and men. Similarly, it is unjust to discriminate against non-human animals because of their species. Their interests, and particularly their interest in not suffering, have to be considered too.

But how do we go about reducing animal suffering? Does this mean that we should become vegetarians and eat no meat? Singer thinks so, but of course this is very controversial in our meat-eating society. In Singer's view, we should stop eating meat to eliminate factory farming or at least to protest against it; we should not treat animals as means to our end (to use Kant's phrase).

Tom Regan takes a different position on the moral status of nonhuman animals. He agrees with Singer that our treatment of animals is wrong and that speciesism is unjust, but to show this he does not want to appeal to any form of utilitarianism. Utilitarianism is not an acceptable moral theory, he argues, because it treats persons and animals as worthless receptacles for valuable pleasure and because it allows immoral actions if they happen to bring about the best balance of total satisfaction for all those affected by the action. Instead of utilitarianism, Regan defends a rights view. On this view, animals have rights based on their inherent value as experiencing subjects of life, and our treatment of animals is wrong because it violates their rights.

Tibor R. Machan defends a position very much like Kant's. In his view, having a moral life and being capable of making moral decisions is a necessary condition for having natural rights to life, liberty, and property. This means that normal human beings with a moral life have rights, but animals have no rights because they have no moral life. Furthermore, Machan believes that there is a hierarchical structure of importance in nature, and that humans are at the top of this structure because they act morally. Animals are not as important because they do not act morally, and this implies that humans are justified in using animals for human purposes.

Mary Anne Warren has a different criticism of the animal rights position. She rejects what she calls Regan's strong animal rights position, which gives animals the same basic moral rights as humans. Her main criticism is that Regan's notion of inherent value is a mysterious nonnatural property that is not adequately explained.

As a result, it fails to produce any clear distinction between those who have rights and those who don't. She calls her own alternative view a weak animal rights theory. On this theory, animals have rights, but they are weaker than human rights. Still, these weak animal rights require us not to make animals suffer and not to kill them without a good reason.

James Rachels is mainly concerned to defend vegetarianism. He gives two arguments, one that appeals to our duty to not waste food when people are starving, and another that appeals to our moral duty to not cause suffering unless there is a good reason. But he also gives a defense of animals' right to life. Given the facts about animals—that they live in communities, communicate with one another, have social relationships, are capable of suffering and happiness—the burden of proof is on those who claim they don't have a right to life. He compares animals with a severely retarded human and asks, "What could be the rational basis for saying that a severely retarded human, who is inferior in every important respect to an intelligent animal, has a right to life but that the animal doesn't?"

Philosophical Issues

What is the criterion of moral standing? Who deserves moral consideration? These are basic issues raised by the readings. Kant says that self-consciousness gives a person moral standing; to use Kant's terminology, a self-conscious being is an end in itself and not just a means. On this criterion, human beings have moral standing as ends, but animals do not, they are mere means to fulfilling human purposes. Or so Kant believed. To be consistent, Kant would have to agree that nonhumans that are self-conscious (for example, angels or chimpanzees that talk) have moral standing, and human beings who are not self-conscious (for example, fetuses) do not have any moral standing.

Machan thinks that having a moral life gives a person moral rights. But as with Kant, human beings who do not have a moral life (fetuses, the severely retarded, and so on) would not have rights on this view, and beings who do have a moral life, who make moral decisions, do have rights. But animals, such as monkeys, who have a social life, care for their young, play social roles, and so on do seem to have a moral life or its equivalent. Does this mean they have rights after all?

The utilitarian criterion of moral standing accepted by Singer and Rachels is sentience or consciousness. Animals are conscious, they are capable of feeling pain or pleasure, so they have moral standing. At least, we have the moral duty to not cause them to suffer without a good reason. But this view is attacked by environmentalists as still another kind of bias—namely "sentientism," the belief that only conscious or sentient beings can have rights or deserve moral consideration. The animal liberation movement has escaped one prejudice, speciesism, only to embrace another one, sentientism. Why not say that nonsentient things, such as forests, have rights too?

Even if animals do have moral standing, is it equal to that of humans? It would be wrong to kill an annoying homeless person, but is it equally wrong to exterminate an annoying rat? It would be wrong to perform experiments on an innocent child, but is it equally wrong to experiment on rabbits if this results in a new treatment for cancer? As for vegetarianism, those who eat meat can insist that their enjoyment outweighs the suffering of the animals they eat. How do we weigh this enjoyment against the suffering of the animals?

Our Duties to Animals

IMMANUEL KANT

For biographical information on Kant, see the reading in the first chapter.

Kant maintains that we have no direct duties to animals because they are not self-conscious. Our duties to animals are merely indirect duties to human beings; that is, the duty to animals is a means of cultivating a corresponding duty to humans. For example, we should not be cruel to animals because this tends to produce cruelty to humans.

BAUMGARTEN SPEAKS OF DUTIES towards beings which are beneath us and beings which are above us. But so far as animals are concerned, we have no direct duties. Animals are not self-conscious and are there merely as a means to an end. That end is man. We can ask, 'Why do animals exist?' But to ask, 'Why does man exist?' is a meaningless question. Our duties towards animals are merely indirect duties towards humanity. Animal nature has analogies to human nature, and by doing our duties to animals in respect of manifestations which correspond to manifestations of human nature, we indirectly do our duty towards humanity. Thus, if a dog has served his master long and faithfully, his service, on the analogy of human service, deserves reward, and when the dog has grown too old to serve, his master ought to keep him until he dies. Such action helps to support us in our duties towards human beings, where they are bounden duties. If then any acts of animals are analogous to human acts and spring from the same principles, we have duties towards the animals because thus we cultivate the corresponding duties towards human beings. If a man shoots his dog because the animal is no longer capable of service, he does not fail in his duty to the dog, for the dog cannot judge, but his act is inhuman and damages in himself that humanity which it is his duty to show towards mankind. If he is not to stifle his human feelings, he must practise kindness towards animals, for he who is cruel to animals becomes hard also in his dealings with men. We can judge the heart of a man by his treatment of animals. Hogarth[1] depicts this in his engravings. He shows how cruelty

Source: Immanuel Kant, "Our Duties to Animals" from *Lectures on Ethics,* trans. Louis Infield (Methuen & Co., 1963), pp. 239–241.

1 Hogarth's four engravings, 'The Stages of Cruelty', 1751.

grows and develops. He shows the child's cruelty to animals, pinching the tail of a dog or a cat; he then depicts the grown man in his cart running over a child; and lastly, the culmination of cruelty in murder. He thus brings home to us in a terrible fashion the rewards of cruelty, and this should be an impressive lesson to children. The more we come in contact with animals and observe their behaviour, the more we love them, for we see how great is their care for their young. It is then difficult for us to be cruel in thought even to a wolf. Leibnitz used a tiny worm for purposes of observation, and then carefully replaced it with its leaf on the tree so that it should not come to harm through any act of his. He would have been sorry—a natural feeling for a humane man—to destroy such a creature for no reason. Tender feelings towards dumb animals develop humane feelings towards mankind. In England butchers and doctors do not sit on a jury because they are accustomed to the sight of death and hardened. Vivisectionists who use living animals for their experiments, certainly act cruelly, although their aim is praiseworthy, and they can justify their cruelty, since animals must be regarded as man's instruments; but any such cruelty for sport cannot be justified. A master who turns out his ass or his dog because the animal can no longer earn its keep manifests a small mind. The Greeks' ideas in this respect were high-minded, as can be seen from the fable of the ass and the bell of ingratitude. Our duties towards animals, then, are indirect duties towards mankind.

Review Questions

1. According to Kant, why don't we have direct duties to animals? What is the difference between animals and humans, in Kant's view?
2. What does Kant mean when he says that our duty to animals is only an indirect duty to humans?

Discussion Questions

1. Comatose people and newborn infants do not seem to be self-conscious. Does this mean we have no direct duties to them? What would Kant say? What is your view?
2. People who hunt and kill deer don't usually do the same to humans. Is this a problem for Kant's view? Why or why not?

All Animals Are Equal

PETER SINGER

For biographical information on Singer, see his reading in Chapter 3.

Singer defines specieism as a prejudice toward the interests of members of one's own species and against those of members of other species. He argues that speciesism is analogous to racism and sexism. If it is unjust to discriminate against women and blacks by not considering their interests, it is also unfair to ignore the interests of animals, particularly their interest in not suffering.

"ANIMAL LIBERATION" may sound more like a parody of other liberation movements than a serious objective. The idea of "The Rights of Animals" actually was once used to parody the case for women's rights. When Mary Wollstonecraft, a forerunner of today's feminists, published her *Vindication of the Rights of Women* in 1792, her views were widely regarded as absurd, and before long an anonymous publication appeared entitled *A Vindication of the Rights of Brutes*. The author of this satirical work (now known to have been Thomas Taylor, a distinguished Cambridge philosopher) tried to refute Mary Wollstonecraft's arguments by showing that they could be carried one stage further. If the argument for equality was sound when applied to women, why should it not be applied to dogs, cats, and horses? The reasoning seemed to hold for these "brutes" too, yet to hold that brutes had rights was manifestly absurd; therefore the reasoning by which this conclusion had been reached must be unsound, and if unsound when applied to brutes, it must also be unsound when applied to women, since the very same arguments had been used in each case.

In order to explain the basis of the case for the equality of animals, it will be helpful to start with an examination of the case for the equality of women. Let us assume that we wish to defend the case for women's rights against the attack by Thomas Taylor. How should we reply?

One way in which we might reply is by saying that the case for equality between men and women cannot validly be extended to nonhuman animals. Women have a right to vote, for instance, because they are just as capable of making rational decisions about the future as

men are; dogs, on the other hand, are incapable of understanding the significance of voting, so they cannot have the right to vote. There are many other obvious ways in which men and women resemble each other closely, while humans and animals differ greatly. So, it might be said, men and women are similar beings and should have similar rights, while humans and nonhumans are different and should not have equal rights.

The reasoning behind this reply to Taylor's analogy is correct up to a point, but it does not go far enough. There *are* important differences between humans and other animals, and these differences must give rise to *some* differences in the rights that each have. Recognizing this obvious fact, however, is no barrier to the case for extending the basic principle of equality to nonhuman animals. The differences that exist between men and women are equally undeniable, and the supporters of Women's Liberation are aware that these differences may give rise to different rights. Many feminists hold that women have the right to an abortion on request. It does not follow that since these same feminists are campaigning for equality between men and women they must support the right of men to have abortions too. Since a man cannot have an abortion, it is meaningless to talk of his right to have one. Since a dog can't vote, it is meaningless to talk of its right to vote. There is no reason why either Women's Liberation or Animal Liberation should get involved in such nonsense. The extension of the basic principle of equality from one group to another does not imply that we must treat both groups in exactly the same way, or grant exactly the same rights to both groups. Whether we should do so will depend on the nature of the members of the two groups. The basic principle of equality does not require equal or identical *treatment;* it requires

Source: Peter Singer, "All Animals Are Equal" from *Animal Liberation* (The New York Review, 1975), pp. 1–22.

equal *consideration*. Equal consideration for different beings may lead to different treatment and different rights.

So there is a different way of replying to Taylor's attempt to parody the case for women's rights, a way that does not deny the obvious differences between humans and nonhumans but goes more deeply into the question of equality and concludes by finding nothing absurd in the idea that the basic principle of equality applies to so-called brutes. At this point such a conclusion may appear odd; but if we examine more deeply the basis on which our opposition to discrimination on grounds of race or sex ultimately rests, we will see that we would be on shaky ground if we were to demand equality for blacks, women, and other groups of oppressed humans while denying equal consideration to nonhumans. To make this clear we need to see first, exactly why racism and sexism are wrong.

When we say that all human beings, whatever their race, creed, or sex, are equal, what is it that we are asserting? Those who wish to defend hierarchical, inegalitarian societies have often pointed out that by whatever test we choose it simply is not true that all humans are equal. Like it or not we must face the fact that humans come in different shapes and sizes; they come with different moral capacities, different intellectual abilities, different amounts of benevolent feeling and sensitivity to the needs of others, different abilities to communicate effectively, and different capacities to experience pleasure and pain. In short, if the demand for equality were based on the actual equality of all human beings, we would have to stop demanding equality.

Still, one might cling to the view that the demand for equality among human beings is based on the actual equality of the different races and sexes. Although, it may be said, humans differ as individuals there are no differences between the races and sexes *as such*. From the mere fact that a person is black or a woman we cannot infer anything about that person's intellectual or moral capacities. This, it may be said, is why racism and sexism are wrong. The white racist claims that whites are superior to blacks, but this is false—although there are differences among individuals, some blacks are superior to some whites in all of the capacities and abilities that could conceivably be relevant. The opponent of sexism would say the same: a person's sex is no guide to his or her abilities, and this is why it is unjustifiable to discriminate on the basis of sex.

The existence of individual variations that cut across the lines of race or sex, however, provides us with no defense at all against a more sophisticated opponent of equality, one who proposes that, say, the interests of all those with IQ scores below 100 be given less consideration than the interests of those with ratings over 100. Perhaps those scoring below the mark, would, in this society, be made the slaves of those scoring higher. Would a hierarchical society of this sort really be so much better than one based on race or sex? I think not. But if we tie the moral principle of equality to the factual equality of the different races or sexes, taken as a whole, our opposition to racism and sexism does not provide us with any basis for objecting to this kind of inegalitarianism.

There is a second important reason why we ought not to base our opposition to racism and sexism on any kind of actual equality, even the limited kind that asserts that variations in capacities and abilities are spread evenly between the different races and sexes: we can have no absolute guarantee that these capacities and abilities really are distributed evenly, without regard to race or sex, among human beings. So far as actual abilities are concerned there do seem to be certain measurable differences between both races and sexes. These differences do not, of course, appear in each case, but only when averages are taken. More important still, we do not yet know how much of these differences is really due to the different genetic endowments of the different races and sexes, and how much is due to poor schools, poor housing, and other factors that are the result of past and continuing discrimination. Perhaps all of the important differences will eventually prove to be environmental rather than genetic. Anyone opposed to racism and sexism will certainly hope that this will be so, for it will make the task of ending discrimination a lot easier; nevertheless it would be dangerous to rest the case against racism and sexism on the belief that all significant differences are environmental in origin. The opponent of, say, racism who takes this line will be unable to avoid conceding that *if* differences in ability do after all prove to have some genetic connection with race, racism would in some way be defensible.

Fortunately there is no need to pin the case for equality to one particular outcome of a scientific investigation. The appropriate response to those who claim to have found evidence of genetically based differences in ability between the races or sexes is not to stick to the belief that the genetic explanation must be wrong, whatever evidence to the contrary may turn up: instead we should make it quite clear that the claim to equality does not depend on intelligence, moral capacity, physical strength, or similar matters of fact. Equality is a moral idea, not an assertion of fact. There is no logically compelling reason for assuming that a factual difference in ability between two people justifies any difference in the amount of consideration we give to their needs and interests. *The principle of the equality of human beings is not a description of an alleged actual equality among humans; it is a prescription of how we should treat humans.*

Jeremy Bentham, the founder of the reforming utilitarian school of moral philosophy, incorporated the essential basis of moral equality into his system of ethics by means of the formula: "Each to count for one and none for more than one." In other words, the interests of every being affected by an action are to be taken into account and given the same weight as the like interests of any other being. A later utilitarian, Henry Sidgwick, put the point in this way: "The good of any one individual is of no more impor-

tance, from the point of view (if I may say so) of the Universe, than the good of any other." More recently the leading figures in contemporary moral philosophy have shown a great deal of agreement in specifying as a fundamental presupposition of their moral theories some similar requirement that operates so as to give everyone's interests equal consideration—although these writers generally cannot agree on how this requirement is best formulated.[1]

It is an implication of this principle of equality that our concern for others and our readiness to consider their interests ought not to depend on what they are like or on what abilities they may possess. Precisely what this concern or consideration requires us to do may vary according to the characteristics of those affected by what we do: concern for the well-being of a child growing up in America would require that we teach him to read; concern for the well-being of a pig may require no more than that we leave him alone with other pigs in a place where there is adequate food and room to run freely. But the basic element—the taking into account of the interests of the being, whatever those interests may be—must, according to the principle of equality, be extended to all beings, black or white, masculine or feminine, human or nonhuman.

Thomas Jefferson, who was responsible for writing the principle of the equality of men into the American Declaration of Independence, saw this point. It led him to oppose slavery even

1 For Bentham's moral philosophy, see his *Introduction to the Principles of Morals and Legislation,* and for Sidgwick's see *The Methods of Ethics* (the passage quoted is from the seventh edition, p. 382). As examples of leading contemporary moral philosophers who incorporate a requirement of equal consideration of interests, see R. M. Hare, *Freedom and Reason* (New York, Oxford University Press, 1963) and John Rawls, *A Theory of Justice* (Cambridge: Harvard University Press, Belknap Press, 1972). For a brief account of the essential agreement on this issue between these and other positions, see R. M. Hare, "Rules of War and Moral Reasoning," *Philosophy and Public Affairs* 1 (1972).

though he was unable to free himself fully from his slaveholding background. He wrote in a letter to the author of a book that emphasized the notable intellectual achievements of Negroes in order to refute the then common view that they had limited intellectual capacities:

> Be assured that no person living wishes more sincerely than I do, to see a complete refutation of the doubts I have myself entertained and expressed on the grade of understanding allotted to them by nature, and to find that they are on a par with ourselves . . . but whatever be their degree of talent it is no measure of their rights. Because Sir Isaac Newton was superior to others in understanding, he was not therefore lord of the property or person of others.[2]

Similarly when in the 1850s the call for women's rights was raised in the United States a remarkable black feminist named Sojourner Truth made the same point in more robust terms at a feminist convention:

> . . . they talk about this thing in the head; what do they call it? ["Intellect," whispered someone near by.] That's it. What's that got to do with women's rights or Negroes' rights? If my cup won't hold but a pint and yours holds a quart, wouldn't you be mean not to let me have my little half-measure full?[3]

It is on this basis that the case against racism and the case against sexism must both ultimately rest; and it is in accordance with this principle that the attitude that we may call "speciesism," by analogy with racism, must also be condemned. Speciesism—the word is not an attractive one, but I can think of no better term—is a prejudice or attitude of bias toward the interests of members of one's own species and against those members of other species. It should be obvious that the fundamental objec-

tions to racism and sexism made by Thomas Jefferson and Sojourner Truth apply equally to speciesism. If possessing a higher degree of intelligence does not entitle one human to use another for his own ends, how can it entitle humans to exploit nonhumans for the same purpose?[4]

Many philosophers and other writers have proposed the principle of equal consideration of interests, in some form or other, as a basic moral principle, but not many of them have recognized that this principle applies to members of other species as well as to our own. Jeremy Bentham was one of the few who did realize this. In a forward-looking passage written at a time when black slaves had been freed by the French but the British dominions were still being treated in the way we now treat animals, Bentham wrote:

> The day may come when the rest of the animal creation may acquire those rights which never could have been withholden from them but by the hand of tyranny. The French have already discovered that the blackness of the skin is no reason why a human being should be abandoned without redress to the caprice of a tormentor. It may one day come to be recognized that the number of the legs, the villosity of the skin, or the termination of the *os sacrum* are reasons equally insufficient for abandoning a sensitive being to the same fate. What else is it that should trace the insuperable line? Is it the faculty of reason, or perhaps the faculty of discourse? But a full-grown horse or dog is beyond comparison a more rational, as well as a more conversable animal, than an infant of a day or a week or even a month old. But suppose they were otherwise, what would it avail? The question is not, Can they reason? nor Can they talk? but, Can they suffer?[5]

In this passage Bentham points to the capacity for suffering as the vital characteristic that gives a being the right to equal consideration. The capacity for suffering—or more strictly, for

---

2 Letter to Henri Gregoire, February 25, 1809.
3 Reminiscences by Francis D. Gage, from Susan B. Anthony, *The History of Woman Suffrage*, vol. 1; the passage is to be found in the extract in Leslie Tanner, ed., *Voices from Women's Liberation* (New York: Signet, 1970).

4 I owe the term "speciesism" to Richard Ryder.
5 *Introduction to the Principles of Morals and Legislation*, chapter 17.

suffering and/or enjoyment or happiness—is not just another characteristic like the capacity for language or higher mathematics. Bentham is not saying that those who try to mark "the insuperable line" that determines whether the interests of a being should be considered happen to have chosen the wrong characteristic. By saying that we must consider the interests of all beings with the capacity for suffering or enjoyment Bentham does not arbitrarily exclude from consideration any interests at all—as those who draw the line with reference to the possession of reason or language do. The capacity for suffering and enjoyment is *a prerequisite for having interests at all,* a condition that must be satisfied before we can speak of interests in a meaningful way. It would be nonsense to say that it was not in the interests of a stone to be kicked along the road by a schoolboy. A stone does not have interests because it cannot suffer. Nothing that we can do to it could possibly make any difference to its welfare. A mouse, on the other hand, does have an interest in not being kicked along the road, because it will suffer if it is.

If a being suffers there can be no moral justification for refusing to take that suffering into consideration. No matter what the nature of the being, the principle of equality requires that its suffering be counted equally with the like suffering—in so far as rough comparisons can be made—of any other being. If a being is not capable of suffering, or of experiencing enjoyment or happiness, there is nothing to be taken into account. So the limit of sentience (using the term as a convenient if not strictly accurate shorthand for the capacity to suffer and/or experience enjoyment) is the only defensible boundary of concern for the interests of others. To mark this boundary by some other characteristic like intelligence or rationality would be to mark it in an arbitrary manner. Why not choose some other characteristic, like skin color?

The racist violates the principle of equality by giving greater weight to the interests of members of his own race when there is a clash between their interests and the interests of those of another race. The sexist violates the principle of equality by favoring the interests of his own sex. Similarly the speciesist allows the interests of his own species to override the greater interests of members of other species. The pattern is identical in each case.

Most human beings are speciesists. Ordinary human beings—not a few exceptionally cruel or heartless humans, but the overwhelming majority of humans—take an active part in, acquiesce in, and allow their taxes to pay for practices that require the sacrifice of the most important interests of members of other species in order to promote the most trivial interests of our own species. . . .

Animals can feel pain. As we saw earlier, there can be no moral justification for regarding the pain (or pleasure) that animals feel as less important than the same amount of pain (or pleasure) felt by humans. But what exactly does this mean, in practical terms? To prevent misunderstanding I shall spell out what I mean a little more fully.

If I give a horse a hard slap across its rump with my open hand, the horse may start, but it presumably feels little pain. Its skin is thick enough to protect it against a mere slap. If I slap a baby in the same way, however, the baby will cry and presumably does feel pain, for its skin is more sensitive. So it is worse to slap a baby than a horse, if both slaps are administered with equal force. But there must be some kind of blow—I don't know exactly what it would be, but perhaps a blow with a heavy stick—that would cause the horse as much pain as we cause a baby by slapping it with our hand. That is what I mean by "the same amount of pain" and if we consider it wrong to inflict that much pain on a baby for no good reason then we must, unless we are speciesists, consider it equally wrong to inflict the same amount of pain on a horse for no good reason.

There are other differences between humans and animals that cause other complications. Normal adult human beings have mental capacities which will, in certain circumstances, lead them to suffer more than animals would in the same circumstances. If, for instance, we decided to perform extremely painful or lethal scientific experiments on normal adult humans, kidnapped at random from public parks for this purpose, every adult who entered a park would become fearful that he would be kidnapped. The resultant terror would be a form of suffering additional to the pain of the experiment. The same experiments performed on nonhuman animals would cause less suffering since the animals would not have the anticipatory dread of being kidnapped and experimented upon. This does not mean, of course, that it would be right to perform the experiment on animals, but only that there is a reason, which is *not* speciesist, for preferring to use animals rather than normal adult humans, if the experiment is to be done at all. It should be noted, however, that this same argument gives us a reason for preferring to use human infants—orphans perhaps—or retarded humans for experiments, rather than adults, since infants and retarded humans would also have no idea of what was going to happen to them. So far as this argument is concerned nonhuman animals and infants and retarded humans are in the same category; and if we use this argument to justify experiments on nonhuman animals we have to ask ourselves whether we are also prepared to allow experiments on humans, on what basis can we do it, other than a barefaced—and morally indefensible—preference for members of our own species?

There are many areas in which the superior mental powers of normal adult humans make a difference: anticipation, more detailed memory, greater knowledge of what is happening, and so on. Yet these differences do not all point to greater suffering on the part of the normal human being. Sometimes an animal may suffer more because of his more limited understanding. If, for instance, we are taking prisoners in wartime we can explain to them that while they must submit to capture, search, and confinement they will not otherwise be harmed and will be set free at the conclusion of hostilities. If we capture a wild animal, however, we cannot explain that we are not threatening its life. A wild animal cannot distinguish an attempt to overpower and confine from an attempt to kill; the one causes as much terror as the other.

It may be objected that comparisons of the sufferings of different species are impossible to make, and that for this reason when the interests of animals and humans clash the principle of equality gives no guidance. It is probably true that comparisons of suffering between members of different species cannot be made precisely, but precision is not essential. Even if we were to prevent the infliction of suffering on animals only when it is quite certain that the interests of humans will not be affected to anything like the extent that animals are affected, we would be forced to make radical changes in our treatment of animals that would involve our diet, the farming methods we use, experimental procedures in many fields of science, our approach to wildlife and to hunting, trapping and the wearing of furs, and areas of entertainment like circuses, rodeos, and zoos. As a result, a vast amount of suffering would be avoided.

So far I have said a lot about the infliction of suffering on animals, but nothing about killing them. This omission has been deliberate. The application of the principle of equality to the infliction of suffering is, in theory at least, fairly straightforward. Pain and suffering are bad and should be prevented or minimized, irrespective of the race, sex, or species of the being that suffers. How bad a pain is depends on how intense it is and how long it lasts, but pains of the same intensity and duration are equally bad, whether felt by humans or animals.

The wrongness of killing a being is more complicated. I have kept, and shall continue to keep, the question of killing in the background because in the present state of human tyranny over other species the more simple, straightforward principle of equal consideration of pain or pleasure is a sufficient basis for identifying and protesting against all the major abuses of animals that humans practice. Nevertheless, it is necessary to say something about killing.

Just as most humans are speciesists in their readiness to cause pain to animals when they would not cause a similar pain to humans for the same reason, so most humans are speciesists in their readiness to kill other animals when they would not kill humans. We need to proceed more cautiously here, however, because people hold widely differing views about when it is legitimate to kill humans, as the continuing debates over abortion and euthanasia attest. Nor have moral philosophers been able to agree on exactly what it is that makes it wrong to kill humans, and under what circumstances killing a human being may be justifiable.

Let us consider first the view that it is always wrong to take an innocent human life. We may call this the "sanctity of life" view. People who take this view oppose abortion and euthanasia. They do not usually, however, oppose the killing of nonhumans—so perhaps it would be more accurate to describe this view as the "sanctity of *human* life" view.

The belief that human life, and only human life, is sacrosanct is a form of speciesism. To see this, consider the following example.

Assume that, as sometimes happens, an infant has been born with massive and irreparable brain damage. The damage is so severe that the infant can never be any more than a "human vegetable," unable to talk, recognize other people, act independently of others, or develop a sense of self-awareness. The parents of the infant, realizing that they cannot hope for any improvement in their child's condition and being in any case unwilling to spend, or ask the state to spend, the thousands of dollars that would be needed annually for proper care of the infant, ask the doctor to kill the infant painlessly.

Should the doctor do what the parents ask? Legally, he should not, and in this respect the law reflects the sanctity of life view. The life of every human being is sacred. Yet people who would say this about the infant do not object to the killing of nonhuman animals. How can they justify their different judgments? Adult chimpanzees, dogs, pigs, and many other species far surpass the brain-damaged infant in their ability to relate to others, act independently, be self-aware, and any other capacity that could reasonably be said to give value to life. With the most intensive care possible, there are retarded infants who can never achieve the intelligence level of a dog. Nor can we appeal to the concern of the infant's parents, since they themselves, in this imaginary example (and in some actual cases) do not want the infant kept alive.

The only thing that distinguishes the infant from the animal, in the eyes of those who claim it has a "right to life," is that it is, biologically, a member of the species Homo sapiens, whereas chimpanzees, dogs, and pigs are not. But to use *this* difference as the basis for granting a right to life to the infant and not to the other animals is, of course, pure speciesism.[6] It is exactly the kind of arbitrary difference that the most crude and overt kind of racist uses in attempting to justify racial discrimination.

This does not mean that to avoid speciesism we must hold that it is as wrong to kill a dog as it is to kill a normal human being. The only position that is irredeemably speciesist is the one that tries to make the boundary of the right to life run exactly parallel to the boundary of our own species. Those who hold the sanctity of life

6 I am here putting aside religious views, for example the doctrine that all and only humans have immortal souls, or are made in the image of God. Historically these views have been very important, and no doubt are partly responsible for the idea that human life has a special sanctity. Logically, however, these religious views are unsatisfactory, since a reasoned explanation of why it should be that all humans and no nonhumans have immortal souls is not offered. This belief too, therefore, comes under suspicion as a form of speciesism. In any case, defenders of the "sanctity of life" view are generally reluctant to base their position on purely religious doctrines, since these doctrines are no longer as widely accepted as they once were.

view do this because while distinguishing sharply between humans and other animals they allow no distinctions to be made within our own species, objecting to the killing of the severely retarded and the hopelessly senile as strongly as they object to the killing of normal adults.

To avoid speciesism we must allow that beings which are similar in all relevant respects have a similar right to life—and mere membership in our own biological species cannot be a morally relevant criterion for this right. Within these limits we could still hold that, for instance, it is worse to kill a normal adult human, with a capacity for self-awareness, and the ability to plan for the future and have meaningful relations with others, than it is to kill a mouse, which presumably does not share all of these characteristics; or we might appeal to the close family and other personal ties which humans have but mice do not have to the same degree; or we might think that it is the consequences for other humans, who will be put in fear of their own lives, that makes the crucial difference; or we might think it is some combination of these factors, or other factors altogether.

Whatever criteria we choose, however, we will have to admit that they do not follow precisely the boundary of our own species. We may legitimately hold that there are some features of certain beings which make their lives more valuable than those of other beings; but there will surely be some nonhuman animals whose lives, by any standards, are more valuable than the lives of some humans. A chimpanzee, dog, or pig, for instance, will have a higher degree of self-awareness and a greater capacity for meaningful relations with others than a severely retarded infant or someone in a state of advanced senility. So if we base the right to life on these characteristics we must grant these animals a right to life as good as, or better than, such retarded or senile humans.

Now this argument cuts both ways. It could be taken as showing that chimpanzees, dogs, and pigs, along with some other species, have a right to life and we commit a grave moral offense whenever we kill them, even when they are old and suffering and our intention is to put them out of their misery. Alternatively one could take the argument as showing that the severely retarded and hopelessly senile have no right to life and may be killed for quite trivial reasons, as we now kill animals.

Since the focus here is on ethical questions concerning animals and not on the morality of euthanasia I shall not attempt to settle this issue finally. I think it is reasonably clear, though, that while both of the positions just described avoid speciesism, neither is entirely satisfactory. What we need is some middle position that would avoid speciesism but would not make the lives of the retarded and senile as cheap as the lives of pigs and dogs now are, nor make the lives of pigs and dogs so sacrosanct that we think it wrong to put them out of hopeless misery. What we must do is bring nonhuman animals within our sphere of moral concern and cease to treat their lives as expendable for whatever trivial purposes we may have. At the same time, once we realize that the fact that a being is a member of our own species is not in itself enough to make it always wrong to kill that being, we may come to reconsider our policy of preserving human lives at all costs, even when there is no prospect of a meaningful life or of existence without terrible pain.

I conclude, then, that a rejection of speciesism does not imply that all lives are of equal worth. While self-awareness, intelligence, the capacity for meaningful relations with others, and so on are not relevant to the question of inflicting pain—since pain is pain, whatever other capacities, beyond the capacity to feel pain, the being may have—these capacities may be relevant to the question of taking life. It is not arbitrary to hold that the life of a self-aware being, capable of abstract thought, of planning for the future, of complex acts of communication, and so on, is more valuable than the life of a being without these capacities. To see the difference between the issues of inflicting pain and taking life, consider how we would choose within our own species. If we had to choose to save the life of a normal human or a mentally defective human, we would probably choose to save the life of the normal human; but if we had to choose between preventing pain in the normal human or the mental defective—imagine that both have received painful but superficial injuries, and we only have enough painkiller for one of them—it is not nearly so clear how we ought to choose. The same is true when we consider other species. The evil of pain is, in itself, unaffected by the other characteristics of the being that feels the pain; the value of life is affected by these other characteristics.

Normally this will mean that if we have to choose between the life of a human being and the life of another animal we would choose to save the life of the human, but there may be special cases in which the reverse holds true, because the human being in question does not have the capacities of a normal human being. So this view is not speciesist, although it may appear to be at first glance. The preference, in normal cases, for saving a human life over the life of an animal when a choice *has* to be made is a preference based on the characteristics that normal humans have, and not on the mere fact that they are members of our own species. This is why when we consider members of our own species who lack the characteristics of normal humans we can no longer say that their lives are always to be preferred to those of other animals. In general, the question of when it is wrong to kill (painlessly) an animal is one to which we need give no precise answer. As long as we remember that we should give the same respect to the lives of animals as we give to the lives of those humans at a similar mental level, we shall not go far wrong.

In any case, the conclusions that are argued for here flow from the principle of minimizing suffering alone. The idea that it is also wrong to kill animals painlessly gives some of these conclusions additional support which is welcome, but strictly unnecessary. Interestingly enough, this is true even of the conclusion that we ought to become vegetarians, a conclusion that in the popular mind is generally based on some kind of absolute prohibition on killing.

Review Questions

1. Explain the principle of equality that Singer adopts.
2. How does Singer define speciesism?
3. What is the sanctity of life view? Why does Singer reject this view?

Discussion Questions

1. Is speciesism analogous to racism and sexism? Why or why not?
2. Is there anything wrong with killing animals painlessly? Defend your view.
3. Do human interests outweigh animal interests? Explain your position.

The Case for Animal Rights

TOM REGAN

Tom Regan is professor of philosophy at North Carolina State University. He has written numerous books and articles, and he has edited several textbooks. His recent books on the subject of animal rights include *All That Dwell Therein: Essays on Animal Rights and Environmental Ethics* (1982) and *The Case for Animal Rights* (1984). Also, he is coeditor of *Animal Rights and Human Obligation,* second edition (1989).

Regan defends the view that animals have rights based on their inherent value as experiencing subjects of a life. He attacks other views, including indirect-duty views, the cruelty-kindness view (as he calls it), and even Singer's utilitarianism. Although he agrees with Singer that our treatment of animals is wrong and that speciesism is unjust, he denies that it is wrong because of animal suffering. Instead he thinks that our treatment of animals is wrong because we violate the rights of animals.

I REGARD MYSELF as an advocate of animal rights—as a part of the animal rights movement. That movement, as I conceive it, is committed to a number of goals, including:

the total abolition of the use of animals in science;

the total dissolution of commercial animal agriculture;

the total elimination of commercial and sport hunting and trapping.

There are, I know, people who profess to believe in animal rights but do not avow these goals. Factory farming, they say, is wrong—it violates animals' rights—but traditional animal agriculture is all right. Toxicity tests of cosmetics on animals violates their rights, but important medical research—cancer research, for example—does not. The clubbing of baby seals is abhorrent, but not the harvesting of adult seals. I used to think I understood this reasoning. Not any more. You don't change unjust institutions by tidying them up.

What's wrong—fundamentally wrong—with the way animals are treated isn't the details that vary from case to case. It's the whole system. The forlornness of the veal calf is pathetic, heart wrenching; the pulsing pain of the chimp with electrodes planted deep in her brain is repulsive; the slow, tortuous death of the raccoon caught in the leg-hold trap is agonizing. But what is wrong isn't the pain, isn't the suffering, isn't the deprivation. These compound what's wrong. Sometimes—often—they make it much, much worse. But they are not the fundamental wrong.

The fundamental wrong is the system that allows us to view animals as *our resources,* here for *us*—to be eaten, or surgically manipulated, or exploited for sport or money. Once we accept this view of animals—as our resources—the rest is as predictable as it is regrettable. Why worry about their loneliness, their pain, their death? Since animals exist for us, to benefit us in one way or another, what harms them really doesn't matter—or matters only if it starts to bother us, makes us feel a trifle uneasy when we eat our veal escalope, for example. So, yes, let us get veal calves out of solitary confinement, give them more space, a little straw, a few companions. But let us keep our veal escalope.

But a little straw, more space and a few companions won't eliminate—won't even touch—the basic wrong that attaches to our viewing and treating these animals as our resources. A veal calf killed to be eaten after living in close confinement is viewed and treated in this way: but so, too, is another who is raised (as they say) 'more humanely'. To right the wrong of our treatment of farm animals requires more than making rearing methods 'more humane'; it requires the total dissolution of commercial animal agriculture.

How do we do this, whether we do it or, as in the case of animals in science, whether and how we abolish their use—these are to a large extent political questions. People must change their beliefs before they change their habits. Enough people, especially those elected to public office, must believe in change—must want it—before we will have laws that protect the rights of animals. This process of change is very complicated, very demanding, very exhausting, calling for the efforts of many hands in education, publicity, political organization and activity, down to the licking of envelopes and stamps. As a trained and practicing philosopher, the sort of contribution I can make is limited but, I like to think, important. The currency of philosophy is ideas—their meaning and rational foundation—not the nuts and bolts of the legislative process, say, or the mechanics of community organization. That's what I have been exploring over the past ten years or so in my essays and talks and, most recently, in my book, *The Case for Animal Rights*. I believe the major conclusions I reach in the book are true because they are supported by the weight of the best arguments. I believe the idea of animal rights has reason, not just emotion, on its side.

In the space I have at my disposal here I can only sketch, in the barest outline, some of the main features of the book. Its main themes—and we should not be surprised by this—involve asking and answering deep, fundamental moral questions about what morality is, how it should be understood and what is the best moral theory, all considered. I hope I can convey something of the shape I think this theory takes. The attempt to do this will be (to use a word a friendly critic once used to describe my work) cerebral, perhaps too cerebral. But this is misleading. My feelings about how animals are sometimes treated run just as deep and just as strong as those of my more volatile compatriots. Philosophers do—to use the jargon of the day—have a right side to their brains. If it's the left side we contribute (or mainly should), that's because what talents we have reside there.

How to proceed? We begin by asking how the moral status of animals has been understood by thinkers who deny that animals have rights. Then we test the mettle of their ideas by seeing how well they stand up under the heat of fair criticism. If we start our thinking in this way, we soon find that some people believe that we have no duties directly to animals, that we owe nothing to them, that we can do nothing that wrongs them. Rather, we can do wrong acts that involve animals, and so we have duties regarding them, though none to them. Such views may be called indirect duty views. By way of illustration: suppose your neighbour kicks your dog. Then your neighbour has done something wrong. But not to your dog. The wrong that has been done is a wrong to you. After all, it is wrong to upset people, and your neighbour's kicking your dog upsets you. So you are the one who is wronged, not your dog. Or again: by kicking your dog your neighbour damages your property. And since it is wrong to damage another person's property, your neighbour has done something wrong—to you, of course, not to your dog. Your neighbour no more wrongs your dog than your car would be wronged if the windshield were smashed. Your neighbour's duties involving your dog are indirect duties to you. More generally, all of our duties regarding animals are indirect duties to one another—to humanity.

How could someone try to justify such a view? Someone might say that your dog doesn't feel anything and so isn't hurt by your neighbour's kick, doesn't care about the pain since none is felt, is as unaware of anything as is your windshield. Someone might say this, but no rational person will, since, among other considerations, such a view will commit anyone who holds it to the position that no human being feels pain either—that human beings don't care about what happens to them. A second possibility is that though both humans and your dog are hurt when kicked, it is only human pain that matters. But, again, no rational person can believe this. Pain is pain wherever it occurs. If your neighbour's causing you pain is wrong because of the pain that is caused, we cannot rationally ignore or dismiss the moral relevance of the pain that your dog feels.

Philosophers who hold indirect duty views—and many still do—have come to understand that they must avoid the two defects just noted: that is, both the view that animals don't feel anything as well as the idea that only human pain can be morally relevant. Among such thinkers the sort of view now favoured is one or other form of what is called *contractarianism*.

Here, very crudely, is the root idea: morality consists of a set of rules that individuals voluntarily agree to abide by, as we do when we sign a contract (hence the name contractarianism). Those who understand and accept the terms of the contract are covered directly; they have rights created and recognized by, and protected in, the contract. And these contractors can also have protection spelled out for others who, though they lack the ability to understand morality and so cannot sign the contract themselves, are loved or cherished by those who can. Thus young children, for example, are unable to sign contracts and lack rights. But they are protected by the contract none the less because of the sentimental interests of others, most notably

their parents. So we have, then, duties involving these children, duties regarding them, but no duties to them. Our duties in their case are indirect duties to other human beings, usually their parents.

As for animals, since they cannot understand contracts, they obviously cannot sign; and since they cannot sign, they have no rights. Like children, however, some animals are the objects of the sentimental interest of others. You, for example, love your dog or cat. So those animals that enough people care about (companion animals, whales, baby seals, the American bald eagle), though they lack rights themselves, will be protected because of the sentimental interests of people. I have, then, according to contractarianism, no duty directly to your dog or any other animal, not even the duty not to cause them pain or suffering; my duty not to hurt them is a duty I have to those people who care about what happens to them. As for other animals, where no or little sentimental interest is present—in the case of farm animals, for example, or laboratory rats—what duties we have grow weaker and weaker, perphaps to vanishing point. The pain and death they endure, though real, are not wrong if no one cares about them.

When it comes to the moral status of animals, contractartianism could be a hard view to refute if it were an adequate theoretical approach to the moral status of human beings. It is not adequate in this latter respect, however, which makes the question of its adequacy in the former case, regarding animals, utterly moot. For consider: morality, according to the (crude) contractarian position before us, consists of rules that people agree to abide by. What people? Well, enough to make a difference—enough, that is, *collectively* to have the power to enforce the rules that are drawn up in the contract. That is very well and good for the signatories but not so good for anyone who is not asked to sign. And there is nothing in contractarianism of the sort we are discussing that guarantees or requires that everyone will have a chance to participate equally in framing the rules of morality. The result is that this approach to ethics could sanction the most blatant forms of social, economic, moral and political injustice, ranging from a repressive caste system to systematic racial or sexual discrimination. Might, according to this theory, does make right. Let those who are the victims of injustice suffer as they will. It matters not so long as no one else—no contractor, or too few of them—cares about it. Such a theory takes one's moral breath away . . . as if, for example, there would be nothing wrong with apartheid in South Africa if few white South Africans were upset by it. A theory with so little to recommend it at the level of the ethics of our treatment of our fellow humans cannot have anything more to recommend it when it comes to the ethics of how we treat our fellow animals.

The version of contractarianism just examined is, as I have noted, a crude variety, and in fairness to those of a contractarian persuasion it must be noted that much more refined, subtle and ingenious varieties are possible. For example, John Rawls, in his *A Theory of Justice,* sets forth a version of contractarianism that forces contractors to ignore the accidental features of being a human being—for example, whether one is white or black, male or female, a genius or of modest intellect. Only by ignoring such features, Rawls believes, can we ensure that the principles of justice that contractors would agree upon are not based on bias or prejudice. Despite the improvement a view such as Rawls's represents over the cruder forms of contractarianism, it remains deficient: it systematically denies that we have direct duties to those human beings who do not have a sense of justice—young children, for instance, and many mentally retarded humans. And yet it seems reasonably certain that, were we to torture a young child or a retarded elder, we would be doing something that wronged him or her, not something that would be wrong if (and only if) other humans with a sense of justice were upset. And since this is true in the case of these humans, we cannot rationally deny the same in the case of animals.

Indirect duty views, then, including the best among them, fail to command our rational assent. Whatever ethical theory we should accept rationally, therefore, it must at least recognize that we have some duties directly to animals, just as we have some duties directly to each other. The next two theories I'll sketch attempt to meet this requirement.

The first I call the cruelty-kindness view. Simply stated, this says that we have a direct duty to be kind to animals and a direct duty not to be cruel to them. Despite the familiar, reassuring ring of these ideas, I do not believe that this view offers an adequate theory. To make this clearer, consider kindness. A kind person acts from a certain kind of motive—compassion or concern, for example. And that is a virtue. But there is no guarantee that a kind act is a right act. If I am a generous racist, for example, I will be inclined to act kindly towards members of my own race, favouring their interests above those of others. My kindness would be real and, so far as it goes, good. But I trust it is too obvious to require argument that my kind acts may not be above moral reproach—may, in fact, be positively wrong because rooted in injustice. So kindness, notwithstanding its status as a virtue to be encouraged, simply will not carry the weight of a theory of right action.

Cruelty fares no better. People or their acts are cruel if they display either a lack of sympathy for or, worse, the presence of enjoyment in another's suffering. Cruelty in all its guises is a bad thing, a tragic human failing. But just as a person's being motivated by kindness does not guarantee that he or she does what is right, so the absence of cruelty does not ensure that he or she avoids doing what is wrong. Many people who perform abortions, for example, are not cruel, sadistic people. But that fact alone does not settle the terribly difficult question of the morality of abortion. The case is no different when we examine the ethics of our treatment of animals. So, yes, let us be for kindness and against cruelty. But let us not suppose that being for the one and against the other answers questions about moral right and wrong.

Some people think that the theory we are looking for is utilitarianism. A utilitarian accepts two moral principles. The first is that of equality: everyone's interests count, and similar interests must be counted as having similar weight or importance. White or black, American or Iranian, human or animal—everyone's pain or frustration matter, and matter just as much as the equivalent pain or frustration of anyone else. The second principle a utilitarian accepts is that of utility: do the act that will bring about the best balance between satisfaction and frustration for everyone affected by the outcome.

As a utilitarian, then, here is how I am to approach the task of deciding what I morally ought to do: I must ask who will be affected if I choose to do one thing rather than another, how much each individual will be affected, and where the best results are most likely to lie—which option, in other words, is most likely to bring about the best results, the best balance between satisfaction and frustration. That option, whatever it may be, is the one I ought to choose. That is where my moral duty lies.

The great appeal of utilitarianism rests with its uncompromising *egalitarianism:* everyone's interests count and count as much as the like interests of everyone else. The kind of odious discrimination that some forms of contractarianism can justify—discrimination based on race or sex, for example—seems disallowed in principle by utilitarianism, as is speciesism, systematic discrimination based on species membership.

The equality we find in utilitarianism, however, is not the sort an advocate of animal or human rights should have in mind. Utilitarianism has no room for the equal moral rights of different individuals because it has no room for their equal inherent value or worth. What has value for the utilitarian is the satisfaction of an individual's interests, not the individual whose

interests they are. A universe in which you satisfy your desire for water, food and warmth is, other things being equal, better than a universe in which these desires are frustrated. And the same is true in the case of an animal with similar desires. But neither you nor the animal have any value in your own right. Only your feelings do.

Here is an analogy to help make the philosophical point clearer: a cup contains different liquids, sometimes sweet, sometimes bitter, sometimes a mix of the two. What has value are the liquids: the sweeter the better, the bitterer the worse. The cup, the container, has no value. It is what goes into it, not what they go into, that has value. For the utilitarian you and I are like the cup; we have no value as individuals and thus no equal value. What has value is what goes into us, what we serve as receptacles for; our feelings of satisfaction have postitive value, our feelings of frustration negative value.

Serious problems arise for utilitarianism when we remind ourselves that it enjoins us to bring about the best consequences. What does this mean? It doesn't mean the best consequences for me alone, or for my family or friends, or any other person taken individually. No, what we must do is, roughly, as follows: we must add up (somehow!) the separate satisfactions and frustrations of everyone likely to be affected by our choice, the satisfactions in one column, the frustrations in the other. We must total each column for each of the options before us. That is what it means to say the theory is aggregative. And then we must choose that option which is most likely to bring about the best balance of totalled satisfactions over totalled frustrations. Whatever act would lead to this outcome is the one we ought morally to perform—it is where our moral duty lies. And that act quite clearly might not be the same one that would bring about the best results for me personally, or for my family or friends, or for a lab animal. The best aggregated consequences for everyone concerned are not necessarily the best for each individual.

That utilitarianism is an aggregative theory—different individuals' satisfactions or frustrations are added, or summed, or totalled—is the key objection to this theory. My Aunt Bea is old, inactive, a cranky, sour person, though not physically ill. She prefers to go on living. She is also rather rich. I could make a fortune if I could get my hands on her money, money she intends to give me in any event, after she dies, but which she refuses to give me now. In order to avoid a huge tax bite, I plan to donate a handsome sum of my profits to a local children's hospital. Many, many children will benefit from my generosity, and much joy will be brought to their parents, relatives and friends. If I don't get the money rather soon, all these ambitions will come to naught. The once-in-a-lifetime opportunity to make a real killing will be gone. Why, then, not kill my Aunt Bea? Oh, of course I *might* get caught. But I'm no fool and, besides, her doctor can be counted on to co-operate (he has an eye for the same investment and I happen to know a good deal about his shady past). The deed can be done . . . professionally, shall we say. There is *very* little chance of getting caught. And as for my conscience being guilt-ridden, I am a resourceful sort of fellow and will take more than sufficient comfort—as I lie on the beach at Acapulco—in contemplating the joy and health I have brought to so many others.

Suppose Aunt Bea is killed and the rest of the story comes out as told. Would I have done anything wrong? Anything immoral? One would have thought that I had. Not according to utilitarianism. Since what I have done has brought about the best balance between totalled satisfaction and frustration for all those affected by the outcome, my action is not wrong. Indeed, in killing Aunt Bea the physician and I did what duty required.

This same kind of argument can be repeated in all sorts of cases, illustrating, time after time, how the utilitarian's position leads to results that impartial people find morally callous. It *is* wrong to kill my Aunt Bea in the name of bringing about the best results for others. A good end does not justify an evil means. Any adequate moral theory will have to explain why this is so. Utilitarianism fails in this respect and so cannot be the theory we seek.

What to do? Where to begin anew? The place to begin, I think, is with the utilitarian's view of the value of the individual—or, rather, lack of value. In its place, suppose we consider that you and I, for example, do have value as individuals—what we'll call *inherent value*. To say we have such value is to say that we are something more than, something different from, mere receptacles. Moreover, to ensure that we do not pave the way for such injustices as slavery or sexual discrimination, we must believe that all who have inherent value have it equally, regardless of their sex, race, religion, birthplace and so on. Similarly to be discarded as irrelevant are one's talents or skills, intelligence and wealth, personality or pathology, whether one is loved and admired or despised and loathed. The genius and the retarded child, the prince and the pauper, the brain surgeon and the fruit vendor, Mother Teresa and the most unscrupulous used-car salesman—all have inherent value, all possess it equally, and all have an equal right to be treated with respect, to be treated in ways that do not reduce them to the status of things, as if they existed as resources for others. My value as an individual is independent of my usefulness to you. Yours is not dependent on your usefulness to me. For either of us to treat the other in ways that fail to show respect for the other's independent value is to act immorally, to violate the individual's rights.

Some of the rational virtues of this view—what I call the rights view—should be evident. Unlike (crude) contractarianism, for example, the rights view *in principle* denies the moral tolerability of any and all forms of racial, sexual and social discrimination; and unlike utilitarianism, this view *in principle* denies that we can justify good results by using evil means that violate an individual's rights—denies, for example, that it could be moral to kill my Aunt Bea to harvest beneficial consequences for others. That would be to sanction the disrespectful treatment of the individual in the name of the social good, something the rights view will not—categorically will not—ever allow.

The rights view, I believe, is rationally the most satisfactory moral theory. It surpasses all other theories in the degree to which it illuminates and explains the foundation of our duties to one another—the domain of human morality. On this score it has the best reasons, the best arguments, on its side. Of course, if it were possible to show that only human beings are included within its scope, then a person like myself, who believes in animal rights, would be obliged to look elsewhere.

But attempts to limit its scope to humans only can be shown to be rationally defective. Animals, it is true, lack many of the abilities humans possess. They can't read, do higher mathematics, build a bookcase or make *baba ghanoush*. Neither can many human beings, however, and yet we don't (and shouldn't) say that they (these humans) therefore have less inherent value, less of a right to be treated with respect, than do others. It is the *similarities* between those human beings who most clearly, most non-controversially have such value (the people reading this, for example), not our differences, that matter most. And the really crucial, the basic similarity is simply this: we are each of us the experiencing subject of a life, a conscious creature having an individual welfare that has importance to us whatever our usefulness to others. We want and prefer things, believe and feel things, recall and expect things. And all these dimensions of our life, including our pleasure and pain, our enjoyment and suffering, our satisfaction and frustration, our continued existence or our untimely death—all make a difference to the quality of our life as lived, as experienced, by us as individuals. As the same is true of those animals that concern us (the ones that are eaten and trapped, for example), they

too must be viewed as the experiencing subjects of a life, with inherent value of their own.

Some there are who resist the idea that animals have inherent value. 'Only humans have such value,' they profess. How might this narrow view be defended? Shall we say that only humans have the requisite intelligence, or autonomy, or reason? But there are many, many humans who fail to meet these standards and yet are reasonably viewed as having value above and beyond their usefulness to others. Shall we claim that only humans belong to the right species, the species *Homo sapiens*? But this is blatant speciesism. Will it be said, then, that all —and only—humans have immortal souls? Then our opponents have their work cut out for them. I am myself not ill-disposed to the proposition that there are immortal souls. Personally, I profoundly hope I have one. But I would not want to rest my position on a controversial ethical issue on the even more controversial question about who or what has an immortal soul. That is to dig one's hole deeper, not to climb out. Rationally, it is better to resolve moral issues without making more controversial assumptions than are needed. The question of who has inherent value is such a question, one that is resolved more rationally without the introduction of the idea of immortal souls than by its use.

Well, perhaps some will say that animals have some inherent value, only less than we have. Once again, however, attempts to defend this view can be shown to lack rational justification. What could be the basis of our having more inherent value than animals? Their lack of reason, or autonomy, or intellect? Only if we are willing to make the same judgment in the case of humans who are similarly deficient. But it is not true that such humans—the retarded child, for example, or the mentally deranged—have less inherent value than you or I. Neither, then, can we rationally sustain the view that animals like them in being the experiencing subjects of a life have less inherent value. *All* who have inherent value have it *equally*, whether they be human animals or not.

Inherent value, then, belongs equally to those who are the experiencing subjects of a life. Whether it belongs to others—to rocks and rivers, trees and glaciers, for example—we do not know and may never know. But neither do we need to know, if we are to make the case for animal rights. We do not need to know, for example, how many people are eligible to vote in the next presidential election before we can know whether I am. Similarly, we do not need to know how many individuals have inherent value before we can know that some do. When it comes to the case for animal rights, then, what we need to know is whether the animals that, in our culture, are routinely eaten, hunted and used in our laboratories, for example, are like us in being subjects of a life. And we do know this. We do know that many—literally, billions and billions—of these animals are the subjects of a life in the sense explained and so have inherent value if we do. And since, in order to arrive at the best theory of our duties to one another, we must recognize our equal inherent value as individuals, reason—not sentiment, not emotion—reason compels us to recognize the equal inherent value of these animals and, with this, their equal right to be treated with respect.

That, *very* roughly, is the shape and feel of the case for animal rights. Most of the details of the supporting argument are missing. They are to be found in the book to which I alluded earlier. Here, the details go begging, and I must, in closing, limit myself to four final points.

The first is how the theory that underlies the case for animal rights shows that the animal rights movement is a part of, not antagonistic to, the human rights movement. The theory that rationally grounds the rights of animals also grounds the rights of humans. Thus those involved in the animal rights movement are partners in the struggle to secure respect for human rights—the rights of women, for example, or minorities, or workers. The animal rights movement is cut from the same moral cloth as these.

Second, having set out the broad outlines of the rights view, I can now say why its implications for farming and science, among other fields, are both clear and uncompromising. In the case of the use of animals in science, the rights view is categorically abolitionist. Lab animals are not our tasters; we are not their kings. Because these animals are treated routinely, systematically as if their value were reducible to their usefulness to others, they are routinely, systematically treated with a lack of respect, and thus are their rights routinely, systematically violated. This is just as true when they are used in trivial, duplicative, unnecessary or unwise research as it is when they are used in studies that hold out real promise of human benefits. We can't justify harming or killing a human being (my Aunt Bea, for example) just for these sorts of reasons. Neither can we do so even in the case of so lowly a creature as a laboratory rat. It is not just refinement or reduction that is called for, not just larger, cleaner cages, not just more generous use of anaesthetic or the elimination of multiple surgery, not just tidying up the system. It is complete replacement. The best we can do when it comes to using animals in science is—not to use them. That is where our duty lies, according to the rights view.

As for commercial animal agriculture, the rights view takes a similar abolitionist position. The fundamental moral wrong here is not that animals are kept in stressful close confinement or in isolation, or that their pain and suffering, their needs and preferences are ignored or discounted. All these *are* wrong, of course, but they are not the fundamental wrong. They are symptoms and effects of the deeper, systematic wrong that allows these animals to be viewed and treated as lacking independent value, as resources for us—as, indeed, a renewable resource. Giving farm animals more space, more natural environments, more companions does not right the fundamental wrong, any more than giving lab animals more anaesthesia or bigger, cleaner cages would right the fundamental wrong in their case. Nothing less than the total dissolution of commerical animal agriculture will do this, just as, for similar reasons I won't develop at length here, morality requires nothing less than the total elimination of hunting and trapping for commercial and sporting ends. The rights view's implications, then, as I have said, are clear and uncompromising.

My last two points are about philosophy, my profession. It is, most obviously, no substitute for political action. The words I have written here and in other places by themselves don't change a thing. It is what we do with the thoughts that the words express—our acts, our deeds—that changes things. All that philosophy can do, and all I have attempted, is to offer a vision of what our deeds should aim at. And the why. But not the how.

Finally, I am reminded of my thoughtful critic, the one I mentioned earlier, who chastised me for being too cerebral. Well, cerebral I have been: indirect duty views, utilitarianism, contractarianism—hardly the stuff deep passions are made of. I am also reminded, however, of the image another friend once set before me— the image of the ballerina as expressive of disciplined passion. Long hours of sweat and toil, of loneliness and practice, of doubt and fatigue: those are the discipline of her craft. But the passion is there too, the fierce drive to excel, to speak through her body, to do it right, to pierce our minds. That is the image of philosophy I would leave with you, not 'too cerebral' but *disciplined passion*. Of the discipline enough has been seen. As for the passion: there are times, and these not infrequent, when tears come to my eyes when I see, or read, or hear of the wretched plight of animals in the hands of humans. Their pain, their suffering, their loneliness, their innocence, their death. Anger. Rage. Pity. Sorrow. Disgust. The whole creation groans under the weight of the evil we humans visit upon these mute, powerless creatures. It *is* our hearts, not just our heads, that call for an end to it all, that demand of us that we overcome, for them, the habits and forces behind their systematic oppression. All great movements, it is written, go through three stages: ridicule, discussion, adoption. It is the realization of this third stage, adoption, that requires both our passion and our discipline, our hearts and our heads. The fate of animals is in our hands. God grant we are equal to the task.

Review Questions

1. According to Regan, what is the fundamental wrong in our treatment of animals?
2. What are indirect-duty views, and why does Regan reject them?
3. What is the cruelty-kindness view? Why isn't it acceptable, according to Regan?
4. What are Regan's objections to utilitarianism?
5. Explain Regan's rights view.
6. What are the implications of Regan's view for science and commercial animal agriculture?

Discussion Questions

1. How would Singer reply to Regan's criticisms of his utilitarianism?
2. What exactly is inherent value and who has it? Do fish and insects have it? How about comatose humans?

Do Animals Have Rights?

TIBOR R. MACHAN

Tibor R. Machan teaches in the School of Business and Economics at Chapman University in Orange, California.

Machan defends the Kantian view that humans have a higher moral status than animals. What distinguishes humans from animals is that humans have a moral life, they act as moral agents and make moral decisions, whereas animals do not have any moral life. In Machan's view, this implies that humans have natural rights to life, liberty, and property, and animals do not have rights. Furthermore, this implies that humans occupy the highest place in a hierarchical structure in nature and animals occupy a lower place, and that humans are justified in using animals for their purposes.

IN RECENT YEARS the doctrine of animals' rights has found champions in important circles where the general doctrine of rights is itself well respected. For example, Professor Tom Regan, in his important book *The Case For Animal Rights* (UC Press, 1983), finds the idea of natural rights intellectually congenial but then extends this idea to cover animals near humans on the evolutionary scale. The tradition from within which Regan works is clearly Lockean, only he does not agree that human nature is distinctive enough, in relevant respects, to restrict the scope of natural rights to human beings alone.

Following a different tradition, namely, utilitarianism, the idea of animal liberation has emerged. And this idea comes to roughly the same thing, practically speaking. Only the argument is different because for utilitarians what is important is not that someone or something must have a specific sphere of dominion but that

they be well off in their lives. So long as the bulk of the relevant creatures enjoy a reasonably high living standard, the moral and political objectives for us will have been met. But if this goal is neglected, moral and political steps are required to improve on the situation. Animal liberation is such a step.

This essay will maintain that animals have no rights and need no liberation. I will argue that to think they do is a category mistake—it is, to be blunt, to unjustifiably anthropomorphize animals, to treat them as if they were what they are not, namely, human beings. Rights and liberty are political concepts applicable to human beings because human beings are moral agents, in need of what Harvard philosopher Robert Nozick calls "moral space," that is, a definite sphere of moral jurisdiction where their authority to act is respected and protected so it is they, not intruders, who govern themselves and either succeed or fail in their moral tasks.

Oddly, it is clearly admitted by most animal rights or liberation theorists that only human beings are moral agents—for example, they never urge animals to behave morally (by, e.g.,

Source: Tibor R. Machan, "Do Animals Have Rights?" from *Public Affairs Quarterly,* Vol. 5, No. 2 (April 1991). Reprinted with permission. Footnotes renumbered.

standing up for their rights, by leading a political revolution). No animal rights theorist proposes that animals be tried for crimes and blamed for moral wrongs.

If it is true that the moral nature of human beings gives rise to the conception of basic rights and liberties, then by this alone animal rights and liberation theorists have made an admission fatal to their case.

Before getting under way I want to note that rights and liberty are certainly not the whole of moral concern to us. There are innumerable other moral issues one can raise, including about the way human beings relate to animals. In particular, there is the question how should people treat animals. Should they be hunted even when this does not serve any vital human purpose? Should they be utilized in hurtful—indeed, evidently agonizing—fashion even for trivial human purposes? Should their pain and suffering be ignored in the process of being made use of for admittedly vital human purposes?

It is clear that once one has answered the question of whether animals have rights (or ought to be liberated from human beings) in the negative, one has by no means disposed of these other issues. In this essay I will be dealing mostly with the issue of animal rights and liberation. Yet I will also touch briefly on the other moral issues just raised. I will indicate why they may all be answered in the negative without it being the case that animals have rights or should be liberated—i.e., without raising any serious political issues.

WHY MIGHT ANIMALS HAVE RIGHTS?

To have a right amounts to having those around one who have the choice to abstain from intruding on one within a given sphere of jurisdiction. If I have the right to the use of our community swimming pool, no one may prevent me from making the decision as to whether I do or do not use the pool. Someone's having a right is a

kind of freedom from the unavoidable interference of moral agents, beings who are capable of choosing whether they will interfere or not interfere with the rights holder.

When a right is considered natural, the freedom involved in having this right is supposed to be justified by reference to the kind of being one is, one's nature as a certain kind of entity. The idea of natural rights was formulated in connection with the issue of the proper relationship between human beings, especially citizens and governments. The idea goes back many centuries. . . .

The major political thinker with an influential doctrine of natural rights was John Locke. In his *Second Treatise on Government* he argued that each human being is responsible to follow the Law of Nature, the source of morality. But to do so, each also requires a sphere of personal authority, which is identified by the principle of the natural right to property—including one's person and estate. In other words, to be a morally responsible being in the company of other persons one needs what Robert Nozick has called "moral space," i.e., a sphere of sovereignty or personal jurisdiction so that one can engage in self-government—for better or for worse. . . .

In our time numerous philosophers and social commentators have made the attempt to demonstrate that if we are able to ascribe basic rights to life, liberty and property to human beings, we can do the same for many of the higher animals. In essentials their arguments can be broken down into two parts. First, they subscribe to Darwin's thesis that no difference of kind, only a difference of degree, can be found between other animals and human beings.[1] Second, even if there were a difference in kind between other animals—especially mammals—and

---

1 Charles Darwin, *The Descent of Man*, Chpts. 3 and 4. Reprinted in Tom Regan and Peter Singer, eds., *Animal Rights and Human Obligations* (Englewood Cliffs, NJ: Prentice-Hall, 1976), pp. 72–81.

human beings, since they both can be shown to have interests (e.g., the avoidance of pain or suffering), for certain moral and legal purposes the difference does not matter, only the similarity does. In connection with both of these arguments the central conclusion is that if human beings can be said to have certain basic rights—e.g., to life, liberty or consideration for their capacity to suffer—then so do (higher) animals.[2]

Now I do not wish to give the impression that no diversity exists among those who defend animal rights. Some do so from the viewpoint of natural rights, treating animals' rights as basic limiting principles which may not be ignored except when it would also make sense to disregard the rights of human beings. Even on this matter there are serious differences among defenders of animals' rights—some do not allow any special regard for human beings,[3] some hold that when it comes to a choice between a person and a dog, it is ordinarily the person who should be given protection.[4] But others choose to defend animal rights on utilitarian grounds—to the extent that it amounts to furthering overall pleasure or happiness in the world, animals must be given equal consideration to what human beings receive. Thus only if there really is demonstrable contribution to the overall pleasure or happiness on earth may an animal capa-

ble of experiencing pleasure or happiness be sacrificed for the sake of some human purpose. Barring such demonstrable contribution, animals and humans enjoy equal rights.[5]

At times the argument for animal rights begins with the rather mild point that "reason requires that other animals are as much within the scope of moral concern as are men" but then moves on to the more radical claim that therefore "we must view our entire history as well as all aspects of our daily lives from a new perspective."[6]

Of course, people have generally invoked some moral considerations as they treated animals—I can recall living on a farm in Hungary when I was 11 and getting all kinds of lectures about how I ought to treat the animals, receiving severe rebuke when I mistreated a cat and lots of praise when I took the favorite cow grazing every day and established a close bond with it over time. Hardly anyone can have escaped one or another moral lecture from parents or neighbors concerning the treatment of pets, household animals, or birds. When a young boy once tried out an air gun by shooting a pigeon sitting on a telephone wire before the apartment house in which he lived, I recall that there was no end of rebuke in response to his wanton callousness. Yet none of those who engaged in the moralizing ever entertained the need to "view our entire history as well as all aspects of our daily lives from a new perspective." Rather they seemed to have understood that reckless disregard for the life or well being of animals shows a defect of character, lack of sensitivity, callousness—realizing, at the same time, that numerous human purposes justify our killing and using animals in the various ways most of us do use them.

And this really is the crux of the matter. But why? Why is it more reasonable to think of animals as available for our sensible use rather than

2 On these points both the deontologically oriented Tom Regan and the utilitarian Peter Singer tend to agree, although they differ considerably in their arguments.

3 Peter Singer holds that "we would be on shaky grounds if we were to demand equality for blacks, women, and other groups of oppressed humans while denying equal consideration to nonhumans." "All Animals Are Equal," op. cit., Regan & Singer, *Animal Rights*, p. 150.

4 Tom Regan contends that "[it] is not to say that practices that involve taking the lives of animals cannot possibly be justified . . . in order to seriously consider approving such a practice [it] would [have to] prevent, reduce, or eliminate a much greater amount of evil . . . there is no other way to bring about these consequences . . . and . . . we have very good reason to believe that these consequences will obtain." "Do Animals Have a Right to Life?" op. cit., Regan & Singer, *Animal Rights,* pp. 204–5.

5 This is the gist of Singer's thesis.

6 Bernard E. Rollin, *Animal Rights and Human Morality* (Buffalo, NY: Prometheus Books, 1981), p. 4.

owed the kind of respect and consideration we ought to extend to other human beings? It is one thing to have this as a common sense conviction, it is another to know it as a sound viewpoint, in terms of which we may confidently conduct ourselves.

WHY WE MAY USE ANIMALS

While I will return to the arguments for animal rights, let me first place on record the case for the use of animals for human purposes. Without this case reasonably well established, it will not be possible to critically assess the case for animal rights. After all, this is a comparative matter—which viewpoint makes better sense, which is, in other words, more likely to be true?

One reason for the propriety of our use of animals is that we are more important or valuable than other animals and some of our projects may require animals for them to be successful. Notice that this is different from saying that human beings are "uniquely important," a position avidly ridiculed by Stephen R. L. Clark, who claims that "there seems no decent ground in reason or revelation to suppose that man is uniquely important or significant."[7] If man were uniquely important, that would mean that one could not assign any value to plants or non-human animals apart from their relationship to human beings. That is not the position I am defending. I argue that there is a scale of importance in nature, and among all the various kinds of being, human beings are the most important—even while it is true that some members of the human species may indeed prove themselves to be the most vile and worthless, as well.

How do we establish that we are more important or valuable? By considering whether the idea of lesser or greater importance or value in the nature of things makes clear sense and applying it to an understanding of whether human beings or other animals are more important. If it turns out that ranking things in nature as more or less important makes sense, and if we qualify as more important than other animals, there is at least the beginning of a reason why we may make use of other animals for our purposes.

That there are things of different degree of value in nature is admitted by animal rights advocates, so there is no great need here to argue about that. When they insist that we treat animals differently from the way we treat, say, rocks or iron ore—so that while we may not use the former as we choose, we may use the latter—they testify, at least by implication, that animals are more important than, say, iron ore. Certainly they invoke some measure of importance or value and place animals higher in line with this measure than they place other aspects of nature. They happen, also, to deny that human beings rank higher than animals, or at least they do not admit that human beings' higher ranking warrants their using animals for their purposes. But that is a distinct issue which we can consider later.

Quite independently of the implicit acknowledgment by animal rights advocates of the hierarchy of nature, there simply is evidence through the natural world of the existence of beings of greater complexity and of higher value. For example, while it makes no sense to evaluate as good or bad such things as planets or rocks or pebbles—except as they may relate to human purposes—when it comes to plants and animals the process of evaluation commences very naturally indeed. We can speak of better or worse trees, oaks, redwoods, or zebras, foxes or chimps. While at this point we confine our evaluation to the condition or behavior of such beings without any intimation of their responsibility for being better or worse, when we start discussing human beings our evaluation

---

7 Stephen R. L. Clark, *The Moral Status of Animals* (Oxford, England: Clarendon Press, 1977), p. 13.

takes on a moral component. Indeed, none are more ready to testify to this than animal rights advocates who, after all, do not demand any change of behavior on the part of non-human animals and yet insist that human beings conform to certain moral edicts as a matter of their own choice. This means that even animal rights advocates admit outright that to the best of our knowledge it is with human beings that the idea of moral goodness and moral responsibility enters the universe.

Clearly this shows a hierarchical structure in nature: some things do not invite evaluations at all—it is a matter of no significance or of indifference whether they are or are not or what they are or how they behave. Some things invite evaluation but without implying any moral standing with reference to whether they do well or badly. And some things—namely, human beings—invite moral evaluation. The level of importance or value may be noted to move from the inanimate to the animate world, culminating, as far as we now know, with human life. Normal human life involves moral tasks, and that is why we are more important than other beings in nature—we are subject to moral appraisal, it is a matter of our doing whether we succeed or fail in our lives.

Now when it comes to our moral task, namely, to succeed as human beings, we are dependent upon reaching sensible conclusions about what we should do. We can fail to do this and too often do so. But we can also succeed. The process that leads to our success involves learning, among other things, what it is that nature avails us with to achieve our highly varied tasks in life. Clearly among these highly varied tasks could be some that make judicious use of animals—for example, to find out whether some medicine is safe for human use, we might wish to use animals. To do this is the rational thing for us to do, so as to make the best use of nature for our success in living our lives. That does not mean there need be no guidelines involved in

how we might make use of animals—any more than there need be no guidelines involved in how we use anything else.

WHY INDIVIDUAL HUMAN RIGHTS?

Where do individual *human* rights come into this picture? The rights being talked of in connection with human beings have as their source, as we have noted earlier, the human capacity to make moral choices. We have the right to life, liberty and property—as well as more specialized rights connected with politics, the press, religion—because we have as our central task in life to act morally. And in order to be able to do this throughout the scope of our lives, we require a reasonably clear sphere of personal jurisdiction—a dominion where we are sovereign and can either succeed or fail to live well, to do right, to act properly.

If we did not have rights, we would not have such a sphere of personal jurisdiction and there would be no clear idea as to whether we are acting in our own behalf or those of other persons. No one could be blamed or praised for we would not know clearly enough whether what the person is doing is in his or her authority to do or in someone else's. This is precisely the problem that arises in communal living and, especially, in totalitarian countries where everything is under forced collective governance. The reason moral distinctions are still possible to make under such circumstances is that in fact—as distinct from law—there is always some sphere of personal jurisdiction wherein people may exhibit courage, prudence, justice, honesty and other virtues. But where collectivism has been successfully enforced, there is no individual responsibility at play and people's morality and immorality is submerged within the group.

Indeed the main reason for governments has for some time been recognized to be nothing other than that our individual human rights should be protected. . . .

WHERE IS THERE ROOM FOR ANIMAL RIGHTS?

We have seen that the most sensible and influential doctrine of human rights rests on the fact that human beings are indeed members of a discernibly different species—the members of which have a moral life to aspire to and must have principles upheld for them in communities that make their aspiration possible. Now there is plainly no valid intellectual place for rights in the non-human world, the world in which moral responsibility is for all practical purposes absent. Some would want to argue that some measure of morality can be found within the world of at least higher animals—e.g., dogs. For example, Rollin holds that "In actual fact, some animals even seem to exhibit behavior that bespeaks something like moral agency or moral agreement."[8] His argument for this is rather anecdotal but it is worth considering:

> Canids, including the domesticated dog, do not attack another when the vanquished bares its throat, showing a sign of submission. Animals typically do not prey upon members of their own species. Elephants and porpoises will and do feed injured members of their species. Porpoises will help humans, even at risk to themselves. Some animals will adopt orphaned young of other species. (Such cross-species "morality" would certainly not be explainable by simple appeal to mechanical evolution, since there is no advantage whatever to one's own species.) Dogs will act "guilty" when they break a rule such as one against stealing food from a table and will, for the most part, learn not to take it.[9]

Animal rights advocates such as Rollin maintain that it is impossible to clearly distinguish between human and non-human animals, including on the grounds of the former's characteristic as a moral agent. Yet what they do to defend this point is to invoke borderline cases, imaginary hypothesis, and anecdotes.

In contrast, in his book *The Difference of Man and the Difference It Makes,* Mortimer Adler undertakes the painstaking task of showing that even with the full acknowledgment of the merits of Darwinian and, especially, post-Darwinian evolutionary theory, there is ample reason to uphold the doctrine of species-distinction—a distinction, incidentally, that is actually presupposed within Darwin's own work.[10] Adler shows that although the theistic doctrine of radical species differences is incompatible with current evolutionary theory, the more naturalistic view that species are superficially (but non-negligibly) different is indeed necessary to it. The fact of occasional borderline cases is simply irrelevant— what is crucial is that the generalization is true that human beings are basically different from other animals—by virtue of "a crucial threshold in a continuum of degrees." As Adler explains:

> . . . distinct species are genetically isolated populations between which interbreeding is impossible, arising (except in the case of polyploidy) from varieties between which interbreeding was not impossible, but between which it was prevented. Modern theorists, with more assurance than Darwin could manage, treat distinct species as natural kinds, not as man-made class distinctions.[11]

Adler adds that "Without the critical insight provided by the distinction between superficial and radical differences in kind, biologists [as well as animal rights advocates, one should add]

---

8 Rollin, *Animal Rights,* p. 14.
9 Ibid.

10 See a discussion of this in Mortimer Adler, *The Difference of Man and the Difference It Makes* (New York: World Publishing Co., 1968), pp. 73ff.
11 Ibid.

might be tempted to follow Darwin in thinking that all differences in kind must be apparent, not real."[12]

Since Locke's admittedly incomplete—sometimes even confusing—theory had gained respect and, especially, practical import (e.g., in British and American political history), it became clear enough that the only justification for the exercise of state power—namely the force of the law—is that the rights of individuals are being or have been violated. But as with all successful doctrines, Locke's idea became corrupted by innumerable efforts to concoct rights that government must protect, rights that were actually disguised special interest objectives—values that some people, perhaps quite legitimately, wanted very badly to have secured for them.

While it is no doubt true that many animal rights advocates sincerely believe that they have found a justification for the actual existence of animal rights, it is equally likely that if the Lockean doctrine of rights had not become so influential, they would now be putting their point

12 Ibid., p. 75.

differently—in a way, namely, that would secure for them what they, as a special interest group, want: the protection of animals they have such love and sympathy for.

CLOSING REFLECTIONS

As with most issues on the minds of many intelligent people as well as innumerable crackpots, a discussion of whether there are animal rights and how we ought to treat animals cannot be concluded with dogmatic certainty one way or the other. Even though those who defend animal rights are certain almost beyond a shadow of doubt, all I can claim is to being certain beyond a reasonable doubt. Animals are not the sort of beings with basic rights to life, liberty and property, whereas human beings, in the main, are just such beings. Yet we know that animals can feel pain and can enjoy themselves and this must give us pause when we consider using them for our legitimate purposes. We ought to be humane, we ought to kill them and rear them and train them and hunt them in a fashion consistent with such care about them as sentient beings.

Review Questions

1. Why does Machan think it is a "category mistake" to say that animals have rights?
2. How does Machan explain the concept of having a right? What is a natural right?
3. According to Machan, what is the two-part argument for saying that animals have rights?
4. Why does Machan believe that humans are more important than animals?
5. According to Machan, what is the source of human rights?
6. Why don't animals have rights in Machan's view?

Discussion Questions

1. Has Machan given a satisfactory reply to the argument that animals have a right not to suffer because they have an interest in not suffering?
2. What is the moral status of human beings who do not have a moral life—for example, the mentally ill? What is Machan's view? What do you think?
3. At the end of his essay, Machan says that we ought to be humane to animals. Doesn't this imply that animals have some rights after all—for example, a right not to suffer?

Difficulties with the Strong Animal Rights Position

MARY ANNE WARREN

For biographical information on Warren, see her reading in Chapter 2.

Warren explains and then attacks Regan's strong animal rights position, the view that nonhuman animals have the same basic moral rights as humans. She makes two criticisms of Regan's position: It rests on an obscure concept of inherent value, and it fails to draw a sharp line between living things which have inherent value and moral rights and other living things which don't have such value or rights. Warren concludes with a defense of the weak animal rights position—that animal rights are weaker than human rights because humans are rational and animals are not.

TOM REGAN HAS PRODUCED what is perhaps the definitive defense of the view that the basic moral rights of at least some non-human animals are in no way inferior to our own. In *The Case for Animal Rights,* he argues that all normal mammals over a year of age have the same basic moral rights.[1] Non-human mammals have essentially the same right not to be harmed or killed as we do. I shall call this "the strong animal rights position," although it is weaker than the claims made by some animal liberationists in that it ascribes rights to only some sentient animals.[2]

I will argue that Regan's case for the strong animal rights position is unpersuasive and that this position entails consequences which a reasonable person cannot accept. I do not deny that some non-human animals have moral rights; indeed, I would extend the scope of the rights claim to include all sentient animals, that is, all those capable of having experiences, including experiences of pleasure or satisfaction and pain, suffering, or frustration.[3] However, I do not think that the moral rights of most non-human animals are identical in strength to those of persons.[4] The rights of most non-human animals may be overridden in circumstances which would not justify overriding the rights of persons. There are, for instance, compelling realities which sometimes require that we kill animals for reasons which could not justify the killing of persons. I will call this view "the weak animal rights" position, even though it ascribes rights to a wider range of animals than does the strong animal rights position.

Source: Mary Anne Warren, "Difficulties with the Strong Rights Position," from *Between the Species* 2, No. 4 (Fall 1987), pp. 433–441.

1 Tom Regan, *The Case for Animal Rights* (Berkeley: University of California Press, 1983). All page references are to this edition.

2 For instance, Peter Singer, although he does not like to speak of rights, includes all sentient beings under the protection of his basic utilitarian principle of equal respect for like interests. (Animal Liberation [New York: Avon Books, 1975], p. 3.)

3 The capacity for sentience, like all of the mental capacities mentioned in what follows, is a disposition. Dispositions do not disappear whenever they are not currently manifested. Thus, sleeping or temporarily unconscious persons or non-human animals are still sentient in the relevant sense (i.e., still capable of sentience), so long as they still have the neurological mechanisms necessary for the occurrence of experiences.

4 It is possible, perhaps probable that some non-human animals—such as cetaceans and anthropoid apes—should be regarded as persons. If so, then the weak animal rights position holds that these animals have the same basic moral rights as human persons.

I will begin by summarizing Regan's case for the strong animal rights position and noting two problems with it. Next, I will explore some consequences of the strong animal rights position which I think are unacceptable. Finally, I will outline the case for the weak animal rights position.

REGAN'S CASE

Regan's argument moves through three stages. First, he argues that normal, mature mammals are not only sentient but have other mental capacities as well. These include the capacities for emotion, memory, belief, desire, the use of general concepts, intentional action, a sense of the future, and some degree of self-awareness. Creatures with such capacities are said to be subjects-of-a-life. They are not only alive in the biological sense but have a psychological identity over time and an existence which can go better or worse for them. Thus, they can be harmed or benefited. These are plausible claims, and well defended. One of the strongest parts of the book is the rebuttal of philosophers, such as R. G. Frey, who object to the application of such mentalistic terms to creatures that do not use a human-style language.[5] The second and third stages of the argument are more problematic.

In the second stage, Regan argues that subjects-of-a-life have inherent value. His concept of inherent value grows out of his opposition to utilitarianism. Utilitarian moral theory, he says, treats individuals as "mere receptacles" for morally significant value, in that harm to one individual may be justified by the production of a greater net benefit to other individuals. In opposition to this, he holds that subjects-of-a-life have a value independent of both the value they may place upon their lives or experiences and the value others may place upon them.

Inherent value, Regan argues, does not come in degrees. To hold that some individuals have

more inherent value than others is to adopt a "perfectionist" theory, i.e., one which assigns different moral worth to individuals according to how well they are thought to exemplify some virtue(s), such as intelligence or moral autonomy. Perfectionist theories have been used, at least since the time of Aristotle, to rationalize such injustices as slavery and male domination, as well as the unrestrained exploitation of animals. Regan argues that if we reject these injustices, then we must also reject perfectionism and conclude that all subjects-of-a-life have equal inherent value. Moral agents have no more inherent value than moral patients, i.e., subjects-of-a-life who are not morally responsible for their actions.

In the third phase of the argument, Regan uses the thesis of equal inherent value to derive strong moral rights for all subjects-of-a-life. This thesis underlies the Respect Principle, which forbids us to treat beings who have inherent value as mere receptacles, i.e., mere means to the production of the greatest overall good. This principle, in turn, underlies the Harm Principle, which says that we have a direct *prima facie* duty not to harm beings who have inherent value. Together, these principles give rise to moral rights. Rights are defined as valid claims, claims to certain goods and against certain beings, i.e., moral agents. Moral rights generate duties not only to refrain from inflicting harm upon beings with inherent value but also to come to their aid when they are threatened by other moral agents. Rights are not absolute but may be overridden in certain circumstances. Just what these circumstances are we will consider later. But first, let's look at some difficulties in the theory as thus far presented.

THE MYSTERY
OF INHERENT VALUE

Inherent value is a key concept in Regan's theory. It is the bridge between the plausible claim that all normal, mature mammals—human or

5 See R. G. Frey, *Interests and Rights: The Case Against Animals* (Oxford: Oxford University Press, 1980).

otherwise—are subjects-of-a-life and the more debatable claim that they all have basic moral rights of the same strength. But it is a highly obscure concept, and its obscurity makes it ill-suited to play this crucial role.

Inherent value is defined almost entirely in negative terms. It is not dependent upon the value which either the inherently valuable individual or anyone else may place upon that individual's life or experiences. It is not (necessarily) a function of sentience or any other mental capacity, because, Regan says, some entities which are not sentient (e.g., trees, rivers, or rocks) may, nevertheless, have inherent value (p. 246). It cannot attach to anything other than an individual; species, eco-systems, and the like cannot have inherent value.

These are some of the things which inherent value is not. But what is it? Unfortunately, we are not told. Inherent value appears as a mysterious non-natural property which we must take on faith. Regan says that it is a *postulate* that subjects-of-a-life have inherent value, a postulate justified by the fact that it avoids certain absurdities which he thinks follow from a purely utilitarian theory (p. 247). But why is the postulate that *subjects-of-a-life* have inherent value? If the inherent value of a being is completely independent of the value that it or anyone else places upon its experiences, then why does the fact that it has certain sorts of experiences constitute evidence that it has inherent value? If the reason is that subjects-of-a-life have an existence which can go better or worse for them, then why isn't the appropriate conclusion that all sentient beings have inherent value, since they would all seem to meet that condition? Sentient but mentally unsophisticated beings may have a less extensive range of possible satisfactions and frustrations, but why should it follow that they have—or may have—no inherent value at all?

In the absence of a positive account of inherent value, it is also difficult to grasp the connection between being inherently valuable and having moral rights. Intuitively, it seems that value is one thing, and rights are another. It does not seem incoherent to say that some things (e.g., mountains, rivers, redwood trees) are inherently valuable and yet are not the sorts of things which can have moral rights. Nor does it seem incoherent to ascribe inherent value to some things which are not individuals, e.g., plant or animal species, though it may well be incoherent to ascribe moral rights to such things.

In short, the concept of inherent value seems to create at least as many problems as it solves. If inherent value is based on some natural property, then why not try to identify that property and explain its moral significance, without appealing to inherent value? And if it is not based on any natural property, then why should we believe in it? That it may enable us to avoid some of the problems faced by the utilitarian is not a sufficient reason, if it creates other problems which are just as serious.

IS THERE A SHARP LINE?

Perhaps the most serious problems are those that arise when we try to apply the strong animal rights position to animals other than normal, mature mammals. Regan's theory requires us to divide all living things into two categories: those which have the same inherent value and the same basic moral rights that we do, and those which have no inherent value and presumably no moral rights. But wherever we try to draw the line, such a sharp division is implausible.

It would surely be arbitrary to draw such a sharp line between normal, mature mammals and all other living things. Some birds (e.g., crows, magpies, parrots, mynahs) appear to be just as mentally sophisticated as most mammals and thus are equally strong candidates for inclusion under the subject-of-a-life criterion. Regan is not in fact advocating that we draw the line here. His claim is only that normal mature mammals are clear cases, while other cases are less clear. Yet, on his theory, there must be such a sharp line *somewhere,* since there are no degrees of inherent value. But why should we believe that there is a sharp line between creatures that are subjects-of-a-life and creatures that are not? Isn't it more likely that "subjecthood" comes in degrees, that some creatures have only a little self-awareness, and only a little capacity to anticipate the future, while some have a little more, and some a good deal more?

Should we, for instance, regard fish, amphibians, and reptiles as subjects-of-a-life? A simple yes-or-no answer seems inadequate. On the one hand, some of their behavior is difficult to explain without the assumption that they have sensations, beliefs, desires, emotions, and memories; on the other hand, they do not seem to exhibit very much self-awareness or very much conscious anticipation of future events. Do they have enough mental sophistication to count as subjects-of-a-life? Exactly how much is enough?

It is still more unclear what we should say about insects, spiders, octopi, and other invertebrate animals which have brains and sensory organs but whose minds (if they have minds) are even more alien to us than those of fish or reptiles. Such creatures are probably sentient. Some people doubt that they can feel pain, since they lack certain neurological structures which are crucial to the processing of pain impulses in vertebrate animals. But this argument is inconclusive, since their nervous systems might process pain in ways different from ours. When injured, they sometimes act as if they are in pain. On evolutionary grounds, it seems unlikely that highly mobile creatures with complex sensory systems would not have developed a capacity for pain (and pleasure), since such a capacity has obvious survival value. It must, however, be admitted that we do not *know* whether spiders can feel pain (or something very like it), let alone whether they have emotions, memories, beliefs, desires, self-awareness, or a sense of the future.

Even more mysterious are the mental capacities (if any) of mobile microfauna. The brisk and efficient way that paramecia move about in their incessant search for food *might* indicate some kind of sentience, in spite of their lack of eyes, ears, brains, and other organs associated with sentience in more complex organisms. It is conceivable—though not very probable—that they, too, are subjects-of-a-life.

The existence of a few unclear cases need not pose a serious problem for a moral theory, but in this case, the unclear cases constitute most of those with which an adequate theory of animal rights would need to deal. The subject-of-a-life criterion can provide us with little or no moral guidance in our interactions with the vast majority of animals. That might be acceptable if it could be supplemented with additional principles which would provide such guidance. However, the radical dualism of the theory precludes supplementing it in this way. We are forced to say that either a spider has the same right to life as you and I do, or it has no right to life whatever—and that only the gods know which of these alternatives is true.

Regan's suggestion for dealing with such unclear cases is to apply the "benefit of the doubt" principle. That is, when dealing with beings that may or may not be subjects-of-a-life, we should act as if they are.[6] But if we try to apply this principle to the entire range of doubtful cases, we will find ourselves with moral obligations which we cannot possibly fulfill. In many climates, it is virtually impossible to live without swatting mosquitoes and exterminating cockroaches, and not all of us can afford to hire someone to sweep the path before we walk, in order to make sure that we do not step on ants. Thus, we are still faced with the daunting task of drawing a sharp line somewhere on the continuum of life forms—this time, a line demarcating the limits of the benefit of the doubt principle.

6 See, for instance, p. 319, where Regan appeals to the benefit of the doubt principle when dealing with infanticide and late-term abortion.

The weak animal rights theory provides a more plausible way of dealing with this range of cases, in that it allows the rights of animals of different kinds to vary in strength. . . .

WHY ARE ANIMAL RIGHTS WEAKER THAN HUMAN RIGHTS?

How can we justify regarding the rights of persons as generally stronger than those of sentient beings which are not persons? There are a plethora of bad justifications, based on religious premises or false or unprovable claims about the differences between human and non-human nature. But there is one difference which has a clear moral relevance: people are at least sometimes capable of being moved to action or inaction by the force of reasoned argument. Rationality rests upon other mental capacities, notably those which Regan cites as criteria for being a subject-of-a-life. We share these capacities with many other animals. But it is not just because we are subjects-of-a-life that we are both able and morally compelled to recognize one another as beings with equal basic moral rights. it is also because we are able to "listen to reason" in order to settle our conflicts and cooperate in shared projects. This capacity, unlike the others, may require something like a human language.

Why is rationality morally relevant? It does not make us "better" than other animals or more "perfect." It does not even automatically make us more intelligent. (Bad reasoning reduces our effective intelligence rather than increasing it.) But it is morally relevant insofar as it provides greater possibilities for cooperation and for the nonviolent resolution of problems. It also makes us more dangerous than non-rational beings can ever be. Because we are potentially more dangerous and less predictable than wolves, we need an articulated system of morality to regulate our conduct. Any human morality, to be workable in the long run, must recognize the equal moral status of all persons, whether through the postulate of equal basic moral rights or in some other way. The recognition of the moral equality of other persons is the price we must each pay for their recognition of our moral equality. Without this mutual recognition of moral equality, human society can exist only in a state of chronic and bitter conflict. The war between the sexes will persist so long as there is sexism and male domination; racial conflict will never be eliminated so long as there are racist laws and practices. But, to the extent that we achieve a mutual recognition of equality, we can hope to live together, perhaps as peacefully as wolves, achieving (in part) through explicit moral principles what they do not seem to need explicit moral principles to achieve.

Why not extend this recognition of moral equality to other creatures, even though they cannot do the same for us? The answer is that we cannot. Because we cannot reason with most non-human animals, we cannot always solve the problems which they may cause without harming them—although we are always obligated to try. We cannot negotiate a treaty with the feral cats and foxes, requiring them to stop preying on endangered native species in return for suitable concessions on our part.

> if rats invade our houses . . . we cannot reason with them, hoping to persuade them of the injustice they do us. We can only attempt to get rid of them.[7]

Aristotle was not wrong in claiming that the capacity to alter one's behavior on the basis of reasoned argument is relevant to the full moral status which he accorded to free men. Of course, he was wrong in his other premise, that women and slaves by their nature cannot reason well enough to function as autonomous moral agents. Had that premise been true, so would

7 Bonnie Steinbock, "Speciesism and the Idea of Equality," *Philosophy* 53 (1978):253.

his conclusion that women and slaves are not quite the moral equals of free men. In the case of most non-human animals, the corresponding premise is true. If, on the other hand, there are animals with whom we can (learn to) reason, then we are obligated to do this and to regard them as our moral equals.

Thus, to distinguish between the rights of persons and those of most other animals on the grounds that only people can alter their behavior on the basis of reasoned argument does not commit us to a perfectionist theory of the sort Aristotle endorsed. There is no excuse for refusing to recognize the moral equality of some people on the grounds that we don't regard them as quite as rational as we are, since it is perfectly clear that most people can reason well enough to determine how to act so as to respect the basic rights of others (if they choose to), and that is enough for moral equality.

But what about people who are clearly not rational? It is often argued that sophisticated mental capacities such as rationality cannot be essential for the possession of equal basic moral rights, since nearly everyone agrees that human infants and mentally incompetent persons have such rights, even though they may lack those sophisticated mental capacities. But this argument is inconclusive, because there are powerful practical and emotional reasons for protecting non-rational human beings, reasons which are absent in the case of most non-human animals. Infancy and mental incompetence are human conditions which all of us either have experienced or are likely to experience at some time. We also protect babies and mentally incompetent people because we care for them. We don't normally care for animals in the same way, and when we do—e.g., in the case of much-loved pets—we may regard them as having special rights by virtue of their relationship to us. We protect them not only for their sake but also for our own, lest we be hurt by harm done to them. Regan holds that such

"side-effects" are irrelevant to moral rights, and perhaps they are. But in ordinary usage, there is no sharp line between moral rights and those moral protections which are not rights. The extension of strong moral protections to infants and the mentally impaired in no way proves that non-human animals have the same basic moral rights as people.

WHY SPEAK OF "ANIMAL RIGHTS" AT ALL?

If, as I have argued, reality precludes our treating all animals as our moral equals, then why should we still ascribe rights to them? Everyone agrees that animals are entitled to some protection against human abuse, but why speak of animal *rights* if we are not prepared to accept most animals as our moral equals? The weak animal rights position may seem an unstable compromise between the bold claim that animals have the same basic moral rights that we do and the more common view that animals have no rights at all.

It is probably impossible to either prove or disprove the thesis that animals have moral rights by producing an analysis of the concept of a moral right and checking to see if some or all animals satisfy the conditions for having rights. The concept of a moral right is complex, and it is not clear which of its strands are essential. Paradigm rights holders, i.e., mature and mentally competent persons, are *both* rational and morally autonomous beings and sentient subjects-of-a-life. Opponents of animal rights claim that rationality and moral autonomy are essential for the possession of rights, while defenders of animal rights claim that they are not. The ordinary concept of a moral right is probably not precise enough to enable us to determine who is right on purely definitional grounds.

If logical analysis will not answer the question of whether animals have moral rights, practical considerations may, nevertheless, incline us to say that they do. The most plausible alternative to the view that animals have moral rights is that, while they do not have *rights,* we are, nevertheless, obligated not to be cruel to them. Regan argues persuasively that the injunction to avoid being cruel to animals is inadequate to express our obligations towards animals, because it focuses on the mental states of those who cause animal suffering, rather than on the harm done to the animals themselves (p. 158). Cruelty is inflicting pain or suffering and either taking pleasure in that pain or suffering or being more or less indifferent to it. Thus, to express the demand for the decent treatment of animals in terms of the rejection of cruelty is to invite the too easy response that those who subject animals to suffering are not being cruel because they regret the suffering they cause but sincerely believe that what they do is justified. The injunction to avoid cruelty is also inadequate in that it does not preclude the killing of animals— for any reason, however trivial—so long as it is done relatively painlessly.

The inadequacy of the anti-cruelty view provides one practical reason for speaking of animal rights. Another practical reason is that this is an age in which nearly all significant moral claims tend to be expressed in terms of rights. Thus, the denial that animals have rights, however carefully qualified, is likely to be taken to mean that we may do whatever we like to them, provided that we do not violate any human rights. In such a context, speaking of the rights of animals may be the only way to persuade many people to take seriously protests against the abuse of animals.

Why not extend this line of argument and speak of the rights of trees, mountains, oceans, or anything else which we may wish to see protected from destruction? Some environmentalists have not hesitated to speak in this way, and, given the importance of protecting such elements of the natural world, they cannot be blamed for using this rhetorical device. But, I would argue that moral rights can meaningfully be ascribed only to entities which have some capacity for sentience. This is because moral rights are protections designed to protect rights holders from harms or to provide them with benefits which matter *to them.* Only beings capable of sentience can be harmed or benefited in ways which matter to them, for only such beings can like or dislike what happens to them or prefer some conditions to others. Thus, sentient animals, unlike mountains, rivers, or species, are at least logically possible candidates for moral rights. This fact, together with the need to end current abuses of animals—e.g., in scientific research . . .—provides a plausible case for speaking of animal rights.

CONCLUSION

I have argued that Regan's case for ascribing strong moral rights to all normal, mature mammals is unpersuasive because (1) it rests upon the obscure concept of inherent value, which is defined only in negative terms, and (2) it seems to preclude any plausible answer to questions about the moral status of the vast majority of sentient animals. . . .

The weak animal rights theory asserts that (1) any creature whose natural mode of life includes the pursuit of certain satisfactions has the right not to be forced to exist without the opportunity to pursue those satisfactions; (2) that any creature which is capable of pain, suffering, or frustration has the right that such experiences not be deliberately inflicted upon it without some compelling reason; and (3) that no sentient being should be killed without good reason. However, moral rights are not an all-or-nothing affair. The strength of the reasons required to override the rights of a non-human organism varies, depending upon—among other things—the probability that it is sentient and (if it is clearly sentient) its probable degree of mental sophistication. . . .

Review Questions

1. Distinguish between what Warren calls the strong animal rights position and the weak animal rights position.
2. What problems does Warren find in Regan's case for the strong animal rights position?
3. Explain Warren's defense of the weak animal rights position.

Discussion Questions

1. Has Warren refuted Regan's strong animal rights position? Does he have an adequate reply?
2. In Warren's view, rationality is essential for having equal basic moral rights. But infants and mentally incompetent humans are not rational; therefore, they do not have moral rights. Does Warren have an acceptable reply to this argument?

Vegetarianism and "the Other Weight Problem"

JAMES RACHELS

For biographical information on Rachels, see the reading in Chapter One.

Rachels gives two arguments for vegetarianism. The first appeals to the moral duty to not waste food. Meat-eating wastes food, and for that reason it is wrong. The second and more compelling argument appeals to the suffering of the animals that are raised and slaughtered for food. According to Rachels, this suffering is not justified by the enjoyment of the way they taste, and therefore it is wrong.

It is now common for newspapers and magazines to carry the ultimate indictment of glutted Americans: ads for weight salons or reducing schemes next to news accounts of starvation in Africa, Latin America, or elsewhere. The pictures of big-bellied children nursing on emptied breasts tell of the other "weight problem."[1]

THERE ARE MORAL PROBLEMS about what we eat, and about what we do with the food we control. In this essay I shall discuss some of these problems. One of my conclusions will be that it is morally wrong for us to eat meat. Many readers will find this implausible and even faintly

Source: James Rachels, "Vegetarianism and 'the Other Weight Problem'" from *World Hunger and Moral Obligation* 1/e (P) by Aiken/LaFollette, Copyright © 1977. Reprinted by permission of Prentice-Hall, Inc., Upper Saddle River, NJ.

1 Coleman McCarthy, "Would we sacrifice to aid the starving?" *Miami Herald*, 28 July 1974, page 2F.

ridiculous, as I once did. After all, meat eating is a normal, well-established part of our daily routines; people have always eaten meat; and many find it difficult even to conceive of what an alternate diet would be like. So it is not easy to take seriously the possibility that it might be wrong. Moreover, vegetarianism is commonly associated with Eastern religions whose tenets we do not accept, and with extravagant, unfounded claims about health. A quick perusal of vegetarian literature might confirm the impression that it is all a crackpot business: tracts have titles like "Victory Through Vegetables" and promise that if one will only keep to a meatless diet one will have perfect health and be filled with wisdom. Of course we can ignore this kind of nonsense. However, there are other arguments for vegetarianism that must be taken seriously. One such argument, which has recently enjoyed wide support, has to do with the world food shortage. I will take up that argument after a few preliminaries.

I

According to the United Nations Food and Agriculture Organization, about 15,000 people die of malnutrition every day—10,000 of them are children. Millions more do not die but lead miserable lives constantly on the verge of starvation. Hunger is concentrated in poor, underdeveloped countries, out of sight of the 70 million Americans who are overweight from eating too much.

Of course, there is some malnutrition in the United States—a conservative estimate is that 40 million Americans are poor enough to qualify for assistance under the Federal Food Stamp Program, although fewer than half that number are actually helped. But it is easy to misinterpret this statistic: while many of these Americans don't get *enough* to eat, neither are they starving. They do not suffer the extreme deprivation

that reduces one's life to nothing more than a continual desperate search for food. Moreover, even the milder degree of malnutrition is an embarrassing anomaly; we are not a poor country, especially not in food. We have an abundance of rich farmland which we use with astonishing efficiency. (Although in some important ways our use of land is very inefficient. I will come to that in a moment.) The "Foodgrain Yield" of American farms is about 3,050 pounds per acre. For comparison, we may note that only Japan does significantly better, with a yield of 4,500 pounds per acre; but in Japan 87 workers per 100 acres are needed to obtain this yield, while in the United States only *one* worker per 100 acres is required![2] If some Americans do not get enough to eat, it is not because we lack the food.

It does not require a very sophisticated argument to show that, if we have an overabundance of food while others are starving, we should not waste our surplus but make it available to those who need it. Studies indicate that the average American family throws out with the garbage about 10 percent of the food it buys.[3] Of course, it would be impractical for us to try to package up our leftover beans and potatoes at the end of each meal and send them off to the poor. But it would not be impractical for us to buy somewhat less, and contribute the leftover money to agencies that would then purchase the food we did not buy and deliver it to those in need.

The argument may be put this way: First, suppose you are about to throw out a quantity of food which you are unable to use, when someone offers to take it down the street to a child who is starving. Clearly, it would be immoral for you to refuse this offer and insist that the food go into the garbage. Second, suppose

2 These figures are based on studies conducted in 1969–1971. They are from James, Grant, "A New Development Strategy," *Foreign Policy*, 12 (1973).
3 One such study is reported in *Time*, 26 January 1976, p. 8.

it is proposed that you *not buy* the extra food, instead give the money to provide for the child. Would it be any less immoral of you to refuse, and to continue to buy unneeded food to be discarded? The only important difference between the two cases is that by giving money, and not leftover food, better nourishment can be provided to the child more efficiently. Aside from some slight inconvenience—you would have to shop a bit more carefully—the change makes no difference to *your* interests at all. You end up with the same combination of food and money in each case. So, if it would be immoral to refuse to give the extra food to the child and insist on throwing it into the garbage, it is also immoral for us to buy and waste food when we could buy less and give the extra money for famine relief.

II

It is sometimes objected that famine-relief efforts are futile because the problems of overpopulation and underdevelopment in some parts of the world are insoluble. "Feed the starving millions," it is said, "and they will survive only to produce more starving millions. When the population in those poor, overcrowded countries has doubled, and then tripled, *then* there will be famine on a scale we have hardly dreamed of. What is needed in those countries is population control and the establishment of sound agricultural systems. But, unfortunately, given the religious, political, and educational situations in those countries, and the general cultural malaise produced by generations of ignorance and grinding poverty, these objectives are impossible to attain. So we have to face the fact that transfusions of food today, no matter how massive, only postpone the inevitable starvation and probably even make it worse."

It must be conceded that, *if* the situation really were this hopeless, then we would have no obligation to provide relief for those who are starving. We are not obligated to take steps that would do no good. What is wrong with this argument is that it paints too gloomy a picture of the possibilities. We have no conclusive evidence that the situation is hopeless. On the contrary, there is good reason to think that the problems can be solved. In China starvation is no longer a serious problem. That huge population is now adequately fed, whereas thirty years ago hunger was common. Apparently, Chinese agriculture is now established on a sound basis. Of course, this has been accomplished by a social regimentation and a denial of individual freedom that many of us find objectionable, and, in any case, Chinese-style regimentation cannot be expected in other countries. But this does not mean that there is no hope for other countries. In countries such as India, birth control programs can help. Contrary to what is popularly believed, such programs are not foredoomed to failure. During India's third "Five Year Plan" (1961–66) the birth rate in Bombay was reduced to only 27 per 1000 population, only a bit higher than the U.S. rate of 23 per 1000.[4] This was the best result in the country, but there were other hopeful signs as well: for example, during the same period the birth rate in a rural district of West Bengal dropped from 43 to 36 per 1000. Experts do not regard India's population problem as hopeless.

It is a disservice to the world's poor to represent the hunger problem as worse than it is; for, if the situation is made to appear hopeless, then people are liable to do nothing. Nick Eberstadt, of the Harvard Center for Population Studies, remarks that:

> Bangladesh is a case in point. The cameramen who photograph those living corpses for your

4 B. L. Raina, "India," in Bernard Berelson, ed., *Family Planning and Population Programs: A Review of World Developments* (Chicago: University of Chicago Press, 1966), pp. 111–22.

evening consumption work hard to evoke a nation of unrecognizable monsters by the roadside. Unless you have been there, you would find it hard to imagine that the people of Bangladesh are friendly and energetic, and perhaps 95% of them get enough to get by. Or that Bangladesh has the richest cropland in the world, and that a well-guided aid program could help turn it from a famine center into one of the world's great breadbaskets. To most people in America the situation must look hopeless and our involvement, therefore, pointless. If the situation is so bad, why shouldn't we cut off our food and foreign aid to Bangladesh, and use it to save people who aren't going to die anyway?[5]

So, even if it is true that shipments of food *alone* will not solve the problems of famine, this does not mean that the problems cannot be solved. Short-term famine-relief efforts, together with longer-range population control programs and assistance to improve local agriculture, could greatly reduce, if not altogether eliminate, the tragedy of starvation.

III

I have already mentioned the waste of food thrown out with the garbage. That waste, as great as it is, is small in comparison to a different sort of waste which I want to describe now.

But first let me tell a little story. In this story, someone discovers a way of processing food so as to give it a radically new texture and taste.

5 Nick Eberstadt, "Myths of the Food Crisis," *The New York Review of Books,* 19 February 1976, p. 32. Eberstadt's article contains a good survey of the problems involved in assessing the world food situation—how bad it is, or isn't. He concludes that the situation is bad, but not at all hopeless. See also various articles, in Philip H. Abelson, ed., *Food: Politics, Economics, Nutrition and Research* (Washington, D.C.: American Association for the Advancement of Science, 1975).

The processed food is no more nutritious than it was unprocessed, but people like the way it tastes, and it becomes very popular—so popular, in fact, that a great industry grows up and almost everyone comes to dine on it several times a week. There is only one catch: the conversion process is extremely wasteful. Seven-eighths of the food is destroyed by the process; so that in order to produce one pound of the processed food, eight pounds of unprocessed food are needed. This means that the new kind of food is relatively expensive and only people in the richer countries can afford to eat much of it. It also means that the process raises moral questions: Can it be right for some people to waste seven-eighths of their food resources, while millions of others are suffering from lack of food? If the waste of 10 percent of one's food is objectionable, the waste of 87.5 percent is more so.

In fact, we do use a process that is just this wasteful. The process works like this: First, we use our farmland to grow an enormous quantity of grain—many times the amount that we could consume, if we consumed it as grain or grain products. But we do not consume it in this form. Instead, we feed it to animals, and then we eat the animals. The process is staggeringly inefficient: we have to feed the animals eight pounds of protein in the form of grain to get back one pound in the form of meat, for a wastage of 87.5 percent. (This is the inefficient use of farmland that I referred to earlier, farmland that could be producing eight pounds of "unprocessed" food produces only one pound "processed.")

Fully one-half of all the harvested agricultural land in the United States is planted with feed-crops. We feed 78 percent of all our grain to animals. This is the highest percentage of any country in the world; the Soviet Union, for example, uses only 28 percent of its grain in this way. The "conversion ratio" for beef cattle and veal calves is an astonishing *21 to 1*—that is, we feed these animals 21 pounds of protein in the form of grain to get back 1 pound in the form of meat. Other animals process protein more efficiently, so that the average conversion ratio is "only" 8 to 1. To see what this means for a single year, we may note that in 1968 we fed 20 million tons of protein to livestock (excluding dairy cattle), in return for which we got 2 million tons of protein in meat, for a net loss of 18 million tons. This loss, in the United States alone, was equal to 90 percent of the world's estimated protein deficit.[6]

If we did not waste grain in this manner, there would clearly be enough to feed everyone in the world quite comfortably. In 1972–1973, when the world food "shortage" was supposedly becoming acute, 632 pounds of grain was produced annually for every person on earth (500 pounds is enough for adequate nourishment). This figure is actually *rising*, in spite of population growth; the comparable figure for 1960 was under 600.[7]

What reason is there to waste this incredible amount of food? Why raise and eat animals, instead of eating a portion of the grain ourselves and using the rest to relieve hunger? The meat we eat is no more nourishing than the grain the animals are fed. The only reason for preferring to eat meat is our enjoyment of its taste; but this is hardly a sufficient reason for wasting food that is desperately needed by people who are starving. It is as if one were to say to a hungry child: "I have eight times the food I need, but I can't let you have any of it, because I am going to use it all to make myself something really tasty."

This, then, is the argument for vegetarianism that I referred to at the beginning of this essay. If, in light of the world food situation, it is wrong for us to waste enormous quantities of food, then it is wrong for us to convert grain protein into meat protein as we do. And if we were to stop doing this, then most of us would have to become vegetarians of at least a qualified sort. I say "of a qualified sort" for two reasons. First, we could still eat fish. Since we do not raise fish by feeding them food that could be consumed by humans, there is no argument against eating fish comparable to this one against eating livestock. Second, there could still be a small amount of beef, pork, etc., produced without the use of feeds suitable for human consumption, and this argument would not rule out producing and eating that meat—but this would be such a small amount that it would not be available to most of us.

This argument against meat eating will be already familiar to many readers; it has been used in numerous books and in magazine and newspaper articles.[8] I am not certain, however, that it is an absolutely conclusive argument. For one thing it may be that a mere *reduction* in the amount of meat we produce would release enough grain to feed the world's hungry. We are now wasting so much food in this way that it may not be necessary for us to stop wasting all of it, but only some of it; so we may be able to go on consuming a fair amount of meat without depriving anyone of food. If so, the argument from wasting food would not support vegetarianism, but only a simple decrease in our meat consumption, which is something entirely different. There is, however, another argument for vegetarianism which I think is conclusive. Unlike the argument from food wastage, this argument does not appeal to the interests of humans as grounds for opposition to meat eating. Instead,

6 The figures in this paragraph are from Frances Moore Lappé, *Diet for a Small Planet* (New York: Ballantine Books, Inc., 1971), part I. This book is an excellent primer on protein.

7 Eberstadt, "Myths of the Food Crisis," p. 34.

8 For example, in Lappé's *Diet for a Small Planet,* and in several of the articles anthologized in Catherine Lerza and Michael Jacobson, eds., *Food for People Not for Profit A Sourcebook on the Food Crisis* (New York: Ballantine Books, Inc., 1975).

it appeals directly to the interests of the animals themselves. I now turn to that argument.

IV

The wrongness of cruelty to animals is often explained in terms of its effects on human beings. The idea seems to be that the animals' interests are not *themselves* morally important or worthy of protection, but, since cruelty to animals often has bad consequences for *humans,* it is wrong to make animals suffer. In legal writing, for example, cruelty to animals is included among the "victimless crimes," and the problem of justifying legal prohibitions is seen as comparable to justifying the prohibition of other behavior, such as homosexuality or the distribution of pornography, where no one (no human) is obviously hurt. Thus, Louis Schwartz says that, in prohibiting the torturing of animals:

It is not the mistreated dog who is the ultimate object of concern. . . . Our concern is for the feelings of other human beings, a large proportion of whom, although accustomed to the slaughter of animals for food, readily identify themselves with a tortured dog or horse and respond with great sensitivity to its sufferings.[9]

Philosophers also adopt this attitude. Kant, for example, held that we have no direct duties to nonhuman animals. "The Categorical Imperative," the ultimate principle of morality, applies only to our dealings with humans:

The practical imperative, therefore, is the following: Act so that you treat humanity, whether in your own person or in that of another, always as an end and never as a means only.[10]

And of other animals, Kant says:

But so far as animals are concerned, we have no direct duties. Animals are not self-conscious, and are there merely as means to an end. That end is man.[11]

He adds that we should not be cruel to animals only because "He who is cruel to animals becomes hard also in his dealings with men."[12]

Surely this is unacceptable. Cruelty to animals ought to be opposed, not only because of the ancillary effects on humans, but because of the direct effects on the animals themselves. Animals that are tortured *suffer,* just as tortured humans suffer, and *that* is the primary reason why it is wrong. We object to torturing humans on a number of grounds, but the main one is that the victims suffer so. Insofar as nonhuman animals also suffer, we have the *same* reason to oppose torturing them, and it is indefensible to take the one suffering but not the other as grounds for objection.

Although cruelty to animals is wrong, it does not follow that we are never justified in inflicting pain on an animal. Sometimes we are justified in doing this, just as we are sometimes justified in inflicting pain on humans. It does follow, however, that there must be a *good reason* for causing the suffering, and if the suffering is great, the justifying reason must be correspondingly powerful. As an example, consider the treatment of the civet cat, a highly intelli-

9 Louis B. Schwartz, "Morals Offenses and the Model Penal Code," *Columbia Law Review,* 63(1963); reprinted in Joel Feinberg and Hyman Gross, eds., *Philosophy of Law* (Encino, Calif. Dickenson Publishing Company, Inc., 1975), p. 156.

10 Immanuel Kant, *Foundations of the Metaphysics of Morals,* trans. Lewis White Beck (Indianapolis: The Bobbs-Merrill Co., Inc., 1959), p. 47.
11 Immanuel Kant, *Lectures on Ethics,* trans. Louis Infield (New York: Harper Torchbooks, 1963), p. 239.
12 Ibid., p. 240.

gent and sociable animal. Civet cats are trapped and placed in small cages inside darkened sheds, where the temperature is kept up to 110°F by fires.[13] They are confined in this way until they finally die. What justifies this extraordinary mistreatment? These animals have the misfortune to produce a substance that is useful in the manufacture of perfume. Musk, which is scraped from their genitals once a day for as long as they can survive, makes the scent of perfume last a bit longer after each application. (The heat increases their "production" of musk.) Here Kant's rule—"Animals are merely means to an end; that end is man"—is applied with a vengeance. To promote one of the most trivial interests we have, thousands of animals are tormented for their whole lives.

It is usually easy to persuade people that this use of animals is not justified, and that we have a moral duty not to support such cruelties by consuming their products. The argument is simple: Causing suffering is not justified unless there is a good reason; the production of perfume made with musk causes considerable suffering; our enjoyment of this product is not a good enough reason to justify causing that suffering; therefore, the use of animals in this way is wrong. At least my experience has been that, once people learn the facts about musk production, they come to regard using such products as morally objectionable. They are surprised to discover, however, that an exactly analogous argument can be given in connection with the use of animals as food. Animals that are raised and slaughtered for food also suffer, and our enjoyment of the way they taste is not a sufficient justification for mistreating them.

Most people radically underestimate the amount of suffering that is caused to animals who are raised and slaughtered for food.[14] They think, in a vague way, that slaughterhouses are cruel, and perhaps even that methods of slaughter ought to be made more humane. But after all, the visit to the slaughterhouse is a relatively brief episode in the animal's life; and beyond that, people imagine that the animals are treated well enough. Nothing could be further from the truth. Today the production of meat is Big Business, and the helpless animals are treated more as machines in a factory than as living creatures.

Veal calves for example, spend their lives in pens too small to allow them to turn around or even to lie down comfortably—exercise toughens the muscles, which reduces the "quality" of the meat, and besides, allowing the animals adequate living space would be prohibitively expensive. In these pens the calves cannot perform such basic actions as grooming themselves, which they naturally desire to do, because there is not room for them to twist their heads around. It is clear that the calves miss their mothers, and like human infants they want something to suck: they can be seen trying vainly to suck the sides of their stalls. In order to keep their meat pale and tasty, they are fed a liquid diet deficient in both iron and roughage. Naturally they develop cravings for these things, because they need them. The calf's craving for iron is so strong that, if it is allowed to turn around, it will lick at its own urine, although calves normally find this repugnant. The tiny stall, which prevents the animal from turning, solves this "problem." The craving for roughage is especially strong since without it the animal cannot form a cud to chew. It cannot be given any straw for bedding, since the animal would be driven to eat it, and that would spoil the

13 Muriel the Lady Dowding "Furs and Cosmetics: Too High a Price?" in Stanley and Roslind Godlovitch and John Harris, eds., *Animals, Men and Morals* (New York: Taplinger Publishing Co., Inc., 1972), p. 36.

14 By far the best account of these cruelties is to be found in Chapter 3 of Peter Singer's *Animal Liberation* (New York: New York Review Books, 1975). I have drawn on Singer's work for the factual material in the following two paragraphs. *Animal Liberation* should be consulted for a thorough treatment of matters to which I can refer here only sketchily.

meat. For these animals the slaughterhouse is not an unpleasant end to an otherwise contented life. As terrifying as the process of slaughter is, for them it may actually be regarded as a merciful release.

Similar stories can be told about the treatment of other animals on which we dine. In order to "produce" animals by the millions, it is necessary to keep them crowded together in small spaces. Chickens are commonly kept eight or ten to a space smaller than a newspaper page. Unable to walk around or even stretch their wings—much less build a nest—the birds become vicious and attack one another. The problem is sometimes exacerbated because the birds are so crowded that, unable to move, their feet literally grow around the wire floors of the cages, anchoring them to the spot. An "anchored" bird cannot escape attack no matter how desperate it becomes. Mutilation of the animals is an efficient solution. To minimize the damage they can do to one another, the birds' beaks are cut off. The mutilation is painful, but probably not as painful as other sorts of mutilations that are routinely practiced. Cows are castrated, not to prevent the unnatural "vices" to which overcrowded chickens are prone, but because castrated cows put on more weight, and there is less danger of meat being "tainted" by male hormones.

> In Britain an anesthetic must be used, unless the animal is very young, but in America anesthetics are not in general use. The procedure is to pin the animal down, take a knife and slit the scrotum, exposing the testicles. You then grab each testicle in turn and pull on it, breaking the cord that attaches it; on older animals it may be necessary to cut the cord.[15]

It must be emphasized that the treatment I am describing—and I have hardly scratched the surface here—is not out of the ordinary. It is typical of the way that animals raised for food are

15 Singer, *Animal Liberation*, p. 152.

treated, now that meat production is Big Business. As Peter Singer puts it, these are the sorts of things that happened to your dinner when it was still an animal.

What accounts for such cruelties? As for the meat producers, there is no reason to think they are unusually cruel men. They simply accept the common attitude expressed by Kant: "Animals are merely means to an end; that end is man." The cruel practices are adopted not because they are cruel but because they are efficient, given that one's only concern is to produce meat (and eggs) for humans as cheaply as possible. But clearly this use of animals is immoral if anything is. Since we can nourish ourselves very well without eating them, our *only reason* for doing all this to the animals is our enjoyment of the way they taste. And this will not even come close to justifying the cruelty.

V

Does this mean that we should stop eating meat? Such a conclusion will be hard for many people to accept. It is tempting to say, "What is objectionable is not *eating* the animals, but only making them suffer. Perhaps we ought to protest the way they are treated, and even work for better treatment of them. But it doesn't follow that we must stop eating them." This sounds plausible until you realize that it would be impossible to treat the animals decently and still produce meat in sufficient quantities to make it a normal part of our diets. As I have already remarked, cruel methods are used in the meat-production industry because such methods are economical; they enable the producers to market a product that people can afford. Humanely produced chicken, beef, and pork would be so expensive that only the very rich could afford them. (*Some* of the cruelties could be eliminated without too much expense—the cows could be given an anesthetic before castration, for example, even though this alone would mean a slight increase in the cost of beef. But others, such as overcrowding, could not be eliminated without really prohibitive cost.) So to work for better treatment for the animals would be to work for a situation in which most of us would *have* to adopt a vegetarian diet.

Still, there remains the interesting theoretical question: *If* meat could be produced humanely, without mistreating the animals prior to killing them painlessly, would there be anything wrong with it? The question is only of theoretical interest because the actual choice we face in the supermarket is whether to buy the remains of animals that are *not* treated humanely. Still, the question has some interest, and I want to make two comments about it.

First, it is a vexing issue whether animals have a "right to life" that is violated when we kill them for trivial purposes; but we should not simply assume until proven otherwise that they *don't* have such a right.[16] We assume that humans have a right to life—it would be wrong to murder a normal, healthy human even if it were done painlessly—and it is hard to think of any plausible rationale for granting this right to humans that does not also apply to other animals. Other animals live in communities, as do humans; they communicate with one another, and have ongoing social relationships; killing them disrupts lives that are perhaps not as complex, emotionally and intellectually, as our own, but that are nevertheless quite complicated. They suffer, and are capable of happiness as well as fear and distress, as we are. So what could be the rational basis for saying that we have a right to life, but that they don't? Or even more pointedly, what could be the rational basis for saying

that a severely retarded human, who is inferior in every important respect to an intelligent animal, has a right to life but that the animal doesn't? Philosophers often treat such questions as "puzzles," assuming that there must be answers even if we are not clever enough to find them. I am suggesting that, on the contrary, there may not be any acceptable answers to these questions. If it seems, intuitively, that there *must* be some difference between us and the other animals which confers on us, but not them, a right to life, perhaps this intuition is mistaken. At the very least, the difficulty of answering such questions should make us hesitant about asserting that it is all right to kill animals, as long as we don't make them suffer, unless we are also willing to take seriously the possibility that it is all right to kill people, so long as we don't make them suffer.

Second, it is important to see the slaughter of animals for food as part of a larger pattern that characterizes our whole relationship with the nonhuman world. Animals are wrenched from their natural homes to be made objects of our entertainment in zoos, circuses, and rodeos. They are used in laboratories not only for experiments that are themselves morally questionable,[17] but also in testing everything from shampoo to chemical weapons. They are killed so that their heads can be used as wall decorations, or their skins as ornamental clothing or rugs. Indeed, simply killing them for the fun of it is thought to be "sport."[18] This pattern of cruel exploitation flows naturally from the Kantian attitude that animals are nothing more than things to be used for our purposes. It is this whole attitude that must be opposed, and not

---

16 It is controversial among philosophers whether animals can have any rights at all. See various essays collected in Part IV of Tom Regan and Peter Singer, eds., *Animal Rights and Human Obligations* (Englewood Cliffs, NJ.: Prentice-Hall, 1976). My own defense of animal rights is given in "Do Animals Have a Right to Liberty?" pp. 205–223, and in "A Reply to VanDeVeer," pp. 230–32.

17 See Singer, *Animal Liberation,* Chap. 2.
18 It is sometimes said, in defense of "non-slob" hunting: "Killing for pleasure is wrong, but killing for food is all right." This won't do, since for those of use who are able to nourish ourselves without killing animals, killing them for food *is* a form of killing for pleasure, namely, the pleasures of the palate.

merely its manifestation in our willingness to hurt the animals we eat. Once one rejects this attitude, and no longer regards the animals as disposable at one's whim, one ceases to think it all right to kill them, even painlessly, just for a snack.

But now let me return to the more immediate practical issue. The meat at the supermarket was not produced by humane methods. The animals whose flesh this meat once was were abused in ways similar to the ones I have described. Millions of other animals are being treated in these ways now, and their flesh will soon appear in the markets. Should one support such practices by purchasing and consuming its products?

It is discouraging to realize that no animals will actually be helped simply by one person ceasing to eat meat. One consumer's behavior, by itself, cannot have a noticeable impact on an industry as vast as the meat business. However, it is important to see one's behavior in a wider context. There are already millions of vegetarians, and because they don't eat meat there *is* less cruelty than there otherwise would be. The question is whether one ought to side with that group, or with the carnivores whose practices cause the suffering. Compare the position of someone thinking about whether to buy slaves in the year 1820. He might reason as follows: "The whole practice of slavery is immoral, but I cannot help any of the poor slaves by keeping clear of it. If I don't buy these slaves, someone else will. One person's decision just can't by itself have any impact on such a vast business. So I may as well use slaves like everyone else." The first thing we notice is that this fellow was too pessimistic about the possibilities of a successful

movement; but beyond that, there is something else wrong with his reasoning. If one really thinks that a social practice is immoral, that *in itself* is sufficient grounds for a refusal to participate. In 1848 Thoreau remarked that even if someone did not want to devote himself to the abolition movement, and actively oppose slavery, ". . . it is his duty, at least, to wash his hands of it, and, if he gives it no thought longer, not to give it practically his support."[19] In the case of slavery, this seems clear. If it seems less clear in the case of the cruel exploitation of nonhuman animals, perhaps it is because the Kantian attitude is so deeply entrenched in us.

VI

I have considered two arguments for vegetarianism: one appealing to the interests that humans have in conserving food resources, and the other appealing directly to the interests of the animals themselves. The latter, I think, is the more compelling argument, and in an important sense it is a deeper argument. Once its force is felt, any opposition to meat eating that is based only on considerations of food wastage will seem shallow in the same way that opposition to slavery is shallow if it is based only on economic considerations. Yet the second argument does in a way reinforce the first one. In this case at least, the interests of humans and nonhumans coincide. By doing what we ought to do anyway—ceasing to exploit helpless animals—we would at the same time increase the food available for hungry people.

19 Henry David Thoreau, *Civil Disobedience* (1848).

Review Questions

1. State and explain Rachels's two arguments about giving food or money to a child who is starving.
2. What objections can be made to famine-relief efforts, and how does Rachels reply to them?
3. Why does Rachels think that meat-eating is wasteful of resources?

4. Explain Rachels's argument for vegetarianism based on the duty to not waste food. Why isn't this argument conclusive?
5. State and explain Rachels's second argument for vegetarianism, the one about the suffering of animals. Why does Rachels believe that this argument is conclusive?
6. Rachels considers an interesting theoretical objection to his argument. What is this objection, and how does Rachels reply to it?

Discussion Questions

1. At the end of his article, Rachels compares meat-eating to slavery. Is this a fair comparison? Why or why not?
2. Do you eat meat? If so, how do you reply to Rachels's arguments?

Problem Cases

1. Killing Chickens

Suppose a farmer raises happy chickens on this farm. They are well fed, they have plenty of room, they have a comfortable place to sleep; in short, they are well cared for and happy. Each year the farmer kills the oldest chickens, the ones that will die of disease or old age. He kills them quickly and with little or no pain. Then he thanks the chickens for their bodies; he is a religious man and believes that the chickens have eternal souls that blissfully unite with the Great Spirit after death and that killing them does not harm the eternal souls. In fact, liberating the chicken souls from their moral bodies is a natural and good thing to do. That done, he carefully prepares the chicken meat and eats it with great relish. He replaces the chickens he kills with new chickens each year so that the chicken population remains stable.

Does this farmer do anything that is morally wrong? Explain your position.

2. The Draize Test

The Draize eye test is used by cosmetic companies such as Revlon and Procter & Gamble to test the eye irritancy of their products—cosmetics, hair shampoos, and so on. The substance to be tested is injected into the eyes of rabbits; more specifically, 0.1 milligrams (a large-volume dose) is injected into the conjuctival sac of one eye of each of six rabbits, with the other eye serving as a control. The lids are held together for one second and then the animal is released. The eyes are examined at 24, 48, and 72 hours to see if there is corneal damage. Although the test is very painful, as you can imagine, anesthetics are not used. The eyes are not washed. Very large doses are used (often resulting in permanent eye damage) to provide a large margin of safety in extrapolating for human response.

Should companies continue to test their new products in this way? Why or why not?

3. Eating Whales

(Reported by Andrew Pollack in *The New York Times,* May 3, 1993.) Eating whale meat is popular in Japan. At the crowded restaurant of Kiyoo Tanahahi in Tokyo, customers dine on whale steak, whale bacon, fried whale, smoked whale, raw whale, and whale tongue. Of course, to satisfy the Japanese demand for whale meat, many whales must be hunted and killed. But the International Whaling Commission, the 39-nation group that regulates whaling, has a moratorium on commercial whaling that has been in effect since 1986. The position of Japan and Norway, the two countries that continue to hunt and kill whales, is that the moratorium is no longer necessary to protect whales. It was originally put in place to protect species of whales endangered by decades of excessive whaling, but according to Japan and Norway, it is no longer needed for certain types of whales. They estimate that there are more than 760,000 minkes (a relatively small whale) in the Southern Hemisphere. Japan claims that killing 2,000 minkes a year has no effect on the total population. Those opposed think that all whales, including the minkes, should be protected. They point out that whales are majestic creatures with high intelligence, and they argue it is morally wrong to kill them. Japan replies that the ban on whaling is just a form of discrimination against Japan and the imposition of one nation's morals on another. Why should Western nations be allowed to kill chickens, cows, and pigs, and Japan not be allowed to kill whales?

What do you think? Should there be a ban on whaling? If so, should Western nations stop killing chickens, cows, and pigs?

Suggested Readings

1. Peter Singer, *Animal Liberation,* second edition (New York Review, 1990), presents the now-classic critique of our treatment of animals together with relevant factual material.
2. Leslie Pickering Francis and Richard Norman, "Some Animals Are More Equal Than Others," *Philosophy* 53 (October 1978), pp. 507–27, agree with Singer that it is wrong to cause animal suffering, but deny that this requires us to adopt vegetarianism or abandon animal experimentation.
3. Roger Crisp, "Utilitarianism and Vegetarianism," *International Journal of Applied Philosophy* 4 (1988), pp. 41–49, argues that utilitarianism morally requires us both to abstain from eating the flesh of intensively reared animals and to eat the flesh of certain nonintensively reared animals. He calls this the Compromise Requirement View.
4. Bonnie Steinbock, "Speciesism and the Idea of Equality," *Philosophy* 53, no. 204 (April 1978), pp. 247–56, presents a defense of speciesism. Although she agrees with Singer that nonhuman suffering deserves some moral consideration, Steinbock denies that this consideration should be equal to that given to humans.
5. R. G. Frey, *Interests and Rights: The Case Against Animals* (Clarendon Press, 1980), argues that animals have neither interests nor moral rights.
6. Joel Feinberg, "The Rights of Animals and Unborn Generations," in *Philosophy and Environmental Crisis,* ed. William T. Blackstone (University of Georgia Press, 1974), analyzes the concept of a right and contends that humans and animals have rights but rocks and

whole species do not. Future generations have rights but only contingent on their coming into existence.

7. H. J. McCloskey, "Moral Rights and Animals," *Inquiry* 22 (Spring/Summer 1979), pp. 25–54, attacks Feinberg's analysis of the concept of a right and presents his own account. According to McCloskey, a right is an entitlement to something and not a claim against someone. In his view, animals do not have rights.

8. James Rachels, *Created from Animals: The Moral Implications of Darwinism* (Oxford University Press, 1990), defends animal rights.

9. Stephen R. L. Clark, *Animals and Their Moral Standing* (Routledge, 1997). This book collects the major writings of Clark on animals. It includes discussions of the rights of wild animals, the problems with speciesism, and the difficulty of calculating costs and benefits.

10. Kerry S. Walters and Lisa Pormess, eds., *Ethical Vegetarianism: From Pythagoras to Peter Singer* (State University of New York Press, 1999). This anthology covers the two-thousand-year Western tradition of vegetarianism beginning with Pythagoras, Seneca, and Plutarch.

11. Frances Moore Lappé, *Diet for a Small Planet,* 20th Anniversary Edition (Ballantine Books, 1992). This is the latest edition of the classic best-selling book that tells you how to be a vegetarian and why you should be one.

12. Daniel A. Dombrowski, *Babies and Beasts: The Argument from Marginal Cases* (University of Illinois Press, 1997), discusses an important argument used to defend animal rights, the argument that there is no morally relevant difference between animals and "marginal humans," such as the severely mentally retarded.

13. Daniel A. Dombrowski, *The Philosophy of Vegetarianism* (University of Massachusetts Press, 1984), presents a history of the arguments for vegetarianism, beginning with Porphyry's *On Abstinence.*

14. Mary Midgley, *Animals and Why They Matter* (University of Georgia Press, 1998), explains why we should have moral concern for animals. Unlike many others, she does not rely on utilitarianism.

15. Josephine Donovan and Carol J. Adams, eds., *Beyond Animal Rights: A Feminist Caring Ethic for the Treatment of Animals* (Continuum Publishers, 1996). This anthology has eight articles that extend the feminist care ethic to the treatment of animals, thus moving beyond the appeal to animal rights.

16. Tom Regan and Peter Singer, eds., *Animal Rights and Human Obligations* (Prentice Hall, 1989). This is a collection of articles on animals that includes discussions of animal rights, the treatment of farm animals, and the treatment of animals in science.

17. Carl Cohen, "The Case for the Use of Animals in Biomedical Research," *The New England Journal of Medicine* 315 (October 2, 1986), defends speciesism and the use of animals in biomedical research. Cohen attacks both Singer and Regan. He argues that speciesism is not analogous to racism and sexism, and that animals have no rights.

18. Barbara F. Orlans, *In the Name of Science: Issues in Responsible Animal Experimentation* (Oxford University Press, 1993), gives a detailed and well-informed discussion of the issues raised by animal experimentation.

19. Barbara Orlans and Rebecca Dresser, *The Human Use of Animals: Case Studies in Ethical Choice* (Oxford University Press, 1997). This book presents various cases of research using animals, including baboon–human liver transplants, cosmetic safety testing, Washoe and other language-using chimpanzees, and monkeys without mothers.

20. Deborah Blum, *The Monkey Wars* (Oxford Unversity Press, 1977), gives detailed information about various animal activists, from the moderate Animal Welfare Institute to the radical Animal Liberation Front (now on the FBI's terrorist list). Among other things, we

find out about Washoe and four other chimpanzees who were trained in the use of sign language.

21. Harlan B. Miller and William H. Williams, eds., *Ethics and Animals* (Humana Press, 1983). This is an anthology dealing with topics such as animal rights, hunting, and animal experimentation.

22. Bernard E. Rollin, *The Unheeded Cry: Animal Consciousness, Animal Pain and Science* (Oxford University Press, 1989), surveys attitudes toward animal consciousness and pain, beginning with George Romanes in the nineteenth century.

Chapter 9

The Environment

Introduction

Factual Background

Environmentalists claim that human beings are rapidly destroying the natural environment; among other things, they say that industrial society is causing global warming, ozone depletion, and acid rain. These are complicated phenomena, however, and not everyone agrees about the causes and effects. Let us confine our attention to two clear cases of environmental harm: the destruction of redwood forests and the extinction of plant and animal species.

Coastal redwoods, or *Sequoia sempervirens,* are rare trees found mostly along the California coast and into southern Oregon. Over a long period of time, they grow to a huge size—the tallest such tree alive today is a 370-foot-tall redwood whose location biologists refuse to disclose, to protect its fragile habitat from visitors.

Despite their obvious beauty, only 4 percent of the original redwood forests remain standing today. Lumber companies have cut down almost all of them to make money. Deforesting is a very profitable business, for at today's prices, a single redwood can contain wood worth hundreds of thousands of dollars.

According to Dr. Reed Noss, codirector of the Conservation Biology Institute and editor of a new book on redwoods to be published in 1999 by Island Press, redwoods that have been cut down are gone forever. They cannot be regrown. The reason for this is a phenomenon called fog drip. When fog rolls into a redwood, water suspended in the fog drips down the tree's limbs, needles, and trunk, soaking the ground with an immense amount of water—the equivalent of a drenching rainstorm. If the redwoods are cut down, then the water in the fog passes right by. Deforested areas warm up and dry out quickly, and they do not get enough water to sustain redwood growth. Once sites are clear cut, they no longer benefit from the fog.

The largest remaining stand of redwoods is about 10,000 acres of ancient forest known as the Headwaters Grove, located more than 225 miles north of San Francisco. Until very recently, the forest was owned by Pacific Lumber. The company planned to clear-cut the forest and had marked the trees to be cut with slashes of blue paint, but they were stopped by radical environmental activists, including members of the group Earth First! The activists blocked logging roads, and even climbed and occupied trees to keep them from being cut.

Environmentalists have been fighting with Pacific Lumber for over twelve years about the fate of the redwoods, as well as the company's plans to log another 20,000 acres of forest. In September 1998, however, the environmentalists won a partial victory. The California legislature voted to purchase the Headwaters Grove from Pacific Lumber for $495 million. Under the legislation, the forest will be set aside forever as a nature preserve, with California paying $245 million and the federal government contributing $250 million.

The destruction of forests affects not only humans but other species of animals and plants as well. According to the World Wildlife Fund (http://www.worldwildlife.org/), about 90 percent of the world's species are found in forested areas. For example, the Headwaters Grove is the habitat of several threatened species, including the coho salmon and the marbled murrelet, a winged relative of the penguin that nests on the wide branches of the old redwoods. But 94 percent of the world's remaining forests are unprotected, and already more than half of the world's forests have been lost, along with their plant and animal life. The World Wildlife Fund estimates that if deforestation continues at the present rate, about one-fifth of all plant and animal species on the planet will be lost in the next twenty years. The Global 2000 Report cited by Rolston also projects a loss of up to 20 percent of the earth's species within a few decades unless present trends are reversed.

The problem is particularly severe in North America, where one-third of all forest ecoregions have extraordinary levels of species. These regions include the entire Pacific coastline between Los Angeles and Alaska, the Appalachian region, the state of Florida, northwest Quebec, and the Yukon Territory. Some of these regions have rich biodiversity. More than half of the world's temperate rain forest occurs along a narrow and fragile coastal band from southern Oregon to British Columbia and Alaska. This rain forest is home to countless species of plants and animals, from salmon and grizzly bears to rare lichens, wild ginseng, and Pacific yew—the bark of which is used to treat some cancers. The complex forests of the Klamath-Siskiyous in northern California support more conifer species and rare plants and animals than any temperate forest in the world, and the southern and central Appalachian temperate forest is one of two such forests in the world with more than 2,500 plant species. Yet 95 percent of these forests ecoregions are unprotected, and three-fourths of them are threatened with extinction.

The Readings

The readings begin with Aldo Leopold's classic view about environmental preservation, a view he calls the land ethic. As Leopold explains it, the land ethic is the result of a natural extension of ethics, an ecological evolution, that begins with a moral concern with individuals (as in the Ten Commandments), moves to relations between the individual and the society (as in the golden rule), and ends up with a moral concern for the land. By "the land" Leopold means not just soils but also waters, plants, and animals, including human beings—all of which form a biotic community. Humans are not the conquerors or owners of this community but citizens of it. According to Leopold, what is right is what tends to preserve the integrity, stability, and beauty of the land, the biotic community, and whatever does not do this is wrong.

J. Baird Callicott discusses conflicts between Leopold's land ethic and two other views, the view that only human beings have moral standing (which he calls ethical humanism and Singer labels speciesism) and the view that extends moral concern to sentient animals but not to the environment. He refers to this view as humane moralism or the animal liberation movement. Callicott sees the animal liberation movement as hostile to Leopold's land ethic. For example, consider hunting, killing, and eating animals. Singer, Regan, and Rachels all agree that this is seriously wrong, but Callicott notes that Leopold was an enthusiastic hunter and eater of animal flesh. Why didn't Leopold care about the suffering of animals? Because from the point of view of his land ethic, the killing and eating of individual animals is morally inconsequential. What matters is not the pain and suffering of individuals but the preservation of the land, including whole species. For this to be accomplished, individual animals must be killed; otherwise, there will be overpopulation and the land will be damaged. Another difference between the animal liberation movement and Leopold's land ethic concerns domestic animals. Singer, Regan, and Rachels agree that domestic animals should not be killed and eaten because this causes more suffering. But Leopold was indifferent, and Callicott explains why. Domestic animals are creations of humans that are a ruinous blight on the landscape, as bad as a fleet of four-wheel-drive off-road vehicles. Unlike wild animals, domestic cattle, sheep, or pigs have no natural place in the environment, and so they contribute to the erosion of the integrity, stability, and beauty of the biotic community. Callicott concludes that when all things are considered, the animal liberation movement is hopelessly impractical, whereas, by contrast, the land ethic is very practical although still hard to implement.

In the 1994 preface to his article, however, Callicott separates his own view from that of Leopold. Unlike Leopold, he now thinks we do have moral responsibilities to domestic animals as members of mixed human-animal communities, and now he thinks that vegetarianism is indicated by the land ethic, since it would be better for the environment if forests were not destroyed to make pasture for cattle. Rather than emphasizing the conflicts between the three views (the land ethic, and individualistic moral humanism and animal liberation), now he thinks that they should unite to oppose activities that are destroying human, mixed, and biotic communities.

Paul W. Taylor's view is different from those of Leopold and Callicott. His respect for nature is a "life-centered system" that is morally concerned with wild living things—namely, plants, animals, whole species, and biotic communities. Thus he is concerned with both individual living things and groups of living things—e.g. whole species and whole forests. He does not seem to be worried about nonliving things such as rivers or rock formations, except perhaps as habitats for living creatures. But like Leopold's, his ethics of respect for nature requires us to see all living things as an interdependent organic whole where humans do not have status superior to other living things. In other words, his view is egalitarian; each organism, species population, and community of life has its own good, and all have equal inherent worth. The problem with this, which Taylor notes at the end of his article, is that his view provides us with no way of resolving conflicts between humans and other living things. After all, what promotes human well-being is often not good for other living things.

Vandana Shiva presents a feminist view of nature based on what she calls the feminine principle. This principle defines growth and productivity in terms of sustaining life and cultural diversity rather than destroying them, where life includes not just human life but the natural environment as well. As such, it is strongly opposed to the patriarchal Western development of Third World countries that in the name of growth and productivity actually destroys the natural environment and harms women by creating new conditions of genuine material poverty. She also attacks the market economy, with its focus on the GNP as a measure of progress. Rather than providing for people's needs and preserving the environment, the market economy generates new and artificial "needs," the satisfaction of which requires more destruction of the environment and more harm to women.

Philosophical Issues

In this chapter the debate continues about who or what is the proper object of moral concern. Is it just human beings, humans and animals, whole species, or biotic communities, such as forests? As Callicott argues in the reading, Leopold seems to hold that our concern should be with the land and not with animals or even humans, but of course this is opposed by Kant and his followers, who insist that only self-conscious and rational beings are the proper objects of moral concern, and by Mill, Bentham, Singer, and other utilitarians, who think that all sentient beings, including animals, should have moral standing.

In the preface to his article, Callicott suggests an interesting solution to the problem. He asks us to think of ourselves as belonging to three different moral communities, each having its own set of peculiar duties and obligations. There is the human community of family, friends, fellow citizens, and so on; the mixed community of humans and animals; and the biotic community as a whole. Callicott thinks these duties and obligations are often convergent and mutually reinforcing, and indeed this may be so. The problem is that Callicott gives no way of resolving conflicts between the different duties and obligations. For example, what would he say to the employee of the lumber company who works to feed her family? Isn't her obligation to take care of her family stronger than her duty to preserve the forests? In general, this problem of conflicts between human interests and duties and environmental preservation seems to remain unresolved in the chapter.

Another issue is whether it even makes sense to say that we have duties to collections of things like species or forests. The standard view held by most philosophers is that we have duties to individuals who have desires, wants, interests, or rights. But a whole species does not have any desires, wants, interests, or rights, and so it can't be the object of moral duty or obligation. In the reading, Rolston tries to answer this objection by suggesting that we should learn to accept value in, and duty to, an informed process that lacks consciousness. But what does this mean? Can we fulfill our duty to this information by preserving the genetic and behavioral information in a computer and destroying the species carrying this information?

What has intrinsic value? This is a basic question raised by the chapter. A standard view is that nature itself has no intrinsic value; it has no value by itself apart from its use. Nature has only instrumental value as something that produces human satisfaction. Imagine a planet overflowing with plant life but with no humans or sentient beings of any kind. Does this planet have any value at all? The standard view says it does not; yet, Leopold, Taylor, Rolston, and others in the chapter seem to hold that such a planet does have intrinsic value or inherent value. The problem is to explain how something could have value without an evaluator.

The Land Ethic

ALDO LEOPOLD

Aldo Leopold was an employee of the United States Forest Service and a professor of Wildlife Management at the University of Wisconsin. Our reading is taken from his classic book about the environment, *A Sand County Almanac* (1947).

Leopold proposes to extend our moral concern beyond humans and human society to the land. As he puts it, the land ethic enlarges the moral community to include soils, waters, plants, and animals—all of which are collectively the land. According to the land ethic, humans are not conquerors of the land, but, rather, biotic citizens of it. What is right is what preserves the integrity, stability, and beauty of the land, and whatever does not do this is wrong.

WHEN GODLIKE ODYSSEUS returned from the wars in Troy, he hanged all on one rope a dozen slave-girls of his household whom he suspected of misbehavior during his absence.

This hanging involved no question of propriety. The girls were property. The disposal of property was then, as now, a matter of expediency, not of right or wrong.

Concepts of right and wrong were not lacking from Odysseus' Greece: witness the fidelity of his wife through the long years before at last his black-prowed galleys clove the wine-dark seas for home. The ethical structure of that day covered wives, but had not yet been extended to human chattels. During the three thousand years which have since elapsed, ethical criteria have been extended to many fields of conduct, with corresponding shrinkages in those judged by expediency only.

THE ETHICAL SEQUENCE

This extension of ethics, so far studied only by philosophers, is actually a process in ecological evolution. Its sequences may be described in ecological as well as in philosophical terms. An ethic, ecologically, is a limitation on freedom of action in the struggle for existence. An ethic,

Source: Aldo Leopold, "The Land Ethic" from *A Sand County Almanac: And Sketches Here and There* by Aldo Leopold. (Oxford University Press, 1966), pp. 217–241. Copyright 1949, 1977 by Oxford University Press, Inc. Used by permission of Oxford University Press, Inc.

philosophically, is a differentiation of social from antisocial conduct. These are two definitions of one thing. The thing has its origin in the tendency of interdependent individuals or groups to evolve modes of cooperation. The ecologist calls these symbioses. Politics and economics are advanced symbioses in which the original free-for-all competition has been replaced, in part, by cooperative mechanisms with an ethical content.

The complexity of cooperative mechanisms has increased with population density, and with the efficiency of tools. It was simpler, for example, to define the antisocial uses of sticks and stones in the days of the mastodons than of bullets and billboards in the age of motors.

The first ethics dealt with the relation between individuals; the Mosaic Decalogue is an example. Later accretions dealt with the relation between the individual and society. The Golden Rule tries to integrate the individual to society; democracy to integrate social organization to the individual.

There is as yet no ethic dealing with man's relation to land and to the animals and plants which grow upon it. Land, like Odysseus' slave-girls, is still property. The land-relation is still strictly economic, entailing privileges but not obligations.

The extension of ethics to this third element in human environment is, if I read the evidence correctly, an evolutionary possibility and an ecological necessity. It is the third step in a sequence. The first two have already been taken. Individual thinkers since the days of Ezekiel and Isaiah have asserted that the despoliation of land is not only inexpedient but wrong. Society, however, has not yet affirmed their belief. I regard the present conservation movement as the embryo of such an affirmation.

An ethic may be regarded as a mode of guidance for meeting ecological situations so new or intricate, or involving such deferred reactions, that the path of social expediency is not discernible to the average individual. Animal instincts are modes of guidance for the individual in meeting such situations. Ethics are possibly a kind of community instinct in-the-making.

THE COMMUNITY CONCEPT

All ethics so far evolved rest upon a single premise: that the individual is a member of a community of interdependent parts. His instincts prompt him to compete for his place in the community, but his ethics prompt him also to cooperate (perhaps in order that there may be a place to compete for).

The land ethic simply enlarges the boundaries of the community to include soils, waters, plants, and animals, or collectively: the land.

This sounds simple: do we not already sing our love for and obligation to the land of the free and the home of the brave? Yes, but just what and whom do we love? Certainly not the soil, which we are sending helter-skelter downriver. Certainly not the waters, which we assume have no function except to turn turbines, float barges, and carry off sewage. Certainly not the plants, of which we exterminate whole communities without batting an eye. Certainly not the animals, of which we have already extirpated many of the largest and most beautiful species. A land ethic of course cannot prevent the alteration, management, and use of these "resources" but it does affirm their right to continued existence, and, at least in spots, their continued existence in a natural state.

In short, a land ethic changes the role of *Homo sapiens* from conqueror of the land-community to plain member and citizen of it. It implies respect for his fellow-members, and also respect for the community as such.

In human history, we have learned (I hope) that the conqueror role is eventually self-defeating. Why? Because it is implicit in such a role that the conqueror knows, *ex cathedra*, just what makes the community clock tick, and just what and who is valuable, and what and who is worthless, in community life. It always turns out that he knows neither, and this is why his conquests eventually defeat themselves.

In the biotic community, a parallel situation exists. Abraham knew exactly what the land was for: it was to drip milk and honey into Abraham's mouth. At the present moment, the assurance with which we regard this assumption is inverse to the degree of our education.

The ordinary citizen today assumes that science knows what makes the community clock tick; the scientist is equally sure that he does not. He knows that the biotic mechanism is so complex that its workings may never be fully understood.

That man is, in fact, only a member of a biotic team is shown by an ecological interpretation of history. Many historical events, hitherto explained solely in terms of human enterprise, were actually biotic interactions between people and land. The characteristics of the land determined the facts quite as potently as the characteristics of the men who lived on it.

Consider, for example, the settlement of the Mississippi valley. In the years following the Revolution, three groups were contending for its control: the native Indian, the French and English traders, and the American settlers. Historians wonder what would have happened if the English at Detroit had thrown a little more weight into the Indian side of those tipsy scales which decided the outcome of the colonial migration into the cane-lands of Kentucky. It is time now to ponder the fact that the cane-lands, when subjected to the particular mixture of forces represented by the cow, plow, fire, and axe of the pioneer, became bluegrass. What if the plant succession inherent in this dark and bloody ground had, under the impact of these forces, given us some worthless sedge shrub, or weed? Would Boone and Kenton have held out? Would there have been any overflow into Ohio, Indiana, Illinois, and Missouri? Any Louisiana Purchase? Any transcontinental union of new states? Any Civil War?

Kentucky was one sentence in the drama of history. We are commonly told what the human actors in this drama tried to do, but we are seldom told that their success, or the lack of it, hung in large degree on the reaction of particular soils to the impact of the particular forces exerted by their occupancy. In the case of Kentucky, we do not even know where the bluegrass came from—whether it is a native species, or a stowaway from Europe.

Contrast the cane-lands with what hindsight tells us about the Southwest, where the pioneers were equally brave, resourceful, and persevering. The impact of the occupancy here brought no bluegrass, or other plant fitted to withstand the bumps and buffetings of hard use. This region, when grazed by livestock, reverted through a series of more and more worthless grasses, shrubs, and weeds to a condition of unstable equilibrium. Each recession of plant types bred erosion; each increment to erosion bred a further recession of plants. The result today is a progressive and mutual deterioration, not only of plants and soils, but of the animal community subsisting thereon. The early settlers did not expect this: on the ciénegas of New Mexico some even cut ditches to hasten it. So subtle has been its progress that few residents of the region are aware of it. It is quite invisible to the tourist who finds this wrecked landscape colorful and charming (as indeed it is, but it bears scant resemblance to what it was in 1848).

This same landscape was "developed" once before, but with quite different results. The Pueblo Indians settled the Southwest in pre-Columbian times, but they happened *not* to be equipped with range livestock. Their civilization expired, but not because their land expired.

In India, regions devoid of any sod-forming grass have been settled, apparently without wrecking the land, by the simple expedient of carrying the grass to the cow, rather than vice versa. (Was this the result of some deep wisdom, or was it just good luck? I do not know.)

In short, the plant succession steered the course of history; the pioneer simply demonstrated, for good or ill, what successions inhered in the land. Is history taught in this spirit? It will be, once the concept of land as a community really penetrates our intellectual life.

THE ECOLOGICAL CONSCIENCE

Conservation is a state of harmony between men and land. Despite nearly a century of propaganda, conservation still proceeds at a snail's pace; progress still consists largely of letterhead pieties and convention oratory. On the back forty we still slip two steps backward for each forward stride.

The usual answer to this dilemma is "more conservation education." No one will debate this, but is it certain that only the *volume* of education needs stepping up? Is something lacking in the *content* as well?

It is difficult to give a fair summary of its content in brief form, but as I understand it, the content is substantially this: obey the law, vote right, join some organizations, and practice what conservation is profitable on your own land; the government will do the rest.

Is not this formula too easy to accomplish anything worthwhile? It defines no right or wrong, assigns no obligation, calls for no sacrifice, implies no change in the current philosophy of values. In respect of land-use, it urges only enlightened self-interest. Just how far will such education take us? An example will perhaps yield a partial answer.

By 1930 it had become clear to all except the ecologically blind that southwestern Wisconsin's topsoil was slipping seaward. In 1933 the farmers were told that if they would adopt certain remedial practices for five years, the public would donate CCC labor to install them, plus the necessary machinery and materials. The offer was widely accepted, but the practices were widely forgotten when the five-year contract period was up. The farmers continued only those practices that yielded an immediate and visible economic gain for themselves.

This led to the idea that maybe farmers would learn more quickly if they themselves wrote the rules. Accordingly the Wisconsin Legislature in 1937 passed the Soil Conservation District Law. This said to farmers, in effect: *We, the public, will furnish you free technical service and loan you specialized machinery, if you will write your own rules for land-use. Each county may write its own rules, and these will have the force of law.* Nearly all the counties promptly organized to accept the proffered help, but after a decade of operation, no *county has yet written a single rule.* There has been visible progress in such practices as strip-cropping, pasture renovation, and soil liming, but none in fencing woodlots against grazing, and none in excluding plow and cow from steep slopes. The farmers, in short, have selected those remedial practices which were profitable anyhow, and ignored those which were profitable to the community, but not clearly profitable to themselves.

When one asks why no rules have been written, one is told that the community is not yet ready to support them; education must precede rules. But the education actually in progress makes no mention of obligations to land over and above those dictated by self-interest. The net result is that we have more education but less soil, fewer healthy woods, and as many floods as in 1937.

The puzzling aspect of such situations is that the existence of obligations over and above self-interest is taken for granted in such rural community enterprise as the betterment of roads, schools, churches, and baseball teams. Their existence is not taken for granted, nor as yet seriously discussed, in bettering the behavior of the water that falls on the land, or in the preserving of the beauty or diversity of the farm landscape. Land-use ethics are still governed wholly by economic self-interest, just as social ethics were a century ago.

To sum up: we asked the farmer to do what he conveniently could to save his soil, and he has done just that, and only that. The farmer who clears the woods off a 75 per cent slope, turns his cows into the clearing, and dumps its rainfall, rocks, and soil into the community creek, is still (if otherwise decent) a respected member of society. If he puts lime on his fields and plants his crops on contour, he is still entitled to all the privileges and emoluments of his Soil Conservation District. The District is a beautiful piece of social machinery, but it is coughing along on two cylinders because we have been too timid, and too anxious for quick success, to tell the farmer the true magnitude of his obligations. Obligations have no meaning without conscience, and the problem we face is the extension of the social conscience from people to land.

No important change in ethics was ever accomplished without an internal change in our intellectual emphasis, loyalties, affections, and convictions. The proof that conservation has not yet touched these foundations of conduct lies in the fact that philosophy and religion have not yet heard of it. In our attempt to make conservation easy, we have made it trivial.

SUBSTITUTES FOR A LAND ETHIC

When the logic of history hunger for bread and we hand out a stone, we are at pains to explain how much the stone resembles bread. I now describe some of the stones which serve in lieu of a land ethic.

One basic weakness in a conservation system based wholly on economic motives is that most members of the land community have no economic value. Wildflowers and songbirds are examples. Of the 22,000 higher plants and animals native to Wisconsin, it is doubtful whether more than 5 percent can be sold, fed, eaten, or otherwise put to economic use. Yet these crea-tures are members of the biotic community, and if (as I believe) its stability depends on its integrity, they are entitled to continuance.

When one of these non-economic categories is threatened, and if we happen to love it, we invent subterfuges to give it economic importance. At the beginning of the century songbirds were supposed to be disappearing. Ornithologists jumped to the rescue with some distinctly shaky evidence to the effect that insects would eat us up if birds failed to control them. The evidence had to be economic in order to be valid.

It is painful to read these circumlocutions today. We have no land ethic yet, but we have at least drawn nearer the point of admitting that birds should continue as a matter of biotic right, regardless of the presence or absence of economic advantage to us.

A parallel situation exists in respect of predatory mammals, raptorial birds, and fish-eating birds. Time was when biologists somewhat overworked the evidence that these creatures preserve the health of game by killing weaklings, or that they control rodents for the farmer, or that they prey only on "worthless" species. Here again, the evidence had to be economic in order to be valid. It is only in recent years that we hear the more honest argument that predators are members of the community, and that no special interest has the right to exterminate them for the sake of a benefit, real or fancied, to itself. Unfortunately this enlightened view is still in the talk stage. In the field the extermination of predators goes merrily on: witness the impending erasure of the timber wolf by fiat of Congress, the Conservation Bureaus, and many state legislatures.

Some species of trees have been "read out of the party" by economics-minded foresters because they grow too slowly, or have too low a sale value to pay as timber crops: white cedar, tamarack, cypress, beech, and hemlock are examples. In Europe, where forestry is ecologically more advanced, the non-commercial tree species are recognized as members of the native forest community, to be preserved as such, within reason. Moreover some (like beech) have been found to have a valuable function in building up soil fertility. The interdependence of the forest and its constituent tree species, ground flora, and fauna is taken for granted.

Lack of economic value is sometimes a character not only of species or groups, but of entire biotic communities: marshes, bogs, dunes, and "deserts" are examples. Our formula in such cases is to relegate their conservation to government as refuges, monuments, or parks. The difficulty is that these communities are usually interspersed with more valuable private lands; the government cannot possibly own or control such scattered parcels. The net effect is that we have relegated some of them to ultimate extinction over large areas. If the private owner were ecologically minded, he would be proud to be the custodian of a reasonable proportion of such areas, which add diversity and beauty to his farm and to his community.

In some instances, the assumed lack of profit in these "waste" areas has proved to be wrong, but only after most of them had been done away with. The present scramble to reflood muskrat marshes is a case in point.

There is a clear tendency in American conservation to relegate to government all necessary jobs that private landowners fail to perform. Government ownership, operation, subsidy, or regulation is now widely prevalent in forestry, range management, soil and watershed management, park and wilderness conservation, fisheries management, and migratory bird management, with more to come. Most of this growth in governmental conservation is proper and logical, some of it is inevitable. That I imply no disapproval of it is implicit in the fact that I have spent most of my life working for it. Nevertheless the question arises: What is the ultimate magnitude of the enterprise? Will the tax base carry its eventual ramifications? At what point will governmental conservation, like the mastodon, become handicapped by its own dimen-

sions? The answer, if there is any, seems to be in a land ethic, or some other force which assigns more obligation to the private landowner.

Industrial landowners and users, especially lumbermen and stockmen, are inclined to wail long and loudly about the extension of government ownership and regulation to land, but (with notable exceptions) they show little disposition to develop the only visible alternative: the voluntary practice of conservation on their own lands.

When the private landowner is asked to perform some nonprofitable act for the good of the community, he today assents only with outstretched palm. If the act costs him cash this is fair and proper, but when it costs only forethought, open-mindedness, or time, the issue is at least debatable. The overwhelming growth of land-use subsidies in recent years must be ascribed, in large part, to the government's own agencies for conservation education: the land bureaus, the agricultural colleges, and the extension services. As far as I can detect, no ethical obligation toward land is taught in these institutions.

To sum up: a system of conservation based solely on economic self-interest is hopelessly lopsided. It tends to ignore, and thus eventually to eliminate, many elements in the land community that lack commercial value, but that are (as far as we know) essential to its healthy functioning. It assumes, falsely, I think, that the economic parts of the biotic clock will function without the uneconomic parts. It tends to relegate to government many functions eventually too large, too complex, or too widely dispersed to be performed by government.

An ethical obligation on the part of the private owner is the only visible remedy for these situations.

THE LAND PYRAMID

An ethic to supplement and guide the economic relation to land presupposes the existence of some mental image of land as a biotic mechanism. We can be ethical only in relation to something we can see, feel, understand, love, or otherwise have faith in.

The image commonly employed in conservation education is "the balance of nature." For reasons too lengthy to detail here, this figure of speech fails to describe accurately what little we know about the land mechanism. A much truer image is the one employed in ecology: the biotic pyramid. I shall first sketch the pyramid as a symbol of land, and later develop some of its implications in terms of land-use.

Plants absorb energy from the sun. This energy flows through a circuit called the biota, which may be represented by a pyramid consisting of layers. The bottom layer is the soil. A plant layer rests on the soil, an insect layer on the plants, a bird and rodent layer on the insects, and so on up through various animal groups to the apex layer, which consists of the larger carnivores.

The species of a layer are alike not in where they came from, or in what they look like, but rather in what they eat. Each successive layer depends on those below it for food and often for other services, and each in turn furnishes food and services to those above. Proceeding upward, each successive layer decreases in numerical abundance. Thus, for every carnivore there are hundreds of his prey, thousands of their prey, millions of insects, uncountable plants. The pyramidal form of the system reflects this numerical progression from apex to base. Man shares an intermediate layer with the bears, raccoons, and squirrels which eat both meat and vegetables.

The lines of dependency for food and other services are called food chains. Thus soil-oak-deer-Indian is a chain that has now been largely converted to soil-corn-cow-farmer. Each species, including ourselves, is a link in many chains. The deer eats a hundred plants other than oak, and the cow a hundred plants other than corn. Both, then, are links in a hundred chains. The pyramid is a tangle of chains so complex as to seem disorderly, yet the stability of the system proves it to be a highly organized structure. Its functioning depends on the cooperation and competition of its diverse parts.

In the beginning, the pyramid of life was low and squat; the food chains short and simple. Evolution has added layer after layer, link after link. Man is one of thousands of accretions to the height and complexity of the pyramid. Science has given us many doubts, but it has given us at least one certainty: the trend of evolution is to elaborate and diversify the biota.

Land, then, is not merely soil; it is a fountain of energy flowing through a circuit of soils, plants, and animals. Food chains are the living channels which conduct energy upward; death and decay return it to the soil. The circuit is not closed; some energy is dissipated in decay, some is added by absorption from the air, some is stored in soils, peats, and long-lived forests; but it is a sustained circuit, like a slowly augmented revolving fund of life. There is always a net loss by downhill wash, but this is normally small and offset by the decay of rocks. It is deposited in the ocean and, in the course of geological time, raised to form new lands and new pyramids.

The velocity and character of the upward flow of energy depend on the complex structure of the plant and animal community, much as the upward flow of sap in a tree depends on its complex cellular organization. Without this complexity, normal circulation would presumably not occur. Structure means the characteristic numbers, as well as the characteristic kinds and functions, of the component species. This interdependence between the complex structure of the land and its smooth functioning as an energy unit is one of its basic attributes.

When a change occurs in one part of the circuit, many other parts must adjust themselves to it. Change does not necessarily obstruct or divert the flow of energy; evolution is a long series of self-induced changes, the net result of which has been to elaborate the flow mechanism and to lengthen the circuit. Evolutionary changes, however, are usually slow and local. Man's invention of tools has enabled him to make changes of unprecedented violence, rapidity, and scope.

One change is in the composition of floras and faunas. The larger predators are lopped off the apex of the pyramid; food chains, for the first time in history, become shorter rather than longer. Domesticated species from other lands are substituted for wild ones, and wild ones are moved to new habitats. In this worldwide pooling of faunas and floras, some species get out of bounds as pests and diseases, others are extinguished. Such effects are seldom intended or foreseen; they represent unpredicted and often untraceable readjustments in the structure. Agricultural science is largely a race between the emergence of new pests and the emergence of new techniques for their control.

Another change touches the flow of energy through plants and animals and its return to the soil. Fertility is the ability of soil to receive, store, and release energy. Agriculture, by overdrafts on the soil, or by too radical a substitution of domestic for native species in the superstructure, may derange the channels of flow or deplete storage. Soils depleted of their storage, or of the organic matter which anchors it, wash away faster than they form. This is erosion.

Waters, like soil, are part of the energy circuit. Industry, by polluting waters or obstructing them with dams, may exclude the plants and animals necessary to keep energy in circulation.

Transportation brings about another basic change: the plants or animals grown in one region are now consumed and returned to the soil in another. Transportation taps the energy stored in rocks, and in the air, and uses it elsewhere; thus we fertilize the garden with nitrogen gleaned by the guano birds from the fishes of seas on the other side of the Equator. Thus the formerly localized and self-contained circuits are pooled on a worldwide scale.

The process of altering the pyramid for human occupation releases stored energy, and this often gives rise, during the pioneering period, to a deceptive exuberance of plant and animal life, both wild and tame. These releases of biotic capital tend to becloud or postpone the penalties of violence.

This thumbnail sketch of land as an energy circuit conveys three basic ideas:

1. That land is not merely soil.
2. That the native plants and animals kept the energy circuit open; others may or may not.
3. That man-made changes are of a different order than evolutionary changes, and have effects more comprehensive than is intended or foreseen.

These ideas, collectively, raise two basic issues: Can the land adjust itself to the new order? Can the desired alterations be accomplished with less violence?

Biotas seem to differ in their capacity to sustain violent conversion. Western Europe, for example, carries a far different pyramid than Caesar found there. Some large animals are lost; swampy forests have become meadows or plowland; many new plants and animals are introduced, some of which escape as pests; the remaining natives are greatly changed in distribution and abundance. Yet the soil is still there and, with the help of imported nutrients, still fertile; the waters flow normally; the new structure seems to function and to persist. There is no visible stoppage or derangement of the circuit.

Western Europe, then, has a resistant biota. Its inner processes are tough, elastic, resistant to strain. No matter how violent the alterations, the pyramid, so far, has developed some new *modus vivendi* which preserves its habitability for man, and for most of the other natives.

Japan seems to present another instance of radical conversion without disorganization.

Most other civilized regions, and some as yet barely touched by civilization, display various stages of disorganization, varying from initial symptoms to advanced wastage. In Asia Minor and North Africa diagnosis is confused by climatic changes, which may have been either the cause or the effect of advanced wastage. In the United States the degree of disorganization varies locally; it is worst in the Southwest, the Ozarks, and parts of the South, and least in New England and the Northwest. Better land-uses may still arrest it in the less advanced regions. In parts of Mexico, South America, South Africa, and Australia a violent and accelerating wastage is in progress, but I cannot assess the prospects.

This almost world-wide display of disorganization in the land seems to be similar to disease in an animal, except that it never culminates in complete disorganization or death. The land recovers, but at some reduced level of complexity, and with a reduced carrying capacity for people, plants, and animals. Many biotas currently regarded as "lands of opportunity" are in fact already subsisting on exploitative agriculture, i.e., they have already exceeded their sustained carrying capacity. Most of South America is overpopulated in this sense.

In arid regions we attempt to offset the process of wastage by reclamation, but it is only too evident that the prospective longevity of reclamation projects is often short. In our own West, the best of them may not last a century.

The combined evidence of history and ecology seems to support one general deduction: the less violent the man-made changes, the greater the probability of successful readjustment in the pyramid. Violence, in turn, varies with human population density; a dense population requires a more violent conversion. In this respect, North America has a better chance for permanence than Europe, if she can contrive to limit her density.

This deduction runs counter to our current philosophy, which assumes that because a small increase in density enriched human life, that an indefinite increase will enrich it indefinitely. Ecology knows of no density relationship that holds for indefinitely wide limits. All gains from density are subject to a law of diminishing returns.

Whatever may be the equation for men and land, it is improbable that we as yet know all its terms. Recent discoveries in mineral and vitamin nutrition reveal unsuspected dependencies in the up-circuit: incredibly minute quantities of certain substances determine the value of soils to plants, of plants to animals. What of the down-circuit? What of the vanishing species, the preservation of which we now regard as an esthetic luxury? They helped build the soil; in what unsuspected ways may they be essential to its maintenance? Professor Weaver proposes that we use prairie flowers to reflocculate the wasting soils of the dust bowl; who knows for what purpose cranes and condors, otters and grizzlies may some day be used?

LAND HEALTH
AND THE A-B CLEAVAGE

A land ethic, then, reflects the existence of an ecological conscience, and this in turn reflects a conviction of individual responsibility for the health of the land. Health is the capacity of the land for self-renewal. Conservation is our effort to understand and preserve this capacity.

Conservationists are notorious for their dissensions. Superficially these seem to add up to mere confusion, but a more careful scrutiny reveals a single plane of cleavage common to many specialized fields. In each field one group (A) regards the land as soil and its function as commodity-production; another group (B) regards the land as a biota, and its function as something broader. How much broader is admittedly in a state of doubt and confusion.

In my own field, forestry, group A is quite content to grow trees like cabbages, with cellulose as the basic forest commodity. It feels no inhibition against violence; its ideology is agronomic. Group B, on the other hand, sees forestry as fundamentally different from agronomy because it employs natural species, and manages a natural environment rather than creating an artificial one. Group B prefers natural reproduction on principle. It worries on biotic as well as economic grounds about the loss of species like chestnut and the threatened loss of the white pines. It worries about a whole series of secondary forest functions: wildlife, recreation, watersheds, wilderness areas. To my mind, Group B feels the stirrings of an ecological conscience.

In the wildlife field, a parallel cleavage exists. For Group A the basic commodities are sport and meat; the yardsticks of production are ciphers of take in pheasants and trout. Artificial propagation is acceptable as a permanent as well as a temporary recourse—if its unit costs permit. Group B, on the other hand, worries about a whole series of biotic side-issues. What is the cost in predators of producing a game crop? Should we have further recourse to exotics? How can management restore the shrinking species, like prairie grouse, already hopeless as shootable game? How can management restore the threatened rarities, like trumpeter swan and whooping crane? Can management principles be extended to wildflowers? Here again it is clear to me that we have the same A-B cleavage as in forestry.

In the larger field of agriculture I am less competent to speak, but there seem to be somewhat parallel cleavages. Scientific agriculture was actively developing before ecology was born, hence a slower penetration of ecological concepts might be expected. Moreover the farmer, by the very nature of his techniques, must modify the biota more radically than the forester or the wildlife manager. Nevertheless, there are many discontents in agriculture which seem to add up to a new vision of 'biotic farming.'

Perhaps the most important of these is the new evidence that poundage or tonnage is no measure of the food-value of farm crops; the products of fertile soil may be qualitatively as well as quantitatively superior. We can bolster poundage from depleted soils by pouring on imported fertility, but we are not necessarily bolstering food-value. The possible ultimate ramifications of this idea are so immense that I must leave their exposition to abler pens.

The discontent that labels itself 'organic farming,' while bearing some of the earmarks of a cult, is nevertheless biotic in its direction, particularly in its insistence on the importance of soil flora and fauna.

The ecological fundamentals of agriculture are just as poorly known to the public as in other fields of land-use. For example, few educated people realize that the marvelous advances in technique made during recent decades are improvements in the pump, rather than the well. Acre for acre, they have barely sufficed to offset the sinking level of fertility.

In all of these cleavages, we see repeated the same basic paradoxes: man the conqueror *versus* man the biotic citizen; science the sharpener of his sword *versus* science the searchlight on his universe; land the slave and servant *versus* land the collective organism. Robinson's injunction to Tristram may well be applied, at this juncture, to *Homo sapiens* as a species in geological time:

> Whether you will or not
> You are a King, Tristram, for you are one
> Of the time-tested few that leave the world,
> When they are gone, not the same place it was.
> Mark what you leave.

THE OUTLOOK

It is inconceivable to me that an ethical relation to land can exist without love, respect, and admiration for land, and a high regard for its value. By value, I of course mean something far broader than mere economic value; I mean value in the philosophical sense.

Perhaps the most serious obstacle impeding the evolution of a land ethic is the fact that our educational and economic system is headed away from, rather than toward, an intense consciousness of land. Your true modern is separated from the land by many middlemen, and by innumerable physical gadgets. He has no vital relation to it; to him it is the space between cities on which crops grow. Turn him loose for a day on the land, and if the spot does not happen to be a golf links or a "scenic" area, he is bored stiff. If crops could be raised by hydroponics instead of farming, it would suit him very well. Synthetic substitutes for wood, leather, wool, and other natural land products suit him better than the originals. In short, land is something he has "outgrown."

Almost equally serious as an obstacle to a land ethic is the attitude of the farmer for whom the land is still an adversary, or a taskmaster that keeps him in slavery. Theoretically, the mechanization of farming ought to cut the farmer's chains, but whether it really does is debatable.

One of the requisites for an ecological comprehension of land is an understanding of ecology, and this is by no means co-extensive with "education"; in fact, much higher education seems deliberately to avoid ecological concepts. An understanding of ecology does not necessarily originate in courses bearing ecological labels; it is quite as likely to be labeled geography, botany, agronomy, history, or economics. This is as it should be, but whatever the label, ecological training is scarce.

The case for a land ethic would appear hopeless but for the minority which is in obvious revolt against these "modern" trends.

The "key-log" which must be moved to release the evolutionary process for an ethic is simply this: quit thinking about decent land-use as solely an economic problem. Examine each question in terms of what is ethically and esthetically right, as well as what is economically expedient. A thing is right when it tends to preserve the integrity, stability, and beauty of the biotic community. It is wrong when it tends otherwise.

It of course goes without saying that economic feasibility limits the tether of what can or cannot be done for land. It always has and it always will. The fallacy the economic determinists have tied around our collective neck, and which we now need to cast off, is the belief that economics determines *all* land-use. This is simply not true. An innumerable host of actions and attitudes, comprising perhaps the bulk of all land relations, is determined by the land-users' tastes and predilections, rather than by his purse. The bulk of all land relations hinges on investments of time, forethought, skill, and faith rather than on investments of cash. As a land-user thinketh, so is he.

I have purposely presented the land ethic as a product of social evolution because nothing so important as an ethic is ever "written." Only the most superficial student of history supposes that Moses "wrote" the Decalogue; it evolved in the minds of a thinking community, and Moses wrote a tentative summary of it for a "seminar." I say tentative because evolution never stops.

The evolution of a land ethic is an intellectual as well as emotional process. Conservation is paved with good intentions which prove to be futile, or even dangerous, because they are devoid of critical understanding either of the land, or of economic land-use. I think it is a truism that as the ethical frontier advances from the individual to the community, its intellectual content increases.

The mechanism of operation is the same for any ethic: social approbation for right actions: social disapproval for wrong actions.

By and large, our present problem is one of attitudes and implements. We are remodeling the Alhambra with a steam-shovel, and we are proud of our yardage. We shall hardly relinquish the shovel, which after all has many good points, but we are in need of gentler and more objective criteria for its successful use.

Review Questions

1. How does Leopold explain his proposed extension of ethics?
2. What is the land ethic, according to Leopold? What is the role of humans in this ethic?
3. According to Leopold, what is wrong with a conservation system based on economic motives?

4. Explain Leopold's image of the biotic pyramid. Where are humans located on the pyramid, and how can they affect it?
5. How does Leopold view the health of the land, and what role should humans play?
6. How does Leopold define right and wrong?

Discussion Questions

1. Are Leopold's definitions of right and wrong acceptable to you? Why or why not?
2. Is hunting compatible with the land ethic? Explain your answer.
3. Do the owners of land have the right to use it as they wish? What would Leopold say? What do you think?

Animal Liberation: A Triangular Affair

J. BAIRD CALLICOTT

J. Baird Callicott is professor of philosophy at the University of Wisconsin, Stevens Point.

The "triangular affair" Callicott discusses is the conflict between three different positions (1) ethical humanists, who accord moral standing to humans only; (2) humane moralists, or animal liberationists, who extend moral standing to animals; and (3) Leopold's land ethic, which gives primary moral concern to the land. He is mainly concerned with defending the land ethic from attacks by animal liberationists. In the course of his defense, he explains why hunting, killing, and eating animals is justified, at least in Leopold's land ethic (but not in his own view, as he explains in the preface), and why he thinks animal liberation, in the final analysis, is "utterly unpracticable." By contrast, he finds the land ethic eminently practicable, although he admits that its implementation would be very difficult, requiring enormous economic reform and a revolution in attitudes and lifestyles.

PREFACE (1994)

I WROTE 'A Triangular Affair' to sharply distinguish environmental ethics from animal libera-

Source: J. Baird Callicott, "Animal Liberation: A Triangular Affair," from *Environmental Ethics*, Vol. 2, No. 4 (Winter 1980). Reprinted with permission. Some of the footnotes have been renumbered.

tion/rights when the former seemed to be overshadowed by the latter. Back in the late 1970s and early 1980s, when the piece was conceived and composed, many people seemed to conflate the two. In my youthful zeal to draw attention to the then unheralded Leopold land ethic, I made a few remarks that in retrospect appear irresponsible.

Most important, I no longer think that the land ethic is misanthropic. 'All ethics so far evolved', Leopold wrote, 'rest upon a single premiss: that the individual is a member of a community of interdependent parts. . . . The land ethic simply enlarges the boundaries of the community to include soils, waters, plants, and animals, or collectively: the land.' The biotic community and its correlative land ethic *does not replace* our several human communities and their correlative ethics—our duties and obligations to family and family members, to municipality and fellow-citizens, to country and countrymen, to humanity and human beings. Rather it *supplements* them. Hence the land ethic leaves our traditional human morality quite intact and pre-emptive.

Second in importance, I now think that we do in fact have duties and obligations—implied by the essentially communitarian premisses of the land ethic—to domestic animals, as well as to wild fellow-members of the biotic community and to the biotic community as a whole. Farm animals, work animals, and pets have long been members of what Mary Midgley calls the 'mixed' community. They have entered into a kind of implicit social contract with us which lately we have abrogated. Think of it this way. Each of us belongs to several hierarchically ordered human communities, each with its peculiar set of duties and obligations; to various mixed human-animal domestic communities, with their peculiar sets of duties and obligations; and to the biotic community, with its peculiar set of duties and obligations (which in sum Leopold called the land ethic). The land ethic no more eclipses our moral responsibilities in regard to domestic animals than it does our moral responsibilities in regard to other people.

Further, I now think that a vegetarian diet is indicated by the land ethic, no less than by the animal welfare ethics. Rainforests are felled to make pasture for cattle. Better for the environment if we ate forest fruits instead of beef. Livestock ruin watercourses and grasslands. And raising field crops for animal feed increases soil erosion and ground-water depletion.

Finally, though certainly I still wish there were far more bears than actually there are, a target ratio of one bear for every two people seems a bit extravagant.

'A Triangular Affair' clearly distinguishes between holistic environmental ethics, on the one hand, and individualistic 'moral humanism' and 'humane moralism', on the other. And that remains a serviceable distinction. Moralists of every stripe, however, must make common cause against the forces that are often simultaneously destroying human, mixed, and biotic communities. The differences between human, humane, and environmental concerns are real, and sometimes conflictive. But just as often they are convergent and mutually reinforcing. And all our ethical concerns can be theoretically unified, I am convinced, by a communitarian moral philosophy, thus enabling conflicts, when they do arise, to be adjudicated rationally.

ENVIRONMENTAL ETHICS AND ANIMAL LIBERATION

Partly because it is so new to Western philosophy (or at least heretofore only scarcely represented) *environmental ethics* has no precisely fixed conventional definition in glossaries of philosophical terminology. Aldo Leopold, however, is universally recognized as the father or founding genius of recent environmental ethics. His "land ethic" has become a modern classic and may be treated as the standard example, the paradigm case, as it were, of what an environmental ethic is. *Environmental ethics* then can be defined ostensively by using Leopold's land ethic as the exemplary type. I do not mean to suggest that all environmental ethics should necessarily conform to Leopold's paradigm, but the extent to which an ethical system resembles Leopold's land ethic might be used, for want of anything better, as a criterion to measure the extent to which it is or is not of the environmental sort.

It is Leopold's opinion, and certainly an overall review of the prevailing traditions of Western ethics, both popular and philosophical, generally confirms it, that traditional Western systems of ethics have not accorded moral standing to nonhuman beings.[1] Animals and plants, soils and waters, which Leopold includes in his community of ethical beneficiaries, have traditionally enjoyed no moral standing, no rights, no respect, in sharp contrast to human persons whose rights and interests ideally must be fairly and equally considered if our actions are to be considered "ethical" or "moral." One fundamental and novel feature of the Leopold land ethic, therefore, is the extension of *direct* ethical considerability from people to nonhuman natural entities.

At first glance, the recent ethical movement usually labeled "animal liberation" or "animal rights" seems to be squarely and centrally a kind of environmental ethics. The more uncompromising among the animal liberationists have demanded equal moral consideration on behalf of cows, pigs, chickens, and other apparently enslaved and oppressed nonhuman animals. The theoreticians of this new hyperegalitarianism have coined such terms as *speciesism* (on analogy with *racism* and *sexism*) and *human chauvinism* (on analogy with *male chauvinism*), and have made animal liberation seem, perhaps not improperly, the next and most daring development of political liberalism. Aldo Leopold also draws upon metaphors of political liberalism when he tells us that his land ethic "changes the role of *Homo sapiens* from conqueror of the land community to plain member and citizen of it."[2] For animal liberationists it is as if the ideological battles for equal rights and equal consideration for women and for racial minorities have been all

but won, and the next and greatest challenge is to purchase equality, first theoretically and then practically, for all (actually only *some*) animals regardless of species. This more rhetorically implied than fully articulated historical progression of moral rights from fewer to greater numbers of "persons" (allowing that animals may also be persons) as advocated by animal liberationists, also parallels Leopold's scenario in "The Land Ethic" of the historical extension of "ethical criteria" to more and more "fields of conduct" and to larger and larger groups of people during the past three thousand or so years.[3] As Leopold develops it, the land ethic is a cultural "evolutionary possibility," the next "step in a sequence."[4] For Leopold, however, the next step is much more sweeping, much more inclusive than the animal liberationists envision, since it "enlarges the boundaries of the [moral] community to include soils, waters, [and] plants . . ." as well as animals.[5] Thus, the animal liberation movement *could* be construed as partitioning Leopold's perhaps undigestable and totally inclusive environmental ethic into a series of more assimilable stages: today animal rights, tomorrow equal rights for plants, and after that full moral standing for rocks, soil, and other earthy compounds, and perhaps sometime in the still more remote future, liberty and equality for water and other elementary bodies.

Put just this way, however, there is something jarring about such a graduated progression in the exfoliation of a more inclusive environmental ethic, something that seems absurd. A more or less reasonable case might be made for rights for some animals, but when we come to plants, soils, and waters, the frontier between plausibility and absurdity appears to have been crossed. Yet, there is no doubt that Leopold sincerely proposes that *land* (in his inclusive sense) be ethically regarded. The beech and chestnut, for

---

1 Aldo Leopold, *A Sand County Almanac* (New York: Oxford University Press, 1949), pp. 202–203.
2 Ibid., p. 204.

3 Ibid., pp. 201–203.
4 Ibid., p. 203.
5 Ibid., p. 204.

example, have in his view as much "biotic right" to life as the wolf and the deer, and the effects of human actions on mountains and streams for Leopold is an ethical concern as genuine and serious as the comfort and longevity of brood hens.[6] In fact, Leopold to all appearances never considered the treatment of brood hens on a factory farm or steers in a feed lot to be a pressing moral issue. He seems much more concerned about the integrity of the farm *wood lot* and the effects of clear-cutting steep slopes on neighboring *streams.*

Animal liberationists put their ethic into practice (and display their devotion to it) by becoming vegetarians, and the moral complexities of vegetarianism have been thoroughly debated in the recent literature as an adjunct issue to animal rights. (No one however has yet expressed, as among Butler's Erewhonians, qualms about eating plants, though such sentiments might be expected to be latently present, if the rights of plants are next to be defended.) Aldo Leopold, by contrast did not even condemn hunting animals, let alone eating them, nor did he personally abandon hunting, for which he had had an enthusiasm since boyhood, upon becoming convinced that his ethical responsibilities extended beyond the human sphere. There are several interpretations for this behavioral peculiarity. One is that Leopold did not see that his land ethic actually ought to prohibit hunting, cruelly killing, and eating animals. A corollary of this interpretation is that Leopold was so unperspicacious as deservedly to be thought stupid— a conclusion hardly comporting with the intellectual subtlety he usually evinces in most other respects. If not stupid, then perhaps Leopold was hypocritical. But if a hypocrite, we should expect him to conceal his proclivity for blood sports and flesh eating and to treat them as shameful vices to be indulged secretly. As it is, bound together between the same covers

with "The Land Ethic" are his unabashed reminiscences of killing and consuming *game*. This term (like *stock*) when used of animals, moreover, appears to be morally equivalent to referring to a sexually appealing young woman as a "piece" or to a strong, young black man as a "buck"—if animal rights, that is, are to be considered as on a par with women's rights and the rights of formerly enslaved races. A third interpretation of Leopold's approbation of regulated and disciplined sport hunting (and *a fortiori* meat eating) is that it is a form of human/animal behavior not inconsistent with the land ethic as he conceived it. A corollary of this interpretation is that Leopold's land ethic and the environmental ethic of the animal liberation movement rest upon very different theoretical foundations, and that they are thus two very different forms of environmental ethics.

The urgent concern of animal liberationists for the suffering of *domestic* animals, toward which Leopold manifests an attitude which can only be described as indifference, and the urgent concern of Leopold, on the other hand, for the disappearance of *species* of plants as well as animals and for soil erosion and stream pollution, appear to be symptoms not only of very different ethical perspectives, but profoundly different cosmic visions as well. The neat similarities, noted at the beginning of this discussion, between the environmental ethic of the animal liberation movement and the classical Leopoldian land ethic appear in light of these observations to be rather superficial and to conceal substrata of thought and value which are not at all similar. The theoretical foundations of the animal liberation movement and those of the Leopoldian land ethic may even turn out not to be companionable, complementary, or mutually consistent. The animal liberationists may thus find themselves not only engaged in controversy with the many conservative philosophers upholding *apartheid* between man and "beast," but also faced with an unexpected dissent from another, very different, system of environmental ethics.

6 Ibid., p. 221 (trees); pp. 129–133 (mountains); p. 209 (streams).

Animal liberation and animal rights may well prove to be a triangular rather than, as it has so far been represented in the philosophical community, a polar controversy.

ETHICAL HUMANISM
AND HUMANE MORALISM

The orthodox response of "ethical humanism" (as this philosophical perspective may be styled) to the suggestion that nonhuman animals should be accorded moral standing is that such animals are not worthy of this high perquisite. Only human beings are rational, or capable of having interests, or possess *self*-awareness, or have linguistic abilities, or can represent the future, it is variously argued. These essential attributes taken singly or in various combinations make people somehow exclusively deserving of moral consideration. The so-called "lower animals," it is insisted, lack the crucial qualification for ethical considerability and so may be treated (albeit humanely, according to some, so as not to brutalize man) as things or means, not as persons or as ends.

The theoreticians of the animal liberation movement ("humane moralists" as they may be called) typically reply as follows. Not all human beings qualify as worthy of moral regard, according to the various criteria specified. Therefore, by parity of reasoning, human persons who do not so qualify as moral patients may be treated, as animals often are, as mere things or means (e.g., used in vivisection experiments, disposed of if their existence is inconvenient, eaten, hunted, etc., etc.). But the ethical humanists would be morally outraged if irrational and inarticulate infants, for example, were used in painful or lethal medical experiments, or if severely retarded people were hunted for pleasure. Thus, the double-dealing, the hypocrisy, of ethical humanism appears to be exposed. Ethical humanism, though claiming to discriminate between worthy and unworthy ethical patients on the basis of objective criteria impartially applied,

turns out after all, it seems, to be *speciesism,* a philosophically indefensible prejudice (analogous to racial prejudice) against animals. The tails side of this argument is that some animals, usually the "higher" lower animals (cetaceans, other primates, etc.), as ethological studies seem to indicate, may meet the criteria specified for moral worth, although the ethical humanists, even so, are not prepared to grant them full dignity and the rights of persons. In short, the ethical humanists' various criteria for moral standing do not include all or only human beings, humane moralists argue, although in practice ethical humanism wishes to make the class of morally considerable beings coextensive with the class of human beings.

The humane moralists, for their part, insist upon *sentience* (*sensibility* would have been a more precise word choice) as the only relevant capacity a being need possess to enjoy full moral standing. If animals, they argue, are conscious entities who, though deprived of reason, speech, forethought or even *self*-awareness (however that may be judged), are capable of suffering, then their suffering should be as much a matter of ethical concern as that of our fellow human beings, or strictly speaking, as our very own. What, after all, has rationality or any of the other allegedly uniquely human capacities to do with ethical standing? Why, in other words, should beings who reason or use speech (etc.) qualify for moral status, and those who do not fail to qualify? Isn't this just like saying that only persons with white skin should be free, or that only persons who beget and not those who bear should own property? The criterion seems utterly unrelated to the benefit for which it selects. On the other hand, the capacity to suffer is, it seems, a more relevant criterion for moral standing because—as Bentham and Mill, notable among modern philosophers, and Epicurus, among the ancients, aver—pain is evil, and its opposite, pleasure and freedom from pain, good. As moral agents (and this seems axiomatic), we have a duty to behave in such a way that the effect of our actions is to promote and procure good, so far as possible, and to reduce and minimize evil. That would amount to an obligation to produce pleasure and reduce pain. Now pain is pain wherever and by whomever it is suffered. As a *moral* agent, I should not consider my pleasure and pain to be of greater consequence in determining a course of action than that of other persons. Thus, by the same token, if animals suffer pain—and among philosophers only strict Cartesians would deny that they do— then we are morally obliged to consider their suffering as much an evil to be minimized by conscientious moral agents as human suffering. Certainly actions of ours which contribute to the suffering of animals, such as hunting them, butchering and eating them, experimenting on them, etc., are on these assumptions morally reprehensible. Hence, a person who regards himself or herself as not aiming in life to live most selfishly, conveniently, or profitably, but rightly and in accord with practical principle, if convinced by these arguments, should, among other things, cease to eat the flesh of animals, to hunt them, to wear fur and leather clothing and bone ornaments and other articles made from the bodies of animals, to eat eggs and drink milk, if the animal producers of these commodities are retained under inhumane circumstances, and to patronize zoos (as sources of psychological if not physical torment of animals). On the other hand, since certain very simple animals are almost certainly insensible to pleasure and pain, they may and indeed should be treated as morally inconsequential. Nor is there any *moral* reason why trees should be respected or rivers or mountains or anything which is, though living or tributary to life processes, unconscious. The humane moralists, like the moral humanists, draw a firm distinction between those beings worthy of moral consideration and those not. They simply insist upon a different but quite definite cut-off point on the spectrum of natural entities, and accompany their criterion with arguments to show that it is more ethically defensible (granting certain assumptions) and more

consistently applicable than that of the moral humanists.

THE FIRST PRINCIPLE
OF THE LAND ETHIC

The fundamental principle of humane moralism, as we see, is Benthamic. Good is equivalent to pleasure and, more pertinently, evil is equivalent to pain. The presently booming controversy between moral humanists and humane moralists appears, when all the learned dust has settled, to be essentially internecine; at least, the lines of battle are drawn along familiar watersheds of the conceptual terrain.[7] A classical ethical theory,

7 John Rodman, "The Liberation of Nature" (p. 95), comments: "Why do our 'new ethics' seem so old? . . . Because the attempt to produce a 'new ethics' by the process of 'extension' perpetuates the basic assumptions of the conventional modern paradigm, however much it fiddles with the boundaries." When the assumptions remain conventional, the boundaries are, in my view, scalar, but triangular when both positions are considered in opposition to the land ethic. The scalar relation is especially clear when two other positions, not specifically discussed in the text, the reverence-for-life ethic and pan-moralism, are considered. The reverence-for-life ethic (as I am calling it in deference to Albert Schweitzer) seems to be the next step on the scale after the humane ethic. William Frankena considers it so in "Ethics and the Environment," *Ethics and Problems of the 21st Century*, pp. 3–20. W. Murry Hunt ("Are *Mere Things* Morally Considerable?" *Environmental Ethics* 2 (1980): 59–65) has gone a step past Schweitzer, and made the bold suggestion that *everything* should be accorded moral standing, pan-moralism. Hunt's discussion shows clearly that there is a similar logic ("slippery slope" logic) involved in taking each downward step, and thus a certain commonality of underlying assumptions among all the ethical types to which the land ethic stands in opposition. Hunt is not unaware that his suggestion may be interpreted as a *reductio ad absurdum* of the whole matter, but insists that that is not his intent. The land ethic is not part of this linear series of steps and hence may be represented as a point off the scale. The principal difference . . . is that the land ethic is collective or "holistic" while the others are distributive or "atomistic." Another relevant difference is that moral humanism, humane moralism, reverence-for-life ethics, and the limiting case, pan-moralism, either openly or implicitly espouse a pecking-order model of nature. The land ethic, founded upon an ecological model of nature emphasizing the contributing roles played by various species in the economy of

Bentham's, has been refitted and pressed into service to meet relatively new and unprecedented ethically relevant situations—the problems raised especially by factory farming and ever more exotic and frequently ill-conceived scientific research employing animal subjects. Then, those with Thomist, Kantian, Lockean, Moorean (etc.) ethical affiliation have heard the bugle and have risen to arms. It is no wonder that so many academic philosophers have been drawn into the fray. The issues have an apparent newness about them; moreover, they are socially and politically *avant garde*. But there is no serious challenge to cherished first principles. Hence, without having to undertake any creative ethical reflection or exploration, or any re-examination of historical ethical theory, a fresh debate has been stirred up. The familiar historical positions have simply been retrenched, applied, and exercised.

But what about the third (and certainly minority) party to the animal liberation debate? What sort of reasonable and coherent moral theory would at once urge that animals (and plants and soils and waters) be included in the same class with people as beings to whom ethical consideration is owed and yet not object to some of them being slaughtered (whether painlessly or not) and eaten, others hunted, trapped, and in various other ways seemingly cruelly used? Aldo Leopold provides a concise statement of what might be called the categorical imperative or principal precept of the land ethic: "A thing is right when it tends to preserve the integrity, stability, and beauty of the biotic community. It is wrong when it tends otherwise."[8] What is especially note-worthy, and that to

which attention should be directed in this proposition, is the idea that the good of the biotic *community* is the ultimate measure of the moral value, the rightness or wrongness, of actions. Thus, to hunt and kill a white-tailed deer in certain districts may not only be ethically permissible, it might actually be a moral requirement, necessary to protect the local environment, taken as a whole, from the disintegrating effects of a cervid population explosion. On the other hand, rare and endangered animals like the lynx should be especially nurtured and preserved. The lynx, cougar, and other wild feline predators, from the neo-Benthamite perspective (if consistently and evenhandedly applied) should be regarded as merciless, wanton, and incorrigible murderers of their fellow creatures, who not only kill, it should be added, but cruelly toy with their victims, thus increasing the measure of pain in the world. From the perspective of the land ethic, predators generally should be nurtured and preserved as critically important members of the biotic communities to which they are native. Certain plants, similarly, may be overwhelmingly important to the stability, integrity, and beauty of biotic communities, while some animals, such as domestic sheep (allowed perhaps by egalitarian and humane herdspersons to graze freely and to reproduce themselves without being harvested for lamb and mutton) could be a pestilential threat to the natural floral community of a given locale. Thus, the land ethic is logically coherent in demanding at once that moral consideration be given to plants as well as to animals and yet in permitting animals to be killed, trees felled, and so on. In every case the effect upon ecological systems is the decisive factor in the determination of the ethical quality of actions. . . .

THE LAND ETHIC AND THE ECOLOGICAL POINT OF VIEW

. . . Since ecology focuses upon the relationships between and among things, it inclines its students toward a more holistic vision of the world.

---

nature, abandons the "higher"/"lower" ontological and axiological schema, in favor of a functional system of value. The land ethic, in other words, is inclined to establish value distinctions not on the basis of higher and lower orders of being, but on the basis of the importance of organisms, minerals, and so on to the biotic community. Some bacteria, for example, may be of greater value to the health or economy of nature than dogs, and thus command more respect.
8 Ibid., pp. 224–225.

Before the rather recent emergence of ecology as a science the landscape appeared to be, one might say, a collection of objects, some of them alive, some conscious, but all the same, an aggregate, a plurality of separate individuals. With this "atomistic" representation of things it is no wonder that moral issues might be understood as competing and mutually contradictory clashes of the "rights" of separate individuals, each separately pursuing its "interests." Ecology has made it possible to apprehend the same landscape as an articulate unity (without the least hint of mysticism or ineffability). Ordinary organic bodies have articulated and discernible parts (limbs, various organs, myriad cells); yet, because of the character of the network of relations among those parts, they form in a perfectly familiar sense a second-order whole. Ecology makes it possible to see land, similarly, as a unified system of integrally related parts, as, so to speak, a third-order organic whole.

Another analogy that has helped ecologists to convey the particular holism which their science brings to reflective attention is that land is integrated as a human community is integrated. The various parts of the "biotic community" (individual animals and plants) depend upon one another *economically* so that the system as such acquires distinct characteristics of its own. Just as it is possible to characterize and define collectively peasant societies, agrarian communities, industrial complexes, capitalist, communist, and socialist economic systems, and so on, ecology characterizes and defines various biomes as desert, savanna, wetland, tundra, wood land, etc., communities, each with its particular "professions," "roles," or "niches."

Now we may think that among the duties we as moral agents have toward ourselves is the duty of self-preservation, which may be interpreted as a duty to maintain our own organic integrity. It is not uncommon in historical moral theory, further, to find that in addition to those peculiar responsibilities we have in relation both to ourselves and to other persons severally, we also have a duty to behave in ways that do not harm the fabric of society *per se*. The land ethic, in similar fashion, calls our attention to the recently discovered integrity—in other words, the unity—of the biota and posits duties binding upon moral agents in relation to that whole. Whatever the strictly formal logical connections between the concept of a social community and moral responsibility, there appears to be a strong psychological bond between that idea and conscience. Hence, the representation of the natural environment as, in Leopold's terms, "one humming community" (or, less consistently in his discussion, a third-order organic being) brings into play, whether rationally or not, those stirrings of conscience which we feel in relation to delicately complex, functioning social and organic systems.

The neo-Benthamite humane moralists have, to be sure, digested one of the metaphysical implications of modern biology. They insist that human beings must be understood continuously with the rest of organic nature. People are (and are only) animals, and much of the rhetorical energy of the animal liberation movement is spent in fighting a rear guard action for this aspect of Darwinism against those philosophers who still cling to the dream of a special metaphysical status for people in the order of "creation." To this extent the animal liberation movement is biologically enlightened and argues from the taxonomical and evolutionary continuity of man and beast to moral standing for some nonhuman animals. Indeed, pain, in their view the very substance of evil, is something that is conspicuously common to people and other sensitive animals, something that we as people experience not in virtue of our metasimian cerebral capabilities, but because of our participation in a more generally animal, limbic-based consciousness. *If* it is pain and suffering that is the ultimate evil besetting human life, and this not in virtue of our humanity but in virtue of our animality, then it seems only fair to promote freedom from pain for those animals who share with us in this mode of experience and to grant them rights similar to ours as a means to this end.

Recent ethological studies of other primates, cetaceans, and so on, are not infrequently cited to drive the point home, but the biological information of the animal liberation movement seems to extend no further than this—the continuity of human with other animal life forms. The more recent ecological perspective especially seems to be ignored by humane moralists. The holistic outlook of ecology and the associated value premium conferred upon the biotic community, its beauty, integrity, and stability may simply not have penetrated the thinking of the animal liberationists, or it could be that to include it would involve an intolerable contradiction with the Benthamite foundations of their ethical theory. Bentham's view of the "interests of the community" was bluntly reductive. With his characteristic bluster, Bentham wrote, "The community is a fictitious *body* composed of the individual persons who are considered as constituting as it were its *members*. The interest of the community then is, what?—the sum of the interests of the several members who compose it."[9] Bentham's very simile—the community is like a body composed of members—gives the lie to his reduction of its interests to the sum of its parts taken severally. The interests of a person are not those of his or her cells summed up and averaged out. Our organic health and well-being, for example, require vigorous exercise and metabolic stimulation which cause stress and often pain to various parts of the body and a more rapid turnover in the life cycle of our individual cells. For the sake of the person taken as whole, some parts may be, as it were, unfairly sacrificed. On the level of social organization, the interests of society may not always coincide with the sum of the interests of its parts. Discipline, sacrifice, and individual restraint are often

9 *An Introduction to the Principles of Morals and Legislation* (Oxford: Oxford University Press, 1823), chap. 1, sec. 4.

necessary in the social sphere to maintain social integrity as within the bodily organism. A society, indeed, is particularly vulnerable to disintegration when its members become preoccupied totally with their own particular interest, and ignore those distinct and independent interests of the community as a whole. One example, unfortunately, our own society, is altogether too close at hand to be examined with strict academic detachment. The United States seems to pursue uncritically a social policy of reductive utilitarianism, aimed at promoting the happiness of all its members severally. Each special interest accordingly clamors more loudly to be satisfied while the community as a whole becomes noticeably more and more infirm economically, environmentally, and politically.

The humane moralists, whether or not they are consciously and deliberately following Bentham on this particular, nevertheless, in point of fact, are committed to the welfare of certain kinds of animals distributively or reductively in applying their moral concern for nonhuman beings. They lament the treatment of animals, most frequently farm and laboratory animals, and plead the special interests of these beings. We might ask, from the perspective of the land ethic, what the effect upon the natural environment taken as whole would be if domestic animals were actually liberated? There is, almost certainly, very little real danger that this might actually happen, but it would be instructive to speculate on the ecological consequences.

ETHICAL HOLISM

Before we take up this question, however, some points of interest remain to be considered on the matter of a holistic versus a reductive environmental ethic. To pit the one against the other as I have done without further qualification would be mistaken. A society is constituted by its members, an organic body by its cells, and the ecosystem by the plants, animals, minerals, fluids, and gases which compose it. One cannot affect a system as a whole without affecting at least some of its components. An environmental ethic which takes as its *summum bonum* the integrity, stability, and beauty of the biotic community is not conferring moral standing on something *else* besides plants, animals, soils, and waters. Rather, the former, the good of the community as a whole, serves as a standard for the assessment of the relative value and relative ordering of its constitutive parts and therefore provides a means of adjudicating the often mutually contradictory demands of the parts considered separately for *equal* consideration. If diversity does indeed contribute to stability (a classical "law" of ecology), then *specimens* of rare and endangered species, for example, have a *prima facie* claim to preferential consideration from the perspective of the land ethic. Animals of those species, which, like the honey bee, function in ways critically important to the economy of nature, moreover, would be granted a greater claim to moral attention than psychologically more complex and sensitive ones, say, rabbits and moles, which seem to be plentiful, globally distributed, reproductively efficient, and only routinely integrated into the natural economy. Animals and plants, mountains, rivers, seas, the atmosphere are the *immediate* practical beneficiaries of the land ethic. The well-being of the biotic community, the biosphere as a whole, cannot be logically separated from their survival and welfare.

Some suspicion may arise at this point that the land ethic is ultimately grounded in *human* interests, not in those of nonhuman natural entities. Just as we might prefer a sound and attractive house to one in the opposite condition so the "goodness" of a whole, stable, and beautiful environment seems rather to be of the instrumental, not the autochthonous, variety. The question of ultimate value is a very sticky one for environmental as well as for all ethics and cannot be fully addressed here. It is my view that there can be no value apart from an evaluator, that all value is as it were in the eye of the be-

holder. The value that is attributed to the ecosystem, therefore, is humanly dependent or (allowing that other living things may take a certain delight in the well-being of the whole of things, or that the gods may) at least dependent upon some variety of morally and aesthetically sensitive consciousness. Granting this, however, there is a further, very crucial distinction to be drawn. It is possible that while things may only have value because we (or someone) values them, they may nonetheless be valued for themselves as well as for the contribution they might make to the realization of our (or someone's) interests. Children are valued for themselves by most parents. Money, on the other hand, has only an instrumental or indirect value. Which sort of value has the health of the biotic community and its members severally for Leopold and the land ethic? It is especially difficult to separate these two general sorts of value, the one of moral significance, the other merely selfish, when something that may be valued in *both ways at once* is the subject of consideration. Are pets, for example, well-treated, like children, for the sake of themselves, or, like mechanical appliances, because of the sort of services they provide their owners? Is a healthy biotic community something we value because we are so utterly and (to the biologically well-informed) so obviously dependent upon it not only for our happiness but for our very survival, or may we also perceive it disinterestedly as having an independent worth? Leopold insists upon a noninstrumental value for the biotic community and *mutatis mutandis* for its constituents. According to Leopold, collective enlightened self-interest on the part of human beings does not go far enough; the land ethic in his opinion (and no doubt this reflects his own moral intuitions) requires "love, respect, and admiration for land, and a high regard for its value." The land ethic, in Leopold's view, creates "obligations over and above self-interest." And "obligations have no meaning without conscience, and the problem we face is the extension of the social conscience from people to land."[10] If, in other words, any genuine ethic is possible, if it is possible to value *people* for the sake of themselves, then it is equally possible to value *land* in the same way.

Some indication of the genuinely biocentric value orientation of ethical environmentalism is indicated in what otherwise might appear to be gratuitous misanthropy. The biospheric perspective does not exempt *Homo sapiens* from moral evaluation in relation to the well-being of the community of nature taken as a whole. The preciousness of individual deer, as of any other specimen, is inversely proportional to the population of the species. Environmentalists, however reluctantly and painfully, do not omit to apply the same logic to their own kind. As omnivores, the population of human beings should, perhaps, be roughly twice that of bears, allowing for differences of size. A global population of more than four billion persons and showing no signs of an orderly decline presents an alarming prospect to humanists, but it is at present a global disaster (the more *per capita* prosperity, indeed, the more disastrous it appears) for the biotic community. If the land ethic were only a means of managing nature for the sake of man, misleadingly phrased in moral terminology, then man would be considered as having an ultimate value essentially different from that of his "resources." The extent of misanthropy in modern environmentalism thus may be taken as a measure of the degree to which it is biocentric. Edward Abbey in his enormously popular *Desert Solitaire* bluntly states that he would sooner shoot a man than a snake.[11] Abbey may not be simply depraved; this is perhaps only his way of dramatically making the point that the human population has become so disproportionate from the biological point of view that if one had to choose between a specimen of *Homo sapiens* and a specimen of a rare

even if unattractive species, the choice would be moot. Among academicians, Garret Hardin, a human ecologist by discipline who has written extensively on ethics, environmental and otherwise, has shocked philosophers schooled in the preciousness of human life with his "lifeboat" and "survival" ethics and his "wilderness economics." In context of the latter, Hardin recommends limiting access to wilderness by criteria of hardiness and woodcraft and would permit no emergency roads or airborne rescue vehicles to violate the pristine purity of wilderness areas. If a wilderness adventurer should have a serious accident, Hardin recommends that he or she get out on his or her own or die in the attempt. Danger, from the strictly human-centered, psychological perspective, is part of the wilderness experience, Hardin argues, but in all probability his more important concern is to protect from mechanization the remnants of wild country that remain even if the price paid is the incidental loss of human life which, from the perspective once more of the biologist, is a commodity altogether too common in relation to wildlife and to wild landscapes."[12] . . .

. . . Modern systems of ethics have, it must be admitted, considered the principle of the equality of persons to be inviolable. This is true, for example, of both major schools of modern ethics, the utilitarian school going back to Bentham and Mill, and the deontological, originating with Kant. The land ethic manifestly does not accord equal moral worth to each and every member of the biotic community; the moral worth of individuals (including, n.b., human individuals) is relative, to be assessed in accordance with the particular relation of each to the collective entity which Leopold called "land."

10 Leopold, *Sand County Almanac,* pp. 223 and 209.
11 Edward Abbey, *Desert Solitaire* (New York: Ballantine Books, 1968), p. 20.

12 Garrett Hardin, "The Economics of Wilderness," *Natural History* 78 [1969]: 173–177. Hardin is blunt: "Making great and spectacular efforts to save the life of an individual makes sense only when there is a shortage of people. I have not lately heard that there is a shortage of people" (p. 176).

There is, however, a classical Western ethic, with the best philosophical credentials, which assumes a similar holistic posture (with respect to the social moral sphere). I have in mind Plato's moral and social philosophy. Indeed, two of the same analogies figuring in the conceptual foundations of the Leopold land ethic appear in Plato's value theory. From the ecological perspective, according to Leopold as I have pointed out, land is like an organic body or like a human society. According to Plato, body, soul, and society have similar structures and corresponding virtues. The goodness of each is a function of its structure or organization and the relative value of the parts or constituents of each is calculated according to the contribution made to the integrity, stability, and beauty of each whole. In the *Republic*, Plato, in the very name of virtue and justice, is notorious for, among other things, requiring infanticide for a child whose only offense was being born without the sanction of the state, making presents to the enemy of guardians who allow themselves to be captured alive in combat, and radically restricting the practice of medicine to the dressing of wounds and the curing of seasonal maladies on the principle that the infirm and chronically ill not only lead miserable lives but contribute nothing to the good of the polity. Plato, indeed, seems to regard individual human life and certainly human pain and suffering with complete indifference. On the other hand, he shrinks from nothing so long as it seems to him to be in the interest of the community. Among the apparently inhuman recommendations that he makes to better the community are a program of eugenics involving a phony lottery (so that those whose natural desires are frustrated, while breeding proceeds from the best stock as in a kennel or stable, will blame chance, not the design of the rulers), the destruction of the pair bond and nuclear family (in the interests of greater military and bureaucratic efficiency and group solidarity), and the utter abolition of private property.

When challenged with the complaint that he is ignoring individual human happiness (and the happiness of those belonging to the most privileged class at that), he replies that it is the well-being of the community as a whole, not that of any person or special class at which his legislation aims. This principle is readily accepted, first of all, in our attitude toward the body, he reminds us—the separate interests of the parts of which we acknowledge to be subordinate to the health and well-being of the whole—and secondly, assuming that we accept his faculty psychology, in our attitude toward the soul—whose multitude of desires must be disciplined, restrained, and, in the case of some, altogether repressed in the interest of personal virtue and a well-ordered and morally responsible life.

Given these formal similarities to Plato's moral philosophy, we may conclude that the land ethic—with its holistic good and its assignment of differential values to the several parts of the environment irrespective of their intelligence, sensibility, degree of complexity, or any other characteristic discernible in the parts considered separately—is somewhat foreign to modern systems of ethical philosophy, but perfectly familiar in the broader context of classical Western ethical philosophy. If, therefore, Plato's system of public and private justice is properly an "ethical" system, then so is the land ethic in relation to environmental virtue and excellence.

REAPPRAISING DOMESTICITY

Among the last philosophical remarks penned by Aldo Leopold before his untimely death in 1948 is the following: "Perhaps such a shift of values [as implied by the attempt to weld together the concepts of ethics and ecology] can be achieved by reappraising things unnatural, tame, and confined in terms of things natural, wild, and free."[13] John Muir, in a similar spirit of reappraisal, had noted earlier the difference

---

13 Leopold, *Sand County Almanac*, p. ix.

between the wild mountain sheep of the Sierra and the ubiquitous domestic variety. The latter, which Muir described as "hooved locusts," were only, in his estimation, "half alive" in comparison with their natural and autonomous counterparts.[14] One of the more distressing aspects of the animal liberation movement is the failure of almost all its exponents to draw a sharp distinction between the very different plights (and rights) of wild and domestic animals. But this distinction lies at the very center of the land ethic. Domestic animals are creations of man. They are living artifacts, but artifacts nevertheless, and they constitute yet another mode of extension of the works of man into the ecosystem. From the perspective of the land ethic a herd of cattle, sheep, or pigs is as much or more a ruinous blight on the landscape as a fleet of four-wheel drive off-road vehicles. There is thus something profoundly incoherent (and insensitive as well) in the complaint of some animal liberationists that the "natural behavior" of chickens and bobby calves is cruelly frustrated on factory farms. It would make almost as much sense to speak of the natural behavior of tables and chairs.

Here a serious disanalogy (which no one to my knowledge has yet pointed out) becomes clearly evident between the liberation of blacks from slavery (and more recently, from civil inequality) and the liberation of animals from a similar sort of subordination and servitude. Black slaves remained, as it were, metaphysically autonomous: they were by nature if not by convention free beings quite capable of living on their own. They could not be enslaved for more than a historical interlude, for the strength of the force of their freedom was too great. They could, in other words, be retained only by a continuous counterforce, and only temporarily. This is equally true of caged wild animals. African cheetahs in American and European

zoos are captive, not indentured, beings. But this is not true of cows, pigs, sheep, and chickens. They have been bred to docility, tractability, stupidity, and dependency. It is literally meaningless to suggest that they be liberated. It is, to speak in hyperbole, a logical impossibility.

Certainly it is a practical impossibility. Imagine what would happen if the people of the world became morally persuaded that domestic animals were to be regarded as oppressed and enslaved persons and accordingly *set free*. In one scenario we might imagine that like former American black slaves they would receive the equivalent of forty acres and a mule and be turned out to survive on their own. Feral cattle and sheep would hang around farm outbuildings waiting forlornly to be sheltered and fed, or would graze aimlessly through their abandoned and deteriorating pastures. Most would starve or freeze as soon as winter settled in. Reproduction which had been assisted over many countless generations by their former owners might be altogether impossible in the feral state for some varieties, and the care of infants would be an art not so much lost as never acquired. And so in a very short time, after much suffering and agony, these species would become abruptly extinct. Or, in another scenario beginning with the same simple emancipation from human association, survivors of the first massive die-off of untended livestock might begin to recover some of their remote wild ancestral genetic traits and become smaller, leaner, heartier, and smarter versions of their former selves. An actual contemporary example is afforded by the feral mustangs ranging over parts of the American West. In time such animals as these would become (just as the mustangs are now) competitors both with their former human masters and (with perhaps more tragic consequences) indigenous wildlife for food and living space.

Foreseeing these and other untoward consequences of immediate and unplanned liberation of livestock, a human population grown morally more perfect than at present might decide that

14 See John Muir, "The Wild Sheep of California," *Overland Monthly* 12 (1874): 359.

they had a duty, accumulated over thousands of years, to continue to house and feed as before their former animal slaves (whom they had rendered genetically unfit to care for themselves), but not to butcher them or make other ill use of them, including frustrating their "natural" behavior, their right to copulate freely, reproduce, and enjoy the delights of being parents. People, no longer having meat to eat, would require more vegetables, cereals, and other plant foods, but the institutionalized animal incompetents would still consume all the hay and grains (and more since they would no longer be slaughtered) than they did formerly. This would require clearing more land and bringing it into agricultural production with further loss of wildlife habitat and ecological destruction. Another possible scenario might be a decision on the part of people not literally to liberate domestic animals but simply to cease to breed and raise them. When the last livestock have been killed and eaten (or permitted to die "natural" deaths), people would become vegetarians and domestic livestock species would thus be rendered deliberately extinct (just as they had been deliberately created). But there is surely some irony in an outcome in which the beneficiaries of a humane extension of conscience are destroyed in the process of being saved.

The land ethic, it should be emphasized, as Leopold has sketched it, provides for the *rights* of nonhuman natural beings to a share in the life processes of the biotic community. The conceptual foundation of such rights, however, is less conventional than natural, based upon, as one might say, evolutionary and ecological entitlement. Wild animals and native plants have a particular place in nature, according to the land ethic, which domestic animals (because they are products of human art and represent an extended presence of human beings in the natural world) do not have. The land ethic, in sum, is as much opposed, though on different grounds, to commercial traffic in wildlife, zoos, the slaughter of whales and other marine mammals, etc.,

as is the humane ethic. Concern for animal (and plant) rights and well-being is as fundamental to the land ethic as to the humane ethic, but the difference between naturally evolved and humanly bred species is an essential consideration for the one, though not for the other.

The "shift of values" which results from our "reappraising things unnatural, tame, and confined in terms of things natural, wild, and free" is especially dramatic when we reflect upon the definitions of *good* and *evil* espoused by Bentham and Mill and uncritically accepted by their contemporary followers. Pain and pleasure seem to have nothing at all to do with good and evil if our appraisal is taken from the vantage point of ecological biology. Pain in particular is primarily information. In animals, it informs the central nervous system of stress, irritation, or trauma in outlying regions of the organism. A certain level of pain under optimal organic circumstances is indeed desirable as an indicator of exertion—of the degree of exertion needed to maintain fitness, to stay "in shape," and of a level of exertion beyond which it would be dangerous to go. An arctic wolf in pursuit of a caribou may experience pain in her feet or chest because of the rigors of the chase. There is nothing bad or wrong in that. Or, consider a case of injury. Suppose that a person in the course of a wilderness excursion sprains an ankle. Pain informs him or her of the injury and by its intensity the amount of further stress the ankle may endure in the course of getting to safety. Would it be better if pain were not experienced upon injury or, taking advantage of recent technology, anaesthetized? Pleasure appears to be, for the most part (unfortunately it is not always so) a reward accompanying those activities which contribute to organic maintenance, such as the pleasures associated with eating, drinking, grooming, and so on, or those which contribute to social solidarity like the pleasures of dancing, conversation, teasing, etc., or those which contribute to the continuation of the species, such as the pleasures of sexual activity and of being parents. The doctrine that life is the happier the freer it is from pain and that the happiest life conceivable is one in which there is continuous pleasure uninterrupted by pain is biologically preposterous. A living mammal which experienced no pain would be one which had a lethal dysfunction of the nervous system. The idea that pain is evil and ought to be minimized or eliminated is as primitive a notion as that of a tyrant who puts to death messengers bearing bad news on the supposition that thus his well-being and security is improved.

More seriously still, the value commitments of the humane movement seem at bottom to betray a world-denying or rather a life-loathing philosophy. The natural world as actually constituted is one in which one being lives at the expense of others. Each organism, in Darwin's metaphor, struggles to maintain its own organic integrity. The more complex animals seem to experience (judging from our own case, and reasoning from analogy) appropriate and adaptive psychological accompaniments to organic existence. There is a palpable passion for self-preservation. There are desire, pleasure in the satisfaction of desires, acute agony attending injury, frustration, and chronic dread of death. But these experiences are the psychological substance of living. To live *is* to be anxious about life, to feel pain and pleasure in a fitting mixture, and sooner or later to die. That is the way the system works. If nature as a whole is good, then pain and death are also good. Environmental ethics in general require people to play fair in the natural system. The neo-Benthamites have in a sense taken the uncourageous approach. People have attempted to exempt themselves from the life/death reciprocities of natural processes and from ecological limitations in the name of a prophylactic ethic of maximizing rewards (pleasure) and minimizing unwelcome information (pain). To be fair, the humane moralists seem to suggest that we should attempt to project the same values into the non-human animal world and to widen the charmed

circle—no matter that it would be biologically unrealistic to do so or biologically ruinous if, per impossible, such an environmental ethic were implemented.

There is another approach. Rather than imposing our alienation from nature and natural processes and cycles of life on other animals, we human beings could reaffirm our participation in nature by accepting life as it is given without a sugar coating. Instead of imposing artificial legalities, rights, and so on on nature, we might take the opposite course and accept and affirm natural biological laws, principles, and limitations in the human personal and social spheres. Such appears to have been the posture toward life of tribal peoples in the past. The chase was relished with its dangers, rigors, and hardships as well as its rewards: animal flesh was respectfully consumed; a tolerance for pain was cultivated; virtue and magnanimity were prized; lithic, floral, and faunal spirits were worshipped; population was routinely optimized by sexual continency, abortion, infanticide, and stylized warfare; and other life forms, although certainly appropriated, were respected as fellow players in a magnificent and awesome, if not altogether idyllic, drama of life. It is impossible today to return to the symbiotic relationship of Stone Age man to the natural environment, but the ethos of this by far the longest era of human existence could be abstracted and integrated with a future human culture seeking a viable and mutually beneficial relationship with nature. Personal, social, and environmental *health* would, accordingly, receive a premium value rather than comfort, self-indulgent pleasure, and anaesthetic insulation from pain. Sickness would be regarded as a worse evil than death. The pursuit of health or wellness at the personal, social, and environmental levels would require self-discipline in the form of simple diet, vigorous exercise, conservation, and social responsibility.

Leopold's prescription for the realization and implementation of the land ethic—the reappraisal of things unnatural, tame, and confined in terms of things natural, wild, and free—does not stop, in other words, with a reappraisal of nonhuman domestic animals in terms of their wild (or willed) counterparts; the human ones should be similarly reappraised. This means, among other things, the reappraisal of the comparatively recent values and concerns of "civilized" *Homo sapiens* in terms of those of our "savage" ancestors. Civilization has insulated and alienated us from the rigors and challenges of the natural environment. The hidden agenda of the humane ethic is the imposition of the anti-natural prophylactic ethos of comfort and soft pleasure on an even wider scale. The land ethic, on the other hand, requires a shrinkage, if at all possible, of the domestic sphere; it rejoices in a recrudescence of wilderness and a renaissance of tribal cultural experience.

The converse of those goods and evils, axiomatic to the humane ethic, may be illustrated and focused by the consideration of a single issue raised by the humane morality: a vegetarian diet. Savage people seem to have had, if the attitudes and values of surviving tribal cultures are representative, something like an intuitive grasp of ecological relationships and certainly a morally charged appreciation of eating. There is nothing more intimate than eating, more symbolic of the connectedness of life, and more mysterious. What we eat and how we eat is by no means an insignificant ethical concern.

From the ecological point of view, for human beings universally to become vegetarians is tantamount to a shift of trophic niche from omnivore with carnivorous preferences to herbivore. The shift is a downward one on the trophic pyramid, which in effect shortens those food chains terminating with man. It represents an increase in the efficiency of the conversion of solar energy from plant to human biomass, and thus, by bypassing animal intermediates, increases available food resources for human beings. The human population would probably, as past trends overwhelmingly suggest, expand in accordance with the potential thus afforded. The net result would be fewer nonhuman beings and more human beings, who, of course,

have requirements of life far more elaborate than even those of domestic animals, requirements which would tax other "natural resources" (trees for shelter, minerals mined at the expense of topsoil and its vegetation, etc.) more than under present circumstances. A vegetarian human population is therefore *probably* ecologically catastrophic.

Meat eating as implied by the foregoing remarks may be more *ecologically* responsible than a wholly vegetable diet. Meat, however, purchased at the supermarket, externally packaged and internally laced with petrochemicals, fattened in feed lots, slaughtered impersonally, and, in general, mechanically processed from artificial insemination to microwave roaster, is an affront not only to physical metabolism and bodily health but to conscience as well. From the perspective of the land ethic, the immoral aspect of the factory farm has to do far less with the suffering and killing of nonhuman animals than with the monstrous transformation of living things from an organic to a mechanical mode of being. Animals, beginning with the Neolithic Revolution, have been debased through selective breeding, but they have nevertheless remained animals. With the Industrial Revolution an even more profound and terrifying transformation has overwhelmed them. They have become, in Ruth Harrison's most apt description, "animal machines." The very presence of animals, so emblematic of delicate, complex organic tissue, surrounded by machines, connected to machines, penetrated by machines in research laboratories or crowded together in space-age "production facilities" is surely the more real and visceral source of our outrage at vivisection and factory farming than the contemplation of the quantity of pain that these unfortunate beings experience. I wish to denounce as loudly as the neo-Benthamites this ghastly abuse of animal life, but also to stress that the pain and suffering of research and agribusiness animals is not greater than that endured by free-living wildlife as a consequence of predation, disease, starvation, and cold—indicating that there is something immoral about vivisection and factory farming which is not an ingredient in the natural lives and deaths of wild beings. That immoral something is the transmogrification of organic to mechanical processes.

Ethical vegetarianism to all appearances insists upon the human consumption of plants (in a paradoxical moral gesture toward those animals whose very existence is dependent upon human carnivorousness), even when the tomatoes are grown hydroponically, the lettuce generously coated with chlorinated hydrocarbons, the potatoes pumped up with chemical fertilizers, and the cereals stored with the help of chemical preservatives. The land ethic takes as much exception to the transmogrification of plants by mechanicochemical means as to that of animals. The important thing, I would think, is not to eat vegetables as opposed to animal flesh, but to resist factory farming in all its manifestations, including especially its liberal application of pesticides, herbicides, and chemical fertilizers to maximize the production of *vegetable* crops.

The land ethic, with its ecological perspective, helps us to recognize and affirm the organic integrity of self and the untenability of a firm distinction between self and environment. On the ethical question of what to eat, it answers, not vegetables instead of animals, but organically as opposed to mechanicochemically produced food. Purists like Leopold prefer, in his expression, to get their "meat from God," i.e., to hunt and consume wildlife and to gather wild plant foods, and thus to live within the parameters of the aboriginal human ecological niche. Second best is eating from one's own orchard, garden, henhouse, pigpen, and barnyard. Third best is buying or bartering organic foods from one's neighbors and friends.

CONCLUSION

Philosophical controversy concerning animal liberation/rights has been most frequently represented as a polar dispute between traditional moral humanists and seemingly *avant garde* humane moralists. Further, animal liberation has been assumed to be closely allied with environmental ethics, possibly because in Leopold's classical formulation moral standing and indeed rights (of some unspecified sort) is accorded nonhuman beings, among them animals. The purpose of this discussion has been to distinguish sharply environmental ethics from the animal liberation/rights movement both in theory and practical application and to suggest, thereupon, that there is an underrepresented, but very important, point of view respecting the problem of the moral status of nonhuman animals. The debate over animal liberation, in short, should be conceived as triangular, not polar, with land ethics or environmental ethics, the third and, in my judgment, the most creative, interesting, and practicable alternative. Indeed, from this third point of view moral humanism and humane moralism appear to have much more in common with one another than either have with environmental or land ethics. On reflection one might even be led to suspect that the noisy debate between these parties has served to drown out the much deeper challenge to "business-as usual" ethical philosophy represented by Leopold and his exponents, and to keep ethical philosophy firmly anchored to familiar modern paradigms.

Moral humanism and humane moralism, to restate succinctly the most salient conclusions of this essay, are *atomistic* or distributive in their theory of moral value, while environmental ethics (again, at least, as set out in Leopold's outline) is *holistic* or collective. Modern ethical theory, in other words, has consistently located moral value in individuals and set out certain metaphysical reasons for including some individuals and excluding others. Humane moralism remains firmly within this modern convention and centers its attention on the competing criteria for moral standing and rights holding, while environmental ethics locates ultimate value in the "biotic community" and assigns differential moral value to the constitutive individuals relatively to that standard. This is perhaps the most fundamental theoretical difference between environmental ethics and the ethics of animal liberation.

Allied to this difference are many others. One of the more conspicuous is that in environmental ethics, plants are included within the parameters of the ethical theory as well as animals. Indeed, inanimate entities such as oceans and lakes, mountains, forests, and wetlands are assigned a greater value than individual animals and in a way quite different from systems which accord them moral considerability through a further multiplication of competing individual loci of value and holders of rights.

There are intractable practical differences between environmental ethics and the animal liberation movement. Very different moral obligations follow in respect, most importantly, to domestic animals, the principal beneficiaries of the humane ethic. Environmental ethics sets a very low priority on domestic animals as they very frequently contribute to the erosion of the integrity, stability, and beauty of the biotic communities into which they have been insinuated. On the other hand, animal liberation, if pursued at the practical as well as rhetorical level, would have ruinous consequences on plants, soils, and waters, consequences which could not be directly reckoned according to humane moral theory. As this last remark suggests, the animal liberation/animal rights movement is in the final analysis utterly unpracticable. An imagined society in which all animals capable of sensibility received equal consideration or held rights to equal consideration would be so ludicrous that it might be more appropriately and effectively treated in satire than in philosophical discussion. The land ethic, by contrast, even though its ethical purview is very much wider, is nevertheless eminently practicable, since, by reference to a single good, competing individual claims may be adjudicated and relative values and priorities assigned to the myriad components of the biotic community. This is not to suggest that the implementation of environmental ethics as social policy would be easy. Implementation of the land ethic would require discipline, sacrifice, retrenchment, and massive economic reform, tantamount to a virtual revolution in prevailing attitudes and life styles. Nevertheless, it provides a unified and coherent practical principle and thus a decision procedure at the practical level which a distributive or atomistic ethic may achieve only artificially and so imprecisely as to be practically indeterminate.

Review Questions

1. Explain the conflict that Callicott sees between the animal liberation movement and Leopold's land ethic.
2. Callicott explores three possible interpretations of Leopold's practice of hunting, killing, and eating animals. What are they?
3. Distinguish between ethical humanism, humane moralism, and the land ethic, as Callicott explains them.
4. According to Callicott, what kind of value does the land ethic place on the land?
5. Explain Callicott's comparison of the land ethic with Plato's moral and social philosophy.
6. Why does Callicott think that the distinction between wild and domestic animals is important? What are the implications of this distinction?
7. How does the land ethic view pain and pleasure, according to Callicott? Why are pain and death good?
8. What is Callicott's view of vegetarianism?
9. Why does he think that the animal liberation movement is, in the final analysis, utterly unpracticable?

Discussion Questions

1. Is the land ethic any more practicable than animal liberation? Explain your answer.
2. How would vegetarians and animal liberationists such as Rachels, Singer, and Regan respond to Callicott? Do they have an adequate response?
3. Callicott quotes Edward Abbey's saying that he would rather shoot a man than a snake, presumably because humans are a threat to the land while snakes are not. Does the land ethic ultimately require the extermination of humans to preserve the land? Why or why not?

The Ethics of Respect for Nature

PAUL W. TAYLOR

Paul W. Taylor is professor of philosophy at Brooklyn College, City University of New York. He is the author of *Respect for Nature* (1986).

Taylor says that his ethics of respect for nature is made up of three basic elements: a belief system, an ultimate moral attitude, and a set of rules of duty and standards of character. The belief system involves a biocentric outlook on nature wherein all living things are interdependent in an organically unified order. Taylor is particularly concerned to defend the implication of this outlook that humans are not superior to other animals in either merit or inherent worth. The ultimate moral attitude involves two basic concepts: that every organism, species population, and community of life has a good of its own, and that all wild living things have inherent worth. The rules of duty include the duty to not harm wild living things and the duty to preserve, promote, and protect what is good for them.

HUMAN-CENTERED AND LIFE-CENTERED SYSTEMS OF ENVIRONMENTAL ETHICS

In this paper I show how the taking of a certain ultimate moral attitude toward nature, which I call "respect for nature," has a central place in the foundations of a life-centered system of en-

Source: Paul Taylor, "The Ethics of Respect for Nature," from *Environmental Ethics* Vol. 3 (Fall 1981), pp. 197–218. Reprinted with permission.

vironmental ethics. I hold that a set of moral norms (both standards of character and rules of conduct) governing human treatment of the natural world is a rationally grounded set if and only if, first, commitment to those norms is a practical entailment of adopting the attitude of respect for nature as an ultimate moral attitude, and second, the adopting of that attitude on the part of all rational agents can itself be justified. When the basic characteristics of the attitude of respect for nature are made clear, it will be seen that a life-centered system of environmental ethics need not be holistic or organicist in its conception of the kinds of entities that are deemed the appropriate objects of moral concern and consideration. Nor does such a system require that the concepts of ecological homeostasis, equilibrium, and integrity provide us with normative principles from which could be derived (with the addition of factual knowledge) our obligations with regard to natural ecosystems. The "balance of nature" is not itself a moral norm, however important may be the role it plays in our general outlook on the natural world that underlies the attitude of respect for nature. I argue that finally it is the good (wellbeing, welfare) of individual organisms, considered as entities having inherent worth, that determines our moral relations with the Earth's wild communities of life.

In designating the theory . . . as life-centered, I intend to contrast it with all anthropocentric views. According to the latter, human actions that affect the natural environment and its nonhuman inhabitants are right (or wrong) by either of two criteria: They have consequences that are favorable (or unfavorable) to human well-being, or they are consistent (or inconsistent) with the system of norms that protect and implement human rights. From this human-centered standpoint it is to humans and only to humans that all duties are ultimately owed. We may have responsibilities *with regard to* the natural ecosystems and biotic communities of our planet, but these responsibilities are in every case based on the contingent fact that our treatment of those ecosystems and communities of life can further the realization of human values and/or human rights. We have no obligation to promote or protect the good of nonhuman living things, independently of this contingent fact.

A life-centered system of environmental ethics is opposed to human-centered ones precisely on this point. From the perspective of a life-centered theory, we have prima facie moral obligations that are owed to wild plants and animals themselves as members of the Earth's biotic community. We are morally bound (other things being equal) to protect or promote their good for *their* sake. Our duties to respect the integrity of natural ecosystems, to preserve endangered species, and to avoid environmental pollution stem from the fact that these are ways in which we can help make it possible for wild species populations to achieve and maintain a healthy existence in a natural state. Such obligations are due those living things out of recognition of their inherent worth. They are entirely additional to and independent of the obligations we owe to our fellow humans. Although many of the actions that fulfill one set of obligations also fulfill the other, two different grounds of obligation are involved. Their well-being, as well as human well-being, is something to be realized *as an end in itself.*

If we were to accept a life-centered theory of environmental ethics, a profound reordering of our moral universe would take place. We would begin to look at the whole of the Earth's biosphere in a new light. Our duties with respect to the "world" of nature would be seen as making prima facie claims on us to be balanced against our duties with respect to the "world" of human civilization. We could no longer simply take the human point of view and consider the effects of our actions exclusively from the perspective of our own good.

THE GOOD OF A BEING AND THE CONCEPT OF INHERENT WORTH

What would justify acceptance of a life-centered system of ethical principles? In order to answer this it is first necessary to make clear the fundamental moral attitude that underlies and makes intelligible the commitment to live by such a system. It is then necessary to examine the considerations that would justify any rational agent's adopting that moral attitude.

Two concepts are essential to the taking of a moral attitude of the sort in question. A being which does not "have" these concepts, that is, which is unable to grasp their meaning and conditions of applicability, cannot be said to have the attitude as part of its moral outlook. These concepts are, first, that of the good (well-being, welfare) of a living thing, and second, the idea of an entity possessing inherent worth. I examine each concept in turn.

(1) Every organism, species population, and community of life has a good of its own which moral agents can intentionally further or damage by their actions. To say that an entity has a good of its own is simply to say that, without reference to any *other* entity, it can be benefited or harmed. One can act in its overall interest or contrary to its overall interest, and environmental conditions can be good for it (advantageous to it) or bad for it (disadvantageous to it). What is good for an entity is what "does it good" in the sense of enhancing or preserving its life and well-being. What is bad for an entity is something that is detrimental to its life and well-being.[1]

We can think of the good of an individual nonhuman organism as consisting in the full development of its biological powers. Its good is realized to the extent that it is strong and healthy. It possesses whatever capacities it needs to successfully cope with its environment and so preserving its existence throughout the various stages of the normal life cycle of its species. The good of a population or community of such individuals consists in the population or community maintaining itself from generation to generation as a coherent system of genetically and ecologically related organisms whose average good is at an optimum level for the given environment. (Here *average good* means that the degree of realization of the good of *individual organisms* in the population or community is, on average, greater than would be the case

under any other ecologically functioning order of interrelations among those species populations in the given ecosystem.)

The idea of a being having a good of its own . . . does not entail that the being must have interests or take an interest in what affects its life for better or for worse. We can act in a being's interest or contrary to its interest without its being interested in what we are doing to it in the sense of wanting or not wanting us to do it. It may, indeed, be wholly unaware that favorable and unfavorable events are taking place in its life. [Trees], for example, have no knowledge or desires or feelings. Yet it is undoubtedly the case that trees can be harmed or benefited by our actions. We can crush their roots by running a bulldozer too close to them. We can see to it that they get adequate nourishment and moisture by fertilizing and watering the soil around them. Thus we can help or hinder them in the realization of their good. It is the good of trees themselves that is thereby affected. We can similarly act so as to further the good of an entire tree population of a certain species (say, all the redwood trees in a California valley) or the good of a whole community of plant life in a given wilderness area, just as we can do harm to such a population or community.

When construed in this way, the concept of a being's good is not coextensive with sentience or the capacity for feeling pain. William Frankena has argued for a general theory of environmental ethics in which the ground of a creature's being worthy of moral consideration is its sentience. I have offered some criticisms of this view elsewhere, but the full refutation of such a position . . . finally depends on the positive reasons for accepting a life-centered theory of the kind I am defending in this essay.[2]

It should be noted further that I am leaving open the question of whether machines—in

---

1 The conceptual links between an entity *having* a good, something being good *for* it, and events doing good *to* it are examined by G. H. Von Wright in *The Varieties of Goodness* (New York: Humanities Press, 1963), chaps. 3 and 5.

2 See W. K. Frankena, "Ethics and the Environment," in K. E. Goodpaster and K. M. Sayre, eds., *Ethics and Problems*

particular, those which are not only goal-directed, but also self-regulating—can properly be said to have a good of their own.[3] Since I am concerned only with human treatment of wild organisms, species populations, and communities of life as they occur in our planet's natural ecosystems, it is to those entities alone that the concept "having a good of its own" will here be applied. I am not denying that other living things, whose genetic origin and environmental conditions have been produced, controlled, and manipulated by humans for human ends, do have a good of their own in the same sense as do wild plants and animals. It is not my purpose in this essay, however, to set out or defend the principles that should guide our conduct with regard to their good. It is only insofar as their production and use by humans have good or ill effects upon natural ecosystems and their wild inhabitants that the ethics of respect for nature comes into play.

(2) The second concept essential to the moral attitude of respect for nature is the idea of inherent worth. We take that attitude toward wild living things (individuals, species populations, or whole biotic communities) when and only when we regard them as entities possessing inherent worth. Indeed, it is only because they are conceived in this way that moral agents can think of themselves as having validly binding duties, obligations, and responsibilities that are *owed* to them as their *due*. I am not at this juncture arguing why they *should* be so regarded; I

consider it at length below. But so regarding them is a presupposition of our taking the attitude of respect toward them and accordingly understanding ourselves as bearing certain moral relations to them. This can be shown as follows:

What does it mean to regard an entity that has a good of its own as possessing inherent worth? Two general principles are involved: the principle of moral consideration and the principle of intrinsic value.

According to the principle of moral consideration, wild living things are deserving of the concern and consideration of all moral agents simply in virtue of their being members of the Earth's community of life. From the moral point of view their good must be taken into account whenever it is affected for better or worse by the conduct of rational agents. This holds no matter what species the creature belongs to. The good of each is to be accorded some value and so acknowledged as having some weight in the deliberations of all rational agents. Of course, it may be necessary for such agents to act in ways contrary to the good of this or that particular organism or group of organisms in order to further the good of others, including the good of humans. But the principle of moral consideration prescribes that, with respect to each being an entity having its own good, every individual is deserving of consideration.

The principle of intrinsic value states that, regardless of what kind of entity it is in other respects, if it is a member of the Earth's community of life, the realization of its good is something *intrinsically* valuable. This means that its good is prima facie worthy of being preserved or promoted as an end in itself and for the sake of the entity whose good it is. Insofar as we regard any organism, species population, or life community as an entity with inherent worth, we believe that it must never be treated as if it were a mere object or thing whose entire value lies in being instrumental to the good of some

---

of the 21st Century (Notre Dame: University of Notre Dame Press, 1979), pp. 3–20. I critically examine Frankena's views in "Frankena on Environmental Ethics," *Monist* (1981): 237–243.

3 In the light of considerations set forth in Daniel Dennett's *Brainstorms: Philosophical Essays on Mind and Psychology* (Montgomery, Vt.: Bradford Books, 1978), it is advisable to leave this question unsettled at this time. When machines are developed that function in the way our brains do, we may well come to deem them proper subjects of moral consideration.

other entity. The well-being of each is judged to have value in and of itself.

Combining these two principles, we can now define what it means for a living thing or group of living things to possess inherent worth. To say that it possesses inherent worth is to say that its good is deserving of the concern and consideration of all moral agents, and that the realization of its good has intrinsic value, to be pursued as an end in itself and for the sake of the entity whose good it is.

The duties owed to wild organisms, species populations, and communities of life in the Earth's natural ecosystems are grounded on their inherent worth. When rational, autonomous agents regard such entities as possessing inherent worth, they place intrinsic value on the realization of their good and so hold themselves responsible for performing actions that will have this effect and for refraining from actions having the contrary effect.

THE ATTITUDE OF RESPECT FOR NATURE

Why should moral agents regard wild living things in the natural world as possessing inherent worth? To answer this question we must first take into account the fact that, when rational, autonomous agents subscribe to the principles of moral consideration and intrinsic value and so conceive of wild living things as having that kind of worth, such agents are *adopting a certain ultimate moral attitude toward the natural world.* This is the attitude I call "respect for nature." It parallels the attitude of respect for persons in human ethics. When we adopt the attitude of respect for persons as the proper (fitting, appropriate) attitude to take toward all persons as persons, we consider the fulfillment of the basic interests of each individual to have intrinsic value. We thereby make a moral commitment to live a certain kind of life in relation to other persons. We place ourselves under the direction of a

system of standards and rules that we consider validly binding on all moral agents as such.[4]

Similarly, when we adopt the attitude of respect for nature as an ultimate moral attitude we make a commitment to live by certain normative principles. These principles constitute the rules of conduct and standards of character that are to govern our treatment of the natural world. This is, first, an *ultimate* commitment because it is not derived from any higher norm. The attitude of respect for nature is not grounded on some other, more general, or more fundamental attitude. It sets the total framework for our responsibilities toward the natural world. It can be justified, as I show below, but its justification cannot consist in referring to a more general attitude or a more basic normative principle.

Second, the commitment is a *moral* one because it is understood to be a disinterested matter of principle. It is this feature that distinguishes the attitude of respect for nature from the set of feelings and dispositions that comprise the love of nature. The latter stems from one's personal interest in and response to the natural world. Like the affectionate feelings we have toward certain individual human beings, one's love of nature is nothing more than the particular way one feels about the natural environment and its wild inhabitants. And just as our love for an individual person differs from our respect for all persons as such (whether we happen to love them or not), so love of nature differs from respect for nature. Respect for nature is an attitude we believe all moral agents ought to have simply as moral agents, regardless of whether or not they also love nature. Indeed, we have not truly taken the attitude of respect for nature ourselves unless we believe this. To put it in a

4 I have analyzed the nature of this commitment of human ethics in "On Taking the Moral Point of View," *Midwest Studies in Philosophy,* vol. 3, *Studies in Ethical Theory* (1978), pp. 35–61.

Kantian way, to adopt the attitude of respect for nature is to take a stance that one wills it to be a universal law for all rational beings. It is to hold that stance categorically, as being validly applicable to every moral agent without exception, irrespective of whatever personal feelings toward nature such an agent might have or might lack.

Although the attitude of respect for nature is, in this sense, a disinterested and universalizable attitude, anyone who does adopt it has certain steady, more or less permanent dispositions. These dispositions, which are themselves to be considered disinterested and universalizable, comprise three interlocking sets: dispositions to seek certain ends, dispositions to carry on one's practical reasoning and deliberation in a certain way, and dispositions to have certain feelings. We may accordingly analyze the attitude of respect for nature into the following components. (a) The disposition to aim at, and to take steps to bring about, as final and disinterested ends, the promoting and protecting of the good of organisms, species populations, and life communities in natural ecosystems. (These ends are "final" in not being pursued as means to further ends. They are "disinterested" in being independent of the self-interest of the agent.) (b) The disposition to consider actions that tend to realize those ends to be prima facie obligatory *because* they have that tendency. (c) The disposition to experience positive and negative feelings toward states of affairs in the world *because* they are favorable or unfavorable to the good of organisms, species populations, and life communities in natural ecosystems.

The logical connection between the attitude of respect for nature and the duties of a life-centered system of environmental ethics can now be made clear. Insofar as one sincerely takes that attitude and so has the three sets of dispositions, one will at the same time be disposed to comply with certain rules of duty (such as nonmaleficence and noninterference) and with standards of character (such as fairness and benevolence) that determine the obligations

and virtues of moral agents with regard to the Earth's wild living things. We can say that the actions one performs and the character traits one develops in fulfilling these moral requirements are the way one *expresses* or *embodies* the attitude in one's conduct and character. In his famous essay, "Justice as Fairness," John Rawls describes the rules of the duties of human morality (such as fidelity, gratitude, honesty, and justice) as "forms of conduct in which recognition of others as persons is manifested."[5] I hold that the rules of duty governing our treatment of the natural world and its inhabitants are forms of conduct in which the attitude of respect for nature is manifested.

THE JUSTIFIABILITY OF THE ATTITUDE OF RESPECT FOR NATURE

I return to the question posed earlier, which has not yet been answered: Why *should* moral agents regard wild living things as possessing inherent worth? I now argue that the only way we can answer this question is by showing how adopting the attitude of respect for nature is justified for all moral agents. Let us suppose that we were able to establish that there are good reasons for adopting the attitude, reasons which are intersubjectively valid for every rational agent. If there are such reasons, they would justify anyone's having the three sets of dispositions mentioned above as constituting what it means to have the attitude. Since these include the disposition to promote or protect the good of wild living things as a disinterested and ultimate end, as well as the disposition to perform actions for the reason that they tend to realize that end, we see that such dispositions commit a person to the principles of moral consideration and intrinsic value. To be disposed to further, as

5 John Rawls, "Justice As Fairness," *Philosophical Review* 67 (1958): 183.

an end in itself, the good of any entity in nature just because it is that kind of entity, is to be disposed to give consideration to *every* such entity and to place intrinsic value on the realization of its good. Insofar as we subscribe to these two principles we regard living things as possessing inherent worth. Subscribing to the principles is what it *means* to so regard them. To justify the attitude of respect for nature, then, is to justify commitment to these principles and thereby to justify regarding wild creatures as possessing inherent worth.

We must keep in mind that inherent worth is not some mysterious sort of objective property belonging to living things that can be discovered by empirical observation or scientific investigation. To ascribe inherent worth to an entity is not to describe it by citing some feature discernible by sense perception or inferable by inductive reasoning. Nor is there a logically necessary connection between the concept of a being having a good of its own and the concept of inherent worth. We do not contradict ourselves by asserting that an entity that has a good of its own lacks inherent worth. In order to show that such an entity "has" inherent worth we must give good reasons for ascribing that kind of value to it (placing that kind of value upon it, conceiving of it to be valuable in that way). Although it is humans (persons, valuers) who must do the valuing, for the ethics of respect for nature, the value so ascribed is not a human value. That is to say, it is not a value derived from considerations regarding human well-being or human rights. It is a value that is ascribed to nonhuman animals and plants themselves, independently of their relationship to what humans judge to be conducive to their own good.

Whatever reasons, then, justify our taking the attitude of respect for nature as defined above are also reasons that show why we *should* regard the living things of the natural world as possessing inherent worth. We saw earlier that, since the attitude is an ultimate one, it cannot be derived from a more fundamental attitude nor shown to be a special case of a more general one. On what sort of grounds, then, can it be established?

The attitude we take toward living things in the natural world depends on the way we look at them, on what kind of beings we conceive them to be, and on how we understand the relations we bear to them. Underlying and supporting our attitude is a certain *belief system* that constitutes a particular world view or outlook on nature and the place of human life in it. To give good reasons for adopting the attitude of respect for nature, then, we must first articulate the belief system which underlies and supports that attitude. If it appears that the belief system is internally coherent and well ordered, and if, as far as we can now tell, it is consistent with all known scientific truths relevant to our knowledge of the object of the attitude (which in this case includes the whole set of the Earth's natural ecosystems and their communities of life), then there remains the task of indicating why scientifically informed and rational thinkers with a developed capacity of reality awareness can find it acceptable as a way of conceiving of the natural world and our place in it. To the extent we can do this we provide at least a reasonable argument for accepting the belief system and the ultimate moral attitude it supports.

I do not hold that such a belief system can be *proven* to be true, either inductively or deductively. As we shall see, not all of its components can be stated in the form of empirically verifiable propositions. Nor is its internal order governed by purely logical relationships. But the system as a whole, I contend, constitutes a coherent, unified, and rationally acceptable "picture" or "map" of a total world. By examining each of its main components and seeing how they fit together, we obtain a scientifically informed and well-ordered conception of nature and the place of humans in it.

This belief system underlying the attitude of respect for nature I call (for want of a better name) "the biocentric outlook on nature." Since it is not wholly analyzable into empirically confirmable assertions, it should not be thought of as simply a compendium of the biological sciences concerning our planet's ecosystems. It might best be described as a philosophical world view, to distinguish it from a scientific theory or explanatory system. However, one of its major tenets is the great lesson we have learned from the science of ecology: the interdependence of all living things in an organically unified order whose balance and stability are necessary conditions for the realization of the good of its constituent biotic communities.

Before turning to an account of the main components of the biocentric outlook, it is convenient here to set forth the overall structure of my theory of environmental ethics as it has now emerged. The ethics of respect for nature is made up of three basic elements: a belief system, an ultimate moral attitude, and a set of rules of duty and standards of character. These elements are connected with each other in the following manner. The belief system provides a certain outlook on nature which supports and makes intelligible an autonomous agent's adopting, as an ultimate moral attitude, the attitude of respect for nature. It supports and makes intelligible the attitude in the sense that, when an autonomous agent understands its moral relations to the natural world in terms of this outlook, it recognizes the attitude of respect to be the only *suitable* or *fitting* attitude to take toward all wild forms of life in the Earth's biosphere. Living things are now viewed as *the appropriate objects of the attitude of respect* and are accordingly regarded as entities possessing inherent worth. One then places intrinsic value on the promotion and protection of their good. As a consequence of this, one makes a moral commitment to abide by a set of rules of duty and to fulfill (as far as one can by one's own efforts) certain standards of good character. Given one's adoption of the attitude of respect, one makes that moral commitment because one

considers those rules and standards to be validly binding on all moral agents. They are seen as embodying forms of conduct and character structures in which the attitude of respect for nature is manifested.

This three-part complex which internally orders the ethics of respect for nature is symmetrical with a theory of human ethics grounded on respect for persons. Such a theory includes, first, a conception of oneself and others as persons, that is, as centers of autonomous choice. Second, there is the attitude of respect for persons as persons. When this is adopted as an ultimate moral attitude it involves the disposition to treat every person as having inherent worth or "human dignity." Every human being, just in virtue of her or his humanity, is understood to be worthy of moral consideration, and intrinsic value is placed on the autonomy and well-being of each. This is what Kant meant by conceiving of persons as ends in themselves. Third, there is an ethical system of duties which are acknowledged to be owed by everyone to everyone. These duties are forms of conduct in which public recognition is given to each individual's inherent worth as a person.

This structural framework for a theory of human ethics is meant to leave open the issue of consequentialism (utilitarianism) versus nonconsequentialism (deontology). That issue concerns the particular kind of system of rules defining the duties of moral agents toward persons. Similarly, I am leaving open [here] the question of what particular kind of system of rules defines our duties with respect to the natural world.

THE BIOCENTRIC OUTLOOK ON NATURE

The biocentric outlook on nature has four main components. (1) Humans are thought of as members of the Earth's community of life, holding that membership on the same terms as apply to all the nonhuman members. (2) The

Earth's natural ecosystems as a totality are seen as a complex web of interconnected elements, with the sound biological functioning of each being dependent on the sound biological functioning of the others. (This is the component referred to above as the great lesson that the science of ecology has taught us.) (3) Each individual organism is conceived of as a teleological center of life, pursuing its own good in its own way. (4) Whether we are concerned with standards of merit or with the concept of inherent worth, the claim that humans by their very nature are superior to other species is a groundless claim and, in the light of elements (1), (2), and (3) above, must be rejected as nothing more than an irrational bias in our own favor. . . .

THE DENIAL
OF HUMAN SUPERIORITY

This fourth component of the biocentric outlook on nature is the single most important idea in establishing the justifiability of the attitude of respect for nature. Its central role is due to the special relationship it bears to the first three components of the outlook. This relationship will be brought out after the concept of human superiority is examined and analyzed.[6]

In what sense are humans alleged to be superior to other animals? We are different from them in having certain capacities that they lack. But why should these capacities be a mark of superiority? From what point of view are they judged to be signs of superiority and what sense of superiority is meant? After all, various nonhuman species have capacities that humans lack. There is the speed of a cheetah, the vision of an

6 My criticisms of the dogma of human superiority gain independent support from a carefully reasoned essay by R. and V. Routley showing the many logical weaknesses in arguments for human-centered theories of environmental ethics. R. and V. Routley, "Against the Inevitability of Human Chauvinism," in K. E. Goodpaster and K. M. Sayre, eds., *Ethics and Problems of the 21st Century* (Notre Dame: University of Notre Dame Press, 1979), pp. 36–59.

eagle, the agility of a monkey. Why should not these be taken as signs of *their* superiority over humans?

One answer . . . is that these capacities are not as *valuable* as the human capacities that are claimed to make us superior. Such uniquely human characteristics as rational thought, aesthetic creativity, autonomy and self-determination, and moral freedom, it might be held, have a higher value than the capacities found in other species. Yet we must ask: valuable to whom, and on what grounds?

The human characteristics mentioned are all valuable to humans. They are essential to the preservation and enrichment of our civilization and culture. Clearly it is from the human standpoint that they are being judged to be desirable and good. It is not difficult here to recognize a begging of the question. Humans are claiming human superiority from a strictly human point of view, that is, from a point of view in which the good of humans is taken as the standard of judgment. All we need to do is to look at the capacities of nonhuman animals (or plants, for that matter) from the standpoint of *their* good to find a contrary judgment of superiority. The speed of the cheetah, for example, is a sign of its superiority to humans when considered from the standpoint of the good of its species. If it were as slow a runner as a human, it would not be able to survive. And so for all the other abilities of nonhumans which further their good but which are lacking in humans. In each case the claim to human superiority would be rejected from a nonhuman standpoint.

When superiority assertions are interpreted in this way, they are based on judgments of *merit*. To judge the merits of a person or an organism one must apply grading or ranking standards to it. (As I show below, this distinguishes judgments of merit from judgments of inherent worth.) Empirical investigation then determines whether it has the "good-making properties" (merits) in virtue of which it fulfills the standards being applied. In the case of humans, merits may be either moral or nonmoral. We can judge one person to be better than (superior to) another from the moral point of view by applying certain standards to their character and conduct. Similarly, we can appeal to nonmoral criteria in judging someone to be an excellent piano player, a fair cook, a poor tennis player, and so on. Different social purposes and roles are implicit in the making of such judgments, providing the frame of reference for the choice of standards by which the nonmoral merits of people are determined. Ultimately such purposes and roles stem from a society's way of life as a whole. Now a society's way of life may be thought of as the cultural form given to the realization of human values. Whether moral or nonmoral standards are being applied, then, all judgments of people's merits finally depend on human values. All are made from an exclusively human standpoint.

The question that naturally arises at this juncture is: Why should standards that are based on human values be assumed to be the only valid criteria of merit and hence the only true signs of superiority? This question is especially pressing when humans are being judged superior in merit to nonhumans. [A] human being may be a better mathematician than a monkey, but the monkey may be a better tree climber than a human being. If we humans value mathematics more than tree climbing, that is because our conception of civilized life makes the development of mathematical ability more desirable than the ability to climb trees. But is it not unreasonable to judge nonhumans by the values of human civilization, rather than by values connected with what it is for a member of *that* species to live a good life? If all living things have a good of their own, it makes sense to judge the merits of nonhumans by standards derived from *their* good. To use only standards based on human values is already to commit oneself to holding that humans are superior to nonhumans, which is the point in question.

A further logical flaw arises in connection with the widely held conviction that humans are *morally* superior beings because they possess, while others lack, the capacities of a moral agent (free will, accountability, deliberation, judgment, practical reason). This view rests on a conceptual confusion. As far as moral standards are concerned, only beings that have the capacities of a moral agent can properly be judged to be *either* moral (morally good) *or* immoral (morally deficient). Moral standards are simply not applicable to beings that lack such capacities. Animals and plants cannot therefore be said to be morally inferior in merit to humans. Since the only beings that can have moral merits *or be deficient in such merits* are moral agents, it is conceptually incoherent to judge humans as superior to nonhumans on the ground that humans have moral capacities while nonhumans don't.

Up to this point I have been interpreting the claim that humans are superior to other living things as a grading or ranking judgment regarding their comparative merits. There is, however, another way of understanding the idea of human superiority. According to this interpretation, humans are superior to nonhumans not as regards their merits but as regards their inherent worth. Thus the claim of human superiority is to be understood as asserting that all humans, simply in virtue of their humanity, have *a greater inherent worth* than other living things.

The inherent worth of an entity does not depend on its merits.[7] To consider something as possessing inherent worth, we have seen, is to place intrinsic value on the realization of its good. This is done regardless of whatever particular merits it might have or might lack, as judged by a set of grading or ranking standards. In human affairs, we are all familiar with the

---

7 For this way of distinguishing between merit and inherent worth, I am indebted to Gregory Vlastos, "Justice and Equality," in R. Brandt, ed., *Social Justice* (Englewood Cliffs, N.J.: Prentice-Hall, 1962), pp. 31–72.

principle that one's worth as a person does not vary with one's merits or lack of merits. The same can hold true of animals and plants. To regard such entities as possessing inherent worth entails disregarding their merits and deficiencies, whether they are being judged from a human standpoint or from the standpoint of their own species.

The idea of one entity having more merit than another, and so being superior to it in merit, makes perfectly good sense. Merit is a grading or ranking concept, and judgments of comparative merit are based on the different degrees to which things satisfy a given standard. But what can it mean to talk about one thing being superior to another in inherent worth? In order to get at what is being asserted in such a claim it is helpful first to look at the social origin of the concept of degrees of inherent worth.

The idea that humans can possess different degrees of inherent worth originated in societies having rigid class structures. Before the rise of modern democracies with their egalitarian outlook, one's membership in a hereditary class determined one's social status. People in the upper classes were looked up to, while those in the lower classes were looked down upon. In such a society one's social superiors and social inferiors were clearly defined and easily recognized.

Two aspects of these class-structured societies are especially relevant to the idea of degrees of inherent worth. First, those born into the upper classes were deemed more worthy of respect than those born into the lower orders. Second, the superior worth of upper class people had nothing to do with their merits nor did the inferior worth of those in the lower classes rest on their lack of merits. One's superiority or inferiority entirely derived from a social position one was born into. The modern concept of a meritocracy simply did not apply. One could not advance into a higher class by any sort of moral or nonmoral achievement. Similarly, an aristocrat held his title and all the privileges that went with it just because he was the eldest son of a titled nobleman. Unlike the bestowing of knighthood in contemporary Great Britain, one did not earn membership in the nobility by meritorious conduct.

We who live in modern democracies no longer believe in such hereditary social distinctions. Indeed, we would wholeheartedly condemn them on moral grounds as fundamentally unjust. We have come to think of class systems as a paradigm of social injustice, it being a central principle of the democratic way of life that among humans there are no superiors and no inferiors. Thus we have rejected the whole conceptual framework in which people are judged to have different degrees of inherent worth. That idea is incompatible with our notion of human equality based on the doctrine that all humans, simply in virtue of their humanity, have the same inherent worth. (The belief in universal human rights is one form that this egalitarianism takes.)

The vast majority of people in modern democracies, however, do not maintain an egalitarian outlook when it comes to comparing human beings with other living things. Most people consider our own species to be superior to all other species and this superiority is understood to be a matter of inherent worth, not merit. There may exist thoroughly vicious and depraved humans who lack all merit. Yet because they are human they are thought to belong to a higher class of entities than any plant or animal. That one is born into the species *Homo sapiens* entitles one to have lordship over those who are one's inferiors, namely, those born into other species. The parallel with hereditary social classes is very close. Implicit in this view is a hierarchical conception of nature according to which an organism has a position of superiority or inferiority in the Earth's community of life simply on the basis of its genetic background. The "lower" orders of life are looked down upon and it is considered perfectly proper that they serve the interests of those belonging to the highest order, namely humans. The intrinsic value we place on the well-being of our fellow humans reflects our recognition of their rightful position as our equals. No such intrinsic value is to be placed on the good of other animals, unless we choose to do so out of fondness or affection for them. But their well-being imposes no moral requirement on us. In this respect there is an absolute difference in moral status between ourselves and them.

This is the structure of concepts and beliefs that people are committed to insofar as they regard humans to be superior in inherent worth to all other species. I now wish to argue that this structure of concepts and beliefs is completely groundless. If we accept the first three components of the biocentric outlook and from that perspective look at the major philosophical traditions which have supported that structure, we find it to be at bottom nothing more than the expression of an irrational bias in our own favor. The philosophical traditions themselves rest on very questionable assumptions or else simply beg the question. I briefly consider three of the main traditions to substantiate the point. These are classical Greek humanism, Cartesian dualism, and the Judeo-Christian concept of the Great Chain of Being.

The inherent superiority of humans over other species was implicit in the Greek definition of man as a rational animal. Our animal nature was identified with "brute" desires that need the order and restraint of reason to rule them (just as reason is the special virtue of those who rule in the ideal state). Rationality was then seen to be the key to our superiority over animals. It enables us to live on a higher plane and endows us with a nobility and worth that other creatures lack. This familiar way of comparing humans with other species is deeply ingrained in our Western philosophical outlook. The point to consider here is that this view does not actually provide an argument *for* human superiority but rather makes explicit the framework of thought that is implicitly used by those who think of humans as inherently superior to nonhumans. The Greeks who held that humans, in virtue of their rational capacities, have a kind of worth greater than any nonrational being, never looked at rationality as but one capacity of living things among many others. But when we consider rationality from the standpoint of the first three elements of the ecological outlook, we see that its value lies in its importance for *human* life. Other creatures achieve their species-specific good without the need of rationality, although they often make use of capacities that humans lack. So the humanistic outlook of classical Greek thought does not give us a neutral (non-question-begging) ground on which to construct a scale of degrees of inherent worth possessed by different species of living things.

The second tradition, centering on the Cartesian dualism of soul and body, also fails to justify the claim to human superiority. That superiority is supposed to derive from the fact that we have souls while animals do not. Animals are mere automata and lack the divine element that makes us spiritual beings. I will not go into the now familiar criticisms of this two-substance view. I only add the point that, even if humans are composed of an immaterial, unextended soul and a material, extended body, this in itself is not a reason to deem them of greater worth than entities that are only bodies. Why is a soul substance a thing that adds value to its possessor? Unless theological reasoning is offered here (which many, including myself, would find unacceptable on epistemological grounds), no logical connection is evident. An immaterial something that thinks is better than a material something that doesn't think only if thinking itself has value, either intrinsically or instrumentally. Now it is intrinsically valuable to humans alone, who value it as an end in itself, and it is instrumentally valuable to those who benefit from it, namely humans.

For animals that neither enjoy thinking for its own sake nor need it for living the kind of life for which they are best adapted, it has no value. Even if "thinking" is broadened to include all forms of consciousness, there are still many living things that can do without it and yet live what is, for their species, a good life. The anthropocentricity underlying the claim to human superiority runs throughout Cartesian dualism.

A third major source of the idea of human superiority is the Judeo-Christian concept of the Great Chain of Being. Humans are superior to animals and plants because their Creator has given them a higher place on the chain. It begins with God at the top, and then moves to the angels, who are lower than God but higher than humans, then to humans, positioned between the angels and the beasts (partaking of the nature of both), and then on down to the lower levels occupied by nonhuman animals, plants, and finally inanimate objects. Humans, being "made in God's image," are inherently superior to animals and plants by virtue of their being closer (in their essential nature) to God.

The metaphysical and epistemological difficulties with this conception of a hierarchy of entities are, in my mind, insuperable. Without entering into this matter here, I point out that if we are unwilling to accept the metaphysics of traditional Judaism and Christianity, we are again left without good reasons for holding to the claim of inherent human superiority.

The foregoing considerations (and others like them) leave us with but one ground for the assertion that a human being, regardless of merit, is a higher kind of entity than any other living thing. This is the mere fact of the genetic makeup of the species *Homo sapiens*. But this is surely irrational and arbitrary. Why should the arrangement of genes of a certain type be a mark of superior value, especially when this fact about an organism is taken by itself, unrelated to any other aspect of its life? We might just as well refer to any other genetic makeup as a ground of superior value. Clearly we are confronted here with a wholly arbitrary claim that can only be explained as an irrational bias in our own favor.

That the claim is nothing more than a deep-seated prejudice is brought home to us when we look at our relation to other species in the light of the first three elements of the biocentric outlook. Those elements taken conjointly give us a certain overall view of the natural world and of the place of humans in it. When we take this view we come to understand other living things, their environmental conditions, and their ecological relationships in such a way as to awake in us a deep sense of our kinship with them as fellow members of the Earth's community of life. Humans and nonhumans alike are viewed together as integral parts of one unified whole in which all living things are functionally interrelated. Finally, when our awareness focuses on the individual lives of plants and animals, each is seen to share with us the characteristic of being a teleological center of life striving to realize its own good in its own unique way.

As this entire belief system becomes part of the conceptual framework by which we understand and perceive the world, we come to see ourselves as bearing a certain moral relation to nonhuman forms of life. Our ethical role in nature takes on a new significance. We begin to look at other species as we look at ourselves, seeing them as beings which have a good they are striving to realize just as we have a good we are striving to realize. We accordingly develop the disposition to view the world from the standpoint of their good as well as from the standpoint of our own good. Now if the groundlessness of the claim that humans are inherently superior to other species were brought clearly before our minds, we would not remain intellectually neutral toward that claim but would reject it as fundamentally at variance with our total world outlook. In the absence of any good reasons for holding it, the assertion of human superiority would then appear simply as the expression of an irrational and self-serving prejudice that favors one particular species over several million others.

Rejecting the notion of human superiority entails its positive counterpart: the doctrine of species impartiality. One who accepts that doctrine regards all living things as possessing inherent worth—the *same* inherent worth, since no one species has been shown to be either "higher" or "lower" than any other. Now we saw earlier that, insofar as one thinks of a living thing as possessing inherent worth, one considers it to be the appropriate object of the attitude of respect and believes that attitude to be the only fitting or suitable one for all moral agents to take toward it.

Here, then, is the key to understanding how the attitude of respect is rooted in the biocentric outlook on nature. The basic connection is made through the denial of human superiority. Once we reject the claim that humans are superior either in merit or in worth to other living things, we are ready to adopt the attitude of respect. The denial of human superiority is itself the result of taking the perspective on nature built into the first three elements of the biocentric outlook.

Now the first three elements of the biocentric outlook, it seems clear, would be found acceptable to any rational and scientifically informed thinker who is fully "open" to the reality of the lives of nonhuman organisms. Without denying our distinctively human characteristics, such a thinker can acknowledge the fundamental respects in which we are members of the Earth's community of life and in which the biological conditions necessary for the realization of our human values are inextricably linked with the whole system of nature. In addition, the conception of individual living things as teleological centers of life simply articulates how a scientifically informed thinker comes to understand them as the result of increasingly careful and detailed observations. Thus, the biocentric outlook recommends itself as an acceptable system of concepts and beliefs to anyone who is clear-minded, unbiased, and factually enlightened, and who has a developed capacity of reality awareness with regard to the lives of individual organisms. This is as good a reason for making

the moral commitment involved in adopting the attitude of respect for nature as any theory of environmental ethics could possibly have.

MORAL RIGHTS AND THE MATTER OF COMPETING CLAIMS

I have not asserted anywhere in the foregoing account that animals or plants have moral rights. This omission was deliberate. I do not think that the reference class of the concept, bearer of moral rights, should be extended to include nonhuman living things. My reasons for taking this position, however, go beyond the scope of this paper. I believe I have been able to accomplish many of the same ends which those who ascribe rights to animals or plants wish to accomplish. There is no reason, moreover, why plants and animals, including whole species populations and life communities, cannot be accorded *legal* rights under my theory. To grant them legal protection could be interpreted as giving them legal entitlement to be protected, and this would be a means by which a society that subscribed to the ethics of respect for nature could give public recognition to their inherent worth.

There remains the problem of competing claims, even when wild plants and animals are not thought of as bearers of moral rights. If we accept the biocentric outlook and accordingly adopt the attitude of respect for nature as our ultimate moral attitude, how do we resolve conflicts that arise from our respect for persons in the domain of human ethics and our respect for nature in the domain of environmental ethics? This is a question that cannot adequately be dealt with here. My main purpose in this paper has been to try to establish a base point from which we can start working toward a solution to the problem. I have shown why we cannot just begin with an initial presumption in favor of the interests of our own species. It is after all within our power as moral beings to place limits on human population and technology with the deliberate intention of sharing the Earth's bounty with other species. That such sharing is an ideal difficult to realize even in an approximate way does not take away its claim to our deepest moral commitment.

Review Questions

1. How does Taylor distinguish between anthropocentric views and the life-centered theory?
2. As Taylor explains it, what two concepts are required by the ultimate moral attitude? Explain these two concepts.
3. What does Taylor mean by inherent worth? Who has it?
4. Explain what is involved in Taylor's respect for nature. How is it different from love of nature?
5. What is the belief system underlying the attitude of respect for nature, according to Taylor?
6. Why aren't humans superior to other animals in capacities, merit, morality, or inherent worth according to Taylor?

Discussion Questions

1. Compare and contrast Taylor's respect for nature with Leopold's land ethic. How are they different? How are they similar?
2. Taylor calls his theory "life-centered." Does this mean that nonliving things such as rivers or rocks have no inherent worth on his view? What do you think?
3. Do Taylor's arguments convince you that humans are not superior to other species, such as deer? Why or why not?
4. In many cases, it seems that what promotes human interests and well-being harms wild living things, such as forests. Does Taylor give us any way of resolving such conflicts between what is good for humans and what is good for wild living things? How should such conflicts be resolved?

Duties to Endangered Species

HOLMES ROLSTON III

Holmes Rolston III is professor of philosophy at Colorado State University. He is the author of *Environmental Ethics* (1988).

Rolston wants to defend the view that we have duties to species of plants and animals, not just because they are valuable to humans as resources, but also because

Source: Holmes Rolston III, "Duties to Endangered Species" from *Environmental Ethics* by Holmes Rolston III, pp. 126–159. Reprinted by permission of Temple University Press.

they constitute valuable forms or essences beyond individuals. The extinction of a species is worse than the killing of an individual because it destroys this form or essence; as Rolston says, it is a kind of superkilling. It is like tearing the pages out of an unread book, written in a language humans can hardly read, about the place where they live. Thus the duty to preserve endangered species, to not superkill them, is stronger than the duty to not kill individual members of a species.

"CERTAINLY . . . the destruction of a whole species can be a great evil." John Rawls, however, advocating his most perceptive contemporary theory of justice, admits that in his theory "no account is given of right conduct in regard to animals and the rest of nature."[1] . . . One searches in vain through several thousand years of philosophy (back at least to Noah!) for any serious reference to endangered species. Previously, humans were seldom able to destroy species; this "great evil" did not threaten, so there are few resources in our heritage with which to confront it. Even the ethics we have so far developed for sentient animals and other organisms has not yet directly addressed obligations concerning species.

But the *Global 2000 Report* projects a massive loss of Earth's species (up to 20 percent) within a few decades if present trends go unreversed.[2] These losses will be about evenly distributed through major groups of plants and animals in the United States and in the world. Congress has lamented, in the Endangered Species Act, the lack of "adequate concern (for) and conser-

vation (of)" species.[3] The act was tougher than was realized by most of those who passed it. The Supreme Court, interpreting the law, said that species are to be conserved with "no exception" at "whatever the cost," their protection overriding even the "primary missions" of federal agencies.[4] That seemed extreme, and the act has been modified. Still, that many do not wish to weaken it much has been shown by its repeated renewal. Articulating an ethic here involves an unprecedented mix of science and conscience.

DUTIES TO PERSONS CONCERNING SPECIES

Some say there are no duties to endangered species, only duties to persons. "The preservation of species," by the usual utilitarian account, reported by Stuart Hampshire, is "to be aimed at and commended only in so far as human beings are, or will be, emotionally and sentimentally interested."[5] Joel Feinberg says, "We do have duties to protect threatened species, not duties to the species themselves as such, but rather duties to future human beings, duties derived from our housekeeping role as temporary inhabitants of this planet."[6] The relation is

1 John Rawls, *A Theory of Justice* (Cambridge, Mass.: Harvard University Press, 1971), p. 512.

A shorter version of this chapter appeared as "Duties to Endangered Species," *BioScience* 35 (1985): pp. 718–26, © AIBS 1985; reprinted in Rolston, *Philosophy Gone Wild* (Buffalo, N.Y.: Prometheus Books, 1986), pp. 206–20. For an introduction to these issues, see Bryan G. Norton, ed., *Preservation of Species* (Princeton, NJ.: Princeton University Press, 1986).

2 Council on Environmental Quality and the Department of State, *The Global 2000 Report to the President* (Washington, D.C.: U.S. Government Printing Office, 1980), vol. 1, p. 37; vol. 2, pp. 327–33.

3 Endangered Species Act of 1973, sec. 2 (a) (1) Public Law 93–205, 87 Stat. 884.

4 *TVA* v. *Hill,* 437 U.S. 153 (1978) at 173, 184, 185.

5 Stuart Hampshire, *Morality and Pessimism* (New York: Cambridge University Press, 1972), pp. 3–4.

6 Joel Feinberg, "The Rights of Animals and Unborn Generations," in W. T. Blackstone, ed., *Philosophy and Environmental Crisis* (Athens: University of Georgia Press, 1974),

three-place. Person A has a duty *to* person B which *concerns* species C, but is not *to* C. Using traditional ethics, we can reapply familiar duties to persons and see whether this exhausts our moral intuitions or leaves a residue of concern. Such a line of argument can be impressive but seems to leave deeper reasons untouched.

Species as Stabilizers and Resources

Persons have a strong duty of nonmaleficence not to harm others and a weaker, though important, duty of beneficence to help others. Arguing the threat of harm, Paul and Anne Ehrlich maintain, in a blunt metaphor, that the myriad species are rivets in the airplane in which humans are flying. Extinctions are maleficent rivet-popping. On the Earthship in which we ride there is considerable redundancy, but humans cannot safely lose 1.5 million species-rivets, and any loss of redundancy is to be deplored. Species, including endangered ones, are stabilizers.[7]

In this model, nonrivet species, if there are any, have no value. Nor is any particular species the object of care. Humans desire only the diversity that prevents a crash. No single thread, but the strength of the fabric is the issue. The care is not for species, not for a breeding population of each kind, but (in Norman Myers's variant metaphor picturing the failing Earthship) for the "sinking ark."[8] To worry about a sinking ark seems a strange twist on the Noah story. Noah built the ark to preserve each species, brought on board carefully, two of each kind. In the Ehrlich/Myers account, the species-rivets are preserved to keep the ark from sinking! The reversed justification is revealing.

On the benefits side, species that are not rivets may have resource value. Wild species can have agricultural, medical, industrial, and scientific uses. Thomas Eisner testified to Congress that only about 2 percent of the flowering plants have been tested for alkaloids, which often have medical uses.[9] North Americans regularly eat almost nothing native to their ecosystem. Elsewhere in the world, loss of the wild stocks of the cultivars leaves Americans genetically vulnerable, so it is prudent to save the native materials. The International Union for the Conservation of Nature and Natural Resources (IUCN) says, "The ultimate protection of nature, . . . and all its endangered forms of life, demands . . . an enlightened exploitation of its wild resources."[10] Myers further urges "conserving our global stock."[11] At first that seems wise, yet later somewhat demeaning for humans to regard all other species as *stock*.

Ingenious biologists and ethicists can stretch the meaning of rivet and resource. On the harm side, the loss of a few species may have no evident results now, but this has destabilizing lag effects generations later. When an extremely cold winter hits, the ecosystem will be thrown into a degenerating spiral. Rare species do not now function significantly in the ecosystem, but they lie in wait as part of the backup resilience. The extinction of nonrivet and nonresource species will affect rivet and resource species. Getting by with a few extinctions lulls humans into thinking that they can get by with more, when in fact the danger increases exponentially with subtractions from the ecosystem. Humans will stumble over the disaster threshold because

---

pp. 43–68, citation on p. 56. Feinberg holds that the duty to preserve species is more important than any rights of individual animals but is not a duty that can property be attributed to species as a whole.

7 Paul Ehrlich and Anne Ehrlich, *Extinction* (New York: Random House, 1981), pp. xi–xiv.

8 Norman Myers, *The Sinking Ark* (Oxford: Pergamon Press, 1979).

9 "Statement of Thomas Eisner," *Endangered Species Act Oversight,* Hearings, 8 and 10 December 1981 (Washington, D.C.: U.S. Government Printing Office, 1982), pp. 295–97.

10 James Fisher, Noel Simon, Jack Vincent, and IUCN staff, *Wildlife in Danger* (New York: Viking Press, 1969), p. 19.

11 Norman Myers, "Conserving Our Global Stock," *Environment* 21, no.9 (November 1979):25–33.

of bad habits formed when these extinctions were not yet harmful. Concern for all species puts up guard rails and provides a margin of safety on a slippery slope.

Species, Science, and Natural History

One should count as resources all those species that generate recreational, aesthetic, and scientific experiences. The rare species fascinate enthusiastic naturalists and are often key scientific study species. They provide entertainments and new knowledge of spaceship Earth, regardless of their stabilizing or economic benefits. One whooping crane in a flock of sandhills perks up a bird watcher's day. A National Science Foundation report advocated saving the Devil's Hole pupfish, *Cyprinodon diabolis,* in a case that went to the Supreme Court, because it and its relatives thrive in hot or salty water.

> Such extreme conditions tell us something about the creatures' extraordinary thermoregulatory system and kidney function—but not enough as yet. . . . They can serve as useful biological models for future research on the human kidney—and on survival in a seemingly hostile environment. . . . Man, in the opinion of many ecologists, will need all the help he can get in understanding and adapting to the expansion of and areas over the Earth.[12]

The Socorro isopod, *Exosphaeroma thermophilum,* has lost its natural habitat and lives only in the drain of an abandoned bath-house at a New Mexico hot springs site. Nevertheless the U.S. Fish and Wildlife Service claims that it "is of particular interest and importance. . . . How this species arrived at its present state of evolutionary adaptation is of concern to isopod specialists, and the concept of landlocked fauna is of concern to biologists as a whole."[13] *Erio-*

gonum gypsophilum is worth saving for a Ph.D. candidate to find out its adaptation to gypsum, even though this could restrict the proposed lake that would threaten its habitat and despite the fact that nothing practical may come from the dissertation. *Shortia galacifolia* is worth saving as a historical souvenir of the excitement of the early American botanists who traded specimens at $50 each.

Destroying species is like tearing pages out of an unread book, written in a language humans hardly know how to read, about the place where they live. We do not know, for instance, whether there are five or ten million species on Earth. We know little about the processes of *ecosystems* evolution as something more than organismic evolution. We do not know whether or how natural selection operates at that level. Biologists are divided over whether interspecific competition is a minimal or a major force in evolution, and sizable natural systems with all their species preserved intact are the likeliest places to settle this debate.

No sensible person would destroy the Rosetta Stone, and no self-respecting humans will destroy the mouse lemur, endangered in Madagascar and thought to be the modern animal nearest to the relatively unspecialized primates from which the human line evolved. Nor should we destroy *Zoonosaurus hazofotsi,* the Madagascar lizard with a third eye atop its head, the pineal eyespot, from which humans might learn about the parallel evolution of sight. Still, following this logic, humans have duties not to the book, the stone, or the species but to ourselves, duties both of prudence and education. Humans need insight into the full text of natural history. They need to understand the evolving world in which they are placed. It is not endangered species but an endangered human future that is of concern.

Such reasons are pragmatic and impressive. They are also moral, since persons are benefited or hurt. But are they exhaustive? Can all duties concerning species be analyzed as duties to persons? Do we simply want to protect these

---

12 National Science Foundation, "The Biology of Aridity," *Mosaic* 8, no. 1 (January/February 1977): 28–35, citation on p. 28.
13 *Endangered Species Technical Bulletin* 3, no. 1 (January 1978): 5.

endangered forms of life *for* exploitation, or do we sometimes want to protect them *from* exploitation? . . .

Human Prudence and Moral Principles

The deeper problem with the anthropocentric rationale, beyond overstatement, is that its justifications are submoral and fundamentally exploitive and self-serving, even if subtly so. This is not true intraspecifically among humans, when out of a sense of duty an individual defers to the values of fellows. But it is true interspecifically, since *Homo sapiens* treats all other species as rivets, resources, study materials, or entertainments. Ethics has always been about partners with entwined destinies. But it has never been very convincing when pleaded as enlightened self-interest (that one ought always to do what is in one's intelligent self-interest), including class self-interest, even though in practice altruistic ethics often needs to be reinforced by self-interest. To value all other species only for human interests is rather like a nation's arguing all its foreign policy in terms of national self-interest. Neither seems fully moral. . . .

It is safe to say that in the decades ahead the quality of life will decline in proportion to the loss of biotic diversity, though it is usually thought that we are sacrificing biotic diversity in order to improve human life. So there is a sense in which humans will not be losers if we save endangered species. There is a sense in which those who do the right thing never lose, even when they respect values other than their own. Slaveowners do not really lose when they free their slaves, since the slaveowners become better persons by freeing their slaves, to whom they can thereafter relate person-to-person. Subsequently, human relationships will be richer. In morality, only the immoral lose—ultimately. Similarly, humans who protect endangered species will, if and when they change their value priorities, be better persons for their admiring respect for other forms of life.

But this should not obscure the fact that humans can be short-term losers. Sometimes we do have to make sacrifices, at least in terms of what we presently value, to preserve species. Moreover, the claim that we are better humans if we protect species is an empirical, statistical claim—true on average, true unless shown otherwise. There might be cases where the worth of a species, coupled with human benefits from respecting it, do not override the human benefits to be gained by sacrificing it. Then humans might be duty-bound to be losers in the sense that they sacrifice values, although they would still be winners for doing the right thing.

Dealing with a problem correctly requires an appropriate way of thinking about it. On the scale of evolutionary time, humans appear late and suddenly. Even more lately and suddenly, they dramatically increase the extinction rate. About 500 species, sub-species, and varieties have been lost in the United States since 1600; the natural rate of extinction would have resulted in about ten.[14] In Hawaii, a bellwether state, half the 2,200 native plants are endangered or threatened; of sixty-eight species of birds unique to the islands, forty-one are extinct or virtually so. In the near future, humans threaten to approach and even exceed the catastrophic rates of the geological past, if indeed we are not doing this already. What is offensive in such conduct is not merely senseless destabilizing, not merely the loss of resources and rivets, but the maelstrom of killing and insensitivity to forms of life and the sources producing them. What is required is not prudence but principled responsibility to the biospheric Earth. . . .

DUTIES TO SPECIES

Humans versus Endangered Species

. . . The obligation to protect humans trumps the obligation to protect *individual* animals and

14 Paul A. Opler, "The Parade of Passing Species: A Survey of Extinctions in the U.S.," *Science Teacher* 43, no. 9 (December 1976): 30–34.

plants, short of extenuating circumstances and even if critical animal and plant goods sometimes outweigh nonbasic humans goods. But it does not follow that the obligation to protect one or even a group of humans trumps the obligation to protect whole *species*. Further, our obligation to protect *existing* lives can be greater than our obligation to bring into existence yet *unborn* lives, and this may offset the otherwise greater obligation to protect humans over animals and plants. It could be more important to protect one million existing species than to bring into existence an additional one million persons—a choice not as farfetched as it may first appear in view of the present pace of tropical deforestation. . . .

A Florida panther, one of about thirty surviving in an endangered subspecies, was mangled when hit by a car. Named Big Guy, he was flown by helicopter to the state university veterinary medical school. Steel plates were inserted in both legs, and the right foot rebuilt. Is this appropriate treatment? Is it something humans ought to do out of justice or benevolence? Because of concern for the individual animal or for the subspecies? Big Guy's story mostly served to bring to focus a bigger issue. He cannot be released into the wild but is being bred and his offspring will be used for experiments to protect his species.

Protecting the panther, Florida's state animal, could cost $112.5 million. The subspecies is peculiarly adapted to the Florida swamps, in contrast with the dry, mountainous areas inhabited by the West's cougars. The panther is nearly extinct because of dwindling habitat, and the last critical habitat—the Big Cypress Swamp, adjacent to the Everglades—is being cut in half by Interstate 75. Florida has argued for spending $27 million (about $1 million per panther) to build forty bridges that will allow the panthers to pass under the high-fenced interstate: both "animal crossings," bridges over dry land, and "extended bridges," bridges over water with spans over land at each end. Otherwise, as Big Guy illustrates, many will be killed by the fast, increasing traffic. Critics—including some federal authorities, who bear 90 percent of the costs—say this is too expensive and won't work. Wildlife biologists claim that it will (as the Alaska pipeline was redesigned to permit caribou migration); they have tracked radiocollared cats and located their routes. . . .

Again, though humans are superior to panthers, the human costs here (about $10 per Floridian, about fifty cents per U.S. citizen) hardly seem high enough to justify the extinction of a sub-species. The loss of limited recreation and sport hunting would be offset by renewed respect for life. Wildlands acquired or protected in an already overcrowded state are valuable with or without the panther. Corridors and crossings that connect otherwise isolated reserves are important for many mammals. The bridges may prove futile, but Americans regularly risk those amounts of money in lotteries. To be gained is the continued existence of an animal handsome enough to be chosen as the state symbol, highly evolved on the top trophic rung of a rare Everglades ecosystem, thought by many to be the most aesthetically exciting animal on the North American continent. In this case too, if in fact humans can be shown to lose, they ought to be the losers in favor of the cat.

Sentient Life versus Endangered Species

A concern for species is not just a way of protecting sentient lives or even individual organisms. The National Park Service allows hundreds of elk to starve in Yellowstone each year, but the starving of an equal number of grizzly bears, which would involve about the same loss in felt experience, would be of much greater concern. Only about 100 whooping cranes remain; to kill and eat them would result in jail sentences. But we kill and eat 100 turkeys without a thought. Something more is at stake ethically than a concern for individual lives. Humans have no duty to deny their ecology and thus do not interrupt spontaneous nature (assume no duty to feed the elk), and humans do sacrifice individual animals and plants to meet their needs. But humans have at least some duty not to cause ecological disruption, a duty not to waste species. . . .

On San Clemente Island, the U.S. Fish and Wildlife Service and the California Department of Fish and Game asked the Navy to shoot 2,000 feral goats to save three endangered plant species: *Malacothamnus clementinus, Castilleja grisea, Delphinium kinkiense.* That would mean killing several goats for each known surviving plant. Isolated from the mainland, the island had evolved a number of unique species. Goats, introduced in the early 1800s, thrived even after humans abandoned them but adversely affected the ecosystem. They have probably already eradicated several never-known species. Following renewed interest in endangered species, officials decided to eliminate the goats. By herding and trapping, 21,000 were removed, but the remaining goats were in inaccessible canyons, which required their being shot from helicopters.

The Fund for Animals filed suit to prevent this, and the court ordered all goats removed. After the shooting of 600 goats, the Fund put political pressure on the Department of the Navy to secure a moratorium on further shooting. Happily, workers for the Fund rescued most of the goats with novel trapping techniques; unhappily, neither they nor others have been able to live-trap them all. The goats reproduce rapidly during any delay, and there are still more than 1,000 on the island.[15]

Despite the Fund's objections, the Park Service did kill hundreds of rabbits on Santa Barbara Island to protect a few plants of *Dudleya traskiae,* once thought extinct and curiously called the Santa Barbara live-forever. This island endemic was once common. But New Zealand red rabbits, introduced about 1900, fed on it; by 1970 no *Dudleya* could be found. With the

15 Details from Jan Larson, Natural Resources Manager, Naval Air Station, North Island, San Diego, California.

discovery in 1975 of five plants, a decision was made to eradicate the rabbits.

Does protecting endangered species justify causing suffering and death? Does the fact that the animals were exotic make a difference? An ethic based on animal rights will come to one answer, but a more broadly based environmental ethic will prefer plant species, especially species in their ecosystems, over sentient animals that are exotic misfits. . . .

Every extinction is a kind of superkilling. It kills forms (*species*), beyond individuals. It kills "essences" beyond "existences," the "soul" as well as the "body." It kills collectively, not just distributively. A duty to a species is more like being responsible to a cause than to a person. It is commitment to an *idea* (Greek, *idea,* "form," sometimes a synonym for the Latin *species*).This duty is a categorical imperative to living categories. It is not merely the loss of potential human information that we lament but the loss of biological information that is present independent of instrumental human uses of it. At stake is something vital, past something biological, and all this is something more than an anthropocentric concern. We are called on, again, objectively to evaluate (appraise the worth of) what we may or may not subjectively value (have a personal preference for).

Much is conserved in Earth's subroutines and cycles (matter, energy, materials); much can be recycled and renewed (water, energy, nutrients); there are many equilibria (food chains, species turnover, natural extinctions with respeciation). But in human-caused extinctions there is the loss of unique biological information, with no conservation by respeciation. A shutdown of the life stream is the most destructive event possible. "Ought species *x* to exist?" is a distributive increment in the collective question, "Ought life on Earth to exist?" Life on Earth cannot exist without its individuals either, but a lost individual is always reproducible; a lost species is never reproducible. The answer to the species question is not always the same as the answer to the collective question, but since life on Earth is an aggregate of many species, the two are sufficiently related that the burden of proof lies with those who wish deliberately to extinguish a species and simultaneously to care for life on Earth.

Every species is a "display" or "show" (also a meaning of the Latin *species*) in the natural history book. These stories are plural, diverse, erratic, but they are not wholly fragmented episodes. The pressures of natural selection pull them into roles into their communities, fit them into niches, give continuity to the stories, and make more unified ecosystemic stories of the many stories. Always, there are themes in their settings, characters moving through space and time, problems and their resolutions, the plotting of life paths. Exceeding the births and deaths of individual members, a specific form of life unfolds an intergenerational narrative. What humans are bound to respect in natural history is not one another's scientific, recreational, or reading material, not rivets in their Earthship, but the living drama, continuing with all its actors. To kill a species is to shut down a unique story, and although all specific stories must eventually end, we seldom want unnatural ends. Humans ought not to play the role of murderers. The duty to species can be overridden—or example, in the case of pests or disease organisms —but a prima facie duty stands nevertheless.

One form of life has never endangered so many others. Never before has this level of question—superkilling by a superkiller—been deliberately faced. Humans have more understanding than ever of the natural world they inhabit and of the speciating processes, more predictive power to foresee the intended and unintended results of their actions, and more power to reverse the undesirable consequences. The duties that such power and vision generate no longer attach simply to individuals or persons but are emerging duties to specific forms of life. If, in this world of uncertain moral convictions, it makes any sense to claim that one ought not to kill individuals without justification, it makes more sense to claim that one ought not to superkill the species without superjustification.

INDIVIDUALS AND SPECIES

Many will be uncomfortable with claims about duties to species because their ethical theory does not allow duty to a collection, only to individuals. Only individuals can inject preferences into the system. As Joel Feinberg writes, "A whole collection, as such, cannot have beliefs, expectations, wants, or desires. . . . Individual elephants can have interests, but the species elephant cannot."[16] That premise underlies Feinberg's conclusion, cited earlier, that duties cannot be to species but must be to future humans, who will have beliefs, desires, and so on. Singer asserts, "Species as such are not conscious entities and so do not have interests above and beyond the interests of the individual animals that are members of the species." That premise supports Singer's conclusion that all our duties must be to sentient beings.[17]

Tom Regan defines the "rights view" as "a view about the moral rights of individuals. Species are not individuals, and the rights view does not recognize the moral rights of species to anything, including survival."[18] Nicholas Rescher says, "Moral obligation is thus always interest-oriented. But only individuals can be said to have interests; one only has moral obligations to particular individuals or particular groups thereof. Accordingly, the duty to save a species is not a matter of moral duty toward it, because moral duties are only oriented to indi-

16 Feinberg, "Rights of Animals and Unborn Generations," pp. 55–56.
17 Peter Singer, "Not for Humans Only: The Place of Non-humans in Environmental Issues," in K. E. Goodpaster and K. M. Sayre, eds., *Ethics and Problems of the 21st Century* (Notre Dame, Ind.: University of Notre Dame Press, 1979), pp. 191–206, citation on p. 203.
18 Tom Regan, *The Case for Animal Rights* (Berkeley: University of California Press, 1983), p. 359.

viduals. A species as such is the wrong sort of target for a moral obligation."[19] But beliefs, desires, conscious awareness, rights, individuality, and so forth, are not the only relevant criteria in an emerging environmental ethic. . . .

Value at the Species Level

There is no value without an evaluator. So runs a well-entrenched dogma in value theory. Humans clearly evaluate their world; sentient animals may do so also. Less clearly, any organism "evaluates" its environment, as when an *Escherichia coli* bacterium prefers glucose over lactose (even though it is programmed to do this genetically). But (some say) no species—whatever "species" exactly is—can evaluate anything, and therefore nothing called "species" can be the holder of intrinsic value, although a collection may be of instrumental value to ("valuable," able to be valued by) bona fide evaluators. Hence, any duties that humans have cannot be to species (though they may concern them) but must be to those evaluators (normally other humans) in whom sooner or later values come to birth.

But we need to revise this logic. Biologists and linguists have learned to accept the concept of information without any subject who speaks or understands. Can environmental ethicists learn to accept value in, and duty to, an informed process in which centered individuality or sentience is absent? Here events can be of value at the specific level, an additional consideration to whether they are beneficial to individuals. The species-in-environment is an interactive complex, a selective system where individuals are pawns on a chessboard. When human conduct endangers these specific games of life, destroying the habitats in which they are played, duties may appear.

19 Nicholas Rescher, "Why Save Endangered Species?" in *Unpopular Essays on Technological Progress* (Pittsburgh, Pa.: University of Pittsburgh Press, 1980), pp. 79–92, citation on p. 83.

The older ethic will say that duties attach to singular lives, most evidently those with a self or some analogue to a self. In an individual organism the organs report to a center; the good of a whole is defended. But the members of a species report to no center. A species has no self. It is not a bounded singular. Each individual has its own centeredness, but the species has no specific analogue to the nervous hookups or circulatory flows that characterize the organism. Like the market in economics, however, an organized system does not have to have a controlling center to have identity. Perhaps singularity, centeredness, selfhood, individuality are not the only processes to which duty attaches.

Having a biological identity reasserted genetically over time is as true of the species as of the individual. In fact, taxonomists can often distinguish two species more readily than two individuals within a species. Uniqueness attaches to the dynamic historical lineage, even if the members also are, in their own ways, idiographic. Individual organisms come and go; the marks of the individual species collectively remain much longer. Biological identity need not attach to the centered organism; it can persist as a discrete, vital pattern over time.

A consideration of species strains any ethic fixed on individual organisms, much less on sentience or persons. But the result can be biologically sounder, though it revises what was formerly thought logically permissible or ethically binding. When ethics is informed by this kind of biology, it is appropriate to attach duty dynamically to the specific form of life. The species line is the more fundamental living system, the whole of which individual organisms are the essential parts. The species too has its integrity, its individuality, its "right to life" (if we must use the rhetoric of rights), and it is more important to protect this than to protect individual integrity. Again and again, processes of value found first in an organic individual reappear at the specific level: defending a particular form of life, pursuing a pathway through the world, resisting death (extinction), regeneration maintaining a normative identity over time, storied achievements, creative resilience learning survival skills. If, at the specific level, these processes are just as evident or even more so, what prevents duties from arising at that level? The appropriate survival unit is the appropriate level of moral concern. . . .

Review Questions

1. According to Rolston, why doesn't the usual utilitarian view recognize any duties to endangered species?
2. Rolston says that other species are viewed as either stabilizers or resources. Explain these two views and why Rolston doesn't accept them.
3. Why does Rolston think that the duty to protect a species outweighs the duty to protect one person or a group of persons?
4. Explain the objection that we have duties only to individuals and not to species. How does Rolston reply to this objection?

Discussion Questions

1. Has Rolston adequately explained the idea of duty to a species? Why or why not?
2. Wouldn't humans benefit from the extinction of certain species—for example, poison ivy and horseflies? If so, why not eliminate them, if that is possible?

Women, Ecology, and Development

VANDANA SHIVA

Vandana Shiva is director of the Research Foundation for Science, Technology and Natural Resource in Dehradun, India. Our reading is taken from her book *Staying Alive: Women, Ecology and Development* (1988).

Shiva begins with an attack on the Western development of Developing World countries. It is really a maldevelopment that applies patriarchal principles of exploitation and domination to nature and women in these countries, with the result that forests are destroyed and women are harmed. Instead of development based on a market economy that produces new conditions of scarcity and poverty to satisfy artificial needs, Shiva recommends a return to the feminine principle that redefines growth and productivity in terms of sustaining all life, including nature, rather than destroying life in the name of progress.

DEVELOPMENT AS A NEW PROJECT OF WESTERN PATRIARCHY

'DEVELOPMENT' WAS TO HAVE BEEN a post-colonial project, a choice for accepting a model of progress in which the entire world remade itself on the model of the colonising modern west, without having to undergo the subjugation and exploitation that colonialism entailed. The assumption was that western style progress was possible for all. Development, as the improved well-being of all, was thus equated with the westernisation of economic categories—of needs, of productivity, of growth. Concepts and categories about economic development and natural resource utilisation that had emerged in the specific context of industrialisation and capitalist growth in a centre of colonial power, were raised to the level of universal assumptions and applicability in the entirely different context of basic needs satisfaction for the people of the newly independent Third World countries. Yet, as Rosa Luxemberg has pointed out, early industrial development in western Europe necessitated the permanent occupation of the colonies by the colonial powers and the destruction of the local 'natural economy.'[1] According to her, colonialism is a constant necessary condition for capitalist growth: without colonies, capital accumulation would grind to a halt. 'Development' as capital accumulation and the commercialisation of the economy for the generation of 'surplus' and profits thus involved the reproduction not merely of a particular form of creation of wealth, but also of the associated creation of poverty and dispossession. A replication of economic development based on commercialisation of resource use for commodity production in the newly independent countries created the internal colonies.[2] Development was thus reduced to a continuation of the process of colonisation; it became an extension of the project of wealth creation in modern western patriarchy's economic vision, which was based on the exploitation or exclusion of women (of the west and non-west), on the exploitation and degradation of nature, and on the exploitation and erosion of other cultures. 'Development' could not but entail destruction for women, nature and subjugated cultures, which is why, throughout the Third World, women, peasants and tribals are struggling for liberation from 'development' just as they earlier struggled for liberation from colonialism.

The UN Decade for Women was based on the assumption that the improvement of women's economic position would automatically flow from an expansion and diffusion of the development process. Yet, by the end of the Decade, it was becoming clear that development itself was the problem. Insufficient and inadequate 'participation' in 'development' was not the cause for women's increasing under-development; it was rather, their enforced but asymmetric participation in it, by which they bore the costs but were excluded from the benefits, that was responsible. Development exclusivity and dispossession aggravated and deepened the colonial processes of ecological degradation and the loss of political control over nature's sustenance base. Economic growth was a new colonialism, draining resources away from those who needed them most. The discontinuity lay in the fact that it was now new national elites, not colonial powers, that masterminded the exploitation on grounds of 'national interest' and

---

Source: Vandana Shiva, "Women, Ecology and Development," from *Staying Alive: Development, Ecology, and Women* (Zed Books, 1988), pp. 1–13. Reprinted with permission.

1 Rosa Luxemberg, *The Accumulation of Capital,* London: Routledge and Kegan Paul, 1951.

2 An elaboration of how 'development' transfers resources from the poor to the well-endowed is contained in J. Bandyopadhyay and V. Shiva, "Political Economy of Technological Polarisations," in *Economic and Political Weekly,* Vol. XVIII. 1982, pp. 1827–32; and J. Bandyopadhyay and V. Shiva, 'Political Economy of Ecology Movements', in *Economic and Political Weekly,* forthcoming.

growing GNPs, and it was accomplished with more powerful technologies of appropriation and destruction.

Ester Boserup[3] has documented how women's impoverishment increased during colonial rule; those rulers who had spent a few centuries in subjugating and crippling their own women into de-skilled, de-intellectualised appendages, disfavoured the women of the colonies on matters of access to land, technology and employment. The economic and political processes of colonial under-development bore the clear mark of modern western patriarchy, and while large numbers of women and men were impoverished by these processes, women tended to lose more. The privatisation of land for revenue generation displaced women more critically, eroding their traditional land use rights. The expansion of cash crops undermined food production, and women were often left with meager resources to feed and care for children, the aged and the infirm, when men migrated or were conscripted into forced labor by the colonisers. As a collective document by women activists, organisers and researchers stated at the end of the UN Decade for Women, 'The almost uniform conclusion of the Decade's research is that with a few exceptions, women's relative access to economic resources, incomes and employment has worsened, their burden of work has increased, and their relative and even absolute health, nutritional and educational status has declined.'[4]

The displacement of women from productive activity by the expansion of development was rooted largely in the manner in which development projects appropriated or destroyed the natural resource base for the production of sustenance and survival. It destroyed women's productivity both by removing land, water and forests from their management and control, as well as through the ecological destruction of soil, water and vegetation systems so that nature's productivity and renewability were impaired. While gender subordination and patriarchy are the oldest of oppressions, they have taken on new and more violent forms through the project of development. Patriarchal categories which understand destruction as 'production' and regeneration of life as 'passivity' have generated a crisis of survival. Passivity, as an assumed category of the 'nature' of nature and of women, denies the activity of nature and life. Fragmentation and uniformity as assumed categories of progress and development destroy the living forces which arise from relationships within the 'web of life' and the diversity in the elements and patterns of these relationships.

The economic biases and values against nature, women and indigenous peoples are captured in this typical analysis of the 'unproductiveness' of traditional natural societies:

> Production is achieved through human and animal, rather than mechanical, power. Most agriculture is unproductive; human or animal manure may be used but chemical fertilizers and pesticides are unknown. . . . For the masses, these conditions mean poverty.[5]

The assumptions are evident: nature is unproductive; organic agriculture based on nature's cycles of renewability spells poverty; women and tribal and peasant societies embedded in nature are similarly unproductive, not because it has been demonstrated that in cooperation they produce *less* goods and services for needs, but because it is assumed that 'production' takes place only when mediated by technologies for commodity production, even when such technologies destroy life. A stable and clean river is not a productive resource in this view: it needs to be 'developed' with dams in order to become so. Women, sharing the river as

3 Ester Boserup, *Womens Role in Economic Development*, London: Allen and Unwin, 1970.
4 Dawn, *Development Crisis and Alternative Visions: Third World Women's Perspectives*, Bergen: Christian Michelsen Institute, 1975, p. 21.

5 M. George Foster, *Traditional Societies and Technological Change*, Delhi: Allied Publishers, 1973.

a commons to satisfy the water needs of their families and society are not involved in productive labor: when substituted by the engineering man, water management and water use become productive activities. Natural forests remain unproductive till they are developed into monoculture plantations of commercial species. Development thus, is equivalent to maldevelopment, a development bereft of the feminine, the conservation, the ecological principle. The neglect of nature's work in renewing herself, and women's work in producing sustenance in the form of basic, vital needs is an essential part of the paradigm of maldevelopment, which sees all work that does not produce profits and capital as non or unproductive work. As Maria Mies[6] has pointed out, this concept of surplus has a patriarchal bias because, from the point of view of nature and women, it is not based on material surplus produced *over and above* the requirements of the community: it is stolen and appropriated through violent modes from nature (who needs a share of her produce to reproduce herself) and from women (who need a share of nature's produce to produce sustenance and ensure survival).

From the perspective of Third World women, productivity is a measure of producing life and sustenance; that this kind of productivity has been rendered invisible does not reduce its centrality to survival—it merely reflects the domination of modern patriarchal economic categories which see only profits, not life.

MALDEVELOPMENT AS THE DEATH OF THE FEMININE PRINCIPLE

In this analysis, maldevelopment becomes a new source of male-female inequality. 'Modernisation' has been associated with the introduction of new forms of dominance. Alice Schlegel[7] has shown that under conditions of subsistence, the interdependence and complementarity of the separate male and female domains of work is the characteristic mode, based on diversity, not inequality. Maldevelopment militates against this equality in diversity, and superimposes the ideologically constructed category of western technological man as a uniform measure of the worth of classes, cultures and genders. Dominant modes of perception based on reductionism, duality and linearity are unable to cope with equality in diversity, with forms and activities that are significant and valid, even though different. The reductionist mind superimposes the roles and forms of power of western male-oriented concepts on women, all non-western peoples and even on nature, rendering all three 'deficient', and in need of 'development'. Diversity, and unity and harmony in diversity, become epistemologically unattainable in the context of maldevelopment, which then becomes synonymous with women's underdevelopment (increasing sexist domination), and nature's depletion (deepening ecological crises). Commodities have grown, but nature has shrunk. The poverty crisis of the South arises from the growing scarcity of water, food, fodder and fuel, associated with increasing maldevelopment and ecological destruction. This poverty crisis touches women most severely, first because they are the poorest among the poor, and then because, with nature, they are the primary sustainers of society.

Maldevelopment is the violation of the integrity of organic, interconnected and interdependent systems, that sets in motion a process of exploitation, inequality, injustice and violence. It is blind to the fact that a recognition of nature's harmony and action to maintain it are preconditions for distributive justice. This is why Mahatma Gandhi said, 'There is enough in

---

6 Maria Mies, *Patriarchy and Accumulation on a World Scale*, London: Zed Books, 1986.

7 Alice Schlegel (ed.), *Sexual Stratification: A Cross-Cultural Study*, New York: Columbia University Press, 1977.

the world for everyone's need, but not for some people's greed.'

Maldevelopment is maldevelopment in thought and action. In practice, this fragmented, reductionist, dualist perspective violates the integrity and harmony of man in nature, and the harmony between men and women. It ruptures the co-operative unity of masculine and feminine, and places man, shorn of the feminine principle, above nature and women, and separated from both. The violence to nature as symptomatised by the ecological crisis, and the violence to women, as symptomatised by their subjugation and exploitation arise from this subjugation of the feminine principle. I want to argue that what is currently called development is essentially maldevelopment, based on the introduction or accentuation of the domination of man over nature and women. In it, both are viewed as the 'other', the passive non-self. Activity, productivity, creativity which were associated with the feminine principle are expropriated as qualities of nature and women, and transformed into the exclusive qualities of man. Nature and women are turned into passive objects, to be used and exploited for the uncontrolled and uncontrollable desires of alienated man. From being the creators and sustainers of life, nature and women are reduced to being 'resources' in the fragmented, anti-life model of maldevelopment.

TWO KINDS OF GROWTH, TWO KINDS OF PRODUCTIVITY

Maldevelopment is usually called 'economic growth', measured by the Gross National Product. Porritt, a leading ecologist has this to say of GNP:

> *Gross* National Product—for once a word is being used correctly. Even conventional economists admit that the hey-day of GNP is over, for the simple reason that as a measure of progress, it's more or less useless. GNP mea-

sures the lot, all the goods and services produced in the money economy. Many of these goods and services are not beneficial to people, but rather a measure of just how much is going wrong; increased spending on crime, on pollution, on the many human casualties of our society, increased spending because of waste or planned obsolescence, increased spending because of growing bureaucracies: it's all counted.[8]

The problem with GNP is that it measures some costs as benefits (e.g. pollution control) and fails to measure other costs completely. Among these hidden costs are the new burdens created by ecological devastation, costs that are invariably heavier for women, both in the North and South. It is hardly surprising, therefore, that as GNP rises, it does not necessarily mean that either wealth or welfare increase proportionately. I would argue that GNP is becoming, increasingly, a measure of how real wealth—the wealth of nature and that produced by women for sustaining life—is rapidly decreasing. When commodity production as the prime economic activity is introduced as development, it destroys the potential of nature and women to produce life and goods and services for basic needs. More commodities and more cash mean less life —in nature (through ecological destruction) and in society (through denial of basic needs). Women are devalued first, because their work cooperates with nature's processes, and second, because work which satisfies needs and ensures sustenance is devalued in general. Precisely because more growth in maldevelopment has meant less sustenance of life and life-support systems, it is now imperative to recover the feminine principle as the basis for development which conserves and is ecological. Feminism as ecology, and ecology as the revival of Prakriti, the source of all life, become the decentred powers of political and economic transformation and restructuring.

8 Jonathan Porritt, *Seeing Green*. Oxford: Blackwell, 1984.

This involves, first, a recognition that categories of 'productivity' and growth which have been taken to be positive, progressive and universal are, in reality, restricted patriarchal categories. When viewed from the point of view of nature's productivity and growth, and women's production of sustenance, they are found to be ecologically destructive and a source of gender inequality. It is no accident that the modern, efficient and productive technologies created within the context of growth in market economic terms are associated with heavy ecological costs, borne largely by women. The resource and energy intensive production processes they give rise to demand ever increasing resource withdrawals from the ecosystem. These withdrawals disrupt essential ecological processes and convert renewable resources into non-renewable ones. A forest for example, provides inexhaustible supplies of diverse biomass over time if its capital stock is maintained and it is harvested on a sustained yield basis. The heavy and uncontrolled demand for industrial and commercial wood, however, requires the continuous overfelling of trees which exceeds the regenerative capacity of the forest ecosystem, and eventually converts the forests into non-renewable resources. Women's work in the collection of water, fodder and fuel is thus rendered more energy and time-consuming. (In Garhwal, for example, I have seen women who originally collected fodder and fuel in a few hours, now travelling long distances by truck to collect grass and leaves in a task that might take up to two days.) Sometimes the damage to nature's intrinsic regenerative capacity is impaired not by over-exploitation of a particular resource but, indirectly, by damage caused to other related natural resources through ecological processes. Thus the excessive overfelling of trees in the catchment areas of streams and rivers destroys not only forest resources, but also renewable supplies of water, through hydrological destabilisation. Resource intensive industries disrupt essential ecological processes not only by their excessive demands for raw material, but by their pollution of air and water and soil. Often such destruction is caused by the resource demands of non-vital industrial products. Inspite of severe ecological crises, this paradigm continues to operate because for the North and for the elites of the South, resources continue to be available, even now. The lack of recognition of nature's processes for survival *as factors in the process of economic development* shrouds the political issues arising from resource transfer and resource destruction, and creates an ideological weapon for increased control over natural resources in the conventionally employed notion of productivity. All other costs of the economic process consequently become invisible. The forces which contribute to the increased 'productivity' of a modern farmer or factory worker for instance, come from the increased use of natural resources. Lovins has described this as the amount of 'slave' labor presently at work in the world.[9] According to him each person on earth, on an average, possesses the equivalent of about 50 slaves, each working a 40 hour week. Man's global energy conversion from all sources (wood, fossil fuel, hydroelectric power, nuclear) is currently approximately 8×10^{12} watts. This is more than 20 times the energy content of the food necessary to feed the present world population at the FAO standard diet of 3,600 cal/day, The 'productivity' of the western male compared to women or Third World peasants is not intrinsically superior; it is based on inequalities in the distribution of this 'slave' labor. The average inhabitant of the USA for example has 250 times more 'slaves' than the average Nigerian. 'If Americans were short of 249 of those 250 'slaves', one wonders how efficient they would prove themselves to be?'

It is these resource and energy intensive processes of production which divert resources away from survival, and hence from women.

9 A. Lovins, cited in S. R. Eyre, *The Real Wealth of Nations*, London: Edward Arnold, 1978.

What patriarchy sees as productive work, is, in ecological terms highly destructive production. The second law of thermodynamics predicts that resource intensive and resource wasteful economic development must become a threat to the survival of the human species in the long run. Political struggles based on ecology in industrially advanced countries are rooted in this conflict between *long term survival options and short term over-production and over-consumption*. Political struggles of women, peasants and tribals based on ecology in countries like India are far more acute and urgent since they are rooted in the *immediate threat to the options for survival* for the vast majority of the people, *posed by resource intensive and resource wasteful economic growth* for the benefit of a minority.

In the market economy, the organising principle for natural resource use is the maximisation of profits and capital accumulation. Nature and human needs are managed through market mechanisms. Demands for natural resources are restricted to those demands registering on the market; the ideology of development is in large part based on a vision of bringing all natural resources into the market economy for commodity production. When these resources are already being used by nature to maintain her production of renewable resources and by women for sustenance and livelihood, their diversion to the market economy generates a scarcity condition for ecological stability and creates new forms of poverty for women.

TWO KINDS OF POVERTY

In a book entitled *Poverty: the Wealth of the People*[10] an African writer draws a distinction between poverty as subsistence, and misery as deprivation. It is useful to separate a cultural conception of subsistence living as poverty from the material experience of poverty that is a result of dispossession and deprivation. Culturally per-

ceived poverty need not be real material poverty: subsistence economies which satisfy basic needs through self-provisioning are not poor in the sense of being deprived. Yet the ideology of development declares them so because they do not participate overwhelmingly in the market economy, and do not consume commodities produced for and distributed through the market *even though they might be satisfying those needs through self-provisioning mechanisms*. People are perceived as poor if they eat millets (grown by women) rather than commercially produced and distributed processed foods sold by global agri-business. They are seen as poor if they live in self-built housing made from natural material like bamboo and mud rather than in cement houses. They are seen as poor if they wear handmade garments of natural fibre rather than synthetics. Subsistence, as culturally perceived poverty, does not necessarily imply a low physical quality of life. On the contrary, millets are nutritionally far superior to processed foods, houses built with local materials are far superior, being better adapted to the local climate and ecology, natural fibres are preferable to man-made fibres in most cases, and certainly more affordable. This cultural perception of prudent subsistence living as poverty has provided the legitimisation for the development process as a poverty removal project. As a culturally biased project it destroys wholesome and sustainable lifestyles and creates real material poverty, or misery, by the denial of survival needs themselves, through the diversion of resources to resource intensive commodity production. Cash crop production and food processing take land and water resources away from sustenance needs, and exclude increasingly large numbers of people from their entitlements to food. 'The inexorable processes of agriculture-industrialisation and internationalisation are probably responsible for more hungry people than either cruel or unusual whims of nature. There are several reasons why the high-technology-export-crop model increases hunger. Scarce land, credit, water and technology are preempted for

10 R. Bahro, From *Red to Green*, London: Verso, 1984, p. 211.

the export market. Most hungry people are not affected by the market at all. . . . The profits flow to corporations that have no interest in feeding hungry people without money.'[11]

The Ethiopian famine is in part an example of the creation of real poverty by development aimed at removing culturally perceived poverty. The displacement of nomadic Afars from their traditional pastureland in Awash Valley by commercial agriculture (financed by foreign companies) led to their struggle for survival in the fragile uplands which degraded the ecosystem and led to the starvation of cattle and the nomads.[12] The market economy conflicted with the survival economy in the Valley, thus creating a conflict between the survival economy and nature's economy in the uplands. At no point has the global marketing of agricultural commodities been assessed against the background of the new conditions of scarcity and poverty that it has induced. This new poverty moreover, is no longer cultural and relative: it is absolute, threatening the very survival of millions on this planet.

The economic system based on the patriarchal concept of productivity was created for the very specific historical and political phenomenon of colonialism. In it, the input for which efficiency of use had to be maximised in the production centres of Europe, was industrial labor. For colonial interest therefore, it was rational to improve the labour resource *even at the cost of wasteful use of nature's wealth*. This rationalisation has, however, been illegitimately universalised to all contexts and interest groups and, on the plea of increasing productivity, labour reducing technologies have been introduced in situations where labor is abundant and cheap, and resource demanding technologies have been introduced where resources are scarce

11 R. J. Barnet, *The Lean Years*, London: Abacus, 1981, p. 171.
12 U. P. Koehn, 'African Approaches to Environmental Stress: A Focus on Ethiopia and Nigeria' in R. N. Barrett (ed.), *International Dimensions of the Environmental Crisis*, Boulder, CO: Westview, 1982, pp. 253–89.

and already fully utilised for the production of sustenance. Traditional economies with a stable ecology have shared with industrially advanced affluent economies the ability to use natural resources to satisfy basic vital needs. The former differ from the latter in two essential ways: first, the same needs are satisfied in industrial societies through longer technological chains requiring higher energy and resource inputs and excluding large numbers without purchasing power; and second, affluence generates new and artificial needs requiring the increased production of industrial goods and services. Traditional economies are not advanced in the matter of non-vital needs satisfaction, but as far as the satisfaction of basic and vital needs is concerned, they are often what Marshall Sahlins has called 'the original affluent society'. The needs of the Amazonian tribes are more than satisfied by the rich rainforest; their poverty begins with its destruction. The story is the same for the Gonds of Bastar in India or the Penans of Sarawak in Malaysia.

Thus are economies based on indigenous technologies viewed as 'backward' and 'unproductive'. Poverty, as the denial of basic needs, is not necessarily associated with the existence of traditional technologies, and its removal is not necessarily an outcome of the growth of modern ones. On the contrary, the destruction of ecologically sound traditional technologies, often created and used by women, along with the destruction of their material base is generally believed to be responsible for the 'feminisation' of poverty in societies which have had to bear the costs of resource destruction.

The contemporary poverty of the Afar nomad is not rooted in the inadequacies of traditional nomadic life, but in the *diversion of the productive pastureland of the Awash Valley*. The erosion of the resource base for survival is increasingly being caused by the demand for resources by the market economy, dominated by global forces. The creation of inequality through economic activity which is ecologically disruptive arises in two ways: first, inequalities in the distribution of privileges make for unequal access to natural resources—these include privileges of both a political and economic nature. Second, resource intensive production processes have access to subsidised raw material on which a substantial number of people, especially from the less privileged economic groups, depend for their survival. The consumption of such industrial raw material is determined purely by market forces, and not by considerations of the social or ecological requirements placed on them. The costs of resource destruction are externalised and unequally divided among various economic groups in society, but are borne largely by women and those who satisfy their basic material needs directly from nature, simply because they have no purchasing power to register their demands on the goods and services provided by the modern production system. Gustavo Esteva has called development a permanent war waged by its promoters and suffered by its victims.[13]

The paradox and crisis of development arises from the mistaken identification of culturally perceived poverty with real material poverty, and the mistaken identification of the growth of commodity production as better satisfaction of basic needs. In actual fact, there is less water, less fertile soil, less genetic wealth as a result of the development process. Since these natural resources are the basis of nature's economy and women's survival economy, their scarcity is im-

poverishing women and marginalised peoples in an unprecedented manner. Their new impoverishment lies in the fact that resources which supported their survival were absorbed into the market economy while they themselves were excluded and displaced by it.

The old assumption that with the development process the availability of goods and services will automatically be increased and poverty will be removed, is now under serious challenge from women's ecology movements in the Third World, even while it continues to guide development thinking in centres of patriarchal power. Survival is based on the assumption of the sanctity of life; maldevelopment is based on the assumption of the sacredness of 'development'. Gustavo Esteva asserts that the sacredness of development has to be refuted because it threatens survival itself. 'My people are tired of development', he says, 'they just want to live.'[14]

The recovery of the feminine principle allows a transcendence and transformation of these patriarchal foundations of maldevelopment. It allows a redefinition of growth and productivity as categories linked to the production, not the destruction, of life. It is thus simultaneously an ecological and a feminist political project which legitimises the way of knowing and being that create wealth by enhancing life and diversity, and which delegitimises the knowledge and practise of a culture of death as the basis for capital accumulation.

13 Gustavo Esteva, 'Regenerating People's Space,' in S. N. Mendlowitz and R. B. J. Walker, *Towards a Just World Peace: Perspectives From Social Movements,* London: Butterworths and Committee for a Just World Peace, 1987.

14 G. Esteva, Remarks made at a Conference of the Society for International Development, Rome, 1985.

Review Questions

1. How does Shiva describe the development of Developing World countries? In particular, how are women, nature, and other cultures treated?
2. Why does Shiva call the so-called development a "maldevelopment"?
3. Shiva identifies several problems with using the GNP as a measure of progress. What are these problems?
4. What is the feminine principle, as Shiva explains it? How does it view productivity, growth, and the market economy?

5. Distinguish between poverty as subsistence living and poverty as deprivation. Why does Shiva think that subsistence living is not really material poverty?

6. According to Shiva, how does the market economy generate new conditions of scarcity and poverty?

Discussion Questions

1. Does the maldevelopment of Developing World countries harm men as well as women? Why or why not?

2. Shiva claims that affluence produces new and artificial needs, or what are often called luxury items. Give some examples. Should people in Western countries give up some or all of these luxury items to preserve the environment? Why or why not?

3. Do you agree that those living at a subsistence level, eating millets rather than beef, are not really poor? Would you be willing to live at a subsistence level to preserve the environment? Explain your answer.

Problem Cases

1. The Burning of Amazon Rain Forests

The tropical forests of the Brazilian Amazon constitute 30 percent of the world's remaining tropical forests, and they are home to one-tenth of all the world's plant and animal species. Yet farmers and cattle ranchers in Brazil are burning the rain forests of the Amazon River to clear the land for crops and livestock. According to the World Wildlife Fund, an estimated 12,350 square miles have been destroyed so far (an area about the size of France), and the burning continues. Conservationists and leaders of rich industrial nations have asked Brazil to stop the destruction. They claim that if the Amazon rain forests are destroyed, more than 1 million species of plant and animal life will vanish forever. This would be a significant loss of the earth's genetic and biological heritage. Furthermore, they are worried about changes in the climate. The Amazon system of forests plays an important role in the way the sun's heat is distributed around the earth because it stores more than 75 billion tons of carbon in its trees. An intact acre of Amazon rain forest sequesters about 1,000 pounds of carbon dioxide annually. Burning the trees of the Amazon forests will produce a dramatic increase in the amount of carbon dioxide in the atmosphere. The trapping of heat by this atmospheric carbon dioxide—the greenhouse effect—will significantly increase the global warming trend.

Brazilians reply that they have a sovereign right to use their land as they see fit. They complain that the rich industrial nations are just trying to maintain their economic supremacy. The Brazilian government claims that the burning is necessary for Brazilian economic development, particularly when Brazil is struggling under a huge load of foreign debt and is in a severe economic crisis. In 1998 the government of Brazil eliminated almost all its environmental protection programs and decided to refuse $25 million in foreign donations for the programs.

Should Brazil continue burning the Amazon rain forests? If not, then what should rich industrial nations do to help Brazil?

2. *Radioactive Waste*

There are two main sources of radioactive waste: used fuel rods from nuclear power plants and the waste from nuclear weapons production. The world has 413 commercial nuclear reactors. The typical nuclear reactor discharges about 30 tons of irradiated fuel annually, and in 1990 the world's accumulation of used fuel was 84,000 tons. Currently, most of the used radioactive fuel is stored in large pools of cooling water alongside nuclear reactors, but this is only a short-term solution, since most of these pools were designed to hold only a few years' worth of waste. More permanent disposal sites must be found.

The radioactive waste is mostly plutonium from fifty-five years of nuclear weapons production at twenty-three sites in the United States. Information about nuclear weapons production in the former Soviet Union is not available at the moment. Currently, it seems that there is no place to store this waste safely. At the Rocky Flats Plant near Boulder, Colorado, more than 29,000 gallons of toxic chemicals are stored in two large tanks and hundreds of barrels. At the Pantex Facility in Amarillo, Texas, toxic chemicals that have been stored in a pit for twenty-six years are leaking into the town's water supply.

One plan is to build a permanent storage site at Yucca Mountain in Nevada. But after the spending of $500 million, the project is bogged down in technical and legal problems. One problem is that there are inadequate safeguards against leaking, and people living in Nevada do not want the storage site there.

A site ready to be used is the Waste Isolation Pilot Plant near Carlsbad, New Mexico. It is a deep underground storage facility carved out of salt beds 2,150 feet below the desert, and it can hold thousands of barrels of radioactive waste from nuclear weapons production. The plan is to keep the material (mostly plutonium) safely sealed away from the environment for at least 10,000 years (although the material will be dangerously radioactive for hundreds of thousands of years). Engineers at the Energy Department claim that the salt formation has a tendency to shift and that this geological pressure will seal cracks in the site, keeping the toxic wastes safely isolated inside.

Critics are not convinced that the site is safe. One problem is that there are extensive oil and gas reserves in the area, which attract drilling that might release the toxic material. There are currently two hundred wells within two miles of the plant, and it is possible that a well might be accidentally drilled directly into the repository. Another problem is that the barrels could corrode. The salt beds contain pockets of water that would migrate toward heat sources such as the nuclear waste. After a few years water could form a brine that would corrode the barrels. To keep this from happening, the Energy Department has decided to fill the empty spaces in the underground chambers with magnesium oxide, a chemical that absorbs waters. Critics doubt, however, that this is a permanent solution to the problem.

The government is ready to open the plant, but opponents argue that a 1991 injunction against burying chemical poisons still applies and that the plant should not be opened.

Should radioactive waste be stored at the New Mexico site? If not, then what should be done with it?

3. The Tongass National Forest

The Tongass National Forest is the largest national forest in the United States and the greatest temperate rain forest on the earth. It is located in Alaska's southern panhandle and covers an area slightly larger than West Virginia (about 17 million acres). It is the home of several endangered species, including the grizzly bear and the bald eagle.

In 1947 the U.S. Congress authorized the Forest Service to sign 50-year contracts with lumber companies that would build pulp mills. In return, the Forest Service would sell Tongass timber at very low prices, about $2 per 1,000 feet. On the open market, the same timber would command much higher prices, over $600 per 1,000 feet. The companies claim that they will pay higher prices under new contracts and that they employ 1,500 people. Critics charge that it is a sweetheart deal that subsidizes the lumber companies at a cost to the taxpayers of over $40 million a year. Worst of all, they say, the lumber companies are destroying 500-year-old trees, great stands of Sitka spruce and hemlock, and eliminating the habitat of the grizzly bears and the bald eagles.

Should the destruction of the Tongass Forest be stopped? Why or why not?

Suggested Readings

1. The World Wildlife Fund website (http://www.worldwildlife.org/) has a wealth of information on endangered species, global warming, endangered seas, forests, and toxic chemicals.
2. Donald VanDeVeer and Christine Pierce, *The Environmental Ethics and Policy Book* (Wadsworth, 1997), covers ethical theory, deep ecology, ecofeminism, activism, and other topics related to environmental preservation.
3. Louis P. Pojman, ed., *Environmental Ethics* (Wadsworth, 1998). This big anthology has eighty-four articles on all aspects of environmental ethics.
4. William F. Baxter, *People or Penguins: The Case for Optimal Pollution* (Columbia University Press, 1974), defends the anthropocentric view that the natural environment, including animals, counts only as a means of producing human benefits; it is not an end in itself and has no value apart from humans.

5. William Godfrey-Smith, "The Value of Wilderness," *Environmental Ethics,* 1 (Winter 1979), pp. 309–19, argues that instrumental justifications for conservation of the wilderness fail to provide a satisfactory rationale. Instead, he proposes a holistic conception of nature based on the intrinsic value of the wilderness.

6. Bernard E. Rollin, "Environmental Ethics," in *Problems of International Justice,* ed. Steven Luper-Foy (Westview Press, 1988), pp. 125–31, maintains that sentient beings, including humans and animals, have intrinsic value and moral rights, but nonsentient things, such as rivers, forests, and species, have only instrumental value.

7. Christopher D. Stone, *Should Trees Have Standing? and Other Essays on Law, Morals, and the Environment* (Oceana Publishers, 1996), argues that natural objects such as trees should be given legal rights and represented by legal friends who protect their interests.

8. Lily-Marlene Russow, "Why Do Species Matter?" *Environmental Ethics* 3 (Summer 1981), pp. 103–12, argues that attempts to give species inherent value are confused. The reason species matter is that individual members of a species have aesthetic value.

9. Alastair S. Gunn, "Why Should We Care About Rare Species?" *Environmental Ethics* 2 (Spring 1989), pp. 17–37, argues that the extermination of rare species is wrong because each species (as well as the ecological whole) has intrinsic value.

10. J. Baird Callicott, "The Search for an Environmental Ethic," in *Matters of Life and Death,* third edition, ed. Tom Regan (McGraw-Hill, 1993), pp. 332–81, argues that ecocentrism, a conceptually developed version of Leopold's land ethic, is the most satisfactory environmental ethic.

11. John Passmore, *Man's Responsibility for Nature* (Scribner's, 1974), maintains that we should not sacrifice art, science, or other human interests for the sake of conservation.

12. Tom Regan, ed., *Earthbound: New Introductory Essays in Environmental Ethics* (Random House, 1984). This is a collection of original essays, including Alastair S. Gunn, "Preserving Rare Species," Annette Baier, "For the Sake of Future Generations," and Mark Sagoff, "Ethics and Economics in Environmental Law."

13. Karen J. Warren, "The Power and the Promise of Ecological Feminism," *Environmental Ethics* 12 (Summer 1990), pp. 125–46. As Warren explains it, ecological feminism, or ecofeminism, sees both the domination of women and the domination of nonhuman nature as the result of an oppressive patriarchal conceptual framework characterized by what she calls the logic of domination.

14. Margarita Garcia Levin, "A Critique of Ecofeminism," in *Environmental Ethics,* second edition, ed. Louis P. Pojman (Wadsworth, 1998), pp. 183–88, attacks Warren's ecofeminism. Levin thinks there are better explanations for the way humans treat nature than Warren's logic of domination.

15. Karen Warren and Nisvan Erkal, eds., *Ecofeminism: Women, Culture, Nature* (Indiana University Press, 1997). This is a collection of articles that address three sets of topics: (1) empirical data about environmental racism, sexism, and classism; (2) the application of ecofeminist insights to various academic disciplines; and (3) philosophical perspectives on ecofeminism.

16. Greta Claire Gaard, ed., *Ecofeminism: Women, Animals, Nature* (Temple University Press, 1993). This is a collection of original articles that present a variety of ecofeminist viewpoints—for example, "Ecology and the Cult of the Romantic" and "For the Love of Nature."

17. Peter C. List, ed., *Radical Environmentalism: Philosophy and Tactics* (Wadsworth, 1993). This is a collection that includes articles on radical environmental views such as ecofeminism and deep ecology. As it is explained by Arne Naess in two articles, deep ecology starts with holism but goes on to recommend a mystical vision of the whole of nature. Also cov-

ered in the book are the tactics of radical environmental groups, such as Earth First!, that engage in nonviolent resistance called monkey wrenching, a term taken from Edward Abbey's book *The Monkey Wrench Gang*.

18. Bill Devall and George Sessions, *Deep Ecology: Living As If Nature Mattered* (Peregrine Smith Books, 1985), present a version of deep ecology that links it to religions such as Buddhism, Taoism, and Native American religion.

19. Jack Turner, *The Abstract Wild* (The University of Arizona Press, 1996). In a series of essays about wild nature and animals, Turner calls for a radical transformation that reveals the wild earth—its mystery, order, and essential harmony.

20. George Sessions, ed., *Deep Ecology for the 21st Century* (Shambhala Press, 1995). This is a collection of articles on deep ecology, including writings by Arne Naess, the founder of the movement.

Index